HANDBOOK OF MENTAL HEALTH INTERVENTIONS IN CHILDREN AND ADOLESCENTS

HANDBOOK OF MENTAL HEALTH INTERVENTIONS IN CHILDREN AND ADOLESCENTS

An Integrated Developmental Approach

Hans Steiner, Editor

JOSSEY-BASS
A Wiley Imprint
www.josseybass.com

Published by Jossey-Bass
A Wiley Imprint
989 Market Street, San Francisco, CA 94103-1741   www.josseybass.com

Jossey-Bass books and products are available through most bookstores. To contact Jossey-Bass directly call our Customer Care Department within the U.S. at 800-956-7739, outside the U.S. at 317-572-3993, or fax 317-572-4002.

Jossey-Bass also publishes its books in a variety of electronic formats. Some content that appears in print may not be available in electronic books.

All figures in Chapter 5 are from *Inborn Errors of Development*, C. J. Epstein, R. Erickson, and A. Wynshaw-Boris, eds. Oxford University Press, 2003.

Library of Congress Cataloging-in-Publication Data

Handbook of mental health interventions in children and adolescents : an integrated
  developmental approach / [edited by] Hans Steiner.—1st ed.
    p. cm.
  Includes bibliographical references and index.
  ISBN 0-7879-6154-X
  1. Child mental health services—Handbooks, manuals, etc. 2. Child
psychotherapy—Handbooks, manuals, etc. 3. Adolescent psychotherapy—Handbooks,
manuals, etc. 4. Developmental psychology—Handbooks, manuals, etc. 5. Mental
illness—Prevention—Handbooks, manuals, etc.   I. Steiner, Hans, 1946–

RJ499.H324 2004
618.92'8914—dc22

                                                                2004040719

Printed in the United States of America
FIRST EDITION
HB Printing   10 9 8 7 6 5 4 3 2 1

To my teachers, who have shown me the way from the very beginning: Gertrud Riedl, Karl Vacek, Viktor Frankl, Ludwig Wittgenstein, Thomas Szasz, Saul Harrison, John R. Searle, and, of course, Charles O. Walton.

—Hans Steiner

CONTENTS

PART TWO: PSYCHOPHARMACOLOGY 245

TABLES, FIGURES, AND EXHIBITS

Tables

Figures

Exhibits

HANDBOOK OF MENTAL HEALTH INTERVENTIONS IN CHILDREN AND ADOLESCENTS

INTRODUCTION

Dr. med. univ. Hans Steiner, James Lock, M.D., Ph.D., Kiki D. Chang, M.D., and Jeffrey J. Wilson, M.D.

We are happy to present you this first edition of the *Handbook of Mental Health Interventions in Children and Adolescents*. Based on the principles of developmental science and evidence-based practice, it is a comprehensive guide to modern mental health interventions as they apply to children and youth who suffer from mental health problems. The organization and structure of this volume sets the *Handbook* apart from other standard texts in the field and is based on our conviction that our field is ready to approach interventions from this new perspective: processes which cause, trigger, and maintain mental health problems. Instead of mapping treatments onto diagnoses, we describe the different treatment modalities, map out the processes that are affected by them, and put these into a developmental context. The *Handbook* does not subscribe to a reductionistic framework, where primacy is assigned to biological interventions.

This book brings together all forms of interventions, ranging from those that target neurons to those that target subcultures. At our present stage of knowledge, it is necessary to include medications, forms of psychotherapy, and methods for environmental manipulation, as they all have been shown to have some efficacy and effectiveness in a wide range of studies in children and adolescents. In approaching interventions from this perspective, we may get closer to answering the question that is so crucial for our field to continue to advance: Why do treatments work and for whom? Simple demonstration that we can be effective is not enough anymore. In approaching interventions from this perspective, we also hope to assist the practitioner in learning more specifics about a particular form of intervention, going a step beyond an introduction to a particular technique: we are helping them on their way to becoming proficient and more expert in a given modality.

How This Book Is Different from Others

In the field of the mental health sciences, we currently have several noted textbooks that approach the topic of mental health interventions based on descriptive diagnosis. We also have a mounting and increasingly sophisticated collection of volumes that offer great detailed information on intervention regarding specific diagnoses and diagnostic clusters. This book is meant to bridge the gap between these two types of volumes. Textbooks are diagnosis-based, generalist in character, and simply list interventions as they have been shown to be effective. Books on a particular intervention or set of interventions are highly focused and specific. This *Handbook* offers a step between the two—offering a deeper understanding of an intervention; it still offers sufficient breadth to do justice to a range of interventions.

This *Handbook* also is intended to show the full range of useful applications of a particular technique without the underlying assumption that solely descriptive diagnostic clusters determine mode of intervention. Rather than being confined by diagnosis, we aim to describe the curative process, the developmental dimensions which affect it, and then secondarily relate intervention to diagnoses, in most cases more than one. In so doing, we hope to direct clinical practice in a direction that is more compatible with evidence-based modern medicine.

Inevitably, this *Handbook* will thus raise new questions regarding the validity of delineating certain types of disorders on a purely descriptive basis, at least in children and adolescents. Approaching psychopathology from the point of view of the developmental sciences commits us to switch from a phenomenologically driven taxonomy to a causal, process-oriented psychopathology. This is important when we work with mental health problems in evolving organisms who can manifest the same problem in very different forms at different ages, and who conversely can respond to injury and threat in a wide range of ways. Appearances may or may not be the unifying feature of a disorder. This approach differs from the prevalent descriptive approach in that it goes beyond mere phenomenology in an effort to establish causal processes that need to be treated successfully to restore health, ensure adaptive adjustment, and provide developmental progression.

Furthermore, we present the entire range of available interventions without prejudging one to be more salient and powerful than the other. Our current state of knowledge regarding the etiology of most mental disorders and the efficacy and efficiency of their treatment prohibits the premature closure of several avenues of intervention. Comparative treatment studies are rare in the treatment of youth. There are only a handful of curative interventions in mental health. Any a priori assumption that psychotherapy, pharmacotherapy, or sociotherapy is the most appropriate is simply not tenable at this stage in the field's development. This, no doubt, will change, but for now, this is a prudent stance to take as we survey the field.

Finally, as much as possible, we base this book on evidence-based practice (Hamburg & Hager, 2002). In the absence of data, we provide a theory or rationale, discuss the putative targets for each intervention, catalogue the developmental influences on these processes, review the available empirical evidence supporting the interventions, and end with a brief description of relevant practice issues from our personal experience.

The Organization

The book opens with a section on developmental science and its implications for mental health interventions (Crain, 2000). We have tried to assemble a distinguished group of basic scientists from the branches of science that are basic to psychopathology from a developmental point of view. We asked them to highlight for us which developments in their respective sciences most likely will have an impact on the field of mental health interventions in the near future. The result is a collection of interesting essays in which the leaders in these sciences attempt to map out research lines for the practitioner to track and follow into the future, as they hold considerable promise to change everyday practice. These chapters all follow a similar outline: definition of the unit of observation, description of developmental changes in this domain, the relationship of this domain to interventions and treatment, and discussion of implications for advances in treatment. We conclude with a chapter outlining the methodological basis for clinical trials and evidence-based practice. This information is vital in helping practitioners decide which interventions are most established and promising of positive outcomes.

We then divide the *Handbook* into three additional sections: Psychopharmacology, Psychotherapy, and Sociotherapy. In each of these sections, we assemble chapters that report in detail on various interventions. The chapters all follow an identical structure: basic rationale and theory for this particular treatment, putative mechanisms of efficacy, developmental influences, putative targets of treatment, empirical support for treatment efficacy and efficiency, personal experience and cases, and future directions. The practitioner should be well prepared in understanding a particular technique, know the empirical database supporting the intervention, and get a glimpse first hand into the expert's practice with this particular technique.

The Psychopharmacology section is formatted much in the same manner as the other sections. Each chapter provides the most up-to-date information regarding psychotropic agents in children, including their putative mechanisms of action, adverse effects, recommended dosing and drug interactions, and empirical evidence for use in pediatric populations. In addition, each author gives his or her expert recommendation for the use of these. First, various treatments for attention-deficit/hyperactivity disorder (ADHD) currently available are discussed, including the stimulants and nonstimulants, such as the alpha-2 agonists, modafinil, antidepressants with ADHD efficacy, and atomoxetine. Some of these treatments, such as the stimulants, have the most efficacy data compared to any other class in child psychiatry. As ADHD is one of the most commonly diagnosed childhood psychiatric disorders, this chapter will appeal to all types of pediatric health care providers. Next, information on the use of novel antidepressants in children and adolescents is given, including the selective-serotonin reuptake inhibitors (SSRIs) and atypical newer antidepressants. As will be discussed, these agents are growing rapidly in popularity, due to the burgeoning evidence for their efficacy in the face of relatively benign adverse effect profiles. Then, the various agents used to treat pediatric anxiety are discussed, some of which overlap with medications already discussed. These medications include the SSRIs, novel antidepressants, alpha-2 agonists, gabapentin, and buspirone. Inclusion of these agents in a chapter dedicated to anxiety treatments underscores the wide spectrum of efficacy of some of these psychotropic agents in children and adolescents. Next, the mood stabilizers are presented, including lithium and the anticonvulsants. While less empirical evidence exists to support the efficacy of these agents as effective mood stabilizers in pediatric populations, these agents are nevertheless being widely used as such. Thus, what empirical data that is known is presented with knowledge that more data from controlled studies will be appearing soon. This is followed by a chapter discussing the typical and atypical antipsychotics. Again, use of these agents is increasing in children and adolescents for various symptoms and diagnoses. Therefore, the data that is presented is crucial to understanding when and how to use these agents in youth. Finally, an issue that is crucial to the success of any pharmacotherapy program is addressed: the context in which the medications are prescribed. A practitioner's relationship to the child, the family, and the schools weighs heavily on the adherence to the medication regimen. Thus, the nature of the information that is imparted to the patients and caregivers, and the manner in which it is shared, are of utmost importance, and these matters are in fact beginning to be studied systematically (Vitiello & Jensen, 1997).

The particular psychotherapies that are included in this Psychotherapy section were chosen to represent the large range of psychotherapy practices common in the United States and the world (Kazdin, 2000). Thus, although it is certainly not a comprehensive compilation, it does offer a practical overview. We wanted to provide a description and the evidential support for therapies that are focused as well as not focused, are appropriate for a range of ages and developmental processes, have both a clinical and empirical base, and are likely to apply to problems common to children and adolescents. Thus, we include various psychodynamic psychotherapies for infants, children, and adolescents, cognitive-behavioral therapy, interpersonal psychotherapy, behavioral analysis, mental skills training, family therapies, and relapse prevention. The chapters in this section provide an excellent look at the present and hint at the future of psychotherapy. They suggest that in all cases, therapies are becoming better defined, that they are more appropriately aligned with patient needs and developmental requirements, that evidence is being gathered to support the intervention approach, and that new and important avenues for applications and development are under way.

In the Sociotherapy section of this handbook, we strive to present several therapies within their social context. Rarely is a child's disorder completely isolated from the environment. In fact, as you will see within this handbook, even the most severe genetic disorders are quite sensitive to environmental manipulations. With the advances in technology within molecular neurobiology, neuroimaging, and neurogenetics, it is too easy at times to lose site of the environments in which all children live. It is at this interface—the proximal zone of development according to Vygotsky (1978)—where each child's unique phenotype is expressed. Identifying this zone, or the area where more proximal risk or resiliency factors have their effect, is an important aspect of assessing where intervention may be successful. Bronfenbrenner and Ceci (1994) reconceptualized the nature-nurture debate in a famous paper in which they developed an empirically testable model that encompasses both distal and proximal risk factors, suggesting that actualized genetic potential can be enhanced through proximal processes and environments. Identifying these processes, through which adaptation and maladaptation occur, are of particular interest developmentally, because of their potential for remediation.

To support socio- and psychotherapies, the practitioner has an ever-growing armamentarium of psychotropic medications to use. This is both a powerful gift and a serious responsibility. These medications, as will be discussed, are often gravely understudied in children and adolescents (Vitiello & Jensen, 1997). The long term, and often short term, adverse effects in youth are not known. As the Hippocratic oath dictates, foremost, do no harm. Yet, with the growing evidence that medications can be extremely effective and at times life-saving agents, to not prescribe them can be doing harm (Perring, 1997). Thus, every qualified practitioner must avail himself or herself of any available information regarding the safety, efficacy, and dosing strategies of relevant psychotropic agents. Here, we have attempted to distill some of the most relevant information regarding the use of these agents in pediatric populations for the mental health practitioner.

In the Sociotherapy section, we will explore common social areas of intervention for child mental health specialists (Vygotsky, 1978). Each of these chapters emphasizes in one way or another where the child meets the world, be it group therapy, hospital bed, or courtroom. In many cases, integrated treatments are emphasized. In the first chapter in this section, Group Psychotherapy and Interventions with Children and Adolescents, helpful tips in leading group psychotherapy for children and adolescents in a variety of contexts are provided. We continue by describing self-help organizations for young patients and their families. The phenomenon of mutual help groups from a "Vygotskian" perspective is discussed. This chapter further emphasizes the interactive processes involved in healing, whether the healing is from psychiatric or medical illness, trauma, or loss. The potential for healing is often a function of the degree to which an intervention is able to take on new life for the child or adolescent in question. Often, integrated interventions are indispensable in allowing this new life to take hold, grow roots, and bloom. Next, a model of inpatient psychotherapy, which integrates many different types of treatment, commonly including group, milieu, individual, and pharmacotherapy, is discussed. In both of these chapters, the environment of the child or adolescent is actively manipulated to produce change through proximal intervention. Three consultation chapters follow: School Consultation and Intervention, Consultation in the Medical Setting: A Model to Enhance Treatment Adherence, and Legal Consultations. In these chapters, practical methods of practicing evidence-based child psychiatry in complex systems are presented by master clinicians and educators. Helping children, adolescents, and their families through these systems is a key aspect of each of these chapters. In Chapter 35, as an example of effective preventive interventions, several evidence-based preventive interventions to reduce high-risk sexual behavior among adolescents, considering both community-based and high-risk samples, are outlined. These interventions may serve as examples for interventions that are central to mental health practice with youth: prevention and early intervention. These clinically based interventions are presented in both theoretical as well as practical terms, designed to aid child mental health professionals in talking with adolescents about highly sensitive material.

We conclude this book with a chapter on integrated treatment. In most cases of children and adolescents, we need to expect to apply a range of techniques, tailored to the problem, the strengths and weaknesses of a particular child, available resources and intended outcomes. All this needs to be done with the intention to be parsimonious and targeted. The chapter introduces definitions relevant to integrated treatment, describes the twelve-year prospective outcome of a small cohort of patients so treated and what can be learned from it. We review available data on the subject (very few directly concerning children and adolescents), drawing on the adult literature as well. We map out rational algorithms to decide on monotherapy or combination treatments. We highlight the importance of an adequate case formulation that weighs the influence of biological, psychological, and social factors in the genesis, precipitation, and maintenance of a particular problem (Steiner & Hayward, 2004). Such an understanding is basic to the development of a coherent rationale for the combined and carefully integrated treatment packages that are commonly applied to mental health problems of youth. The chapter should leave practitioners well prepared to practice what they preach.

Acknowledgments

In this effort, we owe much to many individuals. First and foremost, we want to acknowledge Alan Rinzler, our fearless editor, who tirelessly helped us achieve our goals. Mme. Claire Remy deserves most of the credit of keeping this enterprise organized, moving forward in a predictable fashion. Her assistance, cheerfully and charmingly given at all times, was a sine qua non for the success of this tome.

Personally, I, Hans Steiner, want to thank my section editors, who have clearly proven once again, that they are among the shining stars of the future of our profession. Without their quickly growing expertise, this volume would not have been possible. I also want to thank all my students and patients, who teach me much more than they realize.

I, Kiki Chang, would like to foremost thank my wife and son, who have been my ardent supporters in many ways, and Dr. Steiner, whose leadership has kept the journey safe, productive, and above all else, fun.

I, James Lock, would like to express my appreciation to my many teachers and in particular for my mentors, Drs. Agras, Steiner, and Kraemer. In addition, the support of my family makes my work possible. My work on this book was partially supported by an NIMH Career Development Award (K-08-MH01457).

I, Jeff Wilson, would like to dedicate my section to all of my mentors, especially Hans Steiner and Ned Nunes, who have taken the time to facilitate my academic aspirations. My development as a clinical researcher is a reflection of their efforts. I would also like to acknowledge the following grants: NIDA grant #DA14532 and a Ruane Scholar's Award from the Ruane Foundation.

References

Bronfenbrenner, U., & Ceci, S. J. (1994). Nature-nurture reconceptualized in developmental perspective: A bioecological model. *Psychological Review, 101*(4), 568–586.

Crain, W. (2000). *Theories of development: Concepts and applications.* Englewood Cliffs, NJ: Prentice Hall.

Hamburg, B., & Hager, M. (Eds). (2002). *Modern psychiatry: Challenges in educating health professionals to meet new needs.* New York: Josiah Macy Foundation.

Kazdin, A. (2000). Developing a research agenda for child and adolescent psychotherapy. *Archives of General Psychiatry, 57,* 829–835.

Perring, C. (1997). Medicating children: The case of Ritalin. *Bioethics, 11*(3–4), 228–240.

Steiner, H., & Hayward, R. C. (2004). *Complexity, continuity and context: Assessing mental health problems from a developmental perspective.* New York: Guilford.

Vitiello, B., & Jensen, P. S. (1997). Medication development and testing in children and adolescents. Current problems, future directions. *Archives of General Psychiatry, 54*(9), 871–876.

Vygotsky, L. S. (1978). *Mind in society.* Cambridge, MA: Harvard University Press.

PART ONE

DEVELOPMENTAL SCIENCE

CHAPTER ONE

THE SCIENTIFIC BASIS OF MENTAL HEALTH INTERVENTIONS IN CHILDREN AND ADOLESCENTS: AN OVERVIEW

Dr. med. univ. Hans Steiner

"Granted that mental processes are caused by brain processes, what exactly are these mental events? . . . Mental states are simply higher level features of the brain . . . *a feature of the entire system, but not a feature of the microcomponents of which the system is composed."*

JOHN SEARLE (1994)

". . . The brain is the organ of the mind, the organ of speech and thought, the organ of politics and of human individuality."

GERALD EDELMAN (1994)

"Introspection cannot teach you a thing about the brain as a physical object, even though consciousness is a property of the brain, and outer perception cannot give you any access to consciousness, even though consciousness is rooted in the observable brain."

COLIN MCGINN (1999)

"The barrenness and confusion of psychology (and psychiatry) cannot be explained by the fact that it is a young science . . . its lack of progress is not explained by the fact that it is comparable to physics in its beginnings. For in psychology (and psychiatry) we have scientific methods, but conceptual confusion."

LUDWIG WITTGENSTEIN (1953)

This chapter and the thirty-sixth are bookends for this entire *Handbook*. In this section and its overview, we will put forth what we think are the most salient developments in the sciences underpinning mental health interventions in children and adolescents. The purpose is not to provide a complete discussion of scientific developments in the mental health sciences, which would be beyond the scope of this volume. Instead, we are providing a snapshot of those areas of scientific inquiry, which at the present time are most relevant to the practitioner. The intent is to orient the practitioner to progress, which has influenced or is about to influence mental health interventions.

Psychiatry has always straddled uneasily the social and biological sciences. At different points in the development of our discipline, we have emphasized and de-emphasized this. Currently, we are in a period of mental health sciences and their applied disciplines where reimbursement pressures and the enormous advances in neuroscience are synergistically creating a subtle or not so subtle pressure to re-ductionistic forms of conceptualizing psychopathology. Such pressures also affect treatment: we are supposed to do more with less, and rely predominantly on med-ications to treat. We think this development will not serve our patients and our professions well. This *Handbook* is intended to be an effective antidote to any such pressures. By giving mental health practitioners access to the full range of ex-citing developments in all the fields relevant to our practice, we hope to give in-centive to practitioners to carefully examine the best available, not just the cheapest interventions. Premature orthodoxy, as we witnessed in the case of psychoanaly-sis in the 1950s, is also ill advised for the biological sciences today as they con-tribute to solving the puzzles of mental health and its disorders.

Figure 1.1 represents an array of levels of abstraction and organization relevant to current clinical practice. Psychopathology, at our current level of understanding, can be caused, precipitated, and maintained by problems origi-nating from any of these levels of abstraction, and interventions targeting any one of these levels can be helpful.

At our current stage of knowledge, we have to embrace this entire range of sciences more explicitly. Additionally, practice needs to be informed by the labo-ratory. And the laboratory needs the feedback of practice. Science proceeds by the valid experiment, which may tell us little about a particular patient. Practice proceeds by the controlled clinical trial, which may not tell us much about a dis-ease process. In contradistinction to a weak bio-psycho-social juxtaposition advo-cated by some, we advocate for a strong integration of these sciences and practice on the basis of developmental principles to guarantee continued and rapid progress (Steiner & Hayward, 2003).

How do we select the sciences that are most relevant for this section? In order to do so, we must describe a model, which defines the boundaries of what is rel-evant and what is not. For the purposes of this book, we use the developmental model of psychopathology. For reasons that should become clear this model has the most promise to be helpful because it most closely reflects the realities a given case represents and the dilemmas a given clinician has to struggle with. We first describe the essential features of the *developmental model,* then discuss briefly the

FIGURE 1.1. LEVELS OF ABSTRACTION AND ORGANIZATION RELEVANT TO MENTAL HEALTH SCIENCE AND PRACTICE FROM THE VIEW OF DEVELOPMENT.

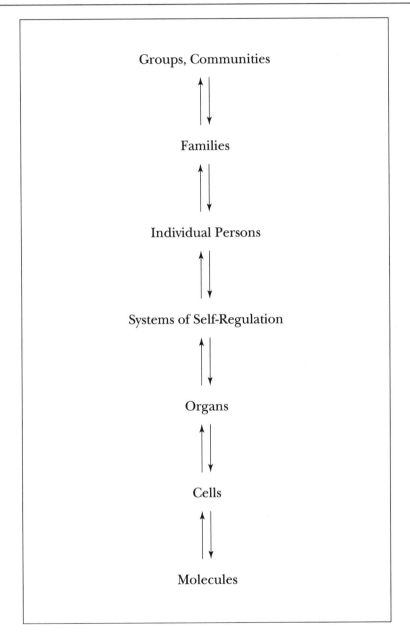

selected areas of scientific inquiry and their most poignant lines of research pertinent to clinical practice. Finally, we outline the principles of evidence-based practice against which any of the following chapters outlining a particular treatment are to be judged in terms of how solidly they are backed up by empirical and clinical facts.

The Developmental Model of Psychopathology

In the past 100 years, the mental health sciences have seen the rise of several developmental theories, as they apply to special domains of functioning (Crain, 2000; Jones & Elcock, 2001; Thomas, 2001). These also have been critiqued in an excellent compendium by Miller (1992). The "big" ones deal with cognition (Piaget, information processing; see Miller, 1992), psychopathology and the human life cycle (Freud & Erickson; see Miller, 1992), learning and adaptation (behaviorism and social learning theory; see Miller, 1992), and animal models of adjustment and adaptation (Bowlby, Lorenz, & Tinbergen; see Miller, 1992). From these theories, we can distill certain characteristics, which are core to a developmental approach, and apply them to our model of psychopathology and treatment. The following list summarizes these characteristics.

The Essence of the Developmental Approach

- Captures change (qualitative/quantitative)
- Builds complexity (systematic, molar, and molecular)
- Examines context (temporal and social)
- Looks for continuities/discontinuities (normality/pathology; isomorphisms/ non-isomorphisms; causal process oriented)
- Historical: pathways and trajectories of change (person + disorder)
- Captures adaptive/maladaptive function (outcomes)
- Is narrative: synthetic across domains (unit of observation = person)

The developmental model of psychopathology first and foremost captures *change* and is interested in defining changing entities. This contrasts sharply with the description of static disease entities. Children and adolescents are involved in dramatic progress and alterations of their competences and levels of abilities at rates that are not paralleled in any later period of humans. This is especially true for adolescence (Steiner, 1996). Change in emotions, cognition, motor skills, and multiple other domains is evident in every individual and poses special demands on what counts as abnormal. Because so little stays the same over time, there is always a question as to whether something is normal or abnormal, a central question to the enterprise of psychopathology. Another question, which the model attempts to address, is how change occurs: in large quantum leaps or in slowly accumulating doses? Quantum leaps can be more easily mistaken as pathology, as the new state seems to appear out of nowhere and is so different from what was just true. A more gradual and slowly accumulating alteration is much less suspect and can be deceptive regarding the severity of the problem it poses.

Inherent in the concept of developmental change are two related concepts: change is in a certain *direction* and occurs in more or less discrete *phases*. Change is usually in the direction toward differentiation and complexity (Werner, 1948) when things go well. This is not the change of entropy, where organization becomes less; it is in the direction of more organization. Change is the product of internal organizational forces, which direct the final outcome. In interaction with experience, though, inherent programmed potential becomes what it appears to be in real life. Implicit in this idea is the concept that even when left to its own devices, the growing organism has a trend toward righting itself, provided conditions are supportive of that, even without intervention. The context is not just important to determine phenotype; it also provides a protective envelope while the disordered person is regaining equilibrium.

As mentioned, also implicit in the concept of internally driven change toward health is the idea that in order for people to become what they are, there is a necessary interaction with the environment. Contextual variables shape the internal program. Psychosocial experiences interact with genetic programs to produce phenotypes. This is true for normal progress, and for the development of psychopathology as well. The model is inherently interactionist, weighing internal, intra-individual variables as much as external forces in the causation, precipitation, and maintenance of psychopathology, as well as in its conceptualization of treatment. This is an important consideration that has implications for the design of interventions aimed at children and adolescents who suffer from psychopathology. The context in which they operate is crucial to their functioning and determines not only how they become disordered, but also how they become well. The psychosocial environment in all its own richness is not a coincidental nuisance variable, but a necessary ingredient for the cause of psychopathology and its treatment. Maybe cancer can be treated in an interpersonal vacuum, but very few mental disorders, especially those in children and adolescents, can.

Change in response to intervention is also understood in more complex ways than in a simple disease model. Because we expect that there will be internal organization and internal forces, which drive the person in a certain direction, we would not expect that response to intervention would always be rapid and uncomplicated. The individual has its own internal set of processes, which equilibrate his or her adjustment. These processes can be cognitive, emotional, neuronal, interpersonal, or otherwise. They are to be taken into account when we apply treatment. Progress in treatment will usually not be linear, but more like a series of equilibrating steps. Repeated applications of interventions are required to move an individual along the path toward healing.

The concept of developmental *phases* is helpful for scientists and practitioners to track what counts for normal and abnormal, and it also occupies a central position in the definition of psychopathology from the developmental perspective (see below, and Mash & Barkley, 1996; Wakefield, 1992). Different phases of development have been described throughout the literature. Unlike in lower level organisms, these phases are often less well defined and contain much overlap. They are helpful though, from a clinical point of view, in constructing multivariate templates for associations to be expected, competencies present or absent. They, therefore, determine the kind of targets present and types of interventions to be planned.

Table 1.1 outlines one possible array of developmental phases we have found quite useful in our practice. It lists the stages of psychosocial development and the critical tasks to be achieved in that particular period. There are many other tasks

TABLE 1.1.   CLINICALLY RELEVANT STAGES OF NORMAL DEVELOPMENT.

Stage of Psychosocial Development	Critical Tasks to Be Achieved
Infancy	Attachment, control over bodily functions, locomotion, speech
Preschool	Separation and expansion of interpersonal orbit, exploration, play as an instrument of knowledge
School-age	Acquisition of skills and knowledge, book-based learning, extra-familial relationships with authority and same-sex peers
Early Adolescence	Pubertal maturation, independence, establishing diverse peer group, exploring sexual components of peer relationships
Late Adolescence	Exit from family, advanced learning, search for partners, managing sexual component of relationships, establishing health habits
Young Adulthood	Establishment of partnerships and family, early career development, refining health habits
Middle Adulthood	Establishing and maintaining a career, growth of own family, mentoring and generativity, maintaining health habits

not listed, pertinent to other domains of functioning, which cannot be listed. The reader is referred to a more complete rendition of this model in Steiner and Hayward (2004).

Implicit in the notion of developmental change is the idea of building *complexity* (Werner, 1948). This means that the model explicitly embraces the concept that our mental functioning becomes more diverse and complicated as we age. Our thinking, emotional life, actions, abilities, and competencies change under the impact of us interacting with our environment. We are learning. We become also more differentiated, specialized, and capable. Psychopathology can manifest itself therefore not only in simple deficits (as a disease model would postulate), but it also can show up as lack of progression and differentiation (a developmental arrest, a "fixation" in analytical language), or as a precocious assumption of complex functions that are not commensurate with what is expected from us, and finally, a loss of complexity of a domain under duress, which can be reversed by appropriate intervention (for example, removal of what impedes progress).

Let us elaborate on a theme which we have briefly touched on above, the importance of *contextual variables* in determining normality, psychopathology, and treatment. Intervening with youth quickly teaches us one thing: humans (especially immature humans) are extraordinarily dependent on their psychosocial context to achieve adaptive functioning and mental health. This has been elegantly discussed and described by Bronfenbrenner and Ceci (1994) and multiple others since then. Social learning theory (Bandura, 1997) deserves perhaps the most credit in calling our attention to the fact that maladaptive behavior not only is sometimes caused by factors in the psychosocial environment, but also precipitated and maintained by the environment. It is not just the individual that needs to be changed in order to allow a child to return to normal functioning. These environmental influences can be so powerful that interventions at the individual level are weak and ineffective despite all best intentions. Even more importantly, in some forms of psychopathology, the adaptive value of the particular problematic mental state or behavior in the repertoire of a given person is such that they will not change it despite the most dire consequences, but rather seek out psychosocial contexts, which more easily accommodate the characteristics in question. A good example: the psychology of the antisocial child, who associates with antisocial peers rather than giving up antisocial exploits. Humans not only carry the results of their deficient interactions with certain environments within them (the definition of psychopathology), but they also appetitively seek out new environments which are in accord with their internal expectancies. Psychopathology has a self-perpetuating quality, which makes it unique in the realm of medicine and the healing arts. Unless one is prepared to encounter this quality and deal with it appropriately, the best laid foundations for recovery will be in vain.

The developmental model also looks for *continuities* across time. As the model deals with rapid change, it cannot be primarily phenomenologically based. Because things can be so different between two ages, yet represent the same phenomenon, the developmental model has to look beneath the surface, and has to attempt to describe what the causal process is that ties together different manifestations of the same psychopathology. The developmental model is intrinsically process oriented, and in that sense pragmatic and close to treatment. Treatment focuses on causal processes that need to be changed to restore normal adjustment. The model's basis in *emergent complexities* admits a range of causal processes in psychopathology, a position that is well suited for our current level of understanding how children become mentally disordered, and how they recover, and what they need to do in order to get well. We will see below that criteria for evidence-based practice demand that one identify processes to be targeted and that such processes play a central role in establishing the efficacy of an intervention.

The model, in looking for continuities, will also acknowledge discontinuities and incomplete manifestations of pre- or post-syndromal psychopathology. This is an important link to other sciences, basic to the mental health domain: epidemiology (Steiner & Hayward, 2004). The study of populations is necessary and important to define the abnormal and the normal. It also defines specific risks and protective factors, which hinder normal development and hinder normal adaptation. Such interests also focus the developmental mental health clinician on early intervention, prevention, community practices, assisting other systems that deal with youth in identifying those who are about to become ill, and helping the system avert the problem by using community-based interventions. The link to public health and systems, which routinely deal with juveniles, is an important one. The mechanisms and strategies, which are effective in influencing these systems either as a consultant or as a participant, are a vital part of developmentally based practice.

Because the model is interested in continuity and phases of growth and influence, the system is also *historical*. The developmental model is interested in pathways and trajectories. This attitude goes well beyond the "history of present illness" found in mainstream medicine, in that it goes beyond a mere symptom tally. It also goes beyond the customary exploration of familial clusters of disorders. Of importance are the special attributes and characteristics of social environments encountered on one's way to maturity, their ability to facilitate growth, and their tendency to impede it. The person's pathways through time are examined in great detail, as they also offer information about the individual and his or her past adaptive success. We chart progress achieved in various domains of functioning (interpersonal, academic-vocational, recreational, and basic biological, just to name a few). We note the successful achievements of each phase and the critical tasks associated with it. And we chart failure of progression even in the absence of symptoms, because such failure is included in the expanded developmental definition of what counts as psychopathology. We will discuss this further.

Because the model is historical, it concerns how a particular individual reconstructs the pathways under discussion. The model is oriented toward personal *narratives,* in that it pays a great deal of attention to how a particular patient describes his or her life and understands it. Our narrations are full of metaphors we live by (Lakoff & Johnson, 1980). In turn, these metaphors determine our reactions and actions. This reconstruction is important for several reasons. On the most basic level, we get a feeling for the more extended and habitual level of functioning. As patients describe these pathways, we appreciate their way of understanding how things go right or wrong in their lives, and what they see as their strengths and weaknesses as people—not just their deficiencies as patients. Building an array of strengths in addition to tallying symptoms is an important preparatory step in setting up interventions. Secondly, the narrative of their lives helps us delineate to what extent patients see themselves as responsible for what is happening to them. Such beliefs often play a central role in the perpetuation of psychopathology, such as in post-traumatic stress disorder (PTSD) (Steiner, 1996). We also get a measure of how the patient assigns blame and culpability to others. This may be particularly important in cases of externalizing disorders. Such an understanding also will help us anticipate roadblocks to treatment in the form of non-compliance and resistance to suggested interventions. Finally, from a pragmatic point of view, their understanding of what happened and what life events intervened, how they relate to what went wrong and what factors hindered and helped their adjustment become a cornerstone for the formulation of a particular case, which subsequently drives the composition of their treatment package. Such a formulation has to take into account an empathic understanding of the patient's perception of the situation in order to maximize the chances that the recommended interventions will be followed and carried out appropriately. This narrative will prepare us for the formulation, including the synthesis of all relevant material in a particular case to a person-specific scenario of how this patient became ill now, what forces put and keep him or her there, and what it will take to get his or her life back on track again. The model forces this synthesis across domains, thus preparing us well for a treatment plan and interventions that stand the greatest chance to be effective.

Having outlined the specific features of the model, we now can turn to a new definition of psychopathology from this particular perspective. Psychopathology is a "harmful dysfunction" (Wakefield, 1992), that is, a "condition that causes harm or deprivation of benefit as judged by social norms (and evolutionary purpose)."

Psychopathology is a process (a dysfunction, not just a tumor) that is harmful to an individual. The process is not just defective; it is dysfunctional, maladaptive. Psychopathology results from the failure of some internal mechanism to perform its natural function—an effect that is part of the evolutionary explanation of the mechanism. The person is symptomatic, but the precise appearance and phenomenology of the pathology is left open, and the dysfunctional process is emphasized. The process leads also to attendant adaptive failure (Mash & Barkley, 1996); it goes beyond symptoms and stalls normal expected progression. This harmful dysfunction has become predominantly internalized, which means it has become highly independent of the context in which it occurs, or it even results in the individual seeking out contexts that fit the harmful dysfunction and that perpetuate its presence (Steiner, 1996). That is, the child will persist doing whatever is maladaptive, regardless of where he or she is or how old he or she is. The net outcome of psychopathology is symptoms (and syndromes) and adaptive failure, which is defined as lack of progression in stage-salient tasks and competencies.

The strong emphasis on process, away from phenomenology, is one of the hallmark features of the model. Most recently, critics of the current diagnostic practices in psychiatry (McHugh, 1998) have also suggested a reorientation of our taxonomies toward causal process. Four pathways are described that might be useful for conceptualizing mental disorders:

- Disease or damage to the brain (for example, mental retardation)
- Weak constitution (bipolar, ADHD)
- Behavior or habits that become a way of life (anorexia nervosa, SAD)
- Reactions induced by external events (PTSD).

We consider this conceptualization a major advance over the current descriptive approach. Whether or not these pathways are sufficient or all necessary remains an issue for empirical research. Viewed from a developmental perspective, though, we must applaud the effort.

The Basic Sciences for Developmental Approaches to Psychopathology

From what we have discussed so far, it should be clear that there is not one science that forms the basis for the developmental clinician. Reaching across the whole span, from culture to molecule, we have to be cognizant that organization at each one of those levels can influence what we see in the consulting room. To represent the entire range of science underpinning mental health would be beyond the scope of this volume. Therefore, we have selected four contributions from sciences that are either revolutionizing our thinking about mental health problems or have great promise to lead to revolutionary changes in our practice over the next five years. Each one of the following chapters describes the contributions of a particular field that might have implications for the causation of psychopathology and, therefore, treatment. Although the gap between these fields and clinical practice is considerable, we would like to give the clinician the opportunity to get acquainted with lines of investigation, which are extremely promising and important.

We first chose a contribution from ethology. We discuss this contribution first, as in some ways this science can be used to study all three therapeutically important spheres (biology, psychology, and sociology) systematically and with fewer constraints than in humans. Furthermore, we can manipulate all these spheres, control their influences, and study effects on the other spheres and specific domains of functioning. By changing patterns of rearing, we can examine influences on stress hormones at the time and in the animal's future (Levine, 1985). By pairing aggressive and anxious animals with calming older ones in ideal habitats, we can examine the influence of "psychotherapy" on temperament and neurophysiology. By controlling breeding behavior, we can examine relative influences of genes and environment (Suomi, 1996) on personality and emotional regulation.

Ethology is the science of observing animals in their natural environment. We can use this intrinsically naturalistic and organism-oriented paradigm to examine specific forces in carefully designed experiments done to gain insights about specific behavior patterns developing, reactions to stressors, and neurophysiological underpinnings of disease states and therapeutic modalities. One of the main advantages of this science for developmentalists is that the methods allow us to collapse time and shrink it to manageable units. By observing animals whose life span is much shorter than ours, we can rapidly gain insight into how certain traits unfold, which variables foster such growth, and which hinder growth. Since the animal, that is, the organism, is usually the unit of observation, the field allows for holistic approaches to diverse sets of very complex phenomena, such as aggression and attachment.

The field has a long and distinguished history of bringing insights to the mental health sciences. The work of Bowlby (1969), McKinney and Bunney (1969), and Suomi (1996) has taught us much about attachment, temperament, stress reactivity, and even therapist models of animals. More recently, ethology is contributing to our understanding of psychopharmacology and neuroscience. Another valuable insight derived from ethology is one regarding methodology: animal behavior, like human behavior, is quite flexible and multivalent, not rigid, hardwired, and completely predictable. It is rare that single behavioral patterns map onto single neural states—animal behavior too is complex, and can relate to many different situations. Animal behavior, like human behavior, must be interpreted in the social context in which it occurs. Insofar as animals do so themselves (and depending on the level of animal, they certainly have to in order to survive), they possess a "mind" and a "psychology" that also allows for detailed studies of particular aspects of psychological functioning. But the methods of this science also have limitations, which must be carefully heeded: animal models often are very distinct from humans and do not lend themselves readily to human comparisons. The chapter by Dr. Lyons addresses the core concepts of ethology, the validity of animal models of behavior, and briefly reviews the utility and limitations of animal research in developmental psychiatry. The following four chapters address content areas that are rapidly becoming vital to our attempts to understand normal development and psychopathology in children and youth: sociology, the study of influences on brain organ formation, molecular neurobiology, and genetics all are accumulating knowledge at an unprecedented pace which shortly should lead to new approaches to treatment.

Dr. Niranjan Karnik discusses the social environment, how we understand it, and how it influences children in health and disorder. Sociology is the study of wide arrays of social, cultural, and environmental factors. Family and friends, in order of immediate relevance, to institutions such as schools and welfare agencies, can be either a precipitant or maintaining factor of psychopathology, and have great potential as treatment or ameliorator. Because children are inherently social beings, and their genetic potential is highly dependent on growth inducing influences, the social environment is essential to the understanding of mental disorder and normal development in humans.

After discussing appropriate current models for conceptualizing the social environment for the work of Uri Bronfenbrenner (Bronfenbrenner & Ceci, 1994), Dr. Karnik divides the social environment into the domains of the family, peer groups and subcultures, the school, mass media, and welfare institutions, selecting these areas because they have an intimate relationship to the clinical sphere, and the high probability that practitioners will have to address questions regarding these social spheres and their relationship to the child or adolescent. These subdivisions also lend themselves to links with the specific methods of treatment that are informed by the sociological base, which are presented in the third section of interventions, as edited by Dr. Wilson.

The chapter introduces us to the methods by which social sciences study cultures, subcultures, and families. Ranging from surveys to experiments and qualitative methods, each has its own contribution to make, and has its limitation. As so often is the case, we need all of these methods to form a comprehensive picture, and each method will shape what we see. Subsequently, we discuss in detail the family, peer groups subcultures, and mass media and their influence on youth, schools and educational systems, welfare institutions, and the juvenile justice system. All of these inherently social institutions have powerful shaping and causal influences on how the lives of young people unfold and how they become disordered.

As children and adolescents are exquisitely dependent on social influences throughout their development in health and disorder, practitioners will ignore the influence of these forces at their own peril. We quickly appreciate how powerful social influences will be when patients describe as the source of their dropping out of treatment or non-compliance with their medication information they have gathered on the Internet, advice they have gotten from their peers, and prohibitions they have received from their families. As Dr. Karnik argues, social history taking must go far beyond the immediate sphere of influence if we want to be accurate in our assessments and maximally beneficial in our interventions. It is a rare practitioner in developmental psychopathology that will not be in contact with schools, welfare systems, and juvenile justice. Skills to consult with these systems in advocating for our patients are core to our professions. And some of the most powerful interventions in psychiatry are socially based, by far exceeding the impact of medications and psychotherapy in terms of immediate impact and net result. Consider the impact of placement in secure custody and seclusion in this regard.

The next chapter by Drs. Remmel and Falvell, two well-known experts in developmental psychology, addresses advances in *cognitive science* pertinent to our field. Connections to clinical practice are immediately apparent. In mental health, psychotherapy always has, and most likely always will, occupy a central place. Pioneered by Freud (1949), we have seen an immense diversification and enrichment in technique and sophistication. Cognitive behavior therapy is among the best-studied and supported intervention techniques in our field, and rivals medications in efficacy. This chapter lays the foundation for our psychotherapy section.

Since its founding days of Piaget (Flavell, Miller, & Miller, 2002) and Vygotsky (1978), the field of cognitive development has moved rapidly during the past ten years. We are increasingly able to study competencies at a younger and younger age by innovative techniques of investigation, which have more closely molded to children's capacity for understanding. This has led to an increasingly fine-grained picture of children's varying levels of knowledge, understanding, and how mental processes change with age. The chapter studies three content areas: core conceptual developments, developments in social cognition, and children's knowledge about the mind. Our appreciation of the newly gained knowledge in all of these is key to matching our interventions to what a young person can handle and utilize. Nobody can doubt anymore that children and adolescents have their own patterns of structuring information that sometimes is highly distinct from that in adults. Their understanding actively shapes what they understand. Much of the therapeutic enterprise is based on our appeal to rational forces, and to appreciate the diversity of the children's capacities is key to our helping them. In order to firmly conclude that we are dealing with resistance to change, defensive behavior, or non-compliance, we first need to make sure that our patients understand what we ask and are able to do what we recommend. These points hardly need elaboration. Another core concept to intervention is the understanding of causality, which varies considerably across the age spans we encounter. Much of therapy appeals to understanding why one thing will lead to another. Variations in the understanding of these chains of events are a core piece of information to consider as we intervene. Children and adolescents also differ from adults in the way they understand hypothetical situations, especially those with multiple facets, which are so often used in treatment. Ever since the pioneering work of Piaget (Flavell, Miller & Miller, 2002), we have come to understand the changes in logical reasoning, which occur as a function of age. While there is some debate as to whether these sequences hold for everyone, we must appreciate the fact that differential logic can be present when different domains of functioning and competencies are discussed. Children also differ from adults in terms of their ability to control, focus, restrain, and inhibit their behavior. Our understanding of this sequence is highly pertinent to behavioral interventions: not all who are restless have ADHD. Finally, the chapter presents a series of discussions on social cognitions highly relevant to the clinical enterprise: self concept, stability of behavior across time, children's understanding of ability, variability in attribution biases, capacity for perspective taking, and awareness that the stream of consciousness has obvious implications for psychotherapeutic technique, especially for those types that seek to work reflectively, rationally, analytically, and introspectively. Many of these insights have accumulated in the past decade, and this chapter will bring them closer to the practitioner, pointing to their current and future relevance. Clearly, the development of cognition is a strong basis for our essential practices.

In the next three chapters, we turn to a discussion of what it is that is in the "black box," and the types of processes that make us able to reflect and be social. As we better understand them, we also will be in a much better position to see the limits of socio- and psychotherapeutic interventions. For many decades, mental health practitioners, especially those from a behaviorist background, thought the contents of our heads to be irrelevant to their science and practice. With the advent of pediatric psychopharmacology, we have learned that this is clearly not so, from a pragmatic perspective. Additionally, we hope that these following three chapters will show us very exciting and new directions in which basic biological research will contribute to our understanding of the causes of and the interventions for psychopathology. These three chapters describe developments in the neurosciences, which directly will relate to our pharmacological treatments as well, and point to some possible interventions that were unimaginable even ten years ago.

The pace of the acquisition of knowledge in the biological neurosciences has quickened in the past ten years and the excitement of the progress has sometimes led to some excessively simplistic demands on our professions. I have heard some colleagues say things like, "If you do not study the genetics of slime molds you are wasting your time in psychiatry," or, "In just a few years we are all going to be geneticists anyway," and mean it. It should be quite obvious for all the foregoing material that this group of authors does not share this perspective. In fact, it is difficult to see at the present time how we can replace our social and cognitive understanding of psychopathology and treatment with that of biology. Only those in the grip of a powerful ideology (Wilson & Herrnstein, 1985) could expect such simplistic reductionism to be valid. Unfortunately, the pressure on medicine and the healing sciences to become increasingly cost effective has combined with such simple-minded solutions to produce such gems as the "med eval" and the "med check," procedures that masquerade as mental health interventions, which in fact are ineffective and sometimes outright dangerous. Our book, as we mentioned, should be an antidote to this attitude and a challenge to managed care and the insurance industry to support not only what is cheap, but also what works.

Drs. Rubenstein and Puelles discuss what we have learned regarding the development of the brain. Employing a series of extremely sophisticated techniques, neuroscientists are now able to map out the wiring diagrams of the brain as it matures. The brain has been called "the most complex organ in the universe," and rightly so (Edelman, 1994). This chapter provides excellent support for this proposition. The connections formed between different brain areas of functioning are the preconditions for developing circuits, which support higher-level functions to be executed. Faulty connections seem to come about through a variety of interferences at the level of neurons in the originating area, the targeted area, and the neuron's dendrites itself. This process is clearly genetically driven, but additionally requires the concerted and integrated action of neural systems. Typically, neural systems are distributed over multiple regions. Some systems are pathways that include predominantly sensory inputs, sensory perception and integration centers, regions that translate sensory stimuli into potential responses, and motor output regions (regions that we would typically associate with stimulus-motor response type sequences). Other systems consist of entirely internal loops, such as the cortex-basal ganglia-thalamus-cortex circuit. These circuits would have, as a predominant task, the internal information processing associated with memory formation, emotional coloring of incoming sensations, and internal thoughts. Loops and systems are usually redundant, a kind of "fail-safe" wiring which helps us survive, but poses problems for scientists who attempt to study processes underlying the formation of these loops. Multiple influences on similar functions are the norm and not the exception, which probably also relates to the fact that our medications are usually not as potent as we would like them to be. If one pathway in the brain is influenced by medication, then there are several alternatives available to bypass whatever influence was externally imposed.

All these brain structures are influenced by other systems that can affect the quality or intensity of the process, such as serotonin, norepinephrine, dopamine, and acetylcholine inputs, and a theme that we will return to in the next chapter on neuronal plasticity. As Rubenstein and Puelles point out, it is highly unlikely that neuropsychiatric disorders will ever be understood solely at the cellular level. Clearly we must ask questions regarding the organization and connection of neurons to understand the development of certain psychopathologies. Another message to be taken from this important summary is that we have barely begun to understand the normal developmental processes that make the brain the organ that it is. We know that multiple factors can interfere with the internally directed organization of the brain as a functional unit, but at the present time we do not know which ones they are and which critical periods they operate in. The challenge for the next five to ten years is to establish them as pathogenetic factors in a variety of psychopathologies. The syndromes for which such information will most likely be relevant are certain pervasive developmental disorders, such as autism and mental retardation, but also more complex psychopathologies such as Asperger's syndrome and psychopathy.

Because of the complexity of the processes that control the normal development of brain function, Rubenstein and Puelles advocate that perhaps one should consider neuropsychiatric disorders in a non-traditional pathophysiological context. Rather than focusing on a disease process affecting a single cell type or organ, one should view the disorder as affecting a neural pathway or a neural circuit. Genetic and other influences should be considered in the pathogenesis of disorders. Our understanding of how perinatal and postnatal influences (such as maternal nutrition, drug exposure, trauma, stress, depression, and subsequent life events) influence the formation of the brain as an organ is almost completely absent at this point. But having arrived at an understanding of how the brain forms under normal conditions, we are now in a much better position to take these next steps.

Two additional chapters then take us to suborganic levels of abstraction. Drs. Post and Post examine molecular and cellular developmental vulnerabilities to the onset of affective disorders in children and adolescents and make some suggestions for several levels of treatment, ranging from disease progression to prevention.

They begin by pointing out that we are just beginning to have an understanding of the cellular-related processes pertinent to emotion, learning, and memory—the kinds of processes that profoundly influence us as we grow and gain experiences, and reorganize ourselves according to what has been learned. The seminal work of Kandel, which earned him the Nobel Prize in medicine, has paved the way for our understanding of these processes (Kandel and Hawkins, 1994). At this point, we assume that the basic wiring of emotional regulation would be extremely plastic and evolve over the course of a child's development. Rather than regarding the brain as a fixed organic entity following a rigidly predetermined pattern of development, it is exquisitely responsive to external input, presumably over one's whole lifetime. This whole line of inquiry is especially pertinent for the study of emotional development. Nerve cells can form new connections and relinquish old ones, dependent on learning and memory. By mapping cellular components, which influence preferential connections in response to exposure to external influences, we begin to appreciate the shaping that takes place—for better or worse—after we are born. The Posts apply this paradigm to the development of affective disorders and anxiety disorders. Discussing pre-clinical data pertinent to affect and affiliation in animals and clinical data in patients with affective and anxiety disorders, this chapter links events at the neuronal level to clinical syndromes. The Posts apply their model to illness progression, as we find in stress responsivity and episode sensitization in bipolar illness. The clinical data are then linked to subhuman data on stimulant-induced behavioral sensitization and electrophysiological kindling in animals, an experimental paradigm, which provides convergent support for the postulated model from the background of experimental science. By using the external drug-use paradigm again, the Posts discuss the impact of such "environmental" factors on gene expression and neuronal development. As work by Beurrier and Malenka (2002) has shown in the case of substance use cravings, we are now in a position to outline the long lasting impact of exogenous substances on neuronal action patterns. The Posts extend these findings to the case of affective regulation and dysregulation, showing that experience can change something as basic as gene expression in the brain. Applying the findings from neurology to the study of affective processes and their disorders, the Posts then show that the phenomenon of *kindling*, which is the stimulation of full-blown nerve discharge after a series of subthreshold stimuli, can also help us understand clinical phenomena such as bipolar disorder and chronic traumatization. Finally, they discuss exciting findings regarding the connections between neonatal stressors and lasting effects on behavior, neuroendocrinology, and substance abuse vulnerability.

In many ways, the findings from this wide range of studies have immediate implications for clinical practice as far as the causes of bipolar illness is concerned. Additionally, there are also implications for therapeutic interventions in this disorder and others, which potentially respond to anticonvulsants and mood stabilizers. There is the exciting possibility that a therapeutic compound may in fact have curative or protective effects, a topic recently summarized by Ketter (2002).

Potentially, psychiatry would be in a position of possessing not just therapeutic or palliative medications (such as stimulants for ADHD or antipsychotics for schizophrenia), but preventive or even curative ones. Posts' discussion also links with the importance of pharmacoprophylaxis in vulnerable individuals with bipolar disorder, a form of tertiary prevention. They are advocating in early and targeted prevention for those at high risk, such as for instance symptomatic, but not syndromally ill bipolar offspring. And they conclude by indicating promising directions for primary prevention in high-risk populations, such as unaffected bipolar offspring. Preventive principles also can be applied to patients with bipolar illness and their offspring when we seek to protect them from substance abuse and its especially deleterious consequences in bipolar illness and interventions for maltreated children. They conclude with a neurobiological overview and integration of the findings in the clinically diverse data sets discussed.

Finally, we examine the role of the gene in the formation of psychopathology. With the mapping of genome, there was much excitement regarding the potential of genetic factors playing a role in much (or even most) of the origin of psychopathology. In a balanced and erudite discussion, Dr. Joachim Hallmayer tells us where we stand in regard to the role of genes in psychopathology and treatment. Although the overall message is cautious and complex, we are beginning to appreciate the contributions of genetics to mental health practices. Changes in available techniques have given us the opportunity to examine gene-expression data that complement gene-sequence data. At the present time, there are many efforts seeking to characterize specific genes, in hopes that such understanding will vastly expand our understanding of health and disease and the practice of medicine.

While there are some examples of interventions, which are based on genetic techniques and successfully studied and marketed, in the area of psychopathology, we have mostly promissory notes. Ultimately, Dr. Hallmayer suggests, the major impacts of this molecular revolution are envisaged to be:

- Using specific genetic indicators to target treatment and to identify individuals at risk for a certain disorder to be able to prevent onset of disorder
- Using genetic studies to predict efficacy of certain medications in individuals (pharmacogenetics)
- Using genes as therapeutic agents to implant corrective genetic material
- Using animal models for studying the genetic contributions to the development of certain disorders.

Introducing us to the types of genetic changes, which are pertinent to our understanding, the chapter leads us to a discussion of single gene disorders, such as Rett syndrome, along with other forms of mental retardation. Dr. Hallmayer then turns to a discussion of genetically complex disorders, such as autism, where we have good reason to believe that multiple genes are involved in creating the problem. Many vexing questions are raised by this discussion, which shows us in impressive detail how far the distance is between the gene and higher levels of complexity affected in a disorder, which is not particularly subtle in its manifestations. Abandoning single gene models leads to questions about how many genes are involved, and how they interact to produce the adverse outcome. On the clinical side, the findings in autism also lead to the expansion of the original diagnostic category into a disease spectrum to account for differential influences of combinations of genes. The chapter continues with a discussion of the implications for therapy for autism. While it is clear from the discussion that direct therapeutic implications will depend on many other unknown factors, we are beginning to see how genetics may play a role in the therapeutics of some disorders in the not so distant future. One such example is the exciting new area of investigation, pharmacogenetics. Clinicians have struggled for many years with the fact that there is a high inter-individual variability in the response to pharmacological drugs, both in terms of side effects and treatment response. Pharmacogenetics seeks to improve our knowledge in regards to who will respond to a particular intervention, in what way and why, based on genetic profiles of relevant nervous system components, such as, for instance, receptors. Other plausible targets for pharmacogenetic studies are variations in enzymes controlling drug absorption and elimination. As in the study of psychopathology and its causes, studies so far have focused on single genes. The technological advance of gene array technology allows characterization of gene expression of thousands of genes in parallel. More multi-targeted studies such as this have considerable promise to improve our currently poor level of understanding of variables that affect efficacious medication treatment.

The chapter then turns to a discussion of gene therapy, where genetic material is inserted into a defective cell in order to treat the problem. For many complex reasons discussed in the chapter, this is not a simple enterprise, but most definitely worthy of pursuing, as once again it offers the chance of curative interventions. Most of the clinical studies in this area are in oncology, and most of those are still in early stages of development (stage I and II), establishing safety, side effects, and tolerability criteria.

In all these chapters, we begin to appreciate the distance between basic science and current clinical practice. However, we can see several important touch points, which show great promise to influence how we will be able to help children and adolescents with mental health problems in new and exciting ways. But, in order to evaluate how adequate and efficacious current techniques of intervention are, we need further tools. The last chapter in this section will provide those. But first we need to briefly establish the current standards for evidence-based practice in medicine. Evidence-based practice has become the standard of the healing sciences in this millennium. Several criteria have been proposed for a practice to be evidence based: we find the ones suggested by Kazdin (2000) to be most helpful. He lists the four requirements for practice to be evidence based, and these criteria show the intrinsically necessary close relationship between basic science and clinical practice.

First, there has to be a *theory linking a particular process to a particular problem.* These theories can originate either in the consulting room or in the laboratory. They can be derived from a series of experiments or a series of patients. An example of a clinically generated theory regarding the origin of anorexia nervosa would be the idea that anorexia nervosa represents an unconscious avoidance of the demands of maturation and adolescence (Steiner & Lock, 1998). An example for a laboratory-generated theory would be that impulsive aggression is caused by a serotonergic neurotransmission deficit. (Swann, et al., 2002). I would characterize the first theory as one of *top down* causation (an attitude, a belief, or a distortion of thinking originates from a high level of complexity in the human mind/brain setup and causes the psychopathological state). The serotonergic theory would be labeled as a *bottom up* process. Both theories lead to testable hypotheses related to intervention and treatment. Given our current state of knowledge, either theory would deserve attention but would lead to quite different interventions. In general, bottom up theories would be easier to test (in animals, for instance) and thus probably lead more rapidly to data. Conversely, theories, which involve highly complex mental states, which occur only in humans, would be more difficult to test for many reasons, some of them ethical. On the other hand, the top down theories might be much more readily applicable to humans, while the external validity of bottom up hypotheses would be at times questionable.

Secondly, there has to be *some research assessing the validity of the proposed mechanism.* In this regard, the serotonergic hypothesis fares much better than the adolescence-avoidance hypothesis. More data in animals and humans confirm the validity of the proposed mechanism (Swann, et al., 2002), although the identity challenge theory is not completely without backing (Steiner & Lock, 1998). It is clear, though, that in both cases, strictly controlled laboratory experiments would be necessary to examine the validity of the particular process.

Thirdly, there should be, according to Kazdin (2000), some preliminary *outcome evidence that treatment along the lines suggested by the hypothesis changes the pathological status* of the patient. In other words, we need to show that by targeting the fears of growing up (presumably by some reflective psychotherapy or perhaps even a desensitization paradigm), we in fact alter the outcome of anorexia nervosa or bulimia. Evidence along these lines exists (Steiner & Lock, 1998). By the same token, we need to show that giving mood stabilizers or SSRIs, thus theoretically enhancing serotonergic neurotransmission, leads to reduction in maladaptive aggression. This is easier and more powerfully shown in animals (Swan, et al., 2002) than in humans (Steiner, et al., 2003), but outcomes are still in line with this theory.

Finally, we need to demonstrate that the *causal process we have postulated for a particular problem is influenced by the treatment we use to target it and changes in that process are connected to the desired outcome.* An elegant body of work in this regard is the work by Patterson's group on coercive behaviors in the genesis and persistence of maladaptive aggression. In this research, it has been convincingly shown that a parent's response to a child's coercive behavior has direct and indirect implications for their antisocial conduct. Altering this causal loop of the parent unwittingly reinforcing coercion and non-compliance changes the child's chance to persist in maladaptive aggression (Patterson, 1986).

A complex series of steps establishes a treatment as evidence based. The proper labels for how treatments are in fact supported would be as follows (*Clinical Evidence*, 2002):

"Beneficial"	Clearly supported effectiveness by evidence from Randomized Controlled Trials (RCT), low risk, high benefit to be expected
"Likely to be beneficial"	Less well supported by RCTs
"Trade off between benefits and harms"	Clinicians and patients should carefully weigh these before applying the treatment
"Unknown effectiveness"	Either insufficient or poor quality empirical support
"Unlikely to be beneficial"	Even less support than in the previous category
"Likely to be ineffective or harmful"	Both of these have been demonstrated clearly in studies

As we will see in the body of this volume, for most interventions we have a long way to go. In order to be able to evaluate how adequately all our available interventions have been tested, we need to become familiar with methods of scientific evaluation, which are particularly pertinent to developmental-based research. The final chapter by Drs. Saxena and Blasey addresses this need. The chapter examines the various designs used in clinical and basic research, illustrating the particular design through a study from the extant literature. Ranging from the "gold standard procedure" (the randomized controlled study to cohort studies), to case control studies, case series, and case reports, the chapter steps us through the advantages and disadvantages of each design. Review papers and meta-analytic techniques used to summarize extensive data from divergent sources are carefully outlined. Special design features, such as longitudinal designs, follow-up studies, and prospective versus retrospective studies are elaborated. Pilot studies are briefly discussed. Multicenter designs and various specific terms we encounter when describing measurements and studies are summarized. The chapter concludes with a careful stepwise dissection of the features of one of the author's favorite studies to illustrate the approach to the scientific literature on a personal level. A useful glossary of commonly encountered terms is appended.

Where Are We, and Where Are We Going?

We have traversed a great distance in this chapter, going from culture to molecule in our search for better ways to help children and adolescents with mental health problems. To summarize all that we will be introduced to in this section is almost impossible. So rich and diverse are the findings in the fields supporting clinicians' endeavors that we have to modestly list them and wait for the near future to provide us with further integration. From my perspective, the diversity, richness, and complexity of facts we have encountered may be overwhelming to those practicing in the consulting room. They certainly are to our trainees and I might add, most of us in academia. From another perspective, we live in very exciting times. Not so long ago, this section in a handbook on treatment would have been either very slender indeed, or very parochial in character. We clearly have departed from the old days of school-driven treatment and thinking. Our continued challenge is not to become prematurely reductionistic while avoiding being confusedly bio-psycho-social.

The developmental model we discussed at the beginning of this chapter will hopefully prevent us from doing either. From its perspective, I see that the evidence supports three major pathways, corresponding to the three major sections in this handbook: psychotherapy, pharmcotherapy, and sociotherapy. At the current state of knowledge in our field, it is impossible to dismiss any of these. As our empirical data base grows, we will hopefully simplify our approaches, but at the same time, we most likely also will stand to gain a whole new array of techniques that are just beginning to be defined and studied, all offering the prospect of reducing human suffering and restoring mental health.

Many questions remain at this stage of knowledge in treatment based on the developmental model. What must be fairly acknowledged is that the empirical data backing up the interventions to be discussed are unevenly distributed. However, at the very least, all of the interventions presented in this volume have a rationale, and sometimes even a more or less sophisticated theory behind them, which allows for the generation of testable hypotheses. Some interventions are standardized, even manualized, in their mode of application; many of them show efficacy, or even effectiveness. As of today, we must keep an open mind regarding all of them and not assume that all can be reduced to one or the other.

The past fifty years have seen a monumental change in the way we think about our mental health and its causes. We have gone from a quasi-disease model of psychic determinism (psychoanalysis) to a black box, environmentalist, continuous trait model (learning theory) back to a phenomenological, typologically based disease model (the *Diagnostic and Statistical Manual of Mental Disorders [DSM]* and the *International Clinical Diagnosis [ICD]*) to a neuroscience-driven reductionism. Each one of these has left its impact on the field, and each has had its modicum of successes; however, none of them have produced any impressive cures or massively effective interventions. Any parochial insistence that one model is superior to the others is ill placed. Pragmatically, we need to track all these models and interventions in their further development and testing in the laboratory and the real world of the consulting room. To uphold our end of the bargain in the dialectical progress of mental health sciences and practice, we need to understand causal processes as best we can, apply the interventions best suited to change them, and show that our approaches work. It is then up to the colleagues in the lab to study why and how exactly they work and, in turn, help us refine how we approach problems in the consulting room.

We (Steiner & Hayward, 2004) conceptualize the progress in solving the mental health problems in youth as dialectic between practitioners and scientists. We approach these problems by studying them scientifically and treating them clinically. At the present time, we are called upon to masterfully select interventions according to problems, blend according to need, and execute to the best of our abilities. This we will discuss in our final chapter on integrating treatment.

References

Bandura, A. (1997). *Self-efficacy in changing societies.* New York: Cambridge University Press.

Beurrier, C., & Malenka, R. (2002). Enhanced inhibition of synaptic transmission by dopamine in the nucleus accumbens during behavioral sensitization to cocaine. *Journal of Neuroscience, 22*(14), 5817–5822.

Bowlby, J. (1969). *Attachment and loss, vol. 1: Attachment.* London: Hogarth.

Bronfenbrenner, U., & Ceci, S. J. (1994). Nature-nurture reconceptualized in developmental perspective: A bioecological model. *Psychological Review, 101*(4), 568–586.

Clinical Evidence: Mental Health. (2002). Issue 7, London: BMJ Publishing Group.

Crain, W. (2000). *Theories of development: Concepts and applications.* Englewood Cliffs, NJ: Prentice Hall.

Edelman, G. (1994). Bright air, brilliant fire: Neurobiology and the mind. In Broadwell, R. D. (Ed.) *Neuroscience, memory, and language.* Decade of the Brain, Vol. 1 (pp. 25–34). Washington, DC: Library of Congress.

Flavell, J. H., Miller, P. H., & Miller, S. A. (2002). *Cognitive development* (4th ed.). Upper Saddle River, NJ: Prentice Hall.

Freud, S. (1949). *An outline of psychoanalysis.* London: Hogarth Press.

Jones, D., & Elcock, J. (2001). *History and theories of psychology: A critical perspective.* New York: Oxford University Press.

Kandel, E., & Hawkins, R. D. (1994). Neuronal plasticity and learning. In Broadwell, R. D. (Ed.) *Neuroscience, memory, and language.* Decade of the brain, Vol. 1 (pp. 45–58). Washington, DC: Library of Congress.

Kazdin, A. (2000). Developing a research agenda for child and adolescent psychotherapy. *Archives of General Psychiatry, 57,* 829–835.

Ketter, T. A. (2002). Predictors of treatment response in bipolar disorders: Evidence from clinical and brain imaging studies. *Journal of Clinical Psychiatry, 63,* 21–25.

Lakoff, G., & Johnson, M. (1980). *Metaphors we live by.* University of Chicago Press.

Levine, S. (1985). A definition of stress? In Moberg G. P. (Ed.) *Animal Stress.* Bethesda, MD: American Physiological Society, 51–69.

Mash, E., & Barkley, R. A. (1996). Child psychopathology. New York: Guilford Press.

McGinn, C. (1999). *The mysterious flame: Conscious minds in a material world.* New York: Basic Books.

McHugh, P. (1998). *The perspectives of psychiatry* (2nd ed.). Baltimore: Johns Hopkins University Press.

McKinney, W. T., Jr., & Bunney, W. E., Jr. (1969). Animal model of depression. I. Review of evidence: Implications for research. *Archives of General Psychiatry, 21*(2), 240–248.

Miller, P. (1992). *Theories of developmental psychology.* New York: Freeman.

Patterson, G. (1986). Performance models for antisocial boys. *American Psychologist, 41*(4), 432–444.

Searle, J. (1994). Some relations between mind and brain. In Broadwell, R. D. (Ed.) *Neuroscience, memory, and language.* Decade of the brain, Vol. 1 (pp. 25–34). Washington, DC: Library of Congress.

Steiner, H. (Ed.). (1996). *Treating adolescents.* San Francisco: Jossey-Bass.

Steiner, H., & Hayward, C. (2004). *Complexity, continuity and context: Developmental approaches to diagnosis and treatment.* New York: Guilford Press.

Steiner, H., & Lock, J. (1998). Eating disorders: A ten year review. *Journal of the American Academy of Child and Adolescent Psychiatry, 37*(4), 352–359.

Suomi, S. (1996). Aging in rhesus monkeys: Different windows on behavioral continuity and change. *Developmental Psychology, 32*(6), 1116–1128.

Swann, A. C., Bjorn, J. M., Moeller, F. G., & Dougherty, D. M. (2002). Two models of impulsivity: Relationship to personality traits and psychopathology. *Biological Psychiatry, 51*(12), 988–994.

Thomas, R. M. (2001). *Recent theories of human development.* Thousand Oaks, CA: Sage.

Venter, J. C., Adams, M. D., Myers, E. W., Li, P. W., Mural, R. J., Sutton, G. G., et al. (2001). The sequence of the human genome. *Science, 291,* 1304–1351.

Vygotsky, L. S. (1978). *Mind in society: The development of higher psychological processes.* Cambridge, MA: Harvard University Press.

Wakefield, J. C. (1992). The concept of mental disorder: On the boundary between biological facts and social values. *American Psychologist, 47,* 373–388.

Werner, H. (1948). Comparative psychology of mental development. Chicago: Follet.

Wilson J., & Herrnstein, R. (1985). *Crime and human nature.* New York: Simon & Schuster.

Wittgenstein, L. (1953). *Philosophical investigations.* Oxford: Blackwell.

CHAPTER TWO

ETHOLOGY

David M. Lyons, Ph.D.

Ethological studies of animal behavior provide insights on aspects of psychiatric disorders that are difficult to investigate in children. Practical limitations and ethical concerns restrict opportunities for prospective controlled studies of behavior, physiology, and brain development in children with psychiatric disorders. This chapter addresses the core concepts of ethology and the validity of animal models of behavior, and briefly reviews the utility and limitations of animal research in developmental psychiatry.

Ethology: Core Concepts and Methods

Ethology arose from the work of biologists who studied animal behavior in Europe during the early twentieth century (Thorpe, 1979). Various forms of behavior were examined in vertebrates and invertebrates. Behavioral diversity was generally viewed in terms of evolution through natural selection and was studied with respect to the environmental contexts in which behavior evolved. In addition to analyzing the functions of behavior and its evolution, ethological research also addressed

This work was supported in part by Public Health Service grant MH47573, DAO16902, the Pritzker Foundation Neuropsychiatric Disorders Research Consortium, and helpful discussions with Alan Schatzberg and William Mason.

immediate causes and development (Tinbergen, 1951). Immediate causation, development, function, evolution, and the relations between these types of analysis were viewed as providing a complete explanation of behavior (Hinde, 1966).

Given their interests in understanding behavior with respect to the environments in which it evolved, ethologists pioneered the creation of methods for direct observational research. This effort produced important advances in sampling procedures (Altmann, 1974) and descriptive taxonomies composed of formally defined units of behavior. These descriptive taxonomies initially were based on the premise, "behavior patterns are not something which animals may do or not do, or do in different ways, according to the requirements of the occasion, but something which animals of a given species 'have got,' exactly in the same manner as they 'have got' claws or teeth of a definite morphological structure" (Lorenz, 1950, p. 238). Ideally, these *"particulate elements* of behaviour" (Lorenz, 1950, p. 238, original emphasis) were described as modal patterns of movement (Barlow, 1977). This basic tenet of classical ethology was succinctly summarized by Tinbergen (1951, p. 7): "Because it is our task to analyze behavior as coordinated muscle activity, the ultimate aim of our description must be an accurate picture of the patterns of muscle action." The task of describing behavior in terms of the visible morphology of muscle movement was viewed as distinguishing ethology as an objective, unbiased, scientific endeavor.

But ethologists soon discovered that modal patterns of movement are often poorly suited for the task of describing what animal behavior is about. Rhesus monkeys, for example, do several different things using the so-called "threat face" display. Depending on the way this behavior is coordinated with aspects of the environmental context, a "threat face" may serve to deter a competitor, recruit an ally, or redirect an incipient attack by another monkey (Anderson & Mason, 1978). In similar fashion, the "head-tossing" display of adult western gulls is used to solicit food from a mate, as a prelude to copulation, or to initiate a change in incubation duties at the nest (Hand, 1985). The "head-bobbing" display of male parakeets, originally classified as a heterosexual courtship behavior, also plays a role in the formation and maintenance of stable relationships among males in large mixed-sex flocks (Stamps, Kus, Clark, & Arrowood, 1990). The lordosis display performed by adult guinea pigs as a pericopulatory behavior is performed by pups during nursing to elicit maternal licking of the anogenital region in order to stimulate micturition (Harper, 1972). These are by no means isolated examples. It is often the case that a given modal pattern of movement may serve more than one function, and that different patterns of movement are used to achieve the same function (Purton, 1978).

During the past thirty years of research, far-reaching and radical changes have occurred in ethological studies of behavior. A shift has occurred away from the illusion of theory-free observation and description, and toward the realization that theory and interpretation cannot be completely removed from the process or the product of observing and describing. A shift has occurred away from the view that behavior is something that animals have, and toward systematic studies in which behavior as goal-directed action is used to describe what animals do. The scope of analysis initially aimed at understanding modal patterns of muscle movement has been broadened to include diverse forms of social power, the creation of friendships, social conventions, conflict resolution, emotional dispositions, payment for labor, jealousy behavior, self-awareness, and psychological well-being. These are a few of the many phenomena now receiving attention from ethologists in departments of biology, zoology, physiology, psychology, psychiatry, and veterinary studies.

Links with Developmental Psychology

John Bowlby (1969) relied on several key concepts and findings from early ethological research to formulate his now classic theory of attachment in human parent-offspring relationships. In keeping with the imprinting process that Lorenz first described for birds, Bowlby noted that human infants also develop a strong preference for being near their principal care-provider. He therefore focused attention on patterns of behavior such as following, touching, clinging, crying, smiling, and non-nutritive suckling used by infant humans and other infant animals to promote parent-offspring proximity. This perspective concurred with seminal studies of "contact comfort" in rhesus monkeys (Harlow & Zimmerman, 1959), and downplayed the significance of feeding behavior in the process of primary drive reduction as formulated by learning theorists.

Bowlby also argued that natural selection favored proximity-promoting behavior because this enhanced infant survival in the environments in which humans evolved (Bowlby, 1969). Contemporary developmental psychologists (Belsky, Steinberg, & Draper, 1991) and psychiatrists (Teicher, Andersen, Polcari, Anderson, & Navalta, 2002) have likewise begun to assimilate from ethology the idea that adaptations are often facultative, and thereby provide flexibility in responding to diverse environmental demands. Contextually contingent adaptations may arise during naturally occurring periods of plasticity in early brain development. Specific aspects of maternal care (Liu et al., 1997), early exposure to patterned light (Katz & Shatz, 1996), auditory stimulation (Moore, 2002), and steroid hormones (Seckl, 2001) are known to exert organizational effects on developing brain systems that last for a lifetime. Early environmental "programming" is viewed as producing adaptive adult phenotypes because many individuals spend their adult life in environments similar to the one in which they were born. Rodent studies suggest that one programming target in the developing mammalian fore-brain is glucocorticoid receptor gene expression, a topic we return to below.

Ethopharmacology and Psychiatry Neuroscience

Ethopharmacology emerged from the view that an intimate familiarity with the behavioral repertoire of a species and its functional significance enables the most reliable and sensitive analysis of drug effects on behavior. In recent years, ethophar-macologists have continued to combine functional perspectives with drug ad-ministration experiments designed to illuminate the mechanisms that mediate complex brain-behavior relationships. Some of the many different forms of be-havior thus far examined by ethopharmacologists include maternal behavior, sex-ual behavior, eating behavior, novelty seeking, anxiety, fear, aggression, and aspects of learning and memory (Blanchard, Yudko, Rodgers, & Blanchard, 1993; Krsiak, 1991; Parmigiani, Ferrari, & Palanza, 1998; Rodgers, 1997). Unfortunately, such studies tend to focus on adults, and child psychiatrists have not fully tapped the enormous potential of animal models in psychiatry neuroscience research.

Two principal types of animal models are used in psychiatry neuroscience. Assay type models are created to screen new drugs for their clinical therapeutic po-tential and need not resemble anything seen in a psychiatric disorder. The validity of animal assay type models is assessed in terms of the ability to predict that a new drug belongs to a class of compounds that elicits a response in the model that drugs not belonging to the class do not produce. For example, passive avoidance deficits in rats induced by olfactory bulbectomy are reversed by many clinically used an-tidepressants, whereas stimulants, neuroleptics, and anticholinergics do not re-produce this effect (Kelly, Wrynn, & Leonard, 1997). New drugs with unknown clinical potential that reverse bulbectomy-induced deficits are taken as candidates for further investigations to determine their utility as antidepressant medications. Assay type models are typically designed to satisfy important practical considera-tions, including simplicity, ease of use, and cost-related economic concerns.

The second principal type of animal model aims to reproduce or simulate conditions of interest in a human psychiatric disorder. Simulation type models are created to investigate the processes underlying psychiatric disorders, and the mech-anisms of action for therapeutic drugs. In addition to the criterion of predictive validity described above for assay type models, animal simulation type models are evaluated for two other aspects of validity.

Face validity refers to phenomenological similarities between a model and the human condition. As originally proposed by McKinney and Bunney (1969), animal models of human mental illness have a high degree of face validity when (1) the model is produced by etiological factors known to produce the human disorder, (2) the model resembles the behavioral manifestations and symptoms of the human disorder, (3) the model has an underlying physiology similar to the human disorder, and (4) the model responds to therapeutic treatments known to be effective in human patients. How these criteria are evaluated and established in animal models of psychiatric disorders is discussed elsewhere in detail (Weiss & Kilts, 1998).

Construct validity refers to the theories linking inferred processes in an animal model to processes that are hypothesized to occur in the human disorder. In order to establish construct validity, a theory for understanding a process underlying a given psychiatric disorder is mapped or shown to be equivalent to the process being studied in the animal model (Sarter & Bruno, 2002). Due to concerns about characterizing the behavior of animals in terms of psychoanalytic constructs and related theories of human mental health, animal models now tend to focus on neurobiological processes as causes of psychiatric disorders. Chief among the advantages offered by the biological approach is that similarities between humans and animals are often homologous at physiological, cellular, and molecular levels due to shared phylogenetic histories.

Features that confer a high degree of validity for animal simulation type models are often undesirable for assay type drug screening tests. Examples include the typical delay in response onset for conventional antidepressant medications, or complex human etiological factors that are difficult and expensive to reproduce in animals. On the other hand, simulation type models that achieve all three aspects of validity may better identify substantively new drugs that differ from those used to establish the assay type model. Excessive reliance on assay type models may also increase the tendency to perpetuate in pharmacotherapies the same side effects as those produced by known medications.

The following section selectively illustrates how animal models are used to investigate the neurobiology of early life stress, novelty seeking, and specific aspects of psychostimulant drug abuse. Other models of developmental psychiatric disorders are summarized elsewhere in several wide-ranging surveys and informative publications (Andres, 2002; Higley, Hasert, Suomi, & Linnoila, 1991; Lipska & Weinberger, 2000; Newport, Stowe, & Nemeroff, 2002).

Neuroadaptations to Early Life Stress

Stressful experiences in adulthood have long been implicated in human drug-seeking behavior and relapse to dependence on psychostimulant drugs. Recent studies have likewise discovered associations between early life stress, drug use onset in children, and neuroadaptations that attenuate hypothalamic pituitary adrenal (HPA) hormone responses to stress (Moss, Vanyukov, Yao, & Kirillova, 1999). Acute stress exposure normally activates hypothalamic release of corticotropin releasing factor (CRF), which stimulates pituitary release of adreno-corticotropic hormone (ACTH), and thereby induces glucocorticoid secretion from the adrenal cortex (cortisol in humans and nonhuman primates; corticosterone in rodents). But chronic or repetitive exposure to stress invokes diverse mechanisms that collectively diminish glucocorticoid biosynthesis and release (Heim, Ehlert, & Hellhammer, 2000). In adulthood, for example, hypocortisolism is evident in people exposed to chronic job stress (Caplan, Cobb, & French, 1979), combat veterans and Holocaust survivors with post-traumatic stress disorder (Yehuda, 1998), and civilians subjected to warfare (Laor et al., 1994). Studies of children have also discovered diminished baseline cortisol concentrations associated with severe conduct disorder (Vanyukov et al., 1993), social deprivation (Carlson & Earls, 1997), and chronically stressful home environments evoked by a substance-abusing parent (Moss et al., 1999). These findings are taken as evidence that hypocortisolism as an aspect of underarousal promotes the development of deviant patterns of sensation-seeking behavior (Moss et al., 1999; Rosenblitt, Soler, Johnson, & Quadagno, 2001; Wang et al., 1997). From this point of view, psychostimulant drug use, risk-taking behavior, and novelty seeking are attempts to alleviate underarousal produced by neuroadaptations to chronic sources of stress.

Similar outcomes in development are produced by exposure of rats to brief repeated periods of human handling and maternal deprivation. Neonatal rats removed from the nest and temporarily deprived of nest-related maternal cues respond with acute behavioral and physiological markers of arousal (Hofer, 1996). When studied as adults, these rats then display diminished corticosterone and ACTH responses to various stressful conditions (Meaney et al., 1996). Diminished pituitary-adrenal hormone responses to stress are mediated in part by enhanced glucocorticoid negative-feedback resulting from increased gene expression for glucocorticoid receptors in the hippocampus (Meaney et al., 1996). This neuroadaptation does not affect baseline corticosterone levels in rats, and in this respect the rat model differs from chronically stressed children who typically exhibit flattened circadian rhythms and diminished baseline levels of cortisol (Gunnar & Vazquez, 2001). Nevertheless, rat pups exposed to early intermittent deprivation respond with diminished stress-levels of corticosterone and ACTH, and more rapidly recover to pre-stress levels of corticosterone relative to non-deprived rats (Meaney et al., 1996).

In addition to diminished stress levels of corticosterone, rat pups exposed to intermittent deprivation subsequently exhibit attenuated place preference conditioning for low but not high doses of amphetamine compared to non-deprived rats (Campbell & Spear, 1999). This finding concurs with numerous reports that diminished stress levels of corticosterone achieved by surgical adrenalectomy or drugs that block glucocorticoid biosynthesis decrease sensitivity to cocaine and other psychostimulants (Marinelli & Piazza, 2002). Despite or because of diminished sensitivity to low doses of psychostimulant drugs, rat pups exposed to intermittent deprivation subsequently self-administer more cocaine at mid- but not low- or high-level doses relative to non-deprived rats (Kosten, Miserendino, & Kehoe, 2000; Matthews, Robbins, Everitt, & Caine, 1999). Intermittently deprived rats also exhibit diminished anxiety and more novelty seeking behavior on the elevated plus-maze, dark-light tests, shuttle-box tests, and the nose-poke hole board (Fernandez-Teruel et al., 2002). These findings are of interest because novelty seeking and psychostimulant drug administration both activate dopamine reward pathways in mesocorticolimbic brain regions (Bardo, Donohew, & Harrington, 1996).

Despite the accumulation of data in rodents, studies of monkeys have failed to find evidence that anti-glucocorticoid treatments exert dose-dependent effects on self-administration of various doses of cocaine (Broadbear, Winger, & Woods, 1999). Anti-glucocorticoid treatments in humans have likewise failed to temper the behavioral, physiological, or subjective effects of psychostimulants in adult human patients and healthy volunteers (Kosten, Oliveto, Sevarino, Gonsai, & Feingold, 2002; Wachtel, Charnot, & de Wit, 2001; Ward, Collins, Haney, Foltin, & Fischman, 1999). These discrepancies may reflect differences in the timing or duration of treatments used to manipulate glucocorticoid levels in humans and monkeys relative to those used in rats (Marinelli & Piazza, 2002). Apart from these issues, there are other concerns resulting from indications that in humans (Volkow & Fowler, 2000) and monkeys (Porrino et al., 2002) drug reward processing generally involves prefrontal cortical brain systems that are not homologous with those found in rodents (Preuss, 1995). Recently, we discovered that intermittent deprivation induces in monkeys long-lasting changes that resemble those found in rats. These and related studies are briefly summarized below.

Maternal Deprivation in Nonhuman Primates

Aside from a limited number of reports on inherited variation in autonomic activity and cerebrospinal fluid monoamine levels, primate research on early life stress has generally focused on severe chronic forms of maternal deprivation (Lyons, 2000). Rhesus macaque monkeys raised without mothers exhibit exaggerated neuroendocrine responses to stress (Chapmoux, Coe, Schanberg, Kuhn, & Suomi, 1989), altered regulation of autonomic activity (Mason, Mendoza, & Moberg, 1991), changes in learning and memory performance (Beauchamp, Gluck, Fouty, & Lewis, 1991; Capitanio & Mason, 2000), fragmented sleep patterns (Kaemingk & Reite, 1987), depression-like behavior (Kraemer, 1997), and excessive consumption of alcohol (Fahlke et al., 2000). Ecologically informed research on maternal availability has likewise identified untoward effects during postnatal development. Bonnet macaque monkeys raised by mothers in variable foraging demand conditions are impaired in social and emotional development (Andrews & Rosenblum, 1994; Rosenblum & Andrews, 1994). These same monkeys exhibit in early adulthood elevated cerebrospinal fluid levels of monoamines, somatostatin, and CRF (Coplan et al., 1996; Coplan et al., 1998).

Recently, we started a series of studies designed to assess less severe forms of early intermittent deprivation. Squirrel monkeys were randomized to three conditions that modified maternal availability. In one condition on five occasions between ten and twenty-one weeks of age, monkeys were periodically separated from groups each comprised of three or four mother-infant pairs (N = 6 male and 7 female infants). Intermittent separations reliably provoke repetitive distress peep-calls, locomotor agitation, and acute elevations in the stress hormone cortisol with baseline levels of these measures restored soon after each social reunion (Coe, Glass, Wiener, & Levine, 1983; Hennessy, 1986). In two other postnatal conditions differences in maternal availability were produced by manipulating the effort required to find food (Lyons, Kim, Schatzberg, & Levine, 1998). Body weights and amounts of food consumed by monkeys maintained continuously for twelve weeks in the high foraging demand condition (N = 7 male and 6 female infants) did not differ significantly from matched controls (N = 7 males and 6 females). But monkey mothers in the high-demand condition spent 60% more time foraging for food, stopped carrying their infant at earlier ages, and infants displayed modest prolonged increases in cortisol levels throughout the twelve-week high-demand foraging condition (Lyons et al., 1998).

Following completion of each postnatal condition at twenty-one weeks of age, all mothers were removed from natal groups after weaning at thirty-six weeks. At this stage of life span development, squirrel monkeys are no longer reliant on maternal care. Puberty occurs at two to three years of age, and the squirrel monkey life span is approximately twenty-one years.

As described elsewhere in greater detail (Lyons, Martel, Levine, Risch, & Schatzberg, 1999), monkeys exposed to intermittent deprivation subsequently responded to the removal of all mothers after weaning with smaller increases in cortisol levels and fewer distress peep-calls. Four years later in early adulthood, all monkeys were administered on two occasions an intravenous injection of CRF preceded by either exogenous cortisol or placebo pretreatment. The intermittently deprived monkeys most clearly showed signs of enhanced glucocorticoid negative-feedback sensitivity as determined by suppression of CRF-stimulated secretion of ACTH induced by pretreatment with exogenous cortisol relative to placebo (Lyons, Yang, Mobley, Nickerson, & Schatzberg, 2000).

The hippocampus plays a well-known role in regulating the HPA-axis stress response (Jacobson & Sapolsky, 1991), but other brain regions are also involved, including the prefrontal cortex (Sullivan & Gratton, 2002). Recently, we discovered that both types of receptor (glucocorticoid and mineralocorticoid) for cortisol are expressed throughout the hippocampus and squirrel monkey prefrontal cortex (Patel et al., 2000). Using magnetic resonance imaging procedures specifically designed for squirrel monkeys, we failed to find evidence for rearing-related differences in adult hippocampal volumes (Lyons, Yang, Sawyer-Glover, Moseley, & Schatzberg, 2001). But right ventromedial prefrontal volumes were 8–14% larger in the monkeys exposed to brief intermittent deprivation (Lyons, Afarian, Schatzberg, Sawyer-Glover, & Moseley, 2002). This effect size is similar to that reported in now classic studies of environmental enrichment and cortical thickness in rats (Rosenzweig & Bennett, 1996). Experience-dependent prefrontal adaptations may contribute to enhanced glucocorticoid negative-feedback regulation of the HPA-axis response if larger prefrontal volumes confer more of both types of receptor for cortisol in this region of the brain (Lyons et al., 2002).

The prefrontal cortex is also involved in novelty detection, attention, working memory, response inhibition, and executive functions. Evidence suggests that ventromedial subregions mediate instrumental goal-directed behavior governed by knowledge of learned contingencies between actions and desired rewards (Roberts & Wallis, 2000). This hypothesis is consistent with electrophysiological studies of reward processing in monkeys (Rolls, 2000; Schultz, Tremblay, & Hollerman, 2000), preliminary evidence that prefrontal lesions impair contingency reward learning in rats (Balleine & Dickinson, 1998), and neuroimaging studies that demonstrate orbitofrontal involvement in human drug addictions (Volkow & Fowler, 2000).

On food-reward learning and memory tests with a series of spatial reversals, we found that intermittently deprived monkeys exhibit perseverative tendencies and continue to select previously rewarded but incorrect locations after each spatial reversal (Lyons & Schatzberg, 2003). As indicated above, the intermittently deprived monkeys also have larger right ventromedial prefrontal cortical volumes (Lyons et al., 2002). Right prefrontal regions in humans mediate inhibitory control of behavior (Garavan, Ross, & Stein, 1999), negative emotion (Canli, Desmond, Zhao, Glover, & Gabrieli, 1998; Davidson, Pizzagalli, Nitschke, & Putnam, 2002), social withdrawal (Fox et al., 1995), and sensitivity to stressful conditions (Kalin, Larson, Shelton, & Davidson, 1998; Sullivan & Gratton, 2002; Wittling & Pfluger, 1990). It is therefore intriguing that early intermittent deprivation elicits a robust stress response, then subsequently leads later in life to diminished anxiety, blunted cortisol stress levels, enhanced glucocorticoid negative-feedback sensitivity, and differences in prefrontal correlates of reward learning and cognitive control.

Given these findings, we recently established another study cohort of monkeys exposed to early intermittent deprivation. Squirrel monkeys randomized to the deprivation condition were separated from four established natal groups once a week for ten total sessions each lasting one hour in duration (n = 4 males and 7 females).

In the non-deprived condition, monkeys were maintained in three undisturbed natal groups each composed of three mother-infant pairs (N = 2 male and 7 female infants). Following completion of these conditions at twenty-seven weeks of age, all monkeys were maintained in natal groups under standard laboratory conditions.

The monkeys were tested at thirty-two weeks of age for rearing-related differences in novelty seeking, baseline levels of plasma cortisol and ACTH, and changes in plasma levels of these hormones evoked by the novelty tests. Plasma levels of cortisol and ACTH were significantly lower at baseline and after the first in a series of novelty tests for the intermittently deprived monkeys relative to non-deprived controls (Parker, Buckmaster, Schatzberg & Lyons, 2003). Diminished cortisol and ACTH responses to novelty in the intermittently deprived monkeys are consistent with diminished stress levels of corticosterone and ACTH in previous studies of intermittently deprived rats (see above). Low baseline levels of cortisol in monkeys exposed to intermittent deprivation likewise concur with reports of hypocortisolism at baseline in children exposed to chronic stress (Carlson & Earls, 1997; Gunnar & Vazquez, 2001; Moss et al., 1999). According to a recent review (Gunnar & Vazquez, 2001), baseline hypocortisolism has been reported in only one other animal model. Our finding that low baseline levels of cortisol in monkeys are associated with low levels of ACTH suggests that central brain mechanisms above the level of the pituitary produce in monkeys a chronic hypocortisolemic state.

The behavior of deprived and non-deprived monkeys did not differ at first during novelty tests, but over repeated involuntary exposures to the novel cage test, intermittently deprived monkeys more rapidly moved away from their mother and made more exploratory contacts with unfamiliar test objects (Parker et al., 2003). Rodent research indicates that forced involuntary exposure to novelty is stressful and may not correspond with performance on tests that assess voluntary novelty seeking behavior. Therefore, we now are investigating in adolescent monkeys voluntary novelty seeking and deprivation-related differences in sensitivity to cocaine. Novelty seeking and drug use onset are common during adolescence in many mammalian species (Spear, 2000). Based on previous findings in rats, our hypothesis predicts that early intermittent deprivation enhances novelty seeking and selectively impairs sensitivity to low but not high doses of cocaine.

Utility and Limitations of Animal Research

Many key symptoms and manifestations of human psychiatric disorders in children cannot be modeled directly in animals. Feelings of worthlessness, impaired verbal recall, and suicidal ideation are obvious examples. The basic core components of contemporary theories for understanding the processes that mediate such symptoms can often be successfully modeled in animals, but doing so runs the risk of modeling flawed theories and faulty theoretical constructs.

Another limitation of animal research is the tendency to isolate and focus on single causal factors for a given disorder. In a few cases one causal factor can perhaps be clearly identified, but often the etiology of psychiatric disorders involves a nexus of proximal and distal risk factors over life span development. Attempts to construct animal models of psychiatric disorders in children based solely on single causal factors may, in fact, be misguided if no single factor alone is sufficiently potent to trigger the disorder in otherwise risk-free individuals. Animal studies that simultaneously model multiple etiological risk factors are now beginning to emerge in developmental neuroscience (for example, Lipska & Weinberger, 2000), and are clearly long overdue.

Beyond the complexities of etiology there are other basic concerns. Prefrontal cortical enlargement and the elaboration of complex cognitive functions over the course of human evolution provide a case in point. The difficulty stems from problems in identifying homologous prefrontal brain regions in human and nonhuman animals (Preuss, 1995).

Despite these and other important limitations, animal research continues to offer crucial opportunities for improving our understanding and treatment of human psychiatric disorders. Prospective longitudinal studies of development are easier to complete in animals because their life span is far shorter than in humans. Carefully controlled animal studies are conducted without the confounds that commonly plague clinical studies of children, such as medical comorbidities and medication effects. Animal research also provides brain tissue of the highest possible quality for cellular and molecular studies. This is essential because opportunities for testing hypotheses with human brain tissue are far less prevalent than in other fields of medicine where biopsies are routinely performed.

Discoveries made in animals have proven useful in generating, testing, and extending current theories and pharmacotherapies for adult patients with psychiatric disorders. Child psychiatrists have just begun to tap the potential of animal models to illuminate disordered brain-behavior relationships and the effects of psychotropic drugs. Such efforts are important because millions of children are prescribed medications designed and tested for use in adults. Psychotropic medications act on brain systems that normally undergo significant developmental changes in the first two decades of life. Interactions between drugs and developing brain systems are important considerations in assessing the efficacy and safety of pharmacotherapies in children, adolescents, and adults. For ethical, methodological, and practical reasons, it is impossible to achieve an adequate understanding of drug effects on developing brain systems based solely on experiments with humans. Animal research will no doubt contribute to future advances in this new area of child and adolescent psychiatry.

References

Altmann, J. (1974). Observational study of behaviour: Sampling methods. *Behaviour, 49*, 227–267.

Anderson, C. O., & Mason, W. A. (1978). Competitive social strategies in groups of deprived and experienced rhesus monkeys. *Developmental Psychobiology, 11*(4), 289–299.

Andres, C. (2002). Molecular genetics and animal models in autistic disorder. *Brain Research Bulletin, 57*(1), 109–119.

Andrews, M. W., & Rosenblum, L. A. (1994). The development of affiliative and agonistic social patterns in differentially reared monkeys. *Child Development, 65,* 1398–1404.

Balleine, B. W., & Dickinson, A. (1998). Goal-directed instrumental action: Contingency and incentive learning and their cortical substrates. *Neuropharmacology, 37*(4–5), 407–419.

Bardo, M. T., Donohew, R. L., & Harrington, N. G. (1996). Psychobiology of novelty seeking and drug seeking behavior. *Behavioural Brain Research, 77*(1–2), 23–43.

Barlow, G. W. (1977). Modal action patterns. In T. A. Sebeok (Ed.), *How Animals Communicate* (pp. 98–134). Bloomington, IN: Indiana University Press.

Beauchamp, A. J., Gluck, J. P., Fouty, H. E., & Lewis, M. H. (1991). Associative processes in differentially reared rhesus monkeys (*Macaca mulatta*): Blocking. *Developmental Psychobiology, 24,* 175–189.

Belsky, J., Steinberg, L., & Draper, P. (1991). Childhood experience, interpersonal development, and reproductive strategy: An evolutionary theory of socialization. *Child Development, 62*(4), 647–670.

Blanchard, R. J., Yudko, E. B., Rodgers, R. J., & Blanchard, D. C. (1993). Defense system psychopharmacology: An ethological approach to the pharmacology of fear and anxiety. *Behavioural Brain Research, 58*(1–2), 155–165.

Bowlby, J. (1969). *Attachment and loss, vol. 1: Attachment.* London: Hogarth.

Broadbear, J. H., Winger, G., & Woods, J. H. (1999). Cocaine-reinforced responding in rhesus monkeys: Pharmacological attenuation of the hypothalamic-pituitary-adrenal axis response. *Journal of Pharmacology & Experimental Therapeutics, 290*(3), 1347–1355.

Campbell, J., & Spear, L. P. (1999). Effects of early handling on amphetamine-induced loco-motor activation and conditioned place preference in the adult rat. *Psychopharmacology, 143*(2), 183–189.

Canli, T., Desmond, J. E., Zhao, Z., Glover, G., & Gabrieli, J. D. (1998). Hemispheric asymmetry for emotional stimuli detected with fMRI. *Neuroreport, 9*(14), 3233–3239.

Capitanio, J. P., & Mason, W. A. (2000). Cognitive style: Problem solving by rhesus macaques (*Macaca mulatta*) reared with living or inanimate substitute mothers. *Journal of Comparative Psychology, 114,* 115–125.

Caplan, R. D., Cobb, S., & French, J. R., Jr. (1979). White collar work load and cortisol: Disruption of a circadian rhythm by job stress? *Journal of Psychosomatic Research, 23*(3), 181–192.

Carlson, M., & Earls, F. (1997). Psychological and neuroendocrinological sequelae of early social deprivation in institutionalized children in Romania. *Annals of the New York Academy of Sciences, 807,* 419–428.

Chapmoux, M., Coe, C. L., Schanberg, S., Kuhn, C., & Suomi, S. J. (1989). Hormonal effects of early rearing conditions in the infant rhesus monkey. *American Journal of Primatology, 19,* 111–117.

Coe, C. L., Glass, J. C., Wiener, S. G., & Levine, S. (1983). Behavioral, but not physiological, adaptation to repeated separation in mother and infant primates. *Psychoneuroendocrinology, 8*(4), 401–409.

Coplan, J. D., Andrews, M. W., Rosenblum, L. A., Owens, M. J., Friedman, S., Gorman, J. M., et al. (1996). Persistent elevations of cerebrospinal fluid concentrations of corticotropin-releasing factor in adult nonhuman primates exposed to early-life stressors: Implications for the pathophysiology of mood and anxiety disorders. *Proceedings of the National Academy of Science, 93,* 1619–1623.

Coplan, J. D., Trost, R. C., Owens, M. J., Cooper, T. B., Gorman, J. M., Nemeroff, C. B., et al. (1998). Cerebrospinal fluid concentrations of somatostatin and biogenic amines in grown primates reared by mothers exposed to manipulated foraging conditions. *Archives of General Psychiatry, 55,* 473–477.

Davidson, R. J., Pizzagalli, D., Nitschke, J. B., & Putnam, K. (2002). Depression: Perspectives from affective neuroscience. *Annual Review of Psychology, 53,* 545–574.

Fahlke, C., Lorenz, J. G., Long, J., Champoux, M., Suomi, S. J., & Higley, J. D. (2000). Rearing experiences and stress-induced plasma cortisol as early risk factors for excessive alcohol consumption in nonhuman primates. *Alcoholism-Clinical and Experimental Research, 24,* 644–650.

Fernandez-Teruel, A., Gimenez-Llort, L., Escorihuela, R. M., Gil, L., Aguilar, R., Steimer, T., et al. (2002). Early-life handling stimulation and environmental enrichment: Are some of their effects mediated by similar neural mechanisms? *Pharmacology, Biochemistry & Behaviour, 73*(1), 233–245.

Fox, N. A., Rubin, K. H., Calkins, S. D., Marshall, T. R., Coplan, R. J., Porges, S. W., et al. (1995). Frontal activation asymmetry and social competence at four years of age. *Child Development, 66*(6), 1770–1784.

Garavan, H., Ross, T. J., & Stein, E. A. (1999). Right hemispheric dominance of inhibitory control: An event-related functional MRI study. *Proceedings of the National Academy of Science of the United States of America, 96*(14), 8301–8306.

Gunnar, M. R., & Vazquez, D. M. (2001). Low cortisol and a flattening of expected daytime rhythm: Potential indices of risk in human development. *Development & Psychopathology, 13*(3), 515–538.

Hand, J. L. (1985). Egalitarian resolution of social conflicts: A study of pair-bonded gulls in nest duty and feeding contexts. *Zeitschrift fur Tierpsychologie, 70,* 123–147.

Harlow, H. F., & Zimmerman, R. R. (1959). Affectional responses in the infant monkey. *Science, 130,* 421–432.

Harper, L. V. (1972). The transition from filial to reproductive function of "coitus-related" responses in young guinea pigs. *Developmental Psychobiology, 5*(1), 21–34.

Heim, C., Ehlert, U., & Hellhammer, D. H. (2000). The potential role of hypocortisolism in the pathophysiology of stress-related bodily disorders. *Psychoneuroendocrinology, 25*(1), 1–35.

Hennessy, M. B. (1986). Multiple, brief maternal separations in the squirrel monkey: Changes in hormonal and behavioral responsiveness. *Physiology & Behavior, 36*(2), 245–250.

Higley, J. D., Hasert, M. F., Suomi, S. J., & Linnoila, M. (1991). Nonhuman primate model of alcohol abuse: Effects of early experience, personality, and stress on alcohol consumption. *Proceedings of the National Academy of Sciences of the United States of America, 88*(16), 7261–7265.

Hinde, R. A. (1966). *Animal behaviour. A synthesis of ethology and comparative psychology.* New York: McGraw-Hill.

Hofer, M. A. (1996). On the nature and consequences of early loss. *Psychosomatic Medicine, 58*(6), 570–581.

Jacobson, L., & Sapolsky, R. (1991). The role of the hippocampus in feedback regulation of the hypothalamic-pituitary-adrenocortical axis. *Endocrine Reviews, 12*(2), 118–134.

Kalin, N. H., Larson, C., Shelton, S. E., & Davidson, R. J. (1998). Asymmetric frontal brain activity, cortisol, and behavior associated with fearful temperament in rhesus monkeys. *Behavioral Neuroscience, 112*(2), 286–292.

Kaemingk, K., & Reite, M. (1987). Social environment and nocturnal sleep: Studies in peer-reared monkeys. *Sleep, 10,* 542–550.

Katz, L. C., & Shatz, C. J. (1996). Synaptic activity and the construction of cortical circuits. *Science, 274*(5290), 1133–1138.

Kelly, J. P., Wrynn, A. S., & Leonard, B. E. (1997). The olfactory bulbectomized rat as a model of depression: An update. *Pharmacology & Therapeutics, 74*(3), 299–316.

Kosten, T. A., Miserendino, M. J., & Kehoe, P. (2000). Enhanced acquisition of cocaine self-administration in adult rats with neonatal isolation stress experience. *Brain Research, 875*(1–2), 44–50.

Kosten, T. R., Oliveto, A., Sevarino, K. A., Gonsai, K., & Feingold, A. (2002). Ketoconazole increases cocaine and opioid use in methadone maintained patients. *Drug & Alcohol Dependence, 66*(2), 173–180.

Kraemer, G. W. (1997). Psychobiology of early social attachment in rhesus monkeys. Clinical implications. *Annals of the New York Academy of Science, 807,* 401–418.

Krsiak, M. (1991). Ethopharmacology: A historical perspective. *Neuroscience & Biobehavioral Reviews, 15*(4), 439–445.

Laor, N., Barber, Y., Selman, A., Schujovizky, A., Wolmer, L., Laron, Z., et al. (1994). Impact of the Gulf War on the anxiety, cortisol, and growth hormone levels of Israeli civilians. *American Journal of Psychiatry, 151*(1), 71–75.

Lipska, B. K., & Weinberger, D. R. (2000). To model a psychiatric disorder in animals: Schizophrenia as a reality test. *Neuropsychopharmacology, 23*(3), 223–239.

Liu, D., Diorio, J., Tannenbaum, B., Caldji, C., Francis, D., Freedman, A., et al. (1997). Maternal care, hippocampal glucocorticoid receptors, and hypothalamic-pituitary-adrenal responses to stress. *Science, 277*(5332), 1659–1662.

Lorenz, K. Z. (1950). The comparative method in studying innate behaviour patterns. *Symposium of the Society for Experimental Biology, 4,* 221–268.

Lyons, D. M. (2000). Primate models, overview. In Fink, G. (Ed.) *Encyclopedia of Stress, Volume 3* (pp. 236–241). San Diego, CA: Academic Press.

Lyons, D. M., Afarian, H., Schatzberg, A. F., Sawyer-Glover, A., & Moseley, M. E. (2002). Experience-dependent asymmetric variation in primate prefrontal morphology. *Behavioural Brain Research, 136*(1), 51–59.

Lyons, D. M., Kim, S., Schatzberg, A. F., & Levine, S. (1998). Postnatal foraging demands alter adrenocortical activity and psychosocial development. *Developmental Psychobiology, 32*(4), 285–291.

Lyons, D. M., Martel, F. L., Levine, S., Risch, N. J., & Schatzberg, A. F. (1999). Postnatal experiences and genetic effects on squirrel monkey social affinities and emotional distress. *Hormones & Behavior, 36*(3), 266–275.

Lyons, D. M., & Schatzberg, A. F. (2003). Early maternal availability and prefrontal correlates of reward-related memory. *Neurobiology of Learning and Memory, 80,* 97–104.

Lyons, D. M., Yang, C., Mobley, B. W., Nickerson, J. T., & Schatzberg, A. F. (2000). Early environmental regulation of glucocorticoid feedback sensitivity in young adult monkeys. *Journal of Neuroendocrinology, 12*(8), 723–728.

Lyons, D. M., Yang, C., Sawyer-Glover, A. M., Moseley, M. E., & Schatzberg, A. F. (2001). Early life stress and inherited variation in monkey hippocampal volumes. *Archives of General Psychiatry, 58*(12), 1145–1151.

Marinelli, M., & Piazza, P. V. (2002). Interaction between glucocorticoid hormones, stress, and psychostimulant drugs. *European Journal of Neuroscience, 16*, 387–394.

Mason, W. A., Mendoza, S. P., & Moberg, G. P. (1991). Persistent effects of early social experience on physiological responsiveness. In Ehara, A., Kimura, R., Takenaka, O., & Iwamoto, M. (Eds.), *Primatology Today* (pp. 469–471). New York: Elsevier.

Matthews, K., Robbins, T. W., Everitt, B. J., & Caine, S. B. (1999). Repeated neonatal maternal separation alters intravenous cocaine self-administration in adult rats. *Psychopharmacology, 141*(2), 123–134.

McKinney, W. T., Jr., & Bunney, W. E., Jr. (1969). Animal model of depression. I. Review of evidence: Implications for research. *Archives of General Psychiatry, 21*(2), 240–248.

Meaney, M. J., Diorio, J., Francis, D., Widdowson, J., LaPlante, P., Caldji, et al. (1996). Early environmental regulation of forebrain glucocorticoid receptor gene expression: Implications for adrenocortical responses to stress. *Developmental Neuroscience, 18*(1–2), 49–72.

Moore, D. R. (2002). Auditory development and the role of experience. *British Medical Bulletin, 63*, 171–181.

Moss, H. B., Vanyukov, M., Yao, J. K., & Kirillova, G. P. (1999). Salivary cortisol responses in prepubertal boys: The effects of parental substance abuse and association with drug use behavior during adolescence. *Biological Psychiatry, 45*(10), 1293–1299.

Newport, D. J., Stowe, Z. N., & Nemeroff, C. B. (2002). Parental depression: Animal models of an adverse life event. *American Journal of Psychiatry, 159*(8), 1265–1283.

Parmigiani, S., Ferrari, P. F., & Palanza, P. (1998). An evolutionary approach to behavioral pharmacology: Using drugs to understand proximate and ultimate mechanisms of different forms of aggression in mice. *Neuroscience & Biobehavioral Reviews, 23*(2), 143–153.

Parker, K. J., Buckmaster, C. L., Schatzberg, A. F., & Lyons, D. M. (2003). Early environmental programming of HPA-axis physiology and emotional reactivity. Manuscript submitted for publication.

Patel, P. D., Lopez, J. F., Lyons, D. M., Burke, S., Wallace, M., & Schatzberg, A. F. (2000). Glucocorticoid and mineralocorticoid receptor mRNA expression in squirrel monkey brain. *Journal of Psychiatric Research, 34*(6), 383–392.

Porrino, L. J., Lyons, D., Miller, M. D., Smith, H. R., Friedman, D. P., Daunais, et al. (2002). Metabolic mapping of the effects of cocaine during the initial phases of self-administration in the nonhuman primate. *Journal of Neuroscience, 22*(17), 7687–7694.

Preuss, T. M. (1995). Do rats have prefrontal cortex? The Rose-Woolsey-Akert program reconsidered. *Journal of Cognitive Neuroscience, 7*(1), 1–24.

Purton, A. C. (1978). Ethological categories of behaviour and some consequences of their conflation. *Animal Behaviour, 26*, 653–670.

Roberts, A. C., & Wallis, J. D. (2000). Inhibitory control and affective processing in the prefrontal cortex: Neuropsychological studies in the common marmoset. *Cerebral Cortex, 10*(3), 252–262.

Rodgers, R. J. (1997). Animal models of 'anxiety': Where next? *Behavioural Pharmacology, 8*(6–7), 477–496, discussion 497–504.

Rolls, E. T. (2000). The orbitofrontal cortex and reward. *Annual Review of Psychology, 51*, 599–630.

Rosenblitt, J. C., Soler, H., Johnson, S. E., & Quadagno, D. M. (2001). Sensation seeking and hormones in men and women: Exploring the link. *Hormones & Behavior, 40*(3), 396–402.

Rosenblum, L. A., & Andrews, M. W. (1994). Influences of environmental demand on maternal behavior and infant development. *Acta Paediatrica Supplement, 397,* 57–63.

Rosenzweig, M. R., & Bennett, E. L. (1996). Psychobiology of plasticity: Effects of training and experience on brain and behavior. *Behavioural Brain Research, 78*(1), 57–65.

Sarter, M., & Bruno, J. P. (2002). Animal models in biological psychiatry. In H. D'haenen, J. A. den Boer & P. Willner (Eds.), *Biological Psychiatry* (pp. 1–8). New York: Wiley.

Schultz, W., Tremblay, L., & Hollerman, J. R. (2000). Reward processing in primate orbitofrontal cortex and basal ganglia. *Cerebral Cortex, 10*(3), 272–284.

Seckl, J. R. (2001). Glucocorticoid programming of the fetus: Adult phenotypes and molecular mechanisms. *Molecular & Cellular Endocrinology, 185,* 61–71.

Spear, L. P. (2000). The adolescent brain and age-related behavioral manifestations. *Neuroscience & Biobehavioral Reviews, 24*(4), 417–463.

Stamps, J., Kus, B., Clark, A., & Arrowood, P. (1990). Social relationships of fledgling budgerigars, Melopsitticus undulatus. *Animal Behaviour, 40,* 688–700.

Sullivan, R. M., & Gratton, A. (2002). Prefrontal cortical regulation of hypothalamic-pituitary-adrenal function in the rat and implications for psychopathology: Side matters. *Psychoneuroendocrinology, 27*(1–2), 99–114.

Teicher, M. H., Andersen, S. L., Polcari, A., Anderson, C. M., & Navalta, C. P. (2002). Developmental neurobiology of childhood stress and trauma. *Psychiatric Clinics of North America, 25*(2), 397–426.

Thorpe, W. H. (1979). *The origins and rise of ethology.* London: Heinemann.

Tinbergen, N. (1951). *The study of instinct.* Oxford: Oxford University Press.

Vanyukov, M. M., Moss, H. B., Plail, J. A., Blackson, T., Mezzich, A. C., & Tarter, R. E. (1993). Antisocial symptoms in preadolescent boys and in their parents: Associations with cortisol. *Psychiatry Research, 46*(1), 9–17.

Volkow, N. D., & Fowler, J. S. (2000). Addiction, a disease of compulsion and drive: Involvement of the orbitofrontal cortex. *Cerebral Cortex, 10*(3), 318–325.

Wachtel, S. R., Charnot, A., & de Wit, H. (2001). Acute hydrocortisone administration does not affect subjective responses to d-amphetamine in humans. *Psychopharmacologia, 153*(3), 380–388.

Wang, S., Mason, J., Charney, D., Yehuda, R., Riney, S., & Southwick, S. (1997). Relationships between hormonal profile and novelty seeking in combat-related post-traumatic stress disorder. *Biological Psychiatry, 41*(2), 145–151.

Ward, A. S., Collins, E. D., Haney, M., Foltin, R. W., & Fischman, M. W. (1999). Blockade of cocaine-induced increases in adrenocorticotrophic hormone and cortisol does not attenuate the subjective effects of smoked cocaine in humans. *Behavioural Pharmacology, 10*(5), 523–529.

Weiss, J. M., & Kilts, C. D. (1998). Animal models of depression and schizophrenia. In A. F. Schatzberg & C. B. Nemeroff (Eds.), *Textbook of Psychopharmacology* (2nd ed., pp. 89–131). Washington, DC: American Psychiatric Press.

Wittling, W., & Pfluger, M. (1990). Neuroendocrine hemisphere asymmetries: Salivary cortisol secretion during lateralized viewing of emotion-related and neutral films. *Brain Cognition, 14*(2), 243–265.

Yehuda, R. (1998). Psychoneuroendocrinology of post-traumatic stress disorder. *Psychiatric Clinics of North America, 21*(2), 359–379.

CHAPTER THREE

THE SOCIAL ENVIRONMENT

Niranjan S. Karnik, M.D., Ph.D.

The social environment encompasses a wide array of social, cultural, and environmental factors. From immediate influences such as the family and friends, to institutions such as schools and welfare agencies, the range and scope of the social environment varies significantly for each child. The social environment, in this regard, can be either a precipitant or maintaining factor of psychopathology, and has great potential as treatment or ameliorator. In several respects, the social environment is essential to understanding children, and cannot be divorced from the life of the child.

While many clinicians would agree that the social environment around children and adolescents is critical for healthy development, the attention to this area of scholarship has often been fragmented and cursory especially in light of the recent and exciting developments in molecular genetics and psychopharmacology that have transformed the field of child and adolescent psychiatry. Nevertheless, attention to social and behavioral interventions will continue to play a lasting role in the treatment of children with psychiatric and pediatric illnesses because social factors consistently and regularly influence and are affected by juveniles and their families.

Understanding Social Environment

Information about the social environment needs to be obtained in depth. Taking a simple, traditional social history is not sufficient to understand the social environment around the child. The clinician may need to delve into details of who the child spends time with, where the child spends his or her days, what the child does for recreation, who constitutes the child's peer group, how the child provides for his or her basic needs, and many other facets of life. Collateral information from parents, welfare authorities, teachers, and relatives may be required to gain a better picture of the social environment around the child.

The goal of this chapter is to provide a clinical and research framework for understanding the social environment, and to highlight key developments from the research literature from across the social and behavioral sciences that influence child and adolescent psychiatry. In constructing this chapter, special attention is given to those developments that might be interesting to the practitioner in the field, and particularly those areas that have implications for interventions in youths. As such, this chapter also provides the basic science knowledge that underpins the later chapters on sociotherapy.

Models for Conceptualizing the Social Environment

Psychiatry and psychology have struggled with how best to account for the social environment. Freud, Erickson, and Piaget all considered aspects of the social environment in establishing their theories of human development. Although they knew that the social environment played a significant role, none of these major theorists of the mind attempted to theorize the social space per se. Instead, they focused on individual pieces of this environment (mother, family, or peers) and looked at how this one factor affected the individual. In light of this, it is important to turn to another set of sciences—those of sociology and social psychology—to better comprehend the social environment.

Urie Bronfenbrenner (1979) is among the most widely known of theorists of the social environment. He divided the social environment into three spheres. The microsystem includes the immediate family, peers, and local social institutions. A step further out from this level leads to the mesosystem in which he placed larger social institutions and broader cultural influences. Finally, there is the macrosystem which includes the global and internal culture, as well as geopolitical events. Bronfenbrenner recognized that many social forces move between and among these levels and he was quite cognizant of the limitations of such a theory.

Along similar lines, Lev Vygotsky (1978) proposed the idea of the zone of proximal development, which he theorized as a time period during which children could be socialized given adequate social interactions. Like Bronfenbrenner, he saw children as situated in multiple spheres of influence with family being closer than other social institutions. Vygotsky's theories stimulated powerful movements within the field of the sociology of education and school-based studies. It occurred in concert with the social constructivist movement within the social sciences, which sought to understand how social forces shape behavior and development.

There are numerous other models that try to capture and conceptualize the social environment. These models all provide useful theories on the ways that the social environment operates and how it affects the lives of children. Nevertheless, the pragmatic value of these models in everyday clinical practice is limited. The ability to take a social and individual history that captures the breadth and scope of these models is unlikely. To make sense of the mass of literature and information, this chapter utilizes a clinical approach that divides the social environment into the domains of the family, peer groups and subcultures, the school, mass media, and welfare institutions. These areas have been selected based on their relationship to the clinical sphere, and the high probability that practitioners will have to address questions regarding these social spheres and their relationship to the child or adolescent. In addition, the domains outlined have significant overlaps with later chapters in this volume on family therapy, preventive interventions, group interventions, self-help groups, and environmental manipulation.

Social Science Methods

The social sciences roughly divide into two broad methodological domains. The quantitative sciences of sociology, demography, and social psychology all make use of empirical data. They generally use existing theories to try to test hypotheses. These techniques often mirror those used in the medical and behavioral sciences in that they often use multivariate regression models, analysis of variance (ANOVA), or order advanced statistical techniques. Although sociologists often make use of survey or questionnaires to test their questions, demographers rely on population data to examine the ways that broad segments of society change. Finally, social psychologists have generally favored experimental testing of social and behavioral experience in the laboratory environment.

The qualitative methods of the social sciences are likely less familiar to readers. Anthropology and field sociology make use of ethnography. This method relies on participant-observation in a single or small number of locales. This places the investigator in a role of directly observing social activity or participating. Such methods have extremely high validity in that they describe the particular social space in significant detail. They also have the powerful potential to be theory generating and to raise new questions from the ground up. In addition, more humanistic sociology and cultural studies make use of interpretive strategies that study cultural productions or artifacts (Denzin, 1997; Denzin & Lincoln, 2000; Grossberg, Nelson, & Treichler, 1992; Treichler, Kramarae, & Stafford, 1985). Such methods, for example, try to look at embedded meanings in writing, literature, art, television, movies or other cultural processes. As with other qualitative techniques, the reliability of these methods may not be high, but their ability to raise important new questions and to explore new avenues for research can be very beneficial.

The Family

The word *family* has its origins in the Latin term *familia*, which means *household*. In many respects, this is a useful way to consider the family. The family is not a fixed object, but instead generally constitutes the adults that form the nucleus around the child and have responsibility to shape the child into a productive member of society. Variations as to what the family around a given children constitutes can vary significantly from the traditional two parents to a grandmother or older sibling. Given the numerous possibilities, practitioners should always inquire about the composition of the family. The family has a unique relationship to child psychiatry because its members form a major avenue for intervention in the child's life, and in most instances the practitioner will need a strong therapeutic alliance with the family to maximize outcomes.

The sociology of the family is one of the oldest fields in the social sciences. It encompasses both the structure and function of family life across the world. One of the major findings of this corpus of literature and research has been that the modern family is tremendously varied and changing.

Historian Stephanie Coontz in her monograph *The Way We Never Were* (1992) argues that our image of the ideal American nuclear family from the 1950s epitomized in television programs such as *Leave It to Beaver* never really existed. Behind the veneer of the Norman Rockwell image of family, many social and interpersonal events were taking place. She argues that alcoholism, domestic abuse, poverty, and reliance on government welfare all characterized the period of the 1950s. She further argues that American society developed a series of myths about the family and ideas of what constituted the core family and family values based on images that were created on television, mass media, and through political campaigns. In *The Way We Really Are* (1997), Coontz extends these arguments and makes the case that the unit of the family is a fragile concept that depends on a series of relationships both interpersonal and with the community and government.

In a related set of arguments, James Garbarino and his colleagues have extended and built upon Urie Bronfenbrenner's ecological view of human development with an impressively prolific series of works (Garbarino, 1982, 1985, 1992, 1995; Garbarino & Bedard, 2001; Garbarino, Eckenrode, Barry, & New York State College of Human Ecology. Family Life Development Center, 1997; Garbarino & Garbarino, 1993). His work on several levels has argued that families and communities can form "toxic environments" within which children have the potential to become highly antisocial. His concept of "toxic environments," although illustrative, also has a pejorative core. Some scholars have resisted this notion because traditional notions and popular culture seem to view the environment as limited to the immediate sphere around the family. Garbarino clearly sees the social environment in much more expansive terms, and it is important to recall that there are structural features that surround and limit the choices that families have. Some authors have begun to term such processes as structural violence (Farmer, 1997).

Sociologist Frank Furstenberg and his colleagues have likewise examined families in the modern era and the exigencies that they face. His recent book *Managing to Make It: Urban Families and Adolescent Success* (Furstenberg, 1999) examines the pathways that lead to positive in the midst of situations which Garbarino would view as toxic. Drawing on ten years of work by the Macarthur Foundation's Network on Successful Adolescence in Disadvantaged Communities, Furstenberg found that the most salient factors appeared to be characteristics of the neighborhood and the style of family management. Two patterns appeared to emerge. In communities with high social capital, families came to rely on strong schools and numerous after-school youth programs. Conversely, when families found themselves in neighborhoods with low social capital and poor community resources, they tended to turn inward and rely on resources and individuals within the family to help guide children through adolescence. Such findings raise important questions about the nature of family support, the ability of public policy to support the functioning of families, and the role that clinicians can play in helping families to use resources around them.

Demography has likewise raised a series of new questions. Shifts in the American population highlight the growth of minorities in the United States, in particular among Latino populations. In addition to these changes, increasing patterns of immigration in the 1960s and 1970s have produced dramatic diversity in the ethnic and racial groups present in the United States. With these changes have come concomitant shifts in the definition of the family. Clinicians need to be aware that the traditional notion of nuclear family may not hold for many ethnic minorities who subscribe to broader notions of family, and that within these families decision-making authority may reside in different individuals than the traditional head of household. One example of this type of phenomenon and the importance of understanding cultural context can be found in Anne Fadiman's well-written and research account of a Hmong child in California (Fadiman, 1997).

Globally, notions of the family are changing as well. The aging trend and increasing life span that characterize Western countries has begun to slowly affect the developing world. The use of vaccinations, increasing access to reliable water supplies, and better food security that have been the cornerstones of the United Nations development effort have in some regions of the world produced remarkable gains. Although poverty and destitution continue to characterize the lives of the vast majority of families, the absolute number of people living into octogenarian levels has increased and it appears that it will continue to do so. This shift of the population into older ages has produced changes in family structures, whereby extended families might now include four generations under one roof. These are important factors for the clinician to keep in mind, because immigrant and refugee families living in the United States may carry with them notions of family that are remarkably different than families in the United States who see the family as defined by the nuclear unit.

Even in the United States, concepts of family are showing tremendous change. Rising divorce rates have resulted in many children having multiple parents (biological as well as stepparents). Depending on the number of divorces that a parent goes through, children may have numerous stepparents. If handled well, these changes can be weathered well by children. Nevertheless, clinicians need to be aware of the additional stress that such changes pose for children. Divorce has traditionally been seen as a negative social force for children. While this may be partially true, recent studies have shown that many of these children do remarkably well. The costs of having children present in the midst of an unhappy or even damaging marital union need to be weighed against the changes required by divorce (Royko, 2000). E. Mavis Hetherington, a long-time scholar of the family, and journalist John Kelly have recently concluded in their book *For Better or for Worse: Divorce Reconsidered* (2002) that children of divorce do experience acute distress and some long-term consequences. They found some increase in rates of psychiatric illness, but did not see the dramatic difference that was believed to be present, and they concluded that the overall trend was that these children recovered well from the acute period. Hetherington believes that the conception that these children do worse has become so engrained in the medical and psychological system that it has become a self-fulfilling prophecy.

Conversely, Judith Wallerstein and colleagues in their book *The Unexpected Legacy of Divorce* (2000) found that although children may not meet criteria for psychiatric illness, they do exhibit high levels of distress when asked about how they feel. She concludes that these children have significant trouble making commitments and engaging in long-term relationships. Between these two camps, it is easy to see that the debate in this realm has become significantly complex. It is no longer a matter of deciding whether divorce is good or bad. Instead, the questions are now about which aspects of divorce benefit or harm children.

In addition to these dramatic changes in the nature of traditional marriage, new types of families have begun to emerge. Single parents, grandparents raising their grandchildren, interracial marriages, and same sex couples are now becoming more commonplace and recognizable forms of families. These new families all have unique challenges to face as children are forced to adapt to these new circumstances. But this process has always been true for families of all types. Clinicians are faced with a complex task of trying to understand the variety of forms that families can take and then understand the needs of children within these new structures. It is essential that clinicians act nonjudgmentally about these forms and assure these families that workable solutions can be found. At the same time, they should not be fearful of making thoughtful and well-reasoned suggestions on ways to improve family life and functioning to enable children to reach their maximum potentials.

Future Directions in Family Studies

The sociology of the family, as a subfield, will continue to struggle with the new forms of families as they emerge and take shape. The literature on children of same-sex couples, for example, has grown substantially (Anderssen, Amlie, & Ytteroy, 2002; Gold, Perrin, Futterman, & Friedman, 1994; Patterson, 1992). The continuing trend in family studies appears to be studies that examine the ways that families develop and maintain themselves, and what structural and institutional processes either assist or inhibit the stability of the family unit. With the advent of new forms of families, we can expect to see a more troubling side, which will be the expected dissolution of some of these families. Just as divorce has become a part of the life trajectory for many who pursue heterosexual unions, some type of separation will inevitably become part of life for the various different forms of family that we see emerging in the late twentieth and early twenty-first centuries. The question of how these dissolutions affect the lives of children will be raised, and family studies scholars will likely engage in the same debate as to the injury that this potentially poses to the child. We can expect to see a growing scholarly study of these phenomena, but should be wary of simplistic accusations or denials, and look for research that paints a more complex and mixed portrait of the effects of these separations on children. Finally, family studies should begin to grapple with the ways that children are resilient in these situations, and the helpful methods that families use to create stability for children in the face of their own relationship changes.

Peer Groups and Subcultures

Peers, or friends, are those children who are of a similar age and developmental stage that children choose to spend time with during their everyday activities. Subcultures are small groups of children or adolescents who have similar interests or shared beliefs. As part of the social environment, peer relationships are often some of the most vexing and challenging aspects for the treating clinician. Parents will often present with their children expressing concerns about the way they are dressing, the friends that they associate with, and how these behaviors lead to conduct difficulties. Parents need to be assured initially that some degree of self-expression and solid peer relations are an accepted and healthy component of normal child and adolescent development. The task for the clinician then becomes one of examining the finer details of the youth's participation in peer groups.

Sociologist Howard Becker touched on some of these issues in his classic study of social deviance and labeling processes in the monograph *Outsiders* (1963). His findings, in keeping within the sociological theories of the time, emphasized the ways that social labels produced a reaction on the part of the subject, and often created circumstances from which antisocial behavior emerged. His argument was rooted in a symbolic interactionist tradition (Becker, McCall, & Society for the Study of Symbolic Interaction, 1990; Denzin, 1992; Denzin & Lincoln, 2000), which sought to challenge established notions that the social world was fixed and predictable, and provided an opening for considering other options. This tradition holds much promise for the future of the sociology of childhood, and its recent advances in theory have the potential to advance our understanding of children's inner lives (Mukherji, 1997; Warner, 1995).

Among the richest recent work on the development of peer culture is an ethnography by Patricia and Peter Adler titled *Peer Power: Preadolescent Culture and Identity* (1998). Both sociologists have had long and respected careers in the field of sociology of childhood and in this volume bring their expertise to the forefront. They document, in their upper-middle class community, the ways that children form social peer groups, the different processes that boys and girls use to establish themselves socially, and the ways that genders interact in the elementary and middle school periods. Their work is rich and detailed but limited to the socioeconomic context that they chose to study. Nevertheless, this type of research adds substantially to that which is currently available and opens new paths for broader studies to explore.

In the wake of the series of school shootings and highly publicized instances of antisocial youth, numerous investigators began looking at peer relations as part of phenomenon leading children to commit unbelievably violent acts. The media and political discourses on these subjects took an apocalyptic tone that saw Goths, video games, music videos, and movies as being the root causes of youth violence. We focus on one strand of this argument for now—peer groups and subcultures. The literature on subcultures is very thin and underdeveloped. This lack of research is largely because youth cultures are constantly in flux, geographically variable, and difficult to study using empiric methods. The U.S. Secret Service, in its study titled the *Safe School Initiative*, failed to find any discernable profile to those who perpetrated violent acts (Vossekuil, 2002). They did find that social isolation, being bullied, and multiple social failures were consistent features of the attackers they studied, but none of these are predictive of this outcome. In other words, although attackers may share certain characteristics, these factors themselves do not lead children to becoming violent. Many children may experience bullying in school, but being bullied does not cause children to become violent in and of itself.

Participation in certain subcultures can cause extreme anxiety for families and communities. Take for instance the Goths, which were widely condemned in the wake of the school shootings. This subculture loosely defines itself by taking an anti-establishment stance. Its members will often wear black clothing and makeup, listen to music like that of Marilyn Manson, and regard themselves as well outside the normative pattern of social interaction. Even these generalizations are problematic, because individuals and groups will vary significantly and there is little to hold these groups together other than a broad ethos. These actions and forms of dress should not be a cause for concern directly, but they should prompt the clinician to explore for any major psychiatric concerns (Boran & Viswanathan, 2000; Lenz, 1973; Pollak, 1974).

Numerous other subcultures exist, and clinicians should be encouraged to explore these groups in their local variants. Even the smallest youth grouping might have created a Web site as a way to express their thoughts and feelings. Clinicians need to be cautious in interpreting these Web pages, because children are apt to create such things for shock value, as a way of testing boundaries. Nevertheless, valuable aspects of the subculture can be discerned and may allow for deeper conversations and interactions with the youth. It may even be useful to have the youth lead the clinician through the available Web resources as a method for opening discussion.

One aspect of youth subcultures that has received substantial scholarly attention has been the process of joining and being part of a gang (Aiken, Rush, & Wycoff, 1993; B. Bjerregaard, 2002; B. E. Bjerregaard, 1991; Bowker & Klein, 1983; Brownfield, Sorenson, & Thompson, 2001; Brownfield & Thompson, 2002;

Chesney-Lind, Shelden, & Joe, 1996; Cureton, 1999; Esbensen & Deschenes, 1998; Hill, Howell, Hawkins, & Battin-Pearson, 1999; Klein, 1966; Maxson, Whitlock, & Klein, 1998; Sirpal, 2002; Vowell & May, 2000; Winfree, Bernat, & Esbensen, 2001). These groups are hardly limited to the urban setting. Rather, they are omnipresent in multiple spheres, geographic settings, and socioeconomic levels, but at varied rates. As with other youth subcultures they are difficult to track and study. Among the most scholarly chroniclers of the ascendancy of gangs in the urban center has been sociologist Elijah Anderson. His work over the past twenty-five years has charted the ways that the street corner, which was once home to the older members of the neighborhood, have gradually given way to a drug and gang culture that used violence as a way to take control of the streets (Anderson, 1978, 1990, 1999). His work points the way for social interventions by under-scoring the importance of social spaces in the functioning of the neighborhood or community.

Club cultures and youth music have likewise become more central to the lives of many young people. As a source of social and peer interactions, these venues provide an outlet for many children to express themselves. Nevertheless, recent reports have begun to suggest that these are also environments that expose children to drugs and alcohol. Recent increases in the use of methylenedioxymethamphetamine (MDMA) and Ketamine, commonly referred to as *Ecstasy* (or *Special K*) should raise concern about how children have access to funds for these drugs and for what reasons they might be seeking to medicate themselves. Despite these concerns, understanding club cultures and the role of music and dance in the lives of youths can be useful. The limited literature in this area is likely outdated by the time it is published (Redhead, Wynne, & O'Connor, 1998) but nonetheless can serve as a starting point. Clinicians should likewise use the Internet as a resource to explore club cultures and become aware of the latest trends in this area of youth culture.

Future Directions for Peer and Subcultures Studies

Much work remains to be done in this area of scholarship. There are exciting developments on the horizon. A few investigators have begun to institute field studies of children and adolescents. Clubs, raves, and bars have become sites for investigators to try to understand the culture of youth.

In addition, we can expect increasing numbers of studies that utilize interpretive and qualitative strategies to examine the ways that children and adolescents express themselves in writing, art, music, and various electronic media. These studies have the potential to help uncover much about how youth culture changes and the best ways to understand these changes as they emerge.

Mass Media and Youth Culture

The effect of mass media on youth is currently one of the most hotly debated areas of psychological research. The two major sides of this debate seem well entrenched and seeming without middle ground. In a widely cited paper, Jonathan Freedman argued that there is little evidence of a correlation between youth violence and television viewing (Freedman, 1984). This paper has been hotly contested by experimental psychologists who claim that the evidence is well established that watching violent programs leads to antisocial behavior (Eron, Huesmann, Lefkowitz, & Walder, 1996; Huesmann, Eron, Berkowitz, & Chaffee, 1992; Huesmann, Moise, & Podolski, 1997; Huesmann, Moise-Titus, Podolski, & Eron, 2003). As with most social phenomena, the relationship is likely between the two poles. It would be foolish to deny any relationship between television viewing and the types of programs that are seen, and the ways that children react to a world around them. The best explanations are that television has an influence both positive and negative, depending on how it is used.

Another area of scholarship, for example, that has demonstrated substantial relationship between mass media and experience is between body image and popular culture. While the media may not cause eating disorders, the popular image of beauty can be heavily influenced by the images around us, and children's ideas can be shaped, in part, by the media around them (Brumberg, 2000; Steiner et al., 2003). Current research supports the idea that children internalize socially sanctioned images of beauty, and that these exert an influence on the ways that juveniles view their own bodies, often in distorted ways. Such social influences appear to be tied, in part, to activity in the serotonin and dopaminergic systems that regulate the pleasure and mood centers in the mind. The precise pathway from social influence to neurochemical action, and the degree of change and influence, have yet to be fully elucidated.

The substantial literature on youth and mass media paints a complex, vivid, and often conflicting portrait. New media transcend beyond television and now include the Internet, e-mail, broadband technology, and multimedia technologies. Postmodernists and cultural studies scholars have tended to view new media rather benignly and generally have argued that the media present opportunities for children and adolescents to present their own narratives regardless of their socioeconomic or cultural status (A. L. Best, 2000; S. Best & Kellner, 1998; Byers, 1998; Downes, 2000; Giroux, 1995, 1996, 2000; Hoechsmann, 2001; Milkie, 1994; Rabinovitz, 1989).

Other empirical studies, especially those utilizing ethnographic and qualitative techniques, have yielded especially interesting results. Vogelgesang found that children developed highly refined decoding skills for understanding these media, and that they concurrently established their own subcultures with ethical and moral norms. He viewed public and political demonizations of new media as being rooted in misunderstandings of child development and interaction with new media (Vogelgesang, 1994, 2000).

Cell phones, pagers, text messaging, and wireless communication must all be considered as part of the new media as well. In many respects, children adopt these technologies rapidly and seamlessly incorporate them into their everyday lives. Young children can be seen riding public transportation and holding a cell phone on which they are rapidly typing messages using the standard telephone keypad. This remarkable adaptation is a facet of youth culture. Clinicians need to be aware of these new technologies because they affect youth culture in a dynamic way and act as a way for children to facilitate peer contacts. Children use phrases drawn from the technological world. For example, a child may ask for the "411," or information in reference to the quick dial code for directory assistance that many cellular phone providers use.

Finally, music has historically been, and continues to be, a key modality through which young people express themselves. Once again, the technology has changed to MP3 players and digital music, and the styles continue to rapidly change. Grunge, rap, acid, house—the names and beats are constantly in flux, but the core content to draw a demarcation between generations continues. Clinicians need to be sensitive to these changes and be willing to engage these forms of expression without being overly judgmental. Parents' concerns about content must be taken seriously, but children's use of this medium to express themselves needs to be weighed as well.

Future Directions for Media Studies

As a discipline, media and communication studies are beginning to become established within the traditional university structure. Combining methods from sociology, cultural studies, art history, history, economics, and philosophy, this discipline has matured into a respected area of research. As a consequence, we can expect to soon see studies that utilize both qualitative and quantitative techniques to study the ways that children are affected by and interact with new and old media.

Given the complexity of mass media, and its omnipresence and continued growth, the future direction of this field will be to develop media literacy and education programs for children. It is important to teach children how to critically evaluate the various media influences around them and be able to select what they find useful and productive.

The School and Educational Sociology

The field of educational sociology, a subfield of sociology that is committed to studying the ways that schools and education systems operate, has undergone remarkable growth and expansion with the proliferation of schools of education within established universities. This shift has given this subfield a strong institutional home and a position from which to influence teachers-in-training. Harvard, Penn, and Columbia all have schools of education which have pushed the boundaries of sociology and the allied social sciences in an attempt to better focus attention on the school as a site of development of children.

Schools are vital sites for the future of child psychiatry. They are one of the key sites for child and adolescent development. The remarkable growth that children experience in the course of education spans well beyond intellectual and academic development to include interpersonal, cultural, sexual, emotional, physical, and social development. The school forms a nexus for child development, intentionally and unintentionally, and consequently can not only be a valuable source of information, but also act as a site of intervention through school consultation psychiatry, which has been well explored in many types of research (Ialongo et al., 1999; Kellam, Koretz, & Moscicki, 1999; Kellam, Ling, Merisca, Brown, & Ialongo, 1998; Kellam, Rebok, Ialongo, & Mayer, 1994; Rebok, Hawkins, Krener, Mayer, & Kellam, 1996; Storr, Ialongo, Kellam, & Anthony, 2002; Werthamer-Larsson, Kellam, & Wheeler, 1991) and is covered later in this volume in greater detail.

Among the most exciting and interesting work in this area centers on the work of Carol Gilligan and her colleagues. Her landmark work *In a Different Voice* (1982) profoundly challenged established notions of pedagogy and education development in children by arguing that girls have different learning styles than boys. Her research was based on detailed and rigorous classroom observations of the behaviors of boys and girls, and their differing responses to varied teaching techniques. She found that girls tended to favor and do better with collaborative, group-oriented teaching methods, whereas boys were apt to be active participants in lectures by asking questions and being aggressive in raising their hands to be recognized. Her work has subsequently been criticized for being overly generalizing, when there may be subpopulations among boys and girls who would benefit from more individualized and tailored strategies. Nevertheless, her work challenged established notions at a critical period, and continues to raise important questions about the methods of teaching in the school environment.

For the clinician, the school is an important source of information on the child, a site of development for the child, and also a potential place for interventions to take place. Schools vary substantially in their capability to provide assistance for children based primarily on the community's financial resources and ability to provide ancillary services. Some schools are able to provide a rich intellectual learning environment, while other schools are riddled with violence, drugs, and a poor learning environment. Although the stereotype suggests that inner-city public schools suffer the most, there is ample evidence to suggest that problems of violence may be much further disseminated into suburban and even rural schools (Hawkins, Miller, & Steiner, 2003). The latter are often more financially deprived than many inner-city schools simply due to the socioeconomics of modern rural life.

In a compelling paper on school violence, Dimitriadis and McCarthy (1999) argue that the modern school has become the site of symbolic and physical violence against children. Such work highlights one pathway that may account for referrals to clinicians for conduct disorders, stress-related symptoms, and other violence-related pathologies. Cameron McCarthy, in particular, has argued that minority children disproportionately suffer in the modern school environment due to structural and historical factors (McCarthy, 1990a, 1990b).

Psychiatric studies of children in school abound on a variety of topics. Recent work has shown that children who exhibit fixed coping patterns are more likely to have more serious psychopathologies (Erickson, Feldman, & Steiner, 1996; Steiner, Erickson, Hernandez, & Pavelski, 2002). In the broader social environment, the experience in school cannot be divorced from peer relations, the family, youth culture, mass media, and culture.

Future Directions for the Sociology of Education

Educational sociology has a great potential to add to the corpus of knowledge on childhood. By studying children in the school context, and observing their behaviors in the educational environment, it is possible to tap into a wide array of knowledge and experience. From a developmental perspective, the school may be one of the key influences, in concert with the family and community, that helps to shape children and their experiences.

For researchers in child psychiatry, it will become increasingly important to build bridges to education researchers, and try to establish concerted scholarly programs that help to build both fields simultaneously. Since the school is often the first place where children display problematic behaviors, it will become increasingly important for researchers to connect their work of training teachers in pragmatic ways so that they can act to help identify children with psychopathologies at early ages and make appropriate referrals for families to follow into the clinical realm.

Welfare and Judicial Institutions

One of the most hotly contested areas of research has to do with the minority of children who become wards of the state, or those children whose behavioral problems escalate to such an extent that they encounter the juvenile justice system. At the heart of these debates is the nature of antisocial behavior and the ways that welfare and judicial institutions can or cannot contain such behaviors.

Welfare institutions charged with the care of juveniles have historically been targets for repeated criticism and calls for reform. These institutions were established in the wake of nineteenth century Progressive Era reforms that redefined childhood as a separate and protected sphere of human development. Such institutions have consistently been under-funded due to a lack of a political base to protect the interests of these institutions and the children who are wards of them.

Rudy Moos has written extensively on the ways that residential communities and programs can assist patients. He has found that focused and specialized treatment facilities have the best outcomes (Moos, 1996, 1998; Moos, Moos, & Andrassy, 1999; Moos, Pettit, & Gruber, 1995; Moos, Pettit, & Gruber, 1995). Earlier literature on the development and establishment of child psychiatry units has found that they can be very productive in creating social communities that are conducive to therapeutic goals (Steiner, 1982; Steiner, Haldipur, & Stack, 1982; Steiner, Marx, & Walton, 1991; Steiner, Walton, & Emslie, 1983). This literature has important lessons for the ways that psychiatric care is structured in welfare institutions. They tend to support the notion that welfare institutions should provide integrated specialty care.

Recent events have highlighted the topic of antisociality among children. Through events like those at Columbine High School in Colorado and Santana High School in California, clinicians and the public have had to face the unsettling fact that children and adolescents are capable of extraordinary antisocial, violent acts. Such antisociality marks one extreme in a spectrum of behavior. Usually, antisocial behavior involves violating the rights of others, and is an aspect of the social development of all children. Through minor transgressions often against family and then possibly the community, children learn the rules of society. During adolescence, behaviors may become more serious and even lead to the involvement of the law enforcement system. Nevertheless, these actions have been found to be rather common with up to one quarter of youth being apprehended by police and convicted of crimes. Antisocial behavior per se does not equate directly with psychopathology. Most forms of juvenile antisocial behavior do not progress to criminality. Despite numerous studies to understand the trajectories that lead to severe antisociality, there is continuing difficulty in distinguishing those youths with a good prognosis from those who will end up in the justice system and perpetrate severe transgressions (Steiner & Karnik, in press).

The development of formal tools to assess children and their risk factors is undoubtedly a productive development in the field. Nevertheless, the ontological basis of such tools has come into question. In particular, Robert Hare and Adele Forth have for some time set out to adapt the Hare Psychopathy Checklist (PCL) for use in juvenile populations (Forth, Hart, & Hare, 1990; Hare, Forth, & Strachan, 1992; Hare, Harpur, Hakstian, Forth, & et al., 1990; Hart, Hare, & Forth, 1994; Widiger et al., 1996). The use of these instruments raises many troubling questions about the use of the diagnostic group of psychopathy or antisocial personality disorder in juvenile populations.

Elizabeth Cauffman and her group at the University of Pittsburgh have been among the articulate challengers of the movement to further develop psychopathy as a category for use in juveniles (Edens, Skeem, Cruise, & Cauffman, 2001). They argue that not only is the category of psychopathy invalidated in juvenile populations, but that its use risks labeling children for a lifetime and setting them on a trajectory from which it will be difficult to change. Hans Steiner and his group at Stanford have likewise joined in this criticism and called for more investigation into the types and subtypes of behaviors that have become blanketed under the rubric of psychopathy (Karnik & Steiner, 2002).

As part of a broader trend among welfare and justice institutions, the use of formal protocols has powerful implications. Particularly with children and adolescents, these protocols and evaluation tests can actually shape experience and label children with disorders that then become difficult to ameliorate or treat (Karnik, 2001).

Steiner and Cauffman (1998), in their review of juvenile forensics, urge child psychiatrists to take a leadership role in helping to treat high-risk children. In this regard, child psychiatrists need to be ever vigilant about the ways that diagnoses and labels developed in the field for clinical use can be used by other entities for non-clinical or non-therapeutic uses. Such actions should not limit clinicians from treating; rather, it is a cautionary tale that the categories we place children in have consequences that can be good and bad.

Future Directions for Welfare and Delinquency Studies

As the field of juvenile forensics continues to develop, the expansion of research on the lives of children in welfare and judicial domains will continue to increase. For example, one area that is gaining remarkable interest is how protective factors often act to prevent children from becoming antisocial. The number of children within the welfare system who, despite significant factors against them, manage to go on to successful and productive lives bears study. This type of research will lead researchers and clinicians to develop a set of interventions that promote positive outcomes and can potentially be adapted to assist all children in the welfare system.

A Prolegomenon for the Study of the Social Environment in Child and Adolescent Psychiatry

The social environment is an essential part of the development of children. Despite the exciting and growing advances in molecular and genetic medicine, we cannot forget that the biological exists within a social environment, and is continually in a dynamic relationship with this environment. Such an understanding requires that we begin to bridge the findings from biology and medicine to the social world. As mental health providers, we limit ourselves tremendously if we rely on purely pharmacological methods. The social world is likely more adaptable and malleable than the biological world because the social world is almost entirely of our own creation. We are beholden to its present structure by virtue of our own history and lack of imagination or commitment.

Future research in this field needs to become more complex and nuanced. It will require researchers to move beyond the traditional methods used in mental health research, and re-establish disciplinary connections to the social sciences and humanities. Such work promises to provide us with multiple investigatory pathways. For example, studying children in multiple contexts (school, home, play, clubs) will require investigators to learn field methods pioneered by anthropologists and sociologists. Likewise, understanding cultural productions made by children (art, drawings, games) will require investigators to adopt methods from literary scholars and art historians. The complexity of the social environment requires methods that can capture these equally complex phenomena so that we can maximize the knowledge base from which to understand the nature of normal and abnormal child and adolescent development.

References

Adler, P. A., & Adler, P. (1998). *Peer power: Preadolescent culture and identity.* New Brunswick, NJ: Rutgers University Press.

Aiken, C., Rush, J. P., & Wycoff, J. (1993). A preliminary inquiry into Alabama youth gang membership. *Gang Journal, 48*(5), 37–47.

Anderson, E. (1978). *A place on the corner.* University of Chicago Press.

Anderson, E. (1990). *Streetwise: Race, class, and change in an urban community.* University of Chicago Press.

Anderson, E. (1999). *Code of the street: Decency, violence, and the moral life of the inner city* (1st ed.). New York: W. W. Norton.

Anderssen, N., Amlie, C., & Ytteroy, E. A. (2002). Outcomes for children with lesbian or gay parents. A review of studies from 1978 to 2000. *Scandinavian Journal of Psychology, 43*(4), 335–351.

Becker, H. S. (1963). *Outsiders: Studies in the sociology of deviance.* London: Free Press of Glencoe.

Becker, H. S., McCall, M. M., & Society for the Study of Symbolic Interaction. (1990). *Symbolic interaction and cultural studies.* University of Chicago Press.

Best, A. L. (2000). *Prom night: Youth, schools, and popular culture.* New York: Routledge.

Best, S., & Kellner, D. (1998). Beavis and Butt-Head: No future for postmodern youth. In J. S. Epstein (Ed.), *Youth culture: Identity in a postmodern world* (pp. 74–99). Malden, MA: Blackwell.

Bjerregaard, B. (2002). Operationalizing gang membership: The impact measurement on gender differences in gang self-identification and delinquent involvement. *Women and Criminal Justice, 51*(1), 79–100.

Bjerregaard, B. E. (1991). The etiology of gang membership: A test of an elaborated social control theory. *Dissertation Abstracts International, A: The Humanities and Social Sciences, 40*(1), 1084-A.

Boran, M., & Viswanathan, R. (2000). Separating subculture from psychopathology. *Psychiatric Services, 51*(5), 678.

Bowker, L. H., & Klein, M. W. (1983). The etiology of female juvenile delinquency and gang membership: A test of psychological and social structural explanations. *Adolescence, 33*(2), 739–751.

Bronfenbrenner, U. (1979). *The ecology of human development: Experiments by nature and design.* Cambridge, MA: Harvard University Press.

Brownfield, D., Sorenson, A. M., & Thompson, K. M. (2001). Gang membership, race, and social class: A test of the group hazard and master status hypotheses. *Deviant Behavior, 49*(3), 73–89.

Brownfield, D., & Thompson, K. (2002). Distinguishing the effects of peer delinquency and gang membership on self-reported delinquency. *Journal of Gang Research, 50*(3), 1–10.

Brumberg, J. J. (2000). *Fasting girls: The history of anorexia nervosa* (1st Vintage Books ed.). New York: Vintage Books.

Byers, M. (1998). Gender/Sexuality/Desire: Subversion of difference and construction of loss in the adolescent drama of My So-Called Life. *Signs, 47*(3), 711–734.

Chesney-Lind, M., Shelden, R. G., & Joe, K. A. (1996). Girls, delinquency, and gang membership. In C. R. Huff, *Gangs in America* (2nd ed., pp. 185–204). Newbury Park, CA: Sage Publications.

Coontz, S. (1992). *The way we never were: American families and the nostalgia trap.* New York: Basic Books.

Coontz, S. (1997). *The way we really are: Coming to terms with America's changing families.* New York: Basic Books.

Cureton, S. R. (1999). Gang membership: Gang formations and gang joining. *Journal of Gang Research, 48*(5), 13–21.

Denzin, N. K. (1992). *Symbolic interactionism and cultural studies: The politics of interpretation.* Oxford, UK, Cambridge, MA: Blackwell.

Denzin, N. K. (1997). *Interpretive ethnography: Ethnographic practices for the 21st century.* Thousand Oaks, CA: Sage Publications.

Denzin, N. K., & Lincoln, Y. S. (2000). *Handbook of qualitative research* (2nd ed.). Thousand Oaks, CA: Sage Publications.

Dimitriadis, G., & McCarthy, C. (1999). Violence in theory and practice: Popular culture, schooling, and the boundaries of pedagogy. *Educational Theory, 49*(1), 125–138.

Downes, L. M. (2000). Lessons for life: Adolescent culture and society in the world of the "true" confessions. (Vol. 48). American Sociological Association.

Edens, J. F., Skeem, J. L., Cruise, K. R., & Cauffman, E. (2001). Assessment of "juvenile psychopathy" and its association with violence: A critical review. *Behavioral Sciences and the Law, 19*(1), 53–80.

Erickson, S. J., Feldman, S. S., & Steiner, H. (1996). Defense mechanisms and adjustment in normal adolescents. *American Journal of Psychiatry, 153*(6), 826–828.

Eron, L. D., Huesmann, L. R., Lefkowitz, M. M., & Walder, L. O. (1996). Does television violence cause aggression? In D. F. Greenberg (Ed.), *Criminal careers* (Vol. 2, pp. 311–321). Brookfield, VT: Dartmouth Publishing Company Limited.

Esbensen, F.-A., & Deschenes, E. P. (1998). A multisite examination of youth gang membership: Does gender matter? *Criminology, 47*(5), 799–827.

Fadiman, A. (1997). *The spirit catches you and you fall down: A Hmong child, her American doctors, and the collision of two cultures* (1st ed.). New York: Farrar, Straus, & Giroux.

Farmer, P. (1997). On suffering and structural violence: A view from below. In A. Kleinman, V. Das, & M. Lock (Eds.), *Social Suffering* (pp. 261–283). Berkeley: University of California.

Forth, A. E., Hart, S. D., & Hare, R. D. (1990). Assessment of psychopathy in male young offenders. *Psychological Assessment, 2*(3), 342–344.

Freedman, J. L. (1984). Effect of television violence on aggressiveness. *Psychological Bulletin, 96*(2), 227–246.

Furstenberg, F. F. (1999). *Managing to make it: Urban families and adolescent success.* University of Chicago Press.

Garbarino, J. (1982). *Children and families in the social environment.* New York: Aldine de Gruyter.

Garbarino, J. (1985). *Adolescent development: An ecological perspective.* Columbus, OH: C.E. Merrill Pub. Co.

Garbarino, J. (1992). *Children and families in the social environment* (2nd ed.). New York: Aldine de Gruyter.

Garbarino, J. (1995). *Raising children in a socially toxic environment* (1st ed.). San Francisco: Jossey-Bass.

Garbarino, J., & Bedard, C. (2001). *Parents under siege: Why you are the solution, not the problem, in your child's life.* New York: Free Press.

Garbarino, J., Eckenrode, J., Barry, F. D., & New York State College of Human Ecology. Family Life Development Center. (1997). *Understanding abusive families: An ecological approach to theory and practice* (1st ed.). San Francisco: Jossey-Bass.

Garbarino, J., & Garbarino, A. C. (1993). *Maltreatment of adolescents* (3rd ed.). Chicago: National Committee to Prevent Child Abuse.

Gilligan, C. (1982). *In a different voice: Psychological theory and women's development.* Cambridge, MA: Harvard University Press.

Giroux, H. A. (1995). Racism and the aesthetic of hyper-real violence: Pulp Fiction and other visual tragedies. *Social Identities, 46*(1), 333–354.

Giroux, H. A. (1996). *Fugitive cultures: Race, violence, and youth.* New York: Routledge.

Giroux, H. A. (2000). Representations of violence, popular culture, and demonization of youth. In S. U. Spina (Ed.), *Smoke and mirrors: The hidden context of violence in schools and society* (pp. 93–105). Lanham, MD: Rowman & Littlefield.

Gold, M. A., Perrin, E. C., Futterman, D., & Friedman, S. B. (1994). Children of gay or lesbian parents. *Pediatrics in Review, 15*(9), 354–358; quiz 358.

Grossberg, L., Nelson, C., & Treichler, P. A. (1992). *Cultural studies.* New York: Routledge.

Hare, R. D., Forth, A. E., & Strachan, K. E. (1992). Psychopathy and crime across the life span. In R. D. Peters, R. J. McMahon, & et al. (Eds.), *Aggression and violence throughout the life span* (pp. 285–300). Thousand Oaks, CA: Sage Publications.

Hare, R. D., Harpur, T. J., Hakstian, A. R., Forth, A. E., et al. (1990). The revised Psychopathy Checklist: Reliability and factor structure. *Psychological Assessment, 2*(3), 338–341.

Hart, S. D., Hare, R. D., & Forth, A. E. (1994). Psychopathy as a risk marker for violence: Development and validation of a screening version of the revised Psychopathy Checklist. In J. Monahan & H. J. Steadman (Eds.), *Violence and mental disorder: Developments in risk assessment* (pp. 81–98). University of Chicago Press.

Hawkins, S., Miller, S., & Steiner, H. (2003). Aggression, psychopathology and delinquency: Influences of gender and maturation. Where did the good girls go? In C. Hayward (Ed.), *Gender differences at puberty* (pp. 93–110). London: Cambridge University Press.

Hetherington, E. M., & Kelly, J. (2002). *For better or for worse: Divorce reconsidered.* New York: W. W. Norton & Company.

Hill, K. G., Howell, J. C., Hawkins, J. D., & Battin-Pearson, S. R. (1999). Childhood risk factors for adolescent gang membership: Results from the Seattle Social Development Project. *Journal of Research in Crime and Delinquency, 48*(2), 300–322.

Hoechsmann, M. (2001). Just do it: What Michael Jordan has to teach us. In D. L. Andrews (Ed.), *Michael Jordan, Inc.: Corporate sport, media culture, and late modern America* (pp. 269–276). Albany, NY: State University New York Press.

Huesmann, L. R., Eron, L. D., Berkowitz, L., & Chaffee, S. (1992). The effects of television violence on aggression: A reply to a skeptic. In P. Suedfeld & P. E. Tetlock (Eds.), *Psychology and social policy* (pp. 191–200). Washington, DC: Hemisphere Publishing Corp.

Huesmann, L. R., Moise, J. F., & Podolski, C.-L. (1997). The effects of media violence on the development of antisocial behavior. In D. M. Stoff, J. Breiling, et al. (Eds.), *Handbook of antisocial behavior* (pp. 181–193). New York: John Wiley & Sons.

Huesmann, L. R., Moise-Titus, J., Podolski, C.-L., & Eron, L. D. (2003). Longitudinal relations between children's exposure to TV violence and their aggressive and violent behavior in young adulthood: 1977–1992. *Developmental Psychology, 39*(2), 201–221.

Ialongo, N. S., Werthamer, L., Kellam, S. G., Brown, C. H., Wang, S., & Lin, Y. (1999). Proximal impact of two first-grade preventive interventions on the early risk behaviors for later substance abuse, depression, and antisocial behavior. *American Journal of Community Psychology, 27*(5), 599–641.

Karnik, N. S. (2001). Between victim and victimizer: The narrow corporeal path of being a foster child. *Children & Youth Services Review, 23*(9–10), 743–759.

Karnik, N. S., & Steiner, H. (2002). *Adolescence, incarceration & experience: Toward a new theory of juvenile psychopathy.* Paper presented at the Annual Meeting of the American Academy of Child and Adolescent Psychiatry, San Francisco.

Kellam, S. G., Koretz, D., & Moscicki, E. K. (1999). Core elements of developmental epidemiologically based prevention research. *American Journal of Community Psychology, 27*(4), 463–482.

Kellam, S. G., Ling, X., Merisca, R., Brown, C. H., & Ialongo, N. (1998). The effect of the level of aggression in the first grade classroom on the course and malleability of aggressive behavior into middle school. *Development and Psychopathology, 10*(2), 165–185.

Kellam, S. G., Rebok, G. W., Ialongo, N., & Mayer, L. S. (1994). The course and malleability of aggressive behavior from early first grade into middle school: Results of a developmental epidemiologically based preventive trial. *Journal of Child Psychology Psychiatry, 35*(2), 259–281.

Klein, M. W. (1966). Factors related to juvenile gang membership patterns. *Sociology and Social Research, 15*(1), 49–62.

Lenz, E. J. (1973). The expression of aggression and the need for social approval in psychopathic, neurotic and subcultural delinquents. *Dissertation Abstracts International, 34*(1-B), 417.

Maxson, C. L., Whitlock, M. L., & Klein, M. W. (1998). Vulnerability to street gang membership: Implications for practice. *The Social Service Review, 21*(2), 70–91.

McCarthy, C. (1990a). Multicultural education, minority identities, textbooks, and the challenge of curriculum reform. *Journal of Education, 172*(2), 118–129.

McCarthy, C. (1990b). *Race and curriculum: Social inequality and the theories and politics of difference in contemporary research on schooling.* Bristol, PA: Falmer Press.

Milkie, M. A. (1994). Social world approach to cultural studies: Mass media and gender in the adolescent peer group. *Journal of Contemporary Ethnography, 43*(1), 354–380.

Moos, R. H. (1996). Understanding environments: The key to improving social processes and program outcomes. *American Journal of Community Psychology, 24*(1), 193–201.

Moos, R. H. (1998). Understanding the quality and outcome of treatment. *Substance Use & Misuse, 33*(14), 2789–2794.

Moos, R. H., Moos, B. S., & Andrassy, J. M. (1999). Outcomes of four treatment approaches in community residential programs for patients with substance use disorders. *Psychiatric Services, 50*(12), 1577–1583.

Moos, R. H., Pettit, B., & Gruber, V. A. (1995). Longer episodes of community residential care reduce substance abuse patients' readmission rates. *Journal of Studies on Alcohol, 56*(4), 433–443.

Moos, R. H., Pettit, B., & Gruber, V. A. (1995). Characteristics and outcomes of three models of community residential care for abuse patients. *Journal of Substance Abuse, 7*(1), 99–116.

Mukherji, C. (1997). Monsters and muppets: The history of childhood and techniques of cultural analysis. In E. Long (Ed.), *From sociology to cultural studies* (pp. 155–184). Malden, MA: Blackwell Publishers.

Patterson, C. J. (1992). Children of lesbian and gay parents. *Child Development, 63*(5), 1025–1042.

Pollak, O. (1974). Youth culture, subcultures, and survival. *Adolescent Psychiatry, 3*, 49–53.

Rabinovitz, L. (1989). Animation, postmodernism, and MTV. *The Velvet Light Trap, 38*(5), 99–112.

Rebok, G. W., Hawkins, W. E., Krener, P., Mayer, L. S., & Kellam, S. G. (1996). Effect of concentration problems on the malleability of children's aggressive and shy behaviors. *Journal of the American Academy of Child and Adolescent Psychiatry, 35*(2), 193–203.

Redhead, S., Wynne, D., & O'Connor, J. (1998). *The clubcultures reader: Readings in popular cultural studies.* Malden, MA: Blackwell.

Royko, D. (2000). *Voices of children of divorce.* New York: St. Martin's Griffin.

Sirpal, S. K. (2002). Familial criminality, familial drug use, and gang membership: Youth criminality, drug use, and gang membership—What are the connections? *Journal of Gang Research, 50*(3), 11–22.

Steiner, H. (1982). The sociotherapeutic environment of a child psychosomatic ward, or is pediatrics bad for your mental health? *Child Psychiatry and Human Development, 13*, 71–78.

Steiner, H., & Cauffman, E. (1998). Juvenile justice, delinquency, and psychiatry. *Child and Adolescent Psychiatric Clinics of North America, 7*(3), 653–672.

Steiner, H., Erickson, S. J., Hernandez, N. L., & Pavelski, R. (2002). Coping styles as corre-
    lates of health in high school students. *Journal of Adolescent Health, 30*(5), 326–335.
Steiner, H., Haldipur, C., & Stack, L. (1982). The acute admission ward as a therapeutic
    community. *American Journal of Psychiatry, 139*, 897–901.
Steiner, H., & Karnik, N. (in press). Child and adolescent antisocial behavior. In B. J. Sadock &
    V. A. Sadock (Eds.), *Kaplan & Sadock's comprehensive textbook of psychiatry.* Philadelphia:
    Lippincott Williams & Wilkins.
Steiner, H., Kwan, W., Shaffer, T. G., Walker, S., Miller, S., Sagar, A., et al. (2003). Risk and
    protective factors for juvenile eating disorders. *European Child & Adolescent Psychiatry, 12
    Suppl 1,* I38–I46.
Steiner, H., Marx, L., & Walton, C. (1991). The ward atmosphere of a child psychosomatic
    unit: A ten-year follow-up. *General Hospital Psychiatry, 13*, 246–252.
Steiner, H., Walton, C. O., & Emslie, G. (1983). A psychosomatic unit for children and
    adolescents: Report on the first year and 10 months. *Child Psychiatry and Human Development,
    14*, 3–15.
Storr, C. L., Ialongo, N. S., Kellam, S. G., & Anthony, J. C. (2002). A randomized controlled
    trial of two primary school intervention strategies to prevent early onset tobacco smoking.
    Drug and Alcohol Dependence, 66(1), 51–60.
Treichler, P. A., Kramarae, C., & Stafford, B. (1985). *For alma mater: Theory and practice in
    feminist scholarship.* Urbana: University of Illinois Press.
Vogelgesang, W. (1994). Youth and media cultures. An ethnographic study of media-
    influenced youth lifestyles. *Kolner Zeitschrift fur Soziologie und Sozialpsychologie, 43*(2), 464–491.
Vogelgesang, W. (2000). Asymmetric styles of perception. How juveniles handle new media
    and why adults don't understand them. *Zeitschrift fur Soziologie der Erziehung und Socialisation,
    48*(5), 181–202.
Vossekuil, B. (2002). *The final report and findings of the safe school initiative: Implications for the preven-
    tion of school attacks in the United States.* Washington, DC: U.S. Secret Service U.S. Depart-
    ment of Education.
Vowell, P. R., & May, D. C. (2000). Another look at classic strain theory: Poverty status,
    perceived blocked opportunity, and gang membership as predictors of adolescent violent
    behavior. *Sociological Inquiry, 48*(3), 42–60.
Vygotsky, L. (1978). *Mind in society: The development of higher psychological processes.* Cambridge,
    MA: Harvard University Press.
Warner, M. (1995). *Six myths of our time: Little angels, little monsters, beautiful beasts, and more* (1st
    Vintage Books ed.). New York: Vintage Books.
Wallerstein, J. (2000). *The unexpected legacy of divorce.* New York: Hyperion.
Werthamer-Larsson, L., Kellam, S., & Wheeler, L. (1991). Effect of first-grade classroom
    environment on shy behavior, aggressive behavior, and concentration problems. *American
    Journal of Community Psychology, 19*(4), 585–602.
Widiger, T. A., Cadoret, R., Hare, R., Robins, L., Rutherford, M., Zanarini, M., et al. (1996).
    DSM—IV antisocial personality disorder field trial. *Journal of Abnormal Psychology, 105*(1),
    3–16.
Winfree, L. T., Jr., Bernat, F. P., & Esbensen, F.-A. (2001). Hispanic and Anglo gang
    membership in two southwestern cities. *The Social Science Journal, 49*(5), 105–117.

CHAPTER FOUR

RECENT PROGRESS IN COGNITIVE DEVELOPMENTAL RESEARCH: IMPLICATIONS FOR CLINICAL PRACTICE

Ethan Remmel, Ph.D., and John H. Flavell, Ph.D.

Cognitive developmental researchers study how children's knowledge and mental processes change with age (Flavell, Miller, & Miller, 2002). Cognitive developmentalists typically seek to describe normative developmental patterns and processes, and rarely stop to consider potential clinical applications of their research. As a result, there is little discussion of clinical implications in the cognitive developmental literature. This chapter attempts to bridge the gap between cognitive developmental research and clinical practice. We review recent research in two broad areas: (1) core conceptual developments, and (2) developments in social cognition. Within each section, we focus on active lines of research with clinical relevance. We discuss how children's cognitive capabilities change with age, and how clinicians may need to tailor their techniques to the child's level of cognitive development.

In the past few decades, developmental theory and clinical psychology have been integrated in the new field of developmental psychopathology (Cichetti & Toth, 1998). However, within the field of developmental psychopathology, the focus has primarily been on social development. Cognitive development has received relatively short shrift (with some exceptions, such as Weisz, 1990). The most extensive discussion to date of cognitive development and child psychotherapy appears in Shirk (1988). Although that volume is still worthwhile reading for practitioners, the research presented is now fifteen years out of date. In this chapter, we update some of the themes raised in that volume and supplement them with more recent research directions.

A better understanding of cognitive development may help clinicians to design and implement more effective interventions. Clearly, children are not just little adults, and clinical practices that may be effective with adults may not be appropriate with children. As cognitive developmentalists, we are prone to believe that cognitive developmental research is vitally important to all types of therapy. Nevertheless, we concede that it is more relevant to some than others. It is probably most relevant to structured psychotherapies, such as cognitive behavioral therapy, and less relevant to expressive-supportive and explorative psychotherapies. However, all forms of therapy assume certain cognitive skills on the part of the client. For example, clients may be expected to reason logically about different alternatives, to reflect upon the causes and consequences of people's actions, to consider other people's perspectives, and to introspect on their own thoughts and feelings. With adults these assumptions may be implicit because the skills are always present and relatively invariant. Clinicians who work with children, on the other hand, need to be explicit about their expectations in order to ensure that they are reasonable for the child's developmental level. As we will see, basic concepts such as causality, the self, and the mind undergo significant change during childhood. Capacities for logical reasoning, conscious control of behavior, and perspective-taking also develop. In general, we cannot assume that children see the world the way we do or think about things the way we do.

We, the authors of this chapter, are cognitive developmentalists, not practicing clinicians. Therefore, we will focus our discussion on our area of expertise: cognitive developmental research. We will attempt to show how a child's level of cognitive development may be relevant to a clinician's approach to treatment, but we will not discuss specific therapeutic techniques or psychological disorders, because they fall outside our expertise. Depending on their theoretical orientations and treatment styles, different clinicians may adjust their techniques in different ways to take account of the child's cognitive developmental level.

Both of the major classic theoretical positions in cognitive developmental psychology, those of Piaget (1970) and Vygotsky (1978), hold that cognitive progress may be stimulated by challenging the child to think just beyond his or her current level of understanding. This principle can be applied to therapeutic progress as well. According to Piaget's theory, information is always actively interpreted in relation to a child's current cognitive structures, rather than passively absorbed. However, information that conflicts with the child's current level of understanding may induce cognitive disequilibrium. The child may restore equilibrium by adjusting his or her cognitive structures, and thereby gaining a higher level of understanding. However, if information is overly discrepant, it will simply be rejected or ignored. In Vygotsky's theory, a child may demonstrate one level of understanding (the "actual level") when working on a problem independently, but a higher level of understanding (the "potential level") when working with the support of a more knowledgeable person. By working together in this intermediate zone, a more knowledgeable person may enable the child to achieve a higher actual level of understanding, as long as the child's potential level of understanding is not exceeded.

These theoretical positions suggest that a moderate level of intellectual challenge is optimal for cognitive growth. This insight is also applicable to clinical practice. By presenting information that challenges a child's current way of thinking, but is not too advanced for the child's current level of development, a supportive therapist may enable the child to achieve a more adaptive way of thinking. Although the child may require scaffolding from the therapist initially, with practice the child should be able to operate at the new level independently.

There is a tendency in the cognitive developmental literature for researchers to compete to demonstrate the earliest possible glimmers of competence in a particular area, under the most simplified and facilitative conditions. This tendency is especially evident since the advent of Piaget's stage theory of cognitive development, as researchers have shown that children are more competent at earlier ages than Piaget's theory predicts. One downside of this tendency is that there is less research than there could be or should be on how competence changes from less mature forms to more mature forms, and how children perform under more typical and ecologically valid conditions. Another downside is that the majority of recent cognitive developmental research focuses on infants and young children rather than on older children and adolescents. In particular, there has been a surge of studies on infant cognition in recent years (see Haith & Benson, 1998, for a review), in part due to the development of new methods such as looking-time measures. Studies of preschoolers are also overrepresented in the literature, in part due to the availability of participants through university laboratory preschools. However, clinicians are less likely to work with infants and very young children than with older children and adolescents, and clinicians are more likely to be interested in typical expected levels of cognitive performance than in "best-case" demonstrations of early competence. Therefore, in this chapter we will try to incorporate research on older children's cognitive performance where available.

Core Conceptual Developments

Certain core conceptual competencies underlie children's cognitive performance across domains. In this section, we review the developmental course of some of these competencies, so that the practicing clinician can get a sense of children's basic cognitive capabilities at different ages.

Children's Understanding of Causality

Clinicians often want children to consider how one thing leads to another, for example, how certain actions have certain consequences. However, this requires children to understand that two different events can be causally linked, that is, that the second event occurs *because* the first event occurred. At what age do children possess this basic concept of causality? Furthermore, at what age are children able to infer such causal relationships from correlations between events? As Hume (1739/1978) observed, experience offers only correlations, nevertheless under some conditions (for example, constant conjunction and spatiotemporal contiguity) adults perceive causality. Do children interpret their experience in the same way?

Evidence suggests that even young infants perceive causal relationships in the physical domain. When one inanimate object collides with another and the second object immediately moves away from the point of contact, infants as young as six months of age appear to infer that the collision caused the movement of the second object (Leslie & Keeble, 1987). However, the same infants do not attribute causality when the second object moves a few moments after the collision. How do we presume to know what preverbal infants think about such events? Infants look longer when the first type of event (immediate reaction) is reversed (that is, the second object now collides with the first object, which immediately moves away) than when the second type of event (delayed reaction) is reversed. The argument is that the infants perceive a reversal of the causal relationship in the first case but not the second, which leads to heightened interest, which leads to longer looking times. If one accepts this argument, it seems that children are capable of understanding causal relationships under some simple conditions very early in life.

How do children fare under more complicated conditions, such as when there are multiple candidate causes for an outcome, some of which may be confounds (that is, merely correlated with true causes)? Research by Gopnik and colleagues suggests that children are able to use covariation information to separate true causes from confounds by three years of age. For example, if three-year-olds observe that one object (object A) is associated with a certain outcome (for example, a machine turns on) in the absence of another object (object B), but object B is only associated with the outcome in conjunction with object A, the children will conclude that object A but not object B causes the outcome (Gopnik, Sobel, Schulz, & Glymour, 2001). As evidence of this understanding, the children will remove object A rather than object B when asked to terminate the effect (turn the machine off). This sort of research indicates that the basic cognitive capacity to infer causal relationships is in place by early childhood. However, the ability to correctly infer causality in more clinically relevant domains, such as interpersonal relationships, may require additional domain-specific knowledge. In other words, clinicians can assume that even young children are capable of understanding cause-and-effect relationships, but clinicians may still need to help children understand how particular causes are related to particular effects in practice.

Children's Understanding of Counterfactuals

Understanding of causality is necessary for reasoning about counterfactuals, that is, for predicting what would happen under hypothetical conditions ("What would happen if X were not the case?"). Counterfactual reasoning is clinically significant because clinicians may want children to consider the ramifications of different alternatives, for example, to imagine the consequences of different courses of action without actually taking those actions. Harris, German, and Mills (1996) have demonstrated that children as young as three years of age engage in counterfactual reasoning under some circumstances. For example, when a person chooses an option (for example, to draw with a pen) that leads to a negative outcome (such as spilled ink), three-year-olds attribute the outcome to the person's decision *only* when the person rejected an alternative option that would have avoided the negative outcome (such as to draw with a pencil). In other words, children of this age are able to consider whether alternative courses of action would have led to the same outcome, and make causal judgments accordingly. Clinicians who may have assumed that young children are incapable of considering hypothetical alternatives may be surprised to learn that young children's causal judgments can be influenced not only by the antecedent-consequent relations that the children actually observe, but also by those that they imagine and contrast with reality.

However, German (1999) suggests that children are more likely to engage in counterfactual reasoning in response to negative outcomes than positive outcomes. That is, negative outcomes naturally prompt children to consider whether alternative choices might have prevented the outcome, whereas positive outcomes are less likely to provoke counterfactual comparisons. In support of this hypothesis, German showed that five-year-olds were likely to consider a rejected course of action causally relevant only when explaining a negative outcome (for example, Sally chooses a sweet rather than a sandwich and ends up hungry). In contrast, children typically considered the actual course of action sufficient to explain a positive outcome (for example, Sally chooses a sandwich rather than a sweet and ends up full). German argues that children do not necessarily consider counterfactuals when making causal judgments. Rather, counterfactuals become causally salient in the context of avoiding an undesired outcome. In a clinical context, children may be more capable of generating and evaluating alternatives when they view the actual situation as unsatisfactory than when they view the actual situation as satisfactory. One implication is that a clinician who wants a child to consider how alternative courses of action could lead to different situations may first need to challenge the child's perception of the current situation as satisfactory.

Children's Capacity for Logical Reasoning

Many clinical practices assume the ability to evaluate propositions and evidence logically. For example, children may be encouraged to recognize inconsistencies in their belief systems and to revise maladaptive beliefs in response to counterevidence. However, research indicates that the basic capacity for logical reasoning undergoes substantial development during childhood. According to Piaget (1970), the final major stage of cognitive development ("formal operations") is achieved around eleven to thirteen years of age, on average. This stage is characterized by the capacity for logical operations on abstract propositions. Piaget argued that, previous to this stage, children's cognition is tied to concrete objects and events. To give a concrete example of this distinction, Osherson and Markman (1975) asked seven-year-old children to evaluate propositions that were logical contradictions (necessarily false, such as "The chip in my hand is white and it is not white.") or logical tautologies (necessarily true, such as "Either the chip in my hand is yellow or it is not yellow."). In either case, the chip was hidden in the experimenter's hand. Most seven-year-olds answered that they could not tell whether the propositions were true or false without actually seeing the chip. That is, they seemed to treat the propositions as empirical hypotheses, which needed to be evaluated against the concrete reality (the color of the chip), even though the propositions could actually be evaluated on purely logical grounds.

As with many aspects of Piaget's theory, subsequent research has demonstrated somewhat earlier competence than Piaget's theory predicts. To borrow terminology from evolutionary theory (phylogeny), individual cognitive development (ontogeny) now appears more like gradualism rather than punctuated equilibrium (that is, periods of relative stasis punctuated by qualitative shifts in reasoning). In a number of areas, children's cognitive performance seems to vary depending on particular features of the context and task, rather than simply reflecting some domain-general level of cognitive development. Young children may demonstrate competence under facilitative conditions, but not under more demanding conditions. For example, Ruffman (1999) found that under facilitative conditions, children demonstrated some understanding of logical contradictions by age six, but not before. Specifically, six-year-olds recognized that it makes less sense for one person to simultaneously make contradictory claims (for example, "Peter is eating an apple, and not only that, Peter is not eating an apple."), than it does for two *different* people to simultaneously make contradictory claims. Children younger than six years recognized when statements were factually implausible

("Peter is eating a television, and not only that, Peter is not eating an apple."), but not when statements were internally inconsistent (as in the first example).

Although the ability to recognize logical inconsistency seems to develop around age six, the ability to test hypotheses in a logical fashion seems to be a later development. That is, even after children are able to evaluate the logical form of a proposition, they still have difficulty selecting appropriate tests to determine the truth of an empirical proposition. Samuels and McDonald (2002) demonstrated that ten-year-olds favor positive tests (those which, if true, would support the hypothesis) over negative tests (those which, if true, would falsify the hypothesis). Although adults also show this sort of positive test bias (Wason, 1960), the bias seems to be stronger in children. In fact, children will often choose a positive test over a negative one even when only the negative test is diagnostic (that is, distinguishes between rival hypotheses). For example, ten-year-olds were familiarized with the properties of three objects and then allowed one question to determine whether a particular one of the objects (the target) was hidden behind a screen. Unlike adults, the children did not reliably recognize that negative diagnostic questions (such as, "Is it heavy?" when only the target object was *not* heavy) would be more informative than positive nondiagnostic questions (such as, "Is it soft?" when another object besides the target was soft). The implication is that children are less likely than adults to seek information that could possibly falsify their current hypotheses. As a result, children may be less likely to independently revise maladaptive beliefs, especially if some evidence is consistent with them. Clinicians may need to help children realize that evidence that seems to support their preconceived notions may also be consistent with other, more adaptive beliefs.

Children's Understanding of Dual Representation

Young children have difficulty understanding that the same thing can sometimes be represented in two different ways simultaneously. Young children tend to believe that things have one essential nature which can be read off of their appearance (Gelman, 2003). However, the world is actually more complicated than that. Some things can be read as symbols for other things. Some things may not be what they seem on the surface. For example, an abusive parent can be a loved and trusted figure, but also a dangerous and feared one. In general, young children have difficulty recognizing and processing this sort of ambiguity. Clinicians should consider this tendency in children's thought, by either pointing out the ambiguity if the child is old enough to understand dual representation, or working around it if not.

For example, a scale model is an object that can be represented in two ways: as an object in its own right, and as a symbol that refers to something else. In a series of important studies, DeLoache and her colleagues (see DeLoache, 2002, for a review) have shown that children do not understand scale models until around three years of age. In a typical study, the child is shown a room and a small three-dimensional scale model of the room, complete with corresponding miniature furniture. The correspondences between the big room and the little room are explicitly highlighted for the child. With the child watching, the experimenter hides a miniature doll in the scale model (for example, behind the miniature couch). The experimenter then tells the child that a real doll is hidden in the same place in the big room. Three-year-olds immediately search behind the real couch, whereas two-and-one-half-year-olds search randomly. However, two-and-one-half-year-olds can use a two-dimensional picture of the big room to guide their search behavior. This may seem somewhat surprising, because to adult eyes a scale model provides more explicit information than a picture. DeLoache argues, however, that the physical salience of the model makes it more difficult for young children to simultaneously view it as a symbol. It is easier for young children to view a picture as a representation, to see "through" the picture to its referent.

However, understanding of dual representation is hardly complete by age three. For example, three-year-olds do not spontaneously make the connection between the big room and the small room. If the correspondence is not highlighted by the experimenter, children do not use the scale model to guide their search behavior until five to seven years of age (DeLoache, 2002). This illustrates the Vygotskian principle that a child's level of cognitive competence is not an absolute quantity that can be measured in isolation. Rather, it varies depending on the social context and the presence and support of knowledgeable others. The clinical implication is that a supportive therapist may be able to point out connections between things that a child would not recognize independently, but that once those connections are made the child may be able to use them to guide his or her own behavior.

DeLoache's research indicates that young children have difficulty viewing an object as itself and also as a representation of something else. Other research indicates that young children also have difficulty viewing the same object as representing two different things. For example, Gopnik and Rosati (2001) showed ambiguous figures such as the famous "duck/rabbit" figure to children aged four to five years. None of the children spontaneously identified both interpretations of the figures. After the alternative interpretations were highlighted by the experimenter, all of the children acknowledged the existence of both interpretations. However, only the five-year-olds reported perceptual reversals, that is, seeing the figure switch from looking like one thing (a duck) to looking like another (a rabbit). These results indicate that once young children assign an interpretation to something, they are unlikely to seek alternative interpretations. Even if alternative interpretations are pointed out to them, such as by a therapist, young children may have difficulty switching back and forth between them. In general, children seem to have difficulty understanding that some objects and events are legitimately ambiguous, that is, they can be interpreted in different but equally valid ways.

While some things in the world are ambiguous, others are downright misleading. Research by author Flavell and his colleagues indicates that children's understanding that appearances and reality can conflict undergoes significant development between ages three and five (Flavell, Green, & Flavell, 1986). For example, when presented with a deceptive object (such as an eraser that looks like a banana), children cannot consistently report that the object looks like one thing but really is another until around age five. Younger children seem to have trouble representing things in two different ways simultaneously, and tend to claim either that the object looks like what it is (the realism error) or that it is what it looks like (the phenomenism error). The ability to reflect upon and talk about the appearance-reality distinction continues to improve during childhood and into early adolescence (Flavell et al., 1986). As a result, clinicians may need to help children realize that appearances can be misleading, for example, that someone can seem nice but actually be mean. Clinicians should not assume, however, that young children are simply slaves to appearance (that is, phenomenists, always believing that things are what they seem to be). In fact, the opposite is sometimes true: children's beliefs about something's real nature can sometimes override their perceptions (for example, realist errors). Both types of error seem to stem from difficulty with dual representation, and clinicians should be on the lookout for each type.

Development of Inhibitory Control

One thing that makes dual representation hard is the need to inhibit one way of seeing something in order to consider another. The ability to inhibit one's initial response to a stimulus improves substantially during early childhood. This has important clinical implications, because one goal of therapy may be to get children to not act upon their first impulse, but to reflect upon their options and select the most adaptive one. Children's capacity for this sort of inhibitory control of their own behavior varies with age. For example, Gerstadt, Hong, and Diamond (1994) gave children, ages three-and-one-half to seven years, an age-appropriate version of the famous Stroop task used with adults (Stroop, 1935). The task required children to say "night" to a picture of the sun and "day" to a picture of the moon and stars (that is, to reverse their natural responses). Performance increased gradually with age, reaching 90% correct by age six or seven. Average response time decreased sharply from three-and-one-half to four-and-one-half, whereupon it leveled off. Children, especially younger children, performed better when they took longer to respond. This suggests that encouraging children, especially younger children, to stop and think before responding to a situation can lead them to make better choices.

The development of inhibitory control is thought to reflect the maturation of prefrontal cortical areas in the brain (Stuss, 1992). Prefrontal cortex is thought to subserve the so-called "executive functions" such as inhibitory control, selective attention, resistance to interference, and so forth. Durston et al. (2002) studied the relationship between inhibitory control and prefrontal activation in children (age six to ten) and adults. Participants were instructed to press a button in response to each of a series of stimuli, but to inhibit response to a particular infrequent stimulus (a "go-no go" task). The adults were both faster and more accurate than the children. Furthermore, accuracy was correlated with changes in prefrontal activity as measured by fMRI. Clinicians should be aware that, due to immature cortical development, children have less capacity to monitor and regulate their behavior than adults do. As a result, it is more difficult for children to consciously override previously learned patterns of behavior.

Developments in Social Cognition

Social cognition refers to thinking and knowledge about the behavior and mental experiences of people. Developments in this area are some of the most relevant for clinical practice. In this section, we review how children's conceptions of self and others change with age and are related to their social behavior and social adjustment.

Development of Self-Concept

One of the most basic developments in social cognition is the development of an understanding of the self as an independent, coherent, and consistent entity (see Harter, 1998, for a review). Many therapeutic approaches seek to foster greater self-understanding, but clinicians should be aware that a child's concept of the self may be very different from that of an adult. For example, young children may not even have a concept of the self as extending through time. Research by Povinelli, Landau, and Perilloux (1996) suggests that young children's self-concept is limited to the present. Children, age two to four years, were videotaped while playing a game with an experimenter. During the course of the game, the experimenter surreptitiously placed a large sticker on the child's head. The child was then shown the videotape, which clearly depicted the marking event. Not until four years of age did children make the connection between their image on the video and their present self, and reach up and remove the sticker. Younger children, however, had no difficulty locating the sticker using live video feedback, indicating that they understood the correspondence between their image and themselves, but only in the present. Povinelli et al. argue that young children could not make the connection between their image in the past and themselves in the present because they do not conceptualize past, present, and future states of the self as an integrated whole. However, Zelazo, Sommerville, and Nichols (1999) argue that the delayed-video paradigm may underestimate children's self-understanding because performance also depends on the child's ability to interpret the video as a representation of a past state of affairs. (See Children's Understanding of Dual Representation, in this chapter.)

Once children form a self-concept, they seem to be motivated to maintain a consistent view of themselves. This desire for self-stability can have clinical implications, however, because if aspects of the self-concept are negative, children may actually seek reinforcement of those aspects. To test this possibility, Cassidy, Ziv, Mehta, and Feeney (2003) measured the perceived self-competence of twelve-year-olds across a range of domains (academic, athletic, social, and so on). For each domain, children also chose whether to hear another person's opinion of why the child might succeed in this domain or another person's opinion of why the child might fail in this domain. Children preferred to hear possible reasons for success in domains in which they felt competent, and possible reasons for failure in domains in which they felt incompetent. Furthermore, both twelve-year-olds and seventeen-year-olds with high overall perceived self-worth chose to hear more positive feedback about their self-worth than did those with low overall perceived self-worth. Cassidy et al. also examined the relationship between depression and feedback-seeking in the seventeen-year-olds. Nondepressed seventeen-year-olds tended to seek positive feedback about their self-worth, whereas depressed seventeen-year-olds actually tended to seek negative feedback about their self-worth. The clinical implications are clear: positive and negative self-images are self-reinforcing. How to break a cycle of negative self-image and negative feedback-seeking is less clear. A clinician could try to show a child how he or she is missing or actively avoiding opportunities for positive feedback. This strategy seems more likely to work with older children and adolescents who are able to reflect upon their own behavior. A clinician could also take advantage of the fact that even a child with low overall self-worth may feel competent in some areas. The clinician could focus on those areas and gradually encourage the child to apply the same sort of positive feedback-seeking attitude to other areas.

Children's Beliefs about Traits and Abilities

One important aspect of the development of a self-concept is an understanding that the self has certain stable characteristics that may differ from those of other people. In particular, children's expectations of consistency in people's behavior across situations tend to increase with age. Adults typically conceptualize such behavioral regularities as due to personality traits: internal psychological dispositions. A number of studies indicate that between five and nine years of age children become more likely to describe themselves and others in trait terms and to consider past behavior as predictive of future behavior. (See Ruble & Dweck, 1995, for a review.) However, some studies indicate that younger children have some understanding of traits. For example, Eder (1989) found that three-and-one-half-year-olds are able to describe their own behavior and that of peers in terms of general tendencies (versus specific instances). However, as with many areas of cognitive development, although children may show some understanding under facilitative conditions at an early age, the ability to apply that knowledge under typical conditions may continue to develop.

Children become more likely to attribute another person's behavior to dispositional factors with age. For example, Aloise (1993) found that, relative to adults, children aged nine to eleven years required more examples of a particular type of behavior before inferring that a person possessed a particular personality trait. In this case, the less mature position may actually be more accurate. Research in social psychology indicates that adults are often too quick to jump to dispositional conclusions and underestimate the importance of situational factors in determining people's behavior (the so-called "fundamental attribution error"; Ross, 1977). Interestingly, this dispositional bias seems to be a cultural rather than a strictly developmental phenomenon. Miller (1984) compared the proportions of dispositional and situational explanations for other people's behavior in American and Indian Hindu adults and children (ages eight, eleven, and fifteen years). At age eight, the proportions were similar in the two cultures. However, dispositional attributions increased with age in the American sample, whereas situational attributions increased with age in the Hindu sample. Clinicians may need to combat the fundamental attribution error in their clients, especially when a client makes negative dispositional attributions about the self or others. The clinician may want to point out situational factors as alternative explanations. One advantage of situational explanations for negative behaviors is that they imply the possibility of more positive behavior under different conditions.

Young children's dispositional attributions tend to be rather global and evaluative (for example, someone is either all good or all bad). With age, children's conceptions of traits become more differentiated (for example, someone may be competent in one domain, but incompetent in another). For example, Stipek and Daniels (1990) found that kindergartners were more likely than older children to believe that if a child was successful in one area (such as academics), then the child would also be successful in all other areas (such as athletics, social behavior, and so on). However, if motivated, kindergartners can make more differentiated judgments. Droege and Stipek (1993) found that kindergartners chose different classmates as play partners versus as teammates for an academic contest, indicating some differentiation between social skills and academic ability (for example, "nice" versus "smart"). As in other areas of cognition, children's understanding seems to vary with the context. The general clinical implication is that younger children are more likely to interpret success in any area as indicating that someone is a good person and failure in any area as indicating that someone is a bad person. Clinicians may want to encourage more differentiated thinking, and especially discourage unwarranted negative global self-evaluations. The Droege and Stipek results suggest that even young children are capable of more differentiated thinking if sufficiently motivated.

Research by Dweck and her colleagues indicates that individual differences in beliefs about ability have serious consequences for motivational and behavioral patterns (see Dweck, 1986, 2002, for reviews). Some children conceptualize ability as a stable trait-like quantity (an "entity theory"), whereas others conceptualize ability as a dynamic process which is revealed in performance and which reflects practice and effort (an "incremental theory"). Children with an entity theory are more vulnerable in the face of adversity, because failure is attributed to inherent internal deficiency. Children with an incremental theory are more resilient in the face of adversity, because failure is attributed to insufficient experience and/or effort. Children with an entity theory are more likely to avoid challenge, due to the risk of negative self-evaluations and unflattering social comparisons. Children with an incremental theory are more likely to seek challenge, as a way to develop competence. In general, Dweck's research shows that entity theories of ability are associated with maladaptive helpless behavior patterns, whereas incremental theories of ability are associated with more adaptive mastery-oriented behavior patterns. The clinical implication is clear: clinicians should encourage incremental conceptions of ability, in which current difficulty in a domain can be overcome by increasing effort and by changing strategies. Research by Dweck and colleagues indicates that adult feedback can modify children's theories of ability (Dweck, 2002, p. 77), suggesting that a supportive therapist could influence children in the incremental direction.

Unfortunately, at least within Western European–American culture, the general developmental trend is in the opposite direction. For example, younger children are more likely than older children to believe that academic ability and social ability can improve with age, effort, or a change of setting (Droege & Stipek, 1993). Older children are more likely to view ability as a stable property of a person, although a person's level of ability may differ in different domains. Younger children tend to define high ability in absolute terms (for example, the ability to do something), whereas older children tend to define high ability in relative terms (for example, the ability to outperform others). Furthermore, younger children tend to overestimate their own ability, whereas older children are more accurate (Stipek & Mac Iver, 1989). In this case, maturity brings vulnerability, as many children will eventually realize that they are below average, which may have negative clinical consequences such as devaluing the self or the domain. As has been noted in other cases, cognitive immaturity can sometimes be adaptive (Bjorklund & Green, 1992). In this case, it may serve to maintain young children's motivation and persistence despite their low levels of ability (in both absolute terms and relative to older children and adults). And in fact children's persistence is often rewarded, as their absolute levels of ability in many areas do improve with age much more rapidly than in adults. Lockhart, Chang, and Story (2002) found that younger children (ages five to six) typically predicted that negative personal characteristics would show large positive changes with age. In contrast, older children (ages seven to nine) typically predicted small positive changes and adults typically predicted no change. All three age groups predicted that positive personal characteristics were not likely to change much with age. Young children seem to believe that everyone grows up to be above average (akin to author Garrison Keillor's mythical Lake Wobegon, except that all the adults are above average rather than all the children). Lockhart et al. suggest that a young child may actually perceive all adults to be above average, because their competence so exceeds the child's. Clinicians should consider that unrealistically positive evaluations and expectations of the self may be maladaptive in adults, but actually adaptive in children (what Lockhart et al. call "protective optimism"). Clinicians should also recognize that the typical developmental course of beliefs about ability in this culture carries clinical risks. With age, children are more likely to identify areas of low competence in themselves and believe that they cannot be changed. This can lead to helpless behavior patterns and perhaps depression or other psychopathology.

Children's Attributional Biases

Social cognition is the application of cognition to the social domain. As such, the study of social cognition incorporates methods and concepts from both cognitive psychology and social psychology. One example of a productive integration of these areas is work by Dodge and his colleagues on social information processing. (See Crick & Dodge, 1994, for a review.) Dodge and colleagues analyze social behavior by using the information-processing paradigm borrowed from cognitive psychology. That is, they break down the process into specific steps, as one would in writing a computer program. Dodge and colleagues are particularly interested in how errors in children's social cognition can lead to maladjusted social outcomes, such as aggressive behavior or peer rejection.

One area that Dodge and colleagues have examined is children's attributions of intent to other people. Here, Dodge and colleagues borrow from attribution theory in social psychology. Attribution theorists study the reasons people give for people's behavior. Attribution theorists have determined that there are characteristic errors in people's attributions. One was discussed in the previous section: the fundamental attribution error (Ross, 1977). Dodge and colleagues have focused on another error found in some children: hostile attributional bias. Hostile attributional bias refers to the tendency of some children to attribute hostile intent to other people in social situations. A number of studies have found that hostile attributional bias predicts aggressive behavior in children. (See Crick & Dodge, 1994, pp. 84–85.) Dodge and colleagues hypothesize that biased information processing leads some children to interpret ambiguous social stimuli (for example, a bump in the school corridor) as intentional provocations rather than benign accidents. This leads such children to select aggressive responses, which may evoke hostility, which reinforces the children's hypervigilance and defensiveness. A recent meta-analysis confirms the association between hostile attribution of intent and aggressive behavior in children (Orobio de Castro, Veerman, Koops, Bosch, & Monshouwer, 2002).

The clinical implication of this research is that interventions that target children's attributional biases may reduce social maladjustment. Hudley and Graham (1993) tested this approach with an attributional intervention for aggressive low-income African-American boys (average age of ten years). The attribution retraining program consisted of twelve sessions over six weeks and encouraged children to consider alternative explanations for ambiguous negative peer interactions (besides peer hostility) and alternative behavioral responses (besides aggression). Children who were randomly assigned to the attribution retraining showed a significant reduction in aggressive behavior, relative to children assigned to either an unrelated training program or a no-treatment control group. The success of the Hudley and Graham program suggests a possible clinical strategy. Careful analysis of a client's social information-processing patterns may reveal biases that have cascading negative effects (to use the computer analogy, bugs in the program that cause the system to crash). Addressing these biases may therefore have cascading positive effects on social adjustment.

Development of Perspective-Taking Ability

An important aspect of social adjustment is the ability to consider other people's perspectives. According to Piaget's theory, this ability develops around seven to eight years of age. Piaget described children younger than this as "egocentric," that is, unable to detach from their own perspectives. As with other areas of cognition, subsequent research has modified Piaget's conclusions in two ways. First, children show some evidence of perspective-taking ability much earlier than Piaget predicted. Second, perspective-taking ability does not develop in one qualitative shift at a certain age. Rather, children develop the ability to consider other people's perspectives in different contexts at different ages.

Children show some understanding that people's desires may differ from their own as early as eighteen months of age. In a study by Repacholi and Gopnik (1997), children watched as the experimenter tasted two types of food (broccoli and goldfish crackers) and expressed pleasure toward one and disgust toward the other. The experimenter then asked (both verbally and via gesture) the child to give her some food. The eighteen-month-olds typically offered the food toward which the experimenter had expressed pleasure, regardless of their own preferences. In contrast, fourteen-month-olds typically responded egocentrically, offering the food that they themselves preferred (almost always the goldfish crackers).

Although understanding of the subjectivity of desires may develop during infancy, understanding of the subjectivity of beliefs does not develop until preschool age. The ability to consider other people's beliefs is typically tested with a "false belief task" (Wimmer & Perner, 1983). In a classic version, the child and another person (call her Sally) see an object placed in one location. Then Sally leaves and the child sees the object moved to a second location. Sally returns and the child is asked where Sally will look for the object. Children older than about age four correctly predict that Sally will look in the first location, because she did not see the object moved, and so has a false belief about its location. In contrast, three-year-olds typically respond egocentrically, predicting that Sally will look in the second location. These children apparently attribute their own knowledge of the object's location to Sally. (See Wellman, Cross, & Watson, 2001, for a recent meta-analysis of this voluminous literature.) Theoretical explanations of young children's failure vary, including inability to simultaneously represent two different beliefs (see Children's Understanding of Dual Representation, in this chapter) and inability to inhibit one's own perspective. (See Development of Inhibitory Control, in this chapter.)

Perspective-taking ability continues to develop after preschool age. Carpendale and Chandler (1996) argue that false belief tasks measure children's understanding that people who perceive different things will believe different things. However, the understanding that two different people can perceive the exact same thing (for example, an ambiguous figure) and form different interpretations of it does not develop until around seven to eight years of age. (See Children's Understanding of Dual Representation, in this chapter.) Elkind (1967) points out that adolescents are egocentric in some ways. For instance, adolescents' preoccupation with themselves leads them to overestimate how much attention other people pay to them (the "imaginary audience" effect). Ross and Ward (1996) discuss egocentric aspects of adult thought ("naïve realism"). Although adults acknowledge other people's perspectives, we tend to discount the fact that our own beliefs are subjective interpretations of reality, rather than objective perceptions. As a result, we tend to view those who disagree with us as ill-informed, irrational, or evil. (See Children's Attributional Biases, in this chapter.) Ross and Ward describe a compelling example of adult egocentrism from a study conducted in their laboratory. In this study, one participant (the tapper) tapped the rhythm of a well-known song on the table and another participant (the listener) tried to guess the song. Tappers (who could hear the melody in their head) estimated that listeners would guess 50% of the songs. In fact, listeners guessed only 2.5% of the songs. This example shows that even adults have trouble taking another person's perspective under some conditions.

What are the clinical implications of research on the development of perspective-taking ability? Some egocentrism is normal, but excessive egocentrism is likely to be maladaptive. Failure to consider other people's perspectives leads to miscommunication, misunderstanding, and ill-will. Some research suggests that discussion of other people's perspectives fosters perspective-taking ability. For example, parental talk about mental states predicts children's understanding of false beliefs (Ruffman, Slade, & Crowe, 2002). Therefore clinicians may promote cognitive development and social adjustment by pointing out differences in people's perspectives. Egocentrism may appear in different forms at different ages, including adulthood. Clinicians themselves are not immune. Acknowledgement of the subjectivity of one's own perspective may help a therapist appreciate the perspective and problems of his or her clients, which may improve communication and strengthen a sense of respect and trust in the therapeutic relationship.

Development of Intuitions about Mental Experiences

A rough distinction can be made between mental states, such as beliefs and attitudes, and conscious mental experiences, such as the experience of having a sudden thought, memory, percept, or feeling. Much of the research on the development of social cognition has dealt with children's developing understanding of mental states; the many studies of children's false belief understanding are familiar examples. However, there have also been a few studies of the development of children's intuitions about mental experiences, especially thinking, attention, and consciousness, mostly by author Flavell and colleagues.

Evidence from these studies has shown that children have acquired some elementary but important knowledge about mental experiences by the end of the preschool period (Flavell, Green, & Flavell, 1995b). They know that only humans and other animates can think. They recognize that thinking is an internal, mental activity; consequently, they understand that a mental image of a dog, unlike a real dog, is internal, private, and intangible. They know that one thinks *about* things—present or absent, real or imaginary. Thus, they know that thinking is some sort of internal, mental activity that people engage in which can have as its content either real or imaginary objects or events. They can also distinguish thinking from other psychological activities that often accompany it and that therefore could be confused with it. For example, even three- and four-year-olds will say that an experimenter who is asked to explain a puzzling sight (a large pear inside a narrow-necked liqueur bottle) and turns away from it to reflect silently is not presently touching, seeing, or talking about the bottle, but is thinking about it. This is an impressive feat in view of the fact that the experimenter does not give the appearance of being psychologically connected to the bottle in any way when facing away from it. Thus, clinicians can count on most preschoolers having at least some basic knowledge in this area.

Despite these important developmental accomplishments, there are a number of commonplace and seemingly obvious intuitions about mental experiences that are mostly acquired later, during middle childhood or adolescence (Flavell, 1999; Flavell, Green, & Flavell, 1995b; Flavell & Miller, 1998). The following are some of these later-developing intuitions, together with some of the research evidence attesting to their development.

1. *When they are awake, people are experiencing a more or less continuous, essentially unstoppable flow of conscious mental content (William James' famous stream of consciousness), even when receiving no significant perceptual input and engaged in no cognitive task.* Several studies indicate that young children are unaware of this important fact about the way our minds work. In one study (Flavell, Green, & Flavell, 1993), for example, three-year-olds, four-year-olds, six- and seven-year-olds, and adults were first given some pretraining on the meaning of "having some thoughts and ideas" (while awake) versus not having any (while sound asleep and not dreaming). Next, one experimenter sat quietly in a chair facing a blank wall, "just waiting." The other experimenter then asked the participants: "How about her mind right now? Is she having some thoughts and ideas right now or is her mind empty of thoughts and ideas?" Empty and nonempty thought bubbles, previously used in the pretraining, were employed to illustrate each option. The percentages of participants saying that the first experimenter was having some thoughts and ideas while waiting were 15%, 35%, 80%, and 95%, from youngest to oldest group. Other studies (Flavell, Green, & Flavell, 1995b) have shown that—surprisingly—some young children may not assume that something must be "going on in a person's mind" or that the person's mind must be "doing something" even when that person is known to be engaged in such obviously (to adults) mind-using activities as listening, talking, or reading.

Another study assessed awareness of the above-mentioned "essentially unstoppable" nature of the stream of consciousness (Flavell, Green, & Flavell, 1998). In this study, five-year-olds, nine-year-olds, thirteen-year-olds, and adults were asked whether a depicted child could go for three days without thinking or wondering about anything if he or she tried really hard. The percentages of participants claiming that the child could not do this were 50%, 90%, 90%, and 100%, from the youngest to oldest group. In their justification for this claim almost one-third of the thirteen-year-olds and over half of the adults seemed to be expressing the intuition that it is the very nature of the mind to be spontaneously active, and therefore one cannot inhibit this activity for long; none of the younger children gave evidence of having this intuition.

These studies suggest that young children are unlikely to wonder spontaneously about the ongoing mental experiences of significant other people (their thoughts, feelings, wishes, and so on), unless the evidence for them is very strong and clear. The reason is that they are not aware that these experiences are inevitable and essentially unceasing in a conscious person. It seems possible, however, that clinicians might be able to find ways to make their young patients more aware of this important fact of mental life.

2. *Attention is selective and limited.* In three studies by Flavell, Green, and Flavell (1995b), four-year-olds revealed a curious limitation in their understanding of how thought or attention is deployed. For example, after having established that a person was currently thinking about one thing, they would often say that the person was also simultaneously thinking about some other, unrelated thing.

In a follow-up study (Flavell, Green, & Flavell, 1995a), children of four, six, and eight years of age were tested for their understanding that a person who is mentally focused on one thing will be devoting little or no simultaneous attention or thought to another, totally irrelevant thing. For example, while one is busy trying to recognize the people in a group photograph one will likely not also be thinking about the photograph's drab frame. Whereas most of the six- and eight-year-olds demonstrated an understanding that task-oriented thought and attention are selectively focused in this way, most of the four-year-olds showed no such understanding. These results suggest that four-year-olds may implicitly conceive of the mind as more analogous to a lamp than a flashlight: that is, they may believe that it is capable of radiating attention or thought in many directions at once, rather than in only one direction at a time. This may make it difficult for them to understand the concept of distraction and the need to defend against it when performing attention-demanding tasks.

3. *When they are deeply asleep and not dreaming, people are not having conscious mental experiences, although they may respond to some stimuli at a subconscious level.* We did four studies investigating the development of an understanding of what it is like,

mentally, to be in a commonly-occurring nonconscious state—namely, in a state of deep, dreamless sleep (Flavell, Green, Flavell, & Lin, 1999). In one, for example, we assessed the willingness of five-year-olds, eight-year-olds, and adults to attribute verbalized, conscious-sounding thoughts to a videotaped sleeping person who was said to be deeply asleep and not dreaming. More than half of the participants in each of the two child groups made this attribution on at least one trial, whereas no adult participant ever did. The adults in this study also showed a much better understanding of levels of consciousness than the children did. When they saw the sleeping individual stir but not wake up in response to a light touch on the nose, they concluded that although the individual did "sort of feel" the touch he or she would not have the highly conscious thought, "Hey, I think someone is tickling my nose right now!" They also often justified this conclusion by saying that the feeling was at a subconscious rather than a conscious level. Thus, just as young children may underestimate the amount of conscious thought in a conscious mind (see 1., above), so also may they overestimate the amount of conscious thought in an unconscious one. These results make it seem unlikely that young children would have any conception of the distinction between conscious and unconscious thoughts, feelings, motives, or other mental processes.

    4. *Mental experiences may cause other mental experiences.* We have been particularly concerned here with the case of thoughts or memories causing emotions. People may suddenly feel sad (or some other emotion) because of something sad that just happened to them. However, they may also suddenly experience a sad feeling merely because they perceive something that triggers a thought or memory of some past event. A third possibility is that an emotion-causing thought or memory may just happen to come to mind, without there being any external reminder. Even very young children are attuned to the first possibility, in which present sad events are construed as triggering present sad feelings directly. Research by Lagattuta, Wellman, and Flavell (1997) and Lagattuta and Wellman (2001) has shown that by age five or earlier, children can also understand the second possibility. Flavell, Flavell, and Green (2001) found that a sensitivity to the third possibility—spontaneous ideation alone triggering feelings—develops still later. In one study, for example, five-year-olds, seven-year-olds, and adults were told a story of a girl lying in bed at night in total darkness (no external cues) who suddenly starts to feel happy. The participants were asked to explain her sudden change of feeling. The percentages of participants who suggested that she must have thought of something happy were 15%, 70%, and 100%, from youngest to oldest group. Young children's limited understanding of how one cognitive event can cue another may help explain their ignorance of the stream of consciousness. Reciprocally, ignorance of the stream of consciousness may impede their understanding of cognitive cueing.

5. *Mental experiences vary considerably in the degree to which they are controllable by the experiencer.* In one study, Flavell, Green, and Flavell (1998) tested five-year-olds, nine-year-olds, thirteen-year-olds, and adults for their understanding that people have limited control over their mental activities and experiences. The experimenter told the participants about a child who, while awaiting a shot in the doctor's office, sees a shot needle. It was emphasized that this child does not want to think about getting a shot and is trying very hard never to do so. Participants were then asked whether or not the child would think about getting a shot while looking at the shot needle, and why. Only the thirteen-year-olds and the adults tended to say the child would. Unlike the two younger groups, they clearly understood that there are severe limits to people's ability to control their own mental activity. They believed that the character in the story would think about getting a shot despite the character's strong wish not to. In their justifications for this view, most of them pointed out that, under the circumstances described in the stories, these mental events would happen automatically and involuntarily; they would not be subject to an individual's control. Further evidence for this developmental trend was obtained in a subsequent investigation (Flavell & Green, 1999). These studies suggest that young children may have difficulty recognizing that people have only limited control over the mental content that streams through their minds and should therefore not feel guilty about experiencing unwanted thoughts and desires.

There is considerable evidence, then, that young children do not have the foregoing intuitions about mental experiences. Why might this be? In order to acquire these intuitions, one may need to pay attention to one's own mental experiences, and we have shown in a number of studies that preschoolers have very limited introspective abilities (Flavell, Green, & Flavell, 1993; 1995b, 1998, 2000; Flavell, Green, Flavell, & Grossman, 1997). As one of many examples, five-year-olds who at the experimenter's instigation had clearly just been thinking silently about which room in their house they keep their toothbrush in, often denied that they had just been thinking; moreover, in those instances when they did say they had been thinking, they often did not mention either a toothbrush or a bathroom when asked what they had been thinking about. In sharp contrast, children of seven or eight years of age were much better than five-year-olds at this and other introspection tasks. Consistent with these results, research by Flavell, Green, Flavell, and Grossman (1997) suggests that preschoolers may not be very aware of their own ongoing inner speech. These findings suggest that therapeutic efforts with young children should take into account their limited ability to notice and reflect on their own inner life—a suggestion that will surely not surprise any experienced clinician!

In this chapter, we summarized research evidence on children's cognitive development that might be of use to clinical practitioners. This evidence offers rough guides to the competencies and knowledge children of various ages would and would not be expected to possess. We hope this evidence may help practitioners avoid both overestimating and underestimating their child clients' capabilities. We conclude with two general suggestions for the reader, both very Piagetian. One is to remember that children will filter what peers, parents, and practitioners say and do to them through whatever knowledge structures they possess and that these may be surprisingly different from those of adults. The other is for you to filter what we have said in this chapter through your own knowledge structures in such a way that it may be translated into sensitive and effective clinical practice. This may mean accepting some of our implications, rejecting others, and modifying still others as your clinical experience dictates.

References

Aloise, P. A. (1993). Trait confirmation and disconfirmation: The development of attribution biases. *Journal of Experimental Child Psychology, 55,* 177–193.

Bjorklund, D. F., & Green, B. L. (1992). The adaptive nature of cognitive immaturity. *American Psychologist, 47,* 46–54.

Carpendale, J. I., & Chandler, M. J. (1996). On the distinction between false belief understanding and subscribing to an interpretive theory of mind. *Child Development, 67,* 1686–1706.

Cassidy, J., Ziv, Y., Mehta, T. G., & Feeney, B. C. (2003). Feedback-seeking in children and adolescents: Associations with self-perceptions, attachment representations, and depression. *Child Development, 74,* 612–628.

Cichetti, D., & Toth, S. L. (1998). Perspectives on research and practice in developmental psychopathology. In W. Damon (Series Ed.) & I. E. Sigel & K. A. Renninger (Vol. Eds.), *Handbook of child psychology, Vol. 4: Child psychology in practice* (5th ed., pp. 479–583). New York: Wiley.

Crick, N. R., & Dodge, K. A. (1994). A review and reformulation of social information-processing mechanisms in children's social adjustment. *Psychological Bulletin, 115,* 74–101.

DeLoache, J. S. (2002). The symbol-mindedness of young children. In W. W. Hartup & R. A. Weinberg (Eds.), *Child psychology in retrospect and prospect* (pp. 73–101). Mahwah, NJ: Erlbaum.

Droege, K. L., & Stipek, D. J. (1993). Children's use of dispositions to predict classmates' behavior. *Developmental Psychology, 29,* 646–654.

Durston, S., Thomas, K. M., Yang, Y., Uluğ, A. M., Zimmerman, R. D., & Casey, B. J. (2002). A neural basis for the development of inhibitory control. *Developmental Science, 5,* F9–F16.

Dweck, C. S. (1986). Motivational processes affecting learning. *American Psychologist, 41,* 1040–1048.

Dweck, C. S. (2002). The development of ability conceptions. In A. Wigfield & J. Eccles (Eds.), *The development of achievement motivation* (pp. 57–88). San Diego, CA: Academic Press.

Eder, R. A. (1989). The emergent personologist: The structure and content of 3 1/2-, 5 1/2-, and 7 1/2-year-olds' concepts of themselves and other persons. *Child Development, 60,* 1218–1228.

Elkind, D. (1967). Egocentrism in adolescence. *Child Development, 38,* 1025–1033.

Flavell, J. H. (1999). Cognitive development: Children's knowledge about the mind. *Annual Review of Psychology, 50,* 21–45.

Flavell, J. H., Flavell, E. R., & Green, F. L. (2001). Development of children's understanding of connections between thinking and feeling. *Psychological Science, 12,* 430–432.

Flavell, J. H., & Green, F. L. (1999). Development of intuitions about the controllability of different mental states. *Cognitive Development, 14,* 133–146.

Flavell, J. H., Green, F. L., & Flavell, E. R. (1986). Development of knowledge about the appearance-reality distinction. *Monographs of the Society for Research in Child Development, 51* (1, Serial No. 212).

Flavell, J. H., Green, F. L., & Flavell, E. R. (1993). Children's understanding of the stream of consciousness. *Child Development, 64,* 387–398.

Flavell, J. H., Green, F. L., & Flavell, E. R. (1995a). The development of children's knowledge about attentional focus. *Developmental Psychology, 31,* 706–712.

Flavell, J. H., Green, F. L., & Flavell, E. R. (1995b). Young children's knowledge about thinking. *Monographs of the Society for Research in Child Development, 60* (1, Serial No. 243).

Flavell, J. H., Green, F. L., & Flavell, E. R. (1998). The mind has a mind of its own: Developing knowledge about mental uncontrollability. *Cognitive Development, 13,* 127–138.

Flavell, J. H., Green, F. L., & Flavell, E. R. (2000). Development of children's awareness of their own thoughts. *Journal of Cognition and Development, 1,* 97–112.

Flavell, J. H., Green, F. L., Flavell, E. R., & Grossman, J. B. (1997). The development of children's knowledge about inner speech. *Child Development, 68,* 39–47.

Flavell, J. H., Green, F. L., Flavell, E. R., & Lin, N. T. (1999). Development of children's knowledge about unconsciousness. *Child Development, 70,* 396–412.

Flavell, J. H., & Miller, P. H. (1998). Social cognition. In W. Damon (Series Ed.) & D. Kuhn & R. S. Siegler (Vol. Eds.), *Handbook of child psychology: Vol. 2. Cognition, perception, and language* (5th ed., pp. 851–898). New York: Wiley.

Flavell, J. H., Miller, P. H., & Miller, S. A. (2002). *Cognitive development* (4th ed.). Upper Saddle River, NJ: Prentice Hall.

Gelman, S. A. (2003). *The essential child: Origins of essentialism in everyday thought.* Oxford, England: Oxford University Press.

German, T. P. (1999). Children's causal reasoning: Counterfactual thinking occurs for "negative" outcomes only. *Developmental Science, 2,* 442–447.

Gerstadt, C. L., Hong, Y. J., & Diamond, A. (1994). The relationship between cognition and action: Performance of children 3 1/2–7 years old on a Stroop-like day-night test. *Cognition, 53,* 129–153.

Gopnik, A., & Rosati, A. (2001). Duck or rabbit? Reversing ambiguous figures and understanding ambiguous representations. *Developmental Science, 4,* 175–183.

Gopnik, A., Sobel, D. M., Schulz, L. E., & Glymour, C. (2001). Causal learning mechanisms in very young children: Two-, three-, and four-year-olds infer causal relations from patterns of variation and covariation. *Developmental Psychology, 37,* 620–629.

Haith, M. M., & Benson, J. B. (1998). Infant cognition. In W. Damon (Series Ed.) & D. Kuhn & R. S. Siegler (Vol. Eds.), *Handbook of child psychology: Vol. 2. Cognition, perception, and language* (5th ed., pp. 199–254). New York: Wiley.

Harris, P. L., German, T., & Mills, P. (1996). Children's use of counterfactual thinking in causal reasoning. *Cognition, 61,* 233–259.

Harter, S. (1998). The development of self-representations. In W. Damon (Series Ed.) & N. Eisenberg (Vol. Ed.), *Handbook of child psychology: Vol. 3. Social, emotional, and personality development* (5th ed., pp. 553–617). New York: Wiley.

Hudley, C., & Graham, S. (1993). An attributional intervention to reduce peer-directed aggression among African-American boys. *Child Development, 64,* 124–138.

Hume, D. (1978). *A treatise of human nature.* Oxford, England: Oxford University Press. (Original work published 1739)

Lagattuta, K. H., & Wellman, H. M. (2001). Thinking about the past: Early knowledge about links between prior experience, thinking, and emotion. *Child Development, 72,* 82–102.

Lagattuta, K. H., Wellman, H. M., & Flavell, J. H. (1997). Preschoolers' understanding of the link between thinking and feeling: Cognitive cueing and emotional change. *Child Development, 68,* 1081–1104.

Leslie, A. M., & Keeble, S. (1987). Do six-month-old infants perceive causality? *Cognition, 25,* 265–288.

Lockhart, K. L., Chang, B., & Story, T. (2002). Young children's beliefs about the stability of traits: Protective optimism? *Child Development, 73,* 1408–1430.

Miller, J. G. (1984). Culture and the development of everyday social explanation. *Journal of Personality and Social Psychology, 46,* 961–978.

Orobio de Castro, B., Veerman, J. W., Koops, W., Bosch, J. D., & Monshouwer, H. J. (2002). Hostile attribution of intent and aggressive behavior: A meta-analysis. *Child Development, 73,* 916–934.

Osherson, D. N., & Markman, E. M. (1975). Language and the ability to evaluate contradictions and tautologies. *Cognition, 2,* 213–226.

Piaget, J. (1970). Piaget's theory (G. Gellerier & J. Langer, Trans.). In P. H. Mussen (Ed.), *Manual of child psychology* (Vol. 1, pp. 703–732). New York: Wiley.

Povinelli, D. J., Landau, K. R., & Perilloux, H. K. (1996). Self-recognition in young children using delayed versus live feedback: Evidence of a developmental asynchrony. *Child Development, 67,* 1540–1554.

Repacholi, B. M., & Gopnik, A. (1997). Early reasoning about desires: Evidence from 14- and 18-month-olds. *Developmental Psychology, 33,* 12–21.

Ross, L. (1977). The intuitive psychologist and his shortcomings: Distortions in the attribution process. In L. Berkowitz (Ed.), *Advances in experimental social psychology* (Vol. 10, pp. 173–220). New York: Academic Press.

Ross, L., & Ward, A. (1996). Naive realism in everyday life: Implications for social conflict and misunderstanding. In T. Brown, E. Reed, & E. Turiel (Eds.), *Values and knowledge* (pp. 103–135). Hillsdale, NJ: Erlbaum.

Ruble, D. N., & Dweck, C. S. (1995). Self-conceptions, person conceptions, and their development. In N. Eisenberg (Ed.), *Review of personality and social psychology: Vol. 15. Social development* (pp. 109–139). Thousand Oaks, CA: Sage.

Ruffman, T. (1999). Children's understanding of logical inconsistency. *Child Development, 70,* 872–886.

Ruffman, T., Slade, L., & Crowe, E. (2002). The relation between children's and mothers' mental state language and theory-of-mind understanding. *Child Development, 73,* 734–751.

Samuels, M. C., & McDonald, J. (2002). Elementary school-age children's capacity to choose positive diagnostic and negative diagnostic tests. *Child Development, 73,* 857–866.

Shirk, S. R. (Ed.). (1988). *Cognitive development and child psychotherapy.* New York: Plenum.

Stipek, D. J., & Daniels, D. H. (1990). Children's use of dispositional attributions in predicting the performance and behavior of classmates. *Journal of Applied Developmental Psychology, 11,* 13–28.

Stipek, D., & Mac Iver, D. (1989). Developmental change in children's assessment of intellectual competence. *Child Development, 60,* 521–538.

Stroop, J. R. (1935). Studies of interference in serial verbal reactions. *Journal of Experimental Psychology, 18,* 643–662.

Stuss, D. T. (1992). Biological and psychological development of executive functions. *Brain and Cognition, 20,* 8–23.

Vygotsky, L. S. (1978). *Mind in society: The development of higher psychological processes.* Cambridge, MA: Harvard University Press.

Wason, P. C. (1960). On the failure to eliminate hypotheses in a conceptual task. *Quarterly Journal of Experimental Psychology, 12,* 129–140.

Weisz, J. R. (1990). Development of control-related beliefs, goals, and styles in childhood and adolescence: A clinical perspective. In J. Rodin, C. Schooler, & K. W. Schaie (Eds.), *Self-directedness: Cause and effects throughout the life course* (pp. 103–145). Hillsdale, NJ: Erlbaum.

Wellman, H. M., Cross, D., & Watson, J. (2001). Meta-analysis of theory of mind development: The truth about false belief. *Child Development, 72,* 655–684.

Wimmer, H., & Perner, J. (1983). Beliefs about beliefs: Representation and constraining function of wrong beliefs in young children's understanding of deception. *Cognition, 13,* 103–128.

Zelazo, P. D., Sommerville, J. A., & Nichols, S. (1999). Age-related changes in children's use of external representations. *Developmental Psychology, 35,* 1059–1071.

CHAPTER FIVE

SURVEY OF BRAIN DEVELOPMENT

John L.R. Rubenstein, M.D., Ph.D., and Luis Puelles,
M.D., Ph.D.

Organization of the Nervous System

The nervous system consists of peripheral and central subdivisions that arise during early embryonic stages. The peripheral nervous system (PNS) is derived from subsets of neural crest cells and from ectodermal placodes (such as olfactory and otic). PNS structures are organized as ganglia (for example, sympathetic, parasympathetic, dorsal root, and enteric) or sensory epithelia (for example, olfactory and otic). The central nervous system (CNS) is derived from the neural plate. CNS structures are categorized according to their location within the neural tube. This chapter will focus on a description of major steps that control development of the CNS and how these steps can be derailed. Major early defects can cause morphologically apparent birth defects, whereas later and subtler defects may not cause anatomical abnormalities, yet may lead to behavioral disturbances. We will begin with a morphological description of CNS development (reviewed in Rubenstein et al., 1998 and in Puelles, 2001).

Induction of the neural plate begins around the onset of gastrulation. It specifies a large region of the embryonic ectoderm to develop into the CNS and PNS. The neural plate has several parts based upon their morphology, position, and molecular constitution, as shown in Figure 5.1. Its lateral edges (or ridges) are continuous with the adjacent non-neural ectoderm. In addition to being the anlage

FIGURE 5.1. LONGITUDINAL AND MORPHOLOGICAL SUBDIVISIONS IN NEURAL PLATE AND NEURULATION STAGE EMBRYOS.

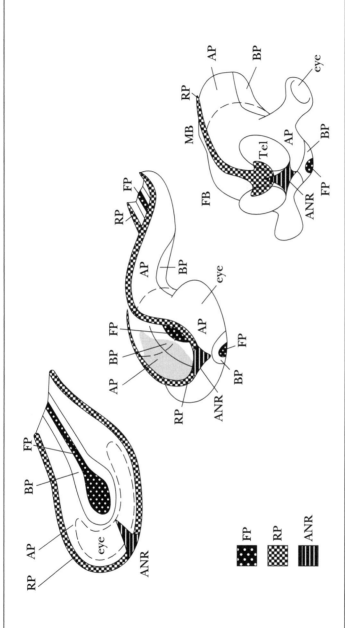

Graphic schematic representation of the neurulation process viewed from the rostrolateral end of the brain. Non-neural structures of the head primordium are not shown. As the borders of the neural plate approach each other and fuse at the dorsal midline, the eye vesicles evaginate and the forebrain and midbrain (delimited by a transverse dash line) gradually acquire their characteristic shape. The schema ends when the telencephalic vesicles (Tel) start to evaginate and the rostral neuropore closes. The fundamental four-tiered longitudinal structure of the CNS has its simplest form at initial neural plate stages. These display the topology of the prospective floor plate (FP), basal plate (BP), alar plate (AP), and roof plate (RF) longitudinal domains, which are continuous from left to right across the midline at the front of the neural plate. The initial eye field, which is conceived to lie within the alar plate, also bridges the rostral midline. The anterior neural ridge (ANR) is postulated as a secondary organizer for the forebrain. We base the blue area on the early expression of Hesx1 and Six3 genes. As neurulation proceeds, the mutual topologic relationships of these domains are not altered. The rostral end of the roof plate will form choroidal tissue at the roof of the III ventricle and the medial wall of the lateral ventricles (Tel). The ANR persists at the telencephalic commissural plate (median septum), the lamina terminalis, and the prospective optic chiasm. The rostralmost floor plate area is the site where the neurohypophysis will develop.

of dorsal parts of the neural tube, this region contains the progenitors of the neural crest. During neurulation (closure of the neural tube; see below), neural crest cells migrate away from the neuroepithelium to form the ganglia of the PNS (sensory, motor, and enteric). In addition to contributing to the PNS, subsets of neural crest differentiate into dermal melanocytes, craniofacial skeletal elements, and additional organ systems.

During neurulation, the lateral edges of the neural plate fuse, and thereby form the roof plate (dorsal midline) of the neural tube (Colas & Schoenwolf, 2001). Disruption of this process leads to neural tube defects such as *exencephaly* (open brain) and *spina bifida* (open spinal cord). Defects in neurulation can be caused by mutations in genes that are expressed in the neural ridge, such as Dlx5 (Depew et al., 1999), or by mutations in genes, such as Apaf1 (Honarpour et al., 2001) that have general effects on the neural tube proliferation/survival.

The rostral edge of the neural plate is characterized by a structure called the anterior neural ridge (ANR). Unlike more caudal parts of the neural ridge, this region produces little or no neural crest (Couly et al., 1998). In addition to contributing to the rostral midline of the brain, the ANR is the anlage of much of the telencephalon (Inoue, Nakamura, & Osumi, 2000; Cobos-Sillero et al., 2001).

The midline of the neural plate has a groove that overlies the axial mesendoderm (prechordal plate and notochord). The middle of this groove will give rise to the floor plate, and the adjacent region becomes the basal plate (that is, the motor-related part of the mature CNS). The region between the prospective basal and roof plates is the anlage of the alar plate (the sensory-related part of the mature CNS). The roof, alar, basal, and floor plates are the principal longitudinal, or dorsoventral, subdivisions of the CNS (Shimamura et al., 1995). At the rostral and caudal limits of the CNS, the left and right parts of the longitudinal subdivisions are continuous across the rostal and caudal midlines. Abnormalities in the induction of these subdivisions in the forebrain cause dysmorphologies, such as *holoprosencephaly* (a severely dysmorphic syndrome with an unpaired forebrain or incompletely separated telencephalic vesicles, often associated with cyclopia).

At the neurulation stage, the CNS is already divided into its major transverse parts: the prosencephalon (forebrain), mesencephalon (midbrain), rhombencephalon (hindbrain), and the spinal cord (Figures 5.2 and 5.3). Smaller transverse units, called neuromeres, subdivide the rhombencephalon and the caudal part of the prosencephalon (this region becomes the caudal diencephalon) (Lumsden & Krumlauf, 1996; Rubenstein et al., 1998). Additional neuromeres in the rostral part of the prosencephalon (secondary prosencephalon) are postulated (Rubenstein et al., 1998; Puelles, 2001). During this period, cervical, rhombic, and

FIGURE 5.2. SUBDIVISIONS IN THE DEVELOPING BRAIN SHOWN IN SAGITTAL AND CORONAL SECTIONS.

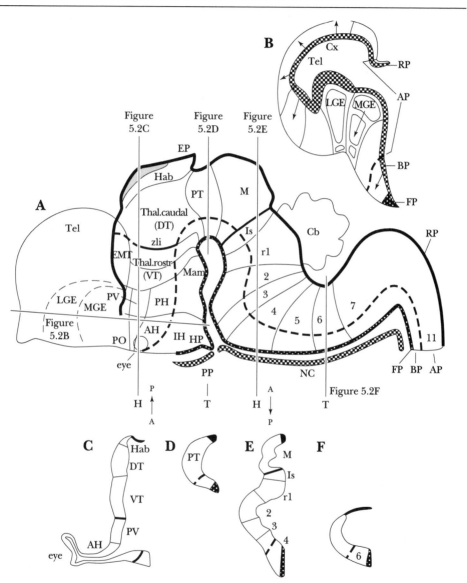

Schema A illustrates the axial flexures produced during early morphogenesis of the neural tube and other associated shape changes (evagination of the telencephalon and protrusion of the cerebellum), jointly with characteristic sectioned appearance at multiple locations (B-F).

FIGURE 5.2. (CONTINUED)

A. The axial dimension is represented jointly by three lines: 1) the floor plate (FP), which ends at the me-dian eminence and neurohypophysis (HP), overlying the prechordal plate axial mesoderm (PP); 2) the alar-basal boundary (BP/AP), which crosses the midline under the optic stalks (eye; also see Figure 5.1); and 3) the roof plate (RP, which stops rostrally at the anterior commissure (not shown). All three are parallel to each other and reveal that the neuraxis is sharply bent ventrally under the pretectum (PT) and the mid-brain (M), as well as under the caudal hindbrain (medulla). There is a dorsal concavity at hindbrain levels, emphasized by cerebellar overgrowth. The hindbrain, composed of an isthmic domain (Is), rhombomeres r1-r6, and pseudorhombomeres 7–11, overlies the notochord (NC). The isthmo-mesencephalic boundary—a secondary organizer domain—is indicated by a thick transverse black line. The diencephalic zona limi-tans intrathalamica (zli)—another presumptive secondary organizer—also appears as a thick black line. Other transverse (interneuromeric) boundaries are represented as thin black lines. The thalamic region of the fore-brain alar plate is divided by the zli into a caudal thalamus (classically known as "dorsal thalamus") and a ros-tral thalamus (classical "ventral thalamus"). The reinterpreted view favored here is consistent with the axial landmarks defined above (FP, AP/BP, RP). The caudal thalamus is capped dorsally by the epithalamus or habe-nular region (Hab) and epiphysis (EP), whereas the rostral thalamus is similarly capped by the eminentia thal-ami at the caudal part of the hemispheric stalk (EMT; it forms a bridge into the telencephalic pallium). Rostral to the thalamus, the large hypothalamic region can be roughly divided in two portions (caudal and rostral; both connect with the telencephalic subpallium—LGE, MGE—dorsalwards). The caudal part of the hypo-thalamus contains the locus of the paraventricular and supraoptic nuclei, the posterior hypothalamus, the subthalamic nucleus and the mammillary complex. The rostral part of hypothalamus contains dorsally the preoptic area (which can also be conceived as a telencephalon impar portion) and the anterior, suprachi-asmatic, retrochiasmatic, and infundibular hypothalamic domains, including the neurohypophysis and median eminence. The optic vesicles evaginate from the alar plate of this rostral hypothalamic region.

Abbreviations

AH	anterior hypothalamus	MGE	medial ganglionic eminence
AP	alar plate	NC	notochord
BP	basal plate	PH	posterior hypothalamus
Cb	cerebellum	PO	preoptic area
Cx	cortex	PP	prechordal plate
DT	dorsal thalamus	PT	pretectum
EMT	eminentia thalami	PV	paraventricular nucleus area
EP	epiphysis	r1-r6	rhombomeres
FP	floor plate	r7-r11	pseudorhombomeres
H	horizontal section plane	RP	roof plate
Hab	habenula	T	transversal section plane
HP	neurohypophysis	Tel	telencephalon
IH	infundibular hypothalamus	Thal.caudal	caudal thalamus
Is	isthmus	Thal.rost.	rostral thalamus
LGE	lateral ganglionic eminence	VT	ventral thalamus
M	midbrain	zli	zona limitans intrathalamica
Mam	mammillary area			

B. A topologically transverse section at the front of the forebrain intersects the telencephalon and the ros-tral hypothalamus (that is, extends from RP to FP; note also the BP/AP boundary). The telencephalon appears divided into four pallial subregions (medial, dorsal, lateral, and ventral pallium—separated by thin lines) and two subpallial domains (LGE and MGE, the primordia for the striatum and pallidum, respec-tively). The pallial domains form largely cortex (isocortex and allocortex), as well as claustral/endopiriform and amygdaloid nuclei (basolateral complex). The arrows represent some of the radial migratory routes of immature neurons, as they move from the progenitor zone (hatched territory adjacent to the ventricle) to the overlaying mantle zone.

FIGURE 5.2. (CONTINUED)

C. A cross-section at early stages through the optic stalk is topologically horizontal to the axial landmarks, and therefore shows periodic outward bulges of the wall separated by ventricular ridges. Most of the section traverses alar plate domains of successive transverse elements of the neural tube. (Compare with A) A more caudal section, across the IH and Mam, would intersect a series of basal plate sectors. This is the sort of morphological evidence that has been adduced for forebrain prosomeres. A number of gene expression domains respect such boundaries.

D. A cross-section through the posterior commissure and pretectum is topologically transverse. Note the relative greater extent of the alar plate relative to the other longitudinal domains.

E. A cross-section through the caudal midbrain (inferior colliculus) is topologically horizontal to the rostral hindbrain and thus again shows a number of bulging areas separated by constrictions, corresponding to hindbrain rhombomeres. Most of the section traverses alar plate domains of successive transverse elements of the neural tube (compare with A).

F. A cross-section through the rostral medulla (rhombomere 6) is again topologically transverse; it illustrates the expanded choroidal roof plate of the hindbrain.

cephalic flexures bend the longitudinal axis of the CNS into its characteristic morphology.

In several brain regions, there is local growth of vesicles. This is particularly prominent in the secondary prosencephalon (Figures 5.1 and 5.2), from which the paired telencephalic and optic vesicles expand. In addition, smaller unpaired outpouchings grow at the dorsal prosencephalic midline (pineal gland and subfornical organ) and the ventral midline (posterior pituitary). Thus, from a morphological point of view, the prosencephalon consists of the diencephalon, optic vesicles, and the telencephalic vesicles. The caudal limit of the diencephalon connects with the mesencephalon (Figures 5.2 and 5.3).

The alar (dorsal) parts of the diencephalon give rise to the pretectum, the epithalamus (habenula), the caudal thalamus (formerly called the dorsal thalamus), the rostral thalamus (formerly called the ventral thalamus: reticular nucleus, zona incerta, and ventral lateral geniculate nucleus) and the alar hypothalamus (includes the preoptic, anterior hypothalamic, and the supraopto-paraventricular areas). The caudal and rostral parts of the thalamus are separated by a cell-poor boundary region known as the zona limitans intrathalamica (ZLI) (Puelles, 1995; Rubenstein et al., 1998; Larsen et al., 2001). The ZLI separates the predominantly inhibitory cell populations in the rostral thalamus from the caudal thalamus, which contains excitatory neurons that project to the cortex.

The basal (ventral) diencephalon caudal to the ZLI contains prerubral (basal) and ventral tegmental (paramedian floor) domains (the nigral tegmentum) that are analogous to the dopaminergic regions of the midbrain tegmentum (substantia nigra and ventral tegmental area).

FIGURE 5.3. FATE MAP OF THE MOUSE NEURAL PLATE.

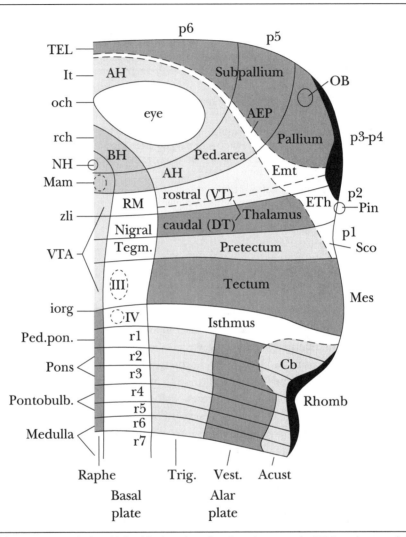

Fate map of the mouse neural plate (right side; based on data from Inoue et al., 2000, and extrapolating some chicken data from Fernandez-Garre et al., 2002; Cobos-Sillero et al., 2001; and Marín & Puelles, 1994). The fate map appears divided in longitudinal domains, corresponding to the early floor, basal, alar, and roof plates (choroidal roof plate in dark gray; see Figure 5.1), as well as in transversal domains (rhombomeres, isthmus, midbrain, prosomeres). The floor region is divided into a prechordal part (NH and Mam) attached to the basal hypothalamus (BH), and an epichordal part. The latter decomposes into two plurisegmental domains: the ventral tegmental area (VTA, underlying the nigral tegmentum in the basal plate) and the hindbrain raphe domain. These two domains are characterized by the formation of dopaminergic and serotoninergic neurons, respectively. The midbrain and isthmic basal plate areas contain the oculomotor and trochlear nuclei (III, IV). The main prospective areas derived from the alar plate are indicated. The alar hypothalamus (AH) surrounds the eye domain and includes caudally the peduncular area (which

FIGURE 5.3. (CONTINUED)

contains the paraventricular nucleus). Rostral to the midbrain, a series of dorsal specialized territories like the subcommissural organ (Sco; under the posterior commissure) and the epithalamus and pineal gland (Eth, Pin) are continuous rostrally with the eminentia thalami (Emt) and anterior entopeduncular area (AEP), which form the so-called hemispheric stalk domains. The Emt borders upon the pallial telencephalon (which includes the olfactory bulb, OB), whereas AEP borders upon the subpallial telencephalon. The neural plate rim rostral to the choroidal roof contains the prospective septal domain. The topologic arrangement of pallium and subpallium in the neural plate shows that the pallium is primarily caudal to the subpallium.

Abbreviations

Acust	cochlear column	och	optic chiasma
AEP	anterior entopeduncular area	p1-p6	prosomeres 1-6
AH	alar hypothalamus	Ped. area	peduncular area
BH	basal hypothalamus	Ped.pon.	pedunculopontine region
Cb	cerebellum	Pin	pineal gland (epiphysis)
DT	dorsal thalamus	Pontobulb	pontobulbar region
Emt	eminentia thalami	r1-r6	rhombomeres
Eth	epithalamus	r7	pseudorhombomere 7
III	oculomotor nucleus	rch	retrochiasmatic area
iorg	isthmic organizer	Rhomb.	rhombencephalon
IV	trochlear nucleus	RM	retromammillary area
It	lamina terminalis	Sco	subcommissural organ
Mam	mammillary area	TEL	telencephalon
Mes	mesencephalon	Trig.	trigeminal column
NH	neurohypophysis	Vest	vestibular column
Nigral Tegm	nigral tegmentum	VT	ventral thalamus
OB	olfactory bulb	VTA	ventral tegmental area
		Zli	zona limitans intrathalamica

The basal diencephalon rostral to the ZLI consists of the basal prethalamus (the traditionally defined posterior hypothalamic and retro[supra]mammillary areas) and the basal hypothalamus (includes mammillary and infundibular hypothalamus: dorsomedial, ventromedial, arcuate areas, and the neurohypophysis).

The telencephalic vesicles are connected to the rostral alar diencephalon through a peduncle (stalk); rostrally the peduncle contains the preoptic and anterior entopeduncular areas, which are substituted caudally by the eminentia thalami (a transitional area placed dorsal to the rostral thalamus along the path of the stria medullaris tract). The eminentia thalami is partially evaginated into the telencephalic medial wall, being continuous across its bulge at the back of the interventricular foramen with the so-called *lamina affixa,* a thin portion of the hemispheric medial wall (concentric to the choroidal fissure of the lateral ventricle); rostrally it limits sequentially along the sulcus terminalis (floor of lateral ventricle) with the anterior entopeduncular area, the medial ganglionic eminence, parts of the amygdala, and finally the hemispheric cortical hem. The eminentia thalami ends dorsally at the rostralmost diencephalic choroidal roof, and the evaginated part ends at the choroidal fissure of the lateral ventricle, all the way to its temporal horn tip. The rostral part of the telencephalic stalk is continuous with the telencephalic subpallium (basal ganglia, extending medially into the septum and the commissural plate), whereas the caudal part of the stalk also contacts the pallium (hippocampal cortex).

The telencephalic subpallium is primarily constituted by the primordia of the striatum and the globus pallidus (Figures 5.2 and 5.3). The pallium has been hypothesized to be organized into the following subdivision: the medial, dorsal, and lateral/ventral pallium (Puelles et al., 2000). These parts correspond to the hippocampus, the isocortex (neocortex), and the olfactory cortex/claustral/endopiriform complex, respectively (Figures 5.2 and 5.4). Each region is further subdivided. For example, the isocortex is composed of multiple motor, sensory, and associative areas. The septum and amygdalar complexes are composed of both pallial and subpallial parts.

The functional organization of structures caudal to the forebrain follow some general principals. Dorsal parts (alar plate) tend to have sensory processing structures. Ventral parts (basal plate) generally have motor processing and output structures (Figure 5.3). For instance, in dorsal parts of the midbrain, the tectum (superior and inferior colliculi) processes visual and auditory information. On the other hand, the ventral midbrain (tegmentum) participates in motor functions through the substantia nigra, the red nucleus and the oculomotor nucleus. The dorsal hindbrain processes craniofacial or global somatic and visceral sensory information (cranial nerve sensory columns and cerebellum), whereas the ventral hindbrain contains cranial nerve motor nuclei and related parts of the reticular formation. Likewise, the dorsal spinal cord (dorsal horn) processes sensory information of the body, whereas the ventral spinal cord contains motor nuclei and integrative local circuits for body musculature and autonomic ganglia control.

Neurons located in an intermediate dorsoventral position in the midbrain/hindbrain reticular formation and in the spinal cord tend to be interneurons that regulate sensory/motor circuitry (that is, postural reflexes and locomotion) and coordinate basic physiological processes such as respiration.

In general, forebrain structures regulate the activity of the brainstem and spinal cord and they analyze information coming from these caudal structures as well as from the retina and olfactory epithelium. Within the forebrain, major circuits interconnect its subdivisions. For instance, dorsal diencephalic elements either relay sensory signals to the telencephalon (the caudal thalamus) or analyze them for suprasegmental reflex actions (pretectum and rostral thalamus). The hypothalamus (a varied set of dorsal and ventral diencephalic nuclei) regulates systemic homeostatic servomechanisms analyzing endogenous humoral signals and various transmitted inputs, and outputs its dynamic state changes through its projections to the brainstem and its neurohumoral control of the pituitary.

While GABAergic and glutamatergic neurons are widely dispersed within the CNS, neurons that use monoamine-type neurotransmitters tend to be clustered as sets of nuclei within the brainstem reticular formation. These types of neurons grow axons that are widely ramified in several parts of the CNS, and serve as neuromodulators of various motor and behavioral states. Dopaminergic neurons are primarily found in the basal plate of the posterior diencephalon and midbrain (that is, the ventral tegmental area and nigral complex, Figure 5.3); serotonergic neurons are present largely in the paramedian basal plate of the hindbrain (raphe nuclei), and most noradrenergic neurons are in the alar plate of the hindbrain. (The locus coeruleus, in rhombomere 1, is the largest collection of these neurons.)

Topologic Model of the CNS

A simplified and unified conception of CNS organization can be conceived using a three-dimensional topologic model, where positions are referred systematically to the brain axis and to the grid of transverse and longitudinal zones in the brain wall; the axis and grid become curved and variously deformed coherently over time, without losing the primary relationships. Anteroposterior and dorsoventral patterning of the neural plate generates a two-dimensional grid of spatial coordinates that subdivide the early CNS primordium into an orthogonal array of differently specified progenitor domains (Figure 5.3). The primordia of some regions that form as secondary fields, such as the telencephalon, appear not to be organized according to a rectilinear grid, or, more probably, its primary grid quickly gets very deformed during the evagination and differential growth of the hemisphere (Cobos-Sillero et al., 2001). Each of these progenitor domains is programmed to produce a given set of neurons and glia that migrate away from the progenitor zone into the mantle zone, to form the laminae and nuclei that constitute the third dimension of the CNS wall (Figure 5.4). Advanced brain morphogenesis results in marked deformation of its wall, causing many of the initial grid lines to adopt curved courses. Various lines of evidence—directional cell migration, axonal growth, and synaptogenetic patterns—suggest that the primitive positional information is maintained by means of radial glia and other mechanisms. This is a strong reason to continue thinking in terms of the deformed grid lines. In some brain regions there is a discrepancy between the *topography* of a brain part (its apparent position relative to external references—its stereotaxic position) and its *topology* (its invariant position relative to internal references, such as the curved longitudinal axis and implicit

FIGURE 5.4. PROLIFERATION AND MIGRATION IN THE DEVELOPING BRAIN.

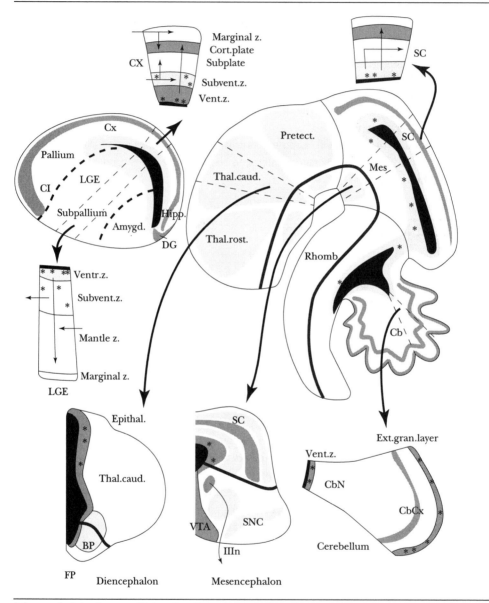

Schema of a lateral parasagittal section through the embryonic mammalian brain, to illustrate the variations in the arrangement and location of the proliferative compartments (ventricular zone, subventricular zone, subpial proliferative zones) and the differentiation compartment (mantle zone, cortical or nuclear). Large arrows point to details of sections at different positions. The most extensive proliferation compartment is the radially organized ventricular zone. This zone, which is derived from the neural tube

FIGURE 5.4. (CONTINUED)

neuroepithelium, is found throughout the CNS, covering all fluid-filled ventricular spaces (small asterisks within indicate ventricularly attached mitoses). The proliferation in the ventricular zone ends earlier in the basal plate than in the alar plate, thus explaining the latter's larger relative growth. There is a second stratum of proliferating and migrating cells, the subventricular zone; this lacks an epithelial organization— no radial elements—and contains extraventricular mitoses (subventricular zone as green areas in the schema; asterisks within these areas represent extraventricular mitoses). The subventricular zone is particularly prominent in the telencephalon, where it is thicker in the subpallium than in the pallium. In most places of the brain, postmitotic neurons and various sorts of glia cells migrate out of the deep proliferative compartments and accumulate after some radial or tangential migration into the mantle zone. Sometimes the mantle zone becomes structured as nuclei, and other times it develops cortical primordia. In that case, a dense cortical plate forms initially, which later differentiates into a number of sublayers. Finally, in some brain regions, superficial (subpial) proliferative zones are established from the migration of ventricular zone progenitors. These cell sources often produce neurons postnatally, even throughout the lifetime of the animal. Examples of such late subpial proliferative zones are the telencephalic source of dentate gyrus (DG) elements and the cerebellar external granular layer.

Abbreviations

Amygd.	amygdala	marginal z.	marginal zone
BP	basal plate	Mes	mesencephalon
CbCx	cerebellar cortex	Pretect.	pretectum
CbN	cerebellar nucleus	Rhomb	rhombencephalon
Cl	claustrum	Cb	cerebellum
Cx	cortex	SC	superior colliculus
DG	dentate gyrus	SNC	substantia nigra compacta
Epithal.	epithalamus	subvent.z.	subventricular zone
ext.gran.layer	external granular layer	Thal.caud.	caudal thalamus
Hipp	hippocampus	Thal.rost.	rostral thalamus
IIIn	oculomotor nerve	vent.z.	ventricular zone
LGE	lateral ganglionic eminence	VTA	ventral tegmental area
mantle z.	mantle zone		

grid lines). For instance, a deformation of the brain wall could result in a topologically dorsal nucleus occupying a topographically ventral position. The model used by us emphasizes the invariant neighborhood relationships (topology) of the histogenic complexes in the neural wall, aiding their comparison at different ages and across species. This model, while perhaps oversimplified, is a useful framework for learning neuroembryology and neuroanatomy.

Molecular Genetics of Brain Development

Due to the application of genetic methods, major advances have been made in elucidating the mechanisms underlying the principal steps in brain development. Here we have chosen to highlight examples that illustrate major principles.

Induction and Anteroposterior Regionalization of the Neural Plate

Neural induction is regulated by the secretion of proteins from organizer tissues that lie adjacent to the anlage of the neural plate. This process involves the specification of neuroepithelial cells from the primitive ectoderm, and is controlled by the activation of receptor tyrosine kinases, perhaps through fibroblast growth factors (FGFs) and or insulin-like growth factors (IGFs) (Streit et al., 2000; Wilson et al., 2000; Pera et al., 2001) and by the inhibition of transforming growth factor-b (TGF-b) signaling through the noggin and chordin proteins that bind to bone morphogenetic proteins (BMPs) (Harland, 2000; De Robertis et al., 2000; Wilson & Edlund, 2001). Furthermore, wingless (WNT) signaling appears to inhibit neural induction in chickens (Wilson et al., 2001).

Early neural induction generates anterior neural plate structures. Anterior specification is controlled by molecules secreted by patterning centers that are adjacent to the anterior neural plate, such as the anterior visceral endoderm and the prechordal mesendoderm (Beddington & Robertson, 1999; Kiecker & Niehrs, 2001). This process depends upon the action of the neural inducing substances in combination with proteins that inhibit signaling through WNT receptors and activin-type TGF-b receptors. For instance, proteins such as Cerberus (which bind BMPs, WNTs, and nodal-type TGF-b proteins) and Dickkopf (which inhibit WNT co-receptors) mediate anterior specification of the neural plate. This process is further controlled through the action of homeobox transcription factors such as Otx2, Lim1, and Hesx1 (Cheah et al., 2000; Acampora et al., 2001; Thomas et al., 2001).

Later stages of neural induction generate posterior neural tissues. The mechanisms that specify posterior fate are less well characterized, but do not seem to require inhibition of WNT-signaling, and appear to involve retinoids and FGFs (Lamb & Harland, 1995; Blumberg et al., 1997; Gavalas & Krumlauf, 2000). Posterior fate is regulated by the Hox family of homeobox genes that are expressed in overlapping patterns along the anteroposterior axis of the CNS (Trainor & Krumlauf, 2000; Barrow et al., 2000; Liu & Joyner, 2001, see Chapter Sixty-Two).

As the anterior and posterior parts of the CNS are formed, two new patterning centers are generated within the neural plate, which regulate subsequent stages of CNS patterning: the anterior neural ridge (ANR) and the isthmus (at the transition between the midbrain and hindbrain). The latter is formed through repressive interactions between the Otx2 and Gbx2 genes (Simeone, 2000; Liu & Joyner, 2001) and the positive action of Pax2 (Ye et al., 2001). These centers express FGF8, and are implicated in specifying anteroposterior position within adjacent areas of the brain (Wilson & Rubenstein., 2000; Nakamura, 2001). They function in part through repressing Otx2 and Emx2 and inducing En1 (Martinez et al., 1999; Crossley et al., 2001; Storm et al., 2003; Garel et al., 2003). The isthmus is essential for formation and patterning of the cerebellum and the midbrain, whereas the ANR plays a similar role in patterning the telencephalon (Shanmugalingam et al., 2000; Storm et al., in press). Later expression of Fgf8 in the rostral midline of the telencephalon is implicated in patterning of the cerebral cortex (Fukuchi-Shimogori & Grove, 2001; Garel et al., in press).

An additional transverse patterning center, the ZLI, forms between the rostral and caudal diencephalon. The ZLI may function as a boundary to restrict the action of patterning signals and later, through the expression of sonic hedgehog and other signals, may pattern adjacent tissues (Shimamura & Rubenstein, 1997; Zeltser et al., 2001).

Further refinement of CNS anteroposterior specification is reflected by the formation of transverse subdivisions, or neuromeres (Figures 5.2 and 5.3). In the hindbrain, the rhombomeres have segment-like properties, as exemplified by restrictions in intra-rhombomeric cell mixing (Lumsden & Krumlauf, 1996; Lumsden, 1999), which is controlled through repulsive actions of cell surface molecules, such as the Eph/Ephrin molecules (Mellitzer et al., 1999). In the forebrain, prosomeres of the caudal diencephalon have similarities and differences with the rhombomeres, perhaps reflecting some development mechanisms that are specific to the forebrain (Puelles & Rubenstein, 1993; Figdor & Stern, 1993; Puelles, 1995, 2001; Larsen et al., 2001).

Neural crest progenitors in the neural ridge are also influenced by CNS regional specification. This has important ramifications for later developmental properties of these cells (Trainor & Krumlauf, 2000). For instance, in the hindbrain and midbrain, subsets of these cells contribute to the head skeleton. Therefore, abnormalities in brain regionalization can cause craniofacial dysmorphologies. Likewise, many genes that regulate brain development are also expressed in facial anlage; thus, brain defects are commonly found when there are craniofacial malformations (Depew et al., 2002).

Dorsoventral Specification of Longitudinal CNS Subdivisions and the Specification of Neuronal Cell Types

During early stages of neural induction, the neural plate has dorsal molecular properties due to the influence of BMPs produced in the neural ridge and adjacent ectoderm (Barth et al., 1999). Then, shortly after anteroposterior specification has begun, involution of the axial mesendoderm under the medial neural plate initiates the process of ventral specification. Substances produced by the prechordal plate and notochord (anterior and posterior parts of the axial mesendoderm) induce expression of transcription factors that confer "ventral" CNS identity to the medial neural plate. *Sonic hedgehog (SHH)* is the best-characterized substance produced by the axial mesendoderm that regulates ventral identity. SHH-mediated ventral specification of the floor and basal plates generates a set of ventral progenitor zones that extend along the CNS. SHH processing during its production includes an autoproteolytic step and esterification with cholesterol and palmitic acid (Nybakken & Perrimon, 2002). Disruption of SHH-signaling results in the loss of ventral CNS tissues, thereby causing CNS disorders such as holoprosencephaly and cyclopia (Roessler & Muenke, 2001).

SHH seems to function as a *morphogen,* a concentration-dependent inducer of cell fate, in the ventral CNS. Decreasing concentrations of SHH induce six major types of neural progenitors (FP, V3, Mn, V2, V1, and V0) in the ventral spinal cord (Briscoe et al., 2000; Marquardt & Pfaff, 2001). Floor plate progenitors (FP) are the ventral-most and lie adjacent to the notochord. V3-V0 progenitors produce distinct types of interneurons, whereas Mn progenitors produce several different types of motor neurons. The formation of sharp domains of transcription factor expression is mediated by mutual repression between SHH-induced transcription factors (such as the Nkx2 and Nkx6 genes) and transcription factors that are not regulated directly by SHH (Pax6 and Irx) (Briscoe et al., 2000). The repression is controlled in part by interactions between the homeodomain proteins with groucho proteins (Muhr et al., 2001).

SHH is not the only substance that generates ventral CNS pattern, as much of this pattern can be formed in mice that lack both SHH and the transcription factor Gli3 (Litingtung & Chiang, 2000; Wijgerde et al., 2002). Gli3 is known to antagonize SHH-signaling; relieving this repression reveals an underlying pattern that must be generated by a yet unknown mechanism that may involve another member of the hegdehog gene family (Wijgerde et al., 2002). Ventral patterning is also regulated by Nodal-type TGF-b proteins in zebrafish (Wilson & Rubenstein, 2000); these genes are presently being investigated for a similar role in mammals.

Patterning of dorsal progenitor zones in the roof and alar plates is controlled by BMPs and WNTs (Lee & Jessell, 1999). In the telencephalon, decreases in BMP signaling leads to expansion of Fgf8 expression (Ohkubo et al., 2002) and loss of the choroid plexus (Hébert et al., 2002). Pervasive defects in the dorsal patterning of the telencephalon, through mutations in Zic2 and TGIF, cause dysmorphic syndromes, such as lobar holoprosencephaly (Wallis & Muenke, 2000).

WNT signaling is largely active in the same dorsal regions where BMP-signaling is occurring. For instance, mutations that reduce WNT signaling in the dorsal telencephalon lead to the deletion of dorsal telencephalic structures (such as the hippocampus) (Galceran et al., 2000; Lee et al., 2000). WNT signaling is also essential at the isthmus for the generation of the cerebellum, where WNT and FGF functions are closely linked (Liu & Joyner, 2001).

The generation of dorsal and ventral progenitors is the first step in the specification of different types of CNS cells. Distinct progenitor domains produce specific types of neurons and glia. For instance, in the spinal cord, V3 progenitors generate V3 interneurons, whereas Mn progenitors generate motor neurons (Briscoe et al., 1999; Briscoe et al., 2000). Thus, specification of dorsoventral progenitor identity is linked to specification of neuronal identity. A similar process takes place in the telencephalon, where Nkx genes specify ventral progenitors and cell types (cholinergic and GABAergic neurons), Gsh genes specify intermediate cell types (GABAergic neurons), and genes such as Gli3, Emx2, and Pax6 are required to specify dorsal cell types (glutamatergic neurons) (Wilson & Rubenstein, 2000; Muzio et al., 2002). Note, however, that this analogy is an oversimplification, as fate maps show that "ventral" parts of telencephalon are topologically anterior to "dorsal" parts of the telencephalon (Cobos-Sillero et al., 2001). During evagination of the telencephalon, topologically anterior parts of the telencephalon secondarily obtain "ventral" molecular properties (Crossley et al., 2001).

Neural Progenitor Cells

A pseudostratified epithelium that lines the ventricular surface of the neural tube, known as the ventricular zone (Figure 5.4), contains the progenitor (neuroepithelial) cells of the developing CNS. At early neural tube stages, the apical surface of neuroepithelial cells maintains contact with the ventricular lumen, and the cells extend a basal process toward the outer or pial surface. After mitosis, the cell nucleus moves, within the neuroepithelial cell body, away from the ventricular lumen. S-phase of the cell cycle takes place when the nucleus is displaced from the lumen; following S-phase, the nucleus moves to the luminal surface, where M-phase of mitosis takes place (Caviness et al., 1995).

Rapid symmetrical mitoses are believed to result in an increase of neural tube surface area, as clearly exemplified by the expansion of the optic and telencephalic vesicles. The mitogenic mechanisms underlying this process are not firmly established, although there is evidence that receptor tyrosine kinase signaling through FGF and EGF receptors participate in regulating proliferation in the embryonic CNS (Korada et al., 2002; Martens et al., 2000). Proliferation in some regions is also controlled by SHH (Wechsler-Reya & Scott 2001) and in other regions by WNT signaling (Galceran et al., 2000; Lee et al., 2000).

Once neurogenesis has begun, asymmetric mitoses are believed to operate in the generation of one progenitor and one immature neuron. The role of asymmetric cell division in controlling neural cell fate is best understood in *Drosophila*, where a number of proteins, including Numb, have key roles (Jan & Jan, 1998).

Numb is also implicated in asymmetric cell division in vertebrates (Shen et al., 2002), where the Numb protein segregates into the immature neuron. Mutations that result in loss of Numb function lead to premature maturation of progenitor cells, suggesting that Numb is required to maintain progenitor cell properties (Petersen et al., 2002).

Neural progenitors have basal processes that extend to the pial surface; these processes become increasingly elongated as the thickness of the neural tube increases during development. Neural progenitors with an elongated basal process are known as radial glia. They were originally thought to be glia because they express some markers found in astrocytes. It is now recognized that "radial glia" in the cerebral cortex can produce both neurons and glia (Noctor et al., 2001; Hartfuss et al., 2001). Radial progenitor cells initially produce neurons; at later developmental stages they produce astrocytes.

As development proceeds, secondary progenitor zones are generated in specific areas of the neural tube. These include the telencephalic subventricular zone, which is composed of proliferating progenitors that are not arranged as an epithelium (Figure 5.4). The subventricular zone is superficial to the ventricular zone and is deep to the differentiating cortical or basal ganglia primordial. Subventricular zones produce neurons at early stages (Anderson et al., 1997) and appear to become primarily gliogenic later (Kakika & Goldman, 1999). Secondary proliferative zones can also form in a subpial location, such as in the cerebellum. Here, the external granule cell layer is a transient progenitor zone that generates granule cells pre- and postnatally (Figure 5.4).

The only parts of the adult mammalian brain that are certain to have active progenitor cells are the subventricular zone of the rostral telencephalon and the dentate gyrus of the hippocampus (Figure 5.4; Luskin, 1998; Palmer et al., 2000; Alvarez-Buylla et al., 2001; Gritti et al., 2002). In the adult CNS, ependymal cells line the ventricle. These cells serve primarily a role as an epithelial barrier, although there is some controversy over whether they may also have neural progenitor properties or not (Alvarez-Buylla et al., 2001; Cassidy & Frisen, 2001).

Differentiation

Differentiation of neurons and glia involves progressive changes in gene expression that define new cell biological states. These processes begin in progenitor cells to alter their mitotic behavior (such as cell cycle rate, symmetrical or asymmetrical divisions), to generate secondary progenitor zones, or to generate progenitors that are programmed to produce different types of neurons or glia (depending on the dorsoventral position).

A major step in differentiation is when progenitor cells are programmed to leave the cell cycle and produce neurons. Neurons do not have the capacity to re-enter the cell cycle (Caviness et al., 1995). The mechanisms that underlie the arrest of neurons at the G0 stage of the cell cycle are poorly understood but involve the retinoblastoma gene (Lee et al., 1994). Once a neuron is born, it usually migrates away from the basal aspect of the progenitor zone toward the mantle zone where they mature (Figure 5.4).

The timing of differentiation is tightly controlled to generate the proper number of neurons at a given developmental stage. This process is regulated in part through lateral inhibitory effects of Notch-signaling (Chitnis, 1995; Henrique et al., 1997). Lateral inhibition occurs when a cell prevents an adjacent cell from differentiating. Conversely, release from lateral inhibition promotes differentiation. Lateral inhibition is promoted when a cell, expressing the Notch protein (a cell surface receptor), is adjacent to a cell expressing a Notch ligand (that is, Delta or Jagged). Mammals have four Notch genes (Notch 1-4) and five DSL ligand genes (Delta1, 3, and 4, Jagged1, and 2) (Lindsell et al., 1996).

Ligand-induced Notch-signaling involves proteolytic cleavage of Notch, which releases its intracellular domain (Notch-IC) and allows its translocation to the nucleus. Notch-IC directly modulates the function of a transcription factor known as CSL (CBF1, Suppressor of Hairless [SuH] or Lag-1). Notch activation of CSL induces the expression of WRPW-bHLH transcription factors (such as Hes genes); these proteins inhibit neuronal differentiation and repress expression of bHLH transcription factors that promote neural differentiation (such as Mash1) (Artavanis-Tsakonas et al., 1999; Robey, 1997). Therefore, an increase in Notch-signaling biases progenitor cells not to differentiate; on the other hand, decreasing Notch-signaling facilitates their maturation.

There are several classes of proneural bHLH genes expressed in the mammalian CNS. In the telencephalon, Mash1 and Olig2 are expressed primarily in the subpallium, whereas Neurogenin 1 and 2 expression is restricted to the pallium (Fode et al., 2000; Lu et al., 2000). Mash1 is required for the expression of Delta in the subpallium; in Mash1 mutants, early-born subpallial cells are not formed and the subventricular zone (SVZ) prematurely differentiates, through precocious expression of the Dlx genes (Casarosa et al., 1999; Horton et al., 1999; Yun et al., 2002). The Dlx1 and Dlx2 homeobox genes are required for late differentiation in the subpallium (Anderson et al., 1997). In the absence of Dlx1 and Dlx2, immature neurons have elevated levels of Hes5 expression, which is indicative of increased Notch-signaling (Yun et al., 2003). Thus both bHLH and homeobox transcription factors participate in mediating the effects of Notch signaling to regulate the differentiation of progenitor cells.

As immature neurons migrate and settle into their final positions, their differentiation is regulated by autonomous and non-autonomous mechanisms. An example of an autonomous mechanism is illustrated by the sequential induction of transcription factors during differentiation. For instance, in the subpallium, while Dlx1 and Dlx2 are expressed primarily in progenitor cells, Dlx5 and Dlx6 are also expressed in postmitotic neurons (Anderson et al., 1997). Dlx1&2 directly regulate the expression of the Dlx5&6 genes (Zerucha et al., 2000); in the absence of Dlx1&2, Dlx5&6 fail to be expressed (Anderson et al., 1997). An example of a non-autonomous mechanism is Notch-mediated lateral inhibition. (See above.)

The molecular mechanisms that regulate motor neuron development provide the best example of how transcription factors define progressively more defined states of differentiation (Jessell, 2000; Lee & Pfaff, 2001). Specification of motor neuron progenitors is regulated by Nkx6.1 and Olig2 (Sander et al., 2000; Mizuguchi et al., 2001; Novitch et al., 2001). These progenitors are then programmed to become either somatic or visceral motor neurons through the action of the MNR2, HB9, and Phox2 homeodomain transcription factors (Tanabe et al., 1998; Arber et al., 1999). Then Lim-homeodomain proteins contribute to specifying how somatic motor neurons become subdivided into different columns (such as medial and lateral) that innervate muscles in different regions of the body (body wall or limbs) (Kania et al., 2000). These genes control the projection pathways that motor neuron axons follow. Within the different columns, ETS transcription factors define motor neuron pools that regulate the branching of motor neuron axons and thereby control the innervation of different groups of muscles within a region (Arber et al., 2000). Subpools of motor neurons that innervate different types of muscles (such as fast, slow, extrafusal, and intrafusal) are defined by yet unknown transcription factors. An ongoing challenge is to identify similar cascades of transcription factors that control the development of neuronal subtypes in all regions of the CNS.

Cell Migration

Neurons and glia migrate away from the progenitor zones in which they were produced via either radial or tangential trajectories (Figures 5.4 and 5.5). There are at least two modes of radial migration. At early stages in development, when the width of the neural tube is relatively small, immature neurons extend a process to the pial surface; the cell body then follows by translocation (Puelles & Bendala, 1978; Nadarajah et al., 2001). At later stages, radially migrating detached neurons use the processes of radial glia as a guidance substrate (Puelles & Bendala, 1978; Gleeson & Walsh, 2000). Tangentially migrating cells follow diverse guidance cues as they move from the primordium where they are generated to their target tissues; finally, in some cases they migrate again radially into their final location (Hatten, 1999; 2002; Marín & Rubenstein, 2001; 2003). It is thought that, in general,

FIGURE 5.5. TANGENTIAL MIGRATION PATHWAYS IN THE DEVELOPING BRAIN.

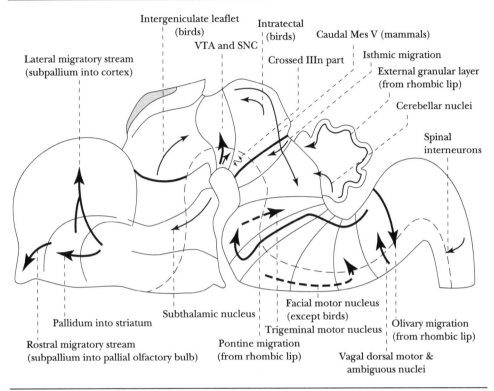

Schema illustrating the location, extent, and topological relationships of the major known cases of tangential neuronal migration in the brain. This schema is based on Figure 5.2 as it regards brain subdivisions, and labels the diverse migratory routes. The crossed oculomotor migration occurs across the ventral midline of the midbrain. It is remarkable that all of these migrations are oriented in three-dimensional space, suggesting that the migratory cells utilize positional information along their trajectory to reach their destination analogous to that used by axons. (See Figure 5.6.)

telencephalic projection neurons follow radial migratory pathways, whereas local circuit neurons tend to follow tangential migrations (Marín & Rubenstein, 2001).

Development of the mouse pallium (cortex) requires both radial and tangential migrations and exemplifies the differential development of projection and local circuit neurons. Pallial projection neurons, which are glutamatergic, are generated by the pallial progenitor zone, whereas most of the eventual pallial local-circuit neurons, which are GABAergic, are generated from subpallial progenitors (Marín & Rubenstein, 2001; Gorski et al., 2002). The radial migration of projection neurons maintains the positional information that their progenitors were exposed to; this could be important for the generation of topographic connectivity maps (Rakic, 2000). It is unclear why the glutamatergic and GABAergic neurons of the pallium are produced by different progenitor zones, but it may be due to the coupling of regional and cell type specification processes described above. Unlike the mouse and chicken, in which the cortical progenitors appear to produce few if any GABAergic neurons, there is evidence that cortical progenitors in humans may produce GABAergic neurons (Letinic et al., 2002).

The molecular mechanisms that regulate neuronal migration are a subject of intense investigation. Most of the studies focused on radial migration in the mammalian neocortex and cerebellum. Here, we will briefly describe cellular and molecular mechanisms in the neocortex. The neocortex is a hexalaminar structure that contains projection neurons with related properties in given layers (McConnell, 1995). The first neurons that reach the cortical mantle are called the primordial cortex or "preplate." Subsequently arriving neurons form the "cortical plate," which splits the preplate into a superficial layer called the marginal zone (layer 1) and a transient deep layer called the "subplate" (Marín-Padilla, 1983; Allendoerfer & Shatz, 1994). As new neurons arrive, they progressively stack inside-out on top of the older cells, building cortical layers 2 through 6; thus, layer 6 neurons are born before layer 2 neurons.

Migration defects of neocortical projection neurons can be classified on the basis of the stage in which radial migration is affected (reviewed in Gleeson & Walsh, 2000; Rice & Curran, 2001). The onset of migration is disrupted by mutations in filamin, an X-linked gene. Filamin encodes an actin-binding protein; defects in its expression lead to ectopic collections of neurons near the ventricle (Gleeson & Walsh, 2000). Mutations in the doublecortin and lis genes disrupt the process of migration and disrupt cortical lamination through altering microtubule function (Gleeson & Walsh, 2000). In humans, they cause smooth brain syndromes (Type I Lissencephalies). Defects in the reelin-signaling pathway lead to an inversion and disorganization of cortical layers. Reelin is a secreted protein produced by Cajal-Retzius cells in the marginal zone. The lipoprotein receptors VLDLR and APOER2 appear to be reelin receptors; they signal through DAB adaptor and CDK5/p35/p39 proteins. Reelin expression is controlled by TBR1 and EMX2; these transcription factors regulate differentiation of Cajal-Retzius cells (Mallamaci et al., 2000; Hevner et al., 2001). The BRN1 and BRN2 transcription factors control p35 and p39 expression (McEvilly et al., 2002).

Type II Lissencephalies are human syndromes in which, like Type I Lissencephalies, the brain lacks gyri and sulci, but the brain also has ectopic collections of neurons and glia in the marginal zone. These dysplasias, which are also known as leptomeningeal glioneural heterotopias, are associated with epilepsy. Mutations in presenilin 1 and a6 integrin lead to neurons migrating out of the brain into the meninges; these mutants phenocopy Type II lissencephalies such as Fukuyama's disease (Gleeson & Walsh, 2000).

The mechanisms that control tangential migrations appear to be extremely diverse (reviewed in Marín & Rubenstein, 2001; 2003; Hatten, 2002). Because these cells travel over long distances, and follow trajectories similar to major axon tracts, it is possible that they use mechanisms that are related to axonal path-finding such as repulsion and attraction. For instance, semaphorin/neuropilin signaling has been implicated in regulating the sorting of tangentially migrating subpallial cells to distinct telencephalic targets (Marín et al., 2001). Likewise, Slit/Robo and Ephrin/Eph signaling are implicated in the tangential migration of precursors for olfactory bulb interneurons (Wong et al., 2001; Conover et al., 2000), although Slit1/2 double mutants show normal tangential migration from the basal ganglia to the cortex (Marín et al., 2003). The tangential migration of neurons of the inferior olivary nucleus is regulated by netrin/DCC signaling (Yee et al., 1999).

Formation and Growth of Dendrites

Each type of neuron has a characteristic dendritic arbor and axonal trajectory. Axons are designed to conduct an axon potential and release neurotransmitters from their terminal, whereas dendrites are designed to receive neurotransmitter signals. Dendrites can have an extremely complex and stereotyped architecture. Here begins a review of some of the salient features of axonal and dendritic development. In addition, a few of the mechanisms that control these processes will be explored.

As a neuron differentiates, it produces multiple thin protrusions called neurites, one of which will become the axon; the others will form dendrites (reviewed in Jan & Jan, 2001). Semaphorins can orient the growth of axons and dendrites in the cerebral cortex. Semaphorin3A, a secreted protein, is an attractant for the apical dendrite and is a repellent for the axon (Polleux et al., 2000). There is evidence that the differential response of the dendrite and axon to semaphorin3A is due to the asymmetric localization of guanylate cyclase within the neuron. This enzyme, which synthesizes cGMP, is preferentially found at the base of the dendrite. It is believed that high concentrations of cGMP lead to an attractant response to semaphorin3A, whereas lower concentrations result in a repulsive response of neural processes (Whitford et al., 2002).

Several mechanisms can regulate the growth and branching of neurites and dendrites. For instance, Notch-signaling inhibits neurite outgrowth (Sestan et al., 1999). Branching of dendrites is regulated by intrinsic factors that change the organization of the cytoskeleton, such as members of the Rho family of small

GTPases (Luo, 2000) and the Plakin cytoskeletal anchor proteins (Gao et al., 1999), and by putative transcription factors (such as Sequoia) that may orchestrate the program of dendritic morphogenesis (Brenman et al., 2001).

Extrinsic mechanisms also regulate dendritic outgrowth and branching, such as Sema3a, BMP7, CPG15, IGFs, and neurotrophins (reviewed in Jan & Jan, 2001; Whitford et al., 2002). Dendritic growth is slowed by increases in neuronal activity that may be mediated through CAMKII (reviewed in Cline, 2001). Dendritic morphogenesis is sensitive to the position of other structures in their environment that arrests the growth of the dendritic tree (the "tiling" process). For instance, mutation of the *Drosophila* Flamingo seven-pass membrane protein, that resembles G-protein receptors, blocks dendritic tiling (Gao et al., 2000).

Dendrites of some types of neurons are covered with small protrusions called spines which are specialized structures for asymmetric excitatory (glutamate-rigic) synapses (Nimchinsky et al., 2002). As such, they contain NMDA- and AMPA-type glutamate receptors as well as other components required for synaptic signaling and plasticity. Symmetric inhibitory (GABAergic) synapses also form on spines. Spine density and size are positively regulated by excitatory neuronal activity. Thus, the development and function of dendritic spines are thought to be essential for the function of neural circuitry.

Spine density is reduced when levels of estrogen, progesterone, and thyroid hormones fall (Nimchinsky et al., 2002). Several mental retardation syndromes such as Down syndrome, Tuberous sclerosis type I, fetal alcohol syndrome, and Fragile X are characterized by having abnormal dendritic spine density and morphology (Nimchinsky et al., 2002). The *Fragile X* gene (FMR1) may be important in mediating dendritic protein synthesis in response to activity (Comery et al., 1997). Spine formation is affected by mutations in *Spinophilin,* which encodes an anchor protein for actin and protein phosphatase (Feng, J. et al., 2000).

Axon Pathfinding and Synapse Formation

Axons grow across considerable distances, follow complex trajectories, and send branches to several target areas where they synapse upon discrete sets of cells (Figure 5.6). To accomplish these tasks, growing axons react to an ordered set of cues provided by their environment, which is regulated by multiple mechanisms. (See reviews by Tessier-Lavigne & Goodman, 1996; O'Leary & Wilkinson, 1999; Brose & Tessier-Lavigne, 2000; Benson et al., 2001; Jacob & Guthrie, 2001).

Tessier-Lavigne and Goodman (1996) describe four general mechanisms that guide axons: "attractive and repulsive cues, which can either be short-range or long-range." The molecular bases for these guidance forces are rapidly being elucidated. However, generalizations about the roles of specific molecules are

FIGURE 5.6. MAJOR AXON PATHWAYS IN THE BRAIN.

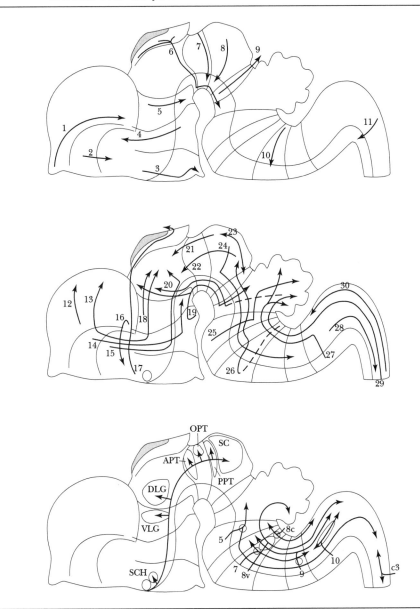

This triple schema illustrates the topological relationships of a number of fiber tracts with the longitudinal and transverse subdivisions of the brain wall. The tracts shown are by no means a complete set, and were selected merely for coverage of different parts of the brain and variety of navigational course. In principle, all brain tracts allow an analogous representation. The general principle illustrated is that, as in the case of tangential migration, axonal navigation tends to respect the primary internal boundaries in the wall,

FIGURE 5.6. (CONTINUED)

so that the course selected at given decision points results in a trajectory that is either parallel or orthogonal to neighboring boundaries. The courses of all these fibers reflect the overall bending of the neural tube axis. Note that several early fiber tracts are elaborated before or during neural tube axial bending, while many others are formed afterward (revealing that the fibers follow intrinsic topological cues that do not change because of morphogenetic deformations).

The upper schema displays tracts (or connections) using mainly a transversal course in different parts of the brain. (See list below for identifications.) The middle schema shows tracts disposed longitudinally, or with mixed longitudinal and transverse sectors in their course. (Contralateral parts of courses appear dashed; see list below for identifications.) The lower schema concentrates on two systems of axons. Rostrally it shows the optic pathway in the forebrain and midbrain, illustrating its overall longitudinal course within the alar plate and a set of retinorecipient fields at different transverse parts of the brain wall. This schema does not imply that each ganglion cell axon from the retina gives collaterals to all retinorecipient nuclei, since there is evidence of some target selectivity. It is noteworthy that the retinotopic projection maps produced along this pathway after synaptogenesis are also aligned with the orthogonal grid of primary brain boundaries. The lower schema shows caudally the characteristic topology in the hindbrain alar plate of the primary sensory afferents from the cranial nerves (and of a cervical spinal nerve). Trigeminal and cervical somatosensory fibers (5, c3), facial, glossopharyngeal and vagal viscerosensory fibers (7, 9, 10) and vestibular and cochlear sensorial fibers (8v, 8c) are represented. In all these cases, again, the primary fibers adopt longitudinal courses along the corresponding plurisegmental sensory column (see Figure 4.3) and will give out collaterals at different transverse levels (again with some target selectivity, as in the retinal fields; details not shown). Note that some nerves contain fibers of different functional modalities (that is, somatosensory and viscerosensory components in 7, 9, and 10), which will each enter into the appropriate column (not shown). The entrance points of the afferents are indicated by circles or ovals.

List of tracts

01	lateral olfactory tract
02	striopallidal projection
03	preoptohypophysary tract
04	subthalamopallidal projection
05	tegmental projection from ventral thalamus
06	habenulointerpeduncular (retroflex) tract
07	posterior commissure
08	crossed tectotegmental tract
09	trochlear nerve
10	cochleo-olivary tract
11	dorsal horn into ventral horn projection
12	claustrocortical projection
13	bi-directional thalamo-cortical connection
14	strionigral tract
15	pallidothalamic (ansa lenticularis) tract
16	stria terminalis
17	stria medullaris
18	reticular nucleus into dorsal thalamus
19	mammillotegmental and mammillothalamic tracts
20	dentato-thalamic tract
21	tectothalamic connection (brachium of superior colliculus)
22	brachium of inferior colliculus
23	tecto-parabigeminal projection
24	tectoreticular tract
25	pontocerebellar tract (brachium pontis)
26	trapezoid body and lateral lemniscus
27	olivo-cerebellar (climbing) fibers
28	reticulospinal tracts
29	dorsal spinocerebellar tract
30	dorsal column tract

List of structures

SCH	suprachiasmatic nucleus
VLG	ventral lateral geniculate nucleus
DLG	dorsal lateral geniculate nucleus
APT	anterior pretectal nucleus
OPT	olivary pretectal nucleus
PPT	posterior pretectal nucleus
SC	superior colliculus
5,7,8v,8c,9,10	trigeminus, facial, vestibular, cochlear, glossopharyngeal, and vagal cranial nerves
c3	third cervical

precarious. For instance, the attractant Netrin1 can be converted into a repellent by Laminin1 (Hopker et al., 1999). These "guidance forces" regulate processes such as growth along the dorsoventral or anteroposterior axes, sprouting of collateral axons, fasciculation with pioneer axons, channeling into narrow passages, crossing midline structures, and choosing synaptic targets.

Many of the choices that an axon makes are generated by the growth cone. The growth cone is at the distal end of immature axons; it integrates environmental signals and generates corresponding modifications of the cytoskeleton that promote either elongation, turning, growth arrest, or retraction of the axon. Once it reaches its target, the growth cone and the targeted cell develop into pre- and postsynaptic structures, respectively.

Here, we will briefly review some of the molecular mechanisms that control axon pathfinding and synapse formation. The growth of commissural axons in the embryonic vertebrate spinal cord illustrates some of the major principals. These sensory neurons lie in the dorsal horn and grow axons that extend ventrally toward the floor plate, where they form a commissure by crossing the ventral midline. On reaching the contralateral side, they coalesce to form a rostral-growing ventral tract that extends to the hindbrain reticular formation. The ventral growth of commissural axons is directed by a family of proteins called netrins that are produced in the ventral spinal cord (Colamarino & Tessier-Lavigne, 1995; Manitt & Kennedy, 2002). In this context, netrins function as chemoattractants for growth cones expressing netrin receptors. (There are at least six genes encoding different types of netrin receptors.) While netrins attract axons, there are repellent agents, such as semaphorins and slits, that focus the axons into incipient tracts (Zou et al., 2000; Plump et al., 2002; Bagri et al., 2002). The receptors for semaphorins are called neuropilins and plexins; the receptors for slits are known as robos.

Transduction of extracellular signals into changes in axon growth and trajectory is mediated in part through cyclic nucleotide second messengers. Growth cone responses to semaphorins, neurotrophin-3, and netrin can be modulated by the levels of cAMP or cGMP (Song et al., 1998). For instance, semaphoring-induced repulsion can be converted to attraction by activation of the cGMP signaling pathways (Song et al., 1998).

Integrins are cell-surface receptors that coordinate the interaction of growing axons and migrating cells with the extracellular matrix molecules such as laminins and fibronectin (Reichardt et al., 1992). Laminins are multi-subunit proteins, parts of which resemble netrins, which regulate diverse processes, including axon growth and synapse formation (Sanes & Lichtman, 2001).

Molecular homophilic interactions are important in mediating mutual adhesion between axons to form axon fascicles (fasciculation), and in forming synapses (Van Vactor, 1998; Kamiguchi et al., 1998; Redies, 2000). These interactions are mediated via cadherins and IgCAMs families. *Cadherins* are calcium-dependent homophilic adhesion proteins. Based on their expression patterns, they are implicated in coordinating modularity and connectivity of brain circuitry (Takeichi et al., 1997; Redies, 2000; Yoon et al., 2000; Redies & Puelles, 2001). Note that IgCAMs are also involved in heterophilic interactions (De Angelis et al., 1999).

Axonal interactions have been implicated in coordinating reciprocal connections, such as the development of connections between specific thalamic nuclei and distinct areas of the neocortex. There is growing evidence that interactions between corticothalamic and thalamocortical axons have a central role in this process (Ghosh & Shatz, 1993; Molnar et al., 1998; Hevner et al., 2001). Furthermore, there is evidence that the pathway through which thalamocortical projections grow to their cortical targets has a key role in controlling the topography of the inputs (Garel et al., 2002).

The formation of topographic synaptic maps in target tissues is regulated by the Eph receptors and their ligands, the Ephrins (Flanagan & Vanderhaeghen, 1998). This is best understood in the formation of retinotopic maps in the superior colliculus (Feldheim et al., 2000; Brown et al., 2000).

Once axons reach their general target area, they search for their specific target, often through the formation of axon branches (Yates et al., 2001). For instance, thalamocortical fibers from the lateral geniculate nucleus (LGN) grow to the visual area of the neocortex. There, they preferentially form stable synapses with the neurons in layer 4 (Sanes & Yamagata, 1999). Within layer 4, a given axon forms synapses with multiple neurons. Activity-dependent competition between the synapses of several axons results in the mature circuitry. For instance, different layers of the LGN process information from either the left or the right eye, or from either X or Y ganglion cell types. Axonal projections from these LGN layers initially overlap within layer 4 of the visual cortex; activity-dependent competition results in the production of alternating stripes of left or right eye innervation within layer 4 (the ocular dominance columns) (Crair et al., 1998; Crowley & Katz, 2000) and a stratification of X versus Y inputs. Thus, the mechanisms underlying synaptic formation, transmission efficiency, and stabilization (known generically as synaptic plasticity) are essential for later stages of neural histogenesis.

The molecular mechanisms that are implicated in regulating how an axon chooses its synaptic partners (for example, other neurons or muscle cells) include many of the same molecules that control axon pathfinding, such as the cadherins, protocadherins, and ephrins (Redies, 2000; Feng, G., et al., 2000; Lee et al., 2001; Benson et al., 2001; Sanes & Lichtman, 2001; Goda, 2002). In the CNS, the initiation of synapse formation appears to be coordinated by interactions between the growth cone and the filipodia of dendrites (Benson et al., 2001), and may be mediated by the cadherins (Goda, 2002) and/or neurexin and neuroligin membrane proteins (Scheiffele et al., 2000).

The complexity of the molecular mechanisms that control the specificity of synapse formation between different targets still evades systematic analysis. In the olfactory bulb, olfactory receptor proteins decorating the afferent axons participate in regulating the specificity of synapse choice (Buck, 2000). In mammals, there are over 1,000 olfactory receptor genes (Mombaerts, 1999); thus, in this case, a large number of distinct molecules control the specificity of synapse formation. It remains to be seen if other complex mechanisms similarly regulate the specificity of synapse formation in other regions of the brain.

Synapse formation is also regulated by adjacent astrocytic glial cells. There is evidence that the astrocytes increase synapse formation by secreting cholesterol-containing lipoproteins (Mauch et al., 2001). This is an intriguing result, because these lipoproteins, or their receptors, are implicated in Alzheimer's disease, as well as in Reelin-signal transduction, and synaptic plasticity (Barres & Smith, 2001).

Once synapse formation is underway, synaptic function depends on the maturation of the molecular machinery that drives the action potential, neurotransmitter/neuropeptide production, release, and signalling. These processes require voltage-gated and ligand-gated channels, ligand-gated receptors, neurotransmitters, neuromodulators, ion and neurotransmitter pumps, and signal-transduction assemblies. Psychoactive medications largely function through their effects on these processes. Several of the genes that cause X-linked forms of mental retardation are implicated in neural activity-dependent processes (Boda et al., 2002).

During development, there are major changes in the electrophysiological response properties of certain neurons to a given neurotransmitter. In rodents, prior to birth GABA acts as an excitatory neurotransmitter, whereas beginning in the neonatal period, GABA obtains its mature function as an inhibitory neurotransmitter (Ben-Ari, 2002). The change in GABA's properties is thought to be mediated by the induction of the KCC2 potassium/chloride pump; its expression results in hyperpolarization when GABA opens chloride channels.

In addition to the physiological changes at the level of individual neurons, synaptic anatomy and physiology of neural assemblies and systems are particularly plastic in the immature brain. It is during this period that there are critical periods in neural plasticity that are required in the formation of specific circuits. Circuit maturation requires a proper balance of excitatory input and local inhibition (Hensch et al., 1998).

Myelination

Many axons in the CNS and PNS are ensheathed by myelinating glial cells, called oligodendrocytes and Schwann cells, respectively (Mirsky & Jessen, 1996). The production of oligodendrocytes has been shown to be restricted to specific loci in the CNS ventricular zone, from where they colonize diverse axon tracts

(Pérez-Villegas et al., 1999; Olivier et al., 2001; Spassky et al., 2001, 2002). Myelination increases the speed at which action potentials are conducted along the axon, and also appears to modulate synaptic function (Ullian & Barres, 1998). Myelination is a protracted process that continues postnatally, and is regulated both by an intrinsic genetic program (Wegner, 2000) and extrinsic factors that include interactions with the axon (Barres & Raff, 1999), and with thyroid hormone and retinoic acid (Barres et al., 1994).

Survival

Neurogenesis and synaptogenesis produce more neurons and synapses than can be assimilated adaptively in the mature brain. Thus, the elimination of neurons and synapses is an important step in sculpting the nervous system (Raff et al., 1993). There are several mechanisms that regulate these processes. In general, the elimination of neurons is controlled by inducing the process of apoptosis (Kuan et al., 2000), which is controlled by a cascade of proteases called caspases (Oppenheim et al., 2001). There are multiple pathways that activate caspases in the developing brain. These include the JNK protein kinases (Kuan et al., 1999), and signals mediated through neurotrophin receptors (Huang & Reichardt, 2001; Sofroniew et al., 2001). Neurons that succeed in forming synapses obtain from the post-synaptic cells trophic substances that promote their survival. For instance, secretion of neurotrophins by postsynaptic cells (such as NGF, BDNF, and NT3) promotes the survival of those neurons that have made a synapse upon them; neurons that fail to form synapses die (Huang & Reichardt, 2001). Neurotrophins signal through receptor tyrosine kinases (Trks) via the mitogen-activated protein (MAP) kinase, and Akt pathways, and through the p75 receptor via the JNK, p53, and NF-kappa B pathways (Kaplan & Miller, 2000). Neurotrophins and other trophic signals tend to have functions that extend beyond survival, as they have roles in the differentiation and morphogenesis of neurons and glia.

Perspective

An animal's behavior is based upon its brain's reactions to external and internal information. Brain function requires the concerted and integrated action of neural systems. Typically, neural systems are distributed over multiple regions. Some systems are pathways that include sensory inputs, sensory perception and integration centers, regions that translate sensory stimuli into potential responses, and motor output regions. Other systems consist of loops, such as the cortex-basal ganglia-thalamus-cortex circuit. These structures are influenced by other systems that can affect the quality and/or intensity of the process, such as serotonin, norepinephrine, dopamine, and acetylcholine inputs. A key challenge to behavioral science and medicine will be to understand the development and function of neural systems, as it is likely that neuropsychiatric disorders will not be understood solely at the cellular level.

Given the molecular complexity of brain development and function, it is surprising that severe developmental neuropsychiatric disorders do not occur at a higher frequency. Perhaps redundancy in the molecular, cellular, and neural systems processes that underlie neural function protect the CNS. It is well known from genetic analyses that gene duplication events have led to a high degree of genetic redundancy in vertebrates. The redundancy has simultaneously allowed for the increased complexity of vertebrates and has protected them against dysfunction when a single gene is defective.

It is perhaps redundancy in the genetics and biology of neural systems that has contributed to impeding our understanding of the genetic basis of neuropsychiatric disorders. This would be consistent with evidence for the polygenic etiology of neuropsychiatric disorders. Thus, even a homozygous state of a loss-of-function mutation may have a subtle phenotype if a redundant gene is active in the same temporal-spatial pattern.

Gene dosage changes that are generated by regulatory processes following fertilization also probably contribute to the complexity of neurogenetic processes. Gene silencing due to X-inactivation or to chromosomal imprinting (based on the parent-of-origin) can have profound effects on brain development and function. Often these processes operate through DNA methylation, which is disrupted by mutation of MECP2, the gene that underlies Rett syndrome and a form of X-linked mental retardation Couvert et al. (2001).

Because of the complexity of the processes that control brain function, perhaps one should consider neuropsychiatric disorders in a non-traditional pathophysiological context. Rather than focusing on a disease process affecting a single cell type or organ, one should view the disorder as affecting a neural pathway or a neural circuit (Rubenstein & Merzenich, 2003). Next, one should consider the possible ways that the efficiency of that pathway/circuit can be altered, as each of those mechanisms could have a similar net result on pathway/circuit function. Thus, a single gene mutation that blocks 50% of the output of the pathway/circuit would have similar phenotype if an individual inherited two genes that each inhibits the pathway by 25%. For instance, consider the case of a disorder of reduced inhibitory tone of the cerebral cortex, which leads to a lower seizure threshold. This syndrome could be caused by a single gene defect that reduces the synthesis of GABA by 50%, or by a combination of two defects which each reduce GABA transmission by 25% (that is, 25% fewer GABAergic neurons are produced during development, and 25% less GABA synthesized by those neurons). Likewise, this view easily incorporates non-genetic mechanisms that alter neural system function. Thus, by considering the genetics, anatomy, and physiology of the processes' underlying behavior, this model may be a useful way to conceptualize neuropsychiatric pathology (Rubenstein & Merzenich, 2003).

In conclusion, the aim of this chapter has been to provide a broad review of basic mechanisms that control brain development. This information should be useful as a foundation for understanding the results from human genetic studies that are identifying genes that contribute to neuropsychiatric disorders. For instance, in the case of autism, recent studies have identified a number of candidate genes (Rubenstein & Merzenich, 2003). The candidate genes include a transcription factor (Arx), an RNA-binding protein (fragile-X gene, FMR1), and neurotransmitter receptors (Glutamate Receptor Ionotropic Kainate 2 gene, and the GABA receptor GABRB3), and tuberous sclerosis tumor suppressor genes (Bolton et al., 2002; Buxbaum et al., 2003; Jamain et al., 2002; Rogers et al., 2001; Turner et al., 2002). The present results are just the tip of the iceberg, and will certainly revolutionize our understanding of human brain function and dysfunction.

References

Acampora, D., Gulisano, M., Broccoli, V., & Simeone, A. (2001). Otx genes in brain morphogenesis. *Progress in Neurobiology, 64,* 69–95.

Allendoerfer, K. L., & Shatz, C. J. (1994). The subplate, a transient neocortical structure: Its role in the development of connections between thalamus and cortex. *Annual Reviews of Neuroscience, 17,* 185–218.

Alvarez-Buylla, A., Garcia-Verdugo, J. M., & Tramontin, A. D. (2001). A unified hypothesis on the lineage of neural stem cells. *Nature Reviews Neuroscience, 2,* 287–293.

Anderson, S. A., Qiu, M., Bulfone, A., Eisenstat, D. D., Meneses, J., Pedersen, R., & Rubenstein, J.L.R. (1997). Mutations of the homeobox genes Dlx-1 and Dlx-2 disrupt the striatal subventricular zone and differentiation of late-born striatal neurons. *Neuron, 19,* 27–37.

Arber, S., Han, B., Mendelsohn, M., Smith, M., Jessell, T. M., & Sockanathan, S. (1999). Requirement for the homeobox gene Hb9 in the consolidation of motor neuron identity. *Neuron, 23,* 659–674.

Arber, S., Ladle, D. R., Lin, J. H., Frank, E., & Jessell, T. M. (2000). ETS gene Er81 controls the formation of functional connections between group Ia sensory afferents and motor neurons. *Cell, 101,* 485–498.

Artavanis-Tsakonas, S., Rand, M. D., & Lake, R. J. (1999). Notch signaling: Cell fate control and signal integration in development. *Science, 284,* 770–776.

Bagri, A., Marin, O., Plump, A. S., Mak, J., Pleasure, S. J., Rubenstein. J. L., & Tessier-Lavigne, M. (2002). Slit proteins prevent midline crossing and determine the dorsoventral position of major axonal pathways in the mammalian forebrain. *Neuron, 33,* 233–248.

Barres, B. A. (1999). A new role for glia: Generation of neurons! *Cell, 97,* 667–670.

Barres, B. A., & Smith, S. J. (2001). Neurobiology. Cholesterol—making or breaking the synapse. *Science, 294,* 1296–1297.

Barres, B. A., Lazar, M. A., & Raff, M. C. (1994). A novel role for thyroid hormone, glucocorticoids and retinoic acid in timing oligodendrocyte development. *Development, 120,* 1097–1108.

Barres, B. A., & Raff, M. C. (1999). Axonal control of oligodendrocyte development. *The Journal of Cell Biology, 147,* 1123–1128.

Barrow, J. R., Stadler, H. S., & Capecchi, M. R. (2000). Roles of Hoxa1 and Hoxa2 in patterning the early hindbrain of the mouse. *Development, 127,* 933–944.

Barth, K. A., Kishimoto, Y., Rohr, K., Seydler, C., Schulte-Merker, S., & Wilson, S. W. (1999). Bmp activity establishes a gradient of positional information throughout the entire neural plate. *Development, 126,* 4977–4987.

Beddington, R. S., & Robertson, E. J. (1999). Axis development and early asymmetry in mammals. *Cell, 96,* 195–209.

Ben-Ari, Y. (2002). Excitatory actions of gaba during development: The nature of the nurture. *Nature Reviews of Neuroscience, 3,* 728–739.

Benson, D. L., Colman, D. R., & Huntley, G. W. (2001). Molecules, maps and synapse specificity. *Nature Reviews of Neuroscience, 2,* 899–909.

Blumberg, B., Bolado, J., Jr., Moreno, T. A., Kintner, C., Evans, R. M., & Papalopulu, N. (1997). An essential role for retinoid signaling in anteroposterior neural patterning. *Development, 124,* 373–379.

Boda, B., Mas, C., & Muller, D. (2002). Activity-dependent regulation of genes implicated in X-linked non-specific mental retardation. *Neuroscience, 114,* 13–17.

Bolton, P. F., Park, R. J., Higgins, J. N., Griffiths, P. D., & Pickles, A. (2002). Neuro-epileptic determinants of autism spectrum disorders in tuberous sclerosis complex. *Brain, 125(Pt. 6),* 1247–1255.

Brenman, J. E., Gao, F. B., Jan, L. Y., & Jan, Y. N. (2001). Sequoia, a tramtrack-related zinc finger protein, functions as a pan-neural regulator for dendrite and axon morphogenesis in Drosophila. *Developmental Cell, 1,* 667–677.

Briscoe, J., Pierani, A., Jessell, T. M., & Ericson, J. (2000). A homeodomain protein code specifies progenitor cell identity and neuronal fate in the ventral neural tube. *Cell, 101,* 435–445.

Briscoe, J., Sussel, L., Serup, P., Hartigan-O'Connor, D., Jessell, T. M., Rubenstein, J. L., et al. (1999). Homeobox gene Nkx2.2 and specification of neuronal identity by graded Sonic hedgehog signalling. *Nature, 398,* 622–627.

Brose, K., & Tessier-Lavigne, M. (2000). Slit proteins: Key regulators of axon guidance, axonal branching, and cell migration. *Current Opinions in Neurobiology, 10,* 95–102.

Brown, A., Yates, P. A., Burrola, P., Ortuno, D., Vaidya, A., Jessell, T. M., et al. (2000). Topographic mapping from the retina to the midbrain is controlled by relative but not absolute levels of EphA receptor signaling. *Cell, 102,* 77–88.

Buck, L. B. (2000). The molecular architecture of odor and pheromone sensing in mammals. *Cell, 100,* 611–618.

Buxbaum, J. D., Silverman, J. M., Smith, C. J., Greenberg, D. A., Kilifarski, M., Reichert J., et al. (2003). Association between a GABRB3 polymorphism and autism. *Molecular Psychiatry, 7,* 311–316.

Casarosa, S., Fode, C., & Guillemot, F. (1999). Mash1 regulates neurogenesis in the ventral telencephalon. *Development, 126,* 525–534.

Cassidy, R., & Frisen, J. (2001). Neurobiology. Stem cells on the brain. *Nature, 412,* 690–691.

Caviness, V. S., Jr., Takahashi, T., & Nowakowski, R. S. (1995). Numbers, time and neocortical neuronogenesis: A general developmental and evolutionary model. *Trends in Neuroscience, 18,* 379–383.

Cheah, S. S., Kwan, K. M., & Behringer, R. R. (2000). Requirement of LIM domains for LIM1 function in mouse head development. *Genesis, 27,* 12–21.

Chitnis, A. B. (1995). The role of Notch in lateral inhibition and cell fate specification. *Molecular and Cellular Neurosciences, 6,* 311–321.

Cline, H. T. (2001). Dendritic arbor development and synaptogenesis. *Current Opinions in Neurobiology, 11,* 118–126.

Cobos-Sillero, I., Shimamura, K., Rubenstein, J.L.R., Martinez, S., & Puelles, L. (2001). Fate map of the avian forebrain at stage 8 with quail-chick chimeras. *Developmental Biology, 239,* 46–67.

Colamarino, S. A., & Tessier-Lavigne, M. (1995). The role of the floor plate in axon guidance. *Annual Reviews of Neuroscience, 18,* 497–529.

Colas, J. F., & Schoenwolf, G. C. (2001). Towards a cellular and molecular understanding of neurulation. *Developmental Dynamics, 221,* 117–145.

Comery, T. A., Harris, J. B., Willems, P. J., Oostra, B. A., Irwin, S. A., Weiler, I. J., et al. (1997). Abnormal dendritic spines in fragile X knockout mice: Maturation and pruning deficits. *Proceedings of the National Academy of Sciences USA, 94,* 5401–5404.

Conover, J. C., Doetsch, F., Garcia-Verdugo, J. M., Gale, N. W., Yancopoulos, G. D., Alvarez-Buylla, A. (2000). Disruption of Eph/ephrin signaling affects migration and proliferation in the adult subventricular zone. *Nature Neuroscience, 3,* 1091–1097.

Couly, G., Grapin-Botton, A., Coltey, P., Ruhin, B., & Le Douarin, N. M. (1998). Determination of the identity of the derivatives of the cephalic neural crest: Incompatibility between Hox gene expression and lower jaw development. *Development, 125,* 3445–3459.

Couvert, P., Bienvenu, T., Aquaviva, C., Poirier, K., Moraine, C., Gendrot, C., et al. (2001). MECP2 is highly mutated in X-linked mental retardation. *Human Molecular Genetics, 10,* 941–946.

Crair, M. C., Gillespie, D. C., & Stryker, M. P. (1998). The role of visual experience in the development of columns in cat visual cortex. *Science, 279,* 566–570.

Crossley, P. H., Martinez, S., Ohkubo, Y., & Rubenstein, J. L. (2001). Coordinate expression of Fgf8, Otx2, Bmp4, and Shh in the rostral prosencephalon during development of the telencephalic and optic vesicles. *Neuroscience, 108,* 183–206.

Crowley, J. C., & Katz, L. C. (2000). Early development of ocular dominance columns. *Science, 290,* 1321–1324.

De Angelis, E., MacFarlane, J., Du, J. S., Yeo, G., Hicks, R., Rathjen, F. G., et al. (1999). Pathological missense mutations of neural cell adhesion molecule L1 affect homophilic and heterophilic binding activities. *European Molecular Biology Organization Journal, 18,* 4744–4753.

Depew, M. J., Liu, J. K., Long, J. E., Presley, R., Meneses, J. J., Pedersen, R. A., et al. (1999). Dlx5 regulates regional development of the branchial arches and sensory capsules. *Development, 126,* 3831–3846.

Depew, M. J., Lufkin, T., & Rubenstein, J.L.R. (2002). Specification of jaw subdivisions by *Dlx* genes. *Science, 298,* 381–385.

De Robertis, E. M., Larrain, J., Oelgeschlager, M., & Wessely, O. (2000). The establishment of Spemann's organizer and patterning of the vertebrate embryo. *Nature Reviews Genetics, 1,* 171–181.

Erskine, L., Williams, S. E., Brose, K., Kidd, T., Rachel, R. A., Goodman, C. S., Tessier-Lavigne, M., & Mason, C. A. (2000). Retinal ganglion cell axon guidance in the mouse optic chiasm: Expression and function of robos and slits. *The Journal of Neuroscience, 20,* 4975–4982.

Feldheim, D. A., Kim, Y. I., Bergemann, A. D., Frisen, J., Barbacid, M., & Flanagan, J. G. (2000). Genetic analysis of ephrin-A2 and ephrin-A5 shows their requirement in multiple aspects of retinocollicular mapping. *Neuron, 25,* 563–574.

Feng, G., Laskowski, M. B., Feldheim, D. A., Wang, H., Lewis, R., Frisen, J., Flanagan, J. G., & Sanes, J. R. (2000). Roles for ephrins in positionally selective synaptogenesis between motor neurons and muscle fibers. *Neuron, 25,* 295–306.

Feng, J., Yan Z., Ferreira, A., Tomizawa, K., Liauw, J. A., Zhuo, M., et al. (2000). Spinophilin regulates the formation and function of dendritic spines. *Proceedings of the National Academy of Sciences USA, 97,* 9287–9292.

Fernández-Garre, P., Rodríguez-Gallardo, L., Gallego-Díaz, V., Alvarez, I., & Puelles, L. (2002). Fate map of the chicken neural plate at stage 4. *Development,129,* 2807–2822.

Figdor, M. C., & Stern, C. D. (1993). Segmental organization of embryonic diencephalon. *Nature, 363,* 630–634.

Flanagan, J. G., & Vanderhaeghen, P. (1998). The ephrins and Eph receptors in neural development. *Annual Reviews of Neuroscience, 21,* 309–345. Review.

Fode, C., Ma, Q., Casarosa, S., Ang, S. L., Anderson, D. J., & Guillemot, F. (2000). A role for neural determination genes in specifying the dorsoventral identity of telencephalic neurons. *Genes & Development, 14,* 67–80.

Fukuchi-Shimogori, T., & Grove, E. A. (2001). Neocortex patterning by the secreted signaling molecule FGF8. *Science, 294,* 1071–1074.

Galceran, J., Miyashita-Lin, E. M., Devaney, E., Rubenstein, J. L., & Grosschedl, R. (2000). Hippocampus development and generation of dentate gyrus granule cells is regulated by LEF1. *Development, 127,* 469–482.

Garel, S., Huffman, K. J., & Rubenstein, J.L.R. (2003). A caudal shift in neocortical patterning in a *Fgf8* hypomorphic mouse mutant. *Development, 130,* 1903–1914.

Garel, S., Yun, K., Grosschedl, R., & Rubenstein, J.L.R. (2002). Topography of connections between the neocortex and thalamus is regulated by intermediate structures. *Development, 129,* 5621–5634.

Gao, F. B., Brenman, J. E., Jan, L. Y., & Jan, Y. N. (1999). Genes regulating dendritic outgrowth, branching, and routing in Drosophila. *Genes & Development, 13,* 2549–2561.

Gao, F. B., Kohwi, M., Brenman, J. E., Jan, L. Y., & Jan, Y. N. (2000). Control of dendritic field formation in Drosophila: The roles of flamingo and competition between homologous neurons. *Neuron, 28,* 91–101.

Gavalas, A., & Krumlauf, R. (2000). Retinoid signalling and hindbrain patterning. *Current Opinions in Genetic Development, 10*(4), 380–386.

Gavalas, A., Trainor, P., Ariza-McNaughton, L., Krumlauf, R. (2001). Synergy between Hoxa1 and Hoxb1: The relationship between arch patterning and the generation of cranial neural crest. *Development, 128,* 3017–3027.

Ghosh, A., & Shatz, C. J. (1993). A role for subplate neurons in the patterning of connections from thalamus to neocortex. *Development, 117,* 1031–1047.

Gleeson, J. G., & Walsh, C. A. (2000). Neuronal migration disorders: From genetic diseases to developmental mechanisms. *Trends in Neuroscience, 23,* 352–359.

Goda ,Y. (2002). Cadherins communicate structural plasticity of presynaptic and postsynaptic terminals. *Neuron, 35,* 1–3.

Gorski, J. A., Talley, T., Qiu, M., Puelles, L., Rubenstein, J.L.R., & Jones, K. R. (2002). Cortical excitatory neurons and glia, but not GABAergic neurons, are produced in the Emx1-expressing lineage. *The Journal of Neuroscience, 22,* 6309–6314.

Gritti, A., Bonfanti, L., Doetsch, F., Caille, I., Alvarez-Buylla, A., Lim, D. A., et al. (2002). Multipotent neural stem cells reside into the rostral extension and olfactory bulb of adult rodents. *The Journal of Neuroscience, 22,* 437–445.

Harland, R. (2000). Neural induction. *Current Opinions in Genetic Development, 10,* 357–362.

Hartfuss, E., Galli, R., Heins, N., & Götz, M. (2001). Characterization of CNS precursor subtypes and radial glia. *Developmental Biology, 229,* 15–30.

Hatten, M. E. (1999). Central nervous system neuronal migration. *Annual Reviews of Neuroscience, 22,* 511–539.

Hatten, M. E. (2002). New directions in neuronal migration. *Science, 297,* 1660–1663.

Hébert, J. M., Mishina, Y., & McConnell, S. K. (2002). BMP signaling is required locally to pattern the dorsal telencephalic midline. *Neuron, 35,* 1029–1041.

Henrique, D., Hirsinger, E., Adam, J., Le Roux, I., Pourquie, O., Ish-Horowicz, D., et al. (1997). Maintenance of neuroepithelial progenitor cells by Delta-Notch signalling in the embryonic chick retina. *Current Biology, 7,* 661–670.

Hensch, T. K., Fagiolini, M., Mataga, N., Stryker, M. P., Baekkeskov, S., & Kash, S. F. (1998). Local GABA circuit control of experience-dependent plasticity in developing visual cortex. *Science, 282,* 1504–1508.

Hevner, R. F., Shi, L., Justice, N., Hsueh, Y., Sheng, M., Smiga, S., et al. (2001). Tbr1 regulates differentiation of the preplate and layer 6. *Neuron, 29,* 353–366.

Honarpour, N., Gilbert, S. L., Lahn, B. T., Wang, X., & Herz, J. (2001). Apaf-1 deficiency and neural tube closure defects are found in fog mice. *Proceedings of the National Academy of Science USA, 98,* 9683–9687.

Hopker, V. H., Shewan, D., Tessier-Lavigne, M., Poo, M., & Holt, C. (1999). Growth-cone attraction to netrin-1 is converted to repulsion by laminin-1. *Nature, 401,* 69–73.

Horton, S., Meredith, A., Richardson, J. A., & Johnson, J. E. (1999). Correct coordination of neuronal differentiation events in ventral forebrain requires the bHLH factor MASH1. *Molecular and Cellular Neurosciences, 14,* 355–369.

Huang, E. J., & Reichardt, L. F. (2001). Neurotrophins: Roles in neuronal development and function. *Annual Reviews of Neuroscience, 24,* 677–736.

Inoue, T., Nakamura, S., & Osumi, N. (2000). Fate mapping of the mouse prosencephalic neural plate. *Development Biology, 219*(2), 373–383.

Jacob, J., Hacker, A., & Guthrie, S. (2001). Mechanisms and molecules in motor neuron specification and axon pathfinding. *Bioessays, 23,* 582–595.

Jamain, S., Betancur, C., Quach, H., Philippe, A., Fellous, M., Giros, B., et al. (2002). Linkage and association of the glutamate receptor 6 gene with autism. *Molecular Psychiatry, 7,* 302–310.

Jan, Y. N., & Jan, L. Y. (1998). Asymmetric cell division. *Nature, 392,* 775–778.

Jan, Y. N., & Jan, L. Y. (2001). Dendrites. *Genes & Development, 15,* 2627–2641.

Jessell, T. M. (2000). Neuronal specification in the spinal cord: Inductive signals and transcriptional codes. *Nature Reviews Genetics, 1,* 20–29.

Kakita, A., & Goldman, J. E. (1999). Patterns and dynamics of SVZ cell migration in the postnatal forebrain: Monitoring living progenitors in slice preparations. *Neuron, 23,* 461–472.

Kamiguchi, H., Hlavin, M. L., Yamasaki, M., & Lemmon, V. (1998). Adhesion molecules and inherited diseases of the human nervous system. *Annual Reviews of Neuroscience, 21,* 97–125.

Kaplan, D. R., & Miller, F. D. (2000). Neurotrophin signal transduction in the nervous system. *Current Opinions in Neurobiology, 10,* 381–391.

Kania, A., Johnson, R. L., & Jessell, T. M. (2000). Coordinate roles for LIM homeobox genes in directing the dorsoventral trajectory of motor axons in the vertebrate limb. *Cell, 102,* 161–173.

Kiecker, C., & Niehrs, C. (2001). The role of prechordal mesendoderm in neural patterning. *Current Opinions in Neurobiology, 11,* 27–33.

Korada, S., Zheng, W., Basilico, C., & Schwartz, M. L., Vaccarino, F. M. (2002). Fibroblast growth factor 2 is necessary for the growth of glutamate projection neurons in the anterior neocortex. *The Journal of Neuroscience, 22,* 863–875.

Kuan, C. Y., Roth, K. A., Flavell, R. A., & Rakic, P. (2000). Mechanisms of programmed cell death in the developing brain. *Trends in Neuroscience, 23,* 291–297.

Kuan, C. Y., Yang, D. D., Samanta Roy, D. R., Davis, R. J., Rakic, P., & Flavell, R. A. (1999). The Jnk1 and Jnk2 protein kinases are required for regional specific apoptosis during early brain development. *Neuron, 22,* 667–676.

Lamb, T. M., & Harland, R. M. (1995). Fibroblast growth factor is a direct neural inducer, which combined with noggin generates anterior-posterior neural pattern. *Development, 121,* 3627–3636.

Larsen, C. W., Zeltser, L. M., & Lumsden, A. (2001). Boundary formation and compartition in the avian diencephalon. *The Journal of Neuroscience, 21,* 4699–4711.

Lee, C. H., Herman, T., Clandinin, T. R., Lee, R., & Zipursky, S. L. (2001). N-cadherin regulates target specificity in the Drosophila visual system. *Neuron, 30,* 437–450.

Lee, E. Y., Hu, N., Yuan, S. S., Cox, L. A., Bradley, A., Lee, W. H., et al. (1994). Dual roles of the retinoblastoma protein in cell cycle regulation and neuron differentiation. *Genes & Development, 8,* 2008–2021.

Lee, K. J., & Jessell, T. M. (1999). The specification of dorsal cell fates in the vertebrate central nervous system. *Annual Reviews of Neuroscience, 22,* 261–294.

Lee, S. K., & Pfaff, S. L. (2001). Transcriptional networks regulating neuronal identity in the developing spinal cord. *Nature Neuroscience,* (Suppl 4), 1183–1191.

Lee, S. M., Tole, S., Grove, E., & McMahon, A. P. (2000). A local Wnt-3a signal is required for development of the mammalian hippocampus. *Development, 127,* 457–467.

Letinic, K., Zoncu, R., & Rakic, P. (2002). Origin of GABAergic neurons in the human neocortex. *Nature, 417,* 645–649.

Li, J. Y., & Joyner, A. L. (2001). Otx2 and Gbx2 are required for refinement and not induction of mid-hindbrain gene expression. *Development, 128,* 4979–4991.

Lindsell, C. E., Boulter, J, diSibio, G., Gossler, A., & Weinmaster, G. (1996). Expression patterns of Jagged, Delta1, Notch1, Notch2, and Notch3 genes identify ligand-receptor pairs that may function in neural development. *Molecular and Cellular Neurosciences, 8,* 14–27.

Litingtung, Y., & Chiang, C. (2000). Specification of ventral neuron types is mediated by an antagonistic interaction between Shh and Gli3. *Nature Neuroscience, 3,* 979–985.

Liu, A., & Joyner, A. L. (2001). Early anterior/posterior patterning of the midbrain and cerebellum. *Annual Reviews of Neuroscience, 24,* 869–896.

Liu, J. P., Laufer, E., & Jessell, T. M. (2001). Assigning the positional identity of spinal motor neurons. Rostrocaudal patterning of Hox-c expression by FGFs, Gdf11, and retinoids. *Neuron, 32,* 997–1012.

Lu, Q. R., Yuk, D., Alberta, J. A., Zhu, Z., Pawlitzky, I., Chan, J., et al. (2000). Sonic hedgehog—regulated oligodendrocyte lineage genes encoding bHLH proteins in the mammalian central nervous system. *Neuron, 25,* 317–329.

Lumsden, A. (1999). Closing in on rhombomere boundaries. *Nature and Cellular Biology, 1,* E83–85.

Lumsden, A., Krumlauf, R. (1996). Patterning the vertebrate neuraxis. *Science, 274,* 1109–1115.

Luo, L. (2000). Rho GTPases in neuronal morphogenesis. *Nature Reviews of Neuroscience, 1,* 173–180.

Luskin, M. B. (1998). Neuroblasts of the postnatal mammalian forebrain: Their phenotype and fate. *The Journal of Neurobiology, 36,* 221–233.

Mallamaci, A., Mercurio, S., Muzio, L., Cecchi, C., Pardini, C. L., Gruss, P., et al. (2000). The lack of Emx2 causes impairment of Reelin signaling and defects of neuronal migration in the developing cerebral cortex. *The Journal of Neuroscience, 20,* 1109–1118.

Manitt, C., Kennedy, T. E. (2002). Where the rubber meets the road: Netrin expression and function in developing and adult nervous systems. *Progress in Brain Research, 137,* 425–442.

Marin, F., & Puelles, L. (1994). Patterning of the embryonic avian midbrain after experimental inversions: A polarizing activity from the isthmus. *Developmental Biology, 163,* 19–37.

Marín, O., Plump., A., Sánchez-Camacho, C., Tessier-Lavigne., M., & Rubenstein, J.L.R. (in press). Attractive and repulsive cues guide interneuron migration to the mammalian cortex: In vivo contribution of Slit1, Slit2 and Netrin1 to neuronal positioning in the telencephalon. *Development.*

Marín, O., & Rubenstein, J. L. (2001). A long, remarkable journey: Tangential migration in the telencephalon. *Nature Reviews of Neuroscience, 2,* 780–790.

Marín, O., & Rubenstein, J.L.R. (2003). Cell migration in the forebrain. *Annual Reviews of Neuroscience.*

Marín, O., Yaron, A., Bagri, A., Tessier-Lavigne, M., & Rubenstein, J. L. (2001). Sorting of striatal and cortical interneurons regulated by semaphorin-neuropilin interactions. *Science, 293,* 872–875.

Marín-Padilla, M. (1983). Structural organization of the human cerebral cortex prior to the appearance of the cortical plate. *Anatomy and Embryology, 168,* 21–40.

Marquardt, T., & Pfaff, S. L. (2001). Cracking the transcriptional code for cell specification in the neural tube. *Cell, 106,* 651–654.

Martens, D. J., Tropepe, V., & van Der Kooy, D. (2000). Separate proliferation kinetics of fibroblast growth factor-responsive and epidermal growth factor-responsive neural stem cells within the embryonic forebrain germinal zone. *The Journal of Neuroscience, 20,* 1085–1095.

Martinez, S., Crossley, P. H., Cobos, I., Rubenstein, J. L., & Martin, G. R. (1999). FGF8 induces formation of an ectopic isthmic organizer and isthmocerebellar development via a repressive effect on Otx2 expression. *Development, 126,* 1189–1200.

Mauch, D. H., Nagler, K., Schumacher, S., Goritz, C., Muller, E. C., Otto, A., et al. (2001). CNS synaptogenesis promoted by glia-derived cholesterol. *Science, 294,* 1354–1357.

McConnell, S. K. (1995). Constructing the cerebral cortex: Neurogenesis and fate determination. *Neuron, 15,* 761–768.

McEvilly, R. J., de Diaz, M. O., Schonemann, M. D., Hooshmand, F., & Rosenfeld, M. G.
(2002). Transcriptional regulation of cortical neuron migration by POU domain factors.
Science, 295, 1528–1532.

Mellitzer, G., Xu, Q., & Wilkinson, D. G. (1999). Eph receptors and ephrins restrict cell
intermingling and communication. *Nature, 400,* 77–81.

Mirsky, R., & Jessen, K. R. (1996). Schwann cell development, differentiation and myelination. *Current Opinions in Neurobiology, 6,* 89–96.

Mizuguchi, R., Sugimori, M., Takebayashi, H., Kosako, H., Nagao, M., Yoshida, S.,
et al. (2001). Combinatorial roles of olig2 and neurogenin2 in the coordinated
induction of pan-neuronal and subtype-specific properties of motoneurons. *Neuron,
3,* 757–771.

Molnar, Z., Adams, R., & Blakemore, C. (1998). Mechanisms underlying the early
establishment of thalamocortical connections in the rat. *The Journal of Neuroscience, 18,*
5723–5745.

Mombaerts, P. (1999). Seven-transmembrane proteins as odorant and chemosensory
receptors. *Science, 286,* 707–711.

Muhr, J., Andersson, E., Persson, M., Jessell, T. M., & Ericson, J. (2001). Groucho-mediated
transcriptional repression establishes progenitor cell pattern and neuronal fate in the
ventral neural tube. *Cell, 104,* 861–873.

Muzio, L., DiBenedetto, B., Stoykova, A., Boncinelli, E., Gruss, P., & Mallamaci, A. (2002).
Conversion of cerebral cortex into basal ganglia in Emx2(-/-) Pax6(Sey/Sey) double-
mutant mice. *Nature Neuroscience, 5,* 737–745.

Nadarajah, B., Brunstrom, J. E., Grutzendler, J., Wong, R. O., & Pearlman, A. L. (2001). Two
modes of radial migration in early development of the cerebral cortex. *Nature Neuroscience,
4,* 143–150.

Nakamura, H. (2001). Regionalisation and acquisition of polarity in the optic tectum. *Progress
in Neurobiology, 65,* 473–488.

Nimchinsky, E. A., Sabatini, B. L., & Svoboda, K. (2002). Structure and function of dendritic
spines. *Annual Review of Physiology, 64,* 313–353.

Noctor, S. C., Flint, A. C., Weissman, T. A., Dammerman, R. S., & Kriegstein, A. R. (2001).
Neurons derived from radial glial cells establish radial units in neocortex. *Nature, 409,*
714–720.

Novitch, B. G., Chen, A. I., & Jessell, T. M. (2001). Coordinate regulation of motor neuron
subtype identity and pan-neuronal properties by the bHLH repressor Olig2. *Neuron, 31,*
773–789.

Nybakken, K., & Perrimon, N. (2002). Hedgehog signal transduction: Recent findings.
Current Opinions in Genetic Development, 5, 503–511.

Ohkubo, Y., Chiang, C., & Rubenstein, J.L.R. (2002). Coordinate regulation and synergistic
actions of BMP4, SHH and FGF8 in the rostral prosencephalon regulate morphogenesis
of the telencephalic and optic vesicles. *Neuroscience, 111,* 1–17.

O'Leary, D. D., & Wilkinson, D. G. (1999). Eph receptors and ephrins in neural development. *Current Opinions in Neurobiology, 9,* 65–73.

Olivier, C., Cobos, I., Perez, Villegas, E. M., Spassky, N., Zalc, B., Martinez, S., et al. (2001).
Monofocal origin of telencephalic oligodendrocytes in the anterior entopeduncular area
of the chick embryo. *Development, 128,* 1757–1769.

Oppenheim, R. W., Flavell, R. A., Vinsant, S., Prevette, D., Kuan, C. Y., & Rakic, P. (2001). Programmed cell death of developing mammalian neurons after genetic deletion of caspases. *The Journal of Neuroscience, 21,* 4752–4760.

Palmer, T. D., Willhoite, A. R., & Gage, F. H. (2000). Vascular niche for adult hippocampal neurogenesis. *The Journal of Comparative Neurology, 425,* 479–494.

Pérez-Villegas, E. M., Olivier, C., Spassky, N., Poncet, C., Cochard, P., Zalc, B., et al. (1999). Early specification of oligodendrocytes in the chick embryonic brain. *Developmental Biology, 216,* 98–113.

Pera, E. M., Wessely, O., Li, S. Y., & De Robertis, E. M. (2001). Neural and head induction by insulin-like growth factor signals. *Developmental Cell, 1,* 655–665.

Petersen, P. H., Zou, K., Hwang, J. K., Jan, Y. N., & Zhong, W. (2002). Progenitor cell maintenance requires numb and numblike during mouse neurogenesis. *Nature, 419,* 929–934.

Plump, A., Lynda, Erskine, L., Sabatier, C., Brose, K., Charles, J., Epstein, Goodman, G., Mason, C. A., & Tessier-Lavigne, M. (2002). Slit1 and Slit2 cooperate to prevent premature midline crossing of retinal axons in the mouse visual system. *Neuron, 33,* 219–232.

Polleux, F., Morrow, T., & Ghosh, A. (2000). Semaphorin 3A is a chemoattractant for cortical apical dendrites. *Nature, 404,* 567–573.

Puelles, L. (1995). A segmental morphological paradigm for understanding vertebrate forebrains. *Brain, Behavior, and Evolution, 46,* 319–337.

Puelles, L. (2001). Brain segmentation and forebrain development in amniotes. *Brain Research Bulletin, 55,* 695–710.

Puelles, L., & Bendala, M. C. (1978). Differentiation of neuroblasts in the chick optic tectum up to the eight day of incubation: A Golgi study. *Neuroscience, 3,* 207–325.

Puelles, L., Kuwana, E., Puelles, E., Bulfone, A., Shimamura, K., Keleher, J., et al. (2000). Pallial and subpallial derivatives in the embryonic chick and mouse telencephalon, traced by the expression of the genes Dlx-2, Emx-1, Nkx-2.1, Pax-6, and Tbr-1. *Journal of Comparative Neurology, 424*(3), 409–438.

Puelles, L., & Rubenstein, J.L.R. (1993). Expression patterns of homeobox and other putative regulatory genes in the embryonic mouse forebrain suggest a neuromeric organization. *Trends in Neuroscience, 16,* 472–479.

Puelles, L., & Verney, C. (1998). Early neuromeric distribution of tyrosine-hydroxylase and dopamine-ß-hydroxylase immunoreactive neurons in human embryos. *The Journal of Comparative Neurology, 394,* 283–308.

Qi, Y., Cai, J., Wu, Y., Wu, R., Lee, J., & Fu, H. (2001). Control of oligodendrocyte differentiation by the Nkx2.2 homeodomain transcription factor. *Development, 128,* 2723–2733.

Raff, M. C., Barres, B. A., Burne, J. F., Coles, H. S., Ishizaki, Y., & Jacobson, M. D. (1993). Programmed cell death and the control of cell survival: Lessons from the nervous system. *Science, 262,* 695–700.

Rakic, P. (2000). Radial unit hypothesis of neocortical expansion. *Novartis Found Symp, 228,* 30–52.

Redies, C. (2000). Cadherins in the central nervous system. *Progress in Neurobiology, 61,* 611–648.

Redies, C., & Puelles, L. (2001). Modularity in CNS development. *Bioessays, 23,* 1100–1111.

Reichardt, L. F., Bossy, B., de Curtis, I., Neugebauer, K. M., Venstrom, K., & Sretavan, D. (1992). Adhesive interactions that regulate development of the retina and primary visual projection. *Cold Spring Harbor Symposia on Quantitative Biology, 57,* 419–429.

Rice, D. S., & Curran, T. (2001). Role of the reelin signaling pathway in central nervous system development. *Annual Reviews of Neuroscience, 24,* 1005–1039.

Robey, E. (1997). Notch in vertebrates. *Current Opinions in Genetic Development, 7*, 551–557.

Roessler, E., & Muenke, M. (2001). Midline and laterality defects: Left and right meet in the middle. *Bioessays, 10*, 888–900.

Rogers, S. J., Wehner, D. E., & Hagerman, R. (2001). The behavioral phenotype in fragile X: Symptoms of autism in very young children with fragile X syndrome, idiopathic autism, and other development disorders. *Journal of Developmental and Behavioral Pediatrics, 22*, 409–417.

Rubenstein, J.L.R., & Merzenich, M. (2003). Neural-system and molecular-genetic model of autism. Manuscript in preparation.

Rubenstein, J.L.R., Shimamura, K., Martinez, S., & Puelles, L. (1998). Regionalization of the prosencephalic neural plate. *Annual Reviews of Neuroscience, 21*, 445–478.

Sander, M., Paydar, S., Ericson, J., Briscoe, J., Berber, E., German, M., et al. (2000). Ventral neural patterning by Nkx homeobox genes: Nkx6.1 controls somatic motor neuron and ventral interneuron fates. *Genes & Development, 14*, 2134–2139.

Sanes, J. R., & Lichtman, J. W. (2001). Developmentinduction, assembly, maturation and maintenance of a postsynaptic apparatus. *Nature Reviews of Neuroscience, 2*, 791–805.

Sanes, J. R., & Yamagata, M. (1999). Formation of lamina-specific synaptic connections. *Current Opinions in Neurobiology, 9*, 79–87.

Scheiffele, P., Fan, J., Choih, J., Fetter, R., & Serafini, T. (2000). Neuroligin expressed in non-neuronal cells triggers presynaptic development in contacting axons. *Cell, 101*, 657–669.

Sestan, N., Artavanis-Tsakonas, S., & Rakic, P. (1999). Contact-dependent inhibition of cortical neurite growth mediated by notch signaling. *Science, 286*, 741–746.

Shanmugalingam, S., Houart, C., Picker, A., Reifers, F., Macdonald, R., Barth, A., et al. (2000). Ace/Fgf8 is required for forebrain commissure formation and patterning of the telencephalon. *Development, 127*, 2549–2561.

Shen, Q., Zhong, W., Jan, Y. N., & Temple, S. (2002). Asymmetric numb distribution is critical for asymmetric cell division of mouse cerebral cortical stem cells and neuroblasts. *Development, 129*, 4843–4853.

Shimamura, K., Hartigan, D. J., Martinez, S., Puelles, L., & Rubenstein, J.L.R. (1995). Longitudinal organization of the anterior neural plate and neural tube. *Development, 121*, 3923–3933.

Shimamura, K., & Rubenstein, J.L.R. (1997). Inductive interactions direct early regionalization of the mouse forebrain. *Development, 124*, 2709–2718.

Simeone, A. (2000). Positioning the isthmic organizer where Otx2 and Gbx2meet. *Trends in Genetics, 16*, 237–240.

Sockanathan, S., & Jessell, T. M. (1998). Motor neuron-derived retinoid signaling specifies the subtype identity of spinal motor neurons. *Cell, 94*, 503–514.

Sofroniew, M. V., Howe, C. L., & Mobley, W. C. (2001). Nerve growth factor signaling, neuroprotection, and neural repair. *Annuual Reviews of Neuroscience, 24*, 1217–1281.

Song, H., Ming, G., He, Z., Lehmann, M., McKerracher, L., Tessier-Lavigne, M., et al. (1998). Conversion of neuronal growth cone responses from repulsion to attraction by cyclic nucleotides. *Science, 281*, 1515–1518.

Spassky, N., de Castro, F., Le Bras, B., Heydon, K., Queraud-LeSaux, F., Bloch-Gallego, E., et al. (2002). Directional guidance of oligodendroglial migration by class 3 semaphorins and netrin-1. *The Journal of Neuroscience, 22*, 5992–6004.

Spassky, N., Olivier C., Cobos, I., LeBras, B., Goujet-Zalc, C., Martinez, S., et al. (2001). The early steps of oligodendrogenesis: Insights from the study of the plp lineage in the brain of chicks and rodents. *Developmental Neuroscience, 23*, 318–326.

Stoeckli, E. T., & Landmesser, L. T. (1998). Axon guidance at choice points. *Current Opinions in Neurobiology, 8,* 73–79.

Storm, E., Rubenstein, J.L.R., & Martin, G. R. (in press). Negative regulation between two FGF signaling pathways as a mechanism for generating distinct phenotypes in response to different levels of FGF8. *Proceedings of the National Academy of Science,* Washington, D.C.

Streit, A., Berliner, A. J., Papanayotou, C., Sirulnik, A., & Stern, C. D. (2000). Initiation of neural induction by FGF signalling before gastrulation. *Nature, 406,* 74–78.

Sun, T., Echelard, Y., Lu, R., Yuk, D. I., Kaing, S., Stiles, C. D., et al. (2001). Olig bHLH proteins interact with homeodomain proteins to regulate cell fate acquisition in progenitors of the ventral neural tube. *Current Biology, 11,* 1413–1420.

Takeichi, M., Uemura, T., Iwai, Y., Uchida, N., Inoue, T., Tanaka T., et al. (1997). Cadherins in brain patterning and neural network formation. *Cold Spring Harbor Symposia on Quantitative Biology, 62,* 505–510.

Tanabe, Y., William, C., & Jessell, T. M. (1998). Specification of motor neuron identity by the MNR2 homeodomain protein. *Cell, 95,* 67–80.

Tessier-Lavigne, M., & Goodman, C. S. (1996). The molecular biology of axon guidance. *Science, 274,* 1123–1133.

Thomas, P. Q., Dattani, M. T., Brickman, J. M., McNay, D., Warne, G., Zacharin, M., et al. (2001). Heterozygous HESX1 mutations associated with isolated congenital pituitary hypoplasia and septo-optic dysplasia. *Human Molecular Genetics, 10,* 39–45.

Trainor, P. A., Krumlauf, R. (2000). Patterning the cranial neural crest: Hindbrain segmentation and Hox gene plasticity. *Nature Reviews of Neuroscience, 1,* 116–124.

Turner, G., Partington, M., Kerr, B., Mangelsdorf, M., & Gecz, J. (2002). Variable expression of mental retardation, autism, seizures, and dystonic hand movements in two families with an identical ARX gene mutation. *American Journal of Medical Genetics, 112,* 405–411.

Ullian, E. M., & Barres, B. A. (1998). The Schwann song of the glia-less synapse. *Neuron, 21,* 651–652.

Van Vactor, D. (1998). Adhesion and signaling in axonal fasciculation. *Current Opinions in Neurobiology, 8,* 80–86.

Wallis, D., & Muenke, M. (2000). Mutations in holoprosencephaly. *Human Mutation, 16,* 99–108.

Wang, K. H., Brose, K., Arnott, D., Kidd, T., Goodman, C. S., Henzel, W., et al. (1999). Biochemical purification of a mammalian slit protein as a positive regulator of sensory axon elongation and branching. *Cell, 96,* 771–784.

Wechsler-Reya, R., & Scott, M. P. (2001). The developmental biology of brain tumors. *Annual Reviews of Neuroscience, 24,* 385–428.

Wegner, M. (2000). Transcriptional control in myelinating glia: Flavors and spices. *Glia, 31,* 1–14.

Whitford, K. L., Dujkhuizen, P., Polleux, F., & Ghosh, A. (2002). Molecular control of cortical dendrite development. *Annual Reviews of Neuroscience, 25,* 127–149.

Wijgerde, M., McMahon, J. A., Rule, M., & McMahon, A. P. (2002). A direct requirement for Hedgehog signaling for normal specification of all ventral progenitor domains in the presumptive mammalian spinal cord. *Genes & Development, 16,* 2849–2864.

Wilson, S. I., & Edlund, T. (2001). Neural induction: Toward a unifying mechanism. *Nature Neuroscience,* (Supp l), 1161–1168.

Wilson, S. I., & Graziano, E., Harland, R., Jessell, T. M., & Edlund, T. (2000). An early requirement for FGF signalling in the acquisition of neural cell fate in the chick embryo. *Current Biology, 10,* 421–429.

Wilson, S. W., & Rubenstein, J. L. (2000). Induction and dorsoventral patterning of the telencephalon. *Neuron, 28,* 641–651.

Wilson, S. I., Rydstrom, A., Trimborn, T., Willert, K., Nusse, R., Jessell, T. M., et al. (2001). The status of Wnt signalling regulates neural and epidermal fates in the chick embryo. *Nature, 411,* 325–330.

Wong, K., Ren, X. R., Huang, Y. Z., Xie, Y., Liu, G., Saito, H. (2001). Signal transduction in neuronal migration roles of gtpase activating proteins and the small gtpase cdc42 in the slit-robo pathway. *Cell, 107,* 209–221.

Xu, Q., Mellitzer, G., & Wilkinson, D. G. (2000). Roles of Eph receptors and ephrins in segmental patterning. *Philosophical Transactions of the Royal Society of London. Series B, Biological Sciences, 355,* 993–1002.

Yates, P. A., Roskies, A. L., McLaughlin, T., O'Leary, D. D. (2001). Topographic-specific axon branching controlled by ephrin-as is the critical event in retinotectal map development. *The Journal of Neuroscience, 21,* 8548–8563.

Ye, W., Bouchard, M., Stone, D., Liu, X., Vella, F., Lee, J., et al. (2001). Distinct regulators control the expression of the mid-hindbrain organizer signal FGF8. *Nature Neuroscience, 4,* 1175–1181.

Yee, K. T., Simon, H. H., Tessier-Lavigne, M., O'Leary, D. M. (1999). Extension of long leading processes and neuronal migration in the mammalian brain directed by the chemoattractant netrin-1. *Neuron, 24,* 607–622.

Yoon, M. S., Puelles, L., & Redies, C. (2000). Formation of cadherin-expressing brain nuclei in diencephalic alar plate divisions. *The Journal of Comparative Neurology, 427,* 461–480.

Yun, K., Fischman, S., Johnson, J., Hrabe de Angelis, M., Weinmaster, G., & Rubenstein, J.L.R. (2003). Modulation of the notch signaling by Mash1 and Dlx1/2 regulates sequential specification and differentiation of progenitor cell types in the subcortical telencephalon. Manuscript submitted for publicaton.

Zeltser, L. M., Larsen, C. W., & Lumsden, A. (2001). A new developmental compartment in the forebrain regulated by lunatic fringe. *Nature Neuroscience, 4,* 683–684.

Zerucha, T. S., Stuhmer, T., Park, B. K., Long, Q., Yu, G., Hatch, G., et al. (2000). A highly conserved enhancer in the Dlx5/Dlx6 intergenic region is the site of cross-regulatory interactions between Dlx genes in the embryonic forebrain. *The Journal of Neuroscience, 20,* 709–721.

Zhou, Q., Choi, G., & Anderson, D. J. (2001). The bHLH transcription factor Olig2 promotes oligodendrocyte differentiation in collaboration with Nkx2.2. *Neuron, 31,* 791–807.

Zou, Y., Stoeckli, E., Chen, H., & Tessier-Lavigne, M. (2000). Squeezing axons out of the gray matter: A role for slit and semaphorin proteins from midline and ventral spinal cord. *Cell, 102,* 363–375.

CHAPTER SIX

MOLECULAR AND CELLULAR DEVELOPMENTAL VULNERABILITIES TO THE ONSET OF AFFECTIVE DISORDERS IN CHILDREN AND ADOLESCENTS: SOME IMPLICATIONS FOR THERAPEUTICS

Robert M. Post, M.D., and Susan L. W. Post, L.C.S.W.

The brain is organized for processing information from the environment in the service of adaptation, survival, and reproduction for the continuation of the species. The basic sensory and motor phenomena involved in reflex and primitive processing of environmental information have been well delineated, but we are just beginning to understand the related processes pertinent to emotion, learning, and memory. The distorted sensory homunculus of the brain is well known for its over-representation of parts of the body that are particularly sensitive to environmental stimuli (such as the face, mouth, and hands) compared with areas wherein precise sensory discrimination is less necessary (such as the trunk, forearms, and thighs).

Our primitive conceptualization of the anatomy of emotion and emotional affiliation is outlined in Figure 6.1, although the disproportionate representation of some pertinent human functions is not schematized. Based on the distortions in the sensory and motor homunculi, we can only surmise that there would be equally disproportionate basic wiring of emotional regulation pertinent to maternal representations and, further, that these would be extremely plastic and evolve over the course of a child's development.

The fine wiring diagram of the brain depends highly on environmental input for its details, if extrapolation from the visual system is appropriate. There, the classical studies of Hubel and Weisel (1979) demonstrated that deprivation of environmental input (for example, suturing one eye shut shortly after birth in the cat)

FIGURE 6.1

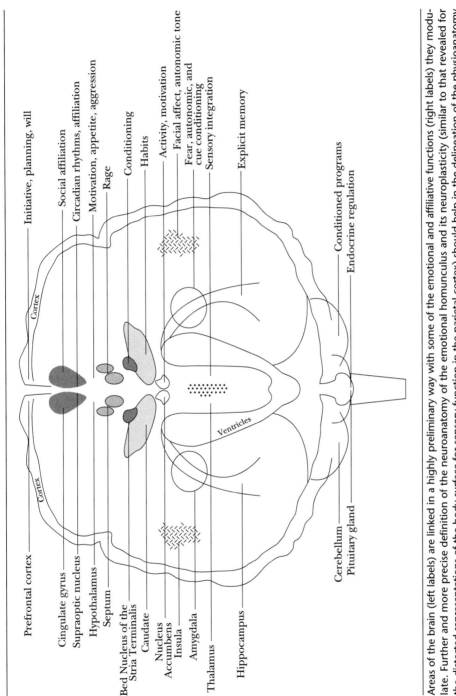

Areas of the brain (left labels) are linked in a highly preliminary way with some of the emotional and affiliative functions (right labels) they modulate. Further and more precise definition of the neuroanatomy of the emotional homunculus and its neuroplasticity (similar to that revealed for the distorted representations of the body surface for sensory function in the parietal cortex) should help in the delineation of the physioanatomy of the major psychiatric illnesses.

results in time-dependent reversible to irreversible changes in the physiological function and anatomy of the visual system. The ocular dominance columns in the occipital cortex that represent the deprived eye shrink in width, whereas those of the undeprived eye expand to occupy the territory that would ordinarily have belonged to the opposite functioning eye. If the deprivation remains long enough, the eye becomes cortically blind and unable to process normal visual information.

The structures mediating and modulating emotional and affiliative behavior are, in addition, subject to modification by the neuroplasticity of experience, learning, and memory. London taxi drivers, for example, have an enlarged size to their hippocampus, an area of the brain crucial for spatial navigation, compared with others less dependent on learning spatial orientation cues (Maguire et al., 2000). The ability of synaptic and nerve cell communications to expand or contract dependent on learning and memory also provides for a wider bi-directional plasticity of the central nervous system (CNS) throughout one's entire life (Malenka, 1994).

Infants born and raised in the infamous Hungarian orphanages of the latter part of the twentieth century (notorious for their lack of stimulation and for the emotional neglect of the children) had a decreased medial temporal lobe size (housing the amygdala and hippocampus) and other critical structures relating to emotion and affiliation. At the same time, we know that emotionally meaningful memories can be indelibly ingrained in the CNS and persist for an individual's lifetime. Thus, psychological and physical traumatic experiences, if either sufficiently severe or repeated, may lead to enhanced connectivity of certain pathways with associated alterations in synaptic function and microanatomy. Thus, with inadequate emotional experience and input, some areas of the brain may show relative atrophy (like the ocular dominance columns of the occipital cortex with visual deprivation), whereas others coding events of particular emotional significance may be over-represented in their circuitry and their memory and impact imprinted in a long-lasting fashion.

The themes of this chapter will alternate between: 1) preclinical data on neurobiology pertinent to affect and affiliation in animals, and 2) clinical phenomena and findings in patients with affective and anxiety disorders. Many of the basic neurobiological findings documented in animals will not yet have been validated in humans. We present this preclinical background literature not to imply that cross-species generalizations are warranted in every instance, but to suggest the plausibility of a whole range of neurobiological alterations that have been documented in lower animals that may, as well, be pertinent to those in humans. We will attempt to highlight wherever possible when the connections are tenuous and when they are well supported by clinical findings.

However, we will assume that the major caveat exists throughout this chapter that phenomena demonstrated in the rodent and other lower experimental animals may or may not have parallel phenomena in the human and nonhuman primate and remain to be studied more fully. In fact, largely based on data from experimental paradigms in animals, we will emphasize the enormous range of contingencies that may influence the response to a given environmental situation based on the individual's genetic vulnerability, earlier prior experience, and a host of modifying factors, including the ability to respond to a stressor and receive social support, that must give us pause in making inferences about human outcomes. These types of complexities in the human would be myriad and might obscure, overwhelm, or reverse well-established principles and paradigms in rodents.

A chapter on molecular and cellular mechanisms must, of necessity, rely on animal studies because, until recently, relatively few CNS molecular events could be explored directly in the awake human brain. In humans, chemicals can be measured in blood and spinal fluid and now directly in specific regions of brain with magnetic resonance spectroscopy (MRS). In addition, hints about regional molecular function have been detected by changes in cerebral activity, as defined by alterations in metabolism and blood flow assessed with positron emission tomography (PET) scans, such that we can now begin to examine regional neural activity in relation to ongoing emotional function. Moreover, in the last several decades there has been an acceleration in the biochemical study of the brain in relation to neuropsychiatric illness based on autopsy specimens from different patient groups and controls.

In many instances, this wide range of techniques has provided preliminary evidence for normal and pathological brain function pertinent to emotional regulation that not only can be directly documented in awake humans, but often parallels related findings in animals. Thus, we can take some comfort from this convergence, even though the animal models of most psychiatric illnesses are not so precise as in many other medical conditions or as one would have hoped. In this chapter, we will focus particularly on the recurrent unipolar and bipolar affective disorders, with only brief comment on posttraumatic stress disorder (PTSD), as these are paradigmatic examples of how genetic and environmental variables may interact in conveying long-term vulnerability to affective dysregulation and how this may be altered by psychopharmacological intervention.

Illness Progression

A century ago, Kraepelin (1921) outlined the basic components of the concepts of stress and episode sensitization in his initial descriptions of unipolar and bipolar illness and their differentiation from schizophrenia. Particularly for bipolar illness, he found that although there was a great variety in subtypes and patterns, there was a general tendency for episodes of affective dysregulation to occur more rapidly over time; that is, on average there was a progressively decreasing well-interval duration between initial episodes compared with later episodes.

At the same time, he noted that unipolar and bipolar affective illnesses were often precipitated by psychosocial stressors related to loss or threat of loss, but these could subsequently occur with less environmental provocation (with anticipated, imagined, or presumably conditioned stressors) and, finally, similar types of episodes could emerge entirely autonomously and without any obvious environmental precipitants. Both of these observations have now been generally validated, both in the early and more modern literature on the course of recurrent affective illness, as we will briefly review below.

Stress and Episode Sensitization

Embedded in Kraepelin's formulations are the essential concepts of stress and episode sensitization. His observations that stressors may be involved in the precipitation of initial episodes, but one can become sensitized to stressors to the point that lesser degrees of or no stress are required, implies an increased responsivity to stressors, that is, a sensitization process rather than the usual adaptation or downregulation of responsivity normally associated with tolerance.

The observations were similar to those in the unmedicated patient (almost always the case in the pre-psychopharmacological era) whereby episodes on average tend to occur with increased rapidity over time, suggesting that prior episodes are somehow facilitating or acting as vulnerability factors for subsequent episodes. Necessary for both types of sensitization are molecular mechanisms for "memory" of the earlier stressors or episode occurrences, so that they could have an impact on subsequent events and alter the stress or episode reactivity of a given individual over long periods of time (years to decades or longer).

Clinical Validation of the Stress Sensitization Phenomenon

A review of the literature in 1992 found that most investigators exploring the topic did, in fact, find stressors were more likely to occur in the first episodes of affective illness compared with subsequent ones (Post, 1992). Several groups have misinterpreted the concept and reported their findings as inconsistent with the stress sensitization phenomena (Hammen & Gitlin, 1997; Hlastala et al., 2000). They found that stressors were likely to initiate even later episodes of affective illness compared with periods that had no stressor involvement. This would actually be the direction predicted by the stress sensitization model, which posits that, based on past experience, patients are becoming more sensitive to stressors rather than less. This increasing sensitivity is seen in the fact that more minor stresses, or, finally, none at all, can "trigger" an episode.

Perhaps the most elegant confirmation of the stress sensitization model is the work of Kendler and associates (2000, 2001) in recurrent unipolar depression (Figures 6.2 and 6.3). They documented that over the first nine episodes of

FIGURE 6.2

Prediction of Major Depression

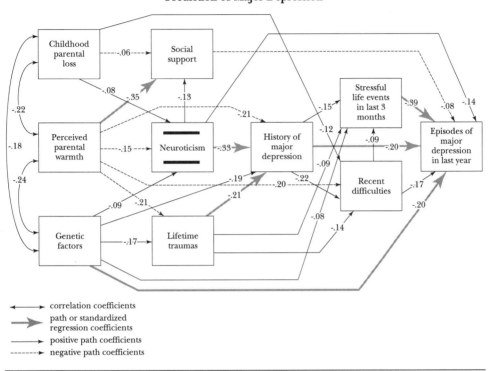

Kendler's path estimates of the best-fitting model of prediction of major depression in 1,360 female twins. Early and recent life events (left, top two boxes) interacting with genetic vulnerability (left, bottom box) predispose to early mild symptoms and episodes (neuroticism box) and more major depression (middle box and last box on right). Episode occurrence further increases vulnerability to recurrence (middle box to last box on right).

Source: American Journal of Psychiatry 150: 1139–1148 (1993). Copyright 1993, the American Psychiatric Association, http://ajp.psychiatryonline.org. Reprinted by permission.

affective illness, there was a close link and then a progressive decrease in the association of stressors to onset of an episode and, with further episodes, the relationship flattened out and remained relatively constant. These investigators also explored the relationship of genetic vulnerability to the stress sensitization concept, and found that with higher degrees of genetic loading for affective illness, individuals reacted as if they were presensitized and needed lesser involvement of stressors to precipitate even the first episodes of illness.

In bipolar illness, we have explored the possible impact of early life stressors on the subsequent course of an illness using a very different strategy. In patients with existing diagnoses of bipolar illness, we examined the retrospective and

FIGURE 6.3(a)

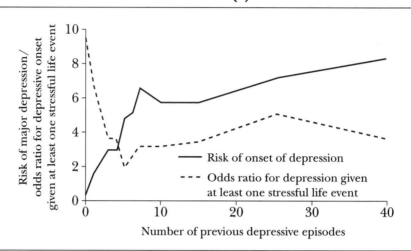

Nature of the relationship between the number of previous depressive episodes and (1) the monthly risk for onset of major depression, and (2) the odds ratio between the occurrence of at least one stressful life event in a month and the probability of a depressive onset in that month.

Source: American Journal of Psychiatry 157: 1243–1251 (2000). Copyright 2000, the American Psychiatric Association, http://ajp.psychiatryonline.org. Reprinted by permission.

FIGURE 6.3(b)

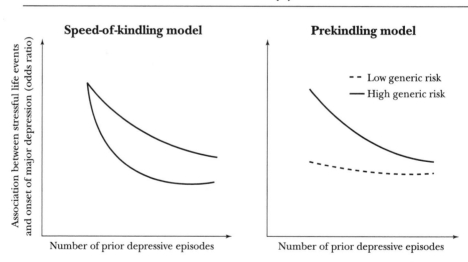

Two hypotheses of how genetic risk influences the reduced association between stressful life events and onset of major depression as the number of prior episodes increases (kindling effect).

Source: American Journal of Psychiatry 158: 582–586 (2001). Copyright 2001, the American Psychiatric Association, http://ajp.psychiatryonline.org. Reprinted by permission.

prospective course of illness in those who did and in those who did not report the occurrence of severe stressors in childhood or adolescence (Leverich et al., 2002). Those patients who reported the early extreme stressors of physical or sexual abuse had experienced a more severe course of bipolar illness prior to study entry (average age 40), and this more severe course (particulary with time depressed) was confirmed with prospective clinician ratings over the following year or more of observation. These individuals were also more likely (compared with those without these early histories) to have more Axis I, Axis II, and Axis III comorbidities. In addition, they were much more likely to have made medically serious suicide attempts. These correlations cannot, of course, give information about causality, although the temporal sequence of events suggests a likely impact of the early stressors, either themselves or through other modifying illness characteristics, that eventuated in a more severe bipolar illness course.

In those studies we also found that those with (compared with those without) these early adverse life experiences reported more negative stressors both at bipolar illness onset and prior to the most recent episode. These data suggest the possibility that these early environmental adversities were later instrumental in generating an increased number of negative, but not positive, life events. Although there are many interpretations of these data, the occurrence of these early life events themselves or as surrogate markers for other vulnerability factors appeared to have a long-lasting influence not only on interactions with the environment, but also on the course of bipolar illness itself. To this extent, these data suggest a long-term impact of these early experiences on a variety of neurobiological processes that could convey these vulnerabilities. Hints about the potential nature of these memory-like processes will be explored from examples from the preclinical literature.

Clinical Evidence for Episode Sensitization

The overwhelming majority of studies examining the interval between the first and second episodes versus the second or third, and so on, suggest a general trend toward a decreasing well-interval between successive episodes (Post, Ketter, Speer, Leverich, & Weiss, 2000). However, it should be emphasized that the episode sensitization concept does not imply that there will be a relentless acceleration of episodes if adequate treatment is not instituted at any point in the illness. What should be noted is that this phenomenon is more likely to occur in instances when either prophylactic pharmacological agents were not available or not widely used between episodes. Episode acceleration might also occur in those with treatment-refractory illness, that is, episodes accelerate despite the patient given agents that were ineffective for episode prevention.

In a recent study, Angst and Sellaro (2000) observed a shortening of the well-interval only between the first three episodes and not subsequent ones, and this has been interpreted by some as lack of validation of the episode sensitization effect, although this is far from clear because these patients were in a variety of naturalistic treatment settings. Moreover, in examining a cohort of treatment-refractory patients admitted to the National Institute of Health, we found that episode sensitization acceleration occurred in only about one-half the patients, whereas others appeared to be sensitized from the outset and began their illness with highly rapid cycling presentations (Roy-Byrne, Post, Uhde, Poreu, & Davis, 1985).

Perhaps the best evidence for episode sensitization comes from the data of Kessing and associates (1998), who examined more that 20,000 patients in the Danish Case Registry. They found that the best predictor of vulnerability recurrence (shorter latency and increased incidence of rehospitalization) was the number of prior hospitalizations (Figure 6.4). This relationship was equally significant for unipolar and bipolar patients and, in this instance, appeared to occur despite whatever treatment was administered in the community, although more detailed analysis of the effect of treatment is now being conducted.

These data are subject to the interpretation that some patients will be predestined to have a more severe and rapidly recurrent course of illness, and these patients would have a more malignant progression of their illness regardless of the occurrence of the episodes themselves. Kessing and associates preliminarily explored this interpretation with complex mathematics and, at least, satisfied themselves that there appeared to be a true impact of episode occurrence rather than the alternative idea of a more ill subgroup from the outset.

Stimulant-Induced Behavioral Sensitization and Electrophysiological Kindling in Animals

Repeated Stimulant Administration

In an effort to begin to explore neural mechanisms that might convey long-lasting increases in behavioral responsivity to a given stimulus over time, we studied two very different animal models (Table 6.1). The first model involved behavioral sensitization to psychomotor stimulants (Post, Weiss, Pert, & Uhde, 1987). In this instance, we found that animals administered the same dose of cocaine on a repeated, intermittent basis had increased behavioral reactivity over time as opposed to decreased reactivity or tolerance. This was manifest in animals having either increases in locomotor hyperactivity or rapid repetitive motor movements of a dysfunctional nature (stereotypies).

One of the more interesting aspects of this phenomenon was that it was context-dependent or conditioned. That is, animals receiving cocaine repeatedly

FIGURE 6.4

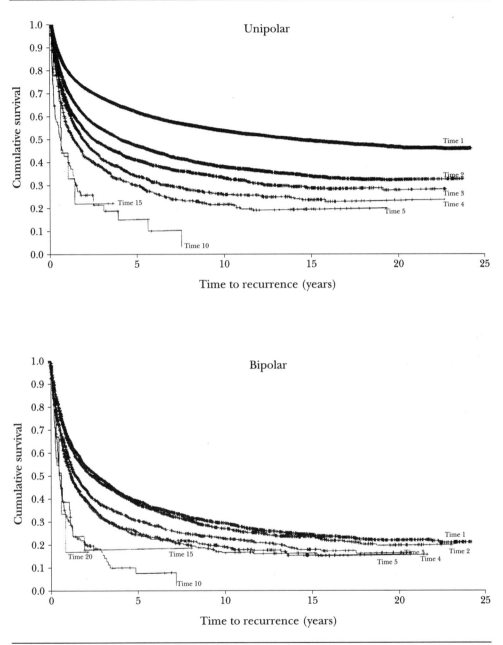

Cumulative survival (probability of remaining well) was calculated using the Kaplan-Meier method for estimation with censored observations. Eight different index admissions (1, 2, 3, 4, 5, 10, 15, and 20) represent the number of prior hospitalizations. For both unipolar (top) and bipolar (bottom) patients, incidence of and latency to relapse varied as a function of the number of prior depressions.

Source: From Kessing et al. 1998, *Br J Psychiatry 172:* 23–28. Copyright 1998, *the British Journal of Psychiatry,* Reprinted by permission.

TABLE 6.1. PHENOMENA IN COURSE OF AFFECTIVE DISORDERS MODELED BY KINDLING AND BEHAVIORAL SENSITIZATION.

Descriptors	Kindling (K)	Sensitization (S)	Phenomenon in Affective Illness
Stressor vulnerability	—	++	Initial stressors early in development may be without effect but predispose to greater reactivity upon rechallenge
Stressor precipitation	++	++	Later stress may precipitate full-blown episode
Conditioning may be involved	—	++	Stressors may become more symbolic
Episode autonomy	++	—	Initially precipitated episodes may occur spontaneously
Cross-sensitization with stimulants	++	++	Comorbidity with drug abuse may work in both directions affective illness ⇆ drug abuse
Vulnerability to relapse	++	++	S and K demonstrate long-term increases in responsivity
Episodes may • become more severe	++	++	S and K both show behavioral evolution in severity or stages
• show more rapid onsets	++	++	Hyperactivity and stereotypy show more rapid onsets
• become spontaneous	+		K seizures evolve to spontaneous seizures
Anatomical and biochemical substrates evolve	++	+	K memory-trace evolves from unilateral to bilateral; S memory trace evolves from midbrain to n. accumbens
IEGs involved	++	++	Immediate Early Genes (IEGs) such as c-fos induced
Alterations in gene expression occur	++	++	IEGs may change later gene expression, for example, peptides over longer time domains
Change in synaptic microstructure occurs	++	—	Neuronal sprouting and cell loss indicate structural changes
Pharmacology differs as function or stage of evolution	++	++	K differs as a function of stage; S differs as a function of development versus expression

in the same environment showed these progressive increases in reactivity, but animals receiving identical doses of cocaine in a different environmental context (home cage) from which they were tested, showed no greater reactivity to cocaine than those pretreated with saline. These data indicated that the sensitization effect to the stimulant was dependent on interaction with the environmental and associated cues and not just the mere presence of cocaine-pretreatment itself in the animal (Pert, 1998; Weiss, Post, Pert, Woodward, & Murman, 1989). It is now thought that the amygdala and nucleus accumbens are responsible for the cued component of sensitization, whereas the extended amygdala or bed nucleus of the stria terminalis is more essential for the environmental context components (Davis, 1998).

Psychomotor-induced behavioral sensitization has a number of properties that make it particularly interesting for its relationship to bipolar illness in general and mania in particular. One of the principal features of mania is increases in psychomotor activity, and this feature is often experienced by individuals experimenting with stimulant substances (such as amphetamine or cocaine). Moreover, many aspects of psychomotor stimulant abuse closely mirror the other symptoms of mania, including euphoria, decreased need for sleep, and even the potential for delusional grandiosity.

Those with more amphetamine or cocaine experience can also begin to have extremely dysphoric components of drug administration, including the development of full-blown panic attacks to doses of cocaine that had apparently been well-tolerated previously. Thus, psychomotor stimulant administration in humans may provide an interesting model for the transition from euphoric to dysphoric mania clinically (Post & Weiss, 1989). Several clinical studies of bipolar patients suggest an increased incidence of dysphoric mania in those with prior substance abuse histories.

Clinically, there can also be a transition from euphoria/dysphoria affective experience to a more full-blown paranoid psychosis, and this, too, appears to occur with increasing duration (if not doses) of psychomotor stimulant administration. A full-blown manic episode may, cross-sectionally, also be very difficult to distinguish from acute paranoid schizophrenia. Thus, the increases in stimulant-induced hyperactivity and stereotypy in animals may, by virtue of the similarities to euphoric and dysphoric mania and paranoid psychosis in clinical substance abuse situations, provide an animal model for manic episode sensitization.

Another key element of stimulant-induced sensitization is its cross-responsivity to many different types of stressors (but not all). Antelman and colleagues (1980) were the first to report that a mild stressor such as tail pinch in the laboratory rat led to increased reactivity to psychomotor stimulants. These observations have now been replicated and extended by many others not only involving amphetamine, but also other psychomotor stimulants such as cocaine, methylphenidate, and a variety of ethologically relevant stressors (Kalivas & Duffy, 1989).

The sensitization model then can be viewed both from the perspective of episode sensitization—the more instances of cocaine administration in the same environment the greater the reactivity—as well as from the perspective that stressors may be able to interact with this process, use common neural substrates, and provide a basis for prior stressors leading to increased episode reactivity (in this case, of the manic variety).

The Impact of Substance Abuse on Neurobiology and Gene Expression

Cocaine and related psychomotor stimulants cause the induction of immediate early genes such as c-fos and Zif268, which then reprogram various circuits in the brain for increased behavioral reactivity (behavioral sensitization, as noted above) (Figure 6.5). Also, there is the induction of increased levels of mRNA and protein for dynorphin and dynorphin (sigma opiate) receptors. This is important because these types of peptides are dysphorogenic and psychotomimetic when administered to humans.

We note the profound changes in neural adaptation that occur with cocaine abuse, which tends to become progressively more associated with dysphoria and paranoia rather than the initial sought-after euphoria. In bringing the brain to a new level of adaptation and homeostasis—referred to as *allostasis* by Koob and Le Moal (2001)—there is not only the increased vulnerability to relapse in drug abuse, but also, in many instances, bi-directional cross-sensitization with stressors.

In this regard, it is of particular interest that both repeated stressors and stimulants can lead to the induction of the transcription factor delta Fos-B, which has, in contrast to most of the other immediate early genes that have a short one- to two-hour existence in the nucleus, a very long life in the nucleus and appears to accumulate with each stressor or drug administration event (Nestler, Barrot, & Self, 2001; Nestler, Kelz, & Chen, 1999). This may thus be one type of molecule that not only "counts" or is a marker of the number of prior stressful or drug experiences, but is also in a position in the nucleus to change what genes are induced (transcribed) or not based on this accumulation of prior events. Experience changes the brain based on changes in gene expression.

We emphasize these neurobiological alterations associated with stimulant abuse as an example of how clinical comorbidities could alter the brain in addition to the primary affective disorders. Bipolar patients with a history of childhood trauma have a higher incidence of substance abuse than those without such histories (Leverich et al., 2002). The acquisition of comorbid substance abuse as an adolescent or adult could have a further adverse effect on the evolution of affective illness by setting up a vicious cycle of stress vulnerability leading to substance abuse relapse and this, in turn, adding to stressor vulnerability via cross-sensitization (Figure 6.5 and Figure 6.6). We have found that comorbid substance abuse is a correlate of a more severe course of bipolar illness.

FIGURE 6.5

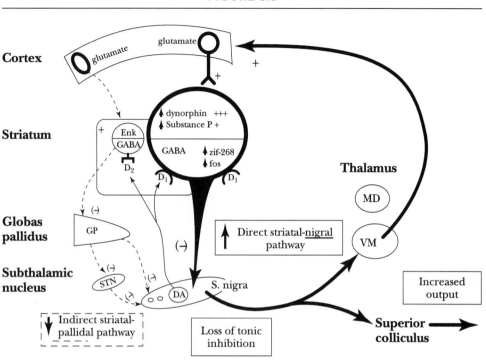

Cocaine Reprograms the Genetic Machinery of the Direct Striatal Output Pathway Leading to Increased Motor Behavior.

Abbreviations

GABA	gamma-aminobutyric acid	MD	medial dorsal nucleus of the thalamus
DA	dopamine	STN	subthalamic nucleus
D1, D2	dopamine receptors	VM	ventromedial nucleus of the thalamus
Enk	enkephalin	S. nigra	substantia nigra
GP	globus pallidus		
Glucocorticoid	glutamate		

Kindled Seizures

We became interested in another model of long-term neural learning and memory based on prior observations by several individuals that repeated administration of the same high doses of cocaine (which were initially subconvulsant) could come to evoke a full-blown seizure after sufficient number of repetitions (Table 6.1). This generation of a seizure from a previous subconvulsant amount of drug appeared to have many similarities to the phenomenon of electrical kindling initially elucidated by Goddard and associates (1969).

FIGURE 6.6

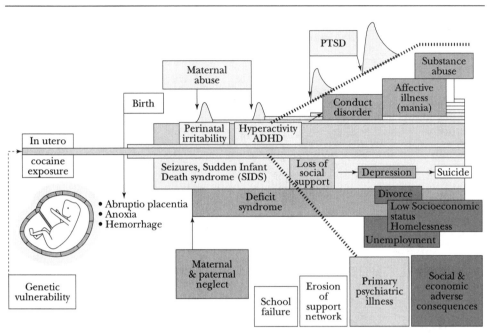

Schematic illustration of the potential sequential, temporal, and cumulative evolution of neurobiological and psychiatric consequences of maternal cocaine abuse during pregnancy and throughout a child's development. Although these hypothetical consequences could be ameliorated by a plethora of interventions, such a deteriorating course could occur based on the clinical literature. At the same time, corrective transgeneration effects also appear possible based on the work of Francis and colleagues (1999).

Abbreviations

ADHD   attention-deficit/hyperactivity disorder

PTSD   post-traumatic stress disorder.

Behavioral and Physiological Progression to Spontaneity. In kindling the amygdala, for example, repeated once-daily stimulation for one second evokes increased responsivity on the electrophysiological and behavioral level, culminating with the development of full-blown major motor seizures to a previously subthreshold stimulation. If one kindles below the amygdala afterdischarge threshold, there is a progressive lowering of this threshold, and then the repeated generation of amygdala afterdischarges (run of spikes) can be seen to increase in duration and complexity and spread to more distant areas of the brain. This physiological progression is associated with the development of progressive behavioral changes (seizure stage evolution). Initially, with amygdala kindling stimulation, one observes no changes or only behavioral arrest with head nodding. This progresses from unilateral tonic-clonic movements of one forepaw to bilateral movements, and then, finally, a full-blown generalized seizure with rearing and falling.

This increase in electrophysiological and behavioral responsivity is a clear manifestation of some kind of neuronal learning and memory mechanism based on the number of prior amygdala stimulations. Most interestingly, if animals are given enough amygdala-kindled stimulations electrically, the kindled seizures are so facilitated that they can begin to occur on their own in the absence of exogenous electrophysiological stimulation, that is, spontaneous seizures (Figure 6.7). The kindling model was thus useful for exploring neural mechanisms not only of increased physiological and behavioral responsivity to the same stimuli over time, but also for examining the transition from triggered to spontaneous episodes.

We are clearly using the kindled seizure model as an analogy, and not with the idea that it is a direct model of affective illness by itself. Kindling has few of the characteristics required of a valid animal model of a neuropsychiatric syndrome. In affective illness versus amygdala kindling, the inducing circumstances (stress versus electrical stimulation) are not the same, the behaviors manifested (affective episodes or seizures) are very different, and the nature of the effective pharmacological interventions differ to some extent (lithium versus anticonvulsants). Obviously, the time domains are completely dissimilar as well, with kindled seizures occurring over a matter of a minute or two and affective episodes lasting weeks to months or longer (Weiss & Post, 1994).

Spatio-temporal Changes in Gene Expression. Nonetheless, even given this lack of precise homologies, some of the principles pertinent to increased responsivity over time, and the transition from precipitated to autonomous episodes, may have important implications for conceptualizing mechanisms underlying the longitudinal course of affective episodes, even if the neural substrates mediating these processes are different. The physiological, biochemical, and molecular alterations accompanying kindling evolution are becoming increasingly clarified.

Concomitant with the spatio-temporal evolution of amygdala kindling at the level of afterdischarges is a similar process that can be observed at the level of gene expression (Figure 6.8). Initial kindled stimulations induce the transcription factor c-fos in brain first unilaterally and then bilaterally in the hippocampus, and then throughout increasing portions of the cortex in association with the development of full-blown seizures. The induction of mRNA for neuropeptides such as thyrotropin releasing hormone (TRH) follows a similar evolution. With initial electrical stimuli, TRH is induced unilaterally and then, upon repeated stimulation, increases in TRH mRNA are seen bilaterally, as readily demonstrated in the dentate granule cells of the hippocampus (Post & Weiss, 1992).

A multitude of other changes occur with the development of full-blown kindling (Figure 6.9), including the induction of corticotropin releasing hormone

FIGURE 6.7

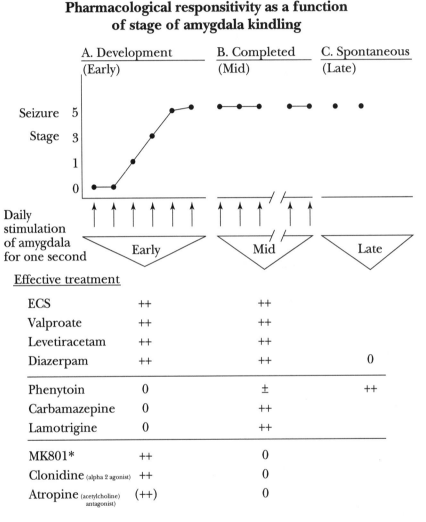

Pharmacological responsitivity as a function of stage of amygdala kindling

Effective treatment	A. Development (Early)	B. Completed (Mid)	C. Spontaneous (Late)
ECS	++	++	
Valproate	++	++	
Levetiracetam	++	++	
Diazerpam	++	++	0
Phenytoin	0	±	++
Carbamazepine	0	++	
Lamotrigine	0	++	
MK801*	++	0	
Clonidine (alpha 2 agonist)	++	0	
Atropine (acetylcholine antagonist)	(++)	0	

* glutamate NMDA$_R$ antagonist

Pharmacological responsivity as a function of stage of kindling. Top: initial stimulations are associated with progressively increasing afterdischarge duration and behavioral seizure stage. Subsequent stimulations (completed) produce reliable generalized motor seizures. Spontaneous seizures emerge after sufficient numbers of triggered seizures have been generated (usually > 100). Bottom: amygdala and local anesthetic kindled seizures show differences in pharmacological responsivity as a function of kindled stage (++, very effective; ±, partially effective; 0, not effective). The double dissociation in response to diazepam and phenytoin in the early versus the late phases of amygdala kindling, as described by Pinel, is particularly striking. Note also that carbamazepine is effective in inhibiting the developmental phase of local anesthetic but not amygdala kindling, whereas the converse is true for the completed phase.

FIGURE 6.8

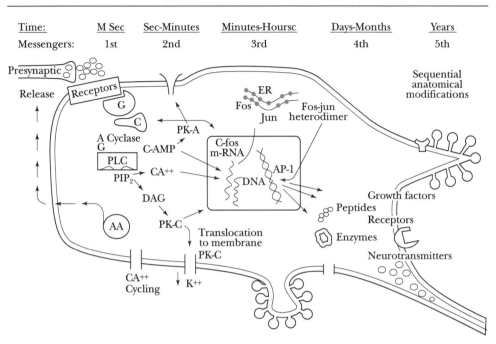

Time:	M Sec	Sec-Minutes	Minutes-Hoursc	Days-Months	Years
Messengers:	1st	2nd	3rd	4th	5th

Neural mechanisms of synaptic plasticity, short- and long-term memory. This schematic of a cell illustrates how transient synaptic events induced by external stimuli can exert longer-lasting effects on neuronal excitability and the microstructure of the brain via a cascade of effects involving alterations in gene transcription. Neurotransmitters activate receptors and second-messenger systems, which then induce IEGs, such as c-fos and c-jun. Fos and Jun proteins are synthesized on the endoplasmic reticulum (ER) and then bind to DNA to further alter the transcription of late effector genes (LEGs) and other regulatory factors, the effects of which could last for months or years.

Abbreviations

PLC   phospholipase C
PIP2   phosphatidyl inositol 4,5-biphosphate
AA   arachidonic acid
DAG   diacylglycerol
PK-C   protein kinase C

AP-1   activator protein 1 (binding site on DNA)
ER   endoplasmic reticulum
PK-A   protein kinase A
LEGs   late effector genes.

(CRH) in cells in the dentate hilus area that had not previously expressed CRH, and of brain-derived neurotrophic factor (BDNF) in the dentate granule cells themselves. This is of particular interest because it has also been observed that these granule cells undergo an increased sprouting with kindling evolution. Thus, repeated stimulation of the brain (using parameters that are very much within the normal physiological range) comes to induce a variety of changes in brain biochemistry based on gene expression and in the cellular function and

FIGURE 6.9

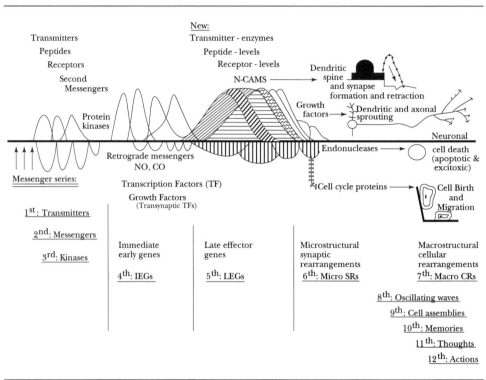

Remodeling the CNS based on experience. This figure portrays an evolving cascade of messenger systems, each with its own complex regulatory mechanisms and cross talk with other systems (not illustrated). In addition to showing IEGs and LEGs, this figure suggests that environmental stimulation can engage mechanisms that change the connectivity of the brain on a biochemical as well as microstructural basis, including cell sprouting, cell migration, or even cell death. These synaptic changes may ultimately be reflected in larger functional units (eighth and ninth messengers) that encode thoughts, memories, and preparation for action.

microanatomy (neural sprouting) as well. With each kindled stimulation, more and more of the brain becomes involved in the physiological, biochemical, and nuclear transcriptional events (Weiss, Clark, Rosen, Smith, & Post, 1995).

Pathological Versus Adaptive Change in Gene Transcription. The kindling model has helped elucidate the principle that many of these changes in gene expression are pertinent to the primary pathological process of kindled "memory trace" evolution, but that other changes are secondary or adaptive and act as endogenous anticonvulsant substances (Figure 6.10). Increased neural responsivity and dentate granule cell sprouting likely represent the primary process of kindling. On the adaptive side, following a kindled seizure there is the induction of mRNA and protein

FIGURE 6.10

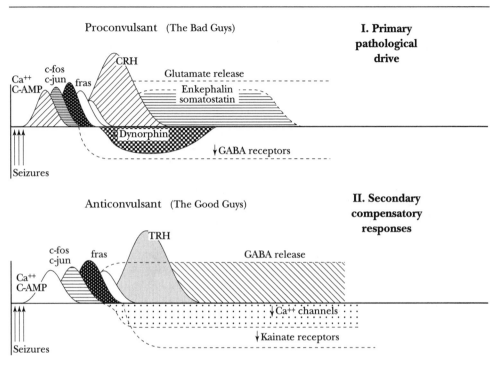

Schematic illustration of potential genomic, neurotransmitter, and peptidergic alterations that follow re-peated kindled seizures. Putative mechanisms related to the primary pathological drive (that is, kindled seizure evolution) are illustrated on top and those thought to be related to the secondary compensatory responses (that is anticonvulsant effects) are shown on the bottom. The horizontal line represents time. Sequential transient increases in second messengers and IEGs are followed by longer lasting alterations in peptides, neurotransmitters, and receptors or their mRNAs, as illustrated above the line, whereas decreases are shown below the line. Given the potential unfolding of these competing mechanisms in the evolution of seizure disorders, the question arises regarding whether or not parallel opposing processes also occur in the course of affective illness or other psychiatric disorders. Endogenous adaptive changes (bottom) may be exploited in the design of the new treatment strategies.

for inhibitory neurotransmitter receptors such as benzodiazepine and GABAA receptors. TRH mRNA and protein is also transiently induced, and TRH is known to have anticonvulsant properties. If TRH is administered bilaterally into the hippocampus, it will attenuate amygdala-kindled seizures.

This idea that the molecular changes following amygdala-kindled seizures can be roughly divided into pathological versus adaptive changes has important consequences for therapeutics (Post & Weiss, 1992; Post & Weiss, 1996). In attempting to inhibit amygdala-kindled seizure evolution, one could theoretically both inhibit the primary pathological processes as well as attempt to enhance the adaptive ones. If a similar division of neurobiological processes occurred with affective episodes, it would be particularly important to discriminate which of the biochemical changes in the illness were part of the primary pathology (to be suppressed) and which were potential endogenous antidepressant substances (to be enhanced). It is interesting that TRH is known to have antidepressant effects when administered intravenously, subcutaneously, or intrathecally (Callahan et al., 1997; Marangell et al., 1997), and thus is a candidate for being an endogenous antidepressant substance (in affective episode recovery) as well as endogenous anticonvulsant substance (in amygdala kindling seizure termination).

Neonatal Stressors and Lasting Effects on Behavior, Neuroendocrinology, and Substance Abuse Vulnerability

Dr. Michael Meaney and Dr. Paul Plotsky have conducted a remarkable series of studies over the past dozen years that have profound implications for many of the themes discussed in this chapter. One of the main themes of their work is that, depending on the type of early environmental events and interactions, one can have a life-long impact on behavior and the neurochemistry of the brain in essentially opposite directions. One type of early experience in the first twelve days of life, that is, a brief fifteen-minute separation of the rat pup (associated with increased maternal licking behavior) can convey a reduction in stress hormones (corticosterone), anxiety behavior, and memory loss in adulthood, whereas three-hour separations (resulting in decreased maternal attention and licking behavior) can produce lasting increases in corticosterone, anxiety behaviors, increased memory loss and hippocampal cell loss as an adult, as well as vulnerability to adopting self-administration of cocaine and alcohol (Figure 6.11) (Huot, Thrivikraman, Meaney, & Plotsky, 2001; Meaney, Aitken, Van Berkel, Bhatnagar, & Sapolsky, 1988; Meaney, Brake, & Gratton, 2002; Plotsky & Meaney, 1993).

In the three-hour maternal deprivation-stressed animals, all of these long-term consequences can be brought back toward normal by treatment with serotonin-selective antidepressants (serotonin selective reuptake inhibitors [SSRIs] such as fluoxetine [Prozac]). However, this does not reverse the underlying molecular alterations and vulnerabilities, because if animals are discontinued from these antidepressants, all of the behavior, neuroendocrine alterations, and vulnerability to substance use returns (Huot et al., 2001; Meaney et al., 2002).

The neurobehavioral mechanisms underlying these long-lasting consequences on brain and behavior are quite remarkable and, to some extent, unexpected. Dr. Plotsky and Dr. Meaney have found that the fifteen-minute separated animals are greeted back by the mother with increased licking and attentive behavior.

FIGURE 6.11

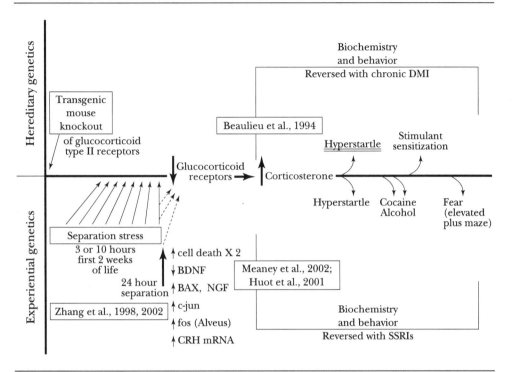

Convergent genetic and environmental models of depression. Either heredity or experiential genetics may lead to compounding behavioral and biochemical end-points similar to those seen in depression and reversible by antidepressants.

DMI	desipramine	
BDNF	brain-derived neurotrophic factor	
NGF	nerve growth factor	

CRH	corticotropin releasing hormone
SSRIs	selective-serotonin reuptake inhibitors

These observations led them to explore whether normal variations in maternal licking behavior were sufficient to induce some of these changes in the offspring. They found that this was true; mothers who were natural low lickers had offspring with the high corticosterone, high anxiety signature, whereas those who were natural high lickers had offspring with the opposite neurobiological set points.

The mechanisms of the alterations in the three-hour separation animals are even more remarkable. They found that the three-hour rat pup separations were associated with increases in agitated and frenetic maternal behavior and an apparent lack of recognition of the pup on return to the cage. This yielded not only decreased licking behavior, but the rat pup was also often unknowingly trampled by the mother during her agitation. If substitute rat pups were provided during the three-hour separation, maternal behavior remained normal and calm and this obviated all of the long-term consequences of the three-hour separation (Caldji et al., 1998). In other words, it was not the three hours of separation in the rat pup that was particularly stressful and enabling all of these long-term consequences on behavior, but it was the consequences to the maternal-infant dyad mediated via alterations in maternal behavior that had long-term consequences for the infant.

The findings that differential maternal high and low licking behavior could induce the long-lasting anxious and endocrine consequences led these investigators to do a cross-fostering study. They took the rat pups from the high licking mothers and had them fostered by low licking mothers. When these infants grew up, they, in fact, had the new high-anxious, high-corticosterone signature of their adoptive mothers and not of their high licking birthing mothers. The opposite was the case when the pups of low licking mothers were cross-fostered with high licking mothers; this was sufficient to change the signature to low corticosterone/ low anxiety. Most remarkably, these investigators were then able to demonstrate that once the endocrine/anxiety signature was changed in this fashion, it would persist in a trans-generational way. That is, when the cross-fostered pups grew up and had offspring of their own, they maintained the signature of their foster parents and not of their initial birth mothers, including lack of proneness to substance self-administration (Francis, Diorio, Liu, & Meaney, 1999).

These data indicate that an important natural difference in maternal rearing behavior, as well as superimposed environmental stressors, can have long-lasting consequences for the organism and can be completely altered transcriptionally by a single change in the environmental conditions (whereas the genetic vulnerabilities remain constant). This set of studies must certainly give one pause in assuming what neurobiological alterations in offspring are or are not genetically mediated. Many apparent genetic traits may turn out to be highly modifiable by environmental circumstances and should be considered as a familial and malleable transmission of a trait rather than a genetic (and invariant) transmission until the genetic "breeding true" mechanism can be proven under appropriate experimental circumstances.

This is not to say that genetic vulnerabilities do not play critical roles in altering neurobiology, but only that one should be cautious in assuming they are not either environmentally mediated or modifiable. In fact, we know that many of these same behaviors can be altered with specific gene manipulations (Figure 6.11). For example, if transgenic animals are bred with a deficient glucocorticoid receptor number, the result is decreased feedback inhibition of corticosterone secretion, and the animals show increased plasma corticosterone and a variety of anxiety-related behaviors including hyper-startle and sensitization to psychomotor stimulants (Francis, Caldji, Champagne, Plotsky, & Meaney, 1999). Interestingly, these genetically altered behaviors and endocrine alterations are also reversible with treatment with antidepressants, in this case, with desmethylimipramine (that is, one acting predominantly on noradrenergic systems). The message from several sets of observations is that genetic vulnerabilities can have long-term consequences for behavior, but that environmental contingencies can also produce comparable changes, and may even predominate in their consequences for the organism. The interaction of both genetic and environmental influences should thus not be underestimated.

Another critical factor for the eventual neurobiological outcome is the timing of these environmental interactions. If animals are exposed to the same repeated separation stressors later in life, similar behavioral and neuroendocrine alterations are not induced. Also, the numbers and durations of repetitions of maternal deprivation stressors may also be crucial to the ultimate outcome.

Dr. Seymour Levine has pioneered studies of the impact of a single twenty-four-hour period of maternal deprivation stress on an animal's immediate and long-term behavior and endocrinology (Levine, Huchton, Wiener, & Rosenfeld, 1991; Rosenfeld et al., 1991). Many of the same changes that are induced with the repeated stressors occur with single one-day maternal deprivation, in particular, increased secretion of glucocorticoids (corticosterone in rats is equivalent to cortisol in humans). Dr. Mark Smith, Dr. Li-Zhin Zhang, and Dr. Guogiang Xing in our laboratory have worked with these animals provided by Seymour Levine and have observed a variety of acute neurobiological perturbations that are of considerable interest. These changes are observed in animals after the single day of maternal separation on the eleventh day of neonatal life and then compared with other animals not undergoing this separation, and all are sacrificed on day twelve (Zhang, Xing, Levine, Post, & Smith, 1998). What is not yet clear in most of the studies using this paradigm is whether these neural alterations are acute and transient or whether they may persist and yield abnormalities in adolescent and adult animals. These studies remain to be performed.

The range of acute neurobiological alterations in the single maternal deprivation stress paradigm is schematized in Figure 6.12 and Figure 6.13. These include decreases in BDNF and calcium-calmodulin kinase II (CaMK-II). These two chemicals are of particular interest because of their diverse roles in CNS neuronal communication and survival, but most importantly, their presence is absolutely necessary for long-term learning and memory. Animals that have these two chemicals genetically knocked-out (an absence of these chemicals in brain) do not show long-term potentiation (LTP) in hippocampal slice preparations (which are considered to be the best model of molecular learning and memory outside the living body), and in accordance with this deficit, these animals are unable to navigate in a Morris water maze,[1] indicating that they are unable to learn and remember in a normal fashion (Frankland, O'Brien, Ohno, Kirkwood, & Silva, 2001; Korte, Kang, Bonhoeffer, & Schuman, 1998; Silva, Stevens, Tonegawa, & Wang, 1992).

Thus, the single-day maternal deprivation experience leads to at least acute deficits in the critical intraneural signaling molecules critical to long-term

FIGURE 6.12

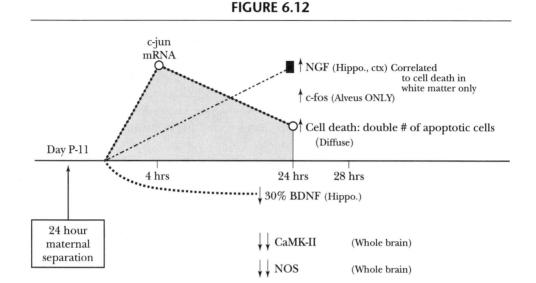

Effects of maternal separation in neonatal rat pups on neurotrophins, transcription factors, and gene expression.

Abbreviations

NGF   nerve growth factor   CaMK-II calcium-calmodulin kinase II
ctx   cortex   NOS   nitric oxide synthase
BDNF brain-derived neurotrophic factor

memory and complex adaptive behavior. BDNF also has been shown to be a critical substance for normal myelination of the brain. As noted below, bipolar illness is characterized by frontal cortical glial as well as neuronal deficits, and, strikingly, a 50% deficit in CaMK-II (Xing et al., 2002). The single day of maternal separation stress also yields increases in nerve growth factor and paradoxically, an approximately doubling of the rate of cell loss by preprogrammed cell death (or *apoptosis*) (Zhang et al., 2002).

Nerve cells die via two separate processes. One is *excitotoxicity*, in which the cell essentially explodes and glial cells migrate into the area and may leave a glial scar. In preprogrammed cell death, the cell commits suicide by active metabolic processes that are programmed into the cellular machinery. During this type of apoptotic cell death, the DNA is enzymatically programmed to be split into little pieces and these and other cellular organelles can be engulfed by glial cells; essentially, the neuron disappears cleanly without a trace in a period of three to five hours. The apoptotic process can be divined by placing a radioactive label on substances that bind to the DNA fragments, however. When this is done, Zhang

FIGURE 6.13

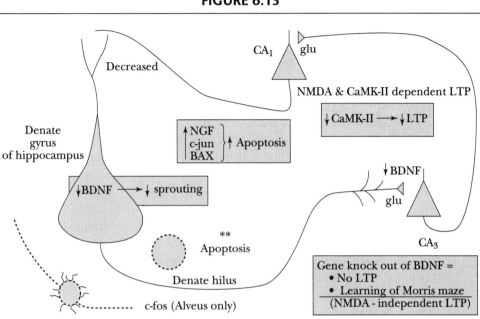

Potential hippocampal effects of neonatal maternal separation.

Abbreviations

BDNF	brain-derived neurotrophic factor	glucocorticoid	glutamate
NGF	nerve growth factor	CaMK-II	calcium-calmodulin kinase II
NMDA	–methyl-D-aspartate	LTP	long-term potentiation

and colleagues have found that the maternal deprivation is associated with a doubling in the rate of cell death throughout the cortex and this involves cell death of both neurons and glia.[2] Could such environmental impacts account for the deficient glial and neural activity and number in bipolar illness?

Figure 6.13 outlines some of the potential acute impact on the hippocampus of the alterations found after a single day of maternal deprivation stress in the rodent.[3] Although we highlight these alterations for their heuristic value, it is again important to emphasize that the question of how long most of these acute perturbations last and what impact they would ultimately have on CNS function in the adult remains to be explored. However, given that some of the perturbations engendered by a single day of maternal deprivation stress persist for a lifetime and that many of the repeated stress paradigms noted above yield changes that persist into adulthood, we take the perspective that it is at least theoretically possible that under the wrong types of environmental circumstances some of these acute perturbations may exert longer-term effects of potential consequence to the organism. Thus, given the range of neurochemical changes induced in the hippocampus by a single day of maternal deprivation stress, one can begin to envision the potential environmental impact on the development of this structure and its functional capacity. We have already seen from the Plotsky and Meaney studies that events early in life can have direct consequences for the rate of age-related memory decline in the adult and loss of hippocampal cellular elements.

We also know that the quality, duration, timing, and repetition of the environmental event (stressor) can alter or completely reverse the valance of the neurobiological changes. This is of particular interest when we consider that the emerging neurobiology of affective and PTSDs in many instances, shows opposite changes, as illustrated in Figure 6.14.

The precipitating events of these two disorders are almost, by definition, different. Those associated with PTSD tend to be of the unexpected horrific variety with the potential for, or threat of, loss of life or limb. In contrast, those typically associated with the onset of affective episodes are those involving loss or the threat of loss, often in the context of relationships with significant others or role success in academic or employment situations.

As illustrated on the left side of Figure 6.14, depressions are often associated with decreased activity in the prefrontal areas of the cortex; in many instances in primary and secondary depression, the degree of decrease is correlated with the severity of depression as rated on the Hamilton Depression Rating Scale. In contrast, in PTSD (Figure 6.14, right side), there may be evidence of cortical and limbic hyperactivity, particularly during the reading of a traumatic script or other re-experiencing phenomena, yet the cortico-limbic-hypothalamic-pituitary-adrenal axis appears to have an opposite set point in the two conditions and somatostatin levels in spinal fluid are opposite as well.

As noted above, depression is associated with hypercortisolism and a decrement in glucocorticoid receptors. In contrast, PTSD is often associated with hypocortisolemia and increased cellular expression of glucocorticoid receptors. Presumably, this expression of glucocorticoid receptors on blood elements reflects what is also occurring in the hippocampus with a deficient negative feedback in affective illness and an excessive one in PTSD. Thus, patients with depression have an increased incidence of escape from dexamethasone (a synthetic steroid that enhances feedback inhibition) suppression whereas those with PTSD have a heightened response and a complete suppression of cortisol secretion following challenge with dexamethasone (Yehuda, 1998). These differential neurobiological elements are also of interest in relation to the apparent similarities of increased CRH in the cerebrospinal fluid (CSF) of many patients with both syndromes. These changes are interestingly mirrored in the findings of increases in brain corticotropin releasing factor (CRF) of the three-hour maternally deprived animals compared with their litter mate controls when studied as adults (Plotsky & Meaney, 1993).

FIGURE 6.14

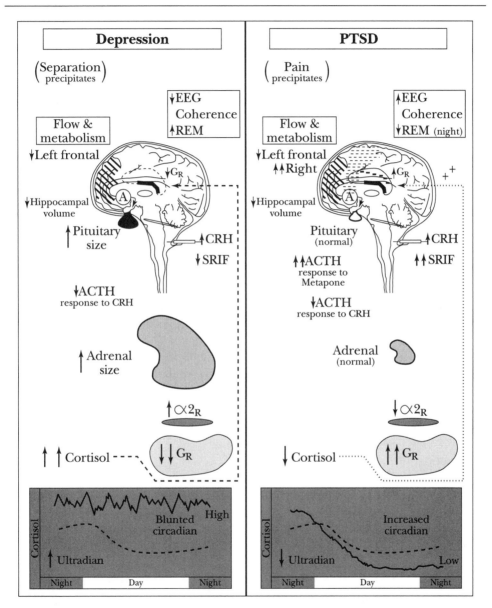

Differences in precipitants, neurophysiology, anatomy, peptides, endocrinology, and circadian rhythms between depression and PTSD.

Abbreviations

EEG	electroencephalogram
REM	rapid eye movement
CRH	corticotropin releasing hormone

SRIF	somatostatin
ACTH	adrenocorticotropin hormone
$\alpha 2_R$	alpha-2 receptors.

FIGURE 6.15

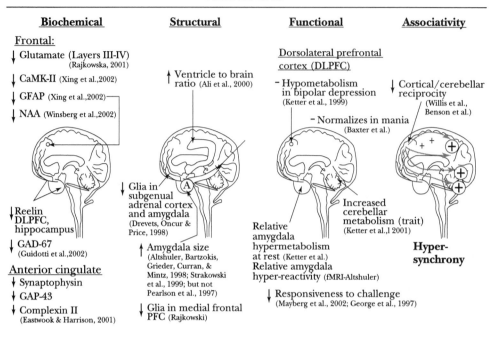

Biochemical, structural, and functional abnormalities in bipolar illness.

Abbreviations

CaMK-II	calcium-calmodulin kinase II	hippo.	hippocampus
GFAP	glial fibrillary acidic protein	GAD-67	glutamic acid decarboxylase-67
NAA	N-acetyl aspartate	GAP-43	growth associated protein-43
pfc	prefrontal cortex	AC	anterior cortex

Some of the other changes noted in brains (Figure 6.15) of those who died after having bipolar illness compared with other ill groups (depression and schizophrenia) and non-psychiatrically ill controls, include: deficits in prefrontal cortical glial number, size, and activity (measured by mRNA and protein levels of glial fibrillary acidic protein [GFAP]); a decreased density of neurons in some cortical layers; a decrement in the cortical developmental protein reelin; a decrease in *GAD67* (but not 65), a marker of one type of inhibitory (GABAergic) intraneuron; and 50% decrements in CaMK-II, the calcium sensory factor recurring for long-term cortically based neurons. The CaMK-II deficits in the prefrontal cortex in bipolar illness could be particularly relevant to some of the neuropsychological and prefrontal cortex-mediated deficits in the illness.

CaMK-II appears to be a central player in learning and memory, as best elucidated at the level of the synapse in the models of LTP and long-term depression (LTD) in amygdala and hippocampal slice preparations (Stevens, Tonegawa, & Wang, 1994). Depending on the quality and quantity of neuronal firing and glutamate release, pre- and post-synaptic responsivity can be altered in a long-lasting fashion. With repeated high-frequency stimulation, LTP results, whereas low intracellular calcium levels achieved with slow firing appear capable of decreasing synaptic excitability and producing LTD (Figure 6.16).

CaMK-II is at the center of this bifurcation, because it "reads" the amount of post-synaptic calcium influx, and its response determines the generation of either LTP or LTD. Although we do not know the consequences of the 50% decrements in CaMK-II found in the adult brains of those with bipolar illness, we know from heterozygote knock-out mice (which also have about a 50% decrease in CaMK-II) that hyperactive behavior occurs, and there are deficits in long-term cortically based (but not hippocampally based) memory.[4] As noted above, it is equally possible that the prefrontal deficits in CaMK-II apparent in bipolar illness could be mediated either through genetic or environmental mechanisms or their interaction.

Clinical Implications for Therapeutic Interventions

Reconceptualization of Recurrent Affective Illness

Given the brief vignettes of the clinical and preclinical data in the literature, it would appear appropriate to reconceptualize the recurrent unipolar and bipolar affective disorders as recurrent, potentially life-threatening illnesses of the brain associated with a series of physiological, neurochemical, and neuroanatomical alterations. This is a different view from that usually inferred from the term "mental" illness, which can imply phenomena of an abstract, ephemeral nature, perhaps ones that the individual could overcome merely with an act of will.

One could consider the recurrent unipolar and bipolar depression more like a malignancy, with the ability to treat it and wipe it out if it is approached appropriately early, but with the potential for malignant transformation if ignored long enough (Post, 1993). Similarly, the affective illnesses tend to recur, sensitize, evolve, and have the potential for their own type of malignant transformation to treatment refractoriness if ignored long enough (Post et al., 1996). Thus, the therapeutic approach should be the same early, aggressive, and sustained intervention as in many malignancies (Post et al., 2001).

One needs to recall that the affective illnesses are potentially lethal by two routes. One is by suicide, and some 10–20% of patients with unipolar and bipolar affective disorder will die of their illness by suicide (Goodwin & Jamison, 1990).

FIGURE 6.16

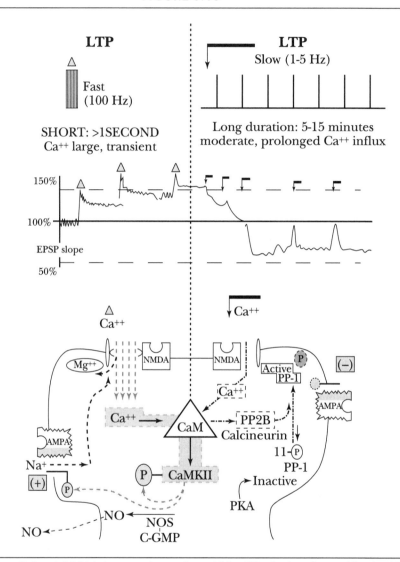

LTP (left side) results from brief, high-frequency bursts of neural firing (▲), allowing a large calcium ion (Ca++) influx through the glutamate NMDA receptor, once it has been depolarized by sodium (Na+) entering via the glutamine AMPA receptor. Long-lasting increases in synaptic responsivity as seen in LTP are shown by the 50% increase in excitation post-synaptic potential (EPSP) slope. LTD (right side) is achieved by low-frequency, prolonged neural firing (1 to 5 Hz) resulting in moderate prolonged Ca++ influx through the NMDA receptor (NMDAR). This can depress synaptic excitability and can depotentiate synapses that have previously been potentiated with LTP. Note: It takes three fifteen-minute trains of 1 Hz firing to reverse the LTP. Calmodulin (CaM) and calcium calmodulin kinase II (CaMK-II) "read" the amount of Ca++ entering the cell. With large Ca++ influxes CaMK-II activates itself with autophosphorylation (-P). This phosphorylates the AMPA receptor which makes it more sensitive to glutamate achieving LTD. With small Ca++ influxes the AMPA receptor is dephosphorylated by phosphatases activated by CaMK-II and excitability is reduced (LTD).

A second, less appreciated route to lethality is that the presence of depression is itself a risk factor for many other medical illnesses such as the occurrence of a heart attack or stroke (Ahrens et al., 1995). There is about a three- to four-fold increased risk of having a heart attack if one is depressed compared with one who is not depressed, and the chances of dying from the heart attack are similarly increased if one is depressed compared with one who is not depressed. It is because of these types of vulnerabilities that it is estimated that untreated recurring unipolar or bipolar depressive illness results in an average of seven years of decreased life expectancy compared with the nondepressed general population. Adequate treatment of the illness with lithium not only tends to reduce the rate of suicide toward that of the general population, but also normalizes excess medical mortality (Muller-Oerlinghausen, Ahrens et al., 1992; Muller-Oerlinghausen, Muser-Causemann, & Volk, 1992).

Positive Effects of Lithium on Neurotrophic Factor Gene Expression

This dual positive role is consistent with a substantial body of evidence emerging in both animals and humans that lithium can exert neurotrophic and neuroprotective properties (Table 6.2). Lithium also increases the production of new neurons that migrate into hippocampus, neurogenesis (Chen, Rajkowska, Du, Seraji-Bozorgzad, & Manji, 2000). Lithium in neural cell cultures increases cell survival factors (like BDNF and BCL-2) and decreases cell death factors (like BAX and P-53), which are involved in the apoptotic cell death pathways (Chen et al., 1999; Chen & Chuang, 1999). These findings are likely to be clinically relevant, because lithium (at usual blood levels achieved in patients) decreases the size and neurological consequences of a stroke in laboratory animals (Nonaka & Chuang, 1998) and decreases the extent of a lesion in animal models of Huntington's disease (Wei et al., 2001). In addition, recent evidence suggests that lithium treatment of patients may increase measures of neuronal integrity such as N-acetyl-aspartate (NAA) levels measured by MRS (Moore et al., 2000) and may even increase the amount of grey matter in the brain as measured with magnetic resonance imaging (MRI) (Moore, Bebchuk, Wilds, Chen, & Manji, 2000).

The antidepressants as a class also appear to exert a variety of positive effects on the brain. Not only do they increase BDNF in the hippocampus (opposite to the effects of stress and glucocorticoids) (Nibuya, Morinobu, & Duman, 1995; Smith, Makino, Kvetnansky, & Post, 1995), but if an animal is stressed during chronic treatment with antidepressants, the stress-induced alterations in BDNF are moderated or inhibited. Thus, it also becomes important to reconceptualize some of the therapeutic approaches to the recurring unipolar and bipolar affective

TABLE 6.2. POTENTIAL NEUROTROPHIC AND NEUROPROTECTIVE EFFECTS OF BIPOLAR ILLNESS, LITHIUM, VALPROATE, AND ANTIDEPRESSANTS.

	Stress	Glucocorticoids	Bipolar Illness	Lithium	Valproate	Antidepressants
Neurotrophic factors						
BDNF	↓	↓		↑		↑ (and block stress effects)
Bcl-2				↑	↑	
Cell death factors						
Bax, p53	↑	↑		↓		
Stroke model						
Severity	↑	↑	(↑, ?)	↓	↓?	
Calcium signaling						
Ca$_i$			↑ Ca$_i$, WBCs	↓		
CaMK-II	↑		↓ PFC CaMK-II	↓		↑
Mineralocorticoid receptors (MR)			↓ MR	↓		↑
New neurons/Glia						
Neurogenesis	↓	↓	(↓ neurons)	↑		↑
Gliagenesis			(↓ glia)	↑		
Neuronal integrity						
NAA (PFC > Hippocampus)	----	----	↓	↓		
Gray matter on MRI			↓	↓		
Clinical suicide	↑	↑	↑↑ incidence	↓	?	↓?
Excess medical mortality if depressed		(↑)	↑ incidence	↓	?	?

Abbreviations: ↑, increase; ↓, decrease; ?, unknown or not definite; BDNF, brain-derived neurotrophic factor; Ca$_i$, intracellular calcium; CaMK-II, calcium calmodulin kinase-II; NAA, N-acetyl-aspartate; PFC, prefrontal cortex; MRI, magnetic resonance imaging; WBCs, white blood cells.

disorders, such as lithium and antidepressants, as agents not only with the potential for side effects, but also with the potential for direct (neuron and glial sparing) therapeutic effects (Table 6.2) on some of the target systems that are altered in these illnesses (Figure 6.15).

In this regard, it will be useful for patients and clinicians to replace the traditional view of lithium as a toxin for the thyroid and kidneys with that of a neuronal and glial growth and protective factor that is capable of preventing or reversing some of the neurobiological abnormalities of affective disorders and their concomitant medical comorbidities.

Maintenance pharmacoprophylaxis (Tertiary Prevention)

We make these suggestions with the hope that they will have an impact on patients' acceptance of long-term prophylactic treatments. Many patients and some professionals believe that discontinuing antidepressants as soon as possible is somehow the preferred approach in dealing with psychotropic medications (those for mental disorders), yet they believe the opposite is true for the treatment of many medical disorders, such as the use of digitalis for congestive heart failure. We would never encourage our patients or family members to undergo a period of digitalis discontinuation to see whether or not it resulted in irreversible heart failure. Yet, it is all too easy for patients, sometimes with the support of others, to consider it appropriate to go off their maintenance antidepressants or lithium, risking potential relapses and even the possibility of becoming treatment refractory.

Keller and colleagues have estimated that each recurrent depression brings with it a 10% risk of a chronic course (Keller & Boland, 1998). We have also seen unipolar patients who are highly responsive to a given antidepressant on multiple occasions continue to stop their medication after they have a remission, and then find that the same antidepressant no longer works for subsequent episodes. A large percentage of patients who discontinue their lithium experience a relapse, and a small percentage may not respond as well as they had previously (Post, Leverich, Altshuler, & Mikalauskas, 1992; Post, Leverich, Pazzaglia, Mikalauskas, & Denicoff, 1993). We have labeled this phenomenon *lithium discontinuation-induced refractoriness* because it appears that if patients had continued their lithium (to which they were having a complete response) they would not have experienced either the relapse off medication or the subsequent loss of response to lithium when it was reinstituted.

Guidelines from most health agencies and psychopharmacological academic groups recommend long-term antidepressant prophylaxis after three prior major depressive episodes. Unipolar patients should be informed that their risk of relapse after discontinuing an effective antidepressant treatment once their depression has remitted is about 50% in the first year, 75% in the second year, and 85% in the third year off treatment, and these relapse rates can be decreased by one-half to two-thirds with continuation of their antidepressant prophylaxis. Similarly, discontinuing effective lithium treatment results in 50% of the patients relapsing in the first five months off treatment and 90% of the patients relapsing in the first year and a half (Suppes, Baldessarini, Faedda, & Tohen, 1991).

If one chooses to stop, or not even begin, effective pharmacoprophylaxis, one is risking not only relapses and the associated morbidity, but also the many secondary potential adverse social, employment, and economic consequences of having a new episode. In addition, the small but real possibility that the illness will not again respond as well as it had previously is rarely entered into the equation. Moreover, the risk of suicide is extraordinarily higher in those discontinuing their lithium compared with those remaining on it, with estimates ranging from seven- to twenty-fold increased risk of suicide in the first year off lithium compared with its continuation (Baldessarini, Tondo, & Hennen, 1999; Baldessarini, Tondo, & Hennen, 2001).

Thus, the recurrent depressive and bipolar illnesses must be de-trivialized so that patients can better understand the benefits of remaining on effective medications versus the potential adverse consequences of discontinuing them. Often, there is the misguided attempt to prove to themselves that they "don't really need them." We should be more explicit in discussing with patients the potential consequences of discontinuation, including that if they have another manic or depressive episode and lose their job, they may also lose their health insurance and then have inadequate access to health care and costly medications, unfortunate circumstances which may yield a new cycle of illness adversity and treatment resistance (Figure 6.17).

This latter route to illness progression is not related to primary treatment-resistance itself, but rather to secondary consequences of preventable relapses and inability to access effective treatment. We consider all of these issues under the rubric of tertiary prevention, that is, preventing new recurrences of full-blown episodes, which can be lifesaving. However, it appears increasingly important to also focus better on secondary prevention and, ultimately, primary prevention as well.

Early Intervention in Those at High Risk (Secondary Prevention)

Secondary prevention refers to intervening early before the illness has reached its full-blown stages and potentially preventing some of the secondary consequences such as comorbid substance abuse to which the adolescent is already highly vulnerable. Depression and bipolar illness often run in families. Until recently, clinicians have neglected to perform careful assessment of affective illnesses in children and adolescents, even though it is known that some children and adolescents are at high risk because one or both parents have an affective disorder. Stigma has

FIGURE 6.17

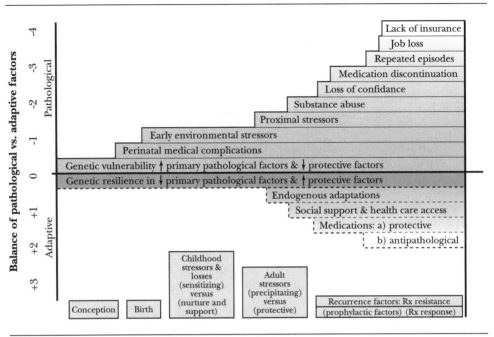

Ratio of pathological versus adaptive factors in determining illness episodes and well intervals.

paradoxically played an enormous role in this regard, as the attempt to prevent stigmatizing a child with an affective illness diagnosis has often been a major motivating factor in not actively seeking out and treating affectively ill children and adolescents. We should take Tipper Gore's lead and treat the affective disorders like any other medical illness. She states: "Yes, any illness that runs in the family, whether it is colon cancer or diabetes or heart disease, you need to talk about it. You need to pay attention to early warning signs that you or your children might have it." In our adult population of patients with bipolar illness, there was an average of a ten-year gap between the onset of first affective symptoms meeting DSM criteria for an affective episode and the onset of first treatment (Suppes et al., 2001). This gap is an enormous public health problem that needs to be addressed from multiple avenues so that it can be corrected.

In childhood-onset unipolar and bipolar illness, parents often appear to be ahead of the medical profession. Surveys have noted that not only do parents want their affectively ill children treated as early as possible, but are also willing to enter them into appropriately designed research studies to better define what are the optimal treatment interventions when there is ambiguity (Post, Leverich, Fergus, Miller, & Luckenbaugh, 2002). The diagnosis and treatment of childhood-onset affective illness is too often confounded by a lack of systematic data, but general principles are beginning to emerge that should encourage earlier, more effective intervention.

Adolescent-onset affective illness should, by itself, be considered a high risk factor for a subsequent substance abuse disorder, and attempts at primary prevention of a substance abuse disorder should be instituted early in the treatment paradigm. Educational approaches, specific role playing of how one can avoid peer pressure, and a variety of other strategies should be considered. This makes sense based on the clinical data available and because of new findings showing that substances of abuse can add to the molecular abnormalities of the primary affective illness (Figure 6.5).

Earliest Intervention in High-Risk Populations

It would also appear appropriate under circumstances of very high risk to attempt to engage in primary prevention of the affective disorder itself, either with psychological interventions or, in some instances, with medications as well. If both parents have an affective disorder (at least one bipolar), the offspring carry a 70% lifetime risk of acquiring an affective disorder (Gershon et al., 1982; Lapalme, Hodgins, & LaRoche, 1997). Intervention at first symptoms, rather than only at or after diagnostic thresholds are reached, should be studied and considered.

The occurrence of a post-partum depression in the mother should be considered as an early risk factor for the newborn infant. Other major depressive or manic episodes in the mothers of young children should likewise be viewed in the same context (that is, potentially having adverse consequences for the children and other family members). Obviously, a first approach to such a problem would be the aggressive treatment of the mother's affective disorder. However, in the face of the reality that such treatment is often delayed, and the onset of a full therapeutic response is often additionally delayed by many months, we suggest that further approaches be considered as well.

If a mother has a broken hip, it is very clear to family members and health care personnel that she needs extra assistance in her usual child-rearing tasks. Many people and, in some instances, several hospital-based agencies would intervene to provide increased help and support. This is highly unlikely to be the case with a moderately to severely depressed mother, yet others in and outside the family need to step in and help provide child care and rearing support.

A depressed or hypomanic parent might not be able to get by without specific help and suggestions about how to manage in the context of an overwhelming affective illness. Interventions of proven value are known and discussed in detail elsewhere in this volume. They should be made part of the standard of care for the depressed mother in general, as part of an effort of primary prevention in children at high risk.

Data suggest that if a mother has made suicide attempts and has been physically or sexually abused, the likelihood increases that her offspring will later become depressed and make a suicide attempt, whether or not they themselves experience such early traumas (Brent et al., 2002). However, if a child does share the same misfortune of early adverse experiences, the chances of an affective illness and subsequent suicide attempts in these children are even more substantial. Such a set of circumstances should trigger early psychotherapeutic interventions and medications when appropriate in the affected child.

Disappointingly, in our adult cohort with bipolar illness, we found that those with a history of early physical or sexual abuse actually had a significantly longer time from first symptoms meeting diagnostic thresholds to first treatment than those who did not report these early adversities (Leverich et al., 2002). Thus, attempts at secondary and tertiary, if not primary, intervention in such instances would appear highly indicated.

Preventing Substance Abuse in Patients and Their Offspring

Similar to the general population, more males with bipolar illness have alcohol abuse problems compared with females; however, females with bipolar illness are at much greater risk (about eight-fold) for alcohol abuse compared with women in the general population. One of the predisposing factors for a higher alcohol abuse rate in women with bipolar illness appears to be the number of prior depressions (Frye et al., in press).

Those with early environmental adversity also appear to be at increased risk for alcohol use and abuse. Ethanol intoxication and withdrawal not only acutely perturb the CNS, but also affect gene expression and have long-term consequences as well. One example is that repeated episodes of alcohol withdrawal can lead to increased seizure vulnerability manifest in the late development of alcohol withdrawal seizures, and to progressive increases in the severity of alcohol withdrawal episodes (beginning with minor anxiety and shakes and culminating in full-blown delirium tremens) (Booth & Blow, 1993).

Kindling of alcohol withdrawal consequences has now been well documented in a variety of preclinical studies that are able to precisely control the amount of alcohol intoxication and number of withdrawals and demonstrate that it is the number of withdrawals rather than the total degree of alcohol intake or severity of a single intoxication that is the crucial variable in the progression of the severity of alcohol withdrawal behaviors and seizures (Ballenger & Post, 1978).

A general family history of alcoholism (but not affective illness) was also associated with an increased incidence of physical or sexual abuse in patients with bipolar illness in our outpatient network (Leverich et al., 2002). Thus, not only should one be careful in eliciting a history of substance abuse in individuals with unipolar and bipolar diagnoses, but one should also be cognizant that a family history of substance abuse in a non-affectively ill parent may be a vulnerability factor for early adverse life experiences for the children in the family. Primary preventive strategies in the child may then be indicated when there is a multiple set of such vulnerabilities.

While most would support such interventional approaches from a psychotherapeutic perspective, the question of when to use medications in children at high (one parent ill) and very high (both parents ill) risk remains much more controversial. It would appear crucial for studies to be performed in order to elucidate whether antidepressant treatment of children with early extreme adversity in the context of a parental history of a primary affective disorder, or a positive family history of a substance abuse disorder, could help prevent the expected high incidence of both affective disorder and secondary substance abuse in the offspring. The preclinical data of Plotsky, Meaney, and associates noted previously not only support such a possibility (that antidepressant treatment of neonatally stressed animals reverses the vulnerability to substance self-administration), but also that a positive effect could be observed transgenerationally. Appropriate clinical trials obviously need to be conducted to expand upon such possibilities.

Even if such clinical studies were positive, one could imagine considerable public controversy around the application of such knowledge. The treatment of full-blown childhood onset bipolar illness (even when it does meet diagnostic thresholds) is already a highly controversial topic, largely because of the absence of controlled data as to how best to proceed (Wozniak, Biederman, & Richards, 2001). Interventions for subthreshold symptomatology in those at very high risk by virtue of a bi-lineal family history for affective disorders would be more controversial, but at least should be studied and considered given the very substantial long-range clinical and biological consequences of full-blown recurrent affective illness.

Practical and Theoretical Considerations

Multiple investigators have shown that interventions for maltreated preschool children in foster care or others at high risk for aberrant behavior and affective disorders can be highly effective (Cicchetti, Rogosch, & Toth, 2000; Fisher, Gunnar, Chamberlain, & Reid, 2000). Fisher et al. (2000) used strategies that emphasized consistent non-abusive discipline, high levels of positive reinforcement, and close monitoring and supervision of the child. Their program included supervision through daily phone contacts, weekly home visits by a consultant, a weekly support group meeting, and twenty-four-hour on-call crisis intervention. The children received services from a behavioral specialist at preschool or daycare and home-based settings, and in a weekly play group program. These interventions resulted in both a mean decrease in early childhood inventory symptom total scores (compared with movement in the opposite direction in the regular foster care control group), and an associated positive change in the caregiver stress scores.

The nature of the optimal program of parental and child support for families in which the mother has an active primary affective disorder and her offspring have a childhood affective syndrome is not entirely clear, but an increased amount of support and intervention would certainly appear indicated, and remains to be better delineated. Where would this type of support come from in the age of managed care, which can often miss long-term benefits in favor of minor short-term gains?

In addition to medications and psychotherapy, the currently depressed mother should receive specific parenting help and support from a trained social worker, psychologist, or other health care worker with knowledge in this area. It is possible that a twenty-four-hour on-call support could be made available through patient advocacy and support groups such as the Depression and Bipolar Support Alliance, the Mental Health Association, and the National Alliance for the Mentally Ill.

In instances when the child presents with a bipolar prodrome or bipolar not otherwise specified (NOS) in addition to full-blown bipolar-I or -II illness, parental support should be upgraded and support should be made a necessary part of the child's therapeutic program. Support should be offered up front in all instances, so that recommendations for such an ameliorative program would not have negative connotations or implications that one was "a bad parent." Instituting the type of program recommended by Ross Greene (1998) or Friedberg and McClure (2002) can be complex and difficult even for the non-depressed parent given the many nonintuitive aspects of the recommendations. Systematically working through these or related therapeutic strategies for the depressed parent would require extra practice, supervision, and follow-up.

Based on the findings of Rutter (1998) and Johnson (2000), it appears that the inability of infants to catch up following severe global early deprivation is directly proportional to the length of the deprivation. This principle would parallel that seen by Hubel and Weisel (1979) in the visual system, wherein the length of time visual input is occluded in proportion to deficits in occipital cortex function, anatomical changes, and irreversibility of vision loss. These data further stress the importance of timely interventions; as deadlines pass, the liabilities may increase, and chances for remediation decrease.

Similarly, in patients with bipolar illness, there appear to be several "dose-response" relationships to the incidence of suicidality. The incidence of serious suicide attempts is approximately 25% in those with no physical or sexual abuse, increases about another 15% in those who had either type of adversity, and doubles (about 55%) in those who have experienced both types of early environmental adversity (Leverich et al., in press). Moreover, there is an additional "dose effect" in terms of the reported frequency (number of instances) of physical abuse during childhood and the incidence of subsequent suicide attempts (Leverich et al., 2002; Leverich et al., in press).

Any type of intervention that can lessen the incidence of verbal abuse and, concomitantly, increase positive touch communications and other measures of comforting and warmth in parents with and without an affective disorder, might have a very dramatic impact on subsequent childhood behavior and adolescent and adult suicidality. Geller et al. (2002) found a relatively poor prognosis in the two-year prospective follow-up of eighty-nine consecutively evaluated subjects averaging 10.9 years of age with a diagnosis of DSM-IV-substantiated mania. Based on naturalistic (but probably not aggressive enough) treatment in the community, only 65.2% of the children had recovered, and of these 55.2% relapsed in the two-year followup. The rate of relapse was associated with the absence of an intact biological family (not easily modifiable) and a low level of maternal warmth (which would be subject to remediation and amelioration through education, training, and other interventions).

Randomized, controlled data (in adults with bipolar illness) are already incontrovertible that a variety of targeted educational, cognitive-behavioral, and family systems psychotherapeutic approaches are clinically and statistically significant adjunctive benefits to ongoing psychopharmacotherapy (Colom et al., 2003; Lam et al., 2003; Miklowitz et al., 2003; Scott & Tacchi, 2002).

Neurobiological Overview and Integration

The first part of this chapter gave examples of how early and late environmental experiences can yield long-term alterations in neurobiology and behavior, focusing primarily on the rodent with single and multiple maternal deprivation stresses, and on cocaine and alcohol self-administration. Each of these has the potential for altering the brain in a long-lasting fashion. Moreover, the Plotsky-Meaney data and those of many other investigators (Table 6.3) have indicated a link between a variety of stressors early in life and neuroendocrine alterations, anxiety-related behaviors, and the subsequent adoption of alcohol and cocaine abuse. These can all be ameliorated with interventions that alter maternal behavior (decreasing agitation by providing her a substitute litter), or with alternative rearing behavior (as evidenced in the cross-fostering studies). Secondary prevention can also be accomplished with treatment with SSRI antidepressants ameliorating many of the neurobiological and behavioral vulnerabilities as well as the proneness to substance abuse.

TABLE 6.3.   RELATIONSHIP OF EARLY AND CONCURRENT STRESSORS TO ACQUISITION, MAINTENANCE, AND REINSTATEMENT OF COCAINE SELF-ADMINISTRATION (IN RODENTS).

Stressor	Age	Cocaine Effect	Authors
Stress	Adult	↑ Acquisition of cocaine self-administration	Piazza et al., 1989
Social stress	Adult	↑ Acquisition of cocaine self-administration	Murphy et al., 1995
Uncontrollable foot-shock	Adult	↑ Cocaine self-administration (only if corticosteriods elevated)	Goeders & Guerin, 1994
Social defeat × 4 (sensitization to stress)	Adult	↑ Cocaine amount (↑binge size) ↑ Motor response to stimulants (that is, cross sensitization)	Covington & Miczek, 2001
Stressors or cocaine cues	Adult	↑ Cocaine lever pressing ↑ Reinstatement of extinguished response	Goeders & Clanfitt, 2002
Three-hour maternal deprivation stress × 7 (neonate)	Stress (neonate) Drug intake (adult)	↑ Alcohol and cocaine self-administration (reversal with antidepressant treatment)	Huot, Thrivikraman, Meaney, & Plotsky, 2001 Meaney, Brake, & Gratton, 2002

FIGURE 6.18

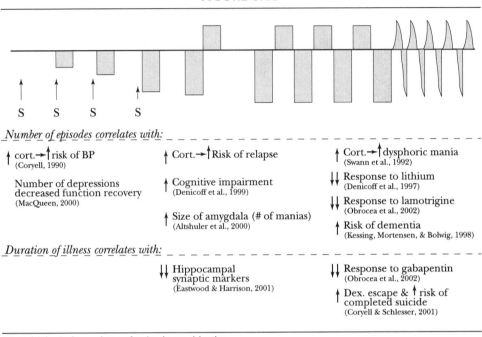

Number of episodes correlates with:

↑ cort.➔↑ risk of BP
(Coryell, 1990)

Number of depressions
decreased function recovery
(MacQueen, 2000)

↑ Cort.➔↑ Risk of relapse

↑ Cognitive impairment
(Denicoff et al., 1999)

↑ Size of amygdala (# of manias)
(Altshuler et al., 2000)

↑ Cort.➔↑ dysphoric mania
(Swann et al., 1992)

↓↓ Response to lithium
(Denicoff et al., 1997)

↓↓ Response to lamotrigine
(Obrocea et al., 2002)

↑ Risk of dementia
(Kessing, Mortensen, & Bolwig, 1998)

Duration of illness correlates with:

↓↓ Hippocampal
synaptic markers
(Eastwood & Harrison, 2001)

↓↓ Response to gabapentin
(Obrocea et al., 2002)

↑ Dex. escape & ↑ risk of
completed suicide
(Coryell & Schlesser, 2001)

Neurobiological correlates of episode sensitization.

Abbreviations

S	stimulus	↓	decreased
cort.	cortisol	dex.	dexamethasone.
↑	increased;		

Environmental experiences can affect neurobiology via changes in gene expression, along with affective episodes or the intake of substances of abuse. As indicated in Figure 6.18, each of these could not only represent accumulating impact on gene expression, but, as noted, each can present an additional vulnerability to stress sensitivity and subsequent substance abuse in a vicious cycle effect.

At the same time, the neurobiological data emphasize the importance of positive factors in preventing or ameliorating the effects of stress on neurobiology and behavior. Here, there is a wealth of opportunities for prevention and intervention that can have positive and indelible effects. Much clinical observation and experience has documented the clinical effects of abuse, on the one hand (Johnson, 2000; MacMillan et al., 2001; Rutter & Maughan, 1997), but equally dramatically, the effect of positive experience in the context of stressors in achieving extraordinary outcomes. Helen Keller, Wilma Rudolph, and Ken Venturi are just a few of the scores of such individuals who have overcome great obstacles in their lives to achieve success.

Born blind and deaf, Helen Keller was able to achieve the penultimate in interpersonal and international communication. Wilma Rudolph was a world class runner and Olympic track and field champion after having childhood polio, and prognostications that she would never walk again. Ken Venturi overcame his severe problem with stuttering to become one of the great sports announcers of our time. People intuitively know of the possibility of these types of transformations, and virtually all parents struggle on a day-to-day basis to make their children repositories of positive learning experiences that will enable them to optimally grow and adapt.

To this extent, the preliminary view of the potential neurobiological and molecular underpinnings of the long-lasting effects of environmental experience on brain and behavior in animals, noted here, perhaps only provides a deeper level of understanding of some of the potential mediating factors involved. Early in the last century Freud predicted the emergence of a scientific psychiatry that subsumed and informed the entire range of psychoanalytic concepts. The field has not yet arrived at such a juncture, but one can begin to glimpse some of the neurobiology mechanisms to which Freud and others have alluded.

While the animal models discussed here are inadequate and one cannot directly extrapolate to the human condition, they may still be useful in the conceptualization of the potential importance of early therapeutic intervention. However imperfect these models are, they are heuristically valuable when we consider the types of molecular mechanisms involved in mediating long-term changes in behavior. These models facilitate clinical hypothesis testing and the design and testing of therapeutic interventions that may help prevent or ameliorate a great amount of human suffering caused by the recurrent affective disorders and the illness by definition based on stressful life events, PTSD.

These types of neurobiological underpinnings of the long-term effects of experience discussed here add a theoretical rationale to the existing strong empirical evidence supporting the importance of attempts at primary and secondary prevention of affective disorders in children and adults. They also raise the paradigm-shifting likelihood that some of our current antidepressant and mood stabilizer psychotropic drugs will be neurotrophic and neuroprotective. As such, some may become suitable for early intervention and even primary prevention in those at high risk.

Endnotes

1. The Morris water maze is one in which animals are placed in milky water so that it is opaque. They readily learn to swim to an underwater platform that enables them to stand, rest, and dry themselves off. Once they learn where this underwater platform is placed, they can then readily and rapidly swim to it on the next day, indicating that they have learned

the position. Animals deficient in CaMK-II or BDNF cannot accomplish this readily learned task, which would obviously have considerable survival value in the wild. Rapidly navigating to a safe place in the environment would be crucial to avoid predators and the like.

2. Why should there be an increase in apoptotic cell death in the CNS when there is an increase in the messenger RNA for nerve growth factor (NGF)? It turns out that the high affinity receptors for NGF have not yet developed in this young animal and the increased NGF acts on a low affinity (p75) receptor, which facilitates apoptosis as opposed to cell protection. This finding illustrates another important principle, that the timing of induction or administration of a given apparent positive or negative growth factor can dramatically change the impact and consequences of it on the organism. In this case, instead of being a nerve growth factor, NGF is a cell death factor when pathologically induced in this period of early development.

3. The tri-synaptic circuitry of the hippocampus is necessary for the encoding of most environmental events into long-term learning and memory. Information comes in to the hippocampus via the proferent path and synapses on the dendrites of the dentate granule cells. These, in turn, synapse on the CA3 pyramidal cells and represent the mossy fibre pathway that also uses the excitatory neurotransmitter glutamate as the major rapid intercellular messenger. However, it is noteworthy that the dentate granular cells via their mossy fibre terminals also release zinc and BDNF along with glutamate. The Schaefer collateral axons of the CA3 neurons in turn synapse on the CA1 pyramidal cells, again using a glutamate synapse. This glutamate synapse is the one that has been most studied in the CNS and it is found to depend on the subtype of receptors called N-methyl-D-aspartate (NMDA) receptors. In contrast, the mossy fibre synapses do not depend on NMDA receptor function. The CA1 cells then exit the hippocampus via the subiculum or another glutamatergic synapse. This series of three glutamatergic hippocampal synapses in a row provides for amplification of messages intended to get into long-term memory.

4. It is interesting that one high-frequency burst of firing leads to short-term potentiation (STP), whereas a series of three high-frequency bursts, particularly if they are given in spaced trials, result in LTP. We know that emotional arousal enhances long-term memory and is a prerequisite for the occurrence of PTSD. The application of the beta receptor agonist isoproterenol leads to a huge multifold potentiation of amygdala-neuronal firing, suggesting that norepinephrine, which is mobilized with alertness, arousal, and anxiety, is important to amygdala-based emotional responsivity and memory. This is of interest in relation to reports that a beta-blocking strategy may be capable of decreasing amygdala activation during the experience of affectively laden events in a laboratory setting and that such an approach with the beta receptor blocker propranolol shows some promise in the immediate posttraumatic period of patients at high risk for PTSD.

It is now clear that the experience of early traumatic events is a marked vulnerability factor in distinguishing which adults will develop PTSD after significant stress as an adult (such as a war experience or a motor vehicle accident), suggesting a behavioral sensitization or kindling-like process that could be occurring over very long time domains in those developing PTSD based on the repetition of traumatic recall and memory circuits. Kindling formally refers to the process eventuating in the development of a full-blown motor seizure to a previously subthreshold stimulus, but we have suggested the utility of the concept that flashbacks of PTSD, which often also evolve from the triggered to spontaneous variety, may usefully be thought of as the kindling of a "memory" seizure. As such, some of the principles pertinent to primary, secondary, and tertiary prophylaxis in kindled seizure evolution may be relevant to those in PTSD, particularly observations of the importance of different pharmacological interventions for different stages of illness evolution, and the importance of early treatment interventions in preventing loss of efficacy from development via tolerance mechanisms.

References

Ahrens, B., Muller-Oerlinghausen, B., Schou, M., Wolf, T., Alda, M., Grof, E., et al. (1995). Excess cardiovascular and suicide mortality of affective disorders may be reduced by lithium prophylaxis. *Journal of Affective Disorders, 33,* 67–75.

Ali, S. O., Denicoff, K. D., Altshuler, L. L., Hauser, P., Li, X., Conrad, A. J., et al. (2000). A preliminary study of the relation of neuropsychological performance to neuroanatomic structures in bipolar disorder. *Neuropsychiatry, Neuropsychology and Behavioral Neurology, 13*(1), 20–28.

Altshuler, L. L., Bartzokis, G., Grieder, T., Curran, J., Jiminez, T., Leight, K., et. al. (2000). An MRI study of temporal lobe structures in men with bipolar disorder or schizophrenia. *Biological Psychiatry, 48*(2), 147–162.

Altshuler, L. L., Bartzokis, G., Grieder, T., Curran, J., & Mintz, J. (1998). Amygdala enlargement in bipolar disorder and hippocampal reduction in schizophrenia: An MRI study demonstrating neuroanatomic specificity. *Archives of General Psychiatry, 55*(7), 663–664.

Angst, J., & Sellaro, R. (2000). Historical perspectives and natural history of bipolar disorder. *Biological Psychiatry, 48,* 445–457.

Antelman, S. M., Eichler, A. J., Black, C. A., & Kocan, D. (1980). Interchangeability of stress and amphetamine in sensitization. *Science, 207,* 329–331.

Baldessarini, R. J., Tondo, L., & Hennen, J. (1999). Effects of lithium treatment and its discontinuation on suicidal behavior in bipolar manic-depressive disorders. *Journal of Clinical Psychiatry, 60*(Suppl 2), 77–84.

Baldessarini, R. J., Tondo, L., & Hennen, J. (2001). Treating the suicidal patient with bipolar disorder. Reducing suicide risk with lithium. *Annals of the New York Academy of Sciences, 932,* 24–38.

Ballenger, J. C., & Post, R. M. (1978). Kindling as a model for alcohol withdrawal syndromes. *British Journal of Psychiatry, 133,* 1–14.

Baxter, L. R., Jr., Schwartz, J. M., Phelps, M. E., Mazziotta, J. C., Guze, B. H., Selin, C. E., et al. (1989). Reduction of prefrontal cortex glucose metabolism common to three types of depression. *Archives of General Psychiatry, 46*(3), 243–250.

Beaulieu, S., Rousse, I., Gratton, A., Barden, N., & Rochford, J. (1994). Behavioral and endocrine impact of impaired type II glucocortoid receptor function in a transgenic mouse model. *Annals of the New York Academy of Sciences, 746,* 388–391.

Booth, B. M., & Blow, F. C. (1993). The kindling hypothesis: Further evidence from a U.S. national study of alcoholic men. *Alcohol and Alcoholism, 28,* 593–598.

Brent, D. A., Oquendo, M., Birmaher, B., Greenhill, L., Kolko, D., Stanley, B., et al. (2002). Familial pathways to early-onset suicide attempt: Risk for suicidal behavior in offspring of mood-disordered suicide attempters. *Archives of General Psychiatry, 59,* 801–807.

Caldji, C., Tannenbaum, B., Sharma, S., Francis, D., Plotsky, P. M., & Meaney, M. J. (1998). Maternal care during infancy regulates the development of neural systems mediating the expression of fearfulness in the rat. *Proceedings of the National Academy of Sciences of the United States of Amercia, 95,* 5335–5340.

Callahan, A. M., Frye, M. A., Marangell, L. B., George, M. S., Ketter, T. A., L'Herrou, T., et al. (1997). Comparative antidepressant effects of intravenous and intrathecal thyrotropin-releasing hormone: Confounding effects of tolerance and implications for therapeutics. *Biological Psychiatry, 41,* 264–272.

Chen, G., Rajkowska, G., Du, F., Seraji-Bozorgzad, N., & Manji, H. K. (2000). Enhancement of hippocampal neurogenesis by lithium. *Journal of Neurochemistry, 75,* 1729–1734.

Chen, G., Zeng, W. Z., Yuan, P. X., Huang, L. D., Jiang, Y. M., Zhao, Z. H., et al. (1999). The mood-stabilizing agents lithium and valproate robustly increase the levels of the neuroprotective protein bcl-2 in the CNS. *Journal of Neurochemistry, 72,* 879–882.

Chen, R. W., & Chuang, D. M. (1999). Long term lithium treatment suppresses p53 and Bax expression but increases Bcl-2 expression. A prominent role in neuroprotection against excitotoxicity. *Journal of Biological Chemistry, 274,* 6039–6042.

Cicchetti, D., Rogosch, F. A., & Toth, S. L. (2000). The efficacy of toddler-parent psychotherapy for fostering cognitive development in offspring of depressed mothers. *Journal of Abnormal Child Psychology, 28,* 135–148.

Colom, F., Vieta, E., Martinez-Aran, A., Reinares, M., Goikolea, J. M., Benabarre, A., et al. (2003). A randomized trial on the efficacy of group psychoeducation in the prophylaxis of recurrences in bipolar patients whose disease is in remission. *Archives of General Psychiatry, 60,* 402–407.

Coryell, W. (1990). DST abnormality as a predictor of course in major depression. *Journal of Affective Disorders, 19*(3), 163–169.

Coryell, W., & Schlesser, M. (2001). The dexamethasone suppression test and suicide prediction. *American Journal of Psychiatry, 158*(5), 748–753.

Covington, H. E., III, & Miczek, K. A. (2001). Repeated social-defeat stress, cocaine or morphine. Effects on behavioral sensitization and intravenous cocaine self-administration "binges." *Psychopharmacology (Berl), 158,* 388–398.

Davis, M. (1998). Are different parts of the extended amygdala involved in fear versus anxiety? *Biological Psychiatry, 44,* 1239–1247.

Denicoff, K. D., Ali, S. O., Mirsky, A. F., Smith-Jackson, E. E., Leverich, G. S., Duncan, C. C., et al. (1999). Relationship between prior course of illness and neuropsychological functioning in patients with bipolar disorder. *Journal of Affective Disorders, 56*(1), 67–73.

Denicoff, K. D., Smith-Jackson, E. E., Disney, E. R., Ali, S. O., Leverich, G. S., & Post, R. M. (1997). Relationship Comparative prophylactic efficacy of lithium, carbamazepine, and the combination in bipolar disorder. *Journal of Clinical Psychiatry, 58*(11), 470–478.

Drevets, W. C., Ongur, D., & Price, J. L. (1998). Neuroimaging abnormalities in the subgenual prefrontal cortex: Implications for the pathophysiology of familial mood disorders. *Molecular Psychiatry, 3*(3), 220–226, 190–191.

Eastwood, S. L., & Harrison, P. J. (2001). Synaptic pathology in the anterior cingulate cortex in schizophrenia and mood disorders. A review and a Western blot study of synaptophysin, GAP-43 and the complexins. *Brain Research Bulletin, 55*(5), 569–578.

Fisher, P. A., Gunnar, M. R., Chamberlain, P., & Reid, J. B. (2000). Preventive intervention for maltreated preschool children: Impact on children's behavior, neuroendocrine activity, and foster parent functioning. *Journal of the American Academy of Child and Adolescent Psychiatry, 39,* 1356–1364.

Francis, D., Diorio, J., Liu, D., & Meaney, M. J. (1999). Nongenomic transmission across generations of maternal behavior and stress responses in the rat. *Science, 286,* 1155–1158.

Francis, D. D., Caldji, C., Champagne, F., Plotsky, P. M., & Meaney, M. J. (1999). The role of corticotropin-releasing factor—norepinephrine systems in mediating the effects of early experience on the development of behavioral and endocrine responses to stress. *Biological Psychiatry, 46,* 1153–1166.

Frankland, P. W., O'Brien, C., Ohno, M., Kirkwood, A., & Silva, A. J. (2001). Alpha-CaMKII-dependent plasticity in the cortex is required for permanent memory. *Nature, 411,* 309–313.

Friedberg, R. D., & McClure, J. M. (2002). *Clinical practice of cognitive therapy with children and adolescents: The nuts and bolts.* New York: Guilford Press.

Frye, M. A., Altshuler, L. L., McElroy, S. L., Suppes, T., Keck, P. E., Jr., Denicoff, K., et al. (in press). Increased risk for alcoholism in women compared to men with bipolar disorder. *American Journal of Psychiatry.*

Geller, B., Craney, J. L., Bolhofner, K., Nickelsburg, M. J., Williams, M., & Zimerman, B. (2002). Two-year prospective follow-up of children with a prepubertal and early adolescent bipolar disorder phenotype. *American Journal of Psychiatry, 159,* 927–933.

George, M. S., Ketter, T. A., Parekh, P. I., Rosinsky, N., Ring, H. A., Pazzaglia, P. J., et al. (1997). Blunted left cingulate activation in mood disorder subjects during a response interference task (the Stroop). *Journal of Neuropsychiatry and Clinical Neuroscience, 9*(1), 55–63.

Gershon, E. S., Hamovit, J., Guroff, J. J., Dibble, E., Leckman, J. F., Sceery, W., et al. (1982). A family study of schizoaffective, bipolar I, bipolar II, unipolar, and normal control probands. *Archives of General Psychiatry, 39,* 1157–1167.

Goddard, G. V., McIntyre, D. C., & Leech, C. K. (1969). A permanent change in brain function resulting from daily electrical stimulation. *Experimental Neurology, 25,* 295–330.

Goeders, N. E., & Guerin, G. F. (1994). Non-contingent electric footshock facilitates the acquisition of intravenous cocaine self-administration in rats. *Psychopharmacology, 114,* 63–70.

Goodwin, F. K., & Jamison, K. R. (1990). *Manic-depressive illness.* New York: Oxford University Press.

Greene, R. (1998). *The explosive child.* New York: HarperCollins.

Guidotti, A., Auta, J., Davis, J. M., Di-Giorgi-Gerevini, V., Dwivedi, Y., Grayson, D. R., et al. (2000). Decrease in reelin and glutamic acid decarboxylase67 (GAD67) expression in schizophrenia and bipolar disorder: A postmortem brain study. *Archives of General Psychiatry, 57*(11), 1061–1069.

Hammen, C., & Gitlin, M. (1997). Stress reactivity in bipolar patients and its relation to prior history of disorder. *American Journal of Psychiatry, 154,* 856–857.

Hlastala, S. A., Frank, E., Kowalski, J., Sherrill, J. T., Tu, X. M., Anderson, B., et al. (2000). Stressful life events, bipolar disorder, and the "kindling model." *Journal of Abnormal Psychology, 109,* 777–786.

Hubel, D. H., & Weisel, T. N. (1979). Brain mechanisms of vision. *Scientific American, 241,* 150–162.

Huot, R. L., Thrivikraman, K. V., Meaney, M. J., & Plotsky, P. M. (2001). Development of adult ethanol preference and anxiety as a consequence of neonatal maternal separation in Long Evans rats and reversal with antidepressant treatment. *Psychopharmacology (Berl), 158,* 366–373.

Johnson, D. E. (2000). Medical and developmental sequellae of early childhood institutionalization in international adoptees from Romania and the Russian Federation.

In C. A. Nelson (Ed.), *The effects of early adversity on neurobehavioral development.* Mahwah, NJ: L Earlbaum Associates.

Kalivas, P. W., & Duffy, P. (1989). Similar effects of daily cocaine and stress on mesocorticolimbic dopamine neurotransmission in the rat. *Biological Psychiatry, 25,* 913–928.

Keller, M. B., & Boland, R. J. (1998). Implications of failing to achieve successful long-term maintenance treatment of recurrent unipolar major depression. *Biological Psychiatry, 44,* 348–360.

Kendler, K. S., Thornton, L. M., & Gardner, C. O. (2000). Stressful life events and previous episodes in the etiology of major depression in women: An evaluation of the "kindling" hypothesis. *American Journal of Psychiatry, 157,* 1243–1251.

Kendler, K. S., Thornton, L. M., & Gardner, C. O. (2001). Genetic risk, number of previous depressive episodes, and stressful life events in predicting onset of major depression. *American Journal of Psychiatry, 158,* 582–586.

Kessing, L. V., Andersen, P. K., Mortensen, P. B., & Bolwig, T. G. (1998). Recurrence in affective disorder. I. Case register study. *British Journal of Psychiatry, 172,* 23–28.

Kessing, L. V., Mortensen, P. B., & Bolwig, T. G. (1998). Clinical consequences of sensitisation in affective disorder: A case register study. *Journal of Affective Disorders, 47*(1–3), 41–47.

Ketter, T. A., Kimbrell, T. A., George, M. S., Dunn, R. T., Speer, A. M., Benson, B. E., et al. (2001). Effects of mood and subtype on cerebral glucose metabolism in treatment-resistant bipolar disorder. *Biological Psychiatry, 49*(2), 97–109.

Ketter, T. A., Kimbrell, T. A., George, M. S., Willis, M. W., Benson, B. E., Danielson, A. et al. (1999). Baseline cerebral hypermetabolism associated with carbamazepine response, and hypometabolism with nimodipine response in mood disorders. *Biological Psychiatry, 46*(10), 1364–1374.

Koob, G. F., & Le Moal, M. (2001). Drug addiction, dysregulation of reward, and allostasis. *Neuropsychopharmacology, 24,* 97–129.

Korte, M., Kang, H., Bonhoeffer, T., & Schuman, E. (1998). A role for BDNF in the late-phase of hippocampal long-term potentiation. *Neuropharmacology, 37,* 553–559.

Kraepelin, E. (1921). *Manic-depressive insanity and paranoia.* Edinburgh: E. S. Livingstone.

Lam, D. H., Watkins, E. R., Hayward, P., Bright, J., Wright, K., Kerr, N., et al. (2003). A randomized controlled study of cognitive therapy for relapse prevention for bipolar affective disorder: Outcome of the first year. *Archives of General Psychiatry, 60,* 145–152.

Lapalme, M., Hodgins, S., & LaRoche, C. (1997). Children of parents with bipolar disorder: A metaanalysis of risk for mental disorders. *Canadian Journal of Psychiatry, 42,* 623–631.

Leverich, G. S., Altshuler, L. L., Frye, M. A., Suppes, T., Keck, P. E., Jr., McElroy, S., et al. (in press). Factors associated with suicide attempts in 648 patients with bipolar disorder in the Stanley Foundation Bipolar Network. *Journal of Clinical Psychiatry.*

Leverich, G. S., McElroy, S. L., Suppes, T., Keck, P. E., Jr., Denicoff, K. D., Nolen, W. A., et al. (2002). Early physical and sexual abuse associated with an adverse course of bipolar illness. *Biological Psychiatry, 51,* 288–297.

Levine, S., Huchton, D. M., Wiener, S. G., & Rosenfeld, P. (1991). Time course of the effect of maternal deprivation on the hypothalamic-pituitary-adrenal axis in the infant rat. *Developmental Psychobiology, 24,* 547–558.

Liotti, M., Mayberg, H. S., McGinnis, S., Brannan, S. L., & Jerabek, P. (2002). Unmasking disease-specific cerebral blood flow abnormalities: Mood challenge in patients with remitted unipolar depression. *American Journal of Psychiatry, 159*(11), 1830–1840.

MacMillan, H. L., Fleming, J. E., Streiner, D. L., Lin, E., Boyle, M. H., Jamieson, E., et al. (2001). Childhood abuse and lifetime psychopathology in a community sample. *American Journal of Psychiatry, 158,* 1878–1883.

MacQueen, G. M., Young, L. T., Robb, J. C., Marriott, M., Cooke, R. G., & Joffe, R. T. (2000). Effect of number of episodes on wellbeing and functioning of patients with bipolar disorder. *Acta Psychiatrica Scandinavia, 101*(5), 374–381.

Maguire, E. A., Gadian, D. G., Johnsrude, I. S., Good, C. D., Ashburner, J., Frackowiak, R. S., et al. (2000). Navigation-related structural change in the hippocampi of taxi drivers. *Proceedings of the National Academy of Sciences of the United States of America, 97,* 4398–4403.

Malenka, R. C. (1994). Synaptic plasticity in the hippocampus: LTP and LTD. *Cell, 78,* 535–538.

Marangell, L. B., George, M. S., Callahan, A. M., Ketter, T. A., Pazzaglia, P. J., L'Herrou, T. A., et al. (1997). Effects of intrathecal thyrotropin-releasing hormone (protirelin) in refractory depressed patients. *Archives of General Psychiatry, 54,* 214–222.

Meaney, M. J., Aitken, D. H., Van Berkel, C., Bhatnagar, S., & Sapolsky, R. M. (1988). Effect of neonatal handling on age-related impairments associated with the hippocampus. *Science, 239,* 766–768.

Meaney, M. J., Brake, W., & Gratton, A. (2002). Environmental regulation of the development of mesolimbic dopamine systems: A neurobiological mechanism for vulnerability to drug abuse? *Psychoneuroendocrinology, 27,* 127–138.

Miklowitz, D. J., Richards, J. A., George, E. L., Frank, E., Suddath, R. L., Powell, K. B., et al. (2003). Integrated family and individual therapy for bipolar disorder: Results of a treatment development study. *Journal of Clinical Psychiatry, 64,* 182–191.

Moore, G. J., Bebchuk, J. M., Hasanat, K., Chen, G., Seraji-Bozorgzad, N., Wilds, I. B., et al. (2000). Lithium increases N-acetyl-aspartate in the human brain: In vivo evidence in support of bcl-2's neurotrophic effects? *Biological Psychiatry, 48,* 1–8.

Moore, G. J., Bebchuk, J. M., Wilds, I. B., Chen, G., & Manji, H. K. (2000). Lithium-induced increase in human brain grey matter. *Lancet, 356,* 1241–1242.

Muller-Oerlinghausen, B., Ahrens, B., Grof, E., Grof, P., Lenz, G., Schou, M., et al. (1992). The effect of long-term lithium treatment on the mortality of patients with manic-depressive and schizoaffective illness. *Acta Psychiatrica Scandinavica, 86,* 218–222.

Muller-Oerlinghausen, B., Muser-Causemann, B., & Volk, J. (1992). Suicides and parasuicides in a high-risk patient group on and off lithium long-term medication. *Journal of Affective Disorders, 25,* 261–269.

Murphy, E. H., Hammer, J. G., Schumann, M. D., Groce, M. Y., Wang, X. H., Jones, L., Romano, A. G., & Harvey, J. A. (1995). The rabbit as a model for studies of cocaine exposure in utero. *Lab Animal Science, 45,* 163–168.

Nestler, E. J., Barrot, M., & Self, D. W. (2001). DeltaFosB: A sustained molecular switch for addiction. *Proceedings of the National Academy of Sciences of the United States of America, 98,* 11042–11046.

Nestler, E. J., Kelz, M. B., & Chen, J. (1999). FosB: A molecular mediator of long-term neural and behavioral plasticity. *Brain Research, 835,* 10–17.

Nibuya, M., Morinobu, S., & Duman, R. S. (1995). Regulation of BDNF and trkB mRNA in rat brain by chronic electroconvulsive seizure and antidepressant drug treatments. *Journal of Neuroscience, 15,* 7539–7547.

Nonaka, S., & Chuang, D. M. (1998). Neuroprotective effects of chronic lithium on focal cerebral ischemia in rats. *Neuroreport, 9,* 2081–2084.

Obrocea, G. V., Dunn, R. M., Frye, M. A., Ketter, T. A., Luckenbaugh, D. A., Leverich, G. S., et al. (2002). Clinical predictors of response to lamotrigine and gabapentin monotherapy in refractory affective disorders. *Biological Psychiatry, 51*(3), 253–260.

Pearlson, G. D., Barta, P. E., Powers, R. E., Menon, R. R., Richards, S. S., Aylward, E. H., Federman, E. B., Chase, G. A., Petty, R. G., & Tien, A. Y. (1997). Medial and superior temporal gyral volumes and cerebral asymmetry in schizophrenia versus bipolar disorder. *Biological Psychiatry, 41,* 1–14.

Pert, A. (1998). Neurobiological substrates underlying conditioned effects of cocaine. *Advances in Pharmacology, 42,* 991–995.

Piazza, P. V., Deminiere, J. M., Le Moal, M., & Simon, H. (1989). Factors that predict vulnerability to amphetamine self-administration. *Science, 245,* 1511–1513.

Plotsky, P. M., & Meaney, M. J. (1993). Early, postnatal experience alters hypothalamic corticotropin-releasing factor (CRF) mRNA, median eminence CRF content and stress-induced release in adult rats. *Molecular Brain Research, 18,* 195–200.

Post, R. M. (1992). Transduction of psychosocial stress into the neurobiology of recurrent affective disorder. *American Journal of Psychiatry, 149,* 999–1010.

Post, R. M. (1993). Malignant transformation of affective illness: Prevention and treatment. *Directions in Psychiatry, 13*(9), 1–8.

Post, R. M., Ketter, T. A., Speer, A. M., Leverich, G. S., & Weiss, S. R. (2000). Predictive validity of the sensitization and kindling hypotheses. In J. C. Soares & S. Gershon (Eds.), *Bipolar disorders: Basic mechanisms and therapeutic implications* (pp. 387–432). New York: Marcel Dekker, Inc.

Post, R. M., Leverich, G. S., Altshuler, L., & Mikalauskas, K. (1992). Lithium-discontinuation-induced refractoriness: Preliminary observations. *American Journal of Psychiatry, 149,* 1727–1729.

Post, R. M., Leverich, G. S., Fergus, E., Miller, R., & Luckenbaugh, D. (2002). Parental attitudes towards early intervention in children at high risk for affective disorders. *Journal of Affective Disorders, 70,* 117–124.

Post, R. M., Leverich, G. S., Pazzaglia, P. J., Mikalauskas, K., & Denicoff, K. (1993). Lithium tolerance and discontinuation as pathways to refractoriness. In N. J. Birch, C. Padgham, & M. S. Hughes (Eds.), *Lithium in Medicine and Biology* (1st ed., pp. 71–84). Lancashire, UK: Marius Press.

Post, R. M., Leverich, G. S., Xing, G., & Weiss, R. B. (2001). Developmental vulnerabilities to the onset and course of bipolar disorder. *Development and Psychopathology, 13,* 581–598.

Post, R. M., & Weiss, S. R. (1989). Sensitization, kindling, and anticonvulsants in mania. *Journal of Clinical Psychiatry, 50*(Suppl), 23–30.

Post, R. M., & Weiss, S. R. (1992). Endogenous biochemical abnormalities in affective illness: Therapeutic versus pathogenic. *Biological Psychiatry, 32,* 469–484.

Post, R. M., & Weiss, S. R. (1996). A speculative model of affective illness cyclicity based on patterns of drug tolerance observed in amygdala-kindled seizures. *Molecular Neurobiology, 13,* 33–60.

Post, R. M., Weiss, S. R., Leverich, G. S., George, M. S., Frye, M., & Ketter, T. A. (1996). Developmental psychobiology of cyclic affective illness: Implications for early therapeutic intervention. *Development and Psychopathology, 8,* 273–305.

Post, R. M., Weiss, S. R., Pert, A., & Uhde, T. W. (1987). Chronic cocaine administration: Sensitization and kindling effects. In A. Raskin & S. Fisher (Eds.), *Cocaine: Clinical and biobehavioral aspects* (pp. 109–173). New York: Oxford University Press.

Rajkowska, G., Halaris, A., & Selemon, L. D. (2001). Reductions in neuronal and glial density characterize the dorsolateral prefrontal cortex in bipolar disorder. *Biological Psychiatry, 49*(9), 741–752.

Rosenfeld, P., Gutierrez, Y. A., Martin, A. M., Mallett, H. A., Alleva, E., & Levine, S. (1991). Maternal regulation of the adrenocortical response in preweanling rats. *Physiology and Behavior, 50*, 661–671.

Roy-Byrne, P., Post, R. M., Uhde, T. W., Porcu, T., & Davis, D. (1985). The longitudinal course of recurrent affective illness: Life chart data from research patients at the NIMH. *Acta Psychiatrica Scandinavica, 71*(Suppl), 1–34.

Rutter, M. (1998). Developmental catch-up, and deficit, following adoption after severe global early privation. English and Romanian Adoptees (ERA) study team. *Journal of Child Psychology and Psychiatry, 39*, 465–476.

Rutter, M., & Maughan, B. (1997). Psychosocial adversities in childhood and adult psychopathology. *Journal of Personality Disorders, 11*, 4–18.

Scott, J., & Tacchi, M. J. (2002). A pilot study of concordance therapy for individuals with bipolar disorders who are non-adherent with lithium prophylaxis. *Bipolar Disorders, 4*, 386–392.

Silva, A. J., Stevens, C. F., Tonegawa, S., & Wang, Y. (1992). Deficient hippocampal long-term potentiation in alpha-calcium-calmodulin kinase II mutant mice. *Science, 257*, 201–206.

Smith, M. A., Makino, S., Kvetnansky, R., & Post, R. M. (1995). Stress and glucocorticoids affect the expression of brain-derived neurotrophic factor and neurotrophin-3 mRNAs in the hippocampus. *Journal of Neuroscience, 15*, 1768–1777.

Stevens, C. F., Tonegawa, S., & Wang, Y. (1994). The role of calcium-calmodulin kinase II in three forms of synaptic plasticity. *Current Biology, 4*, 687–693.

Strakowski, S. M., DelBello, M. P., Sax, K. W., Zimmerman, M. E., Shear, P. K., Hawkins, J. M., et al. (1999). Brain magnetic resonance imagining of structural abnormalities in bipolar disorder. *Archives of General Psychiatry, 56*(3), 254–260.

Suppes, T., Baldessarini, R. J., Faedda, G. L., & Tohen, M. (1991). Risk of recurrence following discontinuation of lithium treatment in bipolar disorder. *Archives of General Psychiatry, 48*, 1082–1088.

Suppes, T., Leverich, G. S., Keck, P. E., Nolen, W. A., Denicoff, K. D., Altshuler, L. L., et al. (2001). The Stanley Foundation Bipolar Treatment Outcome Network. II. Demographics and illness characteristics of the first 261 patients. *Journal of Affective Disorders, 67*, 45–59.

Swann, A. C., Stokes, P. E., Casper, R., Secunda, S. K., Bowden, C. L., Berman, N., et al. (1992). Hypothalamic-pituitary-adrenocortical function in mixed and pure mania. *Acta Psychiatrica Scandinavia, 85*(4), 270–274.

Wei, H., Qin, Z., Senatorov, V. V., Wei, W., Wang, Y., Qian, Y., et al. (2001). Lithium suppresses excitotoxicity-induced striatal lesions in a rat model of Huntington's disease. *Neuroscience, 106*, 603–612.

Weiss, S. R., Clark, M., Rosen, J. B., Smith, M. A., & Post, R. M. (1995). Contingent tolerance to the anticonvulsant effects of carbamazepine: Relationship to loss of endogenous adaptive mechanisms. *Brain Research Brain Research Reviews., 20*, 305–325.

Weiss, S. R., & Post, R. M. (1994). Caveats in the use of the kindling model of affective disorders. *Toxicology and Industrial Health, 10*, 421–447.

Weiss, S. R., Post, R. M., Pert, A., Woodward, R., & Murman, D. (1989). Context-dependent cocaine sensitization: Differential effect of haloperidol on development versus expression. *Pharmacology, Biochemistry, and Behavior, 34*, 655–661.

Winsberg, M. E., Sachs, N., Tate, D. L., Adalsteinsson, E., Spielman, D., & Ketter, T. A. (2000). Decreased dorsolateral prefrontal N-acetyl aspartate in bipolar disorder. *Biological Psychiatry, 47*(6), 475–481.

Wozniak, J., Biederman, J., & Richards, J. A. (2001). Diagnostic and therapeutic dilemmas in the management of pediatric-onset bipolar disorder. *Journal of Clinical Psychiatry, 62*(Suppl 14), 10–15.

Xing, G. Q., Russell, S., Hough, C., O'Grady, J., Zhang, L., Yang, S., et al. (2002). Decreased prefrontal CaMKII α mRNA in bipolar illness. *NeuroReport, 13,* 501–505.

Yehuda, R. (1998). Psychoneuroendocrinology of post-traumatic stress disorder. *Psychiatric Clinics of North America, 21,* 359–379.

Yehuda, R. (2000). Biology of posttraumatic stress disorder. *Journal of Clinical Psychiatry, 61*(Suppl 7), 14–21.

Zhang, L. X., Levine, S., Dent, G., Zhan, Y., Xing, G., Okimoto, D., et al. (2002). Maternal deprivation increases cell death in the infant rat brain. *Developmental Brain Research, 133,* 1–11.

Zhang, L. X., Xing, G. Q., Levine, S., Post, R. M., & Smith, M. A. (1998). Effects of maternal deprivation on neurotrophic factors and apoptosis-related genes in rat pups. *Society for Neuroscience Abstracts, 24,* 451.

CHAPTER SEVEN

GENETICS AND PSYCHOPATHOLOGY: HOW FAR HAVE WE COME AND WHERE ARE WE GOING?

Joachim Hallmayer, M.D.

In 2001, the first draft of the complete sequence of the human genome was published (Lander et al., 2001; Venter et al., 2001), paving the way for the second wave of the genomics revolution: large-scale ribonucleic acid (RNA) assays and gene-expression-microarray studies, providing gene-expression data that complement gene-sequence data and help our understanding of the molecular basis of health and disease. Enormous efforts are under way to characterize the function of each individual gene. It is predicted by many researchers that the combination of genomics, proteomics, and multi-marker approach and single nucleotide polymorphisms will revolutionize the praxis of medicine.

The Promise of the Human Genome Project

The anticancer drug Herceptin has been described as a "glimpse of medicine's future" (Service, 2003). It is a highly specialized medicine intended only for a subgroup of women with breast cancer. The basis for the selection of patients for treatment is the status of the type I receptor tyrosine kinase HER-2 in breast carcinomas (Bartlett, Mallon, & Cooke, 2003). In the future, drugs targeted to disease-specific gene and protein defects that will require co-approval of diagnostic and therapeutic products by regulatory agencies (Ross & Ginsburg, 2003) will be the rule. The spectacular results published in the use of proteomic patterns diagnostics in a variety of cancers (reviewed in Wulfkuhle, Liotta, & Petricoin, 2003) support the notion that we are on the edge of a revolution in the field of molecular medicine.

From a therapeutic standpoint, the major impacts of this molecular revolution are envisaged to be

1. Therapy linked to molecular indicators of the disease
   a. Targeted treatment approach
   b. Identification of individuals susceptible to the disorder for preventative intervention
2. Pharmacogenetics, the study of variations in genes coding for proteins interacting with drugs, will allow prediction of side effects as well as the efficacy of a treatment on an individual basis
3. Gene therapy in a more narrow sense, meaning the direct transfer of genetic material
4. Development of animal models and a better understanding of the pathophysiology of a disorder

The following chapter will provide an overview of some of the approaches taken to achieve the first and third impacts. The impact of findings from molecular genetics on the development of animal models and our knowledge of pathophysiology is disease-specific and beyond the scope of this chapter.

Molecular Indicators and Psychopathology

The underlying basis for future drug developments is the discovery of disease-specific gene and protein defects, or gene expression patterns. For example, a primary mutation of an oncogene or a tumor suppressor gene results in a cancer phenotype by changing the expression patterns of thousands of genes. DNA and RNA microarrays allow us to determine the expression level of every gene in a given cell population (Polyak & Riggins, 2001). Comparing gene expression patterns of cancer cells and their normal counterparts is an extremely powerful tool for determining cancer- and tissue-specific gene expression patterns. It is this link between changes in gene expression, which can be rapidly screened and integrated in the therapeutic protocol, and the phenotype of a cancer cell, which promises to lead to the marriage of diagnostic and prognostic markers and therapeutic targets.

The central question, therefore, in the case of psychiatric disorders becomes whether or not we can pinpoint the genetic factors underlying human behavior in such a way that they can be useful as prognostic and diagnostic markers. For single gene disorders, progress has been rapid and striking advances have been made. Positional cloning has led to the discovery of about 1,200 genes associated with Mendelian diseases (Botstein & Risch, 2003) and it is to be expected that genes associated with the remaining disorders will be discovered in the near future. The model used for the discovery in these disorders is based on the assumption that the spread of the trait in families is synonymous with the transmission of a single molecular defect. Many of the genes found influence behavior and we are beginning to have a better understanding of how individual genes influence psychopathology. However, besides single gene disorders, there are well-defined genetic abnormalities that involve several genes and may tell us how to better understand gene-gene interactions. In order to get a better grasp of the complex relationship between genes and behavioral phenotype, it is helpful to look at some examples of disorders for which the underlying genes are known.

Types of Genetic Changes

The simplest form of a genetic change leading to a disorder is a substitution of one of the nucleotides for another in the DNA. This is the most common kind of change observed. Not all single base pair changes lead to a change of an amino acid in a protein, because several triplets correspond to the same amino acid. Another possible change is the insertion or deletion of one or more nucleotides, the consequences of which are much more drastic. Nucleotides are read successively and the insertion or deletion of one nucleotide leads to a misreading of the message from this point onward. Chromosomal aberrations involve the loss, addition, or displacement of a major part of the chromosome or a whole chromosome, and different types of chromosomal aberrations have been observed. A *deletion* is defined as a missing section of a chromosome. If a section is duplicated, it is defined as a *duplication. Inversion* designates a section of a chromosome that is rotated by 180 degrees. If a chromosome segment is transferred from one place to the other, it is called a *translocation.* Finally, the presence of an extra chromosome or the absence of a chromosome is referred to as *aneuploidy.* When one chromosome is lost, it is called a *monosomy* and when one is added, a *trisomy.*

Examples of Single Gene Disorders

Fragile X Syndrome. Fragile X syndrome is the most common inherited form of mental retardation, affecting about 1:4000 males and 1:8000 females worldwide (Turner, Webb, Wake, & Robinson, 1996). Mental retardation, macroorchidism, and connective tissue dysplasia with a long, narrow face are the characteristic features of the syndrome (Curry et al., 1997). Broad-developmental delay in the areas of language, motor, and cognitive abilities is common (Kau, Meyer, & Kaufmann, 2002). Besides these classical symptoms, many patients show a variety of cognitive, neurological, and behavioral problems, none of which are observed in all patients: seizures, social anxiety, stereotypy, short-term memory deficits, hypersensitivity to sensory stimuli, hyperactivity, attention deficits, and autistic-like symptoms (Hagerman, 2002). The cause of fragile X syndrome is expansions of a CGG repeat which is located in the 5'-untranslated region of the fragile X mental retardation gene 1 (FMR1) (Oberle et al., 1991; Vincent et al., 1991). In normal individuals, a stable repeat of five and fifty CGG trinucleotides is found. An intermediate increase in length of up to 200 such repeats occurs in some individuals. The mechanism for this increase is not known, but the consequence of these "premutations" is that they are highly instable and tend to expand in the next generations. An expansion to more than 200 repeats is considered to be a full mutation. Such full mutations cause over 95% of cases with fragile X syndrome. Women carrying a full mutation are generally less severely affected than males (Abrams et al., 1994). Until recently, such premutation carriers were thought to be asymptomatic. More detailed investigation, however, revealed a more complex picture. In males, essential tremor (Leehey et al., 2003) and a neurodegenerative syndrome, chiefly characterized by intention tremor, parkinsonism, and generalized brain atrophy deficits (Hagerman et al., 2001) have been reported. In females, premature ovarian failure has been associated with premutations (Sherman, 2000).

In recent years, the biochemical consequences of the triplet repeat expansion have been extensively studied (for review, see Todd & Malter, 2002; Hoogeveen, Willemsen, & Oostra, 2002). An increase-of-repeat length above 200 or greater leads to a hypermethylation of the FMR1 gene and histone deacetylation, the result of which is the absence of the FMR1 protein (Verheij et al., 1993). The silencing of FMR1 expression in the brain is thought to be responsible for the observed mental retardation. It has been suggested that FMR1 protein expression is a prognostic indicator in males with fragile X syndrome (Tassone et al., 1999). The FMR1 protein belongs to the class of RNA binding proteins and modulates the translation of proteins encoded by these RNA ligands (O'Donnell & Warren, 2002). Studies of FMR1 knockout mice strongly suggest that the FMR1 protein is involved in the regulation of multiple biological pathways (Miyashiro et al., 2003). Differences in the phenotype of patients with fragile X syndrome may be related to the variability of expression patterns of a whole range of mRNAs and their corresponding proteins (Grossman et al., 2003). The expressions of these proteins are likely to be influenced by genetic variations in the coding regions as well as possible environmental factors.

Rett Syndrome. Rett syndrome is characterized by normal development for the first months followed by developmental regression. In classical Rett syndrome, at five and forty-eight months head growth decelerates and previously acquired purposeful hand skills are lost. This is accompanied by the development of stereo-typic hand movements, loss of social engagement, appearance of poorly coordi-nated gait or trunk movements, and severely impaired receptive language with severe psychomotor retardation (DMS-IV). Classical Rett syndrome has been reported almost exclusively in females. Amir et al. (1999) reported mutations in the gene coding for the methyl-CpG-binding protein 2 (MeCP2) located on Xq28 in patients with Rett syndrome. The relationship between MeCP2 and Rett syndrome has been confirmed by numerous studies (Amir et al., 2000; Amano, Nomura, Segawa, & Yamakawa, 2000; Auranen et al., 2001; Bienvenu et al., 2000; Bourden et al., 2001; Buyse et al., 2000; Cheadle et al., 2000; Hoffbuhr et al., 2001; Huppke, Held, Hanefield, Engel, & Laccone, 2002; Nielsen et al., 2001; Obata et al., 2000; Vacca et al., 2001; Wan et al., 1999; Xiang et al., 2000). About 60–80% of patients with Rett syndrome carry a mutation in the MeCP2 gene. Since the seminal paper by Amir et al. (1999), mutations in the MeCP2 gene have been reported in a variety of disorders, including non-progressive encephalopa-thy (Imessaoudene et al., 2001), nonspecific mental retardation (Winnepenninckx, Errijgers, Hayez-Delatte, Reyniers, & Frank Kooy, 2002; Couvert et al., 2001; Orrico et al., 2000), atypical Rett syndrome (Inui et al., 2001), autism (Lam et al., 2000), and Angelman syndrome (Watson et al., 2001), as well as mildly affected females and normal carrier females (Villard et al., 2000; Wan et al., 1999).

Prader-Willi and Angelman Syndromes. Angelman syndrome and Prader-Willi syndrome are the most prominent examples for imprinting disorders. The genetic abnormality of Prader-Willi and Angelman syndromes (PWS and AS, respectively) are linked to the same region of chromosome 15q11-q13. Genetically, Prader-Willi syndrome is caused by the loss of the expression of normally active paternally in-herited genes in this region, whereas Angelman syndrome is the result of the loss of maternal expression of a single gene in this region, called UBE3A. (For review, see Vogels & Fryns, 2002; Nicholls & Knepper, 2001.) Most commonly in patients with Prader-Willi syndrome, a small interstitial deletion of the paternal chromosome is found. In patients with Angelman syndrome, in about 70% of cases the same region is deleted on the maternal chromosome. Despite the overlap of the disease-causing gene, the phenotypes of both syndromes are extremely different.

The characteristic clinical symptoms of Prader-Willi syndrome include hypotonia, developmental disability, dysmorphic facial features, hypothalamic dysfunction with short stature, obesity, small hands and feet, and hypogonadism. Severe temper tantrums, obsessive-compulsive mannerisms, and hyperphagia resulting in life-threatening obesity if left uncontrolled are part of the typical behavioral phenotype. In a population-based study of Prader Willi syndrome, out of twenty-five patients aged eighteen years or older, seven (28%) had severe affective disorder with psychotic features (Boer et al., 2002). Mild to moderate mental retardation is common with relative weaknesses in short-term memory and relative strengths on tasks that assess attention to visual detail, visual-motor coordination, perceptual planning, and spatial organization. In a study by Dykens (2002), patients with Prader-Willi syndrome were on par with normal peers on word searches and outperformed them on the jigsaw puzzles.

Clinically, the characteristics of AS (for review, see Clayton-Smith & Laan, 2003) include developmental delay, severe mental retardation with a lack of speech, dysmorphic facial features, hypopigmentation with fair hair and blue eyes, movement ataxia, hyperactivity, and seizures. Behaviorally, AS is associated with hyperactivity, aggressive behavior, and abnormal happiness with excessive inappropriate laughter. Hand flapping movements are common. AS children also have a preference to play with water and enjoy turning pages (Clayton-Smith, 1993). A large variation of symptoms in AS has been observed and not all children exhibit all the symptoms described.

Single Genes and Developmental Psychopathology. The phenotype representing closest a specific behavioral disorder is non-syndromal mental retardation. Syndromal types of mental retardation are characterized by external features, neurological signs, and/or metabolic anomalies (Tariverdian & Vogel, 2000). Over 800 disorders fall into this category. The non-syndromal types do not show such specific features and mental retardation is the only indicator. Non-syndromal mental retardation is recognized as a genetic disorder only if it is present in families. Since males outnumber females by about 25%, most of the genes are assumed to be located on the X-chromosome. It has been estimated that about 20–25% of the severe forms of mental retardation and 5–10% of the milder forms are genetic in origin. In recent years, numerous causative mutations have been found for both syndromal and non-syndromal mental retardation (Chiurazzi, Hamel, & Neri, 2001; Chelly & Mandel, 2001) and with the human genome sequence available, this process will speed up even further. More detailed studies of the phenotype-genotype relationship revealed, in many cases of non-syndromal mental retardation, milder clinical abnormalities and the disorder had to be reclassified as a syndromal form (Frints, Froyen, Marynen, & Fryns, 2002).

Fragile X syndrome is the prototype for the group of syndromal mental retardation. The fragile X mutation belongs to a group of mutations characterized by expansion of repeating triplets of nucleotides. Triplet repeat disorders are all conditions affecting the central nervous system. What they have in common is that the severity of the phenotypic expression and penetrance appears to be related to the extent of the triplet expansion. However, repeat length is only one of the factors. Males with the full mutation have been reported being normal (Smeets et al., 1995; De Vries et al., 1996) or being only minimally affected (McConkie-Rosell et al., 1993; Hagerman et al., 1994; Wang, Taylor, & Bridge, 1996). The causative link of expansion of an unstable (CGG)n repeat within the promoter region of the human FMR1, methylation, transcription silencing, loss of FMR protein, and development of the clinical features of fragile X syndrome can be influenced by a number of unknown factors. Tassone et al. (2001) showed that fragile X males with methylated full mutation alleles have significant levels of FMR1 messenger RNA and concluded that the absence of FMRP may be due to posttranscriptional events. As a consequence, any therapy that targets solely the reactivation of the gene itself and does not correct the defect in translation may be doomed to fail.

The genetics of Rett syndrome is very different from those of fragile X. The vast majority of the mutations found in the MECP2 gene occur de novo and 95% originate on the paternal chromosome (Girard et al., 2001; Trappe et al., 2001). As in fragile X, the relationship between phenotype and the type and location of mutation is modified by a number of unknown factors. In females, one of the contributing factors is X-inactivation. MeCP2 binds to methylated CpG dinucleotides throughout the genome and silences the transcription of downstream genes. Shahbazian, Antalffy, Armstrong, and Zoghbi (2002) studied the pattern of MeCP2 localization in the central nervous system in mice and humans during development and could show a correlation of MeCP2 expression and neuronal maturation. Their interpretation of the temporal pattern was that MeCP2 represses genes that are important during neuronal development but detrimental for mature neurons. If this hypothesis turns out to be correct, this would offer a unique opportunity for preventative interventions. The isolation and characterization of the proteins, which are affected by MeCP2, will be essential for the development of future therapeutic targets. The recent development of a mouse model with a truncating mutation similar to those found in some Rett patients will certainly facilitate future research (Shahbazian, Young, et al., 2002).

Disease-causing MeCP2 mutations are nucleotide substitutions, deletions, and duplications and have been found scattered all along the MeCP2 gene (Bourdon et al., 2001). The spectrum of phenotypes seems to be influenced by the location, the mutation type (truncation mutations are associated with a more severe phenotype [Cheadle et al., 2000; Huppke et al., 2002]) and modulated by the X inactivation pattern (Hoffbuhr et al., 2001; Weaving et al., 2003). The variability of the phenotype is the result of a complex interaction between these factors as well as environmental contributors.

Finally, Prader-Willi and Angelman syndromes are part of a large group of disorders that have been called "genomic" (Lupski, 1998) and originate from genomic rearrangements. In most cases they are the consequence of nonallelic homologous recombination between low-copy repeats or duplicons. The result is a change of genome organization and often loss or gain of genomic segments. The striking differences in the phenotype between Prader-Willi and Angelman syndromes are not due to differences in the genes involved, but to the parental origin of defect. The term *epigenetic* encompasses "changes in the genetic material that alter gene expression in a manner that is heritable during somatic cell division, but that is nonmutational" (Tycko & Ashkenas, 2000). The most widely studied epigenetic mechanism resulting in heritable inactivation of genes is DNA methylation (Robertson & Wolffe, 2000). Differential DNA methylation is also known as genomic imprinting, or the differential marking of maternally and paternally inherited alleles of genes during gametogenesis. On fertilization, this leads to differential expression during development. Expression is thus monoallelic, with one parental allele being expressed, the other silenced. It is estimated that about 0.1% of all genes is imprinted (Reik & Dean, 2001). Maternal and paternal contributions to the embryonic genome in mammals are not equivalent and both are required in order to complete normal embryogenesis (McGrath & Solter, 1984). Most of the forty imprinted genes identified in humans are expressed in the brain (Davies, Isles, & Wilkinson, 2001).

Recent experimental studies in the mouse have directly indicated an important role for imprinting in regulating brain development and behavior. The majority of paternally expressed genes enhance fetal growth, whereas maternally expressed genes suppress growth (Reik & Dean, 2001). Keverne, Fundele, Narasimha, Barton, and Surani (1996) showed in chimeric mice that duplicated maternal and paternal genomes contribute unevenly to the formation of the nervous system. Cells that have duplicated paternal genomes contributed more to the cortex and striatum, whereas cells containing a duplicated maternal genome contribute more to the hypothalamus. Based on these studies, the authors suggested that genomic imprinting might be responsible for the evolutionarily recent and rapid non-linear expansion of the brain, especially the cortex.

The above-mentioned examples demonstrate that the correlation between genotype and phenotype is often incomplete, with only a subset of all mutations reliably predicting the phenotype. Intrafamilial phenotypic variability has been reported in many Mendelian diseases. The phenotypic effect of a defect in a single gene is modified by unique genetic, epigenetic, and environmental contributions, and single-gene disorders in the true sense are rare and "simple Mendelian traits are, in fact, complex traits" (Dippel & McCabe, 2000). This variability of the phenotype will be a challenge for the development of treatments linked to molecular indicators. The emerging phenotype is a complex interaction of which only a small number of players is known. A better understanding of the molecular and cellular basis by which modifier genes exert their influence and how they interact with environmental factors will be crucial for development of interventions in human diseases (Nadeau, 2001).

Genetically Complex Disorders

The most common medical disorders with a genetic component are not inherited in a Mendelian fashion, but are influenced by multiple genetic and environmental factors and are called *complex traits*. Coronary heart disease, asthma, diabetes, and most of the psychiatric disorders such as schizophrenia and bipolar disorder belong to this group. Traits influenced by genetic factors can be conceptualized on a continuum between classical single gene (Mendelian) and complex inheritance (Badano & Katsanis, 2002). The position of any given disorder on this continuum depends on the strength of the effect, the number of genes involved, and the extent of environmental influences. It is generally assumed that the majority of behavioral traits are on the complex end of the continuum, that is, oligogenic and polygenic inheritance and strong environmental influences, and are therefore among the most difficult to study using molecular techniques.

Twin and family studies suggest a substantial genetic component for many child psychiatric disorders (for review, see Rutter, MacDonald, et al., 1990; Rutter, Silberg, O'Connor, & Simonoff, 1999) including Tourette's syndrome, ADHD, affective disorders, obsessive-compulsive disorder, dyslexia, conduct disturbance, and juvenile delinquency. Of all child psychiatric disorders, autism is the most strongly genetically influenced and the search for autism-susceptibility genes has recently received a lot of attention.

Genetics of Autism. Autism is the core type of pervasive developmental disorder (PDD), and is diagnosed with reference to a triad of symptoms: (a) language impairments, (b) social interaction deficits, and (c) presence of stereotyped and repetitive behaviors. The onset of autism occurs within the first three years of life. About 70% of children with autism test within the mentally retarded range. Estimates of prevalence rates for autism and autism-spectrum disorders vary substantially between different studies (for overview, see Fombonne, 1999). More recent studies reported autism to occur in about 10 to 20 per 10,000 children (Chakrabarti & Fombonne, 2001; Gillberg & Wing, 1999) compared with earlier reports, which estimated the prevalence to be about 4 to 5 per 10,000 (Fombonne, 1999). This has led to speculation that the incidence of autism is increasing.

The descriptive epidemiology of autism is still in its infancy. Croen, Grether, and Selvin (2002) carried out, by far, the largest study to date on the association between selected infant and maternal characteristics and autism risk. Consistent with previous reports, they observed a dramatic male excess (4:1) for autism overall (Gillberg & Wing, 1999) and a decreasing male-to-female ratio with decreasing IQ (Nordin & Gillberg, 1996; Sponheim & Skjeldal, 1998; Lord & Schopler, 1985; Lord, Schopler, & Revicki, 1982; Tsai & Stewart, 1983; Wing, 1981; Steffenburg & Gillberg, 1986). Risk increased as maternal age and maternal education increased. These results are in line with previous studies showing an increased risk for autism with increasing maternal age (Finegan & Quarrington, 1979; Treffert, 1970; Hoshino, Kumashiro, Yashima, Tachibana, & Watanabe, 1982; O'Moore, 1972; Gillberg, 1980). The risk increase for multiple births compared to singletons (RRa = 1.7, 95% CI 1.4–2.0) in the study by Croen et al. (2002) was substantially less than the one reported by Greenberg, Hodge, Sowinski, and Nicoll (2001). The high proportion of twins found in affected-sibling-pair studies by Greenberg et al. (2001) and Betancur, Leboyer, and Gillberg (2002) can be adequately explained by the high ratio of concordance rates in monozygotic (MZ) twins versus siblings and the distribution of family size in the population studied (Hallmayer et al., 2002).

Although autism was once considered to have little, if any, genetic contribution to its etiology, the last decade of family and twin studies has provided support for a strong genetic basis. Estimates of the prevalence of autism in the siblings of probands with autism in studies utilizing direct assessment have been between 1 to 6% (August, Stewart, & Tsai, 1981; Baird & August, 1985; Bolton et al., 1994; Gillberg, Gillberg, & Steffenburg, 1992; Ritvo et al., 1989; Szatmari et al., 1993; Tsai, Stewart, & August, 1981). These figures may underestimate the true recurrence risk, as some parents of children with a diagnosis of autism may decide to have no more children or have just one more child (Jones & Szatmari, 1988; Gillberg et al., 1992). Szatmari, Jones, Zwaigenbaum, and MacLean (1998) calculated the combined sibling risk of the family studies published so far to be 2.2%. Even though this recurrence rate in siblings is modest, it is considerably above the general population prevalence.

There are three general population-based twin studies of autism, all of which show a much higher MZ than dizygotic (DZ) concordance. A study carried out in Scandinavia (Steffenburg et al., 1989) is the only one with nearly complete ascertainment of twins. The authors reported twin concordance rates of 90% in MZ twins and of 0% in DZ twins. The most recent study (Bailey et al., 1995) is an extension of an earlier study by Folstein and Rutter (1977) in which concordance rates were 73% in MZ twins, compared with 0% in DZ twins. Taken together, these studies argue for a substantial MZ to DZ concordance ratio. Besides these population-based studies, a study by Ritvo, Freeman, Mason-Brothers, Mo, and Ritvo (1985) found 95% MZ concordance and 24% DZ concordance; this study was based on a sample drawn from an advertisement, which may have led to inflated concordance rates. Based on family and twin studies, the heritability has been estimated to be greater than 90% with environmental factors playing a modifying role (Bailey, Phillips, & Rutter, 1996). This makes autism the most strongly genetically influenced of all multifactorial child psychiatric disorders (Rutter, Silberg, O'Connor, & Simonoff, 1999).

A number of studies have attempted to determine the mode of inheritance of autism. Jorde et al. (1991) performed complex segregation analysis on 185 nuclear families from Utah, which included 209 affected subjects. All single major locus models were rejected, while a model specifying only the sibling correlation was not. The polygenic model predicted a significantly lower likelihood, with heritability estimated at 100%. Pickles et al. (1995), applying latent class analysis using data from the family history study of Bolton et al. (1994) and the twin study of Bailey et al. (1995), supported a multiple-locus model of inheritance with three loci giving the best fit.

The Broader Phenotype. Although autism is defined in terms of a triad of behavioral characteristics, there are many children who have autistic-like features that are not severe or wide-ranging enough to merit a diagnosis of autism. The label "Asperger's syndrome" has been coined for high-functioning cases in which the child's language milestones are normal but there is social impairment and stereotyped behaviors and interests. "Pervasive developmental disorders—not otherwise specified" (PDD–NOS) is another label given to children who meet fewer than the six diagnostic criteria needed for a diagnosis of autistic disorder. The term "autism spectrum disorder" (ASD) is frequently used to include those with autism, Asperger's syndrome, and PDD–NOS.

In families that have more than one affected child, the patterns of specific characteristics, symptoms, and/or behaviors are often dissimilar and high intrafamilial variability is common. However, exceptions in the areas of communication and repetitive behaviors have been reported. In a study of a sample of thirty-seven multiple-incidence autism families, Spiker et al. (1994) found the strongest similarities among siblings for ritualistic behavioral symptoms. MacLean et al. (1999) investigated forty-six sibling pairs who had PDD. There was no familial aggregation of PDD subtype, whereas measures of verbal/nonverbal status, nonverbal IQ, and adaptive behaviors in socialization and communication showed a moderate degree of familial resemblance. In the British twin study (LeCouteur et al., 1996), increased similarity for nonverbal IQ was reported within MZ twins. Using a substantially larger sample of 212 multiplex families (457 affected individuals) Silverman et al. (2002) replicated these findings. Repetitive behaviors, nonverbal communication, and verbal/nonverbal status showed all greater similarity within siblings. A follow-up study by Spiker, Lotspeich, Dimiceli, Myers, and

Risch (2002) investigated the behavioral phenotypic variability and similarity of 351 siblings with autism in 171 multiplex families using cluster analysis and correlations. No evidence of discrete behaviorally defined subgroups of affected individuals was detected. Rather, the clusters could be characterized along a single, heritable, continuous severity dimension.

Many first-degree relatives of autistic probands have deficits in one or two of the three symptom areas, which are qualitatively similar but milder than seen in autistic disorder. (For example, see Bolton et al., 1994.) For example, social deficits below the threshold for the full diagnosis of autism aggregate significantly in family members of autistic probands (Wolff, Narayan, & Moyes, 1988; Bailey et al., 1995; Piven, Palmer, Jacobi, Childress, & Arndt, 1997). This suggests that what is inherited is broader than autism as it is currently defined, and studies have identified a broader autism phenotype (BAP) in 15–45% of family members of people with autism (Bailey, Palferman, Heavey, & Le Couteur, 1998). The BAP is highly heritable: 92% of MZ pairs in a recent twin study were concordant for a broader spectrum of related cognitive or social abnormalities compared with only 10% of DZ pairs (Le Couteur et al., 1996). Most studies find that the rate of the BAP is higher in male than female relatives of people with autism (Bailey et al., 1998; Baron-Cohen, Wheelwright, Skinner, Martin, & Clubley, 2001; Piven et al., 1997). Moreover, the symptoms of adults with the broader phenotype echo the triad of symptoms seen in autism (Folstein & Rutter, 1988; Landa et al., 1992). Thus, in order to identify the broader autism phenotype in twins, we will need to examine traits that are commonly present in children with autistic disorder.

However, the BAP goes beyond milder subclinical behaviors. Cognitive differences have been described in relatives of autistic probands. Some studies indicate that siblings of children with autism have lower scores on intelligence tests and other cognitive measures than siblings of typically developing children and siblings of children with other forms of delay (August et al., 1981; Leboyer, Plumet, Goldblum, Perez-diaz, & Marchaland, 1995; Minton, Campbell, Green, Jennings, & Sammit, 1982).

The Search for Autism Susceptibility Genes. Attempts to find the gene or genes conferring a higher risk for developing autism have not resulted in unambiguous identification of a specific gene location on a specific chromosome to date (Auranen et al., 2000; Barrett et al., 1999; Bass et al., 1998; Buxbaum et al., 2001; Hallmayer et al., 1996; IMGSAC, 1998, 2001; Liu et al., 2001; Phillipe et al., 1999; Risch et al., 1999; Shao et al., 2002). Interpretations of results from linkage and association studies have been largely debated. Comparable studies that looked for genes in other psychiatric disorders such as schizophrenia and bipolar disorder have led to similar debates.

Epidemiological studies have consistently demonstrated a higher prevalence of autism in boys; male gender is the strongest known risk factor for autism. The most straightforward explanation for the observed sex differences would be a gene located on the X chromosome causing autism. However, results from linkage studies using affected sibling pairs with autism (Hallmayer et al., 1996; Risch et al., 1999; IMGSAC, 1998, 2001; Buxbaum et al., 2001; Liu et al., 2001; Schutz et al., 2002) are not compatible with a gene of moderate to strong effect on the X chromosome. Smaller gene effects cannot be excluded, nor can the possibility of several genes located on the X chromosome contributing to the increased risk of males to develop autism.

Buxbaum et al. (2001) stratified affected families according to the proband's language difficulties in their linkage study and found that most of the evidence for linkage on chromosome 2q was from families with significant language delay. Similar results were obtained by Bradford et al. (2001) in regards to their positive findings on chromosome 7 and 13. Alarcon, Cantor, Liu, Gilliam, and Geschwind (2002) performed nonparametric linkage analysis for three traits derived from the Autism Diagnostic Interview (ADI): "age at first word," "age at first phrase," and a composite measure of "repetitive and stereotyped behavior." The strongest quantitative trait locus (QTL) evidence was found on chromosome 7q for age at first word.

Complex Disorders—How Many Genes? Two extreme possibilities have been juxtaposed in regard to the way alleles influence common disease (Chakrabarti, 1999). The first model, which is favored by most researchers, presupposes that selection against mutations in complex disorders is so weak that it can be ignored. Based on this assumption, the genetic factors underlying common diseases will be alleles that are themselves quite common in the population (Lander et al., 1996; Chakrabarti, 1999). This model is commonly referred to as the "common allele common disease hypothesis."

The prototype for the common allele common disease hypothesis is the Apolipoprotein E4 (ApoE4) allele. The frequency of the ApoE4 allele in different human populations ranges between 0.1 and 0.4. The ApoE4 allele has been implicated in multiple disorders, such as coronary heart disease, Alzheimer's disease, and sleep apnea (Marin et al., 1998; Kadotani et al., 2001; Strittmatter et al., 1993). Despite the large number of linkage and association studies carried out, however, we have few examples of frequent alleles that underlie common disorders (Goldstein & Chikhi, 2002).

The second model (Pritchard, 2001) predicts, that complex diseases might be due to loci with a high overall mutation rate and that the total frequency of susceptibility mutations may be quite high with extensive allelic heterogeneity at many of these loci (Pritchard, 2001). Most variants in the coding region of genes are relatively infrequent (Glatt & Freimer, 2001) and the allele frequencies of functional polymorphisms are low. The frequency of the mutations in the population will be influenced by the disease risk associated and how much reproduction will be reduced. Early onset disorders will therefore be further skewed towards the lower frequency range (Botstein & Risch, 2003).

In the case of autism, Risch et al. (1999) analyzed the excess sharing in their affected sibling pairs across the entire genome and concluded that it is most compatible with a model specifying a large number of loci (perhaps ≥ 15). However, taking into account the skewed distribution of the recurrence risk ratio (λ_s), Pritchard (2001) suggested a model of 100 loci with the expected λ_s values for the top 15 loci in the range of 1.04 to 3.89. Early onset disorders such as autism may have alleles more skewed towards the lower frequency range (Botstein & Risch, 2003) and a model of a large number of rare alleles may be more realistic.

Implications for Therapy. One likely scenario is that child psychiatric disorders are influenced by a large number of mutations in a host of different genes. As pointed out by a number of geneticists (Badano & Kastanis, 2002; Dipple & McCabe, 2000; Scriver & Waters, 1999), the border between monogenic and multifactorial is far from clear-cut and many single-gene disorders have much in common with so-called genetically complex disorders. Genes from complex disorders will overlap with genes associated with classical Mendelian disorders such as Rett syndrome. Mutations associated with a severe outcome are the first to be identified. As demonstrated by Pritchard (2001), loci with high mutation rates will contribute disproportionately to the genetic variance. Those loci with the strongest effect (λ_s) will have high mutation rates. Such loci will show a close relationship between the genotype and the phenotype; however, allelic heterogeneity may restrict molecular indicators to a relatively small subgroup of patients.

Despite many attempts, linkage studies have been largely negative for psychiatric disorders. It is very unlikely that the clinical phenotype can be explained by mutations involving only a small number of genes. A combination of mutations in different genes predisposes an individual to develop a certain disorder. Several predisposing mutations contribute to the risk increase. Each individual carries a certain risk and the distribution of the liability can best be described as a normal distribution. A range of factors modifies the liability and, above a certain threshold value, the manifest clinical disorder becomes apparent (multifactorial threshold model, Gottesman & Shields, 1967).

As the example of autism indicates, what is inherited is not a predisposition toward a specific clinical syndrome as such, but the genetic liability encompasses a range of behavioral and cognitive characteristics. This is not surprising, because the biological effects of these genes are likely to involve multiple intermediate steps, thus resulting in a very complex relationship between genes and phenotype in autism. The pathway from gene to behavior must include a range of processes at neuronal and neural circuitry levels. From a genetic standpoint, this would suggest that different aspects of the autism phenotype are influenced by different loci. This raises the possibility that a specific gene may be associated with a neurocognitive deficit that does not inevitably lead to the full autistic syndrome, but substantially increases the risk of autism, especially if it occurs in association with other genetic or environmental risk factors.

Terms such as *level II indicators, endophenotype,* or *correlated phenotypes* are currently used to describe this intermediate level (for review, see Gottesman & Gould, 2003). Endophenotypes have been described for a number of psychiatric disorders including schizophrenia, mood disorders, autism, and attention-deficit disorder. The genetic investigation of these endophenotypes will allow us to reconstruct the genetic background of psychiatric disorders. For studying complex genetic disorders, a phenotype based on overt clinical psychiatric symptoms may well be suboptimal.

The implications of the models discussed for therapy are manifold. Only in a subset of patients will there be a clear relationship between the genotype and the resulting clinical phenotype. This may be an obstacle to the development of genetic therapies. However, comprehensive analysis of gene expression may uncover common pathways underlying more specific clinical outcomes. The discovery of such pathways in the case of child psychiatric disorders will have to take into account the specific cell-type as well as developmental expression patterns in the brain. Progress will depend strongly on the development of appropriate animal models.

For the majority of susceptibility genes, the predictive value will be small and a molecular test will provide only an estimate of the increase in risk. Future therapeutic approaches will depend strongly on the discovery of co-factors. Certain combinations of susceptibility alleles may provide one way forward. As important will be to study gene environment interactions more closely. For example, it has long been known that children who are maltreated are more likely to develop conduct disorder and antisocial personality disorder. In a recent study of maltreated children, Caspi et al. (2002) reported that a functional polymorphism in the gene encoding the neurotransmitter-metabolizing enzyme monoamine oxidase A (MAOA) was associated with reduced violent behavior in boys. How the experiences of maltreatment interact with the MAOA genotype and then have an impact on violent behavior is unknown. What is clear, however, is, that the relationship between genes and environment is dynamic and genetic effects change during the course of development. The genetic effect of antisocial behavior is both modified by gender (Jacobson, Prescott, & Kendler, 2002) and age (Lyons et al., 1995). Developmental timing has a significant impact upon the nature of the genetic effects observed.

Therapy should not be restricted to the disorder as such, but should take into account the neurocognitive impairments underlying the disorder. The endophenotype of autism includes problems recognizing facial affect. Similarly, sustained attention deficits have been shown to be markers of genetic susceptibility to develop schizophrenia (for review, see Chen & Faraone, 2000). Attention deficits have been shown to be related to chronic social difficulties in patients with schizophrenia. Combining molecular markers for higher susceptibility to develop a disorder with a treatment approach targeted to the neurocognitive impairments may positively affect long-term outcome.

Pharmacogenetics

The inter-individual variability in the response to pharmacological drugs and the occurrence of adverse drug effects is a major clinical problem in the treatment of patients diagnosed with a mental disorder. The consequence of poor response or the development of side effects is often noncompliance. The aim of pharmacogenetics research is to better understand the effects of genetic variations on drug response. Pharmacogenetics is not a new science, but goes back to the 1950s (Weber, 2001). In post-genome terminology, pharmacogenetics is often referred to as *pharmacogenomics*, which emphasizes the now available technology enabling researchers to study whole genomes or proteins (Basile, Masellis, Potkin, & Kennedy, 2002).

Prime candidates for pharmacogenetic studies are variations in enzymes controlling drug absorption and elimination. Polymorphisms associated with higher drug concentrations or their metabolites in the blood are prime candidates for being related to toxic reactions. Among the best-studied drug-metabolizing enzymes is cytochrome P450 CYP2D6, which has been implicated in the metabolism of about 100 drugs (for review, see Bertilsson, Dahl, Dalén, & Al-Shurbaji, 2002; Staddon, Arranz, Mancama, Mata, & Kerwin, 2002). Enzyme activity is highly variable and more than seventy allelic variants have been described. CYP2D6 activity ranges from complete deficiency to ultrarapid metabolizers (Sachse, Brockmöller, Bauer, & Roots, 1997). Deficiency is inherited as an autosomal recessive trait. An increased risk of developing drug induced adverse reactions in poor metabolizers, such as tardive dyskinisia, has been reported in a number of studies (Jaanson et al., 2002; Andreassen MacEwan, Gulbrandsen, McCreadie, & Steen, 1997; Armstrong, Daly, Blennerhasset, Ferrier, & Idle,1997; Arthur, Dahl, Siwers, & Sjoqvist, 1995; Kapitany et al., 1998). Nikoloff et al. (2002) found the genetic effect to be restricted to males, whereas Lam et al. (2001) to females. Negative studies have also been published (Mihara et al., 2002; Ohmori et al., 1999).

Polymorphisms in other cytochrome P450 enzymes have also been studied. Basile et al. (2000) found a positive association of a genetic variation in the P450 1A2 CYP1A2 gene and the development of tardive dyskinesia in patients treated with typical antipsychotics. Besides enzymes controlling the absorption and metabolism of drugs, variation of genes coding for proteins influencing neurotransmission have been widely studied. Several polymorphisms within serotonergic and dopaminergic pathways have been shown to influence the response to clozapine (for review, see Mancama, Arranz, & Kerwin, 2002). Variations in the 5HT(2A) receptor gene may influence individual responses to risperidone (Lane et al., 2002).

Winsberg and Comings (1999) tested for a possible relationship between the alleles of the D2 (DRD2), D4 (DRD4), and dopamine transporter (DAT1) genes with the behavioral outcome of methylphenidate therapy. Poor outcome after methylphenidate therapy was significantly associated with homozygosity of the 10-repeat allele at the dopamine transporter gene locus. Roman et al. (2002) replicated these finding in a recent study.

Our current understanding of the role of genetic variations in drug response is limited. Studies so far have been concentrated on single genes and a restricted number of variations. Gene array technology allows characterization of gene expression of thousands of genes in parallel, profiles that are induced or repressed by drugs. Similarly, high-throughput methods for single nucleotide polymorphism (SNP) genotyping enable screening of thousands of genes simultaneously. The lack of any comparable high-throughput phenotype measures is a major obstacle. The analysis of such large datasets are still in its infancy and it will take some time for pharmacogenomics to have an impact on the general clinical day-to-day activities.

Gene Therapy

The aim of *gene therapy* is to transfer genes into a cell to correct the defect involved in the disease. The basic principle is to introduce DNA into a specific cell population by a carrying vector. DNA does not pass the cell membranes by itself and genetic material must be transported into the cell. Because of the blood-brain barrier, this poses special problems for brain cells. There are also many different cell types in the brain. Expression of a molecule in the wrong cells can produce grave consequences, and delivery of the gene or genes to specific cell types in the brain is essential (Benitez & Segovia, 2003). Despite recent reports that new neocortical neurons throughout adulthood are added (Gould, Reeves, Graziano, & Gross, 1999), the vast majority of neurons in the brain are not undergoing cell division and therefore some of the most effective vectors, such as modified retroviruses, cannot be employed. To overcome these problems, researchers have explored a number of approaches (for review, see Sapolsky, 2003). For example, Tuszynski et al. (2002) are using an ex vivo nerve growth factor (NGF) gene delivery (autologous fibroblasts genetically modified to secrete human NGF) in a clinical trial for Alzheimer's disease. Other promising delivery systems are DNA incorporated into liposomes and vectors based on neurotropic viruses. Viral delivery systems have the advantage of providing higher transfection efficiency, whereas non-viral delivery systems are less toxic and less immunogenic. There may well be no perfect single vector for the delivery of DNA to the nervous system, and it is likely that several modes of gene delivery will be necessary for successful gene therapies of the CNS (Costantini, Bakowska, Breakefield, & Isacson, 2000).

Clinical research in gene therapy is in its early stage (Lyngstadaas, 2002). Cancer is by far the most studied group of disorders (about 70% of studies), followed by monogenic, infectious, and cardiovascular diseases. The vast majority of studies are on safety, applicability, and toxicity. The clinical effect of gene therapy in phase I and II trials has been limited. Certain forms of cardiovascular diseases and cancers are promising candidates for larger phase III trials. The result of the first phase III, multicenter, randomized, open-label, controlled trial in the treatment of 248 patients with newly diagnosed, previously untreated glioblastoma multiforme (GBM) was disappointing (Rainov, 2000). No differences in median survival could be found between the groups. One major problem was the extremely poor levels of transduction efficiency in this trial (Wang, Tai, Kasara, & Chen, 2003).

The most dramatic success of gene therapy so far has been reported for severe combined immunodeficiency (SCID) (Hacein-Bey-Abina, Fischer, & Cavazzana-Calvo, 2001; Hacein-Bey-Abina et al., 2002). Out of nine patients with typical SCID-X1 diagnosed within the first year of life, eight patients were doing well and living in a normal environment. However, during the treatment, two patients developed a T-cell lymphoma and are undergoing chemotherapy (French Gene Therapy Group, 2003; Gansbacher, 2003). The most likely cause of the cancer is the retroviral vector used in the study to transfer the corrected gene into the cells. In order to ensure the safety of future trials, it will be essential to systematically study the cancerogenic potential of the vectors used.

To summarize, gene therapy is still an experimental procedure. The potential of serious side effects limits clinical trials to diseases with a predictable severe outcome. In light of this and our lack of understanding of gene regulation (including tissue-specific control of gene expression), gene therapy in the brain will remain a domain of basic research for quite some time.

The second wave of the genomic revolution will undoubtedly have a major impact on treatment in psychiatry. Although it may be a long way until direct gene therapy becomes a realistic option for psychiatric disorders, the development of pharmacogenomics will soon lead to the ability to predict patients' response to treatment and vulnerability to adverse effects. Advances in molecular genetics will also change the way we conceptualize disorders and, as a result, targeted therapies will be developed. The use of animal research will be essential in discovering pathways to specific genetic mutations, which will guide the development of new drugs. Most important, however, we need to better understand how genes influence behavior in humans. Studies need to take into account gene-gene and gene-environment interactions and new models must be developed. Only by integrating approaches from different disciplines can psychiatry take full advantage of the rapid progress in molecular medicine.

References

Abrams, M. T., Reiss, A. L., Freund, L. S., Baumgardner, T. L., Chase, G. A., & Denckla, M. B. (1994). Molecular-neurobehavioral associations in females with the fragile X full mutation. *American Journal of Medical Genetics, 51,* 317–327.

Alarcon, M., Cantor, R. M., Liu, J., Gilliam, T. C., the Autism Genetic Resource Exchange Consortium, & Geschwind, D. H. (2002). Evidence for a language quantitative trait locus on chromosome 7q in multiplex autism families. *American Journal of Human Genetics, 70,* 60–71.

Amano, K., Nomura, Y., Segawa, M., & Yamakawa, K. (2000). Mutational analysis of the MECP2 gene in Japanese patients with Rett syndrome. *Journal of Human Genetics, 45,* 231–236.

Amir, R. E., Van den Veyver, I. B., Schultz, R., Malicki, D. M., Tran, C. Q., Dahle, E. J., et al. (2000). Influence of mutation type and X chromosome inactivation on Rett syndrome phenotypes. *Annals of Neurology, 47,* 670–679.

Amir, R. E., Van den Veyver, I. B., Wan, M., Tran, C. Q., Francke, U., & Zoghbi, H. Y. (1999). Rett syndrome is caused by mutations in X-linked MECP2, encoding methyl-CpG-binding protein 2. *Nature Genetics, 23,* 185–188.

Andreassen, O. A., MacEwan, T., Gulbrandsen, A. K., McCreadie, R. G., & Steen, V. M. (1997). Non-functional CYP2D6 alleles and risk for neuroleptic-induced movement disorders in schizophrenic patients. *Psychopharmacology (Berlin), 131,* 174–179.

Armstrong, M., Daly, A. K., Blennerhassett, R., Ferrier, N., & Idle, J. R. (1997). Antipsychotic drug-induced movement disorders in schizophrenics in relation to CYP2D6 genotype. *British Journal of Psychiatry, 170,* 23–26.

Arthur, H., Dahl, M. L., Siwers, B., & Sjoqvist, F. (1995). Polymorphic drug metabolism in schizophrenic patients with tardive dyskinesia. *Journal of Clinical Psychopharmacology, 15,* 211–216.

August, G. J., Stewart, M. A., & Tsai, L. (1981). The incidence of cognitive disabilities in the siblings of autistic children. *British Journal of Psychiatry, 138,* 416–422.

Auranen, M., Nieminen, T., Majuri, S., Vanhala, R., Peltonen, L., & Järvelä, I. (2000). Analysis of autism susceptibility gene loci on chromosomes 1p, 4p, 6q, 7q, 13q, 15q, 16p, 17q, 19q and 22q in Finnish multiplex families. *Molecular Psychiatry, 5,* 320–322.

Auranen, M., Vanhala, R., Vosman, M., Levander, M., Varilo, T., Hietala, M., et al. (2001). MECP2 gene analysis in classical Rett syndrome and in patients with Rett-like features. *Neurology, 56,* 611–617.

Badano, J. L., & Katsanis, N. (2002). Beyond Mendel: An evolving view of human genetic disease transmission. *Nature Reviews Genetics, 3,* 779–789.

Bailey, A., Le Couteur, A., Gottesman, I., Bolton, P., Simonoff, E., Yuzsa, E., et al. (1995). Autism as a strongly genetic disorder: Evidence from a British twin study. *Psychological Medicine, 25,* 63–77.

Bailey, A., Palferman, S., Heavey, L., & Le Couteur, A. (1998). Autism: The phenotype in relatives. *Journal of Autism and Developmental Disorders, 28,* 369–392.

Bailey, A., Phillips, W., & Rutter, M. (1996). Autism: Towards an integration of clinical, genetic, neuropsychological, and neurobiological perspectives. *Journal of Child Psychology and Psychiatry, 37,* 89–126.

Baird, T. D., & August, G. J. (1985). Familial heterogeneity in infantile autism. *Journal of Autism and Developmental Disorders, 15,* 315–321.

Baron-Cohen, S., Wheelwright, S., Skinner, R., Martin, J., & Clubley, E. (2001). The autism-spectrum quotient (AQ): Evidence from Asperger syndrome/high-functioning autism, males and females, scientists and mathematicians. *Journal of Autism and Developmental Disorders, 31,* 5–17.

Barrett, B., Landa, R., Beck, J. C., Braun, T. A., Casavant, T. L., Childress, D., et al. (1999). An autosomal genomic screen for autism. Collaborative linkage study of autism. *American Journal of Medical Genetics, 88,* 609–615.

Bartlett, J., Mallon, E., & Cooke, T. (2003). The clinical evaluation of HER-2 status: Which test to use? *Journal of Pathology, 199,* 411–417.

Basile, V. S., Masellis, M., Potkin, S. G., & Kennedy, J. L. (2002). Pharmacogenomics in schizophrenia: The quest for individualized therapy. *Human Molecular Genetics, 11,* 2517–2530.

Basile V. S., Özdemir, V., Masellis, M., Walker, M. L., Meltzer, H. Y., Lieberman, J. A., et al. (2000). A functional polymorphism of the cytochrome P450 1A2 (CYP1A2) gene: Association with tardive dyskinesia in schizophrenia. *Molecular Psychiatry, 5,* 410–417.

Bass, M. P., Wolpert, C. M., Menold, M. M., Donnelly, S. L., Ravan, S. A., Hauser, E. R., et al. (1998). Genomic screen for autistic disorder. *American Journal of Human Genetics, 63*(Suppl), A281.

Benitez, J. A., & Segovia, J. (2003). Gene therapy targeting in the central nervous system. *Current Gene Therapy, 3,* 127–145.

Bertilsson, L., Dahl, M. L., Dalén, P., & Al-Shurbaji, A. (2002). Molecular genetics of CYP2D6: Clinical relevance with focus on psychotropic drugs. *British Journal of Clinical Pharmacology, 53,* 111–122.

Betancur, C., Leboyer, M., & Gillberg, C. (2002). Increased rate of twins among affected sibling pairs with autism. *American Journal of Human Genetics, 70,* 1381–1383.

Bienvenu, T., Carrié, A., de Roux, N., Vinet, M. C., Jonveaux, P., Couvert, P., et al. (2000). MECP2 mutations account for most cases of typical forms of Rett syndrome. *Human Molecular Genetics, 9,* 1377–1384.

Boer, H., Holland, A., Whittington, J., Butler, J., Webb, T., & Clarke, D. (2002). Psychotic illness in people with Prader Willi syndrome due to chromosome 15 maternal uniparental disomy. *Lancet, 359,* 135–136.

Bolton, P., Macdonald, H., Pickles, A., Rios, P., Goode, S., Crowson, M., et al. (1994). A case-control family history study of autism. *Journal of Child Psychology and Psychiatry, 53,* 877–900.

Botstein, D., & Risch, N. (2003). Discovering genotypes underlying human phenotypes: Past successes for mendelian disease, future approaches for complex disease. *Nature Genetics, 33*(Suppl), 228–237.

Bourdon, V., Philippe, C., Labrune, O., Amsallem, D., Arnould, C., & Jonveaux, P. (2001). A detailed analysis of the MECP2 gene: Prevalence of recurrent mutations and gross DNA rearrangements in Rett syndrome patients. *Human Genetics, 108,* 43–50.

Bradford, Y., Haines, J., Hutcheson, H., Gardiner, M., Braun, T., Sheffield, V., et al. (2001). Incorporating language phenotypes strengthens evidence of linkage to autism. *American Journal of Medical Genetics, 105,* 539–547.

Buxbaum, J. D., Silverman, J. M., Smith, C. J., Kilifarski, M., Reichert, J., Hollander, E., et al. (2001). Evidence for a susceptibility gene for autism on chromosome 2 and for genetic heterogeneity. *American Journal of Human Genetics, 68,* 1514–1520.

Buyse, I. M., Fang, P., Hoon, K. T., Amir, R. E., Zoghbi, H. Y., & Roa, B. B. (2000). Diagnostic testing for Rett syndrome by DHPLC and direct sequencing analysis of the MECP2 gene: Identification of several novel mutations and polymorphisms. *American Journal of Human Genetics, 67,* 1428–1436.

Caspi, A., McClay, J., Moffitt, T. E., Mill, J., Martin, J., Craig, I. W., et al. (2002). Role of genotype in the cycle of violence in maltreated children. *Science, 297,* 851–854.

Chakrabarti, S., & Fombonne, E. (2001). Pervasive developmental disorders in preschool children. *JAMA: The Journal of the American Medical Association, 285,* 3093–3099.

Chakrabarti, A. (1999). Population genetics—making sense out of sequence. *Nature Genetics, 21*(Suppl), 56–60.

Cheadle, J. P., Gill, H., Fleming, N., Maynard, J., Kerr, A., Leonard, H., et al. (2000). Long-read sequence analysis of the MECP2 gene in Rett syndrome patients: Correlation of disease severity with mutation type and location. *Human Molecular Genetics, 9,* 1119–1129.

Chelly, J., & Mandel, J. L. (2001). Monogenic causes of X-linked mental retardation. *Nature Reviews. Genetics, 2,* 669–680.

Chen, W. J., & Faraone, S. V. (2000). Sustained attention deficits as markers of genetic susceptibility to schizophrenia. *American Journal of Medical Genetics, 97,* 52–57.

Chiurazzi, P., Hamel, B. C., & Neri, G. (2001). XLMR genes: Update 2000. *European Journal of Human Genetics, 9,* 71–81.

Clayton-Smith, J. (1993). Clinical research on Angelman syndrome in the United Kingdom: Observations on 82 affected individuals. *American Journal of Medical Genetics, 46,* 12–15.

Clayton-Smith, J., & Laan, L. (2003). Angelman syndrome: A review of the clinical and genetic aspects. *Journal of Medical Genetics, 40,* 87–95.

Costantini, L. C., Bakowska, J. C., Breakefield, X. O., & Isacson, O. (2000). Gene therapy in the CNS. *Gene Therapy, 7,* 93–109.

Couvert, P., Bienvenu, T., Aquaviva, C., Poirier, K., Moraine, C., Gendrot, C., et al. (2001). MECP2 is highly mutated in X-linked mental retardation. *Human Molecular Genetics, 10,* 941–946.

Croen, L. A., Grether, J. K., & Selvin, S. (2002). Descriptive epidemiology of autism in a California population: Who is at risk? *Journal of Autism and Developmental Disorders, 32,* 217–224.

Curry, C. J., Stevenson, R. E., Aughton, D., Byrne, J., Carey, J. C., Cassidy, S., et al. (1997). Evaluation of mental retardation: Recommendations of a Consensus Conference: American College of Medical Genetics. *American Journal of Medical Genetics, 72,* 468–477.

Davies W., Isles, A. R., & Wilkinson, L. S. (2001). Imprinted genes and mental dysfunction. *Annals of Medicine, 33,* 428–436.

De Vries, B. B., Jansen, C. C., Duits, A. A., Verheij, C., Willemsen, R., van Hemel, J. O., et al. (1996). Variable FMR1 gene methylation of large expansions leads to variable phenotype in three males from one fragile X family. *Journal of Medical Genetics, 33,* 1007–1010.

Dipple, K. M., & McCabe, E. R. (2000). Phenotypes of patients with "simple" Mendelian disorders are complex traits: Thresholds, modifiers, and systems dynamics. *American Journal of Human Genetics, 66,* 1729–1735.

Dykens, E. M. (2002). Are jigsaw puzzle skills 'spared' in persons with Prader-Willi syndrome? *Journal of Child Psychology and Psychiatry, and Allied Disciplines, 43,* 343–352.

Finegan, J. A., & Quarrington B. (1979). Pre-, peri-, and neonatal factors and infantile autism. *Journal of Child Psychology and Psychiatry, and Allied Disciplines, 20,* 119–128.

Folstein, S. E., & Rutter, M. L. (1977). Infantile autism: A genetic study of 21 twin pairs. *Journal of Child Psychology and Psychiatry, and Allied Disciplines, 18,* 297–321.

Folstein, S. E., & Rutter, M. L. (1988). Autism: Familial aggregation and genetic implications. *Journal of Autism and Developmental Disorders, 18,* 3–30.

Fombonne, E. (1999). The epidemiology of autism: A review. *Psychological Medicine, 29,* 769–786.

French Gene Therapy Group. (2003). French gene therapy group reports on the adverse event in a clinical trial of gene therapy for X-linked severe combined immune deficiency (X-SCID). Position statement from the European Society of Gene Therapy. *The Journal of Gene Medicine, 5,* 82–84.

Frints, S. G., Froyen, G., Marynen, P., & Fryns, J. P. (2002). X-linked mental retardation: Vanishing boundaries between non-specific (MRX) and syndromic (MRXS) forms. *Clinical Genetics, 62,* 423–432.

Gansbacher, B. (2003). Report of a second serious adverse event in a clinical trial of gene therapy for X-linked severe combined immune deficiency (X-SCID). Position of the European Society of Gene Therapy (ESGT). *The Journal of Gene Medicine, 5,* 261–262.

Gillberg, C. (1980). Maternal age and infantile autism. *Journal of Autism and Developmental Disorders, 10,* 293–297.

Gillberg, C., Gillberg, I. C., & Steffenburg, S. (1992). Siblings and parents of children with autism: A controlled population-based study. *Developmental Medicine and Child Neurology, 34,* 389–398.

Gillberg, C., & Wing, L. (1999). Autism: Not an extremely rare disorder. *Acta Psychiatrica Scandinavica, 99,* 399–406.

Girard, M., Couvert, P., Carrie, A., Tardieu, M., Chelly, J., Beldjord, C., et al. (2001). Parental origin of de novo MECP2 mutations in Rett syndrome. *European Journal of Human Genetics, 9,* 231–236.

Glatt, C. E., & Freimer, N. B. (2002). Association analysis of candidate genes for neuropsychiatric disease: The perpetual campaign. *Trends in Genetics, 18,* 307–312.

Goldstein, D. B., & Chikhi, L. (2002). Human migrations and population structure: What we know and why it matters. *Annual Review of Genomics and Human Genetics, 3,* 129–152.

Gottesman, I. I., & Gould, T. D. (2003). The endophenotype concept in psychiatry: Etymology and strategic intentions. *American Journal of Psychiatry, 160,* 636–645.

Gottesman, I. I., & Shields. (1967). A polygenic theory of schizophrenia. *Proceedings of the National Academy of Sciences USA, 58,* 199–205.

Gould, E., Reeves, A. J., Graziano, M. S., & Gross, C. G. (1999). Neurogenesis in the neocortex of adult primates. *Science, 286,* 548–552.

Greenberg, D. A., Hodge, S. E., Sowinski, J., & Nicoll, D. (2001). Excess of twins among affected sibling pairs with autism: Implications for the etiology of autism. *American Journal of Human Genetics, 69,* 1062–1067.

Grossman, A. W., Churchill, J. D., McKinney, B. C., Kodish, I. M., Otte, S. L., & Greenough, W. T. (2003). Experience effects on brain development: Possible contributions to psychopathology. *Journal of Child Psychology and Psychiatry, and Allied Disciplines, 44,* 33–63.

Hacein-Bey-Abina, S., Fischer, A., & Cavazzana-Calvo, M. (2001). Gene therapy of X-linked severe combined immunodeficiency. *International Journal of Hematology, 76,* 295–298.

Hacein-Bey-Abina, S., Le Deist, F., Carlier, F., Bouneaud, C., Hue, C., De Villartay, J. P., et al. (2002). Sustained correction of X-linked severe combined immunodeficiency by ex vivo gene therapy. *New England Journal of Medicine, 346,* 1185–1193.

Hagerman, R. J. (2002). The physical and behavioral phenotype. In Hagerman, R. J. (Ed.), *Fragile X syndrome: Diagnosis, treatment, and research* (3rd ed., pp. 3–109). Baltimore: Johns Hopkins University Press.

Hagerman, R. J., Hull, C. E., Safanda, J. F., Carpenter, I., Staley, L. W., & O'Connor, R. A., et al. (1994). High functioning fragile X males: Demonstration of an unmethylated fully expanded FMR-1 mutation associated with protein expression. *American Journal of Medical Genetics, 51,* 298–308.

Hagerman, R. J., Leehey, M., Heinrichs, W., Tassone, F., Wilson, R., Hills, J., et al. (2001). Intention tremor, parkinsonism, and generalized brain atrophy in male carriers of fragile X. *Neurology, 57,* 127–130.

Hallmayer, J., Glasson, E. J., Bower, C., Petterson, B., Croen, L., Grether, J., et al. (2002). On the twin risk in autism. *American Journal of Human Genetics, 71,* 941–946.

Hallmayer J., Hebert, J. M., Spiker, D., Lotspeich, L., McMahon, W. M., Petersen, P. B., et al. (1996). Autism and the X chromosome. Multipoint sib-pair analysis. *Archives of General Psychiatry, 53,* 985–989.

Hoffbuhr, K., Devaney, J. M., LaFleur, B., Sirianni, N., Scacheri, C., Giron, J., et al. (2001). MeCP2 mutations in children with and without the phenotype of Rett syndrome. *Neurology, 56,* 1486–1495.

Hoogeveen, A. T., Willemsen, R., & Oostra, B. A. (2002). Fragile X syndrome, the Fragile X related proteins, and animal models. *Microscopy Research and Technique, 57,* 148–155.

Hoshino, Y., Kumashiro, H., Yashima, Y., Tachibana, R., & Watanabe, M. (1982). The epidemiological study of autism in Fukushima-ken. *Folia Psychiatrica et Neurologica Japonica, 36,* 115–124.

Huppke, P., Held, M., Hanefeld, F., Engel, W., & Laccone, F. (2002). Influence of mutation type and location on phenotype in 123 patients with Rett syndrome. *Neuropediatrics, 33,* 63–68.

Imessaoudene, B., Bonnefont, J. P., Royer, G., Cormier-Daire, V., Lyonnet, S., Lyon, G., et al. (2001). MECP2 mutation in non-fatal, non-progressive encephalopathy in a male. *Journal of Medical Genetics, 38,* 171–174.

International Molecular Genetic Study of Autism Consortium (IMGSAC) (1998). A full genome screen for autism with evidence for linkage to a region on chromosome 7q. *Human Molecular Genetics, 7,* 571–578.

International Molecular Genetic Study of Autism Consortium (IMGSAC) (2001). A genomewide screen for autism: Strong evidence for linkage to chromosomes 2q, 7q, and 16p. *American Journal of Human Genetics, 69,* 570–581.

Inui, K., Akagi, M., Ono, J., Tsukamoto, H., Shimono, K., Mano, T., et al. (2001). Mutational analysis of MECP2 in Japanese patients with atypical Rett syndrome. *Brain & Development, 23,* 212–215.

Jaanson, P., Marandi, T., Kiivet, R. A., Vasar V., Vään S., Svensson, J. O., et al. (2002). Maintenance therapy with zuclopenthixol decanoate: Associations between plasma concentrations, neurological side effects and CYP2D6 genotype. *Psychopharmacology (Berlin), 162,* 67–73.

Jacobson, K. C., Prescott, C. A., & Kendler, K. S. (2002). Sex differences in the genetic and environmental influences on the development of antisocial behavior. *Development and Psychopathology, 14,* 395–416.

Jones, M. B., & Szatmari, P. (1988). Stoppage rules and genetic studies of autism. *Journal of Autism and Developmental Disorders, 18,* 31–40.

Jorde, L. B., Hasstedt, S. J., Ritvo, E. R., Mason-Brothers, A., Freeman, B. J., Pingree, C., et al. (1991). Complex segregation analysis of autism. *American Journal of Human Genetics, 49,* 932–938.

Kadotani H., Kadotani, T., Young, T., Peppard, P. E., Finn, L., Colrain, I. M., et al. (2001). Association between apolipoprotein E epsilon4 and sleep-disordered breathing in adults. *JAMA: The Journal of the American Medical Association, 285,* 2888–2890.

Kapitany, T., Meszaros, K., Lenzinger, E., Schindler, S. D., Barnas, C., Fuchs, K., et al. (1998). Genetic polymorphisms for drug metabolism (CYP2D6) and tardive dyskinesia in schizophrenia. *Schizophrenia Research, 32,* 101–106.

Kau, A. S., Meyer, W. A., & Kaufmann, W. E. (2002). Early development in males with Fragile X syndrome: A review of the literature. *Microscopy Research and Technique, 57,* 174–178.

Keverne, E. B., Fundele, R., Narasimha, M., Barton, S. C., & Surani, M. A. (1996). Genomic imprinting and the differential roles of parental genomes in brain development. *Developmental Brain Research, 92,* 91–100.

Lam, C. W., Yeung, W. L., Ko, C. H., Poon, P.M.K., Tong, S.-F., Chan, K.-Y., et al. (2000). Spectrum of mutations in the MeCP2 gene in patients with infantile autism and Rett syndrome. *Journal of Medical Genetics, 37,* E41.

Lam, L. C., Garcia-Barcelo, M. M., Ungvari, G. S., Tang, W. K., Lam, V. K., Kwong, S. L., et al. (2001). Cytochrome P450 2D6 genotyping and association with tardive dyskinesia in Chinese schizophrenic patients. *Pharmacopsychiatry, 34,* 238–241.

Landa, R., Piven, J., Wzorek, M. M., Gayle, J. O., Chase, G. A., & Folstein, S. E. (1992). Social language use in parents of autistic individuals. *Psychological Medicine, 22,* 245–254.

Lander, E. S., Linton, L. M., Birren, B., Nusbaum, C., Zody, M. C., Baldwin, J., et al. (2001). International Human Genome Sequencing Consortium. Initial sequencing and analysis of the human genome. *Nature, 409,* 860–921.

Lane, H. Y., Chang, Y. C., Chiu, C. C., Chen, M. L., Hsieh, M. H., & Chang, W. H. (2002). Association of risperidone treatment response with a polymorphism in the 5HT(2A) receptor gene. *American Journal of Psychiatry, 159,* 1593–1595.

Leboyer, M., Plumet, M. H., Goldblum, M. C., Perez-diaz, F., & Marchaland, C. (1995). Verbal versus visuospatial abilities in relatives of autistic females. *Developmental Neuropsychology, 11,* 139–155.

Le Couteur, A., Bailey, A., Goode, S., Pickles, A., Robertson, S., Gottesman, I., et al. (1996). A broader phenotype of autism: The clinical spectrum in twins. *Journal of Child Psychology and Psychiatry, and Allied Disciplines, 37,* 785–801.

Leehey, M. A., Munhoz, R. P., Lang, A. E., Brunberg, J. A., Grigsby, J., Greco, C., et al. (2003). The fragile X premutation presenting as essential tremor. *Archives of Neurology, 60,* 117–121.

Liu, J., Nyholt, D. R., Magnussen, P., Parano, E., Pavone, P., Geschwind, D., et al. (2001). The Autism Genetic Resource Exchange Consortium. A genomewide screen for autism susceptibility loci. *American Journal of Human Genetics, 69,* 327–340.

Lord, C., & Schopler, E. (1985). Differences in sex ratios in autism as a function of measured intelligence. *Journal of Autism and Developmental Disorders, 15,* 185–293.

Lord, C., Schopler, E., & Revicki, D. (1982). Sex differences in autism. *Journal of Autism and Developmental Disorders, 12*, 317–330.

Lupski, J. R. (1998). Genomic disorders: Structural features of the genome can lead to DNA rearrangements and human disease traits. *Trends in Genetics, 14*, 417–422.

Lyngstadaas, A. (2002). Status and potential of gene therapy in clinical medicine. Assessment of an emerging health technology through systematic survey of clinical gene therapy protocols and published results. *International Journal of Technology Assessment in Health Care, 18*, 645–674.

Lyons, M. J., True, W. R., Eisen, S. A., Goldberg, J., Meyer, J. M., Faraone, S. V., et al. (1995). Differential heritability of adult and juvenile antisocial traits. *Archives of General Psychiatry, 52*, 906–915.

MacLean, J. E., Szatmari, P., Jones, M. B., Bryson, S. E., Mahoney, W. J., Bartolucci, G., et al. (1999). Familial factors influence level of functioning in pervasive developmental disorder. *Journal of the American Academy of Child and Adolescent Psychiatry, 38*, 746–753.

Mancama, D., Arranz, M. J., & Kerwin, R. W. (2002). Genetic predictors of therapeutic response to clozapine: Current status of research. *CNS Drugs, 16*, 317–324.

Marin, D. B., Breuer, B., Marin, M. L., Silverman, J., Schmeidler, J., Greenberg, D., et al. (1998). The relationship between apolipoprotein E, dementia, and vascular illness. *Atherosclerosis, 140*, 173–180.

McConkie-Rosell, A., Lachiewicz, A. M., Spiridigliozzi, G. A., Tarleton, J., Schoenwald, S., Phelan, M. C., et al. (1993). Evidence that methylation of the FMR-I locus is responsible for variable phenotypic expression of the fragile X syndrome. *American Journal of Human Genetics, 53*, 800–809.

McGrath, J., & Solter, D. (1984). Completion of mouse embryogenesis requires both the maternal and paternal genomes. *Cell, 37*, 179–183.

Mihara, K., Kondo, T., Higuchi, H., Takahashi, H., Yoshida, K., Shimizu, T., et al. (2002). Tardive dystonia and genetic polymorphisms of cytochrome P4502D6 and dopamine D2 and D3 receptors: A preliminary finding. *American Journal of Medical Genetics, 114*, 693–695.

Minton, J., Campbell, M., Green, W. H., Jennings, S., & Samit, C. (1982). Cognitive assessment of siblings of autistic children. *Journal of the American Academy of Child Psychiatry, 21*, 256–261.

Miyashiro, K. Y., Beckel-Mitchener, A., Purk, T. P., Becker, K. G., Barret, T., Liu, L., et al. (2003). RNA cargoes associating with FMRP reveal deficits in cellular functioning in Fmr1 null mice. *Neuron, 37*, 417–431.

Nadeau, J. H. (2001). Modifier genes in mice and humans. *Nature Reviews. Genetics*, 165–174.

Nicholls, R. D., & Knepper, J. L. (2001). Genome organization, function, and imprinting in Prader-Willi and Angelman syndromes. *Annual Review of Genomics and Human Genetics, 2*, 153–175.

Nielsen, J. B., Henriksen, K. F., Hansen, C., Silahtaroglu, A., Schwartz, M., & Tommerup, N. (2001). MECP2 mutations in Danish patients with Rett syndrome: High frequency of mutations but no consistent correlations with clinical severity or with the X chromosome inactivation pattern. *European Journal of Human Genetics, 9*, 178–184.

Nikoloff, D., Shim, J. C., Fairchild, M., Patten, N., Fijal, B. A., Koch, W. H., et al. (2002). Association between CYP2D6 genotype and tardive dyskinesia in Korean schizophrenics. *The Pharmacogenomics Journal, 2*, 400–407.

Nordin, V., & Gillberg, C. (1996). Autism spectrum disorders in children with physical or mental disability or both. I: Clinical and epidemiological aspects. *Developmental Medicine and Child Neurology, 38*, 297–313.

Obata, K., Matsuishi, T., Yamashita, Y., Fukuda, T., Kuwajima, K., Horiuchi, I., et al. (2000). Mutation analysis of the methyl-CpG binding protein 2 gene (MECP2) in patients with Rett syndrome. *Journal of Medical Genetics, 37,* 608–610.

Oberle, I., Rousseau, F., Heitz, D., Kretz, C., Devys, D., Hanauer, A., et al. (1991). Instability of a 550-base pair DNA segment and abnormal methylation in fragile X syndrome. *Science, 252,* 1097–1102.

O'Donnell, W. T., & Warren, S. T. (2002). A decade of molecular studies of fragile X syndrome. *Annual Review of Neuroscience, 25,* 315–338.

Ohmori, O., Kojima, H., Shinkai, T., Terao, T., Suzuki, T., & Abe, K. (1999). Genetic association analysis between CYP2D6 *2 allele and tardive dyskinesia in schizophrenic patients. *Psychiatry Research, 87,* 239–244.

O'Moore, M. (1972). A study of the aetiology of autism from a study of birth and family characteristics. *Journal of the Irish Medical Association, 65,* 114–120.

Orrico, A., Lam, C., Galli, L., Dotti, M. T., Hayek, G., Tong, S. F., et al. (2000). MECP2 mutation in male patients with non-specific X-linked mental retardation. *FEBS Letters, 481,* 285–288.

Philippe, A., Martinez, M., Guilloud-Bataille, M., Gillberg, C., Råstam, M., Sponheim, E., et al. (1999). Genome-wide scan for autism susceptibility genes. Paris Autism Research International Sibpair Study. *Human Molecular Genetics, 8,* 805–812.

Pickles, A., Bolton, P., Macdonald, H., Bailey, A., Le Couteur, A., Sim, C. H., et al. (1995). Latent-class analysis of recurrence risks for complex phenotypes with selection and measurement error: A twin and family history study of autism. *American Journal of Human Genetics, 57,* 717–726.

Piven, J., Palmer, P., Jacobi, D., Childress, D., & Arndt, S. (1997). Broader autism phenotype: Evidence from a family history study of multiple-incidence autism families. *American Journal of Psychiatry, 154,* 185–190.

Polyak, K., & Riggins, G. J. (2001). Gene discovery using the serial analysis of gene expression technique: Implications for cancer research. *Journal of Clinical Oncology, 19,* 2948–2958.

Pritchard, J. K. (2001). Are rare variants responsible for susceptibility to complex diseases? *American Journal of Human Genetics, 69,* 124–137.

Rainov, N. G. (2000). A phase III clinical evaluation of herpes simplex virus type 1 thymidine kinase and ganciclovir gene therapy as an adjuvant to surgical resection and radiation in adults with previously untreated glioblastoma multiforme. *Human Gene Therapy, 11,* 2389–2401.

Reik, W., & Dean, W. (2001). DNA methylation and mammalian epigenetics. *Electrophoresis, 22,* 2838–2843.

Risch, N., Spiker, D., Lotspeich, L., Nouri, N., Hinds, D., Hallmayer, J., et al. (1999). A genomic screen of autism: Evidence for a multilocus etiology. *American Journal of Human Genetics, 65,* 493–507.

Ritvo, E. R., Freeman, B. J., Mason-Brothers, A., Mo, A., & Ritvo, A. M. (1985). Concordance for the syndrome of autism in 40 pairs of afflicted twins. *American Journal of Psychiatry, 142,* 74–77.

Ritvo, E. R., Jorde, L. B., Mason-Brothers, A., Freeman, B. J., Pingree, C., Jones, M. B., et al. (1989). The UCLA-University of Utah epidemiologic survey of autism: Recurrence risk estimates and genetic counseling. *American Journal of Psychiatry, 146,* 1032–1036.

Robertson, K. D., & Wolffe, A. P. (2000). DNA methylation in health and disease. *Nature Reviews. Genetics, 1,* 11–19.

Roman, T., Szobot, C., Martins, S., Biederman, J., Rohde, L. A., & Hutz, M. H. (2002). Dopamine transporter gene and response to methylphenidate in attention-deficit/hyperactivity disorder. *Pharmacogenetics, 12,* 497–499.

Ross, J. S., & Ginsburg, G. S. (2003). The integration of molecular diagnostics with therapeutics. Implications for drug development and pathology practice. *American Journal of Clinical Pathology, 119,* 26–36.

Rutter, M., MacDonald, H., Le Couteur, A., Harrington, R., Bolton, P., & Bailey, A. (1990). Genetic factors in child psychiatric disorders—II. Empirical findings. *Journal of Child Psychology and Psychiatry, 31,* 39–83.

Rutter, M., Silberg, J., O'Connor, T., & Simonoff, E. (1999). Genetics and child psychiatry: II Empirical research findings. *Journal of Child Psychology and Psychiatry, 40,* 19–55.

Sachse, C., Brockmöller, J., Bauer, S., & Roots, I. (1997). Cytochrome P450 2D6 variants in a Caucasian population: Allele frequencies and phenotypic consequences. *American Journal of Human Genetics, 60,* 284–295.

Sapolsky, R. M. (2003). Gene therapy for psychiatric disorders. *American Journal of Psychiatry, 160,* 208–220.

Schutz, C. K., Polley, D., Robinson, P. D., Chalifoux, M., Macciardi, F., White, B. N., et al. (2002). Autism and the X chromosome: No linkage to microsatellite loci detected using the affected sibling pair method. *American Journal of Medical Genetics, 109,* 36–41.

Scriver, C. R., & Waters, P. J. (1999). Monogenic traits are not simple: Lessons from phenylketonuria. *Trends in Genetics, 15,* 267–272.

Service, R. F. (2003). Genetics and medicine: Recruiting genes, proteins for a revolution in diagnostics. *Science, 300,* 236–239.

Shahbazian, M. D., Antalffy, B., Armstrong, D. L., & Zoghbi, H. Y. (2002). Insight into Rett syndrome: MeCP2 levels display tissue- and cell-specific differences and correlate with neuronal maturation. *Human Molecular Genetics, 11,* 115–124.

Shahbazian, M. D., Young, J., Yuva-Paylor, L., Spencer, C., Antalffy, B., Noebels, J., et al. (2002). Mice with truncated MeCP2 recapitulate many Rett syndrome features and display hyperacetylation of histone H3. *Neuron, 35,* 243–254.

Shao, Y., Wolpert, C. M., Raiford, K. L., Menold, M. M., Donnelly, S. L., Ravan, S. A., et al. (2002). Genomic screen and follow-up analysis for autistic disorder. *American Journal of Medical Genetics, 114,* 99–105.

Sherman, S. L. (2000). Premature ovarian failure in the fragile X syndrome. *American Journal of Medical Genetics, 97,* 189–194.

Silverman, J. M., Smith, C. J., Schmeidler, J., Hollander, E., Lawlor, B. A., Fitzgerald, M., et al. (2002). Symptom domains in autism and related conditions: Evidence for familiality. *American Journal of Medical Genetics, 114,* 64–73.

Smeets, H. J., Smits, A. P., Verheij, C. E., Theelen, J. P., Willemsen, R., van de Burgt, I., et al. (1995). Normal phenotype in two brothers with a full FMR1 mutation. *Human Molecular Genetics, 4,* 2103–2108.

Spiker, D., Lotspeich, L., Kraemer, H. C., Hallmayer, J., McMahon, W., Petersen, P. B., et al. (1994). Genetics of autism: Characteristics of affected and unaffected children from 37 multiplex families. *American Journal of Medical Genetics, 54,* 27–35.

Spiker, D., Lotspeich, L. J., Dimiceli, S., Myers, R. M., & Risch, N. (2002). Behavioral phenotypic variation in autism multiplex families: Evidence for a continuous severity gradient. *American Journal of Medical Genetics, 114,* 129–136.

Sponheim, E., & Skjeldal, O. (1998). Autism and related disorders: Epidemiological findings in a Norwegian study using ICD-10 diagnostic criteria. *Journal of Autism and Developmental Disorders, 28,* 217–227.

Staddon, S., Arranz, M. J., Mancama, D., Mata, I., & Kerwin, R. W. (2002). Clinical applications of pharmacogenetics in psychiatry. *Psychopharmacology (Berlin), 162,* 18–23.

Steffenburg, S., & Gillberg, C. (1986). Autism and autistic-like conditions in Swedish rural and urban areas: A population study. *British Journal of Psychiatry, 149,* 81–87.

Steffenburg S., Gillberg, C., Hellgren, L., Andersson, L., Gillberg, I. C., Jakobsson, G., et al. (1989). A twin study of autism in Denmark, Finland, Iceland, Norway and Sweden. *Journal of Child Psychology and Psychiatry, and Allied Disciplines, 30,* 405–416.

Strittmatter, W. J., Saunders, A. M., Schmechel, D., Pericak-Vance, M., Enghild, J., Salvesen, G. S., et al. (1993). Apolipoprotein E: High-avidity binding to β-amyloid and increased frequency of type 4 allele in late-onset familial Alzheimer disease. *Proceedings of the National Academy of Sciences of the United States of America, 90,* 1977–1981.

Szatmari, P., Jones, M. B., Tuff, L., Bartolucci, G., Fisman, S., & Mahoney, W. (1993). Lack of cognitive impairment in first-degree relatives of children with pervasive developmental disorders. *Journal of the American Academy of Child and Adolescent Psychiatry, 32,* 1264–1273.

Szatmari, P., Jones, M. B., Zwaigenbaum, L., & MacLean, J. W. (1998). Genetics of autism: Overview and new directions. *Journal of Autism and Developmental Disorders, 28,* 351–368.

Tariverdian, G., & Vogel, F. (2000). Some problems in the genetics of X-linked mental retardation. *Cytogenetics and Cell Genetics, 91,* 278–284.

Tassone, F., Hagerman, R. J., Ikle, D. N., Dyer, P. N., Lampe, M., Willemsen, R., et al. (1999). FMRP expression as a potential prognostic indicator in fragile X syndrome. *American Journal of Medical Genetics, 84,* 250–261.

Todd, P. K., & Malter, J. S. (2002). Fragile X mental retardation protein in plasticity and disease. *Journal of Neuroscience Research, 70,* 623–630.

Trappe, R., Laccone, F., Cobilanschi, J., Meins, M., Huppke, P., Hanefeld, F., et al. (2001). MECP2 mutations in sporadic cases of Rett syndrome are almost exclusively of paternal origin. *American Journal of Human Genetics, 68,* 1093–1101.

Treffert, D. A. (1970). Epidemiology of infantile autism. *Archives of General Psychiatry, 22,* 431–438.

Tsai, L., Stewart, M. A., & August, G. (1981). Implication of sex differences in the familial transmission of infantile autism. *Journal of Autism and Developmental Disorders, 11,* 165–173.

Tsai, L. Y., & Stewart, M. A. (1983). Etiological implication of maternal age and birth order in infantile autism. *Journal of Autism and Developmental Disorders, 13,* 57–65.

Turner, G., Webb, T., Wake, S., & Robinson, H. (1996). Prevalence of fragile X syndrome. *American Journal of Medical Genetics, 64,* 196–197.

Tuszynski, M. H., Thal, L., U. H-S., Pay, M. M., Blesch, A., Conner, J., et al. (2002). Nerve growth factor gene therapy for Alzheimer's disease. *Journal of Molecular Neuroscience, 19,* 207–208.

Tycko, B., & Ashkenas, J. (2000). Epigenetics and its role in disease. *The Journal of Clinical Investigation, 105,* 245–246.

Vacca, M., Filippini, F., Budillon, A., Rossi, V., Mercadante, G., Manzati, E., et al. (2001). Mutation analysis of the MECP2 gene in British and Italian Rett syndrome females. *Journal of Molecular Medicine, 78,* 648–655.

Venter, J. C., Adams, M. D., Myers, E. W., Li, P. W., Mural, R. J., Sutton, G. G., et al. (2001). The sequence of the human genome. *Science, 291,* 1304–1351.

Verheij, C., Bakker, C. E., de Graaff, E., Keulemans, J., Willemsen, R., Verkerk, A. J., et al. (1993). Characterization and localization of the FMR-1 gene product associated with fragile X syndrome. *Nature, 363,* 722–724.

Villard, L., Kpebe, A., Cardoso, C., Chelly, P. J., Tardieu, P. M., & Fontes, M. (2000). Two affected boys in a Rett syndrome family: Clinical and molecular findings. *Neurology, 55,* 1188–1193.

Vincent, A., Heitz, D., Petit, C., Kretz, C., Oberle, I., & Mandel J. L. (1991). Abnormal pattern detected in fragile-X patients by pulsed-field gel electrophoresis. *Nature, 349,* 624–626.

Vogels, A., & Fryns, J. P. (2002). The Prader-Willi syndrome and the Angelman syndrome. *Genetic Counseling (Geneva, Switzerland), 13,* 385–396.

Wan, M., Lee, S. S., Zhang, X., Houwink-Manville, I., Song, H. R., Amir, R. E., et al. (1999). Rett syndrome and beyond: Recurrent spontaneous and familial MECP2 mutations at CpG hotspots. *American Journal of Human Genetics, 65,* 1520–1529.

Wang, W. J., Tai, C. K., Kasahara, N., & Chen, T. C. (2003). Highly efficient and tumor-restricted gene transfer to malignant gliomas by replication-competent retroviral vectors. *Human Gene Therapy, 14,* 117–127.

Wang, Z., Taylor, A. K., & Bridge, J. A. (1996). FMR1 fully expanded mutation with minimal methylation in a high functioning fragile X male. *Journal of Medical Genetics, 33,* 376–378.

Watson, P., Black, G., Ramsden, S., Barrow, M., Super, M., Kerr, B., et al. (2001). Angelman syndrome phenotype associated with mutations in MECP2, a gene encoding a methyl CpG binding protein. *Journal of Medical Genetics, 38,* 224–228.

Weaving, L. S., Williamson, S. L., Bennetts, B., Davis, M., Ellaway, C. J., Leonard, H., et al. (2003). Effects of MECP2 mutation type, location and X-inactivation in modulating Rett syndrome phenotype. *American Journal of Medical Genetics, 118A,* 103–114.

Weber, W. W. (2001). The legacy of pharmacogenetics and potential applications. *Mutation Research, 479,* 1–18.

Wing, L. (1981). Sex ratios in early childhood autism and related conditions. *Psychiatry Research, 5,* 129–137.

Winnepenninckx, B., Errijgers, V., Hayez-Delatte, F., Reyniers, E., & Frank Kooy, R. (2002). Identification of a family with nonspecific mental retardation (MRX79) with the A140V mutation in the MECP2 gene: Is there a need for routine screening? *Human Mutation, 20,* 249–252.

Winsberg, B. G., & Comings, D. E. (1999). Association of the dopamine transporter gene (DAT1) with poor methylphenidate response. *Journal of the American Academy of Child and Adolescent Psychiatry, 38,* 1474–1477.

Wolff, S., Narayan, S., & Moyes, B. (1988). Personality characteristics of parents of autistic children: A controlled study. *Journal of Child Psychology and Psychiatry, and Allied Disciplines, 29,* 143–153.

Wulfkuhle, J. D., Liotta, L. A., & Petricoin, E. F. (2003). Early detection: Proteomic applications for the early detection of cancer. *Nature Reviews Cancer, 3,* 267–275.

Xiang, F., Buervenich, S., Nicolao, P., Bailey, M. E., Zhang, Z., & Anvret, M. (2000). Mutation screening in Rett syndrome patients. *Journal of Medical Genetics, 37,* 250–255.

CHAPTER EIGHT

RESEARCH METHODOLOGY IN CLINICAL TRIALS

Kirti Saxena, M.D., and Christine Blasey, Ph.D.

The purpose of this chapter is to facilitate clinicians' knowledge of the standards for evidence-based practice, which are outlined in Chapter 1. It is to assist the practitioner in sorting through good and bad papers. We present a succinct summary of the types of methods used in clinical trials, discuss their advantages and disadvantages, and end with a definition of useful terms. All this is intended to put the clinician in a better position to judge the adequacy of the data backing up a particular intervention.

Evidence-based medicine is the process of finding, appraising, and applying evidence from research to the care of individual patients. On one hand, employing evidence-based medicine places responsibility on the clinician for knowing how to access relevant research and for evaluating the effectiveness of various treatments. On the other hand, there is a burden on clinical researchers to conduct studies with results that are relevant, accessible, and can be easily incorporated into the clinician's decision-making process. When the clinician is aware of the variety of research designs and the associated strengths and limitations, he or she will be better equipped to evaluate studies, which will likely lead to a more informed, accurate clinical decision.

Types of Studies

The first step of evidence-based medicine is to be familiar with study designs and research definitions.

There are two basic types of studies, a survey and an experimental design. In a survey, the researcher observes and then gathers data. Examples of surveys include cross-sectional studies, prospective studies, and retrospective studies. In contrast, in an experimental approach, the researcher manipulates variables and then observes the effects, as with clinical trials.

Specifically, the types of studies we will examine in this chapter are

- Randomized controlled study (RCT)
- Cohort study
- Case control study
- Case series and case study
- Systematic review and meta-analysis
- Longitudinal study
- Cross-sectional study
- Prospective study
- Retrospective study

Before going into the details of each study, let us review what a researcher thinks about while designing a study. When formulating a study design, the following queries are posed:

- What is the research question? It must be clear and specific.
- How will this study be conducted? Will it be a survey or an experimental study?
- Who will be the study subjects?
- How many subjects are to be studied?
- What is the method of treatment or intervention?
- What do we hypothesize the outcomes to be? For example, will the study result in stabilization, recovery, remission, and so on?
- How are outcomes to be measured?

Description of Studies

The following is a summary of the different types of studies, which includes an example of each study and a discussion of its advantages and disadvantages.

Randomized Controlled Study

A *randomized controlled study* typically compares an experimental treatment to standard treatment or to a placebo. Generally, there are at least two groups, referred to as the treatment group and control group. The treatment group receives the treatment under investigation, and the control group receives no treatment, a placebo, or a standard treatment of usual care. Important ethical decisions are made to determine whether the control group will receive a placebo or standard care (Kraemer, 2000). Patients are *randomly assigned* to condition/treatment groups, such that every subject has equal probability of receiving treatment or control condition. Random assignment of patients reduces the risk of experimenter bias and reduces spurious differences between groups at the beginning of study (baseline). Having a control group enables the researcher to compare the effectiveness of treatment over time with alternative treatments. This is the gold standard in medical and behavioral science research.

Many randomized controlled studies (RCSs) are *double blind*. In a double-blind study, neither the subject nor the clinician knows whether the subject is receiving placebo or the treatment of interest. For example, in a drug study, all subjects take pills of the same size, color, and shape and *neither* the subject *nor* the clinician knows which is the drug being studied or which is the placebo. A double-blind study is the most rigorous clinical research design because, in addition to the randomization of subjects, which reduces the risk of bias, it intends to eliminate the placebo effect which is a further challenge to the validity of a study. The *placebo effect* can be conceptualized as follows: when subjects believe they are receiving a new experimental treatment, they tend to be more optimistic about the outcome, minimize symptoms, take better care of themselves, and comply better with the conditions of the experiment. Under double-blind procedures, the drug and placebo doses are coded (using numbers or letters), and the code is not broken until evaluation data has been analyzed.

Advantages of Randomized Controlled Studies

- Random assignment results in a high probability that the differences between the two groups can be attributed to treatment.
- There is unbiased distribution of confounding variables. (Unmeasured factors may also explain the results of the experiment. For example, in a drug study looking at the effect of a drug, a confounding variable is the subject knowing he has received a new drug. Thus, the question is, is he improved because of the drug or is this a placebo effect?)
- It is more likely that the clinician and subjects can be blinded to the treatment.
- Randomization and blinding procedures reduce the likelihood of confounding variables, which tends to simplify statistical analyses.

Disadvantages of Randomized Controlled Studies

- It is expensive and time-consuming.
- Recruitment may be difficult, as patients may not want a placebo.
- Ethical issues may arise, such as that of having a bipolar subject on a placebo.

Example of a Randomized Controlled Study

Title: A Double-Blind, Randomized, Placebo-Controlled Study of Quetiapine as Adjunctive Treatment for Adolescent Mania (Delbello et al., 2002).

Research question/hypothesis: It was hypothesized that divalproex in combination with quetiapine would be more effective than divalproex alone for treating mania associated with adolescent bipolar disorder. It was also hypothesized that quetiapine would be well tolerated.

What is the hypothesis based on? A review of the literature showed that controlled investigations of atypical antipsychotics are efficacious for the treatment of mania in adults, children, and adolescents. Thus, the addition of an atypical antipsychotic to a mood stabilizer may decrease manic symptoms and improve response. The authors reviewed the literature, explained why they suggest that alternative pharmacological options for the treatment of pediatric mania are needed, and discussed why they decided to choose quetiapine.

Research design: A double-blind, randomized, placebo-controlled study.

Study subjects: Thirty adolescents with bipolar disorder, type 1, aged twelve to eighteen years.

Method: Random assignment to six weeks of combination treatment with quetiapine or placebo.

Outcome measures: Change from baseline to end point in Young Mania Rating Scale scores.

Variants of the randomized controlled study are crossed and nested designs.

Crossed Designs

In a *crossed design*, each subject participates in each level of the treatment conditions. For example, on the first day of an experiment on children with ADHD, the subjects are divided into half with one half getting Ritalin and the other half on no medication. A measure of ADHD symptoms is taken for each subject. On the second day, the conditions are reversed; that is, the subjects who received Ritalin are now not given the medication. The size of the effect will be the difference in ADHD symptoms on the days with and without medication. The distinguishing feature of crossed designs is that each subject will have more than one score. The effect occurs within each subject, thus these designs are sometimes referred to as *within subjects'* designs.

Advantages of Crossed Design

- They generally require fewer subjects, because each subject is used a number of times in the experiment.
- They are more likely to result in a significant effect.

Disadvantages of Crossed Design

The researcher must be concerned about carry-over effects, in which techniques learned in the first part of the study may influence the overall results of the study. For example, one group receives cognitive behavioral therapy (CBT) for eight weeks and the other group receives treatment as usual. When switching groups, the experience with CBT may lead to better resolution of symptoms in the group that underwent CBT initially and is now receiving treatment as usual.

Example of a Crossed Design Study

Title: A Double-Blind, Crossover Trial of Methylphenidate Versus Dexamphetamine in Children With Attention Deficit Hyperactivity Disorder (Efron et al., 1997).

Research question/hypothesis: This study set out to compare systematically methylphenidate (MPH) and dexamphetamine (DEX) in a sample of children with ADHD.

What is the hypothesis based on? MPH and DEX are the two stimulants prescribed frequently and have been shown to have similar types of positive effects in children with ADHD. However, it is not known whether one is more efficacious than the other in terms of probability of producing a positive response, magnitude of response, quality of improved performance, or side-effect profile.

Research design: This study used a double-blind, crossed design.

Study subjects: A total of 125 subjects between the ages of five and fifteen years, meeting *DSM-IV* criteria for ADHD.

Method: Subjects were randomized to receive either DEX or MPH for the first two weeks of the study. After a twenty-four-hour washout period, they were crossed over to receive the other stimulant for the third and fourth weeks. Both drugs were presented in identical form. The investigators, families, subjects, and teachers were blind to the randomization order throughout the study period.

Outcome measures: Four measures of response to stimulant medication were used: Conners' Parent Rating Scale-Revised, Conners' Teacher Rating Scale-Revised, Parental Global Perceptions Questionnaire, and Continuous Performance Test.

Nested Designs

In a *nested design*, each subject receives one, and only one, treatment condition. An example is, an experiment performed on a single day, with half the individuals receiving Ritalin and half without receiving any medication. The size of effect in this case is determined by comparing ADHD between the two groups. The major distinguishing feature of nested designs is that each subject has a single score. The effect, if any, occurs between groups of subjects and thus the name between subjects is given to these designs. The relative advantages and disadvantages of nested designs are opposite those of crossed designs. As individuals are measured only once, carry-over effects is not a problem. The number of subjects needed to discover effects is greater than with crossed designs.

Example of a Nested Design Study

Title: A comparison of practice outcomes of graduates from traditional and non-traditional medical schools in Australia (Pearson et al., 2002).

Research question/hypothesis: The primary aim of the study was to compare the practice outcomes of doctors who graduated from a non-traditional, problem-based medical school (University of Newcastle) with those of graduates from a traditional program (University of Sydney), matched randomly on the background characteristics of graduation year, age, gender, and rural primary and secondary school education. Our secondary aim was to differentiate admission from curricular influences by comparing the outcomes of Newcastle and Sydney graduates who entered medical school under similar admission criteria ("traditional academic" entry).

Why is this question relevant? Over the last twenty years, medical schools internationally have adopted alternative admission procedures and curricular approaches. The traditional profile of medical students as high school graduates with records of exceptionally high academic performance is losing prominence, and problem-based learning is at the forefront of curricular reform. In this climate of educational change, outcome evaluation becomes imperative.

Research design: Nested case-control analysis in a retrospective cohort study.

Study subjects: Doctors who were registered with the New South Wales Medical Board in 1998 formed the sample population. Eligible subjects were doctors from the first sixteen graduating years of the Bachelor of Medicine program at the University of Newcastle (1983–98 inclusive) and doctors who graduated from the University of Sydney in the same years.

Method: At the time of the survey, 752 Newcastle and 2995 Sydney graduates were registered. Each graduate was allocated a unique identification code. Subjects were forwarded an information sheet and questionnaire. A follow-up reminder letter was sent to all graduates approximately one month after the initial mailing. A final reminder letter and a copy of the questionnaire were sent to graduates who had not returned the questionnaire four weeks later. This procedure of repeated mailings was used to maximize response.

Outcome measures: Current main occupation (clinician or other), clinical career choice (family medicine and psychiatry or other specialties), practice location (urban or rural) and employment sector (public or private).

Cohort Study

A *cohort study* is one in which patients who presently have a certain condition and/or receive a particular treatment are followed over time and compared with another group that is not affected by the condition under investigation. The main problem with cohort studies is that they can end up taking a very long time, since the researchers have to wait for the conditions of interest to develop. Another disadvantage with long studies is that things tend to change over the course of the study. People die, move away, or develop other conditions, new and promising treatments arise, and so on. Even so, cohort studies involve far fewer statistical problems and generally produce more reliable answers.

In a *fixed cohort,* a group of individuals is recruited and enrolled at a uniform point in the natural history of a disease or by some defining event. An example is, the first manic episode in an adolescent. In an *open cohort,* a group of individuals is recruited and enrolled through a mechanism that allows for migration of people in and out. Individuals are defined by characteristics other than disease, for example, geographic location or administrative unit such as an outpatient clinic.

Advantages of Cohort Studies

- Is ethically safe.
- Can demonstrate temporal relationship between exposure and disease.
- Allows direct measurement of incidence of disease in exposed and unexposed populations.
- Administratively easier and cheaper than randomized controlled trials.

Disadvantages of Cohort Studies

- Controls may be difficult to identify.
- Exposure may be linked to a hidden confounder.
- Blinding is difficult.

- Randomization not present.
- For rare disease, large sample sizes or long follow-up is necessary.

Example of a Cohort Study

Title: Age-of-onset Classification of Conduct Disorder Reliability and Validity in a Prospective, Cohort Study (Sanford et al., 1999).

Research question/hypothesis: To test in a prospective clinical *cohort study* the reliability and validity of the age-of-onset subtyping of conduct disorder.

What is the hypothesis based on? For a subclassification system to be useful, it should be evaluated across settings and longitudinal data should be used to confirm that it does provide useful information about prognosis and treatment.

Research design: Prospective, cohort study

Study subjects: The sample was drawn from consecutive referrals (aged thirteen to eighteen years) to psychiatric outpatient clinics and inpatient units of four hospitals.

Method: Sampling was conducted during two separate nine-month periods (1990–91 and 1992–93) in order to study the clinical course of both clinical depression (CD) and major depressive disorder (MDD). There were two steps in arriving at the initial sample (time 0). First, consenting subjects were screened using the CD and depressive disorders sections of the Diagnostic Interview Schedule for Children–Revised (DISC-R). All those who met DSM-III-R criteria for either CD or MDD by either informant were included. Second, these subjects were reassessed two to four weeks later with the complete version of the DISC-R, Peabody Picture Vocabulary Test (PPVT), Social Adjustment Inventory for Children and Adolescents, and other interviews and questionnaires. A subsample composed of only those subjects accrued during the initial sampling period (1990–91) was reassessed at two years (time 2) and at three years (time 3) (adolescent informant only). Subjects accrued during the second sampling period (1992–93) were not followed beyond one year.

During the two sampling periods, a total of 385 referrals were eligible for study (239 during 1990–91 and 146 during 1992–93). Of these, 284 underwent screening. Two hundred forty-eight (87%) subjects screened positive and were eligible for reassessment two to four weeks later, while thirty-six (13%) screened negative for CD or MDD by either informant and were excluded. Eleven more subjects were lost, and thirteen subjects with psychotic disorders were excluded, leaving 224 subjects (time 0). These subjects were eligible for follow-up at one year but an additional seven were not traced or refused, leaving 217 subjects (211 subjects with adolescent informant data, 197 subjects with parent informant data) (time 1). By time 3, many of the adolescents had left home, and because of limited resources it was no longer feasible to assess parents. Overall, there was 31%

attrition from identification of potential subjects to time 1 follow-up. However, this was chiefly due to the high initial refusal rate (accounting for a 26% subject loss), which is common in clinic-based studies. Only 5% of consenters were lost to the study over the first year. Of those followed up with at time 2 and time 3, an additional 7% were lost or refused participation.

This is an example of difficulties encountered with subjects over a period of time.

Outcome measures: Social Adjustment Inventory for Children and Adolescents, Peabody Picture Vocabulary Test.

Case Control Study

Case control studies are studies in which patients who already have a certain condition are compared with people who do not.

Advantages of Case Control Studies

- They can be done quickly.
- Researchers do not need special methods, control groups, and so on.
- They are quick and cheap.
- Only feasible method for very rare disorders or those with long lag between exposure and outcome.
- Fewer subjects needed than cross-sectional studies.

Disadvantages of Case Control Studies

- Reliance on recall or records to determine exposure status.
- Selection of control groups is difficult.

Example of a Case Control Study

Title: Case Control Study of Attention-Deficit Hyperactivity Disorder and Maternal Smoking, Alcohol Use, and Drug Use During Pregnancy (Biederman et al., 2002).

Research question/hypothesis: To address the putative association between ADHD and prenatal exposure to maternal cigarette smoking, drugs of abuse, and alcohol, attending to potential confounding by familial ADHD, maternal depression, conduct disorder, and indicators of social adversity in the environment.

What is the hypothesis based on? ADHD is a common childhood psychiatric disorder with a prevalence of 3 to 5% in the United States. Both genes and environmental risk factors influence the etiology of ADHD. Prenatal exposure to alcohol and drugs of abuse may also be associated with symptoms of ADHD. The relationship between ADHD and maternal smoking during pregnancy needs to be revisited with attention to potential confounders. The authors have based their research question a thorough review of the literature.

Research design: This was a retrospective, hospital-based, case control study. The data from two identically designed hospital-based case-control family studies of ADHD were combined. The first study ascertained families on the basis of a male case or control child aged six to seventeen years at the time of ascertainment. The second ascertained families on the basis of a female case or control child also aged six to seventeen years at the time of ascertainment. These samples were not significantly different on any demographic variables, except that the female subjects were slightly older than the male subjects.

Study subjects: This study was conducted with 280 ADHD cases and 242 non-ADHD controls of both genders.

Method: The data from two identically designed hospital-based case-control family studies of ADHD were combined. The first study ascertained families on the basis of a male case or control child aged six to seventeen years at the time of ascertainment. The second ascertained families on the basis of a female case or control child also aged six to seventeen years at the time of ascertainment. These samples were not significantly different on any demographic variables, except that the female subjects were slightly older than the male subjects.

Outcome measures: Psychiatric assessments of children and adolescents relied on the Schedule for Affective Disorders and Schizophrenia for School-Age Children-Epidemiologic version (K-SADS-E) and diagnostic assessments of parents relied on direct interviews with each parent using the Structured Clinical Interview for DSM-III-R (SCID).

Case Series and Case Study

Case series and *case reports* consist either of collections of reports on the treatment of individual patients, or of reports on a single patient. Since they use no control group with which to compare outcomes, it is impossible to know whether the patient's condition is linked to any of the observed outcomes. *Case studies* are often rich in detail and have tutorial value, and are thus often used in medicine, psychiatry, and neurology to illustrate the factors, development, and consequences of a disease or injury.

Example of a Case Study
Title: Bibliotherapy and Extinction Treatment of Obsessive-Compulsive Disorder in a Five-Year-old Boy (Tolin, 2001).

What is the hypothesis of this case report? Obsessive-compulsive disorder (OCD) is a chronic anxiety disorder marked by recurrent, distressing thoughts, and repetitive behaviors or mental acts. Studies have shown a prevalence of approximately 1% in children and adolescents. There is no record in the current literature of the cognitive-behavioral treatment of very young (that is, younger than seven years old) children with OCD. The purpose of the present case report is to describe the case of a five-year-old boy with OCD and to report on his treatment with cognitive-behavioral–based bibliotherapy and parent-directed extinction.

Research design: This case report describes a five-year-old boy with severe OCD.

Method: Treatment consisted of parent-and teacher-directed extinction of compulsive reassurance-seeking, and bibliotherapy with an age-appropriate book on OCD.

Outcome measure: Children's Yale-Brown Obsessive Compulsive Scale (CY-BOCS), National Institute of Mental Health (NIMH) Global, and Clinical Global Impression (CGI) scores.

Systematic Review and Meta-Analysis

A *systematic review* is a comprehensive survey of a topic in which all of the primary studies of the highest level of evidence have been systematically identified, appraised, and then summarized according to an explicit and reproducible methodology. Specific headings for specific types of reviews (academic, literature, multicase, reported cases, and tutorial) are also available. A *meta-analysis* is a survey in which the results of all of the included studies are similar enough statistically that the results are combined and analyzed as if one study. Advantage: In general, a good systematic review or meta-analysis is a better guide to practice than an individual article.

Disadvantages of Systematic Review
It's rare that the results of the different studies precisely agree, and often the number of patients in a single study is not large enough to come up with a decisive conclusion.

Studies that show some kind of positive effect tend to be published more often than those that do not. This effect is known as *publication bias*.

Example of a Systematic Review
Title: Psychopharmacologic Strategies for the Treatment of Aggression in Juveniles (Steiner et al., 2003).

Relevance of topic: Maladaptive aggression in youth has a complex relationship with psychopathology, as there are several syndromes that contain maladaptive aggression in their definition, most notably oppositional defiant disorder

(ODD) and conduct disorder (CD). However, problems with aggression also appear in a wide range of other disturbances, such as bipolar disorder, PTSD, and mood disorders, to name a few. Additionally, aggression is normative, serves an adaptive purpose, and can be situationally induced. These complexities need to be addressed carefully before maladaptive aggression can be targeted psychopharmacologically.

Research design: Systematic review

Method: The literature on the psychopharmacology of maladaptive aggression in youth is summarized and concluded with a discussion of specific strategies to deal with acute, subacute, and chronic aggression.

Example of a Meta-Analysis

Title: Psychopharmacology and Aggression. A meta-analysis of stimulant effects on overt/covert aggression-related behaviors in ADHD (Connor et al., 2002).

Research design/hypothesis: The objective was to determine by meta-analysis the effect size for stimulants on overt and covert aggression-related behaviors in children with ADHD, separately from stimulant effects on the core symptoms of ADHD.

Relevance of this meta-analysis: Studies document that children with ADHD and aggression, oppositional defiant disorder, or conduct disorder do not differ in their response to stimulants on the core symptoms of ADHD as compared with nonaggressive children with ADHD. Far fewer studies have directly investigated the effects of stimulants on aggression-related behaviors within the context of ADHD. Given the importance of aggression-related behaviors in influencing ADHD symptom severity, impairment, clinical referral patterns, and longitudinal outcome, it would be important to know whether stimulants exert clinical benefits on this domain of behavior separate from effects exerted on the core symptoms of ADHD.

Method: A literature search was completed to identify reports in which stimulants were used to treat aggression-related behaviors in youths with ADHD. A review of the literature from 1970 to 2001 revealed twenty-eight studies meeting inclusion/exclusion criteria for meta-analysis.

Longitudinal Studies versus Cross-Sectional Studies

Longitudinal studies are ones in which variables relating to an individual or group of individuals are assessed over a period of time. These studies are often expensive, difficult to conduct, and have many drop outs. A randomized, controlled clinical trial can be longitudinal. *Cross-sectional studies* are ones in which the presence or absence of disease or other health-related variables is determined in each member of the study population or in a representative sample at one particular time. This contrasts with longitudinal studies, which are followed over a period of time.

Advantages of a Cross-Sectional Study

Cheap

Simple

Ethically safe

Disadvantages of a Cross-Sectional Study

Establishes association at most

Confounders may be unequally distributed

Group sizes may be unequal

The advantages and disadvantages of longitudinal studies are the opposite of those for cross-sectional studies.

Example of a Longitudinal Study

Title: Longitudinal Study of Maternal Depressive Symptoms and Child Well-Being (Luoma et al., 2001).

Research question/hypothesis: To investigate whether prenatal, postnatal, and/or current maternal depressive symptoms are associated with a low level of psychosocial functioning or a high level of emotional/behavioral problems in school-age children.

What is the hypothesis based on? There is still a lack of longitudinal research concerning the associations of postnatal depression with the child's functioning and psychopathology in later childhood. It is not known whether the reported consequences of postnatal depression for a child have long-term continuity or whether they are compensated along with the maternal recovery. There are still very few studies on the significance of the timing of maternal depression, given that there may be particularly vulnerable periods in child development. There is clearly a lack of research on the possible effects of maternal prenatal depression on the child's mental health.

Research design: This study is part of a prospective longitudinal study.

Study subjects: The original sample of 349 mothers was collected in 1989–90 in Tampere, Finland. Of the 270 mother–child pairs at the latest stage of the study in 1997–98, 188 mother–child pairs participated and 147 were included.

Method: The sample was collected from all maternity health clinics in the city of Tampere during a six-month period in 1989–90. The depressive symptoms of the mothers were screened by means of questionnaires during late pregnancy (T_1) and three times postnatally (T_2 = during the first week, T_3 = 2 months, and T_4 = 6 months after delivery). A subgroup of these mothers was screened for depressive symptoms at the second stage of the follow-up study in 1994–95 (T_5, not included in this report). At the third stage of the follow-up study, a postal survey was conducted during the period of November 1997 to April 1998 (T_6).

Outcome measures: The associations between maternal depressive symptoms at different points in time and the level of children's psychosocial functioning and problems reported on the Child Behavior Checklist and Teacher's Report Form were examined.

Example of a Cross-Sectional Study

Title: Prescribing of Psychotropic Medications for Children by Australian Pediatricians and Child Psychiatrists (Efron et al., 2003).

Research Question/Hypothesis: To describe the pattern of prescribing of psychotropic medications for Australian children.

What is the hypothesis based on? Australian pediatricians and child and adolescent psychiatrists (child psychiatrists) are seeing increasing numbers of children with severe and complex behavior disturbance. Medication is a commonly used treatment modality. This situation is of concern because for many psychotropic medications it is not clear that the benefits outweigh the potential harms in children. The aim of this study, therefore, was to describe the pattern of prescribing of psychotropic medication for Australian children by all registered general pediatricians and child psychiatrists, both to document current practice and also to identify possible areas of concern to inform training, practice, and research.

Research design: Australia-wide cross-sectional postal survey conducted in 2000.

Method: A postal survey of all 604 general pediatricians and 267 child psychiatrists in Australia was undertaken in November 2000. Contact addresses for practitioners were obtained through the Royal Australasian College of Physicians (Pediatrics and Child Health Division) and the Royal Australian and New Zealand College of Psychiatrists (Faculty of Child and Adolescent Psychiatry), both of whom endorsed the study. A second survey was posted to initial nonresponders after two months.

Study subjects: Australian children

Outcome measures: Questionnaire filled in by the practitioners.

Prospective Studies versus Retrospective Studies

A *prospective study* is the observation of a population for a sufficient number of persons over a sufficient number of years to generate incidence or mortality rates subsequent to the selection of the study group.

A *retrospective study* describes events that have already occurred. Patients with the disease are assigned to the study group; patients without the disease are controls. An attempt is made to identify variables that may have led to the condition under study. Data are obtained after the fact and, therefore, without making an intervention.

Advantages: There are significant advantages to a *retrospective* study. They are relatively inexpensive, they can be used as preliminary data to define the ultimate prospective study, they are convenient, they can be done at one's convenience as it does not rely upon study patients to appear and agree to be studied.

Disadvantages: The problems with a retrospective study are due to the fact that data are retrieved rather than recorded as they occur. The data might be obtained from chart review or patient interview or survey. Unrecognized group differences and bias are problems.

A retrospective study is a study that looks back in time. In contrast, a prospective study looks forward in time.

Title: A Retrospective Study of High-IQ Adolescents and Adults (Piven et al., 1996).

Research question/hypothesis: The course of behavioral change in autistic behaviors has received little attention in previous research, but is a potentially important parameter for study in autism.

What is the hypothesis based on? For several reasons, examination of the course of behavioral change is a potentially important area of study in autism. First, description of the expected continuities and discontinuities of autistic symptoms between childhood and later ages has practical value in clarifying the diagnosis of autism in adults and helping to make predictions about future behavior. Second, clarification of the evolution of autistic features over time may provide clues to the fundamental psychological mechanisms and core features of this disorder. Finally, the identification of subgroups of autistic individuals, defined by having differing behavioral trajectories, may prove to have some biological significance.

Research design: Retrospective study

Method: Autistic behaviors were systematically examined in thirty-eight high-IQ adolescent and adult autistic individuals at their current age (thirteen through twenty-eight years) and retrospectively at age five years using a standardized interview for autism.

Study subjects: Thirty-eight autistic adolescents and adults (twenty-seven males; eleven females) participated in this study.

Outcome measures: Behaviors compared over time were assessed systematically using a standardized, semistructured interview.

Prospective Study

Title: Anxious Children in Adulthood: A Prospective Study of Adjustment (Last et al., 1997).

Research question/hypothesis: To prospectively examine psychosocial functioning in young adulthood for children and adolescents with anxiety disorders.

What is the hypothesis based on? Information regarding the long-term psychosocial effects of childhood and adolescent anxiety disorders is limited.

Research design: Prospective study

Method: Children and adolescents (aged five to seventeen years) were recruited for participation in these studies in the mid to late 1980s. During the fall of 1995, subjects then age eighteen or older were recontacted and asked to participate in a telephone interview. A comparison group of never-psychiatrically-ill (NPI) youngsters were recruited from the community during the same time period and were matched as closely as possible for age and sex to the youngsters with anxiety disorders. The comparison children were required to have no history of a DSM-III-R diagnosis or mental health contact of any kind.

Study subjects: Subjects included 101 young adults (age range eighteen to twenty-six years, mean = 21.92, SD = 2.36) who had participated previously, as children and adolescents, in large-scale family and follow-up studies of anxiety disorders in children.

Outcome measures: Semistructured interviews

Multicenter Studies

Multicenter studies are controlled studies that are planned and carried out by several cooperating institutions to assess certain variables and outcomes in specific patient populations. An example would be a multicenter study of the effects of divalproex sodium in children and adolescents with bipolar disorder.

Title: Efficacy of Paroxetine in the Treatment of Adolescent Major Depression: A Randomized, Controlled Trial (Keller et al., 2001).

Research Design/Hypothesis: To compare paroxetine with placebo and imipramine with placebo for the treatment of adolescent depression. The treatment of depression in adolescents is an area of burgeoning interest.

What is the hypothesis based on? Few well-controlled, large-scale, randomized clinical trials have been conducted in this population. Since the selective serotonin reuptake inhibitors (SSRIs) became commercially available, the safety, tolerability, and efficacy of these agents in treating major depression in adolescents have been noted in several open-label reports.

Research design: This was an eight-week, multicenter, double-blind, randomized, parallel-design comparison of paroxetine with placebo and imipramine with placebo in adolescents with major depression.

Method: The trial was conducted at ten centers in the United States and two in Canada. Four hundred twenty-five subjects were screened for eligibility, and 275 subjects were randomly assigned to experimental treatment.

Subjects: Male and female subjects, aged twelve through eighteen years, fulfilling the *DSM-IV* criteria for a current episode of major depression of at least eight weeks in duration were enrolled.

Outcome measures: HAM-D depressed mood item, K-SADS-L depressed mood item, and CGI score.

Pilot Study

A *pilot study* is a preliminary trial of an experimental procedure intended to reveal deficiencies and provide information on the behavior likely to occur in the main study. Pilot studies can help you pick up *ceiling* and *floor effects* as well as things like, checking that questions and instructions are comprehensible.

Title: School-Based Treatment for Anxious African-American Adolescents: A Controlled Pilot Study (Ginsburg & Drake, 2002).

Research question: To evaluate the feasibility and effectiveness of a school-based group CBT for anxiety disorders with African-American adolescents.

What is the hypothesis based on? Low-income African-American adolescents were selected for this study because they continue to be an underserved population in general, and in the pediatric anxiety literature in particular. Thus, it is important to determine whether an empirically supported intervention designed to reduce anxiety is effective for this population.

Research design: A controlled pilot study

Method: Twelve adolescents (mean age = 15.6 years) with anxiety disorders were randomly assigned to CBT ($n = 6$) or a group attention-support control condition (AS-Control; $n = 6$). Both groups met for ten sessions in the same high school.

Study subjects: Twelve adolescents (mean age = 15.6 years) with anxiety disorders

Outcome measures: At pre- and post-treatment, diagnostic interviews were conducted and adolescents completed self-report measures of anxiety.

Personal Experience

Here is how I evaluate a study and decide if it is relevant to my clinical practice:

Title: Fluoxetine for Acute Treatment of Depression in Children and Adolescents: A Placebo-Controlled, Randomized Clinical Trial (Emslie et al., 2002).

Does the question in the study interest me and is it timely?

This is a relevant topic of interest for practicing pediatric psychiatrists. Studies of psychopharmacological agents for treatment of childhood mood disorders are in great need. Hence, this is a timely topic.

Is the discussion of the background of the study understandable, concise, and to the point?

Yes, the study talks about previous clinical trials in childhood depression and explains the relevance of performing this clinical trial, as follows: Depression occurs in approximately 2% of children and 4% to 8% of adolescents, with MDD being twice as prevalent in adolescent girls as in adolescent boys . Much has been written about the use of antidepressants in children with various mood and anxiety disorders, but there have been few adequately powered, controlled clinical trials in the area of MDD. Controlled studies of tricyclic antidepressant treatment for children and adolescents with depression failed to produce a replicable pattern of efficacy. In a controlled, double-blind clinical trial, venlafaxine was not superior to placebo for treatment of depression in children and adolescents. Efficacy of fluoxetine in the treatment of pediatric depression has been demonstrated in a double-blind, placebo-controlled study. This study demonstrated that a fixed dose (20 mg/day) of fluoxetine was efficacious and well tolerated. Other reports have indicated that children and adolescents may require fluoxetine doses greater than 20 mg/day. One naturalistic study indicated that doses lower than 20 mg may be effective for some adolescents.

Does the study have a sound design, or if there are limitations to the design, are they defendable because the study addresses a difficult problem or population?

The design of the study is well explained:

A multiphase study was designed to examine efficacy and tolerability of various dosing strategies for fluoxetine treatment of depressed children and adolescents. The initial phase, reported in Emslie's article (Emslie et al., 2002), was designed to confirm a previous report that 20 mg of fluoxetine was effective and well-tolerated for acute treatment of pediatric MDD.

To obtain the most reliable assessment of patients' condition, this study incorporated an extensive diagnostic evaluation period requiring three independent diagnostic interviews (visits 1, 2, and 3 [week -3, -2, and -1]). The interviews were conducted by three different interviewers, at least one who was a psychiatrist. Other interviewers were qualified and experienced pediatric health care professionals. Each interviewer had access to information from previous interviews for each patient. This was done to ensure the accuracy and completeness of the information gathered during the evaluation process. Final diagnoses were determined after visit 3. Patients and their parent(s) or guardian(s) were interviewed separately. No drug was administered during the evaluation period. This was followed by a single-blind, one-week, placebo lead-in period (between visits 3 and 4 [week -1 and week 0]). Patients who responded during this period (defined as $\geq 30\%$ decrease in Children's Depression Rating Scale–Revised [CDRS-R] or a Clinical Global Impression [CGI] Improvement score of 1 or 2) were discontinued from the study. Those who did not respond during the placebo lead-in were assigned to treatment groups by means of a computer-generated randomization sequence. Randomization was stratified by gender and age category across investigative sites.

Patients in the placebo treatment group were instructed to take three capsules, which contained placebo, once daily for nine weeks. Patients in the fluoxetine treatment group were also instructed to take three capsules daily. For the first week, these consisted of two placebo capsules and a capsule containing 10 mg of fluoxetine. For weeks 2 through 9, one capsule contained placebo and two capsules contained 10 mg of fluoxetine each.

After receiving study medication, patients returned for efficacy and adverse event assessments at weeks 1, 2, 3, 5, 7, and 9 (visits 5 through 10).

Limitations to the study have been explained. Patients who enrolled in this study were predominantly white. Although no significant differences between whites and nonwhites were observed, the number of nonwhites was too small to conclude that fluoxetine efficacy and safety are constant across ethnic groups. Information about patients' socioeconomic status was not collected during this trial; therefore, we cannot conclude that fluoxetine efficacy and safety were constant across socioeconomic groups.

Adequacy of analysis and presentation of results—is it understandable?

For a clinician, who may not be well versed in statistics, this is the hardest part of evaluating a study. Either one has to familiarize oneself with statistical terms, or otherwise ask a statistician for help.

Does the discussion adequately summarize the results?

For me, this is the most helpful part of the article. This article is clear about the results of the study and even gives further clinical implications.

Fluoxetine was well tolerated and effective in a double-blind, placebo-controlled study evaluating nine weeks of acute therapy with 20 mg of fluoxetine daily in 219 child and adolescent outpatients with MDD. A dosage 20 mg of fluoxetine daily was more effective than placebo for the treatment of depression, as demonstrated by significantly greater improvement in the CDRS-R score. During the first week of treatment, fluoxetine-treated patients received 10 mg of fluoxetine daily. Because fluoxetine was statistically, significantly superior to placebo within one week, it is possible that 10 mg daily may be an effective dose for MDD in some young patients. Further study is necessary to confirm this finding.

Fluoxetine was associated with statistically, significantly greater improvement at the end point in all four CDRS-R subscores than was placebo. Fluoxetine was also significantly superior to placebo on global measures of improvement (CGI-Improvement) and disease severity (CGI-Severity). Significantly more fluoxetine-treated than placebo-treated patients met remission criteria at the endpoint.

A statistically, significantly greater number of fluoxetine-treated patients than placebo-treated patients had a CDRS-R score improvements of greater than or equal to 20%, 40%, 50%, or 60%.

This study is relevant to my clinical practice, and I will consider the results of this study the next time I see a child or adolescent with depression.

Definitions

The terminology relevant to research methodology are defined as follows:

Between-subject designs: The comparison is between different groups of subjects, a control group and a treatment group. Subjects are assigned randomly to groups.

Blinding: A trial is fully blinded if all the people involved are unaware of the treatment group to which trial participants are allocated until after the interpretation of results. This includes trial participants and everyone involved in administering treatment or recording trial results.

Ceiling effect: Measurement failures in which the majority of subjects score 100% correct because the task is too easy.

Confounding: A confounding variable is a variable that offers an alternative explanation for the results of the experiment. For example, in a drug study looking at the effect of a drug, a confounding variable will be the subject knowing he has received a new drug. So, the question is, is he improved because of the drug or is this a placebo effect? Confounding can affect either independent or dependent variables and causes problems in interpreting which variable caused the experimental effect to occur.

(The confounding variable can also be labeled the "nuisance variable.") There are statistical ways of controlling the nuisance variable when you analyze your data, but it is always best to identify any confounding variables *before* you begin your experiment and try to control for them in the experimental design.

Controls: In a randomized controlled trial (RCT), controls refer to the participants in its comparison group. They are allocated either to placebo, no treatment, or a standard treatment.

Control group: A group that is not exposed to the experimental manipulation with the experimental group.

Counterbalancing: Varying the order in which treatments are applied between subjects in a within-subjects design. Any technique used to vary systematically the order of conditions in an experiment to distribute the effects of time of testing (for example, fatigue) so they are not confounded with conditions.

Demand characteristics: Beliefs about expected performance created by an experimental procedure. Subjects naturally try to work out how they are expected to behave and any clues they pick up from the experimental task will probably affect what they do. Compliant subjects will try to produce what they think is the expected behavior, whereas others may seek to defy expectation. An example would be in the amount of space left in a questionnaire, if there was a large space for an answer, the subjects might be expected to write a large amount. Demand characteristics are better eliminated.

Dependent variable: These are variables that are measured by the experimenter to determine if the independent variable had the intended effect. Normally, they are responses of the subjects. For example, in a drug study, did the increased dose of the drug decrease the depressive symptoms of subjects', as was hypothesized?

Effect size: In medical literature, the term effect size refers to a variety of measures of treatment effect.

Experimental study: A study in which the investigator studies the effect of intentionally altering one or more factors under controlled conditions.

Factorial design: Experimental design in which every combination of conditions occurs with equal frequency. Factorial designs are appropriate when experimental conditions might affect each other (an "interaction"). There are usually an equal number of subjects randomly assigned to each condition.

Floor effect: Measurement failure in which the majority of subjects score very poorly because the task is too difficult.

Hypothesis: Implication of a theory derived for the purpose of testing the theory. A hypothesis is always a prediction and is therefore expressed in the future tense.

Independent variable: These are variables that an experimenter manipulates. For example, in a drug study, subjects are given varying dosages of the drug being studied. The experimenter is manipulating this variable (dose of drug).

Likelihood ratio: The ratio of the probability that an individual with the target condition has a specified test result to the probability that an individual without the target condition has the same specified test result.

Negative likelihood ratio: The ratio of the probability that an individual with the target condition has a negative test result to the probability that an individual without the target condition has a negative test result.

Odds: The odds of an event happening is defined as the probability that an event will occur, expressed as a proportion of the probability that the event will not occur.

P value: The probability that an observed or greater difference occurred by chance. If this probability is less than 0.05, then the result is conventionally regarded as being "statistically significant."

Positive likelihood ratio: The ratio of the probability that an individual with the target condition has a positive test result to the probability that an individual without the target condition has a positive test result.

Publication bias: Occurs when the likelihood of a study being published varies with the results it finds.

Quasi randomized: A trial using a method of allocating participants to different forms of care that is not truly random (for example, allocation by date of birth).

Reliability: Refers to the repeatability of an experimental result. If a test is reliable, then it is likely to provide the same results when given to a subject for the second time.

Sensitivity: The chance of having a positive test result given that you have a disease.

Specificity: The chance of having a negative test result given that you do not have a disease.

Subject report: This is either requested from, or provided by, a subject, who provides information concerning their behavior in the experiment. It is supplemental to any experimental measures and can provide insight into why the person is responding the way they are or how they feel. It is particularly useful in the pilot study stage of an investigation.

Within-subject design: The comparison is within subjects. Each subject is administered the control condition and each level of treatment. Keep in mind the possible effects of the order in which the different condition is presented. For example, one group receives cognitive behavioral therapy (CBT) for eight weeks and the other group receives treatment as usual. When switching groups, the experience with CBT may lead to better resolution of symptoms with treatment as usual, in the group that underwent CBT initially.

Validity: Refers to the ability of a test to measure what it claims to measure.

References

Biederman, J., Faraone, S. V., Sayer, J., and Kleinman, S. (2002). *Journal of the American Academy of Child and Adolescent Psychiatry, 41*(12), 1391–1392.

Connor, D. F., et al. (2002). Psychopharmacology and aggression. I: A meta-analysis of stimulant effects on overt/covert aggression-related behaviors in ADHD. *Journal of the American Academy of Child Adolescent Psychiatry, 41*(3), 253–261.

Connor, D. F., Glatt, S. J., Lopez, I. D., Jackson, D., & Melloni, R. H. (2002). Psychopharmacology and Aggression. I: Meta-Analysis of Stimulant Effects on Overt/Covert Aggression-Related behaviors in ADHD. *Journal of the American Academy of Child and Adolescent Psychiatry, 41*(3), 253–261.

Delbello, M. P., et al. (2002). A double-blind, randomized, placebo-controlled study of quetiapine as adjunctive treatment for adolescent mania. *Journal of the American Academy of Child and Adolescent Psychiatry, 41*(10), 1216–1223.

Efron, D., et al. (1997). Methylphenidate versus dexamphetamine in children with attention deficit hyperactivity disorder: A double-blind, crossover trial. *Pediatrics, 100*(6), E6.

Efron, D., et al. (2003). Prescribing of psychotropic medications for children by Australian pediatricians and child psychiatrists. *Pediatrics, 111*(2), 372–375.

Emslie, G. J., et al. (2002). Fluoxetine for acute treatment of depression in children and adolescents: A placebo-controlled, randomized clinical trial. *Journal of the American Academy of Child and Adolescent Psychiatry, 41*(10), 1205–1215.

Ginsburg, G. S., & Drake, K. L. (2002). *Journal of the American Academy of Child and Adolescent Psychiatry, 41*(7), 768–775.

Keller, M. B., et al. (2001). Efficacy of paroxetine in the treatment of adolescent major depression: A randomized, controlled trial. *Journal of the American Academy of Child and Adolescent Psychiatry, 40*(7), 762–772.

Kraemer, A. C. (2000). Statistical analysis to settle ethical issues. *Archives of General Psychiatry, 57*(4), 311–317.

Last, C. G., et al. (1997). Anxious children in adulthood: A prospective study of adjustment. *Journal of the American Academy of Child and Adolescent Psychiatry, 36*(5), 645–652.

Luoma, I., et al. (2001). Longitudinal study of maternal depressive symptoms and child well-being. *Journal of the American Academy of Child and Adolescent Psychiatry, 40*(12), 1367–1374.

Markinson, A. (2002). SUNY Downstate Medical Center Evidence-Based Medicine Course. Retrieved from http://servers.medlib.hscbklyn.edu/ebm/toc.html

Pearson, S. A., et al. (2002). A comparison of practice outcomes of graduates from traditional and non-traditional medical schools in Australia. *Medical Education, 36*(10), 985–991.

Piven, J., et al. (1996). Course of behavioral change in autism: A retrospective study of high-IQ adolescents and adults. *Journal of the American Academy of Child and Adolescent Psychiatry, 35*(4), 523–529.

Sackett, D. L., Straus, S., Richardson, S., Rosenberg, W., & Haynes, R. B. (2000). Evidence-based medicine: How to practice and teach. *EBM*, 2nd Edition. London: Churchhill Livingstone.

Sackett, D. L. (1996). Evidence-based medicine: What it is and what it isn't. *British Medical Journal, 312,* 71–72. Retrieved from http://www.library.utoronto.ca/medicine/ebm

Sanford, M., et al. (1999). Age-of-onset classification of conduct disorder: Reliability and validity in a prospective cohort study. *Journal of the American Academy of Child and Adolescent Psychiatry, 38*(8), 992–999.

Steiner, H., Saxena, K., & Chang, K. (2003). *CNS Spectr., 8*(4), 298–308.

Swann, A. C., Bjorn, J. M., Moeller, F. G., & Dougherty, D. M. (2002). Two models of impulsivity: Relationship to personality traits and psychopathology. *Biological Psychiatry, 51,* 988–994.

Tolin, D. F. (2001). Case Study: Bibliotherapy and extinction treatment of obsessive-compulsive disorder in a 5-year-old boy. *Journal of the American Academy of Child and Adolescent Psychiatry, 40*(9), 1111–1114.

Turgay, A., Binder, C., Snyder, R., et al. (2002). Long-term safety and efficacy of risperidone for the treatment of disruptive behavior disorders in children with subaverage IQs. *Pediatrics, 110,* e34.

Vitaro, F., Brendgen, M., & Tramblay, R. (2002). Reactively and proactively aggressive children: Antecedent and subsequent characteristics. *Journal of Child Psychology Psychiatry, 43,* 495–505.

Vitiello, B., & Stoff, D. M. (1997). Subtypes of aggression and their relevance to Child Psychiatry. *Journal of the American Academy of Child and Adolescent Psychiatry, 36,* 307–315.

Websters Dictionary. 10th ed. Springfield, MA: Merriam-Webster. (1993). 23.

PART TWO

PSYCHOPHARMACOLOGY

CHAPTER NINE

PEDIATRIC PSYCHOPHARMACOLOGY: AN OVERVIEW

Kiki D. Chang, M.D.

We are undergoing another revolution in psychiatry as it relates to psychopharmacology. This first revolution occurred in the mid-twentieth century, when medications such as chlorpromazine allowed for the successful treatment and rehabilitation of hundreds of thousands of patients with psychotic and affective disorders. The advent of lithium and tricyclic antidepressants came afterwards, followed by the introduction of selective-serotonin reuptake inhibitors (SSRIs) and atypical antipsychotics in the 1980s. The current revolution involves the use of these and newer agents in the pediatric population.

Psychotropic Medications: An Increase in Use in Children

We are now treating more children than ever with psychotropic medications, for conditions ranging from ADHD to autism to mood disorders. Between 1987 and 1996, psychotropic prescriptions written for children and adolescents in two Medicaid and one HMO databases increased 200–300% (Zito et al., 2003). During that time, 6% of youths in the databases had been prescribed at least one psychotropic medication. Stimulant and antidepressant prescriptions have also increased in *preschoolers* over the same time (Zito et al., 2000). This explosion in pediatric psychopharmacology has likely arisen partly from a combination of positive events: (1) the increasing realization that children may have or develop primary "brain disorders" that are not due simply to parenting, transient developmental factors, or situational events, (2) the increase in research in pediatric psychiatry, helping to establish reliable methodologies for diagnosing such disorders, and (3) the advent of more effective medications that have fewer adverse effects. However, negative factors undoubtedly have been involved as well: (1) the financial pressures of U.S. health care leading to shorter patient visits, less psychotherapy, and more psychopharmacology, (2) the unavailability of sufficient psychotherapy visits for patients with lower socioeconomic status, leading to over treatment with psychotropics, (3) a national shortage of child and adolescent psychiatrists, resulting in children with psychiatric disorders needing to be cared for by more primary care physicians, who may be prescribing much of the psychotropics to children and adolescents.

The Need for Testing in Younger Age Groups

Therefore, as is typical of revolutions, this change has not gone quietly unnoticed by concerned parental and political groups. Much of the concern arises from well-founded arguments that the majority of these medications were first developed for use in adults and have not been adequately tested for efficacy or safety in children. In 1994, fluoxetine, sertraline, and methylphenidate were among the top ten of any type of drug prescribed off-label to children and adolescents (Pina, 1997). The U.S. government has been taking steps to address these concerns. In 1997, Section 111 of the U.S. Food and Drug Administration (FDA) Modernization Act allowed pharmaceutical companies to extend medication patents by six months (for a total of five years and six months) if studies were done in pediatric populations using that medication (U.S. FDA, 1997). In 1998, the Pediatric Rule stipulated that the FDA had the authority to require that certain new medications having potential pediatric use be tested adequately in children before an FDA indication would be given (U.S. FDA, 1998). This rule should have partially addressed the lack of information on pediatric use by requiring that manufacturers of certain products provide sufficient data to support pediatric use for the claimed indications. For example, in 2000 zipraisadone was the first new psychotropic medication to include such pediatric safety and efficacy data in its application for FDA approval. However, the Pediatric Rule was successfully challenged in court. On October 17, 2002, the U.S. District Court for the District of Columbia ruled that the FDA did not have the authority to issue the Pediatric Rule and barred the FDA from enforcing it. Although the U.S. government decided not to pursue an appeal in the courts, the Department of Health and Human Services announced that it would seek rapid legislation giving the FDA the authority to require pharmaceutical manufacturers to conduct appropriate pediatric clinical trials.

Additionally, the FDA Modernization Act was reborn in early 2002 as the Best Pharmaceuticals for Children Act (BPCA) (U.S. FDA, 2002). The BPCA reauthorized the existing economic incentive of extended patent protection for pharmaceutical companies that conduct pediatric studies requested by the FDA. Drugs that have been granted pediatric exclusivity so far include buspirone, citalopram, fluoxetine, fluvoxamine, gabapentin, midazolam, nefazodone, paroxetine, sertraline, and venlafaxine (U.S. FDA, 2003). However, this act includes only drugs with existing patents or exclusivity. For these drugs, this incentive has resulted in a significant increase in the number of pediatric studies performed. Unfortunately, many medicines used in children are not eligible for this kind of incentive, as they no longer have patent protection or exclusivity. Therefore, the BPCA also provides a new mechanism to help study these types of products, providing for a listing of candidate drugs and federally funded testing of these drugs. Among the first twelve listed in January 2003 were lithium and lorazepam (Kirchstein, 2003).

These legislative acts have and will continue to spur an increase in pediatric safety and efficacy data regarding psychotropics. Furthermore, in 1999 the National Institute of Mental Health (NIMH) established seven Research Units on Pediatric Psychopharmacology (RUPPs), a network of sites funded by the NIMH to study the effects and safety of psychotropic medications in children. Many private foundations and funding agencies have also begun to support child psychiatric research. The result is that we are learning more about child psychiatric disorders and psychopharmacology than ever before, and we are beginning to establish empirical data to support the widespread clinical use of psychotropics in children and adolescents.

Differences from Adults

This research of psychotropic use in pediatric populations is needed, as children are clearly not simply miniature adults. First, children may differ greatly in their pharmacokinetic profiles from adults. For example, certain medications, such as atomoxetine, have volumes of distribution based largely on body mass and are therefore prescribed according to weight. Yet lithium dosages in children often approach or surpass those in adults, due to higher glomerular filtration rates in children and possibly more efficient intracellular sodium pump mechanisms (Tueth, Murphy, & Evans, 1998). Second, children and adolescents are rapidly undergoing psychosocial and physical development, and these concerns need to be heeded when prescribing them medications. Developmental concerns include increasing dosage of some medications as body mass increases, considering psychological and physical effects of adverse effects (acne, weight gain, cognitive impairment, sexual side effects, hormonal effects) relevant to each developmental stage, and understanding the potentially powerful effect of needing to take medications on the family and school environment of the child. Third, because of brain developmental differences, medications that work in adults may not necessarily do so in children, and vice versa. The tricyclic antidepressants (TCAs) are an excellent example: while effective in adult depression, they are not as effective in childhood depression, possibly due to relatively immature norepinephrine systems in children (Geller, Reising, Leonard, Riddle, & Walsh, 1999).

Therefore, we still have much to learn. Mood stabilizers have not been studied in a systematic fashion in children and adolescents. The use of SSRIs and novel antidepressants in preschool-aged children have not been studied. Atypical antipsychotics, while presumed safer than the older generation of antipsychotics, have limited data in children, especially long-term data. The study of the interaction of psychotropic medication with normal development—physical, social, and mental—is sorely lacking as well. Nevertheless, it appears that this revolution has allowed for successful treatment of more children than ever, for a wide spectrum of disorders, allowing for restoration of normal development for hundreds of thousands of children.

The Choice to Medicate

However, for each child, the role of psychopharmacology in their overall treatment should be carefully considered. Foremost, a thorough evaluation of the child in the context of the presenting problem is necessary. Family, school, and social environments need to be assessed. Semi-structured diagnostic interviews, not often performed in the clinical setting, may help in avoiding overlooking a crucial component to the story. Medications should not usually be prescribed reflexively to symptomatology; in many cases, medications are not initially indicated. Exceptions include emergency situations, where acute management of aggression, suicidality, or psychosis is warranted. After these considerations, however, use of medications should be carefully considered. Does this condition warrant psychopharmacology? What is the empirical evidence? What are the potential risks and benefits? How will medications fit into the overall treatment plan? Practitioners and critics alike should also remember that despite possible adverse effects, *not* prescribing medications may be dangerous as well.

Medications often work faster and are less expensive treatments for certain situations. For example, the multimodal treatment study of AHDH (MTA study) clearly demonstrated that even compared to the most structured and carefully designed behavioral treatment program for ADHD, methylphenidate is still superior for treating the core symptoms of ADHD (Jensen et al., 2001). However, ADHD may be the most carefully studied psychiatric condition in children, with the longest track record of effective and safe treatments. For other conditions, such as oppositional defiant disorder, conduct disorder, PTSD, and certain anxiety disorders, it is less clear that medications are more beneficial than psychosocial therapies. In many cases, however, medications may serve to lessen acute symptomatology to help improve the response to psychotherapy. As a concrete example, if a child with social phobia or selective mutism is too anxious to tolerate a group or individual psychotherapeutic situation, medication treatment may decrease the anxiety level so that participation in the psychotherapeutic process is possible. More abstractly, an adolescent who is so depressed that concentration and motivation are affected may not do well in individual therapy until an antidepressant ameliorates these symptoms.

Therefore, the recent rise of the use of psychiatric medications in children should by no means imply that medications should supplant psychotherapeutic forms of treatment. Rather, psychopharmacology should be used to work together with psychotherapy in a synergistic way, allowing for psychotherapy to be more effective. And vice versa, psychotherapeutic interventions such as psychoeducation and CBT should be applied to the use of psychotropic medications in order to fully inform parents and children and increase adherence to prescribed regimens. This crucial involvement of psychotherapy in the psychopharmacologic treatment of children is discussed in Chapter 15 by Joshi and colleagues.

How Should Medication Be Used?

Aside from psychotherapeutic concerns, the specific manner in which medications are currently used to treat children with psychiatric disorders is an interesting one. Psychotropic medications are used in children in a palliative and therapeutic, not curative, manner. For example, in the case of ADHD, stimulants are prescribed to treat existing symptoms of inattention and hyperactivity. When these medications are not given, the symptoms return. This may continue until after puberty, when often ADHD symptoms lessen and in many cases medications are no longer needed. This scenario is different from those involving antibiotics or anti-cancer agents, which are often used in a curative fashion for relatively short durations. In most cases, psychotropics are prescribed for much longer. However, it is often unclear exactly how long it is necessary to continue these medications, as maintenance studies in pediatric populations are lacking. Another example: a fourteen-year-old girl experiences a major depressive episode, which turns out not to be her first. She is successfully treated with an antidepressant and remains symptom-free for six months. Should the medication be stopped? Reduced in dose? Continued? Although it has been recommended by the American Academy of Child and Adolescent Psychiatry that antidepressants be continued for six to twelve months after the initial depressive episode in children (Birmaher, Brent, & Benson, 1998), the data are lacking to support this. A conservative approach would be to continue treatment perhaps longer, to ensure normal psychosocial development by decreasing the risk of relapse. Another model supports continued treatment during periods of high relapse risk such as transitions into high school or college.

This model raises another potential application of psychotropics, that of preventative treatment, whether it is to prevent a recurrent or first episode. As mentioned earlier, the prophylactic nature of stimulants is very acute: as ADHD is not episodic, one is not necessarily preventing future symptoms as much as treating them. In the cases of episodic disorders, such as mood and anxiety disorders, the question of prophylaxis becomes important. Would an SSRI during times of trauma reduce or prevent symptoms of PTSD from appearing (Martenyi, Brown, Zhang, Koke, & Prakash, 2002)? Should relatives of schizophrenic probands, with subsyndromal symptomatology, or adolescents with early signs of schizophrenia be treated with antipsychotics (Cannon et al., 2002; Tsuang, Stone, Tarbox, & Faraone, 2002)? Should mood stabilizers be given to children with family histories of bipolar disorder *before* their first manic episode (Chang, Steiner, Dienes, Adleman, & Ketter, 2003)? These applications for psychotropics are the new frontier. The potential for prevention of mental illness, especially in children, is tantalizing. Research is beginning to demonstrate potential neuroprotective qualities of some psychotropic medications (Manji, Moore, & Chen, 2000). However, the physical and mental risks of taking psychotropics are still unclear, and weigh heavily when considered only against potential future benefit. Because of our limitations regarding understanding of neurobiological and phenomenological prodromes to full psychiatric disorders, it is currently impossible to identify children who will later develop the full disorder with absolute certainty (Chang et al., 2003; Erlenmeyer-Kimling, 2000). Thus, the field of prevention of psychiatric illness awaits further research regarding identification of these prodromes.

Organization and Content of Part Two

What the field does know so far regarding the use of psychotropic medication in youth, we have attempted to present here. Part Two of this *Handbook* is organized primarily according to type of medication, rather than psychiatric disorder. We are realizing that psychotropic medications are largely non-disorder specific, that they have a wide spectrum of activity, and may be useful in multiple conditions. The exception is Chapter 11, which was included to provide discussion of agents that may have a more narrow spectrum of use (benzodiazepines, buspirone) as well as those with wider spectrums (SSRIs). We will present by type of medication, mechanism of action, indications for use, and adverse effect profile, basic pharmacokinetics and interactions. Studies concerning the use of the medication in children and adolescents will be presented. Finally, in each chapter, the expert use recommendations by each author will be given.

The bulk of each chapter concerns the most up-to-date empirical knowledge of pediatric psychopharmacology. Some of this information is gleaned from studies in adults, and this data is presented, but sparingly. Instead, we have attempted to be as current as possible and present the available empirical data regarding the use of psychotropics in children and adolescents. As previously mentioned, in this field we are often lacking the gold standard studies—that of randomized double-blinded placebo-controlled studies. Nevertheless, in an attempt to catch up with real-world practices, we have included material from recent conferences and scientific presentations that may not yet have met the rigor of peer-reviewed journals. This information will, it is hoped, serve to inform both the clinician and academician of the most current appropriate uses of these medications in a pediatric population.

Omissions

In our effort to be precise, thorough, and clinically relevant, we could not be comprehensive by including discussion of all psychotropic agents used in children. The reader may notice that certain medications are not discussed in detail. For example, we do not discuss the use of primary sleeping agents here (for example, zolpidem, zaleplon). These medications have not been studied in children and very little is known about their pediatric use. On the other hand, much more is known about the use of TCAs in children. However, due to the relative inefficacy of TCAs in treating childhood depression (Keller et al., 2001), and to the adverse effect profiles and cardiac safety concerns (Geller et al., 1999), these agents are quickly disappearing from the pediatric armamentarium. TCAs may still be useful in treating enuresis, refractory ADHD (see Chapter 10), and some anxiety disorders (see Chapter 11), and so we discuss these uses. Similarly, monoamine oxidase inhibitors (MAOIs) are rarely used in children and adolescents, as they are rarely used in adults; therefore, we do not discuss their use here. However, with the advent of reversible MAOIs, perhaps there eventually will be a resurgence in the use of these agents in pediatric populations.

There are other agents that have been studied somewhat in childhood psychiatric conditions. Naltrexone may (Kolmen, Feldman, Handen, & Janosky, 1995, 1997) or may not (Feldman, Kolmen, & Gonzaga, 1999; Willemsen-Swinkels, Buitelaar, & van Engeland, 1996) be effective in reducing aggressive and self-injurious behaviors and increasing communication skills in autistic children. Nimodipine (Davanzo, Krah, Kleiner, & McCracken, 1999) may aid in treating children with treatment-refractory bipolar disorder. Other case reports pertaining to novel treatments of children periodically surface in the psychiatric literature. However, such case report data are not usually generalizable and are difficult to interpret for clinical practice. Therefore, we do not include further discussion of these more peripheral agents here. We also do not discuss the use of "natural" or "herbal" treatments, such as St. John's Wort, valerian, kava kava, or omega-3 fatty acids. Although parental administration of these compounds to their children is growing, very little data is currently available to guide the clinician as to the proper use of these agents in children and adolescents.

Although we have attempted to include discussion in each chapter of the most recently available psychotropic medications in the United States, new medications are rapidly appearing from the development pipeline, and there will undoubtedly be new psychotropic medications as we go to press.

We have also avoided strict treatment algorithms, aside from individual authors' expert recommendations. Why? Head to head studies directly comparing efficacy and safety of medications within classes or indications have been few in psychiatry, and very scant in pediatric populations. This type of study is crucial for developing treatment guidelines. Furthermore, algorithms quickly become obsolete with new studies and new medications appearing every year. Also, try as we might to pigeon-hole humans into distinct psychiatric categories, disorders are usually as heterogenous as humans themselves, and thus it is hard to make algorithms that are meaningful for large segments of the population, especially children in which much more data are required to make these algorithms. Finally, individual medications may have utility in multiple types of disorders. It would be both unwieldy and unwise to create treatment guidelines for every psychiatric disorder and disorder subtypes present in children. Nevertheless, treatment guidelines for various childhood psychiatric conditions are available elsewhere in the literature.

Real-World Pharmacotherapy

Additionally, in the "real world," combination pharmacotherapy is often required. Monotherapy would usually be preferred due to less chance of drug interactions and decreased burden on the developing brain. However, often single agents are either not entirely effective or do not address comorbid conditions. Until agents are developed to treat the underlying brain conditions, rather than addressing clusters of symptoms that are our DSM diagnoses, we are left to do the best we can with combining existing medications to treat essentially symptoms. Combination strategies are beginning to be studied in a methodical manner—such as combining two mood stabilizers (Chapter 13), adding stimulants (Chapter 10) or antipsychotics (Chapter 14) to mood stabilizers. More studies are needed regarding combinations or augmentation strategies of antidepressants.

A case example may help to illustrate the need for this type of data. FDG is a twelve-year-old boy with bipolar disorder Not Otherwise Specified (NOS), ADHD, tics, and PDD NOS. His most problematic behaviors are aggression, impulsivity, distractibility, and self-injurious behaviors. He also exhibits anxiety in social situations and depressive periods of crying and withdrawal. Finally, he has periodically had a facial tic, which has been exacerbated in the past by psychostimulant trials. He is currently taking divalproex (for mood stabilization), risperidone (to decrease aggression and self-injurious behaviors), clonidine (for ADHD symptoms), buproprion (for ADHD symptoms and depressive symptoms), and fluvoxamine (for anxiety). This is not an unusual situation—parents belonging to the Child and Adolescent Bipolar Foundation reported that 57% of their children were taking three or more different medications daily (Hellander, personal communication, 2003). Additionally, 64% of these children had tried more than six different psychotropic medications (Hellander, 2003). Very little is known about the safety or efficacy of these types of medication combinations. Therefore, researchers still have much to accomplish to help inform this type of real-world practice.

◆ ◆ ◆

We hope this section will aid clinicians in a logical and methodical way to develop their own appropriate evidence-based algorithms for treating the wide spectrum of childhood psychiatric disorders and symptoms. It is our responsibility to ensure that our children are treated safely, effectively, and above all according to the highest standards that available empirical evidence can give us.

References

Birmaher, B., Brent, D., & Benson, R. S. (1998). Practice parameters for the assessment and treatment of children and adolescents with depressive disorders. *Journal of the American Academy of Child and Adolescent Psychiatry, 37*(10 Suppl), 63S–83S.

Cannon, T. D., Huttunen, M. O., Dahlstrom, M., Larmo, I., Rasanen, P., & Juriloo, A. (2002). Antipsychotic drug treatment in the prodromal phase of schizophrenia. *American Journal of Psychiatry, 159*(7), 1230–1232.

Chang, K. D., Steiner, H., Dienes, K., Adleman, N., & Ketter, T. A. (2003). Bipolar offspring: A window into bipolar disorder evolution. *Biological Psychiatry, 53,* 945–951.

Davanzo, P. A., Krah, N., Kleiner, J., & McCracken, J. (1999). Nimodipine treatment of an adolescent with ultradian cycling bipolar affective illness. *Journal of Child and Adolescent Psychopharmacology, 9*(1), 51–61.

Erlenmeyer-Kimling, L. (2000). Neurobehavioral deficits in offspring of schizophrenic parents: Liability indicators and predictors of illness. *American Journal of Medical Genetics, 97*(1), 65–71.

Feldman, H. M., Kolmen, B. K., & Gonzaga, A. M. (1999). Naltrexone and communication skills in young children with autism. *Journal of the American Academy of Child and Adolescent Psychiatry, 38*(5), 587–593.

Geller, B., Reising, D., Leonard, H. L., Riddle, M. A., & Walsh, B. T. (1999). Critical review of tricyclic antidepressant use in children and adolescents. *Journal of the American Academy of Child and Adolescent Psychiatry, 38*(5), 513–516.

Jensen, P. S., Hinshaw, S. P., Swanson, J. M., Greenhill, L. L., Conners, C. K., Arnold, L. E., et al. (2001). Findings from the NIMH Multimodal Treatment Study of ADHD (MTA): Implications and applications for primary care providers. *Journal of Developmental and Behavioral Pediatrics, 22*(1), 60–73.

Keller, M. B., Ryan, N. D., Strober, M., Klein, R. G., Kutcher, S. P., Birmaher, B., et al. (2001). Efficacy of paroxetine in the treatment of adolescent major depression: A randomized, controlled trial. *Journal of the American Academy of Child and Adolescent Psychiatry, 40*(7), 762–772.

Kirchstein, R. L. (2003). List of drugs for which pediatric studies are needed. *Federal Register, 68,* 2789–2790.

Kolmen, B. K., Feldman, H. M., Handen, B. L., & Janosky, J. E. (1995). Naltrexone in young autistic children: A double-blind, placebo-controlled crossover study. *Journal of the American Academy of Child and Adolescent Psychiatry, 34*(2), 223–231.

Kolmen, B. K., Feldman, H. M., Handen, B. L., & Janosky, J. E. (1997). Naltrexone in young autistic children: Replication study and learning measures. *Journal of the American Academy of Child and Adolescent Psychiatry, 36*(11), 1570–1578.

Manji, H. K., Moore, G. J., & Chen, G. (2000). Clinical and preclinical evidence for the neurotrophic effects of mood stabilizers: Implications for the pathophysiology and treatment of manic-depressive illness. *Biological Psychiatry, 48*(8), 740–754.

Martenyi, F., Brown, E. B., Zhang, H., Koke, S. C., & Prakash, A. (2002). Fluoxetine v. placebo in prevention of relapse in post-traumatic stress disorder. *The British Journal of Psychiatry, 181,* 315–320.

Pina, L. M. (1997). Center IDs top 10 drugs used off-label in out-patient setting. *News Along the Pike, 3*(1), 6–7.

Tsuang, M. T., Stone, W. S., Tarbox, S. I., & Faraone, S. V. (2002). An integration of schizophrenia with schizotypy: Identification of schizotaxia and implications for research on treatment and prevention. *Schizophrenia Research, 54*(1–2), 169–175.

Tueth, M. J., Murphy, T. K., & Evans, D. L. (1998). Special considerations: Use of lithium in children, adolescents, and elderly populations. *Journal of Clinical Psychiatry, 59*(Suppl 6), 66–73.

United States Federal Drug Administration (U.S. FDA). (1997). FDA Modernization Act of 1997. Retrieved from http://www.fda.gov/cdrh/modact97.pdf

United States Federal Drug Administration (U.S. FDA). (1998). Regulations requiring manufacturers to assess the safety and effectiveness of new drugs and biological products in
pediatric patients. Retrieved from http://www.fda.gov/ohrms/dockets/98fr/120298c.pdf

United States Federal Drug Administration (U.S. FDA). (2002). An Act to amend the Federal
Food, Drug, and Cosmetic Act to improve the safety and efficacy of pharmaceuticals for
children. Retrieved from http://www.fda.gov/cder/pediatric/PL107-109.pdf

United States Federal Drug Administration (U.S. FDA). (2003). Approved Active Moieties to
Which FDA has Granted Pediatric Exclusivity for Pediatric Studies under Section 505A of
the Federal Food, Drug, and Cosmetic Act. Retrieved from http://www.fda.gov/cder/
pediatric/exgrant.htm

Willemsen-Swinkels, S. H., Buitelaar, J. K., & van Engeland, H. (1996). The effects of
chronic naltrexone treatment in young autistic children: A double-blind placebo-
controlled crossover study. *Biological Psychiatry, 39*(12), 1023–1031.

Zito, J. M., Safer, D. J., dosReis, S., Gardner, J. F., Boles, M., & Lynch, F. (2000). Trends in
the prescribing of psychotropic medications to preschoolers. *Journal of the American Medical
Association, 283*(8), 1025–1030.

Zito, J. M., Safer, D. J., DosReis, S., Gardner, J. F., Magder, L., Soeken, K., et al. (2003).
Psychotropic practice patterns for youth: A 10-year perspective. *Archives of Pediatrics and
Adolescent Medicine, 157*(1), 17–25.

CHAPTER TEN

PSYCHOSTIMULANTS, ATOMOXETINE, AND ALPHA-AGONISTS

Shashank V. Joshi, M.D.

The stimulant medications continue to be the most commonly prescribed agents in child and adolescent psychiatry in the United States (Safer & Zito, 1999). A vast body of literature exists to support their use, and recently, there has been a marked increase in the types of stimulant compounds available (Wender, 2002). Amphetamines are the prototypical agent, and have been prescribed in the United States since 1887. They were initially used in the treatment of asthma as an alternative to ephedrine (Alles, 1928). In 1937, Dr. Charles Bradley was the first to systematically document the use of psychostimulants in the treatment of children with hyperactivity. He noted marked improvements in school performance and behavior (Bradley, 1937). However, it was not until the 1950s and 1960s that work was done to develop these medications further, and with the introduction of methylphenidate (MPH), there has been a steady interest in the regular use and study of these medications. Methylphenidates and amphetamines currently represent the mainstay of treatment for ADHD in children and teenagers.

Other medications that have been used in ADHD treatment in children and teens include the tricyclic antidepressants (TCAs), which despite a substantial database are relegated to second or third line agents due to side effects. The TCAs and atypical/newer antidepressants, such as bupropion and venlafaxine, are discussed

Sincere thanks to Shalini Joshi, M.A., Lic.S.W., for her assistance in reviewing and preparing this manuscript.

elsewhere in this book. Atomoxetine (Strattera) was approved in January 2003 for the treatment of ADHD in children, teens, and adults. It will be discussed later in this chapter, as will the alpha-adrenergic agents clonidine and guanfacine.

Medications

Both the psychostimulants and atomoxetine are thought to exert their mechanisms of action on the catecholamines dopamine (DA) and/or norepinephrine (NE) by reuptake inhibition, enhanced release, or a combination of these (Bymaster, Katner, & Nelson, 2002; Greenhill, Pliszka, Dulcan, & the Workgroup on Quality Issues, 2002). Bupropion (Wellbutrin) is also thought to act by this mechanism, though its clinical effects on ADHD symptoms are not as robust (Pliszka & the Texas Consensus Conference Panel on Medication Treatment of Childhood Attention-Deficit/Hyperactivity Disorder, 2000a, 2000b). Amphetamines (AMPH) seem to affect many aspects of release, uptake, and storage, while methylphenidates (MPH) act primarily presynaptically to prevent reuptake of dopamine and norepinephrine though the inhibition of the DA transporter protein (Elia, Borcherding, & Potter, 1990).

Amphetamine Preparations

Chemical Properties and Putative Mechanisms of Efficacy. Amphetamine preparations exist in both *d*- and *d*-/*l*-forms. Dexedrine (*d*-amphetamine, DEX) has been in widespread use, and Adderall has now become the most popular of the amphetamine compounds (Safer & Zito, 1999). Its four different salts include *d*-amphetamine saccharate, *d*-amphetamine sulfate, *l*-amphetamine aspartate, and *l*-amphetamine sulfate.

Methamphetamine (Desoxyn) is longer acting, but is rarely prescribed due to its high abuse potential. The common unifying theme among all of the stimulants is the phenylethylamine backbone, typical of agents used in the treatment of ADHD. Although it is a centrally acting compound, minor modifications can provide a host of biological actions, including decongestant, anorectic, antidepressant, and hallucinogenic effects (Glennon, 1987; Fawcett & Busch, 1998). (Please see the chemical makeup of pychostimulant drugs in Figure 10.1.)

Stimulants are so described primarily because of their direct effects on DA, particularly in areas of the brain such as the prefrontal cortex and nucleus accumbens. They are classified as Schedule II by the FDA, the most restrictive class felt to be medically useful (Hyman, Arana, & Rosenbaum, 1995; Rosenberg, Holttum, & Gershon, 1994). Agents with either indirect DA effects (atomoxetine) or milder direct effects (bupropion) have not been given this classification

FIGURE 10.1. PSYCHOSTIMULANT DRUGS.

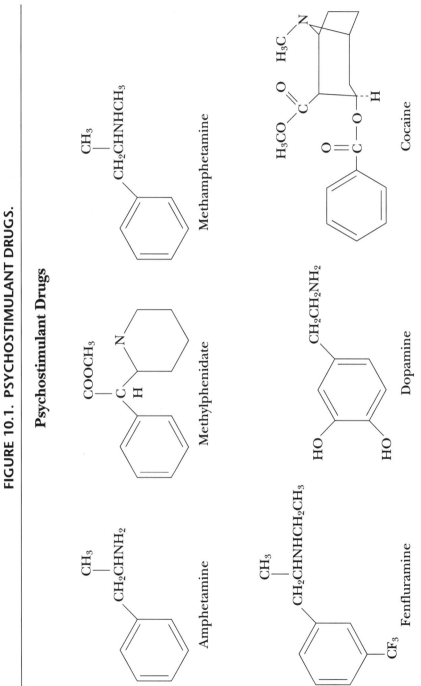

Psychostimulant Drugs

(Schedule II) by the FDA. A nonstimulant classification may be attributed largely to its lack of abuse potential, and/or its lack of activity in the nucleus accumbens. The stimulants have unique pharmacokinetic properties, in that they are rapidly absorbed, go through first pass metabolism, and have a duration of action of three to five hours for short acting agents, and up to twelve hours for longer acting preparations. All agents have a behavioral half life ($T_{1/2}$), which refers to duration of behavioral effect, and a pharmacologic half life, or the time it takes for 50% of the medication to be metabolically degraded. For a review of the current preparations, please see Tables 10.1 and 10.2, as well as the very useful articles by Adesman (2003) or by Howe and Findling (2003). The benefits of stimulants have been shown in many short-term, and some longer-term (one to two years) trials (Greenhill & Osman, 1999) for the treatment of ADHD. Major improvements typically occur in the core symptoms of ADHD (inattention, distractibility, impulsivity, hyperactivity), with secondary improvements in some of the non-core symptoms (social skills, peer relationships, family interactions). Stimulants may be especially useful when comorbid disorders are present (anxiety, depression, or conduct disorder) (Greenhill et al., 2002). Other proven benefits of stimulants occur in the treatment of narcolepsy and certain medical-psychiatric conditions discussed below, though there are only a few randomized controlled trials (Greenhill et al., 2002). In addition to its potent central stimulant effects, amphetamines also have some important adverse peripheral effects. For example, their noradrenergic actions on alpha and beta receptors seem to account for an association with blood pressure elevation (Hoffman & Lefkowitz, 1990).

TABLE 10.1. AMPHETAMINE PREPARATIONS.

Brand name	Type	Dosage forms (mg)	Est. duration (hrs)	Max daily dose (mg) Range 0.15–1.5 mg/kg/day
Generic	IR	5,10,20	3–6	40*
Dexedrine	IR	5,10,20	3–6	40*
	Spansules (ER)	5,10,20	6–8	
Adderall	IR	5,10,15,20	6–8	40*
	XR**	5,10,15,20	8–12	

Source: Chart adapted from Glen R. Elliott, Ph.D., M.D.

*Some patients will tolerate higher doses.

**50% "immediate-release beads" active in first four hours, remainder are released in second four hours.

TABLE 10.2.   METHYLPHENIDATE PREPARATIONS.

Brand	Type	Dosage forms (mg)	Est. duration (hrs)	Max daily dose (mg) Range 0.3– 2 mg/kg/day
Generic	IR	5,10,20	2.5–4	60*
Ritalin	IR	5,10,20	2.5–4	60*
	SR	20	6–?	
	LA[†]	20,30,40	10–12	
Methylin	IR	5,10,20	2.5–4	60*
	ER	5,10,20	6–8	
Focalin	IR	2.5,5,10	3–5	20
Metadate	ER	10,20	6–8	60*
	CD[††]	20	8–12	
Concerta	ER[†††]	18,27,36,54	10–12	54

Source: Chart adapted from Glen R. Elliott, Ph.D., M.D.

*Some patients will tolerate higher doses.

**Methypatch expected in 2004.

[†]50% immediate release beads, 50% delayed release beads; first peak in 1 hour; second peak in 6 hours.

[††]30% immediate release beads, 70% delayed release beads; first peak in 1.5 hours; second peak in 4.5 hours.

[†††]22% immediate release coat, 78% delayed osmotic release mechanism; first peak in 1–2 hours to second peak in 6 to 7 hours.

Dosing and Pharmacokinetics. The recommended dose range for amphetamine preparations in pediatric patients is 0.15 to 1.5 mg/kg/day, with a target maximum dose of 40 mg per day. (See Table 10.2 for a guideline regarding doses.) Some patients may require and tolerate higher doses. Most of the common side effects are dose-related, and generally occur about equally with both methylphenidate and amphetamines. There are some noteworthy differences, however. For instance, there are some data (albeit a small amount) suggesting that certain problems may be more apparent with amphetamines, such as growth velocity deceleration and insomnia (Arnold, 2000), which appears to be dose-related. Also, amphetamine preparations may actually prevent absence seizure activity (three-cycle per second "spike & wave" discharges) in some patients, thus making them especially useful in children at risk for seizures (Green, 2001; McBride, Wang, & Torres, 1986; Weiner, 1980). (Note: Though the manufacturer's insert lists lowered seizure threshold as a possible side effect, very little published data exists to support this (Gucuyener et al., 2003; McBride, 1986).

The immediate release (IR) amphetamines appear to be similar in their kinetics in both teens and children (Swanson, Wigal, & Greenhill, 1998), though teens may derive benefits from lower, weight-adjusted doses, compared to younger children (Findling, Short, & Manos, 2001). They are rapidly absorbed directly from the gastrointestinal (GI) tract (Hoffman & Lefkowitz, 1990). Behavioral effects peak one to two hours after administration, lasting for four to six hours. Peak effects correspond to peak plasma levels, and appear in two to three hours. Although the clearance duration is twelve to twenty hours, the behavioral duration is two to six hours. Newer amphetamine compounds appear to have a faster onset (less than one hour), with cognitive and behavior effects lasting from eight hours (Adderall), to twelve hours (Adderall XR). Refer to Table 10.1 for a summary of available preparations and dosing parameters.

Metabolism. Although amphetamines are extensively metabolized in the liver through the cytochrome P450 enzyme 2D6, it does not appear to have clinically significant interactions with the serotonin reuptake inhibitors (DeVane, 1992; Markowitz, Morrison, & DeVane, 1999), even those that are potent inhibitors of this micromosal enzyme system. As amphetamines are a basic compound, urinary excretion depends greatly on urine pH. Acidification of the urine results in a shortened plasma half life and increased amphetamine clearance. This property makes urine acidification strategies useful in amphetamine toxic situations (Caldwell & Sever, 1974; Goff & Ciraulo, 1991; Masand & Tesar, 1996; Wilens & Spencer, 2000). Hence, patients who report decreased stimulant efficacy should be asked about excessive vitamin C intake (Wilens & Spencer, 2000).

Adverse Effects and Contraindications. As the vast majority of these are similar to those seen with methylphenidate, this will be covered in the next section. Please see Figure 10.2 for some differences that have been noted among stimulant types.

FIGURE 10.2. CHEMICAL MAKEUP OF ATOMOXETINE.

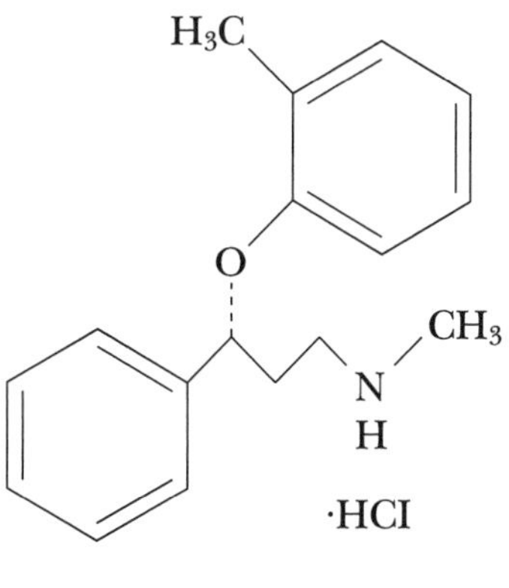

Methylphenidates

Chemical Properties and Putative Mechanisms of Efficacy. Properties of methylphenidate are similar to those of amphetamine and dexedrine, with a few important differences. Though methylphenidate, for example, inhibits presynaptic DA reuptake, its far lesser abuse potential compared to street drugs with similar mechanisms may be related to its slower clearance from the plasma (Volkow, Wang et al. 1998; Volkow, Ding et al. 1995).

Dosing and Pharmacokinetics. As with amphetamine/dexedrine, absorption of methylphenidate is rapid (first pass metabolism). There do not appear to be major interactions with CYP2D6 inhibitors, despite its metabolism there as a substrate. Shorter acting methylphenidate preparations are given two to three times daily, due to the short duration of action of two to four hours. Longer acting preparations are designed to be administered once in the morning, and designed to have a behavioral duration of eight to twelve hours. (Please see Table 10.2 for specifics of doses available, half-lives, and daily dose ranges.)

It should be noted that pemoline, which is not included in the chart, continues to be used in special circumstances, and is available in 18.75, 37.5, and 75 mg tablets. Its half life is about seven to eight hours in children and eleven to thirteen hours in adults, reaching C_{max} (peak levels) in one to four hours after ingestion.

Of the three general types of stimulants, methylphenidate, amphetamine/dexedrine, and pemoline, methylphenidate seems to have the best uptake into the central nervous system (Elia, 1991; Wilens & Spencer, 2000), which may account for the least problematic side effect profile related to peripheral effects (Caldwell & Sever, 1974; Masand & Tesar, 1996; Wilens & Spencer, 2000). Pemoline has the slowest absorption of the three, in part due to its poor lipid and aqueous solubility (Sallee, Stiller, & Perel et al., 1985; Wilens & Spencer, 2000).

Adverse Effects Profile. Adverse effects may be seen in 20% (or more) of children, but most are neither problematic nor long-term (Dulcan, 1990; Masand & Tesar, 1996). The most common ones include headache, stomachache, appetite suppression, sleep problems, irritability, "zombie effect," tachycardia, blood pressure increases, tics, dysphoric mood, height-velocity slow down, and rarely, psychosis. Most of these effects tend to be dose related, which is why it is important to start with a low dose and proceed with titration slowly.

For a discussion of the height velocity issue, see Joshi (2002) for a brief review of some of the seminal articles in the literature on the relationship between psychostimulants and growth suppression. Essentially, although this side effect is potentially problematic in less than 10% of all children, and may in fact be due to the effects of ADHD itself (independent of the effect of psychostimulants), growth parameters should be carefully monitored at regular intervals. The aforementioned side effects should be explained to parents, with special mention about their generally temporary nature. Each of these, if persistent, can often be managed by some simple measures. For example, headache may be managed with acetaminophen, ibuprofen, or lowering of the dose. A switch to a different preparation, proprietary form, or even type of stimulant may be warranted if these side effects continue. Stomachache and appetite suppression may be managed by taking the medication with meals (or after meals). Also, a high-calorie snack may be given at night. Medication holidays should be considered for those patients who continually experience appetite suppression, despite modifications. For the most part, food should not affect absorption, although Concerta (OROS-MPH) may be better absorbed following a fatty meal, compared to Adderall (immediate release preparation) (Auiler, Liu, Lynch, & Gelotte, 2002). Sleep difficulties may require giving the medication earlier in the day, or a switch to a different preparation. Please see Table 10.3 for a summary of strategies on dealing with adverse effects.

TABLE 10.3. MANAGEMENT OF COMMON STIMULANT-INDUCED ADVERSE EFFECTS.

Adverse effect	Management
insomnia	Administer earlier in day Change to shorter acting agents Give last dose no later than mid-afternoon (before 3:30 PM) Consider adjunctive agents (trazodone, mirtazapine, alpha-agonists with caution)
decreased appetite, nausea, weight loss	Administer with meals Give a larger snack/mini-meal at bedtime Caloric enhancers (Boost, Ensure) Change preparation
irritability	Assess timing of phenomena (during peak or withdrawal phase) Reduce dose/change to longer acting preparation Evaluate comorbid symptoms (mood disorder)
rebound phenomena	Overlap stimulant dosing (give small amount of IR dose in the afternoon) Change to longer acting preparation Consider alternative or adjunctive treatment
headaches	Change brand, or change stimulant type
"zombie effect"	Lower dose, change stimulant type May need to switch to non-stimulant
height-velocity slowing	Weekend/vacation holidays Lower dose Consider non-stimulant

Adapted from Greenhill, 2002

Drug Interactions/Contraindications

Contraindications: These apply to both types of stimulants in primary clinical use (Amphetamine/dexedrine, and methylphenidate) and include a previous sensitivity to these agents, a history of glaucoma, symptomatic cardiovascular disease, clinically important hypertension, or hyperthyroidism. Additionally, care should be used if there is a history of substance abuse by the patient or any member of his or her household. Stimulants are not to be used in patients already taking a monoamine oxidase inhibitor (MAOI), or with a history of active psychosis. As outlined in the American Academy of Child and Adolescent Psychiatry (AACAP) Practice Parameters (Greenhill et al., 2002), the FDA packaging lists many other potential contraindications, not all of which have an empirical basis. For example, recent data indicate that the presence of tics or Tourette syndrome alone is not sufficient reason to withhold stimulants (Gadow, Sverd, & Sparfkin, 1995). Finally, although methylphenidate is not approved for use in children under six, there are at least eight published studies documenting their efficacy. In contrast, d-amphetamine and pemoline both have approval down to age three, despite the lack of any published controlled studies in children this young (Greenhill et al., 2002).

Indications: The following are known indications for stimulants, and have been derived from the Practice Parameters for the use of Stimulants, developed by the AACAP. These parameters are classified according to the degree of importance or certainty of each recommendation. "Minimal standards" (MS) are so designated because of a clear evidence base or a consistent clinical consensus, and would be considered a standard of care. These standards are expected to be applied in more than 95% of cases. The parameter states that when and if the practitioner chooses to stray from this standard or modify it in some way, these changes should be documented in the medical record with the reasons for the decision. "Clinical guidelines ("CG") are based on a smaller amount of clinical studies or strong clinical consensus. They apply about 75% of the time. These should be strongly considered by clinicians, but they need not be uniformly applied in all cases. "Options" (OP) are those practices considered acceptable standards, but are not required to be carried out in all cases. They generally have a weaker evidence base, but are nonetheless accepted as conventional wisdom, and clinicians should be aware of what they are. Finally, "Not endorsed" (NE) refers to practices that are considered to be ineffective, and are therefore not recommended based on data available at the time of publication of the Practice Parameters (February 2002).

All children, teens, and adults should undergo a thoughtful and thorough evaluation prior to receiving a diagnosis and subsequent treatment. This includes a comprehensive history of both psychiatric and medical symptoms and treatments, as well as a detailed developmental, school, family, and social/environmental history. Furthermore, this history is best obtained from at least two adults in the child's life, preferably from two different settings (such as home and school or daycare). Next, it is important to document which DSM-IV TR criteria are met, as well as what other target symptoms exist. If, after this workup (which may take three to four hours in total), a definitive diagnosis is not arrived at, but symptoms exist within the ADHD or other (see subsequent list) categories, a trial of psychostimulants may still be indicated. Parents should be given the option of other treatment modalities (such as behavioral treatment and parent support) in all cases of disruptive behavior disorders. The following is a list of indications for the use of stimulants:

- ADHD, as documented by DSM-IV TR criteria, and without comorbid conditions.
- ADHD with certain comorbid conditions, such as conduct disorder: substantial impairment must occur across settings in order to justify treatment.

For adolescents, the clinician needs to monitor use of other medications, especially non-prescribed drugs of abuse. In these cases, it may be useful to contract with the teen regarding the use of illicit substances, thus returning a sense of control over some of the decision-making in a troubled teen's life (CG).

- Narcolepsy, as defined by excessive daytime sleepiness with recurrent sleep attacks and cataplexy.
- Apathy due to a general medical condition, though doses are typically lower than those used in the treatment of ADHD.
- These agents may be especially useful in patients with traumatic brain injuries or degenerative neurological processes who exhibit apathy or some of the core symptoms of ADHD, such as impulsiveness, distractibility, inattention, or problematic impulsivity (OP).
- Adjuvant use: Low dose stimulants may be helpful to those patients who suffer from severe psychomotor retardation secondary to an illness itself, sedative effects from certain agents (such as pain medications), or side effects from therapeutic medical agents (such as chemotherapy). Case reports indicate success at improving energy level, overall functioning, appetite, and alertness (Breitbart, 1998).
- Treatment refractory depression: These agents may be used to augment agents already in-use, such as TCAs. Doses are typically lower than those used in ADHD.

Clinical Efficacy: The largest of the longer-term studies was a fourteen-month multi-site prospective study sponsored by the NIMH, the Multimodal Treatment of ADHD (MTA) study (MTA Cooperative Group, 1999). This was a randomized, six-site clinical trial of four different interventions, n = 579, with children aged 7 to 9.9 years diagnosed with ADHD-combined type (ADHD-CT). The results of this study indicated that medication management (alone or in combination with other modes of parent/behavioral therapy) resulted in substantial improvements in the symptoms and sequelae of ADHD compared to a non-standardized community control group, termed "usual community care." The majority of children enrolled in the study received methylphenidate, although alternative medications were used when necessary. An important result from the study was, that for the core symptoms of ADHD as listed in DSM-IV TR, medication treatment alone would likely suffice. However, parent management and behavior components may be of essential importance for the non-core symptoms (problems with social skills, peer and family relationships, comorbid mental health problems). Practically speaking, although more common in non-referred samples, "garden variety" (non-comorbid) ADHD may account for less than 20% of all referred cases to academic medical center sites in child psychiatry (S. Faraone, Ph.D., personal communication, 2001). (Note: It should be remembered that the "medication management only" arm of this treatment consisted of monthly visits with an academic child psychiatrist for thirty-minute sessions. Aspects of this intervention included regular psychoeducation and parent support components.)

Methylphenidate for Children with ADHD and Tics. Although there have been numerous controlled studies (Castellanos, Giedd, & Elia et al., 1997; Gadow et al., 1995; Gadow, Nolan, & Sverd, 1992; Konkol, Fischer, & Newby, 1990; Sverd, Gadow, & Nolan et al., 1992) showing that psychostimulants can be very effective for core symptoms of ADHD, aggression, and social skills deficits in children with Tourette's syndrome or chronic tics, clinicians are still urged to proceed with caution by some authorities (Cohen & Leckman, 1988; Leckman et al., 1997; Riddle et al., 1995; Sverd, 1999). Based on the available data, and with the knowledge that tics may be associated with ADHD (even without stimulant medication), the AACAP Practice Parameters (Greenhill et al., 2002) urge that a trial of psychostimulant begin with proper informed consent. If tics worsen, one can move to another stimulant type. If the symptoms of ADHD improve, and tics remain the same, the clinician, patient, and family must determine which symptoms are most problematic, and treat accordingly. Alternate agents, such as alpha-agonists (guanfacine, clonidine) or D2 antagonists (risperidone, ziprasidone, haloperidol, pimozide) may be considered as additions to treat tics. Other strategies include a lowering of the stimulant dose, which may become more possible with a second medication in the regimen, or a switch to a nonstimulant as monotherapy, such as atomoxetine, atypical antidepressant (bupropion, venlafaxine), or tricyclic antidepressant.

Developmental Issues

Preschool

Because of developmental variabilities, ADHD can sometimes be hard to diagnose in younger children. Still, there is evidence that DSM-IV criteria are valid for children as young as four (Lahey, 1998). Wilens and Spencer (2000) reviewed the eight published placebo-controlled studies in this age group, and found that the majority showed improvement in school behavior, while displaying a lack of significant problems during unstructured activities such as recess (Barkley, 1988; Barkley, Karlsson, & Strzelecki et al., 1984; Conners, 1975; Cunningham, Siegel, & Offord, 1985; Mayes, Crites, & Bixler et al., 1994; Musten, Firestone, & Pisterman et al., 1997; Schleifer, Weiss, & Cohen et al., 1975). Dose ranges were 0.3 mg/kg to 1.0 mg/kg/day.

Musten and colleagues (1997) studied the effects of methylphenidate in thirty-one preschoolers aged four to six years, using doses of 0.3 and 0.5 mg/kg twice daily. Twenty-six (84%) of the subjects were also diagnosed with comorbid oppositional disorder, and six (19%) with conduct disorder. They found a dose-dependent improvement in attention, academic improvement, and impulse control, with the greatest improvements at higher doses. Though side effects were noted with much greater frequency at the higher doses as well, the authors recommended using the higher doses because of best results overall (Green, 2001; Musten et al., 1997).

School-Age (Preteens). As Wilens and Spencer (2000) have noted in their review, over 200 controlled trials in this age group have consistently demonstrated a 60–70% response rate on multiple cognitive and behavioral measures if one stimulant is tried, and up to 85% if a second stimulant of another type is tried (Arnold, 2000; Klein, 1987; Spencer, Biederman, & Wilens et al., 1996; Swanson, McBurnett, & Christian et al., 1995). A consistently low placebo response rate was also observed in these trials.

Adolescence. There have been four open and six controlled trials of stimulants in adolescents with ADHD, with results showing an overall response rate of about 75% (Wilens & Spencer, 2000; Bostic, Biederman, & Spencer et al., 2000; Brown & Sexson, 1988; Coons, Klorman, & Borgstedt, 1987; Kloorman, Coons, & Borgstedt, 1987; Lerer & Lerer, 1977; MacKay, Beck, & Taylor, 1973; Safer & Allen, 1975; Smith, Pelham, & Gnagy et al., 1998; Varley, 1983). As is the case with other pediatric studies, stimulants appear to be safe and efficacious in adolescents, and improvement in symptoms seems to be dose-dependent.

Adults. There have been ten controlled studies of stimulants to date in adults. Results have been equivocal, with an overall response rate of 25–73%, and about one-third of patients reporting significant side effects. Wilens and Spencer (2000) have reviewed these papers, and propose that low doses, improper diagnoses, and high rates of comorbidity may have contributed to the variability in responses. A higher abuse potential than that seen in the pediatric population has fueled the search for non-stimulant medication options for adult ADHD.

Clinical Use Guidelines

As previously mentioned, a thorough history should be done to elicit prior use of all medications and responses. A baseline cardiovascular assessment should be done, preferably by the prescriber for best continued follow-up. Blood pressure, height, weight, and complete neurologic exam are also highly recommended, and this is the practice followed by most providers. At the Stanford University Clinic, height is measured every three months and plotted on a growth chart; weight, blood pressure, and pulse are taken at each visit; and BP/pulse are done any time there is a dose change. Use a recommended starting dose, and this will depend on which particular medicine is being used. Some data (especially early data from the 1970s) have shown that appetite suppression and sleep may be more affected by amphetamine/dexedrine preparations. Though methylphenidate might (rarely) lower the seizure threshold, the presence of seizure disorder alone is not a sufficient contraindication to its use. Still, it may be wise to stabilize the seizure disorder first, before treating with stimulants. (Please see Table 10.4 for a comparison of methylphenidate and amphetamine.) If bipolar symptoms are also present, they should be stabilized first, as stimulants may potentially cause or exacerbate mania (Pliszka, 2003). Both methylphenidate and amphetamine preparations appear to be equally effective, though Adderall may have a slight edge in head-to-head studies over standard release methylphenidate (Faraone, Biederman, & Roe, 2002). For methylphenidates, the recommended starting dose is 5 mg, once or twice daily, or 0.3 mg/kg/day divided to a dose of twice daily (BID). The dose is then steadily increased to maximum effect, with target doses in the range of 0.3–2 mg/kg/day. Data on medication titrations show that absolute numbers are generally adequate as guidelines for dosing, and are preferred over weight-based dosing, especially for children and adolescents over 25 kg. This allows for minimal chances for "underdosing." Still, weight-based dosing may be useful for smaller children in order to minimize side effects. If a weight-based approach is used, plan to use the target

TABLE 10.4.   RELATIVE ADVANTAGES OF METHYLPHENIDATE AND AMPHETAMINE IN THE TREATMENT OF ADHD.

Methylphenidate	Amphetamine
Better Continuous Performance Task (CPT) response	Adderall may have better effect size, compared to standard release MPH
Possibly better with comorbid Tourette's syndrome	Higher proportion of patients with good or excellent response
Possibly better with comorbid learning disability (LD)	May be better with high IQ
Less anorexia and weight loss	
Less temporary slowing of height velocity in low doses	Adderall may have slightly delayed onset compared to MPH
Lower street value and abuse potential	Slightly anticonvulsant in lower doses; may be safer when there is a history of seizures
More longer acting forms available; two of the longer acting preparations may be taken apart and sprinkled on food just prior to taking	Shorter acting form of Adderall is double-scored, for easy titration; Adderall XR may be sprinkled on food just prior to administration

Source: Data adapted from Arnold, 1999; Swanson, Wigel, & Greenhill, 1998; Manos, Short, & Findling, 1999; Pliszka, Browne, Olvera, & Wynne, 2000.

dose in the range of 0.3 to 2 mg/kg/day, divided into one to three doses for older children (those greater than 25 kg). We recommend lower doses for children less than 25 kg, in the range of 0.3 mg to 1 mg/kg/day). As of September 2003, the maximum recommended dose for methylphenidate preparations is 60 mg (or 54 mg for Concerta [OROS-MPH]). Amphetamine preps are thought of as 1.5 to 2 times as potent as methylphenidate preps. Accordingly, the corresponding dose is one-half to two-thirds of an MPH dose, and this works out to roughly 0.15 to 1.5 mg/kg/day, with the max daily dose being 40 mg. The usual starting dose is 2.5 mg one to three times per day. We recommend a starting dose of 2.5 mg only on the first day as a test dose. As a general rule, the AACAP Practice Parameters (Greenhill et al., 2002) recommend giving no more than single doses of 15 mg methylphenidate or 10 mg amphetamine/dexedrine for children under 25 kg. A clinical guideline is to use no more than 25 mg for any single dose for methylphenidate, if multiple doses are given during the day. At the Stanford University Clinic, we strongly concur with the Practice Parameters that "if there is no help at the top dose, more is not likely to be helpful (but could bring about more side effects)." There are some teens and adults who will tolerate and require higher doses, such as 40 mg of Adderall-XR in the morning. A consistent and regular dose titration schedule should be aimed for. So, for example, if the desired response is not seen, doses should be increased gradually, 5 to 10 mg per week of methylphenidate, and 2.5 to 5 mg per week of amphetamine/dexedrine. A fixed dose schedule may also be used, in which a child gets exposure to his or her "best dose," which can be deduced at the end of such a trial (typically one month or so, as in the MTA study) (MTA Cooperative Group, 1999). Parents must also be informed regarding the method of evaluating drug response, and, importantly, strategies for managing treatment-emergent side effects. (See Table 10.3.) Pemoline's starting dose is typically 18.75 mg in the morning, and the dose is titrated to up to 75 mg daily. The maximum daily dose is 112.5 mg. Due to concerns about fulminant hepatic failure, however, pemoline has fallen out of favor with most clinicians. Still, it is included here for completeness, and because some patients and families feel that pemoline is the best agent for their child. If this medication is chosen, informed consent is a must, as is monitoring every two weeks of certain liver function tests, such as ALT and AST.

Treatment is commonly divided into titration and maintenance phases. The former is usually thought of as the first two to four weeks, while the latter is considered to have started once the patient has been maintained on a therapeutic dose over time. Continued follow-up is best done on a monthly basis to assess response of core symptoms, overall psychological functioning, and presence of side effects, especially growth and cardiovascular parameters.

Atomoxetine. Atomoxetine was the first non-stimulant approved for the treatment of ADHD in children and teens, and the first agent approved for use in adult ADHD.

Mechanism of Action. Atomoxetine is a highly selective norepinephrine reuptake inhibitor (SNRI), with a binding affinity (Ki) of 5. For comparison, Table 10.5 illustrates Ki's for other agents. Note that the Ki of fluoxetine for serotonin is 7.

TABLE 10.5.   AFFINITY OF ATOMOXETINE AND OTHER UPTAKE INHIBITORS FOR HUMAN MONOAMINE TRANSPORTER.

Compound	Norepinephrine	Serotonin Ki, nM	Dopamine
Atomoxetine	5	77	1451
Reboxetine	11	440	>10000
Desipramine	3.8	179	>10000
Methylphenidate	339	>10000	34
Bupropion	>10000	>10000	562
Imipramine	98	19	>10000
Fluoxetine	1022	7	4752

Note: The lower the Ki, the *greater* the affinity.

Source: Adapted from Bymaster et al., 2002.

According to animal data, despite its noradrenergic selectivity it may in fact have potent pro-dopaminergic activity in the prefrontal cortex, with little or no activity in the nucleus accumbens (Bymaster et al., 2002).

Empirical Support. As of this writing, much of the experience thus far comes from the Eli Lilly database (4,800 studied patients as of March 2003). Scientific and initial anecdotal inquiry indicate promise for its use as an alternative to stimulants in children and teens, with comparability in effectiveness to methylphenidate in one investigation (Kratochvil, 2002).

In this study, 228 patients with ADHD were randomized in open label fashion, to receive either atomoxetine (n = 184) or methylphenidate (n = 44). The researchers reported significant improvement in both groups of patients for inattentive and hyperactive-impulsive symptom clusters, using the DuPaul ADHD Rating Scale (DuPaul et al., 1996). The authors propose atomoxetine's safety profile to be superior to that of other effective nonstimulants, such as desipramine.

Michelson, Allen, Busner and associates (2002) examined the efficacy of once-daily atomoxetine in a multi-site randomized placebo-controlled study. Children and teens with ADHD (n = 171, age six to sixteen years) were assigned to receive either six weeks of treatment with atomoxetine, or with placebo. Results showed significant improvements in the atomoxetine treatment group over the placebo-treated group, with an effect size of 0.71, on investigator, parent, and teacher rating scales. Furthermore, drug-specific effects were not only evident in the late afternoon and evening periods, but also seemed to have a "carry-over" effect into the next morning. Discontinuation from adverse effects was considered low (less than 3%) for both treated groups, and no serious safety concerns were observed.

Michelson, Faries, Wernicke and associates (2001) prospectively studied 297 children and teens, ages eight to eighteen, who were randomly assigned to placebo or atomoxetine. The latter group was tried on three different weight-adjusted doses, 0.5 mg/kg/day, 1.2 mg/kg/day, or 1.8 mg/kg/day, for a period of two months. Parent and investigator scales included the ADHD Rating Scale (ADHD-RS), Connors Parent Rating Scale (CPRS), Children's Depression Rating Scale, Revised (CDRS-R), and Child Health Questionnaire (CHQ). Results were significantly better for the atomoxetine group on core symptoms of ADHD, and on selected measures of social and family functioning, such as "ability to meet psychosocial role expectations" and "parental impact." Discontinuation secondary to adverse effects was less than 5% for all three dosing-regimen groups. The authors concluded that atomoxetine was superior to placebo in reducing ADHD symptoms and in improving some "non-core" symptoms of ADHD (aspects of social and family functioning), and is best utilized at a target dose of 1.2 mg/kg/day.

Finally, Michelson, Adler, Spencer and colleagues (2003) studied 536 adults with ADHD for ten weeks in two prospective placebo-controlled studies (n = 280 and n = 256), using the Connors Adult ADHD Rating Scales and Sheehan Disability Scale as the main outcome measures. Results showed that atomoxetine was efficacious (superior to placebo) for both inattentive and hyperactive-impulsive symptoms, and was generally well tolerated. Interestingly, Sheehan Disability scores showed significant improvements for the atomoxetine group in study I, but were not replicated in study II. The authors called for further studies to investigate social and occupational function in adults with ADHD to understand these complex domains better. Atomoxetine may quickly become a first-line treatment for adults with ADHD, given its current status as the sole FDA-approved agent for this condition.

Dosing and Pharmacokinetics. Atomoxetine may be given either once daily or twice daily. The recommended starting dose is 0.5 mg/kg/day, with a gradual increase over three days to 1.2 mg/kg/day, and a maximum daily dose of 100 mg. Caution should be exercised when other medications are already in use, as combination therapy has not been systematically studied as of the date this writing. Although its serum $T_{1/2}$ is approximately five hours, it may have a duration of effect of up to twenty-four hours. Once administered, its release is immediate, with the time to maximum concentration (T_{max}) in one to two hours when given on an empty stomach. Food does not alter the AUC, but does decrease the maximum concentration (C_{max}) and T_{max}. It goes through an extensive first pass metabolism, and is a substrate of CYP2D6.

Adverse Events Profile. The most common side effects reported in children and adolescents were decreased appetite, dyspepsia, dizziness, and mood changes. Most of these may be managed by giving the medicine either with food, or by dividing the total daily dose (TDD) into two doses. Cardiovascular parameters should be assessed at baseline, as there is an association with mild elevations in blood pressure and pulse. Patients with bipolar disorder were excluded from pre-marketing studies, so effects in this population have yet to be understood.

Drug Interactions. Caution must be exercised when administering a known CYP2D6 inhibitor (such as fluoxetine or paroxetine) with atomoxetine. Studies done with extensive metabolizers and poor metabolizers of CYP2D6 agents showed a mild elevation in the incidence of side effects for poor metabolizers but no major dose adjustments were necessary overall.

Clinical Indications. Atomoxetine is indicated for the treatment of adult, adolescent, and childhood ADHD. It may also have some antidepressant properties, according to the Eli Lilly Company, given its prominent NE enhancing properties. On the other hand, crying (2%), irritability (11%), and mood swings (2%) were reported as treatment-emergent side effects from atomoxetine in children and teens in one pre-marketing study (n = 547), though it rarely led to withdrawal from the nine-week study (Strattera package insert).

Developmental Issues. Overall, beneficial and side effects were similar in all three age groups studied. Exceptions to this included adult males over forty-five reporting sexual problems (not found in other age groups), mostly erectile dysfunction. The drug has been studied in children six years and older.

Clinical Experience. We have found that it may be of special use for cases in which there is patient or family hesitancy to use stimulants, or a history of tics, drug abuse, or psychotic vulnerabilities. Among the commonly reported side effects, we have found somnolence, dyspepsia, and dizziness to be usually responsive to a change to BID dosing with food, to QHS (bedtime) dosing, and/or to slow upward titrations in dosing.

The Alpha-Adrenergic Agonists

Chemical Makeup. Clonidine molecule

Mechanism of Action. The alpha-2 agonists, clonidine and guanfacine, have been used for many years to treat ADHD, especially in the presence of comorbid tics, or to help ease sleep onset in those children having insomnia from stimulant treatment. These agents are thought to affect central pre- and post-synaptic alpha-2 adrenergic receptors, thereby acting as cognitive and attentive enhancers through mediation of norepinephrine (Scahill, Chappell, & Kim et al., 2001; Stahl, 2000). Though their mechanisms are similar, there are subtle but important differences in their receptor activities. Clonidine has more potent alpha 1, alpha 2B, alpha 2C activity, and more beta-adrenergic, histamininergic, 5-HT, beta-endorphin, and DA effects than its cousin, guanfacine. The alpha 2B receptor appears to be responsible for the sedative effects more common with clonidine (Arnsten, Steere, & Hunt, 1996). (Please see Figure 10.3 for a diagram of the Clonidine Molecule.)

FIGURE 10.3. CHEMICAL MAKEUP OF THE CLONIDINE MOLECULE.

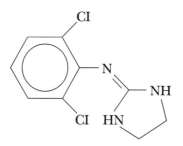

Empirical Support. While four previous studies (two controlled, one open, one retrospective review) had shown predominantly sedative effects on hyperactive-impulsive symptoms of ADHD, some had also shown possible cognitive enhancing effects on the prefrontal cortex (Hunt, Minderaa, & Cohen, 1985; Hunt, 1987; Steingard, et al., 1993; Plizska, 2003). The combination of methylphenidate and clonidine has been actively debated previously (Swanson, Connor, & Cantwell, 1999; Wilens & Spencer, 1999). Proponents cite the favorable tolerability and complementary side effect profiles, while detractors point out that despite its wide use, its lack of systematic study and reports of four sudden deaths and two Apparent Life Threatening Events (ALTEs) on the combination should caution providers against its use. Two recently published studies have systematically evaluated this combination. Connor, Barkley, and Davis (2000) examined twenty-four children with ADHD and comorbid ODD in a study comparing clonidine alone, methylphenidate alone, or the combination, for a period of three months. Children were randomized among the three groups, for a total of eight per group, and there was no placebo arm. Based on parent and teacher ratings of oppositionality and verbal aggression, all three groups showed about equal decreases in aggression. No major safety issues surfaced during this short study.

A larger study (n = 136) examined similar interventions but with a different population (patients with ADHD and comorbid tic disorder) (Tourette's Syndrome Study Group, 2002). Subjects were children ages seven to fourteen who were randomized to methylphenidate, clonidine, the combination, or to placebo in a four-month parallel group design. Results of parent and teacher ratings showed favorable results for the three non-placebo interventions, with the methylphenidate/clonidine combination being superior to both methylphenidate alone and clonidine alone for treating ADHD and tics. Tolerability of the combination was generally good, but sedation was a problem in those treated with clonidine only or the clonidine/methylphenidate combination. Clonidine dosages averaged 0.25 mg/day for the clonidine alone group and 0.28 mg/day for the clonidine/methylphenidate group. Methylphenidate dosages averaged 25.7 mg/day for methylphenidate alone group and 26.1 mg/day for the clonidine/methylphenidate group. Study medications were tolerated well, except that sedation was common in subjects receiving clonidine. No major safety issues surfaced during this study.

Guanfacine. Hunt, Minderaa, and Cohen (1985) were among the first to report guanfacine's usefulness in open studies (Pliszka et al., 2003b), and cited its potentially greater utility than clonidine due to less sedation, bradycardia, and hypotensive effects. More recently, Lawrence Scahill and colleagues (2001) at Yale found guanfacine to be superior to placebo in a prospective randomized double-blind study of thirty-four subjects with ADHD and mild tics. The eight-week study used doses of 1 to 3 mg Total Daily Dose (TDD), and measured pre- and post-intervention scores on the CGI and parent/teacher rating scales. Effect size was relatively weak compared to stimulants, but was similar to that reported for clonidine, with about a 33% response rate for children with ADHD and various tic disorders.

Dosing and Pharmacokinetics. Dosing may vary by disorder and by age. General guidelines are to stay aware of a ten-fold difference between the two agents, and begin with a night dose of 0.05 mg of clonidine or 0.5 mg of guanfacine. Slow titration upward may be pursued to a range of 0.05 to 0.1 mg three to four times a day (TID-QID) for clonidine (TDD 0.15 to 0.4 mg), or 0.5–1.5 mg BID-TID for guanfacine (TDD 1.5–4.5). Higher doses may be tolerated, but are associated with more side effects, most of which are dose-related.

For clonidine, peak plasma levels occur at three to five hours, with a $T_{1/2}$ of twelve to sixteen hours. However, Leckman et al. (1985) found that clonidine's $T_{1/2}$ varies by age, and report it to be only four to six hours in prepubertal children. About 50% is excreted unchanged by the kidneys within twenty-four hours, and the other 50% is metabolized by the liver (Green, 2001).

Guanfacine's peak is within one to four hours post-ingestion, with a plasma $T_{1/2}$ of seventeen hours, and more rapid metabolism in younger children as well (Green, 2001). It is excreted mainly through the kidneys, and steady state is achieved in about four days.

For Tourette's syndrome specifically, Bruun (1983) recommends beginning clonidine at 0.025 mg BID for children seven and under, and 0.05 mg BID for older children and teens. A very gradual increase of 0.05 mg per week is continued, to a target range of 0.25 to 0.45 mg/day, in TID-QID fashion to minimize sedation.

Adverse Effects. Common side effects of both agents include dry mouth, fatigue, dizziness, constipation, weakness, bradycardia, hypotension, and sedation. The last three are clinically more frequent for clonidine. Another important side effect is depression, reported in 5% of children in Hunt's 1991 study of clonidine (Green, 2001). A case of severe depression in apparent response to clonidine, 0.2 mg TDD, was reported by McCracken and Martin (1997) in an eight-year-old boy with autism. The symptoms remitted immediately following clonidine discontinuation. Other rare but important side effects of the alpha-agonists have included precocious puberty with clonidine (Levin, Burton-Teston, & Murphy, 1993), and manic episodes with guanfacine (Horrigan & Barnhill, 1995, 1998; Levin et al., 1993). Rebound hypertension and anxiety or nervousness may occur with abrupt withdrawal of alpha-agonists. Thus, gradual tapering is recommended in patients treated for more than one month, at a reduction rate of about 0.05 mg every three to five days for clonidine, and 0.5 mg every three to five days for guanfacine. In general, the tablet seems to be a more reliable method of delivery for psychiatric purposes (Green, 2001), though Comings (1990) proposes that the patch be considered (and cut with scissors to tailor dose, if necessary) if the oral dose is ineffective. Hunt (1987) found that some of the subjects in his study who required TDDs of 0.2 mg orally (p.o.), required 0.3 mg of the patch for equal effect.

Interactions. Due to their primarily renal excretion, there are no appreciable cytochrome P450 concerns with alpha-agonists. However, Cantwell, Connor, and Swanson (1997) have recommended the following guidelines for clonidine, which include screening for pre-existing cardiac disease (and proceeding with caution after cardiac consultation and clearance), close monitoring of pulse and blood pressure (pre-treatment, and with dose changes), slow titrations in doses, and baseline EKGs. These are done to be aware of baseline bradycardia or AV conduction problems such as heart block or prolonged QRS interval.

Indications. Although guanfacine and clonidine do not have FDA-approved indications other than for hypertension, they have been used in child and adolescent psychiatry for treating tics (Tourette's syndrome or other tic disorders), ADHD with or without tics, sleep disturbance associated with psychostimulants, impulse control problems, aggression, and PTSD symptoms. (See Chapter 11, "Medications for Pediatric Anxiety" in this book for a further discussion of alpha-agonists for anxiety symptoms.)

Developmental Considerations. Lee (1997) reported benefits of low dose guanfacine for very young children (two to three year olds) with ADHD symptoms. Doses of 0.25 to 0.50 mg BID helped to decrease symptoms of aggression and destructiveness, while improving behavioral symptoms overall. Side effects were minimal, and included mild sedation. The author advises practitioners to use psychotropic medication in this age group only after a thorough psychiatric and medical workup, and where the benefits of medication will far outweigh the risks of not trying medication.

Expert Guidelines

We have found these agents to be useful in all of the previously described clinical circumstances, especially in small doses throughout the day, and also for children with autistic disorder or PDD who may not tolerate other agents for impulse control, or for children under six for whom parents may be wary of psychostimulant use. There may be special utility for these agents in other selected populations (H. Kranzler, M.D., personal communication, 1997), such as in combination with atypical antipsychotic agents for school-age children with severe aggression or impulse control problems who have psychotic vulnerabilities (where stimulants are to be avoided). Older children seem less able to tolerate the sedative effects of guanfacine and (especially) clonidine, so divided doses using smaller doses at each administration become especially important. We concur with authors who recommend obtaining baseline EKGs, especially to rule out pre-existing pathology. Also, because complicated patients often need to be treated with increasing numbers of medications, they are likely to be on at least one medication already that can affect EKG parameters. When an alpha-agonist is added to a regimen, it may, in fact, be the "third agent," and aside from systematic study with clonidine and methylphenidate, little is known about cardiac effects of multi-drug regimens.

Other agents that have proven useful for ADHD but are not covered in this chapter include MAOIs, tricyclic antidepressants, venlafaxine, propranolol, and buspirone. For excellent discussions of these agents in ADHD, see Green (2001), Pliszka (2003), Popper (2000), and Cantwell (1996).

Future Directions

Several newer agents for ADHD are currently under development. Ortho-Noven Pharmaceuticals is in Phase III development of a methylphenidate patch. As it cannot be extracted or snorted, it may provide a crucial innovation in delivery systems to deal with a commonly problematic side effect in adult patients (methylphenidate abuse). It may also be helpful in the treatment of ADHD in young children who are unwilling or unable to swallow tablets. It is expected to be released in 2004 (Sane & McGough, 2002).

The H3 receptor antagonist GT-2331 (Perceptin) may also have some DA-, NE-, and acetylcholine (Ach-) enhancing properties, and the histaminergic system is known to be involved in vigilance, attention, and cognition (Laws, Heil, Bickel, Faries, & Badger, 2001; Leurs, Blandina, Tedford, & Timmerman, 1998). Gliatech, the drug's maker, reports that it is safe and well-tolerated as a once-daily medication in phase I trials. Phase II trials are currently under way with adult subjects (Schweitzer & Holcomb, 2002; Wesnes, Garratt, Wickens, Gudgeon, & Oliver, 2000).

An (R)-sibutramine (Meridia) metabolite, marketed by Sepracor, is currently being evaluated as both a potential ADHD treatment and useful medication for depression (Wesnes et al., 2000). It has reuptake properties for DA, NE, and 5-HT. Recent data suggest effectiveness in targeting the attentional problems of ADHD and improving attention on a vigilance task. It also showed improvements in postural control, which may have special significance in ADHD, given recent findings regarding cerebellar abnormalities in children and adults with ADHD (Schweitzer & Holcomb, 2002; Tedford, Pawlowski, Khan, Phillips, & Yates, 1996; Wesnes et al., 2000). Research done so far indicates that sibutramine has little to no abuse potential, and may have utility in reducing attentional problems that are alcohol-induced.

Modafinil (Provigil), approved for the treatment of narcolepsy, has been recently studied for use in ADHD. It is a schedule IV substance that seems to work through activation of the hypocretin-orexin system in the hypothalamus, an area thought to be involved in the mediation of wakefulness and vigilance (Young, 2003; Sigel, 2000). It also appears to have a direct effect on the dopamine transporter (Wiser et al., 2001).

Two investigators (Rugino & Copley, 2001; Taylor & Russo, 2000) have found positive effects for modafinil, with hyperactive and impulsive symptoms responding better than inattentiveness. Both studies were noteworthy for modafinil's tolerability and effectiveness. Rugino and Copley (2001) reported positive overall effects in an open-label study ($n = 11$) with children. However, even though improvements on parent and teacher ratings were statistically significant, endpoints were still in the impaired range. Results from double-blind placebo controlled studies in adults with ADHD have been mixed (Cephalon Inc., 2000; Taylor & Russo, 2000).

Menza, Kaufmann, and Castellanos (2000) studied seven patients with depressive disorder and found that in low doses as an adjunctive treatment, all patients achieved full or partial remission of their symptoms. Modafinil, like sibutramine, has thus far shown minimal-to-no abuse potential. More controlled studies are planned.

Finally, two reports by Wilens (Wilens et al., 1999; Wilens, Biederman, Wong, Spencer, & Prince, 2000) have shown evidence for the use of donepezil (Aricept) as a cognitive enhancer for patients who have ADHD, especially those with executive function deficits. An open series was conducted with five youths, aged eight to seventeen years, all of whom demonstrated improvement (Wilens, Biederman, Wong, et al., 2000). A cholinergic agonist, ABT-418, no longer being developed, found similar effects when Ach was enhanced (Abbott Laboratories, 1998; Schweitzer & Holcomb, 2002). Side effects included syncope, vertigo, depression, asthenia, and anxiety. Despite these, there was minimal dropout from the study, and it was well tolerated in a study by Winblad et al. (2001).

◆ ◆ ◆

The pharmacologic agents and approaches discussed in this chapter have been drawn from a fast growing literature, along with the author's clinical experience and colleagues' wisdom.

Undoubtedly, continued research will reveal greater understanding of the mechanisms of ADHD, which will then spur more effective and specifically targeted agents to treat this disorder across the lifespan. Until then, clinicians may be comforted by the fact that with careful application of principles gained from the currently existing literature, this functionally disabling disorder can be treated effectively and safely with many different medication options as part of the overall treatment approach.

References

Abbott Laboratories. (1998). Drug Development Pipeline: ABT-418.

Adesman, A. R. (2003). New medications for treatment of children with attention/deficit hyperactivity disorder: Review and commentary. *Pediatric Annals, 31*(8), 516–522.

Alles, G. A. (1928). The comparative physiological action of phenylethanolamine. *Journal of Pharmacology and Experimental Therapy, 32,* 121–128.

Arnold, E. L. (2000). Methylphenidate versus amphetamine: A comparative review. In L. Greenhill & B. Osman (Eds.), *Ritalin: Theory and practice* (pp. 127–139). Larchmont, NY: Mary Ann Liebert, Inc.

Arnsten, A. F., Steere, J. C., & Hunt, R. D. (1996). The contribution of alpha-2 noradrenergic mechanisms of prefrontal cognitive function. Potential significance for ADHD. *Archives of General Psychiatry, 53,* 448–455.

Auiler, J. F., Liu, K., Lynch, J. M., & Gelotte, C. K. (2002). Effect of food on early drug exposure from extended-release stimulants: Results from the Concerta, Adderall XR Food Evaluation (CAFE) study. *Current Medical Research and Opinion, 18*(5), 311–316.

Barkley, R. A. (1988). The effects of methylphenidate on the interactions of preschool ADHD children with their mothers. *Journal of the American Academy of Child and Adolescent Psychiatry, 27,* 336–341.

Barkley, R. A., Karlsson, J., & Strzelecki, E., et al. (1984). Effects of age and Ritalin dosage on mother-child interactions of hyperactive children. *Journal of Consulting and Clinical Psychology, 52,* 750–758.

Bostic, J. Q., Biederman, J., & Spencer, T., et al. (2000). Pemoline treatment of adolescents with attention-deficit/hyperactivity disorder: A ten-week controlled trial. *Journal of Child and Adolescent Psychopharmacology, 10*(3), 205–216.

Bradley, C. (1937). The behavior of children receiving benzedrine. *American Journal of Psychiatry, 94,* 577–585.

Breitbart, W. (1998). Psychotropic adjuvant analgesics for pain in cancer and AIDS. *Psycho-Oncology, 7*(4), 333–345.

Brown, R. T., & Sexson, S. B. (1988). A controlled trial of methylphenidate in black adolescents. *Clinical Pediatrics, 27,* 74–81.

Bruun, R. (1983). TSA medical update: Treatment with clonidine. *Tourette Syndrome Association Newsletter.*

Bymaster, F. P., Katner, J. S., & Nelson, D. L. (2002). Atomoxetine increases extracellular levels of norepinephrine and dopamine in prefrontal cortex of rat: A potential mechanism for efficacy in attention-deficit/hyperactivity disorder. *Neuropsychopharmacology, 27*(5), 699–711.

Caldwell, J., & Sever, P. S. (1974). The biochemical pharmacology of abused drugs. *Clinical Pharmacology and Therapeutics, 16,* 625–638.

Cantwell, D. P. (1996). Attention deficit disorder: A review of the past 10 years. *Journal of the American Academy of Child and Adolescent Psychiatry, 35*(8), 978–987.

Cantwell, D. P., Connor, D. F., & Swanson, J. (1997). Case study: Adverse response to clonidine. *Journal of the American Academy of Child and Adolescent Psychiatry, 36,* 539–544.

Castellanos, F. X., Giedd, J. N., & Elia, J., et al. (1997). Controlled stimulant treatment of ADHD and comorbid Tourette's syndrome: Effects of stimulant and dose. *Journal of the American Academy of Child and Adolescent Psychiatry, 36,* 1–8.

Cephalon Inc. (2000). *Cephalon reports no benefit from Provigil in study of adults with ADHD: Plans for label expansion into other indications on track [press release].* Westchester, PA.

Cohen, D. J., & Leckman, J. F. (1988). Commentary. *Journal of the American Academy of Child and Adolescent Psychiatry, 28,* 580–582.

Comings, D. E. (1990). *Tourette syndrome and human behavior.* Duarte, CA: Hope Press.

Conners, C. K. (1975). Controlled trial of methylphenidate in preschool children with minimum brain dysfunction. In Gittelman-Klein (Ed.), *Recent advances in child psychopharmacology* (pp. 65–78). New York: Human Sciences Press.

Connor, D. F., Barkley, R. A., & Davis, H. T. (2000). A pilot study of methylphenidate, clonidine, or the combination in ADHD comorbid with aggressive oppositional defiant disorder or conduct disorder. *Clinical Pediatrics (Phila.), 39,* 15–25.

Coons, H. W., Klorman, R., & Borgstedt, A. D. (1987). Effects of methylphenidate on adolescents with a childhood history of attention deficit disorder: II. Information processing. *Journal of the American Academy of Child and Adolescent Psychiatry, 26,* 368–374.

Cunningham, C. E., Siegel, L., & Offord, D. (1985). A developmental dose-response analysis of the effects of methylphenidate on the peer interactions of attention deficit disordered boys. *Journal of Child Psychology and Psychiatry, 26,* 955–971.

DeVane, C. L. (1992). Pharmacokinetics of the selective serotonin reuptake inhibitors. *Journal of Clinical Psychiatry, 53,* 13–20.

Dulcan, M. K. (1990). Using psychostimulants to treat behavioral disorders of children and adolescents. *Journal of Child and Adolescent Psychopharmacology, 1,* 7–20.

DuPaul, Power, Anastopoulos, Reid, McGoey, & Ikeda. (1996). ADHD Rating Scale-IV: Parent and Child Versions.

Elia, J. (1991). Stimulants and antidepressant pharmacokinetics in hyperactive children. *Psychopharmacology Bulletin, 27,* 411–415.

Elia, J., Borcherding, B. G., & Potter, W. Z., et al. (1990). Stimulant drug treatment of hyperactivity: Biochemical correlates. *Clinical Pharmacological Therapy, 48,* 57–66.

Faraone, S. V., Biederman, J., & Roe, C. (2002). Comparative efficacy of Adderall and methylphenidate in attention-deficit/hyperactivity disorder: A meta-analysis. *Journal of Clinical Psychopharmacology, 22*(5), 468–473.

Fawcett, J., & Busch, K. A. (1998). Stimulants in psychiatry. In A. F. Schatzberg & C. B. Nemeroff (Eds.), *Textbook of psychopharmacology* (pp. 503–522). Washington, D.C.: American Psychiatric Press, Inc.

Findling, R. L., Short, E. J., & Manos, M. J. (2001). Developmental aspects of psychostimulant treatment in children and adolescents with attention-deficit hyperactivity disorder. *Journal of the American Academy of Child and Adolescent Psychiatry, 40*(12), 1441–1447.

Gadow, K., Sverd, J., & Sparfkin, J., et al. (1995). Efficacy of methylphenidate for attention-deficit hyperactivity disorder in children with tic disorder. *Archives of General Psychiatry, 52,* 444–455.

Gadow, K., Nolan, E. E., & Sverd, J. (1992). Methylphenidate in hyperactive boys with comorbid tic disorder: II. Short-term behavioral effects in school settings. *Journal of the American Academy of Child and Adolescent Psychiatry, 31,* 462–471.

Glennon, R. A. (1987). Psychoactive phenylisopropylamines. In H. Y. Meltzer (Ed.), *Psychopharmacology: The Third Generation of Progress* (pp. 1627–1634). New York: Raven Press.

Goff, D. C., & Ciraulo, D. A. (1991). Stimulants. In D. A. Ciraulo (Ed.), *Clinical Manual of Chemical Dependence* (pp. 233–257). Washington, D.C.: American Psychiatric Press.

Green, W. H. (2001). *Child & adolescent clinical psychopharmacology.* Philadelphia: Lippincott Williams & Wilkins.

Greenhill, L., & Osman, B. (1999). *Ritalin: Theory and practice* (2nd ed.). New York: Mary Ann Liebert, Inc.

Greenhill, L. L., Pliszka, S. R., Dulcan, M. K., & the Workgroup on Quality Issues. (2002). Practice parameter for the use of stimulant medications in the treatment of children, adolescents and adults. *Journal of the American Academy of Child and Adolescent Psychiatry, 41*(Suppl. 2), 26S–49S.

Gucuyener, K., Erdemoglu, A. K., Senol, S., Serdaroglu, A., Soysal, S., & Kockar, A. I. (2003). Use of methylphenidate for attention-deficit hyperactivity disorder in patients with epilepsy or electroencephalographic abnormalities. *Journal of Child Neurology, 18*(2), 109–112.

Hoffman, B. B., & Lefkowitz, R. J. (1990). Catecholamines and sympathomimetic drugs. In A. G. Gillman, T. W. Rall, & A. S. Nies (Eds.), *The pharmacological basis of therapeutics.* (pp. 187–220). New York: Pergamon Press.

Horrigan, J. P., & Barnhill, L. J. (1995). Guanfacine for treatment of ADHD in boys. *Journal of Child and Adolescent Psychopharmacology, 5,* 215–223.

Horrigan, J. P., & Barnhill, L. J. (1998). Does guanfacine trigger mania in children? [letter]. *Journal of Child and Adolescent Psychopharmacology, 8,* 149–150.

Howe, D. D., & Findling, R. L. (2003). New pharmacologic treatments for Attention Deficit/Hyperactivity Disorder. *Contemporary Psychiatry, 2*(3), 1–10.

Hunt, R. D. (1987). Treatment effects of oral and transdermal clonidine in relation to methylphenidate: An open pilot study in ADD-H. *Psychopharmacology Bulletin, 23,* 111–114.

Hunt, R. D., Minderaa, R. D., & Cohen, D. J. (1985). Clonidine benefits children with attention deficit disorder and hyperactivity: Report of a double-blind placebo-controlled crossover trial. *Journal of the American Academy of Child and Adolescent Psychiatry, 24,* 617–629.

Hyman, S. E., Arana, G. W., & Rosenbaum, J. F. (1995). *Handbook of psychiatric drug therapy.* Boston: Little, Brown and Company.

Joshi, S. V. (2002). ADHD, growth deficits, and relationships to psychostimulant use. *Pediatrics in Review, 23*(2), 67–68.

Klein, R. (1987). Pharmacotherapy of childhood hyperactivity: An update. In H. Y. Meltzer (Ed.), *Psychopharmacology: The third generation of progress* (pp. 1215–1225). New York: Raven Press.

Kloorman, R., Coons, H. W., & Borgstedt, A. D. (1987). Effects of methylphenidate on adolescents with a childhood history of attention-deficit disorder: I, Clinical findings. *Journal of the American Academy of Child and Adolescent Psychiatry, 26,* 363–367.

Konkol, R., Fischer, M., & Newby, R. (1990). Double-blind, placebo-controlled stimulant trial in children with Tourette's syndrome and ADHD: Abstract. *Annals in Neurology, 28,* 424.

Kratochvil, C. J., et al. (2002). Atomoxetine and methylphenidate treatment in children with ADHD: A prospective, randomized, open-label trial. *Journal of the American Academy of Child and Adolescent Psychiatry, 41*(7), 776–784.

Lahey, B. B., et al. (1998). Validity of DSM-IV attention-deficit/hyperactivity disorder for younger children. *Journal of American Academy of Child and Adolescent Psychiatry, 37*(7), 695–702.

Laws, H. F., Heil, S. H., Bickel, S., Faries, D., & Badger, G. (2001). *Subjective responses to LY139603 (Tomoxetine) and methylphenidate.* Paper presented at the 41st Annual NCDEU Meeting, Phoenix, AZ.

Leckman, J. F., Detlor, J., Harcherik, D. F., Stevenson, J., Ort, S. I., & Cohen, D. J. (1985). Short- and long-term treatment of Tourette's syndrome with clonidine: A clinical perspective. *Neurology, 35,* 343–351.

Leckman, J. F., Peterson, B. S., Anderson, G. M., Arstein, A.F.T., Pauls, D. L., & Cohen, D. J. (1997). Pathogenesis of Tourette's syndrome. *Journal of Child Psychology and Psychiatry, 38,* 119–142.

Lee, B. (1997). Clinical experience with guanfacine in 2- and 3-year old children with ADHD. *Infant Mental Health Journal, 18*(3), 300–305.

Lerer, R. J., & Lerer, M. P. (1977). Responses of adolescents with minimal brain dysfunction to methylphenidate. *Journal of Learning Disabilities, 10,* 223–228.

Leurs, R., Blandina, P., Tedford, C., & Timmerman, H. (1998). Therapeutic potential of histamine H, receptor agonists and antagonists. *Trends in Pharmacological Science, 19,* 177–183.

Levin, E. D., & Rezvani, A. H. (2000). Development of nicotinic drug therapy for cognitive disorders. *European Journal of Pharmacology, 393,* 141–146.

Levin, G. M., Burton-Teston, K., & Murphy, T. (1993). Development of precocious pubertyin two children treated with clonidine for aggressive behavior. *Journal of Child and Adolescent Psychopharmacology, 3,* 127–131.

MacKay, M. C., Beck, L., & Taylor, R. (1973). Methylphenidate for adolescents with minimal brain dysfunction. *New York State Journal of Medicine, 73,* 550–554.

Markowitz, J., Morrison, S., & DeVane, C. L. (1999). Drug interactions with psychostimulants. *International Clinical Psychopharmacology, 14,* 1–18.

Manos, M. J., Short, E. J., & Findling, R. L. (1999). Differential effectiveness of methylphenidate and Adderall in school-age youth with attention-deficit/hyperactivity disorder. *Journal of the American Academy of Child and Adolescent Psychiatry, 38,* 813–819.

Masand, P. S., & Tesar, G. E. (1996). Use of stimulants in the medically ill. *Psychiatric Clinics of North America, 19,* 515–547.

Mayes, S., Crites, D., & Bixler, E., et al. (1994). Methylphenidate and ADHD: Influence of age, IQ, and neurodevelopmental status. *Developmental Medicine in Child Neurology, 36,* 1099–1107.

McBride, M. C., Wang, D. D., & Torres, C. (1986). Methylphenidate in therapeutic doses does not lower seizure threshold. *Annals in Neurology, 20,* 428.

McCracken, J. T., & Martin, W. (1997). Clonidine side effect [Letter]. *Journal of the American Academy of Child and Adolescent Psychiatry, 36,* 160–161.

Menza, M. A., Kaufmann, K. R., & Castellanos, A. (2000). Modafinil augmentation of antidepressant treatment in depression. *Journal of Clinical Psychiatry, 61,* 378–381.

Michelson, D., Adler, L., Spencer, T., Reimherr, F., West, S., Allen, A., Kelsey, D., Wernicke, J., Dietrich, A., & Milton, D. (2003). Atomoxetine in adults with ADHD: Two randomized, placebo-controlled studies. *Biological Psychiatry, 53*(2), 112–120.

Michelson, D., Allen, A. J., Busner, J., Casat, C., Dunn, D., Kratochvil, C., Newcorn, J., Sallee, F., Sangal, R., Saylor, K., West, S., Kelsey, D., Wernicke, J., Trapp, N., & Harder, D. (2002). Once-daily atomoxetine treatment for children and adolescents with attention-deficit/hyperactivity disorder: A randomized, placebo-controlled study. *American Journal of Psychiatry, 159*(11), 1896–1901.

Michelson, D., Faries, D., Wernicke, J., Kelsey, D., Kendrick, K., Sallee, F., Spencer, T., & the Atomoxetine ADHD study group. (2001). Atomoxetine in the treatment of children and adolescents with attention-deficit/hyperactivity disorder: A randomized, placebo-controlled, dose-response study. *Pediatrics, 108*(5), E83.

MTA Cooperative Group. (1999). A 14-month randomized clinical trial of treatment strategies for attention-deficit/hyperactivity disorder. *Archives of General Psychiatry, 56,* 1073–1986.

Musten, L. M., Firestone, P., Pisterman, S., et al. (1997). Effects of methylphenidate on preschool children with ADHD: Cognitive and behavioral functions. *Journal of the American Academy of Child and Adolescent Psychiatry, 36,* 1407–1415.

Pliszka, S. R. (2003). Non-stimulant treatment of attention-deficit/hyperactivity disorder. *CNS Spectrums, 8*(4), 253–258.

Pliszka, S. R., & the Texas Consensus Conference Panel on Medication Treatment of Childhood Attention-Deficit/Hyperactivity Disorder. (2000a). The Texas children's medication algorithm project: Report of the Texas consensus conference panel on medication treatment of childhood attention-deficit/hyperactivity disorder. Part I. *Journal of the American Academy of Child and Adolescent Psychiatry, 39,* 908–919.

Pliszka, S. R., & the Texas Consensus Conference Panel on Medication Treatment of Childhood Attention-Deficit/Hyperactivity Disorder. (2000b). The Texas children's medication algorithm project: Report of the Texas consensus of conference panel on medication treatment of childhood attention-deficit/hyperactivity disorder. Part II. *Journal of the American Academy of Child and Adolescent Psychiatry, 39,* 920–927.

Pliszka, S. R., Browne, R. G., Olvera, R. L., & Wynne, S. K. (2000). A double-blind, placebo-controlled study of Adderall and methylphenidate in the treatment of attention-deficit/hyperactivity disorder. *Journal of the American Academy of Child and Adolescent Psychiatry, 39,* 619–626.

Popper, C. W. (2000). Pharmacologic alternatives to the psychostimulants for the treatment of attention-deficit/hyperactivity disorder. *Child and Adolescent Psychiatric Clinics of North America, 9*(3), 605–646.

Riddle, M. A., Lynch, K. A., Scahill, L., DeVries, A., Cohen, D. J., & Leckman, J. F. (1995). Methylphenidate discontinuation and reinitiation during long-term treatment of children with Tourette's disorder and attention-deficit/hyperactivity disorder: A pilot study. *Journal of Child and Adolescent Psychopharmacology, 5,* 205–214.

Rosenberg, D. R., Holttum, J., & Gershon, S. (1994). *Textbook of pharmacotherapy for child and adolescent psychiatric disorders* (pp. 19–54). New York: Brunner/Mazel Publishers.

Rugino, T. A., & Copley, T. C. (2001). Effects of modafinil in children with attention-deficit/hyperactivity disorder: An open-label study. *Journal of the American Academy of Child and Adolescent Psychiatry, 40,* 230–235.

Safer, D., & Zito, J. (1999). Pharmacoepidemiology of methylphenidate and other stimulants for the treatment of ADHD. In L. Greenhill & B. Osman (Eds.), *Ritalin: Theory and practice* (pp. 7–26). New York: Mary Ann Liebert, Inc.

Safer, D. J., & Allen, R. P. (1975). Stimulant drug treatment of hyperactive adolescents. *Dis Nerv Syst, 36,* 454–457.

Sallee, F., Stiller, R., Perel, J., et al. (1985). Oral pemoline kinetics in hyperactive children. *Clinical Pharmacology and Therapeutics, 37,* 606–609.

Sane, N., & McGough, J. (2002). MethyPatch Noven. *Current Opinion in Investigational Drugs, 3*(8), 1222–1224.

Scahill, L., Chappell, P. B., Kim, Y. S., Schultz, R., Katsovich, L., Shepherd, E., Arnsten, A., Cohen, D., & Leckman, J. (2001). A placebo-controlled study of guanfacine in the treatment of attention-deficit hyperactivity disorder. *American Journal of Psychiatry, 158,* 1067–1074.

Schleifer, N., Weiss, G., Cohen, N., et al. (1975). Hyperactivity in preschoolers and the effect of methylphenidate. *American Journal of Orthopsychiatry, 45,* 38–50.

Schweitzer, J. B., & Holcomb, H. H. (2002). Drugs under investigation for attention-deficit/hyperactivity disorder. *Current Opinion in Investigational Drugs, 3*(8), 1207–1211.

Smith, B., Pelham, W. E., Gnagy, E., et al. (1998). Equivalent effects of stimulant treatment for attention-deficit/hyperactivity disorder during childhood and adolescence. *Journal of the American Academy of Child and Adolescent Psychiatry, 37,* 314–321.

Spencer, T., Biederman, J., Wilens, T., et al. (1996). Pharmacotherapy of attention deficit disorder across the life cycle. *Journal of the American Academy of Child and Adolescent Psychiatry, 35,* 409–432.

Stahl, S. M. (2000). *Essential psychopharmacology: Neuroscientific basis and practical applications* (2nd ed.). New York: Cambridge University Press.

Steingard, R., Biederman, J., Spencer, T., Wilens, T., & Gonzalez, A. (1993). A comparison of clonidine response in the treatment of attention-deficit hyperactivity disorder with and without co-morbid tic disorders. *Journal of American Academy of Child and Adolescent Psychiatry, 32,* 350–353.

Sverd, J. (1999). Methylphenidate treatment for children with attention deficit hyperactivity disorder and tic disorder: Inadvisable or indispensable? In L. Greenhill & B. Osman (Eds.), *Ritalin: Theory and Practice* (pp. 301–319). Larchmont, NY: Mary Ann Liebert, Inc.

Sverd, J., Gadow, K., Nolan, E. E., et al. (1992). Methylphenidate in hyperactive boys with comorbid tic disorder. I. *Advanced Neurology, 58,* 271–281.

Swanson, J., Connor, D. F., & Cantwell, D. P. (1999). Combining methylphenidate and clonidine: Ill-advised, and negative rebuttal [Debate forum]. *Journal of the American Academy of Child and Adolescent Psychiatry, 38,* 614–622.

Swanson, J., McBurnett, K., Christian, D., et al. (1995). Stimulant medications and the treatment of children with ADHD. *Advances in Clinical Child Psychology, 17,* 265–322.

Swanson, J., Wigal, S., Greenhill, L., et al. (1998). Objective and subjective measures of the pharmacodynamic effects of Adderall in the treatment of children with ADHD in a controlled laboratory classroom setting. *Psychopharmacology Bulletin, 34,* 55–60.

Taylor, F. B., & Russo, J. (2000). Efficacy of modafinil compared to dextroamphetamine for the treatment of attention-deficit/hyperactivity disorder in adults. *Journal of Child and Adolescent Psychopharmacology, 10,* 311–320.

Tedford, C. E., Pawlowski, G. P., Khan, M. A., Phillips, J. G., & Yates, S. L. (1996). Cognition and locomotor activity in the developing rat: Comparisons of histamine H, receptor antagonists and ADHD therapeutics. *Abstract Soc Neurosci, 22*(Abs. 18.3).

Tourette's Syndrome Study Group. (2002). Treatment of ADHD in children with tics: A randomized controlled trial. *Neurology, 58,* 527–536.

Varley, C. K. (1983). Effects of methylphenidate in adolescents with attention deficit disorder. *Journal of the American Academy of Child Psychiatry, 22,* 351–354.

Volkow, N., Wang, G., Fowler, J., Gatley, J., Logan, J., Ding, Y-S., Hitzemann, R., & Pappas, N. (1998). Dopamine transporter occupancies in the human brain induced by therapeutic doses of oral methylphenidate. *American Journal of Psychiatry, 155,* 1325–1331.

Volkow, N. D., Ding, Y., Fowler, J. S., Wang, G. J., Logan, J., Gatley, J., Dewey, S., Ashby, C., Liebermann, J., Hitzemann, R., & Wolf, A. (1995). Is methylphenidate like cocaine? *Archives of General Psychiatry, 52,* 456–463.

Weiner, N. (1980). Norepinephrine, epinephrine, and the sympathomimetic amines. In A. G., Gilman, L. S. Goodman, & A. Gilman (Eds.), *Goodman and Gilman's The pharmacological basis of therapeutics* (pp. 138–175). New York: Macmillan.

Wender, E. H. (2002). Managing stimulant medication for attention-deficit/hyperactivity disorder: An update. *Pediatric Review, 23*(7), 234–236.

Wesnes, K. A., Garratt, C., Wickens, M., Gudgeon, A., & Oliver, S. (2000). Effects of sibutramine alone and with alcohol on cognitive function in healthy volunteers. *British Journal of Clinical Pharmacology, 49,* 110–117.

Wilens, T., Biederman, J., Spencer, T., Bostic, J. Q., Prince, J., & Monuteaux, B. A. (1999). A pilot controlled clinical trial of ABT-418, a cholinergic agonist, in the treatment of adults with attention-deficit/hyperactivity disorder. *American Journal of Psychiatry, 156,* 1931–1937.

Wilens, T., Biederman, J., Wong, J., Spencer, T., & Prince, J. (2000). Adjunctive donepezil in attention-deficit/hyperactivity disorder youth: Case series. *Journal of Child and Adolescent Psychopharmacology, 10,* 217–222.

Wilens, T., & Spencer, T. (1998). Pharmacology of amphetamines. In R. Tarter, R. Ammerman, & P. Ott (Eds.), *Handbook of substance abuse: Neurobehavioral pharmacology* (pp. 501–513). New York: Plenum Press.

Wilens, T., & Spencer, T. (1999). Combining methylphenidate and clonidine: A clinically sound medication option, and affirmative rebuttal [Debate forum]. *Journal of American Academy of Child and Adolescent Psychiatry, 38,* 614–622.

Wilens, T. E., & Spencer, T. J. (2000). The stimulants revisited. *Child and Adolescent Psychiatric Clinics of North America, 9*(3), 573–603.

Winblad, B., Engedal, K., Soininen, H., Verhey, F., Waldemar, G., Wimo, A., et al. (2001). A 1-year randomized, placebo-controlled study of donepezil in patients with mild to moderate attetion deficit. *Neurology, 57,* 489–495.

CHAPTER ELEVEN

MEDICATIONS FOR PEDIATRIC ANXIETY

Margo Thienemann, M.D.

This chapter focuses on medications used to treat symptoms of pediatric anxiety. Anxiety troubles many children and adolescents, manifesting as constellations of fearful thoughts and worries, physical symptoms (such as shakiness, stomachache, and muscle tension) and behaviors of avoidance and protest. As many as 15% of children suffer from an anxiety disorder as a primary or additional psychiatric condition (Costello, Angold, Burns, & Erkanli,1966). Except for obsessive compulsive disorder, where pharmacological trials are numerous, empirical evidence for treating anxiety with cognitive behavioral therapy outweighs evidence for pharmacological treatment. Nevertheless, medications are often used when the youth are too anxious to participate in cognitive behavioral therapy or when clinicians lack appropriate therapeutic expertise or resources. The following chapter aims to inform the clinician about medications used for pediatric anxiety and the most effective ways of employing them, based on empirical data and clinical experience.

As is true in other areas of child treatment when empirical evidence is inadequate, practitioners often use pharmacological agents off-label when they can determine a rationale or extrapolate from experience with adult patients. Currently, the clinical use of medication to treat anxiety symptoms far outpaces the proven and approved indications. The Food and Drug Administration (FDA) Modernization Act of 1997 provided a market incentive for drug manufacturers to conduct studies on the health benefits of new and existing drugs to children. If the FDA determined that a new (or already marketed drug) would produce health benefits in a pediatric population, and the manufacturer completed a study to that effect, then the manufacturer was eligible for an additional six months of market exclusivity in that sale of that drug (U.S. FDA, 1997). This act, passed in response to the dearth of drug labeling and information available to pediatricians and other health professionals, led to an increase in studies of marketed drugs from eleven in the seven years prior to the act to about forty-six in the three years that followed. This author hopes that the reader will use up-to-date research to inform his or her choices in the pharmacological arm of treatment planning.

Medications

Research on medications for childhood anxiety disorders has primarily targeted either obsessive-compulsive disorder (OCD) or symptoms of the other anxiety disorders presenting in youth. These disorders include selective mutism, separation anxiety disorder, social anxiety disorder, generalized anxiety disorder, panic disorder, agoraphobia, school refusal (although not a DSM-IVTR disorder), and post-traumatic stress disorder. Because some medications used for treating anxiety are also used for other conditions and will not be discussed elsewhere in this *Handbook*, some discussion of empirical evidence on pediatric use of these compounds for other disorders will be included. The chapter discusses use and evidence for use of tricyclic antidepressants, serotonin reuptake inhibitors, a serotonin norepinephrine-reuptake inhibitor, buspirone, benzodiazepines, alpha-agonists, antihistamines, beta blockers, and gabapentin.

Tricyclic Antidepressants

The tricyclic antidepressants are indicated for relief of symptoms of depression in adults. Imipramine and clomipramine are the tricyclics with the most evidence for efficacy for treating anxious children. Imipramine may also be useful as temporary adjunctive therapy in reducing enuresis in children aged five years and older, after possible organic causes have been excluded by appropriate tests. Imipramine is available in 10-mg, 25-mg, 50-mg, and 75-mg pills. Clomipramine, FDA-approved for treatment of OCD and for treatment of depression, is available in 25-mg, 50-mg, and 75-mg capsules.

Although a number of studies tested the tricyclic antidepressants for efficacy in treatment of childhood anxiety, early studies were equivocal. Troublesome methodologic issues included small sample sizes and failure to monitor blood drug levels, which vary widely between individuals. Since sudden death was reported in several children treated with desipramine (Riddle, Geller, & Ryan, 1993), fewer clinicians and families choose these agents. A recent study, however, compared treatment of school-refusing children in cognitive with and without the tricyclic antidepressant imipramine and found those in the combined treatment group had better outcomes (Bernstein et al., 2000). Furthermore, clomipramine has demonstrated efficacy in treating child and adolescent OCD. Therefore, these tricyclic antidepressant agents may continue to be used clinically despite their adverse effect potential.

Mechanism of Action. The tricyclic antidepressants block the presynaptic reuptake and inactivation of norepinephrine and serotonin at the nerve terminal, potentiating their action and, over time, decreasing the synthesis and metabolism of these neurotransmitters. The clinical activity of these antidepressants likely follows from alterations in receptor sensitivity or density. Therefore, improvement of symptoms takes weeks. These compounds have varying affinity to alpha-adrenergic, histaminic, and muscarinic receptors, which leads to adverse effects.

Dosing and Pharmacokinetics. The tricyclics are rapidly absorbed from the gastrointestinal tract, reaching peak plasma concentration within two to eight hours. Their half life is approximately twenty-four hours. The medications are largely bound to plasma proteins, with the non-bound portion available to the brain. Tricyclics undergo hepatic metabolism via demethylation, hydroxylation, and glucuronide conjugation, using the cytochrome P450 system for hydroxylation, as do many other psychoactive medications. Genetics determine metabolic rates, which vary so much that children taking the same dose of medication may differ thirty-fold in blood levels (Green, 1995). Of Caucasians, 5–10% are slow hydroxylators and 15–30% of Asians carry a cytochrome P450 isoenzyme 2C19 phenotype, causing them to be slow metabolizers of tricyclic antidepressants. Because of this, they require much lower doses of medication.

Dosing of tricyclics should proceed, guided by knowledge of the narrow therapeutic index for this class of medication. A normal electrocardiogram (EKG) should be obtained and a history of individual and family heart disease ruled-out before initiating treatment to ensure that heart abnormalities, which could predispose the patient to arrythmia, are not present. The physician must be aware of any other medications being taken. Dosage should start low and be increased approximately weekly, with EKG and vital-sign monitoring at each dose elevation. Drug level monitoring may be helpful in determining cause of lack of response or suspected drug-drug interactions.

If withdrawal from tricyclic antidepressants is not gradual, flu-like symptoms, gastrointestinal symptoms, headache, and lethargy occur, as do vivid dreams and nightmares.

Adverse Effects Profile. The tricyclic antidepressants interact with a number of neuronal receptors, leading to multiple potential adverse effects. Anticholinergic muscarinic symptoms include dry mouth (and subsequent tooth decay), dry eyes, blurred
vision, sinus tachycardia, urinary retention, constipation, and cognitive dysfunction.
Alpha-adrenergic effects include postural hypotension, dizziness, and drowsiness.
Dopiminergic and histaminergic effects may include extrapyramidal movements,
sedation, and weight gain. Analysis of compliance with medication treatment in
adolescents participating in an imipramine clinical trial for depression and anxiety in adolescents revealed that adverse effects did not cause drop out. Rather, medication noncompliance was associated with oppositional defiant disorder and low
measured family function (Bernstein, Anderson, Hektner, & Ralmuto, 2000).

Clomipramine and the other tricyclic antidepressants may cause a lowering
of the seizure threshold, necessitating careful attention to rule out a history of previous seizure disorder when considering treatment.

The tricyclics influence heart rate and conduction. Routinely, heart rate is
increased. Each of the cardiac conduction intervals may be prolonged, which may
predispose the heart to arrhythmia. In a prospective study of twenty-five pediatric
patients, noninvasive data were collected while children took imipramine at doses
up to 5 mg/kg/day or a serum level of 150 to 250 ng/ml. Two children were
excluded secondary to resting EKG or Holter monitor abnormalities. The
examiners found consistent, but clinically nonsignificant, resting EKG changes
during treatment (Fletcher, Wiggins, & Williams, 1993).

Sudden death has occurred in several children while taking desipramine. While
careful review of the cases suggested that the deaths were idiosyncratic and possibly unrelated to the medication, the clinician is advised to monitor cardiac variables carefully. Determining dose by patient age or size is not adequate, for studies
have demonstrated a poor correlation between dose of tricyclic antidepressant and
serum level. One study of two individuals (one seven years old) attributed sudden
death to accumulation of medication due to the child having a slow-metabolizer
phenotype (Swanson et al., 1997). See Table 11.1 for guidelines. Tricyclic antidepressants may be fatal if taken in overdose, primarily due to cardiac effects.

Drug Interactions and Contraindications. Additive effects of sedation and
dulled cognition may occur when tricyclics are administered with other sedative
medications. Medications metabolized by the cytochrome P450 system influence the metabolism of tricyclics. For example, in one report, combining
clomipramine with a serotonin reuptake inhibitor (each metabolized by the same
cytochrome P450 isoenzyme) for treating seven children with obsessive-compulsive
disorder resulted in two having prolongation of the QTc interval on EKG, and
two having tachycardia (Figueroa, Rosenberg, Birmaher, & Keshavan, 1988).

TABLE 11.1. PHYSIOLOGICAL PARAMETERS FOR TRICYCLIC USE.

PR interval	less than or equal to 210 milliseconds
QRS interval	widening to no more than 30% over baseline
QTc interval	less than 450 milliseconds
Heart rate	no more than 130 beats/minute
Systolic blood pressure	no more than 130 mm HG
Diastolic blood pressure	no more than 85 mm Hg

Source: Elliott & Popper, 1990.

Selective-Serotonin Reuptake Inhibitors

The selective-serotonin reuptake inhibitors (SSRIs) available in the United States now include fluoxetine (Prozac), sertraline (Zoloft), fluvoxamine (Luvox), paroxetine (Paxil), citalopram (Celexa) and its S-isomer, escitalopram (Lexapro). Fluoxetine (Prozac) comes in capsules of 10, 20, and 40 mg and Prozac Weekly capsules of 90 mg, as well as a titratable oral solution of 20 mg/5 ml. Fluoxetine is indicated for depression, OCD, bulimia nervosa, and premenstrual dysphoric disorder in adults and for OCD and depression in children and adolescents. Sertraline (Zoloft), which is available in tablets of 25, 50, and 100 mg and an oral solution of 20mg/ml, is indicated for depression, OCD, panic disorder, post-traumatic stress disorder (PTSD), and premenstrual dysphoric disorder and for OCD and PTSD in children and adolescents. Fluvoxamine, indicated for OCD, is available as tablets of 25, 50, and 100 mg. Paroxetine (Paxil) comes in tablets of 10, 20, 30, and 40 mg; in a sustained release preparation, Paxil CR, in 12.5, 25, and 37.5 mg tablets; and in an oral suspension of 10 mg/5 ml. Paroxetine is indicated for depression, OCD, panic disorder, social phobia, generalized anxiety disorder, and PTSD. Citalopram (Celexa) comes in tablets of 10, 20, and 40 mg and an oral solution of 10 mg/5 ml and is indicated for depression. Escitalopram (Lexapro) comes in 5-, 10-, and 20-mg tablets and is also indicated for depression (Ables & Baughman, 2003).

Introduced after the tricyclic antidepressants, the SSRIs have become more popular than their predecessors because of efficacy, ease of use, and wider safety profile. Of family physicians or pediatricians surveyed in North Carolina, 72% had prescribed one of these agents for a child or adolescent (Rushton, Clark, & Freed, 2000).

Chemical Makeup. The SSRIs vary in their structure, despite similarities in action. Paroxetine, sertraline, and escitalopram are single isomers. Fluoxetine and citalopram are racemic mixtures and fluvoxamine has no optically active forms. The compounds differ in their affinity to serotonin, norepinephrine, and dopamine receptors and in their half lives. SSRIs are generally more selective for serotonin receptors than the tricyclic antidepressants are.

Mechanism of Action. As do the tricyclic antidepressants, the SSRIs inhibit reuptake of serotonin into the neuron and thus make the neurotransmitter available in the synapse. The long-term result of SSRI treatment likely involves desensitization of serotonin receptors (including pre-synaptic autoreceptors) in various brain areas. This leads to a modified rate of neuronal firing and to therapeutic response (Potter, Husseini, & Rudorfer, 2001).

Some investigators have measured changes in brain areas concomitant with and following SSRI treatment. A volumetric imaging study of twenty-one children aged eight to seventeen with OCD showed decreased thalamic volume and decreased obsessive compulsive symptom severity with paroxetine treatment (Gilbert et al., 2000). In eight patients with OCD aged eight to seventeen, caudate glutaminergic concentrations as measured by single photon emission computer tomography (SPECT) scanning decreased after twelve weeks of paroxetine use. Authors concluded that paroxetine treatment may mediate a serotonergically modulated reduction in caudate glutamate (Rosenberg et al., 2000).

Dosing and Pharmacokinetics. The SSRIs and their active metabolites vary in their half lives: fluoxetine, forty-eight to seventy-two hours; norfluoxetine (its metabolite), seven to nine days; citalopram, thirty-six hours; sertraline and paroxetine, twenty-four hours; and fluvoxamine, sixteen hours (necessitating twice-per-day dosing). The medications are protein-bound and accumulate in fatty tissue. A pharmacokinetic study found absorption of fluvoxamine to be similar in adolescents and adults, but the steady-state plasma concentrations in children six to eleven years old were two to three times higher than in older individuals (Cheer & Figgitt, 2002). The authors therefore recommended a maximum fluvoxamine dose for children of 200 mg per day and for adolescents of 300 mg per day.

SSRIs are enzymatically degraded in the liver by the cytochrome P450 system, in which isoenzymes are designated by cytochrome number, family number 1 through 4, subfamily number A through E, and specific enzyme number. Each SSRI is metabolized by and is a competitive inhibitor of one or more isoenzymes. Many of the SSRIs are metabolized by the CYP1A2, CYP2C9, CYP2C19, CYP2D6, and CYP3A isoenzymes. Individual patients may be fast and slow metabolizers of the SSRIs based on genetic polymorphism of these isoenzymes.

Because of this metabolic system, the clinician must be mindful of possible drug-drug interactions when using SSRIs. Competition between two medications for use of the same metabolic enzymes may cause the level of a drug to rise. Other medications may cause the induction of a metabolic isoenzyme, causing the level of an SSRI drug to fall. The wise clinician will refer to a list of drugs metabolized by the cytochrome P450 system when prescribing these medications. Interactions may occur with such commonly used substances as erythromycin, cigarettes, carbamazepine, and antipsychotics.

Adverse Effects Profile. Side effects of the SSRIs fall into the general categories of gastrointestinal, activation, and apathy. Serotonergic receptors are present throughout the gastrointestinal tract, leading to possible side effects of dyspepsia, nausea, emesis, diarrhea, and decreased or increased appetite. Paroxetine, in particular, may be better tolerated when taken with food. Therapy with SSRIs may be associated with weight gain or loss. Recently, Weintrob published four case reports of children who experienced a decrease in growth rate during SSRI therapy. This was postulated to be secondary to suppression of growth hormone secretion (Weintrob et al., 2002).

Activation, in the forms of akathisia, frontal lobe disinhibition, or hypomania is a common side effect of SSRI treatment of children. Riddle, in 1990, reported that 50% of youth demonstrated motor restlessness, sleep disturbance, social disinhibition, and subjective sense of excitation when treated with fluoxetine. These symptoms decreased with medication discontinuation or a drop in dose (Riddle et al., 1991).

This class of medication may cause motor restlessness. In a study of adults taking SSRIs, 45% suffered from akathisia, 28% from dystonia, 14% from parkinsonism, and 11% tardive dyskinesia-like symptoms, but findings were confounded because more than half took other, additional medications (Leo, 1996).

Frontal lobe dysfunction symptoms may occur late in therapy with SSRIs. Subtle symptoms in this category include apathy, poor motivation, and indifference. Patients may not be aware of these sometimes disabling symptoms. Although this syndrome may appear to be a manifestation of depressed mood, increasing the antidepressant would exacerbate the problem.

More overt frontal lobe symptoms may present as self-injurious behavior. In 1991, King and colleagues reported that self-injurious behavior began or intensified in six of forty-two subjects treated with fluoxetine for OCD (King et al., 1991). In this author's clinical experience, some patients taking SSRIs began to bite their fingers, toes, and inner cheeks, or burned and cut their skin. When the dose was decreased, these behaviors abated. After the introduction of SSRIs, early reports questioned the medication's contribution to increased suicidality, perhaps secondary to behavioral disinhibition. However, analysis of case reports in adolescents and large meta-analysis in adults have not attributed increase in suicidal ideation or behavior to the SSRIs (Walsh & Dinan, 2001).

Despite gradual dose elevation and conservative dosing, children and adolescents treated with antidepressants may become hypomanic or manic. In case reports, subjects treated with SSRIs for anxiety or depression have been reported to have experienced a pathological mood elevation (Grubbs, 1997; Kat, 1996; Heimann & March, 1996). Symptoms have included impulsivity, grandiosity, pressured speech, and behavioral disinhibition. Attention to family history, close monitoring with awareness of this risk, and possible pretreatment with a mood stabilizing medication may avoid kicking off a cycling mood disorder.

Other potential adverse effects of this category of medication include decreased seizure threshold, bruising, bleeding, and sexual dysfunction. Although one would not encourage an adolescent to become sexually active, warning teenagers about reversible sexual side effects of decreased arousal, anorgasmia, and delayed or inhibited ejaculation in advance and informing them of potential remedies may avoid later non-compliance.

If an SSRI with a short half life is discontinued too rapidly, an uncomfortable discontinuation syndrome may follow within days. This withdrawal has been described most frequently with paroxetine. Symptoms include flu-like dizziness, nausea, headache, and sensory disturbance. Additionally, hypomania, mood change, aggression, and suicidality (perhaps secondary to a functionally hyposerotonergic state) have been described.

Drug Interactions and Contraindications. As mentioned above, treating a child or adolescent with more than one medication that is protein bound or metabolized by the same enzyme may cause drug levels to rise to toxic levels. In one reported case, a thirteen-year-old boy experienced serotonin syndrome while taking sertraline 37.5 mg and erythromycin for Pediatric Autoimmune Neuropsychiatric Syndrome Associated with Streptococcal (PANDAS) infection. He experienced nervousness, panic, restlessness, irritability, intermittent agitation, paresthesias, tremulousness, decreased concentration, and confusion. Seventy-two hours after discontinuing the medications, he felt calmer, less confused, and less irritable. His serotonin syndrome-like symptoms resulted because both sertraline and erythromycin are bound to alpha-1 glycoprotein and metabolized by and affect the same cytochrome P450 isoenzyme (Lee & Lee, 1999).

Buspirone

Chemical Makeup. Buspirone, an azapirone compound initially developed as an antipsychotic drug, is unlike any other drug used to treat child anxiety. Evidence supporting the use of buspirone in children and adolescents is meager, but does suggest possible utility for improving symptoms of anxiety disorders, aggression, attention, and deficit disorder and for helping children with developmental and autistic disorders. Buspirone is indicated for the management of anxiety disorders with or without accompanying depression in adults. It is available in doses of 5, 10, and 15 mg.

Mechanism of Action. Buspirone stimulates 5HT1A (auto-)receptors and suppresses serotonin over-activity. Although buspirone affects noradrenergic and dopamineregic activity also, animal studies suggest that buspirone improves anxiety through its serotonergic influence. Unlike benzodiazepines, buspirone does not interact with GABA receptors (Ninan, Cole, & Yonders, 2001).

Dosing and Pharmacokinetics. A dose-escalation study recently explored the pharmacokinetics of buspirone in children and adolescents. In an open label, multi-site study, thirteen children, twelve adolescents, and fourteen adults took 5 to 30 mg of buspirone twice daily over three weeks. Buspirone was rapidly absorbed, reaching peak levels at one hour and having a half life of one to two and a half hours. Concentrations peaked highest in the youngest subjects, so that typical doses of buspirone ranged up to 30 mg per day in children and 60 mg per day in adolescents in divided doses (Salazar et al., 2001).

Unlike benzodiazepines, therapeutic effects lag for weeks after reaching target dose. The medication must be taken regularly and in divided doses to sustain its effect. These factors have likely tempered buspirone's popularity.

Adverse Effects Profile. In general, therapy with buspirone is safe and well tolerated. Unlike the benzodiazepines, buspirone does not cause sedation or muscle relaxation or impair psychomotor functioning. Buspirone has no cross-tolerance with alcohol or benzodiazepines, no abuse potential, and no withdrawal or rebound symptoms.

Adverse events associated with buspirone treatment in children have been reported. In the above cited pharmacokinetic study, side effects included light-headedness in 68%, headache in 48%, and dyspepsia in 20% of subjects. One of twenty-two children with pervasive developmental disorder treated with buspirone in an open trial developed involuntary movements (Buitelaar, van der Gaag, & van der Hoeven, 1998). In an open-label trial of buspirone for hospitalized children with anxiety and moderately severe aggression, twenty-five prepubertal children were titrated up to 50 mg buspirone per day (mean 28 mg/day) over six weeks. Six discontinued buspirone: four due to increased aggression and agitation, and two due to mania (Pfeffer, Jiang, & Domeshek, 1997). A number of other cases of mania attributed to buspirone therapy have also been reported.

Drug Interactions and Contraindications. Buspirone is metabolized by the cytochrome P450 system in the liver, using the isoenzyme CYP3A. This enzyme metabolizes more drugs, including the other anxiety medications, SSRIs and benzodiazepines, than any other. Fluoxetine, fluvoxamine, and grapefruit juice inhibit the enzyme's action, so each of these may also decrease elimination of buspirone.

A drug interaction of buspirone may be used to an advantage. Some report that it may reverse sexual dysfunction caused by SSRIs.

Venlafaxine

Venlafaxine extended-release is FDA-approved for the treatment of depression and generalized anxiety disorder in adults. The long-acting preparation is available in three dosage strengths: 37.5 mg, 75 mg, and 150 mg, each designed for once-daily administration. It is also available as a five-hour half life preparation in doses of 25, 37.5, 50, 75, and 100 mg.

Chemical Makeup. Venlafaxine is has a novel bicyclic structure, unlike the tricyclics or serotonin reuptake inhibitors.

Mechanism of Action. Venlafaxine and its active metabolite inhibit neuronal reuptake of serotonin and norepinephrine. While it has a weak affinity to dopaminergic neurons, venlafaxine does not interact with muscarinic, cholinergic, histaminic, or alpha-adrenergic receptors.

Dosing and Pharmacokinetics. Venlafaxine undergoes first-pass metabolism to its active metabolite, O-desmethylvenlafaxine, in the liver, using cytochrome P450 isoenzyme 2D6. The respective half lives are four and ten hours in adults. Elimination then proceeds via the kidneys. Protein binding is not extensive (Kent & Gorman, 2001).

Adverse Effects Profile. Nausea is the most common side effect from venlafaxine. In a study of children treated for generalized anxiety disorder with venlafaxine, the adverse events reported twice as often as placebo included asthenia, anorexia, pain, and somnolence (Rynn, Kunz, Lamm, Nicolacopoulos, & Jenkins, 2002).

Drug Interactions and Contraindications. Although venlafaxine is metabolized by the P450 enzyme system, it is reported to be a weaker enzyme inhibitor than fluoxetine or paroxetine (Kent & Gorman, 2001).

Benzodiazepines

The benzodiazepines may be helpful as short-term agents when beginning other therapies for anxiety disorders. Potential abuse and dependence potential limit their long-term use. Clonazepam is indicated for panic disorder in adults and for some seizure disorders. It is available in 0.5-, 1-, and 2-mg tablets. Alprazolam is indicated for anxiety disorder and panic disorder in adults and comes in 0.25-, 0.5-, 1-, and 2-mg tablets.

Chemical Makeup. Benzodiazepines alprazolam and clonazepam have been studied in anxious children and adolescents. Each of these compounds contains two benzyl groups and a ring having nitrogen molecules.

Mechanism of Action. The benzodiazepines are agonists of the main inhibitory neurotransmitter system: the gamma amino butyric acid (GABA) benzodiazepine chloride receptor complex. Stimulation of the GABA receptor increases opening of the chloride channel and decreases neuronal excitability. Stimulation of benzodiazepine-GABA receptors in the limbic centers by benzodiazepine medication decreases anxiety.

Dosing and Pharmacokinetics. In general, benzodiazepines are well absorbed and exert noticeable symptomatic effects within hours after ingestion. The fact that it may be perceived that symptoms change within hours of taking the medication increases its potential for abuse. Because benzodiazepine half lives vary widely, it may appropriately be exploited in clinical use. Half lives in adults for the most commonly used benzodiazepines are: clonazepam, nineteen to sixty hours; lorazepam, eight to twenty-four hours; and alprazolam, nine to twenty hours (although the effective half life is shorter). Because of alprazolam's short half life, withdrawal between doses may mimic an exacerbation of anxiety. Common doses for children and adolescents are: clonazepam, 0.25 mg once or twice per day, up to 1 TID; lorazepam, 0.5 to 1 mg TID; and alprazolam, 25 mg TID.

Adverse Effects Profile. Although the benzodiazepines are usually safe and well tolerated, treatment with these agents is associated with a risk of dependence, behavioral disinhibition, cognitive impairment, and mood changes. The most common side effects of the benzodiazepines are sedation, tiredness, drowsiness, decreased ability to concentrate, and poor coordination. Students taking benzodiazepines should be aware that they may be impaired by anterograde amnesia. Clinical lore posits that children and adolescents may paradoxically become disinhibited, irritabile, exited, aggressive, and hostile from treatment with benzodiazepine anxiolytics. However, a retrospective study of adult psychiatric inpatients treated with alprazolam, clonazepam, or no benzodiazepine found no increase in behavioral disturbances (Rothschild, Shindul-Rothschild, Viguera, Murray, & Brewster, 2000). Overdose with the benzodiazepine compounds may be dangerous or, when taken with other medications, fatal. Depending on the dose and other substances taken concomitantly, outcome ranges from confusion and slurred speech to ataxia, drowsiness, dyspnea, hyporeflexia, coma, respiratory depression, seizures, and death.

Flumazenil is a competitive agonist of benzodiazepines that can be used to identify or reverse coma secondary to benzodiazepine overdose (Weinbroum et al., 1996). Debate has arisen regarding flumazenil use after deaths associated with status epilepticus occurred. The seizures may have followed acute benzodiazepine withdrawal after bolus administration of flumazenil. In the case of ingestion of multiple substances, benzodiazepine withdrawal may have lead to acute exposure to an epileptogenic agent (such as tricyclic antidepressant) without the antileptic benzodiazepine (Boccuzzi-Chmura & Robertson, 1996).

If benzodiazepines are discontinued abruptly, a withdrawal syndrome may ensue. Withdrawal symptoms include insomnia, dizziness, headache, nausea, vertigo, tinnitis, blurred vision, tremor, hypotention, hyperthermia, neuromuscular irritability, delirium, hallucinations, and seizures. Therefore, in a patient who has been maintained on benzodiazepines for an extended period, medication should be tapered slowly. The existence of dependency and withdrawal argues for using these medications as short-term agents.

Drug Interactions Contraindications. The benzozdiazepines have additive sedative effects with other medications and substances, including alcohol. Increased benzodiazepine levels may be seen with cimetitdine, disulfiram, erythromycin, estrogens, isoniazid, and fluoxetine. Decreased levels may result from co-therapy with carbamazepine. Antacids decrease the absorption, and smoking induces metabolism of benzodiazepine compounds.

Alpha-Adrenergic Agonists

Clonidine is FDA-approved for the treatment of hypertension. It is available as a transdermal patch (film, extended release: 0.1 mg/24 hrs, 0.2 mg/24 hrs, 0.3 mg/24 hrs), injection: 0.1 mg/ml and tablets 0.1 mg, 0.2 mg, 0.3 mg. Guanfacine hydrochloride tablets (1 mg, 2 mg) are indicated in the management of hypertension.

Chemical Makeup and Mechanism of Action. Because they act upon the noradrenergic system, and the noradrenergic system is implicated in generation and maintenance of anxiety disorders, the alpha-adrenergic agonists have begun to have been explored as anxiolytics. The alpha-adrenergic agonists have been used by some in treating individuals with post-traumatic stress disorder (Viola et al., 1997). The alpha-adrenergic agonists interact with presynaptic alpha-2 autoreceptors to suppress cell firing, inhibiting norepinephrine release and downregulating the central noradrenergic system (Newcorn et al., 1998). If, in states of fear and anxiety, necessary modulating feedback to the noradrenergic neurons in the locus coeruleus is disturbed, then activating the normally inhibiting autoreceptors may help normalize the equilibrium and improve symptoms. Clonidine and guanfacine are the currently alpha-2 agonists that are available, but they are not FDA-approved for psychiatric indications.

Dosing and Pharmacokinetics. Clonidine has a half life of eight to twelve hours, with behavioral effects evident from three to six hours. Therefore, it should be given in divided doses, either three or four times per day. Both an oral and a transdermal patch form of medication are available. The patch offers the potential advantage of approximately weekly versus three-times-per-day dosage. While the manufacturer recommends not cutting the patch, some in clinical practice do this to adjust dose. Disadvantages to the patch include dermatitis at the site of the patch and having the patch come off.

Because guanfacine has a longer half life (seventeen hours) than clonidine, it may be more conveniently dosed twice per day. Because of greater selectivity for the alpha-2 adrenergic receptor, guanfacine has fewer side effects of sedation and hypotension. Despite less empirical evidence supporting its use, these qualities make it an attractive therapeutic choice.

Both clonidine and guanfacine should be begun at a low dose at night to minimize potential side effects of sedation and hypotension. For clonidine, it is recommended to start at 0.05 mg at night and increase gradually up to therapeutic effect or approximately 3 mg/day. Using guanfacine, begin with 0.5 mg at night and increase to therapeutic effect or approximately 3 mg/day. Therapeutic effects may not be apparent for several weeks.

Adverse Effects Profile. Potential side effects of the alpha-adrenergic blockers include dry mouth, drowsiness, dizziness, sedation, weakness, fatigue, hypotension, and cardiac effects. The cardiac effects reported when clonidine has been used with other medications have included bradycardia, dysrhythmia, first degree heart lock, supraventricular premature complexes, nonspecific intraventricular conduction delay, T wave abnormality, and possible anterior ischemia (Chandran, 1994; Dawson, Vander Zanden, Werkman, Washington, & Tyma, 1989). A twenty-two-year-old woman experienced transient abnormalities of cardiac conduction upon accidental overdosage of clonidine (Williams, Krafcik, Potter, Hooper, & Hearne, 1977). Because these medications decrease vascular tone, if they are discontinued abruptly blood pressure may increase markedly. Therefore, it is recommended that one slowly taper the medications in discontinuing them.

Metabolism. Clonidine is eliminated 65% by the kidneys and 35% by the liver.

Drug Interactions and Contraindications. In children and adolescents with both attention-deficit/hyperactivitiy disorder (ADHD) and tic disorders, clonidine has frequently been prescribed together with methylphenidate. In 1999, questions were raised about the safety of this combination of medication following the sudden deaths of four children (Wilens et al., 1999). However, review of the cases and of the experience with this medication combination has allayed this concern (Wilens & Spencer, 1999).

Antihistamines

Hydroxyzine has shown efficacy in treating anxiety in adults. It is an antihistamine indicated for symptomatic relief of anxiety and tension associated with psychoneurosis and as an adjunct for organic disease states in which anxiety is manifested, in allergic puritis and urticaria, and as a sedative for premedication and following general anesthesia. It is available as 10-, 25-, 50-, and 100-mg tablets, an oral suspension of 25 mg/5 ml, and in an intramuscular injection.

Chemical Composition. Hydroxyzine is 1-(p-chorobenzhydryl) 4-[2-(2-hydroxyethoxy)-ethyl] piperazine dihydrochloride.

Mechanism of Action. Hydroxyzine is an antagonist of histamine. It has antihistaminic, antiemetic, and skeletal muscle relaxant properties. Its mechanism of action in anxiety has not been studied, but may help anxiety secondary to its sedating properties.

Dosing and Pharmacokinetics. Oral hydroxyzine is rapidly absorbed from the gastrointestinal tract. Clinical effects may be evident within fifteen to thirty minutes.

Adverse Effects Profile. Hydroxyzine may cause drowsiness and dry mouth. More rarely, paradoxical agitition, tolerance, or involuntary motor movements and seizures have been reported (Ninan et al., 2001). In one study, adverse effects in adults treated with hydroxyzine for anxiety included transitory sleepiness (36% of the cases), weakness (18%), headache (6%), changes of both appetite (6%) and body mass (6%), and slight mucosa dryness (2%). In one case urticaria bullosa occurred, requiring discontinuation of medication (Bobrov et al., 1998).

Beta Blockers

Because the noradrenergic system is involved in anxiety and anxiety disorders, beta-adrenergic blockers such as propranolol have been explored as possible interventions for anxiety disorders. Propranolol is indicated for the treatment of hypertension, some cardiac arrhythmias, myocardial infarction, migraine prophylaxis, essential tremor, hypertrophic subaortic stenosis, and pheochromocytoma. Immediate release propranolol is available in 10-, 20-, 40-, 60-, and 80-mg tablets and in an injectable solution. Long-acting propranolol is available in 60-, 80-, 90-, 120-, 160-mg capsules, in a concentrate of 80 mg/ml, and oral solutions of 4 mg/ml and 8 mg/ml.

Mechanism of Action. Beta adrenoreceptors couple to guanosine triphosphate (GTP)-binding regulatory proteins. It is uncertain whether it is central, peripheral, or both actions of beta blocking drugs that are responsible for anxiolytic action. When beta blockers work centrally, their influence on the noradrenergic receptors in the locus coeruleus and amygdala may be responsible. Effects on peripheral sympathetic receptors may decrease physical symptoms of anxiety, such as tremor, sweating, and tachycardia, secondarily influencing cognition and symptoms of anxiety.

Interestingly, beta blockers may prevent development of anxiety symptoms via an additional proposed mechanism. Because the presence of epinephrine strengthens memory consolidation and fear conditioning, blocking the action of epinephrine with a b-adrenergic blocker may avert the development of PTSD (Pittman et al., 2002).

Dosing and Pharmacokinetics. Some beta blockers are lipophilic and able to cross the blood-brain barrier. Propranolol and metoprolol are lipophilic beta blockers, while nadolol and atenolol are not lipophilic and may work only peripherally. No controlled studies have defined a recommendation for dosing beta blockers for pediatric use in anxiety. In one study, low dose propranolol decreased, but high dose increased, spontaneous firing of single neurons in the central nucleus of the amygdala (Simson, Naylor, Gibson, Schneider, & Levin, 2001). This study suggests that appropriate dosing may be critical for clinical response.

Adverse Effects Profile. Beta-blocking agents may have adverse CNS and somatic side effects. Somatic effects may include sedation, dizziness, nausea, fatigue, Raynaud's phenomena, hypotension, bronchoconstriction, and bradycardia. In a study of healthy adults treated for four days with propranolol 40 or 80 mg/day or placebo, subjects rated tension, depression, total mood disturbance, fatigue, and confusion as greater on propranolol than on placebo (Head, Kendall, Ferner, & Eagles, 1996). In a randomized controlled eight-week double-blind cross-over study of adults taking beta blockers (propranolol or atenolol) for blood pressure control, cognitive function did not change on seven of nine tests administered. Performance was impaired on digit cancellation, but was improved on a trail making test (Palac et al., 1990).

That beta blockers have adverse effects on the CNS was suggested by a discontinuation study of lipophilic beta blockers in seventeen adults. After stopping the medication, subjects showed improved sleep, dreams, concentration, memory, and energy. Atenolol did not cause CNS effects, but metoprolol did (Kirk & Cove-Smith, 1983).

Drug Interactions and Contraindications. The use of beta blockers is relatively contraindicated in patients with asthma due to possible bronchoconstriction, with diabetes due to masking of physical symptoms of hypoglycemia, and with abnormal heart function. Additive effects with other medications that lower blood pressure may occur. Blood levels of medications also metabolized by the cytochrome P450 isoenzymes 2C9 and 2D6 (including, among others, tricyclic antidepressants and serotonin reuptake inhibitors) may be increased.

Gabapentin

Gabapentin is indicated as adjunctive therapy in the treatment of partial seizures with and without secondary generalization in adults with epilepsy. It is available in 100-, 300-, and 400-mg capsules.

Chemical Makeup. Gabapentin is an amino acid and novel anticonvulsant that has shown promise in treating some anxiety disorders.

Mechanism of Action. The mechanism of gabapentin's effects on anxiety are not known. Some have proposed that gabapentin interacts with the l-amino acid transporter, increases GABA synthesis, alters GABA release, interacts with calcium and sodium channels, or alters monoamine neurotransmitter release and serotonin blood levels (Pande et al., 2000).

Metabolism. Gabapentin is not appreciably metabolized in humans and is eliminated from the systemic circulation by renal excretion as unchanged drug. Gabapentin elimination half life is 5 to 7 hours and is unaltered by dose or following multiple dosing.

Dosing and Pharmacokinetics. In two studies of adults with social phobia and panic disorder, doses of gabapentin ranged from 600 to 3600 mg/day. Subjects began with 300 mg gabapentin twice per day, then three times per day by the end of week one. If symptoms persisted and adverse effects were not present, the dose was raised no faster than 300 mg/day up, to 3,600 mg/day (Pande, 2000).

Adverse Effects Profile. In adult subjects with panic disorder, only 12% of those on gabapentin versus 4% on placebo withdrew secondary to adverse effects. These included dizziness, somnolence, and ataxia (Pande et al., 2000).

Empirical Data

Tricyclic Antidepressants

The tricyclic antidepressants have not demonstrated effectiveness in treatment of children with depression. Meta-analytic study has indicated that they may have a moderate effect in treating depression in adolescents (Hazell, O'Connell, Heathcote, & Henry, 2002). Some controlled studies have shown tricyclics effective for some anxiety disorders or effective in conjunction with other interventions. Empirical evidence for treating anxiety disorders and symptoms of anxiety in other diagnostic categories is presented below.

Clomipramine is effective for treating children and adolescents with OCD. In 1985, Flament and colleagues performed a double-blind controlled ten-week study of clomipramine in nineteen children with OCD (Flament et al., 1985). At a mean dosage of 141 mg/day, those taking clomipramine showed significant improvement. The degree of improvement did not correlate with plasma concentration of the drug or its metabolites.

Leonard treated forty-eight child and adolescent subjects with OCD in a ten-week double-blind cross-over trial of clomipramine and desipramine (Leonard et al., 1989). Mean doses were, for clomipramine 150 +/− 532, and desipramine 153 +/− 55 mg. Clomipramine was clearly superior to desipramine. Neither age of onset, duration or severity of illness, nor plasma drug concentrations predicted outcome.

Several studies examined tricyclic antidepressants in controlled trials of children with separation anxiety and school refusal. Variable results likely related to study methodology. Gittelman-Klein and Klein (1973) compared the outcomes of thirty-five subjects with separation anxiety treated with imipramine (100 to 200 mg/day) to those treated with placebo and behavioral therapy. After six weeks, 81% of those taking imipramine versus 47% taking placebo had returned to school.

Using relatively low dose (40 to 75 mg/day) clomipramine, Berney and colleagues treated fifty-one school subjects with either clomipramine or placebo, each with concomitant individual and parent therapy. Evaluation at twelve weeks revealed no significant difference between the groups (Berney et al., 1981).

In 1990, Bernstein and colleagues compared eight weeks of treatment with imipramine (50 to 175 mg/day) with alprazolam 0.75 to 4 mg/day or placebo for twenty-four school-refusing youths with anxiety and or depression. Subjects also received weekly individual therapy and a behavioral school reentry plan (Bernstein, Garfinkel, & Borchardt, 1990). Significant differences between the groups were not demonstrated, but with this sample size and concomitant therapy, differences would need to be great to reach statistical significance.

In a differently designed study, Klein and colleagues treated twenty children aged six to fifteen years for one month with vigorous behavior therapy for school refusal. Those who failed to improve with this intervention entered a double-blind trial of imipramine or placebo. Neither therapy was superior (Klein, Kopelwicz, & Kanner, 1992).

Bernstein and colleagues compared eight weeks of treatment with placebo or imipramine plus CBT for school refusing adolescents with comorbid anxiety and major depressive disorders (Bernstein et al., 2000). Sixty-three subjects entered and forty-seven completed the study. School attendance improved significantly and improved faster for those taking imipramine than for placebo, with 70% of imipramine group subjects attending school in the final week versus 28% in the placebo group. Medication was dosed and adjusted on the basis of blood imipramine level to maintain it within the range of 150 to 300 micrograms per liter. At the end of the study, the imipramine dose averaged $182 +/- 50$ mg/day, with average blood level of $151 +/- 90$ micrograms per liter.

Children with autism demonstrate some symptoms that appear like anxiety symptoms, including social withdrawal, reduced spontaneous interaction, and repetitive, compulsive behavior. Gordon and colleagues performed a double-blind comparison of clomipramine and desipramine in twelve subjects and another ten-week double-blind cross-over comparison of clomipramine and placebo in twelve different subjects (Gordon, State, Nelson, Hamburger, & Rapoport, 1993). Clomipramine was superior to placebo in reducing autistic withdrawal, rhythmic motions, abnormal object relations, unspontaneous relation to examiner, under-productive speech, anger, uncooperativeness, hyperactivity, and OCD behavior. Clomipramine was superior to desipramine in reducing autistic symptoms, anger and uncooperativeness. Both drugs were superior to placebo for hyperactivity. Doses for clomipramine and desipramine were increased until positive effects, side effects, or a maximum dose of 5 mg/kg or 250 mg/day were reached. Average doses were 152 and 127 mg/day for clomipramine and desipramine, respectively.

The tricyclic antidepressants may help improve the course of acute stress disorder in pediatric patients. In a randomized double-blind study, twenty-five pediatric burn patients aged two to nineteen with acute stress disorder were treated for seven days with either imipramine (1 mg/kg) or chloral hydrate (Robert,

Blakeney, Villareal, Bosenberg, & Meyer, 1999). Imipramine was more effective than chloral hydrate, with ten of twelve responding.

Serotonin Reuptake Inhibitors

Obsessive Compulsive Disorder. More information exists on medication for children with OCD than for any other anxiety disorder. Double-blind placebo-controlled studies lasting from months to slightly more than one year demonstrate that the serotonin reuptake inhibitor class of antidepressant medication is safe and effective in treating symptoms of OCD in children. Well-designed studies of fluoxetine (Riddle, Scahill, & King, 1992; Black & Uhde, 1994; Geller et al., 2001; Liebowitz et al., 2002), sertraline (March et al., 1998; Cook et al., 2001) and fluvoxamine (Riddle, 2001) have been published. These investigations, involving more than 600 subjects, have found medication superior to placebo and have found the medications tolerable for most. On the whole, response rate (which has been defined differently in different studies, but often by a 25% improvement in Yale-Brown Obsessive Compulsive Scale [Y-BOCS] rating) has been 60% for medication and 25% for placebo. The most common side effects have been headache, abdominal discomfort, behavioral activation, and sleep disturbance.

An open-label extended trial of citalopram suggested its possible utility in treating OCD. Thirty subjects were treated with a flexible dose of citalopram (20 to 70 mg/day, mean 46.5) and monitored for one to two years. All had individual CBT, with a mean number of sixteen sessions. Over one year, 70% had more than a 35% decrease in symptom rating. No subject dropped out because of serious side effects. Common side effects included dry mouth, nausea, headache, and insomnia, most of which disappeared after ten weeks. Sexual dysfunction in 10–12% and sedation in 20% persisted (Thomsen, Ebbesen, & Persson, 2001).

Other Anxiety Disorders. In 1992, a placebo controlled study of fifteen subjects with social phobia and mutism demonstrated superiority for fluoxetine treatment (Black & Uhde, 1994)

A multi-center randomized placebo-controlled trial of fluvoxamine for anxious children (Walkup et al., 2001) was performed by the Research Units on Pediatric Psychopharmacology Anxiety Treatment Study group. Following a three-week psycho-educational lead-in phase, 128 children aged six to seventeen and diagnosed with generalized anxiety, social anxiety, separation anxiety, or agoraphobia, underwent an eight-week trial of fluvoxamine. Subjects with histories of previous use of a serotonin reuptake inhibitor, OCD, PTSD, mood disorders, Tourette's syndrome, pervasive developmental disorder (PDD), conduct disorder, suicidality, or current use of a stimulant medication were excluded. Ratings on the Pediatric Anxiety Rating Scale (clinician-administered) and Clinical Global Impressions–Improvement Scale (CGI) (clinician-rated) demonstrated significant differences between fluvoxamine and placebo. Of those on fluvoxamine, 79% were classified as responders (improved to symptom-free on the CGI) versus 29% of those on placebo. The final dose of fluvoxamine was 5.9+/−2.8 mg/kg (maximum 200 mg/day for children, 300 mg/day for adolescents). The most frequent adverse effects included abdominal discomfort (49% on medication versus 28% on placebo) and increased motor activity (8% versus 1.4%). Only 8% discontinued fluvoxamine because of adverse effects.

A small study of fluoxetine observed its effects on obsessions, compulsions, and Tourette's syndrome (TS) (Scahill et al., 1997). Five TS subjects with OCD, six subjects with obsessive-compulsive features, and three subjects with TS without obsessive-compulsive symptoms, aged eight to thirty-three years old participated in a twenty-week, fixed-dose (20 mg/day), double-blind, placebo-controlled crossover trial of fluoxetine. Fluoxetine was associated with improvement in obsessive-compulsive symptoms in some patients with TS, but did not appear to be effective for tics. The most common side effect was transient behavioral activation, which occurred in about half of the subjects and was more common in children.

A small, double-blind controlled study of another serotonin reuptake inhibitor, sertraline, was published in 2002. Twenty-two boys and girls with generalized anxiety disorder underwent a two-week screen and then a nine-week trial of placebo or medication. Concurrent psychotherapy, except for CBT, was allowed. Subjects receiving sertraline (up to 50 mg/day) had greater reduction in anxiety symptoms than those on placebo. Moreover, an analysis separating those low on depression ratings from those high in depression ratings suggested that improvement in anxiety was not merely secondary to an improvement in depressive symptoms. Those on placebo suffered adverse effects consistent with generalized anxiety disorder symptoms: dizziness, nausea, and stomach pain with an incidence of three to tenfold greater than those on medication. For subjects taking medication, versus placebo, side effects included dry mouth (55% versus 27%), drowsiness (73% versus 45%), leg spasms (36% versus 9%), and restlessness (55 versus 27%) (Rynn et al., 2002).

Paroxetine was investigated for pediatric social anxiety disorder in 319 subjects. Subjects were randomized to receive paroxetine, 10 to 50 mg/day or placebo for sixteen weeks. Of subjects taking paroxetine, 78% were defined as responders to medication versus 38% taking the placebo. The most common adverse effects reported by those on medication were headache (38%), infection (20%), respiratory disorder (15%), abdominal pain (15%), asthenia (15%), insomnia (14%), somnolence (13%), and rhinitis (10%) and nausea (10%) (Wagner, Rynn, Dibbekktm, Kabdaym, & Wohlberg, 2002). In an open label follow-up study of 226 of these subjects, investigators reported continued improvement of symptoms and tolerability of medication. Headache, nausea, and insomnia were the only side effects present in more than 10% of subjects (Wagner et al., 2002).

Venlafaxine

Venlafaxine has shown effectiveness for the treatment of generalized anxiety disorder in children and adolescents. Two multicenter, eight-week, double-blind flexible dose studies in 175 children and 145 adolescents compared venlafaxine extended release versus placebo. Those taking medication reported improved symptoms and were more frequently rated as responders by clinicians (69% versus 48% for placebo). The adverse events reported twice as often for venlafaxine than for placebo were asthenia, anorexia, pain, and somnolence (Rynn et al., 2002).

Benzodiazepines

A few, small studies of benzodiazepines have been conducted with children who have anxiety disorders. Two double-blind placebo-controlled studies of alprazolam for anxiety had ambiguous outcomes. A three-way double-blind trial of alprazolam (mean dosage of 1.4 mg/day), imipramine (mean dosage of 135 mg/day) and placebo given for eight weeks to children and adolescents with anxiety and/or depression showed a trend for advantage for the medications but was not statistically significant (Bernstein, Garfinkel, & Borchardt, 1989). A double-blind study of alprazolam (mean dosage of 1.6 mg/day) versus placebo in thirty children and adolescents with overanxious or avoidant disorder did not demonstrate a significant difference in outcomes (Simeon et al., 1992).

A four-week double-blind, cross-over study of clonazepam (dosages of 0.5 to 2.0 mg/day) versus placebo in fifteen children with separation anxiety showed no advantage for the medication (Graae, Milner, Rizzotto, & Klein, 1994). Clonazepam did show benefit in the treatment of adolescents with panic disorder in a double-blind placebo-controlled study (Riddle et al., 1999).

Buspirone

Open trials of buspirone have had varying results. An open trial of buspirone (mean of 18.6 mg/day) in fifteen anxious children aged six to fourteen found significant improvement with minimal side effects (Simeon, 1993). Another open-label trial used busipirone in twenty-five prepubertal psychiatric inpatients with anxiety and moderately aggressive behavior and found benefit for few subjects. Over three weeks, subjects' doses were titrated up to a maximum of 50 mg/day, then maintained for six weeks. Twenty-five percent of subjects developed either increased agitation and aggression or mania. Despite improvements in depressive and anxious symptoms, authors reported that only three children improved sufficiently enough to be maintained on buspirone (Pfeffer et al., 1997).

An open-label trial of buspirone was performed in twenty-two subjects with pervasive developmental disorders aged six to seventeen. The mean dose of buspirone was 15 to 45 mg/day and duration of treatment was six to eight weeks. Nine subjects had marked and seven had moderate positive response (by clinician rating). Although side effects were minimal, one subject developed a movement disorder (Buitelaar, van der Gaag, & van der Hoeven, 1998).

Hydroxyzine

Two well-designed studies have compared hydroxyzine to other anxiolytics in adults with generalized anxiety disorder.

A three-month multicenter, randomized, double-blind, placebo-controlled trial compared hydroxyzine, bromazepam, and placebo in adults. After two weeks of single-blind run-in placebo, 334 adult subjects with generalized anxiety disorder underwent twelve weeks of double-blind randomized treatment, and four weeks of single-blind run-out placebo. The Hamilton anxiety score (HAM-A), Clinical Global Impressions-Severity (CGI-S) scale score scale, and Hospital Anxiety and Depression scale score, and responder and remission rates were significantly more improved in subjects treated with hydroxyzine than placebo. The mean $+/-$ standard deviation (SD) change in HAM-A scores from baseline to endpoint was -12.16 ($+/-7.74$) for hydroxyzine and -9.64 ($+/-7.74$) for placebo (p $=$ .019) (Llorca et al., 2002; Lader & Scotto, 1998)

In another double-blind, parallel group study, the efficacy of hydroxyzine, buspirone, and placebo were compared. Two hundred forty-four patients with generalized anxiety disorder in primary care took hydroxyzine (12.5 mg morning and mid-day, 25 mg evening), buspirone (5 mg morning and mid-day, 10 mg evening) or placebo (three capsules/day) for four weeks, preceded by a one-week single-blind placebo run-in and followed by a one-week single-blind placebo administration. At thirty-five days, a significant difference between hydroxyzine and placebo on the Hamilton Anxiety Scale (10.75 versus 7.23 points, respectively) was found.

Beta Blockers

Open trials for youth with anxiety who were treated with propranolol have been positive. An open-label off-on-off design study tested propranolol in eleven children with acute PTSD. Propranolol was administered in TID doses from

0.8 mg/kg/day to 2.5 mg/kg/day over two weeks. Dose increase was limited by sedation, decreased blood pressure, or slowed pulse in three children. Significant improvement was seen with active treatment, with symptoms returning after termination (Famularo, Kinscherff, & Fenton, 1988).

In another open trial, propranolol up to 30 mg/day helped thirteen of fourteen adolescents with hyperventilation syndrome (Joorabchi, 1977). A case study of three children with severe school refusal who were treated with propranolol demonstrated hastened time to school return, without bothersome side effects. Authors noted that the medication helped alleviate somatic anxiety symptoms (Fourneret, Descombre, de Villard, & Revol, 2001.)

Adult studies of use of beta blockers for situational anxiety show positive findings as well. A prospective, double-blind, randomized study of fifty-three patients planning day surgery received 10 mg of propranolol or placebo on the day of surgery. Anxiety and depression scores were lower for those pretreated with propranolol (Mealy, Ngeh, Gillin, Fitzpatrick, Keane, & Tanner, 1996). One hundred other surgery patients were randomized in a double-blind fashion to receive either bopindolol (a beta blocker), lorazepam, butalbital, or placebo. Those taking the beta blocker had less anxiety, better sleep, and better performance on a game of manual skill (Chierichetti, Moise, Galeone, Fiorella, & Lazzari, 1985).

Acute treatment with beta blockers also may temper the course of PTSD. A controlled study of thirty-eight adults exposed to an emotionally arousing slide show showed that those pretreated with 40 mg of propranolol had less recall of the arousing story (Reist, Duffy, Fujimoto, & Cahill, 2001). In another study, adult emergency room patients treated with a ten-day course of propranolol 40 mg QID or placebo beginning within six hours of trauma in a double-blind manner found that those on the beta blocker demonstrated less physiologic response to script-driven imagery of their traumatic event three months later (Pittman et al., 2002).

Gabapentin

Gabapentin has demonstrated efficacy and safety in a controlled study of adults with social phobia, but not with panic disorder (Pande et al., 2000). A case report described two adolescents with severe school refusal who responded to gabapentin. The first had failed treatment with paroxetine, venlafaxine, methylphenidate, carbamazepine, valproic acid, and ziprasidone. He responded when gabapentin 600 mg BID was added to hydroxazine 100 mg BID. The second case, failing treatment with an even greater number of medications, responded to 2,000 mg/day of gabapentin (Durkin, 2002).

Alpha-Adrenergic Agonists

Evidence is scant for prescribing the alpha-adrenergic agonists for pediatric anxiety disorders. Clonidine is frequently used as a preanesthetic agent for sedation and anxiety management. A randomized control compared clonidine, midazolam (a benzodiazepine), and placebo for children undergoing tonsillectomy. In this group of 134 subjects, midazolam was the superior agent (Fazi, Jantzen, Rose, Kurth, & Watcha, 2001). However, in a comparison of clonidine, morphine, midazolam, and placebo for 150 patients (adults) undergoing facial surgery, clonidine matched midazolam for anxiety control, morphine for pain control, and was superior in terms of side effects (Beer et al., 2001). Controlled studies have demonstrated clonidine to be effective in treating symptoms of tics, attention deficit disorder, and aggression in children (Gaffney et al., 2002).

Expert Recommendations

Given the current state of evidence for treatment of anxiety disorders with medication, the clinician will need to combine knowledge with clinical judgement to treat children who require medication when the few FDA-approved medications are inappropriate or do not work for a particular patient. For treatment of each of the DSM-defined anxiety disorders, SSRIs are currently the first medication choice. For the tricyclic antidepressants, clomipramine as monotherapy or carefully administered as an augmenting agent, may help when SSRIs have not. Adding an atypical antipsychotic, such as risperidone, or the benzodiazepine, clonazepam, is another augmentation strategy that helps with OCD symptoms. For school refusal, the evidence supports the use of imipramine in combination with CBT.

When anxiety is accompanied by aggression or a developmental disorder, buspirone may be effective, alone, or with an SSRI. For those with concomitant ADHD and anxiety, venlafaxine may be an efficient treatment. The hyperarousal of PTSD may respond to clonidine, the hyperactivity to stimulant medication.

◆ ◆ ◆

Evidence continues to grow in support of the use of medications in treating children and adolescents with anxiety disorders. The tricyclic antidepressants, serotonin reuptake inhibitors, and venlafaxine have the most robust support, but benzodiazepines, buspirone, beta blockers, alpha-adrenergic agonists, hydroxyzine, and gabapentin have promise. This all must be said in context of knowledge about *all* therapies for pediatric anxiety: CBTs have "established" status and should be used as first choice (Ollendick & King, 1998). Analysis of and intervention around family and environmental factors contributing to anxiety is important. Medication may be used when children are too anxious to attempt CBT as an aid to begin the work. In severe cases, medication requirements persist, but medication alone should not be considered sufficient treatment for childhood anxiety disorders.

References

Ables, A. Z., & Baughman, O. L. (2003). Antidepressants: Update on new agents and indications. *American Family Physician, 67*(3), 547–554.

Beer, G. M., Spicher, I., Siefert, B., Emanuel, B., Kompatscher, P., & Meyer, V. E. (2001). Oral premediation for operations on the face under local anesthesia: A placebo-controlled double-blind trial. *Plastic and Reconstructive Surgery, 108*(3), 637–643.

Berney, T., Kolvin, I., Bhate, S. R., Garside, R. F., Jeans, J., Kay, B., & Scarth, L. (1981). School phobia: A therapeutic trial with clomipramine and short-term outcome. *British Journal of Psychiatry, 138*, 110–118.

Bernstein, G. A., Anderson, L. K., Hektner, J. M., & Ralmuto, G. M. (2000). Imipramine compliance in adolescents. *Journal of the American Academy of Child and Adolescent Psychiatry, 39*(3), 284–291.

Bernstein, G. A., Borchardt, C. M., Perwein, A. R., Crosby, R. D., Kushner, M. G., Thuras, P. D., Last, C. G., et al. (2000). Imipramine plus cognitive-behavioral therapy in the treatment of school refusal. *Journal of the American Academy of Child and Adolescent Psychiatry, 39*(3), 2844–2891.

Bernstein, G. A., Garfinkel, B. D., & Borchardt, C. M. (1989). Comparative studies of pharmacotherapy for school refusal. *Journal of the American Academy of Child and Adolescent Psychiatry, 29*, 773–781.

Bernstein, G. A., Garfinkel, B. D., & Borchardt, C. M. (1990). Comparative studies of pharmacotherapy for school refusal. *Journal of the American Academy of Child and Adolescent Psychiatry, 29*, 773–781.

Black, B., & Uhde, T. W. (1994). Treatment of elective mutism with fluoxetine: A double-blind, placebo-controlled study. *Journal of the American Academy of Child and Adolescent Psychiatry, 33*(7), 1000–1006.

Bobrov, A. E., Babin, A. G., Gladyshev, M. A., Piatnitskii, N.I.U., Bakalova, E. A., & Abolmasova, O. B. (1998). [Atarax in treatment of anxiety in outpatient clinic]. *Zh Neurol Psikhiatr Im SS Korsakova, 98*(2), 31–33.

Boccuzzi-Chmura, L., & Robertson, D. C. (1996). Flumazenil (Romazicon) and the patient with benzodiazepine overdose: Risk versus benefits. *Journal of Emergency Nursing, 22*(4), 330–333.

Bolton, J., Moore, G. H., MacMillan, S., Stewart, C. M., & Rosenberg, D. R. (2001). Case study: Caudate glutamatergic changes with paroxetine persist after medication discontinuation in pediatric OCD. *Journal of the American Academy of Child and Adolescent Psychiatry, 40*(8), 903–906.

Buitelaar, J. K., van der Gaag, R. J., & van der Hoeven, J. (1998). Buspirone in the management of anxiety and irritability in children with pervasive developmental disorders: Results of an open-label study. *Journal of Clinical Psychiatry, 59*(2), 56–59.

Chandran, K. S. (1994). ECG and clonidine. *Journal of the American Academy of Child and Adolescent Psychiatry, 33*(9), 1351–1352.

Cheer, S. M., & Figgitt, D. P. (2002). Spotlight on fluvoxamine in anxiety disorders in children and adolescents. *CNS Drugs, 16*(2), 139–144.

Chierichetti, S. M., Moise, G., Galeone, M., Fiorella, G., & Lazzari, R. (1985). Beta-blockers and psychiatric stress: A double-blind, placebo-controlled study of bopindolol vs lorazepam and butalbital in surgical patients. *International Journal of Clinical Pharmacology, Therapy and Toxicaology, 23*(9), 510–514.

Cook, E. H., Wagner, K. D., March, J. S., Biederman, J., Landau, P., Wolkow, R., & Messig, M. (2001). Long-term sertraline treatment of children and adolescents with obsessive-compulsive disorder. *Journal of the American Academy of Child and Adolescent Psychiatry, 40*(10), 1175–1181.

Costello, E. J., Angold, A., Burns, B. J., & Erkanli, A. (1996). The Great Smoky Mountains study of youth. Goals, design, methods, and the prevalence of DSM-III-R disorders. *Archives of General Psychiatry, 53*(12), 1129–1136.

Dawson, P. M., Vander Zanden, J. A., Werkman, S. L., Washington, R. L., & Tyma, T. A. (1989). Cardiac dysrhythmia with the use of clonidine in explosive disorder. *DICP, 23*(6), 465–466.

Durkin, J. P. (2002). Gabapentin in complicated school refusal. *Journal of the American Academy of Child and Adolescent Psychiatry, 41*(6), 632–633.

Elliott, G. H., & Popper, C. W. (1990/1991). Tricyclic antidepressants: The QT interval and other cardiovascular parameters. *Journal of Child and Adolescent Psychopharmacology, 1*(3), 187–189.

Emslie, G. J., Rush, J., Weinberg, W. A., Kowatch, R. A., Hughes, C. W., Carmody, T., Rintelmann, J., et al. (1997). A double blind, randomized, placebo-controlled trial of fluoxetine children and adolescents with depression, *Archives of General Psychiatry, 5*, 1031–1037.

Famularo, R., Kinscherff, R., & Fenton, T. (1988). Propranolol treatment for childhood post-traumatic stress disorder, acute type. A pilot study. *American Journal of Diseases of the Child, 142*, 1244.

Fazi, L., Jantzen, E. C., Rose, J. B., Kurth, C. K., & Watcha, M. F. (2001). A comparison of oral clonidine and oral midazolam as preanesthetic medications in the pediatric tonsillectomy patient. *Anesthesia and Analgesia, 92*(1), 56–61.

Figueroa, Y., Rosenberg, D. R., Birmaher, B., & Keshavan, M. S. (1988). Combination treatment with clomipramine and selective serotonin reuptake inhibitors for obsessive-compulsive disorder in children and adolescents. *The Journal of Child and Adolescent Psychopharmacology, 8*(1), 61–67.

Flament, M. F., Rapoport, J. L., Berg, C. J., Sceery, W., Kilts, C., Mellsrrom, B., et al. (1985). Clomipramine treatment of childhood obsessive-compulsive disorder. A double-blind controlled study. *Archives of General Psychiatry, 42*(10), 977–983.

Fletcher, S. E., Wiggins, D. M., & Williams, E. (1993). Prospective study of the electrocardiographic effects of imipramine in children. *Journal of Pediatrics, 122*(4), 652–654.

Fourneret, P., Descombre, H., de Villard, R., & Revol, O. (2001). Interest in propranolol in the treatment of school refusal anxiety: About three clinical observations. *Encephale, 27*(6), 578–584.

Gaffney, G. R., Perry, P. J., Lund, B. C., Bever-Stille, K. A., Arndt, S., & Kuperman, S. (2002). Risperidone versus clonidine in the treatment of children and adolescents with Tourette's syndrome. *Journal of the American Academy of Child and Adolescent Psychiatry, 41*(3), 330–336.

Geller, D. A., Hoog, S. L., Heiligenstein, J. H., Ricardi, R. K., Tamura, R., Kluszynski, S., et al. (2001). Fluoxetine treatment for obsessive-compulsive disorder in children and adolescents: A placebo-controlled clinical trial. *Journal of the American Academy of Child and Adolescent Psychiatry, 40*(7), 773–779.

Gilbert, A. R., Moore, G. J., Keshavan, M. S., Paulson, L. A., Nareula, V., MacMaster, F. P., et al. (2000). Decrease in thalamic volumes of pediatric patients with obsessive-compulsive disorder who are taking paroxetine. *Archives of General Psychiatry, 57*(5), 449.

Gittelman-Klein, R., & Klein, D. F. (1973). Controlled imipramine treatment of school phobia. *Archives of General Psychiatry, 25,* 204–207.

Gordon, C. T., State, R. C., Nelson, J. E., Hamburger, S. D., & Rapoport, J. L. (1993). A double-blind comparison of clomipramine and of desipramine in autistic disorder. *Archives of General Psychiatry, 50*(6), 441–447.

Graae, F., Milner, J., Rizzotto, L., & Klein, R. G. (1994). Clonazepam in childhood anxiety disorders. *Journal of the American Academy of Child and Adolescent* Psychiatry, *33,* 372–376.

Green, W. H. (1995). *Child and adolescent clinical psychopharmacology* (2nd ed.). Philadelphia: Williams and Wilkins.

Grubbs, J. H. (1997). SSRI-induced mania. *Journal of the American Academy of Child and Adolescent Psychiatry, 36*(4), 445.

Hazell, P., O'Connell, D., Heathcote, D., & Henry, D. (2003). Tricyclic drugs for depression in children and adolescents. *Cochrane Database of Systematic Reviews,* (2), *CD002317.*

Head, A., Kendall, M. J., Ferner, R., & Eagles, C. (1996). Acute effects of beta blockade and exercise on mood and anxiety. *British Journal of Sports Medicine, 30*(3), 238–242.

Heimann, S. W., & March, J.S. (1996). SSRI-induced mania. *Journal of the American Academy of Child and Adolescent Psychiatry, 35*(1), 4.

Joorabchi, B. (1977). Expressions of the hyperventilation syndrome in childhood: Studies in management, including an evaluation of the effectiveness of propranolol. *Clinical Pediatrics, 16*(12), 1110–1115.

Kat, H. (1996). More on SSRI-induced mania. *Journal of the American Academy of Child and Adolescent Psychiatry, 35*(8), 975.

Keller, M. B., Ryan, N. D., Strober, M., Klein, R. G., Kutcher, S. P., Birmaher, B., et al. (2001). Efficacy of paroxetine in the treatment of adolescent major depression: A randomized, controlled trial. *Journal of the American Academy of Child and Adolescent Psychiatry, 40*(7), 762–772.

Kent, J. M., & Gorman, J. M. (2001). Venlafaxine. In A. Schatzberg and C. B. Nemeroff (Eds.), *Essentials of clinical psychopharmacology* (pp. 103–107). Anesthesia and Critical Care Software.

King, R. A., Riddle, M. A., Chappell, P. B., Hardin, M. T., Anderson, G. M., Lombroso, P., et al. (1991). Emergence of self-destructive phenomena in children and adolescents during fluoxetine treatment. *Journal of the American Academy of Child and Adolescent Psychiatry, 30*(2), 179–186.

Kirk, C. A., & Cove-Smith, R. (1983). A comparison between atenolol and metoprolol in respect of central nervous system side effects. *Postgraduate Medical Journal, 59* (Suppl 3), 161–163.

Klein, R. G., Kopelwicz, H. S., & Kanner, A. (1992). Imipramine treatment of children with separation anxiety. *Journal of the American Academy of Child and Adolescent Psychiatry, 31*(1), 21–28.

Lader, M., & Scotto, J. C. (1998). A multicentre double-blind comparison of hydroxyzine, buspirone and placebo in patients with generalized anxiety disorder. *Psychopharmacologia, 139*(4), 402–406.

Lee, D. O., & Lee, C. D. (1999). Serotonin syndrome in a child associated with erythromycin and sertraline. *Pharmacotherapy, 19*(7), 894.

Leo, R. J. (1996). Movement disorders associated with the serotonin selective reuptake inhibitors. *Journal of Clinical Psychiatry, 57*(10), 449–454.

Leonard, H. L., Swedo, S. E., Rapoport, J. L., Koby, E. V., Lenanae, M. C., Cheslow, D. L., et al. (1989). Treatment of obsessive-compulsive disorder with clomipramine and desipramine in children and adolescents. A double-blind crossover comparison. *Archives of General Psychiatry, 46*(12),1088–1092.

Liebowitz, M. R., Turner, S. M., Piacentini, J., Beidel, D. C., Clarvit, S. R., Davies, S. O., et al. (2002). Fluoxetine in children and adolescents with OCD: A placebo-controlled trial. *Journal of the American Academy of Child and Adolescent Psychiatry, 41*(12), 1431–1438.

Llorca, M., Spadone, C., Sol, O., Danniau, A., Bougerol, T., Corruble, E., et al. (2002). Efficacy and safety of hydroxyzine in the treatment of generalized anxiety disorder: A 3-month double-blind study. *Journal of Clinical Psychiatry, 63*(11), 1020–1027.

March, J. S., Biederman, J., Wolkow, A. R., Sufferman, A., Mardekian, J., Cook, E. H., et al. (1998). Sertraline in children and adolescents with obsessive-compulsive disorder: A multicenter randomized controlled trial. *Journal of the American Medical Association, 280,* 1752.

Mealy, K., Ngeh, N., Gillin, P., Fitzpatrick, G., Keane, F. B., & Tanner, A. (1996). Propranolol reduces the anxiety associated with day case surgery. *European Journal of Surgery, 162*(1), 11–14.

Newcorn, J. H., Schulz, K., Harrison, M., DeBellis, M. D., Udarbe, J. K., Halperin, J. M. (1998). Alpha-adrenergic agonists. Neurochemistry, efficacy and clinical guidelines for use in children. *Pediatric Clinics of North America, 45*(5), 1099–1122.

Ninan, P. T., Cole, J. O., & Yonders, K. A. (2001). Nonbenzodiazepine anxiolytics, tricyclics and tetracyclics. In A. F. Schatzberg & C. B. Nemeroff, *Essentials of clinical psychopharmacology* (pp. 93–103). Washington, D.C.: APA Press.

Ollendick, T. H., & King, N. J. (1998). Empirically supported treatments for children with phobic and anxiety disorders: Current status. *Journal of Clinical Child Psychology, 27*(2), 156–167.

Palac, D. M., Cornish, R. D., McDonald, W. J., Middaugh, D. A., Howieson, D., & Bagby, S. P. (1990). Cognitive function in hypertensives treated with atenolol or propranolol. *Journal of General Internal Medicine, 5*(4), 310–318.

Pande, A. C., Davidson, J. R., Jefferson, J. W., Janney, C. A., Katzelnick, D. J., Weisler, R. H., et al. (1999). Treatment of social phobia with gabapentin: A placebo-controlled study. *Journal of Clinical Psychopharmacology, 19*(4), 341–348.

Pande, A. C., Pollack, M. H., Crackatt, J., Greiner, M., Chouinard, G., Lydiard, R. B., et al. (2000). Placebo-controlled study of gabapentin treatment of panic disroder. *Journal of Clinical Psychopharmacology, 20*(4), 467–471.

Pfeffer, C. R., Jiang, H., & Domeshek, L. F. (1997). Buspirone treatment of psychiatrically hospitalized prepubertal children with symptoms of anxiety and moderately severe aggression. *Journal of Child and Adolescent Psychopharmacology, 7*(3), 145–155.

Pittman, R. K., Sanders, K. M., Zusman, R. M., Healy, A. R., Cheema, F., Lasko, N. B., et al. (2002). Pilot study of secondary prevention of post-traumatic stress disroder with propranolol. *Biological Psychiatry, 51*(2), 1809–1892.

Potter, W. Z., Husseini, K. M., & Rudorfer, M. V. (2001). Tricyclics and tetracyclics. In A. F. Schatzberg & C. B. Nemeroff, *Essentials of Clinical Psychopharmacology* (pp. 5–27). Washington D. C.: APA Press.

Reist, C., Duffy, J. G., Fujimoto, K., Cahill, L. (2001). Beta-adrenergic blockade and emotional memory in PTSD. *International Journal of Neuropsychopharmacology, 4*(4), 377–383.

Riddle, M. A., Bernstein, G. A., Cook, E. H., Leonard, H. L., March, J. S., Swanson, J. M. (1999). Anxiolytics, adrenergic agents, and naltrexone. *Journal of the American Academy of Child and Adolescent Psychiatry, 38*(5), 546–556.

Riddle, M. A., Geller, B., & Ryan, N. (1993). Another sudden death in a child treated with desipramine. *Journal of the American Academy of Child and Adolescent Psychiatry, 32*(4), 792–797.

Riddle, M. A., King, R. A., Herdin, M., et al. (1991). Behavioral side effects of fluoxetine in children and adolescents. *Journal of Child and Adolescent Psychopharmacology, 1*, 193.

Riddle, M. A., Reeve, E. A., Yaryura-Tobias, J. A., Yang, H. M., Clahorn, J. L., Gaffney, G., et al. (2001). Fluvoxamine for children and adolescents with obsessive-compulsive disorder: A randomized, controlled, multicenter trial. *Journal of the American Academy of Child and Adolescent Psychiatry, 40*(2), 222–229.

Riddle, M. A., Scahill, L., King, R. A., Hardin, M. T., Anderson, G. M., Ovt, S. I., et al. (1992). Double-blind, crossover trial of fluoxetine and placebo in children and adolescent with obsessive-compulsive disorder. *Journal of the American Academy of Child and Adolescent Psychiatry, 31*, 1062.

Robert, R., Blakeney, P. E., Villareal, C., Bosenberg, L., & Meyer, W. J. (1999). Imipramnine treatment in pediatric burn Patients with symptoms of acute stress disorder: A pilot study. *Journal of the American Academy of Child and Adolescent Psychiatry, 38*(7), 8733–8782.

Rosenberg, D. R., MacMaster, F. P., Keshavan, M. S., Fitzgerald, K. D., Stewart, C. M., & Moore, G. J. (2000). Decrease in caudate glutamatergic concentrations in pediatric obsessive-compulsive disorder patients taking paroxetine. *Journal of the American Academy of Child and Adolescent Psychiatry, 39*(9), 1096–1103.

Rothschild, A. J., Shindul-Rothschild, Viguera, A., Murray, M., & Brewster, S. (2000). Comparison of the frequency of behavioral disinhibition on alprazolam, clonazepam, or no benzodiazepine in hospitalized psychiatric patients. *Journal of Clinical Psychopharmacology, 20*(1), 7–11.

Rushton, J. L., Clark, S. J., & Freed, G. L. (2000). Pediatrician and family physician prescription of selective serotonin reuptake inhibitors. *Pediatrics, 105*(6), E82.

Rynn, M.A., Kunz, N., Lamm, L., Nicolacopoulos, E., Jenkins, L. (2002). Venlafaxine XR for treatment of GAD in children and adolescents. *Proceedings of the American Academy of Child and Adolescent Psychiatry*, p. 91.

Rynn, M. A., Siqueland, L., & Rickels, K. (2001). Placebo-controlled trial of sertraline in the treatment of children with generalized anxiety disorder. *American Journal of Psychiatry, 158*(12), 2008–2114.

Salazar, D. E., Frackiewicz, E.A.J., Dockens, R., Killia, G., Fulmor, I. E., Uderman. H. D., et al. (2001). Pharmacokinetics and tolerability of buspirone during oral administration to children and adolescents with anxiety disorder and normal healthy adults. *Journal of Clinical Pharmacology, 41*(12), 1351.

Scahill, L., Riddle, M. A., King, R. A., Hardin, M. T., Rasmusson, A., Makuch, R. W., et al. (1997). Fluoxetine has no marked effect on tic symptoms in patients with Tourette's syndrome: A double-blind placebo-controlled study. *Journal of Child and Adolescent Psychopharmacology, 7*(2), 75–85.

Simeon, J. G. (1993). Use of anxiolytics in children. *Encephale, 19*(2), 71–74.

Simeon, J. G., Fergason, H. B., Knott, V., Roberts, N., Gauthier, B., Dubois, C., et al. (1992).Clinical, cognitive and neurophysiological effects of alprazolam in children and adolescents with overanxious and avoidant disorders. *Journal of the American Academy of Child and Adolescent Psychiatry, 31*, 29–33.

Simson, P. E., Naylor, J. C., Gibson, B., Schneider, A. M., & Levin, D. (2001). Dose-sensitive excitation and inhibition of spontaneous amygdala activity by propranolol. *Pharmacology, Biochemistry and Behavior, 69*(1–2), 85–92.

Swanson, J. R., Jones, G. R., Krasselt, W., Denmark, L. N., & Ratti, F. (1997). Death of two subjects due to imipramine and desipramine metabolite accumulation during chronic therapy: A review of the literature and possible mechanisms. *Journal of Forensic Sciences, 42*(2), 335–339.

Thomsen, P. H., Ebbesen, C., & Persson, C. (2001). Long-term experience with citalopram in the treatment of adolescent OCD. *Journal of the American Academy of Child and Adolescent Psychiatry, 40*(8), 895–902.

United States Federal Drug Administration (U.S. FDA). (1997). FDA Modernization Act of 1997. From http://www.fda.gov/cdrh/modact97.pdf

Viola, J., Ditzler, T., Batzer, W., Harazin, J., Adams, D., Lettich, L., et al. (1997). Pharmacological management of post-traumatic stress disorder: Clinical summary of a five-year retrospective study, 1990–1995. *Military Medicine, 162*(9), 616–619.

Wagner, K. D., Rynn, M., Dibbekktm, C., Kabdaym, P. O., & Wohlberg, A. C. (2002). Long-term safety and tolerability of sertraline in major depression (Abstracts). *Proceedings of the American Academy of Child and Adolescent Psychiatry*, p. 94.

Walkup, J. T., Labellarte, M. J., Riddle, M. A., Pine, D. S., Greenhill, L., Klein, R., et al. (2001). Fluvoxamine for the treatment of anxiety disorders in children and adolescents. *New England Journal of Medicine, 344*(17), 1279–1285.

Walsh, M. T., & Dinan, T. G. (2001). Selective serotonin reuptake inhibitors and violence: A review of the available evidence. *Acta Psychiatrica Scandinavica, 104*(2), 84–89.

Weinbroum, A., Rudick, V., Sorkind, P., Nevo, Y., Halpern, P., Geller, E., et al. (1996). Use of flumazenil in the treatment of drug overdose: A double-blind and open clinical study in 110 patients. *Critical Care Medicine, 24*(2), 199–206.

Weintrob, N., Cohen, D., Klipper-Aurbach, Y., Zadik, Z., & Dickerman, Z. (2002). Decreased growth during therapy with selective serotonin reuptake inhibitors. *Archives of Pediatric Adolescent Medicine, 156*(7), 696–701.

Wilens, T. E., Swanson, J. M., Connor, D. F., Cantwell, D., & Spencer, T. J. (1999). Combining methylphenidate and clonidine: A clinically sound medication option. *Journal of the American Academy of Child and Adolescent Psychiatry, 38*(5), 614–622.

Williams, P. L., Krafcik, J. M., Potter, B. B., Hooper, J. H., & Hearne, M. (1977). Cardiac toxicity of clonidine. *Chest, 72*(6), 784–785.

CHAPTER TWELVE

ANTIDEPRESSANTS: SSRIs AND NOVEL ATYPICAL ANTIDEPRESSANTS—AN UPDATE ON PSYCHOPHARMACOLOGY

Graham J. Emslie, M.D., Andrew M. Portteus, M.D., M.P.H., E. Chandini Kumar, B.A., and Judith H. Hume, M.S.

Since the release of fluoxetine in the United States in 1988, the newer antidepressants, particularly selective-serotonin reuptake inhibitors (SSRIs), have become a first-line treatment for affective disorders, anxiety disorders, and impulse control disorders. Global sales of antidepressants grew by 18% in 2000, to $13.4 billion. Antidepressants comprised 4.2% of all audited global pharmaceutical sales, and ranked third worldwide in therapy class of drugs. North America was the dominant market, accounting for 74.6% of sales and a 19% growth rate. In 2002, $9.9 billion dollars was spent on SSRIs and novel atypical antidepressants (IMS Health, 2002). Antidepressant prescriptions appear to be growing both in adult and pediatric markets, with the estimated annual rate of antidepressant use by children being 1.0 per 100 persons (Olfson et al., 2002).

Potential clinical uses of antidepressants in pediatric populations may include depression, dysthymia, generalized anxiety disorder (GAD), separation anxiety with school avoidance, social anxiety disorder (SAD), obsessive-compulsive disorder (OCD), and OCD spectrum disorders such as trichotillomania, panic disorder (PD), post-traumatic stress disorder (PTSD), selective mutism, attention-deficit/ hyperactivity disorder (ADHD), weight maintenance in eating disorders, self-injurious behavior, and features of autism. The Food and Drug Administration (FDA) has identified the need for further child and adolescent research of new and existing medications. Accordingly, manufacturers are identifying a growing market and there will likely be a large increase in the number of antidepressant indications in this population. As clinical practice in pediatric psychiatry precedes the development of new treatment interventions through clinical research, it makes apparent the need of research data to support this level of drug use (Popper, 1992).

This chapter reviews the use of SSRIs and novel antidepressants in pediatric populations. The evidence base for the use of these medications is presented as well as limits in the evidence for medication currently used in clinical practice. Pharmacokinetic profiles are discussed, potential side effects, and adverse events are reviewed, and dosing guidelines are presented to assist health care providers in the use of antidepressant medications among children and adolescents. The information included here was gathered from medication package inserts, pharmaceutical prescribing information resources, the *Physician's Desk Reference* (2002), recent abstracts from relevant scientific conferences, and from a literature review using a MEDLINE search.

Table 12.1 lists the SSRIs and novel atypical antidepressants, including their FDA-approved treatment indications.

TABLE 12.1. ANTIDEPRESSANT INDICATIONS.

Medication	Trade Name	Drug Class	FDA Approved Indication
Fluoxetine	Prozac	SSRI	Depression*
			OCD*
			Bulimia
	Serafem		PMDD
Paroxetine	Paxil	SSRI	Depression
			OCD
			PD
			SAD
			GAD
			PTSD
Sertraline	Zoloft	SSRI	Depression
			OCD**
			PMDD
			PD
			PTSD
Citalopram	Celexa	SSRI	Depression
Escitalopram	Lexapro	SSRI	Depression
Fluvoxamine	Luvox	SSRI	OCD***
Bupropion	Wellbutrin	NDRI	Depression
Mirtazapine	Remeron	NaSSA	Depression
Nefazodone	Serzone	SARI	Depression
Trazodone	Desyrel	SARI	Depression
Venlafaxine	Effexor	SNRI	Depression
Venlafaxine	Effexor	XR	GAD

*Also approved for use in children and adolescents (7–17 years old).

**Also approved for use in children and adolescents (6–18 years old).

***Also approved for use in children and adolescents (8–17 years old).

Selective-Serotonin Reuptake Inhibitors

The selective-serotonin reuptake inhibitors (SSRIs) available in the United States are fluoxetine, sertraline, paroxetine, fluvoxamine, citalopram, and escitalopram. Together, they cover indications for FDA-approved advertising for major depression and anxiety disorders in adult patients. Furthermore, case reports and research studies suggest that these medications may be useful in the treatment of a number of additional adult disorders. While many are pursuing FDA approval, at this time, only the SSRIs fluvoxamine, sertraline, and fluoxetine have FDA indications in children and adolescents. All three are approved for treatment of child and adolescent OCD, with fluoxetine having an additional indication for pediatric depression (FDA, 2003). However, extensive use of SSRIs in pediatric clinical practice has been extrapolated from clinical trials, case reports, adult indications, and pharmacologic theory. Due to positive outcomes in clinical trials, SSRIs as a whole are considered to be the first line of treatment for pediatric depression and a wide array of pediatric anxiety disorders.

Fluoxetine Hydrochloride (Prozac)

Chemical Makeup. Fluoxetine hydrochloride (Prozac) is an antidepressant chemically unrelated to tricyclic, tetracyclic, or other available antidepressant agents, designated (±)–N-methyl-3-phenyl-3-[(α, α, α-trifluoro-p-tolyl)oxy] propylamine hydrochloride. The FDA has approved the use of fluoxetine for the treatment of adult depression, OCD, bulimia, and premenstrual dysphoric disorder (PMDD). In January of 2003, fluoxetine was approved to treat children and adolescents seven to seventeen years of age for depression and OCD. This was the first SSRI approved for treatment of pediatric depression (FDA, 2003).

Mechanism of Action. The SSRIs in general have been named for their effect of selective inhibition of serotonin reuptake into the neuronal presynaptic terminal, which increases the concentration of serotonin at the synaptic cleft. While they do not appear to have significant clinical effect on other neurotransmitters, higher clinical doses have been shown to also inhibit the reuptake of norepinephrine, and to some degree, dopamine. Site action of fluoxetine appears to occur at the serotonin reuptake pump in the central nervous system (CNS). Fluoxetine binds to muscarinic, histamanergic, serotonergic, and alpha-1 adrenergic receptors significantly less than tricyclic antidepressants.

Pharmacokinetics. Metabolism occurs by the P450 2D6 system in the liver. Active and inactive metabolites are excreted by the kidneys. Peak plasma levels are achieved six to eight hours after ingestion. Elimination half life is twenty-four to seventy-two hours for the parent compound after acute administration and four to six days for the parent compound after chronic administration. Elimination half life is four to sixteen days for the active metabolite norfluoxetine after acute and chronic administration. Time to achieve steady-state plasma levels is four to five weeks. Protein binding is 94.5%. Absorption and bioavailability is not significantly affected by food. Fluoxetine exhibits non-linear pharmacokinetics. A lower or less frequent dose is recommended in patients with liver disease. Use of a lower or less frequent dose is not routinely necessary in patients with renal impairment.

Dosing. Initiation of treatment is generally recommended at 10 to 20 mg/day as a once daily dose, although 5 mg may be preferable in causing fewer side effects in some patients (Riddle et al., 1992; Boulos, Kutcher, Gardner, & Young, 1992). The average steady-state concentrations are one-and-a-half to two times higher in adolescents, largely explained by differences in weight. Low doses with oral solution may be recommended in very young patients. Patients with anxiety symptoms should be started at lower doses and titrated upwards as clinically indicated and as tolerated. Depression is generally treated in a range of 20 to 40 mg/day with a maximum of 60 mg/day. Treatment of obsessive-compulsive spectrum disorders often requires high doses at 40 to 60 mg/day. Similarly, eating disorders are generally treated at higher doses. Patients with mental retardation and pervasive developmental disorders may respond at low doses and may experience activation at higher doses. Therapeutic effect may not be maximized until four to six weeks of treatment, with some patients showing maximum improvement at ten weeks.

Adverse Effects Profile. Fluoxetine is generally well tolerated. Most adverse effects are mild to moderate, affecting the gastrointestinal (GI) tract and CNS. Controlled clinical trials in children ages eight to eighteen show that the most common side effects were nausea, diarrhea, dry mouth, weight loss, anxiety, headache, nervousness, insomnia, drowsiness, dizziness or lightheadedness, fatigue or asthenia, and excessive sweating.

In addition, there may be some behavioral activation characterized by hyperactivity, sleeplessness, a feeling of being excited, and a subtle increase in impulsivity. In a double-blind trial of fluoxetine by Emslie et al. (1997), three out of forty-eight (6%) subjects (one child and two adolescents) randomized to fluoxetine were discontinued from the study because of manic-like symptoms. Jain, Kaplan, Gadde, & Wadden et al. (1992) reported that 28% of subjects discontinued fluoxetine treatment because of increased irritability and hypomanic-like symptoms. Riddle, King, and colleagues (1990) reported the highest rate of behavioral side effects during fluoxetine treatment in children and adolescents with

OCD and depression. In this trial, 50% developed behavioral side effects characterized by motor restlessness, sleep disturbance, social disinhibition, or a subjective sense of excitation.

During premarketing clinical trials in a patient population composed primarily of unipolar depressives, hypomania or mania occurred in approximately 1% of fluoxetine-treated patients. The incidence in a general patient population that might also include bipolar depressives is unknown. The likelihood of hypomanic or manic episodes may be increased at the higher dosage levels. Such reactions require a reduction in dosage or discontinuation of the drug.

For patients with diabetes, fluoxetine may alter glycemic control. Hypoglycemia has occurred during therapy with fluoxetine, and hyperglycemia has developed following discontinuation of the drug. As is true with many other types of medication when taken concurrently by patients with diabetes, insulin and oral hypoglycemic dosage or both may need adjustment when therapy with fluoxetine is instituted or discontinued.

Drug Interactions and Contraindications. The risk of using fluoxetine hydrochloride (HCl) in combination with other CNS-active drugs has not been systematically evaluated. Like a number of other SSRIs and the tricyclics, fluoxetine is metabolized by the P450 2D6 enzyme system. Accordingly, there is a potential interaction with all other drugs that are metabolized by this system.

Approximately 7% of the normal population has a genetic defect that leads to reduced levels of activity of the cytochrome P450 isoenzyme P450 2D6.

If prescribing a concomitant medication that is predominantly metabolized by the P450 2D6 system and that has a relatively narrow therapeutic index for a patient who is currently on fluoxetine or who has taken it in the previous five weeks, it is advisable to initiate therapy at the low end of the dose range, to titrate conservatively and to closely monitor clinical status.

> Anticonvulsants—Elevated plasma levels of anticonvulsants and toxicity have been reported in patients taking phenytoin or carbamazepine in combination with fluoxetine.
>
> Antipsychotics—Elevated blood levels of haloperidol and clozapine have been observed in patients receiving concomitant fluoxetine, and a single case report has suggested possible additive effects of pimozide and fluoxetine, resulting in bradycardia.
>
> Benzodiazepines—The half life of concurrently administered diazepam may be prolonged in some patients. Co-administration of alprazolam and fluoxetine has resulted in increased alprazolam plasma concentrations

and in further psychomotor performance decrement due to increased alprazolam levels.

Lithium—Lithium levels should be monitored when these drugs are administered concomitantly, as there have been reports of both increased and decreased lithium levels as well as cases of lithium toxicity and increased serotonergeric effects.

Tryptophan—There are reports of adverse effects (AEs) in patients receiving fluoxetine HCl in combination with tryptophan, including agitation, restlessness, and gastrointestinal distress.

Other Antidepressants—The dose of tricyclic antidepressant (TCA) may need to be reduced and plasma TCA concentrations may need to be monitored temporarily when fluoxetine is co-administered or has been recently discontinued.

Atomoxetine—Because fluoxetine (like paroxetine and quinidine) is a strong CYP 2D6 inhibitor, co-administration of these two medications may increase the atomoxetine level.

Fluoxetine HCl should not be used in combination with a monoamine oxidase inhibitor (MAOI), nor should it be administered to any patient who has received an MAOI within the preceding fourteen days. Because fluoxetine and its major metabolite have very long elimination half lives, a minimum of thirty-five days (five weeks) should be allowed to elapse after stopping fluoxetine before starting an MAOI. If fluoxetine has been prescribed chronically or at higher doses, this time period should be even longer (PDR, 2002).

Fluoxetine should be used with caution in patients with impaired liver function. Breastfeeding is not recommended if taking fluoxetine because fluoxetine is secreted in breast milk. Patients receiving warfarin therapy should receive careful coagulation monitoring when fluoxetine is initiated or stopped because altered anticoagulant effects, including increased bleeding, have been reported when fluoxetine is co-administered with warfarin. There have been rare reports of prolonged seizures in patients on fluoxetine receiving electroconvulsive therapy (ECT) treatment.

Empirical Data

Depression. The first controlled trial to demonstrate an antidepressant medication treatment to be superior to placebo in treating depression in children and adolescents was by Emslie and colleagues (1997). In this study of ninety-six patients (ages eight to eighteen) with major depressive disorder (MDD), 56% of those randomized to fluoxetine versus 33% of those randomized to placebo were considered "Much Improved" on the clinical global impressions (CGI) rating scale (CGI = 2) or "Very Much Improved" (CGI = 1) following eight weeks of treatment. In a study replicating these findings, 219 children and adolescents (ages eight to seventeen) with MDD were randomized to nine weeks of treatment in a multisite study of fluoxetine versus placebo. Similar to the initial study, 52% versus 37%, respectively, were considered much or very much improved at the end of nine weeks of treatment (Emslie, Heiligenstein, et al., 2002).

OCD. Double-blind trials have also been conducted for other disorders to demonstrate the effectiveness of fluoxetine over placebo. Riddle and associates (1992) reported on a double-blind placebo-controlled cross-over trial of fluoxetine in fourteen children and adolescents with OCD. The subjects on fluoxetine showed a significant decrease (44%) in the Children's Yale-Brown Obsessive Compulsive Scale (CY-BOCS) total score compared to a nonsignificant decrease in those on placebo. In a larger, multi-site, double-blind study, Geller and colleagues (2001) compared fluoxetine to placebo in 103 children and adolescents (ages seven to seventeen) with OCD. Fluoxetine was associated with greater improvement in CY-BOCS scores (p = .026) than placebo. In addition, fluoxetine was well tolerated and had a similar rate of discontinuation as placebo.

Anxiety Disorders. Although its indicated use in pediatric populations is approved for only two disorders, many clinical trials have shown efficacy in treatment with fluoxetine across a wide spectrum of psychiatric conditions. In an open-label study, Birmaher, Waterman, Ryan, Cully, and associates (1994) reported on twenty-one children and adolescents with overanxious disorder, social phobia, or separation anxiety who had been unresponsive to previous pharmacological or psychosocial treatments. Subjects were treated openly with fluoxetine for up to ten months. Of those subjects, 81% showed moderate to marked improvement in anxiety symptoms and no significant side effects were reported. Two other open-label studies (Dummit, Klein, Tancer, Asche, & Martin, 1996; Fairbanks et al., 1997) and one double-blind, placebo-controlled study (Black & Uhde, 1994) showed that children and adolescents with anxiety disorders improved when treated with fluoxetine.

In a small, double-blind, placebo-controlled study of fluoxetine in selective mutism (Black, Uhde, & Tancer, 1992), four of six subjects responded after twelve weeks. This study followed a case report by Black and Uhde (1992) and another case report (Motavalli, 1995) from Europe. In a nine-week open trial of fluoxetine (10 to 60 mg) in twenty-one children (aged five to fourteen years) with selective mutism, 76% were considered to be improved, with decreased anxiety and increased speech (Dummit et al., 1996).

Behavioral Disorders. Case reports and open medication trials have suggested fluoxetine in low doses may decrease behavioral problems in some pediatric patients with pervasive developmental disorders (PDD) and mental retardation. However, no randomized placebo-controlled studies have verified a positive response in this age group. Cook, Rowlett, Jaselskis, and Leventhal (1992), in an open-label study, assessed perseverative behaviors ranging from self-injurious behavior to complex rituals. Ten of sixteen subjects with mental retardation (age 7.3 to 52 years) and fifteen of twenty-three subjects with autism (age 7.0 to 28 years) had significant improvement in CGI ratings of Clinical Severity when treated with fluoxetine in doses that ranged from 20 mg every other day to 80 mg/day. However, restlessness, hyperactivity, and agitation were seen in some patients. In an open-label study of thirty-seven children (age 2.25 to 7.75 years), DeLong, Teague, and Kamran (1998) gave fluoxetine at doses ranging from 0.2 to 1.4 mg/kg/day and found improvement in behavioral, cognitive, affective, social, and language areas. Of the thirty-seven children, eleven had an excellent clinical response and eleven others had a good response. Agitation, hyperactivity, and aggression were seen in some patients, leading to medication discontinuation.

In a retrospective chart review of seven patients (ages nine to twenty) with autistic disorder given fluoxetine 20 to 80 mg/day, improvement in irritability, lethargy, stereotypy, and inappropriate speech were reported. However, four patients experienced increased hyperactivity. A six-month open-label trial of fluoxetine in six patients with autism (ages four to seven) titrated to final doses of 15 to 20 mg/day, showed improvement in ritualistic behaviors, motor stereotypies, social functioning, and interest in the environment in the five completers (Fatemi, Realmuto, Khan, & Thuras,1998). Most common side effects were impulsivity, restlessness, sleep disturbances, and loss of appetite (Peral, Alcami, & Gilaberte, 1999). Eleven children with PDD completing an open-label, year-long trial of fluoxetine demonstrated marked or moderate improvement. Communication, attention, stereotypies, and repetitive behaviors improved. Most common adverse events were increased impulsivity, restlessness, sleep disturbance, and loss of appetite (Alcami, Peral, & Gilaberte, 2000).

Some open studies have suggested fluoxetine may be useful for treating mood and behavioral symptoms in patients with ADHD and comorbid internalizing or externalizing disorders. Barrickman, Noyes, Kuperman, Schumacher, and Verda (1991) treated nineteen children with comorbid conduct disorder or oppositional defiant disorder (ODD) and found a 58% response rate. Gammon and Brown (1993) added fluoxetine to methylphenidate for thirty-two children (ages nine to seventeen) with ADHD and at least one additional comorbid disorder who did not have adequate therapeutic response to methylphenidate alone. Comorbidities included dysthymia (78%), ODD (59%), major depressive disorder (MDD) (18%), anxiety disorders (18%), and conduct disorder (13%). After eight weeks, all participants showed statistically significant improvements in attention, behavior, and affect. Children with the greatest impairments showed the most significant improvement (Gammon and Brown, 1993). Double-blind, placebo-controlled studies need to be conducted in these populations before the efficacy of SSRIs in ADHD can be determined. Findling (1996) reported a case series of seven pediatric (ages ten to sixteen) and four adult (ages thirty-eight to forty-four) patients with depression and ADHD, treated with fluoxetine or sertraline monotherapy. All eleven patients showed improvement in depression; however, none showed improvement in ADHD. Co-administration of psychostimulant was deemed necessary and effective in treating both ADHD and depressive symptoms.

Other Disorders. It has been hypothesized that a disturbance of serotonin activity may create vulnerability for core features of anorexia nervosa and bulimia nervosa (Kaye, Gendall, & Strober, 1998). SSRIs have been shown to be of some benefit in reducing symptoms of bulimia nervosa and binge eating disorder in adults, independent of their antidepressant effects (Kaye et al., 1998; Bacaltchuk & Hay, 2001). Some studies (Peterson & Mitchell, 1999) have suggested that high doses (60 mg fluoxetine) are superior to low doses (20 mg fluoxetine). However, antidepressants have been shown to be less likely than CBT to achieve remission of symptoms (Peterson & Mitchell, 1999). Studies have failed to establish benefits of SSRIs in the active treatment of anorexia nervosa (Attia, Haiman, Walsh, & Flater, 1998; Strober, Pataki, Freeman, & DeAntonio, 1999; Ferguson, La Via, Crossan, & Kay, 1999). However, it has been shown that fluoxetine may be useful in improving outcome and preventing relapse of patients with anorexia nervosa after weight restoration has been achieved (Kaye, Nagata, & Weltzin, et al., 2001). Studies have shown SSRIs can be useful in treating depressive and obsessive symptoms in anorectic patients (Fassino, Leombruni, & Daga, et al., 2002). Effects in pediatric patients have not been established in placebo controlled trials and must be extrapolated from adult literature.

In one study of Tourette's syndrome (TS), fourteen subjects (ages eight to thirty-three) were enrolled in a twenty-week, double-blind, placebo-controlled cross-over trial of fluoxetine (20 mg). After eight weeks of treatment, fluoxetine improved obsessive-compulsive symptoms in the group initially randomized to fluoxetine (n = 6; p = .04), although this finding was not significant in the cross-over group (n = 8; p = .06). However, there was no improvement in tics (Scahill, Riddle, et al., 1997). On the other hand, two open trials of fluoxetine have demonstrated some improvement in motor and vocal tics (Como & Kurlan, 1991; Riddle, Hardin, et al., 1990). Similarly, in a study by Kurlan, Como, Deeley, McDermtrott, and associates (1993), of eleven children with TS and obsessive-compulsive symptoms, the fluoxetine-treated group trended toward improvement in severity of tics, but not obsessive-compulsive symptoms.

Sertraline Hydrochloride (Zoloft)

Chemical Makeup. Sertraline is chemically unrelated to any other antidepressants. Approved for treatment of adult depression, OCD, PMDD, and panic disorder, in June of 1997 it was also approved by the FDA for treatment of OCD in children ages six- to eighteen-years-old.

Mechanism of Action. The effect of sertraline is presumably linked to its inhibition of CNS neuronal uptake of serotonin. Very weak effects on norepinephrine and dopamine reuptake exist. Chronic administration is thought to down-regulate norepinephrine receptors. In vitro, sertraline has no significant affinity for alpha-1, alpha-2, or beta adrenergic; cholenergic; GABA; dopaminergic; histaminergic; 5HT1A, 5HT1B, or 5HT2 serotonergic; or benzodiazepine receptors.

Pharmacokinetics. Metabolism is influenced by first-pass breakdown, where sertraline undergoes N-demethylation. Both the drug and its less active metabolite undergo oxidative deamination followed by reduction, hydroxylation, and glucuronide conjugation. The drug and its metabolites are excreted in about equal amounts in the feces and urine, with little or no active drug excreted by the kidneys. A lower or less frequent dose is recommended in patients with liver disease. Use of a lower or less frequent dose is not routinely necessary in patients with renal impairment. Pediatric patients may metabolize sertraline with slightly greater efficiency than adults. However, when corrected for weight, pharmacokinetic properties have been shown in some studies not to correlate with age (Alderman, Wolkow, Chung, & Johnston, 1998; March et al., 1998).

Peak plasma levels are achieved after 4.5 to 8.4 hours after ingestion. Elimination half life is 26 hours for the parent compound and 62–104 hours for the major metabolite N-desmethylsertraline, which is substantially less active than the parent compound. Time to achieve steady-state plasma levels is approximately seven days. Absorption and bioavailability is slightly affected by food, with peak blood levels being reached more quickly with a meal. However, no dosage adjustments are necessary and the compound may be taken with or without food. Protein binding is 98%.

Dosing. Initiation of treatment is recommended at 12.5 to 50 mg/day as a once daily dose. Patients with anxiety symptoms should be started at the lower end of the dosing spectrum and titrated upwards as clinically indicated and as tolerated. Depression is generally treated in a range of 50 to 150 mg/day with a maximum of 200 mg/day. Treatment of obsessive-compulsive spectrum disorders often requires high doses at 100 to 200 mg/day. Patients with mental retardation and

PDDs may respond at low doses and may experience activation at higher doses. Therapeutic effect may not be maximized until four to six weeks of treatment, with some patients showing maximum improvement at ten weeks. Sertraline is available in 25-, 50-, and 100-mg tablets and a 20-mg/mL liquid oral solution.

Adverse Effects Profile. Sertraline hydrochloride is generally well tolerated. The most commonly reported side effects associated with use of sertraline are nausea, insomnia, diarrhea, ejaculatory delay, and sleepiness. In a placebo-controlled trial of children and adolescents (six to seventeen years), the most commonly reported side effects were insomnia, nausea, agitation, and tremor (March et al., 1998). Additional side effects reported for children and adolescents include excessive movement, twitching, fever, weight loss, impaired concentration, nosebleeds, easy bruising, excited behavior, and rapid mood swings. In an open-label trial (McConville et al., 1996), of adolescents twelve to eighteen years, the most common side effects at twelve weeks were insomnia, drowsiness, weight change, nightmares, loss of appetite, and headache.

Drug Interactions and Contraindications. Use of sertraline concurrently with any MAOI is contraindicated. MAOIs should be discontinued for a minimum of fourteen days before beginning administration of sertraline. Sertraline has not been evaluated in patients with seizure disorder, but a seizure incidence of 0.2% has been reported, and accordingly, sertraline should be introduced with caution in patients with seizure disorder. Sertraline oral concentrate is contraindicated with Antabuse (disulfuram) due to the alcohol in the concentrate. Several cases of hyponatremia have been reported with use of sertraline; however, they appear reversible upon discontinuation of sertraline (Taylor & McConnell, 1995; Kessler & Samuels, 1996; Liu, Mittman, Knowles, & Shear, 1996).

Empirical Data

Depression. A multi-site study of sertraline versus placebo in 376 children and adolescents (ages six to seventeen) with MDD reported that 63% of subjects randomized to sertraline were considered much or very much improved, compared to 53% on placebo (p = .049; Wagner & Wohlberg, 2002). Additionally, a number of small, open-label studies have supported the use of sertraline for the treatment of pediatric depression (Tierney, Joshi, Llinas, Rosenberg, & Riddle, 1995; McConville et al., 1996; Ambrosini et al., 1999). To date, the number of studies examining the use of pharmacotherapy for dysthymia is limited. A six-month open-label study of sertraline was conducted in adolescents, age twelve- to eighteen-years-old, diagnosed with MDD or dysthymic disorder (DD). Evaluated at week six, the DD group achieved maximal response (100%) on the Hamilton Depression Rating Scale (HAM-D) and the CGI (75%). However, rates did not remain as elevated by week twenty-four, as 66.7% of DD study completers showed response to treatment (Nixon, Milin, Simeon, Cloutier, & Spenst, 2001). Sertraline was shown to be safe and well tolerated, showing evidence of clinical response and improvement for dysthymia, particularly in the acute phase. Long-term response to treatment of dysthymic disorder still remains an area needing further study in children and adolescents.

OCD Spectrum Disorders. In a double-blind, multi-site trial 187 children and adolescents, ages six to seventeen, were treated with either sertraline or placebo for OCD. For those on the active drug, medication was titrated up to 200 mg/day during the first four weeks, followed by eight weeks of continued treatment at that dose. Sertraline showed greater improvement than placebo on the CY-BOCS (p = .005) and the NIMH Global Obsessive Compulsive Scale (NIMH GOCS) (p = .02). CGI-I ratings at study end point indicated 42% of patients receiving sertraline were very much, or much improved, versus 26% of patients receiving placebo (March et al., 1998). Significant difference in efficacy between treatments was seen by week three and persisted throughout the remainder of the study, thus finding sertraline to be safe and effective treatment for childhood and adolescent OCD. In a five-week study of sixty-one children and adolescent patients with OCD, doses were titrated to 200 mg/day, with significant decreases in OCD symptoms (Alderman et al., 1998).

Five outpatients with selective mutism were treated with no drug, followed by placebo, followed by sertraline 50 mg/day followed by sertraline 100 mg/day. In a double-blind trial, four of five subjects were speaking within a few days of starting sertraline. Two subjects no longer met criteria after ten weeks and their disorder was markedly improved at twenty weeks (Carlson, Kratochwill, & Johnston, 1999).

Developmental Disorders. In a clinical sample of six to twelve year olds with autistic disorder, Steingard, Zimnitsky, Demaso, Bauman, and Bucci (1997) reported that eight of nine patients showed clinically significant improvement in transition-induced behavioral deterioration when given sertraline 25 to 50 mg daily. The improvement persisted over several months of follow-up in six of the responders; however, three of the patients showed only transient improvement. Behavioral deterioration was seen in two children when the dose was raised to 75 mg. Two children with Asperger's syndrome (ages six and thirteen years) showed improvement in anxiety and repetitive behavior with low dose sertraline (25 and 50 mg, respectively). One patient did not tolerate a higher dose.

Fluvoxamine Maleate (Luvox)

Chemical Makeup. Fluvoxamine maleate is chemically unrelated to other SSRIs. It belongs to a new chemical series, the 2-aminoethyl oxide ethers of aralkylketones. Luvox is FDA-indicated to treat both adults and children with OCD. It received pediatric approval on March 25, 1997 and has shown safety and tolerability in both populations.

Mechanism of Action. As with the rest of the SSRIs, fluvoxamine inhibits the neuronal uptake of serotonin in brain neurons. In vitro studies have shown no significant affinity for histaminergic, alpha- or beta-adrenergic, muscarinic, or dopaminergic receptors.

Pharmacokinetics. Metabolism occurs extensively in the liver by oxidative demethylation and deamination. Nine metabolites have been identified; primary metabolites are essentially inactive. Smokers metabolize fluvoxamine maleate about 25% faster than non-smokers. A 30% decrease in fluvoxamine clearance is associated with hepatic dysfunction. No accumulation has been seen in renally impaired patients.

The absolute bioavailability of fluvoxamine maleate is 53%, and not significantly affected by food. Peak plasma levels occur between three and eight hours after ingestion. Elimination half life at steady state is 15.6 hours in young adults taking 100 mg/day. Fluvoxamine has non-linear pharmacokinetics. Protein binding is approximately 80%.

Dosing. Initiation of treatment is recommended at 25 to 50 mg/day at bedtime. Treatment of obsessive-compulsive spectrum disorders often requires 50 to 300 mg/day divided into twice daily dosing.

Fluvoxamine maleate is available in 25-, 50-, and 100-mg tablets.

Adverse Effects Profile. The most frequently reported side effects associated with use of fluvoxamine are sleep difficulties (either feeling unusually tired or sleepy, or insomnia), dry mouth, nervousness, tremor, nausea, upset stomach, loss of appetite, vomiting, abnormal ejaculation, asthenia, and sweating. In an open-label trial of adolescents, ages thirteen to eighteen years, sleep difficulties, hyperactivity, agitation, excitement, and anxiety occurred initially but were mild and transient in most cases (Apter et al., 1994).

Drug Interactions and Contraindications. There are many potential interactions of other drugs with fluvoxamine, especially with drugs that inhibit or are metabolized by cytochrome P450 isoenzymes. Concurrent administration with benzodiazepines or diazepam is not recommended. Both plasma levels and half life of alprazolam were approximately doubled when given concurrently with fluvoxamine. Accordingly, if administered concurrently, the dose of alprazolam should be reduced by 50% and titrated down to the lowest effective dose.

Concurrent administration of fluvoxamine with terfenadine, astemizole, or cisapride is contraindicated. Fluvoxamine has the potential to be a powerful inhibitor of the P450 3A4 isoenzyme. This could cause increased levels of these drugs, and could result in QT interval lengthening (associated with some types of ventricular tachycardia and fatalities).

Concurrent administration of fluvoxamine with MAOIs is contraindicated, and a minimum of fourteen days should be observed after discontinuing an MAOI before fluvoxamine is administered.

Empirical Data. In 2001, a definitive study of fluvoxamine in OCD was completed (Riddle et al., 2001). The study was a multi-site, randomized, double-blind, placebo-controlled study of fluvoxamine with seventeen sites and 120 subjects (ages eight to seventeen) with OCD. CY-BOCS scores were significantly different between fluvoxamine and placebo ($p < 0.05$) at weeks one through six and week ten. The same p value was noted for all secondary outcome measures at all visits as well. Such significance accounted for a 25% decrease in CY-BOCS, scores, indicating response from 42% of subjects treated with fluvoxamine in comparison to 26% randomized to placebo (Riddle et al., 2001).

Walkup and associates (2001), conducting a randomized, placebo-controlled trial, found fluvoxamine to be an effective treatment for 128 children and adolescents (six to seventeen years old) with social phobia, separation anxiety, or generalized anxiety disorder. In that study, 76% of the fluvoxamine group had a CGI score of much improved or better compared with 29% of the placebo group.

In a double-blind, placebo-controlled study, thirty-four children (ages five to eighteen) with autism, Asperger's syndrome, and other PDD showed poor tolerance and little benefit from fluvoxamine (25 to 250 mg/day) (McDougle, Kresch & Posey, 2000). In this sample, only one patient showed significant clinical improvement and fourteen patients showed adverse effects including insomnia, agitation, aggression, hyperactivity, anxiety, and increased rituals. Eighteen autistic patients participated in a double-blind trial of fluvoxamine, showing significant improvements in eye contact and language usage. CGI scores improved in approximately half of the patients (Fukuda, Sugie, Ito, & Sugie, 2001).

Paroxetine Hydrochloride (Paxil)

Chemical Makeup. Paroxetine hydrochloride (Paxil) is the hydrochloride salt of a phenylpiperidine compound, chemically unrelated to other antidepressants. It is used to treat depression and anxiety disorders, and is approved for such in adults.

Although clinical data suggests efficacious use in the pediatric population for these same disorders, paroxetine has yet to receive FDA approval in this age group.

Mechanism of Action. The effect of paroxetine is believed to be related to its being a highly potent selective inhibitor of serotonin reuptake in CNS neurons. There is only a very weak effect on norepinephrine or dopamine reuptake by paroxetine. Some muscarinic receptor binding suggests potential for some anticholinergic effects. Paroxetine has little affinity for muscarinic, alpha-1, alpha-2, beta adrenergic, dopamine, 5HT1, 5HT2, and histamine H1 receptors.

Pharmacokinetics. Metabolism occurs extensively in the liver, in part by the 2D6 enzyme system. The principal metabolites have only one-fiftieth the potency of the parent compound in serotonin reuptake inhibition. Peak plasma levels occur in five to six hours and elimination half life is approximately twenty-one hours in adults. A study of thirty children showed a slightly shorter half life of 11.1 ± 5.2 hours, yet steady-state plasma levels were still achieved with once a day dosing (Findling et al., 1999). Time to achieve steady-state usually occurs within ten days. Pharmacokinetics are nonlinear for paroxetine. Absorption and bioavailability are slightly increased with food but paroxetine can be administered with or without food with no dosage adjustment. Approximately two-thirds of the drug is excreted in urine and one-third of the drug excreted in feces, primarily as metabolites. Increased plasma concentration of paroxetine occurs with renal and hepatic impairment. Initial dose reductions are recommended in patients with severe renal or hepatic impairment. Protein binding is 93–95%.

Dosing. Initiation of treatment is recommended at 10 to 20 mg/day as a once-daily dose. Patients with anxiety symptoms should be started at low doses and titrated upwards as clinically indicated and as tolerated. Depression is generally treated in a range of 20 to 40 mg/day with a maximum of 60 mg/day. Treatment of obsessive-compulsive spectrum disorders often requires high doses at 40 to 60 mg/day. Patients with mental retardation and PDDs may respond at low doses and may experience activation at higher doses. Therapeutic effect may not be maximized until four to six weeks of treatment, with some patients showing maximum improvement at ten weeks.

Paroxetine hydrochloride is available in 10-, 20-, 30-, and 40-mg tablets; a 12.5- and 25-mg controlled release; and a 10-mg/5 mL liquid oral solution.

Adverse Effects Profile. In clinical trials, between 16% and 20% of patients discontinued taking paroxetine hydrochloride for the following reasons: headache, weakness (asthenia), sweating, nausea, decreased appetite, sleepiness (somnolence), dizziness, insomnia, tremor, nervousness, and ejaculatory disturbance and other male genital disorders.

As with all antidepressants, paroxetine should be used cautiously in patients with a history of mania. During premarketing testing of immediate-release paroxetine, seizures occurred in 0.1% of paroxetine-treated patients, a rate similar to that associated with other antidepressants. Paroxetine should be used cautiously in patients with a history of seizures and discontinued in any patient who develops seizures.

There have been concerns about a potential increased risk of suicidal ideation and suicide attempts in depressed children and adolescents taking paroxetine. In an analysis of over 1,000 pediatric patients with depression, suicidal thoughts and attempts were higher in children and adolescents taking paroxetine than those taking placebo (3.2% versus 1.5%). This has led to an ongoing evaluation of the safety of this medication in youth by the FDA. On June 19, 2003, the FDA recommended that paroxetine not be used in children and adolescents under the age of 18 for the treatment of major depression. The FDA reports that the data does not clearly establish an association between the use of paroxetine and suicidality, and the need for additional data and data analysis has been emphasized.

As with all other SSRIs, there have been reports of hyponatremia in patients taking paroxetine HCl. The majority of patients who have experienced this side effect were elderly, and some were taking diuretics or were otherwise volume depleted. In all cases, the hyponatremia appeared to be reversible when paroxetine HCl was discontinued (Liu, et al., 1996; Strachan & Shepherd, 1998; Fabian et al., 2002).

There have been reports of abnormal bleeding (mostly mild bleeding disorders, such as ecchymosis and purpura) associated with use of SSRIs, including paroxetine treatment (Ottervanger, Stricker, Huls, & Weeda, 1994; Abajo, Rodríguez, & Montero, 1999). While a causal relationship to paroxetine is unclear, it is possible that platelet serotonin depletion may cause impaired platelet aggregation and contribute to such occurrences.

Drug Interactions and Contraindications. Because of a possibility for serious, life-threatening reactions when administered simultaneously with an MAOI, the use of paroxetine in combination with an MAOI is contraindicated. It is recommended that a minimum of fourteen days elapse after stopping treatment with an MAOI before starting treatment with paroxetine, and at least fourteen days should be allowed after stopping paroxetine before starting an MAOI.

Paroxetine HCl is secreted in breast milk and, accordingly, nursing is not recommended while taking this drug.

Empirical Data. In a large, multi-site study (Keller, Ryan, & Strober, et al., 2001), 275 adolescents (ages twelve to eighteen) with MDD were randomized to paroxetine, imipramine, or placebo for an eight-week acute trial. Paroxetine was superior in efficacy to placebo (66% versus 48%), but imipramine, a tricyclic antidepressant (TCA), (52%) was not, with efficacy defined as an end point CGI improvement score of much or very much improved. This study provides additional support for the efficacy of SSRIs in the treatment of adolescent MDD, and reinforces the suggestions that TCAs are not effective in depressed children and adolescents as a group, but may have a role in specific individuals.

Although, to date, no acute controlled studies have been reported with paroxetine in pediatric OCD, a few open studies bear mentioning. In a twelve-week, open-label study of paroxetine in children and adolescents (ages eight to seventeen) with OCD, CY-BOCS scores decreased significantly (p = .0005). In this study, no patients were discontinued due to side effects (Rosenberg, Stewart, Fitzgerald, Tawile, & Carroll, 1999). In a larger, multi-site trial of paroxetine, 335 children and adolescents (ages eight to seventeen) were treated openly with paroxetine for sixteen weeks, followed by a double-blind discontinuation phase for responders. During the acute phase, 86% of subjects completing sixteen weeks of treatment responded to treatment. Furthermore, paroxetine was shown to reduce the rate of relapse as compared to placebo during the continuation phase (34.7% versus 43.9%) (Emslie et al., 2000).

Citalopram Hydrobromide (Celexa)

Chemical Makeup. Citalopram hydrobromide is a racemic bicyclicphthalane derivative that is chemically unrelated to other antidepressants.

Mechanism of Action

Mechanism of action is thought to be related to potentiation of serotonergic activity in the CNS resulting from the inhibition of CNS neuronal reuptake of serotonin. Citalopram is a highly selective-serotonin reuptake inhibitor, with minimal effects on norepenephrine or dopamine reuptake.

Pharmacokinetics

Peak plasma levels occur at about four hours. Elimination half life is about thirty-five hours. Time to achieve steady state is approximately one week. Pharmacokinetics are linear. Metabolism occurs primarily by N-demethylization in CYP3A4 and CYP2C19 enzyme systems in the liver. The parent compound is at least eight times more potent than its metabolites, which do not play a clinically significant role.

Citalopram oral clearance was reduced by 37%, and half life was doubled in patients with reduced hepatic function. In patients with mild to moderate renal impairment, no adjustment in dose is recommended. Absorption is not affected by food. Protein binding is about 80%.

Dosing

Initiation of treatment is recommended at 10 to 20 mg/day as a once-daily dose. Patients with anxiety symptoms should be started at low doses and titrated upwards as clinically indicated and tolerated. Depression is generally treated in a range of 20 to 40 mg/day with a maximum of 60 mg/day. Treatment of obsessive-compulsive spectrum disorders often requires high doses at 40 to 60 mg/day. Patients with mental retardation and PDDs may respond at low doses and may experience activation at higher doses. Therapeutic effect may not be maximized until four to six weeks of treatment, with some patients showing maximum improvement at ten weeks.

Citalopram hydrobromide is available in 20- and 40-mg tablets and a 10-mg/5 mL (10 mg/tsp.) liquid oral solution.

Adverse Effects Profile

During short-term (six to eight weeks) placebo-controlled phase III trials of citalopram HBr, approximately 16% of patients taking citalopram discontinued treatment due to adverse events, as opposed to a discontinuation rate of 7.7% for placebo-treated patients. The most frequent adverse events reported with citalopram versus placebo in clinical trials were nausea (21% versus 14%), dry mouth (20% versus 14%), somnolence (18% versus 10%), insomnia (15% versus 14%), increased sweating (11% versus 9%), tremor (8% versus 6%), diarrhea (8% versus 5%), and ejaculation disorder (6% versus 1%). Incidence of somnolence, increased sweating, and fatigue were dose-related.

Citalopram decreases heart rate by approximately 5 bpm (beats per minute) in patients under sixty years of age. Following the initial drop, heart rate remains decreased but stable over prolonged periods of time (up to one year in over 100 younger patients and over 50 elderly patients). The effect is reversible within approximately a week after stopping treatment. Decreases in heart rate do not appear to be dose-related and are independent of gender. The differences in heart rates between citalopram and placebo-treated patients are statistically significant, with EKG parameters, including QT interval, unaffected.

Patients receiving citalopram also reported disorders related to sexual functioning. Reported incidence of ejaculation disorders (primarily ejaculation delay and ejaculation failure), and impotence in male depressed patients receiving citalopram (n = 404) was 3.7%, 6.2%, and 3.2%, respectively. In female depressed patients receiving citalopram (n = 623), the reported incidence of decreased libido and anorgasmia was 1.3% and 1.1%, respectively.

Patients who abruptly discontinued treatment with citalopram after eight weeks of treatment have reported discontinuation syndrome. Symptoms included a higher incidence of anxiety, emotional indifference, impaired concentration, headache, migraine, paresthesia, and tremor than was seen in patients who continued on citalopram. Although it is not known whether gradual discontinuation will prevent the discontinuation symptoms, it is recommended that the dosage of citalopram be tapered off over one to two weeks.

Drug Interactions and Contradictions. It is recommended that this drug not be used in combination with an MAOI. A minimum of fourteen days should elapse after stopping citalopram before administering an MAOI, and fourteen days should elapse after stopping an MAOI before administering citalopram.

Empirical Data. Wagner, Robb, Findling, and Tiseo (2001) reported on a multisite, double-blind, placebo-controlled study of citalopram in 174 children and adolescents (ages seven to seventeen) with MDD. In this study, a significant difference was seen between the active treatment group and the placebo group within one week of beginning treatment, with mean Children's Depression Rating Scale–Revised (CDRS–R) scores showing significant decreases between baseline ($p < 0.02$ at week one), and the end of the study ($p < 0.04$ at week eight). At week eight, the difference in response rate between placebo (24%) and citalopram (36%) was statistically significant ($p < 0.05$).

In a small, open trial of citalopram, twenty-three children and adolescents with OCD (ages nine to eighteen) were treated for ten weeks. Over 75% showed marked (greater than 50% reduction in CY-BOCS) or moderate (20–50% reduction) improvement in OCD symptoms. None of the subjects discontinued due to adverse events, and all adverse events were minor and transient (Thomsen, 1997).

In the adolescent population, eight patients with moderate to severe PTSD, in a twelve-week open-label trial, were treated with a fixed dose (20 mg/day) of citalopram (Seedat, Lockhat, Kaminer, Zungu-Dirwayi, & Stein, 2001). Core cluster symptoms showed clinically significant statistical improvement by week twelve with a 38% reduction in rater scores from baseline to end point. However, there is much need for further investigation in double-blind, placebo-controlled trials in the pediatric population.

A retrospective chart review of seventeen outpatients suggested citalopram to be a helpful and well-tolerated treatment for depression and anxiety in pediatric patients (Baumgartner, Emslie, & Crismon, 2002). A six-week open trial of twelve youth showed reductions in impulsive aggression (Armenteros & Lewis, 2002). In this study, ten of seventeen patients with PDDs showed improvement in aggression and anxiety when treated with citalopram, although two patients showed increased aggression.

Escitalopram Oxalate (Lexapro)

Chemical Makeup. Escitalopram is the single isomer of citalopram. It is the active S-enantiomer of citalopram's racemic mixture, with potent and highly selective-serotonin reuptake inhibition due to the application of chiral chemistry.

Mechanism of Action. Escitalopram is one hundred times more potent in its execution than its stereoisomer. It has low or no affinity for neurotransmitter receptors or for dopamine and norepinephrine transporters.

Pharmacokinetics. The drug is rapidly and almost fully absorbed following administration. Maximum blood levels are achieved after five hours, and steady-state levels reached after seven to ten days of dosing. Its bioavailability is approximately 80% and is not affected if taken with food. Protein binding, about 56%, is comparatively low in relation to the binding of the other SSRIs. Elimination is biphasic, and the terminal half life ranges from twenty-seven to thirty-two hours. Three cytochrome P450 isoenzymes mediate its metabolism in the liver, through multiple and parallel pathways. When administered as either a single or multiple dose ranging from 10 to 30 mg daily, escitalopram exhibits linear, dosepro-portional kinetics.

Dosing. Recommended initial dosing of the drug is 10 mg/day in adults. If clinically indicated, the dose can be titrated up to 20 mg, but a minimum of a week should occur before this dose change. Escitalopram should be taken once daily, in the morning or evening, with or without food.

Escitalopram oxalate is available in 5-, 10-, and 20-mg tablets.

Adverse Effects Profile. Escitalopram is well tolerated by most people. The most commonly reported side effects in adults are nausea, insomnia, fatigue, drowsiness, increased sweating, and problems with ejaculation (delayed ejaculation). Most adverse events are mild to moderate.

Drug Interactions and Contraindications. As with other SSRIs, caution is indicated in the co-administration of TCAs with escitalopram. Because escitalopram is the active isomer of racemic citalopram (Celexa), the two drugs should not be co-administered. Escitalopram is contraindicated in patients taking MAOIs or in patients with a hypersensitivity to escitalopram oxalate. At least fourteen days should elapse between discontinuation of an MAOI and initiation of escitalopram. Similarly, at least fourteen days should be allowed after stopping escitalopram before starting an MAOI.

Empirical Data. As the newest SSRI, escitalopram has shown to be an effective treatment for panic disorder in adults (Wade, 2002; Burke, 2002; Lepola, 2003). Stahl and colleages report on a double-blind, placebo-controlled trial in 237 adult patients having a DSM-IV diagnosis of panic disorder with or without agoraphobia. Based on results of efficacy, measures of 125 patients assigned to the active drug, escitalopram in comparison to placebo significantly reduced panic attack frequency. They reported having 1.61 less panic attacks a day, 50.4% of patients experiencing zero panic attacks, in comparison to the 38.6% in the placebo arm (p $<=$ 0.05 versus placebo). Improvement in symptomatology was seen by week four, as indicated by the Quality of Life (QOL) scale. At a median dose of 10 mg/day, significantly greater mean changes (p $<$ .01) from baseline to end point included improvement on items such as overall life satisfaction, social and family relations, the ability to function in daily life, and an overall sense of well being (Stahl, Gergel, & Dayong, 2002). There has been no reported empirical data of escitalopram use in children or adolescents.

Novel Antidepressants

Also widely used in clinical practice are the novel atypical antidepressants, which differ from the SSRIs in their neurotransmitter mechanisms. Included within this class are the dual reuptake inhibitors such as bupropion, a norepinephrine and dopamine reuptake inhibitor (NDRI), mirtazapine, a noradrenergic and specific serotonergic antidepressant (NaSSA), and venlafaxine, a serotonin/norepinephrine reuptake inhibitor (SNRI). Both nefazodone and trazodone exhibit mixed mechanisms as serotonin antagonists and reuptake inhibitors (SARIs), behaving primarily as antagonists with weaker reuptake inhibition. While all have FDA approval in adults for the treatment of depression, there are currently no approved indications for the treatment of child and adolescent disorders. Just as with SSRIs, this class of drug has expanded its therapeutic use beyond that of the mood disorders.

Bupropion Hydrochloride (Wellbutrin)

Chemical Makeup. Bupropion hydrochloride is a structure closely resembling diethylpropion, related to phenylethylamines, and is an antidepressant of the aminoketone class. It is chemically unrelated to tricyclics, tetracylics, SSRIs or other known antidepressant agents. It is a racemic mixture, but the enantiomers have not been studied individually.

Mechanism of Action. The neurochemical mechanism responsible for the antidepressant effect of bupropion is not known. Bupropion is classified as an *NDRI*; however, it is a relatively weak uptake inhibitor of norepinephrine, serotonin, and dopamine. It does not inhibit monoamine oxidase.

Pharmacokinetics. Peak plasma concentrations of bupropion are achieved approximately within two hours, followed by a biphasic decline. Within an eight to twenty-four hour range, the terminal phase has a mean half life of fourteen hours. The distribution phase's mean half life is three to four hours. Steady-state plasma concentrations are reached within eight days, and elimination half life is 21 ± 9 hours after chronic dosing. The drug is extensively metabolized in humans with three active metabolites formed. Following chronic dosing within ranges of 300 to 450 mg/day, bupropion and its metabolites exhibit linear kinetics.

Dosing. Treatment with the standard release preparation is usually initiated at 100 mg twice a day. Dosage has not been established for individuals under eighteen years of age. After the fourth day of treatment, bupropion may be increased to 100 mg three times a day. Agitation, motor restlessness, and insomnia frequently occur at the start of treatment. Initiating treatment at low doses, and making slow incremental dosage increases, may help minimize these effects. Also, avoiding bedtime dosing may help reduce the potential for insomnia. The maximum daily dose should not exceed 450 mg. A single dose within a four-hour time period should not exceed 150 mg.

Treatment with the sustained release preparation is usually initiated at 100 mg or 150 mg in the morning. After four or more days of treatment, an additional 100 or 150 mg dose may be added. An eight-hour interval between doses is recommended. Dosage may be increased to 200 mg twice a day as clinically indicated, for a 400-mg maximum daily dose.

Bupropion hydrochloride is available in 75- and 100-mg immediate release tablets and 100- and 150-mg sustained release tablets.

Adverse Effects Profile. Seizures have been associated with the use of bupropion (Wellbutrin, Wellbutrin SR, and Zyban SR). Seizures appear to be dose-related.

At a dose of 300 mg/day, the chance of having a seizure is approximately 1 in 1000, but at a dose of 400 mg/day, the chance increases to 4 in 1000. The chance of having a seizure is increased for individuals with a history of seizure or seizure disorder (such as epilepsy), as well as for those individuals with a current or prior diagnosis of an eating disorder (such as bulimia or anorexia nervosa).

The most commonly reported adverse events associated with use of bupropion hydrochloride are dry mouth, insomnia, agitation, headache, nausea, vomiting, constipation, and tremor. Furthermore, although it may cause weight gain in some individuals, Bupropion more often causes weight loss. In adults taking this medication, it is estimated that 28% lose at least 5% of their body weight (Jain et al., 2002).

Drug Interactions and Contraindications. There is little information on the interactions of bupropion hydrochloride with other drugs. Known hypersensitivity to bupropion hydrochloride and seizure disorders are contraindications. Concurrent administration of bupropion with any drug that reduces seizure threshold is a relative contraindication. Other contraindications include administering bupropion hydrochloride concurrently with an MAOI, as MAOIs may increase the acute toxicity of bupropion. A minimum of fourteen days off MAOIs should be observed before introducing treatment with bupropion. Due to its extensive metabolism, the potential for drug interactions is found particularly with agents that are metabolized by the cytochrome P4502D6 isoenzyme (Rotzinger, Bourin, Akimoto, Coutts, & Baker, 1999).

The CYP2D6 enzyme does not metabolize bupropion. Nevertheless, bupropion and morpholinol, its metabolite, inhibit the CYP2D6 enzyme in vitro, and accordingly, extreme caution should be exercised when prescribing bupropion for any patient who is concurrently taking a drug metabolized by the CYP2D6 enzyme (Hesse, Venkatakrishnan, Court, et al., 2000). Bupropion is contraindicated for patients with a current or prior diagnosis of bulimia or anorexia nervosa and for those patients taking any drug that reduces seizure threshold. Bupropion is also contraindicated for individuals who are abruptly discontinuing use of alcohol or sedatives (including benzodiazepines).

Empirical Data. Bupropion has not been evaluated in randomized controlled clinical trials for the treatment of depression or smoking cessation in children or adolescents; however, bupropion is approved for treatment of these disorders in adults.

In contrast to SSRIs, the novel antidepressant bupropion has evidence from double-blind, placebo-controlled studies to support its use in the treatment of ADHD. The magnitude of clinical improvement appears to be less than for standard stimulants; thus, bupropion appears to be a useful second-line treatment for children and adolescents with ADHD. Casat, Pleasants, Schroeder, and Parler (1989) in a double-blind study, administered bupropion to twenty children and placebo to ten children diagnosed with ADHD. Improvement in overall clinical presentation and symptom severity was reported by physician ratings. Improvement in hyperactivity was reported by teacher ratings. However, there were no differences between placebo and active treatment on parent behavior ratings or laboratory cognitive measures. The effect size as reported by Connors Teachers Rating Scale appeared less robust than that of stimulants. Clay Gualtieri, Evans, and Gullion (1988) reported similar results from a double-blind, placebo-controlled study of thirty children treated with optimal doses of bupropion at 100 to 250 mg/day. It was noted that some children responded to bupropion who had not previously shown a good response to stimulants. Conversely, some stimulant-naive patients who failed bupropion therapy responded to methylphenidate. Further, it was the authors' clinical impression that children with prominent conduct disorder symptoms responded particularly well. In a single-blind, placebo-controlled study, Simeon, Ferguson, and Fleet (1986) showed significant improvements in teacher and parent ratings of inattentiveness and hyperactivity after eight weeks of bupropion (50 to 150 mg/day) in seventeen preadolescents with ADHD. In a double-blind, placebo-controlled study of fifteen outpatients (ages seven to sixteen), Barrickman and colleagues (1991) found bupropion (50 to 200 mg/day) to be as effective as methylphenidate (20 to 60 mg/day), but with non-significant trends suggesting superiority of stimulant. Bupropion appeared less well tolerated.

A multi-site, randomized, double-blind comparison of bupropion (n = 72) and placebo (n = 37) in children (ages 6 to 12) with ADHD and without MDD demonstrated improvements in parents' and teachers' ratings (Conners et al., 1996). However, at the end of the study, teacher's ratings showed no significant difference between treatment and placebo groups. EEGs at day twenty-eight, compared to baseline, found that six patients in the bupropion group developed EEG abnormalities, three of whom had spike and wave discharges, but none of whom with clinical seizure activity (Conners et al., 1996).

Some studies have looked at bupropion in patients with ADHD and comorbid conditions. Daviss and associates (2001) evaluated twenty-four adolescents (ages eleven to sixteen) with ADHD and depression or dysthymia. Clinicians rated 58% as responders for depressive and ADHD symptoms, 29% responders for depression only, and 4% responders for ADHD only. Statistically significant improvements were seen in parents' and childrens' ratings of depressive symptomatology. Statistically significant improvements in ADHD were reported in parents' but not teachers' ratings. Functional impairment improved significantly from enrollment. Riggs, Leon, Mikulich, and Pottle (1998) evaluated thirteen non-depressed adolescent males with comorbid substance abuse and conduct disorder, treated with bupropion (final dose 300 mg/day). Mean ADHD symptoms decreased by 13% and mean CGI improved by 39%, both statistically significant. Bupropion appears effective, especially at low doses, for the treatment of ADHD, but improvements may be less robust than with stimulants.

No controlled clinical trials of bupropion have been reported in children and adolescents who have other psychiatric disorders.

Venlafaxine Hydrochloride (Effexor)

Chemical Makeup. Venlafaxine hydrochloride is a structurally novel antidepressant chemically distinct from other available antidepressants, classified as an SNRI.

Mechanism of Action. Its antidepressant effects are presumably related to potent inhibition of the reuptake of serotonin and norepinephrine and weak inhibition of the reuptake of dopamine in CNS neurons. It does not have significant affinity for muscarinic, histaminergic, or alpha-1 adrenergic receptors.

Pharmacokinetics. Elimination half life is approximately eleven hours. Steady-state serum concentrations are achieved within approximately three days of multi-dose administration. Venlafaxine and its principle active metabolite *o*-demethylvenlafaxine exhibit linear pharmacokinetics. Protein binding is approximately 27–30%. The drug is absorbed well and extensively metabolized in the liver. Renal elimination of venlafaxine and its metabolites is the primary route of excretion. Food has no significant effect on absorption or bioavailability.

Dosage adjustment is recommended for patients with liver disease, as hepatic cirrhosis has been shown to prolong elimination and decrease clearance of this drug. Also, dosage adjustment is necessary for patients with renal disease and in dialysis patients, as elimination is prolonged and clearance is reduced.

Dosing. Initiation of treatment at 75 mg/day in two to three divided doses is recommended for the standard release preparation. If clinically indicated, the dose may be increased to 225 mg/day for moderately depressed patients and up to 375 mg/day in severely depressed patients. Increments of up to 75 mg should be made at intervals of at least four days. Administration with food may enhance tolerability. Initiation of treatment with extended release capsules is recommended at 37.5 mg/day to 75 mg/day. Based on clinical indication, doses may be titrated to 225 mg/day. Dose increases may be made in 75-mg increments as needed per day, and should be made at intervals no less than four days because steady-state plasma levels are generally achieved by day four. Capsules should be swallowed whole and should not be broken.

Venlafaxine hydrochloride is available in 25-, 37.5-, 50-, 75-, and 100-mg tablets and 37.5-, 75-, and 150-mg extended release tablets.

Adverse Effects Profile. Venlafaxine has a high clinical trials dropout rate due to side effects. Clinical trials show that the most common adverse events included weakness (asthenia), weight loss, excessive muscular activity (hyperkinesias), and sleepiness (somnolence). Changes in appetite and weight, including treatment-emergent anorexia, have been reported in patients treated with venlafaxine for several weeks. Significant weight loss, especially in underweight depressed patients, may be an undesirable result of venlafaxine treatment. CNS adverse events include somnolence, insomnia, dizziness, nervousness, dry mouth, anxiety, and activation of mania or hypomania. In pediatric clinical trials, increased reports of hostility and suicide-related adverse events such as suicidal ideation and self-harm, have been observed.

EKG changes (mean heart rate increased by four beats per minute compared with baseline but no treatment-emergent conduction abnormalities) have been reported in adult patients taking venlafaxine. Sustained blood pressure elevations of patients receiving venlafaxine have been reported. The incidence of sustained increases in blood pressure at doses greater than 300 mg/day has not been fully evaluated. Regular blood pressure monitoring is recommended.

Discontinuation effects of venlafaxine HCl have not been systematically evaluated in controlled clinical trials. Nevertheless, a retrospective survey of new events occurring during taper or following discontinuation revealed the following six events that occurred at an incidence of at least 5% and for which the incidence for venlafaxine HCl was at least twice the placebo incidence: asthenia, dizziness, headache, insomnia, nausea, and nervousness. Therefore, it is recommended that the dosage be tapered gradually and the patient monitored.

Drug Interactions and Contradictions. Venlafaxine administered under steady-state conditions at 150 mg/day in twenty-four healthy subjects decreased total oral-dose clearance of a single 2-mg dose of haloperidol by 42%, which resulted in a 70% increase in haloperidol. In addition, the haloperidol Cmax increased 88% when co-administered with venlafaxine, but the haloperidol elimination half life ($T_{1/2}$) was unchanged. The mechanism explaining this finding is unknown.

The effects of combined use of venlafaxine and MAOIs have not been evaluated in humans or animals. Because of a possibility for serious, life-threatening reactions when administered simultaneously with an MAOI, it is recommended that venlafaxine HCl not be used in combination with an MAOI. It is recommended that a minimum of fourteen days elapse after stopping treatment with an MAOI before starting treatment with venlafaxine. Based on the half life of venlafaxine HCl, at least seven days should be allowed after stopping venlafaxine HCl before starting an MAOI.

For patients with pre-existing hypertension, and for patients with hepatic dysfunction, the interaction associated with the concomitant use of venlafaxine hydrochloride and cimetidine is not known and potentially could be pronounced. Therefore, caution is advised with such patients. As with all antidepressants, venlafaxine HCl should be used cautiously in patients with a history of mania or hypomania, as activation could occur.

Empirical Data. In a double-blind, placebo-controlled, six-week study of thirty-three youth ages eight to seventeen meeting DSM-IV criteria for major depression, benefits from venlafaxine could not be established. Patients showed significant improvement over time, which could not be attributed to the effects of active medication. The low doses used, the short length of treatment, and the small sample size may have been limiting factors (Mandoki, Tapia, Tapia, & Sumner, 1997). Controlled trials of venlafaxine for the treatment of pediatric depression, social anxiety disorder, generalized anxiety disorder, and panic disorder are ongoing or recently completed, and results have not yet been published.

Ten subjects with autism were treated with a low dose of venlafaxine (6.25 to 50 mg/day). Six of ten completers were found to be much or very much improved on the CGI. Improvement was noted in repetitive behaviors and restrictive interests, social deficits, communication and language function, inattention, and hyperactivity (Hollander, Kaplan, Cartwright, & Reichman, 2000).

Some preliminary data (Findling, Schwartz, Flannery, & Manos, 1996; Olvera, Pliszka, Luh, & Tatum, 1996) and open studies of adults with ADHD suggest that venlafaxine may play a role in the treatment of ADHD symptomatology. Olvera and colleagues (1996) enrolled sixteen non-depressed subjects (ages eight to sixteen) in an open-label trial of venlafaxine with a target dose of 75 mg/day. Six subjects did not complete the study, three due to behavioral activation. Impulsivity and hyperactivity showed statistically significant improvement on the Connors Parent Rating Scale. Conduct and cognitive factors did not improve (Olvera et al., 1996). Double-blind, placebo-controlled trials are necessary before the efficacy of venlafaxine as a treatment for ADHD can be determined.

Mirtazapine (Remeron)

Chemical Makeup. Mirtazapine belongs to the piperazino-azepine group of compounds and has a tetracyclic chemical structure. It is a racemic mixture and is classified as an NaSSA.

Mechanism of Action. As with other antidepressants, its mechanism is unknown. However, in preclinical trials, mirtazapine has been shown to act at central presynaptic alpha-adrenergic inhibitory autoreceptors and heteroreceptors as an antagonist, thus enhancing central noradrenergic and serotonergic activity. It is a potent antagonist of histamine, 5-HT2 and 5-HT3 receptors, a moderate peripheral alpha-1 antagonist, and a moderate antagonist at muscarinic receptors, but has no affinity for the 5-HT1A and 5-HT1B receptors.

Pharmacokinetics. Mirtazapine is quickly and completely absorbed following administration and peak plasma concentrations are reached within about two hours. Half life of the drug is about twenty to fourty hours. Food has negligible effect on absorption; no dose adjustments are required when taken with food. Major pathways of metabolism and biotransformation are demethylation and hydroxylation followed by glucuronide conjugation. Absolute bioavailability of mirtazapine is about 50% and protein binding approximately 85%. Plasma levels are linearly related to dose over the dose range of 15 to 80 mg.

Dosing. Initial dosing of 7.5 to 15 mg at bedtime is recommended. Effective doses usually range from 15 to 45 mg in adults. More sedation may be seen at lower doses.

Mirtazapine is available in 15-, 30-, and 45-mg tablets and 15-, 30-, and 45-mg soluble tablets.

Adverse Effects Profile. Mirtazapine has fewer side effects than many of the other anti-depressants. It is generally well tolerated. The most commonly reported side effects for patients taking mirtazapine are drowsiness (daytime sleepiness), increased appetite, weight gain, and dizziness. Although drowsiness is reported by more than half of patients taking mirtazapine, drowsiness is reported to decrease in intensity over time, even as dosages increase. Another concern with mirtazapine is weight gain. Nutt (2002) reviewing safety aspects of mirtazapine, felt that weight gain was the most commonly reported side effect, but noted that evidence suggests this is not a significant problem in long-term treatment. Other side effects may also lessen in severity, or completely resolve, with prolonged use of the drug.

Drug Interactions and Contraindications. Use of other drugs that cause drowsiness (antihistamines, prescription painkillers) may increase somnolence and impair motor or coordination skills. Use of mirtazapine with CNS stimulants may cause an increase in agitation or even mania, especially in bipolar patients.

In clinical trials, 2 of 2,796 persons treated with mirtazapine developed agranulocytosis, and a third person (0.1%) developed severe neutropenia (Buck, 2000). These potentially dangerous decreases in white blood cell counts were reversed, and the individuals recovered, after mirtazapine was discontinued. However, it should be noted that any patient who develops a sore throat, fever, inflammation of the mouth, or other signs of infection should discontinue treatment with mirtazapine under the supervision of a doctor.

Simultaneous administration with an MAOI is contraindicated, and a minimum of fourteen days should be observed after stopping an MAOI before administering mirtazapine; also, a minimum of fourteen days should elapse after stopping mirtazapine before beginning an MAOI.

Empirical Data. Serotonergic agents have been proposed as the first line of treatment for child and adolescent PTSD based on the extrapolation from the adult literature and psychobiological theory. However, for those patients who do not tolerate SSRIs or do not reach a therapeutic level of symptom remission, novel antidepressants, such as mirtazapine, may provide some benefit. In an eight-week adult study of PTSD (Connor, Davidson, Weisler, & Ahearn, 1999), six outpatients were treated up to 45 mg/day of mirtazapine. Global rating by assessors demonstrated an improvement of 50% or more in half of the sample. Further study is warranted.

Twenty-six subjects with PDD (ages 3.8 to 23.5 years) participated in a naturalistic, open-label trial of mirtazapine, 7.5 to 45 mg/day (Posey, Guenin, Kohn, Swiezy, & McDougle, 2001). Nine of twenty-six subjects (34.6%) were responders, based on improvement in a variety of symptoms including aggression, self-injury, irritability, hyperactivity, anxiety, depression, and insomnia. Core symptoms of social or communication impairment were not improved. Adverse effects were minimal and included increased appetite, irritability, and transient sedation.

Studies of mirtazapine in children and adolescents with other psychiatric disorders are ongoing or recently completed, and results are not yet published.

Nefazodone Hydrochloride (Serzone)

Chemical Makeup. Nefazodone is a phenylpiperazine antidepressant whose chemical structure is unrelated to SSRIs, tricyclics, tetracyclics, or MAOIs. Like trazodone, it is classified as an SARI.

Mechanism of Action. While the mechanism of action is unknown, it is believed that SARIs have mixed mechanisms. Studies have shown nefazodone to inhibit the neuronal uptake of serotonin and norepinephrine. However, this reuptake inhibition appears to be weak, while the drug primarily functions as an antagonist. At central 5-HT2 receptors, nefazodone has shown to antagonize alpha1-adrenergic receptors. With alpha-2- and beta-adrenergic, 5HT1A, cholinergic, dopaminergic, or benzodiazepine receptors, no significant affinity has been found.

Pharmacokinetics. Nefazodone is absorbed quickly and completely, with its bioavailability at a low 20% due to the need for extensive metabolism. Peak plasma concentrations occur in about an hour, with a half life of two to four hours. Its kinetics are nonlinear for dose and time, with Cmax and Area Under the Curve (AUC) increasing more than proportionally with multiple dosing over time in comparison to single dosing.

The drug is metabolized by n-dealkylation and aliphatic and aromatic hydroxylation in the liver. Less than 1% of the unchanged drug is secreted in urine. Protein binding to human plasma proteins in vitro is high at 99%. Food will delay the absorption of the drug and causes its bioavailibility to decrease by 20%.

Dosing. Initiation of treatment at 100 mg twice a day is recommended. The effective daily dose for most patients is 300 to 600 mg/day in twice daily, divided doses. Incremental increases of 100 to 200 mg/day should be made at intervals of greater than seven days. In adolescent populations, doses are tolerated up to 600 mg/day, with the average effective dose around 200 mg BID.

Nefazodone hydrochloride is available in 50-, 100-, 150-, 200-, and 250-mg tablets.

Adverse Effects Profile. Nefazodone hydrochloride is generally well tolerated, with mild side effects. In an eight-week open-label study of children and adolescents (seven- to sixteen-years-old), the most commonly reported side effects in children (ages seven to twelve) were headache, nausea, vomiting, and decreased appetite; the most common side effects in adolescents (ages thirteen to sixteen) were headache, asthenia, and sedation (Findling et al., 2000). Overall, the most common side effects reported by individuals treated with nefazodone are dry mouth, constipation, light-headedness, blurred or abnormal vision, and confusion. Side effects associated with discontinuation include nausea, dizziness, insomnia, asthenia, and agitation.

When prescribing nefazodone, however, physicians should be aware of the black box warning of hepatotoxicity issued for this drug. In patients treated with nefazodone, there have been cases of life-threatening hepatic failure. Therefore, treatment should not be initiated in patients with active liver disease or elevated serum transaminases at baseline. Patients should be educated on the symptoms of liver dysfunction (such as jaundice, anorexia, GI complaints, and malaise) so they may alert their doctor immediately if any occur. In the event a patient experiences signs or symptoms of liver failure, nefazodone treatment should be discontinued.

Drug Interactions and Contraindications. Nefazodone inhibits CYP3A4, and therefore serious or life-threatening cardiac electroconductivity abnormalities could result if nefazodone were taken concurrently with terfenadine, astemizone, cisapride, or pimozide. Use of nefazodone concurrently with any MAOI is contraindicated. MAOIs should be discontinued for a minimum of fourteen days before beginning administration of nefazodone.

Nefazodone administered concurrently with triazolobenzodiazepines may result in significant increases in serum levels of these drugs, although the serum levels of nefazodone will not be affected. Dose reductions of triazolobenzodiazepines can be calculated and recommended (for example, a 50% reduction in dose of alprazolam is recommended if nefazodone is administered concurrently with alprazolam; a 75% reduction in dose of triazolam is recommended when nefazodone is administered concurrently). Nevertheless, concurrent administration of these medications may not be feasible because commercial preparations are often not available in sufficiently small doses.

Empirical Data. Mixed-mechanism antidepressants have limited efficacy data in the pediatric age group. In an eight-week open-label trial of twenty-eight children and adolescents (ages seven to sixteen) diagnosed with MDD, nefazodone was found to be well tolerated and effective. Completion of the study showed improvement in the CDRS-R scores by week one, CGI-severity scores by week two, and increase (denoting improvement) in the Clinical Global Assessment Score (CGAS) by the end of the study (Findling et al., 2000). Similarly, a large, multi-site trial comparing nefazodone and placebo in 195 adolescents (ages twelve to seventeen) with MDD, adolescents randomized to nefazodone initially received 100 mg/day in equally divided doses, and were titrated by 100 mg/week to targeted total daily doses of 300 to 400 mg based on tolerability and clinical response. At week eight the nefazodone group was superior to placebo on CGI response rate (65% versus 46%, $p = 0.005$), HAM-D (-10.0 versus -8.2, $p = 0.023$), and CGAS (17.2 versus 13.0, $p = 0.020$). Nefazodone was safe and well tolerated in this trial, with the rate of discontinuation for adverse events similar between the treatment groups (Emslie, Findling, Rynn, Marcus, Fernandes, & D'Amico, 2002). Pediatric case studies of nefazodone in children with mood disorders have also been positive (Wilens, Spencer, Biederman, & Schleifer, 1997; Domon & Anderson, 2000).

Although SSRIs have been deemed most effective in treating PTSD, adult literature also has shown clinical improvement when treated with a mixed-mechanism antidepressant. Davidson, Weisler, Malik, and Connor (1998) treated seventeen private-practice patients with nefazodone of up to 600 mg/day for twelve weeks. Final outcome showed statistically significant improvement of symptoms for all clusters, with a response rate of 60% at end point. For those individuals who may demonstrate intolerance to side effects of SSRIs, or a limited response when treated, the novel antidepressants are postulated to be effective in treating PTSD. Unfortunately, pediatric data is limited. However, with the black box warning, it is unlikely that any new trials of nefazodone will be conducted in children and adolescents at this time.

Trazodone Hydrochloride (Desyrel)

Chemical Makeup. Trazodone HCl is an antidepressant chemically unrelated to tricyclic, tetracyclic, or other known antidepressant agents.

Mechanism of Action. It is classified as a serotonin antagonist and reuptake inhibitor (SNRI). However, this reuptake inhibition is weak, as the drug acts primarily as an antagonizer. Although the mechanism is not fully known, it has been shown to potentiate behavioral changes induced by 5-hydroxytryptophan (PDR, 2002).

Pharmacokinetics. When taken with food, trazodone will be absorbed 20% more than if taken on an empty stomach. Maximum serum levels will be reached by two hours instead of one. This appears to lessen the likelihood of developing light-headedness or dizziness effects from the drug (PDR, 2002).

The drug undergoes biphasic elimination through the liver and kidney. The first phase half life is between three and six hours, followed by a second phase with an approximate five- to nine-hour half life.

Dosing. It is recommended that for children six to eighteen years of age dosing should begin with 1.5 to 2 mg/kg/day in divided doses. The dosage should be initiated at a low level and increased gradually at three- to four-day intervals to a maximum of 6 mg/kg/day, noting the clinical response and any evidence of intolerance. Occurrence of drowsiness may require the administration of a major portion of the daily dose at bedtime or a reduction of dosage. Symptomatic relief may be seen during the first week, with optimal antidepressant effects typically evident within two weeks. Of those who respond to trazodone HCl, 25% require more than two weeks (up to four weeks) of drug administration. Due to this sedation, trazodone is rarely used for the treatment of depression in pediatric populations. It is, however, sometimes used in low doses at bedtime to promote sleep. Recommended initial dose is 25 to 50 mg at bedtime, and this may be increased to 100 mg, as needed.

Trazodone hydrochloride is available in 50- and 100-mg tablets and 150- and 300-mg divided dose tablets.

Adverse Effects Profile. The most commonly reported side effects for patients taking trazodone hydrochloride are drowsiness, dizziness or lightheadedness, dry mouth, and nausea or vomiting. Trazodone has been associated with the occurrence of priapism. In approximately 33% of reported cases of priapism, surgical intervention was required and in a portion of these cases permanent impairment of erectile functioning or impotence results. Male patients with prolonged or inappropriate erections should immediately discontinue trazodone and consult their doctor or go to an emergency room.

Drug Interactions and Contraindications. The effects of the interactions of trazodone and MAOIs are unknown, and accordingly trazodone should not be administered with MAOIs.

Empirical Data. Most studies of trazodone in children and adolescents are as adjunctive treatment. Zubieta and Alessi (1992) reported an open study of twenty-two inpatients ranging between five and twelve years of age, diagnosed with disruptive and behavioral mood disorders often with comorbidity. Six of the patients continued on their neuroleptic drugs for psychotic symptoms during their trial of trazodone. Dosing was initiated at 50 mg at bedtime and then titrated after a week to the maximum dose tolerated and administered three times a day. Thirteen children were denoted as responders, receiving a mean dose of 185 ± 117 mg/day for approximately 27 ± 13 days (Zubieta & Alessi, 1992).

Trazodone was evaluated in combination with haloperidol in an open-label trial in ten pediatric patients with Tourette's and chronic tic syndrome. A mean reduction of symptoms was found (58.9%) on the Yale Global Tic Severity Scale with clinically significant difference between the baseline and end point treatment conditions (Saccomani, Rizzo, & Nobili, 2000).

A retrospective chart review of adolescents with insomnia associated with depressive disorders assessed the relative effectiveness of fluoxetine and trazodone in promoting sleep. Median time to insomnia resolution was two days in the trazodone group and four days in the fluoxetine group. Although statistically significant, the authors concluded that the difference was not clinically significant in the management of insomnia associated with depressive disorders in adolescents (Kallepalli, Bhatara, Fogas, Tervo, & Misra, 1997).

Ghaziuddin and Alessi (1992) noted the successful use of trazodone to control aggressive behavior in adults, due to the relationship of the aggression expression and decreased levels of serotonin in the CNS. In addition, case reports and open trials of adult patients with OCD have shown efficacious response when treated with trazodone (Pigott, L'Heureux, Rubenstein, Bernstein, et al., 1992). However, empirical evidence is lacking for the treatment in the pediatric population across psychiatric disorders, making great the need for double-blind placebo-controlled trials in order to determine efficacy and safety in treatment of children and adolescents.

Table 12.2 lists the formulations for the antidepressants covered in this chapter. Table 12.3 shows the common adverse effects associated with each antidepressant.

TABLE 12.2. ANTIDEPRESSANT FORMULATIONS.

	Capsules			Tablets	Liquid
Buproprion					
Wellbutrin	—	—	75 mg	Gold	—
	—	—	100 mg	Red	—
Wellbutrin SR	—	—	100 mg	Turquoise	—
	—	—	150 mg	Grey	—
Zyban SR	—	—	150 mg	Purple	—
Citalopram HBr					
Celexa	—	—	20 mg	Pink	10 mg/5 mL
	—	—	40 mg	White	—
Escitalopram					
Lexapro	—	—	5 mg	White or off-white	—
	—	—	10 mg	Scored	—
	—	—	20 mg	Scored	—
Fluoxetine					
Prozac	10 mg	Lime green	10 mg	Green elliptical	20 mg/5 ml
	20 mg	Green & Yellow	—	—	—
	40 mg	Green & Orange	—	—	—
Prozac Weekly	90 mg	Green & White	—	—	—
Sarafem	10 mg	Lavender	—	—	—
	20 mg	Lavender + pink	—	—	—
Generic	10 mg	—	10 mg	—	—
	40 mg	—	20 mg	—	—
Fluvoxamine					
Luvox	—	—	25 mg	White	—
	—	—	50 mg	Gold	—
	—	—	100 mg	Tan	—
Mirtazapine					
Remeron	—	—	15 mg	Yellow	—
	—	—	30 mg	Red	—
	—	—	45 mg	White	—
Nefazadone HCl					
Serzone	—	—	50 mg	Deep pink	—
	—	—	100 mg	White (small)	—
	—	—	150 mg	Pink	—
	—	—	200 mg	Yellow	—
	—	—	250 mg	White (big)	—
Paroxetine HCl					
Paxil	—	—	10 mg	Gold	10 mg/ 5mL
	—	—	20 mg	Pink	—
	—	—	30 mg	Violet blue	—
	—	—	40 mg	Green	—

(Continued)

TABLE 12.2. ANTIDEPRESSANT FORMULATIONS (*CONTINUED*).

	Capsules		Tablets		Liquid
Sertraline HCl					
Zoloft	—	—	25 mg	Green	20 mg/ml
	—	—	50 mg	Blue	—
	—	—	100 mg	Yellow	—
Trazodone					
Desyrel	—	—	50 mg	—	—
	—	—	100 mg	—	—
Venlafaxine HCl					
Effexor	—	—	25 mg	Pink	—
	—	—	37.5 mg	Pink	—
	—	—	50 mg	—	—
	—	—	75 mg	—	—
	—	—	100 mg	—	—
Effexor XR	37.5 mg	Grey & peach	—	—	—
	75.0 mg	Peach	—	—	—
	150 mg	Brown	—	—	—

Expert Recommendations

The available research information on the efficacy and safety of antidepressants in a variety of disorders has increased exponentially in the past five years. Similarly, there has been an increase in the number of prescriptions written in the pediatric age group for antidepressants. An interesting recent observation is that the suicide rate in adolescent males has decreased by about one-third in parallel with the increase in use of SSRI medications. Whether these two phenomena are causally related continues to be debated.

Continued research is needed to demonstrate safety and efficacy in youth. In the past, clinicians have relied on adult data to guide treatment decisions. However, as seen with the TCAs, which have established efficacy in adults, but not in children and adolescents (Hazell et al., 1995; Kutcher et al., 1994), results from adult trials may not be applicable to the younger population. Furthermore, safety concerns are heightened in children and adolescents. For example, there has been recent speculation about growth attenuation in pediatric patients on SSRIs (Weintrob, Cohen, & Klipper-Aurback, 2002). Such concerns would not be raised in adult populations, and therefore investigation into such issues will require research in the pediatric population.

To date, research has demonstrated safety and efficacy of several SSRIs in treating depression and anxiety disorders. Additional research has attempted to

TABLE 12.3. ADVERSE EFFECTS OF ANTIDEPRESSANTS.

SSRIs	Agitation/ insomnia	Anti-cholinergic	GI effects	Orthostatic hypotension	Sedation	Sexual dysfunction	Dosage forms	Usual adult daily dosage	Comments
Citalopram (Celexa)	Low	None	High	None	Low	Very high	T,L	20–60 mg/day	SSRIs overall: low end of dose range effective for most patients; much safer in overdose than TCAs; not necessary to titrate from smaller starting doses as necessary with TCAs; except for citalopram, variable and significant inhibitory effect on hepatic P450 enzymes; caution when co-prescribed with drugs that undergo extensive hepatic metabolism and have narrow therapeutic index; effective for panic disorder, OCD, bulimia nervosa, social phobia, PTSD, and premenstrual dysphoria.
Escitalopram (Lexapro)		None	Moderate	None			T	5–10 mg/day	
Fluoxetine (Prozac)	Very high	None	High	None	None	Very high	C,T,L	10–80 mg/day	
Fluvoxamine (Luvox)	Low	None	High	None	Moderate	Very high	T	100–300 mg/day	
Paroxetine (Paxil)	Low	Low	High	None	Low	Very high	T,L	20–60 mg/day	
Sertraline (Zoloft)	Moderate	None	Very high	None	Very low	Very high	T	50–200 mg/day	
Others									
Buproprion (Wellbutrin, Wellbutrin SR)	High / Moderate	None / None	Moderate / Moderate	None / None	None / None	None / None	T / SR	150–450 mg/day / 150–400 mg/day	Wellbutrin/Zyban: used for stopping smoking. Avoid use in patients with seizure disorders. Effexor: also effective for GAD. Mirtazapine: less sedation at doses >15 mg/day; weight gain. Trazodone: not well tolerated at antidepressant dosage; commonly used as hypnotic; priapism rare.
Desyrel (Trazodone)	None	Very low	Moderate	Very high	Very high	None	T	200–600 mg/day	
Mirtazapine (Remeron)	None	None	Very low	None	High	None	T	15–45 mg/day	
Nefazodone (Serzone)	Very low	None	Moderate	Low	High	None	T	300–600 mg/day	
Venlafaxine (Effexor, EffexorXR) SSNRI	Moderate	None	Very high	Very low	Low	High	C(XR)T	75–375 mg/day	

Note: anticholinergic effects = dry mouth, blurred vision, urinary retention, constipation disseminate research findings to clinical practice. An example of this has been the development of a treatment algorithm for depression in children and adolescents treated in the public mental health sector (Hughes et al., 1999). The treatment algorithm was developed from a consensus conference of experts, clinicians, administrators, and consumers. In addition, the algorithm addresses treatment of depression in the context of common comorbid conditions, such as ADHD and anxiety disorders. Treatment recommendations are divided into strategies and tactics.

A strategy is the "what to do" of the treatment and tactic is the "how to do it." Strategies and tactics provide guidelines based on empirical research data. The strategies for the treatment of depression include an evaluation component, then recommendations on when to initiate medication, as well as recommendations about which types of medications to use and the goals of treatment. Several components of this algorithm are worth highlighting. Prior to initiating medication, accurate diagnosis and assessment of psychosocial context of the disorder is essential. Also important is the beginning of development of a strong therapeutic alliance.

From the consensus conference, consumers (both parents and adolescents) were particularly vocal about the need for education and involvement in the decision-making process, particularly on whether to initiate medication or start with specific psychotherapy. Based on available research, the consensus was that if medication was initiated, that monotherapy is preferred over multiple medications, and that for depression in this age group, SSRIs would be the first line of treatment. If the depression is severe enough to require medication, then visits should be weekly or every other week to increase the likelihood of adherence to treatment and to monitor for safety, as side effects (leading to potential stopping of treatment) tend to occur early in treatment.

Although research is available on acute treatment, little is available on longer-term treatment. The goals of all treatment, however, are initially to achieve remission of symptoms and not just response. Continuation treatment is needed to stabilize the gains made in acute treatment, and maintenance treatment may be needed to prevent recurrence in some patients.

Although these treatment guidelines were developed specifically for depression, many of the issues addressed are generally applicable to other disorders (such as anxiety disorders, ADHD, and so on). Similar recommendations have already been published for management of aggression (Schur et al., 2002). What these treatment algorithms demonstrate is that although clinical research is essential to provide the basic information needed to inform decision making, data from clinical trials is not the only information that clinicians utilize in decision making. Algorithms provide a synthesis of available clinical research information to assist clinicians. Regardless of what medications are shown to be effective in research, treatment adherence remains the biggest factor in determining outcome in clinical practice. Recent research is beginning to explore psychoeducational approaches to improving adherence and hence improve outcome. Finally, treatment guidelines provide a framework to identify areas of need for future research (such as the relative efficacy of psychotherapy and psychopharmacology).

◆ ◆ ◆

Clearly, we are seeing a significant increase in the use of psychotropic medication in children. Antidepressants are a large part of this increase. Research often lags behind the clinical use for these compounds, and until recently, there was little controlled clinical data on antidepressant treatment for children and adolescents. Studies of the acute effectiveness and safety of newer antidepressants in children have rapidly increased, with many research studies of antidepressants for a variety of disorders recently completed or ongoing, thus likely influencing the increased rate of prescriptions among use.

Yet, the need for continued research in pediatric antidepressant use is critical, as the potential efficacy of these medications for a range of disorders is significant. They are widely used in children and adolescents not only by child and adolescent psychiatrists, but also by primary care physicians and physician extenders, with potential effectiveness in depression, anxiety disorders, Tourette's, behavior disorders, and possibly some developmental disorders. Many of the applications for which they are prescribed are not FDA-approved, but are extrapolated from double-blind studies, open-label studies, case reports, clinical experience, adult indications, and psychopharmacologic theory. At present, only fluoxetine, sertraline, and fluvoxamine have FDA indications in children and adolescents with OCD, and fluoxetine for pediatric depression.

Because acute data are just now being published, long-term treatment has yet to be evaluated in this population. Now that several of these antidepressants have demonstrated short-term efficacy, long-term continuation trials are needed to determine optimal length of treatment.

Furthermore, studies of safety are needed. It remains unclear how antidepressant treatment influences long-term development. Pharmacokinetic data are also needed in the pediatric population, as these data are not easily extrapolated from adults.

Although information from adults can suggest potential areas of possible efficacy in disorders that are similar in children and adolescents, efficacy, safety, and pharmacokinetic information specific to children and adolescents is necessary for the delivery of high quality patient care in this age group. To date, most studies assessing the use of antidepressants in youth have evaluated their efficacy and safety in the short term. Studies assessing long-term safety, augmentation, and combination strategies are the next step in the quest for evidence-based treatment of youth.

References

Abajo, F. J., Rodríguez, L.A.G., & Montero, D. (1999). Association between selective serotonin reuptake inhibitors and upper gastrointestinal bleeding: Population based case-control study. *British Medical Journal, 319*(7217), 1106–1109.

Alcami, P. M., Peral, G. M., & Gilaberte, I. (2000). Open study of fluoxetine in children with autism. *Actas Esp Psiquiatr, 28*(6), 353–356.

Alderman, J., Wolkow, R., Chung, M., & Johnston, H. E. (1998). Sertraline treatment of children and adolescents with obsessive-compulsive disorder or depression: Pharmacokinetics, tolerability, and efficacy. *Journal of the American Academy of Child and Adolescent Psychiatry, 37,* 386–394.

Ambrosini, P. J., Wagner, K. D., Biederman, J., Blick, I., Tan, C., Elia, J., et al. (1999). Multicenter open-label sertraline study in adolescent outpatients with major depression. *Journal of the American Academy of Child and Adolescent Psychiatry, 38,* 566–572.

Apter, A., Ratzone, G., King, R. A., Weizman, A., Iancu, I., Binder, M., et al. (1994). Fluvoxamine open-label treatment of adolescent inpatients with obsessive-compulsive disorder or depression. *Journal of the American Academy of Child and Adolescent Psychiatry, 33,* 342–348.

Armenteros, J. L., & Lewis, J. E. (2002). Citalopram treatment for impulsive aggression in children and adolescents: An open pilot study. *Journal of the American Academy of Child and Adolescent Psychiatry, 41*(5), 522–529.

Attia, E., Haiman, C., Walsh, T., & Flater, S. R. (1998). Does fluoxetine augment the inpatient treatment of anorexia nervosa? *American Journal of Psychiatry, 155*(4), 548–551.

Bacaltchuk, J., & Hay, P. (2001). Antidepressants versus placebo for people with bulimia nervosa. *Cochrane Database Syst Rev,* (4), CD003391.

Barrickman, L., Noyes, R., Kuperman, S., Schumacher, E., & Verda, M. (1991). Treatment of ADHD with fluoxetine: A preliminary trial. *Journal of the American Academy of Child and Adolescent Psychiatry, 30,* 762–767.

Baumgartner, J. L., Emslie, G. J., & Crismon, M. L. (2002). Citalopram in children and adolescents with depression or anxiety. *The Annals of Pharmacotherapy, 36,* 1692–1697.

Benoit, M. (2003). FDA action on Paxil. American Academy of Child and Adolescent Psychiatry. Retrieved from http://www.aacap.org/Announcements/Paxil.htm

Birmaher, B., Waterman, G. S., Ryan, N., Cully, M., et al. (1994). Fluoxetine for childhood anxiety disorders. *Journal of the American Academy of Child and Adolescent Psychiatry, 33,* 993–999.

Black, B., & Uhde, T. W. (1992). Elective mutism as a variant of social phobia. *Journal of the American Academy of Child and Adolescent Psychiatry, 31,* 1090–1094.

Black, B., Uhde, T. W. (1994). Treatment of elective mutism with fluoxetine: A double blind placebo study. *Journal of the American Academy of Child and Adolescent Psychiatry, 33,* 1000–1006.

Black, B., & Uhde, T. W., & Tancer, M. E. (1992). Fluoxetine for the treatment of social phobia. *Journal of the American Academy of Child and Adolescent Psychiatry, 29,* 36–44.

Boulos, C., Kutcher, S., Gardner, D., & Young, E. (1992). An open naturalistic trial of fluoxetine in adolescents and young adults with treatment-resistant major depression. *Journal of Child and Adolescent Psychopharmacology, 2,* 103–111.

Burke, W. J., Gergel, I., Bose, A. (2002). Fixed-dose trial of the single isomer SSRI escitalopram in depressed outpatients. *Journal of Clinical Psychiatry, 63*(4), 331–336. Retrieved from http://www.ncbi.nlm.nih.gov/entrez/query.fcgi?cmd-Retrieve&db-PubMed&list_uids-12000207&dopt-Abstract

Carlson, J. S., Kratochwill, T. R., & Johnston, H. F. (1999). Sertraline treatment of 5 children diagnosed with selective mutism: A single-case research trial. *Journal of Child and Adolescent Psychopharmacology, 9,* 293–306.

Casat, C. D., Pleasants, D. Z., Schroeder, D. H., & Parler, D. W. (1989). Bupropion in children with attention deficit disorder. *Psychopharmacology Bulletin, 25,* 198–201.

Clay, T. H., Gualtieri, C. T., Evans, R. W., & Gullion, C. M. (1988). Clinical and neuropsychological effects of the novel anti-depressant bupropion. *Psychopharmacology Bulletin, 24,* 143–148.

Como, P. G., & Kurlan, R. (1991). An open-label trial of fluoxetine for obsessive-compulsive disorder in Gilles de la Tourette's syndrome. *Neurology, 41*(6), 872–874.

Conners, C. K., Casat, C. D., Gualtieri, C. T., Weller, E., Reader, M., Reiss, A., et al. (1996). Bupropion hydrochloride in attention deficit disorder with hyperactivity. *Journal of the American Academy of Child and Adolescent Psychiatry, 34,* 1314–1321.

Connor, K. M., Davidson, J. R., Weisler, R. H., & Ahearn, E. (1999). A pilot study of mirtazapine in post-traumatic stress disorder. *International Clinical Psychopharmacology, 14*(1), 29–31.

Cook, E. H., Rowlett, R., Jaselskis, C., & Leventhal, B. L. (1992). Fluoxetine treatment of children and adults with autistic disorder and mental retardation. *Journal of the American Academy of Child and Adolescent Psychiatry, 31,* 739–745.

Davidson, J.R.T., Weisler, R. H., Malik, M. L., & Connor, K. M. (1998). Treatment of posttraumatic stress disorder with nefazodone. *International Clinical Psychopharmacology, 13*(3), 111–113.

Daviss, W. B., Bentivoglio, P., Racusin, R., Brown, K. M., Bostic, J. Q., & Wiley, L. (2001). Bupropion sustained release in adolescents with comorbid attention-deficit/hyperactivity disorder and depression. *Journal of the American Academy of Child and Adolescent Psychiatry, 40*(3), 307–314.

DeLong, G. R., Teague, L. A., & Kamran, M. M. (1998). Effects of fluoxetine treatment in young children with idiopathic autism. *Developmental Medicine and Child Neurology, 40,* 551–562.

Domon, S. E., & Andersen, M. S. (2000). Nefazodone for PTSD. *Journal of the American Academy of Child and Adolescent Psychiatry, 39*(8), 942–943.

Dummit, E. S. III, Klein, R. G., Tancer, N. K., Asche, B., & Martin, J. (1996). Fluoxetine treatment of children with selective mutism: An open trial. *Journal of the American Academy of Child and Adolescent Psychiatry, 35,* 615–621.

Emslie, G. J., Findling, R. L., Rynn, M. A., Marcus, R. N., Fernandes, L. A., D'Amico, M. F., et al. (2002). Efficacy and safety of nefazadone in the treatment of adolescents with major depressive disorder. NCDEU 42nd Annual Meeting, Boca Raton, FL.

Emslie, G. J., Heiligenstein, J. H., Wagner, K. D., Hoog, S. L., Ernest, D. E., Brown, E., et al. (2002). Fluoxetine for acute treatment of depression in children and adolescents: A placebo-controlled, randomized clinical trial. *Journal of the American Academy of Child and Adolescent Psychiatry, 41*(10), 1205–1214.

Emslie, G. J., Rush, A. J., Weinberg, W. A., Kowatch, R. A., Hughes, C. W., Carmody, T., et al. (1997). A double-blind, randomized, placebo-controlled trial of fluoxetine in children and adolescents with depression. *Archives of General Psychiatry, 54,* 1031–1037.

Emslie, G. J., Wagner, K., Riddle, M., Birmaher, B., Geller, D., Rosenberg, D., et al. (2000). Efficacy and safety of paroxetine in juvenile OCD. Abstracted in the 47th Annual Scientific Proceedings of the Annual Meeting. *American Academy of Child and Adolescent Psychiatry,* New York.

Fabian, T. J., Amico, J. A., Kroboth, P. D., Mulsant, B. H., Reynolds, C. F. III , & Pollock, B. G. (2002). Paroxetine-induced hyponatremia in older depressed patients: A prospective study. Abstracted in the NCDEU 42nd Annual Meeting, Boca Raton, FL.

Fairbanks, J. M., Pine, D. S., Tancer, N. K., Dummit E. S. III, Kenetgen, L. M., Martin, J., et al. (1997). Open fluoxetine treatment of mixed anxiety disorders in children and adolescents. *Journal of Child and Adolescent Psychopharmacology, 7,* 17–29.

Fassino, S., Leombruni, P., Daga, G. A., et al. (2002). Efficacy of citalopram in anorexia nervosa: A pilot study. *European Neuropsychopharmacology, 12,* 453–459.

Fatemi, S. H., Realmuto, G. M., Khan, L., & Thuras, P. (1998). Fluoxetine in treatment of adolescent patients with autism: A longitudinal open trial. *Journal of Autism and Developmental Disorders, 28*(4), 303–307.

Ferguson, C. P., La Via, M. C., Crossan, P. J., & Kaye, W. H. (1999). Are serotonin selective reuptake inhibitors effective in underweight anorexia nervosa? *International Journal of Eating Disorders, 25,* 11–17.

Findling, R. L. (1996). Open-label treatment of comorbid depression and attention-deficit disorder. *Journal of Child and Adolescent Psychopharmacology, 6*(3), 165–175.

Findling, R. L., Preskorn, S. H., Marcus, R. N., Magnus, R. D., D'Amico, R., Marathe, P., et al. (2000). Nefazodone pharmacokinetics in depressed children and adolescents. *Journal of the American Academy of Child and Adolescent Psychiatry, 39,* 1008–1016.

Findling, R. L., Reed, M. D., Myers, C., O'Riordan, M. A., Fiala, S., Branicky, L., et al. (1999). Paroxetine pharmacokinetics in depressed children and adolescents. *Journal of the American Academy of Child and Adolescent Psychiatry, 38,* 952–959.

Findling, R. L., Schwartz, M. A., Flannery, D. J., & Manos, M. J. (1996). Venlafaxine in adults with attention-deficit/hyperactivity disorder: An open clinical trial. *Journal of Clinical Psychology, 57*(5), 184–189.

Food and Drug Administration. (FDA). (2003). FDA Talk Paper, 1, 1–2. FDA web site T03–01.

Food and Drug Administration. (FDA). (1998). Regulations requiring manufacturers to assess the safety and effectiveness of new drugs and biological products in pediatric patients: Final rule. 63 (Dec. 2): 66631–72.

Food and Drug Administration Modernization Act of 1997. (1997). 27 USC 321.

Fukuda, T., Sugie, H., Ito, M., & Sugie, Y. (2001). Clinical evaluation of treatment with fluvoxamine, a selective serotonin reuptake inhibitor in children with autistic disorder. *No To Hattatsu, 33*(4), 314–318.

Gammon, G. D., & Brown, T. E. (1993). Fluoxetine and methylphenidate in combination for treatment of attention deficit disorder and comorbid depressive order. *Journal of Child and Adolescent Psychopharmacology, 3,* 1–10.

Geller, D. A., Hoog, S. L., Heiligenstein, J. H., Ricardi, R. K., Tamura, R., Kluszynski, S., Jacobson, J. G., Fluoxetine Pediatric OCD Study Team. (2001). Fluoxetine treatment for obsessive-compulsive disorder in children and adolescents: A placebo-controlled clinical trial. *Journal of the American Academy of Child and Adolescent Psychiatry, 40*(7), 773–779.

Ghaziuddin, N., & Alessi, N. E. (1992). An open clinical trial of trazodone in aggressive children. *Journal of Child and Adolescent Psychopharmacology, 2,* 291–297.

Hazell, P., O'Connell, D., Heathcote, D., Robertson, J., & Henry, D. (1995). Efficacy of tricyclic drugs in treating child and adolescent depression: A meta-analysis. *British Medical Journal, 310*(6984), 897–901.

Hesse, L. M., Venkatakrishnan, K., Court, M. H., et al. (2000). CYP2B6 mediates the in vitro hydroxylation of bupropion: Potential drug interactions with other antidepressants. *Drug Metabolism & Disposition, 28*(10), 1176–83.

Hollander, E., Kaplan, A., Cartwright, C., & Reichman, D. (2000). Venlafaxine in children, adolescents, and young adults with autism spectrum disorders: An open retrospective clinical report. *Journal of Child Neurology, 15*(2), 132–135.

IMS Health. Retrieved January 2002, from http://www.ims-global.com

Jain, U., Birmaher, B., Garcia, M., Al-Shabbout, M., & Ryan, N. (1992). Fluoxetine in children and adolescents with mood disorders: A chart review of efficacy and adverse effects. *Journal of Child and Adolescent Psychopharmacology, 2,* 259–265.

Jain, A. K., Kaplan, R. A., Gadde, K. M., Wadden, T. A., et al. (2002). Bupropion SR vs. placebo for weight loss in obese patients with depressive symptoms. *Obesity Research, 10*(10), 1049–1056.

Kallepalli, B. R., Bhatara, V. S., Fogas, B. S., Tervo, R. C., & Misra, L. K. (1997). Trazodone is only slightly faster than fluoxetine in relieving insomnia in adolescents with depressive disorders. *Journal of Child and Adolescent Psychopharmacology, 7*(2), 97–107.

Kaye, W. H., Gendall, K., & Strober, M. (1998). Serotonin neuronal function and selective serotonin reuptake inhibitor treatment in anorexia and bulimia nervosa. *Biological Psychiatry, 44*(9), 825–838.

Kaye, W. H., Nagata, T., Weltzin, T. E., et al. (2001). Double-blind placebo-controlled administration of fluoxetine in restricting- and restricting-purging-type anorexia nervosa. *Biological Psychiatry, 49,* 644–652.

Keller, M. B., Ryan N. D., Strober, M., et al. (2001). Efficacy of paroxetine in the treatment of adolescent major depression: A randomized, controlled trial. *Journal of the American Academy of Child and Adolescent Psychiatry, 40,* 762–772.

Kessler, J., & Samuels, S. C. (1996). Sertraline and hyponatremia. [Letter] *New England Journal of Medicine, 335*(7), 524.

Kurlan, R., Como, P. G., Deeley, C., & McDermott, M., et al. (1993). A pilot controlled study of fluoxetine for obsessive-compulsive symptoms in children with tourette's syndrome. *Clinical Neuropharmacology, 16*(2),167–172.

Kutcher, S., Boulos, C., Ward, B., Marton, P., Simeon, J., Ferguson, H. B., et al. (1994). Response to desipramine treatment in adolescent depression: A fixed-dose, placebo-controlled trial. *Journal of the American Academy of Child and Adolescent Psychiatry, 33*(5), 686–694.

Lepola, U. M., Loft, H., & Reines, E. H. (2003). Escitalopram (10–20 mg/day) is effective and well tolerated in a placebo-controlled study in depression in primary care. *International Clinical Psychopharmacology, 18*(4), 211–217. Retrieved from http://www.ncbi.nlm.nih.gov/entrez/query.fcgi?cmd-Retrieve&db-PubMed&list_uids-12817155&dopt-Abstract

Liu, B. A., Mittmann, N., Knowles, S. R., & Shear, N. H. (1996). Hyponatremia and the syndrome of inappropriate secretion of antidiuretic hormone associated with the use of selective serotonin reuptake inhibitors: A review of spontaneous reports. *Canadian Medical Association Journal, 155*(5), 519–527.

Mandoki, M. W., Tapia, M. R., Tapia, M. A., & Sumner, G. S. (1997). Venlafaxine in the treatment of children and adolescents with major depression. *Psychopharmacology Bulletin, 33,* 149–154.

March, J. S., Biederman, J., Wolkow, R., Safferman, A., Mardekian, H., Cook, E. H., et al. (1998). Sertraline in children and adolescents with obsessive-compulsive disorder: A multicenter randomized controlled trial. *Journal of the American Medical Association, 280,* 1752–1756.

McConville, B. J., Minnery, K. L., Sorter, M. T., West, S. A., Friedman, L. M., & Christian, K. (1996). An open study of the effects of sertraline on adolescent major depression. *Journal of Child and Adolescent Psychopharmacology, 6,* 41–51.

McDougle, C. J., Dresch, L. E., & Posey, D. J. (2000). Repetitive thoughts and behavior in pervasaive developmental disorders: Treatment with serotonin reuptake inhibitors. *Journal of Autism and Developmental Disorders, 30*(5), 427–435.

Motavalli, N. (1995). Fluoxetine for (s)elective mutism. *Journal of the American Academy of Child and Adolescent Psychiatry, 33,* 1000–1006.

Nixon, M. K., Milin, R., Simeon, J. G., Cloutier, P., & Spenst, W. (2001). Sertraline effects in adolescent major depression and dysthymia: A six-month open trial. *Journal of Child and Adolescent Psychopharmacology, 11*(2), 131–142.

Nutt, D. J. (2002). Tolerability and safety aspects of mirtazapine. *Human Psychopharmacology, 17*(1), 37–41.

Olfson, M., Marcus, S. C., Druss, B., Elinson, L., Tanielian, T., & Pincus, H. A. (2002). National trends in the outpatient treatment of depression. *Journal of the American Academy of Child and Adolescent Psychiatry, 41*(7), 837.

Olvera, R. L., Pliszka, S. R., Luh, J., & Tatum, R. (1996). An open trial of venlafaxine in the treatment of attention-deficit/hyperactivity disorder in children and adolescents. *Journal of Child and Adolescent Psychopharmacology, 6,* 241–250.

Ottervanger, J. P., Stricker, B. H., Huls, J., & Weeda, J. N. (1994). Bleeding attributed to the intake of paroxetine. *American Journal of Psychiatry, 151*(5), 781–782.

Peral, M., Alcami, M., & Gilaberte, I. (1999). Fluoxetine in children with autism. *Journal of the American Academy of Child and Adolescent Psychiatry, 38,* 1472–1473.

Peterson, C. B., & Mitchell, J. E. (1999). Psychosocial and pharmacological treatment of eating disorders: A review of research findings. *Journal of Clinical Psychology, 55*(6), 685–697.

Physician's desk reference (PDR). (56th ed.). (2002). Montvale, NJ: Medical Economics Co.

Pigott, T. A., L'Heureux, F., Rubenstein, C. S., Bernstein, S. E., et al. (1992). A double-blind, placebo controlled study of trazodone in patients with obsessive-compulsive disorder. *Journal of Clinical Psychopharmacology, 12*(3), 156–162.

Popper, C. W. (1992). Are clinicians ahead of researchers in finding a treatment for adolescent depression? [Editorial] *Journal of Child and Adolescent Psychopharmacology, 2,* 1–3.

Posey, D. J., Guenin, K. D., Kohn, A. E., Swiezy, N. B., & McDougle, C. J. (2001). A naturalistic open-label study of mirtazapine in autistic and other pervasaive developmental disorders. *Journal of Child and Adolescent Psychopharmacology, 11*(3), 267–277.

Riddle, M. A., Hardin, M. T., et al. (1990). Fluoxetine treatment of children and adolescents with tourette's and obsessive compulsive disorders: Preliminary clinical experience. *Journal of the American Academy of Child and Adolescent Psychiatry, 29*(1), 45–48.

Riddle, M. A., King, R. A., Hardin, M. T., Scahill, L., Ort, S. I., Chappel, P., et al. (1990). Behavioral side effects of fluoxetine in children and adolescents. *Journal of Child and Adolescent Psychopharmacology, 1,* 193–198.

Riddle, M. A., Reeve, E. A., Yaryura-Tobias, J. A., Yang, H. M., Claghorn, J. L., Gaffney, G., et al. (2001). Fluvoxamine for children and adolescents with obsessive-compulsive disorder: A randomized, controlled, multicenter trial. *Journal of the American Academy of Child and Adolescent Psychiatry, 40*(2), 222–229.

Riddle, M. A., Scahill, I., King, R. A., Hardin, M. T., Anderson, G. M., Ort, S. I., et al. (1992). Double-blind, crossover trial of fluoxetine and placebo in children and adolescents with obsessive-compulsive disorder. *Journal of the American Academy of Child and Adolescent Psychiatry, 31,* 1062–1069.

Riggs, P. D., Leon, S. L., Mikulich, S. K., & Pottle, L. C. (1998). An open trial of bupropion for ADHD in adolescents with substance use disorders and conduct disorder. *Journal of the American Academy of Child and Adolescent Psychiatry, 37*(12), 1271–1278.

Rosenberg, D. R., Stewart, C. M., Fitzgerald, K. D., Tawile, V., & Carroll, E. (1999). Paroxetine open-label treatment of pediatric outpatients with obsessive-compulsive disorder. *Journal of the American Academy of Child and Adolescent Psychiatry, 38,* 1180–1185.

Rotzinger, S., Bourin, M., Akimoto, Y., Coutts, R. T., & Baker, G. B. (1999). Metabolism of some "second"- and "fourth"-generation antidepressants: Iprindole, viloxazine, bupropion, mianserin, maprotiline, trazodone, nefazodone, and venlafaxine. *Cellular and Molecular Neurobiology, 19*(4), 427–442.

Saccomani, L., Rizzo, P., & Nobili, L. (2000). Combined treatment with Haloperidol and Trazodone in patients with tic disorders. *Journal of Child and Adolescent Psychopharmacology, 10*(4), 307–310.

Scahill, L., Riddle, M. A., et al. (1997). Fluoxetine has no marked effect on tic symptoms in patients with tourette's syndrome: A double-blind placebo-controlled study. *Journal of Child and Adolescent Psychopharmacology, 7*(2), 75–85.

Schur, S. B., Sikich, L., Findling, R. L., Malone, R. P., Crismon, M. L., & Derivan, A. (2002). Treatment recommendations for the use of antipsychotics for aggressive youth (TRAAY). Part I: A review. *Journal of the American Academy of Child and Adolescent Psychiatry, 42*(2), 132–144.

Seedat, S., Lockhat, R., Kaminer, D., Zungu-Dirwayi, N., & Stein, D. J. (2001). An open trial of citalopram in adolescents with post-traumatic stress disorder. *International Clinical Psychopharmacology, 16*(1), 21–25.

Simeon, J. G., Ferguson, H. B., & Fleet, J.V.W. (1986). Bupropion effects in attention deficit and conduct disorder. *Canadian Journal of Psychiatry, 31,* 581–585.

Stahl, S. M., Gergel, I., & Dayong, L. (2002). Escitalopram in the treatment of panic disorder. Abstracted in NCDEU 42nd Annual Meeting, Boca Raton, FL.

Steingard, R. J., Zimnitsky, B., DeMaso, D. R., Bauman, M. L., & Bucci, J. P. (1997). Sertraline treatment of transition-associated anxiety and agitation in children with autistic disorder. *Journal of Child and Adolescent Psychopharmacology, 7,* 9–15.

Strachan, J., & Shepherd, J. (1998). Hyponatraemia associated with the use of selective serotonin reuptake inhibitors. *Australian New Zealand Journal of Psychiatry, 32*(2), 295–298.

Strober, M., Pataki, C., Freeman, R., & DeAntonio, M. (1999). No effect of adjunctive fluoxetine on eating behavior or weight during the inpatient treatment of anorexia nervosa: An historical control study. *Journal of Child and Adolescent Psychopharmacology, 9*(3), 195–201.

Taylor, I. C., & McConnell, J. G. (1995). Severe hyponatraemia associated with selective serotonin reuptake inhibitors. *Scottish Medical Journal, 40*(5), 147–148.

Thomsen, P. H. (1997). Child and adolescent obsessive-compulsive disorder treated with citalopram: Findings from a open trial of 23 cases. *Journal of Child and Adolescent Psychopharmacology, 7,* 157–166.

Tierney, E., Joshi, P. T., Llinas, J. F., Rosenberg, L.L.A., & Riddle, M. A. (1995). Sertraline for major depression in children and adolescents: Preliminary clinical experience. *Journal of Child and Adolescent Psychopharmacology, 5,* 13–27.

U.S. Food and Drug Administration. (2003). FDA issues public health advisory entitled: Reports of Suicidality in pediatric patients being treated with antidepressant medications for major depressive disorder (MDD). Retrieved from http://www.fda.gov/bbs/topics/ANSWERS/2003/ANS1256.html

U.S. Food and Drug Administration. (2003). FDA statement regarding the anti-depressant Paxil for pediatric population. Retrieved from http://www.fda.gov/bbs/topics/ANSWERS/2003/ANS1230.html

Wade, A., Michael Lemming, O., & Bang, Hedegaard, K. (2002). Escitalopram 10 mg/day is effective and well tolerated in a placebo-controlled study in depression in primary care. *International Clinical Psychopharmacology, 17*(3), 95–102. Retrieved from http://www.ncbi.nlm.nih.gov/entrez/query.fcgi?cmd-Retrieve&db-PubMed&list_uids-11981349&dopt-Abstract

Wagner, K. D., Robb, A. S., Findling, R., & Tiseo, P. F. (2001). Citalopram treatment of pediatric depression: Results of a placebo-controlled trial. Sponsored by Hirschfeld RMA. Presented at American College of Neuropsychopharmacology, Waikoloa, HI.

Wagner, K. D., & Wohlberg, C. J. (2002). Efficacy and safety of sertraline in the treatment of pediatric major depressive disorder (MDD). Presented at the American Psychiatric Association 155th Annual Meeting, Philadelphia, PA.

Walkup, J. T., Labellarte, M. J., Riddle, M. A., Pine, D. S., Greenhill, L., Klein, R., et al. (2001). Fluvoxamine for the treatment of anxiety disorders in children and adolescents. *New England Journal of Medicine, 344*(17), 1279–1285.

Weintrob, N., Cohen, D., Klipper-Aurback, Y., et al. (2002). Decreased growth during therapy with selective serotonin reuptake inhibitors. *Archives of Pediatric and Adolescent Medicine, 156,* 696–701.

Wilens, T. E., Spencer, T. J., Biederman, J., & Schleifer, D. (1997). Case study: Nefazodone for juvenile mood disorders. *Journal of the American Academy of Child and Adolescent Psychiatry, 36,* 481–485.

Zubieta, J. K., & Alessi, N. E. (1992). Acute and chronic administration of trazodone in the treatment of disruptive behavior disorders in children. *Journal of Clinical Psychopharmacology, 12,* 346–351.

CHAPTER THIRTEEN

MOOD STABILIZERS: USE IN PEDIATRIC PSYCHOPHARMACOLOGY

Kiki D. Chang, M.D., and
Diana I. Simeonova, Dipl.-Psych.

The term *mood stabilizer* carries multiple connotations. Some feel that a mood stabilizer is an agent that is effective in treating at least one mood state of bipolar disorder and that does not exacerbate the other mood state (Keck & McElroy, 2003). For example, lithium is effective for acute mania and does not exacerbate depression. Yet others argue that mood stabilizers should have proven efficacy in preventing relapse in the maintenance treatment of bipolar disorder. Perhaps the ideal mood stabilizer would have acute and maintenance efficacy for both mania and depression. Nevertheless, due to the increasing use and efficacy of these agents for conditions outside of bipolar disorder, they may eventually be renamed to more specifically describe their actions. For now, the class of mood stabilizers usually refers to those medications that are useful in treating bipolar disorder, such as lithium, and anticonvulsants, but not including antipsychotics.

Lithium was the first of these agents to be discovered. Thus, being the oldest, lithium has had the most reported use in child psychiatric conditions. Despite this fact, there are relatively few well-controlled studies of lithium in pediatric populations in the literature. Therefore, one would correctly expect that the anticonvulsants, as relatively newer agents, have even less preponderance of well-controlled studies in children. However, with the growing support for pediatric psychopharmacological research (see Chapter 9), there are increasing numbers of studies of anticonvulsants for the treatment of pediatric psychiatric disorders under way.

In this chapter, we will present the various mood stabilizers, including anti-convulsants that have potential mood stabilization properties, and discuss what empirical data exists for their use in child psychiatry. As will be seen, while the older, more established agents, such as lithium, valproate, and carbamazepine, have more data on the efficacy in treating psychiatric conditions, there are also more data on adverse effects. This is typical of how psychotropic agents develop after becoming available for use: there is first great promise and burgeoning efficacy data, with little known of long- or short-term adverse effects. Then the longer the drug is used, the more is known about both its positive and negative effects. Thus, it should be remembered that while the older agents appear to have more serious potential for adverse effects, they are better studied, and the newer agents simply have not yet had the same level of scrutiny. With these limitations in mind, we will end this chapter by discussing our currently recommended approaches to using these agents in pediatric populations.

Lithium

Lithium is the oldest and first mood stabilizer to be used successfully for mania. It has been approved by the United States Federal Drug Administration (FDA) since 1974 for the treatment of mania in adults and children over twelve-years-old.

Chemical Makeup

Lithium is available as 150-mg or 300-mg tabs and 150-mg, 300-mg, or 600-mg capsules. Lithium citrate is available in suspension form of 300 mg/5 mL. There are also slow-release preparations that may aid in BID dosing and possibly decrease gastrointestinal (GI) side effects (Eskalith CR in 450-mg tabs and Lithobid in 300-mg tabs).

Mechanism of Action

Lithium's exact mechanism of action is unknown. It is a monovalent cation that had been used as a panacea for a wide variety of conditions in the nineteenth and early twentieth centuries, including gout, arthritis, and "moodiness." Lithium augments 5-hydroxytryptamine function by increasing tryptophan uptake. Regarding second-messenger systems, lithium inhibits inositol monophosphate, decreasing intracellular myoinositol and reducing levels of cyclic AMP. It also inhibits protein kinase C and upregulates the neuroprotective protein Bcl-2 (Manji, Moore, & Chen, 1999). Furthermore, grey matter increases have been seen directly (via MRI) and indirectly (via magnetic resonance spectroscopy) in bipolar patients treated with lithium (Moore, Bebchuk, Hasanat et al., 2000; G. J. Moore, Bebchuk et al., 2000).

Dosing and Pharmacokinetics

Dosing is titrated to achieve serum levels of 0.6 to 1.2 mEq/L (Weller, Weller, & Fristad, 1986), based on levels found to be effective in adults with mania. Recommended serum lithium levels are based on adult data and are from 0.8 to 1.2 mEq/L for acute mania. Maintenance levels may be in the 0.6 to 1.0 mEq/L range. It is important to note that due to increased glomerular filtration rates, children may need dosing approximating that of adults to achieve similar serum levels. Recent brain imaging data suggest that children have lower brain to serum ratios of lithium levels (Moore et al., 2002)—that is, children may have more efficient sodium pumps in the brain that expel lithium—therefore, it is possible that children may require higher serum lithium levels to achieve clinical efficacy. This, however, remains to be studied. Brain levels in adults may need to be at least 0.2 mEq/L to have therapeutic effects (Kato, Shioiri, Inubushi, & Takahashi, 1993).

Nomograms have been developed that may be used to load the initial dose, in cases of acute mania such as one that requires hospitalization. These nomograms involve starting with a 600-mg dose (300-mg in preschoolers) and checking a serum level twenty-four hours later to guide subsequent dosing (Cooper, Bergner, & Simpson, 1973). In an outpatient or less acute setting, to decrease adverse effects lithium can be started at 150 mg to 300 mg daily, and titrated to 450 mg to 900 mg in BID dosing. (Target is 30 mg/kg/day.) Pharmacokinetics are similar for lithium in children under twelve-years-old as in adults, with a trend toward a shorter elimination half life and a higher total clearance (Vitiello et al., 1988).

Lithium is well absorbed in the GI system. It is not protein-bound and its half life is approximately eighteen to twenty-four hours. Lithium is not metabolized and is excreted unchanged by the kidneys.

Adverse Effects Profile

The most common adverse effects of lithium reported in children include polyuria, tremor, acne, weight gain, and nausea (Tueth, Murphy, & Evans, 1998). Particularly relevant to the treatment of bipolar disorder is the possibility of lithium-induced hypothyroidism. Lithium is concentrated in the thyroid and by various mechanisms may decrease secretion of thyroid hormone and induce a hypothyroid state (Lazarus, 1998). One study reported subclinical hypothyroidism in 39% of patients with mood disorders taking lithium (Deodhar, Singh, Pathak, Sharan, & Kulhara, 1999). Subclinical hypothyroidism refers to thyroid index abnormalities (such as a high thyroid stimulating hormone [TSH] or low free thyroxine [T4]) in the absence of *physical* symptoms of hypothyroidism. Subclinical hypothyroidism may be found at higher rates in adults with rapid cycling bipolar disorder (Bauer,

Whybrow, & Winokur, 1990; Cowdry, Wehr, Zis, & Goodwin, 1983) and mixed manic states (Chang et al., 1998) regardless of lithium treatment. Subsequent treatment with thyroxine in these adults has been shown to decrease rapid-cycling (M. S. Bauer & Whybrow, 1990). However, thyroid replacement has not been as well studied in children with bipolar disorder (BD), with only two positive case reports of efficacy (Davanzo & McCracken, 2000; Weeston & Constantino, 1996). Furthermore, it is not clear if long-term lithium exposure increases the chance of developing hypothyroidism after initial exposure (Bocchetta et al., 2001).

Other adverse effects include cognitive impairment, polydipsia, enuresis, and sedation. Lithium may have teratogenic effects—historically it has been linked to Ebstein's anomaly, a cardiac malformation, in 1% of cases of prenatal use. However, more recent data suggest that the actual incidence may be less than 0.1% (Cohen, Friedman, Jefferson, Johnson, & Weiner, 1994). Lithium may also have cardiac effects, particularly on sinus node dysfunction. However, EKG monitoring is required only if there is a pre-existing or suspected underlying cardiac condition.

As lithium has been in use for many years, there are some long-term data regarding possible renal adverse effects. Therefore, it is recommended to obtain baseline laboratories, including a complete blood count (CBC), renal panel, and TSH, and in adolescent females, a β-hCG. If cardiac abnormalities are suspected, an EKG is indicated. Serum lithium levels as well as a renal panel, CBC, and TSH should be drawn every six months when the dose is stabilized and rechecked with changes in dose or clinical status. The half life of lithium is twelve to twenty-seven hours, and so levels should be checked four to five days after a stable dose has been achieved.

Drug Interactions and Contraindications

Lithium levels may be increased by medications that affect glomerular filtration rate, including thiazide diuretics, non-steroidal anti-inflammatory drugs (NSAIDS), ACE inhibitors, as well as dehydration and renal disease (Wang & Ketter, 2002). Levels may be decreased by osmotic diuretics, methylxanthines (caffeine, theophylline), and during pregnancy or mania.

Empirical Data

Lithium has been studied for pediatric mania more than other medications. In the first published double-blind placebo-controlled study of a mood stabilizer in pediatric BD, Geller and colleagues (Geller, Cooper, Sun et al., 1998) reported on twenty-five adolescents with BD, or major depressive disorder (MDD) and strong family histories of BD, treated with either lithium or placebo over a six-week period. Six out of thirteen adolescents taking lithium had a significant decrease in manic symptoms, compared to only one out of twelve on placebo. In this study, substance abuse was also significantly decreased in the lithium group. Multiple open studies of lithium have also supported its efficacy in pediatric BD (DeLong, 1978; Hassanyeh & Davison, 1980; Hsu, 1986; Kowatch et al., 2000; McKnew et al., 1981; Strober et al., 1988; Varanka, Weller, Weller, & Fristad, 1988) (See Table 13.1.)

In one open prospective trial of lithium in hundred acutely manic adolescents, sixty-three subjects met response criteria on at least a 33% decrease in the YMRS score and a 1 or a 2 on the CGI-I by week four (Kafantaris, Coletti, Dicker, Padula, & Kane, 2003). Furthermore, twenty-six subjects achieved "remission" by week four, defined as a YMRS of less than 7. No variables could be detected that predicted response status.

TABLE 13.1.   STUDIES OF LITHIUM IN PEDIATRIC BIPOLAR DISORDER.

Year	First Author	Ages (years)	Disorder	Improved	
1980	Hassanyeh	13–15	Bipolar	6/7	(86%)
1981	McKnew	6–12	Cyclothymia	2/2	(100%)
			Other	0/4	(0%)
1986	Hsu	14–19	Bipolar	11/14	(79%)
1987	DeLong	3–20	Bipolar	39/59	(66%)
1988	Varanka	6–12	Psychotic Mania	11/11	(100%)
1988	Strober	13–17	Bipolar	34/50	(68%)
1998	Geller	12–18	Bipolar/MDD	6/13	(46%)
2000	Kowatch	6–18	Bipolar I and II	5/13	(38%)
2003	Kafantaris	12–18		63/100	(63%)
			TOTAL	177/273	(65%)

TABLE 13.2.   STUDIES OF DIVALPROEX MONOTHERAPY IN PEDIATRIC BIPOLAR DISORDER.

Year	First Author	Ages (years)	Disorder	# Improved	
1994	West	12–17	Bipolar	9/11	(82%)
1995	Papatheorodou	12–20	Bipolar	12/15	(80%)
2000	Kowatch	6–18	Bipolar I and II	8/15	(53%)
2002	Wagner	7–19	Bipolar I and II	22/36	(61%)
			TOTAL	51/77	(66%)

Despite its history of high efficacy in classic adult euphoric mania, lithium monotherapy may still be ineffective in up to 40% of adults with classic mania (Calabrese & Woyshville, 1995). Furthermore, patients with mixed mania or rapid cycling may have even lower response rates to lithium (Calabrese & Woyshville, 1995; Prien, Himmelhoch, & Kupfer, 1988). This may be a significant limitation, as these states are commonly seen in pediatric forms of bipolar disorder (Findling et al., 2001; Geller et al., 1995). Strober and colleagues identified adolescents with BD having a prepubertal onset of any psychiatric disorder (Strober et al., 1988) and specifically attention-deficit/hyperactivity disorder (ADHD) (Strober et al., 1998) as more likely to be non-responsive to lithium. Other possible risk factors for lithium nonresponse in children include mixed states (Himmelhoch & Garfinkel, 1986) and presence of a comorbid personality disorder (Kutcher, Marton, & Korenblum, 1990).

Lithium has been used for the maintenance treatment of bipolar disorder, but the empirical evidence for this is not so clear. In ten maintenance studies including a placebo arm, 34% of patients taking lithium and 81% of patients taking placebo experienced relapses (Sachs & Thase, 2000). However, these have been mostly older studies (before 1980) and used cohorts who responded initially to lithium monotherapy. A study of adolescents with BD taking lithium found 92% of those discontinuing lithium to have a manic relapse within eighteen months, compared to 38% of those who continued lithium (Strober, Morrell, Lampert, & Burroughs, 1990). Other than in this study by Strober and colleagues, maintenance treatment with lithium has not been studied in children or adolescents.

Data from research in adult major depression support the efficacy of lithium added to antidepressants for refractory MDD (Bauer et al., 2000; Wilkinson, Holmes, Woolford, Stammers, & North, 2002). There have been reports in the literature of lithium having a similar augmentation effect in adolescents when combined with tricyclic antidepressants (Ryan, Meyer, Dachille, Mazzie, & Puig-Antich, 1988; Strober, Freeman, Rigali, Schmidt, & Diamond, 1992) and with venlafaxine (Walter, Lyndon, & Kubb, 1998). One might surmise that children and adolescents at genetic risk for development of BD presenting with depression would respond to lithium treatment. However, lithium monotherapy was no better than placebo in a study of depressed prepubertal patients with strong family histories of BD (Geller, Cooper, Zimerman et al., 1998).

Lithium has also been studied somewhat for the treatment of aggression associated with mental retardation (McCracken & Diamond, 1988; Tyrer, Walsh, Edwards, Berney, & Stephens, 1984), autism, and conduct disorder (Campbell et al., 1995).

Carbamazepine

Carbamazepine was approved by the United States FDA in 1968 for the treatment of neuralgia, and in 1974 and 1978 as an anticonvulsant in adults and children over six years, respectively. There are no FDA-approved psychiatric indications.

Chemical Makeup

Carbamazepine is a tricyclic anticonvulsant, resembling imipramine in structure. The medication is available as 100-mg and 200-mg tabs, and as a 100-mg/5-mL suspension. There are also slow release preparations that may aid in BID dosing. Tegretol XR uses an osmotic pump delivery system (OROS) and is available in 100-, 200-, and 400-mg tabs. Carbatrol uses a beaded delivery system, with different release times for each of three different beads. It is available in 200- and 300-mg capsules.

Mechanism of Action

As with most anticonvulsants, the mechanism of action is unknown. Carbamazepine blocks norepinephrine reuptake, but only 25% as much as imipramine (Purdy, Julien, Fairhurst, & Terry, 1977). It indirectly decreases GABA turnover and decreases brain glutamate levels. Carbamazepine (CBZ) may be especially effective at inhibiting neuronal discharge in limbic areas, including amygdalar-thalamo-cortical pathways (Evans & Gualtieri, 1985).

Dosing and Pharmacokinetics

Dosing is titrated to achieve serum levels of 4 to 12 ug/ml. These levels are based on the effective levels for control of epilepsy. Children six- to twelve-years-old may be started at 100 mg BID with an eventual target dose of 10 to 20 mg/kg/day, divided BID or TID. In adolescents, 400 to 1400 mg/day divided BID or TID is the recommended dose to achieve therapeutic serum levels of carbamazepine.

Carbamazepine is unevenly absorbed, with 80% bioavailability; 75% is protein bound. Carbamazepine is a strong enzyme inducer and inhibitor. It is extensively metabolized by the P450 system (3A3/4, 2C8) in the liver to carbamazepine-10, 11-epoxide (CBZ-E), an active metabolite. It induces its own metabolism, and so serum levels may be expected to decrease after three to five weeks of treatment. Therefore, serum levels should be checked one month after initiation and the dosage adjusted as necessary. The half life is initially twenty-five to sixty-five hours, which decreases to nine to fifteen hours after autoinduction occurs.

It is recommended that baseline laboratories be obtained, including CBC with differential, TSH, and liver function tests for all patients. In addition, a β-hCG should be obtained for sexually active females. Serum carbamazepine levels as well as liver function tests, CBC, and TSH should be drawn every three to six months when the dose is stabilized and rechecked with changes in dose. As the half life of carbamazepine is about twenty-four hours before autoinduction, serum levels should be checked four to five days after a stable dose has been achieved.

Adverse Effects Profile

The most common adverse effects of carbamazepine reported in children include sedation, dizziness, ataxia, blurred vision, nausea, and vomiting. Carbamazepine may lower plasma thyroxine. The most serious adverse effects are leukopenia and rash. Benign leukopenia may occur in one out of ten patients, but progression to aplastic anemia may occur in one out of 100,000 patients. Rash may also occur in one out of ten patients, but progression to Stevens-Johnson syndrome may occur in one out of 100,000 patients. For these reasons, it is recommended to monitor for low white blood cell (WBC) counts (or to monitor clinically for fever, bruising, or frequent infections) and rash. If either develops, more careful monitoring or discontinuation of carbamazepine is recommended.

There have also been case reports of mania (Pleak, Birmaher, Gavrilescu, Abichandani, & Williams, 1988; Reiss & O'Donnell, 1984) and tics (Evans & Gualtieri, 1985) caused by carbamazepine in children and adolescents.

Drug Interactions and Contraindications

Carbamazepine may lower levels of the following medications: antipsychotics (including haloperidol, olanzapine, risperidone, zipraisidone, clozapine), lamotrigine, valproate, topiramate, tiagabine, tricyclic antidepressants bupropion, mirtazipine, oral contraceptives, warfarin, and zonisamide.

The following medications may raise carbamazepine levels: azole antifungals, cimetidine, clarithrimycin, erythromycin, fluoxetine, fluvoxamine, nefazadone, omeprazole, and verapamil. Phenytoin may lower CBZ levels, while Valproate may increase levels of the carbamazepine epoxide.

Empirical Data

Carbamazepine has been reported effective in treating mania in adults in monotherapy (Ballenger & Post, 1980; Okuma, 1983) and as an adjunctive treatment to lithium (Bocchetta, Chillotti, Severino, Ardau, & Del Zompo, 1997). It is less clear if carbamazepine is as effective as lithium for maintenance therapy (Greil, Kleindienst, Erazo, & Muller-Oerlinghausen, 1998; Keck, Jr. & McElroy, 2002); however, for rapid cycling BD, it may be effective when added to lithium (Denicoff et al., 1997). Carbamazepine had become a mainstay of treatment for adult mania, but its use has since declined compared to lithium and valproate, likely due to its drug interactions and potentially serious, albeit rare, adverse effects. However, the positive effects of carbamazepine in BD had set the stage for valproate and the current wave of interest in anticonvulsants as mood stabilizers.

A recent placebo-controlled study using Carbatrol demonstrated superiority to placebo in treating adults with mania (Weisler, 2002). In this study, 204 patients with mixed or manic BD were randomized to Carbatrol or placebo for three weeks. Out of the 204 patients, 96 completed the study, with more subjects on Carbatrol than placebo (42% versus 22%) having at least a 50% decrease in Young Mania Rating Scale (YMRS) scores. Main adverse effects experienced by patients in the Carbatrol group were dizziness, nausea, and somnolence, with no differences in the number of serious adverse events (four) between the groups.

There is some empirical data to support the use of carbamazepine as a mood stabilizer in children. Carbamazepine has not been well studied in pediatric BD with case reports and studies of patients with mixed diagnoses contributing to the extant literature. Cases of successful treatment of adolescents with BD have been reported with carbamazepine monotherapy (Woolston, 1999) and adjunctive therapy with lithium (Hsu, 1986). Kowatch and colleagues found open carbamazepine monotherapy to be effective in treating four of thirteen (31%) children and adolescents with mania (Kowatch et al., 2000). Due to the relative lack of studies and greater potential for serious adverse effects such as neutropenia or aplastic anemia, carbamazepine has become a second or third line medication for pediatric BD. However, given its long track record of safety in pediatric epilepsy and efficacy in past adult bipolar trials, it would be useful to have additional studies of carbamazepine in pediatric BD.

Carbamazepine has been investigated in prepubertal conduct disorder, specifically to decrease aggressive behaviors. An open, uncontrolled study of ten patients found carbamazepine useful (Kafantaris et al., 1992), but another study of twenty-two patients found carbamazepine no better than placebo for treating aggression in prepubertal conduct disorder (Cueva et al., 1996).

In open studies, carbamazepine has been effective in improving childhood hyperactivity, aggression, dysphoria, and poor concentration (Remschmidt, 1976). A meta-analysis of studies using carbamazepine to treat behavioral problems in children, including three double-blind placebo-controlled studies, supported the efficacy of carbamazepine in treating ADHD symptoms such as hyperactivity, impulsivity, and inattention (Silva, Munoz, & Alpert, 1996).

Valproate

Valproate was approved by the United States FDA for use in adults with partial and complex seizures in 1978.

Chemical Makeup

Valproate is an eight-carbon branched-chain fatty acid. Divalproex sodium is the conjugated form of valproic acid marketed as Depakote, which is often preferred due to causing decreased GI disturbance. Divalproex is available in 125-mg sprinkles; 125-, 250-, and 500-mg tabs, and 250- and 500-mg extended release tabs (Depakote-ER). It is also available in intravenous formulation (Depacon), which is usually used for acute seizure control. Generic valproic acid is available as 250-mg capsules or a 250-mg/5 mL syrup.

Mechanism of Action

Valproate blocks sodium channels and modulates gamma-amino-butyric-acid (GABA) function. There is interesting recent data on its effect on inhibiting protein kinase C, an effect it shares with lithium (Manji, Moore, & Chen, 2000). Valproate may also affect other second-messenger systems, promote neuroprotective proteins, and inhibit apoptotic proteins (Manji et al., 2000).

Dosing and Pharmacokinetics

Valproate is readily absorbed by the GI system. Peak serum levels are obtained two to four hours after administration; food delays this to five to six hours. The half life is eight to sixteen hours in children and adolescents. It is highly protein bound and extensively metabolized in the liver (Cloyd, Fischer, Kriel, & Kraus, 1993). Valproate may have "sublinear kinetics," resulting in greater dose increases needed at higher doses to achieve serum-level increases (Wang & Ketter, 2002).

The recommended dosage in pediatric patients is 15 to 20 mg/kg/day in two to three divided doses. Dosing may be initiated by loading at 15 mg/kg/day, which should achieve a serum level of 50 to 120 mcg/ml by day five. Overweight children may have higher than therapeutic serum levels and more adverse effects if loaded at 15 mg/kg/day (Good, Feaster, & Krecko, 2001). The therapeutic range for mania, based on adult studies, is 50 to 100 mcg/ml. However, a more optimum range for manic adults and adolescents may be 75 to 120 mcg/ml (Chang & Ketter, 2001). On an outpatient or less urgent basis, in order to decrease adverse effects, dosing may be initiated at 125 to 250 mg QHS, and increased by 125 to 250 mg every three to four days to achieve desired serum levels. Typical maintenance doses in children and adolescents range from 375 mg/day to 2,000 mg/day. Based on five half lives achieving a serum steady-state, serum levels should be checked five days after a stable dose is achieved.

Depakote ER should be dosed at approximately 20% higher doses than divalproex, as serum levels are generally 10–20% lower (Dutta et al., 2002). Depakote ER may be more tolerable secondary to less GI adverse effects and less weight gain. However, Depakote ER has not yet been studied in acute mania and has been FDA approved only for the treatment of migraine headaches at this time.

Baseline chemistries should be obtained before administration of divalproex, including CBC with differential, liver enzymes, and amylase in all patients. In post-menarchal females, a β-hCG should be obtained. Serum levels, liver enzymes, and CBC should be rechecked every three months for the first six months, then every three to six months thereafter.

Adverse Effects Profile

The most common adverse effects reported in children and adolescents are nausea, sedation, tremor, dizziness, and weight gain (McDougle, Stern, & Bangs, 2001). Less frequently, hair loss and thrombocytopenia may occur. Hepatotoxicity, while rare, may be fatal and has been mostly reported in children under two years taking other anticonvulsants concurrently (Bryant & Dreifuss, 1996). Similarly, pancreatitis is an uncommon side effect but may progress to fulminant, life-threatening pancreatitis. Thus, valproate carries a black box warning mandated by the FDA to monitor carefully for abdominal pain and early signs of pancreatitis, which includes checking a serum amylase level at the first sign of significant abdominal pain. Valproate has also been associated with a 1.5% risk of neural tube defects in babies born to mothers taking the drug while pregnant, thought to be secondary to reduction of serum folate levels (Samren et al., 1997).

Relevant to the treatment of adolescent females, there has been concern about the possibility of polycystic ovary syndrome (PCOS) due to a report of a higher incidence of polycystic ovaries (PCO) in epileptic women taking divalproex compared to women taking other antiepileptics (Isojarvi, Laatikainen, Pakarinen, Juntunen, & Myllyla, 1993). However, it is not clear if this finding was due to a direct effect of divalproex or to other possible explanations, including obesity leading to increased peripheral estrogen conversion to testosterone or direct hormonal effects of the particular seizure disorders in those women taking divalproex (Isojarvi et al., 1996). More importantly, the presence of PCO is not necessarily pathologic, as they occur in 17–22% of the female population, and up to 25% of women with PCO diagnosed by ultrasound have no endocrine or menstrual difficulties (Ernst & Goldberg, 2002). More recent studies found no increased incidence of PCOS in women with epilepsy taking divalproex compared to other antiepileptics (Bauer, Jarre, Klingmuller, & Elger, 2000) or in women with BD taking divalproex compared to lithium (Rasgon et al., 2000). Menstrual irregularities in the women with BD were also found to have preceded treatment with mood stabilizers (Rasgon et al., 2000). Therefore, although it appears that women with seizure disorders, and possibly BD, may have higher incidences of PCO, it is not currently clear that there is a true association between PCOS and divalproex therapy.

Drug Interactions and Contraindications

VPA is a weak inhibitor, and thus may raise levels of CBZ-E, LTG, tricyclic antidepressants, and benzodiazepines. Due to protein-binding interactions, VPA may increase free diazepam, CBZ, tiagabine, and warfarin. VPA levels may be decreased by CBZ, phenytoin, and increased by cimetidine, erythromycin, phenothiazines, and fluoxetine. VPA is relatively contraindicated in children under six-years-old, in patients with uncontrolled medical illness, and in co-administration with clonazepam (Davanzo & McCracken, 2000).

Empirical Data

Valproate has established efficacy in the treatment of acute mania in adults (Bowden et al., 1994). Furthermore, a maintenance study has suggested that valproate is superior to placebo or lithium in preventing depressive episodes in BD, but it has not yet been shown to be a superior prophylaxis for mania (Bowden et al., 2000). Valproate may also be more effective than lithium for mixed states and rapid-cycling BD in adults (Calabrese, Markovitz, Kimmel, & Wagner, 1992; Calabrese, Rapport, Kimmel, Reece, & Woyshville, 1993).

There have been no published placebo-controlled studies of valproate in children and adolescents who have BD. Numerous open data, however, support its acute efficacy in this population. There have been three case series of adolescents with BD treated with divalproex, two of which included some of the same patients (Papatheodorou & Kutcher, 1993; Papatheodorou, Kutcher, Katic, & Szalai, 1995; West, Keck, & McElroy, 1994). The largest of these series studied fifteen adolescents and young adults, fifteen- to twenty-years-old, over a seven-week open divalproex trial (Papatheodorou et al., 1995). All subjects required additional medications for acute symptom management. At the end of the trial, eight subjects were considered markedly improved and four moderately improved.

In an open study of forty-two children and adolescents with BD randomized to either lithium, divalproex, or carbamazepine, six out of fifteen subjects responded to divalproex monotherapy (Kowatch et al., 2000). In this trial, the authors noted that the divalproex group would often show worsening mood and behavior symptoms at three weeks of treatment. However, if parents tolerated this period, by week four these symptoms generally resolved and patients continued to improve afterward (Kowatch et al., 2000). In another study of open divalproex monotherapy, twenty-two out of forty patients with mania (61%), aged seven- to nineteen-years-old, responded over two to eight weeks, as measured by a 50% decrease in Mania Rating Scale (MRS) scores. The next phase of the study was to be a double-blind randomized discontinuation phase, but too few patients remained in this phase for statistical analysis (Wagner et al., 2002). The most common adverse effects during this study were headache, nausea, vomiting, and somnolence.

Valproate has also been used as the initial mood stabilizer in add-on studies in patients with pediatric BD. DelBello and colleagues studied the use of quetiapine versus placebo administered adjunctively to divalproex in thirty inpatient adolescents with mania. Subjects were loaded on divalproex 20 mg/kg/day and either quetiapine or placebo was added. Over six weeks, both groups showed significant improvement. The divalproex and quetiapine group, however, had a significantly greater reduction in manic symptoms and a higher percentage of responders as determined by Clinical Global Impression-Change (CGI-C) and a 50% reduction in YMRS score (DelBello, Schwiers, Rosenberg, & Strakowski, 2002). Final valproate serum levels were 102 to 104 ug/mL and mean quetiapine dose was 432 mg/day. The divalproex and quetiapine group had greater sedation. Scheffer and colleagues studied the use of adjunctive Adderall versus placebo in children and adolescents with bipolar I or II disorder and ADHD (Schaeffer & Kowatch, 2002). In the first phase of the study, thirty out of forty patients were successfully stabilized on open VPA. Main adverse effects were GI upset, bruising (without thrombocytopenia), and hair loss, mostly in girls.

Divalproex has been more effective than lithium for treating mixed mania or rapid-cycling states in adults (Calabrese et al., 1993). Although it is not clear if this finding extends to pediatric BD, a historical case control comparison done by Strober and colleagues indicated a greater risk of relapse for adolescents with mixed mania on lithium compared to divalproex (Davanzo & McCracken, 2000). However, divalproex added to lithium may be more effective than either agent alone. In a sample of 102 children and adolescents (mean age 10.8 years) with bipolar I and II disorder, 44% were stabilized on a combination of open lithium and divalproex (Findling, McNamara, Gracious, Youngstrom, Stansbrey, et al. 2003). Of those who discontinued this first phase of the study, 41% was due to noncompliance, 28% was due to unstable mood, 24% was due to lithium intolerance, and 6% was due to divalproex intolerance. Weight gain was noted to be 0.30 kg/wk over the first eight weeks, and then 0.18 kg/wk thereafter. In the second phase of the study, subjects who responded to combination therapy in the first phase were then randomized to discontinue either lithium or divalproex, in a 1:1 blinded manner. In this phase, 75% of subjects dropped out, primarily due to unstable mood, and of the completers, 49% relapsed anyway. There were no significant differences between survival rates in the divalproex and lithium groups.

Divalproex has also been reported as effective in treating putative prodromal symptoms of pediatric BD (Chang, Dienes, Blasey, Steiner, & Ketter, 2003). In this report, Chang and colleagues studied twenty-four children and adolescents who were the offspring of at least one parent with bipolar disorder and who had either a mood or behavioral disorder, but not fully developed bipolar disorder, and at least mild affective symptoms. After twelve weeks of open divalproex monotherapy, 78% of the patients responded, with the majority showing improvement by week three. However, another similar, but placebo-controlled, study found that divalproex and placebo equally led to improvement of affective symptoms in adolescents with cyclothymia or BD not otherwise specified who were bipolar offspring. Notably, though, divalproex was superior to placebo in a subset of patients who had very strong family histories of bipolar disorder (Findling, 2002a; Findling, Gracious, McNamara, & Calabrese, 2000). These results are similar to those of a study of divalproex for bipolar II depression, in which twelve out of nineteen adults responded to open divalproex monotherapy. Those who were medication-naïve tended to respond more favorably (nine out of eleven) than those who were not (three out of eight) (Winsberg, DeGolia, Strong, & Ketter, 2001). Therefore, divalproex may have mood-stabilizing effects in children and adults with underlying bipolar diatheses.

Divalproex has been less studied in very young children. One case series described good response to valproate in nine young children (ages two- to seven-years-old) with symptoms suggestive of mania (Mota-Castillo et al., 2001).

Divalproex has been studied somewhat in juvenile populations with conduct disorders and behavioral problems. In an open (Donovan et al., 1997) and a placebo-controlled study (Donovan et al., 2000), divalproex demonstrated efficacy in treating adolescents with "explosive behavior" and "mood lability." These subjects met criteria for conduct disorder (CD) and oppositional defiant disorder (ODD) and in addition had significant temper outbursts (fighting, property destruction, or rage attacks) and irritability, lasting for at least one year. In the placebo-controlled study, 80% of subjects responded to divalproex, compared to 0% of subjects taking placebo (Donovan et al., 2000). Mean serum level after six weeks of treatment was 82.2 ug/mL. Adverse effects were described as minimal, with only increased appetite noted in 20% of subjects. In a seven-week trial of adolescents with CD randomized to either high-dose (1,000 mg/day) or low-dose (125 mg/day) divalproex, those in the high-dose group had a better response rate of 53% compared to 8%, based on blinded Clinician Global Impression—Improvement (CGI-I) ratings (Steiner, Petersen, Saxena, Ford, & Matthews, in press). Furthermore, those with a reactive, affective-based aggression, rather than a predatory-type, responded better regardless of condition (52% response rate versus 18%, respectively) (Remsing, Chang, Saxena, Silverman, & Steiner, 2002).

Divalproex has also been used with some success in treating children with mental retardation and mood symptoms (Kastner, Friedman, Plummer, Ruiz, & Henning, 1990; Whittier, West, Galli, & Raute, 1995). In an open study of fourteen patients with autism, ages five to forty years, Hollander and colleagues reported a 71% response rate to adjunctive or monotherapy with divalproex as determined by CGI-I scores of "much" or "very much improved" (Hollander, Dolgoff-Kaspar, Cartwright, Rawitt, & Novotny, 2001). Improvements were noted in the areas of affective instability, impulsivity, and aggression. Controlled studies of valproate in children with mental retardation or pervasive developmental disorders have not yet been conducted.

Gabapentin

Gabapentin was approved by the United States FDA in 1993 for the adjunctive treatment of refractory partial complex seizures in adults and subsequently for the treatment of postherpetic neuralgia.

Chemical Makeup

Gabapentin is an anticonvulsant that is structurally similar to GABA and l-leucine. The medication is available as 100-, 300-, and 400-capsules; 600-, and 800-mg tabs, and a 250-mg/5 mL oral solution.

Mechanism of Action

The exact mechanism of action for gabapentin is unknown. It modulates sodium channels, resulting in an increase in glial release of GABA. It does not interact directly with GABA receptors. Alteration in brain amino acid levels may also contribute to its anticonvulsant effect. Gabapentin furthermore increases GABA turnover and increases whole blood serotonin (McLean, 1995).

Dosing and Pharmacokinetics

The current recommended dosage in pediatric patients is 10 to 15 mg/kg/day dividing TID to start, and titrated up to a target dose of 25 to 60 mg/kg/day. Usual adult maintenance doses are 1,800 to 4,800 mg/day, given TID or QID. Children under five-years-old may need approximately a 30% increase in dosage to obtain similar serum levels as older children (Haig et al., 2001).

Gabapentin is well absorbed in the GI tract, but absorption becomes saturated with individual doses greater than 900 mg; therefore, it is usually administered BID to QID. Food has no effect on the bioavailability. Gabapentin is not significantly protein-bound, is not metabolized, and is excreted unchanged in the urine. Half life in adults is six to seven hours.

Adverse Effects Profile

Gabapentin is generally well tolerated in children and adults. The most common adverse effects are somnolence, dizziness, ataxia, peripheral edema, nystagmus, and fatigue. There have been case reports of gabapentin causing irritability and worsening aggressive behavior in some children (Lee et al., 1996). In case reports and open trials, patients given gabapentin have also had manic reactions (Leweke, Bauer, & Elger, 1999; Short & Cooke, 1995).

Drug Interactions and Contraindications

There are virtually no significant drug interaction concerns with gabapentin. One exception is that antacids may decrease gabapentin levels by 20%.

Empirical Data

There are some case reports and open studies suggesting the utility of gabapentin as adjunctive and monotherapy in adults with mania (Erfurth, Kammerer, Grunze, Normann, & Walden, 1998; Ghaemi & Goodwin, 2001; Schaffer & Schaffer, 1999; Vieta et al., 2000; Wang et al., 2002). However, in a large (n = 116) placebo-controlled study of gabapentin add-on therapy for bipolar patients over sixteen years old, gabapentin was inferior to placebo for reducing manic and depressive symptoms (Pande et al., 2000). Furthermore, gabapentin was no better than placebo in a six-week study of thirty-one adults with treatment-refractory BD (Frye et al., 2000). Gabapentin has been reported useful as an adjunctive treatment or in monotherapy for depressive symptoms of adults with BD (Ghaemi & Goodwin, 2001; Wang et al., 2002). In one of these studies, Wang and colleagues added gabapentin (mean final dose = 1,725 mg/day) to mood stabilizers or antipsychotics in twenty-two adults with bipolar depression. They reported an overall decrease in 28-item HAM-D scores of 53%, from 32.5 +/−7.7 at baseline to 16.5 +/−12.8 at week twelve. Fifty-five percent of patients had moderate to marked improvement (HAM-D decrease > 50%), with HAM-D scores decreasing 78%, while 36% of patients remitted (HAM-D < 9). However, no placebo-controlled studies of gabapentin in bipolar depression have yet been conducted.

There are no placebo-controlled studies of gabapentin in children and/or adolescents with bipolar disorder. Gabapentin appears to be generally well tolerated in children and adolescents (Khurana et al., 1996; McLean, 1995) and has been reported in case reports to be useful in a child (Hamrin & Bailey, 2001) and an adolescent with BD (Soutullo, Casuto, & Keck, 1998). The dosing in these reports ranged from 200 mg to 1500 mg/day. However, there have been reports of adverse behavioral effects in children, including irritability and worsening of aggressive behavior (Lee et al., 1996).

Gabapentin may also be useful in adults with social phobia (Pande et al., 1999), panic disorder (Pande et al., 2000), chronic pain (Backonja & Glanzman, 2003; Mellegers, Furlan, & Mailis, 2001), and insomnia. However, its use in children for these indications has not been studied.

Lamotrigine

Lamotrigine (LTG) was approved by the United States FDA in 1994 for the adjunctive treatment of refractory partial complex seizures and for monotherapy of seizures resulting from Lennox-Gastaut syndrome (in both adults and children as young as 2 years of age). LTG was approved in 2003 for the maintenance treatment of adults with bipolar I disorder to delay the time to occurrence of mood episodes.

Chemical Makeup

Lamotrigine is a phenyltriazine, unrelated in structure to other anticonvulsants. The medication is available as 25-, 100-, 150-, and 200-mg tabs, and as 2-, 5-, and 25-mg chewable tabs.

Mechanism of Action

The exact mechanism of action of LTG is unknown. Similar to topiramate, it also blocks voltage-sensitive sodium channels, resulting in inhibition of glutamate release. LTG also inhibits serotonin reuptake.

Dosing and Pharmacokinetics

The current recommended dosage in pediatric patients under twelve-years-old is 1 to 5 mg/kg/day in two divided doses. To achieve this dose, lamotrigine should be slowly titrated, beginning with 0.6 mg/kg/day for two weeks, and then

TABLE 13.3. RECOMMENDED TITRATION AND DOSING FOR LAMOTRIGINE IN ADOLESCENTS AND CHILDREN.

		Weeks 1–2	Weeks 3–4	Maintenance
Adults/adolescents: (>12 y.o.)		25 mg/day	50 mg/day	100–200 mg/day
	+VPA	12.5 mg/day	25 mg/day	50–100 mg/day
	+CARB	50 mg/day	100 mg/day	200–400 mg/day
Children: (<12 y.o.)		0.6 mg/kg/day	1.2 mg/kg/day	1–5 mg/kg/day
	+VPA	0.2 mg/kg/day	0.5 mg/kg	1–5 mg/kg/day
	+CARB	2 mg/kg/day	5 mg/kg/day	5–15 mg/kg/day

1.2 mg/kg/day for two more weeks before reaching the recommended 1 to 5 mg/kg/day dosage. (See Table 13.3.) However, if valproate is administered concurrently, the dose should be adjusted downward by up to two-thirds due to enzyme inhibition by valproate. Conversely, due to enzyme induction by carbamazepine, the dose of lamotrigine should be increased two-fold when given with carbamazepine (Table 13.3).

In adults and adolescents (over twelve-years-old), the dosing recommendation is to start at 25 mg/day for two weeks, increase to 50 mg/day for two more weeks, and then adjust gradually to achieve a target dose of 100 to 200 mg/day. Again, with concurrent valproate the dose should be halved, and with concurrent carbamazepine the dose should be doubled. There are no indications that blood levels of lamotrigine correlate with clinical efficacy, so unlike for valproate, lithium, or carbamazepine, blood levels are not necessary to obtain.

This dosage adjustment is very important, especially in the case of concomitant valproate administration. The normal half life of lamotrigine in adults is twenty-four to thirty-five hours. However, with concurrent valproate, the half life doubles in adults, and in children may reach up to forty-four to ninty-four hours (Garnett, 1997). Lack of adjusting for concurrent valproate administration may have resulted in a high incidence of serious rash, especially in children, in early use of lamotrigine (Messenheimer, Giorgi, & Risner, 2000).

In addition to careful titration, adherence to antigen precautions may decrease risk of rash. These precautions involve not using other new medications, foods, cosmetics, detergents, soaps, or deodorants for the first two months. Patients should also not begin LTG within two weeks of a viral syndrome or rash (Wang & Ketter, 2002).

In adult bipolar studies, generally effective doses have been in the 100 to 300 mg/day range, usually divided BID.

Lamotrigine is well absorbed in the GI tract, with no first-pass metabolism. Its absorption is unaffected by food. Lamotrigine is 55% protein-bound.

Adverse Effects Profile

Lamotrigine is generally well tolerated in children and adults. In open add-on studies of over 500 pediatric patients, the most common adverse effects were somnolence (17.8%), infection (17.6%), rash (16.9%), and vomiting (15.8%). In placebo-controlled trials involving children and adolescents (n = 359), adverse effects that occurred significantly more frequently than compared to placebo were dizziness (13.7% versus 3.5%), ataxia (10.7% versus 2.9%), nausea (9.5% versus 1.8%), and tremor (9.5% versus 1.2%) (Messenheimer, 2002).

Rash has been the most common reason for medication discontinuation. Because of incidence of serious rash in pre-marketing data leading to Stevens-Johnson syndrome or toxic epidermal necrolysis (TEN) in 1.0% of children and 0.3% of adults (Dooley et al., 1996; Guberman et al., 1999), lamotrigine carries a black box warning mandated by the U.S. FDA stating that lamotrigine should be used carefully in children under sixteen years old. However, substantial post-marketing data has reported an estimated incidence of serious rash in just 3 out of 10,000 pediatric patients who are "new users" (Messenheimer, 2002). The higher incidence of serious rash in past studies is thought to have been due to higher initial dosing and more rapid titration than the current dosing guidelines, lack of dose adjustment with concomitant valproate administration, and a definition of "serious rash" as any rash leading to discontinuation from a clinical trial (Messenheimer et al., 2000). However, despite the much lower incidence of rash since 1998, any rash accompanied by eye, mouth, or bladder discomfort, indicating possible involvement of mucous membranes, should result in an emergency dermatological assessment.

There have been case reports of acute hepatic failure in adults and children who were taking other anticonvulsants and whose dosages of lamotrigine were titrated up fairly rapidly (Fayad, Choueiri, & Mikati, 2000). There also have been case reports of lamotrigine causing motor and vocal tics in children, particularly those with language deficiencies (Sotero de Menezes, Rho, Murphy, & Cheyette, 2000).

Drug Interactions and Contraindications

As noted above, lamotrigine levels are affected by carbamazepine and valproate. Sertraline may also increase lamotrigine levels (Kaufman & Gerner, 1998; Wang & Ketter, 2002). Lamotrigine may decrease serum valproate levels slightly, but it is unclear if it does so to any clinically significant level (Mataringa, May, & Rambeck, 2002).

Empirical Data

Open and blinded, controlled studies of lamotrigine have supported its efficacy in BD. A naturalistic study of open lamotrigine added to other mood stabilizers in seventeen adults with bipolar I or II disorder reported 65% to have a good response to lamotrigine, with improvement in both depressive and manic symptoms (Suppes et al., 1999). In a study of 195 adults with bipolar depression, lamotrigine at 100 mg/day was superior to placebo over seven weeks in alleviating depressive symptoms (51% response versus 26% response, respectively) (Calabrese et al., 1999). In another study of 182 adults with rapid-cycling BD, lamotrigine monotherapy was superior to placebo in maintaining remission at six months (41% response versus 26% response, respectively) (Calabrese et al., 2000). No serious rashes occurred in either of these studies.

In a six-week placebo-controlled cross-over study of lamotrigine monotherapy in thirty-one adults with acute mania, 52% of patients responded to lamotrigine compared to only 23% to placebo, as measured by CGI-I (Frye et al., 2000). Mean dose of lamotrigine at six weeks was $274 +/\pm 128$ mg/day. Lamotrigine was generally well-tolerated, except for one patient who developed a rash after completing the study, progressing to TEN and requiring hospitalization, after which the patient recovered fully. Mean weight change (-0.96 kg) was no different from placebo. These studies support the efficacy of lamotrigine in adults with bipolar mania and/or depression.

The FDA approved LTG for maintenance therapy of BD in part due to a study of euthymic patients with BD who were recently hypomanic or manic, and who were then gradually switched to LTG monotherapy. One hundred seventy-five patients were successfully switched in an open fashion and then randomized to lamotrigine (100 to 400 mg daily), lithium (0.8 to 1.1 mEq/L), or placebo as double-blind maintenance treatment for up to eighteen months. Both LTG and lithium were superior to placebo in delaying the time needed for clinical intervention for any mood episode (mania or depression). Lamotrigine was especially effective in preventing depressive relapse, a finding that supports its consideration as an antidepressant in BD that generally does not exacerbate mania as SSRIs and TCAs can.

There are no placebo-controlled studies of lamotrigine in children and/or adolescents with BD. One open-label study of adjunctive lamotrigine treatment for refractory bipolar depression or rapid-cycling included seven adolescents (Kusumakar & Yatham, 1997). In this six-week open trial, 72% of subjects responded by week four and 63% were considered to be in remission by week six. The main adverse effects were headache (in five subjects) and tremor (in three subjects). No rash was noted in this study, despite a more aggressive titration schedule than is currently recommended. (Some subjects were also taking valproate.)

A few other pediatric uses have been investigated. In one case report, lamotrigine was useful in decreasing irritability, insomnia, and self-injurious behavior in an eighteen-year-old woman with mental retardation (Davanzo & King, 1996). However, in a study of autistic children, lamotrigine was equal to placebo in reducing autistic symptoms (aggression, self-injury) over eight weeks. Lamotrigine was titrated to 5 mg/kg/day, without any rash occurrence. Further studies of lamotrigine for pediatric psychiatric conditions appear warranted.

Levetiracetam

Levetiracetam, (Keppra) was approved by the United States FDA in 1999 for the treatment of partial-onset seizures in adults.

Chemical Makeup

Levetiracetam, a second-generation antiepileptic drug, is a pyrrolidine acetamide, which is chemically unrelated to other existing anticonvulsant drugs. It is available as 250-, 500-, and 750-mg tablets for oral administration.

Anecdotal evidence indicates that levetiracetam might be efficacious in the treatment of psychiatric disorders in adults and in children but as yet there is no sufficient support from clinical trials.

Mechanism of Action

The specific mechanism of action of levetiracetam is unknown, but it does not appear to have direct influence on inhibitory and excitatory neurotransmission. Levetiracetam seems to modulate $GABA_A$ and glycine receptors through an allosteric mechanism, which enhances chloride flux and stimulates inhibitory transmission. Also, second messenger systems, ion channels, glutamate receptors, GABA transaminase, or glutamate decarboxylase are not affected by levetiracetam (Wang & Ketter, 2002).

Dosing and Pharmacokinetics

Pellock and colleagues (2001) evaluated the pharmacokinetic characteristics of levetiracetam and its major inactive, acidic metabolite, ucb L057, in twenty-four pediatric patients (ages six to twelve) with partial seizures in an open-label, single-dose study. Peak plasma concentration of levetiracetam was reached within two hours of oral administration of a single dose of 20 mg/kg, while its metabolite ucb L057 peaked at four hours after administration. The elimination half life of levetiracetam was approximately six hours, independent of gender. The half life of ucb L057 was about eight hours. Plasma half life in adults is also generally six to eight hours. However, body clearance of levetiracetam is 30–40% higher in children than adults. Therefore, higher doses of levetiracetam for pediatric patients are suggested. A daily maintenance dose equivalent to 130–140% of the usual adult dose (1,000 to 3,000 mg/day) in two divided doses, on a weight normalized level (mg/kg/day), is recommended for children with epilepsy (Pellock et al., 2001). Ongoing clinical trials in children are using doses of 20 to 60 mg/kg/day.

Levetiracetam is rapidly and completely absorbed after oral administration, with absolute bioavailability of 100%. The pharmacokinetic profile is linear and there is no effect of food on extent of absorption. Peak plasma concentrations in adults are achieved in about one hour after administration. Levetiracetam is less than 10% protein-bound and, unlike some other antiepileptic drugs, it is not metabolized in the liver by the action of cytochrome P450 processes (Patsalos, 2000). About 66% is excreted unchanged in the urine and 24% is excreted as inactive metabolites, the major of which is an enzymatic hydrolysis product, ucb L057 (Wang & Ketter, 2002).

Adverse Effects Profile

Levetiracetam has a generally well-tolerated safety profile. Adverse events are mainly CNS-related and are mild or moderate in intensity. Most frequently reported adverse reactions with incidences higher than placebo are somnolence, asthenia, infection, and dizziness (Betts, Waegemans, & Crawford, 2000) as well as headache, flu syndrome, and rhinitis (Cereghino et al., 2000). Also, agitation, anxiety, depression, and psychosis have been reported with levetiracetam use in adults (Wang & Ketter, 2002).

Five pediatric patients out of twenty-four reported adverse events in a pharmacokinetic study of levetiracetam (Pellock et al., 2001). These included abnormal air conduction in the left ear, diarrhea, lethargy, decreased appetite, and dizziness. Similarly, an open-label study of ten autistic children showed mild to moderate adverse events such as rash, headache, stomach ache, vomiting, diarrhea, and somnolence. Only one subject required withdrawal from the study because of an adverse reaction (Rugino & Samsock, 2002).

Drug Interactions and Contraindications

Data from placebo-controlled clinical trials shows that levetiracetam has no drug interactions with other anticonvulsants, does not affect their plasma concentration, and its pharmacokinetics are not altered by other antiepileptic drugs. Furthermore, levetiracetam does not affect the pharmacokinetic properties of oral contraceptives, digoxin, or warfarin (Wang & Ketter, 2002). Evidence from combination therapy in animal models demonstrates that the co-administration of levetiracetam with valproate, clonazepam, phenobarbital, carbamazepine, and phenytoin enhances anticonvulsant potency (*Levetiracetam: Combination therapy with other antiepileptic drugs in animal models*, 2001).

Empirical Data

There is a paucity of reports addressing the potential efficacy of levetiracetam in the treatment of psychiatric disorders. Open-label levetiracetam monotherapy was used in the treatment of acute mania and subthreshold depression in a forty-two-year-old white male diagnosed with bipolar I disorder. The initial dose of 500 mg/day was increased over a five-week period to 2,500 mg/day and no adverse events were reported. Despite unplanned drug discontinuation for approximately one week and re-emergent mania, the patient's mood was rapidly stabilized after reintroduction of levetiracetam. There was significant improvement in symptoms as measured by the YMRS and the HAM-D.

Evidence for use and efficacy of levetiracetam in the treatment of pediatric psychiatric disorders is small. Levetiracetam was administered for an average of four weeks in an open-label study in ten autistic boys (ages four to ten) (Rugino & Samsock, 2002). Initial medications used for behavioral control, but not medications administered for medical problems, were withdrawn before the beginning of the trial. By using a variety of standardized measurement tools, the researchers found that levetiracetam treatment (13 to 54 mg/kg) resulted in statistically significant improvements in inattention, hyperkinesis, impulsivity, and mood instability in these children. Aggressive behaviors seemed to be exacerbated in pediatric patients who were withdrawn from medications prescribed specifically to treat aggression, such as risperidone, carbamazepine, and desipramine. All other autistic children showed significant reduction in aggression behaviors, as measured by the Achenbach Aggression scale.

Oxcarbazepine

The United States FDA approved oxcarbazepine in 2000 for the treatment of partial seizures in adults and in children ages four to sixteen.

Chemical Makeup

Oxcarbazepine (Trileptal), an anticonvulsant medication, is a 10-keto derivative of carbamazepine. It possesses a similar therapeutic profile as carbamazepine, but it has more favorable pharmacokinetic and safety characteristics, and a different metabolism. Oxcarbazepine is available as 150-, 300-, and 600-mg tablets for oral administration.

Evidence from open trial data indicates that oxcarbazepine exerts antimanic efficacy in adult bipolar patients, as well as antidepressant-like effect in animal models. Furthermore, oxcarbazepine appears to be useful in the treatment of panic disorder. However, limited data has been published on its use in the treatment of psychiatric problems in children and adolescents.

Mechanism of Action

The specific mechanism of action of oxcarbazepine is unclear. In vitro studies suggest that oxcarbazepine and its major active metabolite 10-monohydroxy derivative (MHD) modulate sodium and calcium channels. These two compounds do not seem to affect brain neurotransmitters or modulate receptors.

Dosing and Pharmacokinetics

In pediatric patients, oxcarbazepine is usually started at a daily dose of 8 to 10 mg/kg given BID and is generally administered in a twice-a-day dosing regimen. It is recommended that oxcarbazepine be titrated to clinical response over the first two weeks of administration. In a multicenter, randomized, placebo-controlled trial Glauser and colleagues (2000) evaluated the efficacy of oxcarbazepine in 267 children with partial seizures (ages three to seventeen). They reported an effective dose range of 6 to 51 mg/kg/day (median 31.4 mg/kg/day) and good tolerability in this sample. In another double-blind controlled clinical trial investigating the efficacy of oxcarbazepine versus phenytoin in children aged five to eighteen, the daily dose varied between 450 and 2,400 mg (Guerreiro et al., 1997). Similarly, a dose range of 30 to 50 mg/kg was reported in an open-label study of 110 children with epilepsy, aged two to twelve (Motte et al., 1995).

The pharmacokinetic profile of oxcarbazepine in children older than eight years of age and in adults is similar. However, clearance in younger children is about 30–40% higher and they need a higher medication dose per body weight than adults. An open trial study of oxcarbazepine in younger children with epilepsy (less than seven years of age) suggests a maintenance dose range of 21 to 83 mg/kg/day (Gaily, Granström, & Lindahl, 1995).

Following oral administration, oxcarbazepine is 96% absorbed and its metabolic pathway involves rapid and cytosolic reduction to an active metabolite, MHD. Oxcarbazepine is excreted in the urine as active MHD (70%), glucuronide conjugates of MHD (20%), and oxcarbazepine glucuronide conjugates. In adults, the elimination half life of oxcarbazepine and MHD is about two hours and nine hours, respectively. Steady-state plasma concentrations of MHD are achieved within two to three days after initiating treatment. The pharmacokinetics of MHD are linear and food has no effect on extent of absorption of oxcarbazepine. About 40% of oxcarbazepine is protein-bound.

Adverse Effects Profile

Clinical trials indicate that adverse events observed in pediatric patients are similar to these seen in adults. In one controlled clinical trial, 91% of children treated with oxcarbazepine and 82% of patients taking placebo experienced mild to moderate adverse events. Adverse reactions were usually associated with the CNS and the digestive system. Compared to the placebo group, the oxcarbazepine group experienced more vomiting (36%), somnolence (35%), dizziness (29%), and nausea (22%) (Glauser et al., 2000). Also, about 11% of pediatric patients participating in several clinical trials terminated treatment because of adverse events. These events generally involved somnolence, vomiting, ataxia, diplopia, dizziness, fatigue, and nystagmus. Furthermore, cognitive impairment such as concentration difficulties, language problems, and psychomotor slowing have been reported to occur during treatment.

A chart-review study conducted by Borusiak, Korn-Merker, Holert, & Boenigk (1998) indicates that children might be at risk for developing clinically significant hyponatremia and hypochloremia during oxcarbazepine treatment. The authors recommend monitoring of sodium levels before and during drug therapy, since these adverse events might take place independent of dose or blood serum levels (Borusiak et al., 1998). In addition, caution is advised when children are treated with combinations of oxcarbazepine and SSRIs because the latter can reduce serum sodium levels as well.

Drug Interactions and Contraindications

Oxcarbazepine has fewer drug interactions compared to traditional antiepileptic drugs. Oxcarbazepine does not show significant drug interactions with warfarin, valproate, cimetidine, erythromycin, and dextroprophoxyphrene (Baruzzi, Albani, & Riva, 1994). However, oxcarbazepine can cause clinically relevant metabolic induction of oral contraceptives similar to other inducing antiepileptic drugs.

Oxcarbazepine inhibits CYP2C19 and induces CYP3A4/5, which could affect plasma concentrations of other drugs. For example, plasma levels of phenytoin may increase by up to 40% during add-on therapy with oxcarbazepine (daily dose greater than 1,200 mg/day). Some inducing antiepileptic drugs (such as carbamazepine and phenytoin) also may decrease the plasma levels of MHD.

Empirical Data

A number of European studies have provided evidence for the antimanic efficacy of oxcarbazepine in the treatment of adult bipolar patients (Cabrera, Mühlbauer, Schley, Stoll, & Müller-Oerlinghausen, 1986; Emrich, 1990; Hummel, et al., 2001; Müller & Stroll, 1984; Velikonja & Heinrich, 1984). In an open-label trial, forty-eight patients with acute mania were treated with oxcarbazepine at a dose range of 600 to 3,000 mg, with 83% showing good clinical improvement (Müller & Stroll, 1984). In another open study, ten patients were treated for manic and schizoaffective symptoms with an add-on dosage of 900 mg/day of oxcarbazepine. While hostile and manic symptoms were reduced, no significant changes were observed in schizophrenic symptoms (Velikonja & Heinrich, 1984). Furthermore, a fifteen-day study compared the effects of oxcarbazepine and haloperidol in the treatment of acute mania (Emrich, 1990). There were nineteen patients in each treatment group who received a mean dose of 2,400 mg/day of oxcarbazepine or a mean dose of 42 mg/day of haloperidol. Of patients in the oxcarbazepine group, 94% showed good to excellent improvement compared to 75% of patients in the haloperidol group. Also, the incidence of adverse events in the haloperidol group was three and a half times higher than in the oxcarbazepine group. In a second study, Emrich (1990) compared the efficacy of oxcarbazepine (n = 28) with lithium (n = 24) in the treatment of adults with acute mania. The mean dose of oxcarbazepine was 1,400 mg/day while the lithium group received a mean dose of 1,100 mg/day. Of patients in the oxcarbazepine group, 93% experienced improvement compared to 92% of patients in the lithium group.

These results are consistent with a number of yet unpublished abstracts in the North American region. In an open-label, ten-week, prospective study of sixty adult patients diagnosed with BD, oxcarbazepine showed comparable efficacy to valproate in the treatment of mania as measured by the Clinician Administered Rating Scale for Mania (CARS-M) (Reinstein, Sonnenberg, Chasanov, Mohan, Patel, Jones et al., 2001). A retrospective review of 200 subjects (ages eleven to eighty-three) titrated to doses ranging from 600 to 3,000 mg/day provided supportive evidence for the antimanic efficacy and tolerability of oxcarbazepine (Reinstein, Sonnenberg, Mohan, Chasanov, Koltun, Reyngold et al., 2002). A second retrospective study reviewed the charts of eighty-seven patients with mood disorders who had failed to improve on or tolerate other antiepileptic drugs

(Nasr & Casper, 2002). A mean dose of 801 mg/day (±359 mg/day) of oxcarbazepine was administered for at least four weeks. Patients showed significant improvement in Clinical Global Impression Scale (CGI-S) scores. Patients who were diagnosed with bipolar II disorder and experienced anger and irritability showed the greatest improvement in mood on the Carroll Depression Rating Scale (CDRS) and the Visual Analogue Scale (VAS) compared to unipolar patients.

Oxcarbazepine has been shown to exert antidepressant-like effects in animal models of depression, such as learned helplessness via the forced swimming test (Beijamini, Skalisz, Joca, & Andreatini, 1998), raising the possibility of such effects in humans. It has been further postulated that the antidepressant effect of oxcarbazepine might be mediated by dopaminergic neurotransmission (Joca, Skalisz, Beijamini, Vital, & Andreatini, 2000). In a twelve-week open-label study, twenty-eight bipolar patients received 300 to 2,400 mg/day of oxcarbazepine in addition to other medications (Munoz, 2002). While fifteen initially manic patients experienced ≥ 50% improvement in YMRS scores within three weeks of beginning treatment, seven initially depressed patients reported ≥ 50% improvement in depressive symptoms within six weeks as measured by the HAM-D. However, one recent naturalistic study of thirteen patients with refractory bipolar disorder, with 69% having predominantly depressive symptoms, provided only limited evidence on the antidepressant efficacy of oxcarbazepine (Ghaemi, Ko, & Katzow, 2002). Moderate improvement was seen in only 16% of patients and mild improvement in 46% as measured by the CGI-I. Seven patients discontinued oxcarbazepine treatment due to side effects such as sedation, cognitive and weight problems, tremor, dizziness, headache, stomach problems, and chest discomfort.

Oxcarbazepine may also be useful in the treatment of panic disorder. One case study reported symptom improvement in a patient experiencing grand mal seizures and comorbid panic disorder. Treatment was initiated with a dose of 600 mg/day and increased to 900 mg/day. Both conditions were relieved by oxcarbazepine (Windhaber, Maierhofer, & Dantendorfer, 1997).

Evidence for use and efficacy of oxcarbazepine in the treatment of children and adolescents with psychiatric disorders is limited. To our knowledge, there is only one relevant publication, a case report of a six-year-old girl diagnosed with bipolar I disorder. The patient was started at 150 mg of oxcarbazepine twice daily in combination with lithium carbonate (150 mg twice daily) and guanfacine (0.5 mg twice daily) (Teitelbaum, 2001). Symptom remission and full mood stabilization occurred within six weeks of initiating treatment with oxcarbazepine. There was also a notable decrease in oppositional behavior and improvement in academic and social functioning. Controlled studies of oxcarbazepine in pediatric psychiatric disorders are warranted.

Tiagabine

Tiagabine (Gabitril) was approved by the FDA in 1997 for the treatment of partial complex seizures in adults and in children as young as twelve years of age.

Chemical Makeup

Tiagabine is a nipecotic acid hydrochloride and a GABA uptake inhibitor in presynaptic neuronal and glial cells (Suzdak & Jansen, 1995). It is available as 2-, 4-, 12-, 16-, and 20-mg tablets for oral administration.

Several open-label studies in adults suggest than tiagabine might be effective in the treatment of BDs including rapid cycling, and in schizoaffective disorder bipolar type. Furthermore, tiagabine seems to be useful as add-on medication in the treatment of post-traumatic stress disorder (PTSD) and in anxiety disorders. To our knowledge, there have been no studies evaluating the use of tiagabine for the treatment of psychiatric disorders in children and adolescents.

Mechanism of Action

Although the precise mechanism of action of tiagabine is not fully understood, it is thought to enhance the activity of GABA by increasing extracellular concentrations of GABA in the brain. Tiagabine also inhibits the major GABA transporter in cortical and hippocampal neurons, GAT-1 (Pellock, 2001). Tiagabine has no significant affinity for other neurotransmitter receptors as well as uptake sites, and it appears to lack affinity for calcium and sodium channels (Suzdak & Jansen, 1995).

Dosing and Pharmacokinetics

In adolescents (ages twelve to eighteen), the recommended initial dose for seizure control is 4 mg once daily. The dose can be increased by 4 mg in the second week and by 4 to 8 mg in the following weeks (up to 32 mg/day). The maximum dosage should be administered in two to four divided doses.

A single-blind European study evaluated the tolerability, safety, and preliminary efficacy of ascending doses (0.25 to 1.50 mg/kg/day) of tiagabine as adjunctive therapy. Tiagabine was administered to fifty-two children (ages two to seventeen) with refractory epilepsy. The initial dosage of 0.25 mg/kg/day was increased at four-week intervals to 0.5, 1.0, and 1.5 mg/kg/day (Uldall, Bulteau, Pedersen, Dulac, & Lyby, 2000). Similarly, one open-label study reported an initial dose of 0.25 mg/kg/day. The dose was increased approximately every two weeks by 0.25 mg/kg and reached up to 1.0 mg/kg/day (Boellner, Gu, & Sommerville, 1996).

Tiagabine is rapidly absorbed and it reaches peak plasma concentrations within two hours after administration (Gustavson & Mengel, 1995). It is 96% protein-bound and it is primary metabolized in the liver by isoform 3A of the hepatic cytochrome P450-system (Brodie, 1995). Only 2% is excreted unchanged in the urine. Absorption and elimination are linear.

Gustavson and colleagues (1997) conducted a single-dose pharmacokinetics study of about 0.1 mg/kg tiagabine in twenty-five children aged three to eleven years. Tiagabine was well tolerated. In the presence of enzyme induction (carbamazepine and phenytoin), the elimination half life was 3.2 hours, while the half life in children receiving valproate was 5.7 hours. Relative to body weight, clearance and volume of distribution were greater in children than adults. When adjusted according to body surface area, these measures were similar for adults and children.

Adverse Effects Profile

Tiagabine is generally well tolerated. Most adverse events are mild or moderate in severity and are associated with the CNS. A single-blind study of children with refractory epilepsy reported mild to moderate adverse events in 39% of children during the single-blind placebo period and in 83% of children during the tiagabine treatment phase. The most common adverse reactions were asthenia (19%), nervousness (19%), dizziness (17%), and somnolence (17%) (Uldall et al., 2000). These results are consistent with adverse events reported by adults with epilepsy participating in placebo-controlled studies (Leppik, 1995) (Uthman et al., 1998). In addition, tiagabine has been reported to cause concentration difficulties, speech or language problems, and confusion.

Drug Interactions and Contraindications

An open-label study of tiagabine in manic adults found loadings doses of 20 mg/day to cause severe side effects, such as epileptic seizures (Grunze et al., 1999). Therefore, it is recommended not to begin treatment of tiagabine with a loading dose. Tiagabine appears to cause a slight decrease (10%) in valproate steady-state plasma concentrations, but does not affect plasma concentrations of other anticonvulsants. Furthermore, phenytoin, carbamazepine, and primidone decrease tiagabine levels, while valproate leads to increase of free tiagabine concentration (Wang & Ketter, 2002).

Empirical Data

Open-label trials suggest that tiagabine might be effective in the treatment of certain psychiatric disorders in adults. One case series of three patients, in which low doses of tiagabine (4 to 12 mg) were added to other medications, reported improvement in two males diagnosed with BD (thirty-nine and twenty-two years of age) and one forty-four-year-old female with schizoaffective disorder bipolar type. In all three cases, there were no adverse events observed (Kaufman, 1998). Another group reported significant improvement in two refractory bipolar patients after low doses of tiagabine were added to the medication regimen (Schaffer & Schaffer, 1999). These results are consistent with a study by Schaffer and colleagues (Schaffer, Schaffer, & Howe, 2002), in which twelve adults diagnosed with bipolar I and II disorder, including rapid cycling, and ten patients diagnosed with BD not otherwise specified (NOS), were treated with adjunctive, open low-dose tiagabine (1 to 8 mg) for six months. Each patient had an unsatisfactory response to other medications including lithium, valproate, carbamazepine, primidone, phenytoin, lamotrigine, gabapentin, topiramate, several antidepressants, benzodiazepines, and antipsychotics. Improvement was shown in 36% of the patients. All fourteen nonresponders discontinued the study because of adverse events, such as increase of hypomanic symptoms, oversedation, cognitive impairment, and headaches. One patient with history of absence seizures controlled with gabapentin experienced breakthrough absence seizures. Adverse effects resolved shortly after discontinuation of tiagabine. In contrast, a two-week open-label study found no antimanic efficacy in eight acutely manic patients, two of whom were treated with tiagabine in monotherapy (Grunze et al., 1999). Also, rapid dosage increases, starting at 20 mg/day and increasing dosage in steps of 5 mg/day, seemed to cause severe adverse reactions. One patient with no previous history of epilepsy experienced a generalized, tonic-clonic epileptic seizure after being given 30 mg/day of tiagabine for three days.

Recent, unpublished open-trial data indicate that tiagabine may be effective in the treatment of PTSD and other anxiety disorders. Doses ranging from 8 to 16 mg/day were administered together with antidepressant drugs to treat symptoms of increased arousal in six adult patients diagnosed with PTSD and a comorbid mood disorder. Clinically significant reduction in impulsivity and aggression symptoms was reported as compared to two patients taking other medications. One control patient was receiving SSRI treatment and the other was treated with an antidepressant and a benzodiazepine (Lara, 2002). In another study, ten patients with anxiety disorders received 2 to 8 mg/day of tiagabine either as monotherapy (n = 5) or in combination with other antianxiety medications (n = 5). Good drug tolerability was reported, as well as a significant improvement in anxiety symptoms as measured by the CGI-C scale (Crane, 2002).

Although open trial data suggest that low-dose tiagabine can be helpful in the treatment of adults with various psychiatric disorders, there are currently no reports of psychiatric efficacy in pediatric populations.

Topiramate

Topiramate (Topamax) was approved by the U.S. FDA in 1996 for the treatment of partial-onset seizures or primary generalized tonic-clonic seizures in adults and in children as young as two years of age.

Chemical Makeup

Topiramate, a sulfamate derivative of the naturally occurring monosaccharide D-fructose, is a structurally novel anticonvulsant that is distinct from other known antiepileptic drugs. It is available as 25-, 100-, and 200-mg tablets and as 15- and 25-mg sprinkle capsules for oral administration.

Mechanism of Action

The exact mechanism of action of topiramate is unknown. It has some similar pharmacological characteristics to valproate and carbamazepine in that topiramate inhibits voltage-activated Sodium channels (Shank, 1998). It also enhances the activity of GABA, the primary inhibitory neurotransmitter in the brain. Topiramate blocks glutamate at non N-methyl-D-aspartate (NMDA) receptors and inhibits some isoenzymes of carbonic anhydrase (CA-II and CA-IV).

Dosing and Pharmacokinetics

The recommended dosage in pediatric patients is 5 to 9 mg/kg/day in two divided doses. However, a study by Schwabe and colleagues (Schwabe & Wheless, 2001) supports a wider dosing range of 2 to 35 mg/kg/day. The researchers obtained topiramate dosing and corresponding serum levels from forty-one children twelve years of age or under with epilepsy. This study suggests that serum levels may be useful in guiding topiramate dosing, especially in young children. However, serum topiramate levels are not routinely obtained in clinical practice. An open-label study of the treatment of pediatric patients with prodromal (subthreshold) symptoms of bipolar I disorder reported initial doses of 25 mg/day, followed by a increase of 25 mg/day as tolerated by patients (Hussain, 2001).

Rosenfeld, Doose, Walker, Baldassarre, and Reife (1999) conducted a pharmacokinetic study of topiramate in eighteen pediatric patients with epilepsy (ages four to seventeen). Clearance was 50% higher in pediatric patients than in adults. The half life of topiramate in adults is about twenty-five hours in the absence of enzyme induction and twelve to fifteen hours in the presence of enzyme induction, which occurs with carbamazepine and phenytoin. Therefore, the half life is approximately half that in pediatric patients. Thus, the steady-state plasma concentration for the same mg/kg dose will be lower in children compared to adults (Rosenfeld et al., 1999). Because the pharmacokinetics of topiramate are linear, plasma concentrations increase in proportion to dosage.

Topiramate is not extensively metabolized and 70% is eliminated unaltered in the urine during monotherapy. Only about 50% is unchanged in urine when topiramate is administered with enzyme inducers (Wang & Ketter, 2002).

Adverse Effects Profile

Topiramate is generally well tolerated. Most adverse events are mild to moderate. and involve the CNS or are associated with weight loss. The latter is a potentially beneficial side effect for patients who experience weight gain while taking other mood stabilizers.

Controlled clinical trials in children (ages two to sixteen) found common adverse effects to be somnolence, weight decrease, fatigue, nervousness, difficulty with concentration or attention, difficulty with memory, and aggression (*Physicians Desk Reference*, 2001). In addition, topiramate has been reported to have cognitive side effects when titrated up rapidly. Studies have found declines in verbal memory and word fluency in healthy young adults (Martin et al., 1999) and psychomotor slowing, subjective dysnomia, and memory problems in adults with epilepsy taking topiramate (Faught, Kuzniecky, & Gilliam, 1997). A ten-year-old boy with refractory BD treated with topiramate experienced cognitive and academic difficulties including spelling, sound reversals, arithmetic problems, and memory deficits (Davanzo et al., 2001). These cognitive adverse reactions have been suggested to interfere with acquisition of language skills. Therefore, the use of topiramate in the preschool population requires careful consideration (Pavuluri, Janicak, & Carbray, 2002).

Drug Interactions and Contraindications

A case series of three children with treatment-refractory epilepsy (Longin, Teich, Koelfen, & Konig, 2002) suggests that topiramate and valproate combination therapy may increase the risk of development of adverse effects associated with valproate such as apathy, hyperammonemia, and hypothermia. Topiramate may moderately increase plasma phenytoin concentrations in some patients. Also, topiramate and zonisamide should not be given concomitantly or with acetazolamide because they both inhibit carbonic anhydrase (Wang & Ketter, 2002).

Empirical Data

Open-label studies indicate that topiramate may be effective as add-on therapy in the treatment of BD in adults and in children. Vieta and associates (2002) evaluated thirty-four treatment-resistant bipolar-spectrum adult patients who received topiramate as adjunctive therapy for manic, depressive, hypomanic, or mixed states. There was a significant reduction in YMRS, HAM-D, and Clinical Global Impression-Severity (CGI-S) scores, with improvement shown in 59% of manic patients and in 55% of depressed patients. Chengappa and colleagues (1999) studied the effects of topiramate administered as adjunctive therapy to other pharmacologic agents in eighteen adults with bipolar I disorder and two adults diagnosed with schizoaffective disorder, bipolar type. Sixty percent were responders to topiramate and experienced decreases in YMRS and Clinical Global Impression-Bipolar (CGI-BP) scores. These results are consistent with several more studies (Bozikas, Petrikis, Kourtis, Youlis, & Karavatos, 2002; Marcotte, 1998; McElroy et al., 2000) as well as some unpublished abstracts that support the effectiveness and safety of adjunctive topiramate therapy in BD (Marcotte & Gullick, 2001; McIntyre, Girgla, Binder, Riccardelli, & Kennedy, 2002). In a small pilot monotherapy study, ten patients hospitalized for acute mania were treated with open topiramate for up to twenty-eight days. Three patients experienced at least 50% improvement in YMRS scores and two patients improved by 25% to 49%. These studies indicate that topiramate may be useful in mono- and adjunctive therapy in adults with acute mania.

There are fewer studies of topiramate in pediatric BD. DelBello and colleagues (2002) conducted a retrospective chart review of twenty-six subjects (mean age 14 ± 3.5 years) diagnosed with bipolar I or II disorder, thirteen of whom had comorbid ADHD. Children and adolescents were treated with topiramate as adjunctive or monotherapy for anywhere from one to thirty months. Significant improvement was experienced in 73% of patients with manic symptoms, 62% had an overall improvement in psychiatric illness, and 38% showed a decrease in ADHD symptom severity. Dosages ranged from 25 to 400 mg/day and no serious adverse events occurred during treatment. In an interesting study design, Hussain (2001) evaluated the efficacy of open topiramate in forty-four children (ages seven to sixteen) with putative prodromal BD. Subjects had a positive family history of BD and were exhibiting subsyndromal manic symptoms such as mood swings and irritability as well as anger, defiance, anxiety, and other behavioral problems. Clinically significant improvement was observed in both depressive and hypomanic symptoms. Of the thirty-three patients completing the one-year trial, all were found to have 70% to 90% symptom reduction. Dosages ranged from 25 to 200 mg/day. Eight subjects discontinued treatment due to adverse reactions such as sedation, confusion, nausea, parasthesia, agitation, and restlessness. Three subjects discontinued treatment due to limited response. No prospective controlled trials of topiramate have been conducted in children and adolescents who have fully syndromal BD.

In addition to BD, topiramate was found to be effective as add-on or monotherapy in an open-label study of thirty-five adults diagnosed with PTSD. In this study,

79% experienced significant suppression of nightmares and 85% experienced a decrease in trauma-related flashbacks (Berlant, 2000). Furthermore, several studies provide some evidence for the effectiveness of topiramate in the treatment of eating disorders and as an antiobesity agent (Appolinario et al., 2001; Hoopes et al., 2002; Hussain, Hussain, & Chaudhry, 2000). In a double-blind, placebo-controlled study of sixty-eight outpatients treated for bulimia nervosa, topiramate treatment was associated with significant reduction of CGI-S scores (Hoopes, 2002). Topiramate was also reported effective for the treatment of premenstrual dysphoric disorder in a case series of eight female patients, especially for those who were overweight (Hussain, Chaudhry, & Hussain, 2000). The effects of topiramate in children and adolescents for these indications are, to date, unstudied.

Expert Use

Our method of use of mood stabilizers and potential mood stabilizers is based on what little empirical data is available in children and adolescents with mood disorders, and based on empirical evidence from studies in adults. Furthermore, as most clinicians do, we have incorporated our clinical experience into our method. We use lithium in all age groups, predominantly for children and adolescents with mania, especially those with euphoric, episodic mania. In cases of antidepressant-refractory depression, we often augment standard treatment with lithium or in cases in which a bipolar depression is suspected, despite no history of mania.

We use divalproex for all forms of mania in children and adolescents, finding special utility in mixed states and rapid cycling, and in combination with lithium. We are frequently asked about our concern with divalproex inducing PCOS in adolescent females. Due to lack of convincing clinical evidence correlating this condition to divalproex, we do not let this affect our decision of whether to use divalproex in females. However, we do present the possibility to parents that research may or may not eventually establish such a link, but state that we have not yet seen PCOS to be a significant acute clinical problem in female patients we treat with divalproex.

We use carbamazepine predominantly in cases of failure to respond to lithium, divalproex, or atypical antipsychotics, or in cases of mood disorders secondary to head trauma or a medical condition. Therefore, we reserve carbamazepine as a second- or third-line agent. Oxcarbazepine may eventually prove to be a useful substitute, due to its lower potential for adverse events, drug interactions, and potential utility as a mood stabilizer in children. However, there is certainly more history of documented efficacy of carbamazepine in pediatric psychiatric conditions.

We have found significant utility of lamotrigine in children and adolescents, at this time mainly in children twelve and above. We titrate dosage carefully and gradually based on current recommendations given previously in this chapter. In this manner, we have not found rash incidence to be problematic. We instead have found lamotrigine to be useful in mixed states, rapid cycling, and bipolar depression in adjunctive treatment and monotherapy.

Topiramate has been anecdotally helpful adjunctively in both depression and mania in adolescent patients in our clinic. However, its major use so far has been as an adjunctive treatment to other mood stabilizers for weight loss. Though largely unstudied systematically, this use of topiramate nevertheless has been useful. Gabapentin has been useful in some cases for mood stabilization as an adjunct to other medications, but we have used it more successfully in cases of anxiety, particularly social phobia, and insomnia. Its tolerability has undoubtedly led to increased usage in BD despite the lack of efficacy data for mood stabilization. We have not yet had significant experience with levetiracetam or tiagabine to comment on their clinical utility in children with mood disorders.

Overall, we find that frequently the agents described in this chapter need to be combined with agents from other classes (atypical antipsychotics, ADHD treatments, antidepressants) to successfully treat the myriad symptoms in children and adolescents with bipolar and other mood disorders. We lament that these practices have not been adequately studied (see Chapter 9), and hope that more "real world" studies of combination pharmacotherapy are performed soon.

Lithium and the anticonvulsants are often used for conditions other than bipolar I or II disorder in our clinic. BD NOS is a growing diagnosis as more children are being included in this category in the community. However, it is unclear precisely what this label means in terms of etiology and treatment. Nonetheless, it appears that various medications may be suitable to treat the symptoms of this disorder, in regard to extreme irritability, impulsivity, or aggression. For example, as found in children with CD (Donovan et al., 2000; Steiner et al., in press) divalproex may have utility in decreasing impulsive reactive aggression, regardless of diagnosis. Therefore, we often will use divalproex as well as atypical antipsychotics such as risperidone in treating irritability and aggression in the context of BD NOS or other disorders.

We often encounter one specific situation in which mood stabilizers may eventually become the standard treatment. This situation involves a child or adolescent who presents with an untreated major depressive episode and has a strong family history of BD, perhaps in one or both parents. Currently, the standard of care is to prescribe an SSRI and monitor closely for any subsequent manic symptoms. However, mood stabilizers may eventually prove to be first-line treatments in such cases, both for acute treatment and prophylaxis of later development of mania. In our clinic, based on early data (Chang et al., 2003; Winsberg et al., 2001), we favor use of mood stabilizers such as divalproex in this population. Future longitudinal studies on children at high risk for BD will help to inform as to the most appropriate pharmacological treatment.

◆ ◆ ◆

We must remember that other than lithium, these "mood stabilizers" were first developed to prevent seizures, not to treat BD specifically. Time and experience has led to discovery of novel uses for these agents, including widespread uses in psychiatry. The challenge, as with any medication, is to determine when the benefits of their use outweigh any potential harm, especially in populations as vulnerable as children.

Some current research has focused on the cellular and neurotransmitter-based mechanisms of action of these agents. Divalproex has been proposed to be an antikindling agent (Stoll & Severus, 1996) and has been shown to prevent the kindling of seizures in laboratory rats given repeated subthreshold electrical stimuli. In other animal studies, both lithium and valproate have been shown to inhibit glycogen synthase kinase-3B (Chen, Huang, Jiang, & Manji, 1999), an enzyme which may be involved in activating proteins involved in neuronal death. Valproate also increases frontal cortex Bcl-2 (Chen, Huang, Zeng, & Manji, 2001; Manji et al., 2000), a neurotrophic and neuroprotective protein that may be the downstream agent of endogenous nerve growth factors. Valproate further activates mitogen-activated protein kinases that mediate the effects of these neurotrophic factors to stimulate neural dendritic growth (Chen, Masana, & Manji, 2000; Manji et al., 2000). Interestingly, omega-3 fatty acids have also been shown to inhibit protein kinase C (Seung Kim, Weeber, Sweatt, Stoll, & Marangell, 2001), and have been proposed to aid in the management of BD (Stoll et al., 1999). Lithium has also been reported to increase cortical levels of N-acetyl-aspartate, a marker of neuronal density (Moore, Bebchuk, Hasanat et al., 2000), as well as increase grey matter volumes as seen by MRI (Moore, Bebchuk, Wilds et al., 2000). These early findings suggest that some of these mood stabilizers may not only exert acute mood stabilization effects through these pathways, but also possess neuroprotective qualities. Thus, their use may eventually extend beyond acute and maintenance treatments to use as prophylactic agents.

Future research needs also include finding agents that fulfill all putative requirements of mood stabilizers: that they work in both acute depression or mania, do not exacerbate the other pole, and successfully prevent future mood episodes (Keck & McElroy, 2003). Study of these ideal agents will hopefully be conducted

TABLE 13.4. MOOD STABILIZER FORMULATIONS.

	Capsules		Tablets		Liquid
Lithium					
Generic	150 mg	—	150 mg	—	—
	300 mg	—	300 mg	—	—
	600 mg	—	—	—	—
Eskalith CR	—	—	450 mg	Yellow	—
Lithobid	300 mg	Peach	—	—	—
Lithium citrate	—	—	—	—	300 mg/5 mL
Carbamazepine					
Generic	—	—	100 mg	—	100 mg/5 mL
	—	—	—	—	—
Tegretol	—	—	100 mg	Pink	100 mg/5 mL
	—	—	200 mg	Pink	—
Tegretol XR	—	—	100 mg	White/orange	—
	—	—	200 mg	White/pink	—
	—	—	400 mg	White/brown	—
Carbatrol	200 mg	Bluish-green/black	—	—	—
	300 mg	Bluish-green/gray	—	—	—
Valproic acid					
Generic	250 mg	—	—	—	250 mg/5 mL
Depakote	125 mg	White/blue	125 mg	Salmon-pink	—
	—	—	250 mg	Cream	—
	—	—	500 mg	Lavender	—
Depakote ER	—	—	250 mg	Brown	—
	—	—	500 mg	Brown	—
Gabapentin					
Neurontin	100 mg	White	600 mg	White	250 mg/5 mL
	300 mg	Yellow	800 mg	White	—
	400 mg	Orange	—	—	—
Lamotrigine					
Lamictal	—	—	2 mg*	White	—
	—	—	5 mg*	White	—
			5 mg	Gray	
	—	—	25 mg*	White	—
	—	—	25 mg	Gray	—
	—	—	100 mg	Peach	—
	—	—	150 mg	Cream	—
	—	—	200 mg	Blue	—
Levetiracetam					
Keppra	—	—	250 mg	Blue	—
	—	—	500 mg	Yellow	—
	—	—	750 mg	Orange	—

(Continued)

TABLE 13.4.   MOOD STABILIZER FORMULATIONS (*CONTINUED*).

	Capsules		Tablets		Liquid
Oxcarbazepine					
Trileptal	—	—	150 mg	Yellow	—
	—	—	300 mg	Yellow	—
	—	—	600 mg	Yellow	—
Tiagabine					
Gabitril	—	—	2 mg	Peach	10 mg/5 mL
	—	—	4 mg	Yellow	—
	—	—	12 mg	Green	—
			16 mg	Blue	
			20 mg	Pink	
Topiramate					
Topamax	15 mg	Gray	25 mg	White	—
	25 mg	Gray	100 mg	Yellow	—
	—	—	200 mg	Salmon	—

*chewable/dispersible tablets.

sooner in pediatric populations than has been for other mood stabilizers in the past. Because of the theorized kindling progression of mood disorders (Post, 1992), it may be even more important to develop agents effective in children and adolescents to prevent or ameliorate a potentially severe and chronic course of mood disorder.

References

Appolinario, J. C., Godoy-Matos, A., Povoa, L. C., Fontenelle, L., Bueno, J. R., Papelbaum, M., et al. (2001). *Topiramate in obese patients with binge eating disorder.* Paper presented at the American Psychiatric Association 2002 Annual Meeting, Philadelphia, PA.

Backonja, M., & Glanzman, R. L. (2003). Gabapentin dosing for neuropathic pain: Evidence from randomized, placebo-controlled clinical trials. *Clinical Therapeutics, 25*(1), 81–104.

Ballenger, J. C., & Post, R. M. (1980). Carbamazepine in manic-depressive illness: A new treatment. *American Journal of Psychiatry, 137*(7), 782–790.

Baruzzi, A., Albani, F., & Riva, R. (1994). Oxcarbazepine: Pharmacokinetic interactions and their clinical relevance. *Epilepsia, 35*(Suppl 3), S14–19.

Bauer, J., Jarre, A., Klingmuller, D., & Elger, C. E. (2000). Polycystic ovary syndrome in patients with focal epilepsy: A study in 93 women. *Epilepsy Research, 41*(2), 163–167.

Bauer, M., Bschor, T., Kunz, D., Berghofer, A., Strohle, A., & Muller-Oerlinghausen, B. (2000). Double-blind, placebo-controlled trial of the use of lithium to augment antidepressant medication in continuation treatment of unipolar major depression. *American Journal of Psychiatry, 157*(9), 1429–1435.

Bauer, M. S., & Whybrow, P. C. (1990). Rapid cycling bipolar affective disorder. II. Treatment of refractory rapid cycling with high-dose levothyroxine: A preliminary study. *Archives of General Psychiatry, 47*(5), 435–440.

Bauer, M. S., Whybrow, P. C., & Winokur, A. (1990). Rapid cycling bipolar affective disorder. I. Association with grade I hypothyroidism. *Archives of General Psychiatry, 47*(5), 427–432.

Beijamini, V., Skalisz, L. L., Joca, S. R., & Andreatini, R. (1998). The effect of oxcarbazepine on behavioural despair and learned helplessness. *European Journal of Pharmacology, 347*(1), 23–27.

Berlant, J. L. (2000). *Topiramate in chronic civilian PTSD: An open-label study of a novel treatment.* Paper presented at the American Psychiatric Association 2000 Annual Meeting, Chicago.

Betts, T., Waegemans, T., & Crawford, P. (2000). A multicentre, double-blind, randomized, parallel group study to evaluate the tolerability and efficacy of two oral doses of levetiracetam, 2000 mg daily and 4000 mg daily, without titration in patients with refractory epilepsy. *Seizure, 9*(2), 80–87.

Bocchetta, A., Chillotti, C., Severino, G., Ardau, R., & Del Zompo, M. (1997). Carbamazepine augmentation in lithium-refractory bipolar patients: A prospective study on long-term prophlyactic effectiveness. *Journal of Clinical Psychopharmacology, 17*(2), 92–96.

Bocchetta, A., Mossa, P., Velluzzi, F., Mariotti, S., Zompo, M. D., & Loviselli, A. (2001). Ten-year follow-up of thyroid function in lithium patients. *Journal of Clinical Psychopharmacology, 21*(6), 594–598.

Boellner, S. W., Gu, Y., & Sommerville, K. W. (1996). Long-term trial of tiagabine (gabitril) for partial seizures in children. *Epilepsia, 37*(Suppl 4), 92.

Borusiak, P., Korn-Merker, E., Holert, N., & Boenigk, H. E. (1998). Hyponatremia induced by oxcarbazepine in children. *Epilepsy Research, 30*(3), 241–246.

Bowden, C. L., Brugger, A. M., Swann, A. C., Calabrese, J. R., Janicak, P. G., Petty, F., et al. (1994). Efficacy of divalproex vs lithium and placebo in the treatment of mania. The Depakote Mania Study Group [Published erratum appears in JAMA 1994 Jun 15, *271*(23), 1830] [See comments]. *Journal of the American Medical Association, 271*(12), 918–924.

Bowden, C. L., Calabrese, J. R., McElroy, S. L., Gyulai, L., Wassef, A., Petty, F., et al. (2000). A randomized, placebo-controlled 12-month trial of divalproex and lithium in treatment of outpatients with bipolar I disorder. Divalproex Maintenance Study Group. *Archives of General Psychiatry, 57*(5), 481–489.

Bowden, C. L., Calabrese, J. R., Sachs, G., Yatham, L. N., Asghar, S. A., Hompland, M. et al. Lamictal 606 Study Group. (2003). A placebo-controlled 18-month trial of lamotrigine and lithium maintenance treatment in recently manic or hypomanic patients with bipolar I disorder. *Archives of General Psychiatry, 60*(4), 392–400.

Bozikas, V. P., Petrikis, P., Kourtis, A., Youlis, P., & Karavatos, A. (2002). Treatment of acute mania with topiramate in hospitalized patients. *Progress in Neuro-Psychopharmacology & Biological Psychiatry, 26*(6), 1203–1206.

Brodie, M. J. (1995). Tiagabine pharmacology in profile. *Epilepsia, 36*(Suppl 6), S7–S9.

Bryant, A. E., III, & Dreifuss, F. E. (1996). Valproic acid hepatic fatalities. III. U.S. experience since 1986. *Neurology, 46*(2), 465–469.

Cabrera, J. F., Mühlbauer, H. D., Schley, J., Stoll, K. D., & Müller-Oerlinghausen, B. (1986). Long-term randomized clinical trial on oxcarbazepine vs lithium in bipolar and schizoaffective disorders: Preliminary results. *Pharmacopsychiatry, 19*, 282–283.

Calabrese, J. R., Bowden, C. L., Sachs, G. S., Ascher, J. A., Monaghan, E., & Rudd, G. D. (1999). A double-blind placebo-controlled study of lamotrigine monotherapy in outpatients with bipolar I depression. Lamictal 602 Study Group. *Journal of the Clinical Psychiatry, 60*(2), 79–88.

Calabrese, J. R., Markovitz, P. J., Kimmel, S. E., & Wagner, S. C. (1992). Spectrum of efficacy of valproate in 78 rapid-cycling bipolar patients. *Journal of Clinical Psychopharmacology, 12*(Suppl 1), 53S–56S.

Calabrese, J. R., Rapport, D. J., Kimmel, S. E., Reece, B., & Woyshville, M. J. (1993). Rapid cycling bipolar disorder and its treatment with valproate. *Canadian Journal of Psychiatry, 38*(3 Suppl 2), S57–61.

Calabrese, J. R., Suppes, T., Bowden, C. L., Sachs, G. S., Swann, A. C., McElroy, S. L., et al. (2000). A double-blind, placebo-controlled, prophylaxis study of lamotrigine in rapid-cycling bipolar disorder. Lamictal 614 Study Group. *Journal of Clinical Psychiatry, 61*(11), 841–850.

Calabrese, J. R., & Woyshville, M. J. (1995). Lithium therapy: Limitations and alternatives in the treatment of bipolar disorders. *Annals of Clinical Psychiatry, 7*(2), 103–112.

Campbell, M., Adams, P. B., Small, A. M., Kafantaris, V., Silva, R. R., Shell, J., et al. (1995). Lithium in hospitalized aggressive children with conduct disorder: A double-blind and placebo-controlled study. *Journal of the American Academy of Child and Adolescent Psychiatry, 34*(4), 445–453.

Cereghino, J. J., Biton, V., Abou-Khalil, B., Dreifuss, F., Gauer, L. J., & Leppik, I. (2000). Levetiracetam for partial seizures: Results of a double-blind, randomized clinical trial. *Neurology, 55*(2), 236–242.

Chang, K. D., Dienes, K., Blasey, C., Steiner, H., & Ketter, T. A. (2003). Divalproex in the treatment of bipolar offspring with mood and behavioral disorders and at least mild affective symptoms. *Journal of Clinical Psychiatry, 53*, 945–951.

Chang, K. D., Keck, P. E., Jr., Stanton, S. P., McElroy, S. L., Strakowski, S. M., & Geracioti, T. D., Jr. (1998). Differences in thyroid function between bipolar manic and mixed states. *Biological Psychiatry, 43*(10), 730–733.

Chang, K. D., & Ketter, T. A. (2001). Special issues in the treatment of paediatric bipolar disorder. *Expert Opinion in Pharmacotherapy, 2*(4), 613–622.

Chen, G., Huang, L. D., Jiang, Y. M., & Manji, H. K. (1999). The mood-stabilizing agent valproate inhibits the activity of glycogen synthase kinase-3. *Journal of Neurochemistry, 72*(3), 1327–1330.

Chen, G., Huang, L. D., Zeng, W. Z., & Manji, H. (2001). Mood stabilizers regulate cytoprotective and mRNA-binding proteins in the brain: Long-term effects on cell survival and transcript stability. *International Journal of Neuropsychopharmacology, 4*(1), 47–64.

Chen, G., Masana, M. I., & Manji, H. K. (2000). Lithium regulates PKC-mediated intracellular cross-talk and gene expression in the CNS in vivo. *Bipolar Disorder, 2*(3 Pt. 2), 217–236.

Chengappa, K. N., Rathore, D., Levine, J., Atzert, R., Solai, L., Parepally, H. et al. (1999). Topiramate as add-on treatment for patients with bipolar mania. *Bipolar Disorder, 1*(1), 42–53.

Cloyd, J. C., Fischer, J. H., Kriel, R. L., & Kraus, D. M. (1993). Valproic acid pharmacokinetics in children. IV. Effects of age and antiepileptic drugs on protein binding and intrinsic clearance. *Clinical Pharmacology & Therapeutics, 53*(1), 22–29.

Cohen, L. S., Friedman, J. M., Jefferson, J. W., Johnson, E. M., & Weiner, M. L. (1994). A reevaluation of risk of in utero exposure to lithium. *Journal of American Medical Association, 271*(2), 146–150.

Cooper, T. B., Bergner, P. E., & Simpson, G. M. (1973). The 24-hour serum lithium level as a prognosticator of dosage requirements. *American Journal of Psychiatry, 130*(5), 601–603.

Cowdry, R. W., Wehr, T. A., Zis, A. P., & Goodwin, F. K. (1983). Thyroid abnormalities associated with rapid-cycling bipolar illness. *Archives of General Psychiatry, 40*(4), 414–420.

Crane, D. L. (2002). *Tiagabine, a selective GABA reuptake inhibitor for the treatment of anxiety.* Paper presented at the American Psychiatric Association Annual Meeting, Philadelphia, PA.

Cueva, J. E., Overall, J. E., Small, A. M., Armenteros, J. L., Perry, R., & Campbell, M. (1996). Carbamazepine in aggressive children with conduct disorder: A double-blind and placebo-controlled study. *Journal of the American Academy of Child and Adolescent Psychiatry, 35*(4), 480–490.

Davanzo, P. A., Cantwell, E., Kleiner, J., Baltaxe, C., Najera, B., Crecelius, G., et al. (2001). Cognitive changes during topiramate therapy. *Journal of the American Academy of Child and Adolescent Psychiatry, 40*(3), 262–263.

Davanzo, P. A., & King, B. H. (1996). Open trial lamotrigine in the treatment of self-injurious behavior in an adolescent with profound mental retardation. *Journal of Child and Adolescent Psychopharmacology, 6*(4), 273–279.

Davanzo, P. A., & McCracken, J. T. (2000). Mood stabilizers in the treatment of juvenile bipolar disorder. Advances and controversies. *Child and Adolescent Psychiatric Clinics of North America, 9*(1), 159–182.

DelBello, M. P., Kowatch, R. A., Warner, J., Schwiers, M. L., Rappaport, K. B., Daniels, J. P., et al. (2002). Adjunctive topiramate treatment for pediatric bipolar disorder: A retrospective chart review. *Journal of Child and Adolescent Psychopharmacology, 12*(4), 323–330.

DelBello, M. P., Schwiers, M. L., Rosenberg, H. L., & Strakowski, S. M. (2002). A double-blind, randomized, placebo-controlled study of quetiapine as adjunctive treatment for adolescent mania. *Journal of the American Academy of Child and Adolescent Psychiatry, 41*(10), 1216–1223.

DeLong, G. R. (1978). Lithium carbonate treatment of select behavior disorders in children suggesting manic-depressive illness. *Journal of Pediatrics, 93*(4), 689–694.

Denicoff, K. D., Smith-Jackson, E. E., Disney, E. R., Ali, S. O., Leverich, G. S., & Post, R. M. (1997). Comparative prophylactic efficacy of lithium, carbamazepine, and the combination in bipolar disorder. *Journal of Clinical Psychiatry, 58*(11), 470–478.

Deodhar, S. D., Singh, B., Pathak, C. M., Sharan, P., & Kulhara, P. (1999). Thyroid functions in lithium-treated psychiatric patients: A cross sectional study. *Biological Trace Element Research, 67*(2), 151–163.

Donovan, S. J., Stewart, J. W., Nunes, E. V., Quitkin, F. M., Parides, M., Daniel, W., et al. (2000). Divalproex treatment for youth with explosive temper and mood lability: A double-blind, placebo-controlled crossover design. *American Journal of Psychiatry, 157*(5), 818–820.

Donovan, S. J., Susser, E. S., Nunes, E. V., Stewart, J. W., Quitkin, F. M., & Klein, D. F. (1997). Divalproex treatment of disruptive adolescents: A report of 10 cases. *Journal of Clinical Psychiatry, 58*(1), 12–15.

Dooley, J., Camfield, P., Gordon, K., Camfield, C., Wirrell, Z., & Smith, E. (1996). Lamotrigine-induced rash in children. *Neurology, 46*(1), 240–242.

Dutta, S., Zhang, Y., Selness, D. S., Lee, L. L., Williams, L. A., & Sommerville, K. W. (2002). Comparison of the bioavailability of unequal doses of divalproex sodium extended-release formulation relative to the delayed-release formulation in healthy volunteers. *Epilepsy Research, 49*(1), 1–10.

Emrich, H. M. (1990). Studies with oxcarbazepine (trileptal) in acute mania. *International Clinical Psychopharmacology, 5*(Suppl. 1), 83–88.

Erfurth, A., Kammerer, C., Grunze, H., Normann, C., & Walden, J. (1998). An open label study of gabapentin in the treatment of acute mania. *Journal of Psychiatric Research, 32*(5), 261–264.

Ernst, C. L., & Goldberg, J. F. (2002). The reproductive safety profile of mood stabilizers, atypical antipsychotics, and broad-spectrum psychotropics. *Journal of Clinical Psychiatry, 63*(Suppl 4), 42–55.

Evans, R. W., & Gualtieri, C. T. (1985). Carbamazepine: A neuropsychological and psychiatric profile. *Clinical Neuropharmacology, 8*(3), 221–241.

Faught, E., Kuzniecky, R. I., & Gilliam, F. (1997). Cognitive adverse effects of topiramate. *Neurology, 48,* A336.

Fayad, M., Choueiri, R., & Mikati, M. (2000). Potential hepatotoxicity of lamotrigine. *Pediatric Neurology, 22*(1), 49–52.

Findling, R. L. (2002). *Evolving maintenance trial designs in pediatric bipolarity.* Paper presented at the 41st Annual Meeting of the American College of Neuropsychopharmacology, San Juan, Puerto Rico.

Findling, R. L., McNamara, N. K., Gracious, B. L., Youngstrom, E. A., Stansbrey, R. J., Reed, M. D., Demeter, C. A., Branicky, L. A., Fisher, K. E., & Calabrese, J. R., (2003). Combination lithium and divalproex sodium in pediatric bipolarity. *Journal of the American Academy of Child and Adolescent Psychiatry, 42*(8), 895–901.

Findling, R. L., Gracious, B. L., McNamara, N. K., & Calabrese, J. R. (2000). The rationale, design, and progress of two novel maintenance treatment studies in pediatric bipolarity. *Acta Neuropsychiatrica, 12,* 136–138.

Findling, R. L., Gracious, B. L., McNamara, N. K., Youngstrom, E. A., Demeter, C. A., Branicky, L. A., et al. (2001). Rapid, continuous cycling and psychiatric co-morbidity in pediatric bipolar I disorder. *Bipolar Disorder, 3*(4), 202–210.

Frye, M. A., Ketter, T. A., Kimbrell, T. A., Dunn, R. T., Speer, A. M., Osuch, E. A., et al. (2000). A placebo-controlled study of lamotrigine and gabapentin monotherapy in refractory mood disorders. *Journal of Clinical Psychopharmacology, 20*(6), 607–614.

Gaily, E., Granström, M., & Lindahl, E. (1995). Oxcarbazepine in early childhood epilepsy. *Epilepsia, 36*(Suppl 3), S118.

Garnett, W. R. (1997). Lamotrigine: Pharmacokinetics. *Journal of Child Neurology, 12*(Suppl 1), S10–15.

Geller, B., Cooper, T. B., Sun, K., Zimerman, B., Frazier, J., Williams, M., et al. (1998). Double-blind and placebo-controlled study of lithium for adolescent bipolar disorders with secondary substance dependency. *Journal of the American Academy of Child and Adolescent Psychiatry, 37*(2), 171–178.

Geller, B., Cooper, T. B., Zimerman, B., Frazier, J., Williams, M., Heath, J., et al. (1998). Lithium for prepubertal depressed children with family history predictors of future bipolarity: A double-blind, placebo-controlled study. *Journal of Affective Disorders, 51*(2), 165–175.

Geller, B., Sun, K., Zimerman, B., Luby, J., Frazier, J., & Williams, M. (1995). Complex and rapid-cycling in bipolar children and adolescents: A preliminary study. *Journal of Affective Disorders, 34*(4), 259–268.

Ghaemi, S., Ko, J. Y., & Katzow, J. J. (2002). Oxcarbazepine treatment of refractory bipolar disorder: A retrospective chart review. *Bipolar Disorder, 4*(1), 70–74.

Ghaemi, S. N., & Goodwin, F. K. (2001). Gabapentin treatment of the non-refractory bipolar spectrum: An open case series. *Journal of Affective Disorders, 65*(2), 167–171.

Glauser, T. A., Nigro, M., Sachdeo, R., Pasteris, L. A., Weinstein, S., Abou-Khalil, B., et al. (2000). Adjunctive therapy with oxcarbazepine in children with partial seizures. The Oxcarbazepine Pediatric Study Group. *Neurology, 54*(12), 2237–2244.

Good, C. R., Feaster, C. S., & Krecko, V. F. (2001). Tolerability of oral loading of divalproex sodium in child psychiatry inpatients. *Journal of Child and Adolescent Psychopharmacology,11*(1), 53–57.

Greil, W., Kleindienst, N., Erazo, N., & Muller-Oerlinghausen, B. (1998). Differential response to lithium and carbamazepine in the prophylaxis of bipolar disorder. *Journal of Clinical Psychopharmacology, 18*(6), 455–460.

Grunze, H., Erfurth, A., Marcuse, A., Amann, B., Normann, C., & Walden, J. (1999). Tiagabine appears not to be efficacious in the treatment of acute mania. *Journal of Clinical Psychiatry, 60*(11), 759–762.

Guberman, A. H., Besag, F. M., Brodie, M. J., Dooley, J. M., Duchowny, M. S., Pellock, J. M., et al. (1999). Lamotrigine-associated rash: Risk/benefit considerations in adults and children. *Epilepsia, 40*(7), 985–991.

Guerreiro, M. M., Vigonius, U., Pohlmann, H., de Manreza, M. L., Fejerman, N., Antoniuk, S. A., et al. (1997). A double-blind controlled clinical trial of oxcarbazepine versus pheny-toin in children and adolescents with epilepsy. *Epilepsy Research, 27*(3), 205–213.

Gustavson, L. E., Boellner, S. W., Granneman, G. R., Qian, J. X., Guenther, H. J., el-Shourbagy, T., et al. (1997). A single-dose study to define tiagabine pharmacokinetics in pediatric patients with complex partial seizures. *Neurology, 48*(4), 1032–1037.

Gustavson, L. E., & Mengel, H. B. (1995). Pharmacokinetics of tiagabine, a gamma-aminobutyric acid-uptake inhibitor, in healthy subjects after single and multiple doses. *Epilepsia, 36*(6), 605–611.

Haig, G. M., Bockbrader, H. N., Wesche, D. L., Boellner, S. W., Ouellet, D., Brown, R. R., et al. (2001). Single-dose gabapentin pharmacokinetics and safety in healthy infants and children. *Journal of Clinical Pharmacology, 41*(5), 507–514.

Hamrin, V., & Bailey, K. (2001). Gabapentin and methylphenidate treatment of a preadoles-cent with attention deficit hyperactivity disorder and bipolar disorder. *Journal of Child and Adolescent Psychopharmacology, 11*(3), 301–309.

Hassanyeh, F., & Davison, K. (1980). Bipolar affective psychosis with onset before age 16 years: Report of 10 cases. *The British Journal of Psychiatry, 137*, 530–539.

Himmelhoch, J. M., & Garfinkel, M. E. (1986). Sources of lithium resistance in mixed mania. *Psychopharmacology Bulletin, 22*(3), 613–620.

Hollander, E., Dolgoff-Kaspar, R., Cartwright, C., Rawitt, R., & Novotny, S. (2001). An open trial of divalproex sodium in autism spectrum disorders. *Journal of Clinical Psychiatry, 62*(7), 530–534.

Hoopes, S. P., Reimherr, F. W., Kamin, M., Karvois, D., Rosenthal, N. E., & Karim, R. (2002). *Topiramate treatment of bulimia nervosa.* Paper presented at the American Psychiatric Association 2002 Annual Meeting, Philadelphia, PA.

Hsu, L. K. (1986). Lithium-resistant adolescent mania. *Journal of the American Academy of Child and Adolescent Psychiatry, 25*(2), 280–283.

Hummel, B., Stampfer, R., Grunze, H., Schlösser, S., Amann, B., Frye, M., et al. (2001). Acute antimanic efficacy and safety of oxcarbazepine in an open trial with on-off-on design. *Bipolar Disorder, 3*(Suppl 1), 43.

Hussain, M. Z. (2001). *Evaluation and intervention of prodromal symptoms of bipolar disorder.* Paper presented at the New Clinical Drug Evaluation Unit, 41st Annual Meeting, Scottsdale, AZ.

Hussain, M. Z., Hussain, S., & Chaudhry, Z. A. (2000). *Topiramate as an anti-obesity agent.* Paper presented at the American Psychiatric Association 2000 Annual Meeting, Chicago.

Hussain, S., Chaudhry, Z. A., & Hussain, M. Z. (2000). *Topiramate in premenstrual dysphoric disorder.* Paper presented at the American Psychiatric Association Annual Meeting, Chicago.

Isojarvi, J. I., Laatikainen, T. J., Knip, M., Pakarinen, A. J., Juntunen, K. T., & Myllyla, V. V. (1996). Obesity and endocrine disorders in women taking valproate for epilepsy [see comments]. *Annals of Neurology, 39*(5), 579–584.

Isojarvi, J. I., Laatikainen, T. J., Pakarinen, A. J., Juntunen, K. T., & Myllyla, V. V. (1993). Polycystic ovaries and hyperandrogenism in women taking valproate for epilepsy. *New England Journal of Medicine, 329*(19), 1383–1388.

Joca, S. R., Skalisz, L. L., Beijamini, V., Vital, M. A., & Andreatini, R. (2000). The antidepressive-like effect of oxcarbazepine: Possible role of dopaminergic neurotransmission. *European Neuropsychopharmacology, 10*(4), 223–228.

Kafantaris, V., Campbell, M., Padron-Gayol, M. V., Small, A. M., Locascio, J. J., & Rosenberg, C. R. (1992). Carbamazepine in hospitalized aggressive conduct disorder children: An open pilot study. *Psychopharmacology Bulletin, 28*(2), 193–199.

Kafantaris, V., Coletti, D. J., Dicker, R., Padula, G., & Kane, J. M. (2003). Lithium treatment of acute mania in adolescents: A large open trial. *Journal of the American Academy of Child and Adolescent Psychiatry, 42*(9), 1038–45.

Kastner, T., Friedman, D. L., Plummer, A. T., Ruiz, M. Q., & Henning, D. (1990). Valproic acid for the treatment of children with mental retardation and mood symptomatology. *Pediatrics, 86*(3), 467–472.

Kato, T., Shioiri, T., Inubushi, T., & Takahashi, S. (1993). Brain lithium concentrations measured with lithium-7 magnetic resonance spectroscopy in patients with affective disorders: Relationship to erythrocyte and serum concentrations. *Biological Psychiatry, 33*(3), 147–152.

Kaufman, K. R. (1998). Adjunctive tiagabine treatment of psychiatric disorders: Three cases. *Annals of Clinical Psychiatry, 10*(4), 181–184.

Kaufman, K. R., & Gerner, R. (1998). Lamotrigine toxicity secondary to sertraline. *Seizure, 7*(2), 163–165.

Keck, P. E., Jr., & McElroy, S. L. (2002). Carbamazepine and valproate in the maintenance treatment of bipolar disorder. *Journal of Clinical Psychiatry, 63*(Suppl 10), 13–17.

Keck, P. E., & McElroy, S. L. (2003). Redefining mood stabilization. *Journal of Affective Disorders, 73*(1–2), 163–169.

Khurana, D. S., Riviello, J., Helmers, S., Holmes, G., Anderson, J., & Mikati, M. A. (1996). Efficacy of gabapentin therapy in children with refractory partial seizures. *Journal of Pediatrics, 128*(6), 829–833.

Kowatch, R. A., Suppes, T., Carmody, T. J., Bucci, J. P., Hume, J. H., Kromelis, M., et al. (2000). Effect size of lithium, divalproex sodium, and carbamazepine in children and adolescents with bipolar disorder. *Journal of the American Academy of Child and Adolescent Psychiatry, 39*(6), 713–720.

Kusumakar, V., & Yatham, L. N. (1997). An open study of lamotrigine in refractory bipolar depression. *Psychiatry Research, 72*(2), 145–148.

Kutcher, S. P., Marton, P., & Korenblum, M. (1990). Adolescent bipolar illness and personality disorder. *Journal of the American Academy of Child and Adolescent Psychiatry, 29*(3), 355–358.

Lara, M. E. (2002). *Adjunctive use of tiagabine with antidepressants in PTSD.* Paper presented at the American Psychiatric Association 2002 Annual Meeting, Philadelphia, PA.

Lazarus, J. H. (1998). The effects of lithium therapy on thyroid and thyrotropin-releasing hormone. *Thyroid, 8*(10), 909–913.

Lee, D. O., Steingard, R. J., Cesena, M., Helmers, S. L., Riviello, J. J., & Mikati, M. A. (1996). Behavioral side effects of gabapentin in children. *Epilepsia, 37*(1), 87–90.

Leppik, I. E. (1995). Tiagabine: The safety landscape. *Epilepsia, 36*(Suppl 6), S10–S13.

Levetiracetam: Combination therapy with other antiepileptic drugs in animal models. (2001). Paper presented at the American Epilepsy Society Annual Meeting, Philadelphia, PA.

Leweke, F. M., Bauer, J., & Elger, C. E. (1999). Manic episode due to gabapentin treatment. *The British Journal of Psychiatry, 175,* 291.

Longin, E., Teich, M., Koelfen, W., & Konig, S. (2002). Topiramate enhances the risk of valproate-associated side effects in three children. *Epilepsia, 43*(4), 451–454.

Manji, H. K., Moore, G. J., & Chen, G. (1999). Lithium at 50: Have the neuroprotective effects of this unique cation been overlooked? *Biological Psychiatry, 46*(7), 929–940.

Manji, H. K., Moore, G. J., & Chen, G. (2000). Clinical and preclinical evidence for the neurotrophic effects of mood stabilizers: Implications for the pathophysiology and treatment of manic-depressive illness. *Biological Psychiatry, 48*(8), 740–754.

Marcotte, D. (1998). Use of topiramate, a new anti-epileptic as a mood stabilizer. *Journal of Affective Disorders, 50*(2–3), 245–251.

Marcotte, D., & Gullick, E. (2001). Long-term treatment with topiramate for bipolar disorder. *Bipolar Disorder, 3*(Suppl 1), 46.

Martin, R., Kuzniecky, R., Ho, S., Hetherington, H., Pan, J., Sinclair, K., et al. (1999). Cognitive effects of topiramate, gabapentin, and lamotrigine in healthy young adults. *Neurology, 52*(2), 321–327.

Mataringa, M. I., May, T. W., & Rambeck, B. (2002). Does lamotrigine influence valproate concentrations? *Therapeutic Drug Monitoring, 24*(5), 631–636.

McCracken, J. T., & Diamond, R. P. (1988). Bipolar disorder in mentally retarded adolescents. *Journal of the American Academy of Child and Adolescent Psychiatry, 27*(4), 494–499.

McDougle, C. J., Stern, A. E., & Bangs, M. E. (2001). Bipolar disorder in children and adolescents, Part II: Valproate and other newer treatments. *International Drug Therapy Newsletter, 36*(1), 1–8.

McElroy, S. L., Suppes, T., Keck, P. E., Frye, M. A., Denicoff, K. D., Altshuler, L. L., et al. (2000). Open-label adjunctive topiramate in the treatment of bipolar disorders. *Biological Psychiatry, 47*(12), 1025–1033.

McIntyre, R. S., Girgla, S., Binder, C., Riccardelli, R., & Kennedy, S. (2002). *Efficacy of topiramate as adjunctive therapy to mood stabilizers in patients with bipolar I or II disorder.* Paper presented at the American College of Neuropsychopharmacology 41st Annual Meeting, San Juan, Puerto Rico.

McKnew, D. H., Cytryn, L., Buchsbaum, M. S., Hamovit, J., Lamour, M., Rapoport, J. L., et al. (1981). Lithium in children of lithium-responding parents. *Psychiatry Research, 4*(2), 171–180.

McLean, M. J. (1995). Gabapentin. *Epilepsia, 36*(Suppl 2), S73–86.

Mellegers, M. A., Furlan, A. D., & Mailis, A. (2001). Gabapentin for neuropathic pain: Systematic review of controlled and uncontrolled literature. *The Clinical Journal of Pain, 17*(4), 284–295.

Messenheimer, J. (2002). Efficacy and safety of lamotrigine in pediatric patients. *Journal of Child Neurology, 17*(Suppl 2), 2S34–32S42.

Messenheimer, J. A., Giorgi, L., & Risner, M. E. (2000). The tolerability of lamotrigine in children. *Drug Safety, 22*(4), 303–312.

Moore, C. M., Demopulos, C. M., Henry, M. E., Steingard, R. J., Zamvil, L., Katic, A., et al. (2002). Brain-to-serum lithium ratio and age: An in vivo magnetic resonance spectroscopy study. *American Journal of Psychiatry, 159*(7), 1240–1242.

Moore, G. J., Bebchuk, J. M., Hasanat, K., Chen, G., Seraji-Bozorgzad, N., Wilds, I. B., et al. (2000). Lithium increases N-acetyl-aspartate in the human brain: In vivo evidence in support of bcl-2's neurotrophic effects? *Biological Psychiatry, 48*(1), 1–8.

Moore, G. J., Bebchuk, J. M., Wilds, I. B., Chen, G., Manji, H. K., & Menji, H. K. (2000). Lithium-induced increase in human brain grey matter. *Lancet, 356*(9237), 1241–1242.

Mota-Castillo, M., Torruella, A., Engels, B., Perez, J., Dedrick, C., & Gluckman, M. (2001). Valproate in very young children: An open case series with a brief follow-up. *Journal of Affective Disorders, 67*(1–3), 193–197.

Motte, J., Arzimanoglou, A. A., Billard, C., Boidein, F., Boulloche, J., Carriere, J., et al. (1995). Open study of tolerability of oxcarbazepine in children. *Epilepsia, 36*(Suppl 3), S118.

Müller, A. A., & Stroll, K. D. (1984). Carbamazepine and oxcarbazepine in the treatment of manic syndromes: Studies in Germany. In H. M. Emrich, T. Okuma, & A. A. Müller (Eds.), *Anticonvulsants in affective disorders* (pp. 139–147). Amsterdam-Oxford-Princeton: Excerpta Medica.

Munoz, R. A. (2002). *Oxcarbazepine for the treatment of bipolar disorder.* Paper presented at the American Psychiatric Association 2002 Annual Meeting, Philadelphia, PA.

Nasr, S. J., & Casper, M. L. (2002). *Oxcarbazepine use in the treatment of mood disorders.* Paper presented at the American Psychiatric Association Annual Meeting, Philadelphia, PA.

Okuma, T. (1983). Therapeutic and prophylactic effects of carbamazepine in bipolar disorders. *Psychiatric Clinics of North America, 6*(1), 157–174.

Pande, A. C., Davidson, J. R., Jefferson, J. W., Janney, C. A., Katzelnick, D. J., Weisler, R. H., et al. (1999). Treatment of social phobia with gabapentin: A placebo-controlled study. *Journal of Clinical Psychopharmacology, 19*(4), 341–348.

Pande, A. C., Pollack, M. H., Crockatt, J., Greiner, M., Chouinard, G., Lydiard, R. B., et al. (2000). Placebo-controlled study of gabapentin treatment of panic disorder. *Journal of Clinical Psychopharmacology, 20*(4), 467–471.

Papatheodorou, G., & Kutcher, S. P. (1993). Divalproex sodium treatment in late adolescent and young adult acute mania. *Psychopharmacology Bulletin, 29*(2), 213–219.

Papatheodorou, G., Kutcher, S. P., Katic, M., & Szalai, J. P. (1995). The efficacy and safety of divalproex sodium in the treatment of acute mania in adolescents and young adults: An open clinical trial. *Journal of Clinical Psychopharmacology, 15*(2), 110–116.

Patsalos, P. N. (2000). Pharmacokinetic profile of levetiracetam: Toward ideal characteristics. *Pharmacological Therapy, 85*(2), 77–85.

Pavuluri, M. N., Janicak, P. G., & Carbray, J. (2002). Topiramate plus risperidone for controlling weight gain and symptoms in preschool mania. *Journal of Child and Adolescent Psychopharmacology, 12*(3), 271–273.

Pellock, J. M. (2001). Tiagabine (gabitril) experience in children. *Epilepsia, 42*(Suppl 3), 49–51.

Pellock, J. M., Glauser, T. A., Bebin, E. M., Fountain, N. B., Ritter, F. J., Coupez, R. M., et al. (2001). Pharmacokinetic study of levetiracetam in children. *Epilepsia, 42*(12), 1574–1579.

Physicians Desk Reference. (55th ed.)(2001). Montvale, NJ: Medical Economics Co.

Pleak, R. R., Birmaher, B., Gavrilescu, A., Abichandani, C., & Williams, D. T. (1988). Mania and neuropsychiatric excitation following carbamazepine. *Journal of the American Academy of Child and Adolescent Psychiatry, 27*(4), 500–503.

Post, R. M. (1992). Transduction of psychosocial stress into the neurobiology of recurrent affective disorder. *American Journal of Psychiatry, 149*(8), 999–1010.

Prien, R. F., Himmelhoch, J. M., & Kupfer, D. J. (1988). Treatment of mixed mania. *Journal of Affective Disorders, 15*(1), 9–15.

Purdy, R. E., Julien, R. M., Fairhurst, A. S., & Terry, M. D. (1977). Effect of carbamazepine on the in vitro uptake and release of norepinephrine in adrenergic nerves of rabbit aorta and in whole brain synaptosomes. *Epilepsia, 18*(2), 251–257.

Rasgon, N. L., Altshuler, L. L., Gudeman, D., Burt, V. K., Tanavoli, S., Hendrick, V., et al. (2000). Medication status and polycystic ovary syndrome in women with bipolar disorder: A preliminary report. *Journal of Clinical Psychiatry, 61*(3), 173–178.

Reinstein, M. J., Sonnenberg, J. G., Chasanov, M. A., Mohan, S. C., Patel, S. A., Jones, L. E., et al. (2001). *Oxcarbazepine and divalproex sodium: A comparison of efficacy and side effects for mania.* Paper presented at the American Psychiatric Association Annual Meeting, New Orleans.

Reinstein, M. J., Sonnenberg, J. G., Mohan, S. C., Chasanov, M. A., Koltun, A., Reyngold, P., et al. (2002). *Review of 200 subjects treated for mania with oxcarbazepine in a hospital setting.* Paper presented at the American Psychiatric Association Annual Meeting, Philadelphia, PA.

Reiss, A. L., & O'Donnell, D. J. (1984). Carbamazepine-induced mania in two children: Case report. *Journal of Clinical Psychiatry, 45*(6), 272–274.

Remschmidt, H. (1976). The psychotropic effect of carbamazepine in nonepileptic patients with particular reference to problems posed by clinical studies in children with behavioural disorders. In W. Birkmayer (Ed.), *Epileptic seizures-behaviour-pain.* Bern, Switzerland: Hans Huber.

Remsing, L., Chang, K. D., Saxena, K., Silverman, M., & Steiner, H. (2002). *Divalproex sodium in conduct disorder: Response rates and aggression.* Paper presented at the American Psychiatric Association Annual Meeting, Philadelphia, PA.

Rosenfeld, W. E., Doose, D. R., Walker, S. A., Baldassarre, J. S., & Reife, R. A. (1999). A study of topiramate pharmacokinetics and tolerability in children with epilepsy. *Pediatrics Neurology, 20*(5), 339–344.

Rugino, T. A., & Samsock, T. C. (2002). Levetiracetam in autistic children: An open-label study. *Journal of Developmental and Behavioral Pediatrics, 23*(4), 225–230.

Ryan, N. D., Meyer, V., Dachille, S., Mazzie, D., & Puig-Antich, J. (1988). Lithium antidepressant augmentation in TCA-refractory depression in adolescents. *Journal of the American Academy of Child and Adolescent Psychiatry, 27*(3), 371–376.

Sachs, G. S., & Thase, M. E. (2000). Bipolar disorder therapeutics: Maintenance treatment. *Biological Psychiatry, 48*(6), 573–581.

Samren, E. B., van Duijn, C. M., Koch, S., Hiilesmaa, V. K., Klepel, H., Bardy, A. H., et al. (1997). Maternal use of antiepileptic drugs and the risk of major congenital malformations: A joint European prospective study of human teratogenesis associated with maternal epilepsy. *Epilepsia, 38*(9), 981–990.

Schaeffer, R., & Kowatch, R. (2002). *Combination pharmacotherapy in pediatric bipolar disorders— treating comorbid ADHD.* Paper presented at the Scientific Proceedings of the 49th Annual Meeting of the American Academy of Child and Adolescent Psychiatry, San Francisco, CA.

Schaffer, C. B., & Schaffer, L. C. (1999). Open maintenance treatment of bipolar disorder spectrum patients who responded to gabapentin augmentation in the acute phase of treatment. *Journal of Affective Disorders, 55*(2–3), 237–240.

Schaffer, L. C., & Schaffer, C. B. (1999). Tiagabine and the treatment of refractory bipolar disorder. *American Journal of Psychiatry, 156*(12), 2014–2015.

Schaffer, L. C., Schaffer, C. B., & Howe, J. (2002). An open case series on the utility of tiagabine as an augmentation in refractory bipolar outpatients. *Journal of Affective Disorders, 71*(1–3), 259–263.

Schwabe, M. J., & Wheless, J. W. (2001). Clinical experience with topiramate dosing and serum levels in children 12 years or under with epilepsy. *Journal of Child Neurology, 16*(11), 806–808.

Seung Kim, H. F., Weeber, E. J., Sweatt, J. D., Stoll, A. L., & Marangell, L. B. (2001). Inhibitory effects of omega-3 fatty acids on protein kinase C activity in vitro. *Molecular Psychiatry, 6*(2), 246–248.

Shank, R. P. (1998). *Rationale for evaluating topiramate in bipolar disorders: Mechanism of action.* Paper presented at the 21st Congress of the Collegium Internationale Neuro-Psychopharmacologicum, Glasgow, UK.

Short, C., & Cooke, L. (1995). Hypomania induced by gabapentin. *British Journal of Psychiatry, 166*(5), 679–680.

Silva, R. R., Munoz, D. M., & Alpert, M. (1996). Carbamazepine use in children and adolescents with features of attention-deficit hyperactivity disorder: A meta-analysis. *Journal of the American Academy of Child and Adolescent Psychiatry, 35*(3), 352–358.

Sotero de Menezes, M. A., Rho, J. M., Murphy, P., & Cheyette, S. (2000). Lamotrigine-induced tic disorder: Report of five pediatric cases. *Epilepsia, 41*(7), 862–867.

Soutullo, C. A., Casuto, L. S., & Keck, P. E., Jr. (1998). Gabapentin in the treatment of adolescent mania: A case report. *Journal of Child and Adolescent Psychopharmacology, 8*(1), 81–85.

Steiner, H., Petersen, M., Saxena, K., Ford, S., & Matthews, Z. in press. A randomized clinical trial of divalproex sodium in severe conduct disorders. *Journal of Clinical Psychiatry.*

Stoll, A. L., & Severus, W. E. (1996). Mood stabilizers: Shared mechanisms of action at postsynaptic signal-transduction and kindling processes. *Harvard Review of Psychiatry, 4*(2), 77–89.

Stoll, A. L., Severus, W. E., Freeman, M. P., Rueter, S., Zboyan, H. A., Diamond, E., et al. (1999). Omega 3 fatty acids in bipolar disorder: A preliminary double-blind, placebo-controlled trial. *Archives of General Psychiatry, 56*(5), 407–412.

Strober, M., DeAntonio, M., Schmidt-Lackner, S., Freeman, R., Lampert, C., & Diamond, J. (1998). Early childhood attention deficit hyperactivity disorder predicts poorer response to acute lithium therapy in adolescent mania. *Journal of Affective Disorders, 51*(2), 145–151.

Strober, M., Freeman, R., Rigali, J., Schmidt, S., & Diamond, R. (1992). The pharmacotherapy of depressive illness in adolescence: II. Effects of lithium augmentation in nonresponders to imipramine. *Journal of the American Academy of Child and Adolescent Psychiatry, 31*(1), 16–20.

Strober, M., Morrell, W., Burroughs, J., Lampert, C., Danforth, H., & Freeman, R. (1988). A family study of bipolar I disorder in adolescence. Early onset of symptoms linked to increased familial loading and lithium resistance. *Journal of Affective Disorders, 15*(3), 255–268.

Strober, M., Morrell, W., Lampert, C., & Burroughs, J. (1990). Relapse following discontinuation of lithium maintenance therapy in adolescents with bipolar I illness: A naturalistic study. *American Journal of Psychiatry, 147*(4), 457–461.

Suppes, T., Brown, E. S., McElroy, S. L., Keck, P. E., Jr., Nolen, W., Kupka, R., et al. (1999). Lamotrigine for the treatment of bipolar disorder: A clinical case series. *Journal of Affective Disorders, 53*(1), 95–98.

Suzdak, P. D., & Jansen, J. A. (1995). A review of the preclinical pharmacology of tiagabine: A potent and selective anticonvulsant GABA uptake inhibitor. *Epilepsia, 36*(6), 612–626.

Teitelbaum, M. (2001). Oxcarbazepine in bipolar disorder. *Journal of the American Academy of Child and Adolescent Psychiatry, 40*(9), 993–994.

Tueth, M. J., Murphy, T. K., & Evans, D. L. (1998). Special considerations: Use of lithium in children, adolescents, and elderly populations. *Journal of Clinical Psychiatry, 59*(Suppl 6), 66–73.

Tyrer, S. P., Walsh, A., Edwards, D. E., Berney, T. P., & Stephens, D. A. (1984). Factors associated with a good response to lithium in aggressive mentally handicapped subjects. *Progress in Neuro-Psychopharmacology & Biological Psychiatry, 8*(4–6), 751–755.

Uldall, P., Bulteau, C., Pedersen, S. A., Dulac, O., & Lyby, K. (2000). Tiagabine adjunctive therapy in children with refractory epilepsy: A single-blind dose escalating study. *Epilepsy Research, 42*(2–3), 159–168.

Uthman, B. M., Rowan, A. J., Ahmann, P. A., Leppik, I. E., Schachter, S. C., Sommerville, K. W., et al. (1998). Tiagabine for complex partial seizures: A randomized, add-on, dose-response trial. *Archives of Neurology, 55*(1), 56–62.

Varanka, T. M., Weller, R. A., Weller, E. B., & Fristad, M. A. (1988). Lithium treatment of manic episodes with psychotic features in prepubertal children. *American Journal of Psychiatry, 145*(12), 1557–1559.

Velikonja, M., & Heinrich, K. (1984). Effects of oxcarbazepine (CG 47.680) on affective and schizoaffective symptoms: A preliminary report. In H. M. Emrich, T. Okuma, & A. A. Müller (Eds.), *Anticonvulsants in affective disorders* (pp. 208–210). Amsterdam: Excerpta Medica.

Vieta, E., Martinez-Aran, A., Nieto, E., Colom, F., Reinares, M., Benabarre, A., et al. (2000). Adjunctive gabapentin treatment of bipolar disorder. *European Psychiatry, 15*(7), 433–437.

Vieta, E., Torrent, C., Garcia-Ribas, G., Gilabert, A., Garcia-Pares, G., Rodriguez, A., et al. (2002). Use of topiramate in treatment-resistant bipolar spectrum disorders. *Journal of Clinical Psychopharmacology, 22*(4), 431–435.

Vitiello, B., Behar, D., Malone, R., Delaney, M. A., Ryan, P. J., & Simpson, G. M. (1988). Pharmacokinetics of lithium carbonate in children. *Journal of Clinical Psychopharmacology, 8*(5), 355–359.

Wagner, K. D., Weller, E. B., Carlson, G. A., Sachs, G., Biederman, J., Frazier, J. A., et al. (2002). An open-label trial of divalproex in children and adolescents with bipolar disorder. *Journal of the American Academy of Child and Adolescent Psychiatry, 41*(10), 1224–1230.

Walter, G., Lyndon, B., & Kubb, R. (1998). Lithium augmentation of venlafaxine in adolescent major depression. *Australian and New Zealand Journal of Psychiatry, 32*(3), 457–459.

Wang, P. W., & Ketter, T. A. (2002). Pharmacokinetics of mood stabilizers and new anticonvulsants. *Psychopharmacology Bulletin, 36*(1), 44–66.

Wang, P. W., Santosa, C., Schumacher, M., Winsberg, M. E., Strong, C., & Ketter, T. A. (2002). Gabapentin augmentation therapy in bipolar depression. *Bipolar Disorder, 4*(5), 296–301.

Weeston, T. F., & Constantino, J. (1996). High-dose T4 for rapid-cycling bipolar disorder. *Journal of the American Academy of Child and Adolescent Psychiatry, 35*(2), 131–132.

Weisler, R. H. (2002, December). *A multicenter randomized, double-blind, placebo-controlled trial of extended-release carbamazepine capsules (Carbatrol) monotherapy in patients with manic or mixed bipolar disorder.* Paper presented at the American Epilepsy Society Annual Meeting, Seattle, WA.

Weller, E. B., Weller, R. A., & Fristad, M. A. (1986). Lithium dosage guide for prepubertal children: A preliminary report. *Journal of the American Academy of Child and Adolescent Psychiatry, 25*(1), 92–95.

West, S. A., Keck, P. E., Jr., & McElroy, S. L. (1994). Open trial of valproate in the treatment of adolescent mania. *Journal of Child and Adolescent Psychopharmacology, 4,* 263–267.

Whittier, M. C., West, S. A., Galli, V. B., & Raute, N. J. (1995). Valproic acid for dysphoric mania in a mentally retarded adolescent [Letter]. *Journal of Clinical Psychiatry, 56*(12), 590–591.

Wilkinson, D., Holmes, C., Woolford, J., Stammers, S., & North, J. (2002). Prophylactic therapy with lithium in elderly patients with unipolar major depression. *International Journal of Geriatric Psychiatry, 17*(7), 619–622.

Windhaber, J., Maierhofer, D., & Dantendorfer, K. (1997). Oxcarbazepine for panic disorder occurring after two grand mal seizures: A case report. *Journal of Clinical Psychiatry, 58*(9), 404–405.

Winsberg, M. E., DeGolia, S. G., Strong, C. M., & Ketter, T. A. (2001). Divalproex therapy in medication-naive and mood-stabilizer-naive bipolar II depression. *Journal of Affective Disorders, 67*(1–3), 207–212.

Woolston, J. L. (1999). Case study: Carbamazepine treatment of juvenile-onset bipolar disorder. *Journal of the American Academy of Child and Adolescent Psychiatry, 38*(3), 335–338.

CHAPTER FOURTEEN

ANTIPSYCHOTIC MEDICATIONS

Sandra DeJong, M.D., Anthony J. Giuliano, Ph.D., and
Jean A. Frazier, M.D.

A ntipsychotics revolutionized the treatment of major mental illness beginning
with their introduction in the 1950s. Their discovery was fortuitous: chlorpromazine was developed as an antihistamine, but its calming properties led to
trials in psychiatric patients with unprecedented success. The last two decades
have seen the rise of "atypical" antipsychotics, which differ from their typical predecessors by having a lower incidence of extra-pyramidal symptoms.

These agents are used to treat psychotic disorders. They also are used as primary agents or adjunctive treatments for a wide variety of psychiatric and
behavioral disorders in children and adolescents, including pervasive developmental disorders, severe anxiety disorders, eating disorders, aggressive behavior,
attention-deficit-hyperactivity disorder, and tic disorders. The number of systematic studies for each indication varies considerably.

This chapter discusses important pharmacological characteristics of both typical and atypical agents (mechanisms of action, side effect profiles, and drug-drug
interactions) using illustrative examples. A review of research supporting their
clinical indications follows with an emphasis on the controlled investigations. In
addition, issues specific to the pediatric population are addressed, offering clinical wisdom regarding antipsychotic use in everyday practice. Finally, some
potential trends for the future are discussed.

Medications

A summary of individual antipsychotic medications is included in Table 14.1.

TABLE 14.1. SUMMARY OF ANTIPSYCHOTICS' PROPERTIES.

Generic Name (tablet dose)	Trade Name	Chemical Class	Adult Half Life	Child Half Life	Receptor Binding	Cytochrome Metabolized By	Other
				Atypicals			
Clozapine (25-, 100-mg tablets)	Clozaril Leponex	Dibenzo-diazepine	4–66 hours (mean = 12)	Unknown	D1-5 especially D4, M1-5, H1, alpha-1, 5HT2A-2C	P4502D6 (genetic polymorphism) 1A2, 2D6, 3A4	97% protein bound NOR > CLZ in children NOR + CLOZ levels should be monitored in children
Olanzapine (2.5-, 5-, 7.5-, 10-mg tablets) disintegrating wafer	Zyprexa Zydis	Thienobenzo-diazepine	21–54 hours	37.2 ± 5.1 hours	5HT2A-2C; D1-4, M1-5, H1, alpha-1	2D6, 1A2	40% first pass metabolism; 93% plasma bound; clearance lower in women, smokers, and Japanese
Risperidone (0.25-, 0.5-, 1-, 2-, 3-, 4-mg tablets) Elixir 1 mg/ml	Risperdal	Benzisoxazole	3–20 hours	Unknown	D2, 5HT2, alpha-1-2, H1	2D6, 3A4	Active metabolite 9hydroxy risperidone
Quetiapine (25-, 100-, 200-, 300-mg tablets)	Seroquel	Dibenzothia-zepine	6 hours	Unknown	5HT1A, 5HT2, D1, D2, H1, alpha-1-2	3A4	83% plasma bound 10–15% decreased bioavailability with food
Aripiprazole (10-, 15-, 20-, 30-mg)	Abilify	Dihydro-carbostyril	75 hours	Unknown	Partial agonist at D2; antagonist at D3, D4. Partial agonist at 5HT1A; antagonist at 5HT2A, 2C and 7. alpha-1. H1, serotonin reuptake site.	2D6, 3A4	Active metabolite dehydroariproazole
Ziprasidone (20-, 40-, 60-, 80-mg capsules) Intramuscular 20-mg/ml	Geodon	Benzisothiazolyl	7 hours	Peak serum concentration after a single dose occurs at 4 hours post dose. Half life unknown.	D2, D3; 5HT2A, 2C and agonist at 1A; alpha-1; H1; inhibits serotonin and NE reuptake.	P4503A4 30% metabolized by this cytochrome P450 system	

Chlorpromazine (10-, 25-, 50-, 100-, 200-mg tablets) Spansules 30-, 75-, 150-mg Ampules for intramuscular injection 1- and 2 ml- 25 mg/ml	Thorazine	Phenothiazine		Unknown	2D6	60 identified metabolites
Fluphenazine (1-, 2.5-, 5-, 10-mg tablets) Decanoate	Prolixin Permitil	Phenothiazine		Unknown	2D6	
Thioridazine (10-, 15-, 25-, 50-, 100-, 150-, 200-mg tablets)	Mellaril	Phenothiazine		Unknown	2D6	
Perphenazine (2-, 4-, 8-, 16-mg tablets) Concentrate 16 mg/1ml	Trilafon	Phenothiazine	9–12 hours	Unknown	2D6	
Trifluoperazine (1-, 2-, 5-, 10-mg tablets) IM 10-mg/ml Concentrate 10 mg/ml- vanilla/banana flavor	Stelazine	Phenothiazine		Unknown		
Mesoridazine (10-, 25-, 50-, 100-mg tablets) Concentrate 25 mg/ml IM- Ampuls 1 ml- 25 mg/ml	Serentil	Phenothiazine	24 hours in studies done in dogs and rabbits	Unknown		

(Continued)

TABLE 14.1. SUMMARY OF ANTIPSYCHOTICS' PROPERTIES (CONTINUED).

Generic Name (tablet dose)	Trade Name	Chemical Class	Adult Half Life	Child Half Life	Receptor Binding	Cytochrome Metabolized By	Other
Haloperidol (0.5-, 1-, 2-, 5-, 10-, 20-mg tablets) Concentrate 2 m/ml IM 1 ml per ampule-5 m/ml Decanoate	Haldol	Butyrophenone	16–35 hours	4–16 hours	D2	2D6, 3A4	One active metabolite
Loxapine (5-, 10-, 25-, 50-mg capsules)	Loxitane	Dibenzoxazepine	4 hours	Unknown			Metabolized and excreted mainly in the first 24 hours
Molindone (5-, 10-, 25-, 50-, 100-mg tablets) concentrate— cherry flavor	Moban, Lidone	Dihydroindolone	Peak blood level achieved within 1.5 hours	Unknown			Reaches peak in 1.5 hours. Pharmacologic effect from a single dose lasts for 24–36 hours.
Pimozide (1-, 2-mg tablets)	Orap	Diphenylbutyl pipe ridine	55 hours after single dose schizophrenia 111—hours Tourette's	66 hours-Tourette's	D2	3A4, 1A2	Two major metabolites have been identified
Thiothixene (1-, 2-, 5-, 10-, 20-mg capsules) IM 5 mg/ml	Navane	Thioxanthene		Unknown		2D6	

Chemical Makeup

The major classes of typical antipsychotic medications are (1) phenothiazines, which include low-potency compounds (chlorpromazine) and high-potency compounds (trifluoperazine and perphenazine), (2) butyrophenones (haloperidol), (3) diphenybutylpiperidine (pimozide), (4) thioxanthenes (thiothixene), (5) indolone derivatives (molindone), and (6) dibenzoxazepines (loxapine, and others). Atypical agents approved for use in the United States are clozapine (a dibenzodiazepine), risperidone (a benzioxazole), olanzapine (a thienobenzodiazepine), quetiapine (adibenzothiazepine), ziprasidone (a benzisothiazolyl), and aripiprazole (a dihydroquinolinone).

Mechanism of Action

Their in-vitro receptor binding properties and in-vivo effects confirm that most antipsychotics block dopamine at the D2 receptor. These agents differ in their relative affinities for the five dopamine receptors (D1, D2, D3, D4, D5) as well as for other receptor types: cholinergic, central alpha-adrenergic (alpha-1), histaminic (H1), and serotonergic (5HT2) (Findling, McNamara, & Gracious, 2003; Shen, 1999; Guerin et al., 1993). Clozapine, for example, has a weak affinity for the D2 receptor but a high affinity for the D4 receptor, which has greater specificity for meso-limbic and meso-cortical tracts. This affinity profile may explain the low incidence of extra-pyramidal side effects seen with this medication. Clozapine also has higher affinities for the 5HT, alpha-1, and H1 receptors than for either D2 or D1 receptors (Schulz, Fleischhaker, & Remschmidt, 1996). Chlorpromazine and thioridazine block alpha-adrenoreceptors more potently than D2 receptors and have a higher 5HT2 blockade than D1 blockade. Finally, aripiprazole, the newest available agent, is unique in its mechanism of action. Not only does this medication block the D2 receptor, but it also is a partial D1 agonist. In addition, it blocks the D3 receptor, and is an antagonist at the 5HT2a receptor, while serving as a partial agonist at the 5HT1a receptor. (See Table 14.1.) The differences in the receptor binding profiles of the various antipsychotics account for their slight differences in efficacy and in their side effect profiles.

Dosing and Pharmacokinetics

Most antipsychotics are readily but incompletely absorbed. Many undergo significant first-pass metabolism. For example, chlorpromazine has a bioavailability of 25–30% due to first-pass metabolism; whereas haloperidol is less likely to be immediately metabolized and has an average bioavailability of about 65% (Katzung, 1992).

Most antipsychotics are very soluble in fat and protein-bound (92–99%). Thus, their volume of distribution tends to be large. Due to their storage in lipid compartments, most agents have a longer duration of action than would be predicted based on their plasma half lives (Katzung, 1992). Most of these medications are extensively metabolized to more polar substances and excreted. Elimination half lives in adults vary from ten to twenty-four hours. Some agents, particularly chlorpromazine, have complex patterns of drug metabolism, resulting in multiple (about sixty for chlorpromazine) identified active metabolites; others, such as haloperidol, have far fewer metabolic steps and fewer (one for haloperidol) active metabolites. (See Table 14.1.)

Unfortunately, there are only a handful of studies of antipsychotic pharmacokinetics that have been done in youths. *Pharmacokinetic (PK) studies* are important, as they inform clinical dosing strategies. Prescriptive practices in child psychiatry historically have been based on data from adult studies; yet, the metabolism and pharmacokinetics of these agents vary considerably over the first two decades of life. Of the typical agents, haloperidol, chlorpromazine, and pimozide have been studied in children (Furlant et al., 1990; Sallee et al., 1987; Morselli, Bianchette, & Dugas, 1982). Most children have a plasma half life on haloperidol that is shorter than in adults (Morselli et al., 1982). In addition, a significant relationship was observed between side effects and haloperidol plasma concentrations (Morselli et al., 1979) with side effects emerging at levels greater than 3 ng/ml and being present in 80% of cases with plasma levels of 9 ng/ml or greater. Haloperidol levels of 1 to 3 ng/ml have been found to have therapeutic results in tics and Tourette's syndrome as well as in stuttering (Morselli, Bianchette, & Dugas, 1983). In psychotic disorders, higher haloperidol levels are necessary (6 to 10 ng/ml) (Morselli et al., 1983). The half life in children ranged from four to sixteen hours and increased with age. In general, children appear to be more sensitive to the action of these medications because both therapeutic and toxic effects are present at levels lower than those in adults (Morselli et al., 1983; Morselli et al., 1982). Similar results have also been demonstrated with chlorpromazine (Meyers, Tune, & Coyle, 1980; Rivera-Calimlim, Griesbach, & Perlmutter, 1979).

PK studies on atypical antipsychotics in children are also relatively sparse. Clozapine plasma levels seem to correlate with clinical response in adolescents with schizophrenia (Piscitelli et al., 1994). In addition, clozapine (CLZ) PK results have been reported (Frazier et al., 2003) in six youths with schizophrenia (ages nine to sixteen years). The mean daily CLZ dose was 200 ± 79.1 mg (range 100 to 300); weight-corrected CLZ dose was 3.4 ± 2.2 mg/kg/day (range 1.43 to 7.62). Its clearance averaged 1.7 L/kg per hour. Norclozapine concentrations (410) exceeded CLZ (289) and clozapine-N-oxide (NOX) (63 ng/ml) and AUC_{0-8h} of NOR (3,356) > CLZ (2,359) > NOX (559 ng/ml-h) (53, 38, and 9%

of total analytes, respectively). In adults, NOR serum concentrations on average are 10–25% < CLZ, differing significantly from the child sample. Dose normalized concentrations of CLZ (mg/kg/day) did not vary with age and were similar to reported adult values. Clinical improvement was seen in five out of six patients and correlated with serum CLZ concentrations. In addition, clinical response *and* total number of side effects correlated with NOR concentrations. The authors proposed that NOR (a neuropharmacologically active metabolite) and free CLZ may contribute to the effectiveness and adverse effects in youth (Frazier et al., 2003).

Like CLZ, risperidone is more rapidly metabolized in young children than in adults (Casaer, Walleghem, Vandenbussche, Huang, & DeSmedt 1994), which might explain the clinical need for the often TID dosing in children. In sharp contrast, one report indicates that in eight youths with schizophrenia (ages ten to eighteen years) olanzapine concentrations were of the same magnitude as for non-smoking adult patients, but twice the typical concentrations in patients that smoke. (Oral clearance was 9.6 ± 2.4 L/hour and half life was 37.2 ± 5.1 hours [Grothe et al., 2000].) The authors recommended a target olanzapine dose of 10 mg/day for most adolescents based on the PK results. Finally, quetiapine and ziprasidone appear to have similar PK results to those in adults (McConville et al., 2000; Sallee, Gilbert, Vinks, Miceli, et al., 2003).

Overall, it is important to note that since the metabolism and disposition of some antipsychotics may be faster in children, a more careful adjustment of daily dosing is indicated. With many of these agents, two or more divided doses are recommended to avoid peak related side effects and fluctuations in serum concentrations. Finally, it is important to consider the age, weight, and psychopathology (and possibly gender) of the patient when choosing a medication and its starting dose. In general, the recommendation is to start at a relatively low dose and to titrate the medication slowly upward.

Adverse Effects

The side effect profile of each of the antipsychotics is related to its relative affinity for different receptors. Each side effect is discussed in Table 14.2.

Extra-Pyramidal Symptoms. Extra-pyramidal symptoms (EPS) include a variety of motor disturbances, including acute dystonias, parkinsonian stiffness, shuffling, and tremor, as well as withdrawal and tardive dyskinesias. There is evidence that children and adolescents are more susceptible to these side effects than adults when typical agents are used (Keepers, Clappison, & Casey, 1983). For example, in a prospective study of treatment with typical antipsychotics (mean duration

TABLE 14.2. SUMMARY OF ANTIPSYCHOTICS, CLINICAL PROFILES.

Generic Name	Dosing Range in Children & Adolescents	Dosing Chlorpromazine Equivalency	Potency	Disorders Studied in Children and Adolescents	Side Effects	Important Medication Interactions
Atypicals						
Clozapine	25–600 mg	100	Low	Treatment-refractory schizophrenia Bipolar disorder Autistic disorder	Agranulocytosis Decreased seizure threshold Hypotension Anticholinergic Drooling Weight gain Sedation Hepatic changes	Other bone marrow suppressors (carbamezapine); other medications that lower seizure threshold; 2D6 inhibitors and inducers
Olanzapine	5–20 mg/day	5	Medium	Schizophrenia Bipolar disorder Pervasive developmental disorder	Somnolence Weight gain Hypotension	
Risperidone	0.5–6.0 mg (available in oral solution)	2	High	Bipolar disorder Pervasive developmental disorder Schizophrenia Tics Aggression in sub-IQ	EPS Increased weight Sedation Increased prolactin Hypotension, if rapidly titrated Hepatic changes	2D6 inhibitors
Quetiapine	25–400 mg in divided doses	100	Low	Psychotic disorder	Cataracts in dogs Sedation Hypotension Increased liver function tests	3A4 inducers; 3A4 inhibitors including ketoconazole, erythromycin
Ziprasidone	20–160 mg/day in divided doses with food	20	Medium	Tics Aggression	QTc prolongation Rash Somnolence Hypotension	
Aripiprazole	5–30 mg/day		High	Psychotic disorder	Activation Insomnia Somnolence	3A4 inducers (carbamazepine); 3A4 inhibitors (fluoxetine, paroxetine)

Typicals

Chlorpromazine	50–500 mg (Available in spansules, ampuls, syrup, suppositories)	100	Low	Schizophrenia Bipolar disorder Aggression	Anticholinergic Hypotension	Agents that are sedating and cause QTc prolongation
Fluphenazine	2–20 mg (Depot available)	3–5	High	Pervasive developmental disorder Tics	Extra-pyramidal side effects	
Thioridazine	50–400 mg (Oral concentrate available)	100	Low	Conduct disorder Schizophrenia	QTc prolongation Retinary pigmentation	Agents that cause QTc prolongation
Perphenazine	8–64 mg (Available in intramuscular preparation)	10	Medium	Schizophrenia Aggression	Anticholinergic Sedation	
Trifluperazine	5–60 mg	3–5	High	Pervasive developmental disorder	Extra-pyramidal side effects	
Mesoridazine	50–400 mg	50	Low	Personality disorder	Anticholinergic Sedation	
Haloperidol	1–15 mg (Intramuscular and depot available)	2–5	High	Autistic disorder Conduct disorder Schizophrenia Tics	Extrapyramidal side effects	
Loxapine	20–160 mg	10–15	Medium	Schizophrenia		
Molindone	20–200 mg	2–5	Medium	Conduct disorder Schizophrenia	Extra-pyramidal side effects—possibly less risk of tardive dyskinesia	
Pimozide	0.5–10 mg	1–2	High	Tics Aggression Schizophrenia	QTc prolongation Extra-pyramidal side effects	
Thiothixene	2–60 mg (Not recommended for under 12)	3–5	High	Schizophrenia	Extra-pyramidal side effects	

49.2 ± 36.2 months) in a diagnostically heterogeneous group of forty-one children and adolescents [males (n = 31); females (n = 10); age range: three–twenty-one years], Gualtieri and colleagues (1984) assessed the occurrence, location, severity and course of tardive dyskinesia (measured via the Abnormal Involuntary Movement Scale [AIMS]) (NIMH, 1985). Fifteen patients developed abnormal movements upon withdrawal of their antipsychotic: three of forty-one subjects developed tardive dyskinesia (two achieved remission within nine months); nine developed withdrawal dyskinesias and three developed ambiguous cases of post-withdrawal dyskinesia. Most abnormal movements involved the face. Only twelve subjects required resumption of neuroleptic treatment. Female patients, taking higher medication doses, were more likely to develop the withdrawal symptoms. Results were compromised by the heterogeneity of the sample and the small number of subjects. In particular, the mean Intelligence Quotient (IQ) of the total group was only 45.5 ± 25.3 and dyskinetic movements (at baseline and on medication) are generally more common in the mentally retarded population. Therefore, the results of this study are not readily generalizable to the IQ-normal psychiatric population (Gualtieri, Quade, Hicks, Mayo, & Schroeder, 1984).

The atypical agents are reputed to cause fewer EPS in both children and adults. However, recent studies suggest that, as with the typical agents, children may have a higher incidence of EPS on these agents relative to adults (Mandoki, 1995; Richardson, Haugland, & Craig, 1991). Clozapine may have the lowest risk of EPS overall; however, it is associated with a dose-related risk of seizures and an increased risk of neutropenia and agranulocytosis in adolescents and adults. In general, side effects on clozapine may be slightly more frequent in the younger age group (Frazier et al., 2003; Kumra et al., 1996; Remschmidt, Schulz, & Martin, 1994).

Disorders of Thermoregulation

Neuroleptic Malignant Syndrome. Another serious potential reaction to antipsychotics is the *neuroleptic malignant syndrome (NMS)*, which is marked by muscle rigidity, delirium, autonomic instability (unstable blood pressure and pulse with diaphoresis and fever) often with elevated creatine phosphokinase (CPK) levels and white blood cell counts and rhabdomyolysis (muscle breakdown). This condition causes a dysfunction in the body's thermoregulatory system.

Overall, NMS has a similar presentation in children as it does in adults. However, NMS may be more difficult to diagnose in children as it is difficult to distinguish from more benign EPS of antipsychotics. In addition, in all age groups, NMS must be distinguished from primary central nervous system (CNS) pathology, concurrent infection, underlying psychosis, and elevated CPK related to injury or intramuscular injections. The syndrome may be related to dose increase rather than to absolute dose. It can be fatal, and treatment involves intensive medical surveillance, immediate discontinuation of the neuroleptic, and aggressive treatment of any medical sequelae such as renal failure due to rhabdomyolysis. NMS can best be avoided by gradual dose titration, wearing sun blocking agents during the summer, and maintaining hydration status (Connor, Fletcher, & Wood, 2001; Kumra et al., 1998; Pearlman, 1986; Gualtieri et al., 1984; Campbell, Greg, & Green, 1983).

Serotonin Syndrome. Clinically similar to NMS, serotonin syndrome results from hyperstimulation of the central and peripheral serotonin receptors, and in most cases results from treatment with a combination of medications that work through the serotonin pathways. Those antipsychotics with a potent 5HT blockade, such as clozapine, are potential causes of this disorder, particularly when combined with other serotonergic agents such as selective-serotonin reuptake inhibitors (SSRIs) and anxiolytics (Godinho, Thompson, & Bramble, 2002).

CNS Effects

Sedation. Sedation is associated with the antihistaminergic properties of antipsychotics and is more common with the low-potency agents such as chlorpromazine, clozapine, olanzapine, and quetiapine (Findling et al., 2003). This side effect is particularly distressing in children and adolescents as level of arousal is directly related to learning and information processing in school.

Cognitive Effects. Although not formally studied, antipsychotics have the potential to cause decreased alertness, cognitive blunting, apathy, and memory deficits. However, the potential improvement in cognitive functioning that is secondary to illness in psychotic subjects treated with antipsychotics must also be recognized (Sikich et al., 1999). In the study reported by Sikich and colleagues (1999), nineteen youth with psychotic disorders were treated with either haloperidol, olanzapine, or risperidone in a double-blind fashion. The results of this study showed a trend for subjects treated with all agents to have positive changes in memory and executive functions. Subjects treated for a more sustained period with atypical antipsychotics but not haloperidol, showed additional modest improvements in psychoeducational performance and fine-motor functions.

Seizures. Patients with certain psychiatric disorders may be at higher risk for epilepsy at baseline. For example, the frequency of epilepsy in schizophrenic patients has been estimated at 1–18% (Hill, 1948; Notkin, 1929). Any known brain damage, such as anoxia at birth or head trauma, may further increase the risk of developing seizures.

Antipsychotic medications can contribute to lowering the seizure threshold. This effect has been recognized since chlorpromazine became available in the mid 1950s, and has been reported in other classes of antipsychotics, including haloperidol (Messing, Closson, & Simon, 1984; Logothetis, 1967).

Of the atypical neuroleptics, clozapine has most clearly been shown to increase the risk of seizures in a dose-related fashion. In adults, doses of clozapine lower than 300 mg/day have a reported seizures rate of 1%, doses between 300 and 600 mg/day of 2.7%, and doses above 600 mg/day of 4.4% (Devinsky, Honigfeld, & Patin, 1991). Severe myoclonus may be a precursor to generalized seizures during clozapine treatment. Some evidence from clinical trials suggests that children and adolescents may be more vulnerable to clozapine-induced seizures. Electroencephalogram (EEG) abnormalities have been described in 10–44% of youths treated with clozapine (Kumra et al., 1996; Frazier et al., 1994; Remschmidt et al., 1994). In general, antipsychotics, particularly clozapine, should be used cautiously in children and adolescents who have a history of known neurologic insult, seizures, or abnormal EEG.

There is only one report of a child having a seizure on any of the newer atypicals. One child was reported to experience a seizure on quetiapine (Martin, Koenig, Scahill, & Bregman, 1999).

Endocrine Side Effects

Prolactinemia. Prolactin, a hormone made in the anterior pituitary, is responsible primarily for breast tissue development and stimulation of lactation. Because prolactin is under inhibitory dopaminergic control via hypothalamic neurons, medications that block D_2 receptors (such as antipsychotics) can secondarily raise prolactin levels.

In a study of the treatment of psychosis in thirty-five youth (mean age 14.1 ± 2.3 years, range 9.1–19) that involved haloperidol, clozapine, and olanzapine, mean prolactin concentration after six weeks of treatment was significantly elevated in all three medication groups. The olanzapine-treated patients had elevated prolactin levels substantially higher than those reported in adult populations (Wudarsky et al., 1999). Those treated with clozapine had prolactin elevation, but the levels remained within the normal range. In another study of twenty subjects (age range 5 to 17 years, mean 13.1 years) treated with risperidone (n = 10), olanzapine (n = 6), or quetiapine (n = 4), prolactin levels were obtained at baseline and after 10.5 ± 2.7 weeks on medication. Endpoint prolactin levels were significantly higher with risperidone (p = 0.004) compared to olanzapine and quetiapine (Saito, Correll, & Kafantaris, 2002). However, data suggest these prolactin elevations may be transient, with levels normalizing over time. Findling and colleagues (2002) studied pooled data from five risperidone treatment studies (both open and double-blind) involving a total of 709 children (aged five to fifteen years) and found elevated prolactin levels (29.4 ± 13.2 ng/ml) during weeks four through seven of treatment. The levels subsequently decreased and normalized within twelve months, with no serious sequelae noted (Findling et al., 2002).

The potential clinical impact of hyperprolactinemia includes menstrual disturbance, galactorrhea, decreased ovarian production of estrogen, and secondary effects of low estrogen such as decreased bone density in females, and impotence and azospermia in males. Such clinical effects suggest the need for greater study of this area in younger populations (Wudarsky et al., 1999). The potential impact of prolactin elevations on growth and development are not well known. However, one study suggested that in youths with schizophrenia treated with typical antipsychotics, there was no significant impact of these agents on pubertal development when these youths were compared to their well siblings and population norms (Frazier et al., 1997). Additionally, Dunbar and colleagues (2002) presented data on the use of risperidone in patients with disruptive behavioral disorders and found that there was no delay in the progression of Tanner staging or in growth in the risperidone-treated youth relative to population norms (Dunbar, Kusumakar, Daneman, & Schulz, 2002).

Diabetes. In general, schizophrenic patients have higher rates of impaired glucose tolerance, insulin resistance, and Type II diabetes mellitus than the general population (Ryan & Thakore, 2002; Mukherjee, Decina, Bocola, Saraceni, & Scapicchio, 1996). This appears to be true even with no prior exposure to antipsychotics (Ryan, Collins, & Thakore, 2003). Recent case reports and one retrospective chart review indicate that in patients with risk factors for diabetes, treatment with novel antipsychotics may hasten the onset of this disorder. In the retrospective chart review, five of thirty-eight (13%) adolescents treated with clozapine had at least one elevated random blood glucose level (Kranzler, Gernino-Rosen, Pattin, & Kumra, 2002). Other epidemiologic data support an association between clozapine, olanzapine, and quetiapine and Type II diabetes (Sernyak, Leslie, Alarcon, Lozonczy, & Rosenheck, 2002). Proposed mechanisms for glucose dysregulation, include weight gain from histamine blockade, alterations in the glucose homeostatic system due to 5HT antagonism, and a prolactin-induced insulin-resistant state. Further studies in children are pending (Sikich et al., 1999). Prudent management includes ongoing consideration of risk factors, patient education, weight monitoring, and quick intervention with diet and exercise (Wirshing, Spellberg, Erhart, Marder, & Wirshing, 1998).

Weight Gain. Almost all antipsychotics have been associated with weight gain, likely due to their H_1 and/or $5HT_2$ antagonism (Sikich et al., 1999; Wirshing et al., 1998; Kelly, Conley, Love, Horn, & Ushcak, 1998). One interesting exception is molindone, which is associated with weight stability or decrease (Gardos & Cole, 1977; Gallant, Bishop, Steele, Bishop, & Guerro-Figueroa, 1973; Clark, Huber, Sakata, Fowles, & Serafetinides, 1970; Escobar et al., 1985; Freeman & Frederick, 1969). Children and adolescents may be more prone than adults toward developing weight gain on antipsychotics (Frazier et al., 2001).

In a twelve-week prospective naturalistic study of twenty-five patients aged five to eighteen years, height, weight, fasting glucose, and lipid profiles were obtained at baseline and monitored monthly thereafter. Patients were treated with either olanzapine (n = 11), risperidone (n = 8), or quetiapine (n = 6). In subjects treated for longer than six weeks, those on olanzapine and risperidone had more weight gain than those on quetiapine (8.2 ± 3.5 kg and 7.4 ± 4.5 kg, versus 4.1 ± 1.8 kg, respectively). Extreme weight gain (that is, greater than a 7% increase in body weight) was documented in 81.0% on olanzapine, 75.0% on risperidone, and 50.0% on quetiapine. In addition, risperidone was associated with significantly more dyslipidemia than olanzapine and quetiapine (66.7%, 9.1%, and 0.0%, respectively) (Correll, Saito, Kafantaris, Kumra, & Malhotra, 2002).

A retrospective chart review of thirty-eight children and adolescents (ten to eighteen years) with treatment-resistant DSM-IV schizophrenia or schizoaffective disorder treated with clozapine over variable time periods (three weeks to eighteen months) found that sixteen of thirty-eight (42%) developed clinically significant obesity and ten of thirty-eight (26%) had at least one episode of elevated triglyceride or cholesterol levels on random monitoring (Kranzler et al., 2002).

The atypicals appear to have a higher risk of weight gain than the typical antipsychotics: a six-month study of adolescents, aged twelve to eighteen years, treated with risperidone (n = 18) were compared to those treated by conventional antipsychotics (n = 23) as well as a control group (n = 19), and found weight gain in both treatment groups, but a significantly higher rate on risperidone [mean of 8.64 kg/3.67 kg/m^2 Body Mass Index (BMI) increase versus 3.03 kg/0.31 kg/m^2 BMI increase] (Kelley et al., 1998). An open twelve-week study comparing weekly weight gain in adolescents and young adults (thirteen to twenty-five-year-olds) treated with risperidone (n = 21), olanzapine (n = 21), and (n = 8) haloperidol found no weight change in the haloperidol group, but significant weight gain in the two other treatment arms. Average weight gain for the olanzapine group was 7.2 ± 6.3 kg (11.1% ± 7.8%) and for the risperidone group 3.9 ± 4.8 kg (6.6% ± 8.6%) (Ratzoni et al., 2002). Finally, a study of ten adolescent male schizophrenic inpatients treated with olanzapine and ten haloperidol-treated matched controls found significantly increased BMI after four weeks on olanzapine treatment but not on haloperidol. Weight gain was attributed to increase in dietary intake, without change in diet composition or resting energy expenditure (which was low at baseline) (Gothelf et al., 2002). In an open six-week trial of fifteen psychotic youth on quetiapine, mean weight gain was 4 kg (Shaw et al., 2001).

The issue of weight gain is a concern because obesity that begins earlier in life tends to persist. Obesity is also associated with medical problems such as Type II diabetes, hypertension, hypertriglycidemia, and orthopedic complications, but also with negative self-esteem, social issues, and medication noncompliance (Allison and Casey, 2001).

Cardiovascular Effects. Orthostatic hypotension, the most common cardiovascular side effect of antipsychotics, is associated with both typical and atypical agents and is particularly problematic with lower-potency medications, including clozapine (Casey, 1997). The postulated mechanism is alpha-1-adrenergic blockade. In addition, reflex tachycardia may result from the hypotension. This side effect may also be due to the anticholinergic properties of some antipsychotics (Gutgesell et al., 1999).

The most serious cardiovascular side effect described about some antipsychotics is the prolongation of the QTc interval on electrocardiogram (EKG), which has the potential of leading to fatal arrhythmias. (In adult males a QTc greater than 0.43 is considered abnormal; in adult females, greater than 0.45; and in children, the EKG normal range is age dependent.) In particular, pimozide (Orap) has a known risk of EKG changes (Opler & Feinberg, 1991). More recently, droperidol and thioridazine have been reported to carry a risk of QTc changes (Reilly, Ayis, Ferrier, Jones, & Thomas, 2000). Thioridazine now carries a black box warning on the package insert and is indicated only for treatment-refractory patients with schizophrenia. In addition, the use of thioridazine, an agent metabolized by the CYP2D6 system, is contraindicated in patients who are poor metabolizers and/or who are taking other medications metabolized by this enzyme family. Finally, there is the potential of QTc prolongation on ziprasidone, which seems to be idiosyncratic and not dose related. There is a warning about QTc prolongation on this medication; however, studies on the QTc prolongation of this agent reveal a modest prolongation of QTc and out of 3,095 patients only two had a QTc prolongation more than 500 msec (Pfizer Inc.).

Although rare, myocarditis and cardiomyopathy have been reported in patients taking clozapine. In addition, these conditions have been seen on other antipsychotics. The etiology is not well understood (Hagg, Spigset, Bate, & Soderstrom, 2001). These conditions should be considered in patients developing dyspnea, fatigue, chest pain, and/or edema.

Ophthalmologic Effects. The anticholinergic effects of neuroleptics can cause acute angle closure (and potential glaucoma) as well as blurred vision due to accommodation difficulties. Pigmentary deposits on the corneal lens have also been reported; in particular, thioridazine has been associated with pigmentary retinopathy at doses above 400 mg/day.

In preclinical trials of quetiapine, an associated risk of cataracts in beagles was reported. Although no cases in humans treated with quetiapine have been reported to date, the clinical recommendation for slit-lamp exam at baseline and during treatment remains (Stip & Boisjoly, 1999). *Clinical practice differs from FDA recommendations.*

Hematological Effects. A variety of blood dyscrasias such as leukopenia have been associated with virtually all antipsychotics. The most clinically significant hematological side effect is the agranulocytosis reported with clozapine in about 3% of adults (Krupp & Barnes, 1992). Occasional cases of agranulocytosis with other antipsychotics have been reported. The incidence of this side effect in children and adolescents is not clear; however, there is a suggestion that children may be more susceptible to moderate neutropenia and perhaps to developing agranulocytosis on clozapine (Frazier et al., 2003; Kumra et al., 1996; Alvir, Lieberman, Safferman, Schwimmer, & Schaaf, 1993). If treated with clozapine, the current monitoring recommendation is for weekly blood draws for the first six months and every other week thereafter if no problems emerge.

Hepatic Effects. Jaundice has been reported with antipsychotic use, particularly with chlorpromazine (Hansen, Casey, & Hoffman, 1997). Although Kumra and colleagues reported that two of thirteen youths treated with risperidone developed liver enzyme abnormalities and steatohepatitis within the context of extreme weight gain (Kumra, Herion, Jacobsen, Briguglia, & Grothe, 1997), a chart review of thirty-eight children and adolescents treated with risperidone at a mean dose of 2.5 mg/day for a mean of 15.2 days reported no significant liver abnormalities (one subject had an increased ALT by 7 units/liter [Szigethy, Wiznitzer, Branicky, Mazwell, & Findling, 1999]). The discrepancy between these two reports may be due to the fact that the case series reported by Kumra and colleagues (1997) consisted of treatment refractory children who had been exposed to multiple agents previously and had severe weight gain. The etiology of the liver enzyme increase in these cases is not clear, but likely due to the weight gain itself rather than due to a direct toxic effect of the medication (Szigethy et al., 1999; Kumra et al., 1997).

Sexual Side Effects. Antipsychotics are associated with a variety of sexual side effects in both men and women. In adolescents, this may become an important issue and could potentially lead to noncompliance. Perhaps the most significant cause of these side effects may be due to an increase in prolactin. Antipsychotics block dopamine and dopamine inhibits prolactin release from the anterior pituitary; thus, the net effect of a medication's antidopaminergic action is to lead to hyperprolactinemia. Other possible etiologic mechanisms for sexual side effects include decreased alpha-1 activity, decreased cholinergic activity, decreased testosterone, and decreased luteinzing hormone releasing hormone pulsatile activity. Specific effects include desire disorders, erection difficulties (including priapism), orgasm irregularities, ejaculation irregularities, menstrual disorders, infertility (due to hypogonadism and spermatogenesis problems), and breast disorders (pain, tenderness, gynecomastia, and galactorrhea) (Crenshaw & Goldberg, 1996). Of note, in adults quetiapine caused the least amount of sexual dysfunction when compared to haloperidol, risperidone, and olanzapine (Bobes et al., 2003).

Anticholinergic Effects. Anticholinergic side effects with antipsychotics are common, particularly on the lower potency agents. These include confusion, decreased learning and memory, dry mouth, constipation, blurry vision with accommodation, urinary retention, and increased heart rate. Anticholinergic medications such as benztropine used to minimize EPS, particularly with the typical neuroleptics, may exacerbate these effects.

Other Effects. Treatment-emergent school phobias, separation anxiety, and obsessive compulsive symptomatology have also been described during antipsychotic treatment in children and adolescents. School phobia occurring during antipsychotic treatment was initially reported with haloperidol and pimozide and is likely pharmacologically mediated (Linet, 1985; Mikkelson, Detlor, & Cohen, 1981). More recently, separation anxiety was reported during treatment with risperidone (Hanna, Fluent, & Fisher, 1999). Treatment-emergent obsessive-compulsive disorder (OCD) was described as occurring in 6% of adolescents suffering from schizophrenia (n = 200) during treatment with atypical antipsychotics (Rabe-Jablonska, 2001).

Drug-Drug Interactions

Interactions with antipsychotics can occur at the pharmacodynamic level, or at the level of drug metabolism and clearance (Meyer, Baldessarini, Goff, & Centorrino, 1996). The net effect of combining various psychotropics with antipsychotics can either be beneficial (as in sedation or mood alteration) or lead to adverse effects.

Many interactions between antipsychotics and other psychotropics occur due to shared metabolism by specific oxidases in the cytochrome P450 (CYP) system. This system consists of over thirty partially described enzymes, classified into three families (1 to 3) and five subfamilies (A to E). Most psychotropic medications are metabolized by four isozymes: CYP1A2, CYP2C, CYP2D6, and CYP3A3/4. At least two of these (CYP1A2 and CYP2D6) are responsible for the metabolism of antipsychotic drugs. Children and adolescents use some of these different isozymes more efficiently than adults do, which might result in developmental differences in metabolic rate of antipsychotic agents (Frazier et al., 2003).

Medications that inhibit these particular isozymes may increase circulating concentrations of antipsychotics to the point of toxicity, thus increasing adverse effects. The selective-serotonin reuptake inhibitor (SSRI) antidepressants are particularly significant in this regard. Prescription of the combination of an SSRI and an antipsychotic that are metabolized through the same isozyme system should be undertaken with caution. For example, paroxetine and fluoxetine are metabolized by CYP2D6 and when combined with agents (such as thioridazine, chlorpromazine, haloperidol, fluphenazine, pimozide, and risperidone) that are metabolized via that cytochrome system, increased antipsychotic levels may result. Fluvoxamine is an inhibitor of CYP1A2, and agents such pimozide, olanzapine, and clozapine are substrates for CYP1A2 (Findling et al., 2003). Other antidepressants, benzodiazepines, and propranolol also can raise antipsychotic levels this way, but to a lesser degree than the SSRIs (Meyer et al., 1996).

Clinical Indications

Antipsychotic prescriptive practice in children, in terms of indication and guidelines, has predominantly been based on data from adult studies. Few systematic studies with sufficient numbers have been done in children and adolescents. Despite the lack of empirical data, antipsychotics are in some children and adolescents irreplaceable for treating disabling conditions that interfere with their functioning.

Psychotic Disorders

Antipsychotic medications have proven effective in adults with psychotic disorders in reducing symptoms, preventing relapse, and improving overall functioning (APA, 1994). Fewer empirical data exist for psychotic children and adolescents; however, the studies that do exist to date complement the adult literature and are encouraging. Target symptoms, which respond to both typical and atypical antipsychotics, are "positive symptoms" (such as delusions, thought disorder, hallucinations, and catatonia). In contrast, "negative symptoms" (such as affective blunting, inattention, apathy, poverty of speech and thought, and poor social functioning) have shown little change or even worsening on the typical agents (Sikich et al., 1999). The atypical agents are at least as effective or, in the case of clozapine especially, more effective than the typicals in treating negative symptoms seen in youths suffering from psychosis (Kumra et al., 1996; Frazier et al., 1994; Remschmidt et al., 1994); Other target symptoms for which antipsychotics are used are agitation and aggression, as well as the neuropsychological deficits seen in patients with chronic psychosis.

Typicals

In 1976, Pool and colleagues compared loxitane, haloperidol, and placebo in a four-week, double-blind study of seventy-five hospitalized adolescents with schizophrenia (age range: thirteen to eighteen years). Average daily dose of loxapine was 87.5 mg and of haloperidol, 9.8 mg. Anticholinergic medications were initiated in thirty-seven of the seventy-five subjects due to side effects. The authors found both agents equally efficacious and superior to placebo (Pool, Bloom, Mielke, Roninger, & Gallant, 1976). Sedation and somnolence were reported in 34% of subjects, twenty-one of twenty-six on loxapine and thirteen of twenty-five on haloperidol. In 1984, Realmuto and colleagues reported on a six-week single-blind study of thiothixene (a high-potency agent) and thioridazine (a low-potency agent) in twenty-one adolescents (mean age 14.6 years) with DSM-III schizophrenia. Mean daily dose of thiothixene was 0.26 mg/kg and thioridazine, 2.57 mg/kg. Standard outcome measures such as the Brief Psychiatric Rating Scale (BPRS) and the Clinical Global Impressions Scale (CGI) were used. Both agents were equally efficacious, leading to a significant reduction in total BPRS scores. Although the authors report significant clinical improvements, the patients remained significantly impaired. The rate of side effects was similar for both agents. However, there were differences in the nature of the side effect profile of these two medications: thiothixene produced more EPS (54% on thiothixene versus 0% on thioridazine) and thioridazine produced more sedation (75% on thioridazine versus 54% on thiothixene) (Realmuto, Erickson, Yellin, Hopwood, & Greenberg, 1984).

Spencer and colleagues (1992) reported the results of a ten-week, double-blind, placebo-controlled study of haloperidol (0.02 to 0.12 mg/kg) in sixteen hospitalized children with DSM-III-R schizophrenia (age range: five to twelve years). Haloperidol was superior to placebo in decreasing symptoms of thought disorder, hallucinations, and persecutory ideation (Spencer et al., 1992). Symptoms and side effects were assessed using standardized rating scales (CGI, Children's Psychiatric Rating Scale (CPRS), and AIMS). Dosage was adjusted individually, with mean optimal dose of 1.92 mg daily. Twelve of sixteen patients (75%) on haloperidol showed marked improvement, while four (25%) showed mild or moderate improvement. Side effects were reported only in the first twelve subjects: eight (75%) had drowsiness, one (8%) had parkinsonian symptoms, and two (17%) experienced acute dystonia. No use of anticholinergic agents was reported.

The above studies suggest that typical antipsychotics are effective in alleviating psychotic symptoms in schizophrenic youth. EPS occurred commonly, particularly with high-potency agents at higher doses. Low-potency agents were associated more with sedation. There are no controlled or systematic long-term follow-up studies; therefore, information regarding long-term efficacy and side effects of these agents in children and adolescents is lacking.

Atypicals

The advent of the atypical antipsychotic medications with the potential of greater efficacy and fewer side effects has been important in the treatment of psychotic youth. The use of these medications in children and adolescents suffering from a variety of diagnoses has become an area of active study.

Clozapine. There have been five open-label studies of clozapine treatment in psychotic youth, all demonstrating that treatment with this medication led to clinical improvement in these youths; however, side effects were a concern (Turetz et al., 1997; Frazier et al., 1994; Remschmidt et al., 1994; Levkovitch, Kaysar, Kronnenberg, Hagai, & Gaoni, 1994; Blanz & Schmidt, 1993). The only published controlled study of an atypical agent (Kumra et al., 1996) was a six-week double blind randomized study comparing clozapine (n = 10) with haloperidol (n = 11) in treatment-refractory youth with DSM-III-R childhood-onset schizophrenia (mean age 14 ± 2.3 years). Dosage increases were individualized. The final mean dose of clozapine was 176 ± 149 mg and of haloperidol was 16 ± 8 mg. Prophylactic benztropine up to 6 mg QD was co-administered with haloperidol and a placebo pill, with clozapine, in a blinded fashion. Outcome measures were the BPRS, the Bunny-Hamburg Psychosis Rating Scale, the CGI, the BPRS-C, the Scale for the Assessment of Positive Symptoms (SAPS), and the Scale for the Assessment of Negative Symptoms (SANS). The Modified Subjective Treatment Emergent Symptoms Scale (STESS), AIMS, and the Simpson-Angus Neurological Rating Scale were used to monitor side effects. Clozapine was significantly better than haloperidol on improving all measures of psychosis, including negative symptoms. Four of the clozapine patients developed neutropenia and two had seizures. One of the haloperidol patients developed NMS. Drowsiness, sedation, and weight gain were common side effects on both agents, but to a lesser extent on haloperidol. No EPS were seen in the patients treated with haloperidol plus benztropine. The treatment-refractory nature of the study group may have introduced some bias in favor of clozapine in this study (given that many of the patients had already had prior unsuccessful trials on haloperidol) and may also account for the relatively high proportion of adverse effects. These youth demonstrated side effects at rates higher than those reported in adults treated with clozapine. Clearly, this study indicates that clozapine does effectively treat both positive and negative symptoms in youths with treatment-refractory schizophrenia, but close monitoring is warranted due to its potential serious side effects (Alvir et al., 1993).

Preliminary data in adults suggests that clozapine may be more effective than other atypicals at preventing suicide in psychotic patients (Meltzer et al., 2003). To date, no such data have been reported in children and adolescents.

Risperidone. Two open trials, two retrospective chart reviews, and five reports on risperidone support its use in psychotic youth. Armenteros and colleagues (1997) reported a six-week open trial using risperidone in ten adolescents (eleven to eighteen years) diagnosed with DSM-IV schizophrenia. The authors found significant improvement on the Positive and Negative Symptom Scale (PANSS), BPRS, and CGI. Five of ten adolescents (50%) developed EPS, one had a reversible oro-facial dyskinesia, eight (80%) had mild somnolence, and eight (80%) experienced weight gain. Overall, the incidence of EPS in this study was higher than reported in adult studies (Marder & Meiback, 1994). However, in this study the dose was rapidly titrated over a three-week period, up to relatively high doses (as high as 9 mg/day with a mean dose as high as 6.6 mg/day). The incidence of EPS was related to higher doses and more rapid titration. Therefore, gradual titration and lower final doses can minimize this uncomfortable side effect (Grcevich, Findling, Rosane, Friedman, & Schulz, 1996; Simeon, Carrey, Wiggins, Milin, & Hosenbocus, 1995).

Olanzapine. Olanzapine is the third FDA-approved atypical agent with documented efficacy and safety for treating psychosis in adults. Structurally similar to clozapine, it has a high affinity for a variety of receptors, including dopamine, serotonin, muscarinic, alpha-adrenergic, and histamine. The anti-serotonergic potency of olanzapine is eight-times greater than its anti-dopaminergic potency. Olanzapine has been studied in the treatment of psychotic youth in three open trials, resulting in somewhat mixed findings. Kumra and colleagues (1998) reported "marginal benefit" in an eight-week open trial of eight adolescents (mean age 15.25 ± 2.31 years) with treatment-refractory DSM-III-R schizophrenia. The starting dose of 2.5 mg QD or QOD, was increased on an individualized basis up to a maximum dose of 20 mg QD. Mean dose at six weeks was 17.5 ± 2.3 mg. Outcome measures included the CGI, the Clinical Global Assessment Scale (CGAS), BPRS, SAPS, SANS, Bunney Hamburg Rating scale, modified STESS, AIMS, Simpson-Angus Neurological Rating Scale. Three patients were much improved, two minimally improved, one minimally worse, one no change, and one much worse (compared with ratings on prior treatment). Four patients discontinued due to insufficient response. The size of the effect was notably less than the similarly designed clozapine study reported above by the same group. Side effects included increased appetite, weight gain (mean 3.4 ± 4.1 kg), nausea or vomiting, headache, somnolence, insomnia, impaired concentration, sustained tachycardia, transient increase in liver enzymes, and increased agitation. There was minimal EPS and no neutropenia, seizures or EEG change.

A second open-label trial with olanzapine in fifteen youths with schizophrenia indicated that all patients improved, with one-third being very much improved (Sholevar, Baron, & Hardie, 2000). In a third open-label trial, Findling and colleagues (2002) reported a prospective study of sixteen adolescents (mean age: 13.8 ± 1.5 years; age range: twelve to seventeen years) with DSM-IV schizophrenia, schizophreniform, or schizoaffective disorder and no history of treatment resistance. Subjects received a mean end-of-study dose of 12.42 mg/day. Significant improvement ($p < .01$) was found on all outcomes measured (CGAS, CGI-severity, PANSS). Most common side effects were increased appetite and sedation. In addition, case reports document mixed findings with olanzapine treatment of psychotic disorders in youth (Krishnamoorthy & King, 1998; Mandoki, 1997).

Others. Of the newer atypicals there is some information on the use of quetiapine and ziprasidone in psychotic youth. An open trial in ten psychotic youth (ages twelve to fifteen years) demonstrated improvement in psychotic symptoms and adequate tolerability of quetiapine in doses ranging from 50 to 800 mg (McConville, Arvanitis, Thyrum, & Smith, 2000). Patel and colleagues (2002) studied ziprasidone in a retrospective chart review in thirteen hospitalized children with a variety of psychiatric diagnoses. Nine of thirteen patients were improved or much improved on the CGI-severity scale at a mean maximum dose of 52.3 mg/day (Patel, Sierk, Dorson, & Crimson, 2002).

Cognitive Issues Secondary to Psychotic Disorders

Cognitive dysfunction is regarded as a core deficit in schizophrenia, and is related more strongly to functional outcomes than positive symptom severity (Brekke, Raine, Ansel, Lencz, & Bird, 1997; Green, 1996; Harvey et al., 1998; Hemsley, 1994). As a result, there is increased interest in the influence of antipsychotic medication on cognition. To date, these studies focus largely on adults; however, their implications may be especially important for the treatment of children, and are an active area of study.

Typicals. Typical antipsychotics have little benefit in the treatment of cognitive impairment found in adults with schizophrenia (Medalia, Gold, & Merriam, 1988; Spohn & Strauss, 1989). In sharp contrast, studies have demonstrated that atypical antipsychotics are superior to conventional antipsychotics in improving cognitive function, independent of improvement in psychiatric (positive) symptoms (Keefe, Silva, Perkins, & Lieberman, 1999).

Clozapine. Relative to haloperidol or to a traditional antipsychotic, a series of prospective studies have documented that clozapine enhances some aspects of cognition: motor and mental speed, visual spatial working memory, and new verbal learning or encoding (Buchanan, Holstein, & Breir, 1994; Hagger et al., 1993; Hoff et al., 1996; Meltzer & McGurk, 1999; Purdon, 1999), often after three to six months of treatment. However, clozapine does not effect a more generalized or broad-based improvement in cognition.

Atypicals. Atypical antipsychotics may have differential effects on cognitive processes. Risperidone has a positive effect on selective attention (alertness), visuomotor tracking, working memory, motor speed, and coordination, and the set-shifting component of executive function (Meltzer & McGurk, 1999; Purdon, 1999). Positive effects on attention (reaction time), motor function, visuo-spatial function, and executive skills have been documented with olanzapine (Meltzer & McGurk, 1999; Purdon, 1999). In a multi-center, random assignment, double-blind comparison study, Purdon and colleagues (1999) differentiated the cognitive gains due to haloperidol (5 to 20 mg; attention), risperidone (4 to 10 mg; new non-verbal learning), and olanzapine (5 to 20 mg; attention, learning, executive, and motor), over twelve months in an early-phase schizophrenia sample. Although improvement was observed at six weeks, the magnitude of change increased further by weeks thirty and fifty-four. The researchers concluded that olanzapine was superior to haloperidol and risperidone in its cognitive benefits.

Sikich and colleagues recently reported on the neurocognitive data obtained through a double-blind study comparing treatment with olanzapine, risperidone, and haloperidol in nineteen youths with psychotic disorders (ages eight to nineteen years) (Sikich et al., 1999). The study had an eight-week acute phase, and for responders, a twelve-week continuation phase. There was a clear trend for subjects treated with either the atypical or typical agents to show early positive changes in memory and executive functions. Subjects who were treated for a more sustained period with atypical antipsychotics but not haloperidol, showed additional modest improvements in psychoeducational performance and fine-motor functions.

The putative basis for the salutary effects of atypical antipsychotics on cognition includes alterations in prefrontal metabolism or neurotransmission, specifically dose-dependent increases in prefrontal cortex dopamine and norepinephrine (Volonte, Monferini, Cerutti, Fodritto, & Borsini, 1997). Further research is needed to clarify the effects of these drugs on cognition in children and adolescents and will have important implications for clinical management.

Mood Disorders

Bipolar Disorder. To date, there are no published randomized, placebo-controlled, double-blind studies examining atypical antipsychotic medications as monotherapy for childhood-onset bipolar disorder. However, a systematic chart review of risperidone treatment added to ongoing pharmacologic treatments in youth with bipolar disorder (n = 28, mean age 10.4 ± 3.8) indicated that once the risperidone was added to their other medications, there was a rapid, robust, and sustained response in controlling manic (82%), psychotic (69%), and aggressive symptoms (82%). The response did not seem to be secondary to the sedative effects of the medication. No EPS or tardive dyskinesia were observed. However, this report was limited due to its retrospective nature, the fact that these children were on multiple agents, and the lack of long-term follow-up (Frazier et al., 1999).

An eight-week prospective, open-label treatment trial of olanzapine monotherapy was conducted in youth with bipolar disorder (Frazier et al., 2001). The study examined twenty-three youths between five and fourteen years of age. Eight of these youths continued to take stimulants for their ADHD symptoms. Twenty-two subjects (96%) completed the study. Olanzapine was associated with significant improvement and a response rate of 61% during this eight-week time frame. Overall, olanzapine was well tolerated, and EPS measures were not significantly different from baseline. Body weight increased significantly during the course of the study (5.0 ± 2.3 kg). There were no differences seen in response rate nor in weight gain in children (n = 8) who remained on stimulants versus those who did not. The results of this study suggested that olanzapine might be effective during the acute treatment phase in youths with acute mania. However, the study is limited because it was an open design, with a relatively small number of subjects, and only eight weeks in duration. The authors concluded that olanzapine may be effective for the acute treatment of mania in youth. In addition, the authors recommended that double-blind studies of a longitudinal nature comparing olanzapine to mood stabilizers be done to more fully determine the safety and efficacy of this agent and to determine if this agent would be effective as first line or as monotherapy for bipolar disorder in youth (Frazier et al., 2001).

DelBello and colleagues examined the addition of quetiapine to divalproex versus divalproex treatment alone for hospitalized manic adolescents with bipolar disorder in a six-week, randomized, placebo-controlled, double-blind study (n = 30; mean age 14 ± 2) (DelBello, Schwiers, Rosenberg, & Strakowski, 2002). Quetiapine (450 mg/day) in combination with divalproex (20 mg/kg/day) was found to be significantly more effective than divalproex alone in the treatment of manic adolescents. The quetiapine-treated group reported mild to moderate sedation, but no subjects developed EKG abnormalities, prolactin elevation, or EPS.

There remains ongoing controversy about whether or not antipsychotics are necessary to treat the psychosis that occurs in youth with bipolar disorder. Some literature has suggested that mood stabilizers alone can be effective (Wagner et al., 2002; Findling et al., 2002; Kowatch et al., 2000; Geller et al., 1998). However, Kafantaris and colleagues systematically evaluated adjunctive haloperidol treatment with lithium in bipolar youth with psychotic features (Kafantaris, Dicker, Coletti, & Kane, 2001). Haloperidol was added after therapeutic lithium levels were obtained, then the haloperidol was discontinued after one week of treatment. The first five study patients with bipolar disorder experienced a quick re-exacerbation of psychotic symptoms and/or agitation.

In another open-label treatment study, Kafantaris and colleagues examined forty-two youths with bipolar disorder with psychotic features (mean age 15.9 years ± 1.9) (Kafantaris, Coletti, Dicker, Padula, & Kane, 2001). Twenty-eight of the subjects completed the study. Lithium was administered with adjunctive haloperidol (n = 15), risperidone (n = 6), olanzapine (n = 3), thiothixene (n = 1), or chlorpromazine (n = 1). There were no significant differences seen in response rate on any of these agents (whether typical or atypical). Nearly all patients had rapid resolution of their psychotic symptoms. In this study, approximately half of the patients were too clinically unstable to discontinue their antipsychotic medication. Furthermore, eight out of the fourteen remaining subjects who qualified for discontinuation of their antipsychotic medication relapsed. The authors concluded that the usual recommendation of limiting antipsychotic treatment to only four weeks duration in patients with psychotic mania might not be sufficient.

Atypical antipsychotics for maintenance treatment of pediatric bipolar disorder has not been well studied. This is an area of much needed research given that atypicals are often being used as monotherapy, as first line acute treatment and in maintenance treatment for pediatric bipolar disorder, without double-blind data to support this clinical practice. In addition, it will be crucial that long-term maintenance studies be undertaken, as it is possible that dosing and use of these agents in acute mania may differ from their use in maintenance treatment (Chang & Ketter, 2000).

Given the paucity of double-blind, long-term treatment studies using antipsychotics in bipolar youths, further studies associated with the medications typically used in the treatment of bipolar disorder are necessary to examine the risk-benefit ratio of adjunctive antipsychotic use in pediatric bipolar disorder and the use of atypical antipsychotics as first-line and as monotherapeutic interventions. It is critical that double-blind studies of mood stabilizers versus atypicals be done to assess the long-term safety and efficacy of these agents in the management of bipolar symptoms in youths. Specific side effects, such as weight gain, including hyperglycemia and Type II diabetes mellitus, EKG abnormalities, prolactin elevation, EPS, and tardive dyskinesia with acute and long-term antipsychotic exposure need to be systematically investigated in these children. In addition, side effects contribute to noncompliance with treatment and, at times, medication discontinuation is seen in as many as 40% of youths with bipolar disorder and 64% of bipolar youths with comorbid externalizing symptoms (Carlson, Lavell, & Bromet, 1999).

Major Depression with Psychotic Features. No controlled trials using typical or atypical antipsychotics in this diagnostic group have been published to date. However, an open-label study of olanzapine monotherapy in children and adolescents with bipolar disorder indicates that depressive symptoms improved in these youths, indicating that further research regarding the use of these agents in depressed youths with psychosis is warranted (Frazier et al., 2001).

Developmental Disorders

Mental Retardation. Historically, antipsychotics have been used in patients with mental retardation to decrease self-injury. Data on the actual efficacy of these agents is quite varied. Thioridazine is perhaps one of the most effective agents in decreasing self-injurious behavior; however, recent concerns about the QTc prolongation limits the use of this agent.

There have been numerous positive, open-label studies or case reports of the use of atypical antipsychotics in the mentally retarded (Findling, Aman, DeSmedt, Derivan, & Nash, 2001; Findling, Fegert, & DeSmedt, 2001; Friedlander, Lazar, & Klancnik, 2001; Hardan, Johnson, Honson, & Hrecznyj, 1996). There also have been four double-blind studies assessing the efficacy and safety of risperidone in the borderline-IQ to moderately mentally retarded populations for disruptive behaviors (Buitelaar van der Gaag, Cohen-Kettenis, & Melman, 2001; Turgay, Aman, Binder, Snyder, & Schulz, 2001; Van Bellinghen & De Troch, 2001; Aman et al., 2000). These studies indicate overall improvement in anxious, hyperactive, and self-injurious behaviors. The mean daily doses in these studies ranged from 1.1 to 2.9 mg of risperidone.

Pervasive Developmental Disorders. A subgroup of children with autistic disorders may benefit from pharmacotherapy, and antipsychotics have been used in this population (Tanguay, 2002).

Several agents have been described in case studies of children with autism (Campbell & Schopler 1989). However, only pimozide and haloperidol have been systematically studied. Four double-blind, placebo-controlled studies support the short-term efficacy and safety of haloperidol in hospitalized autistic children (Anderson et al., 1989; Anderson et al., 1984; Campbell et al., 1978; Cohen et al., 1980). In addition, Perry and colleagues showed that children who benefited from acute haloperidol treatment continued to have long-term benefit (Perry et al., 1989). Haloperidol did not negatively affect IQ (Shell et al., 1987). Two studies reported enhanced facilitated learning in a computerized laboratory in autistic individuals treated with haloperidol (Anderson et al., 1984; Campbell et al., 1978). Therapeutic doses ranged from 0.25 to 4.0 mg/day in children aged 2.3 to 8 years. There was a reduction of both core and associated symptoms of autism (Anderson et al., 1989, Locascio et al., 1991). Acute side effects occurred only in those above therapeutic doses, and sedation was the most common side effect. Older children had a greater response to haloperidol. The most significant negative side effect of haloperidol in this population is either tardive or withdrawal dyskinesias (Armenteros, Adams, Campbell, & Eisenberg, 1995; Campbell, Grega, Green, & Bennett, 1983; Malone, Ernst, Locascio, & Campbell, 1991). However, the incidence of dyskinesias in this population, even in the antipsychotic naïve exceeds that in the IQ-normal population (Meiselas et al., 1989).

In a double-blind, multi-center trial, both haloperidol and pimozide reduced problematic behaviors in children with pervasive developmental disorder (PDD) (Naruse et al., 1982).

There is only one report of the use of clozapine in autistic disorder (Zuddas, Ledda, Fratta, Muglia, & Cianchetta, 1996). Three children with marked hyperactivity, fidgetiness, or aggression demonstrated improvement after three months of treatment at doses up to 200 mg/day. However, side effects and the obligatory weekly blood draw make this agent one that should be used only in the most severe, treatment-refractory cases.

Potenza and colleagues (1999) reported on a twelve-week open-label prospective trial of olanzapine in eight patients with DSM-IV autism or PDD, NOS (50% males; below the age of nineteen). Diagnosis was confirmed by the Autism Diagnostic Interview and Autism Diagnostic Observation Schedule. Patients also met cut-offs for severity on the CGI-severity scale, Yale-Brown Obsessive Compulsive Scale Compulsion Subscale (YBOCS-Cs), the Self-Injurious Behavior Questionnaire (SIB-Q), or the Ritvo-Freeman Real-Life Rating scale (RF). Olanzapine was initiated at 2.5 mg/day and adjusted individually, with a endpoint mean dose of 7.8 ± 4.7 mg/day (range 5 to 20 mg/day). No other psychotropic medications were used. Outcome measures were the YBOCS-Cs, SIB-Q, Vineland Adaptive Behavior Scale Maladaptive Behavior subscales, CGI, RF, and Visual Analog Scale (VAS). One child dropped out due to lack of response. Six out of the remaining seven subjects were considered responders. Adverse effects included weight gain (n = 6) and sedation (n = 3). Mean weight gain was 8 kilograms. Two responders discontinued treatment at weeks fourteen and twenty, respectively, because of adverse effects (weight gain).

An open pilot comparison of olanzapine to haloperidol (mean dose 1.6 ± 0.9 mg/day) in eleven children with PDD showed that both agents were effective in reducing problematic behaviors such as social withdrawal, hyperactivity, anger, lability, and stereotypic behaviors. The olanzapine-treated group gained significantly more weight (Malone, Cater, Sheikh, Choudhury, & Delaney, 2001).

An open-label trial of risperidone in children with autism spectrum disorders showed improvement in repetitive behavior, aggression, impulsivity, and some elements of social relatedness; however, there were no statistically significant changes in outcome measures assessing social relatedness or language (McDougle et al., 1997). A more recent open-label trial of risperidone (mean dose 1.2 mg/day) in twenty-one children (mean age 7.1 years) with autism (DSM-IV) found significant improvement on the CGI and Children's Psychiatric Rating Scale. However, two of thirteen (15.4%) treated long term developed mild, transient withdrawal dyskinesias when risperidone was discontinued. No child developed dyskinesias while on risperidone (Malone, Maislin, Choudhury, Gifford, & Delaney, 2002).

A large-scale controlled study of risperidone in behaviorally disturbed children with subaverage IQs has been recently reported (Snyder et al., 2002). This trial began with a one-week, single-blind placebo run-in period followed by a six-week double-blind, placebo-controlled period. A total of 110 children with IQs ranging from thirty-six to eighty-four and with a score of ≥ 24 on the Conduct Problem subscale of the Nisonger Child Behavior Rating Form (NCBRF) were enrolled. Eighty percent had a diagnosis of ADHD. Risperidone doses ranged from 0.02 to 0.06 mg/kg/day. Outcome measures included the NCBRF, Aberrant

Behavior Checklist, Behavior Problems Inventory, CGI, modified California Verbal Learning Test, and a continuous performance task. The authors reported significant improvement on risperidone in outcome measures with no cognitive deterioration as measured by cognitive scales. The most common side effects included somnolence (41.5%), headache (17.0%), increased appetite (15.5%), and dyspepsia (15.51%). EPS were reported in seven (13.2%) of the risperidone-treated group and three (5.3%) of the placebo-treated group.

In an open trial in autistic boys suffering from outbursts, risperidone significantly decreased aggression, explosivity, and self-injury (Horrigan & Barnhill, 1997).

Anxiety Disorders

Antipsychotic medications have been studied in adults with anxiety disorders, particularly severe obsessive-compulsive disorder (OCD), as augmentation to treatment with selective-serotonin reuptake inhibitors. Haloperidol and risperidone have been shown to be potentially helpful in adults (McDougle, Epperson, Pelton, Wasylink, & Price, 2000; McDougle et al., 1994; McDougle et al., 1990). Recent open studies and case series indicate that quetiapine may also be helpful in the adult patient with severe OCD (Denys van Megan, & Westenberg, 2003).

Aggression

Typical Antipsychotics. Antipsychotics are commonly used to treat aggression. Typical agents such as haloperidol, thioridazine, and chlorpromazine are labeled for the treatment of "severe explosive behaviors" in pediatric patients. Several studies have demonstrated the efficacy of typical neuroleptics (haloperidol, molindone, thioridazine) in decreasing aggression in youths (Pappadopulos et al., 2003; Schur et al., 2003; Campbell et al., 1984; Greenhill, Solomon, Pleak, & Ambrosini, 1985; Gittleman-Klein, Klein, Katz, Saraf, & Pollack, 1976).

Atypicals. Risperidone, olanzapine, and haloperidol have been studied for aggression in the pediatric population. An outpatient, clinic, retrospective chart review of risperidone treatment (added to the ongoing medication regimen) in twenty-eight children with bipolar disorder (mean age 10.4 ± 3.8 years) found that 57% of the children showed a robust improvement in aggression, mania, and psychosis within the first month of treatment (Frazier et al., 1999). The medication was generally well tolerated.

An open trial assessing the effectiveness of risperidone in reducing aggression in eleven youths (5.5- to 16-years-old) with concurrent affective symptoms reported improvement in eight of eleven (73%) of the children (Schreier, 1998).

Several additional open-label trials of risperidone for the treatment of aggressive youths demonstrated a decrease in aggression (Buitelaar, 2000). Buitelaar (2001) administered risperidone to hospitalized aggressive subjects (age range ten to eighteen years) and all patients had some reduction in aggression: fourteen of twenty-six (54%) had marked reduction and ten had a moderate reduction (Buitelaar, van der Gaag, Cohen-Kettenis, & Melman, 2001).

In an open trial of olanzapine monotherapy in youths with bipolar disorder, mania, psychosis, depression, and aggression, all improved (Frazier et al., 2001).

In emergency situations with aggressive, out-of-control youth, administration of intramuscular (IM) preparations of antipsychotic agents might be indicated in order to calm the patient and to ensure the safety of not only the individual, but also those in the immediate environment. Although the administration of benzodiazepines in these situations is generally preferable, IM antipsychotics may be necessary. If antipsychotics are necessary, haloperidol at 0.5 to 5 mg (given with anticholinergics) given every one to two hours as needed for acute behavioral dyscontrol may be necessary. In addition, agents like perphenazine are available in IM preparations and may be preferable in children due to its medium potency and slightly decreased risk of causing acute dystonic reactions. However, EPS are a potential concern.

IM preparations of some of the atypical agents are currently under investigation. In situations where a patient is willing to take medications by mouth, risperidone in doses of 0.25 to 0.5 may be helpful (Frazier, 2003). Ziprasidone also comes in an IM preparation (20 mg/ml) and risperidone IM preparation looks promising and may soon be available. Neither of these agents have been studied in children.

Tics

Typicals. Some antipsychotics have been shown to be effective in the treatment of severe tic disorders, including Tourette's syndrome. Pimozide and haloperidol were first shown to be effective, but there are concerns regarding the risk of EPS with these agents (Shapiro et al., 1989).

Haloperidol is usually initiated with an evening dose of 0.25 mg and if tolerated another 0.25 mg can be added in the morning after five to seven days, if necessary. The dose can be raised by 0.25 mg thereafter every five days until there is symptomatic control. Total daily doses of 0.75 to 2.5 mg are typically effective.

Pimozide is typically initiated in the evening at a dose of 0.5 mg and titrated upward every five days to a total dose of 2 to 4 mg/day, given in divided doses.

Atypicals. Three atypical neuroleptics, risperidone, olanzapine, and ziprasidone, have been shown to be effective in controlling tics in prospective studies with small numbers of subjects (Gaffney et al., 2002; Onofrj, Paci, D'Andreamatteo, & Toma, 2000; Sallee et al., 2000; Lombroso, Scahill, King, & Lunch, 1995). In a double-blind comparison of risperidone and clonidine in twenty-one subjects (aged seven to seventeen years), risperidone was equally effective to clonidine as measured by the Yale Global Tic Severity Scale (YGTSS). The most common adverse event with both treatments was sedation (Gaffney et al., 2002). The olanzapine study was conducted with adults with Tourette's syndrome (ages nineteen to forty) and in comparison to pimozide, olanzapine 10 mg was superior to 2 mg of pimozide and olanzapine 5 mg was superior to 4 mg of pimozide (Onofrj et al., 2000). Interestingly, all patients opted for olanzapine treatment at the end of the study. In a double-blind, placebo-controlled study of twenty-eight patients (ages seven to seventeen) with Tourette's syndrome or chronic tic disorder, ziprasidone was associated with improvement in tic severity and frequency (Sallee et al., 2000). Side effects of ziprasidone included sedation, insomnia, and akathisia. There were no significant cardiac conduction effects.

Dose ranges for risperidone for tic disorders generally range from 1 to 3 mg in twice daily dosing regimens. Olanzapine doses ranged from 2.5 to 20 mg. Effective ziprasidone mean dose was 28.2 ± 9.6 mg/day in two divided doses.

Attention-Deficit/Hyperactivity Disorder

Antipsychotics are used clinically to treat the child with severe symptoms of attention-deficit/hyperactivity disorder (ADHD) who have been relatively treatment-resistant to more usual agents. However, there are few controlled studies assessing the safety and efficacy of these agents in ADHD youth, which have shown that these agents may be effective in decreasing hyperactivity and impulsivity (Simeon, Milin, & Walker, 2002; Pliszka et al., 2000; Gittleman-Klein et al., 1976).

Eating Disorders

A handful of case reports suggests that atypical antipsychotics may be helpful in the treatment of severe eating disorders, but these findings need to be substantiated by controlled, systematic studies (Fisman, Steele, Short, Byrne, & Lavalle, 1996).

Psychopharmacology, when used is only one arm of a multidisciplinary team approach to these patients.

Post-traumatic Stress Disorder

Although atypical antipsychotics are being used clinically in youth suffering from post-traumatic stress disorder (PTSD), there are no systematic studies assessing their use for this indication.

Personality Disorders

One double-blind, placebo-controlled study of mesoridazine (Serentil) over six weeks in thirty adolescent patients with various personality disorders was conducted. The average daily dose for the mesoridazine group (n = 15) was 27.3 mg in the first week and 44.7 mg in the sixth. Mesoridazine was significantly better than placebo in treatment of anxiety, depression, and hostility (Barnes, 1977).

Stuttering

Many medications have been used with limited success in the treatment of stuttering, which is a disruption in the normal fluency of speech. Two antipsychotics that have been shown to have efficacy for adults in double-blind studies are haloperidol and risperidone. (Maguire, Gottshchalk, Riley, Franklin, Bechtel, & Ashurst, 1999; Murray, Kelly, Campbell, & Stefanik, 1977). The haloperidol trial was a three-month, double-blind, cross-over design and included twenty-six adults. Eighteen of the adults completed the trial and eleven showed reduced dysfluencies, increased speed of speaking, and a reduced secondary struggle phenomenon. Side effects were common on doses of 3 mg (Maguire et al., 1999). In another study of adults with stuttering, eight out of sixteen subjects were randomized to risperidone (0.5 to 2 mg/day) for six weeks. Five of the eight responded to 0.5 mg/day with stuttering recurring at higher doses. Overall, there was a decrease in the percent of syllables stuttered and in overall stuttering severity (Murray et al., 1977).

Lavid and colleagues (1999) described three cases of children and adolescents with stuttering who successfully responded to olanzapine (dose range 2.5 to 5 mg) (Lavid, Franklin, & Maguire, 1999).

Developmental Issues

Few studies have examined the impact of antipsychotics on normal growth and development. One retrospective analysis of pooled data from five trials of risperidone for disruptive behavior disorders in 709 children and adolescents (five- to fifteen-years-old) assessed growth and maturation over a twelve-month period and found no evidence for delayed puberty or stunted growth (Dunbar et al., 2002).

Clinical Expertise

Despite a relative lack of controlled clinical evidence, antipsychotics continue to be used in children and adolescents for a wide variety of clinical indications. In addition to the psychiatric uses already mentioned, they are used in general pediatrics as antiemetics and preanesthetics (Campbell, Rapaport, & Simpson, 1999; Findling, Schulz, Reed, & Blumer, 1998). Their use merits some caution given the range and potential severity of side effects.

Before beginning therapy with an antipsychotic, certain baseline measures should be considered. For the typicals, particularly those with known potential QTc prolongation (pimozide and thioridazine), an EKG should be done. A baseline AIMS should be administered. Weight, height, and vital signs should be recorded. For typical antipsychotics, baseline complete blood count and liver function tests are recommended. For atypical neuroleptics, liver function tests, complete count including white blood cell count and absolute neutrophil count are recommended. Assessing baseline prolactin, glucose, triglycerides, and cholesterol may be helpful in the ongoing monitoring of patients on these agents. In addition, monitoring for EPS and other side effects should be done. Finally, in the event that clozapine is used, a baseline EEG is recommended. A baseline slit-lamp eye exam is recommended by the FDA prior to initiating quetiapine.

Deciding on an agent of choice involves a number of factors: past response to medication, including past side effects or treatment-refractory status; familial response to medication; side-effect risk profile of the patient and the medication; medical history of the patient; history of medication compliance (for example, requirement for a depot preparation); medication expense and insurance issues; and potential interactions with concurrent medications.

A few brief examples may help illustrate these points. A patient with a known personal or family history of obesity or diabetes may not be a candidate for those atypicals associated with weight gain. In these cases, the clinician may wish to consider medications that are associated with less or no weight gain, such as quetiapine, ziprasidone, aripiprazole, or molindone. In the case of treatment-refractory status, clozapine may need to be considered unless there is a significant history of seizure risk, head injury, abnormal EEG, or hematological problems. In a young male whose risk for EPS including acute dystonias may be highest, the atypical agents would be preferable over the typicals. If a patient has severe illness and a history of noncompliance, or is on court-mandated treatment, a medication that is available intramuscularly, including depot preparations such as prolixin or haloperidol, may need to be considered.

If the patient is new to antipsychotics and there are no known specific risk factors in the individual or family, a reasonable approach would be to begin with a low-dose atypical agent and titrate the dose up slowly (every few days) until a reasonable target dose is reached. For example, with risperidone, an initial dose for the treatment of psychosis might be 0.5 mg BID (twice daily) with gradual titration up to 4 mg in divided doses, and then hold the dose for about six weeks to evaluate efficacy. Monitoring should be weekly for the acute treatment phase (about eight weeks). If there is a good therapeutic response, the maintenance phase of treatment should include at least monthly monitoring. After a reasonable period of time of symptomatic stability (about six to twelve months in a youth with schizophrenia), one could very gradually decrease the dose to determine the lowest effective dose required to maintain symptom remission.

While monotherapy remains the preferential mode of treatment to minimize side effects and medication interactions, some severely psychotic patients may require the use of two antipsychotics simultaneously. In addition, other kinds of medication, such as anxiolytics, sleep medications, and mood agents often need to be used. Polypharmacy brings with it an increased risk of medication interactions, serotonin syndrome, and other side effects, and must be undertaken judiciously.

With patients who have any severe psychiatric disorder, particularly bipolar disorder and schizophrenia, who do not respond to appropriate trials of at least two antipsychotics, and who may be considered treatment-refractory, a reasonable approach is to step back and re-evaluate the diagnosis, which should include a more rigorous work-up for possible organic causes. In the case of psychotic disorders in youth, organic causes include Lyme disease or other CNS infections; metabolic problems including mitochondrial disorders; degenerative brain disorders, including white matter degeneration (such as metachromatic leukodystrophy or arylsulfatase deficiency); or structural brain pathology, such as tumors.

Constant monitoring of side effects, including height and weight and body mass index, EKG as indicated, and AIMS exams, is necessary. In the case of clozapine, prescribers must register all clozapine-treated patients with the national clozapine registry and report weekly white blood cell counts (WBCs) and absolute neutrophil counts; once six months of normal values has been established, WBC monitoring may be decreased to biweekly. Side effects in general are best approached by minimizing the risk through lowest possible dosing, gradual titrations, and so on. Side effects may need to be treated with additional medications. EPS may be treated by using antiparkinsonian agents such as amantadine, benztropine, diphenhydramine, or procyclidine. Akathisia may be treated with clonazepam, propranol, benztropine, or diphenhydramine. There is some evidence that vitamin E can be helpful in both the prevention and treatment of tardive dyskinesia, although the data are mixed. (See Table 14.3.)

In the case of neuroleptic malignant syndrome, the most critical step is making the correct diagnosis. Once achieved, treatment consists of immediate discontinuation of the neuroleptic and administering medically supportive measures (that is, reduce the fever, hydrate intravenously) and bromocriptine (Silva, Munoz, Alpert, Perlmutter, & Diaz, 1999). Similarly, serotonin syndrome must be promptly recognized, the combination of serotonergic medications stopped, and supportive measures administered.

For hyperprolactinemia, there is some evidence that increased levels will stabilize over time. Dopamine agonists such as bromocriptine can help to lower prolactin levels, but such an intervention should be taken judiciously, particularly in the psychotic patient, as this type of intervention can exacerbate psychotic symptomatology.

Seizures or risk of seizures in patients treated with clozapine or other antipsychotics known to decrease the seizures threshold may require special monitoring. EEGs may be need to be obtained occasionally. In the case of clozapine, low to medium doses (lower than 600 mg/day in adolescents) and slow upward titration may minimize the risk. Epileptic patients on clozapine may require higher dosages of their anticonvulsant medication. If a patient develops seizures during clozapine treatment, the dose should be reduced at least until the seizure activity is stabilized and an anticonvulsant is added and therapeutic doses are achieved. Because carbamazepine can lower white-blood-cell counts, it is contraindicated in combination with clozapine. Most often valproic acid and gabapentin are utilized in conjunction with clozapine.

Because of the potential cardiovascular side effects related to the use of psychotropic drugs, the American Heart Association (AHA) has drawn up a series of guidelines for cardiovascular monitoring of children and adolescents (Gutgesell et al., 1999). For most antipsychotics, with the exception of molindone (which has no known cardiovascular side effects), the AHA recommends (1) baseline history and physical with attention to cardiac symptoms, medication use, and family history; (2) updated history at subsequent visits, including new medications, cardiac symptoms, and repeat blood pressure and pulse; (3) avoiding concomitant medications that are metabolized by or inhibit the P450 enzyme system; (4) checking baseline EKG before initiating phenothiazine therapy and again when steady state is achieved. If resting heart rate is higher than 130 beats per minute, if the PR interval is greater that 200 milliseconds, if the QRS interval is greater than 120 milliseconds, or if the QTC interval is greater than 460 milliseconds, or if symptoms such as palpitations, near-syncope, or syncope occur, alternative therapy and pediatric cardiology consultation should be considered.

TABLE 14.3. ANTIPSYCHOTIC-RELATED SIDE EFFECTS AND THEIR CLINICAL MANAGEMENT.

Organ System	Side Effect	Receptor Likely Responsible	Clinical Management
Neurological	EPS Neuroleptic malignant syndrome Serotonin syndrome Sedation and other cognitive effects Seizures	Dopaminergic Histaminic	Maintain baseline and dose-increase Abnormal Involuntary Movement Scale and monitoring for akathisia using Barnes Akathisia Scale Use antiparkinsonian agents (such as benztropine) Avoid polypharmacy if possible EEG at baseline and therapeutic dosage
Endocrine	Increased prolactin Diabetes	Dopamine 2	Obtain prolactin levels in symptomatic patients Monitor glucose and HbA1C at baseline and regularly if weight gain is significant
Cardiovascular	Dizziness Hypotension QTc prolongation Tachycardia Shortness of breath Myocarditis clozapine	Alpha-1 adrenergic Muscarinic	History and physical at baseline EKG at baseline and at therapeutic dosage Blood pressure and pulse monitoring at baseline and with dose increases
Dermatologic	Allergic reactions, Photosensitivity Skin discoloration Alopecia	Receptor not identified	Instruct patient to report any rash immediately Use sun protection and avoid exposure
Oral and GI	Weight gain Dry mouth Cavities Constipation Hypersialorrhea	Histaminic Serotonergic Muscarinic	Monitor weight with every visit Monitor cholesterol and triglycerides Recommend sugarless gum or hard candy Regular dental checks Nutritional and exercise counseling proactively

System	Effects	Receptor	Management
Ophthalmologic	Blurry vision Acute angel closure Pigmentary deposits ?Cataracts (quetiapine)	Muscarinic	Routine eye examinations Slit-lamp exam at baseline and every 6 months if on quetiapine
Hematologic	Agranulocytosis Leukopenia Neutropenia	Receptor not identified	Complete blood count with differential at baseline and as needed for symptom development Weekly blood counts for clozapine-treated patients with national registry recording
Hepatic	Elevated transaminases	Receptor not identified	Check liver function tests at baseline and subsequently if significant weight gain
Sexual	Anorgasmia Impotence Priapism Reduced libido	Dopamine	Change medication
General	Thermoregulation Dehydration	Receptor not identified	Avoid sun exposure Use sun protection Ensure adequate ventilation in residence Hydrate adequately (suggest electrolyte-rich drinks)
Urological	Urinary retention	Muscarinic	Ask about urinary symptoms Decrease dose

Clinical suggestions for monitoring for or decreasing antipsychotic side effects are as follows. For weight gain, weight needs to be monitored and nutritional consultation may be necessary. Prudent diet and exercise are highly recommended. Some practitioners have used topiramate for weight control. (See Chapter 13.) Similarly, the risk of diabetes requires selection of an agent that has not been associated with significant glucose dyscontrol if at all possible and monitoring fasting glucose. If a patient has gained a significant amount of weight, obtaining an insulin level might be helpful to assess whether the patient has developed insulin resistance. In those with developing glucose dyscontrol and/or insulin resistance, obtaining an endocrinologic consultation is recommended and switching agents, if at all possible, is recommended. Anticholinergic side effects may be minimized by avoiding the use of anticholinergic adjuvant medications. Ophthalmologic, hematologic, and hepatic side effects should be monitored via exam, history, and appropriate blood monitoring. In the event that these side effects persist despite lowering the dose of the agent, and are severe, agents should be switched and the appropriate consultation with specialists obtained.

In general, patients and their parents should be advised to adhere to good sleep habits, maintain adequate hydration, eat healthy, well-balanced diets, and get regular exercise. These youths should also be supported in staying away from illegal substances and in those who have struggled with substance abuse, to maintain sobriety. If children or adolescents who are on antipsychotic agents spend a fair amount of time outdoors, particularly in warmer climates and during the summer, they should be advised to apply sunscreen.

Given the nature of adolescence as a developmental stage, as well as the lack of insight that accompanies psychotic disorders, medication noncompliance can become an issue. Developing a good alliance with the patient and his or her parents, including an empathic, direct, and nonjudgmental approach is crucial to maximize compliance. Additional treatment modalities, such as individual therapy, cognitive behavioral therapy, substance abuse treatment, family therapy, peer support groups, and individual therapy play important roles, as do social rehabilitation efforts such as vocational training, social skills development, clubhouse participation. They are all vital in reframing a life in which severe psychopathology has reset the equilibrium and in providing psychoeducation to a family that may be the patient's key support.

At times, legal issues emerge. For example, in the case of an adolescent refusing treatment, parents may need to seek emergency custody and court-mandated treatment if safety is an issue and the patient is deemed incompetent to make his or her own decisions.

◆ ◆ ◆

Antipsychotics are widely used in child psychiatry to treat a variety of disorders and behavioral disturbances. Despite their wide-spread clinical use, there is a relative paucity of data, based on long-term double-blind studies to guide prescriptive practice. Atypical antipsychotics are being utilized much more than typical agents due to their lower incidence of EPS, including tardive dyskinesia. However, these newer agents have their attendant liabilities as well. The most significant side effect seen in youth with these agents is weight gain. Clearly, further research is indicated on the use of these agents in youth. Antipsychotics can vastly help children and adolescents suffering from major mental illness. However, these agents should be used for well-formulated diagnoses and with clear target symptoms that will allow for judicious monitoring of response over time.

Future Directions

Aripiprazole is a newly released atypical neuroleptic considered the next generation of antipsychotics because it is a dopamine antagonist and a partial dopamine agonist—that is, it occupies the receptor but does not fully block its stimulation. Because it also is a partial agonist of the 5HT(1A) receptor, it has been called the first dopamine-serotonin system stabilizer (Jordan, Koprivica, & Chen et al., 2002; Carson et al., 2001) Aripiprazole has been shown effective (comparable to risperidone and haloperidol and superior to placebo) in alleviating positive and negative symptoms in adults. It has a seventy-two-hour half life. Early trials suggest that the medication is well tolerated, and does not appear to induce weight gain. In adults with bipolar disorder, aripiprizole was found superior to placebo in treating acute manic or mixed states, with a response rate (greater than 50% decrease in YMRS) of 42%, versus 21% for placebo (Keck et al., 2003). The dosage used was 30 mg/day, with the most common adverse effects being headache (36%), nausea (23%), dyspepsia (22%), and somnolence (20%). Aripiprazole has not yet been systematically studied in pediatric populations. Another new agent, amisulpride, is a substituted benzamide that seems to be effective in doses between 400 mg/day and 800 mg/day in the treatment of positive and negative psychotic symptoms. It has "dual dopamine blockade" and is in theory an antipsychotic at high doses while disinhibitory at low doses. It acts preferentially on presynaptic dopamine receptors to increase dopaminergic transmission. Interestingly, it does not have affinity for serotonergic, alpha-adrenergic, H1 histaminergic, or cholinergic receptors. One study documents its prescription in children (Toren, Laor, & Weizman, 1998).

Prevention appears to be an increased direction in the future. Researchers worldwide are studying the feasibility and efficacy of identifying and treating "at risk" populations, particularly those at risk for developing bipolar disorder and schizophrenia spectrum disorders (Yung et al., 2002; McGorry, Yung, & Phillips, 2001; Jablensky, 2000; Johnstone et al., 2000; Phillips et al., 1999). Interest in more explicitly identifying and treating the negative symptoms of psychotic disorders is growing. Functional impairment and quality of life are receiving new emphasis (Heinrichs, Hanlon, & Carpenter 1984). In addition, adjunctive medications for concomitant issues are being studied. For example, treatment of the cognitive deficits using agents such as the acetylcholine esterase inhibitors (traditionally used in Alzheimer's) and the stimulants (traditionally used in ADHD) is being explored. Adjunctive treatment with neurotrophic factors and other neuronal regulators is also being explored (Strous et al., 2003). New technologies in the treatment of brain disorders, including transcranial magnetic stimulations, are also being studied (Hoffman et al., 2003). Nonpharmacological treatment such as cognitive-behavioral therapy and psychosocial rehabilitation in psychotic youths is increasingly emphasized (Garety, Fowler, & Kuipers, 2000; Engelhardt & Rosen, 1976). Finally, novel methods of managing antipsychotic side effects are being explored (Poyurovsky et al., 2003).

The long-term impact of finding better treatments for major mental illness may be to reduce morbidity and mortality as well as the significant cost associated with having these illnesses. Future developments in antipsychotic medications will undoubtedly help society reach these goals.

References

Allison, D. B., & Casey, D. E. (2001). Antipsychotic-induced weight gain: A review of the literature. *Journal of Clinical Psychiatry, 62*(Suppl 7), 22–31.

Alvir, J. M., Lieberman, J. A., Safferman, A. Z., Schwimmer, J. L., & Schaaf, J. A. (1993). Clozapine-induced agranulocytosis. Incidence and risk factors in the United States. *New England Journal of Medicine, 329*(3), 162–167.

Aman, M. G., Findling, R. L., Derivan, A., Merriman, U., & the Conduct Study Group. (2000). Risperidone versus placebo for severe conduct disorder in children with mental retardation. *Poster presented at 40th Annual Meeting of the New Clinical Drug Evaluation Unit.* Boca Raton, FL.

American Psychiatric Association. (1994). Diagnostic and statistical manual of mental disorders. (4th Ed.). Washington, D.C.: *American Psychiatric Association.*

Anderson, L. T., Campbell, M., Grega, D. M., Perry, R., Small, A. M., & Green, W. H. (1984). Haloperidol in infantile autism: Effects on learning and behavioral symptoms. *American Journal of Psychiatry, 141,* 1195–1202.

Anderson, L. T., Campbell, M., Adams, P., Small, A. M., Perry, R., & Shell, J. (1989). The effects of haloperidol on discrimination learning and behavioral symptoms in autistic children. *Journal of Autism and Developmental Disorders, 19,* 227–239.

Armenteros, J. L., Adams, P. B., Campbell, M., & Eisenberg, Z. W. (1995). Haloperidol related dyskinesias and pre- and perinatal complications in autistic children. *Psychopharmacology Bulletin, 31,* 363–369.

Armentaros, J. L., Whitaker, A. H., Welikson, M., Steedge, D. J., & Gorman, J. (1997). Risperidone in adolescents with schizophrenia: An open pilot study. *Journal of the American Academy of Child and Adolescent Psychiatry, 36,* 694–700.

Barnes, R. J. (1977). Mesoridazine in personality disorders—a controlled trial in adolescent patients. *Diseases of the nervous system, 38,* 258–264.

Blanz, B., & Schmidt, M. H. (1993). Clozapine for schizophrenia. *Journal of the American Academy of Child and Adolescent Psychiatry, 32,* 223–224.

Bobes, J., Garc A-Portilla, M. P., Rejas, J., Hernandez, G., Garcia-Garcia, M., Rico-Villademoros, F., et al. (2003). Frequency of sexual dysfunction and other reproductive side-effects in patients with schizophrenia treated with risperidone, olanzapine, quetiapine, or haloperidol: The results of the EIRE Study. *Journal of Sex and Marital Therapy, 29*(2), 125–147.

Brekke, J. S., Raine, A., Ansel, M., Lencz, T., & Bird, L. (1997). Neuropsychological and psychophysiological correlates of psychosocial functioning in schizophrenia. *Schizophrenia Bulletin, 23,* 19–28.

Buchanan, R. W., Holstein, C., & Breier, A. (1994). The comparative efficacy and long term effect of clozapine treatment on neuropsychological test performance. *Biological Psychology, 36,* 717–725.

Buitelaar, J. K. (2000). Open-label treatment with risperidone of 26 psychiatrically hospitalized children and adolescents with mixed diagnoses and aggressive behavior. *Journal of Child and Adolescent Psychopharmacology, 10,* 19–26.

Buitelaar, J. K., van der Gaag, R. J., Cohen-Kettenis, P., & Melman, C. T. (2001). A randomized controlled trial of risperidone in the treatment of aggression in hospitalized adolescents with subaverage cognitive abilities. *Journal of Clinical Psychiatry, 62,* 239–248.

Buitelaar, J. K., van der Gaag, R. J., Cohen-Kettenis, P., & Melman, C.T.M. (2001). A randomized controlled trial of risperidone in the treatment of aggression in hospitalized adolescents with subaverage cognitive abilities. *Journal of Clinical Psychiatry, 62,* 239–248.

Campbell, M., Anderson, L. T., Meier, M., Cohen, I. L., Small, A. M., Samit, C., et al. (1978). A comparison of haloperidol and behavior therapy and their interaction in autistic children. *Journal of the American Academy of Child and Psychiatry, 17,* 640–655.

Campbell, M., Grega, D. M., Green, W. H., & Bennett, W. G. (1983). Neuroleptic-induced dyskinesias in children. *Clinical Neuropharmacology, 6,* 207–222.

Campbell, M., Greg, D. M., & Green, W. H. (1983). Neuroleptic induced dyskinesias in children. *Clinical Neuropharmacology, 6,* 207–222.

Campbell, M., Rapoport, J. L., & Simpson, G. M. (1999). Antipsychotics in children and adolescents. *Journal of the American Academy of Child and Adolescent Psychiatry, 38,* 537–545.

Campbell, M., Small, A. M., Green, W. H., Jennings, S. J., Perry, R., Bennett, W. G., et al. (1984). Behavioral efficacy of haloperidol and lithium carbonate. A comparison in hospitalized aggressive children with conduct disorder. *Archives of General Psychiatry, 41,* 650–656.

Campbell, M., & Schopler, E. (1989). Pervasive developmental disorders. In *Treatment of psychiatric disorders: A task force report of the American Psychiatric Association.* (Vol. 1, pp. 201–217), Washington, D.C.: American Psychiatric Association.

Carlson, G. A., Lavell, J., & Bromet, E. J. (1999). Medication treatment in adolescents vs. adults with psychotic mania. *Journal of Child and Adolescent Psychopharmacology, 9,* 221–231.

Carson, W. H., Jr., Saha, A. R., Alig., M., Dunbar, G. C., & Ingenito, G. (2001). Aripiprazole and risperidone versus placebo in schizophrenia and schizoaffective disorder. [Abstract NR263]. Presented at *American Psychiatric Association Annual Meeting,* New Orleans, LA.

Casear, P., Walleghem, D., Vandenbussche, I., Huang, M. L., & DeSmedt, F. (1994). Pharmacokinetics and safety of risperidone in autistic children [Abstract]. *Pediatric Neurology, 11,* 89.

Casey, D. E. (1997). The relationship of pharmacology to side effects. *Journal of Clinical Psychiatry, 58*(Suppl. 10), 55–62.

Chang, K. D., & Ketter, T. A. (2000). Mood stabilizer augmentation with olanzapine in acutely manic children. *Journal of Child and Adolescent Psychopharmacology, 10,* 45–49.

Clark, M. L., Huber, W. K., Sakata, K., Fowles, D. C., & Serafetinides, E. A. (1970). Molindone in chronic schizophrenia. *Clinical Pharmacology and Therapeutics, 11,* 680–688.

Cohen, I. L., Campbell, M., Posner, D., Triebel, D., Small, A. M., & Anderson, L. T. (1980). A study of haloperidol in young autistic children: A within-subjects design using objective rating scales. *Psychopharmacology Bulletin, 6,* 63–65.

Connor, D. F., Fletcher, K. E., & Wood, J. S. (2001). Neuroleptic-related dyskinesias in children and adolescents. *Journal of Clinical Psychiatry, 62,* 967–974.

Correll, C. U., Saito, E., Kafantaris, V., Kumra, S., & Malhotra, A. (2002). Atypical antipsychotics: Nutritional and metabolic effects on children and adolescents. [Abstract] *Scientific Proceedings from the Annual Meeting of the American Academy of Child and Adolescent Psychiatry* (p. 89). NRA. 8.

Crenshaw, T. L., & Golberg, J. P. (1996). Sexual pharmacology: Drugs that affect sexual function. In T. L. Crenshaw & J. P. Goldberg (Eds.), *Antipsychotics/Neuroleptics* (pp. 307–316). New York: WW Norton.

Delbello, M., Schwiers, M., Rosenberg, H. L., & Strakowski, S. (2002). A double-blind, randomized, placebo-controlled study of quetiapine as adjunctive treatment for adolescent mania. *Journal of the American Academy of Child and Adolescent Psychiatry, 41,* 1216–1223.

Denys, D., van Megan, H., & Westenberg, H. (2003). Quetiepine addition to serotonin reuptake inhibitor treatment in patients with treatment refractory obsessive compulsive disorder. Open-label study. *Journal of Clinical Psychiatry, 63,* 200–203.

Devinsky, O., Honigfeld, G., & Patin, J. (1991). Clozapine-related seizures. *Neurology, 41*(3), 369–371.

Dunbar, F., Kusumakar, V., Daneman, D., & Schulz, M. (2002). Growth and sexual maturation during treatment with risperidone. *New Research Posters, AACAP Scientific Proceedings* (p. 89).

Engelhardt, D. M., & Rosen, B. (1976). Implications of drug treatment for the social rehabilitation of schizophrenic patients. *Schizophrenia Bulletin, 2,* 454–462.

Escobar, J. I., Mann, J. J., Keller, J., Wilkins, J., Mason, B., & Mills, M. J. (1985). Comparison of injectable molindone and haloperidol followed by oral dosage forms in acutely ill schizophrenics. *Journal of Clinical Psychiatry, 6*(Suppl. 8), 15–19.

Findling, R. L. (2002). Combination pharmacotherapy in pediatric bipolar disorders. [Abstract] *Scientific Proceedings of the 49th Annual Meeting of the American Academy of Child and Adolescent Psychiatry* (p. 33).

Findling, R. L., Aman, M. G., DeSmedt, G., Derivan, A., & Nash, P. L. (2001). Long-term safety and efficacy of risperidone in children with significant conduct problems and borderline IQ or mental retardation. *Poster presented at Annual Meeting of the American Psychiatric Association,* New Orleans, LA.

Findling, R. L., Fegert, J. M., & DeSmedt, G. (2001). On behalf of the International Disruptive Behavior Disorder Study Group. Risperidone in children and adolescents with severe disruptive behaviors and subaverage IQ. *Poster presented at 40th Annual Meeting of the American College of Neuropsychopharmacology,* Waikoloa, HI.

Findling, R. L., Kusumakar, V., Danerman, D., Moshang, T., De Smedt, G., & Binder, C. (2002). Prolactin levels in children after long term treatment with risperidone. [Abstract] *American Academy of Child and Adolescent Psychiatry Scientific Proceedings* (p. 88). NRA1.

Findling, R. L., McNamara, N., Demeter, C., & Schulz, S. (2002). Olanzapine in adolescents with a psychotic illness. [Abstract] *Scientific Proceedings of the Annual Meeting of the American Academy of Child and Adolescent Psychiatry* (p. 88). NR A2.

Findling, R. L., McNamara, N. K., & Gracious, B. L. (2003). Antipsychotic agents: Traditional and atypical. In A. Martin, L. Scahill, D. S. Charney, & J. F. Leckman (Eds.), *Pediatric psychopharmacology principles and practice* (pp. 328–340). New York: Oxford University Press.

Findling, R. L., Schulz, S. C., Reed, M. D., & Blumer, J. L. (1998). The antipsychotics. A pediatric perspective. *Pediatric Clinics of North America, 45,* 1205–1232.

Fisman, S., Steele, M., Short, J., Byrne, T., & Lavallee, C. (1996). Case study: Anorexia nervosa and autistic disorder in an adolescent girl. *Journal of the American Academy of Child and Adolescent Psychiatry, 35,* 937–940.

Frazier, J. (2003). Agitation and aggression. In A. Martin, L. Scahill, D. S. Charney, & J. F. Leckman, *Pediatric psychopharmacology: Principles and practice* (pp. 671–685). New York: Oxford Press.

Frazier, J. A, Alaghband-Rad, J, Jacobsen, L., Lenane, M. C., Hamburger, S., Albus, K., et al. (1997). Pubertal development and onset of psychosis in childhood onset schizophrenia. *Psychiatric Research, 70,* 1–7.

Frazier, J. A., Biederman, J., Tohen, M., Feldman, P. D., Jacobs, T. G., Toma, V., et al. (2001). A prospective open-label treatment trial of olanzapine monotherapy in children and adolescents with bipolar disorder. *Journal of Child and Adolescent Psychopharmacology, 11*(3), 239–250.

Frazier, J. A., Cohen, L. G., Jacobsen, L., Grothe, D., Flood, J., Baldessarini, R. J., et al. (2003). Clozapine serum concentrations in children and adolescents with childhood-onset schizophrenia. *Journal of Clinical Psychopharmacology, 23,* 87–91.

Frazier, J. F., Gordon, C. T., McKenna, K., Lenane, M. C., Jih, D., & Rapoport, J. L. (1994). An open trial of clozapine in 11 adolescents with childhood-onset schizophrenia. *Journal of the American Academy of Child and Adolescent Psychiatry, 33,* 658–663.

Frazier, J. A., Meyer, M. C., Biederman, J., Wozniak, J., Wilens, T., Spencer, T., et al. (1999). Risperidone treatment for juvenile bipolar disorder: A retrospective chart review. *Journal of the American Academy of Child and Adolescent Psychiatry, 38,* 960–965.

Freeman, H., & Frederick, A. N. (1969). Comparison of trifluoperazine and molindone in chronic schizophrenic patients. *Current Therapeutic Research, 11,* 670–676.

Friedlander, R., Lazar, S., & Klancnik, J. (2001). Atypical antipsychotic use in treating adolescents and young adults with developmental disabilities. *Canadian Journal of Psychiatry, 46,* 741–745.

Furlant, M., Benetello, P., Baraldo, M., Zara, G., Montanari, G., & Donzelli, F. (1990). Chlorpromazine disposition in relation to age in children. *Clinical Pharmacokinetics, 18,* 329–331.

Gaffney, G. R., Perry, P. J., Lund, B. C., Bever-Stille, K. A., Arndt, S., & Kuperman, S. (2002). Risperidone versus clonidine in the treatment of children and adolescents with Tourette's syndrome. *Journal of the American Academy of Child and Adolescent Psychiatry, 41,* 330–336.

Gallant, D. M., Bishop, M. P., Steele, C. A., Bishop, G., & Guerro-Figueroa, R. (1973). Molindone: A crossover evaluation of capsule and tablet formulations in severely ill schizophrenic patients. *Current Therapeutic Research, 15,* 915–918.

Gardos, G., & Cole, J. O. (1977). Weight reduction in schizophrenics by molindone. *American Journal of Psychiatry, 134,* 302–304.

Garety, P. A., Fowler, D., & Kuipers, E. (2000). Cognitive-behavioral therapy for medication resistant symptoms. *Schizophrenia Bulletin, 26,* 73–86.

Geller, B., Cooper, T., Sun, K., Zimmerman, B., Frazier, J., Wiliams, M., et al. (1998). Double-blind and placebo-controlled study of lithium for adolescent bipolar disorders with secondary substance dependency. *Journal of the American Academy of Child and Adolescent Psychiatry, 37,* 171–178.

Gittlemann-Klein, R., Klein, D. F., Katz, S., Saraf, K., & Pollack, E. (1976). Comparative effects of methylphenidate and thioridazine in hyperkinetic children. *Archives of General Psychiatry, 33,* 1217–1231.

Godinho, E. M., Thompson, A. E., & Bramble, D. J. (2002). Neuroleptic withdrawal versus serotonergic syndrome in an 8-year-old child. *Journal of Child and Adolescent Psychopharmacology, 12,* 265–270.

Gothelf, D., Falk, B., Singer, P., Kairi, M., Phillip, M., Zigel, L., et al. (2002). Weight gain associated with increased food intake and low habitual activity levels in male adolescent schizophrenic inpatients treated with olanzapine. *American Journal of Psychiatry, 159,* 1055–1057.

Grcevich, S. J., Findling, R. L., Rosane, W. A., Friedman, L., & Schulz, S. C. (1996). Risperidone in the treatment of children and adolescents with schizophrenia: A retrospective study. *Journal of Child and Adolescent Psychopharmacology, 6,* 251–257.

Greenhill, L. L., Solomon, M., Pleak, R., & Ambrosini, P. (1985). Molindone hydrochloride treatment of hospitalized children with conduct disorder. *Journal of Clinical Psychiatry, 46,* 20–25.

Green, M. F. (1996). What are the functional consequences of neurocognitive deficits in schizophrenia? *American Journal of Psychiatry, 153,* 321–330.

Grothe, D. R., Calis, K. A., Jacobsen, L., Kumra, S., DeVane, C. L., Rapoport, J. L., et al. (2000). Olanzapine pharmacokinetics in pediatric and adolescent inpatient with childhood-onset schizophrenia. *Journal of Clinical Psychopharmacology, 20,* 220–225.

Gualtieri, C. T., Quade, D., Hicks, R. E., Mayo, J. P., & Schroeder, S. R. (1984). Tardive dyskinesia and other clinical consequences of neuroleptic treatment in children and adolescents. *American Journal of Psychiatry, 141,* 20–23.

Guerin, P., Barthelemy, C., Garreau, B., Heraut, J., Muh, J. P., & Lelor, G. (1993). The complexity of dopamine receptors and psychopharmacotherapy in children. *Acta Paedopsychiatrics, 56,* 139–151.

Gutgesell, H., Atkins, D., Barst, R., Buck, M., Franklin, W., Humes, R., et al. (1999). AHA scientific statement: Cardiovascular monitoring of children and adolescents receiving psychotropic drugs. *Journal of the American Academy of Child and Adolescent Psychiatry, 38,* 1047–1050.

Hagg, S., Spigset, O., Bate, A., & Soderstrom, T. G. (2001). Myocarditis related to clozapine treatment. *Journal of Clinical Psychopharmacology, 21,* 382–388.

Hagger, C., Buckley, P., Kenny, J. T., Friedman, L., Ubogy, D., & Meltzer, H. (1993). Improvement in cognitive functions and psychiatric symptoms in treatment-refractory schizophrenic patients receiving clozapine. *Biological Psychology, 34,* 702–712.

Hanna, G. L., Fluent, T. E., & Fischer, D. J. (1999). Separation anxiety in children and adolescents treated with risperidone. *Journal of Child and Adolescent Psychopharmacology, 9,* 277–283.

Hansen, T. E., Casey, D. E., & Hoffman, W. F. (1997). Neuroleptic intolerance. *Schizophrenia Bulletin, 23*(4), 567–582.

Hardan, A., Johnson, K., Honson, C., & Hrecznyj, B. (1996). Case study: Risperidone treatment of children and adolescents with developmental disorders. *Journal of the American Academy of Child and Adolescent Psychiatry, 35,* 1551–1556.

Harvey, P. D., Howanitz, E., Parrella, M., White, L., Davidson, M., Mohs, R. C., et al. (1998). Symptoms, cognitive functioning, and adaptive skills in geriatric patients with lifelong schizophrenia: A comparison across treatment sites. *American Journal of Psychiatry, 155,* 1080–1086.

Heinrichs, D. W., Hanlon, T. E., & Carpenter, W. T., Jr. (1984). The quality of life scale: An instrument for rating the schizophrenic deficit syndrome. *Schizophrenia Bulletin, 10,* 388–398.

Hemsley, D. R. (1994). Cognitive disturbance as the link between schizophrenic symptoms and their biological basis. *Neurology and Psychiatry Brain Research, 2,* 163–170.

Hill, D. (1948). The relationship between schizophrenia and epilepsy. *Folia Psychiatrica, Neurologica et Neurochirurgica Neederlandica, 51,* 95–111.

Hoff, A. L., Faustman, W. O., Wieneke, M., Espinoza, S., Costa, M., Wolkowitz, O., et al. (1996). The effects of clozapine on symptom reduction, neurocognitive function, and clinical management in treatment-refractory state hospital schizophrenic inpatients. *Neuropsychopharmacology, 15,* 361–369.

Hoffman, R. E., Hawkins, K. A., Gueorguiva, R., Boutros, N. N., Rachid, F., Carroll, K., et al. (2003). Transcranial magnetic stimulation of left temporopareital cortex and medication-resistance auditory hallucinations. *Archives of General Psychiatry, 60,* 49–56.

Horrigan, J. P., & Barnhill, L. J. (1997). Risperidone and explosive aggressive autism. *Journal of Autism and Developmental Disorders, 27,* 313–323.

Jablensky, A. (2000). Prevalence and incidence of schizophrenia spectrum disorders: Implications for prevention. *Australia & New Zealand Journal of Psychiatry, 34,* S26-S34, discussion S35-B.

Johnstone, E. C., Abukmeil, S. S., Bryne, M., Clafferty, R., Grant, E., Hodges, A., et al. (2000). Edinburgh high risk study-findings after four years: Demographic, attainment and psychopathological issues. *Schizophrenia Research, 46,* 1–15.

Jordan, S., Koprivica, V., Chen, R., et al. (2002). The antipsychotic aripiprazole is a potent partial agonist at the human 5-HT1A- receptor. *European Journal of Pharmacology, 441,* 137–140.

Kafantaris, V., Coletti, D. J., Dicker, R., Padula, G., & Kane, J. M. (2001). Adjunctive antipsychotic treatment of adolescents with bipolar psychosis. *Journal of the American Academy of Child and Adolescent Psychiatry, 40,*1448–1456.

Kafantaris, V., Dicker, R., Coletti, D. J., & Kane, J. M. (2001). Adjunctive antipsychotic treatment is necessary for adolescents with psychotic mania. *Journal of Child and Adolescent Psychopharmacology, 11,* 409–413.

Katzung, B. G. (1992). Basic and clinical pharmacology (5th Ed.). East Norwalk, CT: Appleton and Lange.

Keck, P., Marcus, R., Tourkodimitris, T., Ali, M., Liebeskind, A., Saha, A., Ingenito, G., & the Aripiprazole Study Group. (2003). A placebo-controlled double-blind study of the efficacy and safety of aripiprazole in patients with acute bipolar mania. *The American Journal of Psychiatry, 160,* 1651–1658.

Keefe, R. S., Silva, S. G., Perkins, D. O., & Lieberman, J. A. (1999). The effects of atypical antipsychotic drugs on neurocognitive impairment in schizophrenia: A review and meta-analysis. *Schizophrenia Bulletin, 5,* 201–222.

Keepers, G. A., Clappison, V. J., & Casey, D. E. (1983). Initial anticholinergic for neuroleptic induced extrapyramidal syndromes. *Archives of General Psychiatry, 40*(10), 1113–1117.

Kelly, D. L., Conley, R. R., Love, R. C., Horn, D. S., & Ushcak, C. M. (1998). Weight gain in adolescents treated with risperidone and conventional antipsychotics over six months. *Journal of Child and Adolescent Psychopharmacology, 8*(3), 151–159.

Kowatch, R. A., Suppes, T., Carmody, T. J., Bucci, J., Hume, J., Kromelis, M., et al. (2000). Effect size of lithium, divalproex sodium, and carbamazepine in children and adolescents with bipolar disorder. *Journal of Child and Adolescent Psychiatry, 39,* 713–720.

Kranzler, H. N., Gernino-Rosen, G., Pattin, R., & Kumra, S. (2002). Treatment-emergent laboratory abnormalities during clozapine treatment of adolescent with schizophrenia. [Abstract] *Scientific Proceedings from the Annual Meeting of the American Academy of Child and Adolescent Psychiatry* (p. 104). NRB31.

Krishnamoorthy, J., & King, B. H. (1998). Open-label olanzapine treatment in five preadolescent children. *Journal of Child and Adolescent Psychopharmacology, 8,* 107–113.

Krupp, P., & Barnes, P. (1992). Clozapine-associated agranulocytosis: Risk and etiology. *The British Journal of Psychiatry, 17*(Suppl), 38–40.

Kumra, S., Frazier, J. A., Jacobsen, L. K., McKenna, K., Lenane, M. C., Hamburger, S., et al. (1996). Childhood-onset schizophrenia: A double-blind clozapine-haloperidol comparison. *Archives of General Psychiatry, 53,* 1090–1097.

Kumra, S., Herion, D., Jacobsen, L. K., Briguglia, C., & Grothe, D. (1997). Case study: Risperidone-induced hepatotoxicity in pediatric patients. *Journal of the American Academy of Child and Adolescent Psychiatry, 36,* 701–705.

Kumra, S., Jacobsen, L. K., & Lenane, M. (1998). Childhood-onset schizophrenia. An open-label study of olanzapine in adolescents. *Journal of the American Academy of Child and Adolescent Psychiatry, 37,* 277–385.

Kumra, S., Jacobsen, L. K., Lenane, M., Smith, A., Lee, P., Malanga, C. J., et al. (1998). Case series: Spectrum of neuroleptic-induced movement disorders and extrapyramidal side effects in childhood-onset schizophrenia. *Journal of the American Academy of Adolescent Psychiatry, 37,* 221–227.

Lavid, N., Franklin, D. L., & Maguire, G. A. (1999). Management of child and adolescent stuttering with olanzapine: Three case reports. *Annals of Clinical Psychiatry, 11,* 233–236.

Levkovitch, Y., Kaysar, N., Kronnenberg, Y., Hagai, H., & Gaoni, B. (1994). Clozapine for schizophrenia. *Journal of the American Academy of Child and Adolescent Psychiatry, 33,* 431.

Lewis, R. (1998). Typical and atypical antipsychotics in adolescent schizophrenia: Efficacy, tolerability, and differential sensitivity to extrapyramidal symptoms. *Canadian Journal of Psychiatry, 4,* 596–604.

Linet, L. S. (1985). Tourettes syndrome, pimozide, and school phobia: The neuroleptic separation anxiety syndrome. *American Journal of Psychiatry, 142,* 613–615.

Locascio, J. J., Malone, R. P., Small, A. M., Kafantaris, V., Ernst, M., Lynch, N. S., et al. (1991). Factors related to haloperidol response and dyskinesias in autistic children. *Psychopharmacological Bulletin, 27,* 119–126.

Logothetis, J. (1967). Spontaneous epileptic seizures and electroencephalographic changes in the course of phenothiazine therapy. *Neurology, 17,* 869–877.

Lombroso, P. J., Scahill, L., King, R. A., & Lynch, K. A. (1995). Risperidone treatment of children and adolescents with chronic tic disorders: A preliminary report. *Journal of the American Academy of Child and Adolescent Psychiatry, 147*, 370–371.

Maguire, G. A., Gottshchalk, L. A., Riley, G. D., Franklin, D. L., Bechtel, R. J., & Ashurst, J. (1999). Stuttering: Neuropsychiatric features measured by content analysis of speech and the effect of risperidone on stuttering severity. *Comprehensive Psychiatry, 40*(4), 308–314.

Malone, R. P., Cater, J., Sheikh, R. M., Choudhury, M. S., & Delaney, M. A. (2001). Olanzapine versus haloperidol in children with autistic disorder: An open pilot study. *Journal of the American Academy of Child and Adolescent Psychiatry, 40*, 887–894.

Malone, R. P., Ernst, K. A., Locascio, J. J., & Campbell, M. (1991). Repeated episodes of neuroleptic-related dyskinesias in autistic children. *Psychopharmacology Bulletin, 27*, 113–117.

Malone, R. P., Maislin, G., Choudhury, M. S., Gifford, C., & Delaney, M. A. (2002). Risperidone treatment in children and adolescents with autism: Short- and long-term safety and effectiveness. *Journal of the American Child and Adolescent Psychiatry, 41*, 140–147.

Mandoki, M. (1997). Olanzapine in the treatment of early-onset-schizophrenia in children and adolescents. *Biological Psychiatry, 41*(Suppl 7), 22.

Mandoki, M. (1995). Risperidone treatment of children and adolescents: Increased risk of extrapyramidal side effects. *Journal of Child and Adolescent Psychopharmacology, 5*, 49–67.

Marder, S. R., & Meiback, R. C. (1994). Risperidone in the treatment of schizophrenia. *American Journal of Psychiatry, 151*, 825–835.

Martin, A., Koenig, K., Scahill, L., & Bregman, J. (1999). Open-label quetiapine in the treatment of children and adolescents with autistic disorder. *Journal of Child and Adolescent Psychopharmacology, 9*, 99–107.

McConville, B., Arvanitis, L., Thyrum, P., & Smith, K. (2000). Pharmacokinetics, tolerability and clinical effectiveness of quetiapine fumarate: An open-label trial in adolescents with psychotic disorders. *Journal of Clinical Psychiatry, 61*, 252–260.

McConville, B. J., Arvanitis, L. A., Thyrum, P. T., Yeh, C., Wilkinson, L. A., Chaney, R. O., et al. (2000). Pharmacokinetics, tolerability, and clinical effectiveness of quetiapine fumarate: An open-label trial in adolescents with psychotic disorders. *Journal of Clinical Psychiatry, 61*, 252–260.

McDougle, C. J., Epperson, C. N., Pelton, G. H., Wasylink, S., & Price, L. H. (2000). A double-blind, placebo-controlled study of risperidone addition in serotonin reuptake inhibitor-refractory obsessive-compulsive disorder. *Archives of General Psychiatry,57*, 794–801.

McDougle, C. J., Goodman, W. K., Leckman, J. F., Lee, N. C., Heninger, G. R., & Price, L. (1994). Haloperidol addition in fluvoxamine-refractory obsessive compulsive disorder: A double-blind, placebo-controlled study in patients with and without tics. *Archives of General Psychiatry, 51*, 302–308.

McDougle, C. J., Goodman, W. K., Price, L. H., Delgado, P. L., Krystal, J. H., Charney, D. S., et al. (1990). Neuroleptic addition in fluvoxamine-refractory obsessive-compulsive disorder. *American Journal of Psychiatry, 147*, 652–654.

McDougle, C. J., Holmes, J. P., Bronson, M. R., Anderson, G. M., Volkmar, F. R., Price, L. H., et al. (1997). Risperidone treatment of children and adolescents with pervasive developmental disorders: A prospective open-label study. *Journal of the American of Child and Adolescent Psychiatry, 36*, 685–693.

McGorry, P. D., Yung, A., & Phillips, L. (2001). Ethics and early intervention in psychosis: Keeping up the pace and staying in step. *Schizophrenia Research, 51*, 17–29.

Medalia, A., Gold, J., & Merriam, A. (1988). The effects of neuroleptics on neuropsychological test results in schizophrenia. *Archives of Clinical Neurology, 3,* 249–271.

Meiselas, K., Spencer, E. L., Oberfield, R., Peselow, E. D., Angrist, B., & Campbell, M. (1989). Differentiation of stereotypies from neuroleptic-related dyskinesias in autistic children. *Journal of Clinical Psychopharmacology, 9,* 207–209.

Meltzer, H. Y., Alphs, L., Green, A. I., Altamura, A. C., Anand, R., Bertoldi, A., et al. (2003). Clozapine treatment for suicidality in schizophrenia. *Archives of General Psychiatry, 60,* 82–91.

Meltzer, H. Y., & McGurk, S. R. (1999). The effects of clozapine, risperidone and olanzapine on cognitive function in schizophrenia. *Schizophrenia Bulletien, 25,* 233–255.

Messing, R. O., Closson, R. G., & Simon, R. P. (1984). Drug-induced seizures: A 10-year experience. *Neurology, 34,* 1582–1586.

Meyer, M. C., Baldessarini, R. J., Goff, D. C., & Centorrino, F. (1996). Clinically significant interactions of psychotropic agents with antipsychotic drugs. *Drug Safety, 15*(5), 336–346.

Meyers, B., Tune, L. E., & Coyle, J. T. (1980). Clinical response and serum neuroleptic levels in childhood schizophrenia. *American Journal of Psychiatry, 137,* 483–484.

Mikkelson, E. J., Detlor, J., & Cohen, D. J. (1981). School avoidance and social phobia triggered by haloperidol in patients with Tourette's disorder. *American Journal of Psychiatry, 138,* 1572–1576.

Morselli, P. L., Bianchette, G., & Dugas, M. (1982). Haloperidol plasma level monitoring in neuropsychiatric patients. *Therapeutic Drug Monitoring, 4,* 51–58.

Morselli, P. L., Bianchette, G., Durand, G., Le Heuzey, M. F., Zarifian, E., & Dugas, M. (1979). Haloperidol plasma level monitoring in pediatric patients. *Therapeutic Drug Monitoring, 1,* 35–46.

Morselli, P. L., Bianchetti, G., & Dugas, M. (1983). Therapeutic drug monitoring of psychotropic drugs in children. *Pediatric Pharmacology, 3,* 149–156.

Mukherjee, S., Decina, P., Bocola, V., Saraceni, F., & Scapicchio, P. L. (1996). Diabetes mellitus in schizophrenic patients. *Comprehensive Psychiatry, 37,* 68–73.

Murray, T. J., Kelly, P., Campbell, L., & Stefanik, K. (1977). Haloperidol in the treatment of stuttering. *British Journal of Psychiatry, 130,* 370–373.

Naruse, H., Nagahata, M., Nakane, Y., Shirahashi, K., Takesada, M., & Yamazaki, K. (1982). A multi-center double-blind trial of pimozide (orap), haloperidol and placebo in children with behavioral disorder, using a crossover design. *Acta Paedopsychiatrica, 48,* 173–184.

National Institute of Mental Health (NIMH). (1985). Special feature: Rating scales and assessment instruments for use in pediatric psychopharmacology research. *Psychopharmacology Bulletin, 21,* 765–770.

Notkin, J. (1929). Epileptic manifestations in the group of schizophrenic and manic-depressive psychoses. *Journal of Nervous and Mental Disorders, 69,* 494–495.

Onofrj, M., Paci, C., D' Andreamatteo, G., & Toma, L. (2000). Olanzapine in severe Gilles de la Tourette syndrome: A 52-week double-blind cross-over study vs. low-dose pimozide. *Journal of Neurology, 247,* 443–446.

Opler, L. A., & Feinberg, S. S. (1991). The role of pimozide in clinical psychiatry: A review. *Journal of Clinical Psychiatry, 52,* 221–233.

Pappadopulos, E., MacIntyre, J. C., Crismon, M. L., Findling, R. L., Malone, R. P., Derivan, A., et al. (2003). Treatment Recommendations for the Use of Antipsychotics for Aggressive Youth (TRAAY), Part II. *Journal of the American Academy of Child and Adolescent Psychiatry, 42,* 145–161.

Patel, N. C., Sierk, P., Dorson, P. G., & Crimson, M. L. (2002). Experience with ziprasidone. [Letter] *Journal of the American Academy of Child and Adolescent Psychiatry, 41,* 495.

Pearlman, C. A. (1986). Neuroleptic malignant syndrome: A review of the literature. *Journal of Clinical Psychopharmacology, 6,* 257–273.

Perry, R., Campbell, M., Adams, P., et al. (1989). Long-term efficacy of haloperidol in autistic children: Continuous vs. discontinuous drug administration. *Journal of the American Academy of Child and Adolescent Psychiatry, 28,* 87–92.

Piscitelli, S. C., Frazier, J. A., McKenna, K., Albus, K. E., Grothe, D. R., Gordon, C. T., et al. (1994). Plasma clozapine and haloperidol concentrations in adolescents with childhood-onset schizophrenia: Association with response. *Journal of Clinical Psychiatry, 55,* 94–97.

Pliszka, S. R., Greenhill, L. L., Crismon, M. L., Sedillo, A., Carlson, C., & Conners, C. K. (2000). The Texas Children's Medication Algorithm Project: Report of the Texas Consensus Conference Panel on Medication Treatment of Childhood Attention-Deficit/Hyperactivity Disorder. Part II: Tactics. Attention-Deficit/Hyperactivity Disorder. *Journal of the American Academy of Child and Adolescent Psychiatry, 39,* 920–927.

Phillips, L., Yung, A. R., Hearn, N., McFarlane, C., Hallgren, M., & McGorry, P. D. (1999). Preventative mental health care: Accessing the target population. *Australia and New Zealand Journal of Psychiatry, 33,* 912–912.

Pool, D., Bloom, W., Mielke, D. H., Roninger, J. J., Jr., & Gallant, D. M. (1976). A controlled evaluation of loxitane in seventy-five adolescent schizophrenic patients. *Current Therapy Research, Clinical and Experimental, 19*(1), 99–104.

Potenza, M. N., Holmes, J. P., Kanes, S. J., & McDougle, C. J. (1999). Olanzapine treatment of children, adolescents, and adults with pervasive developmental disorders: An open-label pilot study. *Journal of Clinical Psychopharmacology, 19,* 37–44.

Poyurovsky, M., Isaacs, I., Fuchs, C., Schneidman, M., Faragian, S., Weizman, R., et al. (2003). Attenuation of olanzapine-induced weight gain with reboxetine in patients with schizophrenia: A double-blind, placebo-controlled study. *American Journal of Psychiatry, 160,* 297–302.

Pfizer, Inc., Geodon package Insert. New York, New York. (2001).

Purdon, S. E. (1999). Cognitive improvement in schizophrenia with novel antipsychotic medications. *Schizophrenia Research, 35,* 54–66.

Rabe-Jablonska, J. (2001). Obsessive-compulsive disorders in adolescents with diagnosed schizophrenia. *Psychiatria Polska, 35,* 47–57.

Ratzoni, G., Gothelf, D., Brand-Gothelf, A., Reidman, J., Kikinzon, L., Gal, G., et al. (2002). Weight gain associated with olanzapine and risperidone in adolescent patients: A comparative prospective study. *Journal of the American Academy of Child and Adolescent Psychiatry, 41*(3), 337–343.

Realmuto, G. M., Erickson, W. D., Yellin, A. M., Hopwood, J. H., & Greenberg, L. M. (1984). Clinical comparison of thiothixene and thioridazine in schizophrenic adolescents. *American Journal of Psychiatry, 141*(3), 440–442.

Reilly, J. G., Ayis, S. A., Ferrier, I. N., Jones, S. J., & Thomas, S. H. (2000). QTc interval abnormalities and psychotropic drug therapy in psychiatric patients. *Lancet, 25,* 1048–1052.

Remschmidt, H., Schulz, E., & Martin, C. L. (1994). An open trial of clozapine in thirty-six adolescents with schizophrenia. *Journal of Child and Adolescent Psychopharmacology, 4,* 31–41.

Richardson, M. A., Haugland, G., & Craig, T. J. (1991). Neuroleptic use, parkinsonian symptoms, tardive dyskinesia, and associated factors in child and adolescent psychiatric patients. *American Journal of Psychiatry, 148,* 1322–1328.

Rivera-Calimlim, L., Griesbach, P. H., & Perlmutter, R. (1979). Plasma chlorpromazine concentrations in children with behavioural disorders and mental illness. *Clinical Pharmacology and Therapeutics, 26,* 114–121.

Ryan, M.C.M., & Thakore, J. H. (2002). Physical consequences of schizophrenia and its treatment: The metabolic syndrome. *Life Sciences, 71,* 239–257.

Ryan, M.C.M., Collins, P., & Thakore, J. (2003). Impaired fasting glucose tolerance in first-episode, drug-naïve patients with schizophrenia. *American Journal of Psychiatry, 160,* 284–289.

Saito, E., Correll, C., & Kafantaris, V. (2002). A prospective study of hyperprolactinemia secondary to atypical antipsychotic agents. [Abstract] *American Academy of Child and Adolescent Psychiatry Scientific Proceedings* (p. 90). NRSA13.

Sallee, F. R., Kurlan, R., Goetz, C. G., Singer, H., Scahill, L., Law, G. (2000). Ziprasidone treatment of children with Tourette's syndrome: A pilot study. *American Journal of Child and Adolescent Psychiatry, 39,* 292–299.

Sallee, F. R., Gilbert, D. L., Vinks, A. A., Miceli, J. J., Robarge, L. & Wilner, K. (2003). Pharmacokinetics of ziprasidone in children and adolescents: Impact of dopamine transmission. *Journal of the American Academy of Child and Adolescent Psychiatry, 42*(8), 902–907.

Sallee, F. R., Pollock, B. G., Stiller, R. L., Stull, S., Everett, G., & Perel, J. M. (1987). Pharmacokinetics of pimozide in adults and children with Tourette's syndrome. *Journal of Clinical Pharmacology, 27,* 776–781.

Schreier, H. A. (1998). Risperidone for young children with mood disorders and aggressive behavior. *Journal of Child and Adolescent Psychopharmacology, 8,* 49–59.

Schulz, E., Fleischhaker, C., & Remschmidt, H. E. (1996). Correlated changes in symptoms and neurotransmitter indices during maintenance treatment with clozapine or conventional neuroleptics in adolescents and young adults with schizophrenia. *Journal of Child and Adolescent Psychopharmacology, 6,* 199–131.

Schur, S. B., Sikich, L., Findling, R. L., Malone, R. P., Crismon, M. L., Derivan, A., et al. (2003). Treatment Recommendations for the Use of Antipsychotics for Aggressive Youth (TRAAY), Part I: A review. *Journal of the American Academy of Child and Adolescent Psychiatry, 42,* 132–144.

Sernyak, M. J., Leslie, D. L., Alarcon, R. D., Lozonczy, M. R., & Rosenheck, R. (2002). Association of diabetes mellitus with use of atypical neuroleptics in the treatment of schizophrenia. *American Journal of Psychiatry, 159,* 561–566.

Shapiro, E., Shapiro, A. K., Fulop, G., Hubbard, M., Mandeli, H., Nordlie, H., et al. (1989). Controlled study of haloperidol, pimozide, and placebo for the treatment of Gilles de la Tourette's syndrome. *Archives of General Psychiatry, 46,* 722–730.

Shaw, J. A., Pascal, S., Sharma, R. P., Rodriguez, R., Lewis, J., Guillen, R., et al. (2001). An open trial of quetiapine in adolescent patients with psychosis. *Scientific Proceedings of the Annual Meeting of the American Psychiatric Association, New Research Poster, 733,* New Orleans.

Shell, J., Spencer, E. K., Curren, E., et al. (1987). Long-term haloperidol administration and intellectual functioning in autistic children. [Abstract] In *Scientific Proceedings, 34th Annual Meeting of the American Academy of Child and Adolescent Psychiatry,* Washington, D.C.

Shen, W. W. (1999). A history of antipsychotic drug development. *Comprehensive Psychiatry, 40,* 401–414.

Sholevar, E. H., Baron, D. A., & Hardie, T. L. (2000). Treatment of childhood onset schizophrenia with olanzapine. *Journal of Child and Adolescent Psychopharmacology, 10,* 69–78.

Sikich, L., Williamson, K., Malekpour, A., Bashford, R., Hooper, S., Sheitman, B., et al. (1999). Double-blind comparison haloperidol, risperidone and olanzapine in psychotic youth. *Annual Meeting of the Academy of Child and Adolescent Psychiatry,* Chicago.

Silva, R. R., Munoz, D. M., Alpert, M., Perlmutter, I. R., & Diaz, J. (1999). Neuroleptic malignant syndrome in children and adolescents. *American Journal Academy of Child and Adolescent Psychiatry, 38,* 187–194.

Simeon, J. G., Carrey, N. J., Wiggins, D. M., Milin, R. P., & Hosenbocus, S. N. (1995). Risperidone effects in treatment-resistant adolescents: Preliminary case reports. *Journal of Child and Adolescent Psychopharmacology, 5,* 69–79.

Simeon, J., Milin, R., & Walker, S. (2002). A retrospective chart review of risperidone use in treatment-resistant children and adolescents with psychiatric disorders. *Progress in Neuro-Psychopharmacology & Biology Psychiatry, 26,* 267–275.

Snyder, R., Turgay, A., Aman, A., Binder, C., Fisman, S., Carroll, A., & the Risperidone Conduct Study Group. (2002). Effects of risperidone on conduct and disruptive behavior disorders in children with subaverage IQs. *Journal of the American Academy of Child and Adolescent Psychiatry, 41,* 1026–1036.

Spencer, E. G., Kafantaris, V., Padron-GayoL, M. V., Rosenberg, C., & Campbell, M. (1992). Haloperidol in schizophrenic children: Early findings from a study in progress. *Psychopharmacology Bulletin, 28*(2), 183–186.

Spohn, H. E., & Strauss, M. E. (1989). Relation of neuroleptic and anticholinergic medication to cognitive functions in schizophrenia. *Journal of Abnormal Psychology, 98,* 367–380.

Stip, E., & Boisjoly, H. (1999). Quetiapine: Are we overreacting in our concern about cataracts (the beagle effect)? *Canadian Journal of Psychiatry, 44,* 503.

Strous, R. D., Maayan, R., Laapidus, R., Stryjer, R., Lustig, M., Kotler, M., et al. (2003). Dehydroepiandrosterone augmentation in the management of negative, depressive and anxiety symptoms in schizophrenia. *Archives of General Psychiatry, 60,* 133–141.

Szigethy, E., Wiznitzer, M., Branicky, L. A., Mazwell, K., & Findling, R. L. (1999). Risperidone-induced hepatotoxicity in children and adolescents: A chart review. *Journal of Child and Adolescent Psychopharmacology, 9*(2), 93–98.

Tanguay, P. E. (2000). Pervasive developmental disorders: A 10-year review. *Journal of the American Academy of Child and Adolescent Psychiatry, 39,* 1079–1095.

Toren, P., Laor, N., & Weizman, A. (1998). Use of atypical neuroleptics in child and adolescent psychiatry. *Journal of Clinical Psychiatry, 59,* 644–656.

Turetz, M., Mozes, T., Toren, P., Chernauzan, N., Yaran-Hegesh, R., Mester, R., et al. (1997). An open trial of clozapine in neuroleptic-resistant childhood—onset schizophrenia. *British Journal of Psychiatry, 170,* 507–510.

Turgay, A., Aman, M., Binder, C., Snyder, R., & Schulz, M. (2001). Risperidone in children with oppositional defiant disorder, conduct disorder, subaverage IQ and comorbid ADHD. *Poster presented at 48th Annual Meeting of the American Academy of Child and Adolescent Psychiatry,* Honolulu, HI.

Van Bellinghen, M., & De Troch, C. (2001). Risperidone in the treatment of behavioral disturbances in children and adolescents with borderline intellectual functioning: A double-blind placebo controlled pilot trial. *Journal of Child and Adolescent Psychopharmacology, 11,* 5–13.

Volonte, M., Monferini, E., Cerutti, M., Fodritto, R., & Borsini, F. (1997). BIMG 80, a novel potential antipsychotic drug: Evidence for multireceptor actions and preferential release of dopamine in prefrontal cortex. *Journal of Neurochemistry, 69,* 182–190.

Wagner, K. D., Weller, E. B., Carlson, G. A., Sachs, G., Biederman, J., Frazier, J. A., et al. (2002). An open-label trial of divalproex in children and adolescents with bipolar disorder. *Journal of the American Academy of Child and Adolescent Psychiatry, 41,*1224–1230.

Wirshing, D. A., Spellberg, B. J., Erhart, S. M., Marder, S. R., & Wirshing, W. C. (1998). Novel antipsychotics and new onset diabetes. *Society of Biological Psychiatry, 44,* 778–783.

Wudarsky, M., Nicolson, R., Hamburger, S. D., Spechler, L., Gochman, P., Bedwell, J., et al. (1999). Elevated prolactin in pediatric patients on typical and atypical antipsychotics, *9*(4), 239–245.

Yung, A. R., Phillips, L. J., Yuen, H. P., Francey, S. M., McFarlane, C. A., Hallgren, M., et al. (2002). Psychosis prediction: 12-month follow up of a high-risk ("prodromal") group. *Schizophrenia Research, 60,* 21–32.

Zuddas, A., Ledda, M. G., Fratta, A., Muglia, P., & Cianchetti, C. (1996). Clinical effects of clozapine on autistic disorder. *American Journal of Psychiatry, 153,* 738.

CHAPTER FIFTEEN

PSYCHOLOGICAL ASPECTS OF PEDIATRIC MEDICATION MANAGEMENT

Shashank V. Joshi, M.D., Leena A. Khanzode, M.D., and Dr. med. univ. Hans Steiner

The offer of treatment to patients is much more than a simple neutral act. It represents an offer of hope and of confidence in things to come (Pruett & Martin, 2003). Everything we do with, and say to, patients and families has important potential meaning (Tasman, Riba, & Silk, 2000), and we must therefore be ever-cognizant of our own unconscious wishes and expectations for a particular treatment (Pruett & Martin, 2003). We may, in fact, share the same "magic cure" fantasies of the perfect potion for what ails our patients (Pruett & Martin, 2003). But while the fields of psychotherapy and sociotherapy openly acknowledge these principles and are prepared to examine latent content, pharmacotherapy is often practiced as if these issues could be ignored. The term *prescription* is somewhat of a misnomer . . . one is never written in a vacuum, devoid of relational and diagnostic context (Pruett & Martin, 2003).

Because psychopharmacological practice is part of psychiatric practice, it requires experience with psychotherapeutic issues and techniques, and skilled practitioners must use these to best identify symptoms and promote adherence. In fact, unless the psychological aspects of care are attended to carefully, pharmacological aspects may be only suboptimal at best (Pillay & Ghaemi, 2002).

We sincerely thank Malathy Sivapalsingam, M.S., P.N.P., for her assistance in reviewing and preparing this manuscript.

In this chapter, we shall attempt to address the following questions:

What are the psychological implications of administering medications? Do such forces powerfully distort, enhance, or even neutralize the effects of medications administered?

Putative Mechanisms of Efficacy

The psychology of psychopharmacology becomes manifest in at least three ways: by the characteristics of the pediatric patient, those of the important adults in that patient's life, and those of the patient's social environment.

Characteristics of the Pediatric Patient

The patient's internal working model of receiving support, help, nurturance, and treatment will be based on previous experiences with caregivers, both within and outside of the family. This may include past relationships with physicians, teachers, and counselors. This transference will, in turn, influence the patient's capacity to form a helping alliance with the physician who administers the medication. Attachment status, age of the child, and past outcomes of interacting with caregivers in times of hurt and need will also influence the formation of the helping alliance. The ultimate goal is to understand these factors in order to create the strongest possible therapeutic alliance to maximally enhance adherence, and ultimately to lead to better clinical outcomes. (Note: We prefer the term *adherence* to *compliance* for many reasons. The former term implies more of a partnership, less of a power differential, and less of a "defensively authoritarian" connotation [Pruett & Martin, 2003]). (For a thorough discussion of this topic, see Ellison, 2000.)

Characteristics of the Important Adults in the Youth's Life

Because children are context-dependent on caregivers and families, especially at young ages, the way their family/school handles the supervision and administration of medication will have profound influences on how well this process will unfold, and how it will facilitate or hinder the child's taking medication under optimal conditions. Adherence is promoted when the teacher or parent avoids backhanded "compliments" such as "You're doing really well today, you must have taken your meds!" The child/teen is likely to attribute success more to his or her inherent abilities, rather than to medication, when adults are attentive to the specific language they use.

School, Peers, and Media Factors

Many pediatric patients will be more likely to accept the idea of having to take medication if there is a connection to a peer or famous person with a similar problem. Media influences may include Internet information (or misinformation), music video depictions of teens with mental health problems, as well as mental illness themes in television, film, or in printed media. It is important to elicit the child or teen's self-perception of what it means to him or her to be taking psychotropic medication.

Barriers to Adherence

The construct, *psychopharmacotherapy*, has been previously described (Pruett & Martin, 2003; Schowalter, 1989), and may be defined as the combined use of psychoactive medication and psychotherapy. Next, we will describe several aspects of this concept as we understand and apply it, some of which have inherent implications not only for pediatric psychopharmacology, but also for medication management with children and teens in general.

The decision to offer medication: Patients, and parents of patients, often wonder why their therapist would consider the use of psychoactive medication. For example, questions such as *Why now? Am I such a failure as patient/parent?* take on crucial relevance, especially if the idea is presented in a non-sensitive manner.

How and when to present the idea of prescribing medication: We prefer to discuss the possibility of a medication intervention at the outset of assessment and treatment plan development. This allows for an open and frank discussion regarding potential benefits and side effects, so as to make the family/child aware of its availability either in the short-term, or in the future. It eases the task of "bringing up medication" as an intervention later in the course of therapy, as it had already been discussed previously. Also, it is ideal to discuss medicinal strategies/medication changes with the primary therapist first, not only in the spirit of collaboration, but also to best convey a unified message to the patient and family.

The act of writing and giving the prescription: Whenever possible, this should be done only after adequate time (sometimes an entire session) has been spent explaining benefits and risks, and answering all questions for both child and parent. We first try to earnestly gauge the developmental level of the child or teen, then tailor an explanation geared to his or her level of sophistication. This means that for most middle and older teens (ages fourteen and above), we are addressing our comments directly to them, and we are also writing and handing the prescriptions directly to *them, rather than to their parents.* This sends a powerful message of our faith in them and in their ability to be "captain of their ship" when it comes to medication. We, the adults in the teen's life, are there to provide coaching, support, and supervision (which includes rule-making and limit-setting; for example, that a teen with attention-deficit/hyperactivity disorder (ADHD) cannot use the car on weekends if he or she chooses to not take medication, because of the higher incidence of accidents for untreated teens).

The meaning of the medication itself, and on the self: Many teens will have preconceived notions about medication, based partly on direct-to-consumer marketing campaigns meant to encourage potential clients to "ask (your) doctor about Zoloft." Other potential barriers to adherence include feeling different or damaged from friends who do not have to take medication, feeling strange or altered when medicine has begun to take effect, feeling like a different person when medicated (and likeable only in this altered state), and seeing the prescriber as an agent of the teen's parents (a possibly irreparable mistake!). Care must be taken to not send a signal that all discomfort must be squelched out through favoring pharmacology over psychotherapy. As Schowalter (1989, p. 683) has noted, "All too often it is unclear whether a medication heals directly or mainly removes obstacles to self-healing."

The *name* of the medicine can have prejudicial effects on attitudes, and hence, adherence. We have experienced both success and failure in this regard. A bright fifteen-year-old boy with bipolar disorder was reluctant to take a medication which made him feel "vilified" (Abilify), while a seventeen-year-old with similar symptoms felt that this drug would "abilify" him to control his mood lability and impulse control problems. A nine-year-old who experienced side effects on all other antipsychotics was eventually convinced to try Geodon for psychotic thinking and impulsive aggression/rage attacks, after his speech therapist helped him connect the idea of taking this medicine with a Pokemon character, Geodude. Placebo (Latin for "I will please") effects must be taken seriously, not only because of their impressive record of having therapeutic effects (Blakeslee, 1998; Park & Covi, 1965; Schowalter, 1997), but also because realistic hope and confidence can be relevant, unignorable, and powerful tools in the process of psychopharmacotherapy (Pruett & Martin, 2003; Schowalter, 1989).

Do children and teens feel "changed" as people? Some patients and families will fear a change in personality, onset of a "zombie effect," or loss of a *joie de vivre* inherent to their child/teen. We are very careful to include this as part of our discussion in the initial assessment phase, and emphasize how the aforementioned changes are unacceptable and/or unnecessary in this day of numerous efficacious agents and a growing empiric database. Others worry that it will alter their perceptions of themselves: "I love my symptoms doc, they make me *myself!*" (Pruett & Martin, p. 418)

Backhanded compliments: Even well-meaning parents, teachers, and other adults need to be reminded about the use of appropriate language when praising or checking for adherence. One approach would be to discreetly keep track of pill counts in the prescription bottle, then to subtly but regularly give appropriate praise (at the appropriate times) for good decision-making, good behavior, compliance with parent requests, getting along with siblings, and so on. They'll likely make the connection on their own, which is often the most effective way to learn.

Transferring medication therapists and *institutional transference:* Do not assume that an effective medication regimen will continue when a resident on rotation for six months leaves. A patient's feelings of loss and abandonment in such a case may be just as important to acknowledge as those of a patient whose psychotherapist leaves for the next assignment. Also, *institutional transference* (feelings that a patient may have toward a new therapist, based on previous experiences with therapists or other personnel from the same institution) must be acknowledged, especially for patients who may have been in a university clinic for many years, and who are used to being "shuffled" from one doctor to the next. Thus, we must remain aware of these factors for successful transitions in care to evolve.

The context and setting of the medication prescription: An observant teen once told a resident of ours about the irony in getting a prescription for Prozac, written by the doctor with a Wellbutrin logo pen, and with titration instructions written on a Depakote notepad. In keeping with the theme that all of our actions have meaning to the patient and family, mindful psychopharmacotherapists should be aware of the subliminal messages they are broadcasting through their nonverbal acts.

When discussing context and setting of the prescription, one must always consider the different levels of parent sophistication, understanding, opposition, or buy-in to treatment. A myriad number of factors can become barriers to successful treatment adherence, including misunderstanding of doses, ambivalence regarding the decision to medicate, guilt about having caused the problem to be addressed (either by genes or poor parenting), Internet or other media-based information, or transference based on past providers (Tasman et al., 2000). We must choose our language carefully, based on who the audience is. Providers ought to be careful not to overuse terms such as "chemical imbalance," as these may be interpreted in different and unpredictable ways (Pruett & Martin, 2003).

The school environment may be a second important context for a child or teen who takes medication. School staff may actually have originated the initial medication consultation. Therefore, it is important for the prescriber to have direct contact with teachers, and in some cases school officials. It may be necessary, for example, to correct the "delusion of precision" that may exist as a collective wish from the school administration (Gutheil, 1977, 1982). Medication may be endowed with the power to specifically and concretely target symptoms in an unambiguously effective manner—if the therapist would simply prescribe them. The school may feel under pressure to medicate these children into docility and compliance, more for reasons of understaffing, overcrowding, academic standards and to quiet other parents who complain, rather than for the best interests of the child (Pruett & Martin, 2003). The successful psychopharmacotherapist always works as part of a team on a particular patient's behalf. This therapist presumes that there is always at least a four-way relationship: client, parent, teacher, and prescriber). The prescriber can and must work with the teacher or school nurse to find ways of gently reminding the child to take medication (for example, coming up with a signal, or giving the student an errand to run at medication time, which allows him to discreetly go to the nurse station for medication).

Even though the need for multiple daily doses has been decreasing with the advent of many once-daily preparations, the reality of having to take medication need not be equated with humiliation.

Developmental Influences

For preschool children, there is complete dependence and trust on parents and caregivers, who in turn must have a thorough understanding of benefits and risks, as well as an ability to ensure adherence through an authoritative parenting style. During the latency (school age) years, there is a transition to having the child assume some responsibility for their own treatment, and resistance should be processed in light of the child's increasing understanding of matters on a higher level. Ultimately, however, the parent or caretaker is still in charge of treatment. Table 15.1 illustrates some commonly held beliefs by children regarding medicine.

In adolescence, as children move toward more independence, there is, an increasing shift toward having them assume more responsibility for their care. Helping parents to avoid intrusive, controlling styles and attitudes, while still maintaining a proper monitoring and supervisory relationship, is the task for prescribers. Clinicians are wise to heed the advice of Pruett and Martin (2003), who stress the importance of the *new developmental terrain* of adolescence that must be negotiated by both client and prescriber. In other words, this uniquely important time may lead patients to ascribe new meanings to medication itself, as well as the act of incorporating a "pill" within themselves (Tasman & Riba, 2000). Any agent in the prepubescent past that may have affected appetite (resultant gain or loss), endocrine function (galactorrhea, amenorrhea), skin appearance (acne), sexual function (genital arousal or dysfunction), mood, alertness, or sleep may now be viewed or experienced in an entirely different light. What might have been tolerable in the past now becomes unacceptable simply because the problems present themselves during a time of "exquisitely sensitive developmental tasks" (Pruett & Martin, p. 419). Teens may manifest simple and overt noncompliance due to ignorance of the importance of medication, general noncompliance because of familial factors

TABLE 15.1. CHILDREN'S CONCEPTS ABOUT MEDICATION.

Physical properties of the medication itself

Name:	May help to enhance or decrease adherence, depending on association (for example, the medicine's name may sound like a superhero or cartoon villain).
Form:	Liquid, tablet, capsule, or injectable form may each carry specific and different meanings (for example, liquid is for "babies," bad-tasting meds or injectables are "punishments"). Special caution must be taken in using injectables with children and teens who have a history of trauma.
Size:	The bigger the pill or mg size, the bigger the problem (and vice versa).
Labeling and printing:	Personalized associations may be made with imprinted numbers or letters.

The need to take medicine
Only kids who are "sick" or "bad" have to take medicine.

Timing of the dose

Frequency:	Greater frequency may be seen as more trouble, or perhaps, more help.
A.M. or P.M.:	A.M. is for school, and may be neglected (with or without prescriber agreement) on weekends; P.M. is for sleeping or dreaming troubles.
During school:	Concern about stigma.
Who administers:	Self-administration is good, mature; teacher/parent administrator is the doctor's agent.

Source: Adapted from Pruett & Martin, 2003.

(parent ambivalence regarding need for medication, family history of poor response or of drug addiction), covert noncompliance due to oppositionality, and intermittent noncompliance because of interference with activities.

A relevant issue for parents and for children and teens of all ages is that of the dosing in milligrams. (See Table 15.1.) A medication that requires *hundreds* of milligrams for effectiveness may be viewed differently by parent, child, or teen, compared to one that requires only a *few* milligrams (Pruett & Martin, 2003).

Putative Targets of Treatment

At the elementary school level, there needs to be "buy in" on the part of the child and the parent. Pruett and Martin (2003) give the example of an eight-year-old child with ADHD who felt that the medicine (methylphenidate, MPH) helped him to stay in control. He conceived of the markings on the tablets as a sort of code, specific for each little monster inside him manifesting as bad behavior. The code would then help blow up the little monsters that might come up during the course of the day.

While he used this specific for MPH, we have seen similar models used for children taking other medications, especially those that need to be given multiple times daily.

With middle- and high-schoolers, as discussed earlier, consider giving the actual prescription document directly to the teen. Even if he or she immediately gives it to the parent, you have communicated your belief that the teen is ready to be in charge of his or her own treatment, though parents still have roles to play (for example, regarding adherence). The pharmacotherapist must ensure that there is adequate, regular, and delineated supervision, for example, by saying, "Your mom will put the medicine out with your cereal every morning. Is that something you'd be OK with?" The older a patient gets, the more there needs to be communication to and from the teen that the intervention is warranted. Other important developmental stage-appropriate tasks include exploration of the teen's feelings regarding the effects of the treatment, and reaction to being identified as someone in need of treatment—that is, deficient; especially with something as central as the brain, which they may conceptualize as the most essential organ of selfhood. Other issues germane to teens may include fears of being altered in uncontrollable ways or of being poisoned, and fears of becoming permanently dependent on an external substance ("a happy pill") or the adults who administer it. Parent concerns include that their child is damaged and that they have had a direct role in that outcome, worries about cost of medication and long-term side effects, and feeling as if they do not have a choice to say "no" to medication if being pressured by the school. Additional issues include trouble seeing some familiar behavior as pathological, and expectations that medication will fix all problems, including those that have resulted from poor parenting or problematic parent-teen relational patterns.

An important and ultimate target of good psychopharmacotherapy, adherence to prescribed medication is a major factor influencing the efficacy of any treatment (Brown & Sammons, 2002). According to this model, the factors affecting adherence in pediatric psychopharmacology are (1) caregivers' attitudes and their roles; (2) medication side effects; (3) treatment accessibility, acceptability, and satisfaction; and (4) therapeutic relationship.

Caregivers' Attitudes and Roles

Because children may be reluctant to use psychotropic medications, it becomes the caregivers' responsibility to administer medications and to arrange all appointments. Thus, parental attitudes influence nearly all aspects of a child's treatment, including efficacy. Often, however, there may be caregiver ambivalence about using psychotropic medication, particularly when a school staff member initiates the referral, and when the child's behavior is not deemed to be a problem at home (Brown & Sammons, 2002). Also, because the level of agreement among child, parent, and teacher reports of certain behavior may be relatively poor (Achenbach, McConaughy, & Howell, 1987), it is incumbent on practitioners to be skilled in obtaining and communicating information across all sources. Phelps, Brown, and Power (2001) advised that clinicians carefully evaluate the attitudes of all significant individuals (caregiver, teacher, and child) because their attitudes are apt to influence adherence to medication protocols. Some research has found that attitudes toward psychotropic medication between caregivers and teachers are similar (Power, Hess, & Bennett, 1995). Attitudes can be modified as follows:

- By encouraging the participation of the caregivers in systematic drug trials, where ongoing efficacy of the drug as well as the side effects are documented (Johnston & Fine, 1993).
- By providing teachers with feedback regarding potential for the response to medication and ongoing treatment efficacy (Power et al., 1995).
- By acknowledging the "Level of Distress" experienced by the caregivers due to their child's symptoms and the adverse effects of the medication, and by using appropriate therapeutic interventions (Ellison, 2001).

Medication Side Effects

Young children lack the cognitive schema to accurately describe the changes (physiological or psychological) or the adverse effects that may be associated with the use of psychotropic medications (Brown & Sawyer, 1998; Zametkin & Yamada, 1999). Hence, it becomes important to obtain this information from the significant adults who may best serve as accurate informants, as described above.

An accurate history is best obtained through following these steps:

Side Effects Education. Educating a patient and parent about side effects prior to treatment allows both client and prescribing physician to anticipate which side effects may occur and how they might be managed (Ellison et al., 2000).

The relevance and clarity of the information is also crucial:

- The parent (and patient, wherever possible) should know the names of the medication (brand and generic)
- The rationale for its use
- How to tell if it is working, what to do if it appears not to be working
- When and how to take it, what to do if a dose is missed
- How long the treatment is expected to continue

- The side effects that the patient likely wants to know about (and any serious ones); possible effects on work or driving, and known drug interactions with alcohol and other drugs

Monitoring Side Effects. Continued monitoring of side effects throughout the treatment can enhance adherence in adult patients (Ellison, 2000). For medication effects to be fully appreciated in pediatric populations, it is necessary that monitoring be based on systematic data from multiple settings (school, home) rather than simply on the clinician's global impression (Aman & Pearson, 1999).

Thus, objective monitoring of medication effects and careful use of caregivers as informants and historians is required.

Objective monitoring can be done by using

- Behavior rating scales. Rating scales are particularly useful in assessing those adverse effects that may not be reported by the caregivers (Brown & Sawyer, 1998).
- Structured interviews. These seem to be the most sensitive to psychotropic drug effects (Brown & Sawyer, 1998).
- Direct observations of the behavior. This provides the clinician with a valid display of a child's behavior in different settings (classroom, playroom, home). Direct observations are particularly sensitive to psychotropic medications in general, and to various doses of medications in particular (DuPaul & Kyle, 1995).
- Other measures. Performance tests (CPT), computerized assessments, and intelligence and achievement tests, but their sensitivity to psychotropic medication seems to be low (Shelton & Barkley, 1995; Brown & Sawyer, 1998).

Treatment Accessibility, Acceptability, and Satisfaction

Among the barriers to treatment adherence identified by Warner and colleagues (1994), the lack of a supportive life routine was most often cited by adult patients in the study as a key factor. Hence, to increase adherence to treatment, it may be very important to examine the accessibility to treatment and continuity of care (Ellison, 2000). Regarding treatment acceptability and satisfaction on the part of the child and her caregivers, Shouten and Duckworth (1999) noted that a host of ethical and legal considerations emerge when psychotropic medications are used to manage children's behavior, including unresolved questions regarding long-term safety and efficacy. Hence, informed consent, the right to refuse treatment, issues of custody, confidentiality, and the patient's best interest should remain as the essential standards of pharmacotherapy practice. Besides parent/caretaker *consent*, it is also important that children give *assent* for medications as a means of fostering a therapeutic alliance and encouraging some degree of autonomy and responsibility for the medication regimen (Brown & Sawyer, 1998; Krener & Mancina, 1994; Shouten & Duckworth, 1999). Krener and Mancina (1994) have observed that including the child or adolescent in the consent process can help to avoid the creation of feelings of coercion on the child's part, and may also serve to enhance the therapeutic goals of the treatment and the developmental interests of the child. Making realistic promises about medication efficacy and safety to children and their families gives them satisfaction, and thus enhances the therapeutic alliance (Shouten & Duckworth, 1999).

Therapeutic Relationship

Adherence to treatment depends on the working relationship, the transference and countertransference relationships with the prescribing clinician, the therapeutic interventions being used, and the "relationship" that the patient carries on with the pills themselves (Ellison, 2000). This may be especially true for teenagers. To promote the working alliance, it is helpful to identify the patient's expectations and wishes for the treatment, and to restate them to ensure that they are correctly understood. Approaches that involve a combination of pharmacotherapy and psychotherapy have consistently been demonstrated to be more acceptable to caregivers and teachers than medication alone (Liu, Robin, Brenner, & Eastman, 1991; Pelham, 1999; Power et al., 1995). Because the psychotherapist is in a powerful position to either strengthen medication adherence or undermine it, a collaboration between prescribing clinician and psychotherapist is of crucial importance (Sederer et al., 1998). Clinicians should share sufficient information about diagnosis, treatment options, rationale for the choices made, and plans for treatment follow-up and session frequency, to allow the psychotherapist to support pharmacotherapy in a knowledgeable manner (Ellison, 2000), and for the pharmacologist, in turn, to support the psychotherapy.

The previous paragraph describes a model wherein the treatment alliance (working alliance) may have indirect effects on adherence to treatment, leading to better outcomes. In fact, important research in adults (Krupnick et al., 1996) indicates that there may be a positive direct effect on better clinical outcomes from the alliance itself (independent of adherence per se). There may be some data in children to support this as well, as Thiruchelvam and associates (2001) have described. In their three-year study of adherence to treatment with stimulants, a response to treatment was not clearly associated with the medication treatment itself, and some patients improved even with suboptimal adherence. Furthermore, adherence itself declined over time (81%, year 1; 67% year 2, 52% year 3), and this coincided with fewer and fewer contacts with research staff (several times per year in year 1, with regular access to the team as needed if questions arose, decreasing to only once per year in years 2 and 3). One interpretation of this is that adherence and outcomes were best in the first year of the study due to the frequency of contact and perceived quality of support from the research team. (Thiruchelvam, et al. 2001)

Empirical Support for Treatment Efficacy

Literature about children is very limited, and a Medline search of years 1966 through 2000 uncovered only seven peer-reviewed articles reporting on adherence or compliance with pediatric psychopharmacology. All of these studies looked at stimulant-compliance among children with ADHD. A brief summary of these studies follows:

Kauffman and colleagues (1981) performed a doubled-blind triple cross-over study comparing compliance between methylphenidate and amphetamine in twelve boys, ages six to twelve years. Compliance rates, as measured by urine drug testing, were 67% and 61%, respectively, and by pill counts, 87% and 82%, respectively. The discrepancy between compliance rates is consistent with other reports in the literature, and highlights the shortcomings of pill counts as an accurate measure of compliance in pediatric populations.

Firestone (1982) randomized seventy-six children with ADHD between ages five and nine years to twelve months of treatment with methylphenidate, with or without four months of weekly behavioral treatment. Medication compliance was gauged by parent report only. At four months, 80% of the children were still taking their medication, and by ten months, this figure dropped to 56%. Of note, less than 10% of parents discussed medication discontinuation with their doctors. Younger parents were more likely to discontinue treatment, but there were no parental personality characteristics that were associated with discontinuation.

Sleator, Ullmann, and von Neumann (1982) interviewed fifty-two children with a mean age of 11.7 years, all of whom had been taking stimulants for at least one year. She found that 42% of the children reported that the medication was helpful, 42% of the children admitted disliking the medication, 62% of the children were known to dislike medication according to parent and teacher reports, 40% of the children acknowledged *attempting* to avoid taking their medication, and 65% of the children actually avoided taking their medication.

Brown, Borden, and Clingerman (1985) randomized thirty children with ADHD, ages six and twelve years, to methylphenidate or placebo treatment. All

Erratum

Chapter 15, *Psychological Aspects of Pediatric Medication Management*, p. 478, under the section entitled "Empirical Support for Treatment Efficacy," please note that the brief summary of these studies is taken from an excellent review by Hack and Chow (2001). We are paraphrasing their report in the next eight paragraphs.

The full reference is:

Hack, S., & Chow, B. (2001). Pediatric psychotropic medication compliance: A literature review and research-based suggestions for improving treatment compliance. *Journal of Child and Adolescent Psychopharmacology*, *11*, 59–67.

children received adjunctive psychological treatment (exact treatment not specified in the paper). Compliance, as measured by pill counts, revealed that 25% of the children who completed the study missed at least two of ten doses prescribed per week. Notably, non-adherent children and their families demonstrated greater pathology, but reported less distress.

In another study, Brown and associates (1987) randomized fifty-eight children with ADHD between ages six and thirteen to methylphenidate or placebo and three months of cognitive behavioral therapy (CBT), or an attention control procedure. Medication compliance was 75% as measured by pill counts. Parental reports overestimated compliance relative to pill counts.

In a third study, Brown and colleagues (1988), randomized seventy-one children with ADHD between ages six and thirteen years to methylphenidate only, to placebo only, to a no pill condition and three months of CBT, or to an attention control group. He then measured compliance by pill counts and therapy sessions attended late or missed. Better compliance was associated with higher rates of perceived self-control, higher Wide Range Achievement Test (WRAT) scores, higher IQ, and milder symptoms.

A study by Johnston and Fine (1993) reported a noncompliance rate of approximately 20% during evaluation, and at six-week and three-month follow-ups, based on multiple compliance measures including missed appointments, pill counts, and teacher, physician and parental reports.

A survey of seventy-seven parents of children with ADHD attending the 1999 U.S. Children and Adults with Attention Deficit Disorder (CHADD) conference revealed that 59% believed that their child's self-esteem had suffered as a result of taking the medication at school, and 68% thought that their child was embarrassed by taking medication. These values were higher for ten- to twelve-year-old children than for other ages.

A recent study by Ibrahim and associates (2002) examined the rate of adherence to prescribed medication in fifty-one children and adolescents ages 7 to 16.6 years, diagnosed with ADHD, and demonstrated compliance rates greater than 70%. The children and their parents were administered a children behavior checklist (CBCL), a teacher report form (TRF) scale, and a compliance-with-treatment opinion and attitude scale. There were very high reports of adherence by children to prescribed medications for ADHD. Correlation between the children's and adolescents' reports, and the parents' reports revealed high agreement at the end of week one, and also at the end of the study (twelve weeks). There were also findings of stability of adherence reports over a three-month period.

The three-year study mentioned previously by Thiruchelvam and associates (2001) examined stimulant adherence in seventy-one children ages six to twelve. This was a prospective placebo-controlled trial of a twelve-month treatment, with subsequent follow-up questionnaires yearly in years two and three. Measures included a Treatment Monitoring Questionnaire (TMQ) for parents and teachers, and a Child Satisfaction Survey (CSS) as a self-report measure for children. The adherence rates were found to be highest in year one (81%), but dropped off over years two and three to 67% and 52%, respectively. Moderators of adherence included teacher-rated severity of ADHD (the more impairment, the better the adherence), presence of oppositional defiant disorder features in the school setting (ODD symptoms at school made it eleven times more likely that a child would have poor adherence), and younger age at baseline (predicted better adherence). Response to treatment at twelve months was not clearly associated with adherence, per se, which points to a possible role for the treatment alliance in the first year of success.

Adolescents may be especially vulnerable to poor adherence (Cromer & Tarnowski, 1989; Sawyer, 1995). Central developmental tasks of adolescence (such as separation and individuation) may lead to arguments about independence between adolescents and their parents, and medication adherence can become the battlefield on which control issues are fought. Also, the defense mechanisms typically used by adolescents (denial and acting out) tend to impede good adherence practices.

Personal Experience and Cases

We have tried to structure our outpatient setting, the Stanford University ADHD Clinic, to ensure that poor adherence issues do not persist, whenever possible. When psychologists and psychology trainees refer cases for psychopharmacologic consultation, and feedback is given in person at a clinic meeting and a brief written report is produced. The psychologically minded pharmacologist (the psychopharmacotherapist) then sees the child or teen every one to two weeks during the initial treatment phase (first month), and spaces visits according to the disorder and target symptoms identified. For uncomplicated, non-comorbid ADHD, stable patients are seen every month for thirty- to sixty-minute sessions. The focus for side-effect monitoring is on growth and cardiovascular parameters, and extra time is scheduled when comorbidity issues are problematic. Once entirely stable, patients are seen every one to three months, and no longer apart than this, in order to best follow the clinical course of both core symptoms and associated psychosocial adjustment, as well as to monitor side effects. Connors forms for parents and teachers are used to objectively track improvements or worsening of symptoms, and supplement interval histories obtained from child or teen, and parent(s). We spend a great deal of time in psycho-education, helping teens (especially) to become familiar with all forms of empirically supported treatments available, Web sites such as CHADD.org, schwablearning.org, and ADD.org, and with useful books to help with school, social, and medication interventions.

◆ ◆ ◆

"Too often a prescription signals the end of an interview rather than the start of an alliance," Blackwell (1973, p. 252).

When thinking about prescribing medication for children and teens, effective medication managers must take into account the myriad factors discussed in this chapter, as well as those discussed in the works of many experts in the field, as outlined in the reference section. Prescribers must quickly attain an understanding of not just the target symptoms, but also the context and setting(s) in which they occur (through home or school contacts and visits, and regular contact with the therapist, parent, and teacher). These principles apply especially in cases of psychopharmacology, but are also applicable for other pharmacotherapies with children and teens. Adherence rates continue to be no more than 50–60%, at best, for all medication therapies, a far less-than-acceptable standard. Acknowledgment of the powerful psychological factors at work will likely enhance therapeutic outcomes through increased adherence and a stronger therapeutic alliance. However, many more prospective studies are needed to better understand these issues.

References

Achenbach, T. M., McConaughy, S. H., & Howell, C. T. (1987). Child/adolescent behavioral and emotional problems: Implications of cross-informant correlations for situational specificity. *Psychological Bulletin, 101,* 213–232.

Aman, M. G., & Pearson, D. A. (1999). Monitoring and measuring drug effects: Part 2 Behavioral, emotional, and cognitive effects. In J. Werry & M. Aman (Eds.), *Practitioner's guide to psychoactive drugs for children and adolescents* (2nd ed., pp. 99–164). New York: Plenum.

Blackwell, B. (1973). Drug therapy: Patient compliance. *New England Journal of Medicine, 289,* 249–252.

Blakeslee, S. (1998). Placebos prove so powerful even experts are surprised; New studies explore the brain's triumph over reality. *The New York Times,* Late Edition—Final, section F, page 1, column 2.

Brown, R. T., Borden, K. A., & Clingerman, S. R. (1985). Adherence to methylphenidate therapy in a population: A preliminary investigation. *Psychopharmacology Bulletin, 21*(1), 28–36.

Brown, R. T., Borden, K. A., Wynne, M. E., Spunt, A. L., & Clingerman, S. R. (1988). Patterns of compliance in a treatment program for children with attention deficit disorder. *Journal of Compliance in Health Care, 3*(1), 23–39.

Brown, R. T., & Sammons, M. T. (2002). Pediatric psychopharmacology: A review of new developments and recent research. *Professional Psychology: Research and Practice, 33*(2), 135–147.

Brown, R. T., & Sawyer, M. G. (1998). *Medications for school-age children: Effects on learning and behavior.* New York: Guilford Press.

Cromer, B. G., & Tarnowski, K. (1989). Noncompliance in adolescents: A review. *Journal of Developmental and Behavioral Pediatrics, 10*(4), 207–215.

DuPaul, G. J., & Kyle, K. E. (1995). Pediatric pharmacology and psychopharmacology. In M. C. Roberts (Ed.), *Handbook of pediatric psychology* (2nd ed., pp. 741–758). New York: Guilford Press.

Ellison, J. M. (2000). Enhancing adherence in the pharmacotherapy treatment relationship. In A. Tasman, M. B. Riba & K. R. Silk (Eds.), *The doctor-patient relationship in pharmacotherapy: Improving treatment effectiveness* (pp. 71–94). New York: Guilford Press.

Firestone, P. (1982). Factors associated with children's adherence to stimulant medication. *American Journal of Orthopsychiatry, 52*(3), 447–457.

Gutheil, T. G. (1977). Improving patient compliance: Psychodynamics in drug prescribing. *Drug Therapy, 7,* 82–95.

Gutheil, T. G. (1982). The psychology of psychopharmacology. *Bulletin of the Menninger Clinic, 46,* 321–330.

Ibrahim, E. S. R. (2002). Rates of adherence to pharmacological treatment among children and adolescents with attention deficit hyperactivity disorder. *Human Psychopharmacological Clinical Exp., 17,* 225–231.

Johnston, C., & Fine, S. (1993). Methods of evaluating methylphenidate in children with attention-deficit hyperactive disorder: Acceptability, satisfaction, and compliance. *Journal of Pediatric Psychology, 18,* 717–730.

Kauffman, R. E., Smith-Wright, D., Reese, C. A., Simpson, R., & Jones, F. (1981). Medication compliance in hyperactive children. *Pediatric Pharmacology, 1,* 231–237.

Krener, P. K., & Mancina, R. A. (1994). Informed consent or informed coercion? Decision-making in pediatric psychopharmacology. *Journal of Child and Adolescent Psychopharmacology, 4,* 183–200.

Krupnick, J., Sotsky, S., Simmens, S., Moyer, J., Elkin, I., Watkins, J., et al. (1996). The role of the therapeutic alliance in psychotherapy pharmacotherapy outcome: Findings in the National Institute of Mental Health Treatment of Depression Collaborative Research Program. *Journal of Consulting and Clinical Psychology, 64*(3), 532–539.

Lui, C., Robin, A. L., Brenner, A., & Eastman, J. (1991). Social acceptability of methylphenidate and behavior modification for treating attention deficit hyperactivity disorder. *Pediatrics. 88,* 560–565.

Park, L. C., & Covi, L. (1965). Nonblind placebo trial: An exploration of neurotic patients' responses to placebo when its inert content is disclosed. *Archives of General Psychiatry, 12,* 336–344.

Pelham, W. E. (1999). The NIMH multimodal treatment study for attention-deficit hyperactivity disorder: Just say yes to drugs alone? *Canadian Journal of Psychiatry, 44,* 981–990.

Phelps, L., Brown, R. T., & Power, T. (2001). *Pediatric psychopharmacology: Combining medical and psychological intervention.* Washington, D.C.: American Psychological Association.

Pillay, S. S., & Ghaemi, S. N. (2002). The psychology of polypharmacy. In S. N. Ghaemi (Ed.), *Polypharmacy in psychiatry* (pp. 299–310). New York: Dekker.

Power, T. J., Hess, L. E., & Bennett, D. S. (1995). The acceptability of interventions of attention deficit disorder among elementary and middle school teachers. *Developmental and Behavioral Pediatrics, 16,* 238–243.

Pruett, K. D., & Martin, A. (2003). Thinking about prescribing: The psychology of psychopharmacology. In A. Martin, L. Scahill, D. S. Charney & J. F. Leckman (Eds.), *Principles and practice of pediatric psychopharmacology* (pp. 417–425). New York: Oxford University Press.

Schowalter, J. E. (1997). *Psychopharmacology: The mind-brain frontier. Paper presented at the Annual Meeting of the American Academy of Child and Adolescent Psychiatry (AACAP)*. Toronto.

Schowalter, J. E. (1989). Psychodynamics and medication. *Journal of the American Academy of Child and Adolescent Psychiatry, 28,* 681–684.

Sederer, L. I., Ellison, J. M., & Keyes, C. (1998). Guidelines for prescribing psychiatrists in consultative, collaborative, and supervisory relationships. *Psychiatric Services, 49,* 1197–1202.

Shelton, T., & Barkley, R. A. (1995). The assessment and treatment of attention and treatment of attention deficit hyperactivity disorder in children. In M. Roberts (Ed.), *Handbook of pediatric psychology* (2nd ed., pp. 663–754). New York: Guilford Press.

Shouten, R., & Duckworth, K. S. (1999). Medicolegal and ethical issues in the pharmacologic treatment of children. In J. Werry & M. Aman (Eds.), *Practitioner's guide to psychoactive drugs for children and adolescents* (2nd ed., pp. 99–164). New York: Plenum.

Sleator, E. K., Ullmann, R. K., & von Neumann, A. (1982). How do hyperactive children feel about taking stimulants and will they tell the doctor? *Clinical Pediatrics, 21*(8), 474–479.

Tasman, A., & Riba, M. B. (2000). Psychological management in psychopharmacologic treatment, and combination pharmacologic and psychotherapeutic treatment. In J. Lieberman & A. Tasman (Eds.), *Psychiatric drugs* (pp. 242–249). Philadelphia: WB Saunders.

Tasman, A., Riba, M. B., & Silk, K. R. (2000). Using the interview to establish collaboration. In A. Tasman, M. B. Riba, & K. R. Silk (Eds.), *The doctor-patient relationship in pharmacotherapy: Improving treatment effectiveness* (pp. 49–69). New York: Guilford Press.

Thiruchelvam, D., Charach, A., & Schachar, R. (2001). Moderators and mediators of long-term adherence to stimulant treatment in children with ADHD. *Journal of the American Academy of Child and Adolescent Psychiatry, 40*(8), 922–928.

Warner, L. A., Silk, K., Yeaton, W. H., & et al. (1994). Psychiatrists' and patients' views on drug information sources and medication compliance. *Hospital and Community Psychiatry, 45,* 1235–1237.

Zametkin, A. J., & Yamada, E. M. (1999). Monitoring and measuring drug effects: Vol. 1 Physical effects. In J. Werry & M. Aman (Eds.), *Practitioner's guide to psychoactive drugs for children and adolescents* (2nd ed., pp. 69–97). New York: Plenum.

PART THREE

PSYCHOTHERAPY

CHAPTER SIXTEEN

PSYCHOTHERAPY IN CHILDREN AND ADOLESCENTS: AN OVERVIEW

James Lock, M.D., Ph.D.

Ⓞ ne of the most effective ways to influence behavior is the use of psychotherapy. Broadly defined, *psychotherapy* is a psychosocial intervention (as opposed to a physiological or pharmacological, or surgical intervention) designed to influence feelings and behaviors. Although this can include interventions as wide ranging as psychoanalysis, hypnosis, behavior modification, and family therapy, the full range of these approaches has not been systematically assessed for their impact on feelings and behaviors. Nonetheless, increasingly, studies of psychotherapy suggest that psychotherapy is effective and may be more effective than other types of interventions for many conditions (Kazdin, 1986, 2000; Luborsky, Singer, & Luborsky, 1975). In this chapter, we review a distinct subset of the range of psychotherapies, with an eye to those that have an established or a developing base of empirical support, and that are most relevant for practitioners who work with children and adolescents.

Why Is Psychotherapy Included?

Some scientists, and even a few clinicians might ask why psychotherapy is included as a major section in a contemporary textbook on child and adolescent psychiatry (Kazdin, 2000). After all, the main focus of research for more than twenty-five years, both clinical and in basic science, has been on biological psychiatry and its applications including psychopharmacology, genetics, and brain abnormalities through various scanning techniques. This is reflected in the major trends of treatment, in which psychopharmacological-agent use in child and adolescent psychiatry has more than doubled in the past decade; in psychiatry training programs, in which courses and supervision in psychotherapy are increasingly marginalized or absent in favor of biologically based intervention training; and, in reimbursement practices, in which psychiatrists are paid more favorably for providing psychopharmacological interventions compared to psychotherapy. There has been significant progress in biological psychiatry and in psychopharmacology in particular, and although child and adolescent research in biological domains still significantly lags behind that of adult psychiatry, advances are being made there at a more rapid rate than in psychotherapy studies. There is much good in this, of course, as there was until the middle of the last century almost a hegemony of psychoanalytic therapy and so the possibility of a more balanced approach to children and adolescents psychiatric needs is indeed needed.

Nonetheless, most clinicians recognize that the hope that medications alone or other biologically based interventions yet to be developed (for example, genetic) will fully address the psychiatric needs of younger patients is misplaced. Not only does such a perspective miss the crucial interaction of biology and environment, but it also places an undue confidence in such interventions. Our understanding of human development and the importance of parents, stress, and peers on the development and maintenance of psychopathology, especially in children and adolescents, argues clearly for the inclusion of interventions that address these factors, none of which are amenable to a purely biological approach (Holmbeck et al., 2000; Kazdin, 2000; Smith, Glass, & Miller, 1980).

On the other hand, it might be argued that indeed we do and will need psychotherapies, but our state of knowledge about them is so limited, that it is not helpful to provide descriptions of interventions with so little evidence. We will address this question more fully later, but the fact remains that psychotherapy is being provided so there is a need to provide information about interventions so commonly practiced. As the chapters in this section illustrate, we do have some very good ideas about how to address a range of problems using psychotherapy, and there is a growing body of evidence that supports some of these interventions.

This section includes many types of psychotherapies. They can be organized into a number of heuristic structures that are useful in understanding what the current state of psychotherapy development is. For example, therapies can be broadly defined into focused and unfocused therapies. *Focused psychotherapies* target a narrow range of behaviors or symptoms, are time-limited, and usually employ quite specific intervention strategies. Examples of focused therapies are behavioral analysis (BA) and cognitive-behavioral therapy (CBT). Unfocused therapies are

FIGURE 16.1. FOCUSED AND UNFOCUSED THERAPIES.

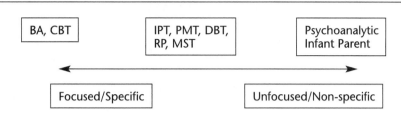

characterized by having broader aims (overall health or development), are usually open-ended in terms of time course, and employ general principles of psychotherapy such as therapeutic alliance and relationship as a primary aspect of the intervention. Examples of these therapies are psychodynamic psychotherapy and infant parent therapy. There are some therapies that lie somewhere in the middle of these two poles; that is, they are somewhat focused, may have a usual time-course, and may employ specific therapies while acknowledging and relying upon the therapeutic relationship to a greater or lesser extent. Such therapies are interpersonal psychotherapy (IPT), dialectical behavioral therapy (DBT), and family-based treatments such as parent management training (PMT).

Another way to group the therapies in this section is by developmental appropriateness. The therapies designed for the youngest patients are BA and IPT. These therapies focus their interventions on specific behaviors and often work exclusively through parents. On the other hand, some therapies are most likely to be developmentally best applied to older children and adolescents. These therapies would include CBT, IPT, mental skills training (MST), and relapse prevention (RP). The reason these therapies are more likely to be appropriate for use with this older age group is that the interventions depend to a greater extent on language, insight, motivation, and the ability to apply what is learned in therapy

FIGURE 16.2. DEVELOPMENTAL APPROPRIATENESS
OF TREATMENTS.

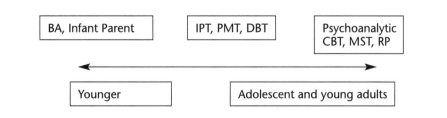

to future situations or problems. There are, of course, psychotherapies that are in between. These therapies tend to depend more on family members or other external structures to heavily support the therapy, but still require more active participation on the part of younger patients. Examples of these therapies are PMT and psychodynamic therapy.

Still another way to group these therapies is by their empirically supported status. Of all the therapies discussed, CBT and PMT are probably the most studied and for which there is the greatest systematic support for their use in specific clinical situations. The least empirically supported therapies are the psychodynamic therapies including psychoanalysis and infant parent training and some of the newer therapies, such as MST and RP. Somewhere in the middle, in terms of evidential support, are IPT and DBT.

FIGURE 16.3. EMPIRICAL SUPPORT FOR TREATMENTS.

A final way that might be used to structure these therapies is on how commonly they are employed. The most commonly employed psychotherapies are psychodynamic and psychoanalytically based interventions. Second would likely be behavioral interventions along the line of behavioral analysis techniques and CBT. The reason for this is that both of these approaches are older than the others and have had considerable lead-time in terms of influencing clinical practice. Importantly, these psychotherapies, particularly CBT, were well-timed for systematic exploration, and as noted above, now probably have the edge in terms of systematic evidence for applicability to a range of clinical problems.

FIGURE 16.4. PRACTICE PATTERNS OF PSYCHOTHERAPY.

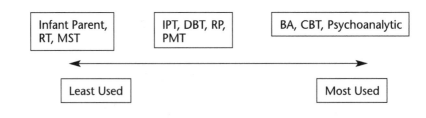

Among the middle group of commonly employed therapies for children and adolescents (at least in the United States) are PMT, IPT, and DBT, in part because these interventions have made only a small impact to date in the overall practice of psychotherapy. On the other hand, these therapies developed a large following in the 1980–1990s and many younger clinicians are well versed in these techniques. Also, in part because they are such relatively new approaches, MST and RP are not commonly employed psychotherapies at this time.

Why Are These Psychotherapies Included?

The particular psychotherapies that are included in this section were chosen to represent the large range of psychotherapy practices in the United States and the world. Thus, although it is certainly not a comprehensive compilation, it does offer a practical overview. We wanted to provide a description and the evidential support for therapies that are focused as well as not focused, are appropriate for a range of ages and developmental processes, have both a clinical and empirical base, and that are likely to apply to problems common to children and adolescents. Of course, we have included in a separate section, the sociotherapies, including group, inpatient, residential, prevention, and self-help psychotherapies.

Why Empirically Based Treatments?

As will be evident in the chapters, the empirical support for most psychotherapies in children and adolescents is modest at best. So why bother with it? First, it is important to acknowledge that there is some evidence for psychotherapy, and in some cases, more evidence than for psychopharmacologic interventions (for example, eating disorders, depression, and anxiety disorders all have a stronger research base that supports psychotherapeutic interventions more than it supports the use of medications in children and adolescents). This is important because there is an impression, albeit a false one, that psychotherapy is an altogether hopeless enterprise from a scientific point of view and that it consists only of personal opinion and belief systems (Kazdin, 2000). This is just not the case. Second, and a point that is related in an opposing way to the first, is that it is important to identify the need to better provide evidence for psychotherapy. The fact that our knowledge base for interventions so commonly applied is so small, will, I hope, provide an impetus for developing and furthering this base. Third, the nature of evidence in psychotherapy is itself an important consideration. What will become evident in the empirical discussion in the chapters is that what is an important outcome (or evidence that a treatment works) is closely tied to the treatment approach itself. This makes general reviews of empirical evidence challenging, especially in younger patients whose developmental trajectories are already uncertain. Finally, and perhaps most importantly, it appears to be important to provide what evidence we have in whatever form it is, in order for clinicians to make the best informed decisions about what therapy to use in a particular case. As with psychopharmacologic agents, therapies do have side effects, unexpected benefits, and causalities. The wise clinician is one that does not follow a single therapy for all, but examines what may be the best psychotherapy for the problems that need to be addressed. No more than one would use an antipsychotic for all mental health problems, so it is unlikely that a one size, one type of therapy is best suited to all conditions. The empirical evidence provided, I hope, will be a guide in this respect.

What's Common Among the Therapies?

As divergent as these therapies are, they also have much in common. I would start by emphasizing that none of the psychotherapies are really "individual" and this is because, as Winnicott wrote many years ago, "there's no such thing as a baby." Or, there's no such thing as a baby on its own. Psychotherapy with children and adolescents depends and utilizes parents and other members of the environment to a greater or lesser extent. Even the most individually based psychodynamic psychoanalytic therapies recognize and include, in both conceptualization and application, parental figures. They may be indirect participants in the therapy compared to their children, but their presence is identified as important because they both support the patient's ability to attend such therapy (through payment, transportation, and so on) as well as provide vital information (about development, current behaviors outside therapy, and more). Interestingly, parents are the primary agents of intervention in several therapies, including infant parent therapy and PMT. In these therapies, the target of the intervention is the child, but the intermediate agent with whom the therapist works primarily are the parents. Even therapies like CBT, MST, and IPT, although practiced primarily as individual therapies in adults, are much less so in younger patients where parents play more active roles in therapy (Holmbeck et al., 2000; Kendall, 1993; Mufson, Moreau, & Weissman, 1994; Mufson, Moreau, Weissman, & Klerman, 1993).

Another common feature of the psychotherapies is the use of the therapeutic relationship. It appears that psychotherapy, of whatever form, is a relationship-based intervention. How the therapeutic relationship supposedly operates varies from transferential (in psychodynamic and infant parent therapy) to psychoeducational in PMT. Nonetheless, it is clear that even though the conceptualization of the therapeutic relationship varies, the general dependence on it does present. This should not be taken as a "win" for psychodynamic therapies over behavioral therapies as such, though some studies have suggested that this therapeutic relationship better predicts outcome than for any specific therapy, because relationships are more basic to human interaction than necessarily transferential (Hartley & Strupp, 1983; Krupnick et al., 1996). Humans are social beings and even the prescribing of medications is a human interaction that is characterized by trust, understanding, and some sense of reciprocity. The therapeutic relationships among the therapies described range from highly transferential (in adolescent psychoanalysis, for example) to highly practical, as in PMT, MST, or RP. Most of the other therapies contain stronger elements of both.

The psychotherapies described all are conceived of in developmental terms. That is, the application of any of the therapies depends on an underlying understanding of child and adolescent development. What this means in practical terms is that therapists who use these therapies are expected to be educated and competent in assessing the common issues of child development and how they inter-relate with the particular therapy they are proposing. Without being educated to the developmental norms of children and adolescents, it would be impossible to know either how to intervene effectively (how to talk to the child or even the parents) or how to evaluate the outcome (what should be expected of a child of this age behaviorally, emotionally, and socially). All the chapters in this psychotherapy section include a special section devoted to how development is taken into consideration in applying particular therapies.

What's Different Among the Therapies?

Even though there are many things in common among the therapies described, many other aspects of the interventions highly differentiate them in terms of theory, style, and desired goals. Theories of psychotherapy are many. Behavioral, or largely behavioral, theories emphasize the predominance of behavior as the leading edge for change of symptoms, both internal and external. The emphasis of the intervention is, of course, highly focused on behavior, its analysis, and then how to change it. Cognitive therapies emphasize the importance of ideas and beliefs on behavior and thus interventions proceed from distorted thoughts, beliefs, and ideas to their impact on behaviors. Neither behavioral nor cognitive therapies depend on unconscious conflict or developmental challenges. Instead, behavioral and cognitive interventions emphasize conscious control and experimentation.

Psychodynamic therapies, in contrast, are based in a theory of the unconscious where conflicts are both inevitable, given the tension between desire and reality, and developmental, based on the passing through of predictable developmental stages and conflicts. Problems arise when conflicts appropriate to a particular developmental stage are not mastered and compromise functioning (psychologically, behaviorally, and socially). Psychodynamic therapies are meant to allow the expression and resolution of unconscious conflict because they provide an opportunity for conflicts to be identified, clarified, and resolved (sometimes by play and others by more conscious understanding via interpretation). Thus, in contrast with behavioral and cognitive approaches, psychodynamic therapy is not about conscious beliefs, but about those out of awareness, and not about changing behaviors intrinsically, but rather about understanding what the behaviors mean and thereby promote change. Although behavioral experimentation and play have some things in common—using action—their purpose and aims are quite different (Lock, 1995). IPT shares many features with psychodynamic therapy, but they are distinguished by IPT's sharply defined here-and-now emphasis, its interpersonal rather than unconscious focus, and its time-limited nature. Thus, although relationships and their dynamics are obvious key components in IPT, the emphasis is on current behaviors and beliefs and their impacts on emotional functioning, which in some ways aligns IPT more with behavioral and cognitive therapies.

PMT is distinguished from traditional schools of family therapy, structural or strategic family therapies, where families were viewed as highly disturbed (Minuchin, Rosman, & Baker, 1978; Palazzoli, 1974; Palazzoli, Boscolo, Cecchin, & Prata, 1980). Instead, PMT emphasizes the strengths of families, and the need for parental involvement to change the child's dysfunctional behaviors. In addition, PMT uses therapists as "expert consultants" as opposed to authority figures or omniscient interpreters of family process. Thus, PMT shares much with CBT and IPT.

The applicability of a kind of psychotherapy to particular diagnoses is another way these therapies can be differentiated. Behavioral analysis, for example, appears to be most appropriate for management of clearly defined and specific behavioral problems and less useful for mood and anxiety problems, in which the problem is more a state of mind or pervasive dysphoric feelings. Psychoanalysis and psychodynamic psychotherapies appear to be useful for less clearly defined problems of emotional development that are on the one hand pervasive, but on the other, not highly specified behaviorally. CBT and IPT appear to be appropriate for common, but not pervasive problems of mood and anxiety. DBT is useful for management of severe and chronic behavioral problems that are relationship-based. RP appears useful for illnesses in which behaviors, particularly impulsive ones, are likely to recur, such as substance abuse, sexual perversion, bulimia nervosa, and gambling.

On the other hand, it is important to take note that, in many ways, all psychotherapies as conceived are not well-aligned with descriptive psychiatric diagnoses. Psychotherapies, even the most specific ones like BA and CBT, are based in general theories applicable across many disorders and developmental needs. As such, psychotherapy as a field finds itself at odds with classification systems. They work in opposite directions. Classification systems seek precision and delimitation. Psychotherapy, while employing precision and focus in its intervention style in many cases, generally aims at much broader problems, such as behavior, cognition, self-efficacy, and conflict. This difference in perspective is natural enough given that classification systems consciously purge themselves of theory, while psychotherapy often begins with it. However, these differences, like many others, are potentially fruitful ones. Psychotherapy will never be atheoretical and classification systems should not be wedded to a single theory, but examining the interaction between diagnostic categories and particular psychotherapies may lead to greater precision in classification because identifying who responds to treatment and who does not would help refine such definitions. In contrast, psychotherapy, when applied to different populations, can potentially identify how that psychotherapy operates so it can be made more generalizable and its underlying theory supported or further clarified.

What's the Future of Psychotherapy?

I like to think that the future of psychotherapy is bright. There are so many avenues for development and I will mention only a few. Near and dear to my heart is the pursuit of evidence for psychotherapy, and I mean for all types of psychotherapy. Our current database is heavily weighted in terms of evidence for specific, focused, and time-limited therapies. These therapies are easier for the researcher to study both practically and financially. However, we need to identify ways to study more unfocused, less specific therapies as well, as there will likely continue to be a plethora of problems and clinical issues that cannot be addressed through specific and focused therapies of short duration. In relation to this latter theme, another important element of research in psychotherapy is related to intensity and duration of psychotherapy. One of the major stumbling blocks to having psychotherapy paid for is that it so often appears open ended and therefore perceived to be an endless money sink to insurers.

Also, in the area of research, it is important that we better understand not only if a particular psychotherapy works, but for whom and how it works (Kraemer, Wilson, Fairburn, & Agras, 2002). This is a study of moderators and mediators of treatment effects. Moderators are baseline characteristics of a patient or patient's environment (such as parental competence) that makes it more likely that a patient will respond to a particular type of psychotherapy more than another is. For example, a patient who is depressed but also has only a single parent may respond better to CBT than family therapy. The assessment of moderators of treatment is important, because it is entirely plausible that an effective treatment for a particular condition on average may not be so for a subgroup of patients. For example, an antihypertensive agent may work in 90% of all patients, but only in 30% of those who are also obese. Obesity might, in such a case, be a moderator of that particular drug effect on hypertension. For psychotherapy, it would not be surprising if we found that CBT and IPT were moderated by age—that is, that younger patients might fare better with another treatment less dependent on psychological insight and self-awareness.

Examining how treatment operates is a study of mediators. A mediator is something that changes early in treatment that is not directly the same as the outcome, but partly explains how that treatment might help. For example, if a patient with bulimia nervosa decreases her restraint and control over eating (dietary restraint) early in treatment, this may lead to a decreased need to binge eat and thus decrease purging as well. In this example, decreased dietary restraint is a mediator of outcome for CBT for bulimia nervosa (Wilson, Fairburn, Agras, Walsh, & Kraemer, 2002). Understanding better how a treatment works helps clinicians and researchers to identify better where treatment should be focused and potentially how to improve and extend the applicability of treatment to other conditions.

Psychotherapy of the future, will, I think, be increasingly specialized and time-limited. There will be continued pressure to decrease cost and to be increasingly efficient in psychotherapy treatments. This will also lead to an increased use of structured interventions, employing manuals in particular. Although manuals can be perceived as too confining, especially for non-specific therapies, they are for a large number of conditions increasingly helpful to clinicians by providing a clear guideline and set of expectations for the course of psychotherapy and treatment response (Lock & Le Grange, 2001; Lock, Le Grange, Agras, & Dare, 2001). Manuals are not lock-step programs usually, but allow considerable flexibility in their application to particular patients and circumstances. Manuals assist in the dissemination of treatments, their training, and their comparability across time and environments. Of course, not all treatments can or should be completely manualized, but the movement to more accurately describe, codify, specify, and define treatments will increase.

Related to manualized treatments is an emerging integrated approach to psychotherapies. With greater sophistication, therapists are beginning to recognize that patients are not as simple as the major diagnosis they sometimes carry. To this end, patients who present with problems of a cognitive nature as well as an interpersonal nature might well benefit from a psychotherapy that integrates principles of both CBT and IPT. For examples, a depressed patient might well make great progress on his cognitive distortions and beliefs, but still have considerable interpersonal problems that might respond better to a different approach, such as IPT. This "modularization" of therapies will allow therapists to create therapies that incorporate the best therapy with the particular needs of a patient. Thus, in the future, therapists may choose from a menu of empirically supported therapy approaches that are then structured to be appropriate for a particular patient's set of psychological needs. Another example of integration is psychotherapy with psychopharmacological interventions. This is common practice, and best evidence suggests that psychotherapy and psychopharmacological interventions are complementary and enhance the efficacy of overall treatment in the case of depression and, probably, anxiety disorders as well.

Although a strong case can and should be made for focused, specific, and time-limited therapies, the several chapters in this section devoted to psychodynamic psychotherapy make a compelling case for the usefulness of such approaches. There will, no doubt, continue to be a need for such treatments because these treatments are among the most flexible, broadly applicable, and acceptable treatments for younger patients and their families. Their flexibility allows for application of techniques and strategies across a wide range of diagnoses and problems. Their lack of specific focus makes them elastic and thereby useful for problems that are more pervasive and that tend to incorporate broad challenges in life. Because psychodynamic therapists are especially attuned to therapeutic relationships and their importance, their interventions are perceived as sensitive and helpful and therefore acceptable. Thus, it is likely that psychodynamic therapy will continue to be a highly valued and useful psychotherapy. The challenge for psychodynamic therapy will be how to better provide evidence of effectiveness of the approach. Development of an empirical base is more difficult for psychodynamic psychotherapies because of the strengths just discussed. It is more challenging to measure outcomes for a psychotherapy that is applicable to many situations, is highly flexible, and depends to such a large extent on the interpersonal skills of the therapist. It may be tempting to try to "simplify" or "focus" psychodynamic therapy to test it. I believe this would be a mistake. These challenges should be taken up and evidence developed to support this form of treatment with its strengths and complexities intact.

◆ ◆ ◆

Something should be said about the future of psychotherapists in psychotherapy. Will we continue to need them? There are provocative data that suggest computer-based psychotherapy and so-called "distant" psychotherapy may be effective and acceptable. These psychotherapies challenge the prevailing notion that the "therapist" or the relationship with the therapist is a key ingredient in psychotherapy. These psychotherapies provide anonymity, low cost, and convenience for patients who are sensitive to these concerns. Anonymity may be particular salient for younger patients who often resist traditional therapy and therapists. Adolescents are increasingly comfortable with technology and the advantages it confers. Low cost appeals to insurers, families, and governments. Convenience applies particularly to those in rural areas or to those who lead pressured lives (which seems to be most everyone now). There are, of course, many limitations to these forms of psychotherapy. Such treatments cannot usually be as flexible, specific, and complicated as interventions provided by a professional in person. Nonetheless, I expect we will see more of these types of interventions, especially for low-level, lower severity problems.

The chapters in this section provide an excellent look at the present and hint at the future of psychotherapy. They suggest that in all cases, therapies are becoming better defined, more appropriately aligned with patient needs and developmental requirements, that evidence is being gathered to support the intervention approach, and that new and important avenues for applications and development are under way.

References

Hartley, D., & Strupp, H. (1983). The therapeutic alliance: Its relationship to outcome in brief psychotherapy. In J. Maslin (Ed.), *Empirical Studies of Psychoanalytic Studies* (Vol. 1, pp. 1–37). Hillsdale, NJ: Erlbaum.

Holmbeck, G., Colder, C., Shapera, W., Westhoven, V., Keneally, L., & Updegrove, A. (2000). Working with adolescents: Guides from developmental psychology. In P. Kendall (Ed.), *Child and adolescent therapy*. New York: Guilford Press.

Kazdin, A. (1986). Comparative outcome studies of psychotherapy: Methodogical issues and strategies. *Journal of Clinical and Consulting Psychology, 54,* 415–424.

Kazdin, A. (2000). Developing a research agenda for child and adolescent psychotherapy. *Archives of General Psychiatry, 57,* 829–835.

Kendall, P. (1993). Cognitive-behavioral therapies with youth: Guiding theory, current status, and emerging developments. *Journal of Clinical and Consulting Psychology, 61,* 235–247.

Kraemer, H., Wilson, G. T., Fairburn, C. G., & Agras, W. S. (2002). Mediators and moderators of treatment effects in randomized clinical trials. *Archives of General Psychiatry, 59,* 877–884.

Krupnick, J., Sotsky, S., Simmens, S., Moyer, J., Elkin, I., Watkins, J., et al. (1996). The role of the therapeutic alliance in psychotherapy and pharmacotherapy outcome: Findings in the National Institute of Mental Health Treatment of Depression Collaborative Research Program. *Journal of Clinical and Consulting Psychology, 64,* 532–539.

Lock, J. (1995). Acting out and the narrative function: Reconsidering Peter Blos's concept of the second individuation process. *American Journal of Psychotherapy, 49,* 548–557.

Lock, J., & Le Grange, D. (2001). Can family-based treatment of anorexia nervosa be manualized? *Journal of Psychotherapy Practice and Research, 10,* 253–261.

Lock, J., Le Grange, D., Agras, W. S., & Dare, C. (2001). *Treatment manual for anorexia nervosa: A family-based approach.* New York: Guilford Press.

Luborsky, L., Singer, B., & Luborsky, L. (1975). Comparative studies of psychotherapies: Is it true that "everyone has won and all must have prizes?" *Archives of General Psychiatry, 32,* 995–1007.

Minuchin, S., Rosman, B., & Baker, I. (1978). *Psychosomatic families: Anorexia nervosa in context.* Cambridge, MA: Harvard University Press.

Mufson, L., Moreau, D., & Weissman, M. M. (1994). Modification of interpersonal psychotherapy with depressed adolescents (IPT-A): Phase I and phase II studies. *Journal of the American Academy of Child and Adolescent Psychiatry, 33,* 695–704.

Mufson, L., Moreau, D., Weissman, M. M., & Klerman, G. (1993). *Interpersonal psychotherapy for depressed adolescents.* New York: Guilford Press.

Palazzoli, M. (1974). *Self-starvation: From the intrapsychic to the transpersonal approach to anorexia nervosa.* London: Chaucer Publishing.

Palazzoli, M., Boscolo, L., Cecchin, G., & Prata, G. (1980). Hypothesizing-circularity-neutrality: Three guidelines for the conductor of the session. *Family Process, 19,* 3–12.

Smith, M., Glass, G., & Miller, T. (1980). *The benefits of psychotherapy.* Baltimore: Johns Hopkins Press.

Wilson, G. T., Fairburn, C. G., Agras, W. S., Walsh, B. T., & Kraemer, H. (2002). Cognitive behavior therapy for bulimia nervosa: Time course and mechanism of change. *Journal of Clinical and Consulting Psychology, 70,* 267–274.

CHAPTER SEVENTEEN

BEHAVIOR ANALYSIS AND CHILD AND ADOLESCENT TREATMENTS

Brandi C. Fink and Linda Lotspeich, M.D.

Behavior analysis is a comprehensive approach to the study of behavior. This approach refers to a more general scientific approach to the study of behavior that includes a systematic body of knowledge, techniques to carry out the analysis of behavior, practical implications for therapeutic interventions, and specific assumptions about how to study behavior. There are two key assumptions underlying the analytic approach to the study of behavior and treatment. The first is that behavior occurs within a context and if one removes a behavior from its context, it becomes meaningless (Kohlenberg & Tsai, 1991). Second, psychological development is viewed as "progressive changes in the interactions between the behaviors of a person and the events in his/her environment" (Bijou & Baer, 1961, 1978). Because behavior analysis is often confused with behavior therapy, this chapter will provide a brief history of the approach, its theoretical assumptions, a summary of the techniques used in conducting a functional analysis, and the methods used in interventions.

Basic Rationale and Theory

Behavior analysis is an approach to the study of behavior and to therapy that has its foundations in the work of John B. Watson. It is also a part of a larger group of learning theory-based approaches that developed as a result of the dissatisfaction with the introspective study of behavior that dominated psychology in the early part of the twentieth century. Watson first argued that the psychodynamic approach was insufficient to study behavior because in his opinion, the mind did not exist and that all psychologists could legitimately study was overt behavior (Smith, 2001; Watson, 1913; 1924). Secondly, Watson argued that if the mind did exist, intrapsychic phenomena could not be reliably measured. Because of these arguments, Watson asserted that psychology should abandon the introspective approach to psychological research in favor of the more precise specification and measurement of overt behavior (Smith, 2001). These two arguments are generally termed *Watsonian metaphysical behaviorism* and *methodological behaviorism,* respectively (Dougher & Hayes, 2000; Smith, 2001).

While Watsonian metaphysical behaviorism never really gained popularity, methodological behaviorism did and quickly became the dominant approach to psychology in the United States. Methodological behaviorism also represented the important relationship between basic theory and applied research. The application of theory to research was also the most notable difference between it and the psychodynamic approaches. Following the application of basic theory to research was the application of research to treatment settings. As a result, in the late 1950s and early 1960s, behavior therapy emerged in two distinct veins. In the United States, applied behavior analysis emerged and closely followed the principles of operant conditioning described by B. F. Skinner (Dougher & Hayes, 2000; Smith, 2001). In Great Britain and South Africa, methodological behaviorism became the dominant approach and followed the principles of stimulus-response learning. This is also the vein that came to be known as "behavior therapy" (Dougher & Hayes, 2000).

Although both of these approaches were strongly empirically grounded, they differed significantly in their focus and philosophy. *Behavior therapists* tended to be clinical psychologists who worked with adults in outpatient settings. They also tended to focus on alleviating problems such as depression and anxiety by helping their patients make new associations. An example of this is in the use of systematic desensitization to alleviate anxiety. *Behavior analysts* tended to be, on the other hand, mostly experimental or developmental psychologists. Behavior analysts also tended to work with children in the school or the group home setting and with institutionalized individuals. Furthermore, behavior analysts relied on parents, teachers, or group home staff to administer direct contingencies of reinforcement such as those found in behavioral contracts, time outs, and token economies. As a result of these treatments, behavioral analysts have gradually become most well known for their successful work with children with developmental disabilities and most notably, less verbal (and even nonverbal) autistic children (Dougher & Hayes, 2000). Behavior analysis has also been the most effective method of behavior control to emerge from psychology with solid evidence supporting its efficacy; a claim that many other approaches have had difficulty making (Smith, 2001).

As mentioned, behavior therapy and behavior analysis also differed in their philosophy. The underlying philosophy of behavior therapy is mechanistic and purports that human system is a sum of independent parts that operate together and that to understand the system, one has to understand each individual part and the principles under which they operate (Dougher & Hayes, 2000). Behavior analysis is, on the other hand, epigenetic in nature and believes that behavior is developmental and situated within a context. A person's behavior is thought to be influenced by his or her personality or disposition, learning history, and the current context within which it is occurring (Dougher & Hayes, 2000; Harrington, Fink, & Dougher, 2001; Hudson, 1999). As such, it is thought to evolve over time and emerge in certain, specific situations.

Despite the emergence of clinical behavior analysis in the 1990s, applied behavior analysis has remained remarkably consistent over the years. Behavior therapy underwent a significant shift, however, during the mid to late 1970s. During this shift, behavior therapy continued to be quite mechanistic, but it adopted the computer as its mechanical metaphor. Also, mediational accounts of behavior change, such as thoughts, began to materialize (Bandura, 1969; 1977). This shift also represented the emergence of the cognitive therapy movement (now referred to as cognitive-behavioral therapy; see Chapter 18) and the orientation toward the detection and alteration of maladaptive thoughts (Meichenbaum, 1977).

Putative Mechanism of Efficacy

Although behavior analysis has its roots in the operant conditioning principles of B. F. Skinner, not all behavior is thought to be the result of operant conditioning. It is important to emphasize that the determinants of a person's behavior are thought to include disposition (personality or temperament), prior learning history, current physiological state, and current contextual factors (Harrington, Fink, & Dougher, 2001; Ross, 1976). As it may be imagined, it is difficult to manipulate the first three determinants so as to alter behavior, but the contextual influences can be manipulated. When they are manipulated in accordance with operant conditioning principles, they form the basis for the therapeutic approach in behavior analysis.

Furthermore, within the principles of operant conditioning, behavior is viewed as occurring between two sets of stimuli: stimuli that precede the target behavior and stimuli that follow the target behavior. The stimuli that precede a target behavior are called *antecedent stimuli* and provide stimulus control or cues for the target behavior. Stimuli that follow a target behavior are called *consequent stimuli* and affect the likelihood of the future occurrence of the behavior. Antecedents and consequences are controlling variables and explain why a person behaves in the manner in which he does.

To elucidate how these variables control behavior, we will first discuss consequences because they have the most powerful control over behavior. Consequences are divided into two primary types: reinforcers and punishers. Reinforcers are consequences that increase the likelihood that a behavior will occur again in the future; more simply, they strengthen the behavior. Reinforcers can also be thought of as good effects or rewards. In addition, reinforcers can occur in two different ways: positive and negative. When discussing positive and negative reinforcers, it is important to emphasize that the term positive means "addition" and not "good" and the term negative means "subtraction" and not "bad." A positive reinforcer is a pleasant stimulus presented after a target behavior that subsequently increases the likelihood that the target behavior will occur again. It is important to note that a reinforcer is defined functionally and entirely by its effects on the target behavior. More explicitly, if a consequence increased or strengthened the behavior, then it is defined as a reinforcer. If the consequence did not lead to an increase in the rate or strength of the behavior, then it cannot be defined as a reinforcer. Positive reinforcers can include anything as abstract and internal as the feeling of accomplishment after mastering a difficult piece on the piano, to something as tangible as a child being taken for ice cream after behaving well in church. In contrast, a negative reinforcer is the removal of an unpleasant stimulus after the occurrence of a target behavior. Examples of negative reinforcement include the reduction of anxiety over attending school by skipping class, the seat belt indicator ceasing to buzz after fastening one's seatbelt, and being exempted from a household chore after good behavior. The negative reinforcement in these examples increase the likelihood that one will continue skipping class, one will continue to fasten one's seatbelt, and one will continue to behave well.

Contrary to reinforcers, punishers are consequences that weaken behavior and decrease the likelihood that a target behavior will occur in the future. Here again, punishment is defined functionally and entirely by its effect on the behavior it follows. Punishment, in this sense, must also be differentiated from the common usage of punishment which generally means retribution and may not necessarily reduce the occurrence of the behavior that preceded it. If the consequence of a behavior does not weaken the behavior, then it cannot be considered a punisher. Furthermore, just as there is positive and negative reinforcement, there is also positive and negative punishment. Positive punishment is the presentation of an unpleasant stimulus as a consequence of a behavior. The natural environment is often a source full of positive punishment. For example, disturbing a beehive often results in the punishment of being stung and not wearing a jacket on a brisk day results in the punishment of becoming cold. A social example of positive punishment is a child being reprimanded after behaving badly. Another, less intuitive, example of a positive punishment is a parent criticizing a child's performance on a task. Instead of working to encourage the child to do a better job in the future, the criticism will actually decrease the likelihood that he or she will attempt anything like it again.

Negative punishment is the removal of a pleasant stimulus as a consequence of a behavior, such as taking away a toy or privilege after a child's misbehavior. Negative punishment can also come in social forms. Consider how, when a person says something insensitive at a party, others turn to join different conversations. The loss of social attention would reduce the occurrence of insensitive comments in the future.

When discussing consequences, it is also important to emphasize that natural consequences are generally more effective in influencing behavior than contrived consequences. In addition, reinforcement generally has a greater influence on behavior than does punishment. Thus, natural positive reinforcement has the strongest influence on behavior. Most individuals that we see, however, are referred for an excess of a problem behavior. How does positive reinforcement result in decreasing problem behavior? Although, we will discuss this in greater detail in the sections addressing strengthening and weakening behavior, we can briefly answer, for now, by pointing out that while punishing undesirable behavior is important, it is even more important to positively reinforce any approximation of a desired behavior in a manner that seems natural and genuine (Kohlenberg & Tsai, 1991). Unnatural rewards or contrived praise may work with young children, but as children develop and learn about life, they may become wary of such unnatural and contrived consequences (Baldwin & Baldwin, 2001). In fact, unnatural and contrived consequences, used in a manipulative manner, can actually increase the frequency of undesired behavior (Baldwin & Baldwin, 2001).

A final point to remember when considering consequences is that close timings between a reinforcer or a punisher and a behavior do not always guarantee operant conditioning, nor do extended timings necessarily prevent it. What is important here is that the consequence is causally related to the behavior. This concept is referred to as "contingency of reinforcement" (Hudson, 1999; Baldwin & Baldwin, 2001). Consequences that accidentally follow a behavior (noncontingent consequences) have little ability to modify the behavior they follow because they are not causally related to it. Humans are the species most capable of determining contingent relationships between behaviors and reinforcers or punishers, in part because of our ability to verbally reconstruct past events

(Baldwin & Baldwin, 2001). In fact, the more that a person engages in such reconstruction of events, the more likely it is that the behavior will be modified, even if the consequences were quite delayed.

Antecedent cues are also important to the theory of behavior analysis, for they may signal the likelihood that a behavior will be reinforced or punished based upon the prior reinforcement or punishment history of that behavior (Hudson, 1999; Baldwin & Baldwin, 2001). Furthermore, it is important to note that antecedent stimuli can include stimuli internal or external to the body. For example, the anxiety that a child who has been teased at school feels before leaving for school is an internal antecedent stimulus that signals that school should possibly be avoided because his prior attendance has been punished by the teasing. An example of an external antecedent stimulus is a child seeing his grandmother and knowing that he can ask her for a cookie because he has been reinforced (given a cookie) in the past when he has asked her for one.

Developmental Influences

As mentioned, one feature of behavior analytic treatment that sets it apart from other modalities is its ideographic approach. In other words, treatments are "tailor made" for each child based upon the principles of operant conditioning and the child's behavioral excesses or deficits. This is also the feature that contributes significantly to the success of behavior analytic treatments. As such, if a thorough assessment and case formulation are completed according to the discussion in the next section, the treatment will be developmentally appropriate for the child.

Two complex psychotherapies have been developed that may not be developmentally appropriate for all children, however. They are acceptance and commitment therapy and functional analytic psychotherapy and will be discussed in greater detail in the section in this chapter on Complex Intervention Procedures. Although both psychotherapies are based on behavior analytic principles and are to be applied in an ideographic manner, they are psychotherapies and require a greater amount of abstraction on the part of the client. As such, these therapies are probably best reserved for adolescents.

Putative Targets of Treatment

Assessment and case formulation are the first steps in applying behavior analytic principles to the modification of the excesses or deficits of a target behavior (Baldwin & Baldwin, 2001; Hudson, 1999). More specifically, assessment and case formulation involve the specification of the behavior, the measurement of the behavior, and the assessment of the function of the behavior (Cooper, Heron, & Heward, 1987; Sulzer-Azaroff & Mayer, 1991; Martin & Pear, 1996). Once assessment and case formulation are completed, one can set about changing the most important antecedents and consequences that control the behavior in question.

Specification of the Behavior

The specification of the target behavior is the first step in the process of assessment and case formulation (Hudson, 1999; Baldwin & Baldwin, 2001). Specification involves a precise, careful and objective definition of the behavior of interest. It is only through the precise definition of the behavior that problems, such as the behavior being interpreted in various ways, are avoided. Because of this, it is important to avoid vague descriptions of the target behavior. For example, to say that Susie is aggressive can mean several things. Without a specification of the behavior, we do not know if she is physically aggressive (hitting her classmates) or if she is verbally aggressive (threatening her classmates). Furthermore, if she is verbally aggressive, it is important to specify exactly what she says to her classmates.

Also useful in the specification of behavior is the identification of chains of behavior. Chains of behavior are smaller operant links that are joined in a stream of activities that comprise the target behavior (Baldwin & Baldwin, 2001). If the target behavior is learning a new dance, the smaller operant links would be the steps that compose the dance. In this example, one can see that a target behavior rarely consists of only one unit of behavior. Usually, it consists of dozens, if not hundreds, of small components that must be chained together to form the target behavior (Baldwin & Baldwin, 2001). Chaining as a method of strengthening behavior will be discussed in greater detail later in the chapter. For now, however, we want to emphasize the usefulness of chaining in the specification of behavior.

Measurement of the Behavior

The measurement of the target behavior is important for two reasons. First, it helps determine whether an intervention is actually required. For example, a parent who is concerned that her child does not play with children after school may worry that she is isolated at school, as well. Upon careful observation, it may be determined that the frequency of her social interaction is within a normal range and an intervention is, therefore, not necessary. The second reason that it is important to precisely measure target behaviors is that the initial measurement will become the baseline against which the success of the intervention is determined.

There are several methods of measuring target behaviors that include frequency counts, duration measures, and permanent product measures (Hudson, 1999). A frequency count involves simply counting the times a behavior occurs within a specified period of time. Frequency counts are appropriate for measuring behaviors that occur quickly and often. In the cases where a behavior is occurring infrequently, but for a longer duration, duration measures would be more appropriate. A duration measure would be appropriate for measuring a behavior such as time spent daydreaming while doing homework. The frequency of such a behavior may be low and not very meaningful, but the duration of such a behavior would indicate to what degree daydreaming may be interfering with the completion of homework. Another measurement that may be appropriate with the homework example is a permanent product measurement. This measurement involves counting the relatively permanent products of a behavior. In the case of homework, pages read or science problems completed would be an appropriate product to measure.

Functional Analysis of Behavior

The final step in the assessment of a target behavior is the completion of a functional analysis, which involves identifying the antecedents and the consequences that are functionally related to the target behavior (Baldwin & Baldwin, 2001; Grant & Evans, 1994; Hudson, 1999; Sulzer-Azaroff & Mayer, 1991). As previously discussed, it is important to distinguish between antecedents and consequences that are functionally (causally) related and those that are simply temporally related. For example, the simple presence of an adult has been found to be an antecedent cue for child misbehavior. Besevegis and Lore (1983) observed children playing under the two conditions of an adult present and an adult absent. When the adult was present, there was significantly more arguing and fighting among the pairs of children than when the adult was absent. In this instance, the adult was the antecedent cue for the increased likelihood of reinforcement for aggression with social attention (the adult stepping in to stop the fighting). Similarly, Iwata et al. (1994) found that social attention was reinforcing self-injurious behavior (SIB) in over two-thirds of the 152 cases analyzed. In these situations, the child's SIB functioned to attract both positive and negative reinforcement from parents and teachers. The positive reinforcement resulted from the social attention the child would receive when engaging in SIB (parents and teachers would attempt to stop the child's SIB). The negative reinforcement resulted from the parents and the teachers lightening their expectations of the child. The parents and teachers would withdraw their demands on the child when the child would begin the self-injurious behavior (for example, remove the request to set the table). As it can be seen, antecedents and consequences that are functionally related to the target behavior can be counter-intuitive. Such instances emphasize the importance of clearly specifying the behavior, measuring the behavior, and completing a functional analysis. Once the antecedents and consequences are identified, they can be modified to strengthen or weaken the specific target behavior to the desired outcome.

Lastly, a functional analysis does not assume that a behavior is, in and of itself, either adaptive or maladaptive (Baldwin & Baldwin, 2001; Grant & Evans, 1994; Hudson, 1999; Sulzer-Azaroff & Mayer, 1991). It simply assumes that behavior lies somewhere along the continuum of adaptive to maladaptive. A behavior is deter-mined to be maladaptive only if the behavior is causing problems for the child and his or her family. Furthermore, any child or adolescent behavioral excess or deficit is a good candidate for a behavioral analytic intervention. Behavioral excesses can include countless difficulties, such as delinquency, overeating, getting angry too often, dominating conversations, phobias, obsessive-compulsive behavior, physical aggression, or overachieving. Behavioral deficits can include limited social abilities, being shy, limited abilities for studying, not getting enough exercise, or not being able to express friendship and love. The goal of behavior analytic treatments is to help people learn how to reduce behavior excesses and gain the skills necessary to overcome behavior deficits (Baldwin & Baldwin, 2001).

In conducting a functional analysis, it is useful to obtain information from as many sources and by as many means as possible. The following are methods commonly used to collect such information.

Interviews. In the behavior analytic approach to intervention and therapy, infor-mation collection generally begins with the interview (Grant & Evans, 1994; Hudson, 1999; Sulzer-Azaroff & Mayer, 1991). In the case of working with children, the interview is usually conducted with someone who knows the child well, such as a parent, but can include teachers and child-care workers, as well. The purpose of the interview is to obtain as much information about the target behavior (such as frequency, duration, severity, and factors that appear to increase and decrease the behavior) as possible. Information regarding the child's likes and dislikes should also be collected, because these will be useful in designing the intervention. If the child has sufficient communication skills, it is useful to conduct an interview with him or her to obtain supplemental information and to understand the child's perspective. It is also during this time that the parents or significant others (teachers, child-care workers) receive instruction on collecting baseline behavior.

Written Materials. Materials assessing child functioning, such as the Child Behavior Checklist (Achenbach & Edlebrock, 1983) can be used to supplement the information gained from the interviews. Considering the significant impact that marital functioning that has on child behavior and adjustment (Belsky & Rovine, 1990; Cowan & Cowan, 1992; Cohn, Silver, & Cowan, 1992; Cowan, Cowan, Shulz, & Heming, 1994; Fainsilber-Katz & Gottman, 1994), it is often useful to assess marital adjustment using measures such as the Short Marital Adjustment Scale (Locke & Wallace, 1959) or the Diadic Adjustment Scale (Spanier, 1982). In addition to providing meaningful information for the case formulation, these measures can also be used after the intervention to assess its success.

Direct Observation of Target Behavior. It is also important when assessing the function of a target behavior to directly observe it. A direct observation of the target behavior is used to gain information regarding the baseline occurrence of the behavior. It is also an essential component of determining the antecedent and consequent stimuli of said behavior. The direct observation of a young child's behavior is typically conducted daily by significant others in the child's life, such as a parent or teacher. When instructing parents and teachers how to conduct a direct observation and to ensure that the information collected is useful, it is important to provide organized charts or recording forms that are easy for the observer to use along with a sufficient amount of practice time in using them. If the materials are too complicated and obtuse, the observers may record only pertinent information when it is convenient to do so and not at its every occurrence.

Adolescents who have been referred to therapy may also be involved in the direct observation of their own behavior using the same direct observation procedures. The adolescent's participation is essential for the direct observation of covert target behaviors, such as his or her own depressive or anxious symptoms. While the best observation is often performed by an independent observer, such as a therapist, the disruptive effect that a new person may have on the natural occurrence of target behavior may actually offset the benefit of an objective observer.

Hypothesis Development. The last step in performing a functional analysis of a target behavior is the development of the hypothesis regarding the function of the behavior. While interviews, written materials, and direct observation will provide extensive information about the target behavior, the identity of the antecedents and consequences that are functionally related to it cannot be precisely known. It is only through the formulation of hypotheses regarding the antecedents and consequences and the systematic testing of those hypotheses by manipulation of antecedents and consequences that stimuli functionally related to the target behavior can be identified. A formulated hypothesis is confirmed only when the desired change in the target behavior is observed. If the behavior remains unchanged or changes in an undesired direction, the therapist must reformulate the hypothesis and test it again.

This hypothesis formulation and testing process is often not well understood, but is essential to the successful implementation of a behavior analytic intervention. Hypothesis testing is also a point in the process at which the operant conditioning principles of behavior analysis and its ideographic approach to intervention are most evident. The hypothesis-testing component of the case formulation process allows one to determine what is punishing and reinforcing to the child. It also underscores the fact that what is punishing or reinforcing for one child may not be for another. To reiterate, one cannot say, "Well, I reinforced the desired behavior, but it did not change." If the behavior did not change then it truly was not reinforced (or punished, as the case may be).

Mechanisms for Change and Intervention Procedures

As mentioned, the behavior analytic approach to behavior change is ideographic in nature. In other words, it reflects the unique characteristics of the individual for whom an intervention is targeted. While interventions must consider such individual characteristics as age, developmental stage, skill level, preferred reinforcers and the like, there are some general behavioral procedures that are routinely used to strengthen or weaken a behavior.

Strengthening Behavior

The methods for strengthening behavior include prompting, shaping, chaining, modeling and the systematic use of reinforcement. In behavior modification, as in everyday life, these procedures are most often present in combinations. Pure examples of these processes are less common, but they will be discussed individually so that the contribution of each to operant conditioning can be more clearly understood. While these modes of learning will be discussed in relation to operant conditioning, it should be noted that they influence respondent (Pavlovian) conditioning, as well.

Systematic Use of Reinforcement. The simplest method for strengthening behavior is called *contingent reinforcement*. Contingent reinforcement involves waiting for a desired behavior to occur and then reinforcing it. Reinforcers are generally broken down into two categories: primary reinforcers and secondary reinforcers. Primary reinforcers are those that do not depend on prior learning for their reinforcing properties and include such things as food and drinks. Secondary reinforcers are those that have become reinforcing based upon some prior learning. Reading books is an example of a secondary reinforcer. One must learn to read before stories become entertaining and thus reinforcing.

As discussed in the section on consequences, another important distinction among reinforcers is whether they are naturally occurring or contrived. Contrived reinforcers are also referred to as artificial reinforcers (Hudson, 1999). Contrived reinforcers would include items that are not usually available, but are purchased or obtained specifically for the purpose of reinforcement, such as a toy or favorite candy. Naturally occurring reinforcers are generally present in a child's environment and can include things such as parental attention or television viewing (Hudson, 1999). The use of natural reinforcers is usually more desirable than the use of contrived reinforcers because natural reinforcers are readily available. The continued use of contrived reinforcers may become impractical. For instance, the expense of purchasing new toys to use as reinforcers.

Lastly, the systematic use of reinforcement to strengthen behavior requires adherence to operant principles of conditioning. Learning will occur most quickly if reinforcement is continuous at first and then once established, thinned. Thinning the reinforcement involves moving to a schedule that reinforces the behavior only intermittently. In doing so, the behavior will become more resistant to extinction (ceasing once reinforcement has stopped).

Prompting. As discussed, the likelihood that a behavior will occur increases if it has been reinforced. If a behavior is not occurring spontaneously, it must be prompted so that it can be reinforced. Learning from prompting occurs in three phases: prompting, reinforcement, and fading. Prompts can be various stimuli that help initiate a behavior, including visual, verbal, and physical stimuli. A visual prompt is, for instance, a note on the refrigerator reminding the child to do something. A verbal prompt is the use of sounds or words to initiate a behavior and can include making an "ssss . . . " sound when helping a child sound out the word "snake." Physical prompts often involve adult assistance in performing a task, such as a parent helping a child hold a spoon when learning to use table utensils to eat.

In addition, prompted behavior will be learned much more efficiently if all prompted responses are reinforced (Baldwin & Baldwin, 2001; Hudson, 1999). A parent who enthusiastically praises her child for using a spoon to eat will find that her child learns the new task much more quickly than when the praise is not used. Reinforcement is crucial to learning prompted behaviors.

Fading is the final step in learning from prompting. As learning occurs, prompts are gradually faded until the desired behavior occurs without them. Fading allows for the target behavior to come under the control of naturally occurring stimuli. Following the example of learning to use a spoon to eat, it would be the presence of the spoon at mealtime that would become the stimulus controlling its use in eating. New behavior is most efficiently learned if fading is adjusted to the child's own pace; it should occur neither too rapidly nor too slowly.

Personal Experience Using Prompting. I recently worked with Tyler, a three-year-old boy with autism who had poor expressive and receptive language abilities. He did not use gestures to communicate. To remedy this I taught him to point to pictures using a type of physical prompt commonly referred to as "hand-over-hand." To do this, I placed my hand over Tyler's hand and moved it through the pointing. In this case, I presented him with a picture of a cat and told Tyler to point to the cat. I then took Tyler's pointer finger and touched the picture. This activity was repeated many times and over several days with different pictures. As this activity was repeated I would first pause before guiding Tyler's finger through the pointing behavior to give him a chance to point independently. To motivate his interest in completing the task, I gave Tyler a piece of cracker each time he pointed to the picture, whether he pointed independently or with the help of the hand-over-hand prompt. Soon he was pointing on his own most of the time. I then increased the complexity of the task by presenting him with two pictures. I now wanted Tyler to point to a specific picture on verbal instructions. At first, Tyler did not understand the task and pointed to both pictures. Since the added complexity was confusing to him, I used the physical prompt of hand-over-hand until he understood that he was to point only to the picture I named. Once he was successful in this, I faded out the use of the physical prompt.

While working with another child with poor language abilities, four-year-old Emma, I had to address an additional problem. Emma liked to handle the pictures and her hands were often on the picture even before I could instruct her to point to them. To solve this problem, I had to first teach Emma to keep her hands in her lap and wait for my instruction. Using hand over hand, I placed Emma's hands in her lap while saying, "hands down." Once Emma's hands were in her lap, I then taught her how to point to a picture, much as I had done with Tyler.

Shaping. Shaping is a procedure by which behavior is changed in a series of steps or successive approximations from its original condition to a later and generally more sophisticated and complex level. Each step in the process requires that the individual meet a slightly higher criterion before the behavior is reinforced. At each step, the behavioral variation that best represents the final desired behavior is reinforced while the poorest variations are allowed to extinguish through non-reinforcement. Because only the best approximations are reinforced and the poorest approximations are ignored, a person learns sophisticated and complex behaviors without failure. Shaping provides significant benefits for a child's sense of mastery and perceived self-efficacy while minimizing the risks of failure and aversive feelings that may become associated with learning if the child is corrected during the process.

Teachers who are effective at shaping watch the variation in each child's behavior and provide positive feedback for the variations that best represent each child's attempts at the end behavior (Baldwin & Baldwin, 2001). For successful learning from shaping to occur, each child's behavior should be compared only to his or her own previous behavior and not to any other child's behavior. This further avoids any feelings of failure and enhances feelings of mastery.

Chaining. Many everyday activities are complex and consist of long chains of behaviors that ultimately lead to reinforcement. Preparing a salad is a good example of such a behavior. There are a number of smaller behaviors that are linked in a behavioral chain that result in an appetizing salad. One must choose the ingredients, wash the vegetables, chop them, and then assemble the salad. Reinforcement for the entire chain will occur only when one is finished and eating the salad. Certainly, making a salad is an adult behavior, but the principles are the same for most complex behaviors in which a child would engage.

Chaining can be either forward or backward and involves strengthening all components of the chain that generate the final behavior. Forward chaining involves focusing on the beginning of the sequence, prompting and reinforcing each step, as necessary, until the segment is mastered. Once mastery is achieved, one progressively moves through the other steps.

Backward chaining involves beginning with the last step of the behavioral chain and working from there backward to finish with the first step of the chain. An example of this concept is demonstrated by O'Brien and Simek (1983). The authors used the principles of backward chaining to teach students golf and compared this method to traditional methods of teaching golf. In this study, the authors began by teaching randomly assigned students how to putt the ball into the cup and worked backward in a series of ten steps to a long backswing. By mastering the last step of putting, the students were also learning all of the principles of body placement and swing involved in a long backswing. When the students who learned to golf by traditional methods were compared to backward-chaining students on a moderately difficult Professional Golfers Association rated 18-hole course, the backward-chaining students' performance was significantly superior. These students averaged 98 strokes and the traditional group averaged 116 strokes (O'Brien & Simek, 1983). Also, four out of the six backward-chaining students broke 100, while only one of the traditionally taught students did (O'Brien & Simek, 1983).

Personal Experience Using Backward Chaining. Molly is a six-year-old girl with borderline IQ and poor motor coordination who frequently had temper tantrums in the morning when it was time to get dressed. Her parents reported that she could complete each task necessary to dress herself, but needed to be prompted and encouraged at each step. If she was left alone in the task she would only get partially dressed because she would become distracted by some other activity. Her parents acknowledged that dressing was difficult for her due to her poor motor coordination but, with effort, she had the necessary skills. I suggested that her parents use the backward chaining technique to divide the task into sequential steps, and then teach the child each step of the task, starting with the last step and working back to the first step.

I instructed Molly's parents to start by ordering her dressing activities into steps, starting with underwear and ending with socks and shoes. Each morning they helped Molly get dressed, always following the same order of steps. At the start the only task Molly was required to perform completely on her own was the last step (putting on her shoes). Once Molly was independently putting on her shoes, she was then required to put on her socks and shoes. Once she mastered each new step, the others were added in a backward order. Because she had mastered the previous steps in the backward chain, she already knew exactly what she had to do next to finish getting dressed each time a new step was added. Her parents informed me that the backward chaining technique helped Molly to stay organized when getting dressed. The memorized sequence of steps helped her in being less distracted by other activities. Molly did not have to stop and think what should happen next and, gradually, the whole process became automatic. She was also more compliant with this training strategy than ones her parents had previously used. This is due to the feelings of mastery that Molly was experiencing from the start because she was able to successfully complete each step.

Modeling. At first glance, modeling (sometimes referred to as observational learning) may resemble visual prompting, but it is more complex than visual prompting. Modeling involves a demonstration of a complex behavior by a model. The observer then attempts to replicate the model's behavior. If the model's behavior is only a few steps ahead of the observer's level of competence, then the new behavior may be replicated after the first attempt. If, however, the model's behavior is several steps ahead of the observer's skill level, the observer may require practice accompanied by reinforcement and corrective feedback from the model until the behavior is mastered.

Weakening Behavior

Although the term reinforcement is generally associated with strengthening behavior, the first two procedures discussed in the weakening behavior category have reinforcement in their titles because these procedures focus on strengthening behaviors other than the undesired target behavior. This, in turn, weakens the undesired behavior. Other weakening procedures discussed will include extinction, time-out, overcorrection, and negative control.

It should also be noted that the weakening procedures presented in this section are discussed in order with Turbull's (1981) principle of least restrictive alternative. The *principle of least restrictive alternative* states that an intervention should use the least aversive procedure available. The procedures of extinction through punishment progress along a continuum of increasing levels of aversiveness. In other words, the intervention should be aversive enough to be effective, but should not be excessive. The principle of least restrictive alternative is in keeping with the ideographic nature of behavior analytic interventions and considers the differing sensitivity levels of children. Many parents will attest that the undesirable behavior of one child may be corrected with a cross look, while another child will require being grounded in order to alter their undesirable behavior.

Differential Reinforcement of Other Behavior. Differential reinforcement of other (DRO) behavior involves reinforcing a child for *any* behavior other than the target behavior and can include just sitting quietly. The DRO procedure does not specify behaviors for reinforcement. What is tantamount for reinforcement to occur with DRO is the absence of the target behavior. A common usage of the DRO procedure is reinforcing the child if the target behavior did not occur within a set amount of time.

DRO schedules are useful in reducing the frequency of problematic behaviors including aggressive and destructive behaviors (Baldwin & Baldwin, 2001; Novak, 1996). They are also quite effective in treating behaviors that have long-term negative consequences for a child's development and socialization, such as self-injurious and strange behaviors (Baldwin & Baldwin, 2001; Iwata, et al., 1994).

Differential Reinforcement of Incompatible Behavior. Differential reinforcement of incompatible (DRI) behavior is a subset of DRO and is remarkably powerful in suppressing undesirable behavior. DRI seeks to reinforce responses that are incompatible with the target behavior. For example, in performing DRI with a child who has problems with aggressiveness and bullying, one would find and reinforce behaviors that are incompatible with those behaviors. These might include cooperative playing, friendliness, and sharing (as discussed in the previous section, the use of prompting, modeling, and so on may be required for the prosocial behavior to be exhibited so that it can be reinforced). The reinforcement of the prosocial behavior drives down the frequency of the antisocial behavior because the two response classes are incompatible. DRI has been shown to be very effective in turning aggressive children and bullies into friendly, cooperative and prosocial children (Kellam, Ling, Meriaca, Brown & Ialongo, 1998; Richman et al., 1997).

Extinction. *Extinction* is a procedure that is based on the operant principle that if a behavior is not reinforced it will weaken and eventually disappear and essentially involves ignoring the undesirable behavior. In using extinction for intervention, it is important to identify that the reinforcement may be maintaining the target behavior. Although extinction can be a powerful tool in ceasing behavior that has previously been positively reinforced, it can be difficult to determine exactly what reinforcement is maintaining the behavior. This is especially true if the reinforcement is intrinsic, occurs intermittently, or comes from several sources. Also, when a behavior is first put on extinction, an extinction burst typically occurs. An extinction burst is an initial increase in the intensity, emotionality, and frequency of the target behavior and is often difficult to tolerate. If the target behavior is consistently ignored, this burst will weaken and the target behavior will be successfully eliminated. Thus, for extinction to be effective, it is absolutely necessary to tolerate the extinction burst. For example, when a child's screaming for cookies (which had previously been reinforced with a cookie) is ignored, the child might first respond with a more intense temper tantrum. If reinforcement (that is, cookie) is given at this stage, then the target behavior will be nearly impossible to extinguish in the future.

Although it may be counter-intuitive, children exhibit many aversive behaviors because they have been reinforced for doing so. For example, children learn to whine, pout, throw tantrums, and shout because they receive the positive reinforcement of social attention or getting what they want. At the same time, parents receive negative reinforcement for paying attention to these behaviors because it helps them escape the child's obnoxious behavior (Baldwin & Baldwin, 2001). Putting behaviors such as these on extinction is a very effective method of intervention. Studies have shown that after the extinction burst, the obnoxious behavior abruptly drops to less than half the prior rate and continues to decline from there (Baldwin & Baldwin, 2001).

Overcorrection. Overcorrection is an intervention comprised of two elements, restitution and positive practice and is best explained using an example. Consider the situation of a child who comes home from school and flings his backpack on an end table, knocking over a lamp in the process. The restitution component of overcorrection would require the child to go back into the living room, remove his bag from the table, replace the tipped-over lamp and replace the broken light bulb. The positive practice component would require the child to reenter the house with his bag and place it in the closet where it belongs. In using overcorrection, it may be necessary for the positive practice component to be repeated on several occasions until the child is doing it automatically.

Punishment

Time-Out. Time-out is a gentle, but very effective, nonviolent form of punishment. It is also a desirable form of punishment because it emphasizes good behavior and the positive consequences associated with it without modeling anger or aggression. In time-out, the consequence of a target behavior is immediate removal of the child from the reinforcement (Novak, 1996). Commonly, time-out involves placing the child in a relatively boring environment. This form of time-out is referred to as exclusionary time-out. A child can also be placed in a nonexclusionary time-out by, for example, placing him or her on the sofa without access to any activities such as toys, TV, computer, and so on. The purpose of time-out is not to isolate the child, but to have the undesired target behavior result in a loss of reinforcement. Also, this procedure is most effective if it is immediate and brief, usually three to five minutes depending upon the age of the child. For time-out to be successful, there are several important elements that must be present. First, the time-out environment must be less reinforcing than the area in which the undesirable behavior occurred. If the child is sent to his or her bedroom and the bedroom is filled with toys and a television, then it will be just as reinforcing as the previous environment and time-out will be ineffective. Secondly, one must consider the child's behavior during the time-out. A child who screams and cries for the entire time-out period and is then released when the predetermined time is up will get the idea that screaming and crying is the way to get released from time-out. It is important to explain to the child that he will be required to sit quietly for a predetermined period of time before being released. This means, of course, that the child may be in time-out for quite a while before this requirement is met. Usually, however, this will occur once or twice before the child learns the rules and settles quickly.

Response Cost. Response cost is another gentle, but effective form of punishment. *Response cost* is punishment by addition (positive punishment) without taking away any reinforcers the way time-out does. Response cost attaches a cost to a target behavior. For example, if a child fights with his brother, he would be punished by having to do an additional household chore. Both time-out and response cost heighten the child's awareness of rewards, services, and privileges that may be taken for granted and has the beneficial effect of helping the child value good things.

Negative Control. Negative control consists of the delivery of an aversive consequence (yelling, spanking, and so on) in the face of a target behavior. While punishment and extinction have been shown to reduce behavior, punishment that is strong and immediate does so much more quickly. For example, the natural consequence of stubbing one's toe when walking down a darkened hall quickly teaches one to turn on the light before embarking down the hall again.

There are many problems with using negative control as a form of punishment, however, and much care must be taken with it because it can often be brutal and dehumanizing. Furthermore, it can produce many undesirable effects. Baldwin and Baldwin (2001) highlight six main problems with using this form of punishment. The first problem is that it often teaches aggression. The recipient of the negative control and onlookers learn, via modeling, that aggression (verbal and physical) is an effective means of dealing with others. Secondly, negative control causes more vigorous responding. Whatever response (crying, talking, hitting) the child was displaying prior to the administration of the aversive consequence, whether the punishment is a harsh criticism or a spanking, is likely to increase in intensity after the punishment. One is also likely to find that the child's behavior becomes more angry and aggressive toward others in these instances. A third problem with negative control is that it has been found to only temporarily suppress undesirable responses or target behaviors and is, therefore, not permanent. A fourth problem with the use of negative control is that it teaches a person to both avoid the punishment and the people who administer the punishment. The child is often motivated to avoid detection and will learn, for instance, to tell more sophisticated lies rather than learn not to lie. Also, once the child has learned to avoid the people who punish him, those people have lost the opportunity to exert positive control. A fifth problem with negative control is that it has been found to condition negative emotions. People who have received frequent punishment in the form of negative control as children learn to respond to a large number of stimuli with negative emotions, such as fear, anxiety, guilt, shame, and bad feelings about themselves. Lastly, negative control can lead to generalized response suppression, resulting in individuals who are highly inhibited, afraid to speak up for themselves, afraid to take the lead, and who are in constant fear of aversive consequences.

Considering the far reaching problems of using negative control, DRO, DRI, extinction, over-correction, and the gentle forms of punishment of time-out and response cost are often more desirable choices for weakening target behavior.

Complex Intervention Procedures

There have been several complex intervention procedures developed using the principles of behavior analysis. These procedures are generally combinations of several of the specific procedures discussed above and include token economies, behavioral contracts, and problem-solving training. Also included in the category of complex intervention procedures are two complex psychotherapies: acceptance and commitment therapy and functional analytic psychotherapy.

Token Economies

A *token economy* is a system in which objects, such as a poker chips, pennies, check marks on a notice board, or gold stars are given to reward or reinforce target behaviors and removed to punish undesirable behaviors. Tokens take on value when they can be exchanged for secondary reinforcers such as extra recess time, snacks, comic books, and toys. Tokens can also be used as secondary punishers. Anyone who has received a traffic or a parking ticket knows that the ticket is a token that precedes the loss of reinforcement (paying the fine) (Baldwin & Baldwin, 2001). We often feel bad as soon as we see the parking ticket under the windshield wiper.

Token economies are often set up in classrooms and reward children for quietly studying, completing homework, and so on. In these settings, tokens are lost for things like disruptive behavior and incomplete assignments. The tokens earned can then be exchanged for extra computer time, extra recess time, or the like. Eisenberger and Selbst (1994) designed a token economy in which fifth and sixth graders were rewarded for creativity and they found that this system significantly increased the children's creativity. Hudson also (1999) notes that the monetary systems of developed countries are, in effect, large-scale token economies.

When designing a token economy, careful and extensive planning must be conducted to ensure that tokens can be only gained through contingent behavior and not through illicit means such as stealing (Hudson, 1999). One must also ensure that the secondary reinforcers are desirable enough to motivate the children and that the most desirable secondary reinforcers are expensive enough to require hard work, but are still accessible (Hudson, 1999).

Behavioral Contracts

Behavioral contracts are agreements, usually written, that detail what reinforcement will be delivered for desirable behavior and what punishment will be delivered for undesirable behavior. Behavioral contracts are often used with children who have behavioral problems at school and can involve an agreement between the teacher and child or an agreement between the parent and child. In the agreement between the teacher and child, the terms are detailed and reinforcement and punishment are delivered by the teacher. In the agreement between the parent and the child the teacher completes a daily report card on the child's behavior in class and the reinforcement and punishment are delivered by the parent at home. Behavioral contracts between parents and a child can also be effectively used to modify the child's behavior at home.

It is essential when establishing a behavioral contract to be as specific as possible about the target behaviors (both desirable and undesirable) and the subsequent reinforcement and punishment. Specificity is necessary to avoid future disputes over what behaviors qualify for reinforcement and punishment under the contract. Also, for a behavioral contract to be effective, it is essential that the person who delivers the consequences be very consistent in doing so. Lastly, behavioral contracts may be most appropriate for older children who can read and abstract sufficiently to understand rule-governed behavior.

Personal Experience Using a Behavioral Contract

David is a ten-year old boy with Asperger's syndrome who was easily distracted and frequently oppositional at school. His mother informed me that she and the school psychologist had developed a behavioral contract for David to help address these problems. They had learned from experience that David really wanted to do well and that he was very sensitive and easily upset when corrected or told he had done something "wrong" or "bad." As a result, his teacher and one-on-one aide tended to frame his behaviors in positive terms. The first step in setting up David's behavioral contract was to solicit his input in developing a list of positively stated target behaviors. This was done with David and his one-on-one aide and was then presented to his teacher for her input. The specific target behaviors were

1. Watch the teacher while she is talking with no more than one reminder.
2. Follow the teacher's direction about assignments with no more than one reminder.
3. Follow the teacher's request to work in a group or with a partner.
4. When not on classroom task, cooperate with the aide and/or allow someone to help him complete his work.

David tended to focus on the here-and-now and had a hard time managing his behaviors over a period of hours. Therefore, the school psychologist divided David's day into three periods: 8:00 a.m. to 10:00 a.m., 10:00 a.m. to noon, and noon to 2:30 p.m. After each period David would meet with his aide and review his target behaviors for that period. David earned twenty cents for each target behavior he was successfully able to complete in the specified time frame. The amount he earned was then recorded on his target behavior form. After school his mother would give him the money he earned that day and he and his mother would discuss how the money would be spent. The discussion had the added benefit of positive social attention from his mother.

Once the behavioral program was implemented, David was better able to focus his attention on meeting his behavior goals. His oppositional behaviors declined and he usually completed his school assignments. I was very impressed with the team approach to David's behavioral contract. This program might well have failed without the commitment and involvement of his parents, his one-on-one aide, his teacher, the school psychologist, and David.

Problem-Solving Training

Problem-solving training is an intervention procedure that is designed to teach children a breadth of problem-solving abilities. Problem-solving training begins with the selection of a particular problem that the child is facing. Once the problem is selected, the child is helped in identifying all of the behavioral options available. The child is then asked to select and try out one of the options. If the selected option is not satisfactory in solving the problem, the trainer and child move onto other options until the problem is satisfactorily solved. The assistance from the trainer is gradually faded as the child moves onto subsequent problems. Problem-solving training is effective because the consequences of the behavioral options chosen are likely to be of a natural nature. Unlike behavioral contracting, the trainer in problem-solving training is not likely to be in control of the consequences the child experiences.

Complex Therapies

Two adult therapies based upon behavior analytic principles are beginning to show promise when used with children. Although a complete discussion of the theories and procedures of each therapy is beyond the scope of this chapter, we would like to highlight a few of the most relevant principles and refer the reader to the appropriate literature for an elaboration of the procedures that accompany the principles.

Acceptance and Commitment Therapy. The first therapy in the category of complex therapies is acceptance and commitment therapy (ACT). ACT is quintessentially behavior analytic in its perspective of thoughts, feelings, and psychological health. Behavior analytic theory defines all things that humans do as behaviors and assumes that they are products of a particular learning history. This definition is not limited to observable behaviors, but also includes thoughts and feelings (Dougher, 1994). Furthermore, because thoughts and feelings are considered to simply be things that one does, they are not given the special status (Dougher, 1994) that they often are in cognitive behavioral therapy (CBT). ACT does not believe that thoughts and feelings (generally, negative) are the causes of suffering or are obstacles to behavior change (Dougher, 1994), but sees the struggle to control them or a person's reaction to them as the source of human distress and suffering. The terms acceptance and commitment in the ACT acronym refer to experiencing the thoughts and feelings that accompany life in this world, understanding them for what they are, and committing to the pursuit of experiences and interactions that give one's life meaning (Dougher, 1994; see Hayes, Jacobson, Follette, & Dougher, 1994, for a detailed description of acceptance and commitment therapy).

Although ACT has been developed and used principally in adult populations, Metzler, Biglan, Noell, Ary, and Ochs (2000) demonstrated that ACT was effective in reducing high-risk sexual behavior in adolescents. The effectiveness of ACT has not been demonstrated with children, and is probably more appropriately used with an adolescent population because ACT techniques rely heavily on the use of abstraction.

Functional Analytic Psychotherapy. Functional analytic psychotherapy (FAP) is another complex treatment based upon behavior analytic principles. FAP focuses on naturally reinforcing client improvements in the therapy session and believes that therapeutic gains made in this manner are more likely to generalize to other areas of a client's life (Kohlenberg & Tsai, 1991). The client-therapist relationship is thought to be a relationship like any other and a setting where client problems are just as likely to occur. FAP has identified three particularly relevant categories of client behavior that are likely to occur in therapy. These behaviors are termed *clinically relevant behaviors* (CRBs) and included the client problems that occur in session, the client improvements that occur in session, and the client's interpretations of his or her own behavior and the causes for it (Kohlenberg & Tsai, 1991). Because CRBs are critical to the effectiveness of this therapeutic approach, FAP requires that the therapist adhere to five technical rules. The first rule stipulates that the therapist watch for all categories of CRBs to occur in session. Secondly, depending upon the severity of a client's life problems, it may be necessary for the therapist to evoke CRBs in session. The therapist is also obligated to reinforce improvements that occur in session through direct and indirect means and avoid using punishment. Fourthly, the therapist is obligated to observe the unintentional, but potentially reinforcing effects of his or her own behavior on client CRBs. Lastly, the therapist is to provide interpretations of variables that affect client behavior, which will help generate more effective rules for the client (Zettle & Hayes, 1982) and increase the client's contact with those variables. (See Kohlenberg & Tsai, 1991, for a detailed discussion of functional analytic psychotherapy.)

Thus far, FAP has been used only in the treatment of depression in an adolescent population (Gaynor & Lawrence, 2002). Therefore, for the present it may not be appropriate for use with younger children.

Empirical Support for Treatment

As mentioned in the introduction, the behavior analytic approach includes assumptions about how to study behavior. In this section, we will discuss this methodology because it is important in understanding how empirical evidence is obtained and reported under this approach. Behavior analysis is concerned with discovering the basic principles behind the behavior of single organisms and, therefore, is not interested in the ways that humans typically behave. As such, single-subject designs (n = 1, within-subject) have been developed to evaluate the effectiveness of behavior analytic treatments. A common misunderstanding about single-subject designs is that it is not possible to make generalizations to the larger population because only a few individuals are used in such studies. This position is valid if the researcher is interested in descriptions of what the typical individual does (Pierce & Epling, 1999). For example, a single-subject design would be inappropriate for evaluating the effects of an advertising campaign to increase sales of a cereal brand.

Because behavior analysts are concerned with the prediction, control, and interpretation of the behavior of single organisms, they are less interested in aggregate or group effects. Generality of findings from a study to other humans is usually demonstrated through replication. In this type of experimental design, an individual is exposed to all values of a variable and then the experiment is run on several participants. Each subsequent participant replicates the experiment and is considered a direct replication. If there are five participants in the study, then the study has been directly replicated five times. Systematic replication is another method of increasing generality. Systematic replication involves systematically altering the procedure in a manner that is logically related to the original research question (Pierce & Epling, 1999).

The most common single-subject research designs used to evaluate behavior analytic treatments are the ABAB and the multiple-baseline designs (Hersen & Barlow, 1984; Hudson, 1999; Kazdin, 1982). The ABAB design consists of a baseline phase, a treatment phase, then a return to the baseline phase, and then another treatment phase. Multiple baseline designs, on the other hand, involve concurrently measuring three target behaviors during the baseline phase and then sequentially introducing the treatment phase for each behavior (Hudson, 1999). Other variations of multiple baseline designs include multiple baselines across behaviors, multiple baselines across subjects, and multiple baselines across settings and follow the general principles of the original multiple baseline design. Generally speaking, for a treatment to be considered effective under this method of research, one must witness a significant shift in the target behavior from that observed during the baseline condition (Pierce & Epling, 1999).

Lastly, because behavior analysis employs a single-subject design to research, it is not conducive to meta-analyses that are typically used to purport the statistical success of a modality. The empirical evidence for behavioral analytic treatments lies in its approach to basic science from which the technology of the treatment is derived. Because behavior analytic treatments are ideographic or custom tailored to each individual and have been applied to nearly every conceivable behavioral excess and deficit, a thorough discussion of the supporting literature beyond what has been done during the discussion of specific techniques is clearly beyond the scope of this chapter. It is safe to say, however, that behavior analysis has found its application in psychopharmacology, psychotherapy, behavior management, and education (Catania, 1984; Smith, 2001).

◆ ◆ ◆

A strength of behavior analysis is that it is a philosophy of science as well as a well-developed methodology. Unlike other systems of psychology, its principles are derived from, not imposed on, research. While it has found application in many areas, it has yet to be applied as fully as possible to complex psychotherapies with children and adolescents. One reason for this may be that behavior analysis explicitly connects behavior to its context and the context for child and adolescent behavior problems may be the family, school, and community. As such, treatments that require familial, school, and community involvement may have been so successful that the demand for the development of individual psychotherapies has been delayed. These psychotherapies hold such promise for internalizing disorders such as anxiety disorders and depression that continued research is certainly warranted.

References

Achenback, T. H., & Edelbrock, C. (1983). *Manual for the child behavior checklist and revised child behavior profile.* Burlington, CT: University Associates in Psychiatry.

Baldwin, J. D., & Baldwin, J. I. (2001). *Behavior principles in everyday life* (4th ed.). Upper Saddle River, NJ: Prentice Hall.

Bandura, A. (1969). *Principles of behavior modification.* New York: Holt, Rinehart & Winston.

Bandura, A. (1977). Self efficacy: Toward a unifying theory of behavior change. *Psychological Review, 84,* 191–215.

Belsky, J., & Rovine, M. (1990). Patterns of marital change across the transition to parenthood: Pregnancy to three years postpartum. *Journal of Marriage and the Family, 52*(1), 5–19.

Besevegis, E., & Lore, R. K. (1983). Effects of an adult's presence on the social behavior of preschool children. *Aggressive Behavior, 9,* 243–252.

Bijou, S. W., & Baer, D. M. (1961). *Child development I: A systematic and empirical theory* (Vol. 1). New York: Appletone-Century-Crofts.

Bijou, S. W., & Baer, D. M. (1978). *Behavior analysis of child development.* Englewood Cliffs, NJ: Prentice-Hall.

Catania, A. C. (1984). The operant behaviorism of B. F. Skinner. *Behavioral and Brain Sciences, 7,* 473–475.

Cohn, D. A., Silver, D. H., & Cowan, C. P. (1992). Working models of childhood attachment and couple relationships. *Journal of Family Issues, 13*(4), 432–449.

Cooper, J., Heron, T., & Heward, W. (1987). *Applied behavior analysis.* Columbus, OH: Merrill.

Cowan, P. A., Cowan, C. P., & Schulz, M. S. (1994). Prebirth to preschool family factors in children's adaptations to kindergarten. In R. D. Parke & S. G. Kellan (Eds.), *Exploring family relationships with other social contexts* (pp. 75–114). Hillsdale, NJ: Erlbaum.

Dougher, M. J. (1994). The act of acceptance. In S. C. Hayes, N. S. Jacobson, V. M. Follette, & M. J. Dougher (Eds.), *Acceptance and change: Content and context in psychotherapy* (pp. 37–45). Reno, NV: Context Press.

Dougher, M. J., & Hayes, S. C. (2000). Clinical behavior analysis. In M. J. Dougher (Ed.), *Clinical behavior analysis* (pp. 11–25). Reno, NV: Context Press.

Eisenberger, R., & Selbst, M. (1994). Does reward increase or decrease creativity? *Journal of Personality and Social Psychology, 66,* 1116–1128.

Fainsilber-Katz, L., & Gottman, J. M. (1994). Patterns of marital interaction and children's emotional development. In R. D. Parke & S. G. Kellan (Eds.), *Exploring family relationships with other social contexts* (pp. 49–74). Hillsdale, NJ: Erlbaum.

Gaynor, S. T., & Lawrence, P. S. (2002). Completmenting CBT for depressed adolescents with Learning through In Vivo Experience (LIVE): Conceptual analysis, treatment description and feasibility study. *Behavioral & Cognitive Psychotherapy, 30*(1), 79–101.

Grant, L., & Evans, A. (1994). *Principles of behavior analysis.* New York: Harper Collins.

Harrington, J. A., Fink, B. C., & Dougher, M. J. (2001). Into the lion's den: Incorporating personality and evolutionary psychology to expand clinical behavior analysis. *International Journal of Psychology and Psychological Therapy, 1*(2), 175–189.

Hersen, M., & Barlow, D. (1984). *Single case experimental designs: Strategies for studying behavior change* (2nd ed.). New York: Pergamon Press.

Hudson, A. (1999). Behavior analysis. In R. Ollendick (Ed.), *Handbook of psychotherapies with children and families* (pp. 181–197). New York: Kluwer/Plenum.

Iwata, B. A., Pace, G. M., Dorsey, M. F., Zarcone, J. R., Vollmer, T. R., Smith, R. G., et al. (1994). The functions of self-injurious behavior: An experimental-epidemiological analysis. *Journal of Applied Behavior Analysis, 27,* 215–240.

Kazdin, A. E. (1987). *Single-case research designs: Methods for clinical and research settings.* New York: Oxford University Press.

Kellam, S. G., Ling, X., Meriaca, R., Brown, C. H., & Ialongo, N. (1998). The effect of the level of aggression on the first grade classroom on the course and malleability of aggressive behavior into middle school. *Development and Psychology, 10,* 165–185.

Kohlenberg, R. J., & Tsai, M. (1991). *Functional analytic psychotherapy: Creating intense and curative therapeutic relationships.* New York, NY: Plenum Press.

Locke, H. J., & Wallace, K. M. (1959). Short marital-adjustment and prediction tests: Their reliability and validity. *Marriage and Family Living, 21,* 251–255.

Martin, G., & Pear, J. (1996). *Behavior modification: What it is and how to do it.* (5th ed.). Englewood Cliffs, NJ: Prentice-Hall.

Meichenbaum, D. H. (1977). *Cognitive-behavior modification: An integrative approach.* New York: Plenum.

Metzler, C. W., Biglan, A., Noell, J. Ary, D., & Ochs, L. (2000). A randomized controlled trial of a behavioral intervention to reduce high-risk sexual behavior among adolescents in STD clinics. *Behavior Therapy, 31,* 27–54.

Novak, G. (1996). *Developmental psychology: Dynamical systems and behavior analysis.* Reno, NV: Context Press.

O'Brien, R. M., & Simek, T. C. (1983). A comparison of behavioral and traditional methods for teaching golf. In G. L. Martin, D. Harycaiko (Eds.), *Behavior modification and coaching: Principles, procedures and research* (pp. 175–183). Springfield, IL: Charles C. Thomas.

Pierce, W. D., & Epling, W. F. (1999). *Behavior analysis and learning* (2nd ed.). Upper Saddle River, NJ: Prentice-Hall.

Richman, D. M., Berg, W. K., Wacher, D. P., Stephens, T., Rankin, B., & Kilroy, J. (1997). Using pretreatment and posttreatment assessments to enhance and evaluate existing treatment packages. *Journal of Applied Behavior Analysis, 30,* 709–712.

Ross, A. O. (1976). *Psychological disorders of children: A behavioral approach.* New York: McGraw-Hill.

Smith, N. W. (2001). *Current systems in psychology: History, theory, research and applications.* Belmont, CA: Wadsworth/Thomson Learning.

Spanier, G. B., & Thompson, L. (1982). A confirmatory analysis of the dyadic adjustment scale. *Journal of Marriage and the Family, 44*(3), 731–738.

Sulzer-Azaroff, B., & Mayer, G. R. (1991). *Behavior analysis for lasting change.* New York: Holt, Rinehart & Winston.

Turnbull, H. R. (1981). *The least restrictive alternative: Principles and practice.* Washington, D.C.: American Association on Mental Deficiency.

Watson, J. B. (1913). Psychology as a behaviorist views it. *Psychological Review, 20,* 158–177.

Watson, J. B. (1924). *Behaviorism.* New York: Norton.

Zettle, R. D., & Hayes, S. C. (1982). Rule governed behavior: A potential theoretical framework for cognitive-behavioral therapy. In P. C. Kendall (Ed.), *Advances in cognitive behavioral research and therapy* (Vol. 1). New York: Academic Press.

CHAPTER EIGHTEEN

COGNITIVE BEHAVIORAL THERAPY WITH CHILDREN AND ADOLESCENTS

Sarah J. Erickson, Ph.D., and Georgianna Achilles, Ph.D.

The guiding theory for cognitive behavioral therapy (CBT) with children and adolescents adopts a developmentally informed problem-solving orientation, addressing cognitive information processing and emotional states, incorporating multiple levels of the child's social and interpersonal environment, and employing structured and performance-based interventions (Kendall, 2000a). The primary goal of CBT is to modify maladaptive emotional, cognitive, and behavioral responses to one's environment (Krain & Kendall, 1999). Both internal and external environments of the child are considered in this framework: therapists assist children in understanding, primarily through experiential procedures, how thoughts, feelings, and behaviors mutually influence each other. In this way, CBT integrates cognitive and behavioral approaches to problem-solving, including cognitive processing (such as generating alternatives, evaluating outcomes) and skill development (such as modeling, role playing, behavioral rehearsal), reinforced by contingencies, feedback, and support to effect cognitive, behavioral, and affective change (Kendall, 1991; Krain & Kendall, 1999).

The CBT model of child and adolescent psychological distress emphasizes the learning process, the influence of environmental contingencies and models, and the individual's cognitive information processing style (Kendall, 2000a). Because maladaptive information processing is conceptualized to be at the core of behavioral and emotional difficulties, CBT therapy incorporates new cognitive schema generation and concomitant behavioral and emotional strategies in constructing new templates of making sense of one's world.

Compared with all other treatment modalities with children and adolescents, therapies that are more structured, such as CBT and behavioral therapy, have amassed the strongest empirical support over the past two decades (Kazdin & Weiss, 1998; Weisz, Weiss, Han, Granger, & Morton, 1995). Relatively structured, brief therapy with measurable, often observable, outcomes is a hallmark of CBT. In fact, the nature of CBT in part explains its impressive standing in outcome research. In addition, the number of published CBT and behavioral therapy outcome studies greatly overshadows the number of all other, less structured, therapy outcome studies.

Putative Mechanisms of Efficacy

Whereas processes of change are the primary foci of all therapies, within CBT these processes include an integration of behaviors, associated cognitions (such as anticipatory cognitions, subsequent attributions, information processing), and emotions. For each problem or disorder experienced by a child, it is essential to address each of these domains, as it is their complex interplay that is believed to result in the disorder. Depending on the developmental level of the child and nature of the disorder, differential attention is given to cognitive techniques (such as cognitive restructuring), behavioral techniques (such as behavioral rehearsal), and emotion management (Kendall, 1993).

The cognitive element of CBT addresses how children think about themselves, their world, and the influence each has on the other. Kendall, Flannery-Schroeder, Panichelli-Mindel, and Gerow (1995) review four components of cognition that together dynamically interact to form individual perceptions and expectations about the world. Cognitive *structure* is the memory storage, processing, and filtering component of cognition. Cognitive *content* refers to the information stored in memory that shapes internal dialogue. Cognitive *process* refers to the perception and interpretation of experiences. Cognitive *products* are the conclusive thoughts that are reached through the interaction of content, structure, and process. Cognitive therapy seeks to modify maladaptive cognition through attention to these multiple domains.

Kendall (1993) enumerates two types of maladaptive cognitions to be addressed in therapy: distortions and deficiencies. *Distortions* refer to misinterpretations of events, experiences, or the environment, whereas *deficits* refer to lapses or difficulties in thinking about the possible consequences of behavior. Cognitive distortions are often present in children with internalizing disorders. In fact, depressive disorders are generally characterized by the specific distortions of attributing negative outcomes to internal, global, and stable causes. Cognitive deficiencies are primarily exhibited by children with externalizing disorders wherein their difficulties often include an inability to take into account the likely consequences of their behavior. Both distortions and deficiencies can co-occur, as in the case of aggressive children who misread the intentions of others, assume more positive consequences, and minimize negative consequences of their behavior (Dodge, 1986; Kendall & McDonald, 1993).

The initial step of most cognitive interventions includes increasing the child's awareness of his or her thoughts and how they influence behavior and emotions (Krain & Kendall, 1999). Children are taught how to monitor their thoughts and how to apply various techniques to alter their thoughts. Cognitive strategies employed with children include problem solving, cognitive restructuring, reframing, and learning new coping skills. A hallmark of most CBT involves problem solving, which includes identifying the problem and the environmental contingencies, identifying possible solutions and their likely outcomes, selecting and implementing a plan, and evaluating the plan. In this framework of learning how to manage difficult situations, children learn how to cope more effectively, generate alternatives, and persist in their efforts toward a given outcome.

The behavioral component of CBT focuses on behavior modification of maladaptive behaviors and skill acquisition of adaptive behaviors. Both internal and external sources of reinforcement are employed toward this aim. Typically, external reinforcement is more prevalent at the beginning of behavior modification, with internal reinforcement gradually taking over external reinforcement over the course of treatment. Attributing success to oneself as opposed to others or the result of medication is important in improving self-confidence and self-esteem, and in maintaining gains achieved through treatment. Behavioral rehearsal, in the form of role playing and modeling, is the primary behavioral method of helping children learn new skills and ways of coping. In role playing, typically the initial form of behavioral rehearsal, the child learns and practices new skills in the safe confines of the therapeutic relationship. The child can either play himself or herself in a difficult situation, or the therapist can play the child, demonstrating an approach to a difficult scenario. In this way, the child solves the problem with the therapist and evaluates his or her efforts without fear of reprisal.

Modeling processes allow children to observe and participate in difficult situations, try alternative efforts, and evaluate their effects. Coping modeling, in which the therapist models addressing problems (cognitive, behavioral, emotional, environmental) impeding a successful outcome, is often more helpful than mastery modeling, in which the therapist demonstrates obtaining the successful outcome (Krain & Kendall, 1999). Coping modeling assists the child in understanding how to solve problems in difficult situations. Modeling can be symbolic (such as watching videotapes of someone performing a difficult task), live (demonstration by the therapist or another child of handling a difficult situation), or participant (the child is with the therapist or another child while they encounter the difficult situation). Participant modeling is the most efficacious form of modeling in that it encourages the child to learn and practice new skills while encountering the difficult situation. To maximize the efficacy of behavioral rehearsal, the child must be attentive, retain the information (that is, learn), practice the targeted behavior, and receive reinforcement (often in the form of praise and positive attributions toward self). These processes can occur only if the child's anxiety is manageable enough to allow him or her to attend to the difficult situation and not only to internal anxiety states.

Thus, in learning how to cope with difficult situations, some children are taught relaxation exercises, such as progressive muscle relaxation, in order to manage their anxiety. Exposure and response prevention may also be employed with anxious children, typically after relaxation training. Exposure tasks increase children's self-confidence by exposing them to feared or anxiety-provoking situations, allowing them to use their newly acquired coping skills, and to experience success in facing difficult situations. Exposure to feared stimuli generally proceeds in a hierarchical fashion, with less feared situations introduced first. For example, exposure typically begins with the child imagining the feared situation, identifying thoughts and feelings, and imagining coping with the anxiety and the situation. Then the child is exposed to real situations and is required to put into practice newly learned coping skills. It is essential that the exposure process is gradual and that the child is well prepared so that he or she experiences success: some anxiety is necessary for motivation and is anticipated during difficult situations, but too much anxiety can impede successful resolution and can even be experienced as traumatic. Response prevention refers to the prevention of responses that decrease anxiety but preclude a child from experiencing success. For example, a child may have coped with anxiety-provoking stimuli by avoidance, thereby limiting the ability to practice coping and achieve a desirable outcome. In the response prevention component of exposure, the child is prevented from avoiding the situation and must employ his or her new skills in order to address anxiety and cope effectively.

Unique to CBT, the therapist's role is to serve as a consultant, diagnostician, and educator to the child and family (Kendall, 1991; Krain & Kendall, 1999). The therapeutic relationship is collaborative, with the therapist assisting in the problem-solving process and outcome evaluation. Instead of simply offering solutions, the therapist acts as a consultant in assisting a child to identify possible solutions, processes in order to achieve a given result, and methods of evaluating the efficacy of such efforts. The therapist's diagnostic role goes beyond assessing DSM criteria and involves a hypothesis-testing approach to understanding the child in his or her environment. Specifically, the CBT therapist gathers and integrates information about the child's behaviors in multiple settings by multiple informants. In general, internal states (such as feelings and a subjective sense of well being or distress) and internalizing disorders (such as anxiety and depressive disorders) are best evaluated by the child, whereas behaviors and externalizing disorders (for example, ADHD, oppositional defiant disorder, and conduct disorder) are best evaluated by informed adults. Ideally, multiple methods (such as observation, parent and teacher reports, child self-assessment, formal testing, and physiological indices if appropriate) are employed in obtaining information. All of this information is then integrated to test hypotheses about the etiology, influences, and consequences of the child's problems, with an eye toward intervention. In addition, the therapist plays the role of educator throughout the therapy process by assisting the child in learning new cognitive and behavioral skills, such as hypothesis testing and social skills, and identifying exactly how thoughts, behaviors, and feelings are related and contributing to the child's difficulties (Krain & Kendall, 1999).

In addition to these features specific to CBT, there are common elements in most therapies that contribute to positive outcomes. Although the vast majority of these qualitative studies are with adults, common therapeutic elements identified in therapy process studies with children include therapist techniques that initiate activities and actively include a child in the therapy process (Stith, Rosen, McCollum, Coleman, & Herman, 1996). Certainly these "common" features are present in CBT with children and may therefore also explain how CBT achieves its desired outcomes.

Developmental Systems Perspective

Across all treatment modalities, placing children's difficulties in a developmental systems framework is essential. Children's diagnostic and intervention guidelines have historically been adevelopmental, resulting from downward extensions of adult diagnostic and intervention approaches. This inherent "developmental uniformity myth" (Kendall, Lerner, & Craighead, 1984) that psychiatric disorders manifest in the same way independent of age and developmental level results in interventions that do not account for developmental issues and changes. In contrast, an organizational perspective on development (Cicchetti, 1993) suggests that as each new stage-related issue emerges, an individual is faced with opportunities for growth and reorganization, as well as for challenges and the possibility of maladaptation. Successful resolution of an earlier stage-related task increases the likelihood of future successful adjustment (Sroufe & Rutter, 1984). In this model of ongoing developmental processes, reorganization, and consolidation, new adaptations or maladaptations can manifest at various times through the life span and interact with the individual's prior developmental organization (Cicchetti & Tucker, 1994). Therefore, an understanding of each child's individual developmental organization is necessary in order to inform therapeutic interventions.

The principles of developmental psychopathology have significant implications for interventions with children and adolescents (Toth & Cicchetti, 1999). CBT addresses developmental influences in its guiding theory and techniques: children are considered within their many interacting and influencing environments and developmental domains. One of the primary goals of CBT is to assist children in maintaining, aligning with, or enhancing normal developmental trajectories (Kendall, 2000a). CBT theory recognizes that it is within the social domain that children interact reciprocally and their functioning is characterized as adaptive or maladaptive. This perspective has implications for assessment, case formulation, and treatment: each child is seen as developing within and influencing his or her multiple environments. Braswell (1991) emphasizes the importance of including parents in therapy in her in-depth discussion of social context in CBT work. Parents have special knowledge about their children that can contribute to therapeutic progress. Also, including parents allows for better understanding of the bi-directional processes between child and parent characteristics (emotional state, perceptions, reactivity) as well as family characteristics (interpersonal dynamics, magnitude of family stress) that can provide useful information regarding factors that influence a child's behavior, cognition, and emotion.

In addition, developmental timing of interventions is an important consideration in CBT. At the most basic level, behavior is the primary focus of treatment with very young children because of their limited developmental competencies. Because causal reasoning, emotion understanding, self-understanding, and language ability all change in content, organization, and structure during development (Toth & Cicchetti, 1999), these factors must be accounted for when providing interventions to children. For example, because young children are unable to relate emotional or behavioral experiences to internal, unobservable, or past events, insight is not a reasonable goal for a young child. Until children have developed a theory of mind, they cannot conceptualize and subsequently alter their thought processes. Instead, CBT treatments for young children focus on current correlates of affect or behavior; and many treatments for this population focus on parent training and behavior management. (See Webster-Stratton, 1998 for an example.) In contrast, when children develop abstract cognitive capacities during early adolescence, cognitions as well as behavior are primary targets of most CBT interventions. Key therapeutic challenges emerging during adolescence often relate to the adolescent's growing autonomy, family conflict, and motivation, wherein adolescents and their parents disagree on whether treatment is needed, who should be included in treatment, the nature of the problem, and goals of treatment. In this way, developmental timing and cognitive as well as psychosocial capacities of children are taken into account in CBT interventions.

For example, in the CB treatment of children with obsessive-compulsive disorder (OCD), a decreased ability to articulate fears and triggers may complicate assessment and the development of an appropriate treatment plan. Also, children are less able to conceptualize the benefit of experiencing anxiety in the present to obtain future benefits. Motivation and compliance may be further restricted by an inability to perceive their anxiety as abnormal, a low frustration tolerance, and poor coping skills (Piacentini, 1999). Treatment protocols have been developed with these cognitive and motivational limitations in mind, and have considered comorbidity and family functioning as well. (See March, Mulle, & Herbel, 1994.)

In addition to sensitivity to the developmental period in which an intervention is employed, interventions may also need to take into account when in childhood a negative, potentially pathology-inducing insult occurred (Toth & Cicchetti, 1999). For example, according to Cicchetti and Toth (1998), if a child suffered sexual abuse when he or she was preverbal, more experiential and less verbally reliant approaches may be most effective because the abuse memory was not verbally encoded. In such an example, information about developmental timing would potentially yield a CBT focus on behavioral mastery and affective states, with relatively less emphasis on cognitions.

Because children have less control over selecting and modifying their environment, it is important to understand the larger context within which a child functions. Social environments, including family, peers, school, and the larger community, not only have considerable impact on a child's current psychological functioning, but may also differentially influence and support a child's therapeutic progress. For example, behaviors that may be considered maladaptive and therefore potential targets for treatment in a school setting, such as noncompliance or fighting, may be reinforced, either consciously or unwittingly, by parents. In this way, the environmental context for the range of childhood behaviors must be considered before a behavior is characterized as maladaptive.

Putative Targets of Cognitive Behavioral Treatment

Cognitive behavioral targets of treatment are formulated with consideration of the nature of the disturbance and related symptomatology, and the age and developmental functioning of the child. In their review of CBT for children,

Braswell and Kendall (2001) identified problem-solving, cognitive restructuring, self-regulation, affective education, relaxation training, modeling, role playing and behavioral contingencies as important treatment elements in targeting maladaptive cognitions, behavior, and affect. Specific treatment components are selected and emphasized to match the diagnostic and developmental needs of the child. For example, because younger children's capacity to reflect on their own thinking is rather limited, treatments for them tend to be more behavioral and less cognitive in nature. Treatments tend to emphasize coping skills and cognitive restructuring for internalizing disorders, and reinforcement contingency and social problem-solving for externalizing disorders (Krain & Kendall, 1999).

Internalizing Disorders

Anxiety Disorders

A well-established CBT approach for treating a variety of anxiety-disordered youth emphasizes the identification of anxious thoughts and feelings, problem-solving skills training for coping with anxiety, and self-evaluation and reward (Howard & Kendall, 1996). Coping skills are enhanced through the use of behavioral techniques such as modeling, role playing, relaxation training, in vivo exposure, and reinforcement contingencies (with an emphasis on social reinforcement). When families are included in treatment, treatment encourages expression of negative affect, discussion of problems, problem-solving, and respect for the child's perspective. A contextual approach to considering the child's expressed anxiety symptoms within the dynamic family and extended system is emphasized. The family is empowered to participate in learning about and supporting the adaptive development of the child (Howard & Kendall, 1996).

Treatment efforts for OCD include the above mentioned targets, but also target obsessive thinking and behavior through exposure and response prevention (ERP). The objective of ERP is to trigger obsessive patterns and prevent the performance of associated compulsions in order to achieve autonomic habituation and dissipation of anxiety (Piacentini, 1999). In a related effort, treatment of phobias target fear, avoidance, and social and problem-solving skill deficits through self-monitoring, fear, and avoidance hierarchies, education, cognitive restructuring, social skill deficits, and problem-solving skill training (Albano, Detweiler, & Logsdon-Conradsen, 1999).

Depression. For treatment of depression, foci include cognitive distortions, social skill and problem-solving deficits, maladaptive attributional styles, poor self-concept, and the use of passive or avoidant coping strategies (Reinecke, Ryan, & DuBois, 1998). These targets are similar to those targeted in anxiety treatment, but the nature of the cognitive distortions and skill deficits are qualitatively different.

Post-traumatic Stress Disorder. When children suffer from traumatic experiences (such as child abuse, violence, disasters, accidents, war, or sudden death of a family member) and either develop or are at risk of developing Post-traumatic Stress Disorder (PTSD), targets of treatment are multi-faceted to address the range of problematic symptomatology that may develop. In addition to general targets of treatment, trauma-specific distortions are targeted (such as feeling they may have caused the event, expectations of bad events in the future). Stress management in the form of relaxation therapy is used to reduce hypervigilance and anxiety. Thought stopping and replacement is used to help the child to recognize and stop negative thoughts and to replace them with more positive thoughts and empowering self-talk. Further, parental involvement provides support for the child, allows family dysfunction to be addressed, and encourages the reinforcement of therapeutic objectives at home (Cohen, Mannarino, Berliner, & Deblinger, 2000).

Eating Disorders. Models for treating eating disorders tend to integrate behavioral techniques for weight gain, cognitive behavioral techniques to modify cognitive distortions, and family components to change existing patterns and support the patient's progress. For example, Robin and colleagues employ the behavioral family systems therapy (BFST) approach to treating adolescents who have anorexia nervosa (Robin, Bedway, Siegel, & Gilroy, 1996). Although this treatment is a behavioral family systems-based treatment, targeting cognitive distortions related to body perceptions and fear of becoming fat is the primary focus of the cognitive component of intervention (Robin et al., 1996).

Externalizing Disorders

Aggression, Anger, and Disorders of Conduct

Targets of treatment for externalizing disorders (oppositional defiant disorder, conduct disorder, ADHD, antisocial behavior, delinquency) often include dysfunctional social-interpersonal cognitive processes, outcome expectations, and reinforcement values in an effort to address anger and aggression (Lochman, Whidby, & Fitzgerald, 2000). Lochman and colleagues (2000) contend that deficits in executive cognitive functioning may be associated with poor self-control, the root of multiple behavioral and psychosocial problems including aggression. In an effort to encourage appropriate self-control, CBT with aggressive children targets perceptual and cognitive processes stemming from perceived threats and frustrations. Specifically, deficient and distorted cognitive processing in response to social conflicts or perceived threats and regulation of anger are foci of intervention. The conceptualization of nonaggressive problem-solving options is encouraged (Braswell & Kendall, 2001). These objectives are emphasized in problem-solving skill training (PSST), an empirically supported CBT protocol.

In addition, parent-focused intervention is becoming recognized as a valuable therapeutic component in targeting maladaptive family patterns that serve to maintain problem behaviors. In parent management training (PMT), parents are trained to identify problem behaviors in systematic terms, to identify within the family maladaptive interactional patterns that reinforce negative child behaviors. They are taught the principles of social learning, behavior modification, and changing well-established patterns to support and reinforce prosocial behavior (Lis, Zennaro, & Mazzeschi, 2001).

Attention-Deficit/Hyperactivity Disorder. Successful models for the treatment of ADHD have primarily emphasized pharmacological intervention and behavioral contingency programs (home and school) that often involve parent training. Foci of behavioral programs include increasing on-task and rule-governed behavior and decreasing impulsivity (Craighead, Craighead, Kazdin, & Mahoney, 1994). However, Hinshaw (2000) considers cognitive components to be a useful adjunct to behavioral models and can be applied, for example, in the improvement of interpersonal skills. Integrative protocols with attention-disordered youth have included problem solving, self-monitoring, and behavioral management techniques (Fonagy, Target, Cottrell, Phillips, & Kurtz, 2002).

Empirical Support

Support for the efficacy of cognitive behavioral treatments with children and adolescents has been established empirically for both internalizing (anxiety, depression, PTSD, and more limited support for eating disorders) (Flannery-Schroeder et al., 1996; Kendall, 2000b) and externalizing disorders (oppositional defiant disorder, conduct disorder, and more limited support for ADHD) (Kendall, 2000b). The following review presents controlled studies offering substantial empirical support for child and adolescent cognitive behavioral treatments. Both individual and group formats are included.

Several notable findings have emerged from broad reviews of child and adolescent therapy interventions. They include the general superiority of individual to group format, behaviorally based protocols to non-behavioral protocols, targeting specific problems to overall adjustment. Older child age and female gender are also associated with better outcomes. Findings for long-term efficacy suggest maintenance of gains at six months post-treatment (Kazdin, 2000; Weisz et al., 1995).

Internalizing Disorders

Empirical Support for Cognitive Behavioral Treatment of Depression

CBT for childhood and adolescent depression enjoys stronger empirical support than any other treatment orientation. Because adolescent depression is more prevalent than child depression, many of the CBT trials include adolescent samples. A review and meta-analysis of empirical studies of adolescent depression conducted between 1970 and 1997 supports the efficacy of CBT for depression and depressive symptoms among adolescents (Reinecke, Ryan, & DuBois, 1998). Studies were included if they employed random assignment of subjects and the use of a control group. Group and individual formats were included. All studies shared common protocol tasks of identifying and modifying distorted thinking and teaching new processing styles. Post-treatment and follow-up data from 217 subjects across six studies were assessed to determine treatment outcome gains and their stability over time. Results reflected moderate to large effect sizes at post-treatment and maintenance of gains at follow-up (Reinecke et al., 1998). Another review of CBT outcome studies with depressed adolescents suggested similar findings, revealing CBT-treated children to be more likely to be in remission from childhood depressive disorder by the end of treatment than inactive treatment comparison groups (Harrington, Whittaker, Shoebridge, & Campbell, 1998).

Recent studies by Brent and colleagues (Brent et al., 1997; Brent et al., 1998; Brent, Kolko, Birmaher, Baugher, & Bridge, 1999) compared CBT to other interventions with depressed adolescents and considered contextual factors related to change. In these studies, CBT, systemic-behavioral family therapy, and nondirective supportive therapy conditions were compared in 107 adolescents. Findings reflected more rapid remission and better clinical remission of depressive symptomatology in the CBT condition than the other two conditions. In addition, level of depression was predictive of clinical remission (Brent et al., 1997). In accounting for contextual factors, the relative power of CBT to effect change was diminished in the presence of maternal depression, and the CBT condition was identified to be particularly helpful for patients with comorbid anxiety (Brent et al., 1998). Later referral for additional follow-up treatment was not predicted by the CBT condition, but was best predicted by severity of depressive symptoms immediately post-treatment, and level of disruptive behavior and family dysfunction (Brent et al., 1999).

Other studies have contributed to our understanding of the influence of contextual factors and individual characteristics on the efficacy of CBT for depression. Southam-Gerow, Kendall, and Weersing (2001) summarized key findings regarding treatment response in depressed adolescents, citing symptom severity and problematic cognitions as the most consistent correlates of poor response. One study found younger age and less social impairment (associated with lower severity of depression) to be associated with greater likelihood of remission (Jayson, Wood, Kroll, Fraser, & Harrington, 1998). Extending treatment or providing booster sessions to non-responders has been found to improve response (Clarke, Rohde, Lewinshon, Hops, & Seely, 1999). An early finding suggested a strong trend towards superiority of including parents in CBT treatment of depression (Lewinsohn, Clark, Hops, & Andrews, 1990), while a more recent study by the same group did not show differential effectiveness (Clarke et al., 1999). In addition, family therapy alone has been indicated as less effective than CBT for depressed adolescents (Brent et al., 1997).

Although most of the empirical support comes from studies conducted with mild to moderately impaired adolescents (Fonagy et al., 2002), empirical efficacy for the use of CBT with depressed children has also recently been supported in controlled studies. Weersing & Weisz (2002) compared symptom trajectories of sixty-seven youth (ages seven to seventeen) treated in community mental health centers (CMHCs) to those receiving CBT in clinical trials. Results suggested that CBT treatments were more effective than CMHC treatments. Shorter length of treatment and ethnic minority status predicted poorer outcomes. After controlling for these factors, CBT remained superior to CMHC treatment (Weersing & Weisz, 2002).

Asarnow, Scott, and Mintz (2002) evaluated the efficacy of a brief combined CB family education intervention for children reporting depressive symptoms. Twenty-three children (fourth through sixth grades) were randomly assigned to treatment or wait-list conditions. At post-treatment, treated children evidenced fewer depressive symptoms, less negative automatic thinking, and fewer internalized approaches to coping. In addition, Weisz and his colleagues (Weisz, Thurber, Sweeney, Proffitt, & LeGagnoux, 1997) identified forty-eight elementary-age children (third through sixth grade) exhibiting clinical levels of depressive symptoms on diagnostic rating scales. Sixteen of the children were administered an eight-session CBT protocol. The remaining children served as the no-treatment control group. The treatment group showed significant symptom remission, about twice the reduction in depression scores as the control group. Furthermore, among the 60% of the treated children available for nine-month follow-up analysis, significant treatment gains were maintained (Weisz et al., 1997).

Empirical Support for Cognitive-Behavioral Treatment of Anxiety Disordered Youth. Cognitive-behavioral and behavioral approaches have received more empirical support than other treatment modalities for the treatment of childhood anxiety disorders (Albano & Kendall, 2002; Ollendick & King, 1998). Kendall and his colleagues have conducted efficacy trials of CBT with a variety of anxiety disordered youth. This series of clinical trials have been conducted with nine- to thirteen-year-olds (Kendall, 1994; Kendall et al., 1997; Kendall & Southam-Gerow, 1996). Protocols involve sixteen to twenty individual sessions, divided into two segments. The first segment is primarily educational, encouraging child recognition of somatic, cognitive, and behavioral aspects of anxiety. The child learns to identify and modify anxiety enhancing cognitive distortions. Alternative solutions are developed that may lead to more adaptive coping. Subsequently, the coping plan is evaluated and children self-reward their efforts. The second segment focuses on the application of new skills in situations specific to the child's anxieties as well as continued self-evaluation and reinforcement aimed at maintenance of coping (Kendall & Treadwell, 1996).

Outcomes for this randomized controlled trial (n = 47) included 60% of treated cases no longer meeting diagnostic criteria post-treatment versus 5% of the wait-list group. Post-treatment gains for the treated group included self-reported anxiety and depression, and behavioral observations of anxious distress. Parents and teachers reported improvements in child internalizing behavior problems, and parents indicated improvements in social and health problems and trait anxiety. Treatment gains were maintained at one-year follow-up (Kendall, 1994). A recent study with a larger sample replicated earlier results: 71% of adolescents no longer met diagnostic criteria for anxiety at the end of treatment, versus 5.8% of the wait-list control group (Kendall et al., 1997).

Not only does CBT appear to be efficacious for anxiety disordered youth, but treatment gains appear to be sustained over time. In a follow-up study (n = 36) of cognitive behavioral treated youth, an average of 3.35 years post-treatment, self and parent report and structured diagnostic interviews indicated that treatment gains were maintained in the population over time on measures of anxiety symptoms (self and parent-report), and self-reported levels of anxious self-talk and depression (Kendall & Southam-Gerow, 1996).

In a more recent study, Lumpkin, Silverman, Weems, Markham, and Kurtines (2002) applied a multiple baseline group cognitive behavioral therapy (GCBT) to a diagnostically heterogeneous, anxiety-disordered group of children and adolescents. Twelve participants ranged in age from six to sixteen years. Post-treatment analyses indicated 50% remission of anxiety symptoms immediately post-treatment, 83% remission at six months, and 75% remission at twelve months.

The findings support the application of GCBT across the range of anxiety disorder diagnoses.

Flannery-Schroeder and Kendall (2000) randomly assigned thirty-seven primarily anxiety-disordered children (ages eight to fourteen) to one of three conditions: individual cognitive-behavioral treatment, group cognitive-behavioral treatment, or a wait-list control group. Treatment included education about emotional, physiological, and cognitive components of anxiety, as well as behavioral and exposure techniques. At immediate post-treatment, a significantly greater proportion of children receiving treatment (73% individual, 50% group) compared to wait-listed controls (8%) exhibited remission from their primary anxiety-related diagnosis. Both individual and group-based improvements were maintained three months post-treatment.

The relative impact of including families in cognitive-behavioral intervention with anxiety disordered youth was explored by Barrett, Dadds, and Rapee (1996). CBT intervention was based on an adaptation of Kendall's model with exposure and cognitive restructuring as the primary components (Kendall & Treadwell, 1996). Seventy-nine subjects, ages seven to fourteen, were randomly assigned to three groups: CBT, CBT with family therapy, and wait-list control group. The family component taught parents skills in problem solving, communication, behavioral contingency management, and modeling appropriate behavior. At post-treatment, the treatment component of CBT and family therapy (84% remission) was superior to CBT only (57% remission) and to the wait-list control (26% remission). Treatment gains were maintained at one-year follow-up. Similarly, Mendlowitz and colleagues (1999, as reviewed in Braswell & Kendall, 2001) reported greater improvements on active coping strategies and parent-rated emotional well-being for anxiety-disordered children in a condition where they and their parents received group treatment compared to conditions of child-only or parent-only group treatment.

Although research examining correlates of treatment response for a variety of childhood disorders is quite limited, one study identified such response correlates in anxiety-disordered youths (Southam-Gerow et al., 2001). One hundred and thirty-five CBT-treated youths were divided into two groups: poor treatment responders and good treatment responders. Correlates of poor response included higher pretreatment internalizing psychopathological tendencies of the child (obtained through maternal and teacher report), higher maternal self-reported depressive symptoms, and older child age.

Empirical Support for CBT with Obsessive-Compulsive Disorder. Fonagy and colleagues (2002) contend that because there are only a few randomized controlled trials of CBT with children who have OCD, the efficacy of CBT for treating OCD has yet to be convincingly demonstrated. In addition, because children with OCD are frequently treated pharmacologically, there are only a couple of small studies that attempt to delineate the effect of pharmacological treatment plus CBT versus pharmacological treatment alone versus CBT alone. Although larger, controlled studies are needed, smaller, primarily naturalistic studies provide optimism regarding the ERP model for children with OCD. One controlled study evaluating the ERP model with OCD youths was conducted by De Hann and colleagues (1997). The ERP model predominantly included behavioral components. The study randomly assigned twenty-two youths (mean age 13.7 years) to one of two twelve-week treatment conditions: ERP or clomipramine only. Although both treatments were effective and exhibited large effect sizes, ERP led to a higher reduction than clomipramine in severity (59.9% versus 33.4%) and occurrence (66.7% versus 50%) of symptoms.

Piacentine (1999) found that 79% of participants were identified as treatment responders in his non-controlled open-trial evaluation of CBT treatment with forty-two OCD youths. The mean percentage of decrease in OCD symptoms was 45%. Significant predictors of successful treatment response included baseline indications of fewer severe obsessions, less anhedonia, higher social functioning, and higher family conflict. Concurrent medication use was not significantly associated with outcome (Piacentine, 1999). This study, in addition to De Haan's (1998) small controlled study, constitute the strongest support for the efficacy of CBT, or behavioral therapy in particular, over medication in the treatment of OCD in youth.

Pilot data from Thienemann and colleagues' (2001) naturalistic, open trial of group CBT provide additional support for the use of group CBT with adolescents suffering from OCD. In this study, adolescents were treated over the course of fourteen weeks with a manualized CBT treatment, and the vast majority of participants had undergone at least one medication trial. Significant clinical and statistical post-treatment improvements were reported (Thienemann, Martin, Cregger, Thompson, & Dyer-Friedman, 2001).

March and colleagues (1994) employed anxiety management (cognitive restructuring, controlled breathing, and relaxation) and behavioral (exposure, response prevention, extinction) techniques with fifteen OCD youths, ages eight to eighteen. Length of treatment varied from three to twenty-one months. All but one of the subjects was on selective-serotonin reuptake inhibitor (SSRI) medication as well. The authors reported a 30% or greater reduction in compulsive symptom scores among twelve subjects by post-treatment, and six were asymptomatic. Treatment gains were maintained at a six-month, post-treatment follow-up.

Empirical Support for CBT with Phobias. Because phobic avoidance is maintained at least in part by maladaptive cognitions (see review by Ollendick & King,

1998), CBT strategies have attempted to modify perceptions and beliefs in an attempt to alleviate fear responses in phobic children. A cognitive-behavioral group therapy model was used to empirically support short-term efficacy of the treatment with thirty-five socially phobic adolescent girls (Hayward et al., 2000). Subjects were randomly assigned to treatment and no-treatment conditions. Significant reductions in anxiety symptoms and diagnostic eligibility were noted in the treated group immediately post-treatment, but the differences were not maintained at one year post-treatment follow-up. However, the treated group did evidence a lowered major depression relapse rate among socially phobic adolescents with a history of major depression.

Another study compared the relative power of (1) child-focused CBT, (2) CBT with parent involvement, and (3) wait-list control conditions to effect change in fifty socially phobic children (ages seven to fourteen). Treatment emphasized social skills, graded exposure techniques, and cognitive restructuring. At post-treatment, children in both treatment conditions evidenced significantly higher rates of diagnostic remission compared to wait-listed children. Social and general anxiety and parent ratings of child social-skill performance improved significantly for treated children. Although there were no significant differences in outcome between parent involvement and child-only treatment conditions, the data showed a trend towards superiority of parental involvement (Spence, Donovan, & Brechman-Toussaint, 2000).

A recent CBT pilot study lends additional support for using CBT with socially phobic adolescents (n = 5). Results were promising, with four out of five adolescents showing sub-clinical levels of social phobia at three-month follow-up (Albano et al., 1999). An earlier study employing group CBT with social phobia treated five adolescents over sixteen sessions and included parents. Following treatment, subjects showed significant improvement in symptoms of anxiety and depression, and one-year follow-up assessments indicated four of the five subjects were in full remission, while one was in partial remission (Albano, Marten, Holt, Heimberg, & Barlow, 1995).

Also, two older studies recently reviewed by Ollendick & King (1998) showed the efficacy of CBT with children who feared the dark. One study identified forty-five children (ages five to six) who had extreme fear of the dark and randomly assigned them to one of three conditions. The groups varied in the type of self-talk children were instructed to use: one emphasized competence and active control, a second emphasized enjoyment of being in the dark (reversing aversive aspects of threatening situation), and a third group simply rehearsed nursery rhymes (neutral). Tolerance to dark was assessed pre- and post-treatment. Outcomes reflected superior results in the competence group versus the other groups on post-treatment fear of the dark (Kanfer, Karoly, & Newman, 1975).

In another study, thirty-three children with nighttime fears were assigned to either a treatment or a wait-list control group. The treatment group children received training in nightly exercises, including relaxation and self-talk reflecting bravery. Parents supervised, monitored, and reinforced their child's progress. After treatment, there were significant improvements in the treatment group's level of nighttime fear. Gains were maintained over time, and persisted even at a three-year follow-up (Graziano & Mooney, 1980).

Trauma and PTSD. The use of CBT treatment for PTSD has received greater empirical support than other theoretical approaches have received (Cohen et al., 2000). In recent years, several studies have examined the validity of CBT models using controlled methodology, and they have favored a multiple-component approach. Intervention components have included: cognitive processing and restructuring, exposure, stress management training, and parental involvement (Cohen et al., 2000). Cohen and colleagues contend that while there is insufficient research to support the efficacy of individual CBT components, there is support for the efficacy of CBT-based interventions to decrease trauma-related symptomology. Support for its efficacy has been gleaned from empirical research with victims of sexual abuse (Cohen & Mannarino, 1996; Cohen & Mannarino, 1998; Deblinger, Lippmann & Steer, 1996; Deblinger, Steer & Lippmann, 1999) earthquake victims (Goenjian, Karayan, Pynoos & Minassian, 1997), and single episode traumas (March, Amaya-Jackson, Marray & Schulte, 1998).

The efficacy of CBT in treating sexually abused children and their nonoffending parents has been evaluated by Deblinger and colleagues (Deblinger et al., 1996; 1999). Four conditions were included in the study. Three conditions involved providing exposure and CBT to the child only, parent only, or the child and parent. The fourth condition was standard community treatment. Results suggested that CBT treatment conditions involving direct treatment to the child (child only, parent and child) were superior to the other two conditions. Child improvement was noted on measures of externalizing behavior problems, depression, and PTSD. Further, parental involvement was associated with the child's decreased behavior problems and depressive symptoms as well as more effective parenting (Deblinger et al., 1996). Treatment gains were upheld at three-month, six-month, one-year, and two-year follow-ups (Deblinger et al., 1999).

Cohen and Mannarino (1996; 1998) compared the efficacy of nondirective supportive therapy (NST) to sexual abuse-specific cognitive behavioral therapy (including cognitive techniques, indirect exposure, stress management, and parental treatment) in sexually abused children and adolescents. Twelve individual sessions were conducted involving the child and nonoffending parent. In their first study, sixty-seven preschool-age children were treated. At post-treatment, significant improvement in the CBT compared with the NST group was evidenced on several outcome measures (Child Behavior Checklist, Child Sexual Behavior Inventory, weekly report of emotional and behavioral symptoms) (Cohen & Mannarino, 1996). In a subsequent study, forty-nine sexually abused children and adolescents (ages seven to fourteen) were treated. Improvements were significantly greater in the CBT group than in the NST group on measures of sexually inappropriate behaviors, depression scores, and social competence (Cohen & Mannarino, 1998).

The efficacy of CBT for single episode trauma has also been demonstrated. Goenjian and associates (1997) compared adolescents who received treatment with a strong cognitive emphasis to those who received no treatment after experiencing an earthquake in Armenia. Treated youths evidenced decreased PTSD symptomology, while depression and PTSD symptoms worsened in the untreated group. March and colleagues (1998) treated youths diagnosed with PTSD from various single exposure traumatic episodes in an eighteen-week CBT-based group format. Fourteen youths were included in the study, ranging in age from ten to fifteen years. At post-treatment, 57% of participants showed diagnostic remission for PTSD, and 86% of subjects had remitted by the six-month follow-up. Depression, anxiety, and anger also improved significantly (March et al., 1998).

Eating Disorders. The most common approach to treating eating disorders is the use of operant techniques to increase weight gain and cognitive techniques to alter distorted and irrational thinking (Fonagy et al., 2002). Robin and colleagues (1996) evaluated the efficacy of behavioral family systems therapy (BFST) to ego-oriented individual therapy (EOIT). This model employs cognitive and behavioral targets in addition to the BFST and EOIT theoretical models. Results suggest that both approaches to treatment were associated with significant improvements on outcome variables such as body mass index, eating attitudes, ineffectiveness, interoceptive awareness, depression, internalizing behavior problems, and self-reported eating-related conflict. In addition, Christie (2000) enumerated or wide array of cognitive behavioral techniques, including clinical examples, in the treatment of children with eating disorders. See Chapter 16 for a review of adolescent eating disorder treatments.

Externalizing Disorders

Aggression, Anger, and Disorders of Conduct

Anger and aggression include tremendous social-interpersonal implications, as peers, teachers, and parents of aggressive children may feel disrupted, helpless, or victimized, and aggressive children may feel disliked and rejected. Early intervention may help to prevent an increasingly pathological trajectory, including disorders of conduct, oppositionality, and deviant behaviors in adolescence and adulthood. Evidence supporting CBT as an effective approach to intervention is considerable, and highlights are presented here. For a more detailed review, see Lochman, Whidby, and Fitzgerald (2000).

Beck and Fernandez (1998) conducted a meta-analysis of anger interventions with children, adolescents, and adults. They included fifty studies, composed of 1,640 subjects. They obtained an overall effect size of 0.70, suggesting that the average subject receiving CBT treatment for anger fared better than 76% of those who did not receive CBT. Another meta-analysis reviewed thirty studies of cognitive behavioral treatment for antisocial youth (ages five to eighteen). Treatment protocols varied by study, but were all guided by CBT principles. The overall effect size was determined to be small to moderate (ES = 0.23). Treatment effect was stronger for older children (older elementary school-age and adolescents). However, variability of treatment effectiveness across studies was substantial. Further consideration of the relative success of specific protocol packages is merited (Bennett & Gibbons, 2000).

Not only have controlled CBT studies provided substantial evidence to support its use with antisocial and aggressive children, but they have demonstrated the importance of including parents in treatment, especially for younger children. For example, Kazdin demonstrated the efficacy of problem-solving skills training (PSST) (Kazdin, Bass, Siegel, & Thomas, 1989) and later added a parent component, parent behavioral management training (PMT) to intervention (Kazdin, Siegel, & Bass, 1992). The combination resulted in significantly enhanced treatment response, generalization, and long-lasting effectiveness. In a study of clinically referred antisocial youth, Kazdin, Bass, Siegel, and Thomas (1989) randomly assigned eighty-four children (ages seven to thirteen) to one of three treatment conditions: (1) PSST, whereby cognitive and behavioral techniques were combined to enhance social problem-solving skills, (2) PSST with in vivo practice (PSST-P), and (3) client-centered relationship therapy (RT), focused on developing rapport and demonstrating warmth, empathy, and unconditional positive regard. Results revealed that the PSST and PSST-P groups improved significantly on measures of antisocial behavior, overall behavior problems, and prosocial adjustment compared to the RT group. At the one-year follow-up, significant treatment gains were retained for PSST and PSST-P groups relative to the RT group.

Subsequently, Kazdin, Siegel, and Bass (1992) demonstrated the utility of combining parent-management training with PSST in the treatment of clinically referred antisocial youth. They examined the relative efficacy of three treatments: PSST, PMT, and PSST with PMT. Ninety-seven children (ages seven to thirteen) were randomly assigned to treatment conditions. In the PSST condition, therapy was administered to children individually, employing cognitive and behavioral techniques to enhance problem solving and interpersonal skills. Parents observed sessions in order to provide assistance and reinforcement outside therapy. In the PMT condition, individual treatment was provided to the parent or guardian, with foci of identifying and monitoring child behavior, teaching the tenets of behavioral contingency, and using role-play and modeling to demonstrate and practice these skills. All groups evidenced significant improvements in child behavioral conduct, prosocial skills, and general functioning immediately post-treatment. The combined PSST and PMT group showed significant improvement relative to the other groups in antisocial and conduct problems, level of parental stress, depression, psychopathology, and family system maintenance. In fact, this combined treatment shifted the greatest number of children into normative ranges of functioning. Child self-reports of aggressive behavior improved significantly for the PSST- only and combined PSST and PMT groups compared to the PMT-only group. PSST was superior to PMT on measures of aggression, delinquent behavior, and conduct problems. Gains were maintained at the one-year follow-up (Kazdin et al., 1992).

The generalized effects of delivering CBT to conduct-disordered youth on parent and family functioning were examined by Kazdin and Wassell (2000). In their study, 250 children ranging in age from two to fourteen years who presented with oppositional, aggressive, and antisocial behavior received variations of CBT. Changes at the level of the child (symptomatology), parents (symptomatology, level of stress), and family (interpersonal relationships, support, family functioning, marital satisfaction) were assessed. Significant improvements were evidenced at each level of analysis (child, parent, family), although children were affected to a greater degree than parents and families. However, maladaptive parent and family characteristics were positively affected by the child-focused interventions.

Anger management training with non-clinical samples has also provided support for the efficacy of CBT. Lochman and colleagues instituted a social-cognitive anger management approach in a school-based Anger Coping Program (fourth- and fifth-grade boys). The eighteen group interventions were considered ideal for providing peer reinforcement and in vivo interpersonal learning and social skill experiences. Tasks included enhancing awareness of cognitive, affective, and physiological processes related to anger, improved ability to reflect and manage anger, and increasing the child's competence in conceptualizing social problems and considering alternative responses (Lochman et al., 2000). Findings support its effectiveness in improving self-esteem, reducing disruptive-aggressive off-task behavior in the classroom, and parent ratings of aggression (Lochman, Burch, Curry, & Lampron, 1984). Three years later, the treatment group maintained improvements on self-esteem and problem solving skills, and also showed lower substance use than untreated controls. However, reductions in aggressive and off-task behaviors were maintained only for boys who received booster treatment (six sessions) during a subsequent school year (Lochman, 1992).

An extended multicomponent version of the Anger Coping Program, the Coping Power treatment program, evidenced improvements in child social competence, information processing and aggressive behavior, and improvements in parenting practices and marital relationships. At a one-year follow-up, gains were maintained, and the highest risk-group exhibited lower substance use rates than the control group (Lochman & Wells, 1996).

Contextual factors hypothesized to influence treatment outcome for antisocial and aggressive youth were examined by Kazdin & Crowley (1997). They hypothesized that cognitive/academic functioning and severity of clinical impairment would serve to moderate treatment response. Participants included 120 youth, ages seven to thirteen years. The children were administered twenty to twenty-five sessions of PSST. Parents were instructed to observe weekly sessions in order to reinforce the problem-solving techniques outside of therapy. Post-treatment measures indicated significant improvement on total behavior problems, adaptive functioning, and social competence. Better treatment outcome was associated with higher reading achievement and academic performance and fewer pretreatment psychiatric symptoms, even when family and contextual factors were controlled. Contextual factors, including lower income and receipt of social assistance, adverse parenting practices, and parent history of antisocial behavior were associated with more child symptoms, greater likelihood of child history of antisocial behavior, and lower child IQ and reading achievement scores (Kazdin & Crowley, 1997).

Attention-Deficit/Hyperactivity Disorder. The most effective treatments for ADHD at this time include pharmacological and behavioral interventions (Craighead et al., 1994; Fonagy et al., 2002; Hinshaw, 2000). Despite initial enthusiasm and the expectation that CBT would be useful for treating ADHD children, several studies failed to support its efficacy. (See reviews by Braswell & Kendall, 2001; Fonagy, et al., 2002; Hinshaw, 2002.) These results may be attributable to the significant neurological underpinnings of the disorder (Braswell & Kendall, 2001). However, research by Hinshaw and colleagues has reported promising effects of CBT on ADHD-related interpersonal challenges when linked to behavioral reinforcement (Hinshaw, 2002).

Hinshaw (1996) evaluated the utility of self-monitoring and self-evaluation training to reduce aggression and enhance social competence and prosocial behaviors among young ADHD males. Hinshaw, Henker, and Whalen (1984a) demonstrated the superiority of a CBT-based self-evaluation in concert with token reinforcement compared to token reinforcement alone in reducing negative social behaviors in a sample of twenty-four hyperactive males (ages eight to thirteen).

These groups were compared across stimulant medicated and non-medicated conditions. On the playground, when children received reinforcement following accurate self-evaluation, the number of negative social interactions was reduced to a significantly greater degree than when they received token reinforcement only. Also, children in the stimulant medication group displayed significantly less negative behavior than non-medicated counterparts. The least amount of negative social interactions occurred among the medicated, reinforced self-evaluation condition.

Support of CBT for anger control among ADHD youth has also been demonstrated. Hinshaw, Henker, and Whalen (1984b) assigned forty-five hyperactive males (ages eight to thirteen years) to one of two studies, each involving a treatment (CBT self-control intervention or empathy enhancement) and a control condition. Each study also included stimulant medication versus placebo conditions. The CBT self-control intervention was superior to empathy training for improvements in general self-control and coping strategies in response to peer provocation. Medication treatment did not improve self-control or coping, but was associated with reductions in behavioral intensity. The CBT plus medication condition was not superior to the CBT treatment alone.

In summary, the use of developmentally sensitive, theoretically driven structured and manual-based cognitive-behavioral protocols have provided promising empirical support for the use of CBT for treating a wide range of child and adolescent disorders. Educating children and adolescents about the dynamic interplay between thoughts, emotions, and behaviors; enhancing problem-solving skills; identifying and correcting cognitive distortions and deficiencies; and increasing emotional awareness constitute important targets of treatments throughout the empirically based literature. Also, the importance of social context and the interaction between the child and his or her environmental systems is an ongoing focus and is central to current and future directions of research (Kendall, 2000a).

Case Presentation

Christina, a sixteen-year-old Laotian American girl, presented to an outpatient clinic with depressive symptoms: depressed mood, anhedonia, hypersomnia, anergia, amotivation, concentration difficulties, and feelings of worthlessness. She denied suicidal ideation. Christina's school performance had previously been characterized by perfectionism, but at intake she reported difficulty concentrating and applying herself to her schoolwork. In addition to academic difficulties, Christina's depressive symptoms caused her clinically significant distress in social and family realms. An evaluation of symptom onset, duration, persistence, and severity revealed that Christina met criteria for dysthymic disorder.

Christina's developmental history was based on Christina's report, the limited information garnered from parents with limited English proficiency, and collateral resources of school records. Prior developmental milestones and tasks appeared to be successfully resolved. There was no evidence of significant developmental issues that would affect the presenting problem with the exception of persistent acculturation issues.

Several salient developmental considerations were targeted in Christina's treatment. First, identity construction, a primary task during adolescence, appeared to be complicated by Christina's cultural identity conflict. While her parents were embedded in their Asian culture and pressured Christina to accept their values and lifestyle, Christina struggled to fit in with peers and be an American. She also wanted to achieve high honors in school and succeed in athletics. Since Christina had undergone puberty, she reported feeling uncomfortable with attention from boys, and had no dating or sexual experience. Christina was attempting to renegotiate family relations by limiting her caretaking role within the family and increasing her autonomy from her family. These efforts were met with family resistance. During the course of treatment, special attention was paid to issues of identity development, increasing autonomy, and risk-taking, particularly in the forms of potential suicidality and self-harm.

While in treatment, Christina attended the tenth grade at a suburban public school. Christina's academic performance had been characterized by straight A's. She reported feeling increased academic pressures coupled with feelings of being overwhelmed, concentration difficulties, and decreased motivation. The semester she began outpatient treatment she received her first B and C in school.

Christina lived with her biological parents and six younger siblings. Her family, of Laotian descent, emigrated from Laos when Christina was four-years-old. Because both parents had limited English proficiency, Christina served as the primary translator and negotiator for them. She was also expected to care for her younger siblings, advocate for them at school, and work in the store. Clearly, these issues all inform a significant need to consider cultural issues in assessing, diagnosing, and treating this patient. Christina had several friends at school, some of whom she spent considerable time with outside of school. However, her social contact was limited by her family responsibilities.

Christina's depressive symptoms appeared and worsened in the context of transitioning from a white family (summer with informal placement family) to her own Laotian American family. Throughout treatment Christina struggled with her identity as a Laotian American, demonstrating an overvaluation of white culture and a devaluation of Laotian culture (representing the Conformity stage of cultural identity development). Conflict with her parents remained high, as they appeared to be "from a different world." Her friends were exclusively white and she sought out a (primarily white) Christian church affiliation whereas her parents were Buddhist. She endorsed dominant cultural images of beauty as well.

The importance of building credibility with Christina's parents was paramount in working with this family. Because of their cultural background and limited formal education, depressive symptoms were conceptualized by them as either physical or spiritual in nature. In addition, their cultural values orientation included a more collectivistic versus individualistic perspective. Hence, family treatment focused on parent education regarding adolescent development and Christina's concomitant needs, including renegotiating Christina's role in the family in behavioral terms.

In summary, the formulation of Christina's presenting depressive symptoms incorporated significant acculturation issues. Triggers identified for symptom development and exacerbation included: returning to her family with concomitant stressors (conflictual external expectations), identity development confusion; increasing school pressures (achievement striving), interest in and attention from boys (threats of sexuality and external evaluative pressures), and persistent cultural pressures.

Christina's underlying discomfort with these multiple changes included significant fears that demands would continue to increase and be overwhelming, with a subsequent loss of highly valued control. Facing family conflict, confusion about where she belonged, and increasing demands and autonomy, Christina struggled with feelings of depression and worthlessness. Notable assets included several stable and supportive friendships, Christina's resourcefulness in accessing additional support, and academic strengths.

CBT goals were divided into short-term (first two to four months) and long-term goals. Short-term goals included: assessing and stabilizing any acute suicidal crisis, and referring Christina to a psychiatrist for an antidepressant medication consultation. Therapy addressed target depressive symptoms with a goal of enhancing mood, self-esteem, and self-efficacy; and decreasing feelings of hopelessness. Christina was also encouraged to mobilize support and collateral resources. This goal was fostered through increasing positive interpersonal interactions, and decreasing social withdrawal. Finally, feelings of shame, low self-esteem, helplessness, and powerlessness and their relationship to cognitions were also included in short-term therapy goals.

Long-term goals included: alleviating depressed mood, restoring interest and pleasure in activities, stabilizing the social support network, addressing underlying issues (such as acculturation issues, negative cognitive schemas, interpersonal patterns), and exploring depressive symptoms in relation to dependency needs, control issues, cultural issues, and sexuality. Ongoing collaboration with Christina's psychiatrist included assisting in the assessment of antidepressant medication efficacy regarding symptom abatement.

Christina's treatment included individual CBT for dysthymia with an integration of developmental and cultural considerations. In fact, cultural and developmental considerations were integrated into case formulation, treatment planning, and ongoing progress evaluation. At the most basic level, because of Christina's feelings of shame and guilt regarding deteriorating academic performance, family disappointment, and "not fitting in," treatment included ongoing monitoring of suicidal ideation. Christina reported at times feeling that she had "let everyone down" and that her family would be "better off without her." The initial stage of treatment included a psychoeducational component targeted to educate both Christina and her family about dysthymia, its course of treatment, and signs of deterioration. In addition to the strong empirical support for CBT with this type of problem, psychoeducational and behavioral treatment components in particular were selected because they were relatively congruent with the family's cultural values.

Treatment components included: identification and self-monitoring of mood, triggers for depressive symptoms, and employing stimulus control procedures in relation to these triggers. Cognitive restructuring efforts targeted beliefs regarding worthlessness, hopelessness, and cultural identity. Through the course of treatment Christina developed and role-played a wider repertoire of coping skills in order to alleviate her depressive symptoms, provide her with a greater sense of control, and increase her problem-solving abilities. Therapy also attempted to facilitate Christina's acculturation process by making explicit her culturally based conflicts and employing cognitive techniques (such as reframing, problem solving, and coping skill enhancement) and behavioral techniques (such as behavioral rehearsal regarding family expectations and time management techniques for increasing academic demands) to address these conflicts. In an effort to enhance Christina's treatment gains, collateral family therapy was also employed. Family therapy included a focus on the conflicts Christina was experiencing, in particular the importance of support and congruent expectations and demands regarding adolescent needs and behavior. Christina and her parents were able to develop a list of agreed-upon expectations regarding Christina's behavior and performance, which served to alleviate the stress of overwhelming expectations and role obligations for her. Cultural values conflict was also addressed in family therapy.

Christina's dysthymic symptoms stabilized at a subclinical level after approximately five months of twice-weekly therapy. Beyond symptom abatement, Christina reported feeling better about her interactions with others, her family relationships, and her academic performance. Christina's therapy then decreased in frequency to weekly, then biweekly, and finally monthly sessions. During this time, Christina was assisted in managing her anxiety regarding her ability to maintain progress with less frequent sessions. A behavioral management plan was put in place for relapse prevention, and Christina was able to consolidate her gains and apply what she learned in therapy to new situations and problems.

Future Directions

The establishment of CBT as an efficacious approach to treating children and adolescents has amassed considerable support during the past several decades. However, future directions call for research to reflect the complexity of human adaptation in study design and implementation. Trends in developmental psychopathology have recognized that adaptation is best understood as a process of bi-directional, continual interaction among individual and contextual systems and system variables at various levels of analysis (behavioral, mental, biological, physical, social, temporal, and cultural aspects of the individual's experience) over time (Cairns, Cairns, Rodkin, & Xie, 1998). In CBT outcome research, attending to the predictive value of individual (temperament, diagnostic comorbidity, developmental level) and contextual characteristics (maternal depression, family conflict, academic functioning) and the bi-directional dynamics between them (family patterns of communication) is needed.

De-aggregation of data to determine individual and family characteristics associated with treatment outcome is an emerging analytical objective that has been recently demonstrated. For example, Brent and colleagues (1998) and Southam-Gerow and colleagues (2001) determined that maternal depression negatively affected the treatment outcome for depressed (Brent et al., 1998) and anxiety-disordered (Southam-Gerow et al., 2001) adolescents. Southam-Gerow and colleagues (2001) also found that higher levels of internalizing pathology and older age predicted poorer outcomes. In the future, examining clustering patterns among variables might be useful for identifying subgroups of youths who may be more or less amenable to treatment.

Similarly, a more complex approach to understanding and describing the efficacy of CBT is a necessary future step. Establishing the differential efficacy of specific CBT protocol components and the optimal length and intensity of treatment is likely to inform more powerful interventions. An interactional approach would recognize the importance of increased attention to treatment components best matched to client characteristics and presenting symptoms (Braswell & Kendall, 2001).

◆ ◆ ◆

Although CBT efficacy has been documented for a variety of disorders, effectiveness has not yet been clearly demonstrated. Many studies have used small sample sizes in clinical settings, comparing CBT to wait-list controls. Larger samples and the greater use of non-clinical settings are needed to establish the generalizability of CBT. Also, some studies have begun to compare the efficacy of CBT to that of other clinical approaches. Continued effort in this direction is needed to identify the relative efficacy of various approaches within diagnostic categories (Reinecke et al., 1998). Furthermore, consideration of financial, therapist, venue, resource, and diversity issues is imperative for successful implementation (Braswell & Kendall, 2001).

Recently, greater effort has been directed to evaluating the influence of parental involvement on treatment outcome (Southam-Gerow & Kendall, 1997). Continued efforts toward determining the conditions under which parent involvement is most beneficial to treatment are needed. For example, determining the most beneficial way to involve parents with respect to format of intervention (group, family), developmental considerations (that is, examining how the influence of parent involvement changes according to developmental level), and characteristics of the child or presenting symptoms would inform current treatment. Also, the role of parental expectations, attitudes, and perceptions and level of additional stressors on treatment outcome is an emerging area of inquiry that deserves further attention (Braswell & Kendall, 2001).

References

Albano, A. M., Detweiler, M. F., & Logsdon-Conradsen, S. (1999). Cognitive-behavioral interventions with socially phobic children. In S. W. Russ & T. H. Ollendick (Eds.), *Handbook of psychotherapies with children and families* (pp. 255–280). New York: Kluwer/Plenum.

Albano, A. M., & Kendall, P. C. (2002). Cognitive behavioural therapy for children and adolescents with anxiety disorders: Clinical research advances. *International Review of Psychiatry, 14,* 129–134.

Albano, A. M., Marten, P. A., Holt, C. S., Heimberg, R. G., & Barlow, D. H. (1995). Cognitive-behavioral group treatment for social phobia in adolescents: A preliminary study. *The Journal of Nervous and Mental Disease, 183,* 649–656.

Asarnow, J. R., Scott, C. V., & Mintz, J. (2002). A combined cognitive-behavioral family education intervention for depression in children: A treatment development study. *Cognitive Therapy and Research, 26*(2), 221–229.

Barrett, P. M., Dadds, M. R., & Rapee, R. M. (1996). Family treatment for childhood anxiety: A controlled trial. *Journal of Consulting and Clinical Psychology, 64,* 333–342.

Beck, R., & Fernandez, E. (1998). Cognitive-behavioral therapy in the treatment of anger: A meta-analysis. *Cognitive Therapy and Research, 22*(1), 63–74.

Bennett, D. S., & Gibbons, T. A. (2000). Efficacy of child cognitive-behavioral interventions for antisocial behavior: A meta-analysis. *Child and Family Behavior Therapy, 22*(1), 1–15.

Braswell, L. (1991). Involving parents in cognitive-behavioral therapy with children and adolescents. In P. C. Kendall (Ed.), *Child and adolescent therapy: Cognitive-behavioral procedures* (pp. 316–351). New York: Guildford Press.

Braswell, L., & Kendall, P. C. (2001). Cognitive-behavioral therapy with youth. In K. S. Dobson (Ed.), *Handbook of cognitive-behavioral therapies* (2nd ed., pp. 246–294). New York: Guildford Press.

Brent, D. A., Holder, D., Kolko, D. A., Birmaher, B., Baugher, D. A., Roth, C., et al. (1997). A clinical psychotherapy trial for adolescent depression comparing cognitive, family, and supportive treatments. *Archives of General Psychiatry, 54,* 877–885.

Brent, D. A., Kolko, D. J., Birmaher, B., Baugher, M., & Bridge, J. (1999). A clinical trial for adolescent depression: Predictors of additional treatment in the acute and follow-up phases of the trial. *Journal of the American Academy of Child and Adolescent Psychiatry, 38,* 263–271.

Brent, D. A., Kolko, D. J., Birmaher, B., Baugher, M., Bridge, J., Roth, C., et al. (1998). Predictors of treatment efficacy in a clinical trial of three psychosocial treatments for adolescent depression. *Journal of the American Academy of Child and Adolescent Psychiatry, 37,* 906–914.

Cairns, R. B., Cairns, B. D., Rodkin, P., & Xie, H. (1998). New directions in developmental research: Models and methods. In R. Jessor (Ed.), *New perspectives on adolescent risk behavior* (pp. 13–40). Cambridge, MA: Cambridge University Press.

Christie, D. (2000). Cognitive behavioral therapeutic techniques for children with eating disorders. In B. Lask, & R. Bryant-Waugh (Eds.), *Anorexia nervosa and related eating disorders in childhood and adolescence* (2nd ed., pp. 205–226). East Sussex, UK: Psychology Press.

Cicchetti, D. (1993). Developmental psychopathology: Reactions, reflections, projections. *Developmental Review, 13,* 471–502.

Cicchetti, D., & Toth, S. L. (1998). Risk, trauma, and processes of memory. *Development and Psychopathology, 10*(4), 589–598.

Cicchetti, D., & Tucker, D. (1994). Development and self-regulatory structures of the mind. *Development and Psychopathology, 6,* 533–549.

Cohen, J. A., Mannarino, A. P., Berliner, L., & Deblinger, E. (2000). Trauma-focused cognitive behavioral therapy for children and adolescents: An empirical update. *Journal of Interpersonal Violence, 15*(11), 1202–1223.

Cohen, J. A., & Mannarino, A. P. (1996). A treatment outcome study for sexually abused preschool children: Initial findings. *Journal of the American Academy of Child and Adolescent Psychiatry, 35,* 42–50.

Cohen, J. A., & Mannarino, A. P. (1998). Interventions for sexually abused children: Initial treatment outcome findings. *Child Maltreatment, 3*(1), 17–26.

Craighead, L. W., Craighead, W. E., Kazdin, A. E., & Mahoney, M. J. (1994). *Cognitive and behavioral interventions: An empirical approach to mental health problems. Part III.* Needham Heights, MA: Allyn & Bacon.

Deblinger, E., Lippmann, J., & Steer, R. (1996). Sexually abused children suffering from posttraumatic stress symptoms: Initial treatment outcome findings. *Child Maltreatment, 1,* 310–321.

Deblinger, E., Steer, R. A., & Lippmann, J. (1999). Two year follow-up study of CBT for sexually abused children suffering posttraumatic stress symptoms. *Child Abuse and Neglect, 23,* 1371–1378.

De Haan, E., Hoogduin, K. A., & Buitelaar, J. K. (1998). Behavior therapy versus clomipramine for the treatment of obsessive-compulsive disorder. *Journal of the American Academy of Child and Adolescent Psychiatry, 37*(10), 1022–1029.

Dodge, K. A. (1986). A social information processing model of social competence in children. In M. Perlmutter (Ed.), *Cognitive perspectives on children's social and behavioral development* (pp. 77–125). Hillsdale: Earlbaum.

Flannery-Schroeder, E., Henin, A., & Kendall, P. C. (1996). Cognitive-behavioral treatment of internalizing disorders in youth. *Behaviour Change, 3*(4), 207–221.

Flannery-Schroeder, E. C., & Kendall, P. C. (2000). Group and individual cognitive-behavioral treatments for youth with anxiety disorders: A randomized clinical trail. *Cognitive Therapy and Research, 24*(3), 252–278.

Fonagy, P., Target, M., Cottrell, D., Phillips, J., & Kurtz, Z. (2002). *What works for whom? A critical review of treatments for children and adolescents.* New York: Guildford Press.

Goenjian, A. K., Karayan, I., Pynoos, R. S., & Minassian, D. (1997). Outcome of psychotherapy among early adolescents after trauma. *American Journal of Psychiatry, 154*(4), 536–542.

Graziano, A. M., & Mooney, K. C. (1980). Family self-control instruction for children's nighttime fear reduction. *Journal of Consulting & Clinical Psychology, 48*(2), 206–213.

Hayward, C., Varady, S., Albano, A. M., Thienemann, M., Henderson, L., & Schatzberg, A. F. (2000). Cognitive–behavioral group therapy for social phobia in female adolescents: Results of a pilot study. *Journal of the American Academy of Child and Adolescent Psychiatry, 39,* 721–726.

Harrington, R., Whittaker, J., Shoebridge, P., & Campbell, F. (1998). Systematic review of efficacy of cognitive behavior therapies in childhood and adolescent depressive disorder. *British Medical Journal, 316,* 1559–1563.

Hinshaw, S. P. (1996). Enhancing social competence: Integrating self-management strategies with behavioral procedures for children with ADHD. In E. D. Hibbs & P. S. Jensen (Eds.), *Psychosocial Treatments for Child and Adolescent Disorders: Empirically Based Strategies for Clinical Practice* (pp. 285–309). Washington, D.C.: American Psychological Association.

Hinshaw, S. P. (2000). Attention-deficit/hyperactivity disorder: The search for viable treatments. In P. C. Kendall (Ed.), *Child and Adolescent Therapy: Cognitive-Behavioral Procedures* (2nd ed., pp. 88–128). New York: Guildford Press.

Hinshaw, S. P., Henker, B., & Whalen, C. K. (1984a). Cognitive-behavioral and pharmacologic interventions for hyperactive boys: Comparative and combined effects. *Journal of Consulting & Clinical Psychology, 52*(5), 739–749.

Hinshaw, S. P., Henker, B., & Whalen, C. K. (1984b). Self-control in hyperactive boys in anger-inducing situations: Effects of cognitive-behavioral training and of methylphenidate. *Journal of Abnormal Child Psychology, 12*(1), 55–77.

Howard, B. L., & Kendall, P. C. (1996). Cognitive-behavioral family therapy for anxiety-disordered children: A multiple-baseline evaluation. *Cognitive Therapy and Research, 20*(5), 423–443.

Jayson, D., Wood, A., Kroll, L., Fraser, J., & Harrington, R. (1998). Which depressed patients respond to cognitive-behavioral treatment? *Journal of the American Academy of Child and Adolescent Psychiatry, 37*(1), 35–39.

Kanfer, F. H., Karoly, P., & Newman, A. (1975). Reduction of children's fear of the dark by competence-related and situational threat-related verbal cues. *Journal of Consulting & Clinical Psychology, 43*(2), 251–258.

Kazdin, A. E. (2000). *Psychotherapy for children and adolescents: Directions for research and practice.* New York: Oxford University Press.

Kazdin, A. E., Bass, D., Siegel, T., & Thomas, C. (1989). Cognitive-behavioral treatment and relationship therapy in the treatment of children referred for antisocial behavior. *Journal of Consulting and Clinical Psychology, 57,* 522–535.

Kazdin, A. E., & Crowley, M. J. (1997). Moderators of treatment outcome in cognitively based treatment of antisocial children. *Cognitive Therapy and Research, 21*(2), 185–207.

Kazdin, A. E., Siegel, T., & Bass, D. (1992). Cognitive problem-solving skills training and parent management training in the treatment of antisocial behavior in children. *Journal of Consulting and Clinical Psychology, 60,* 733–747.

Kazdin, A. E., & Wassell, G. (2000). Therapeutic changes in children, parents, and families resulting from treatment of children with conduct problems. *Journal of the American Academy of Child & Adolescent Psychiatry, 39*(4), 414–420.

Kazdin, A. E., & Weiss, J. R. (1998). Identifying and developing empirically supported child and adolescent treatments. *Journal of Consulting and Clinical Psychology, 66,* 19–36.

Kendall, P. C. (1991). Guiding theory for therapy with children and adolescents. In P. C. Kendall (Ed.), *Child and adolescent therapy: Cognitive behavioral procedures* (pp. 3–22). New York: Guildford Press.

Kendall, P. C. (1993). Cognitive-behavioral strategies with youth: Guiding theory, current status, and emerging developments. *Journal of Consulting and Clinical Psychology, 61,* 235–247.

Kendall, P. C. (1994). Treating anxiety disorders in children: Results of a randomized clinical trial. *Journal of Consulting and Clinical Psychology, 62,* 100–110.

Kendall, P. C. (2000a). *Child and adolescent therapy: Cognitive behavioral procedures.* New York: Guildford Press.

Kendall, P. C. (2000b). Guiding theory for therapy with children and adolescents. In P. C. Kendall (Ed.), *Child and adolescent therapy* (2nd ed., pp. 3–30). New York: Guildford Press.

Kendall, P. C., Flannery-Schroeder, E., Panichelli-Mindel, S. M., & Gerow, M. A. (1995). Cognitive-behavioral therapies with children and adolescents: An integrative overview. In H.P.J.G. van Bilsen & P. C. Kendall (Eds.), *Behavioral approaches for children and adolescents: Challenges for the next century* (pp. 1–18). New York: Plenum Press.

Kendall, P. C., Flannery-Schroeder, E., Panicheli-Mindel, S. M., Southam-Gerow, M., Henin, A., & Warman, M. (1997). Therapy for youths with anxiety disorders: A second randomized clinical trial. *Journal of Consulting and Clinical Psychology, 65,* 366–380.

Kendall, P. C., Lerner, R., & Craighead, W. (1984). Human development and intervention. *Child Development, 55,* 71–82.

Kendall, P. C., & McDonald, J. P. (1993). Cognition in the psychopathology of youth and implications for treatment. In K. S. Dobson & P. C. Kendall (Eds.), *Psychopathology and cognition* (pp. 387–427). San Diego: Academic Press.

Kendall, P. C., Panichelli-Mindel, S. M., & Gerow, M. A. (1995). Cognitive-behavioral therapies with children and adolescents. An integrative overview. In H.P.J.G. van Bilsen et al. (Eds.), *Behavioral Approaches for Children and Adolescents* (pp. 1–17). New York: Plenum Press.

Kendall, P. C., & Southam-Gerow, M. A. (1996). Long-term follow-up of a cognitive-behavioral therapy for anxiety-disordered youth. *Journal of Consulting and Clinical Psychology, 64*(4), 724–730.

Kendall, P. C., & Treadwell, K.R.H. (1996). Cognitive-behavioral treatment for childhood anxiety disorders. In E. D. Hibbs & P. S. Jensen (Eds.), *Psychosocial treatments for child and adolescent disorders: Empirically based strategies for clinical practice* (pp. 23–41). Washington, D.C.: American Psychological Association.

Krain, A. L., & Kendall, P. C. (1999). Cognitive behavioral therapy. In S. W. Russ & T. H. Ollendick (Eds.), *Handbook of psychotherapies with children and families* (pp. 121–135). New York: Kluwer.

Lis, A., Zennaro, A., & Mazzeschi, C. (2001). Child and adolescent empirical psychotherapy research. *European Psychologist, 6*(1), 36–64.

Lochman, J. E. (1992). Cognitive-behavioral intervention with aggressive boys: Three-year follow-up and preventive effects. *Journal of Consulting and Clinical Psychology, 60,* 426–432.

Lochman, J. E., Burch, P. R., Curry, J. F., & Lampron, L. B. (1984). Treatment and generalization effects of cognitive behavioral and goal-setting interventions with aggressive boys. *Journal of Consulting and Clinical Psychology, 52,* 915–916.

Lochman, J. E., & Wells, K. C. (1996). A social-cognitive intervention with aggressive children: Prevention effects and contextual implementation issues. In R. D. Peters & R. J. McMahon (Eds.), *Preventing childhood disorders, substance use, and delinquency* (pp. 111–143). Thousand Oaks, CA: Sage.

Lochman, J. E., Whidby, J. M., & Figzgerald, D. P. (2000). Cognitive-behavioral assessment and treatment with aggressive children. In P. C. Kendall (Ed.), *Child and adolescent therapy* (2nd ed., pp. 31–87). New York: Guildford Press.

Lumpkin, P. W., Silverman, W. K., Weems, C. F., Markham, M. R., & Kurtines, W. M. (2002). Treating a heterogeneous set of anxiety disorders in youth with group cognitive behavioral therapy. A partially nonconcurrent multiple-baseline evaluation. *Behavior Therapy, 33*(1), 163–177.

March, J., Amaya-Jackson, L., Murray, M. C., & Schulte, A. (1998). Cognitive-behavioral psychotherapy for children and adolescents with posttraumatic stress disorder after a single-incident stressor. *Journal of the American Academy of Child and Adolescent Psychiatry, 37*(5), 585–593.

March, J., Mulle, K., & Herbel, B. (1994). Behavioral psychotherapy for children and adolescents with OCD. *Journal of the American Academy of Child and Adolescent Psychiatry, 33,* 333.

Ollendick, T. H., & King, N. J. (1998). Empirically supported treatments for children with phobic and anxiety disorders. *Journal of Clinical Child Psychology, 27,* 156–167.

Piacentini, J. (1999). Cognitive behavioral therapy of childhood OCD. *Child and Adolescent Psychiatric Clinics of North America, 8*(3), 599–615.

Reinecke, M. A., Ryan, N. E., & DuBois, D. L. (1998). Cognitive-behavioral therapy of depression and depressive symptoms during adolescence: A review and meta-analysis. *Journal of the American Academy of Child and Adolescent Psychiatry, 37*(1), 26–34.

Robin, A. L., Bedway, M., Siegel, P. T., & Gilroy, M. (1996). Therapy for adolescent anorexia nervosa: Addressing cognitions, feelings and the family's role. In D. Hibbs & P. S. Jensen (Eds.), *Psychosocial treatments for child and adolescent disorders: Empirically based strategies for clinical practice* (pp. 239–266). Washington, DC: American Psychological Association.

Southam-Gerow, M. A., & Kendall, P. C. (1997). Parent-focused and cognitive-behavioral treatments of antisocial youth. In D. M. Stoff & J. Breiling (Eds.), *Handbook of antisocial behavior* (pp. 384–394). New York: Wiley.

Southam-Gerow, M. A., Kendall, P. C., & Weersing, V. R. (2001). Examining outcome variability: Correlates of treatment response in a child and adolescent anxiety clinic. *Journal of Community Psychology, 30*(3), 422–436.

Spence, S. H., Donovan, C., & Brechman-Toussaint, M. (2000). The treatment of childhood social phobia: The effectiveness of a social skills training-based, cognitive behavioural intervention, with and without parent involvement. *Journal of Child Psychology and Psychiatry and Allied Disciplines, 41,* 713–726.

Sroufe, L. A., & Rutter, M. (1984). The domain of developmental psychopathology. *Child Development, 55,* 17–29.

Stith, S. M., Rosen, K. H., McCollum, E. E., Coleman, J. U., & Herman, S. A. (1996). The voice of children: Preadolescent children's experiences in family therapy. *Journal of Marital and Family Therapy, 22*(1), 69–86.

Toth, S. L., & Cicchetti, D. (1999). Developmental psychopathology and child psychotherapy. In S. W. Russ & T. H. Ollendick (Eds.), *Handbook of psychotherapies with children and families* (pp. 15–44). New York: Kluwer.

Webster-Stratton, C. L. (1998). Preventing conduct problems in Head Start children: Strengthening parenting competencies. *Journal of Consulting and Clinical Psychology, 66,* 715–730.

Weisz, J. R., Thurber, C. A., Sweeney, L., Proffitt, V. D., & LeGagnoux, G. L. (1997). Brief treatment of mild-to-moderate child depression using primary and secondary control enhancement training. *Journal of Consulting and Clinical Psychology, 65,* 703–707.

Weisz, J. R., Weiss, B., Han, S. S., Granger, D. A., & Morton, T. (1995). Effects of psychotherapy with children and adolescents revisited: A meta-analysis of treatment outcome studies. *Psychological Bulletin, 117,* 450–468.

CHAPTER NINETEEN

PSYCHOTHERAPEUTIC INTERVENTIONS IN INFANCY AND EARLY CHILDHOOD

Marina Zelenko, M.D.

O ver the last several decades, there has been growing recognition of the importance of mental health in infancy and early childhood. The need to attend to mental health issues in early childhood is underscored by the fact that severe psychological difficulties, such as depression, anxiety, post-traumatic stress disorder, and others can develop in infancy and early childhood (Luby & Morgan, 1997; Zeanah, Boris, & Scheeringa, 1997). It is well known that negative early childhood experiences, such as early childhood maltreatment or other psychological traumas, can have a profound impact on the child's later mental health and development (Rutter, Kreppner, O'Connor, & English and Romanian Adoptees study team, 2001; Schore, 2001). Mental health problems that developed in early childhood often tend to persist and may lead to more severe and entrenched difficulties as the child gets older (Richman, Stevenson, & Graham, 1982; Shaw, Owens, Vondra, Keenan, & Winslow, 1996). The past history of psychiatrically disturbed school-age children often reveals early childhood problems that were not diagnosed and addressed because the child was "too young." Thus, early recognition and timely interventions addressing emotional, behavioral, and relationship problems in young children are necessary to optimize the children's

I wish to thank Dr. Anne Benham for her assistance with the preparation of this chapter.

healthy development and to prevent later difficulties (Briggs-Gowan, Carter, Moye Skuban, & McCue Horwitz, 2001).

The transactional model of early childhood development emphasizes that the child's development progresses via reciprocal interactions between the child's constitutional propensities and the caregiving environment (Sameroff & Chandler, 1975). The caregiving environment is a complex psychosocial construct that incorporates the multitude of social, cultural, family, marital, and individual caregiver's factors (Cicchetti, Toth, Bush, & Gillespie, 1988). These environmental factors affect the child through innumerous continuous interactions with the child's caregiver, that is, through the child-caregiver relationship.

The child's constitutional characteristics invariably contribute to and shape the environment and the relationship system as the caregiver adjusts caregiving efforts according to the child's characteristics (Sroufe, 1990). Infant research has shown that the young child is a communicative, participatory, and both relationship- and reality-oriented person who from the first weeks of life is capable of making various distinctions, expressing preferences, and exercising the capacity for mutuality and reciprocal relationships (Stern, 1985). While the child's constitutional characteristics unfold within the relationship, the constitutional characteristics themselves may be transformed by the environment and the relationship. For example, with a young child who is easily over-aroused, the caregiver may be prompted to modulate stimulation or to smooth transitions, depending on what intervention is likely to prevent or relieve the over-arousal. With consistent and sensitive sensory modulation by the caregiver, the over-aroused young child in time may develop sufficient arousal tolerance and self-modulating capacity. Thus, the child's particular behavioral or developmental outcome evolves as a result of reciprocal interactions between the constitutional and environmental factors in the context of the infant-caregiver relationship (Sroufe, 1997).

In addition to being a medium by which the environment and the child influence each other, the child-caregiver relationship is also the immediate context for the child's development progress. The younger the child is, the more influential the child-caregiver relationship is in the child's behavior and development. The essential premise of the critical importance of the child-caregiver relationship in the child's outcome is a foundation for all therapeutic interventions in this population. The famous quip by Winnicot, "I have never seen *a baby*" (Winnicot, 1960/1965) emphasizes the fact that a young child does not exist in isolation, but is embedded in the family system. By implication, is it equally true that there is no such a thing as *a parent* (Lieberman & Pawl, 1993) because one can only be a parent if there is (or has been) a child. Thus, although the identified patient in mental health evaluation and treatment is usually a young child, therapeutic interventions are directed not only at the child, but also at the caregivers, child-caregiver relationship, and the entire cultural, social, family, marital, and parenthood constellation.

The ultimate goal of the interventions is to assist the young child to achieve optimal functioning. This goal is pursued via multifaceted interventions that use joint work with caregivers and their children (Lieberman & Pawl, 1993). The therapeutic approaches may include concrete assistance and advice to the caregiver and education of the caregiver on how to address a particular symptom. The interventions may also include insight-oriented therapy, supportive, or behavioral therapy. The therapeutic approaches are often defined by the young age of the child and associated developmental, relational, and systemic issues rather than by the child's particular clinical problem. Considering the pivotal power of the child-caregiver's relationship in the child's functioning, the interventions are often based on the assumption that a nurturing and stimulating caregiving environment, the caregiver's own psychological well being, adequate parenting skills, and appropriate developmental expectations tailored to the constitutional characteristics and needs of the particular child will improve the child's symptoms and behavior and optimize the child's developmental path.

Putative Mechanisms of Efficacy

Perhaps the most important therapeutic factor that defines the ultimate outcome of the intervention is the development of the working alliance between the caregiver and the therapist. The caregiver's experience of the nurturing and respectful relationship with the therapist coalesces with the caregiver's new knowledge, self-understanding, and understanding of the child. This complicated process, created by the caregiver and the therapist, can lead to enduring changes in the caregiver's and the child's experience of each other, in the quality of their relationship, and in the child's functioning (Lieberman & Pawl, 1993).

Working Alliance with the Caregiver

The therapeutic alliance between the caregiver and the therapist is a basic catalyst for therapeutic change and a primary vehicle for utilizing therapy. The special significance of the working alliance with the caregiver in early childhood interventions is underlined by the fact that, although the carrier of the presenting symptom usually is the child, it is the caregiver who actually possesses the power to help the child to change behaviors. This is quite different from individual psychotherapy situations in which the identified patient presents himself or herself for treatment supposedly looking for the therapeutic change. The notion that changes in the *caregiver's* thinking, attitude, or behavior toward the child might have therapeutic influence *on the child* is an intricate message that the caregiver should be ready to hear from the therapist. On one hand, this message emphasizes the caregiver's role and empowers the caregiver. On the other hand, it implies that the caregiver's earlier approaches were not optimal and needed to be changed, which might be perceived by the caregiver as a blame for the child's symptom.

While the therapist, by definition has a role of an expert in the relationship with the caregiver, the way in which this expertise is delivered becomes an essential aspect of the work, because it may determine whether or not the caregiver agrees to participate in the treatment (Pawl & Lieberman, 1997). The ability of the therapist to establish a rapport that allows the caregiver to minimize defensiveness and resistance and to accept his or her role in the therapeutic process is essentially a core of all interventions in early childhood.

Not only does this rapport make the therapeutic process possible, but also the therapist's relationship with the caregiver itself may be an important mutative factor in the caregiver's relationship with the child (Lieberman & Pawl, 1993). The therapist's attitude and behavior must convey basic positive regard, feeling of respectful partnership, support, accommodation, and concern. This relationship with the therapist may provide the caregiver with a "corrective experience" (Alexander, 1956), which contrasts with the caregiver's unconscious expectations of abandonment, punishment, or criticism that the caregiver might have experienced in the past. When the therapist's behavior consistently fails to confirm these expectations and exposes the caregiver to a nurturing and empathic relationship, this new experience becomes gradually internalized and incorporated into the caregiver's internal representation of self and the child (Pawl & Lieberman, 1997).

Further, the caregiver's relationship with the therapist parallels aspects of the caregiver-child relationship. Therefore, in the relationship with the caregiver, the therapist should foster the aspects that are desirable in the caregiver-child relationship (Lieberman & Pawl, 1993). The therapist strives to help the caregiver feel heard, supported, and respected and this is how the child should feel in the relationship with the caregiver. Winnicot's (1971) clever paraphrase of Socrates, "I am seen, so I exist" emphasizes the important role of positive emotional mirroring of the caregiver's experience by the therapist that is transferred to the caregiver-child relationship in the therapeutic process. This notion is supported by research that has shown that the caregivers who developed a strong positive relationship with the therapist tended to be more empathic to their children (Lieberman, Weston, & Pawl, 1991).

There are various factors that may facilitate or impede the establishment of the working alliance with the caregiver (Seligman & Pawl, 1985). The first factor that comes to the clinician's attention is the caregiver's understanding and feelings regarding the reason and the necessity for mental health services (Lieberman & Pawl, 1993). Caregivers are much more likely to have an open and accepting attitude towards the therapist and treatment when they are concerned about the child's symptoms and seek treatment on their own. When the caregivers are urged to seek treatment by social agencies that express more concern about the child than the caregivers themselves, the clinician should expect some reluctance to engage in the therapeutic process. It is unfortunate that the later referrals often reflect the most serious concerns regarding the child's safety and well being (Pawl & Lieberman, 1997). It also happens at times that the caregiver states that although a pediatrician referred the family to psychiatry, there is "nothing wrong" with the child. Insisting on the caregiver's commitment to the treatment when the caregiver denies the presence of the problem would preclude the development of the rapport and, therefore, would defy the purpose. In our clinic, we have found that offering a consultation in order to explore the referring provider's concern often helps with the initial engagement of the caregiver.

If the caregiver agrees that there is a problem, it is always necessary to ask about the *caregiver's* treatment expectations and goals (McDonough, 2000). Letting the caregiver identify the problem and treatment goals enhances the caregiver's motivation and engagement and, thus, facilitates the working alliance (McDonough, 2000). When the clinician follows the caregiver's lead, the caregiver is likely to feel understood and heard by the clinician (Seligman & Pawl, 1985). We found that it is helpful to convey to the caregiver that the therapeutic intervention is undertaken to address the needs of *the child and the family* rather than those of school or other involved agencies.

Perhaps the most powerful positive factor in the establishment of the therapeutic rapport with the caregiver is the working assumption that the identified patient is *not the caregiver but the child*. Vast majority of caregivers are devoted to their children's healthy development and would strive to help them. This is an exceptionally powerful clinical leverage. In our clinical work, we found that re-formulating the situation in terms of the child *experiencing difficulties*, rather than bringing them on, dramatically changes the dynamics and almost always guarantees enhancement of the therapeutic alliance. For example, a two-year-old child with aggressive outbursts who is considered a tyrant of the family may be presented as a young child who is feeling unable to control his strong negative impulses and is greatly suffering from frequent overflow of his unbearable emotions. Not only does this approach force the caregiver to acknowledge and validate the child's emotional experience, which is an accomplishment in itself, but it also brings the caregiver and the therapist together in search for things the caregiver can do to alleviate the child's distress.

Transference phenomena, as in any psychotherapy, can serve as an impediment, facilitator, or an opportunity for the development of the working alliance. Previous negative experiences with mental health professionals or social agencies and the caregiver's own difficult childhood experiences may render the caregivers reluctant to engage in yet another relationship with a "helper." The clinicians should be aware that their interventions are often perceived and experienced through the template of the caregivers' past histories. The transference issues should always be carefully and sensitively attended to, including in therapies where the focus is on supportive or educational efforts. Even in relatively structured situations, such as pediatric offices, social services agencies, or parenting classes, interventions may be more effective when the clinicians orient their approaches to the caregivers' specific experiences. This helps the caregivers to be more accepting of the assistance offered to them and also allows the clinicians to clarify their own occasional feelings of anger or frustration, which may interfere with providing the assistance (Seligman & Pawl, 1985).

In addition to the efforts on the part of the therapist, the establishment of the working alliance requires the willingness and the ability of the caregiver to participate in the process. The caregiver might have no control over the source of problem or no motivation to try to exercise control over it. A family's difficult socio-economic condition is a particularly salient issue in programs working with impoverished populations (Lieberman, Silverman, & Pawl, 2000). Childcare, housing, and transportation problems, acute economic insecurity, joblessness, or long hours of hard and unrewarding work make it difficult for even the best-intentioned caregivers to engage in emotionally and practically demanding treatment. Differences in financial situation, education, and ethnicity between the clinician and the family may create feelings of resentment and suspicion, which also impede the establishment of the working alliance (Seligman & Pawl, 1985). Often, the caregivers fear that if their parenting skills are evaluated negatively, the child protective services will be involved to remove the child. Clinicians working with impoverished inner-city populations know that in spite of all their consistent and sensitive efforts, which often include home visitations and concrete assistance, the working alliance at times fails to develop due to the multitude of psychosocial obstacles.

Caregivers' emotional investment in their children makes it possible to utilize joint therapy even with caregivers who might be unlikely candidates for more conventional individual treatments. Low educational level, social marginality, and inability to be introspective, which impede successful involvement in individual therapy, do not seem to interfere when it comes to the treatment on the child's behalf (McDonough, 2000).

Caregiver's psychopathology itself does not predict disturbed parenting (Sameroff, Seifer, & Zax, 1982) or poor therapeutic response (Cramer, 1995). Caregivers suffering from severe depression or personality disorders may still be emotionally invested in their children and capable of using treatment (Fraiberg, 1980; Zelenko & Benham, 2000). Understanding the caregiver's psychopathology helps to anticipate difficulties in the therapeutic process and informs clinical decisions. For example, caregivers with serious narcissistic personality disorder may be unable to tolerate the therapist's attention to the child and may perceive any comment about the child-rearing as criticism or insult. Caregivers with concrete thinking styles may need expressions of empathy and support conveyed through actions and concrete assistance rather than words, while caregivers with low self-esteem might not perceive themselves as deserving of care and attention (Pawl & Lieberman, 1997). Perhaps the most difficult obstacle to the development of the therapeutic alliance, and, thus, to treatment, is the caregiver's drug use. Unless the caregiver is not using drugs and is actively engaged into a recovery program, the attempts to establish alliance and implement therapy are usually futile (McDonough, 1995).

Therapeutic Formats

The therapeutic formats and the role of the therapist vary depending on the particular interventional approach. Most often, the treatment includes joint meetings of the therapist with the caregiver(s) and the child. This setting works best with preverbal children whose reactions and demands can be incorporated smoothly into the therapeutic work with the caregivers (Pawl & Lieberman, 1997). The basic idea underlying this approach is that the presence of both the caregiver and the child offers the unique opportunity to observe actual interactions and to discuss and reflect on the immediate experience and spontaneous emotions. This opportunity would not be available during individual sessions with either the caregiver or the child when these experiences and emotions would be recalled and perhaps edited.

Depending on the age of the child, family compositions, and other factors, variations of this format may be utilized. With older children, the treatment may include alternating joint caregiver-child sessions with sessions with the caregiver only. This is because the caregiver may need at times to talk about life events, feelings, and experiences that should not be discussed in the child's presence or because the child's presence may inhibit the caregiver' expressiveness. In addition, toddlers and older children often demand much attention and make it difficult for the caregiver and the therapist have a conversation without frequent interruptions. The caregiver and the therapist should work together to design the right arrangement to support the therapeutic work (Lieberman & Pawl, 1993).

Therapist's Role

The presence of both the caregiver and the child creates a complex and demanding psychodynamic in the room (Pawl & Lieberman, 1997). The therapist not only holds conversations with the caregivers and observes the situation, but also at times is engaged in direct interactions with the child. This requires the therapist to predict and understand the effect of these interactions on the caregiver as well as the effect of the interactions with the caregiver on the child. Considering a potential for envy, jealousy, or competition between the caregiver and the child for the therapist's attention or between the therapist and the caregiver for the child's attention, the therapist should be keenly attuned to careful balancing of the individual needs of the participants in this three-way communication. Cramer (1995) suggests that the therapist should attempt to divide attention between the caregiver and the child in both verbal and behavioral interactions. Most of the therapist's speech is usually addressed to the caregiver but according to the child's ability to speak and comprehend, the therapist should address the child as well so the child feels included. The therapist often responds to the child's invitations to play but Cramer (1995) advises that the therapist should not initiate the engagement unless the caregiver is also involved in the play to avoid competitive feelings on the caregiver's part. On the emotional level, the therapist should be careful not to become too much involved in the caregiver's experience and not to exclude the child from the evolving understanding of the situation. On the other hand, the therapist's strong identification with the child's experience may hinder the therapist's empathical attunement to the caregiver's feelings.

The physical presence of the child also creates a unique opportunity for the therapist to identify and name the child's experience and provide a new, more objective meaning to the child's behavior. The caregivers tend to assign (or project) meanings to the child's behavior that can only be clarified when the therapist has the opportunity to observe the actual situation. One humorous example of the merging of the child's and the caregiver's experience in the caregiver's mind would be a statement by one of the caregivers in our clinic. She was drinking a cup of hot coffee while her eight-month-old son was comfortably sleeping next to her. When her face started turning red and sweaty, she took off her jacket and then started undressing the baby saying, "He is getting too hot."

Bringing in and clarifying the child's experience is an important therapeutic task in all types of interventions. For example, in psychodynamic therapies, the therapist attempts to disentangle the child's experience from the caregiver's perceptions. When a mother says about her six-month-old son, "He looks exactly like his abusive father, the same angry face," the therapist tries to free the baby from his father's negative shadow in the mother's mind and to help the mother consider other reasons for the "angry" face, such as hunger or colic (Fraiberg, 1980).

In more behavioral and educational approaches, the therapist also spends a great deal of time identifying and naming the child's experience. Demonstrating to the caregiver the child's developmental strengths and vulnerabilities as in the Behavioral Pediatric Approach (Brazelton, 1982) or providing Interactional Guidance (McDonough, 1995), the therapist "speaks" for the child, making the child's immediate experience and feelings pronounced and hopefully heard by the caregiver. How would the six-month-old boy with "angry face" express hunger or pain? Would abdomen massages or changes in the body position be helpful? What would be his optimal feeding schedule and composition of the meals? These questions and answers to them are based on the identification and validation of this particular child's experience and feelings and serve to help the caregiver to recognize and respect the individuality of the young child. As one of the mothers who came to our clinic for help said about her infant son, "I thought you just feed and change them (*babies*); I did not know that they understand, but now I see that he is a little person."

In any therapeutic approach, if the therapist identifies the young child's experience as one of abuse and neglect, this should be immediately addressed. Failure to do so on the therapist's part so would mean colluding with the abuse and legitimizing it (Pawl & Lieberman, 1997).

To help the caregiver and the child to enjoy interactions with each other more is another task applicable to all interventions with young children and their families. To be able to enjoy being a caregiver of this particular child is a basic prerequisite for a healthy caregiver-child relationship. This is not necessarily about the unconditional love that the majority of caregivers experience toward their children, but more about innumerable day-to-day interactions that may bring much frustration and irritation even in the most loving caregivers. Along with addressing a particular symptom or complex psychosocial situation, perhaps one of the most powerful therapeutic interventions would be to help the caregiver and the child enjoy each other and experience positive emotions about each other. If this is achieved, the problems will become more amenable. Pointing out that the child is strongly attached to and very fond of the caregiver (Lieberman & Pawl, 1997); demonstrating to the caregiver particular strengths and achievements of the child that the caregiver might be proud of (Brazelton, 1982); reinforcing interactions that are enjoyable to both the caregiver and the child and nourishing the caregiver's feelings of competency and pride in self (McDonough, 2000)—all of these interventions utilized in different therapeutic modalities serve, among other goals, to make the caregiver and the child happier in their roles.

Another overarching principle of therapeutic interventions with young children and their families is to empower caregivers in their caregiving role. Embracing the position that the caregivers are doing the best they know how to do (McDonough, 2000) is necessary because it helps to develop a therapeutic alliance, provides the caregiver with positive relationship experiences, and conveys respect and support, which hopefully then will be conveyed to the child (Lieberman & Pawl, 1993). There are also simpler reasons why empowering the caregivers is so important. First, the caregivers are most likely indeed doing the best they know how to do. Second, the caregivers' feelings of expertise and competency make the parenting less stressful and more enjoyable. Finally, it is the caregiver who knows and loves the child the most, lives with the child, goes through all wonders and pains of raising the child, is ultimately responsible for the child, and has an ultimate power to help the child. As much as we would like to believe in our therapeutic influence, it is the caregiver, not the therapist, who provides continuous life-long interventions. The therapist's role, thus, is to join the caregiver and to assist in this formidable task.

Developmental Influences

Parents of very young children rarely think of a psychiatric consultation. They are more likely to voice their worries with their pediatrician, who works closely with the family and who might suggest psychiatric involvement. The reason for these referrals usually is a concern about the child's development, behavior, or emotions that make the child different from other children. These may include somatic complaints that do not seem to have an identified medical cause, failure to develop skills expected for the age, or failure to relate to others appropriately, including lack of social relatedness, aggression, or withdrawal. The younger the child is, the more often the concerns are of physiological nature, such as problematic feeding, sleeping, or irritability. During the second year of life and later, when children start attending group settings, issues of socialization and emotional and behavioral regulation become more salient.

A distinct, rapidly growing group of clients in young child mental health are foster and adoptive families, who might be concerned with issues of the children's attachment to new caregivers and/or developmental and socio-emotional consequences of early psychological trauma and early social deprivation, as in children who were adopted from orphanages (Rutter, Kreppner, O'Connor, & English and Romanian Adoptees study team, 2001). Sometimes, the families are referred for psychiatric intervention by social agencies. The reason for these referrals is often a concern regarding the caregiving environment, the caregiver's parenting skills and the quality of the caregiver-child relationship, custody issues, or possible child maltreatment.

The goal of the intervention may be to address the child's symptom, to improve the child's behavior and relationships, or to optimize the child's development. Clearly defined symptoms and mutually agreed upon therapeutic goals and outcome measures facilitate the monitoring of the therapeutic progress and assessing the results of the intervention (McDonough, 2000). For instance, if the mother reports that her two-year-old son is "aggressive," it is necessary to ask her to describe the behavior in concrete terms and give examples of the child' aggressive behavior, its circumstances, antecedents, and consequences. The decrease in number or length of angry outbursts per day or a number of days without the outbursts per week could be a concrete measurable therapeutic goal for this youngster. The treatment outcome may be defined not only by catching up with developmental and behavioral "norms," but also by the trajectory of the child's own developmental curve and how quickly it is approaching the target "norm."

Considering the critical influence of the child-caregiver's relationship in the child's functioning, enhancement of the caregiving environment and improvement of the quality of the child-caregiver relationship may be also an important goal of the intervention. In situations of possible child maltreatment, the quality of the child-caregiver relationship is usually the primary focus of the intervention. The therapeutic focus may shift in the process of the therapy, for example, from the child's behavior to the caregiving environment or child-caregiver interactions.

Young children's relatively limited cognitive abilities and language skills present a salient developmental influence in therapeutic work with this population. These limitations often restrict the young child's ability to verbalize thoughts and feelings. Most often, young children express themselves behaviorally. Thus, in the process of mental health evaluation and treatment, a lot of emphasis is placed on direct observation of the child's behavior and interactions (Benham, 2000).

Another reason why direct observation is so important is the fact that due to the young child's developmental limitations, most of the initial information about the child's functioning is conveyed to the clinician through the caregiver's report that represents the caregiver's perception of the child. Although caregiver's reports are often reliable (Carter, Little, Briggs-Gowan, & Kogan, 1999; Olson, Bates, Sandy, & Lanthier, 2000), they are likely to be affected by variety of environmental and individual factors and systematic personal biases such as the parents' expectations, mood, or attributions about the child (Briggs-Gowan, Carter, & Schwab; Stone, 1996; Eddy, Dishio, & Stoolmiller, 1998; Fergusson, Lynskey, & Horwood, 1993). It is also not unusual to have two different caregivers (for example, a mother and a grandmother) present conflicting reports regarding behaviors of the same young child. Behaviors in early childhood are often relationship-specific (Zeanah, Boris, & Scheeringa, 1997) and the child's behavior may indeed be different with different caregivers. Direct observation of the child's behavior with different caregivers helps to clarify to what extent the child's behavior is consistent across the relationships, to reveal the caregivers' biases, and to achieve more objective understanding of the child's behavior (Zelenko, in press).

Psychopathology in early childhood is inseparably intertwined with the child's development (Rutter & Sroufe, 2000). The ubiquitous presence of the developmental issues in young child psychopathology has numerous implications for assessment and treatment. Working with young children, the clinician at all times should be aware of the child's normal rapid maturational processes and be ready to assess the quickly changing child's presentation against age, gender, and cultural norms. The same behaviors may have different meaning depending on the age, gender, or cultural background of the child. What is seen as problematic at one age or in a particular cultural group may not be perceived as a problem at another age or in another culture (Ollendick & King, 1990). Moreover, behavioral manifestations of young children's emotional experiences evolve with age and display "age trends" (Edelbrock, 1984). For example, anxiety is often elicited by a stranger approach or by separation from the caregiver during the first two years of life; animals or darkness may elicit the same emotion later.

Rapid normal developmental changes in early childhood necessitate continuous reassessment of the young child's presentation throughout the treatment process. A powerful impetus of normal development and learning supports some progress over time in all young children, with or without interventions. The momentum of development appropriately used in the intervention greatly facilitates the treatment process and is in part responsible for the dramatic therapeutic changes frequently seen in young children and their families. The remarkable plasticity of the psychological make-up of children in the first years of life and their great receptivity to caregiver's influences are likely to be among the reasons for the therapeutic progress (Cramer, 1995).

Putative Targets of Treatment

In the early years of infant mental health, interventions with young children and their families were defined in four primary types: supportive psychotherapy, developmental guidance, psychodynamic infant-parent therapy, and social support, including concrete advice and assistance (Fraiberg, 1980). *Developmental guidance* provides information about age-appropriate behaviors and concerns and suggests optimal caregiving responses based on the individual caregiver's situation and understanding of the strengths and vulnerabilities of the child and of the caregiver-child relationship. *Psychodynamic infant-parent therapy* involves understanding of the caregiver's current reactions in the context of the caregiver's early experiences and intrapsychic conflicts (Pawl & Lieberman, 1997).

These classic therapeutic modalities could be briefly illustrated by examples from therapeutic work with a five-month-old infant with failure to thrive and his family. The supportive psychotherapy approach would be to provide emotional support and validation of the experience to the young mother who is overwhelmed with taking care of the demanding child. Concrete advice and assistance would include facilitation of the social services providing baby food and transportation to the pediatrician's appointments. The developmental guidance approach would include educating the mother about amount of nutrition and optimal feeding schedule appropriate for a five-month-old child, including pointing out the necessity of the additional feeding during the night. Finally, psychodynamic infant-parent therapy would focus on helping the mother to recognize that her reluctance to get up in the middle of the night to provide an additional feeding to the hungry baby stems from her unresolved resentment toward her own mother who was abusive and neglectful.

In contemporary literature, emotional support is often seen not as separate therapeutic modality but rather the overarching attitude the therapist brings to all interventions (Pawl & Lieberman, 1997). Didactic teaching and education also has a role in some interventional approaches (Brazelton, 1982; McDonough, 1995). As discussed earlier, the manner in which the therapist's expertise is delivered is critically important in the development of the working alliance and, thus, in the treatment outcome. Often, the caregivers ask the therapist's advice about how to solve a specific problem. Although it is imperative that the caregiver's question is answered in full (McDonough, 2000), the process of answering is equally important. Pawl and Lieberman (1997) suggest that rather than offering information right away, the therapist should first ask about the caregiver's experience regarding the problem, what had been tried, and what had happened. This conversation allows the therapist to offer advice based on the detailed knowledge of the individual situation rather than reflecting an "expert's" view of how *all children should be raised* (Pawl & Lieberman, 1997). This approach in answering the caregiver's questions also serves to convey the therapist's respect for the caregiver's experience and expertise.

The choice of the appropriate intervention is guided by several factors. Considerations of appropriateness and optimal timing apply to all interventions. As in any psychotherapy, some clients, because of their cognitive make-up or personality characteristics, are reluctant to engage in psychological exploration and prefer an educational or behavioral approach while others respond better to psychodynamic interventions. Further, caregivers who are not ready to do exploratory work in the beginning of the treatment may be more open to it later on when the working alliance and trust with the clinician is well established. Offering concrete assistance could be good for a caregiver who is overwhelmed with the situation or needs concrete proof that the therapist indeed intends to help. For others, offers of concrete assistance may be infantalizing or may demonstrate the therapist's lack of trust in the caregiver's abilities (Pawl & Lieberman, 1997).

This choice also is influenced by the desired outcome, whether it is to address a concrete symptom or behavior of the child, optimize the child's development, or improve the child-caregiver relationship problem underlying the child's difficulty. Multiple-problem families usually need a range of various services to be integrated into the treatment plan. In addition to the dyadic therapies, the treatment plan may include individual therapy for the caregivers, marital therapy, or other psychosocial interventions. Certainly, to design a comprehensive treatment plan, the therapist should be aware in detail of the caregiving environment and family situation and psychological strengths and vulnerabilities of the caregivers. Therapist's own preference and comfort with one or another type of intervention are also important and often define the direction of the treatment. The clinician should recognize his or her limitations and lack of experience in other types of intervention and provide appropriate referral for the family as indicated.

Mental health professionals working with young children and their families know well that therapeutic interventions with this population are usually multimodal (Leifer, Wax, Lebental-Belfer, Fouchia, & Morrison, 1989; Lieberman, Silverman, & Pawl, 2000; Pawl & Lieberman, 1997). Often, depending on the immediate needs of the situation, the therapist engages in the most appropriate therapeutic mode, whether it is discussing feeding schedule or providing emotional comfort. Although one or another modality might predominate, the intervention usually fluidly combines elements of all modalities, which all are considered equally important components of the therapeutic process (Pawl & Lieberman, 1997).

Basic Model of Interventions with Young Children and Their Families

The multimodal multilayer psychotherapeutic work with young children and their families varies a great deal depending on the desired outcome, psychosocial context, availability of resources, and training and preferences of the therapists. These numerous defining factors make it difficult to structure and manualize the interventions. To organize the existing clinical experience and provide theoretical and clinical guidance to different modalities of interventions with young children and their families, Stern-Bruschweiler and Stern (1989) developed a basic interactional model.

In this model, the child-caregiver relationship is presented as a dynamic system with multiple, active, interdependent, and mutually influencing elements (Stern, 1995). These elements include actual behaviors in the dyad as well as the caregiver's and the child's mental representations of self, the other, and the relationships between self and the other. The actual behaviors and mental representations in the child-caregiver dyad are in a constant dynamic interaction. The caregiver's representations of the child and the relationship influence the caregiver's actual behaviors with the child. Similarly, the child's representations of the caregiver and the relationship influence the child's actual behaviors with the caregiver. At the same time, actual behaviors of the caregiver and the child toward each other influence their mental representations.

Because all elements of this system are interconnected, a successful therapeutic intervention directed at any of the behavioral or representational elements ultimately changes other elements and the entire system. This model explains why both behavioral and psychodynamic interventions may be equally effective in improving the child-caregiver relationship and, ultimately, the child's overall outcome (Robert-Tissot, Cramer, Stern, Serpa, Bachmann, Palacio-Espasa et al., 1996). Both psychodynamic and behavioral interventions change the dynamic relationship system, only through different "points of entry." While behavioral interventions are focused more on the change of actual behaviors in the dyad, psychodynamic interventions are directed more at changing mental representations of self, the other, and the relationship. Strictly speaking, because of the systemic reciprocal influences, none of the interventions could be considered "purely" psychodynamic or behavioral.

Psychodynamic Infant-Parent Therapies

The focus of psychodynamic infant-parent psychotherapies is mainly on the caregiver's mental representations of the child, self, and the relationship. These mental representations develop as a result of the caregiver's past and present experiences. They are conveyed to the child through multiple everyday interactions and to a significant extent define the caregiving relationship and the caregiving environment, thus greatly influencing the child's well being, development, and behavior. According to the basic model, positive changes in the caregiver's mental representations lead to positive changes in the caregiver's actual behavior toward the child and, thus, result in positive changes in the entire relationship system, including the child's behavior and mental representations (Stern-Bruschweiler & Stern, 1989; Stern, 1995). Examples of psychodynamic infant-parent therapies are classic infant-parent therapy (Fraiberg, 1980) and its contemporary developments, including therapy currently practiced at the San Francisco Infant-Parent

Program (Lieberman, Silverman, & Pawl, 2000), brief psychoanalytically oriented psychotherapy (Cramer & Stern, 1988), the "Watch, Wait, and Wonder" technique (Muir, 1992), and techniques utilizing video feedback as a psychodynamic therapeutic tool (Zelenko & Benham, 2000).

Classic Psychodynamic Infant-Parent Therapy and Its Current Approaches

In classic psychodynamic infant-parent therapy, the role of the caregiver's past and current representations of the child, self, and the relationship with the child are seen as central in conceptualizing the pathogenesis of the problem (Fraiberg, 1980). The caregiver's mental representations, including wishes, fears, and fantasies about the child, are unknowingly played out in child-caregiver interactions. The caregiver's perceptions of the child's personality and behavior are colored and distorted by the caregivers' past experience, which obscures the child's selfhood. Thus, the child serves as a transference object for the caregiver's mental representations and unresolved inner conflicts.

The goal of the therapy is to free the child from the caregiver's inner conflicts and to change the caregiver's mental representations to be more positive and objective (Pawl & Lieberman, 1997). The source of clinical information in the classic psychodynamic infant-parent therapy is mostly the caregiver's narrative, which includes perceptions, description, and interpretation of the problems. Listening to this narrative, the therapist tries to uncover the conflicting themes from the caregiver's past that are reactivated and enacted in the current child-caregiver relationship. The therapist works to bring these themes into the caregiver's awareness and to help the caregiver to create meaningful links between the past and the present. Disentangling the current child-caregiver relationship from the past relationships should eventually lead to insight and therapeutic change. The main therapeutic methods employed in classic psychodynamic infant-parent therapy are interpretation and clarification.

The young child's physical presence during the therapeutic session is a central ingredient of the psychodynamic infant-parent therapy because it provides both context and material for eliciting and addressing the caregiver's mental representations and allows the disentangling real experiences from the perceptual disturbances resulting from the caregiver's past. The baby's real affective and emotional contributions allow for therapeutic interpretations in the immediacy of the moment while the therapist helps the caregiver to construct new, more objective and positive meaning to the child's behavior. A classic example of this approach is presented by S. Fraiberg and her colleagues in the famous paper "Ghosts in the nursery," which describes psychotherapeutic work with an adolescent mother whose behaviors towards her child were greatly influenced by her own unresolved childhood conflicts (Fraiberg, Adelson & Shapiro, 1980).

Current approaches to psychodynamic infant-parent therapy give less primacy to conflict analysis and to clarifying links between the past and present. Similar importance is attributed to the corrective attachment experience provided by the therapeutic relationship and to the transformational power of learning and practicing reciprocal, mutually satisfying interactions (Lieberman, Silverman, & Pawl, 2000). Informed by the latest developments in infant research and relational theories, current approaches acknowledge the contribution of the infant to the relationship and emphasize the importance of the explicit emotional support and responsiveness on the part of the therapist. As in classic psychodynamic infant-parent therapy, much attention is paid to positive reconstructing of the caregiver's negative attributions regarding the child because they may be expressed through behaviors that impel the child to identify with the negative attributions and to internalize them into the child's sense of self (Cramer, 1995; Lieberman, 1999; Silverman & Lieberman, 1999).

The Watch, Wait, and Wonder Technique

In a psychodynamic "infant-led" therapeutic technique, "Watch, Wait, and Wonder" (Muir, 1992), the primary therapeutic action takes place in the psychological space between the infant and the mother. The source of clinical information in this technique is maternal emotional experiences during her observations of her child's spontaneous activity.

The mother is instructed to become an inobtrusive observer of her infant and only to interact at the infant's initiative. The mother's experience of the infant's spontaneous undirected activity inevitably stirs up her past feelings and memories. During the infant-mother interaction, the clinician does not intrude, direct, or interfere. Later, the mother makes observations about her infant's activity and talks about her emotional experience. The role of the clinician is to provide a safe and containing setting in which the mother can explore her thoughts and feelings and make links between her own childhood experiences and the current relationship with the child (Muir, 1992).

Behavioral Therapies

The focus of behavioral techniques is primarily on the caregiver's and the child's behaviors. The goal is to optimize these behaviors by changing them to be more appropriate and positive. According to the basic model, positive changes in the child's and caregiver's behaviors lead to positive change in their mental representations of self, relationships, and the other and thus result in positive changes in the entire relationship system (Stern-Bruschweiler & Stern, 1989; Stern, 1995). Examples of techniques directed mainly at behaviors include the Interactional Coaching and Guidance approaches (Field, 1982; McDonough, 2000), Behavioral Pediatric approach (Brazelton, 1982), and others.

Interactional Guidance

In the *Interactional Guidance technique* (McDonough, 1995; McDonough, 2000), the focus of the intervention is the interactional behaviors of the caregiver toward the child. This technique was designed to meet the needs of the families that had not been engaged successfully in previous treatments. These are the families overburdened by multiple environmental, psychological, and social risks, including poverty, family conflict, poor education, large family size, history of family mental illness, substance use, and limited social support. The interventions are problem-focused; the program provides practical assistance and concrete suggestions and offers extended follow-up services at the completion of the treatment. The basic idea of the approach is to enhance the individual family strengths and competencies (McDonough, 2000).

The main source of clinical material is the videotaped dyadic interaction. Families are seen weekly for ten to twelve hourly sessions. The sessions are conducted in a specially designed play room with developmentally appropriate toys. Initially, the caregiver is asked to have a ten- to twenty-minute free-play interaction with the child. The play is videotaped. Immediately after the play session, the caregiver and the therapist review and discuss the tape. The therapist seeks out the caregiver's behaviors that can be positively interpreted and reinforced and then expanded upon and elaborated with relevant information and advice.

The following example illustrates this approach. A child with sensory hypersensitivity pushed away a musical toy that the caregiver introduced with a loud noise and offered to the child. The caregiver put the musical toy down and seemed unsure what to do next while the child reached for a non-sound toy and started playing. Reviewing the tape with the caregiver, the therapist positively reinforces the fact that the caregiver did not pursue a play with the musical toy and let the child make his or her own choice. Complemented on the ability to respond to the child's sensory hypersensitivity, the caregiver is more open to the information and advice. The therapist then discusses the meaning and clinical presentation of sensory hypersensitivity. Using concrete examples from everyday life, the therapist discusses how important it is to follow the child's tolerance of physical stimuli and not to overstimulate the child.

Videotaping in this technique allows ongoing examination of the dyadic interactions and gives the caregivers an opportunity to get immediate feedback regarding their behavior and its effect on the child. Videotaping is also used to review progress across the sessions. At the end of the treatment, the caregivers are given an edited tape with the positive changes as an example of their sensitive and positive caregiving. The caregiver can share the videotape with other caregivers and use it as a source of validation of the caregiver's attempt to restructure previous ways of thinking or behaving (McDonough, 1995).

In the Interactional Guidance approach, the therapist avoids criticism and behavioral modeling in order to support the caregiver's expertise in caring for the child. The therapeutic methods employed in this technique are positive reinforcement, education, and advice. The primary implicit message to the caregiver is: "Having seen your relationship with the baby and having learned from you about the problems, I believe that you already have a foundation for improving things because you are able to be a good, loving, and sensitive parent" (McDonough, 2000, p. 429).

Behavioral Pediatric Approach

The focus of *Behavioral Pediatric* intervention is primarily on the caregiver's behaviors but also on the caregiver's mental representations of the child. The main source of information in this approach is the child's spontaneous and elicited behaviors. Clinical work of Brazelton and his colleagues presents a classic illustration of this technique (Brazelton, 1982). Using the Neonatal Assessment Scale (Brazelton, 1973), the clinician conducts the assessment of the child in the caregiver's presence. During the assessment, the clinician demonstrates to the caregiver the limitations and capacities of the young child. This new information helps the caregiver to adjust the caregiving behaviors to fit better to the child's interactive capacities. It also helps to adjust the caregiver's attributions and expectations about the child's behavior and development, that is, to change the caregiver's mental representations. Therapeutic methods employed in this approach include education, advice, positive reinforcement, and modeling. The role of the clinician in this approach is one of an expert and teacher (Stern-Bruschweiler & Stern, 1989).

In the case of the hypersensitive child described above, the therapist interacts with the child in the caregiver's presence to demonstrate to the caregiver the child's abilities and limits in tolerating different sensory stimuli. By interacting with the child, the clinician also shows to the caregiver the types of caregiving responses that help to prevent and alleviate sensory overstimulation. These may include limiting the intensity or length of the stimulation or restricting the stimulation to only one sensory domain, for example, auditory or tactile.

Empirical Support for Treatment Efficacy

Clinicians working with young children and their families are frequently privileged to observe quite dramatic positive changes in the course of the therapeutic process. This therapeutic response implements brief therapeutic formats (ten to twelve sessions) that have proven to be successful (Cramer, 1995; Cramer, & Stern, 1988; Robert-Tissot, Cramer, Stern, Serpa, Bachmann, Palacio-Espasa, et al., 1996).

As we discussed earlier, the relatively rapid therapeutic response could be due to the momentum of normal development, to the remarkable plasticity of the neurological and psychological makeup of children in the first years, and their great receptivity to the caregiver's influences. Cramer (1995) asserts that a large proportion of the infants, with the exception of those with pervasive developmental disorder (PDD) and severe gross deprivation, are able to respond well to short-term psychotherapy.

Another powerful factor is the equally remarkable ability of the caregivers to change (Cramer, 1995). The caregivers who often are reluctant to change for their own sake are usually emotionally invested in their children and willing to put much effort for the sake of the children if the children are suffering (Pawl & Lieberman, 1997). In addition, the extended postpartum period renders the new mother's hormonal and psychic functioning unstable and susceptible to rapid changes. Considering maternal receptivity and the infant's sensitivity to changes mediated by modifications in the mother's affect and behavior, it is not surprising that the early mother-child relationship is in a state of flux and is highly responsive to external influences, including therapeutic interventions (Cramer, 1995).

From the psychodynamic point of view, the responsiveness to therapeutic interventions in this population also could be explained by the fact that the caregiver's transference of past experiences is directed more toward the infant rather then toward the therapist. Compared to individual therapy, this may ease the establishment of the caregiver-therapist working alliance and thus facilitate therapeutic progress (Cramer, 1995).

There have been several published reports addressing the effectiveness of the psychotherapeutic interventions with young children and their families. They include studies assessing outcome of a particular therapeutic intervention (Fraiberg, Lieberman, Pekarsky, & Pawl, 1981; Lieberman, Weston, & Pawl, 1991; Cramer, & Stern, 1988) and studies comparing the outcome of different therapeutic approaches (Cohen, Lojkasek, Muir, Muir, & Parker, 2002; Cohen, Muir,

Parker, Brown, Lojkasek, Muir et al., 1999; Heinicke & Ramsey-Klee, 1986; Robert-Tissot et al., 1996).

An early study (Fraiberg, Lieberman, Pekarsky, & Pawl, 1981) assessed the effectiveness of the classic infant-parent therapy in a sample of fifty mother-infant dyads (children younger than three years of age) that were referred for treatment because of the relationship difficulties. The outcome measures included infant physical health and socio-emotional, cognitive, and motor functioning and the quality of parenting, including adequacy of physical caregiving environment, ability to read the child's signals, and emotional availability. After the treatment, about 90% of the infants improved in their functioning and 86% of parents improved in their parenting skills.

Lieberman, Weston, and Pawl (1991) assessed the results of infant-parent therapy in 100 poor, Spanish-speaking mothers and their infants. After the therapy, the dyads with insecure attachment improved in goal-corrected partnership, child avoidance, resistance, and anger at mother, and maternal responsiveness to the child. The major factor predicting positive outcome was the mother's ability to make use of the therapeutic relationship to explore her feelings about herself and her child and to increase her self-knowledge and understanding of the child. Mothers who developed a strong positive relationship with the therapist tended to be more empathic to their infants. At the same time, the regularity of attendance of the treatment sessions was not associated with improved outcome. These findings emphasize the crucial importance of the quality of the caregiver-therapist relationship in promoting the therapeutic change, as compared to mere fact of meeting with the therapist (Lieberman, Weston, & Pawl, 1991).

Infant-parent interventions have been applied with preschoolers who witnessed severe domestic violence showed notable improvement in quality of the child-mother interaction as well as in the child's cognitive performance and behavior (Lieberman, Van Horn, Grandison, & Pekarsky, 1997).

Meta-analysis of a wide variety of early educational and behavioral intervention programs suggests their comparable positive effect (Heinicke & Ramsey-Klee, 1986). Consistent with the basic model (Stern-Bruschweiler & Stern, 1989), it has been shown that different modalities of therapy may be equally effective in addressing the child's symptom and improving the caregiver-child relationship (Robert-Tissot et al., 1996). An appropriate match between the treatment choice and characteristics of the particular family is likely to be an important mediating variable in the treatment outcome. For example, brief insight-oriented infant-parent therapy showed good results in educated, sophisticated caregivers, whereas the Interactional Guidance approach was effective in caregivers with less education, more concrete cognitive makeup, and an impoverished psychosocial situation (McDonough, 2000; Cramer, 1995).

An outcome study was conducted comparing two forms of mother-infant therapy that showed that valuable changes can be obtained both at the level of the child's symptom removal and improvement in the quality of interactions and relationships (Robert-Tissot et al., 1996). Seventy-five mother-infant dyads (infants less than thirty months old) were assessed prior to ten-week treatment and randomly assigned to either brief psychodynamic mother-infant psychotherapy or the Interactional Guidance therapy. Results indicate a significant reduction in infants' symptoms and increase in harmony of the dyadic interactions for both therapeutic interventions. The most robust changes were related to the removal of the infants' functional symptoms, such as sleep or eating problems, while behavioral symptoms, such as aggression, changed less. The mothers became less intrusive and the infants became more cooperative. Decrease in the infant's negative affect was related to more positive maternal representation of the infant and self. The mothers' self-esteem significantly grew and negative affects (anxiety and distress) decreased. The improvements lasted as least several months, with some further positive improvement detected at the six-month follow-up. No major difference in outcome was found between the effects of the two forms of intervention. Another interesting finding in this study was that the mothers' pretreatment heightened score on the Beck Depression Inventory was not associated with poor treatment response. The mother's depressed affect moderately improved after the therapy but the main therapeutic effect seem to be a disengagement of the infant from pathogenic influences linked to maternal depression (Cramer, 1995).

In another study comparing effectiveness of two therapeutic techniques, fifty-eight mothers and infants (aged ten to thirty months) participated in the Watch, Wait, and Wonder (WWW) therapy and more traditional mother-infant psychodynamic psychotherapy (PPT) (Cohen, Lojkasek, Muir, Muir, & Parker, 2002; Cohen, Muir, Parker, Brown, Lojkasek, Muir et al., 1999). Results indicated positive effects observed from the beginning to the end of treatment in both treatment groups. Both WWW and PPT were successful in reducing infant-presenting problems, decreasing parenting stress, and reducing maternal intrusiveness and mother-infant conflict. The positive changes were maintained or improved further at the six-month follow-up. Decreased maternal depression, gains in infant cognitive development and emotion regulation, and improved infant-mother attachment security or organization had been observed in both treatment groups but emerged earlier in the WWW group.

Personal Experiences and Cases

In our clinic, we developed a psychodynamic therapeutic technique that employs videotaping of the dyadic interactions and subsequent viewing and discussion of the videotape with the caregiver (Zelenko & Benham, 2000). Before the play session, the mother is instructed to play with the child as she normally would at home. The therapist, similar to the WWW method, is not active during this session to facilitate more spontaneous interactions between the child and the parent. This session is videotaped. During the next session, the mother and the therapist review the videotape together. The therapist lets the mother make her own observations about any particular episode or the session as whole. The mother and the therapist discuss the mother's thoughts and feelings regarding the tape, which helps the mother make links between her childhood experience and present behaviors with the child.

In our experience, the use of replay of videotaped child-caregiver interactions allows fast access to the caregiver's early memories and internal representations, provides voluminous emotionally charged material for exploration, and facilitates the development of the therapeutic relationship by providing the therapist and the caregiver with a better understanding of the dyadic dynamics and giving both of them a feeling of mutual intimate experience. Videotape replay provides the caregiver with a unique opportunity to observe her own nonverbal behaviors during interactions with the child. These behaviors (expressions of the eyes, fleeting facial expressions, gestures) are enacted mental representations, wishes, fears, and fantasies (Cramer & Stern, 1988; Stern, 1995). Bringing the overt behaviors into consciousness facilitates the caregiver's awareness of the underlying mental representations. Videotape replay also allows the caregiver to observe self-behaviors in a safe distance from the immediate experience and thus helps to decrease defensiveness and improve objectivity of the observations. In addition, watching oneself in a caregiver role promotes identification with the child, and not only facilitates the caregiver's access to her own childhood memories, but also leads to better understanding of the child's immediate experience with the caregiver. The following case illustrates the application of the videotape replay technique in psychodynamic infant parent therapy (Zelenko & Benham, 2000).

Case Illustration

Brian, an eleven-month-old Caucasian boy, was born to a single, unemployed twenty-eight-year-old mother. The mother was diagnosed with borderline personality disorder and had a history of depression. Since birth, Brian had had feeding difficulties with frequent vomiting and poor weight gain. The medical staff felt that the mother was at times uncooperative and did not provide appropriate care for the boy. Per the Child Protective Services, at the age of six months the child was removed from the mother and placed in foster care. The mother's involvement with the child during the foster placement was limited to weekly one-hour supervised visits. During the following six months in the foster care Brian continued to have similar feeding difficulties and demonstrated similarly poor weight gain. The court ultimately decided to reunite the child with the mother while requesting psychological support to the dyad.

Brian and his mother attended weekly therapy sessions during the first six months; later the frequency of the sessions was decreased. Approximately every fourth session was videotaped and then discussed with the mother. Before the play session, the mother was instructed to play with Brian as she normally would at home. During the next meeting, the mother and the therapist reviewed the videotape together and discussed it. The following episodes are excerpts from the discussion sessions.

Episode 1 Videotape Replay

Brian is sitting on the floor with the dollhouse. He is trying to open the door of the dollhouse. The mother is sitting on the floor in front of Brian; her head and face are over the dollhouse, very close to Brian. The mother quickly opens and closes the door that Brian was working on and then opens and closes other doors saying quickly and loudly "open, close, open, close." Brian looks away. He then takes a little toy hummer and starts playing with it. The mother tries to attract Brian's attention by showing him a little doll and asking Brian to show the body parts on the doll. Brian takes the doll from the mother, puts it inside the house, and moves back from the mother dragging the house along.

Discussion

Therapist: How did it feel to you?

Mother: I do not know, I am closing these doors . . . And he is interested in the hammer . . . It is like, Mom, I do not want the doll, I want the hammer. I guess, I did not get it . . . I do not know . . . It is strange, I feel like my mother . . . She had good qualities, I do not want to say she was a bad mother, but I do not want to be like her and I can see it . . .

Therapist: What is it that reminds you of your mother?

Mother: Because . . . Okay, my mother always told what toys we should play with . . . And I can see, I am doing the same thing and I do not like that . . . Just realizing . . . This is not a good thing (*laughs*).

Therapist: Why are you are laughing? Are you feeling uncomfortable?

Mother: Well . . . It was not like my mother was a bad mother . . . I felt that my mom, which was not her fault, she loved me a lot . . . But she did not teach me the skills I needed to learn. I know them now but I did not know then . . . I do not want to, I am nervous about falling into that, that scares me, that is why I laugh, yes, I feel very uncomfortable, I do not want to be like my mother.

Therapist: Watching yourself with Brian makes you think about your mother?

Mother: She had wonderful qualities. She was a wonderful woman . . . The only thing I did not like that she chose what we wore. This went until high school, farther than high school. I do not want to be like my mother . . . I always felt she was overbearing but I can see now I am turning like her. My mom . . . she meant well . . . I do not think she realized the damage she caused, that is what it is . . . It makes me very nervous.

This video replay stimulated discussions regarding maternal past and its possible influence on maternal current attitudes and behaviors toward Brian. The process encouraged multiple maternal insights and itself became a foundation for a solid therapeutic alliance. We felt that the format allowed the mother to have more control over the therapeutic process by choosing the topic for the discussion based on the impressions of the videotape. This approach also allowed the mother to identify herself with worrisome aspects of the interaction (being intrusive, overbearing), which itself was an effective intervention. Not only did this process facilitate important therapeutic insights, but it also helped to minimize maternal feelings of being criticized by the therapist, which is one of the major hindrances in the development of the therapeutic alliance.

The following excerpt is from the session videotaped four months after the beginning of the therapy. It demonstrates significant improvement in the dyadic interactions, which now are more reciprocal and obviously enjoyable to both participants. The mother's behavior shows respect for Brian's physical and emotional space and willingness to follow his lead. The discussion brought into light many salient therapeutic issues that we addressed earlier in this chapter, including the mother's need to be "seen" and preferred by the child, her difficulties understanding Brian's behaviors and tendency to interpret them negatively, her still unresolved early childhood conflicts and fear of abandonment, and merging of Brian's and her own experience in her mind.

Episode 2 Videotape Replay, Four Months Later

Brian is playing in the toy kitchen. The mother is sitting on the floor several feet from him. She asks him what he is doing. Brian shows her a serving spoon, pretends to try food from it and makes a "yummy" sound. The mother smiles and repeats the sound. Brian laughs and shakes the spoon in front of his face. The mother picks up another spoon and shakes it the way Brian did it. Brian hides his spoon behind the kitchen cabinet. Mother "searches" for it, finally finds it and

gives it back to Brian. Brian hides it again, Mother finds it again; both are looking at each other and laughing.

Discussion

Therapist: Do you remember how it felt to you?

Mother: I think we communicated, for once we communicated . . . I think I felt
included. We never did before . . . before, I kind of took over, did not let
him do his own thing; he wanted to do his own thing . . .

Therapist: Was it a feeling before that you were not included? That Brian did not
include you?

Mother: You know . . . With everything that happened, yes, I think so. That he
did not like me, that he did not know me anymore. Now I know . . . He
lights up like a Christmas tree when he sees me . . . Even though he did
before, I was so worried, I thought, he was not going to love me, he was
going to love the foster mother more than he loved me. He is older now.
When he was a baby, he was crying and stuff, I did not know . . . I did
not understand . . . But now I know, he knows who his mother is. And I am
going to watch him as a hawk. When I was a kid, my mom had her back
towards the ocean and I went to the ocean. I got picked up by a surfer,
on the surfboard. This is a very scary thought, I could have been dead. I
remember it so vividly, I was two years old and my mother did not even
know I was gone. I mean, poor kid. And I still think, I never want to be
that kind of the mother, I want to know at all times where my son is . . .

Future Directions

Considering the significance of early mental health for the children's developmental outcome and later behavioral and socioemotional adjustment, and in view
of the proven effectiveness of the psychotherapeutic interventions with young children and their families, broader implementation of such interventions is clearly indicated. The multitude of developmental, environmental, and relational therapeutic
issues renders therapeutic work with young children and their families multimodal
and multilayered. This often necessitates interdisciplinary and interagency efforts
on the part of therapeutic and social institutions. At the same time, the diversity of
training backgrounds and philosophical and practical approaches among professionals involved in work with this population makes systemic implementation of the
complex programs challenging. The major research and administrative direction in
the field's evolution at this time is the development of structured, manualized, and
coordinated interventions that could be implemented by mental health professionals

with diverse backgrounds. More intensive implementation of brief therapy formats and the use of videotaping to facilitate the therapeutic progress will help to make the treatment programs more time- and cost-effective.

References

Alexander, F. (1956). *Psychoanalysis and psychotherapy*. New York: Norton.

Benham, A. L. (2000). The observation and assessment of young children including use of the Infant-Toddler Mental Status Exam. In Zeanah (Ed.), *Handbook of infant mental health*, (2nd ed., pp. 249–265). New York: Guildford Press.

Brazelton, T. B. (1973). Neonatal behavioral assessment scale. Philadelphia: J. B. Lippincott.

Brazelton, T. B. (1982). Joint regulation of neonate-parent behavior. In E. Tronick (Ed.), *Social interchange in infancy* (pp. 7–22). Baltimore, MD: University Park Press.

Briggs-Gowan, M. J., Carter, A. S., Moye Skuban, E., & McCue Horwitz, S. (2001). Prevalence of social-emotional and behavioral problems in a community sample of 1- and 2-year-old children. *Journal of the American Academy of Child and Adolescent Psychiatry, 40*(7), 811–819.

Briggs-Gowan, M., Carter, A., & Schwab-Stone, M. (1996). Discrepancies among mother, child, and teacher reports: Examining the contribution of maternal depression and anxiety. *Journal of Abnormal Psychology, 24,* 749–765.

Carter, A. S., Little, C., Briggs-Gowan, M. J., & Kogan, N. (1999). The Infant Toddler Socio-Emotional Assessment (ITSEA): Comparing parent ratings to laboratory observations of task mastery, emotion regulation, coping behaviors, and attachment status. *Infant Mental Health Journal, 20*(4), 375–392.

Cicchetti, D., Toth, S. L., Bush, M. A., & Gillespie, J. F. (1988). Stage-salient issues: A transactional model of intervention. In E. D. Nannins & P. A. Cowan (Eds.) *Developmental psychopathology and its treatment. New directions of child development.* San Francisco: Jossey-Bass.

Cohen, N. J., Lojkasek, M., Muir, E., Muir, R., & Parker, C. (2002). Six-month follow-up of two mother-infant psychotherapies: Convergence of therapeutic outcomes. *Infant Mental Health Journal, 23*(4), 361–380.

Cohen, N. J., Muir, E., Parker, C. J., Brown, M., Lojkasek, M., Muir, R., et al. (1999). Watch, wait and wonder: Testing the effectiveness of a new approach to mother-infant psychotherapy. *Infant Mental Health Journal, 20*(4), 429–451.

Colombo, J., & Fagan, J. (Eds.). (1990). *Individual differences in infancy: Reliability, stability, and prediction.* Hillsdale, NJ: Lawrence Erlbaum.

Cramer, B. (1995). Short-term dynamic psychotherapy for infants and their parents. *Child and Adolescent Psychiatric Clinics of North America, 4,* 649–660.

Cramer, B., & Stern, D. N. (1988). Evaluation of changes in mother-infant brief psychotherapy. *Infant Mental Health Journal, 9,* 20–45.

Eddy, J. M., Dishio, T., & Stoolmiller, M. (1998). The analysis of intervention change in children and families: Methodological and conceptual issues embedded in intervention studies. *Journal of Abnormal Child Psychology, 26,* 53–71.

Edelbrock, C. S. (1984). Developmental considerations. In T. H. Ollednick & M. Hersen (Eds.), *Child behavioral assessment: Principles and procedures.* Elmstrod, NY: Pergamon Press.

Fergusson, D., Lynskey, M., & Horwood, L. (1993). The effects of maternal depression on maternal ratings of child behavior. *Journal of Abnormal Child Psychology, 21,* 245–271.

Field, T. M. (1982). Interactional coaching for high-risk infants and their parents. *Prevention and Human Service, 1,* 5–24.

Fraiberg, S. (1980). Clinical studies in infant mental health. New York: Basic Books.

Fraiberg, S., Adelson, E., & Shapiro, V. (1980). Ghosts in the nursery: A psychoanalytic approach to the problems of impaired infant-mother relationships. In S. Fraiberg (Ed.), *Clinical studies in infant mental health* (pp. 64–195). New York: Basic Books.

Fraiberg, S., Lieberman, A. F., Pekarsky, J., & Pawl, J. (1981). Treatment and outcome in an infant psychiatry program. *Journal of Preventive Psychiatry, 1*(1), 89–111.

Heinicke, C. M., & Ramsey-Klee, D. M. (1986). Outcome of child psychotherapy as a function of frequency of session. *Journal of the American Academy of Child and Adolescent Psychiatry, 25*(2), 247–253.

Lieberman, A. F., & Pawl, J. H. (1993). Infant-parent psychotherapy. In C. H. Zeanah (Ed.), *Handbook of infant mental health* (1st ed., 427–442). New York: Guildford Press.

Lieberman, A. F., Silverman, R., & Pawl, J. H. (2000). Infant-parent psychotherapy: Core concepts and current approaches. In C. H. Zeanah (Ed.), *Handbook of infant mental health* (2nd ed., 472–484). New York: Guildford Press.

Lieberman, A. F. (1999). Negative maternal attributions: Effects on toddlers' sense of self. *Psychoanalytic Inquiry, 19*(5), 737–756.

Lieberman, A. F., Van Horn, P. Grandison, C. M., & Pekarsky, J. H. (1997). Mental health assessment of infants, toddlers, and preschoolers in a service program and a treatment outcome research program. *Infant Mental Health Journal, 18*(2), 158–170.

Lieberman, A. F., Weston, D. R., & Pawl, J. H. (1991). Preventive intervention and outcome with anxiously attached dyads. *Child Development, 62,* 199–209.

Leifer, M., Wax, L. C., Lebental-Belfer, L., Fouchia, A., & Morrison, M. (1989). The use of multitreatment modalities in early interventions: A quantitative case study. *Infant Mental Health Journal, 10,* 100–116.

Luby, J. L., & Morgan, K. (1997). Characteristics of an Infant/Preschool psychiatric clinic sample: Implications for clinical assessment and nosology. *Infant Mental Health Journal, 18,* 209–220.

McDonough, S. (1995). Promoting positive early parent-infant relationships through interaction guidance. *Child and Adolescent Psychiatric Clinics of North America, 4,* 661–673.

McDonough, S. (2000). Interactional guidance: An approach for difficult-to-engage families. In C. H. Zeanah (Ed.), *Handbook of infant mental health,* 2nd ed., 485–493. New York, Guildford Press.

Muir, E. (1992). Watching, waiting, and wondering: Applying psychoanalytic principals to mother-infant intervention. *Infant Mental Health, 13,* 319–328.

Ollendick T., & King, N. (1991). Developmental factors in child behavioral assessment. In P. R. Martin (Ed.), *Handbook of behavior therapy and psychological science: An integrative approach* (pp. 57–72). New York: Pergamon Press.

Olson, S. L., Bates, J. E., Sandy, J. M., & Lanthier, R. (2000). Early developmental precursors of externalizing behavior in middle childhood and adolescence. *Journal of Abnormal Psychology, 28*(2), 119–133.

Pawl, J. H., & Lieberman A. E. (1997). Infant-parent psychotherapy. In J. N. Noshpitz (Ed.), *Handbook of child and adolescent psychiatry, volume 1. Infants and preschoolers: Development and syndromes* (pp. 339–351). New York: Wiley.

Richman, N., Stevenson, J., & Graham, P. (1982). *Preschool to school: A behavioral study.* London: Academic Press.

Robert-Tissot, C., Cramer B., Stern, D. N., Serpa, S. R., Bachmann, J-P., Palacio-Espasa, F., et al. (1996). Outcome evaluation in brief mother-infant psychotherapy: Report on 75 cases. *Infant Mental Health Journal, 17,* 97–114.

Rutter, M. L., Kreppner, J. M., O'Connor, T. G., & English and Romanian Adoptees study team (2001). Specificity and heterogeneity in children's responses to profound institutional privation. *British Journal of Psychiatry, 179,* 97–103.

Rutter, M. L., & Sroufe, L. A. (2000). Developmental psychopathology: Concepts and challenges. *Development and Psychopathology, 12,* 265–296.

Sameroff, A. J., & Chandler, M. J. (1975). Reproductive risk and the continuum of caretaking casuality. In F. D. Horowitz (Ed.), *Review of child developmental research* (Vol. 4). University of Chicago Press.

Sameroff, A. J., Seiffer, R., & Zax, M. (1982). Early development of children at risk for emotional disorders. *Monographs of the Society for Research in Child Development, 47*(7, Serial No. 199).

Schore, A. N. (2001). The effects of early relational trauma on right brain development, affect regulation, and infant mental health. *Infant Mental Health Journal, 22*(1–2), 201–269.

Seligman, S. P., & Pawl, J. H. (1985). Impediments to the formation of the working alliance in infant-parent psychotherapy. In J. D. Call, E. Galeston, & R. L. Tyson (Eds.), *Frontiers of infant psychiatry* (Vol. 2, pp. 232–237). New York: Basis Books, Inc.

Shaw, D. S., Owens, E. B., Vondra, J. I., Keenan, K., & Winslow, E. B. (1996). Early risk factors and pathways in the development of early disruptive behavioral problems. *Development and Psychopathology, 8,* 679–699.

Silverman, R. C., & Lieberman, A. F. (1999). Negative maternal attribution, projective identification and the intergenerational transmission of violent relational patterns. *Psychoanalytic Dialogues, 9,* 166–186.

Sroufe, L. A. (1990). Pathways to adaptation and maladaptation: Psychopathology as developmental deviation. In D. Cicchetti (Ed.), *Rochester Symposium on Developmental Psychopathology: Vol. 1. The emergence of discipline,* 13–40. Hillsdale, New Jersey, Erlbaum.

Sroufe, L. A. (1997). Psychopathology as an outcome of development. *Development and Psychopathology, 9,* 251–268.

Stern, D. N. (1985). *The interpersonal world of the infant.* New York: Basic Books.

Stern, D. N. (1995). *The motherhood constellation.* New York: Basic Books.

Stern-Bruschweiler, N., & Stern, D. N. (1989). A model for conceptualizing the role of the mother's representational world in various mother-infant therapies. *Infant Mental Health Journal, 10,* 142–156.

Winnicot, D. W. (1965). The theory of the parent-infant relationship. In D. W. Winnicot (Ed.), *The maturational processes and the facilitating environment* (pp. 37–55). New York: International Universities Press (Original work published 1960).

Winnicot, D. W. (1971). *Playing and reality.* New York: Tavistock Publications.

Zeanah, C. H., Boris, N. W., & Scheeringa, M. S. (1997). Psychopathology in infancy. *Journal of Child Psychology and Psychiatry, 38,* 81–99.

Zelenko, M. (In press). Observation in infant and toddler mental health assessment. In R. Del Carmen-Wiggins & A. Carter (Eds). *Handbook of infant and toddler mental health assessment.* New York: Oxford University Press.

Zelenko, M., & Benham, A. (2000). Videotaping as a therapeutic tool in psychodynamic infant-parent therapy. *Infant Mental Health, 21*(3), 192–203.

CHAPTER TWENTY

PSYCHODYNAMIC THERAPY WITH ADOLESCENTS

Michael J. Loughran, Ph.D.

There exists one real cure for adolescence, and only one. The cure for adolescence belongs to the passage of time and to the gradual maturation processes. This process cannot be hurried or slowed up, though indeed it can be broken into and destroyed, or it can wither up from within, in psychiatric illness (Winnicott, 1965a, p. 79).

Psychodynamic psychotherapy with adolescents, while flexible and varied in its techniques, is based on psychoanalytic theory. Psychoanalysis is both a theory of the mind and a theory of clinical practice. From their origin in the singular genius of Freud over a hundred years ago, both tracks are continually evolving. These two tracks constitute separate but interrelated lines of development: an advance in one invites a re-thinking and a refinement in the other. These advances come both from within the psychoanalytic world, by theorists inspired by clinical insight, and from without as contributions from science, philosophy, and literature constantly enrich psychoanalytic thinking.

The contemporary psychoanalytic theory of the mind is the most elegant and complex model we have of psychic life. It outlines psychological development from infancy through adulthood in terms of both conscious and unconscious aspects of mental functioning. Psychoanalytic theory explains how intrapsychic organization evolves out of the complex interplay between the individual's nature and the caregiving environment (Abrams & Solnit, 1998). At its heart, the traditional psychoanalytic model is a model of conflict. The ego psychological model imagined conflict in terms of patterns of opposing forces between three hypothesized structures or systems in the mind—id, ego, superego—and reality. In this view, we live in the clash between our basic libidinal and aggressive drives, represented in the mind as wishes, and the secondary claims of social reality. This concept of conflict tied to the structural model is thought to best explain neurotic psychopathology. It has been supplemented in contemporary, object relations theories by the concept of deficit (Greenberg & Mitchell, 1983). The concept of *deficit* suggests that unmet developmental needs for phase-specific modes of relationship explain more primitive forms of pathology better than conflicts thought of solely in terms of wishes related to the drives (Killingmo, 1989). This advance has greatly refined psychoanalytic conceptions of the mechanisms both of pathology and of psychic change in therapy, and has led to the development of new therapeutic techniques. These new formulations of technique, in turn, have broadened the range of pathology psychoanalytic approaches can treat.

Historically, psychodynamic psychotherapy has been the most commonly used approach for treating disturbed adolescents. This treatment uses an integrated approach that focuses on helping the individual adolescent and the key adults in the adolescent's life. Psychodynamic psychotherapy differs from behavioral therapies, which are interested only in the removal of symptoms but not in their origin, and from family systems approaches that focus more on the current interpersonal aspects of the symptoms than on their origin and meaning in the intrapsychic life of the individual patient.

This chapter begins with an overview of the basic rationale and theory of the psychodynamic approach, followed by a discussion of the putative mechanisms of efficacy involved in the principles of psychoanalytic practice. The developmental influences on these mechanisms are examined in an outline of the psychoanalytic understanding of adolescence as a transitional stage of development. A review of the empirical support for psychodynamic treatment of adolescents follows. Then an outline is presented of conducting treatment from initial evaluation and treatment planning through termination. The chapter concludes with a discussion of future directions.

Basic Rationale and Theory

A discussion of the therapeutic action of the psychodynamic approach, of how this treatment helps disturbed adolescents, requires consideration of the mechanisms that underlie psychic change. To limit repetition, the reader is referred to Fonagy's listing in Chapter 21 of the core assumptions underlying the psychoanalytic approach.

The psychoanalytic tradition is identified with the view that change is best pursued by focusing on intrapsychic change in the individual patient. Most of its techniques are defined and discussed in terms of their use in individual psychotherapy or psychoanalysis. The psychoanalytic model of the mind, however, focuses on how intrapsychic organization develops within a context of interpersonal attachment. Consistent with this, a treatment approach with adolescents focused solely on individual intrapsychic change is incomplete (Szapocznik et al., 1989). To be effective, it must be integrated with a focus on the modifications, guided by the psychoanalytic understanding of development, needed in the interpersonal context of family and parents in which the adolescent's life is embedded (Bleiberg, 2001; Bloch, 1995). Many adolescent treatments fail not because of inadequate individual psychotherapeutic technique, but because caregivers are not involved in the treatment enough to support the treatment and the process of change in their adolescents. Regular meetings with parents have to be built into the treatment plan. A therapeutic alliance with the adolescent aimed at enhancing self-regulation and awareness of self and others must be matched by an alliance to help parents be both more reflective and more in charge of parenting. Adolescents call upon parents to redefine their continuing emotional and psychological availability, and to understand their adolescents enough to provide them with what they need.

The abbreviated aim of broadening the adolescent's understanding of how his or her mind works is frequently cited as central to the psychodynamic approach. This implies the more specific goal of strengthening the ego in its self-regulating, self-observing, and synthesizing functions. From the developmental perspective, treatment aims at helping the adolescent resume development by removing obstacles that interfere with its progression. This developmental goal broadens the focus on individual change to include effecting change as well in the "facilitating environment" of parents and families.

Putative Mechanisms of Efficacy

How does the psychodynamic process, based on a psychoanalytic model of the mind, bring about change in the internal world of the adolescent? What carries the therapeutic action?

The two basic mechanisms underlying change in psychodynamic psychotherapy are (1) resolving unconscious conflict, and (2) strengthening mental processes. There are two categories of technique generally related to these two mechanisms. These two categories are (a) interpretive techniques aimed at promoting insight, and (b) techniques that focus on the relational experience in treatment

(Jones, 1997). These latter techniques fall under the rubric of "developmental help" or "containment" and aim at establishing mental processes such as thinking and the capacity to mentalize. In good analytic work, interpretation and containment are often intertwined, but each is selectively in the foreground at different clinical moments based on the present capacities and immediate needs of the patient (Lafarge, 2000).

Putative Targets of Treatment

Interventions Differentiating Neurotic from Developmental Disturbance

These two different mechanisms of change and two categories of technique differentially apply to the treatment of adolescent patients who present at different levels of ego functioning. Psychoanalytic theory has historically framed this distinction between different levels of ego functioning in terms of neurotic disturbance for those with intact egos and developmental disturbance for those with ego deficits (Edgcumbe, 1993; A. Freud, 1958). Over the past few decades, psychoanalytic clinical theory has broadened its scope of treatable patients beyond those with neurotic disturbance to include patients stuck at lower or more primitive levels of ego development who do not respond well to a strictly insight-oriented approach. This reflects a shift in psychoanalytic interest over the past thirty years from oedipal conflict to pre-oedipal development (Greenberg & Mitchell, 1983).

Treatment of higher functioning adolescents with intact egos focuses on gaining insight through interpretation into unconscious "intersystemic" conflicts between the ego and id and superego demands. For example, a fifteen-year-old adolescent with an intact ego and a high level of functioning came into treatment some months after his parents separated. An excellent student, he was suddenly unable to do any schoolwork and was frequently leaving school mid-day to return home. In therapy, he came to understand how doing well in school represented a feared oedipal victory in outdistancing his father and winning his mother. His mother had contributed to his anxiety by turning to him for emotional closeness as she criticized his father. Interpretation of resistance, transference, and his conflicted feelings in response to his parents' marital problems, resulted in insights that explained and resolved his anxiety and work inhibition. His higher level of ego functioning, specifically his ability to represent his thoughts and feelings, made it possible for him to utilize this type of insight-oriented treatment approach. Many such adolescents with neurotic problems have relatively good reflective capacities, founded on "good enough" early attachment relationships and on the adequate mentalizing capacities of an early caregiver (Fonagy & Perron, 2002). Neurotic adolescents are thought to have achieved relatively stable differentiation between self-representation and object-representation, and to rely predominantly on repression as a mechanism of defense (Kernberg, 1975).

Clinical intervention with lower functioning adolescents, in contrast, focuses on treating defects in the ego itself. With patients at lower levels of ego functioning, psychological disturbance results from deficits within the ego, in its self-regulating and organizing functions, rather than from intersystemic conflicts, for instance, between the ego and superego. Deficits in ego functioning manifest in such adolescents in poor judgment, poor reality testing, poor control over affect and impulse, a diffuse sense of identity, and reliance on primitive defenses such as splitting to protect the ego. This serious level of disorder requires intensive intervention over long periods as treatment must focus on engaging the absent or significantly deficient mental processes on which ego functioning is based. These adolescents lack the reflective capacities for symbolic thought that are needed to create mental representations of affects, of aspects of bodily experience, of cause and effect, and of interactions between self and object (Edgcumbe, 1983). The ego was injured before it had developed the ability to mentally represent the self and object as separate. Fonagy describes this level of disorder as centering on an insufficient capacity for mentalization. He defines this capacity as involving "both a self-reflective and an interpersonal component that ideally provides the individual with a well-developed capacity to distinguish inner from outer reality, . . . and intrapersonal mental and emotional processes from interpersonal communications" (Fonagy et al., 2002, p. 25). Interpretive work is inappropriate when this capacity for representing is absent. In pathology based on such deficit, it is not a matter of defending oneself against anxiety connected with forbidden object-directed needs, as in the case in conflict. What is defended against is anxiety of fragmentation, of losing one's own feeling of identity (Killingmo, 1989). These patients need a therapy that promotes a practicing and developing of those functions of thinking and feeling and knowing which did not develop normally, and which underlie object relations and such key ego functions as affect tolerance, impulse control, and reality testing (Fonagy & Moran, 1991; Smith, 1993). Therapy must activate the patients' capacity to find meaning in their own behavior and that of others (Blieberg, 2001, p. 153).

In helping self-reflection and self-regulation that never developed adequately, the therapist is intervening in a manner that parallels the container/contained aspects of an early developmental interaction (Bion, 1959). The more disturbed adolescent must rely on the therapist's imaginative capacity to receive and process primitive emotional experience (Lafarge, 2000). At this lower level of ego functioning, the adolescent's slow internalization of these containing and organizing aspects of the therapeutic relationship, rather than insight, carries the therapeutic action and corrects early developmental disturbance. The mechanism of change centers on techniques that encourage development of these functions of feeling and thinking, and on identification with or internalization of the therapist's way of thinking and responding.

Fonagy and his colleagues have recently advanced the traditional view of dividing the treatment of neurotic conflict or developmental disturbance by similarly delineating two models of therapeutic action. Fonagy labels these models the representational model and the mental process model (Fonagy et al., 1993). The therapeutic action in the representational model is carried by the reintegration of repudiated mental representations of self and object. In the latter model, the mental process of representing is undeveloped or defensively inhibited, sometimes to the point that certain experiences cannot be thought, felt, or remembered. In the mental process model of treatment, the therapeutic action is carried by the stimulation and modification of these impaired mental processes.

These distinctions between models of therapeutic action, conflict resolution versus developmental help or containment, are reminiscent of a traditionally conceptualized continuum of techniques from exploratory techniques on one end to supportive techniques on the other. Many of what were once considered merely supportive techniques can be better understood from a contemporary perspective in terms of developmental help or containment. Many ego-supportive techniques such as hospitalization, placement in a different school, or the use of medication represent containment when the adolescent's inner controls over impulsive, non-reflective, destructive action are insufficient. Such responses create a better "hold" for the adolescent in treatment that, along with techniques that promote self-reflection, may help the adolescent mentally process internal experience (Bleiberg, 2001).

Developmental Influences

An Age Between: Adolescence as a Transitional Stage of Development

Psychoanalysis from its beginning was revolutionary in understanding adult disturbance in terms of early developmental experience. The developmental perspective, inherent to this theory, is central to work with adolescents in a number of ways. Adolescent conflict is developmental in nature. The psychoanalytic explanation of adolescent conflict is embedded in its model of the structural changes that must unfold, and the tasks that must be mastered, for this stage of development to progress normatively. Central to this understanding is the idea that a break or serious deviation in the process of development is itself the pathology during adolescence (Laufer & Laufer, 1984). This is true whether breakdown is due to current dynamic conflicts, ego weakness tied to earlier developmental disturbances (Blos, 1967), or current failure of the adolescent's attachment system to provide needed support and sponsorship for development (Bloch, 1995; Fonagy et al., 2002).

The psychodynamic approach also asserts that the therapeutic relationship is developmental in nature. In many ways, the clinician's provision of holding, containing, and organizing functions, which lies at the heart of the therapeutic interaction, parallels early caregiver-child interactions (Abrams, 1990; Modell, 1976; Winnicott, 1965b, 1975). These aspects of psychodynamic technique, centered on emotional attunement in the treatment relationship, aim at getting development back on track by helping the adolescent expand and consolidate reflective and self-regulating capacities.

Adolescence is one of the most radical of all the developmental periods. Potentially disorienting and profound changes require a massive reappraisal in every sphere of internal and external life. The adolescent's sense of self has to integrate and adapt to all the physical changes in appearance, size, and sexuality, to the changing character of relationships with parents and peers, to radically new desires, and to new capacities to think and understand oneself and the world. Ideally, the losses involved in these changes and in the ending of childhood are balanced by the adolescent's sense of discovery and new synthesis in an expanded internal and interpersonal world (Gitelson, 1943). Developmental turbulence is reflected in the frequent observation that no time in the life cycle combines regression and growth to the extent that occurs normatively in adolescence. This is partly due to the antagonistic aims of this period, such as those between active and passive wishes, between defiance and dependence, and between wishes to grow up and wishes to return to the safety of childhood (Blos, 1962, 1967; A. Freud, 1958; Winnicott, 1965a). Regression takes place during adolescence on every line of development of ego functioning and defense (A. Freud, 1965). More disturbed adolescents have more severe regressions, for instance in the developmental lines of self-object differentiation, magical thinking, and levels of defense. Even for normal adolescents, disharmony seems a basic fact during these years as one's self seems frequently out of balance.

The impact on parents and other adults echo the bewildering changes happening within the adolescent as issues of control and autonomy reverberate through families and communities. Contemporary western culture, fascinated with adolescence, alternates between envying and disapproving, and between idealizing and demonizing the young (Anthony, 1970). The part played by the environment during adolescence is immensely significant (Winnicott, 1965a).

The *classical psychoanalytic view* of normal adolescence has been amended in a number of significant ways. Originally, adolescence was conceived of as a period of tremendous turmoil and of ego and affective instability (Geleerd, 1957). Empirical research has corrected the excesses of this position (Masterson, 1972; Offer, 1969; Offer & Offer, 1975), suggesting that extreme upset is not universal and that adolescent personality upheaval can be reflected primarily in manageable, non-debilitating rebellion and mood swings. There is still general agreement and empirical support, however, that some degree of regression, turmoil, and rebellion seems to be part of the optimal accomplishment of the tasks of adolescence (Peskin, 1972).

Other corrections of traditional psychoanalytic views of adolescence challenge the culturally and perhaps gender biased over-emphasis on individuation, independence, separation, and autonomy in our theories. Contemporary theorists emphasize for adolescence of both genders, across sociocultural differences, the interdependence of individuation and connectedness. Seeing individuation and attachment as dialectic counterparts leads to the conclusion, supported by clinical experience, that adolescent separation from parents proceeds optimally on the basis of secure attachment (Blatt & Blass, 1990; Bleiberg, 1988; Bloch, 1995; Fonagy et al., 2002; Gilligan, 1982; Jordan, 1993). The individual adolescent may *feel* free and independent but, as Winnicott asserts, "the individual seen as an autonomous unit is in fact never independent of environment" (Winnicott, 1971a, p. 139). It is more accurate clinically to think of adolescents changing their relationships with parents, in the direction of balancing needs for both individuation and connectedness, than to think of these changes in terms of their "breaking ties." Despite defensive stances, adolescents wish to retain positive relationships with their parents as they strive to complete development (Bloch, 1995). The most serious adolescent psychopathology occurs when internally separating from parents is avoided or is undermined because it is internally experienced as a threat of losing the object or the object's love (Masterson, 1972).

Psychoanalytic theory conceptualizes this radical period of development as consisting of three overlapping phases: early, middle, and late (Esman, 1985). Each phase is characterized by specific changes in object relations that tie into (a) the structural changes of adolescence, and (b) specific tasks requiring mastery for development to progress normally (Blos, 1962, 1967; A. Freud, 1957, 1966).

Structural Changes of Adolescence

Blos argues that the key to understanding the surface manifestations of change during adolescence can be found in the structural changes that underlie a second separation-individuation process (Blos, 1962, 1967, 1970). These structural changes can best be explained using the language of Freud's structural model consisting of the hypothesized mental structures of id, ego, and superego.

Latency, the period preceding adolescence, from approximately six-and-a-half to ten years, is seen as a period in normal development of relative harmony between these psychic systems. The acquisition of repression at the "resolution" of the Oedipus complex anchors a period of defensive stability buttressed by the latency child's new reliance on internalized parental standards in his superego (Loewald, 1975; Sandler, 1968; Wieder, 1978). This breathing space provided by latency, however, is soon swept away by hormonal changes at puberty as the child enters early adolescence (A. Freud, 1966). At puberty, the whole tenor and texture of inner life changes for the early adolescent (Harley, 1970). A central problem is that puberty reanimates unconscious sexual and aggressive wishes that now seem more possible to gratify due to physical maturation. This intensification threatens repression, and the adolescent ego must turn to more primitive defenses such as regression, displacement, acting out, and body language to defend its integrity.

Returning to Blos' formulation, much of the behavioral unrest in early adolescence is due to a weakening of the ego in its efforts to mediate between id impulses and the demands of the outer world. This is due to two main structural factors. The first is the quantitative upsurge in drives. The upsurge in drives results in regression to instinctual anxiety, and to a recathexis of all the libidinal and aggressive modes of gratification experienced during the early childhood years. The partial success of the id over the ego manifests in increased impulsivity, and in defensive regression to oral, anal, and phallic exhibitionistic behaviors. In psychoanalytic theory, adolescence represents a transition between this diffuse infantile sexuality and genitally centered adult sexuality. Genital trends ultimately predominate. At first, however, increased genital pleasure threatens repression, causing a defensive use of regression to earlier modes. Eating disorders, for instance, can be understood in terms of both displacement of conflict and regression to an oral level as a defense against the anxieties stimulated by unconscious genital wishes and reanimated oedipal dynamics. Stronger aggressive drives also threaten defenses. In the face of this upsurge of both libidinal and aggressive drives, and the resultant intensification of unconscious fantasies, the ego has to redouble its defensive efforts (A. Freud, 1958).

The second factor contributing to ego weakness is the decrease in the power and efficacy of the superego. This is due to a devaluing of the mental representations of the parents and their internalized moral equivalents in the superego. The early adolescent treats the superego with suspicion as an incestuous object (A. Freud, 1958). This decrease in the superego's power to come to the aid of the ego manifests in breakdowns in self-control and judgment. Estrangement from the superego and the reworking of the superego during adolescence are major foci of adolescent psychotherapy.

Structurally, according to Blos, during middle adolescence the ego is expanding in strength in its mediating role. The consolidation of cognitive development, with the advance to formal operational thinking, aids the ego immensely in its functioning (Overton et al., 1992; Piaget, 1975). This increased capacity for reflection enlarges the scope of trial and error, which now can take place in thought. This new cognitive capacity aids affect development as middle adolescents have greater conscious awareness of increasingly complex and subtle affective states and have expanded capacities to think about their own feelings and those of others. This greatly aids the ability to differentiate internal experience from external perception, and to move from the narcissistic relating characteristic of early adolescence to now more mature and mutually caring relationships. This greater self-awareness, aided by active experimentation with different roles in middle adolescence, serves the process of identity formation as defined by Erikson and empirically validated by Marcia (Erikson, 1979; Marcia, 1966).

By late adolescence, the ego has developed more stability in its habitual ways of handling inner and outer demands. Favored defenses and compromises between the psychic systems shape character. The reworking of the superego ideally results in clearer and more consistent standards.

Developmental Tasks of Adolescence

Interwoven with these structural changes, each of the three phases of adolescence involves mastering specific developmental tasks. Early adolescence centers on two tasks: coming to terms with a changed body image, and beginning the process of psychological disengagement from the parents of childhood.

Regarding the first task, the maturational events of puberty sharpen the distinction between the sexes and facilitate the delineation of the body image features of one's own sexuality. This contributes to the gradual construction of a feminine or masculine self-representation (Harley, 1970). Menarche, for example, serves as a nidus around which a revised body image is built. The young adolescent girl must integrate her body as feminine, as sexually mature, and as potentially childbearing. Reactions to these changes in body image, conflicts around discrepancies with an ideal body, and heightened awareness of intense, new sexual thoughts and feelings all contribute to disturbing states of mind for both genders at this age and may even precipitate serious pathological response. The acting out seen in risk-taking behavior has been empirically shown to be related to uneven rates of physical maturation within adolescent peer groups (Ponton, 1997), and can be related to the underlying fantasies about early or late physical development. Clinical experience shows that any adolescent who differs in any way from the "visibly average" is at risk.

The second task of early adolescence, the separation process, involves a gradual, step-by-step, internal and external moving away. This involves a moving away both from reliance on the protection and comfort of the idealized and omnipotent parents internalized during childhood, and a giving up of the parents as oedipal love objects. The regressive pull of pre-oedipal and oedipal wishes is strong, as is the anxiety these wishes stimulate. Adolescents concretely avoid parents, and displace their intense hunger for them onto transitory, idealized, narcissistic love relationships. Separating from parents involves for all adolescents a partial relinquishment of needed identifications (object relinquishment), and a search for new, extrafamilial love objects in peers and valued adults (object finding). Object choices are largely made on a narcissistic basis in early adolescence, as the self is especially vulnerable in this move away from the narcissistic supplies of parental approval. This normative increase in narcissism manifests in adolescence in states of self-absorbed moodiness and in what Elkind termed "egocentrism" (Elkind, 1967).

It is of enormous clinical importance to understand that there is a continuum in adolescents' abilities to disengage, and in their parents' ability to emotionally support this second separation-individuation. Clinically, the separation process is the key developmental challenge of adolescence, and the one that can painfully reveal significant developmental weakness. On the healthier end of a clinical continuum, disengagement from internalized parents proceeds without internal breakdown or external eruptions (Offer, 1969; Offer & Offer, 1975). On the other end of this continuum, the task of separating from parents lays bare the serious pathology associated with earlier developmental arrest (Masterson, 1972; Rinsley, 1980). Here the dialectic between separation and connection can be seen clearly, as adolescents cannot pursue separation without breakdown unless internal connection with parents and their support can be counted on (Bloch, 1995; Fonagy et al., 2002; Loughran, 1989). In separating, the adolescent must be able to keep alive an internal image of the good object or else the goal of separation itself must be given up and the separating self destroyed. Clinically, in adolescent suicidality, it is often the separating and abandoned self that is the focus of what the adolescent feels he or she needs to kill. The adolescent, not unlike the toddler, needs to return again and again to the security of the relationship with the parent, however ambivalently regarded, and then to separate in wider and wider circles without a sense of abandonment (Mahler et al., 1975).

The two tasks in the middle phase of adolescence, according to Blos, are a new searching for relationship with extrafamilial love objects, and the establishment of an irreversible sexual identity. The ego grows in strength and identity as the self comes into slightly better focus during middle adolescence. As a result, the narcissistic use of the object characteristic of early adolescence decreases and the capacity for true caring increases. The acceleration of the process of object-relinquishment and object-finding leads to the dominance of two broad affective states in middle adolescence: mourning and being in love (A. Freud, 1958). The capacity to mourn is essential to the liberation from the incestuous ties to the parents and is a prerequisite to the adolescent's ability to give up various aspects of infantile omnipotence and to diminish grandiose views of the self. Regarding sexual identity, classical theory argues that the universal bisexuality of previous phases of development is repressed in middle adolescence, as those tendencies that are ego-alien threaten to disrupt the unity of the ego or self-image. There is a move toward a final sexual orientation and away from the pregenital and bisexual positions.

The developmental task of late adolescence focuses on the consolidation and stabilization of these structural changes in the personality. The ego, by late adolescence, normally has established habitual ways of dealing with impulses as well as with demands from the outer world. The scope and functioning of the autonomous ego is enlarged, and the id is less preemptory. Ego functions are more stable as one sees better regulation of affective states and self-esteem, greater frustration tolerance and ability to delay gratification, and greater stability of reality testing. The ego assesses the external world more realistically. Self-reflective functioning is more consistent, which limits ego regression to action and body language. Ego defenses are normally now less extreme and less rigid in defending the integrity of the ego because repression is more available. The flexibility of defenses determines whether character is adaptive or maladaptive at the end of adolescence. Pathological outcome is evident when defenses such as omnipotence, denial, splitting, and projective identification become rigid and stable aspects of personality. Normal adolescents increasingly surrender narcissistic preoccupations as they turn toward the outer world as a source of pleasure and mastery. Superego development has likewise progressed as one observes in the late adolescent a clearer and more consistent value system. Ideally, the superego is more moderate in its guiding and protective, as well as prohibiting, roles (Schafer, 1960). In the area of object relations, there are more stable, integrated, and realistic perceptions of self and objects, which results in increased capacity for empathy and intimacy. As disengagement gets consolidated, another rapprochement can be observed as the closeness with parents is less threatening to the adolescent.

The psychoanalytic map of adolescent development thus postulates that personality development, which has largely emerged through the dialogue between caregiver and child, makes a qualitative shift by the end of adolescence. While additional developmental challenges are posed by such life events as marriage, parenting, and aging, the basic, organized capacities and patterns of an individual's experiencing, coping, and relating that exist at the end of adolescence are thought to endure through adulthood.

Treating young patients while they are still immersed in these fluid adolescent processes constitutes an extraordinary opportunity to affect developmental outcome. There are numerous implications of the psychoanalytic understanding of this developmental phase for the psychotherapeutic treatment of adolescents and their families.

Empirical Support for Psychodynamic Therapy with Adolescents

The effectiveness of psychotherapy must be measured by its ability to improve patient functioning and to maintain that improvement after the therapy ends. Empirical support for the effectiveness of the psychodynamic approach falls short compared to the evolution of its techniques and their prevalent use in diverse settings and contexts (Bleiberg, 2001; Weisz et al., 1998). While one of the goals of treatment research is to provide firm empirical footing for clinical practice, psychodynamic psychotherapy with adolescents has generally not been evaluated in well-designed studies. The reader is encouraged to review Fonagy's discussion in Chapter 19 of empirical support of psychodynamic therapies along with these additional comments focused specifically on adolescent treatment.

The psychoanalytic tradition's claim to legitimacy relies heavily on the case study approach that, while rich and evocative, resists objective assessment (Bleiberg, 2001). Single case investigations have yielded profound clinical insights but need to be supplemented by other confirmatory empirical procedures in order to not be dismissed as merely anecdotal. Data from single cases is more suitable for generating theories and hypotheses than for evaluating those theories as guides for intervention. Fonagy argues that clinical research must address the somewhat loose relationship that exists between psychodynamic theory and technique, as the same theory can generate different techniques and the same technique may be justified by different theories (Fonagy, 2002; Wallerstein, 1989). Fonagy also points out the problems in the predominant epistemic strategy in case reports that merely enumerate instance after instance of clinical observations consistent with a theoretical premise (Fonagy, 2002). Psychodynamic therapists and psychoanalysts, on the other hand, are justifiably antagonistic to research methods that threaten essential elements of the psychotherapeutic process (Fonagy & Target, 1996). It is also difficult to reconcile the experience of intensively treating an individual with the attempt to stand back and identify patterns across large numbers of cases in a manner that can be analyzed quantitatively. Perhaps these difficulties are reflected in the alarming finding that psychodynamic treatment of children and adolescents is evaluated in less than 5% of all child and adolescent psychotherapy outcome studies (Kazdin, 1993). This paucity of studies, combined with specific methodological defects of studies of alternate approaches, has created the erroneous impression that psychodynamic therapy for children and adolescents is less effective than newer treatments (Shirk & Russell, 1992).

Although vigorous efforts in the past twenty-five years have been brought to assess the effectiveness of adult psychodynamic therapy (Hartley & Strupp, 1983; Luborsky, et al., 1981), psychodynamic child and adolescent therapy research lags behind (Barnett, Docherty, & Frommelt, 1991; Kazdin, 1993). Part of this deficit in our knowledge base of adolescent psychotherapy stems from the fact that many of the studies done in the 1960s and 1970s do not meet current methodological standards (Barrnett et al., 1991). Even more recent studies that evaluate treatment effectiveness have predominantly grouped children and adolescents together, rarely making age and stage distinctions despite the fact that play therapy techniques predominate in the treatment of children but not in the treatment of adolescents. Global research questions such as "Is psychodynamic psychotherapy effective?" are less useful than a more focused inquiry: "Which techniques are effective when used with what kind of patients with what kind of problems as practiced by what sort of therapists?" (Barrnett et al., 1991, p. 2). Various methodological issues include the need to address different treatment responses according to diagnostic category, developmental stage of patients, inclusion/exclusion criteria, control groups, outcome measurement, specifics of the intervention employed, and specific patient, therapist, and process variables relevant to adolescent therapy outcome (Barrnett et al., 1991). Most reviews of existing research agree that there are too few studies available, and too many methodological limitations exist, to make broad conclusions either about individual treatments for a given clinical problem or the factors that moderate treatment outcome for adolescents.

A major effort to investigate which aspects of psychodynamic child and adolescent techniques are effective for which types of psychological disturbances is the work of Peter Fonagy and his colleagues (Fonagy & Moran, 1991; Fonagy & Target, 1996; Fonagy et al., 2000; Fonagy et al., 2002). In a chart review of 763 case records at a psychoanalytic clinic in England on all outcome criteria, the probability of reliable improvement decreased with age, regardless of severity and diagnosis, with only 40% of adolescents moving into the normal range of functioning. This remained statistically significant even when dropouts were excluded. Attrition was highest among adolescents, although those in intensive treatment and whose parents were engaged in regular guidance sessions were much less likely to drop out. Also, in contrast to younger children, who did better in treatment that occurred four to five times per week, it appeared adolescents benefited as much or more from non-intensive treatment. Only 34% of latency children showed reliable improvement in non-intensive treatment, while 65.6% of the adolescents did. These findings seem to argue against intensive therapy and in favor of less intensive treatment during adolescence, as the regression and dependency involved combat the strong developmental need for independence and separation. Adolescent anxiety disorders with specific symptoms were associated with a good prognosis, even if the primary diagnosis was of a different type, such as disruptive disorder. This interesting finding suggests a particular strength in the psychodynamic approach in resolving anxiety, and reveals what may constitute a substantial developmental handicap for adolescents who defensively succeed in being free from anxiety. This study found that those who did not respond well to psychoanalytic treatment were children with pervasive developmental disorders (such as autism) or mental retardation, where the mental processes that need to be engaged in this treatment approach may be stunted. Adolescents with serious conduct disorders or ADHD also did not respond well to traditional psychoanalytically informed techniques, especially if non-intensive. One striking finding of this study was that, of the emotional disorders, adolescent depression, in contrast to the adult outcome literature, seemed relatively resistant to psychodynamic help. The authors suggest that childhood depression might indicate a deeper and more widespread disturbance.

Personal Experiences and Case Material

What follows is a practical outline of conducting a psychodynamic treatment with an adolescent and his or her parents. This outline is simplified to allow a general discussion of how to apply core psychodynamic principles and techniques across the range from neurotic to developmentally disturbed adolescents (Bleiberg, 2001; Bloch, 1995; Edgcumbe, 1993; Lamb, 1986; Levy-Warren, 1996; Maenchen, 1970; Masterson, 1972; Meeks & Bernet, 1990; Miller, 1983; Mishne, 1986; Settlage, 1974; Steiner, 1996). Adapting these ideas to various settings and reality conditions, while requiring modification, should not undermine their usefulness. This outline starts with initial evaluation and treatment planning, discusses beginning treatment in terms of establishing a therapeutic alliance and dealing with resistance, then outlines a method of containment and interpretation in working with transference and countertransference in the middle phase of treatment, and concludes with a discussion of termination.

Initial Evaluation and Treatment Planning

The goals of an initial evaluation are (1) to determine the nature of adolescent's current difficulties, and (2) to assess how the adolescent and the family will hold up their end of a plan of treatment. In evaluating the nature of the adolescent's difficulties, psychodynamic therapy goes beyond arriving at a psychiatric diagnosis. It requires assessing the overall state of the intactness and adaptation of the adolescent, as well as a more specific evaluation of particular ego functions. Manifest symptomatology is thought to express an underlying vulnerability in the regulatory and adaptive activities of the self. Similar symptoms such as inattentiveness in school can stem from diverse pathologies. To sort out this complexity, thorough evaluation requires a careful gathering of information from multiple dimensions: the biological or constitutional, the psychological, and the sociocultural. The sources for data include clinical interviews with the adolescent and parents and, as needed, psycho-educational testing and reports from pediatricians, teachers, and probation officers. At the end of the evaluation, the clinician should arrive at a dynamic formulation that links surface symptoms with underlying causes, and should recommend a treatment plan to the adolescent and the family that flows from this formulation.

There are no set rules as to the form that the evaluation should take. The initial interviews should permit enough contact with the adolescent and the family to answer one's diagnostic questions. Ideally, your recommendations for treatment should not surprise the adolescent or the family. By the end of the evaluation, you have established your understanding of the problems together, and sufficiently demonstrated each person's contribution to the problems and their strengths in contributing to their solution (Meeks & Bernet, 1990).

In terms of mechanics, who does one see first in the family? The form the evaluation takes is often dictated by the circumstances and the particular preferences and skills of the evaluator. When a family is in the midst of a life-threatening crisis, it often makes sense to conduct a conjoint family session first. Otherwise, many psychodynamic therapists tend to see the parents first with early adolescents because early adolescents tend to have more difficulty with self-disclosure and with identifying problems. They tend to see middle or late adolescents first because they are more able to speak for themselves and more sensitive to questions involving confidentiality. In outpatient settings, the decision of who to see first is often discussed with the parents during initial phone contact as the therapist gets an initial description of the problems. Important diagnostic information is revealed even as you set up these first interviews. The therapist gathers impressions of how effective and how empathic the parents are, and how clearly they communicate their concerns to the adolescent.

It is important in the first individual session with the adolescent to establish a natural flow of talk. One should be sensitive to the narcissistic vulnerability with which most adolescents enter therapy. The therapist should define the purpose of the first session and help the adolescent to identify and express his or her initial reactions. Due to wanting to keep anxiety within manageable limits, long silences are best avoided in initial interviews, even if the clinician has to carry the conversation. You want the adolescent to perceive you as genuine, direct, honest, and wanting to help. Many adolescents do not come to therapy having expressed motivation, so it is often helpful to explore who initiated the contact, what the concerns were, and whether the adolescent agrees that there is reason for concern. Adolescents in initial interviews can attempt to get the therapist to ally against parents. This can usually be handled by exploring the adolescent's feelings toward the parents and interpreting how it might be difficult for the adolescent at this point to both be in such conflict with parents, and to look for himself or herself from an outside perspective. What you can do is promise that the adolescent will be the first to hear your conclusions as to the nature of the problems and what you think needs to be done about them.

In these unhurried initial meetings, adolescents should feel as free as possible to tell you or not tell you what they wish about relationships, family history, school and social life, and personal thoughts, feelings, or behaviors that define or concern them. The issue of confidentiality, and its limits, often needs to be explained early on. Its guarantee is limited to not repeating what the adolescent says, and to not conveying facts about behaviors to others without the adolescent's permission. Most adolescents seem to easily accept that confidentiality is limited when life is endangered, and when sexual or physical abuse is reported.

Limits to confidentiality get especially difficult to define for the adolescent around issues of drug and alcohol abuse. Getting accurate information about drug involvement sometimes has to wait until trust is better established. I have found an effective approach to questioning in this area that focuses on transference. This approach explores the adolescents' experience of being left on their own without adult help in dealing with a problem often out of their control. A series of questions can be asked about the choices the adolescent is faced with in leaving the therapist in the dark or not about their drug behavior. These questions can be framed in terms of what it would be like if the therapist just stood aside not offering help, versus taking effective action based on clinical experience in helping other adolescents facing the same situation. Psychoanalytic psychotherapists have to be ready to accept that when it comes to serious drug and alcohol abuse that threatens life, let alone an attempt at therapy, symptom relief is primary and often its achievement preliminary to any more exploratory treatment. Treatment of serious drug dependence often requires an initial period in which treatment is involuntary and focused solely on gaining control and establishing sobriety.

The observational capacity and attentiveness of the therapist is of obvious importance in the initial meeting with the adolescent. This goes beyond gathering factual information and involves how the therapist allows what the adolescent communicates verbally and nonverbally to have an emotional impact. The aesthetic of an adolescent emerges from the impact he or she has on the observer. The nonverbal includes behaviors as well as the physical appearance of the adolescent. Our adolescent patients often communicate a great deal about current identifications through "self symbols" such as haircuts, clothing styles, piercing, and so on.

Attentiveness in a psychoanalytic sense also involves a particular kind of listening. If one works from a model of intervention that focuses upon unconscious aspects of mental functioning, one listens differently. There is latent content involving unconscious fantasy underneath the manifest level of the stories the adolescent patient tells us. Hearing manifest content simply as objectively factual would destroy its psychic value and real meaning to the adolescent, and would constitute a form of resistance in the therapist to the emotional impact of the unconscious. One listens to material as one would to a dream, or as a child therapist would track a child's play. One listens for metaphors, for disowned aspects of emotional experience, for descriptions of dramas that are taking place with internal objects (Casement, 1985). Internal forces within the adolescent shape what he or she remembers and reports. Does the adolescent tell stories of interactions in which objects can be relied on, or do these objects always leave, not understand, or attack?

There are different aspects of the psychoanalytic therapist's effort to imagine the inner world of a patient (Lafarge, 2000). The first involves a tracking and interpreting of verbally elaborated feelings, beliefs, and fantasies. A second aspect is the therapist's reception and transformation of more primitive emotional experiences that may not be verbally represented in the patient's mind. The adolescent often communicates unbearable aspects of experience through projective identification, that is, by making the therapist feel something. Here, again, there is a parallel between the psychoanalytic process and early developmental interaction with a caregiver as container. The mother lets in her infant's crying, makes sense of it, says, "You're hungry," and feeds her child. The therapist similarly must be able to tolerate and hold unbearable thoughts and feelings our adolescent patients project into him or her. An adolescent I treated entered therapy with a need, out of fear of abandonment, to defensively idealize a non-custodial father who treated him sadistically. I treated my countertransference reactions to this patient's painful stories of mistreatment as emotions to register, metabolize, and contain for this adolescent. This patient had to first be made ready in the therapy before I could interpretively return to him these disavowed feelings and aspects of self and object representations. I thus started with containment, and only slowly started clarifying and interpreting his need for defense in the face of anxiety. I began showing him how he was letting me know how important it was to be understanding of his father so as to preserve the tie to the father. He was able to start looking at his own critical feelings only after we understood the nature of his anxiety that this father would abandon him. In doing this, he resolved his depression and reliance on marijuana. The main point is that in any successful treatment, accurate understanding and interpretation implies a deep relatedness, a holding-the-adolescent-in-mind.

During the initial evaluation, meeting separately with parents is invaluable. It offers a chance for the therapist, in addition to gathering information, to often begin helping parents shift from reacting to, to understanding their adolescent. Assessment of the reflective capacities of the parents is critical (Fonagy et al., 1993). One starts the interview with the parents by asking for descriptions of current problems and concerns. A careful accounting of when these problems started often reveals a defended against correspondence between an event or shift in the family and the onset of problems with the adolescent. The therapist learns a great deal in these parental interviews about the history of the parent-child relationship, including parental hopes and anxieties for the adolescent. It is extremely important to explore in detail the parents' style of discipline and whether they set clear, firm, non-vindictive limits. Adolescents need strong objects to support development. I have found few parents with symptomatic adolescents that set appropriate limits with their teenagers. Winnicott took an important step in helping our understanding of the adolescent's need for limits. He disagreed with Freud's conception of destructiveness as motivated by the wish to eliminate external obstacles to satisfaction. Winnicott saw destruction as inviting opposition. This is what adolescents need from parents to reinforce the boundary between self and other and between fantasy and actual consequences—to set limits and survive the adolescent's angry reactions to those limits (Rappaport, 1998; Winnicott, 1971b). Appropriate limit-setting establishes the parents as strong objects outside the adolescent's omnipotent control. If the parents cannot do this, adolescents will act out until some external authority, such as the police, respond to this need.

Taking a careful developmental history deepens this refocusing on understanding as parents link current difficulties with earlier developmental processes. Often, changes in the relationship with parents at entry into adolescence precipitated the difficulties. It often proves helpful to learn if the parents identify themselves or one of their own siblings with their adolescent. One mother recently discussed during evaluation of her young adolescent son her experience of sexual molestation by her older brother when he was a teenager. Exploring this was obviously critical in understanding her son's neurotic conflicts around aggression and sexuality.

Family interviews during the evaluation process often reveal patterns of interaction that otherwise remain hidden. It is important in these sessions to focus more on the process of how the family handles conflict than on the content. In doing this, strengths as well as weaknesses can be identified. The evaluative family interview is not the time to work through problems, but rather an opportunity to observe and demonstrate interactional patterns.

The purpose of a post-diagnostic session is to summarize the understanding you have evolved together of the core problems, to make the treatment recommendations, and to state your prognosis if the recommendation is followed and if it is not (Meeks & Bernet, 1990). Post-diagnostic sessions can be done with the adolescent and parents together or separate. Choice of modality should flow from a well-documented and careful assessment. The intensity of intervention in terms of frequency of sessions per week must also be presented at the end of the evaluation. Multiple interventions—family treatment, couple treatment for the parents, medication, group treatment—are not uncommon in clinical practice due to the intrapsychic-interpersonal complexity and the comorbidity of adolescent psychopathology. A treatment contract with the family basically outlines what must be done for the treatment to be successful. It is important for the parents to understand how they will be helped in parenting, and how the adolescent is to come to treatment for his or her own problems. The therapist's conviction that a specific level of care, from frequency of outpatient sessions to residential or hospital care, must be clearly explained to the adolescent and parents as being essential to treatment success.

Beginning Treatment

The psychodynamic approach to adolescent psychotherapy centers in the beginning phase of treatment on (1) promoting a therapeutic alliance, and (2) dealing with initial resistances to entering treatment.

The therapist begins with an adolescent by attempting to create a therapeutic space to explore his or her mind within the context of the treatment relationship (Bronstein & Flanders, 1998). This space is often talked about in terms of transitional space in the sense of stepping back and mentally playing with thoughts and meaning, and with the fantasies that accompany experience. This stepping back, because it helps secure the difference between fantasy and reality, frees the adolescent's imagination to explore central fantasies and to question his or her more irrational thoughts, feelings, reactions, and motives. If this boundary between inner and outer is not clear, as is true for more disturbed adolescents, consciously becoming aware of a fantasy is too threatening. Because fantasies are experienced as real events in the unconscious, exploration and play in therapy must be resisted by more disturbed patients to prevent primitive anxiety from overwhelming ego defenses.

Establishing a Therapeutic Alliance

Creating this space has often been identified in the psychoanalytic literature with the effort to establish a therapeutic alliance with the adolescent (Meeks & Bernet, 1990). Therapeutic alliance consists of the therapist and the adolescent working to put together an evolving picture of the adolescent's internal situation. From the first moment with an adolescent, the therapist begins building such an alliance by addressing nearly every comment to the adolescent's observing ego. Directing comments to this emerging capacity for self-observation initiates the process of the adolescent shifting from action to thought and verbalization, thus strengthening internal controls. The therapeutic alliance is established by assisting the adolescent in understanding the link between feelings, thoughts, and behavior in the present.

An initial part of forming an alliance involves helping adolescents observe, label, and understand their emotions. The focus on surface affect includes differentiating between emotions, and understanding the relationship between certain behaviors and such internal states as anxiety or frustration. In therapy, adolescents learn how certain emotions have clear signal functions, and lead to specific self-protective measures. Thus, before identifying repudiated affects, one often has to help adolescents first start understanding how ideas and circumstances can make them feel certain things. This understanding helps them start to modulate their affective responses. They also learn that they have a range of emotions, not just from negative to positive, but from emotions that are simple reflexes to more elaborated and cognitively complex emotional experiences such as envy or love. They explore as well how their emotions give them valuable insights into their values.

A frequent focus in the initial phase of treatment is that of helping the adolescent identify which emotions are the most threatening, and how these emotions frequently prompt them to retreat from reflective functioning. A turning point recently in the treatment of a severely acting out adolescent centered on her simple insight that it was not that she lacked guilt or a sense of right and wrong, which she had previously insisted upon, but that she had little tolerance for guilt as an emotion. Another fourteen-year-old adolescent came to treatment unable to access any feelings of loss in response to repeated separations tied to foster care placement when her mother returned to prison. We began with an exploration of how important it had been for her to not feel anything. Her self-destructive acting out decreased as this relatively intact adolescent began talking about the decision to "shut off" at age eight all her loving and angry feelings for a drug-addicted mother she once could depend on. Ongoing treatment allowed her to preserve a complex representation of herself and her mother from different developmental periods, which helped make more feeling in the present and in the transference tolerable.

Another step in enhancing self-observation and reflective function involves the tendency of all adolescents to act rather than to feel. Some adolescents, especially those with severe personality disorders, particularly borderline adolescents, need considerable help in curbing their impulsivity. During the beginning stage of therapy, the therapist explores strategies to help the adolescent channel impulsive behavior into more adaptive forms of conduct, and increase control over the expression of feelings in self-defeating or self-destructive actions. The message in beginning treatment is that stepping back and using talk and imagination and humor can offer a way to slowly manage the overwhelming emotional states that coerce the adolescent into taking such action. Bleiberg makes the point that with adolescents who have severe personality disorders, impulsivity can actually increase early in treatment when the attachment to the therapist starts to grow (Bleiberg, 2001, p. 186). Building a therapeutic alliance thus goes hand in hand in the early phase of treatment with such patients with helping them gain better self-control. In addition to offering interpretations that link behaviors with warded-off ideas and feelings, the therapist uses supportive techniques such as offering concrete suggestions for expanding self-control, and encouraging and praising more delay and more affect and anxiety tolerance. All these serve the aim of developmental work. At times, one also needs to establish a "contract for safety" in an agreement that the adolescent will call the therapist before acting on cutting or suicidal impulses. Offering to serve as an auxiliary ego in this way can be one part of a "crisis plan" with adolescents for those moments when they feel unsafe or out of control. There is also room for a psycho-educational approach of sharing information in such areas as trauma response syndromes or hyperactivity.

Bleiberg suggests that an additional step in enhancing reflective function involves helping adolescent patients become aware of the mental states of others (Bleiberg, 2001). The achievement of a capacity to mentally represent states of one's own mind as well as the mental states of others is a significant developmental advance in the organization of experience. The term "a theory of mind" designates this psychic capacity to formulate accounts to explain the self's and the object's attitudes, emotions, and behaviors. Not all adolescents enter psychotherapy with this capacity to reflect on or conceive of mental states in others and in themselves (Meeks & Bernett, 1990). The development of this capacity is a key focus in psychotherapy with developmentally disturbed adolescents. Every therapy, however, must help adolescents identify distorted views of others, and see how they tend to react to these perceptions before testing them out in reality. For example, aggressive adolescents tend to interpret ambiguous situations, in which the intention of others is unclear, as hostile. This distortion can precipitate an aggressive response on the part of the adolescent as he or she can justify aggressive acts as retaliation. These distortions are, therefore, potential points of intervention. Elkind focused on the egocentric tendency of all adolescents to relate to peers as if to an "imaginary audience" constructed of equal parts of perception, wish, projection, and anxiety (Elkind, 1967). In psychodynamic treatment, perceptual distortions in relationships are explored as transferences or displacements of internal representations of aspects of self and others into current relationships. For instance, it is common in work with early adolescents to demonstrate to them how they misperceive their parents as controlling when often the parents are set up by the adolescent to be anxious about some aspect of their behavior. The perception of the parent as critical and controlling then shifts from being a projection of the adolescent's super-ego conflicts, to a more reality-based perception of the adults as anxious and needing to be able to trust the adolescent. In the early phase of treatment, therapists can also begin to outline the shape of the adolescents' transference to the therapist by showing the patients patterns in how they expect the therapist to respond.

The capacity for self-observation during adolescence is unstable even in adolescents on the healthier end of the spectrum. Meeks, in his seminal contribution on the therapeutic alliance with adolescents, defines the observing ego as that capacity for reflection without self-judgement and without action. This is especially important in early treatment as adolescent propensities toward self-criticism, and toward acting in order to avoid feeling, both interfere significantly with reflective capacities. Once established, the very existence of a treatment alliance has a substantial, inherent, and immediate ego-supportive value to the adolescent patient. In contrast, Meeks describes so-called "unholy alliances" with the id, with pathological ego defenses, and with the superego, that significantly interfere with the treatment of adolescents (Meeks & Bernet, 1990). A therapist who forms an alliance with the adolescent's id weakens the patient's inner controls. An alliance with pathological ego defenses such as intellectualization leaves the adolescent untouched by the therapy. Lastly, an alliance with the superego can produce a lessening of acting-out behavior by producing guilt, with little gain in maturation.

Working with Resistance

Another main focus in the beginning phase of a psychodynamic therapy is dealing with resistance. Resistance is a particular kind of defense that is a core therapeutic issue in all treatment (Settlage, 1974). Working with resistance involves helping the adolescent develop awareness of, understand, and work through his or her initial fears and self-protective reactions to treatment. *Resistance* can be defined as anything the patient does that serves as an obstacle to self-awareness. Resisting protects by forestalling the experience of an unacceptable thought or painful affect. Anything can be used as resistance: being late or always being on time, being silent or talking excessively, or rejecting or agreeing with everything the therapist says.

The technical problem many have in working with resistance is tied up in how the word resistance itself has an adversarial connotation. An adversarial view leads the therapist to attempt to get the adolescent patient to stop resisting through coercion or humiliation. In contrast, Schafer defines what he calls an "affirmative approach" to resistance which, if undertaken by the therapist, avoids many of the early impasses in treating adolescents (Schafer, 1983). The affirmative approach seeks to understand resistance as something puzzling or unintelligible that needs to be understood, rather than as a force that opposes treatment. This shift from delivering a "cut it out" message to adopting a more neutral, open, and curious stance promotes alliance by establishing a safe, unhurried, non-coercive, and non-judgmental quality to the work. The first tenet of defense analysis is to respect the ego's need for defense by addressing the positive side of the defense in the spirit of "Why might you want to do this?" (Settlage, 1974). This promotes a feeling of security that the defense is being understood rather than taken away. The second tenet of defense analysis is to interpret the defense and what it defends against simultaneously. To be complete, a resistance interpretation must include a tentative statement about the anxiety being defended against. The form for this might be: "I think you are more comfortable doing x because of your worry about y."

Concept of Analytic Neutrality

The analysis of resistance ties into the psychoanalytic concept of neutrality. This is one of the core principles of technique that distinguishes the psychoanalytic method from behavioral or family systems approaches. In clinical practice, neutrality means that the therapist does not unilaterally try to make anything happen in the therapy with the adolescent. Instead, the therapist simply tries to invite the adolescent to understand the necessity of doing specifically what he or she is doing. The therapist does not try to coerce the adolescent who is late to sessions to be on time, or who is silent at the beginning of sessions to speak. Neutrality in the face of such resistance consists of the stance, "You have your reasons. Let's try to understand them." The psychoanalytic principle of neutrality is not equivalent to the therapist's disengagement in the face of situations in which one has to take a stand, or to an outdated and stilted caricature of the therapist as a purely objective observer.

Neutrality is very difficult to maintain with adolescents when acting out can create within therapists a reactive anxiety and feeling of urgency that can disrupt analytic listening and lead to attempts by the therapist to direct or control, rather than understand, the behavior (Chused, 1990). Borderline adolescents, for instance, who frequently injure themselves and threaten suicide stir up powerful reactions in those who treat them (Kernberg, et al., 2000; Masterson, 1972). Therapists must struggle against these coercive patterns of experience to contain, tolerate, and reflect on the intense feelings that precipitated the acting out in order to create in these moments an opportunity for therapeutic intervention. The main point here is that an affirmative approach to resistance, tied to this contemporary understanding of neutrality, are essential elements in preserving the therapist's freedom to think in difficult treatment situations with adolescents (Ogden, 1995). If resistance is managed properly, the therapist can create the sense of therapeutic space for the adolescent early in treatment that helps the adolescent begin developing a receptivity to his or her own mind.

Ongoing Treatment

There is a form of listening within psychoanalysis described as "evenly suspended," in which the therapist is simply listening and not bothering about whether he or she is keeping anything specific in mind or not. Each session with an adolescent should begin this way, with an attempt to listen freshly and to temporarily set aside favored hypotheses about the adolescent. This protects against the therapy becoming focused on what you already know about the adolescent. In ongoing treatment, while a return to this kind of listening is important, the therapist actively develops hunches and hypotheses with the adolescent about what is going on. Developing a way of talking with the adolescent, labeling emotions, clarifying thoughts, and communicating understanding in the form of developed themes dominates ongoing treatment. After an initial phase of treatment, there should be evidence of at least the beginnings of a therapeutic alliance. Such evidence would include the adolescent demonstrating the tendency to reflect on affective experience, to explore emotional origins of behavior, to recognize and discuss affects that emerge during sessions, to accept ambivalence as an internal reality, and to react with curiosity to interpretations (Meeks & Bernet, 1990).

Interpretation

Communicating understanding is usually done in the form of interpretations. Interpretation is a true statement about the adolescent patient's mental life. Clinical theory suggests certain rules governing interpretations. For the most part, one wants to work from the surface and first address defense and the anxiety about warded off ideas, affects, or impulses. One would tend to interpret the avoidance or the fear, for instance, of an aggressive wish rather than interpret the unconscious wish directly. Working from the surface also implies that the first step toward making an interpretation is to point to something observable to which you think the adolescent should pay attention. This step, technically referred to as clarification, is like shining a light on a behavior that is often a repeated, characteristic way the adolescent responds to something. For instance, a resistance interpretation might take the simple first step of inviting the adolescent to pay attention to a behavior in a session. A very disturbed adolescent fifteen-year-old young man with a single-parent mother with a history of repeated hospitalizations for psychotic depression, early in therapy would come to sessions with a large quantity of health food that he would spend the entire session eating voraciously. Starting on the surface, I began by observing that he seemed more comfortable in our sessions if he ate. This led to a discussion of how healthy the food always was. Many, many issues were associated with this oral behavior. A key fantasy emerged only gradually of this young man's belief that healthy food would give him muscles that would serve as a boundary between inside and outside, a second skin (Bick, 1968), and would better contain his feeling terrified of getting close to anyone. By the middle phase of psychotherapy, the therapist has built up a history of identifying such characteristic forms of resistance and central patterns of anxiety and conflict in relationships. Empirical research has validated the central importance for clinical treatment of identifying such central patterns of conflict (Jones, 1997; Luborsky, 1984; Strupp & Binder, 1984; Weiss & Sampson, 1986).

The Transference-Countertransference Interplay

The focus on the transference-countertransference interplay further distinguishes psychodynamic therapy from all other approaches. The centrality of attachment and relatedness in theory and practice is consistent with a focus on transference as perhaps the most powerful tool a therapist has to understanding and demonstrating unconscious mental functioning to a patient. Working with transference and countertransference with adolescents deepens the therapeutic relationship and makes it a useful lens into dynamics that otherwise can only be examined indirectly.

There are disagreements within the field as to how focused psychotherapy with an adolescent should be on the transference relationship. One side of the argument seems to center on concerns that it is contraindicated developmentally to invite adolescents into a too dependent or regressive a transference experience. Some also point out how a focus on transference interpretations confuses psychotherapy with psychoanalysis, and somehow limits the "timely help" of more supportive activities in adolescent treatment such as offering encouragement and making concrete suggestions (Lamb, 1986). These concerns seem misleading. Transference is universal in relationships, and evident in every treatment relationship. The real question is how to best focus on its presence in psychotherapy with an adolescent. We must be aware, for instance, that we may be viewed by our adolescent patients as extensions of the parents, as "reflecting old superego standards and a perpetuation of dependence" (Harley, 1970, p. 103). One difference in working with adolescents versus adults in terms of interpreting transference is how much less genetic material is emphasized with an adolescent. Hansi Kennedy pointed out how adolescents are often absorbed by their current difficulties and apprehensions about the future and tend to be comparatively uninterested in the past (Kennedy, 1979).

Focusing on transference is, in fact, often avoided because of the therapist's anxiety. Transference assaults the therapist's identity by constantly casting and recasting the therapist as objects in the patient's psychic life. This is a lot to go through a few times an hour. The rationale for focusing on the transference is that it is frequently the most alive, in-the-moment aspect of affective experience between patient and therapist. An in-the-room focus on the transference to the therapist does not, however, preclude an examination of transference in relation to other people in the adolescent's environment. It enriches and enlivens it. A focus on transference very simply allows the examination with the adolescent of aspects of current and past, self and object experiences that are transferred into the safety of the patient-therapist relationship. Interpreting transference follows the same rules of interpretation in general. One starts with the surface, with fears and defense, then makes connections to past experience only after initial work at clarifying just what the transference reaction is.

Very closely aligned with the focus on transference is the usefulness of the therapist's countertransference in guiding treatment. Again, adolescent patients can place powerful demands on the emotional resources, boundaries, ethics, and technical skills of therapists. Defensive reactions can easily replace the therapist's preferred mode of a more reflective, neutral stance. We can lose our reflective capacities in a way that mirrors a parallel loss of the adolescent's. Therapists can start feeling defeated, helpless, and weak, or terrified, bored, irritated, and enraged. Adolescent therapists often struggle, as well, with countertransference reactions to parents, and can fall into a mode of trying, overtly or covertly, to rescue their adolescent patients from disturbed families. Countertransference identification with the adolescent against parents is common, especially at the beginning of one's career. The point in working with countertransference reactions is to discern what our reactions tell us about our patients. This requires a developed ability to filter out what in our reactions reflects our own unresolved past conflicts or our own narcissism.

Use of the Therapist as a "Real Object"

Working with lower functioning adolescents requires different techniques, as these patients cannot use interpretations of transference as higher functioning adolescents can. The distorted internal models of relationship in lower functioning patients cannot be resolved by interpretation alone. Bleiberg refers to the importance, in his discussion of the treatment of adolescents with personality disorders, of the adolescent patient actually experiencing a "representational mismatch" between what they expect from past experience and what they actually experience with the therapist (Bleiberg, 2001; Horowitz, 1987). Such "developmental help" involves the therapist as more of a real object and as an object of identification than as a transference object (Edgcumbe, 1993). In these treatments, the agent of change is not a transference interpretation but the new experience with the therapist as "usably different" real object who, for instance, responds to provocation with an attempt to understand rather than with rejection or abandonment (Winnicott, 1971b).

Termination of Treatment

In psychodynamic psychotherapy with adolescents, termination ideally is the process that begins with the achievement of the goals mutually agreed upon by patient and therapist. These goals include symptom relief and resolution of the underlying causes. Often in work with adolescents the treatment stops for reasons other than it coming to this ideal point of resolution. Adolescents frequently move away to move on with their lives. These endings technically constitute interruptions more than terminations and have to be dealt with as such. Any ending of treatment, however initiated, needs to focus on helping the adolescent to consolidate gains made and to work through the dynamics set in motion by the anticipation of the loss of the relationship with the therapist.

Termination implies that the adolescent patient has internalized the functions provided by the therapist, and that as a result the concrete person of the therapist can be given up. The therapy, in a sense, never stops but the therapist is no longer needed. As noted above, however, our theories are culturally bound and tend to valorize separation and independence. Even in cases of higher functioning adolescents, a healthy need for the concrete person of the therapist may re-emerge. It is not necessarily a sign of failure of a treatment if at a later point an adolescent needs to return.

Time itself always seems very present in work with adolescents. Its passage seems palpable. This is perhaps partly due to adolescent immersion in developmental processes that seem to rush them past new milestones on a "ready or not" basis. For an adolescent, therefore, ending the relationship with the therapist stimulates thoughts and feelings about other losses, both the developmental and the traumatic losses that are specific to the adolescent's life history. It is common that the exploration of experiences of previous losses helps the adolescent understand not just his or her suffering, but his or her strengths and the central value of deep relationship.

Similarly, termination involves a mourning response in adolescent patients, as well as feelings of relief and pride in the accomplishment of an important task. The feeling of expanded ego mastery at the end of a successful treatment often serves as the basis of the adolescent experiencing a new level of connection, self-esteem, and self-confidence in being able to handle life's challenges.

Future Directions

Adherents of the psychoanalytic approach to the treatment of adolescents argue that this approach is effective in the treatment of a wide range of disorders, and for many disorders may constitute the treatment of choice. The problem is that this argument at present is not backed by sufficient evidence, and relies too heavily on reports of anecdotal clinical observation and statements of analytic authority. Critics who want treatment to be evidence based, and who increasingly look to competing "symptom removal" approaches, are not convinced by those who point to the complex elegance of the psychoanalytic theory of mind and to the historical and ongoing evolution of psychoanalytic technique.

Many have convincingly argued that psychoanalytic practitioners need to embrace a research agenda that would require improved manualization of treatment techniques with children and adolescents and routine observation and measurement of both treatment process and outcome (Emde & Fonagy, 1997; Fonagy & Perron, 2002; Gabbard et al., 2002; Jones, 1997). This suggests a change in the stance of analysts and therapists toward psychoanalytic knowledge itself, a move toward replacing statements of belief derived from clinical experience with an openness to systematic inquiry. We have to re-examine our relationship to our theories. These theories serve important holding and containing functions for our clinical anxiety, but should be subject to constant rethinking guided by empirical studies of effectiveness. Our theories cannot be the epistemic justification for clinical practice. The international psychoanalytic community is already engaged in such study as to the process and outcome factors that best explain and promote therapeutic action in psychoanalytic treatment (Fonagy & Perron, 2002; Jones, 1997). The resistance to efforts in this direction could be minimized by a more rigorous integration of research methods into one's early training.

Increased scientific inquiry might open our field to integrate findings from other disciplines into the psychoanalytic theory of mind, just as we have done with the findings of academic psychologists on infant development. Perhaps the biological and psychological sciences can be better joined, especially with all the advances in neurocognitive science in understanding the brain functions involved in the subjective experience of emotions and meaning making (Kandel, 1998). Given the fact that the part played by the environment during adolescence is immensely significant, and is largely ignored in our thinking of clinical practice, it would also behoove psychoanalytic theorists to develop a more sophisticated understanding of the influence of the sociocultural environment on adolescent development and breakdown.

Developing a manualized form of a standardized psychodynamic therapy with adolescents would be a useful step, albeit a very challenging one. The question of what constitutes standardized psychodynamic therapy with adolescents must be broad enough, however, to encompass the flexibility of techniques and approaches psychodynamic therapists actually use in treatment. Clinical techniques must also address the differences in treating adolescents in different phases of this critical developmental stage.

◆ ◆ ◆

The psychoanalytic approach offers unique advantages in the treatment of adolescent disorders. Its strength lies in its being grounded in a comprehensive understanding of adolescent development and breakdown, and in its formulation of the analytic process, which addresses the complementary roles of interpretation and containment. This enables psychoanalytic theory to serve as a guide in treating different levels of pathology, from neurotic disorder to developmental disturbance. The range of intensive to non-intensive interventions, from analysis to once weekly psychotherapy, gives this approach a flexibility that seems well-suited to adolescents. The limitation of the psychodynamic approach lies in its needing to engage certain mental processes which may not be present in certain disorders or with specific patients. Its effectiveness has been oversold in the past as a treatment for severe mental illnesses like schizophrenia and manic depression, and its techniques seem poorly suited for adolescents with pervasive developmental disorders (such as autism), mental retardation, or severe ADHD (Fonagy & Target, 1996).

Perhaps, similar to our adolescent patients, those of us in the psychoanalytic community can honor our past in all its depth and richness and, at the same time, accept and successfully struggle with the developmental challenges that lie ahead.

References

Abrams, S. (1988). The psychoanalytic process in adults and children. *Psychoanalytic Study of the Child, 43,* 245–261.

Abrams, S. (1990). The psychoanalytic process: The developmental and the integrative. *Psychoanalytic Quarterly, 59,* 650–677.

Abrams, S., & Solnit, A. J. (1998). Coordinating developmental and psychoanalytic processes. *Journal of the American Psychoanalytic Association, 46,* 85–103.

Anderson, R., & Dartington, A. (Eds.). (1998). *Facing it out: Clinical perspectives on adolescent disturbance.* New York: Routledge.

Anthony, E. J. (1970). The reactions of parents to adolescents and to their behavior. In E. J. Anthony & T. Benedek (Eds.), *Parenthood: Its psychology and psychopathology* (pp. 307–324). Boston: Little, Brown, & Company.

Barrnett, R. J., Docherty, J. P., & Frommelt, G. M. (1991). A review of child psychotherapy research since 1963. *Journal of the American Academy of Child and Adolescent Psychiatry, 30,* 1–14.

Bick, E. (1968). The experience of the skin in early object relations. *International Journal of Psycho-Analysis, 49,* 484–486.

Bion, W. R. (1959). Attacks on linking. *International Journal of Psycho-Analysis, 40,* 308–315.

Blatt, S. J., & Blass, R. B. (1990). Attachment and separateness: A dialectical model of the products and processes of development throughout the life cycle. *Psychoanalytic Study of the Child, 45,* 107–127.

Bleiberg, E. (1988). Adolescence, sense of self, and narcissistic vulnerability. *Bulletin of the Menninger Clinic, 52,* 211–228.

Bleiberg, E. (2001). *Treating personality disorders in children and adolescents: A relational approach.* New York: Guilford Press.

Bloch, H. S. (1995). *Adolescent development, psychopathology, and treatment.* Madison, CT: International Universities Press.

Blos, P. (1962). *On adolescence: A psychoanalytic interpretation.* New York: The Free Press.

Blos, P. (1967). The second individuation process of adolescence. *Psychoanalytic Study of the Child, 22,* 162–186.

Blos, P. (1970). *The young adolescent: Clinical studies.* New York: The Free Press.

Bronstein, C., & Flanders, S. (1998). The development of a therapeutic space in a first contact with adolescents. *Journal of Child Psychotherapy, 24,* 5–36.

Casement, P. J. (1985). *Learning from the patient.* New York: Guilford Press.

Chused, J. F. (1990). Neutrality in the analysis of action-prone adolescents. *Journal of the American Psychoanalytic Association, 38,* 679–703.

Dahl, H. (1988). Frames of mind. In H. Dahl, H. Kachele, & H. Thoma (Eds.), *Psychoanalytic process research strategies* (pp. 51–66). New York: Springer Verlag.

Edgcumbe, R. (1993). Developmental disturbances in adolescence and their implications for transference and technique. *Bulletin of the Anna Freud Centre, 16,* 107–210.

Elkind, D. (1967). Egocentrism in adolescence. *Child Development, 38,* 1025–1034.

Emde, R. N., & Fonagy, P. (1997). An emerging culture for psychoanalytic research? Editorial. *International Journal of Psycho-Analysis, 78,* 643–661.

Erikson, E. (1979). The concept of ego identity. In A. Esman (Ed.), *The psychology of adolescence* (pp. 178–195). New York: International Universities Press.

Esman, A. (1985). A developmental approach to the psychotherapy of adolescents. *In Adolescent Psychiatry* (Vol. 13, pp. 119–133). University of Chicago Press.

Fonagy, P. (1991). Thinking about thinking: Some clinical and theoretical considerations in the treatment of a borderline patient. *International Journal of Psycho-analysis, 72,* 639–656.

Fonagy, P. (Ed.). (2002). *An open door review of outcome studies in psychoanalysis* (2nd rev. ed.). London: International Psychoanalytic Association.

Fonagy, P., Edgcumbe, R., Moran, G., Kennedy, H., & Target, M. (1993). The roles of mental representation and mental processes in therapeutic action. *Psychoanalytic Study of the Child, 48,* 9–47.

Fonagy, P., Gergely, G., Jurist, E. L., & Target, M. (2002). *Affect regulation, mentalization, and the development of the self.* New York: Other Press.

Fonagy, P., & Moran, G. (1991). Understanding psychic change in child psychoanalysis. *International Journal of Psycho-Analysis, 78,* 15–22.

Fonagy, P., & Perron, R. (2002). Epistemological and methodological background. In P. Fonagy, H. Kachele, R. Frause, E. Jones, R. Perron, J. Clarkin, A. J. Gerber, & E. Allison (Eds.), *An open door review of outcome studies in psychoanalysis* (pp. 1–64). London: International Psychoanalytical Association.

Fonagy, P., Steele, M., Moran, G. S., Steele, H., & Higgitt, A. (1993). Measuring the ghost in the nursery: An empirical study of the relation between parents' mental representations of childhood experiences and their infants' security of attachment. *Journal of the American Psychoanalytic Association, 41,* 957–989.

Fonagy, P., & Target, M. (1996). Predictors of outcome in child psychoanalysis: A retrospective study of 763 cases at the Anna Freud Centre. *Journal of the American Psychoanalytic Association, 44,* 27–77.

Freud, A. (1958). Adolescence. *Psychoanalytic Study of the Child, 13,* 255–278.

Freud, A. (1965). *Normality and pathology in childhood: Assessments of development.* New York: International Universities Press.

Freud, A. (1966). *The ego and the mechanisms of defense* (Rev. ed.). New York: International Universities Press.

Freud, S. (1917). Mourning and melancholia. In J. Strachey (Ed. & Trans.), The standard edition of the complete psychological works of Sigmund Freud (Vol. 14, pp. 239–258). London: Hogarth Press.

Gabbard, G. O., Gunderson, J. G., & Fonagy, P. (2002). The place of psychoanalytic treatments within psychiatry. *Archives of General Psychiatry, 59*(6), 505–510.

Geleerd, E. (1957). Some aspects of psychoanalytic technique in adolescence. *Psychoanalytic Study of the Child, 12,* 263–282.

Gilligan, C. (1993). *In a different voice: Psychological theory and women's development.* Cambridge, MA: Harvard University Press.

Gitelson, M. (1943). Character synthesis: The psychotherapeutic problem of adolescence. *American Journal of Orthopsychiatry, 18,* 422–436.

Greenberg, J. R., & Mitchell, S. A. (1983). *Object relations in psychoanalytic theory.* Cambridge, MA: Harvard University Press.

Harley, M. (1970). On some problems of technique in the analysis of early adolescents. *Psychoanalytic Study of the Child, 25,* 99–121.

Hartley, D. G., & Strupp, H. H. (1983). The therapeutic alliance: Its relationship to outcome in brief psychotherapy. In J. M. Masling (Ed.), *Empirical studies of psychoanalytical theories* (Vol. 1, pp. 7–11). Hillsdale, NJ: Analytic Press.

Hauser, S. T., & Smith, H. F. (1991). The development and experience of affect in adolescence. *Journal of the American Psychoanalytic Association, 39,* 131–165.

Horowitz, L. M., Rosenberg, S. E., Ureno, G., Kalehzan, B. M., & O'Halloran, P. (1989). Psychodynamic formulation, consensual response method, and interpersonal problems. *Journal of Consulting and Clinical Psychology, 57,* 599–606.

Horowitz, M. J. (1987). *States of mind: Configurational analysis of individual psychology* (2nd ed.). New York: Plenum Press.

Inhelder, B., & Piaget, J. (1958). *The growth of logical thinking from childhood to adolescence.* (A. Parsons & S. Milgram, Trans.). New York: Basic Books. (Original work published 1955).

Jones, E. E. (1997). Modes of therapeutic action. *International Journal of Psycho-Analysis, 78,* 1135–1150.

Jordan, J. V. (1993). The relational self: Implications for adolescent development. In S. E. Feinstein (Ed.), *Adolescent psychiatry* (pp. 228–239). University of Chicago Press.

Kandel, E. R. (1998). A new intellectual framework for psychiatry. *American Journal of Psychiatry, 155,* 457–469.

Kazdin, A. E. (1993). Psychotherapy for children and adolescents: Current progress and future research directions. *American Psychologist, 48,* 644–657.

Kennedy, H. (1979). The role of insight in child analysis: A developmental viewpoint. *Journal of the American Psychoanalytic Association, 27* (Suppl.), 9–28.

Kernberg, O. F. (1975). *Borderline conditions and pathological narcissism.* New York: Jason Aronson.

Kernberg, P. F., Weiner, A. S., & Bardenstein, K. K. (2000). *Personality disorders in children and adolescents.* New York: Basic Books.

Killingmo, B. (1989). Conflict and deficit: Implications for technique. *International Journal of Psycho-Analysis, 70,* 65–79.

Lafarge, L. (2000). Interpretation and containment. *International Journal of Psycho-Analysis, 81,* 67–84.

Lamb, D. (1986). *Psychotherapy with adolescent girls* (2nd ed.). New York: Plenum Press.

Laufer, M. (1968). The body image, the function of masturbation, and adolescence. *Psychoanalytic Study of the Child, 23,* 114–137.

Laufer, M., & Laufer, E. (1984). *Adolescence and developmental breakdown.* New Haven, CT: Yale University Press.

Levy-Warren, M. H. (1996). *The adolescent journey: Development, identity formation, and psychotherapy.* Northvale, NJ: Aronson.

Loewald, H. (1975). The waning of the Oedipus complex. *Journal of the American Psychoanalytic Association, 27,* 751–775.

Loughran, M. (1989). *Emotional disengagement from fathers as a factor affecting the postdivorce adjustment of young adolescent sons.* Unpublished doctoral dissertation, Smith College School for Social Work, Northampton, MA.

Luborsky, L. (1984). *Principles of psychoanalytic psychotherapy: A manual for supportive-expressive treatment.* New York: Basic Books.

Luborsky, L., Crits-Cristoph, P., Mintz, J., & Auerbach, A. (1981). *Who will benefit from psychotherapy? Predicting therapeutic outcomes.* New York: Basic Books.

Maenchen, A. (1970). On the technique of child analysis in relation to stages of development. *Psychoanalytic Study of the Child, 25,* 175–208.

Mahler, M. S., Pine, F., & Bergman, A. (1975). *The psychological birth of the human infant.* New York: Basic Books.

Marcia, J. E. (1966). Development and validation of ego-identity status. *Journal of Personality and Social Psychology, 3,* 551–558.

Masterson, J. F. (1972). *Treatment of the borderline adolescent: A developmental approach.* New York: Wiley-Interscience.

Meeks, J., & Bernet, W. (1990). *The fragile alliance: An orientation to the psychiatric treatment of the adolescent.* Malabar, FL: Robert Kreiger Publishing Company.

Miller, D. (1983). *The age between: Adolescence and therapy.* Northvale, NJ: Jason Aronson.

Modell, A. H. (1976). The holding environment and the therapeutic action of psychoanalysis. *Journal of the American Psychoanalytic Association, 24,* 285–307.

Offer, D. (1969). *The psychological world of the teen-ager: A study of normal adolescent boys.* New York: Basic Books.

Offer, D., & Offer, J. B. (1975). *From teenage to young manhood: A psychological study.* New York: Basic Books.

Ogden, T. (1995). Analyzing forms of aliveness and deadness of the transference-countertransference. *International Journal of Psycho-Analysis, 76,* 695–709.

Overton, W. F., Steidl, J. H., Rosenstein, D., & Horowitz, H. A. (1992). Formal operations as the regulatory context in adolescence. In S. Feinstein (Ed.), *Adolescent psychiatry* (pp. 502–513). University of Chicago Press.

Peskin, H. (1972). Multiple predictions of adult psychological health from preadolescent and adolescent behaviors. *Journal of Consulting and Clinical Psychology, 38,* 155–160.

Piaget, J. (1975). The intellectual development of the adolescent. In A. H. Esman (Ed.), *The psychology of adolescence* (pp. 104–108). New York: International Universities Press.

Ponton, L. E. (1997). *The romance of risk: Why teenagers do the things they do.* New York: Basic Books.

Rappaport, D. (1998). Destruction and gratitude: Some thoughts on the "The use of the object." *Contemporary Psychoanalysis, 34*(5), 369–378.

Renik, O. (1990). Comments on the clinical analysis of anxiety and depressive affect. *Psycho-analytic Quarterly, 59,* 226–248.

Rinsley, D. (1980). *Treatment of the severely disturbed adolescent.* New York: Jason Aronson.

Sandler, J. (1968). On the concept of the superego. *Psychoanalytic Study of the Child, 15,* 128–162.

Schafer, R. (1960). The loving and beloved superego. *Psychoanalytic Study of the Child, 25,* 163–188.

Schafer, R. (1983). The analysis of resisting. In *The analytic attitude* (pp. 162–182). New York: Basic Books.

Settlage, C. F. (1974). The technique of defense analysis in the psychoanalysis of an early adolescent. In M. Harley (Ed.), *The analyst and the adolescent at work* (pp. 3–39). New York: Quadrangle.

Shirk, S. R., & Russell, R. L. (1992). A reevaluation of estimates of child therapy effectiveness. *Journal of the American Academy of Child and Adolescent Psychiatry, 31,* 703–709.

Smith, S. (1993). Problems with affect tolerance in the analysis of an adolescent girl. *Child analysis: Clinical, theoretical, applied* (Vol. 4, pp. 75–98). Cleveland, OH: Center for Research in Child Development.

Strupp, H. H., & Binder, J. L. (1984). *Psychotherapy in a new key: A guide to time-limited dynamic psychotherapy.* New York: Basic Books.

Szapocznik, J., Rio, A., Murray, E., Cohen, R., Scopetta, M., Rivas-Valquez, A., et al. (1989). Structural family versus psychodynamic child therapy for problematic Hispanic boys. *Journal of Consulting and Clinical Psychology, 57,* 571–578.

Wallerstein, R. S. (1989). Psychoanalysis: The common ground. Paper presented at the Fifth Congress of the International Psychoanalytic Association, Rome, Italy.

Weiss, J., & Sampson, H. (1986). *The psychoanalytic process: Theory, clinical observations, and empirical research.* New York: Guilford Press.

Weisz, J. R., Huey, S. J., & Weersing, V. R. (1998). Psychotherapy outcome research with children and adolescent: The state of the art. *Advances in Clinical Child Psychology, 20,* 49–91.

Wieder, H. (1978). Psychoanalytic treatment of preadolescents. In J. Glenn (Ed.), *Child analysis and therapy* (pp. 237–259). Northvale, NJ: Jason Aronson.

Winnicott, D. W. (1965a). Adolescence: Struggling through the doldrums. In *The family and individual development* (pp. 79–87). London: Tavistock Publications.

Winnicott, D. W. (1965b). The theory of the parent-infant relationship. In *The maturational processes and the facilitating environment: Studies in the theory of emotional development* (pp. 37–55). London: Hogarth Press.

Winnicott, D. W. (1971a). *Playing and reality.* London: Tavistock Publications.

Winnicott, D. W. (1971b). The use of an object and relating through identifications. In *Playing and reality* (pp. 86–94). London: Tavistock Publications.

Winnicott, D. W. (1975). Transitional objects and transitional phenomena. In *Through paediatrics to psycho-analysis* (pp. 229–242). New York: Basic Books.

CHAPTER TWENTY-ONE

PSYCHODYNAMIC THERAPY WITH CHILDREN

Peter Fonagy, Ph.D., F.B.A.

Psychodynamic psychotherapy covers a wide range of treatment approaches. These range from child psychoanalysis (Sandler, Kennedy, & Tyson, 1980), through once weekly individual therapy (Kernberg, 1995), group implementation (Rose, 1972), family based implementations (Selvini Palazzoli, Boscolo, Cecchin, & Prata, 1978) and many others. Psychodynamic therapies in themselves differ in terms of the use made of expressive versus supportive techniques (Luborsky, 1984), the emphasis placed on play (Schaefer & Cangelosi, 1993; Simon, 1992) or drama (Johnson, 1982). In addition, there are major theoretical divisions that overlap in part with issues of technique originating from different understandings of the nature of development and psychopathology (King & Steiner, 1991).

Psychodynamic approaches, however, share an understanding of psychological abnormality as being a consequence of conflicting motivational states. Such states are often seen to be unconscious and the conflict created seems to be intrapsychic. (See Brenner, 1982.) This is not invariably the case, as approaches emphasizing interpersonal rather than intrapsychic conflicts have been gaining ground in contemporary psychodynamic theorization (Jacobs & Wachs, 2002; Klerman, Weissman, Rounsaville, & Chevron, 1984). Psychodynamic treatment is considered to be therapeutic because it helps individuals to build on their inherent capacities for understanding and emotional responsiveness. This is facilitated by a therapeutic relationship, and in particular by the therapist's communication of her understanding of the patient's conflicting motivations and responses to these conflicts. (For reasons of simplicity, therapists will be referred to generically as "she" and patients as "he.") Via such intervention and the improved self-understanding and self-regulatory capacity that follows, the patient may be enabled to arrive at more adaptive solutions than the rather limited strategies that brought him to seek psychological help.

Putative Mechanisms of Efficacy

Notwithstanding the theoretical heterogeneity of psychoanalytically based therapeutic approaches, there is probably a core set of assumptions to which all psychodynamic therapists would, to a greater or lesser extent, subscribe. These can be basically summarized as follows.

The Notion of Psychological Causation

This is not an assumption concerning the psychogenic nature of psychological disturbance, but rather refers to the preferred level of conceptualization for psychodynamic clinicians. Whether psychological problems are genetically or socially determined, psychodynamic therapists assume that the representation of past experience, its interpretation and its meaning, whether conscious or unconscious, determine children's reaction to the external world and their capacity or lack of capacity to adapt to it. This formulation does not imply lack of respect for other levels of analysis of childhood psychological problems, the biological, the sociocultural or the systemic. Rather, psychological difficulties are conceived of as meaningful organizations of a child's conscious or unconscious beliefs, thoughts, and feelings whatever the root cause of such maladaptive organizations, and therefore they are assumed to be accessible to psychotherapeutic intervention.

The Assumption of Unconscious Mental Processes

Psychodynamic clinicians assume that the explanation of conscious ideation and intentional behavior requires the assumption of complex mental processes functioning outside of awareness. Although psychodynamic clinicians probably no longer think in terms of "an unconscious," in the sense of a physical space where forbidden or repudiated feelings and ideas are stored, they assume that nonconscious, narrative-like experiences analogous to conscious fantasies associated with potential wishes for gratification or safety, profoundly influence children's behavior, their capacity to regulate affect, and to adequately handle their social environment. For example, an unconscious repudiated feeling of being held and kept safe may paradoxically underpin an exaggerated belief in self-sufficiency.

The Assumption of a Representational Model of the Mind

In common with cognitive scientists, psychodynamic therapists assume that the experience of self with others is internalized, and forms the basis for relatively enduring representational structures of social and interpersonal interactions. These representational structures determine interpersonal expectations and shape the mental representation of the self.

The Pathogenic Significance of Conflict

Intrapsychic conflict (incompatible wishes, affects, or ideas) is assumed to be ubiquitous in development. It is seen as the cause of displeasure as well as an absence of safety. Adverse environments tend to intensify conflicts as well as undermine the development of capacities that may help the child to deal with conflicts in ordinary life. For example, the loss of a caregiver or severe neglect or abuse may aggravate a natural predisposition to relate with mixed feelings to the caregiver, as well as reducing the child's competence to resolve such incompatible ideas.

The Assumption of Psychic Defenses

It is assumed that children rapidly develop an unconscious capacity to modify unacceptable or dangerous ideas, desires, or affects by resorting to a set of mental operations that have in common the function of distorting these mental states in a direction of reducing their capacity to generate anxiety, distress, or displeasure. Like all mental operations, defenses have a developmental or maturational hierarchy. More complex defenses, such as intellectualization or humor, come into effect relatively late in development or perhaps never. Simpler processes such as projection (attribution of the self's state to the other), denial (refusing to acknowledge self-states), or splitting (simultaneously holding opposite-valence self-states but experiencing them only sequentially) are available to the child from a relatively early stage.

The Assumption of Complex Meanings

Psychodynamic therapists assume that children's communication within the treatment context has meanings beyond that intended by the child. Likewise, children's symptoms might carry multiple meanings reflecting the nature of the child's internal representations of themselves and others. Within a classical formulation, symptoms express a combination of a wish as well as the child's attempt to erect a defensive, self-protective set of mental operations to protect themselves from conscious awareness of that wish. The therapist's task is to make appropriate links between the child's behaviors in different contexts that may show the child that the behavior that is seemingly bizarre, confusing, frightening, or even self-destructive has a meaningful and even rational facet when looked at from a different perspective or in a different context. Elaborating and clarifying such meaning structures may be seen as the essence of psychodynamic psychotherapy.

The Assumption of Transference Displacement

It is generally accepted that internalized representations of interpersonal relationships originally in the child-parent relationship can determine the child's behavior with others in the outside world, also become active in the context of the therapeutic relationship. The displacement of patterns of expectation from important others in the child's life to the therapist serves as a window on the child's internal world. This function becomes all the more important because the relative neutrality and ambiguity of the therapeutic relationship encourages externalizations of repudiated aspects of past relationships (Tyson & Tyson, 1986). The situation becomes more complicated because the child's verbal and nonverbal behavior must naturally have an impact on the therapist's experience. However, modern psychodynamic therapists tend to make extensive use of their subjective reactions to help them understand the roles that they are implicitly asked by the child to play. By this indirect route, the therapist is able to gain a view of the child's internal struggles and representations of both themselves and others.

The Therapeutic Aspect of the Relationship

Psychodynamic therapists assume that, in addition to new understanding and insight that the child might gain through the experience of therapy, aspects of the relationship with a supportive, respectful, and empathic adult will also have benefits for the child's capacities for understanding emotional responsiveness. In particular the therapist's interest in the child's mental states, talk and play, thoughts and feelings, and the therapist's commitment to find meaning even in the disruptive or distressing aspects of the child's behavior provides him with an opportunity to reflect upon and reorganize experiences and identify more adaptive solutions to the interpersonal and intrapsychic conflicts he faces.

Developmental Influences

Psychoanalytic Views of Development and Developmental Influences

Freud's psychosexual theory of development (1905) was revolutionary in presenting a predominantly developmental view of adult psychopathology, in that he begun to construct an understanding of adult disturbances in terms of infantile and early childhood experience. Abraham (1979) etched in the details of the model, identifying specific links between character formation, neurosis, and psychosis on the one hand and instinctual development on the other. Contemporary followers of Freud had a variety of theoretical preoccupations, but all were based on developmental formulations.

Many psychoanalytic theories have continued this developmental emphasis. Anna Freud (1946) provided a developmental model of ego defenses and later (1965) a comprehensive model of psychopathology based on the dimensions of normal and abnormal personality development. Melanie Klein (1975), influenced by Ferenczi and Abraham, was a pioneer in linking interpersonal relationships to instinctual developmental factors to provide a radically different perspective both on severe mental disorders and on child development. Meanwhile, in the United States Heinz Hartmann with Ernst Kris and Rudolph Lowenstein (1946) provided an alternative, equally developmentally oriented framework, focusing on the evolution of mental structures (id, ego, superego) necessary for adaptation, and elaborated on the common developmental conflicts between mental structures in early childhood. Margaret Mahler and her colleagues (1975) provided psychoanalysts in the North American tradition with a dynamic map of the first three years of life, and opportunities for tracing the developmental origins of severe character disorders. Psychoanalytic object relations theory had a uniquely developmental emphasis. Fairbairn (1952) traced the development of object-seeking from immature to mature dependence; Jacobson (1964) explored the development of representations of self and other. Kernberg (1975) drew on previous work by Klein, Hartmann, and Jacobson to produce a developmental model of borderline and narcissistic disturbances; Kohut (1977) constructed a model of narcissistic disturbances based on presumed deficits of early parenting.

Unfortunately, early theories have not been supplanted by later formulations and most psychoanalytic writers assume that a number of explanatory frameworks are necessary in order to account for the relationship of development and psychopathology. (See Sandler, 1983.) So-called neurotic psychopathology is presumed to originate in later childhood at a time when there is self-other differentiation and when the various agencies of the mind (id, ego, superego) have been firmly established. The structural frame of reference (Arlow & Brenner, 1964) is most commonly used in developmental accounts of these disorders. Personality or character disorders, as well as most non-neurotic psychiatric disorders, are most commonly looked at in frameworks developed subsequent to structural theory.

The Evolution of Psychoanalytic Child Psychotherapy

Freud was an acute observer of the behavior of young children. He used his observations to support and elaborate his assumptions about infantile mental processes. (See for example Freud, 1900; 1909; 1920; 1926.) Although these observations were detailed and accurate, he was skeptical about their value in clinical work with psychologically disordered children. It was Hug-Helmuth (1920) who first used the play of children as part of an insight-oriented technique. She saw the child's play in a therapeutic context as providing insight into the child's unconscious sexual fantasies, which could then be interpreted with similar results as interpretations of adults' unconscious motives.

The true originators of psychodynamic psychotherapy for children were Anna Freud (1946) and Melanie Klein (1932). They evolved somewhat different, yet in important ways compatible, approaches that enabled psychodynamic clinicians to work with children. Klein's approach was based on the assumption that children's play was essentially the same as the free association of adults. She saw such play as motivated by unconscious fantasies activated principally by specific aspects of the relationship with the therapist. It therefore required interpretation, or at least clarification, if the child's anxiety was to be addressed by the therapist. The principal focus of Klein's therapeutic work was the interpretation of the child's deeply unconscious concerns related to destructive and sadistic impulses.

Kleinian technique with children has changed considerably since the early days. Modern Kleinians (DeFolch, 1988; O'Shaughnessy, 1988) would not frequently give direct interpretations of deeply unconscious material. Bion (1959) emphasized the importance of "containment," that is, the therapist's capacity to understand and accept the child's projections. This may be critical in normal development (in the caregiver) as well as in the therapist's experience of the countertransference (Fonagy, Gergely, Jurist, & Target, 2002).

Anna Freud's approach (see Edgcumbe, 2000) was deeply rooted in the developmental context of the child's efforts to achieve a reasonable adaptation to a social and an internal environment. She was reluctant to make assumptions concerning the meaning of the child's play and, in comparison with Melanie Klein, approached the work of interpretation far more gradually. She assumed that changes in the child's environment brought about by communicating to caregivers an understanding of the child's problems derived from therapy, might have equal if not greater long-term benefit for the child's functioning. Her emphasis was on conflicts arising from the child's sexual impulses rather than, as was Klein's, on innate aggression. The essential aspect of her technique was the interpretation of the child's strategies of adapting to conflict, the interpretation of defense, and only through this the anxieties that brought them into play. The therapeutic goal is less the achievement of the integration of a fragmented sense of self and object, but rather the developmental goal of returning the child to a normal path of maturation. Consequently, she was far more accepting of supportive and educational techniques to address the child's poorly developed ego functions (Pine, 1985).

The third important strand in the development of psychodynamic technique originates in the work of Donald Winnicott (1965; 1971). While influenced by Klein in his model of childhood pathology, his technique, in common with Anna Freud, emphasized the importance of a holding environment as well as the importance of play. Play was seen not simply as a vehicle for communicating unconscious fantasy, but as an activity that is uniquely generative of human development. One of Winnicott's major contributions is his description of a "transitional space" between self and object where the subjective object and the truly objective other could be simultaneously seen (Winnicott, 1971). This duality of representation created an important bridge between psychodynamic thinking and interpersonalist approaches such as that of Sullivan (1953). Within the interpersonal approach, the therapist becomes an active and real participant in the therapeutic situation (Altman, 1992; 1994; Warshaw, 1992).

These trends evolved to some degree independently in different parts of the world. While Kleinian thinking dominated the United Kingdom and, to some degree, Latin America, it was the work of Anna Freud that was most readily integrated into psychodynamic ideas in the United States and some parts of Europe. More recently, interpersonal approaches to psychodynamic therapy have taken hold in many treatment centers in the United States, anticipated partly by self-psychological (Kohutian) therapeutic orientation as well as the integration of Winnicottian object relations approaches. There has also been considerable cross fertilization of psychoanalytic psychodynamic techniques, even in the more committed Kleinian (such as Alvarez, 1993) and Anna Freudian (such as Bleiberg, Fonagy, & Target, 1997) traditions.

Putative Targets of Treatment

Differentiating Disorders of Mental Representation and Disorders of Mental Process in Children: A Heuristic to Guide Treatment Interventions

While psychoanalytic theories have achieved a reasonable level of sophistication and complexity, the relationship between theory and practice has widened and the way in which foundations of pathology could be linked to therapeutic approaches has come to be increasingly obscure (Fonagy, 1999). In order to address the challenge represented by this gap, and as part of an effort to manualize psychodynamic child therapy, we proposed a clinical heuristic to facilitate the bringing together of formulation, models of therapy, and technique in psychodynamic child therapy. We have elaborated two psychoanalytic models of childhood disturbance, to clarify why it is that children with different forms of pathology require different therapeutic techniques, and the nature of therapeutic action in each case (Fonagy, Moran, Edgcumbe, Kennedy, & Target, 1993).

The first model, the *representational model,* concerns the exclusion from consciousness of threatening ideas and feelings and the distortions of mental content brought about by the defenses that permit this exclusion. The concept of mental representation has been successfully used to clarify the nature of certain childhood disturbances and psychic change in the psychoanalytic treatment of children. Mental representation is a theoretical construct that psychoanalysts may use to understand and explain the inner world of patients (Jacobson, 1964; Sandler & Rosenblatt, 1962). It is axiomatic that human thought and action must involve a "representational system." It is misleading to use representation in the sense of a symbol that "stands for" some external reality. Rather, mental representations are better conceived of as patterns of mental activation, as links between the component features of representations. They not only store our past experience, but also guide our perception and influence our experience of our external and internal worlds.

Significant figures are "represented" in the sense that we construct mental models that integrate numerous attributes into a single system. Connections between attributes may be based on experience or the activation of attributes by wishes, fantasies, fears, or other affective structures with the capacity to distort the internal organization of mental life. Both others and the self may be represented in numerous ways as person schemas, as representations of frequently encountered patterns of relationships, as assumptions of functions frequently associated with the person, as representations of typical interpersonal interactions, and so on.

Mental representation may be considered a dynamic (motivationally relevant) construct insofar as it is inextricably linked to emotional experience.[1] The motivational properties of drive states and intrapsychic conflicts at the level of psychic structure are experienced in terms of both conscious and unconscious, positive and negative, emotional states (Sandler, 1972). Many psychoanalytic theories of developmental disturbance speak to distortions of mental representations, conscious and unconscious, caused by various forms of intra-psychic conflict. Such representations come to be split off and isolated, forming a separate structure that undermines the coherent functioning of the child's mind. Depression, for example, may be helpfully conceptualized as the tension created by the discrepancy between an "ego-ideal" and self-representation. Mental representations, however, cannot be separated from the psychological processes that generate and organize them. Just as it is necessary to think of light in terms of both particles and waves, one cannot conceive of mental life other than in terms of both mental representations and the mental processes that create and operate upon them. The second therapeutic model, the *mental process model*, focuses on the pathological effects of the inhibition of developing psychological processes. In using the term "inhibition of mental processes," we are describing the situation in which a whole class or category of mental representations appears to be absent from a patient's mental functioning. We assume that the situation comes about as an attempt by the child to protect his mental functioning from specific, extremely painful, mental representations, which occurred as a result of using a particular mental process. In such cases, the mental representations that generate displeasure may be too central to be isolated from the core of the representational system which may become part of consciousness. For example, experiences of the mother's feeling states (say her depression) cannot be ignored by the child, so he might inhibit aspects of his own capacity to empathically experience the emotional state of another person. The child therefore disengages or inhibits the entire mental process that creates that class of mental representations. This second, mental process model may help to explain how and why psychotherapy benefits those whose pathology resides within the ego, pathology that has been described in the past under headings such as ego deficit, ego restriction, or developmental pathology (Freud, 1965). It draws attention to the therapeutic effects of engaging previously inhibited mental processes in the here-and-now of the psychoanalytic encounter.

The models identify two distinct, potentially pathological, means available to the child to deal with psychological conflict. These strategies have in common the function of reducing displeasure by the constriction of conscious mental life. Incompatible wishes may generate uncomfortable affective states (anxiety, guilt), which in turn lead to the wish to reduce the incompatibility. This may be accomplished through mental adaptation of one or both wishes (such as the defensive distortion of turning a wish into its opposite), or a fundamental interference with affective or cognitive mental processes related to the conflict (such as inhibition of imaginative capacity).

Differences in Client Groups Treated According to the Mental Representation and Mental Process Models

Broadly speaking, children whose disorder is best conceptualized in terms of the mental representation model tend to correspond to what has traditionally been regarded as the neurotic category. Traditionally psychodynamic therapists have worked with relatively less severely disturbed young people. The criteria of suitability for psychodynamic child psychotherapy have been identified by Hoffman (1993), Glenn (1978), Sandler and Tyson (1980), and others as the following:

1. Good verbal skills and psychological mindedness, that is, the ability to conceive of behavior as mediated by mental states (thoughts and feelings). Equally important here is the child's capacity to tolerate awareness of conflicts and anxieties, particularly those previously kept unconscious, without risking substantial disorganization or disintegration of the personality.
2. A supportive environment that is able to sustain the child's involvement in an intense and demanding long-term interpersonal relationship. Particularly important here is the willingness of parents to respect the boundaries of the child's therapy and promote the child's commitment to the treatment.
3. It is assumed that successful treatment depends on internal conflicts being the cause of the child's disturbance.
4. Further, traditionally psychotherapists were reluctant to treat children with major developmental deficits (ego deviations) that were not the result of unconscious conflict and therefore could not be seen as resolvable through insight.
5. As the child's motivation for treatment stems from anxiety, guilt, or other unpleasant affects, these experiences are often seen as essential to ensuring the child's commitment to the treatment as well as a sense of agency (a sense of responsibility for their problems and actions).
6. It is assumed that a capacity to form relationships and develop trust must be present in order for psychodynamic therapy to operate.

This description corresponds to what has traditionally been referred to as neurotic disturbance. For example, Tyson (1992) describes neurosis as characterized by (1) a predominance of internalized conflicts producing symptoms, (2) a capacity for affect regulation, and (3) a capacity for self-responsibility. Kernberg (1975) has added to this list the predominance of repression as a mechanism of defense. However, neurosis is a term largely discredited in modern descriptive psychiatry as lacking in clarity and reliability and probably also over-inclusive and based on an outmoded theory of psychological disorder.

There is evidently a group of children commonly treated by psychodynamic psychotherapy who do not meet the criteria as described above. We have described this group in our retrospective examination of case records at the Anna Freud Centre (Fonagy & Target, 1996a; 1996b). Other descriptions by Cohen and colleagues (1994), Towbin and colleagues (1993), and Bleiberg (1987; 1994) have arrived at strikingly similar descriptions. This group of children appears to suffer from a variety of deficiencies of psychological capacities, indicated, for example, by lack of control over affect, lack of stable self and other representations, and diffusion of their sense of identity. These individuals may be most helpfully seen as suffering from defensive inhibition or distortion of *mental processes* rather than just the mental representations that such processes generate. Thus, for this group of children, a wide variety of situations is likely to bring about maladaptive functioning, as the very capacities that may be involved in achieving adaptive functioning are impaired.

Historically, patients suffering from disorders of mental processes were most readily recognized by their failure to respond positively to insight-oriented interpretation-focused psychotherapy, and by their very slow rate of improvement in psychodynamic therapy. Often, the serious and immutable character of their disturbance was not easily detected during the diagnostic assessment, and the children could not be placed in any recognized diagnostic category. They might even have enough areas of good functioning and an overall level of adaptation such that they appeared only mildly disturbed. In other children, borderline, narcissistic, or autistic features were evident.

The internal world of patients with major developmental disturbance may be chaotic and confused, lacking firm boundaries between self and objects. There may be ego deficits, poor defenses, overwhelming affects, overexcitability, lack of internal safety, poor frustration tolerance or poor impulse control. Viewed externally, the child's relationships tend not to be age appropriate; peer relationships are frequently deficient and the child's capacity for awareness of other people and their needs is limited. The child may see the other as only there to meet his need. Self-esteem is often visibly poor because the self-representation is damaged or characterized by defensive grandiosity. There may be problems in cognitive functioning such as magical thinking, limited attention span, memory problems, poor perception of causality, and understanding of other people's intentions. Verbal understanding and expression of emotions seems frequently to be lacking. Often, developmental problems, such as severe learning difficulties with or without IQ deficit, accompany emotional complaints.

We assume that the development of specific mental processes is defensively inhibited by the child as an attempt to cope with specific traumata or environmental pressures. For example, parents may themselves be inadequate or infantile and quite inappropriate in their way of relating to the child, unaware of the child's developmental capacities. The parents' handling of the child may be in some way disturbed: it may be inconsistent, excessively overindulgent or over-stimulating, or insufficiently protective from hostile siblings or other common dangers. Parents often experience specific difficulty in addressing the child's affects appropriately. For example, an anxious mother may be incapable of providing an adequate model of the regulation of affect; or a severely depressed mother may be unable to respond to the child's needs and demands. Frequently, there are family secrets, necessitating the suppression of curiosity and understanding in the child. Sometimes there are overtly frightening aspects in the child's environment, such as a psychiatrically ill parent, or an overtly abusive one. Extreme aggressiveness in a parent may be mirrored in the child's behavior; alternatively the child may become withdrawn and inhibited. Often families have been broken up by divorce or separation, and sometimes mutual recrimination between parents has escalated to violence, or an atmosphere of confession and manipulation, which can lead to a shutting down of attempts to understand. There may also be constitutional inadequacies in the child, but it is often difficult to distinguish those that may be genetically based or the aftereffects of a severe illness, from those deriving from very early traumatic handling or pressures in the parent-child relationship. In a significant minority of cases, organic reasons exist for the difficulties (such as neurological problems or severe physical illness compromising normal developmental processes).

Important considerations from the point of view of psychotherapeutic technique arise out of the distinction between disorders of mental representation and disorders of mental process. Disorders of mental representation are well served by a primarily interpretive therapeutic process that aims at addressing distorted ideas and integrating repudiated or incoherent notions of self and other. The reintegration of split off (repressed), often infantile but troublesome ideas, into the child's developmentally appropriate mental structures is the therapeutic aim (Abrams, 1988). For the group of patients whose disorder is a mental process disturbance, this kind of approach has limited usefulness. There is a need for promoting, strengthening or disinhibiting mental processes that may have been disengaged (decoupled) or distorted for defensive or constitutional biological reasons. These children may, for example, need assistance in labeling and verbalizing affects and ideas, revalidating affect, directing their attention, understanding the feelings of others, retaining a more stable image of their attachment figure—just being more realistic in their expectations of their own competence. Much of psychodynamic intervention aimed at the so-called neurotic patient may change the organization or the shape of the child's mental representation (Sandler & Rosenblatt, 1962). To regenerate mental processes, an alternative set of psychodynamic techniques, emphasizing a developmental approach, are necessary. Our review of current therapeutic approaches will be based around this distinction.

Empirical Support for Psychodynamic Therapies

Psychoanalytic psychotherapy is a clinical intervention, although some psycho-analysts may wish to maintain that it should be considered outside the medical frame of reference. Over the past decade, all aspects of medicine have come under scrutiny, where those purchasing, directing, or using medical services expressed an explicit wish to know what evidence is available to support the choice of specific procedures under specific conditions (Sackett, Rosenberg, Gray, Haynes, & Richardson, 1996). Clinical judgment is no longer accepted as sufficient grounds for offering any medical treatment. Recommendations at national policy as well as local health-care-provider level are expected to be based upon evidence of effectiveness. We may have major concerns about the simplistic application of the principles of evidence-based medicine to the complex problems of mental health, which the clinical challenges of mental disorders present. These objections have been frequently stated (Goldfried & Wolfe, 1996) and will not be repeated here. At the end of the day, notwithstanding the difficulty of measuring outcomes in mental health, or even the specific problems of ownership of outcomes in child mental health (child, parent, school, and so on), or the vexed question of the ethics of randomization in psychosocial treatment research and a myriad of other dif-ficulties, professional ethics will soon mandate that health care workers desist from procedures unless these are of known effectiveness (that is, demonstrated to be effective in randomized controlled trials). As the evidence-based movement gath-ered momentum in most Western countries over the past decades, new paradigms for collecting evidence for treatment effectiveness emerged, such as pragmatic trials, effectiveness research, and qualitative research methodologies. These have augmented rather than replaced information from randomized controlled trials (Fonagy, in press). However, the current view of evidence in mental health is some-what more ecumenical than has been the case in the past. Different kinds of evidence are required to answer different kinds of clinical and research questions (Kazdin & Kendall, 1998). The collecting of systematic information on psy-chodynamic treatments is long overdue. The evidence available often does not meet the most stringent requirements of evidence-based medicine (Gabbard, Gunderson, & Fonagy, 2002). Historically, there has been opposition to outcomes research from those with a psychodynamic orientation. Systematic data collection, however, is increasingly seen as being compatible with psychoanalytic ideas, particularly as the evidence that is collected in many instances showed the psychodynamic approach to be comparable to physical treatments or other psy-chosocial approaches (Fonagy, 2002).

There is little research available on the outcome of psychodynamic treatment (Kazdin, 2003; Weisz, Weiss, Morton, Granger, & Han, 1992). The most extensive study of intensive psychodynamic treatment was a chart review of more than 700 case records at a psychoanalytic clinic in the United Kingdom (Fonagy & Target, 1994, 1996b; Target & Fonagy, 1994a, 1994b). The observed effects of psychodynamic treatment were relatively impressive, particularly with younger children and those with emotional disorder diagnoses or those with disruptive disorder whose symptom profile included anxiety. Children with pervasive developmental disorders or mental retardation appeared to respond poorly to psychodynamic treatment. There was some evidence that more intensive treatment was desirable for children with emotional disorders whose symptomatology was relatively severe or pervasive.

Some smaller scale studies demonstrated that psychodynamic therapy could bring about improvement in aspects of psychological functioning beyond psychiatric symptomatology. Heinicke (1965; Heinicke & Ramsey-Klee, 1986) demonstrated that general academic performance was superior at a one-year follow-up in children who were treated more frequently in psychodynamic psychotherapy. Moran and Fonagy (Fonagy & Moran, 1990; Moran, Fonagy, Kurtz, Bolton, & Brook, 1991; 1987) demonstrated that children with poorly controlled diabetes could be significantly helped with their metabolic problems by relatively brief, intensive psychodynamic psychotherapy. Lush and colleagues (1991) in a naturalistic study offered preliminary evidence that psychodynamic therapy was helpful for children with a history of severe deprivation who were fostered or adopted. Improvements were noted only in the treated group. Negative findings were, however, reported by Smyrnios and Kirkby (1993). In this study, no significant differences were found at follow-up between a time-limited and a time-unlimited psychodynamic therapy group and a minimal contact control group.

All these studies suffer from severe methodological shortcomings. These include, in different studies: (1) small sample size, (2) non-standardized, perhaps unreliable assessment procedures, (3) non-random assignment, (4) non-independent or over-narrow assessments of outcome, (5) lack of full specification of the treatment offered, and (6) the absence of measures of therapist adherence, and so on.

Better evidence is available for the success of therapeutic approaches that can be considered indirect implementations of psychoanalytic ideas. Kolvin et al., for example (Kolvin et al., 1981) demonstrated that psychodynamic group therapy had relatively favorable effects when compared with behavior therapy and parent counseling, particularly on long-term follow-up. Similar encouraging results have been reported in a smaller-scale study by Lochman and colleagues (1993). A sobering finding is reported by Szapocznik and colleagues (1989) treating disruptive adolescents using individual psychodynamic therapy or structural family therapy. Both forms of treatment led to significant gains. But on one-year follow-up, while the child's functioning remained improved for both groups, family functioning had deteriorated in the individual therapy group. Interpersonal psychotherapy, although not a psychodynamic treatment (Klerman et al., 1984), incorporates interpersonal psychodynamic principles. Mufson and colleagues (1993) have manualized this therapy for depressed adolescents Interpersonal Psychotherapy—Adolescent version (IPT–A), and a clinical RCT has been reported (Mufson, Weissman, Moreau, & Garfinkel, 1999). This included forty-eight referred adolescents with major depression, of whom thirty-two completed the protocol. The majority of drop-outs came from the control condition, which was used for "clinical monitoring," effectively as a waiting list. An intent-to-treat analysis showed that 75% of patients treated with IPT–A recovered, as judged by Hamilton Rating Scale scores, in comparison with 46% of those in the control group. Other studies have also found IPT to be effective for adolescents, more so on some dimensions than was CBT (Rosselló & Bernal, 1999), and sertraline (Santor & Kusumakar, 2001).

An important study from the University of Pisa (Muratori, Picchi, Bruni, Patarnello, & Romagnoli, 2003) looked at the effectiveness of an eleven-session treatment program for fifty-eight children with anxiety disorder or dysthymic disorder. The treatment was structured, focal psychodynamic psychotherapy, including both family and individual sessions. The control group was referred for community treatment. Measures were taken at baseline, six months (end of treatment for the experimental group), and two-year follow-up. The two key measures were the Clinical Global Assessment Score (CGAS) (completed by a blind, independent interviewer who interviewed both child and parent), and Children Behavior Checklist (CBCL) completed by the parents. The results revealed a significant difference between the groups, only at follow-up, on both the CGAS and CBCL scales. In addition, the authors report a significantly lower level of service usage in the experimental group during the follow-up period. This study is unique in providing a well-matched control group, in assessing the effectiveness of psychodynamic psychotherapy.

Personal Experience and Case Material

Child psychodynamic therapy uses the tools evolved for psychodynamic therapy for adults. This is not unique to a psychodynamic approach. Adult cognitive-behavioral therapists similarly extend therapeutic strategies from adult work to work with children (such as Kendall, 1991). In psychotherapy for children, it is possible to classify interventions into categories such as supportive, summary statements, clarifications, and interpretations. Naturally, with younger patients the manner of application of these tools may be different. Developmental considerations drive the work of child therapists, thus judging how to communicate an idea to a child in a way that is understandable and helpful requires an intuition of the cognitive maturity of the client, which ultimately is more a matter of experience than of learning and knowledge. There are two aspects that do differentiate work with a young person from work with a mature individual. First, as Anna Freud pointed out (Freud, 1965), the task of the therapist is to unleash a powerful natural force for healing: development. Developmental continuity and developmental discontinuity exist side by side (Emde, 1988) and psychopathology often persists because it is normal development and thus the opportunity for a felicitous developmental discontinuity that is lost. Getting the developmental process under way may indeed be all that a particular treatment might require. Second, and related to this, is what we know about the process of development itself. As Linda Mayes has pointed out, there are very few good theories of development as such. Particularly in the psychodynamic domain, we have only sparse understanding of what aspect of an intervention might advance a child to the next developmental phase. Broadly leaning on Vygotsky's suggestions, child therapists offer their interventions with the aim of providing a scaffolding for the child's evolving mental capacities; that is, they simultaneously challenge the child's understanding and lead him to advance to the next developmental level.

Therapeutic Approaches to Disorders of Mental Representation

We can identify three mechanisms of therapeutic action through changes in mental representations: integration, elaboration, and the genesis of new representational structures.

Integration. The first aspect of therapeutic action concerns the enhancing effect of the therapist's interventions on the integrity of the child's mental representations. We conceive of mental representations as being either partially or fully activated, depending on the proportion of the features defining it that are active concurrently. Consistent with current knowledge of the functioning of the brain (Edelman, 1987; Edelman, 1989; Rumelhart & McClelland, 1986), we might expect that each activation of the representation strengthens the links between aspects in such a way that subsequent partial activation is more likely to lead to the activation of the entire representation. The internal cohesion or integration of the representation will thus improve with repeated activation.

For example, imagine a child who feels somewhat rejected, angry, and hurt following the therapist's brief absence from sessions while at a conference. As he begins to talk of distances and gaps, his associative links allow the therapist to identify in an affectively meaningful way his perception of her as being too far away to be accessible. Thus, this partially activated representation of the therapist influences associations and play. But the therapist has to spell out the idea, often in several guises, for the child to be able to begin to integrate it into his current thinking. As a mental representation is brought from a preconscious to a conscious state, we assume that a transformation takes place that enhances the internal coherence and boundaries of components of the representation, a process which may be labeled integration. This consolidation of a representation in consciousness by interventions that address non-conscious subjective experience is thought of as a prototypical form of therapeutic action. It is thought to have the effect of further delineating mental representations, and allowing them to be more readily called upon in different contexts.

While some components of representations need to be made explicit and coherent, others are so tightly integrated that they become fully activated even from very partial cues. The extensive repetition of a particular pattern of activation in thought or in reality can establish powerful links between features of a representation, leading to such highly integrated representations. Because of the strong links between its features such representations are very readily activated and thus impose themselves on a wide variety of experiences. Mental representations have the potential to aggregate experience and the most readily accessible representations need not correspond to actual occurrences. For example, a child's representation of his mother lying down, claiming to be tired, which he enacts in a session, may or may not correspond to a memory of her retreating to her bed and expressing a wish to die. Nevertheless, the features of passivity, inaccessibility, the expression of hopelessness, and seeking attention may be underlying invariants of the child's experience with her across many different situations, leading to this powerful, highly integrated representation of overwhelming emotional salience. Reflecting on such a representation increases its differentiation and reduces its dominance over the representational system. Changes to such representational prototypes are the hallmark of therapeutic action and success.

Elaboration. Reflection, instigated by psychotherapy, works through the elaboration of mental representations. Elaboration establishes relationships among mental representations and creates the kind of network of relations that is basic to the process of understanding. "Understanding" an idea may amount to placing that idea in appropriate relation to the family of ideas that are articulated with it. The majority of interpretative work in psychotherapy may be seen as having as its primary aim the making of new links between representational structures so that the influence of more childlike mental structures is curtailed. The process of elaborating well-integrated representations will then define larger representational units, which in their turn will require to be bounded and integrated.

The Genesis of New Representational Structures. The integration of poorly articulated representations, and the elaboration of the relationship between representations within a system, combine over time to facilitate the child's unique contribution to the therapeutic process. The therapist's interpretation does not create new representational structures. It merely points to particular internal or external experiences and may speculate as to why they were "difficult" or "dangerous." Once anxiety concerning feelings and ideas has been addressed and elaborated in the context of other experiences, it then becomes possible for the child to initiate the change in his mental representational system in a form which takes account of the previously unacceptable experience. The therapeutic situation enables the patient to create the new mental representation. In particular, "working within the transference" focusing comments and discourse on current (here and now) experience enhances the potential of the therapeutic situation to present the patient directly with novel emotional perspectives and thus maximize the opportunity to bring about a self-initiated change in psychic structure.

Techniques Pertinent to the Representational Model

Prototypically psychodynamic child psychotherapy aims to address non-conscious aspects of the child's representational systems, identifying and healing splits, pointing out distortions and putative psychological reasons for these. For example, the child may unconsciously represent his father as cruel and rageful, a representation distorted by the child's unconscious aggression, a feeling experienced as dangerous paradoxically because of the father's perceived vulnerability and weakness. Further, it is anticipated that these distortions have a developmental dimension whereby ideas or feelings more appropriate to an earlier stage of development are likely to confuse the child's current perceptions (Abrams, 1988). The separation (repression, denial, displacement) of such early ideas is assumed to be defensive. For example the perception of a caregiver as cruel and destructive may be based on an infantile perception of that parent. As a consequence of the pain associated with this perception at odds with seeing him as a loving father, this aspect is never integrated into the evolving representation of the father in the child's mind. It exists as a separate, yet disturbing idea. The child may react to the presence of such a representation as potentially painful and incompatible with his perception of his parent as loving and affectionate. By displacing this perception onto others who he then perceives as frightening he may, for example, exaggerate the subjective likelihood that burglars or other intruders might attack him and his family. Of course, if these ideas are based on the externalization of his aggressive feelings towards the father, then it is feelings about the father that have to be addressed in the context of the therapy.

The therapist, using the child's verbalization, non-verbal play, dream reports, or other behaviors, attempts to create a model of the child's conscious and unconscious thoughts and feelings. On the basis of this model, the therapist assists the child to acquire an understanding of his irrational or at times inappropriate feelings and beliefs. This kind of understanding may, under ideal conditions, result in the integration of developmentally earlier modes of thinking into a more mature and age appropriate framework. The structure of the treatment appears to be relatively unimportant. Some therapists use toys or games, others more readily engage children in a process of self-exploration. In most contexts the therapist works to draw attention to determinants of the child's behavior outside the child's conscious awareness. Therapists tend to use material of the child's fantasy and play in conjunction with other information they have obtained about the child (parental reports, school reports) to construct a plausible picture in their minds of the child's current emotional concerns. The most common foci of psychodynamic child therapists tend to be the child's concerns about his body, anxieties about conscious or unconscious destructive or sexual impulses, and concerns about relationships with or between caregivers or siblings or peers. These are indeed frequently, potentially, bothersome aspects of human development but clinical experience has shown that specific foci for clinical concern (which varies greatly by the training and orientation of the psychoanalytic therapist) matters less than the broad framework within which the child's mental experience becomes the focus of adult interest, reflection, understanding, and elaboration.

A range of standard techniques is used by psychodynamic therapists. These have been systematized on the basis of empirical studies by Paulina Kernberg (1995) who observed a number of somewhat overlapping but reliably distinguishable categories of interventions. These include:

- *Supportive interventions* aimed at reducing the child's anxiety or increasing his sense of competence and mastery using suggestion, reassurance, empathy, or the provision of information.
- *Summary statements* or paraphrases of the child's communication to that point that support and develop the therapeutic exchange with the child. For example, in the opening phase of treatment, the child may enact a scene with toy animals in which one is placed alone behind a fence while all the others are together on the other side. The therapist may try an exploratory interpretation such as, "That one looks lonely—I wonder if he feels scared." Later in treatment, when there has been material about things the child ostensibly feels guilty about, she might identify the animal as standing for the child being punished: "Perhaps you are afraid that you'll be shut out like that when you do bad things." Or, if she knows more by then about links with the child's history she

might say, "Perhaps you felt shut out when your baby brother was born and everyone seemed to love him more than they loved you."

- *Clarifications* of the child's verbalization or affect. These help prepare the child for interpretation or simply direct his attention to noticeable aspects of his behavior, such as a repeated tendency to behave in self-defeating, self-destructive ways. Clarification is the therapist's attempt to get clear something she has not understood, the child has not understood, or both, by asking a question or suggesting a link. In the example above, she might say, for example, "I don't understand why that animal has to be apart from the others, do you?" She hopes the child will respond with *his* idea of the reasons. Or, if she thinks the fenced animal represents the child's initial reaction to being alone with her in the treatment room, she might say, "Perhaps you believe your family sent you to me because they want to get rid of you. But I think they want me to help you feel better."

- *Interpretation* is the way in which the therapist conveys her understanding of the child's behavior in the session; she adds meaning to what the child is consciously saying or doing by linking it with unconscious ideas and feelings in order to bring these to the child's awareness. Interpretation focuses attention on the child's internal representational world and on the mental processes involved in creating and maintaining that world. The therapist forms working hypotheses about the unconscious components of the child's difficulties that might helpfully be addressed. By making explicit various aspects of the child's functioning and internal world, the therapist helps him in the process of recognition, the first step in self-initiated change of the representational world. In formulating an interpretation, the therapist is well advised to concentrate her attention on the therapeutic situation itself, in which evidence is most likely to become available. While the therapist may often be able to identify significant connections between the child's behavior in therapy and what the therapist knows about the child's past experience, interpretations, at least in the early phase of treatment, are best restricted to the child's current feelings and conflicts, as these are brought into the consulting room. The ultimate aim of the therapist is to provide the child with an emotionally meaningful comprehensive understanding of the connections between past experiences and current methods of coping with conflict.

Kernberg (1995) distinguishes between three kinds of interpretation: (1) interpretations of defense, (2) interpretations addressing repudiated wishes, and (3) reconstructive interpretations. The first of these draws the child's attention to actual exclusion of certain ideas from awareness. This focuses attention on certain contents, but also invites the child to consider alternative strategies for coping with or expressing these ideas or feelings. It is usually more readily acceptable for the child to interpret defenses before the wishes or impulses against which the child is defending. Bypassing the defenses with a direct interpretation of an unconscious wish ignores the fact that the child needs his defenses and has good reason for erecting them: he feels guilty about them, ashamed in front of the therapist, anxious about losing his parents' love and approval, or most likely a combination. Interpretation of the wish alone can, therefore, feel to him like an accusation. A child with low self-esteem can similarly feel criticized and denigrated if he is given no credit for trying to curb his wishes and impulses. To take an example of a child who complains of his little brother's interference with his toys, and his mother's failure to stop this, direct interpretation simply of the wish to attack or get rid of his little brother might make the child feel the therapist is accusing or criticizing. This might raise his anxiety or lower his self-esteem, perhaps pushing him to fear alienation from the therapy. If the therapist speaks first of how hard the struggle must sometimes be to be kind and loving to a brother who is such a nuisance, especially when "Mummy doesn't help," the child is more likely to feel his efforts are appreciated. This usually helps him to tolerate exploring his unconscious (often nearly conscious) wishes.

The second kind of interpretation generally aims to explain the child's behavior in terms of a putative non-conscious wish. Most frequently, the need for defense is explained in terms of the presence of an unconscious wish. For example, the therapist might say, "I think you tend to forget your dreams because in these dreams you are able to think about how angry you feel with your father and that you wish to punish him in cruel ways for how he has treated you."

Reconstructive interpretations aim not only to explain a current state of affairs in the child's mind, but also to give an account of how this may have come about. The reconstruction of early experience in this context is somewhat controversial. Although psychodynamically oriented psychotherapists frequently assume that the representation the child constructs of them is powerfully influenced by the child's prior experiences with caregivers, it does not by any means invariably follow that these experiences find direct expression in such representations. For example, a child might see the therapist as a critic who persistently undermines the child's sense of confidence and well being. He is thus evidently externalizing an internal representational figure who constantly bombards the self with disparagement and criticism. Such a representation may well be the product of defensive maneuvers rather than an indication of the presence of a severely critical adult figure in the child's past. Thus, the therapist might safely interpret that, "I think you are worried about my criticizing you because there is a voice inside your head that constantly says that you are such a naughty child that nobody could love you." It would probably be unwise to assume, however, that such a critical figure was actually part of the child's earlier experience. Such an "internal object" is far more likely to be a split-off part of the child's self-representation that may indeed be based on the internalization of an actually destructive and aggressive caregiver, or it may be a disowned destructive or aggressive part of the child, separated precisely because the perceived kindness of the actual parent made such aggressive impulses seem totally unacceptable and intolerable to the child. In either case, what needs to be addressed in reconstructive interpretations is how unacceptable a child finds even a small amount of residual aggression and destructiveness that has remained as part of the self structure. The unacceptability of such feelings towards the therapist/father and how the child's anxieties about, say, burglars link to his image of father responding to his angry feelings. Through verbalization of these defensive aspects, the child is gradually able to modify his internal standards for acceptable ideas and feelings and take on board (introject) the destructive aggression as part of his self-representation, leading to greater integration and flexibility in his psychic functioning.

Thus, the therapist's interventions tend mostly to combine a focus on defenses, wishes, and past or current experience. What all such interventions have in common is a focus on the child's emotional experience in relation to these domains. The therapeutic action of child psychoanalytic psychotherapy is assumed to be "work in the transference" (Strachey, 1934). The child's interaction with the therapist becomes increasingly invested with affect as the therapy progresses, as internal representations of relationships find expression in the relationship with the therapist. "Working through," helping the child to understand his reactions to the therapist in terms of anxieties, conflicts and defenses, is regarded as the essence of therapeutic work. The development of the transference is facilitated by (1) the therapist's neutrality, (2) emotional availability (attunement to the child's predicament), (3) encouragement to freely express thoughts and feelings, (4) the regularity and consistency of the therapeutic structure, and (5) the child's underlying perception of the therapist as a benign figure (Chethik, 1989). The transference relationship offers a window on both the nature of the child's relationship with the caregiver, as experienced by the child, and aspects of the child's experience of himself—particularly those aspects that the child experiences as unacceptable and wishes quickly to externalize on to the figure of the therapist. The role in which she finds herself enables the therapist to learn about the child's internal world. Distorted mental representations are identified, clarified, and understood and ideally reintegrated with the mature aspects of the child's thinking (Abrams, 1988).

For example, Steven, a shy, frightened, and withdrawn boy, aged eight, who was referred because of his depression, developed an exceptionally acrimonious relationship with his therapist. The therapist frequently found herself shamed and ridiculed, endlessly failing in the tasks set by the child, accused of being stupid and so on. The child simultaneously bullied and patronized the therapist. The therapist gently showed the child how he often considered himself not to be good enough and placed himself in situations where this would be all too evident. Gradually, the idea was presented that being insignificant and "no-good" was preferable (safer) because it avoided the even more unpleasant possibility of observing that the therapist or his parents might be disappointed with him. His guilt feelings about his cruel and aggressive feelings toward his younger brother, whose birth precipitated his depressive episode, played a critical part in this feeling that he was "bound to disappoint everyone he knew."

Termination of the treatment is signaled by (1) symptomatic improvement, (2) improved family and peer relationships, (3) the ability to take advantage of normal developmental opportunities, (4) the ability to deal with new environmental stressors, and (5) the ability to use the therapy more effectively (experience the therapy as helpful, allow the therapist's interpretive work to continue, express feelings more readily, show gratitude as well as criticism and anger, show insight, humor, and healthy self-mockery, and so on) (Kernberg, 1995). "Traditional" psychodynamic treatment of this sort is rarely prolonged; much may be achieved in once-weekly meetings over one year, although treatment length is often eighteen months to two years (Fonagy & Target, 1996b).

Therapeutic Approaches Addressing Disorders of Mental Process

In therapeutically addressing mental process disturbances, the child's active mental involvement is elicited by the therapist's focus on the preconscious mental content of the child. This mental involvement gradually brings about a reactivation of inhibited mental processes and thus leaves the child open to a gradual restructuring of distorted mental representations through further therapeutic work. In order to link the therapist's interpretation to his current mental state, the patient will be obliged to use his inhibited mental capacity. In the best of situations, the patient's mental work recapitulates that of the therapist, albeit within the limitations set by the child's level of development. The patient's observation of the therapist's use of the capacity may encourage him to reactivate inhibited modes of mental function. In this context, the interpretation does not need to be totally accurate in order to be effective, although one may assume that accurate interpretations are more likely to be inherently challenging for the patient and thus lead to his greater mental involvement.

The use of the term "developmental help" has been useful to describe this aspect of our work with children (for example, Kennedy & Moran, 1991), but it has not sufficiently clarified what the "help" consists of. The notion of unused inhibited mental processes offers a conceptual bridge between psychotherapeutic work with children and adults and makes clear that developmental therapy does not imply gratification or education, but true psychodynamic work.

Techniques Pertinent to the Mental Process Model

The treatment of disorders of mental process is composed of a range of techniques that address delays and deficiencies in specific areas of psychological development. Essentially, the therapist begins by performing mental functions, of which the child is incapable, or by showing the child ways of performing these functions until such time as the child can take over and do it himself. These interventions are used with pathologies traditionally defined as ego defects, deficiencies in relationships, or developmental disturbances, pathologies understood here as *mental process disturbances.*

The techniques used have sometimes been labeled remedial education or ego-support. There has been controversy over including such work among psychotherapeutic techniques, because the therapist appeared to be stepping out of the therapeutic role to become an educator, an ego-auxiliary, a parent-substitute by whom the child could feel nurtured, with whom he could identify and from whom he could learn. For children with developmental disorders these techniques are essential and have to be so intertwined with interpretative techniques, that they cannot but be regarded as a legitimate and essential part of psychodynamic therapeutic technique.

All patients are assumed to experience developmental disturbances to some degree. Some of these disturbances are transient manifestations of normal developmental stresses, and disappear in the natural course of development. Some respond relatively quickly to interpretation. Some are more intransigent and respond only to the techniques of developmental therapy.

The techniques of developmental therapy are those that

(1) First and foremost, provide the safe place and relationship within which the child can dare to change or wish to be different. This is crucial in cases where the child has adapted to an environment perceived as dangerous or destructive in which improvement in his functioning would not be welcome. It is especially important when the child has so thoroughly internalized the noxious environment that his internal representations and relationships are largely engaged in reproducing it, with little room for identification with alternative modes of relating and functioning; or when his own capacities are perceived as so weak that he despairs of achieving any change or improvement.

(2) Make up for some deficits in the parenting the child has received by providing him with the missing elements. These might include explanations of reality

events, help in understanding cause and effect (including other people's affective reactions), support in learning to control his feelings and behavior, suggestions or demonstrations of how to manage difficulties he encounters, and so on; whatever will improve areas of deficient functioning and thereby increase the child's sense of competence. Encouragement and praise to boost his self-esteem goes alongside this.

(3) Stimulate delayed or stunted developmental processes by drawing the child's attention to what is missing, and encouraging his interest and wish to achieve better functioning.

(4) Later on, use interpretation to provide the understanding of the dynamics that could help the child understand his own role in the creation of his developmental difficulties as well as confronting the role played by his environment. In developmental therapy, interpretation rarely concerns "unconscious" material repudiated because of guilt or anxiety. It might, however, concern elements of the mental world normally part of conscious experience but outside the conscious experience of the child with such conflict-driven developmental problems. It is used in varying measure according to the child's capacity to use it; the important difference from classical technique is the addition of active educational, supportive, explanatory, and modeling techniques.

The therapist's aim is to free the inhibition of mental processes and aid their development. This task tends to be conceptualized in different ways and each formulation is tied to a slightly different emphasis in technique. While there is no general agreement yet on which of these techniques is most important, they are far from being mere additions to the therapeutic armamentarium of child therapists; the formal acceptance of their importance in most cases by these therapists is relatively recent. Thus, the general themes outlined below give an indication of the main areas of focus for those providing developmental therapy for the child. In each individual case technique is adjusted according to which aspect of the child's disturbance is the focus at any given moment.

The Therapist as New Object. There is general agreement that the therapist as a real person who develops an intimate relationship with the child is of central relevance to developmental therapy. It is important that the child sees the therapist as someone who can understand and help him. This has been formulated in past accounts as providing "auxiliary ego support." This includes numerous functions, such as affect-regulation and behavioral control, facilitating communication, reality testing, and memory. When these functions have been partly set aside by the child in the face of relationships perceived by the child as threatening, the child cannot benefit from the therapist's demonstration of these mental functions unless she can be experienced as a secure and reliable figure, "a benign object." The safety of the relationship provides the child with an important object for identification and internalization. As the child responds to treatment, the need for the provision of these functions decreases correspondingly.

It is hard to operationalize which aspects of the therapist's behavior may ensure that she is experienced as a benign object because her behavior has to match the differing needs of each child. Certainly tolerance, calmness, a nonpersecutory stance, firmness and confidence in managing wild behavior, consistency, and above all a genuine acceptance of the child are extremely important. The specific content of an interpretation is sometimes less important for the child than the general experience of being understood and accepted. Verbalization of the child's sense of lack of safety is perhaps the most important single interpretation to such children to ensure they experience being accepted. This may be done directly through interpretations at appropriate times when the child appears to feel in danger. Sometimes the child cannot accept direct interpretation, and in these cases safety may be communicated symbolically, by acting, for example, as the rescuer in the child's ongoing war games.

John (aged five) was awkward and clumsy and had several major accidents during his therapy. In the third month of therapy he broke his collarbone, and returned to therapy after a two-week absence, his play frantic and out of control. He was extremely aggressive, and became more controlled only after these feelings were talked about a great deal. He began to fall during sessions, and sometimes seemed to be consciously testing the therapist: would she protect him from falling? The therapist focused on his underlying anger at her (and his mother) for not looking after him well enough. When, a few months later, he fell down the stairs of a bus, he again began to enact this in sessions, but could also speak of "mummies who don't look after their babies properly."

Communication and Thinking. Children with developmental disturbances often have difficulties in communicating with others. This tends to manifest quickly in the therapy. The therapist has to use considerable ingenuity to establish a mode of communication that enables the child to express his feelings and experiences, and to understand the therapist. Sometimes the child initiates an activity that the therapist can recruit into the service of communication. Sometimes the therapist has to introduce a way of communicating. For example, David, a ten-year-old boy, perceived his therapist as frightening and potentially violent. Interpretations of David's projection of his aggressive wishes onto the therapist were rarely effective in stopping his attacks and he often had to be restrained. More helpful was a game that emerged in the second year of treatment, and which David wished to repeat day after day for months. The game consisted of David and his therapist making notes on "what I think you think I am thinking about you today." Increasingly, he would call for a round of the game at times of heightened anxiety. The content of the notes he and the therapist wrote evolved to include a large variety of feelings, wishes, and fantasies. David became better able to differentiate fears and wishes within himself and between himself and his therapist.

Commonly used modes of communicating include play with family dolls, drawing and painting; using play-dough; creating scenes with model animals, people, and vehicles; and dramas with hand puppets. The range of individual inventions is infinite, however, and may include things that happen to be in the treatment room but are not intended as play material, such as potted plants (which can be tended, destroyed, observed to grow or wilt) or minute bits of fluff from curtains (which can be discovered, lost, found again, and preserved).

The therapist may have to struggle to understand what the child is communicating, and often verbalizes her own thinking and puzzlement about what is going on, as well as providing a verbal narrative to accompany the play or activity as she understands it. This verbalization is important because it models the thinking capacity that the child lacks, as well as gives meaning to the child's behavior. Children who cannot communicate with others also cannot reflect upon their experiences, so both have to be learned via identification with the therapist.

Children whose development from somatic to psychic expression is delayed or deviant may have little mentalizing capacity and instead experience thoughts and feelings as bodily states. The therapist may need to link external signs of emotion to internal states in a way that would not be necessary for other children, for example by drawing attention to the child's gestures or flushed face as indications of feeling angry. Similarly, the therapist may help the child recognize physical cues of other people's mental states.

Intrapsychic Organization, Affect Regulation, and Impulse Control. One of the aims of psychodynamic interventions in developmental therapy is to make sense of the child's disorganized internal state for both the child and the therapist. The therapist aims to enhance the child's reflective processes by encouraging the observation and labeling of somatic and psychological experiences, initially focusing on states being felt in the immediate situation. She constantly makes comments that convey her understanding of the internal state of the child. At first these are kept very simple, perhaps verbalizing a feeling and linking it with a possible cause, such as "how horrible it feels not to be sure if your Mummy is coming back." or "You are feeling so frustrated with me, you want to tear everything up." These are the kinds of partial interpretations that the therapist hopes in due course to incorporate into a more complete interpretation that would link cause and effect in the transference with a reconstruction of the origin of such feelings. When working with children whose disturbance includes a large element of process disorder, the therapist may have to go relatively slowly, making sure that the child understands and confirms the simpler ideas and links before she attempts anything more complex, such as trying to make sense of the child's fantasies. These fantasies are often not unconscious yet are totally confusing for the child and need to be labeled and verbalized before their origins can be explored.

Affect regulation is an important aim of developmental work. It can be assisted by the verbalization and labeling of affect, and by explaining to the child possible reasons for his feelings, for example that his aggressive attacks are reactions to his sense of being threatened and endangered. Placing emotional relations into a meaningful causal sequence assists self-regulation through anticipation of actions. Some children need interpretations related to the way in which they use affective states in order to block other feelings. For example, the child may use manic excitement to block out feelings of sadness. The therapist tries to help the child recognize anxious feelings before they get out of control, initially by using her own facial expressions, behavior, and words to demonstrate her sense of what the child is feeling, or by drawing the child's attention to cues in his own behavior that can be used to predict rising anxiety. If the child is unable to tackle a task because of overwhelming fear, she may help him break down the task into manageable bits, as well as help him comprehend what causes his fear and work out whether that fear is justified.

Karen Weise (1995) describes her treatment of John, a five-year-old child. John moved from furious physical attacks on her at the end of sessions, to being able to put his feelings into words. Initially, when she tried to prepare him for the end of the session, he would dash out of the room without saying good-bye, or would start destroying the room. For some time she suggested to him that his aggression was because he did not want her to leave. After two months, at the end of the session John lassoed her foot, and was thrilled when she said that she understood that he wanted her to stay. Gradually, he became able to verbalize as well, and after a year he more often responded with, "I don't want you to go!" or "Come back! Don't leave me all alone!" and was able to talk about how this felt.

Similar work is needed for children whose capacities for impulse control are deficient. The therapist may initially have to provide the control herself by "setting limits." She tells the child what he may and may not do in his sessions, explaining that she will not let him hurt himself or her, or damage things in the room. She may actively explain this as part of her way of caring for him, or she may leave that implicit. She will suggest to the child ways he might use to control himself.

Overall, the therapist looks for strategies, which the child can develop with her help, for channeling impulses into socially acceptable forms of behavior, and increasing control over expression of feeling in action. The therapist may also need to devise strategies to help the child cope with low frustration tolerance and inability to delay gratification. Such strategies often have to precede or accompany exploratory work on such inner states as low self-esteem or feeling unloved, which may be causing or contributing to the low frustration tolerance or inability to delay gratification.

Self and Object Relationships. Modifications of technique are needed by children whose capacity to maintain object relations is limited and who cannot maintain a memory of the therapist as a thinking, helpful figure in her absence. In these cases, the child may need direct help in coping with separations, perhaps by practicing leaving the therapist and returning to her during the session, or by enacting separations with toys, and imagining how the actors feel. The child gradually learns some sense of control over separations and therefore has less need to blot out of consciousness the image of the absent object.

Some children avoid psychological contact with the therapist, as with all objects, because of a basic perception of objects as incomprehensible, unpredictable, and frightening. The therapeutic situation, by its very nature, compels the child to become aware of the mental state of another person. Often the therapist has to make extensive use of her own emotional reactions to the patient (her countertransference) in finding non-threatening ways of making contact with the child. Often she tries to focus the child's attention on her own mental state rather than commenting on the child's intentions, beliefs, and desires. She tries to help the child make sense of the interaction between them and to sort out accurate perceptions from misperceptions. She offers the child a safe relationship within which to learn what another person thinks and feels, and against which to check his own expectations.

Some very deprived children enter treatment lacking the most elementary social skills, which compound their difficulties in being accepted. The therapy can be used as an arena in which social skills (such as exchanging greetings) may be practiced. This is not simply an instance of "social skills training," because the target is not just the acquisition of the skill, but rather an understanding as to why the skill is important, how the child's behavior affects others, and how they may be modified in order to make the child feel more acceptable.

Alongside the child acquiring knowledge of the other, developmental therapy aims to enhance the child's self-representation. Interpretations are very frequently focused on the child's thoughts and feelings about himself, especially on moments when his self-esteem plummets, or when disintegration threatens. The therapist attempts to differentiate aspects of the child's perception of himself. For example, the therapist may try to help the child distinguish a helpless baby from a big boy part of the child's self-representation. The image of the baby offers the child a way of distancing the helplessness from the center of his self-representation, yet helps him in understanding his reactions, feelings, and defenses. The therapist at times needs to enter a fantasy world of the child, frequently populated by omnipotent objects. Within that world she may be able to question the child's omnipotence and gradually reduce and ameliorate the grandiosity of his self representation. Throughout, the therapist is sympathetic with the child's difficulty to achieve self-management and self-regulation, and attempts to enhance his capacity to achieve self-control. For example, the therapist may talk to the child about being "a boss" of himself.

Six-year-old Pedro had taken on the role of an omnipotent but uncontrolled mechanical object. He was the most powerful train engine in the world. He proved his strength by climbing and jumping on the high window sill, whistling like a train, pulling the curtains down and threatening to jump out of the window (as it was impossible for such a powerful train to be damaged). His therapist suggested that really powerful vehicles had brakes and part of his strength was being able to start and stop under at his own command. Pedro took eagerly to the game of stopping and starting, allowing more space for the therapist to speak. She subsequently introduced the idea of a mechanic who was very clever at understanding how the train worked, and what could go wrong, so that he could prevent breakdowns and damage. Pedro was able to use this bridge between psychological and physical reality to gain much greater recognition and control of his feelings.

Developmental Help as Practice. In many children with developmental disorders, past experiences or current environment inhibit the child's capacity to acquire certain new skills. In some children, the very act of learning seems to be compromised. The therapist uses the therapeutic situation to practice skills likely to facilitate the process of learning in other situations. Sometimes it is enough to offer the child materials to explore and experiment with or she may show him how something works. In these ways, the therapist may encourage curiosity and facilitate a more open attitude to new experiences. Some children cannot readily use such opportunities, because their experience of maltreatment, or the confusing behavior of psychiatrically disordered parents makes them mistrustful of offers to experiment. Such children may be unable to play, because they cannot distinguish "pretend" from real, and therefore cannot use play as a means of practicing, exploring, and mastering the external world or their own feelings and wishes. The therapist has to help such children learn to play by offering a safe context, different from the child's expectations.

The therapist tried to reach Eric, a seven-year old, through the language of gesture: she demonstrated her understanding of his internal state of almost intolerable tension by puffing herself up and mimicking an explosion. Both Eric and the therapist could laugh at this imitation. The idea of thinking about other people was introduced slowly. The therapist played the "church-steeple and people" game, using her clasped, outwardly turned hands to show that inside physical objects were live people. The game acquired particular significance for Eric, perhaps because he experienced his hands as frequently out of control. Later the therapist was able to represent single characters with the index and middle fingers of her hand. At first, the fingers just rushed away from one another over the edges of the table, illustrating Eric's panic at human contact and the disorganization and chaos that ensued. Later, the fingers acquired personal identities: self and other. For example, when Eric arrived for his session in tears because he had been left behind in a race with his brother, the fingers enacted the race, and the little boy crying. Once Eric understood the explanation about the sadness of the little boy who feels he is being left behind and may get lost, he wanted to hear it many times: "Tell me again why he is crying."

Eric spent a lot of time contemplating what the therapist thought of him over the weekend. This did not appear to be an indication of Eric's attachment to the therapist, but rather his desperate need to be thought about since he, alone, could not think about his mental states. He became attached to her, not as an independent psychic entity, but rather, as a reflective part of himself. For some time in his treatment, this capacity was restricted to the physical environment of the consulting room. Indeed, Eric showed no interest in or even recognition of his therapist if they met on the street, or even in the clinic outside the consulting room. He expressed no personal interest in her life. Only when his treatment progressed quite substantially did he show any interest in her as a person, and ask her one day, "How old are you? Do you like porridge?"

It is important to note that the therapist's target is very rarely a simple behavioral one, such as the child acquiring a specific skill. Rather, by creating an emotional context that legitimizes exploration, the therapist hopes to facilitate the emergence of mental capacities that underlie social behavior. Normally, this emotional climate is available to the child and the learning of these skills occurs naturally. Developmental therapy functions to create in the therapeutic relationship a social context within which normal maturational processes may manifest themselves.

Limitations. The psychoanalytic model of developmental disturbance is still developing as is the range of techniques to deal with such disturbance. Classical interpretative interventions play a part in the treatment of developmental pathology, but special techniques are also needed that require more from the therapist than being a transference object. Techniques are often idiosyncratic both to the therapist and to the child. Much depends on the goodness of fit between patient and therapist. Children whose developmental deficiencies or delays are widespread and severe may be beyond the reach of even the most skillful and inspired therapist. Yet, the lack of efficacy of short-term therapies, combined with

the general recognition of the chronicity and severity of developmental disturbances inclines clinicians toward intensifying their efforts of early intervention
(Siegel, 1999; Solomon & Siegel, 2003).

In general, success is greater with younger children because treatment ante-
dates the firm localization of enduring structures and enables the maximization
of the natural operation of brain plasticity. Further, early intervention ensures that
disturbances can be tackled before there are too many interacting repercussions
on other areas of development. Because the work required in developmental therapy is so intricate and extensive, it really needs long and intensive treatment for
severely and even moderately disturbed children. Less severely disturbed children,
especially very young ones, can be helped in less intensive therapy, particularly if
it can be of long duration (at least two or three years).

Future Directions

Psychoanalytic treatments for children are not sufficiently persuasive to placate
critics of the approach. Psychoanalytic therapists, however, retain a unique and
potentially crucial role for treating certain forms of disorder. By placing the focus
of explanation into an intrapsychic domain that is not necessarily compatible with
controlled observations and testable hypotheses, psychoanalysis has deprived itself
of the interplay between data and theory that has contributed so much to the
growth of modern science. In the absence of data, psychoanalysts of the past have
been forced to fall back upon either the indirect evidence of clinical observation
or to argument by authority. In several publications, we have suggested that psychodynamic therapists and psychoanalysts should now wholeheartedly embrace
a research agenda that would open their discipline to the possibility of evidence
inconsistent with their expectations (Emde & Fonagy, 1997; Fonagy & Perron,
2002; Gabbard et al., 2002). Without opening up fully to systematic inquiry, it is
hard to envision how both critics and advocates of psychoanalytic therapy will
have the opportunity to rethink that which they believe they already know.

To achieve a systematic reconsideration of psychoanalytic ideas of therapy,
developments will have to occur in training, measurement, and in general stance
toward knowledge among psychoanalytically oriented clinicians. First, psychoanalytic child therapists will need to acquire research training in order for them to describe more systematically key aspects of the intervention. Methods of observation
will need to be refined in order to label and extract the effective components of the
complex interventions that psychoanalytic therapists undertake. Intensive single-
case studies will be helpful here and the long-term nature of psychoanalytic intervention is a helpful feature (Moran & Fonagy, 1987). Ultimately, this will lead to

improved manualization of psychodynamic treatment, routine observations of the actual process rather than impressionistic clinical accounts. Second, measurement techniques will need to be developed that capture what is unique about both the process of psychodynamic psychotherapy and the aspects of the outcome of psychotherapy that are indeed unique to psychoanalytic therapy. Here, we have been particularly interested in the long-term impact of psychoanalytic psychotherapy, particularly in the case of severe psychological disturbance (Target & Fonagy, in press). We have argued that psychoanalytic psychotherapy was particularly useful in cases of significant developmental difficulties, especially when examined in the context of long-term developmental outcomes. Finally, from the point of view of a changed attitude, a number of modifications of prevailing ways of working for psychodynamic clinicians are urgently required:

1. Moving from global to specific constructs that allow for cumulative data-gathering.
2. Routinely considering alternative accounts, which would fill the void created by the absence of the tradition of what might be called "comparative psychoanalytic studies."
3. Increasing psychoanalytic sophistication concerning social influences.
4. Ending the splendid isolation of psychoanalysis by undertaking active collaboration with other disciplines. Instead of fearing that fields adjacent to psychoanalysis might destroy the unique insights offered by clinical work, we need to embrace the rapidly evolving "knowledge chain" focused at different levels of the study of brain-behavior relationship, which as Kandel (1998, 1999) points out, may be the only route to the preservation of the hard-won insights of psychoanalysis.
5. Refining treatment models using the psychoanalytic theory of the mind in combination with methods evolved in classical psychoanalytically oriented therapy to develop new protocols for conditions that currently resist psychosocial and simple pharmacological treatments.

◆ ◆ ◆

In combination, these developments should breathe new life into a tradition that has in some ways been handicapped by its history, particularly its past successes. Understandably, those who were responsible for the great achievements of the heyday of psychoanalytic therapy have been reluctant to facilitate change when this may imply abandoning hard-won insights and the achievement of creative understandings. Particularly in the absence of challenging new data, the psychoanalytic tradition turned inward over the second half of the twentieth century.

Fortunately, in aiming to rise to the challenge of developing psychopharmacology and alternative psychosocial approaches, it has been revitalized and is now moving beyond its historic boundaries. In many ways, child psychotherapy has led and perhaps will continue to lead the way in adding fresh insights and treatment models because, like their clients, psychoanalytic child psychotherapists are also perhaps more willing to play than their adult therapist counterparts.

Endnote

1. Emotional experience is constructed out of mental representations. The separation of thinking and affect may be possible only at the level of common parlance, based on and restricted to, phenomenal experience. Affective valuations are associated with all types of representational content (such as beliefs, expectations, associations, wishes, desires).

References

Abraham, K. (1979). *Selected papers of Karl Abraham.* New York: Brunner/Mazel.

Abrams, S. (1988). The psychoanalytic process in adults and children. *Psychoanalytic Study of the Child, 43,* 245–261.

Altman, N. (1992). Relational perspectives on child psychoanalytic psychotherapy. In N. J. Skolnick & S. C. Warshaw (Eds.), *Relational perspectives in psychoanalysis* (pp. 175–194). Hillsdale, NJ: Analytic Press.

Altman, N. (1994). The recognition of relational theory and technique in child treatment. Special Issue: Child analytic work. *Psychoanalytic Psychology, 11,* 383–395.

Alvarez, A. (1993). *Live company.* London: Routledge.

Arlow, J. A., & Brenner, C. (1964). *Psychoanalytic concepts and the structural theory.* New York: International University Press.

Bion, W. R. (1959). Attacks on linking. *International Journal of Psychoanalysis, 40,* 308–315.

Bleiberg, E. (1987). Stages in the treatment of narcissistic children and adolescents. *Bulletin of the Menninger Clinic, 51,* 296–313.

Bleiberg, E. (1994). Borderline disorders in children and adolescents: The concept, the diagnosis, and the controversies. *Bulletin of the Menninger Clinic, 58,* 169–196.

Bleiberg, E., Fonagy, P., & Target, M. (1997). Child psychoanalysis: Critical overview and a proposed reconsideration. *Psychiatric Clinics of North America, 6,* 1–38.

Brenner, C. (1982). *The mind in conflict.* New York: International Universities Press.

Chethik, M. (1989). *Techniques of child therapy: Psychodynamic strategies.* New York: Guilford Press.

Cohen, D. J., Towbin, K. E., Mayes, L., & Volkmar, F. (1994). Developmental psychopathology of multiplex developmental disorder. In S. L. Friedman & H. C. Haywood (Eds.), *Developmental follow-up: Concepts, domains and methods* (pp. 155–182). New York: Academic Press.

DeFolch, T. E. (1988). Guilt bearable or unbearable: A problem for the child in analysis. Special Issue: Psychoanalysis of children. *International Review of Psycho-Analysis, 15,* 13–24.

Edelman, G. M. (1987). *Neural Darwinism: The theory of neuronal group selection.* New York: Basic Books.

Edelman, G. M. (1989). *The remembered present: A biological theory of consciousness.* New York: Basic Books.

Edgcumbe, R. (2000). *Anna Freud: A view of development, disturbance and therapeutic techniques.* London: Routledge.

Emde, R. N. (1988). Development terminable and interminable II. Recent psychoanalytic theory and therapeutic considerations. *International Journal of Psycho-Analysis, 69,* 283–286.

Emde, R. N., & Fonagy, P. (1997). An emerging culture for psychoanalytic research? Editorial. *International Journal of Psycho-Analysis, 78,* 643–651.

Fairbairn, W.R.D. (1952). *An object-relations theory of the personality.* New York: Basic Books, 1954.

Fonagy, P. (1999). The relation of theory and practice in psychodynamic therapy. *Journal of Clinical Child Psychology, 28,* 513–520.

Fonagy, P. (2002). The outcome of psychoanalysis: The hope for the future. In S. Priebe & M. Slade (Eds.), *Evidence in mental health care* (pp. 177–185). London: Routledge.

Fonagy, P. (in press). How can psychotherapy practice be informed by research findings? The pros and cons of evidence-based psychotherapy. *World Psychiatry.*

Fonagy, P., Gergely, G., Jurist, E., & Target, M. (2002). *Affect regulation, mentalization and the development of the self.* New York: Other Press.

Fonagy, P., & Moran, G. S. (1990). Studies on the efficacy of child psychoanalysis. *Journal of Consulting and Clinical Psychology, 58,* 684–695.

Fonagy, P., Moran, G. S., Edgcumbe, R., Kennedy, H., & Target, M. (1993). The roles of mental representations and mental processes in therapeutic action. *The Psychoanalytic Study of the Child, 48,* 9–48.

Fonagy, P., & Perron, R. (2002). Epistemological and methodological background. In P. Fonagy, H. Kachele, R. Krause, E. Jones, R. Perron, J. Clarkin, A. J. Gerber, & E. Allison (Eds.), *An open door review of outcome studies in psychoanalysis* (pp. 1–64). London: International Psychoanalytical Association.

Fonagy, P., & Target, M. (1994). The efficacy of psychoanalysis for children with disruptive disorders. *Journal of the American Academy of Child and Adolescent Psychiatry, 33,* 45–55.

Fonagy, P., & Target, M. (1996a). A contemporary psychoanalytical perspective: Psychodynamic developmental therapy. In E. Hibbs & P. Jensen (Eds.), *Psychosocial treatments for child and adolescent disorders: Empirically based approaches* (pp. 619–638). Washington, DC: American Psychiatric Association and National Institutes of Health.

Fonagy, P., & Target, M. (1996b). Predictors of outcome in child psychoanalysis: A retrospective study of 763 cases at the Anna Freud Centre. *Journal of the American Psychoanalytic Association, 44,* 27–77.

Freud, A. (1946). *The ego and the mechanisms of defence.* New York: International Universities Press.

Freud, A. (1946). *The psychoanalytic treatment of children.* London: Imago Publishing.

Freud, A. (1965). *Normality and pathology in childhood: Assessments of development.* Madison, CT: International Universities Press.

Freud, S. (1900). The interpretation of dreams. In J. Strachey (Ed.), *The standard edition of the complete psychological works of Sigmund Freud* (Vol. 4, 5, pp. 1–715). London: Hogarth Press.

Freud, S. (1905). Three essays on the theory of sexuality. In J. Strachey (Ed.), *The standard edition of the complete psychological works of Sigmund Freud* (Vol. 7, pp. 123–230). London: Hogarth Press.

Freud, S. (1909). Analysis of a phobia in a five-year-old boy. In J. Strachey (Ed.), *The standard edition of the complete psychological works of Sigmund Freud* (Vol. 10, pp. 1–147). London: Hogarth Press.

Freud, S. (1920). Beyond the pleasure principle. In J. Strachey (Ed.), *The standard edition of the complete psychological works of Sigmund Freud* (Vol. 18, pp. 1–64). London: Hogarth Press.

Freud, S. (1926). The question of lay analysis. In J. Strachey (Ed.), *The standard edition of the complete psychological works of Sigmund Freud* (Vol. 20, pp. 179–258). London: Hogarth Press.

Gabbard, G. O., Gunderson, J. G., & Fonagy, P. (2002). The place of psychoanalytic treatments within psychiatry. *Archives of General Psychiatry, 59*(6), 505–510.

Glenn, J. (1978). *Child analysis and therapy.* New York: Aronson.

Goldfried, M. R., & Wolfe, B. E. (1996). Psychotherapy practice and research: Repairing a strained alliance. *American Psychologist, 51,* 1007–1016.

Hartmann, H., Kris, E., & Loewenstein, R. (1946). Comments on the formation of psychic structure. *The Psychoanalytic Study of the Child, 2,* 11–38.

Heinicke, C. M. (1965). Frequency of psychotherapeutic session as a factor affecting the child's developmental status. *The Psychoanalytic Study of the Child, 20,* 42–98.

Heinicke, C. M., & Ramsey-Klee, D. M. (1986). Outcome of child psychotherapy as a function of frequency of sessions. *Journal of the American Academy of Child Psychiatry, 25,* 247–253.

Hoffman, L. (1993). An introduction to child psychoanalysis. *Journal of Clinical Psychoanalysis, 2,* 5–26.

Hug-Helmuth, H. (1920). Child psychology and education. *International Journal of Psycho-Analysis, 1,* 316–323.

Jacobs, L., & Wachs, C. (2002). *Parent therapy: A relational alternative to working with children.* New York: Jason Aronson.

Jacobson, E. (1964). *The self and the object world.* New York: International Universities Press.

Johnson, E. (1982). Principles and techniques in drama therapy. *International Journal of Arts and Psychotherapy, 9,* 83–90.

Kandel, E. R. (1998). A new intellectual framework for psychiatry. *American Journal of Psychiatry, 155,* 457–469.

Kandel, E. R. (1999). Biology and the future of psychoanalysis: A new intellectual framework for psychiatry revisited. *American Journal of Psychiatry, 156,* 505–524.

Kazdin, A. E. (2003). Psychotherapy for children and adolescents. *Annual Review of Psychology, 54,* 253–276.

Kazdin, A. E., & Kendall, P. C. (1998). Current progress and future plans for developing effective treatments: Comments and perspectives. *Journal of Clinical Child Psychology, 27,* 217–226.

Kendall, P. C. (Ed.). (1991). *Child and adolescent therapy: Cognitive-behavioral procedures.* New York: Guilford Press.

Kennedy, H., & Moran, G. (1991). Reflections on the aims of child psychoanalysis. *The Psychoanalytic Study of the Child, 46,* 181–198.

Kernberg, O. F. (1975). *Borderline conditions and pathological narcissism.* New York: Jason Aronson.

Kernberg, P. F. (1995). Child psychiatry: Individual psychotherapy. In H. I. Kaplan & B. J. Sadock (Eds.), *Comprehensive textbook of psychiatry* (6th ed., pp. 2399–2412). Baltimore, MD: Williams & Wilkins.

King, P., & Steiner, R. (1991). *The Freud-Klein controversies: 1941–45.* London: Routledge.

Klein, M. (1932). *The psycho-analysis of children.* London: Hogarth Press.

Klein, M. (1975). A contribution to the psychogenesis of manic-depressive states. *Love, guilt and reparation: The Writings of Melanie Klein, Volume I* (pp. 236–289). London: Hogarth Press.

Klerman, G. L., Weissman, M. M., Rounsaville, B. J., & Chevron, E. S. (1984). *Interpersonal psychotherapy of depression.* New York: Basic Books.

Kohut, H. (1977). *The restoration of the self.* New York: International Universities Press.

Kolvin, I., Garside, R. F., Nicol, A. R., MacMillan, A., Wolstenholme, F., & Leitch, I. M. (1981). *Help starts here: The maladjusted child in the ordinary school.* London: Tavistock.

Lochman, J. E., Coie, J. D., Underwood, M. K., & Terry, R. (1993). Effectiveness of a social relations intervention program for aggressive and nonaggressive, rejected children. *Journal of Consulting and Clinical Psychology, 61,* 1053–1058.

Luborsky, L. (1984). *Principles of psychoanalytic psychotherapy: A manual for supportive-expressive (SE) treatment.* New York: Basic Books.

Lush, D., Boston, M., & Grainger, E. (1991). Evaluation of psychoanalytic psychotherapy with children: Therapists' assessments and predictions. *Psychoanalytic Psychotherapy, 5,* 191–234.

Mahler, M. S., Pine, F., & Bergman, A. (1975). *The psychological birth of the human infant: Symbiosis and individuation.* New York: Basic Books.

Moran, G., & Fonagy, P. (1987). Psycho-analysis and diabetic control: A single-case study. *British Journal of Medical Psychology, 60,* 357–372.

Moran, G., Fonagy, P., Kurtz, A., Bolton, A., & Brook, C. (1991). A controlled study of the psychoanalytic treatment of brittle diabetes. *Journal of the American Academy of Child and Adolescent Psychiatry, 30,* 926–935.

Mufson, L., Moreau, D., Weissman, M. M., & Klerman, G. L. (1993). *Interpersonal psychotherapy for depressed adolescents.* New York: Guilford Press.

Mufson, L., Weissman, M. M., Moreau, D., & Garfinkel, R. (1999). Efficacy of interpersonal psychotherapy for depressed adolescents. *Archives of General Psychiatry, 56,* 573–579.

Muratori, F., Picchi, L., Bruni, G., Patarnello, M., & Romagnoli, G. (2003). A two-year follow-up of psychodynamic psychotherapy for internalizing disorders in children. *Journal of the American Academy of Child and Adolescent Psychiatry, 42*(3), 331–339.

O'Shaughnessy, E. (1988). W. R. Bion's theory of thinking and new techniques in child analysis. In E. B. Spillius (Ed.), *Melanie Klein today: Developments in theory and practice. Vol. 2: Mainly practice* (pp. 177–190). London: Routledge.

Pine, F. (1985). *Developmental theory and clinical process.* New Haven, CT: Yale University Press.

Rose, S. D. (1972). *Treating children in groups.* London: Jossey-Bass.

Rosselló, J., & Bernal, G. (1999). The efficacy of cognitive-behavioral and interpersonal treatments for depression in Puerto Rican adolescents. *Journal of Consulting and Clinical Psychology, 67,* 734–745.

Rumelhart, D. E., & McClelland, J. L. (1986). *Parallel distributed processing.* Cambridge, MA: MIT Press.

Sackett, D. L., Rosenberg, W. M., Gray, J.A.M., Haynes, R. B., & Richardson, W. S. (1996). Evidence based medicine: What it is and what it isn't. *British Medical Journal, 312,* 71–72.

Sandler, J. (1972). The role of affects in psychoanalytic theory. In J. Sandler (Ed.), *From safety to superego: Selected papers of Joseph Sandler* (pp. 285–300). New York: Guilford Press.

Sandler, J. (1983). Reflections on some relations between psychoanalytic concepts and psychoanalytic practice. *International Journal of Psycho-Analysis, 64,* 35–45.

Sandler, J., Kennedy, H., & Tyson, R. (1980). *The technique of child analysis: Discussions with Anna Freud.* London: Hogarth Press.

Sandler, J., & Rosenblatt, B. (1962). The concept of the representational world. *The Psychoanalytic Study of the Child, 17,* 128–145.

Santor, D. A., & Kusumakar, V. (2001). Open trial of interpersonal therapy in adolescents with moderate to severe major depression: Effectiveness of novice IPT therapists. *Journal of the American Academy of Child and Adolescent Psychiatry, 40*(2), 236–240.

Schaefer, C. E., & Cangelosi, D. M. (Eds.). (1993). *Play therapy techniques.* Northway, NJ: Aronson.

Selvini Palazzoli, M., Boscolo, L., Cecchin, G., & Prata, G. (1978). *Paradox and counter-paradox.* New York: Aronson.

Siegel, D. J. (1999). *The developing mind: Toward a neurobiology of interpersonal experience.* New York: Guilford.

Simon, M. R. (1992). *The symbolism of style: Art as therapy.* London: Routledge.

Smyrnios, K. X., & Kirkby, R. J. (1993). Long-term comparison of brief versus unlimited psychodynamic treatments with children and their parents. *Journal of Consulting and Clinical Psychology, 61,* 1020–1027.

Solomon, M., & Siegel, D. J. (2003). *Healing trauma: Attachment, mind, body and brain.* New York: Norton.

Strachey, J. (1934). The nature of the therapeutic action of psychoanalysis. *International Journal of Psycho-Analysis, 50,* 275–292.

Sullivan, H. S. (1953). *The interpersonal theory of psychiatry.* New York: Norton.

Szapocznik, J., Rio, A., Murray, E., Cohen, R., Scopetta, M., Rivas-Valquez, A., et al. (1989). Structural family versus psychodynamic child therapy for problematic Hispanic boys. *Journal of Consulting and Clinical Psychology, 57,* 571–578.

Target, M., & Fonagy, P. (1994a). The efficacy of psychoanalysis for children: Developmental considerations. *Journal of the American Academy of Child and Adolescent Psychiatry, 33,* 1134–1144.

Target, M., & Fonagy, P. (1994b). The efficacy of psychoanalysis for children with emotional disorders. *Journal of the American Academy of Child and Adolescent Psychiatry, 33,* 361–371.

Target, M., & Fonagy, P. (in press). Attachment theory and long-term psychoanalytic outcome. In M. Leuzinger-Bohleber (Ed.), *The pluralism of sciences: The psychoanalytic method between clinical, conceptual and empirical research.* London: Karnac.

Towbin, K. E., Dykens, E. M., Pearson, G. S., & Cohen, D. J. (1993). Conceptualising "borderline syndrome of childhood" and "childhood schizophrenia" as a developmental disorder. *Journal of the American Academy of Child and Adolescent Psychiatry, 32,* 775–782.

Tyson, P. (1992). *Neurosis in childhood and in psychoanalysis.* Paper presented at the Annual Meeting of the American Psychoanalytic Association, Washington, DC.

Tyson, R. L., & Tyson, P. (1986). The concept of transference in child psychoanalysis. *Journal of the American Academy of Child Psychiatry, 25,* 30–39.

Warshaw, S. C. (1992). Mutative factors in child psychoanalysis: A comparison of diverse relational perspectives. In N. J. Skolnick & S. C. Warshaw (Eds.), *Relational perspectives in psychoanalysis* (pp. 141–173). Hillsdale, NJ: Analytic Press.

Weise, K. (1995). The use of verbalisation in the management of feelings and behaviour: A therapeutic intervention in the nursery. *The Bulletin of the Anna Freud Centre, 18,* 35–47.

Weisz, J. R., Weiss, B., Morton, T., Granger, D., & Han, S. (1992). *Meta-analysis of psychotherapy outcome research with children and adolescents.* Los Angeles: University of California.

Winnicott, D. W. (1965). *The maturational process and the facilitating environment.* London: Hogarth Press.

Winnicott, D. W. (1971). *Playing and reality.* London: Tavistock.

CHAPTER TWENTY-TWO

DIALECTICAL BEHAVIOR THERAPY FOR SUICIDAL ADOLESCENTS: AN OVERVIEW

Alec L. Miller, Psy.D., Elizabeth E. Wagner, Ph.D., and Jill H. Rathus, Ph.D.

This chapter outlines our application of Dialectical Behavior Therapy (DBT) for suicidal adolescents who meet criteria for borderline personality disorder (BPD) or who have borderline features. We divide this chapter into six sections. Section I provides the basic rationale, theory, and putative mechanisms of efficacy for our application of DBT to suicidal, multi-problem adolescents. Section II outlines the developmental influences in our adaptation of DBT. In Section III we detail the putative targets of treatment found in our application of DBT with suicidal adolescents. In Section IV we review the empirical data for DBT. Section V presents a detailed case presentation and in Section VI we conclude with a discussion of future directions for this treatment approach. We hope this chapter will be useful to clinicians working to address the complexity of problems that characterize suicidal adolescents.

Basic Rationale, Theory, and Putative Mechanisms of Efficacy

As adolescents enter puberty, they encounter myriad physical, cognitive, social, and emotional changes. Challenges and changes specific to their developmental level can exacerbate emerging psychiatric difficulties. For example, adolescents typically live with parents, and the quality of their relationship with their parents mediates many developmental outcomes. Further, adolescents are physically and cognitively maturing, demanding more autonomy, and trying on new behaviors to fit their adult-like bodies and minds, without the benefit of adult experience. Through school achievement and peer group membership, adolescents are in the process of forming an identity, which can be compromised by difficulties encountered at this time. The additional challenges presented by this stage of development require a treatment that responds to adolescents' developing cognitive, emotional, and behavioral capacities.

The development of psychosocial treatments should be informed by both the nature of the target problems and the developmental level of the specific population. In adapting DBT for adolescents (Miller, Rathus, Linehan, Wetzler, & Leigh, 1997), we made several changes based on developmental considerations (for example, simplifying skills handouts, adding new skills, and including parents in skills training), while maintaining the essence of DBT (principles, skills, format, targets, and strategies).

For comprehensive coverage of standard DBT, including a manual for running the behavioral skills group, we refer the reader to the original text and manual by Linehan (1993a; 1993b). Although we describe an outpatient DBT program, practitioners have adapted the treatment for a variety of other settings including adolescent and inpatient units (Katz, Gunasekara, & Miller, 2002; Bohus et al., 2000; Swenson, Sanderson, & Linehan, in press), day treatment or partial hospitalization programs (Simpson et al.,1998), residential treatment facilities (Swenson, under review), or even school settings (Sally et al., 2002).

Linehan developed DBT (Linehan, 1993a; 1993b; Linehan, Armstrong, Suarez, Allmon, & Heard, 1991) for the treatment of adult chronically parasuicidal patients diagnosed with BPD. The term *parasuicide* was introduced by Kreitman (1977) and defined as (1) any nonfatal, intentional self-injurious behavior resulting in tissue damage, illness, or risk of death, or (2) any ingestion of substances of non-prescribed drugs, or of prescribed drugs taken in excess of prescription with clear intent to cause bodily harm or death. Thus, when we use the term parasuicide, we are referring to any acute, intentional self-injurious behavior resulting in physical harm, with or without intent to die. DBT was the first empirically supported psychosocial treatment for this multiple-problem population. The treatment weaves standard cognitive behavioral interventions with Eastern contemplative practice (essentially psychological and behavioral versions of meditation). This cognitive behavioral treatment is distinguished by its balancing of delineated validation and acceptance strategies with more traditional problem-solving and behavior change techniques, and its hierarchically ordered treatment targets within specified stages. However, at its core, DBT remains a behavioral approach, and it shares underlying treatment assumptions with other behavioral treatments, including (1) focus upon current rather than historical determinants of behavior, (2) emphasis on overt behavior change as the main criterion by which treatment should be evaluated, (3) specification of treatment in objective terms so as to make replication possible, (4) reliance upon basic research in psychology as a source of hypotheses about treatment and specific therapy techniques, and (5) specificity in defining, treating, and measuring the target problem in therapy (Kazdin, 1978). DBT is based on a dialectical world view and on the biosocial theory of BPD; these theories inform both the clinicians' understanding of the borderline diagnosis and the clinicians' moment-to-moment interactions in session.

Dialectical World View

A dialectical philosophy provides the theoretical foundation of DBT treatment strategies. This dialectical philosophy views reality as an interrelated system, with opposing internal forces, and in a state of continuous change. *Dialectics* refers further to the multiple tensions that emerge in treating the suicidal patient with BPD. The core dialectic in DBT involves accepting patients exactly as they are in the moment (including teaching the patient self-acceptance) while working to help them change. In a treatment style characterized by movement, speed, and flow, the therapist helps the patient synthesize these opposing internal forces so she can find her own "middle path."

The individual therapist employs a dialectical focus on two levels. First, within therapeutic interactions, the therapist balances change and acceptance, flexibility and stability, and challenging and nurturing to maintain a collaborative relationship with the patient. Second, the therapist teaches and models dialectical thinking and behavior for the patient and employs specific dialectical strategies to highlight contradictions in the patient's behavior and thinking by offering opposite or alternative positions.

Biosocial Theory of BPD

DBT is based on Linehan's (1993a) biosocial theory in which BPD is viewed primarily as a dysfunction of the emotion regulation system. Consistent with this model is the notion that most dysfunctional behavior in individuals with BPD (such as self-injury, substance abuse, violent acts) can be viewed as either a direct consequence of emotion dysregulation or as a means of re-regulation. For example, in an abandonment panic, an emotionally dysregulated patient might lash out physically against her partner (a direct consequence of emotional dysregulation) or might ingest substances to try to ease her panic and sadness (as a means of re-regulating). Thus, parasuicidal or other dysfunctional behaviors are considered maladaptive attempts at problem-solving, in which the problem to be solved is generally the management of painful affective states.

According to the theory, the etiology of this dysfunction lies in the transaction between a biologically emotionally vulnerable individual and an environment that is a poor fit with this vulnerability (one that is invalidating). Emotionally vulnerable individuals are biologically predisposed to be highly sensitive (that is, they have a low threshold for having an emotional reaction) and reactive (they have a "big" or intense reaction) to emotional stimuli, as well as to have a slow return to emotional baseline. An invalidating environment chronically and pervasively communicates that the individual's responses are incorrect, faulty, inappropriate, or otherwise invalid. For example, if a parent says, "You're being silly and making a big deal out of nothing," in response to her daughter's statement that she is upset at not making the softball team, that parent is invalidating her daughter's feelings. The environment may begin as invalidating or may become invalidating as, over time, it itself is stressed by the emotional variations of the individual. This transactional model highlights how the individual reciprocally influences the environment, just as the individual is continually influenced by the environment.

The biosocial theory is useful to clinicians and patients in several ways. First, it promotes compassion for the patient instead of pejorative interpretations of patients' behaviors (as in "blaming the victim"). Second, by highlighting biological influences and inadequate learning experiences, it can provide psycho-education for patients and families. Third, it supports the treatment focus on skill acquisition to modulate extreme emotions, reduce emotion vulnerability, and reduce maladaptive mood-dependent behaviors while learning to validate emotions, thoughts, and behaviors.

Developmental Influences

We have adapted DBT for suicidal adolescents with borderline personality features; most of the modifications have been described elsewhere (Miller, Rathus, Linehan, Wetzler, & Leigh, 1997; Miller, 1999; Rathus & Miller, 2000). In brief, these modifications involve (1) shortening the first phase of treatment from one year to twelve, and most recently, sixteen weeks—not only do many of these teens not require the same length of treatment as adults with BPD, but also shorter treatments help foster early commitment with this age group; (2) including parents in the skills training group both to enhance generalization and maintenance of skills by teaching family members who can potentially serve as coaches to the adolescents, and to improve the adolescents' often dysfunctional, invalidating home environments; (3) including parents or other family members by having family therapy sessions when familial issues seem paramount; (4) providing skills coaching for the family member(s) attending the skills training group to foster skills generalization for them as well; (5) reducing the number of skills taught in order to facilitate learning the content within a shorter time period; (6) simplifying the language on the skills handouts to make them developmentally appropriate for adolescents; and (7) forming a set of supplementary dialectical dilemmas and secondary behavioral treatment targets.

Based on her clinical experience working with chronically parasuicidal patients diagnosed with BPD, Linehan (1993a) described six maladaptive behavior patterns that characterize these patients. (See Linehan 1993a for extensive review.) Each pattern represents an aspect of the transaction between an emotionally vulnerable individual and his or her invalidating environment. Over time, the individual with BPD learns to alternate between one behavioral pattern that under-regulates emotion and another that over-regulates emotion. The fluctuations between polarities are hypothesized to occur because the tension or discomfort of each extreme triggers its opposite or complementary pattern. These patterns are specifically addressed as secondary treatment targets in DBT because they may be functionally related to the primary target problems of borderline patients and may present significant obstacles to therapeutic change. We have identified several dialectical dilemmas that exist among adolescents and their family members. They include, but are not limited to, excessive leniency versus authoritarian control, normalizing pathological behaviors versus pathologizing normative behaviors, and forcing autonomy versus fostering dependence (Rathus & Miller, 2000). Thus, the challenge for the patient, the family members, and the therapist involves finding the synthesis of these extreme behavioral styles.

Putative Targets of Treatment

For Whom Is the Treatment Intended?

DBT for adolescents has been applied to teenagers with various psychological and behavioral problems in a wide range of treatment settings including outpatient, inpatient, residential, day treatment, and juvenile detention centers. Due to space limitations, we review only our outpatient model here. Entry criteria for our DBT outpatient program is as follows: thirteen to nineteen years of age, suicidality (defined as current suicidal ideation or parasuicidal behavior within the previous sixteen weeks), and borderline personality features (patients meet full criteria or exhibit at least three DSM-IV symptoms). Exclusion criteria include active psychosis and mental retardation. Primary comorbid diagnoses are common and frequently include mood, anxiety, substance-use, eating, learning, and disruptive behavior disorders. Our patients are diverse in terms of ethnicities and socio-economic levels, and range from low-income, minority families living in the inner city to middle- and upper-middle-class majority-group families from the suburbs.

Who Is the Treatment Team?

The treatment team should include, at minimum, three mental health professionals trained in DBT and, preferably, experienced in treating adolescents. Family therapy experience is enormously helpful but not required. We work in a multidisciplinary outpatient DBT team that includes psychologists, psychologists-in-training, psychiatrists, psychiatry residents and fellows, and social workers. Other disciplines, for example, nurses, case workers, or mental health aids, can participate also. Ideally, at least one member of the team (likely the team leader) will have completed a ten-day training course).

What Does the Treatment Look Like Over Time?

We begin treatment with an in-depth intake evaluation that confirms the preliminary clinical diagnosis and provides the basis for assignment to DBT treatment. This evaluation takes several hours and sometimes requires two separate visits. After assignment to DBT, adolescents begin Phase I of treatment, which lasts sixteen weeks and consists of participation in five concurrent treatment modes described in the Treatment Modes and Functions section. Adolescents and their families receive an overview of DBT at their first multi-family skills training group. Patients graduate from Phase I when they complete the sixteen weeks of treatment. Adolescents are then to attend Phase II of DBT. Phase II, the Graduate Group, is a sixteen-week maintenance phase of treatment that includes weekly group therapy, telephone consultation with the group co-leaders, and family therapy as needed. Patients can contract for one or more additional sixteen-week courses of this group provided they can identify and express commitment toward specific goals.

What Is the Attendance Policy?

In DBT the attendance policy is articulated clearly and followed consistently. Specifically, patients can miss three sessions of any modality. If patients miss four sessions of a single modality (that is, individual or multi-family skills group), they are considered to have "dropped out" of treatment. The policy is not intended to be punitive, but rather to increase compliance through clear and consistent contingencies. We find that many of the patients who are referred to our outpatient program from other clinics are not accustomed to contingencies around attendance to therapy appointments; consequently, our therapists need to clearly and repeatedly review the rationale for this policy. Therapists work hard to help patients overcome potential and actual impediments to the policy.

Treatment Modes and Functions

Effective treatment of suicidal patients who have multiple problems requires that the therapist provide comprehensive treatment structured so that highest-order priorities are addressed systematically. In DBT, comprehensive treatment involves five functions (Linehan, 1993a). In standard DBT, these five functions are (1) enhancing the patient's capabilities, (2) improving the patient's motivation to change, (3) ensuring that new capabilities are generalized from therapy to the patient's everyday life, (4) enhancing the therapist's capabilities and motivation to treat patient effectively, and (5) structuring the environment to support the patient's and therapist's capabilities. In outpatient DBT, these five functions are assigned to concurrent modes of outpatient treatment, including individual therapy, multi-family skills training group, telephone consultation, and therapist consultation meetings. These modes may also occur with ancillary treatments, for example, pharmacotherapy, self-help groups, or acute hospitalizations. The primary therapist (that is, the individual therapist) ensures that the system as a whole is providing each function.

In DBT for adolescents, the patient commits to sixteen weeks of twice-weekly therapy that targets the five functions (Miller, 1999) across the five modes of treatment:

Function 1: learning new skills delivered primarily in a psycho-educational multi-family skills training group. Five sets of skills are taught in the skills training group: mindfulness skills to address the confusion about oneself, emotion-regulation skills to address emotional instability, distress tolerance skills to target impulsivity, interpersonal-effectiveness skills to address interpersonal problems, and walking the middle path skills to target adolescent family conflicts and dilemmas.

Function 2: working one-to-one with a therapist to reduce factors that interfere with the ability to use skills (that is, increasing motivation) both in individual and family sessions.

Function 3: ensuring that generalization occurs via in vivo interventions (phone consultation when in crisis or in-vivo individual, group, or family therapy interactions).

Function 4: participating in a weekly therapist consultation meeting that provides both technical help and emotional support to assist therapists in performing DBT competently.

Function 5: providing (1) the various additional interventions that may be needed to structure the environment, including collateral family sessions or meetings with other treatment providers or school personnel so that the patient does not have to get worse to get additional help, and (2) the necessary structure in the DBT program (such as time for supervision and consultation meetings) for therapists to deliver the treatment effectively and competently and so as not to burn out.

Treatment Stages and Primary and Secondary Behavioral Targets

DBT is organized into treatment stages that parallel the stage of disorder (Linehan, in press), with a hierarchy of treatment targets within stages. Thus, the extent of disordered behavior (severity of dysfunction, complexity of other problems, comorbid disorders) determines the focus of treatment both over the course of treatment as well as within a given treatment interaction. Each of the four stages of treatment in DBT has specific treatment targets. Treatment stages include (1) Pretreatment, which aims to orient and gain commitment to treatment, (2) Stage 1, which aims to establish safety and treat behavioral dyscontrol, (3) Stage 2, which aims to decrease post-traumatic stress and emotionally process the past, (4) Stage 3, which aims to increase respect for self and work on individual goals, and (5) Stage 4, which aims to increase hedonic capacity. Given the brief nature of our program, we limit the treatment focus primarily to

Pretreatment and Stage 1 targets. Treatment targets in DBT refer to a set of behaviors to increase or decrease. Secondary treatment targets include DBT targets originally developed for adults and those we have developed for adolescents (Rathus & Miller, 2000).

Primary Behavioral Targets
Pretreatment Targets. Pretreatment targets involve orienting the client to DBT and securing the client's commitment to engage in treatment, reduce parasuicide, and work toward long-term goals.

Stage 1 Targets
Decreasing Life-Threatening Behaviors. DBT targets suicide-related behaviors as the highest priority in DBT. Treating parasuicidal behavior and acute suicidal ideation takes precedence over all other targets. If a patient is likely to put a gun to her own or someone else's head before the next contact, the therapist does what is needed to prevent this before addressing less imminently threatening problems. The rationale is straightforward: the patient must be alive for the next session for ongoing therapy to be possible.

DBT views suicidal behavior as maladaptive problem-solving behavior, with unbearable emotional pain being the central problem. DBT helps patients build a meaningful life and replace maladaptive problem-solving attempts with effective problem-solving behavior. DBT explicitly asserts the goal of being a life enhancement program designed to help patients construct a life worth living, rather than being a suicide prevention program. The skills and strategies employed in DBT help adolescents cope with or change the many life stressors, crises, relationship difficulties, school-related problems, and dysfunctional behavior patterns that can exacerbate or maintain these and other problems that often lead to the desire to end one's life. Thus, the therapist avoids colluding with the patient in seeing suicide as a viable choice, while helping her to expand her options for effective problem solving.

DBT targets the following categories of suicidal behavior: (1) suicidal crisis behaviors, (2) parasuicidal behaviors, (3) suicidal ideation or communication, (4) suicide-related expectancies and beliefs, and (5) suicide-related affect. DBT uses the term parasuicide in lieu of the term suicide gesture. Labeling the self-injurious behavior a suicide gesture often leads to premature judgment of function (for example, to manipulative others), without proper assessment.

Decreasing Therapy Interfering Behaviors. Suicidal adolescents often experience repeated therapy failures, primarily because of their high treatment drop-out rate (Trautman, Steward, & Morishima, 1993). Problems in therapy involve motivational difficulties, relational or other behavioral difficulties that reduce the therapist's motivation to treat, or client behaviors that punish effective therapist behaviors and reinforce ineffective behaviors. Thus, second to suicidal behaviors, DBT targets client and therapist behaviors that interfere with therapy as well as client and therapist behaviors that enhance effective therapy. Decreasing therapy-interfering behaviors supersedes targets related to the patient's quality of life. Again, the rationale, which is shared with the patient, is straightforward: if the patient drops out of therapy, discussion of other issues becomes impossible; the patient who is not receiving therapy can obviously no longer benefit from therapy.

Decreasing Behaviors That Interfere with the Quality of Life. Suicidal adolescents often engage in behaviors that, although not directly life threatening, interfere with building a life worth living. These behaviors may be related to dysfunctional interpersonal relationship interactions (for example, staying in abusive relationships or alienating caregivers), school- or work-related dysfunction (cutting classes, failing exams or courses), impulsive behaviors (anger outbursts, sexual promiscuity), substance abuse and related behaviors (violence, gang membership), mental-health related dysfunctional behaviors (repeated hospitalizations, emergency room visits), other Axis I or Axis II diagnostic symptom patterns (depression, social phobia), problems in maintaining physical health (not following necessary medication regimens, such as insulin for diabetes), and behaviors that interfere with long-term goals (extreme behavioral passivity, dropping out of high school, getting pregnant).

Treatment Modes

Individual Therapy

DBT individual outpatient therapy with adolescents consists of sixteen weeks of fifty- to sixty-minute weekly sessions. The individual therapist is the "primary" therapist for that patient and oversees the entire treatment plan and all the providers. In individual therapy, adolescents learn to apply skills taught in the multi-family behavioral skills group to their own lives. The individual therapist balances problem-oriented change strategies (standard cognitive behavioral techniques including behavioral analyses, contingency management, cognitive modification, and exposure to emotional cues), irreverent communication strategies, and consultation to the patient strategies with environmental interventions and acceptance strategies (that is, core validation strategies; reciprocal communication strategies) in session to "drag out" clients' more skillful responses to replace maladaptive responses.

The problem focus of each individual DBT session is determined jointly by both the patient's behavior since the last session and where it falls on the target behavioral hierarchy. For example, if the adolescent has engaged in parasuicidal acts or high-risk suicidal threats since the last session, the first task in session is to conduct a behavioral and solution analysis of that target behavior. A behavioral analysis is a step-by-step examination of a problem behavior, including an exhaustive description of the moment-to-moment chain of environmental and behavioral events, including the antecedents and consequences of the target behavior. During the behavioral analysis, the therapist identifies emotions, cognitions, and skill deficits as well as behavioral and environmental factors that interfere with more adaptive solutions. The solution analysis identifies more effective behaviors the patient could have used and is encouraged to use next time.

During all sessions, the therapist actively teaches and reinforces adaptive behaviors, including those that occur within the therapeutic relationship, while consistently withholding reinforcement for maladaptive behaviors (those that are targeted for change). Between sessions, the patient is strongly encouraged to use phone consultation with the individual therapist to help solve problems during crises, increase skills generalization, or to repair the relationship with the therapist.

Family Therapy

Given that much turmoil in the lives of suicidal adolescents involves their primary support system, we often include family members in some individual sessions (typically at least three to four sessions of the adolescent's sixteen individual therapy sessions). This occurs when (1) a family member provides a central source of conflict, (2) a family crisis needs immediate attention, (3) the therapist determines that treatment would be enhanced by orienting a family member (who is not attending the skills group) to an aspect of treatment, or (4) contingencies at home both reinforce dysfunctional behavior and are too powerful for the patient to ignore or avoid. It is preferable for the same family members to attend these sessions for both treatment continuity and to maximize the probability of follow-through with agreements made and skills learned in these sessions.

These "family sessions" largely retain their DBT structure. Generally, the sessions are conducted with only the adolescent for the first twenty to thirty minutes and with both the adolescent and the family member for the remainder of the session. The first part of the session (1) allows time to review the patient's diary card, and (2) gives the adolescent an opportunity to prepare for the family session. This includes identifying goals for the family session and conducting role plays with the therapist in which the adolescent can practice and receive feedback. For example, the adolescent might practice making requests or saying no in the family session. The second part of the session includes both the adolescent and the family member. The therapist and family set the session agenda together and, as needed, the therapist highlights rules, identifies central issues, and employs skill-enhancement/generalization and problem-solving approaches.

The therapist balances supporting the adolescent with direct validation and solving problems with family members. While DBT therapists assume that the adolescents with BPD or BPD behavior patterns are in tremendous pain as they are currently living their lives, they assume also that families of these adolescents are experiencing tremendous pain as well. There is often shame and feelings of failure on the part of the parents or caregivers. Parents often experience intense fears for the safety of their adolescents and feelings of guilt about their participation in the process. Additionally, families often bring a history of prior treatment failures or experiences of being blamed by therapists for their adolescents' problems. Therefore, while the therapist provides in-vivo coaching in assertive communication and listening skills during the family session, he or she emphasizes validation of both the adolescent and family members. The therapists may intervene with the environment more than in DBT for adults; this balance is necessary given that the treatment is short-term and that many adolescents continue to reside in an invalidating atmosphere with parents who likely need coaching in applying the DBT skills to family interactions. If the family sessions include relatives who do not participate in the skills group, then the therapist or adolescent provides an in-session orientation to DBT principles or to skills.

Multi-Family Skills Training Group

DBT's overarching goal is to build a life worth living. Thus, the therapist works both to reduce the aforementioned target behaviors and, simultaneously, to increase behavioral skills. The multi-family skills training group is the primary forum for the acquisition and strengthening of these skills, while the individual and family therapy sessions help the client generalize the skills to the situations they encounter in their lives.

The skills taught in DBT correspond directly to Linehan's reorganization of DSM-IV BPD symptoms (Linehan, 1993a). According to this reorganization, the symptoms fall into areas of dysregulation across four domains. DBT for adolescents maintains this conceptualization of suicidal and parasuicidal multi-problem adolescents, even when full criteria for BPD is not met. The areas of dysfunction and the corresponding skill modules follow:

1. Self Dysregulation   Core Mindfulness Skills
2. Interpersonal Dysregulation   Interpersonal Effectiveness Skills
3. Behavioral and Cognitive Dysregulation   Distress Tolerance Skills
4. Emotional Dysregulation   Emotion Regulation Skills
5. Adolescent Family Dilemmas   Walking the Middle Path Skills

Core mindfulness skills involve increased awareness of the present moment and of aspects of the self and environment. Specifically, the adolescent may have difficulty experiencing or identifying what she feels, why one feels the way she does, or identifying a stable sense of self. Moreover, the adolescent may report a pervasive sense of emptiness and have problems maintaining her feelings, opinions, or decisions around others. Teaching suicidal teens how to nonjudgmentally observe and describe what they are feeling and thinking in the moment may be one of the most difficult, but also the most critical, skills for suicidal teens to learn. The interpersonal effectiveness skills address patients' difficulties in maintaining consistent and rewarding relationships. These adolescents typically have intense, unstable relationships, and often experience panic-type anxiety and dread over relationships ending. In addition, they may stay in abusive relationships because of an intense fear of being alone. Interpersonal problems are typically the primary precipitating event in suicidal behaviors in our inner-city population, as well as among suicidal adolescents in general (Lewinsohn, Rohde, & Seeley, 1996). The distress tolerance skills address impulsivity by teaching adolescents how to effectively distract and soothe themselves while considering pros and cons of their actions. These skills typically replace some of the following behaviors: self-inflicted cutting or burning, overdosing, engaging in physical fights, abusing alcohol or drugs, engaging in unprotected or promiscuous sex, cutting classes, and school truancy. Emotion regulation skills address extreme emotional sensitivity, rapid, intense mood changes, as well as unmodulated emotional states characterized by chronic depression, anxiety, or problems with either overcontrolled or undercontrolled anger. Identifying and labeling emotions, learning how to increase positive emotions, and reducing vulnerability to negative emotions are a few of the emotion regulation skills. Walking the middle path skills address nonbalanced thinking and behaviors among teens and family members. These skills involve learning about principles of behavior change, validation, and finding the middle path between common dialectical dilemmas in these families (such as authoritarian control versus excessive leniency).

Secondary Behavioral Targets. The secondary behavioral targets in DBT are addressed throughout treatment rather than within a particular stage. These targets are based on a set of dialectical dilemmas, or behavior patterns characterized by vacillation between polarities. Each pattern represents an aspect of the transaction between an emotionally vulnerable individual and her invalidating environment. Over time, the individual with BPD learns to alternate between one behavioral pattern that under-regulates and another that over-regulates emotions. It is hypothesized that the fluctuations between polarities occur because of the strong tension and discomfort the patient experiences at either pole. These fluctuations are significant obstacles to therapeutic change. Thus, the treatment targets involve finding the synthesis of these extreme behavioral styles. While Linehan's (1993a) original dialectical dilemmas and secondary targets are applicable to this younger population (for an extended discussion of standard DBT dialectical dilemmas and targets see Linehan, 1993a; Koerner, Miller, & Wagner, 1998), we found that to successfully treat the primary target problems among adolescents, additional behavior patterns specific to adolescents and their families required further attention and intervention. Suicidal adolescents, along with their parents and therapists, commonly vacillate and become polarized along three dimensions: (1) excessive leniency versus authoritarian control, (2) pathologizing normative behaviors versus normalizing pathological behaviors, and (3) fostering dependency versus forcing autonomy. In essence, the secondary targets in DBT aim to enhance dialectical behavior patterns, that is, to help suicidal adolescents with borderline traits and their family members change their extreme behavioral patterns into a more balanced lifestyle. Regardless of the stage of therapy, the emphasis is on increasing the ability of these patients and their family members to "walk the middle path" and resolve the many dialectical tensions inherent in their emotions, thoughts, and actions.

Telephone Consultation

The individual therapist receives telephone calls or pages from the patient for (1) coaching skills during in vivo problematic situations, (2) repairing the relationship alliance, and (3) reporting good news. Family members in the multi-family skills group are instructed to call the skills group leaders for telephone consultation for purposes of skills generalization (as opposed to other purposes such as repairing the relationship, or sharing good news). When one of the skills group leaders is the child's primary therapist, the parents may call only the other group leader; this avoids placing the therapist in a potentially compromised position.

Therapist Consultation Meeting

The adolescent DBT therapist consultation team is a weekly ninety-minute meeting that begins with a brief mindfulness exercise to cue a DBT mind set and enhance therapists' skills in leading mindfulness exercises. We then set the meeting agenda by asking therapists about themselves and their patients according to the following DBT hierarchy of targets: (1) suicidal crises, (2) therapist burnout, (3) client and therapist therapy interfering behaviors, (4) good news, (5) quality-of-life-interfering behaviors, (6) summary of the previous skills group and patient graduate group, and (7) administrative issues. The above agenda is covered in the first hour of the meeting; didactics are covered during the last half hour of the meeting and may include a review of skills being taught in group currently, skills practice, videotapes, or other new teaching materials and exercises.

The primary goals of the consultation meeting are to help therapists remain effective and motivated in delivering DBT. Further, the treatment explicitly acknowledges and strives to address the stress and burnout that can occur when working with a suicidal, borderline population. The team members accomplish this through remoralizing and re-energizing therapists and helping therapists to maintain a dialectical position in treatment. Overall, the consultation team "treats" the DBT therapists with the DBT treatment. As in treating patients, treating the therapist occurs in the context of balancing validation with problem-solving strategies. Therapist trainees receive an additional hour per week of individual or dyadic supervision from intensively trained senior therapists.

Patient Graduate Group

Upon graduation from Phase I of the DBT program, patients and family members receive a graduation certificate, and individual therapy, multi-family skills group, and telephone consultation with the individual therapist end. In Phase II of treatment, the adolescent is invited to join the "Graduate Group," which is composed of adolescent graduates and two therapists. The primary goals of the Graduate Group are to prevent relapse by reinforcing the progress made in the first sixteen weeks and to facilitate generalization of patients' behavioral skills. This treatment phase is less time intensive, consisting of ninety-minute groups once per week for sixteen weeks with the opportunity to contract for an additional sixteen weeks if the adolescent is able to identify clear treatment goals. The ninety-minute format of the Graduate Group is as follows:

(1) Mindfulness Practice (five minutes): Each meeting starts with a different adolescent or group therapist leading the mindfulness exercise. This provides adolescents the opportunity to be creative in their mindfulness exercise, practice taking on the role of "leader," and increase generalization of mindfulness skills in their daily lives.

(2) Check-in/Virtual Diary Card (ten minutes): One problem inherent in a group therapy format compared to individual therapy is that therapists are less likely to obtain consistent reporting about suicidal ideation and self-harm urges and behaviors unless there is a semi-structured assessment. Consequently, in the graduate group, therapists learn how each individual is functioning in the previous seven days with a virtual diary card. A group leader asks each member to rate the following behaviors on a scale of 0 to 5 based on the previous week (responses are documented): depression, anger, self-harm thoughts, self-harm actions (yes or no), suicidal thoughts, suicidal actions (yes or no), current self-harm thoughts or suicidal thoughts, list any positive emotions and rate intensity, list which specific skills were used, compliance with pharmacotherapy (yes or no).

(3) Skill Review (fifteen minutes): Adolescents teach their peers a DBT skill. The specific skill taught is based on group consensus.

(4) Snack Break (five minutes): We have arrived at a dialectical synthesis regarding the snacks we provide: we offer both healthy food, which exemplifies healthy choices and skillful eating, as well as junk food, which serves as a reinforcer for some of our adolescents.

(5) Consultation and Problem-Solving (fifty minutes): The primary objective here is to provide consultation to adolescents regarding management of their current life problems. Adolescents are coached to frame their discussion so as to encourage feedback, and each adolescent receives equal time for consultation. The group provides heavy doses of validation and positive reinforcement to each

member, which then provides the foundation for the groups' subsequent constructive criticism and direct feedback. Group leaders model appropriate use of validation, other important interpersonal skills (such as listening and not interrupting, asking questions, and using a respectful tone of voice and good eye contact), and the use of reinforcement.

(6) Closing Observation (five minutes): This last activity of each group involves each group member sharing one non-judgmental observation about the day's group. The function of the closing observation is to help the patients practice mindfulness skills, return to wise mind, and practice self- and other-validation skills as well as reinforcement skills. The patient consultation group leaders take responsibility for telephone consultation; each co-leader becomes primary co-leader for half of the group members and provides telephone consultation and as-needed individual or family sessions for those patients. The therapist consultation team and ancillary treatments, as needed, continue. Ideally, these patients will begin to rely on one another after the group ends, having become less reliant on the adult therapists.

Empirical Support for DBT

DBT with Adults

DBT is the first empirically supported psychosocial treatment for chronically parasuicidal adult women diagnosed with borderline personality disorder. In a randomized, controlled one-year treatment trial, DBT subjects showed significant reductions in anger, suicide attempts, and other parasuicidal acts (both in frequency and medical risk), and number of inpatient psychiatric days, as well as improvement in social adjustment and treatment compliance (Linehan et al., 1991). Results were generally maintained at one-year follow-up (Linehan, Heard, & Armstrong, 1993; Linehan, Tutek, Heard, & Armstrong, 1994). Promising results have been obtained also in the application of DBT to women diagnosed with both a substance use disorder and BPD (Linehan et al., 1999; Linehan et al., in press). Partial replications by other investigators, at other sites and in other countries, have lent further support to DBT as an effective treatment for this population (Bohus et al., 2000; Koons et al., 2001; McCann & Ball, 1996; Stanley, Ivanoff, Brodskly, Oppenheim, & Mann, 1998; Verheul, 2003).

Regarding cost-effectiveness, the Mental Health Center of Greater Manchester New Hampshire obtained overall reductions in service use and cost by integrating DBT into their clinical program (Potenza, 1998). They found that for the first fourteen subjects to complete the one-year program, hospital costs declined from $453,000 to $83,000. This resulted in a reduction in total costs by more than 50%, from $645,000 in the year prior to program entry to $273,000 at the completion of the one-year program. Thus, greater than a 50% reduction in total costs was achieved despite the increase in number of outpatient visits (which tripled) and cost of outpatient visits (which rose from a total of $49,000 to $141,000). The Center's substantial reduction in overall service use and cost despite the substantial increase in number and cost of outpatient visits highlights the necessity of comprehensive evaluation of service cost and utilization with BPD clients. These findings have implications for providers and their administrators as well as patients. In our current health care climate, any effective treatments that also reduce cost are extremely relevant to providers and their administrators. These data are also relevant to patients since they may deplete their insurance benefits due to repeated hospitalizations and ER visits. The American Psychiatric Association honored the Center's achievements with DBT in 1998 with the prestigious Gold Award for the best small community-based mental health program.

DBT with Adolescents

Based on our initial outcome data, DBT also appears to be a promising treatment for suicidal and depressed adolescents with borderline personality features. Our pilot data indicate that the short-term treatment program retains multi-problem teens in outpatient care and decreases inpatient hospitalizations (Rathus & Miller, 2002). In this quasi-experimental pilot investigation of suicidal adolescent outpatients diagnosed with borderline personality traits, we compared DBT (n = 29) to treatment as usual (TAU, n = 82). The pilot sample was composed primarily of an ethnic minority, largely Hispanic, population. This is important given both the dearth of behavior therapy and research with culturally diverse populations as well as Hispanic high school students' status of having the highest suicide attempt rate as compared to other ethnic groups. DBT participants received twelve weeks of twice weekly therapy consisting of individual therapy, a multi-family skills training group, and telephone consultation as needed. TAU participants received twelve weeks of twice weekly supportive-psychodynamic individual therapy plus weekly family therapy. At post-treatment, compared with TAU, the DBT group had significantly fewer psychiatric hospitalizations during treatment and a significantly higher rate of treatment completion. Examining pre-post change within the DBT group, there were significant reductions in suicidal ideation, general psychiatric symptoms, and symptoms of borderline personality disorder. Based on our pilot data, we view DBT as a promising treatment for suicidal adolescents with borderline personality traits.

Employing our adaptation of DBT for adolescents, Fellows obtained impressive results with her adolescent population in New Hampshire. She and her colleagues evaluated twenty-three patients who completed their sixteen-week open program. They examined three outcome measures: inpatient psychiatric days, emergency service contracts, and days of respite bed usage during three time periods—six months prior to treatment, during treatment, and six-months post-treatment. DBT patients showed significant reductions in all three costly services. For example, prior to treatment, the group had 539 inpatient psychiatric days, compared to 40 days during DBT treatment and 11 days during the six months post-treatment (Fellows, personal communication, July, 1999). Other researchers (Katz, Gunasekara, Cox, & Miller, 2003) have obtained results that support the efficacy of DBT applied to suicidal adolescent inpatients.

Personal Experiences and Cases

Introduction

"Theresa," our composite client, is a fifteen-year-old Hispanic female referred to our adolescent outpatient DBT program by her high school counselor, after her vice principal discovered she had been self-injuring daily by cutting herself with razor blades. Theresa is a ninth grader who lives with her mother, mother's boyfriend, and sister. Upon evaluation, she presented with depressive symptoms including depressed and irritable mood, poor concentration, initial insomnia, poor appetite, psychomotor retardation, feelings of worthlessness, and recurrent suicidal ideation. Theresa said she had experienced these symptoms "as long as I can remember," however she noted they had worsened substantially over the past month. Further, Theresa endorsed multiple symptoms of BPD including affective instability, a pattern of unstable interpersonal relationships, severe dissociative symptoms, chronic feelings of emptiness, suicidal ideation and threats, and parasuicidal behavior. Theresa received the following DSM-IV, Axis I diagnosis based on the Kiddie-SADS (Schedule for Affective Disorders and Schizophrenia for school-aged children) semi-structured interview: major depressive disorder, recurrent, moderate; dysthymic disorder; eating disorder, NOS; and cannabis abuse. On Axis II, based on the SCID-II, Theresa met criteria for BPD.

Theresa's psychiatric history included feeling depressed "as long as I can remember" and engaging in multiple parasuicidal behaviors since age twelve, including burning herself with cigarettes and lighters and cutting herself with various "sharps" (razors, scissors, knives) on her arms and legs. The self-injury was typically superficial; however, on two occasions within the past year self-inflicted cuts on her legs required sutures. Both incidents precipitated week-long psychiatric hospitalizations. Theresa endorsed suicidal intent on both occasions, reporting that she couldn't "take the pain any longer." Theresa also described a history of relationship patterns characteristic of BPD including chronic conflict with her mother that escalated often into "screaming matches and silent treatments for days" and intense friendships formed quickly and then ended precipitously following a perceived infraction or rejection. Theresa had been treated in several local outpatient clinics and with several different antidepressants; Theresa reported no therapeutic response to either psychotropic medications or previous psychotherapies.

Family psychiatric history included mother with major depression and father with bipolar disorder and history of polysubstance dependence.

Upon her entry into our program, Theresa was living with her mother, her mother's boyfriend, and her seventeen-year-old sister. Her parents were divorced and her biological father had been released from prison recently and was living locally for the first time in over ten years. Her father stated he wanted to develop a relationship with Theresa; however, Theresa reported she "wasn't interested . . . he wasn't around all those years and he didn't care about me . . . why would he now?" Theresa reported experiencing chronic tension and conflict with her mother and described her as someone who "can't understand me and doesn't care about me."

Phase One

Pretreatment and Commitment

Theresa agreed to participate in DBT, which included sixteen weeks of the following weekly sessions: individual therapy (one hour), multi-family skills group (two hours), family sessions as needed (folded into individual treatment), and PRN telephone coaching provided by the individual therapist for Theresa and by the multi-family skills training group leader for Theresa's mother. The individual therapist oriented Theresa to DBT over the initial sessions. The skills group leaders oriented Theresa and her mother to DBT in their initial group meeting, providing an overview of the structure and philosophy of our DBT treatment program and working to enhance their motivation for treatment. Initially, Theresa told her individual therapist that her life was "fine," she had "no problems," and she "didn't need treatment." The therapist used both commitment strategies and the stylistic strategy of irreverence to encourage Theresa to acknowledge that her life really was not "fine" and that if she wanted her life to improve, she needed to acknowledge her problems and try new behaviors. For example, the therapist used the commitment strategy of highlighting freedom to choose and absence of alternatives to highlight both Theresa's freedom to choose whether she would participate in treatment as well as the realistic consequences of either choice.

Specifically, Theresa was free to choose a lifetime of coping by parasuicide, however, she would need to choose another therapy because a required goal of DBT is reduction of parasuicide. When Theresa said, "I have to cut myself; I can't help it." Her therapist used the communication strategy of omnipotence and said, "I know that if you participate fully in DBT, I will teach you how to stop cutting yourself." After several sessions, Theresa was able to begin to articulate her problems, and Theresa and her therapist agreed on treatment goals by session three. Theresa's treatment goals were folded into the DBT Stage 1 Target areas.

Target 1: reducing suicidality, such as parasuicidal behaviors and chronic suicidal ideation.

Target 2: reducing treatment-interfering behaviors such as missing sessions, not completing therapy homework assignments, and noncollaborative behaviors

Target 3: reducing quality-of-life interfering behaviors, such as depression, anxiety, substance use, conflicts at home and in peer relationships

Target 4: increasing behavioral skills, such as core mindfulness, distress tolerance, emotion regulation, interpersonal effectiveness, and walking the middle path skills.

Stage 1: Safety and Security. During Stage 1, when the patient has severe behavioral dyscontrol, the primary focus of interventions is to establish behavioral control.

Individual Therapy. In individual therapy, Theresa completed a diary card weekly to monitor dysfunctional behaviors and DBT skills practiced. Dysfunctional behaviors were addressed by conducting a behavioral analysis.

Over the course of the sixteen weeks of Phase I DBT, Theresa showed good behavioral compliance with consistent attendance in individual, family, and multifamily skills group sessions as well as consistent completion of her homework and diary card. Further, Theresa demonstrated an intellectual understanding of all the skills when in session. However, initially it appeared that she had difficulty consistently translating that intellectual knowledge into an ability to use the skill effectively in a moment of crisis (e.g., urge to self harm). She would often injure herself and conclude the skill "didn't work." Repeated behavioral analyses in individual therapy clarified that, in moments of crisis, Theresa *thought* about the skill she might use however did not actually *employ* the skill. Thus, Theresa concluded the skill "didn't work" when she had not actually used it. The therapist had Theresa practice skills in session to facilitate generalization of Theresa's skill use. The therapist began each individual session with a brief mindfulness exercise and had Theresa engage other skills as needed throughout the session. This in-vivo practice enabled Theresa to give feedback to her therapist on the effectiveness of the skill and her therapist to give immediate feedback and coaching to Theresa on her use of the skill.

Target 1. For the first several weeks of treatment, Theresa experienced chronic suicidal ideation and engaged in self-mutilative behavior (that is, self-inflicted cuts on arms and legs). When Theresa had engaged in a parasuicidal act in the previous week or experienced acute suicidal ideation, her individual therapist always addressed it in the subsequent individual therapy session with a behavioral analysis, given that parasuicidal behaviors and acute suicidal ideation take precedence over other target behaviors. However, in contrast to acute suicidal ideation, Theresa's habitual or chronic low-level suicidal ideation (two on a five-point scale) was not always addressed directly because this would have eliminated discussion of almost everything else. Although any change in Theresa's chronic suicidal ideation was always addressed, her chronic low-level ideation was addressed indirectly by working on enhancing her quality of life. DBT considers ongoing suicidal ideation to be an outcome of low-quality lives and therefore believes the focus of treatment should be on enhancing quality of life.

Theresa and her therapist completed the following behavioral analysis (BA) on an incident of Theresa's self-injury. The therapist first elicited from Theresa a clear description of the target behavior (which was a superficial cut on her forearm with a razor). The therapist then elicited from her several vulnerability factors (fatigue from insomnia the previous two nights, chronic anger regarding ongoing invalidation by her mother) and precipitating events (an argument with her mother) that had contributed to her problematic behavior. The connections between her thoughts ("My mother always yells at me I can't take this. . . . Hurting myself will help me let go of this anger."), emotions (intense anger at her mother for not understanding her), and actions (cutting herself) were made explicit. Additionally, specific intervening variables were identified in the chain analysis. These variables included Theresa's deficits in emotion regulation and distress tolerance skills. The behavioral analysis helped Theresa perceive how her problematic behavior of self-injury was negatively reinforced by the consequence of temporary avoidance of her negative emotion of anger. The behavioral analysis also helped her identify positive reinforcers of her self-injury, such as the increased attention she received from her mother. Her therapist emphasized with Theresa the negative consequences of her actions, which included scars on her arms, the aversive aspect of tediously conducting a behavioral analysis, jeopardizing the tenuous trust she was developing with her mother, and the decreased sense of competency (she was not employing skills previously mastered), to highlight factors that might decrease her problematic behaviors in the future. The therapist provided a solution analysis to help Theresa develop alternative pathways for managing similar problems in the future. Together, Theresa and her therapist identified specific skills (mindful-ness skills, acting opposite of the current emotion) Theresa could use the next time a similar situation arose. Theresa was also encouraged to make better use of phone consultations with the individual therapist as needed.

Target 2. The second behavioral target in individual therapy is to reduce behaviors, either the patient's or the therapist's, that interfere with treatment. Theresa engaged in multiple Target 2 behaviors throughout treatment. Superficially, Theresa was extremely compliant and apparently competent. She attended both individual therapy and multi-family skills group consistently, arrived on time, and completed her homework. However, Theresa was also consistently noncollaborative. Although she "showed up" each week both to individual and to group, she reported often that everything was "fine" and that she had "no problems." She completed her diary card weekly, but it reflected primarily "zeros" in terms of emotional experience. Although she was physically present during individual therapy, she became increasingly withdrawn (responded to questions with "I don't know"; slouched in her chair, and exhibited poor eye contact) as her therapist tried to elicit her active participation in session.

Target 3. Theresa had multiple quality-of-life issues that required a subhierarchy to help organize the treatment. The first targeted behavior within quality-of-life issues is substance abuse. After Theresa's therapist explained that regular cannabis use can exacerbate depression, Theresa agreed to work to decrease her cannabis use. Other Target 3 behaviors, listed in order of priority, included decreasing symptoms of depression, decreasing conflict with her mother, and improving her attendance at school.

Target 4. Target 4 is to increase behavioral skills. It was crucial that Theresa learn, and then generalize, the behavioral skills, given that these are the behaviors that replace the maladaptive behaviors identified in the first three targets. Theresa seemed to learn the skills easily. She was able to define them and provide relevant examples of how her peers might use particular skills in a given crisis situation. Further, she was able to complete her homework with relevant examples of skill use in her own life.

Multi-Family Skills Group. Theresa attended the multi-family skills group with her mother. Four other teens and their parents participated. The skill modules taught included core mindfulness, distress tolerance, emotions regulation, interpersonal effectiveness, and walking the middle path skills. At the end of the sixteen weeks, Theresa was able to recite many of the skills in the five skill modules, but did not appear to generalize or incorporate all the skills into her daily repertoire. Theresa did use some skills (such as pleasant activities, increased self-validation, radical acceptance), which seemed to help reduce her depression. Theresa and her mother made some progress in reducing their ongoing conflicts. Initially, Theresa's mother focused almost exclusively on criticizing Theresa's behavior and judgment. In particular, she accused Theresa of trying to manipulate people with her self-injurious behaviors. ("She hurts herself over nothing . . . she just doesn't want to have to listen to anyone.") Over time, with coaching from the group leaders, her mother made some progress in learning to validate the feelings driving Theresa's self-injury and provide coaching suggestions for managing her urges to self-injure ("I would be angry too if the teacher had said something like that to me . . . how about if we get out of the house for a bit and walk to the corner store together?"). Her mother also learned to use interpersonal effectiveness skills to help her effectively engage her daughter's participation in household chores while treating her daughter respectfully and maintaining their relationship.

Both Theresa and her mother completed the sixteen-week multi-family skills training and each received a diploma at the DBT graduation ceremony. The graduation ceremony takes place during the second half of the skills group meeting. Each group member says good-bye to the graduating member and the graduating member says good-bye to each member of the group. Theresa was able consistently to offer insightful and radically genuine feedback on her peers' progress and ongoing challenges.

Family Therapy. Theresa and her mother participated in four family sessions over the course of the sixteen weeks to work more directly on the chronic conflict between Theresa and her mother and contingencies at home that reinforced Theresa's dysfunctional behavior. (For example, Theresa received intermittent increased warmth and attention from her mother when she self-injured.)

Telephone Consultation. Initially, Theresa did not make use of the telephone coaching for help in managing her urges to self-injure because she feared she would "bother" her therapist. The therapist shaped Theresa's use of the telephone coaching by scheduling several practice pages. Specifically, Theresa and her therapist agreed upon both a date and a time Theresa would page her therapist. The practice pages exposed Theresa to the anxiety provoking behavior of paging her therapist and enabled her to learn that her therapist was not bothered but was instead pleased Theresa was asking for help skillfully. After a few practice pages, Theresa was able to independently page her therapist for coaching prior to self-injury, and she experienced the naturally reinforcing consequence of helpful coaching during the ten-minute coaching call.

Therapist Consultation Group. The therapist consultation meetings included all DBT treatment providers in the outpatient DBT program, including individual therapists, skills trainers, and pharmacotherapists. The meeting provides both technical help and emotional support to assist therapists in conducting DBT competently with these difficult suicidal patients. In these meetings Theresa's therapist received support and feedback on how to cope with Theresa's noncollaboration (that, initially, she would not call for coaching prior to self-injury) and her intermittent report that "everything's fine," despite the chronic chaos in her life.

Phase Two

Upon graduation from Phase I of DBT, Theresa elected to enter the optional sixteen-week graduate group. Theresa attended the graduate group consistently and continued to work collaboratively with the group leaders and her peers on reducing self-harm, her urges to purge, and building a life worth living.

Case Conclusion

Theresa and her mother both completed the sixteen-week treatment and each received a diploma. Theresa had learned many of the skills in the five modules and had incorporated many of these skills in her daily repertoire. Upon discharge, Theresa no longer met DSM criteria for major depression, no longer used cannabis, and her eating disorder symptoms had diminished greatly. Her BPD symptoms diminished also (only one incident of self-harm behavior during the last five weeks of therapy, better affect regulation according to reports of both her therapist and her mother, and improved interpersonal relationships according to her self report). Further, Theresa acknowledged feeling more certain about her feelings and her values. Theresa continued to report some fluctuations in her mood, however, she reported also that she was better able to regulate her emotions overall. During the final four weeks of therapy, she did not exhibit any maladaptive or parasuicidal behaviors and denied suicidal ideation.

Future Directions

DBT was originally developed by Linehan for the treatment of chronically parasuicidal adult outpatients diagnosed with BPD. In less than a decade, this treatment approach, which is backed by solid research with adults and promising data with adolescents, has had a substantial impact on the field of mental health. In contrast to standard CBT, DBT includes a flexible principle-based rather than manual-based set of interventions, the notion of a dialectical world view, a biosocial theory of borderline personality disorder, specified treatment functions and modes, the concept of stage of disorder, a hierarchy of treatment targets, an integration of acceptance and validation strategies with change strategies, and a significant emphasis on the therapeutic relationship. DBT also employs a specific set of commitment strategies, it targets therapy-interfering behaviors, and the DBT therapist requires the adolescent to page for coaching when in crisis; all strategies were intended to engage and retain the patient in treatment and to further generalize the patient's skills.

◆ ◆ ◆

DBT has been applied to adolescents in outpatient, inpatient, day hospital, residential, juvenile detention center, and school settings. Hence, in addition to applying DBT to the suicidal adolescent with borderline personality features, DBT has also been used to target adolescents with various psychiatric and behavioral disorders, including substance-abuse, depression, dissociation, eating disordered behaviors, conduct disorders, and violent and aggressive behaviors, to name a few. Clearly, more research is required with multi-problem adolescents in various settings before more definitive conclusions can be made regarding DBT's efficacy and effectiveness with this age group.

References

Bohus, M., Haaf, B., Stiglmayer, C., Pohl, U., Bohme, R., & Linehan, M. M. (2000). Evaluation of inpatient dialectical behavior therapy for borderline personality disorder—A prospective study. *Behavior Research and Therapy, 38,* 875–887.

Katz, L. Y., Gunasekara, S., Cox, B. J., & Miller, A. L. (2003). Dialectical behavior therapy for suicidal adolescent inpatients: A pilot study. Manuscript submitted for publication.

Katz, L. Y., Gunasekara, S., & Miller, A. L. (2002). Dialectical behavior therapy for suicidal adolescent inpatients and outpatients. *Annals of Adolescent Psychiatry, 26,* 161–178.

Kazdin, A. E. (1978). *History of behavior modification: Experimental foundations of contemporary research.* Baltimore, MD: University Park Press.

Koerner, K., Miller, A. L., & Wagner, A. W. (1998). Dialectical behavior therapy: Part I. Principle based intervention with multi-problem patients. *Journal of Practical Psychiatry and Behavioral Health, 4,* 28–36.

Koons, C. R., Robins, C. J., Tweed, J. L., Lynch, T. R., Gonzalez, A. M., Morse, J. Q., et al. (2001). Efficacy of dialectical behavior therapy in women veterans with borderline personality disorder. *Behavior Therapy, 32,* 371–390.

Kreitman, N. (1977). *Parasuicide.* Chichester, U.K.: Wiley.

Lewinsohn, P. M., Rohde, P., & Seeley, J. R. (1996). Adolescent suicidal ideation and attempts: Prevalence, risk factors, and clinical implications. *Clinical Psychology: Science and Practice, 3*, 25–46.

Linehan, M. M. (1993a). *Cognitive behavioral therapy of borderline personality disorder.* New York: Guilford Press.

Linehan, M. M. (1993b). *Skills training manual for treating borderline personality Disorder.* New York: Guilford Press.

Linehan, M. M., Armstrong, H. E., Suarez, A., Allmon, D., & Heard, H. L. (1991). Cognitive behavioral treatment of chronically parasuicidal borderline patients. *Archives of General Psychiatry, 48*, 1060–1064.

Linehan, M. M., Dimeff, L. A., Reynolds, S. K., Comtois, K. A., Shaw Welch, S., Heagerty, P., et al. (in press). Dialectical behavior therapy versus comprehensive validation plus 12-step for the treatment of opioid dependent women meeting criteria for borderline personality disorder. *Drug and Alcohol Dependence.*

Linehan, M. M., Heard, H. L., & Armstrong, H. E. (1993). Naturalistic follow-up of a behavioral treatment for chronically parasuicidal borderline patients. *Archives of General Psychiatry, 50*, 971–974.

Linehan, M. M., Schmidt, H., Dimeff, L. A., Craft, J. C., Kanter, J., & Comtois, K. A. (1999). Dialectical behavior therapy for patients with borderline personality disorder and drug-dependence. *American Journal of Addiction, 8*, 279–292.

Linehan, M. M., Tutek, D. A., Heard, H. L., & Armstrong, H. E. (1994). Interpersonal outcome of cognitive behavioral treatment for chronically suicidal borderline patients. *American Journal of Psychiatry, 151*, 1771–1776.

McCann, R. A., & Ball, E. M. (1996). *Skills training manual for treating forensic patients.* Unpublished manuscript.

Miller, A. L. (1999). Dialectical behavior therapy: A new treatment approach for suicidal adolescents. *American Journal of Psychotherapy, 53*, 413–417.

Miller, A. L., Rathus, J. H., Linehan, M. M., Wetzler, S., & Leigh, E. (1997). Dialectic behavior therapy for suicidal adolescents. *Journal of Practical Psychiatry and Behavioral Health, 3*, 78–86.

Potenza, D. (1998). Integrating dialectical behavior therapy into a community mental health program. *Psychiatric Services, 49*, 1338–1340.

Rathus, J. H., & Miller, A. L. (2000). DBT for adolescents: Dialectical dilemmas and secondary treatment targets. *Cognitive and Behavioral Practice, 7*, 425–434.

Rathus, J. H., & Miller, A. L. (2002). Dialectical behavior therapy adapted for suicidal adolescents. *Suicide and Life Threatening Behavior, 32*, 146–157.

Sally, M., Jackson, L., Carney, J., Kevelson, J., & Miller A. L. (2002). *Integrating DBT skills training groups in an underperforming high school.* Poster session presented at the 7th annual meeting of the International Society for the Improvement and Teaching of DBT, Reno, NV.

Stanley, B., Ivanoff, A., Brodsky, B., Oppenheim, S., & Mann, J. (1998). Comparison of DBT and "treatment as usual" in suicidal and self-mutilating behavior. *Proceedings of the 32nd Association for the Advancement of Behavior Therapy Convention*, Washington, D.C.

Trautman, P., Stewart, N., & Morishima, A. (1993). Are adolescent suicide attempters noncompliant with outpatient care? *Journal of the American Academy of Child and Adolescent Psychiatry, 32*, 89–94.

Verheul, R., van den Bosch, L. M., Koeter, M.W. J., de Ridder, M.A. J., Steijnen, T., van den Brink, W. A. (2003). A 12-month randomized clinical trial of dialectical behavior therapy for women with borderline personality disorder in the Netherlands. *The British Journal of Psychiatry, 182*, 135–140.

CHAPTER TWENTY-THREE

INTERPERSONAL PSYCHOTHERAPY FOR THE TREATMENT OF ADOLESCENT DEPRESSION: A GUIDE TO TECHNIQUES AND IMPLEMENTATION

Jami F. Young, Ph.D., and Laura Mufson, Ph.D.

Interpersonal psychotherapy for depressed adolescents, or IPT–A, is an adaptation of interpersonal psychotherapy (IPT). IPT is a brief treatment that was developed and tested for depressed adults (Weissman, Markowitz, & Klerman, 2000). IPT is based on the premise that depression, regardless of its etiology, occurs in an interpersonal context. Thus, the focus of treatment is on the patients' depressive symptoms and the interpersonal context in which these symptoms occur. The theoretical roots of this treatment can be found in the teachings of Harry Stack Sullivan and other interpersonal theorists who argued that interpersonal interactions form the basis of personality (Sullivan, 1953). As a result, treatment needs to address the individual's interpersonal interactions, as well as the individual's symptoms and behaviors.

Research supports an interpersonal approach to the conceptualization and treatment of depression (Hammen, 1999; Joiner, Coyne, & Blalock, 1999). Several studies have demonstrated that depression is associated with significant interpersonal problems in adolescents (Lewinsohn et al., 1994; Puig-Antich et al., 1993). More specifically, interpersonal events have been implicated as both predictors and sequelae of adolescent depression in both community and clinical samples (Hammen, 1999; Lewinsohn et al., 1994; Puig-Antich et al., 1993; Sheeber, Hops, Alpert, Davis, & Andrews, 1997). For instance, Lewinsohn and colleagues (1994), in a prospective study of depression in a community-based sample of adolescents, found that family and peer support were significantly associated with past, current, and future depression. In a clinical sample, Puig-Antich and colleagues (1993) found that adolescents with a current depressive disorder had more negative family and peer relations than non-depressed adolescents. These findings point to the importance of focusing on interpersonal events and interpersonal skills when treating adolescent depression, as is done in IPT–A.

Putative Mechanisms

IPT–A works by addressing the interpersonal problems that are causing or contributing to the adolescent's depression. The treatment posits that improving the interpersonal context will lead to an improvement in depressive symptoms. Thus, both the diagnosis and treatment are focused on the individual's interpersonal interactions and how these interactions affect the adolescent's mood and other depressive symptoms. Adolescents' interpersonal problems generally fall into one of five categories: grief, interpersonal disputes, role transitions, interpersonal deficits, or single-parent families.

During treatment, the therapist identifies maladaptive interpersonal patterns that are related to the adolescent's depression (that is, identifies an interpersonal problem area), makes these patterns explicit to the patient, and helps the patient disrupt these patterns during the course of treatment (Kiesler, 1991). Addressing the interpersonal problem leads to a positive change in the feedback that the adolescent gets from significant others. As a result, the adolescent develops a sense of agency in relationships, improves his or her self-view, and begins to feel better.

The targets and mechanisms of IPT–A differ somewhat for the different problem areas. For example, if an adolescent presents a conflict with a parent, the therapist and patient discuss the factors contributing to the conflict, and then the therapist helps the adolescent learn more adaptive ways to communicate with parents to resolve the conflict, including clarification of the issues, negotiation, and other problem-solving strategies. This decrease in conflict results in a decrease in depressed mood and other symptoms, as well as gives the adolescent a sense of mastery and control. Each problem area and its associated treatment strategies are discussed later in the chapter.

Developmental Influences

Based on the success of IPT with adults (Weissman et al., 1979; Elkin et al., 1989), the similarities between depressive symptoms in adults and adolescents (Ryan et al., 1987), and the interpersonal literature discussed above, IPT has been adapted to treat adolescent depression. IPT–A is developmentally relevant for adolescents who are becoming increasingly focused on the status and terms of their relationships. IPT–A addresses developmental issues that are pertinent to adolescence, including the development of romantic relationships, separation from parents, experiencing the death of a loved one, and negotiating peer relationships.

A number of alterations have been made to the IPT manual to increase the model's appropriateness for the treatment of adolescent depression. First, a parent component has been added to the treatment protocol. Although IPT–A is an individual treatment, some degree of involvement on the part of the parent or guardian is usually indicated to ensure the success of the treatment. Although we recommend parental attendance at each phase of treatment, especially the initial and termination phases, parent involvement in IPT–A is flexible and can range from no involvement to attendance at several sessions. The degree of parental involvement is discussed and negotiated between the therapist and the adolescent during the course of treatment, with the support and cooperation of the parents.

Second, the techniques used to decrease depressive symptoms and improve interpersonal functioning have been geared toward adolescents. Techniques employed specifically with adolescents include giving them a rating scale from 1 to 10 to rate their depressed mood so it is more concrete and easier for them to monitor improvement; doing more basic social skills work; conducting explicit work on perspective-taking skills to counteract adolescent black-and-white thinking about solutions to problems; and learning how to negotiate parent-child tensions. Third, IPT–A added a fifth problem area, "single-parent family," based on the frequency of single-parent families, its empirically demonstrated connection to depressive symptoms, and the interpersonal challenges and difficulties that can be associated with this living situation (Aseltine, 1996; Cornwell, Eggebeen, & Meschke, 1996; Spruijt & de Goede, 1997). Finally, strategies were developed for dealing with specific issues that may arise in the course of treating adolescents, including school refusal, physical or sexual abuse, involvement of child protective agencies, and suicidality.

IPT–A is an outpatient treatment designed for adolescents with non-psychotic, unipolar depression. It is not indicated for adolescents who are mentally retarded, currently in crisis, actively suicidal or homicidal, psychotic, or bipolar. In addition, when an evaluation uncovers that an adolescent is using alcohol or drugs on a regular basis, the clinician needs to make a decision about whether the substance use is severe enough to warrant substance abuse treatment before addressing the depression. In general, IPT–A is not recommended for adolescents who are actively abusing substances.

Among teens with non-psychotic unipolar depression, our clinical experience has shown us that adolescents who are motivated to be in treatment derive greater benefit from treatment. Since the adolescent and clinician regularly review the patient's depressive symptoms and link these symptoms to interpersonal events, IPT–A is best suited for adolescents who acknowledge that they are depressed and are able to agree with the therapist that at least one interpersonal problem exists. Adolescents whose families are supportive of treatment are more likely to have positive treatment outcomes, although family involvement is not a requirement for treatment.

Putative Targets of Treatment

Interpersonal Problem Areas

As stated before, each individual is conceptualized as having one or more of five interpersonal problem areas: grief, interpersonal disputes, role transitions, interpersonal deficits, and single parent-families. In the sections that follow, we briefly discuss each problem area. A more detailed discussion of each problem area can be found in the IPT–A manual (Mufson, Moreau, Weissman, & Klerman, 1993).

Grief. Many bereaved adolescents experience some depressive symptoms including dysphoria, anhedonia, and appetite disturbance. IPT–A is appropriate if the adolescent's grief is prolonged and results in significant depressive symptoms and associated impairment in functioning. It is particularly useful for those adolescents who have experienced a significant disruption in their support network as a result of the death or who had a conflictual relationship with the deceased, as these situations have been identified as risk factors for more complicated bereavement (Clark, Pynoos, & Goebel, 1994). IPT–A helps the adolescent mourn the loss of a loved one, while encouraging the adolescent to develop other relationships that can help fill some of the voids left by the death.

Interpersonal disputes. A dispute involving interpersonal roles exists when one individual and a significant other (or others) have nonreciprocal expectations about the relationship (Klerman, Weissman, Rounsaville, & Chevron, 1984). Adolescents frequently have disputes with their parents or guardians around issues such as authority, sexuality, money, and the adolescent's increasing autonomy. Disputes do not necessarily lead to adolescent depression. However, when these disputes become chronic and unmanageable, they can become more stressful and can act as a precipitant of depression. Conversely, adolescents who are experiencing depression may become more irritable or may have other symptoms that make them particularly ill-equipped to manage interpersonal conflict. In such cases, the dispute may exacerbate the adolescent's depression. Although disputes between adolescents and parents are often the focus of treatment, adolescents may also present with disputes with other people in their lives (such as peers or teachers) that can be addressed in treatment. The goal of treatment is to help resolve the dispute if possible and, if not, to help the adolescent develop strategies to better cope with the relationship.

Role transitions. Role transitions are changes that occur due to a person's progression from one social role to another. Role transitions can be predictable as in normal developmental shifts that occur at different stages in adolescence, or they can be more unexpected, such as a change associated with a life stressor, such as moving or having a parent fall ill. Certain adolescents may feel unable to meet the increased responsibilities associated with a role transition, resulting in depression and impairment in interpersonal functioning. A transition is especially problematic if it occurs too rapidly, is experienced as a loss by the individual, is associated with secondary changes or stressors, or is met by the inflexibility of either the adolescent or significant others in the adolescent's life. Treatment is focused on helping the adolescent develop the skills needed to manage her new role more successfully.

Interpersonal deficits. Interpersonal deficits are the identified problem area in which an adolescent lacks the social skills needed to have positive relationships with family members and friends due to prolonged social isolation. Adolescents with this problem area often experience loneliness and decreased self-confidence and self-esteem, which can lead to or exacerbate feelings of depression. The depression can lead to further social withdrawal and isolation, leading to further deficits in interpersonal skills. IPT–A is best suited to adolescents whose interpersonal deficits are less pervasive and/or a consequence of either their depression or a specific stressor. The goal of treatment is to help the adolescent develop the skills needed to have more satisfying interpersonal relationships.

Single-parent families. Although single-parent family status itself is not a problem, the underlying circumstances such as parental absence or abandonment, parental divorce, or parental separation can precipitate or exacerbate depression. Depending on a number of factors, such as the family context or the presence of additional stressors, some adolescents will have more difficulty with this situation than others. This problem area differs from some of the others in that the problem is often outside of the adolescent's control, such as failure of parents to comply with a custody agreement, but affects his or her well being. Treatment helps the adolescent better cope with this living situation and its associated problems.

Course of IPT–A

IPT–A is a time-limited treatment. It is designed as a once weekly, twelve-session treatment. If a crisis occurs, or additional sessions are warranted for other reasons, treatment can be extended to sixteen sessions. In certain settings, a more flexible schedule may be necessary. For instance, in the school study just completed, adolescents received IPT–A for eight consecutive weeks. The remaining four sessions were more flexible, depending on the individual patient's need, school schedule, and so on, and were conducted over an additional eight-week time period.

IPT–A is divided into three phases: (1) the initial phase, (2) the middle phase, and (3) the termination phase. The general structure of the sessions is consistent throughout treatment, regardless of the treatment phase. At the beginning of each session, the clinician assesses the patient's depressive symptoms, noting any changes that occurred over the course of the week and linking changes in depressive symptoms to interpersonal events that occurred during the course of the week. Following the review of symptoms, the session progresses to the tasks particular to that phase of treatment, whether that be conducting the interpersonal inventory, focusing on a particular interpersonal event, or discussing the patient's warning signs of depression. This structure ensures that the treatment focuses on issues related to the identified problem area.

Throughout treatment, both the therapist and patient play an active role in the sessions. The therapist is responsible for assessing depressive symptoms, inquiring about the patient's interpersonal relationships, linking the adolescents' symptoms to her interpersonal functioning, and guiding the work on the particular problem area. The patient is expected to discuss interpersonal relationships, work with the therapist to find solutions to the interpersonal problem area, and practice new interpersonal techniques. In addition, as treatment progresses, the adolescent is asked to bring in particular interpersonal events that occurred during the previous week to address in treatment.

Initial Phase

The initial phase of IPT–A typically consists of the first four sessions. We recommend that the parent(s) participate in, at least, one session during the initial phase of treatment, most typically the first session. There are several objectives for this phase of treatment: (1) confirm the depression diagnosis, (2) educate the patient and family about depression and assign patient the "limited sick role," (3) explain theory and goals of IPT–A, (4) Conduct the interpersonal inventory in order to relate the depression to the interpersonal context, (5) identify the interpersonal problem area(s), and (6) make a treatment contract.

Confirm the depression diagnosis. Although the diagnostic assessment is typically conducted before beginning IPT–A, it is important to confirm the depression diagnosis in the first session. Using a clinical interview, the clinician should assess the patient's current depressive symptoms, history of depressive symptoms, as well as other symptoms, such as mania, psychosis, substance abuse, or suicidality, which might make IPT–A an inappropriate treatment for that patient. As discussed earlier, during ensuing sessions, the therapist conducts somewhat briefer assessments in order to evaluate any change in symptoms.

Education about depression and assigning the "limited sick role." Another important goal of the first session is to educate the patient and parent(s) about depression. This follows directly from the review of symptoms and involves educating the adolescent and parents about the symptoms and behaviors associated with depression. Many parents do not associate their child's increased irritability with depression. Other parents think that their child is doing worse in school because he or she does not care about doing well. By educating the patient and parents about the depression, the clinician provides a context for these symptoms. Part of the education component is likening depression to a medical illness that can be treated. This medical model of depression is helpful to the family for a number of reasons: it decreases the stigma associated with depression, it takes the blame off the patient or others for causing the depression, and it provides an optimistic prognosis for the patient improving over time.

The last part of the educational component involves assigning the patient the *limited sick role*. This involves discussing with patient and parents that similar to someone with a medical illness, adolescents with symptoms of depression may not be able to do things as well as before the depression. However, despite it being more difficult to do certain things such as concentrate in school or continue extracurricular activities, it is important for the patient to do as much as possible. This differs from adult IPT in which the patient is given the sick role (not the limited sick role) and is encouraged to scale back on activities until he or she feels better. The reason for this difference is that, developmentally, it is very important for an adolescent to be in school. Thus, the goal is to get the adolescent back to a regular school schedule and attendance as soon as possible, while acknowledging that he or she might not do as well as he or she did previous to the depression.

Explain the theory and goals of IPT–A. At the beginning of treatment, the therapist defines the structure and context of the treatment, including the brief, time-limited nature of IPT–A, the roles of the therapist and patient, and the theory behind IPT–A. In particular, the patient and family are told that IPT–A is based on the premise that depression occurs in an interpersonal context. That is, regardless of the etiology of the depression, depression affects our relationships and our relationships affect our mood. Thus, the focus of treatment will be on improving the child's relationships with the hope that this will lead to improvements in mood. As a result of this discussion, the patient and parents understand why the treatment focuses on the patient's relationships, as opposed to other parts of the patient's life. The discussion of the theory and structure of the therapy makes the course of treatment more predictable and decreases the likelihood of dropout. In addition, this discussion helps enlist the parents as collaborative therapists in treating the adolescent's depression.

Conduct the interpersonal inventory. Much of what is described above occurs in the first session or two. The remainder of the initial phase of treatment is focused on conducting the interpersonal inventory, an interpersonal assessment of the patient's most important relationships. Similar to placing an emphasis on the assessment of the patient's symptoms, IPT–A emphasizes the importance of assessing the patient's interpersonal functioning. The goal of the interpersonal inventory is to identify those interpersonal issues that are most closely related to the onset or persistence of the patient's depression. Although the primary informant for the interpersonal inventory is the adolescent, parents can also provide information about the adolescent's relationships.

During the interpersonal inventory, the therapist asks the patient to identify important people in his or her life. Following this, the therapist asks detailed questions about each relationship, including the frequency, content, and context of contacts; positive and negative aspects of the relationship; how the relationship has changed since the patient became depressed; and the patients goals for changing the relationship over the course of treatment. While conducting the interpersonal inventory, the therapist should also probe for any significant life events that may be related to the depression.

Identify the interpersonal problem area(s). On the basis of the interpersonal inventory, the therapist helps the adolescent understand the relationship between interpersonal events and her depressive symptoms. The therapist identifies common themes or problems in the various relationships (such as, the patient has difficulty letting others know how she feels and, as a result, feels like she is not having her needs met), and, together with the adolescent, chooses one of the five interpersonal problem areas that will be the focus of treatment. While it is most common to identify one interpersonal problem area to address in treatment, there are times when two problem areas are identified. In this case, part of the treatment contract (see below) will involve discussing how the two problem areas will be addressed during the course of treatment.

Making the treatment contract. Once the problem area has been identified, the patient and therapist establish a verbal treatment contract. In this contract, the adolescent's and family's roles in treatment are specified, the focus of treatment (the identified problem area) is highlighted, and practical details regarding the treatment are reviewed. While discussing the treatment contract, the therapist stresses to the patient that, in order for treatment to be most helpful, she needs to bring in information about interactions that occurred in her relationships. In addition, the patient is informed that the parent might be invited into treatment to work on the identified problem area. The structure of treatment also is reviewed at this time. In particular, the therapist emphasizes the importance of the adolescent coming to treatment on time and calling to cancel if necessary. It is useful in this discussion to highlight the number of sessions that have elapsed and the number of sessions that remain. This contract is both helpful for the treatment and serves as a model of clarity in communication and expectations.

Middle Phase

The middle phase of IPT–A consists of sessions five through eight or nine. During the middle phase of treatment, the therapist and patient begin to work directly on one or two of the designated problem areas. The tasks associated with the middle phase are (1) monitoring depressive symptoms, (2) considering adjunctive medication, (3) clarifying the interpersonal problem, (4) identifying effective strategies to deal with the problem, and (5) implementing the interventions. During this phase of treatment, the therapist gives continuous feedback about the use of strategies and observed changes in the patient's functioning. In addition, interpersonal style in the session is discussed as it relates to interactions that occur outside of the session.

General Techniques. Although some of the techniques vary depending on the problem area being addressed, several techniques are used across multiple problem areas. These general techniques will be discussed in more detail before outlining the techniques that are particular to the specific problem areas.

Linking affect with interpersonal events. An important technique in IPT–A is to link affect with interpersonal events. This is done both in the beginning of the session when reviewing symptoms, as well as during the remainder of the session. There are typically two types of patients: those who discuss events that have occurred without any discussion of affect and those who report feeling a certain way but who have no clear insight into the possible cause of their mood. For both types of patients, it is beneficial to link any interpersonal events with their mood. For instance, if a patient comes in and reports worsening sadness and irritability, it is important to link that change to any events that occurred in the previous week. It may be necessary to review the week in great detail in order to uncover what event(s) may have been responsible for the change in mood. Conversely, if a patient comes in and reports a fight with her mom, it is important for the therapist to ask the patient how this event made the patient feel and whether or not the event affected the patient's depressive symptoms. This serves to both educate the patient about the link between interpersonal events and one's mood, as well as make the patient more comfortable with and adept at identifying and communicating about his or her feelings.

Communication analysis. Communication analysis is a hallmark of the middle phase of treatment. Whenever the patient brings in an interpersonal event that occurred during the week, it is helpful to analyze the communication. The goals of communication analysis are to help the adolescent recognize the impact of his or her words on others, the feelings he or she conveys verbally and nonverbally, the feelings generated by the communication, and how modifying the communication might affect both the outcome of the interaction and the patient's associated feelings. This involves getting detailed information about the conversation such as: How did the discussion start? When did the conversation take place? Where did it happen? What exactly did the adolescent say? What did the person say back? How did that make the adolescent feel? What happened next? Is that the outcome the adolescent wanted?

Once the therapist has a clear understanding of the communication, it is useful to discuss how altering the communication at various points might have led to a different outcome, beginning with any ideas the adolescent may have about what she could have done or said differently. For instance, not approaching someone when they are busy doing something else might have led to a better conversation or starting the conversation calmly may have made the other person more willing to compromise. Once more adaptive communication strategies have been identified, it is helpful to role-play the communication using these techniques. When practicing these techniques in session or at home, it is best to start with a topic that is manageable and has a high likelihood of success. This will generate hope in the adolescents that these strategies can help facilitate change in their relationships.

Decision analysis. Once the patient and therapist have a better understanding of the interpersonal problem area, including any communication issues, it is useful to conduct a decision analysis to determine what the best course of action is. Decision analysis in IPT–A closely resembles problem-solving techniques used in other therapies, but is focused on addressing interpersonal problems. Decision analysis includes selecting an interpersonal situation that is causing the patient concern, encouraging the adolescent to generate possible solutions, evaluating the pros and cons of each solution, selecting a solution to try first, and role-playing the interaction needed for the chosen solution. The following session, the therapist and adolescent should review the interaction, examining possible reasons for its success or failure. Similar to communication analysis, the therapist should guide the adolescent to begin with a manageable problem and then progress to more difficult situations as treatment progresses.

Role-playing. Role-playing follows directly from both communication analysis and decision analysis. In both instances, it is helpful for the patient and therapist to role-play the interpersonal interaction for the patient to feel more comfortable using the skills or strategies in real life. In order for the role-play to be most useful, it is important not to simply talk about what it would be like to do something, but to actually act it out. Adolescents may be initially uncomfortable with the role-plays. To make the adolescent more comfortable, it is helpful if the role-play is structured so she knows what to expect. In addition, an adolescent may be more willing to role-play if she is allowed to choose which role to play first. During the role-play, it is important to have different outcomes to the interpersonal interaction, both positive and negative, so the patient can become more adept at handling different types of situations.

Problem-Area Specific Techniques. While the above techniques can be applied across multiple problem areas, the middle phase of treatment also uses techniques specific to the identified problem area. Goals and techniques of the middle phase are discussed below for each problem area.

Grief. According to IPT–A, it is important for the adolescent to discuss his or her loss in significant detail, including her relationship with the deceased. During this process, the therapist encourages the adolescent to identify and express feelings associated with the relationship and the loss. Over the course of the grief work, the adolescent is encouraged to create a more realistic memory of the deceased individual and of the relationship. In addition, the therapist helps the adolescent find a way to honor the memory of the deceased while engaging in other relationships. As treatment progresses, the therapist encourages the adolescent to develop new relationships or further develop established relationships to help replace the support and roles that were lost. This typically involves exploring the adolescent's fears about developing new relationships, as well as actively rehearsing skills needed to develop relationships or engage in new activities.

Interpersonal disputes. When an adolescent presents with an interpersonal dispute, it is important to clarify the dispute and any differences in expectations that may be contributing to the dispute. The therapist works with the adolescent and the other person if possible to modify communication patterns and expectations about the relationship. Because the conflict often involves a parent, the parent is invited into treatment to address the conflict. However, this problem area can be addressed with an adolescent alone when necessary. If a resolution seems impossible, the therapist works with the adolescent to develop strategies for coping with relationships that cannot be changed. It is helpful to point out that, although the relationship cannot be changed completely, simply decreasing the frequency of conflict can result in improved mood. In addition, when appropriate, the therapist encourages the adolescent to seek out other adaptive relationships that may address the adolescent's emotional needs more effectively.

Role transitions. Treatment of this problem area typically begins by identifying and defining the role transition. This is followed by a discussion about what the transition means to the adolescent, demands associated with this role change, and gains and losses associated with the transition. In addition, the therapist helps the adolescent learn other skills that are necessary to manage the new role. If the role transition in any way involves the adolescent's family, they should be involved in some of the treatment sessions whenever possible. If family members are having difficulty with the transition (for example, parents who are not allowing their child to socialize with peers), then treatment can address these difficulties.

Interpersonal deficits. In IPT–A, treatment of interpersonal deficits involves reviewing past significant relationships, with a focus on repetitive interpersonal problems that have occurred in these relationships. The therapist helps adolescents to recognize the relationship between their depression and their interpersonal problems. For instance, a therapist working with an adolescent who has difficulty interacting with peers might point out that the adolescent's social isolation leads to an increase in depressive symptoms, which in turn leads to an increase in social isolation. Following this, the therapist introduces new strategies for handling interpersonal relationships. These strategies are then practiced in role-plays. For example, a middle session might involve having the adolescent practice starting a conversation, asking questions to continue the conversation, asking a friend to do something, telling a parent how he or she feels, and so on. The adolescent would then be encouraged to try these strategies outside of the session and report on how it went the following week. Family members may be involved in treatment, particularly to help support the adolescent as she develops and practices these skills.

Single-parent families. Treatment for the single-parent family typically begins by helping adolescents recognize the relationship between their depressive symptoms and their family situation. For instance, if an adolescent's parents frequently argue about child support and place the adolescent in the middle, the therapist would help the adolescent identify the link between this difficult situation and his or her symptoms. In addition, the therapist helps the adolescent learn skills needed to communicate with family members to clarify expectations about the relationships, define roles in the new family structure, and solve problems about various issues that arise. Involvement of the parent(s) in treatment sessions can be very helpful.

Termination Phase

In many ways, the termination phase of IPT–A (sessions nine or ten through twelve) is similar to the termination process of other treatments. The objectives for this phase of treatment include (1) reviewing the adolescent's warning symptoms of depression, (2) reviewing strategies that were successful for improving relationships, (3) reviewing changes in the adolescent and/or family, (4) antici-pating potential future situations that may be difficult for the adolescent and reviewing strategies for managing those situations, (5) discussing feelings about ending treatment, (6) discussing skills or strategies that the adolescent can continue to work on once treatment ends, and (7) discussing the possibility of recurrence of depression and strategies for managing such a recurrence.

During the termination phase, it is important to review the course of the patient's depressive symptoms and how these symptoms have changed. It is also useful to highlight the association between depressive symptoms and the identi-fied interpersonal problem area(s) and the strategies that have proved most help-ful to the patient. Because depression is a recurrent illness, it is important to discuss the warning signs of depression for that particular adolescent and what he or she can do to address these symptoms if they return. It is also useful to meet with the patient's parent(s) during the termination phase to review progress made, warning signs for recurrence of symptoms, plans to manage future stressors, and further treatment options or referrals if these are needed.

Empirical Support for Treatment Efficacy

Dr. Mufson and her colleagues have conducted an open clinical trial, a controlled clinical trial, and an effectiveness study of IPT–A. In the open trial, fourteen twelve-to eighteen-year-olds who were referred to a hospital outpatient clinic due to depressive symptoms or who responded to an advertisement for the treatment of adolescent depression were treated with IPT–A. Adolescents experienced a signif-icant decrease in depressive symptoms and psychological distress following treatment, and none of the adolescents met criteria for a DSM-III-R depression diagnosis at the end of treatment. Adolescents also demonstrated significant improvement in their general functioning at home and at school (Mufson et al., 1994).

The next study was a randomized, controlled trial comparing IPT–A to clin-ical monitoring in a sample of clinic-referred depressed adolescents (Mufson, Weissman, Moreau, & Garfinkel, 1999). Adolescents with a diagnosis of major depressive disorder (MDD) who were not currently suicidal or psychotic and were not diagnosed with a chronic medical illness, bipolar I or II, conduct disorder, sub-stance abuse disorder, eating disorder, or obsessive-compulsive disorder were eli-gible to participate. Forty-eight adolescents were randomized to IPT–A or clinical monitoring. Treatment in both conditions was provided for twelve weeks.

Adolescents in IPT–A had weekly forty-five-minute therapy sessions with ad-ditional parent sessions during the initial and termination phase, and when needed in the middle phase of treatment. Adolescents in the clinical monitoring condition received once-monthly thirty-minute sessions with a therapist with the option for a second session each month. They were also seen bi-monthly by the independent evaluator. During the one week of the month without a face-to-face meeting, the therapists contacted the adolescent by phone to assess clinical status and safety.

For both the completer and the intent-to-treat samples, IPT–A patients reported significantly fewer depressive symptoms on the Hamilton Depression Rating Scale and the Beck Depression Inventory. Using standards for recovery set forth by the National Collaborative Study for the Treatment of Depression (Elkin et al., 1989), significantly more IPT–A patients met the recovery criteria for major depression as compared to control patients. IPT–A also resulted in improved over-all social functioning and improved functioning in the domains of peer and dating relationships (Social Adjustment Scale-Self Report Version). These improvements were significantly greater in the IPT–A condition than in the clinical monitoring condition. IPT–A patients also demonstrated better skills than control patients in certain areas of social problem-solving skills on the Social Problem-Solving Inventory–Revised.

A second research group also has conducted studies of IPT for depressed adolescents using a different modification of the adult manual tailored to the Puerto Rican culture. Rosselló and Bernal (1999) compared IPT versus cognitive-behavioral therapy (CBT) versus wait list for depressed teens. IPT and CBT resulted in a greater reduction in depressive symptoms than the wait list condition. IPT was significantly better than the wait list condition at increasing self-esteem and improving social adaptation.

Dr. Mufson and colleagues recently completed an effectiveness study of IPT–A in the school-based health clinics in the New York metropolitan area. This effectiveness study was a randomized controlled trial comparing the outcome of IPT–A to treatment as it is usually provided in the school-based health clinics. School-based health clinics were selected because they offer a community-based setting for providing care to adolescents. Preliminary analyses of the school data suggest that the results from the efficacy study are generalizable to a community-based setting.

Personal Experiences and Cases

We have treated and supervised the treatment of a large number of depressed adolescents using IPT–A in both research and clinical settings. Our clinical experience with IPT–A confirms the efficacy data discussed above. While the treatment does not work for everybody, many adolescents show large improvements in depressive symptoms and interpersonal functioning. In addition, the adolescents often report that they enjoyed the treatment and its focus on relationships.

The following is a fictional case to illustrate the different phases of IPT–A. Jessica is a fifteen-year-old girl who was referred for treatment by her pediatrician for possible depression. Jessica lives with her mother, stepfather, and brother. On evaluation, her depressive symptoms included sadness, irritability, initial insomnia (one and half to two hours to fall asleep), poor concentration, fatigue, poor self-esteem, and passive suicidal thoughts that consisted of periodic thoughts of wishing she were dead. Jessica's depressive symptoms began about nine months before assessment. Jessica's grades had deteriorated in the previous several months and she recently started cutting class to hang out with friends. About a year ago, Jessica started fighting more with her mother. Conflict centered around Jessica wanting to spend more time with friends. Based on a clinical evaluation, Jessica was diagnosed with a major depressive episode and was referred for IPT–A.

Initial phase of IPT–A: The first session of IPT–A began with the therapist meeting with Jessica alone to confirm the depression diagnosis using the Hamilton Rating Scale for Depression. The therapist then met with Jessica's mother, Mrs. Martin, alone to get her view of Jessica's symptoms and interpersonal relationships. Next, the therapist met with Jessica and Mrs. Martin together to educate them about Jessica's symptoms of depression and put the depression in the context of a medical illness that could be treated. In addition, the therapist assigned Jessica the limited sick role, with a focus on encouraging Jessica to stay in school during the day despite her difficulty concentrating and her desire to socialize with peers. The therapist had Mrs. Martin sign a release to allow the therapist to talk to school personnel about Jessica's attendance and academic difficulties. The session ended by the therapist explaining the theory and structure of IPT–A.

The remainder of the initial phase of treatment was spent conducting the interpersonal inventory. Jessica identified a number of people who were important to her including her mother, her stepfather, her younger brother, two close girl friends, and her grandmother, who lived nearby. When discussing her mother, Jessica described their relationship as very conflictual of late. In particular, she stated that she and her mother seemed to fight about everything because, according to Jessica, Mrs. Martin did not want her to grow up. The fights focused on Jessica spending time with friends, wanting to go out on the weekends, and Jessica spending too much time on the phone. Since the depression began, Jessica described herself as being increasingly irritable with her mother and stated that she spent more time in her room in order to avoid arguing with her mother.

During the rest of the interpersonal inventory, Jessica reported that her stepfather and grandmother frequently took her mother's side in arguments, leading Jessica to feel alone and unsupported in her family. Since Jessica became depressed, she reported being increasingly annoyed with her brother, with increased conflict over little things, such as watching television. The review of her peer relationships revealed that although Jessica continued to spend time with peers in school, she had become more withdrawn and quiet when she was with them. This, combined with her mother's strictness, led to increased social isolation in the past several months.

After the interpersonal inventory, the therapist made a treatment contract with Jessica that her primary problem area seemed to be a role dispute with her mother, with a secondary problem area of a role transition, given that the conflict with her mother primarily focused on Jessica's transition to adolescence and her increasing desire for autonomy. The therapist and Jessica discussed how Jessica's depression increased her irritability with her mom, leading to an increase in conflict. The increase in conflict, in turn, led to an increase in Jessica's depression, which resulted in her becoming more withdrawn. This withdrawal prevented Jessica from getting the support she needs from peers and other family members. The therapist outlined the goals of the middle phase of treatment, including helping Jessica communicate better with her mother and getting more support from her friends and other family members.

Middle phase of IPT–A. During the middle phase of treatment, the therapist worked with Jessica to get a better understanding of her conflict with her mother. This involved analyzing in detail several arguments that Jessica had with her mother during the middle phase. Communication analysis focused on examining how and what Jessica communicated to her mother and how the communications made Jessica feel. Through this analysis, it became apparent that Jessica would explode at her mother when her mother restricted her social interactions. During these arguments, Jessica would typically say something she regretted and end up feeling sad and angry. The therapist and Jessica discussed how Jessica could abstain from talking to her mother when angry and instead arrange a time later when she could calmly discuss her feelings. They also discussed how Jessica might express to her mother that she understood her mother's reasons for being strict while expressing how this strictness made Jessica feel. The therapist and Jessica then role-played these communication techniques. Jessica was asked to try this at home, but came back stating that it ended in an argument, with Jessica running to her room and slamming her door.

To facilitate improved communication with her mother, the therapist invited Mrs. Martin to come in for a collateral session. The session began with the therapist meeting with Mrs. Martin alone to place Jessica's desire to spend time with peers in the context of normal adolescence. Following this, the therapist met with Jessica and Mrs. Martin together, during which Jessica practiced communicating with her mother about wanting to spend more time with friends. During this conversation, Jessica was able to express to her mother that she often felt left out because she was not able to go out like her friends. Unlike in the past, when this type of discussion quickly escalated into an argument, Jessica and Mrs. Martin were able to discuss this calmly. In addition, Mrs. Martin was able to express some of her concerns about what might happen to Jessica if she were allowed to go out. Jessica began to understand her mother's point of view and they were able to compromise that Jessica could spend time with her friends on the weekends, during the day.

During this phase of treatment, the therapist also worked with Jessica to help her reach out more to her friends and grandmother who, in the past, were a source of support for Jessica. This included having Jessica talk to her grandmother about her depression and some of the difficulties she was having with her mother. Although Jessica's grandmother generally agreed with Mrs. Martin, she was able to see Jessica's point of view, which helped Jessica feel less isolated from her family. As these changes in Jessica's relationships occurred, her depressive symptoms improved. The therapist highlighted the link between Jessica's improved relationships and improved mood.

Termination phase of IPT–A. During the termination phase, the therapist reviewed with Jessica the strategies that had been most effective in dealing with her mother, including expressing her feelings in a calm way, showing Mrs. Martin that she understood her perspective, and solving problems with her mother about possible compromises to their disagreements. In addition, the therapist again highlighted for Jessica that, as she was able to talk more with her friends and grandmother about how she was feeling, she started to feel better. This led to a discussion of the strategies that Jessica could continue to use once treatment ended, both with her mother and with other people in her life. Jessica and the therapist also reviewed Jessica's warning symptoms of depression so that Jessica would be able to identify a relapse if it were to occur and to seek help if needed. Lastly, they discussed Jessica's feelings about ending treatment and evaluated the need for further treatment.

Future Directions

In the research realm, we are currently conducting a small, pilot, randomized trial comparing a group model of IPT–A (IPT–AG) to individual IPT–A. The feasibility and acceptability of IPT–AG has been tested in two open trials. It appears that, based on adolescent reports, our clinical impressions, and limited data, adolescents find IPT–AG acceptable and helpful. The current investigation will provide preliminary efficacy data for the group format. In addition, we are conducting a small, open trial of a modified version of group IPT, Interpersonal Therapy–Adolescent Skills Training (IPT–AST), as an indicated prevention intervention in the schools. IPT–AST follows the format of IPT–AG, but focuses more on psycho-education and skill-building that can be applied to multiple relationships, rather than a particular problem area. Soon, we hope to pursue a controlled trial comparing IPT–A to medication, as well as a follow-up study to establish whether IPT–A has long-term effects on depression and interpersonal functioning, particularly given the high rates of recurrence in adolescents. This will indicate whether continuation or maintenance IPT–A is needed to bolster the long-term effects.

◆ ◆ ◆

In the clinical realm, we continue to treat depressed adolescents with IPT–A and to train clinicians in this treatment. We believe that IPT–A is a viable alternative to cognitive behavior therapy and medication for the treatment of adolescent depression, and may be particularly appropriate for adolescents who present with interpersonal problems.

References

Aseltine, R. (1996). Pathways linking parental divorce with adolescent depression. *Journal of Health & Social Behavior, 37,* 133–148.

Clark, D., Pynoos, R., & Goebel, A. (1994). Mechanisms and processes of adolescent bereavement. In R. Haggerty (Ed.), *Stress, risk, and resilience in children and adolescents: Processes, mechanisms, and interventions* (pp. 100–145). Cambridge, UK: Cambridge University Press.

Cornwell, G., Eggebeen, D., & Meschke, L. (1996). The changing family context of early adolescence. *Journal of Early Adolescence, 16,* 141–488.

Elkin, I., Shea, M. T., Watkins, J. T., Imber, S. D., Sotsky, S. M., Collins, J. F., et al. (1989). National Institute of Mental Health Treatment of Depression Collaborative Research Program: General effectiveness of treatments. *Archives of General Psychiatry, 46,* 971–983.

Hammen, C. (1999). The emergence of an interpersonal approach to depression. In T. Joiner & J. Coyne (Eds.), *The interactional nature of depression: Advances in interpersonal approaches* (pp. 22–36). Washington, DC: American Psychological Association.

Joiner, T., Coyne, J., & Blalock, J. (1999). On the interpersonal nature of depression: Overview and synthesis. In T. Joiner & J. Coyne (Eds.), *The interactional nature of depression: Advances in interpersonal approaches* (pp. 3–20). Washington, DC: American Psychological Association.

Kiesler, D. (1991). Interpersonal methods of assessment and diagnosis. In C. R. Snyder & D. R. Forsyth (Eds.), *Handbook of social and clinical psychology: The health perspective* (pp. 438–468). Elmsford, NY: Pergamon Press.

Klerman, G. L., Weissman, M. M., Rounsaville, B. J., & Chevron, E. S. (1984). *Interpersonal Psychotherapy of Depression.* New York: Basic Books.

Lewinsohn, P. M., Roberts, R. E., Seeley, J. R., Rohde, P., Gotlib, I. H., & Hops, H. (1994). Adolescent psychopathology: II. Psychosocial risk factors for depression. *Journal of Abnormal Psychology, 103,* 302–315.

Mufson, L., Moreau, D., Weissman, M. M., & Klerman, G. L. (1993). *Interpersonal psychother-apy for depressed adolescents.* New York: Guilford Press.

Mufson, L., Moreau, D., Weissman, M. M., Wickramaratne, P., Martin J., & Samoilov, A. (1994). The modification of interpersonal psychotherapy with depressed adolescents IPT–A: Phase I and Phase 11 studies. *Journal of the American Academy of Child and Adolescent Psychiatry, 33,* 695–705.

Mufson, L., Weissman, M. M., Moreau, D., & Garfinkel, R. (1999). Efficacy of interpersonal psychotherapy for depressed adolescents. *Archives of General Psychiatry, 56,* 573–579.

Puig-Antich, J., Kaufman, J., Ryan, N. D., Williamson, D. E., Dahl, R. E., Lukens, E. (1993). The psychosocial functioning and family environment of depressed adolescents. *Journal of the American Academy of Child and Adolescent Psychiatry, 32,* 244–253.

Rosselló, J., & Bernal, G. (1999). The efficacy of cognitive-behavioral and international treat-ments depression in Puerto Rican adolescents. *Journal of Consulting and Clinical Psychology, 67*(5), 734–745.

Ryan, N. D., Puig-Antich, J., Ambrosini, P., Rabinovich, H., Robinson, D., Nelson, B., et al. (1987). The clinical picture of major depression in children and adolescents. *Archives of General Psychiatry, 44,* 854–861.

Sheeber, L., Hops, H., Alpert, A., Davis, B., & Andrews, J. (1997). Family support and con-flict: Prospective relations to adolescent depression. *Journal of Abnormal Child Psychology, 25,* 333–344.

Spruijt, E., & de Goede, M. (1997). Transitions in family structure and adolescent well-being. *Adolescence, 32,* 898–911.

Sullivan, H. S. (1953). *The interpersonal theory of psychiatry.* New York: W.W. Norton.

Weissman, M. M., Markowitz, J. C., & Klerman, G. L. (2000). *Comprehensive guide to interper-sonal psychotherapy.* New York: Basic Books.

Weissman, M. M., Prusoff, B. A., DiMascio, A., Neu, C., Goklaney, M., & Klerman, G. L. (1979). The efficacy of drug and psychotherapy in the treatment of acute depressive episodes. *American Journal of Psychiatry, 136,* 555–558.

CHAPTER TWENTY-FOUR

RELAPSE PREVENTION FOR SUBSTANCE USE DISORDERS: ADAPTING THE ADULT-BASED PARADIGM FOR YOUTH

John F. Kelly, Ph.D., and Stephen W. Tracy, M.A.

Since its inception in the late 1970s and early 1980s, the relapse prevention (RP) paradigm has gained widespread acceptance and been applied broadly across many aspects of treatment for various psychopathologic conditions. (See Wilson, 1992.) The original conceptual frameworks grew out of, and had their strongest influence in, the treatment of substance use and other addictive disorders, which often are characterized as chronically relapsing conditions (SAMHSA, 2002). For this reason, the focus in the current chapter will be within this domain. Although several psychobiological and psychological models have been proposed, few have gained widespread acceptance. (For a review, see Connors, Maisto, & Donnovan, 1996.) We begin the current chapter by reviewing the two most prominent RP models and examining how well such models, or aspects of them, apply to youth. Specifically, we highlight life-stage developmental differences between youth and adults and how such differences affect the appropriateness of these paradigms for understanding and treating youth substance-related problems. Next, we review the empirical support for this approach with youth, and subsequently

This work was supported in part by the Department of Veterans Affairs Quality Enhancement Research Initiative, Mental Health Strategic Health Care Group, and Health Services Research and Development Service. The views expressed are those of the authors and do not necessarily represent the views of the Department of Veterans Affairs.

present a case study of RP principles and practices in action. In the final section, we make recommendations for future directions.

Each year, approximately 1.6 million individuals in the United States receive substance use disorders (SUD) treatment, about 140,000 of whom are adolescents (SAMHSA, 2001). However, despite intensive treatment efforts, relapse rates are high and relapse occurs quickly following the cessation of treatment (Brown et al., 1989; Hunt et al., 1971). One reason for the rapid assimilation of the RP paradigm is its emphasis on the essential difficulty of the addictive behavior change process: not *initial* change, but rather the *maintenance* of initial change; a stark phenomenon humorously exemplified by a quote attributed to author Mark Twain, "Quitting smoking is easy—I've done it hundreds of times."

The term "relapse prevention" is used broadly to describe a variety of practices intended to "prevent relapse." However, RP, as originally proposed by Marlatt and Gordon (1985), consists of a specific and elaborate approach to addictive behavior change that is grounded in social learning theory. It is not a school of "therapy," on its own, but rather a conceptual framework that provides a detailed explication of a specific stage in the addictive-behavior change process, upon which cognitive and behavioral therapeutic strategies may be brought to bear.

At about the same time in the early 1980s Gorski and Miller (1982) published a text entitled *Staying Sober: A Guide for Relapse Prevention* that described a different conceptualization and approach to RP. Gorski and Miller's model was initially derived more atheoretically by using inductive methods and emphasizes a more dynamic process conceptualization of relapse. It also has intuitive appeal and has gained widespread acceptance in the treatment community.

Two Prominent RP Models

Marlatt and Gordon

The model proposed by Marlatt and Gordon (1985) draws heavily on constructs derived from social learning theory (SLT) (Bandura, 1977a). Indeed, some have viewed this RP model as a cogent summary of SLT as applied to alcohol and other drug-related problems (Abrams & Niaura, 1987). In this context, RP is defined as "a self-management program designed to enhance the maintenance stage of the habit-change process." The habit-change process itself can be divided along the lines of the stages of change as proposed by Prochaska and DiClemente (1982): precontemplation, contemplation, determination/preparation, action, maintenance, and relapse. An individual in the *precontemplation stage* is unaware of a problem themselves, although others are concerned about their behavior; an individual in the *contemplation stage* begins to recognize the possible existence of a problem with subsequent ambivalence. The *determination stage* is characterized by a conviction for the need to change followed by a commitment to engage in action. During the *action stage,* the strategies or plans are implemented. The *maintenance stage* is characterized by continued recognition that the fluctuating nature of motivation involves constant vigilance. The *relapse stage* is seen as a part of the process of change and will occur until sufficient experience and learning has taken place for an individual to remain in the maintenance stage and to exit the cycle.

Within the Marlatt and Gordon RP framework, an important distinction is made regarding the nature of the resumption of the target behavior. Often in the addiction field, both novice and experienced clinicians and researchers view a relapse as a return to substance use of any kind. However, in this RP conceptualization a distinction is made between a lapse and a relapse: a *lapse* is considered an initial, short-lived, period of substance use, which may or may not deteriorate into a more prolonged/intensive episode, or *relapse*, depending on individual cognitive interpretations and behavioral responses.

Related to this distinction, and deemed of critical importance, is whether individuals attempting to change addictive behaviors view the maintenance phase of change as one of gradual improvement or of gradual decline. For example, if one holds a view of gradual decline, then an individual is likely to view treatment effects as initially strong with the probability of relapse increasing as time since treatment increases. If, on the other hand, one holds a view of gradual improvement, the probability of relapse would be high early on as the individual engages in a series of "learning trials" in which new coping strategies are practiced and improved. This latter view appears more in keeping with the research data, which has shown that approximately two-thirds of treated individuals, across a broad range of addictive substances, return to at least some use within the first ninety days post-treatment, most within the first month (Hunt, Barnett & Branch, 1971).

Relapse following an initial change attempt appear to be preceded by certain common antecedents. Based on a study involving 311 initial relapse episodes described by adults attempting to change a range of addictive or compulsive behaviors (such as alcohol use, smoking, heroin use, gambling, or overeating), it was found that nearly three-quarters of the episodes could be attributed to three broad high-risk domains defined as: interpersonal conflict (16% of relapses; for example, arguments with significant others or employers), negative emotional states (35% of relapses; for example, bored, angry, depressed, anxious), and social pressure (20% of relapses; for example, direct or indirect social pressure to return to substance use; Cummings, Gordon, & Marlatt, 1980). However, subsequent research suggests types of high-risk relapse situations may not generalize across substances, gender, or other variables such as age, but rather, be moderated by a variety of factors (Peters & Schonfeld,1993; Annis, 1990).

Three important aspects of Marlatt and Gordon's conceptualization are that errors or lapses are very likely early following a change attempt; that relapses are most often preceded by intra-personal factors; and, that an error or lapse need not become a disaster or full-blown relapse.

Gorski and Miller

In the late 1970s, through his work with chronic alcohol-dependent relapsers, addictions counselor Terry Gorski formulated an approach to relapse prevention known as "relapse prevention planning" (Gorski & Miller, 1982). Through detailed observations and interviews with 118 alcohol-dependent individuals, he began to recognize certain commonalities across cases. Specifically, he observed a dynamic, process-oriented deterioration culminating finally in a return to substance use. One thing noted by Gorski was that these individuals did not lack motivation for change; they did not lack the willingness to obtain and access counseling, treatment, or self-help groups such as Alcoholics Anonymous meetings, but yet returned to use. Gorski, in collaboration with Merlene Miller, published *Staying Sober: A Guide for Relapse Prevention* in 1986, which explicated in more detail this approach to RP. One important difference between this model and Marlatt and Gordon's paradigm is that this model is derived from work with patients with substance use disorders (SUDs) only, while Marlatt and Gordon's model is influenced by observations made with a variety of habit disorders, including compulsive eating, gambling, and smoking. This may be one reason why Gorski's model more strongly emphasizes neurophysiological and biobehavioral sequelae, because these consequences were more likely apparent among the chronic alcohol and drug users influencing Gorski's conceptualization than among individuals with gambling addictions or eating disorders that were included in Marlatt's conceptualization.

The elaborate, richly conceptual, and empirically based model espoused by Marlatt and Gordon, is in contrast to the largely atheoretically derived model of Gorski and Miller's, although the latter model has become more strongly allied with a disease-model framework. Nevertheless, the model itself is clearly a holistic one, emphasizing biological, psychological, and social factors and related to developmental models of recovery (Brown, 1985). Such models assume successful completion of tasks associated with one stage before proceeding to the next. (For example, one needs to recognize the existence of a SUD problem and become medically stabilized before one can begin the tasks associated with early recovery.)

Putative Mechanisms of Efficacy

Marlatt and Gordon

A critical assumption of Marlatt and Gordon's model is that an individual has made a voluntary choice to abstain from (or change) addictive behavior. Given this degree of motivational readiness, an individual is purported to increase in confidence or "self-efficacy" to remain abstinent the longer that goal is achieved, until a high-risk relapse situation is encountered. These "high risk" situations are described as any situation that "poses a threat to an individual's sense of control and increases the risk of potential relapse."

According to Marlatt and Gordon's model, if, in encountering a high-risk situation an individual is able to cope effectively with it (such as discuss and resolve disagreement with an employer) a sense of mastery or control begins to grow, leading to increased confidence or self-efficacy (Bandura, 1977b) and a lower likelihood of relapse. If, on the other hand, an individual encountering a high-risk situation feels unable to cope, there will be a consequent decrease in perceived confidence or self-efficacy, and an increased probability of an initial lapse. The likelihood of an initial lapse is further increased if, on entering a high-risk situation without an adequate coping repertoire (or is unable to use an adaptive coping response due to fear or anxiety), the same individual also holds positive outcome expectancies about the effects of the substance ("I know a drink or two will help me out here") or target behavior he is trying to avoid.

According to this RP theory, whether or not an initial lapse progresses into a full-blown relapse will depend on an individuals' beliefs about its cause, and how that individual reacts to it. This notion is referred to as the abstinence violation effect (AVE). If, following a period of abstinence, there is a resumption of the old behavior, an individual may continue in the behavior and resurrect the old self-image in, "This just proves I am an alcoholic so what's the use?" Second, a lapse can become a relapse by attributing it to an internal, personal, stable, negative quality ("This just goes to show how weak I really am") rather than viewing it as an opportunity to cope with a difficult situation.

Gorski and Miller

From the Gorski and Miller perspective, the purported reason for relapse is due to a combination of mistaken beliefs about the recovery and relapse process coupled with a lack of awareness and inability to manage the abstinence-based symptoms associated with post-acute withdrawal (PAW).

PAW is a syndrome with a neurobiological basis, resulting from the chronic use of alcohol or other drugs (Gorski, 1979). Following acute withdrawal and detoxification, these PAW symptoms can last many months but are proposed to reach peak intensity within the first six months following initiation of abstinence, with residual effects lasting possibly for years, depending on the nature of the central nervous system (CNS) damage. PAW primarily affects higher level cognitive functioning, such as memory and abstract reasoning, but is also linked to heightened stress sensitivity. The presence of such symptoms is thought to compromise adaptive decision making, leading to inadequate coping efforts. This, in turn, leads to negative emotional consequences and eventually to resumption of substance use. The severity of the PAW an individual experiences is purported to be related to the extent of CNS damage incurred as a result of use and the degree of psychosocial stress experienced in recovery.

There are six major types of PAW symptoms within this RP framework: inability to think clearly, memory problems, emotional overreactions or numbness, sleep disturbances, physical coordination problems, and stress sensitivity. The topography of the PAW syndrome falls into one of four possible sub-typed categories: regenerative PAW (fairly steady improvement with abstinence), degenerative PAW (fairly steady decline with abstinence), stable PAW (symptoms have only minor fluctuation, but remain largely the same), and intermittent PAW (symptoms come and go, but gradually decline with abstinence). The successful management of these PAW symptoms, thus, is a critical aspect of this RP model. PAW is purported to be controlled by the patient's learning of more adaptive ways of managing stress.

Another major component of this approach to RP is dispelling mistaken beliefs about relapse, particularly with regard to the dynamic nature of the relapse process itself and associated relapse warning signs. In Gorski's clinical observations and interviewing he was able to derive a set of thirty-seven relapse warning signs from 118 case histories he had examined in the early 1970s. These warnings signs were obtained from detailed interviews with patients regarding the temporal sequence of events that led to a resumption of use. He then further divided these thirty-seven signs to occur along developmental stages involving eleven phases (Gorski & Miller, 1986, pp. 139–156). These are broadly defined as a progression from internal (high stress sensitivity; sleep, thought, and memory problems), through external dysfunction (return of denial, avoidance and defensiveness, crisis building), and finally, loss of control (option reduction, depression, loss of behavioral control, return to active alcohol or other drug use).

Developmental Influences

Both Marlatt and Gordon's and Gorski and Millers' RP conceptualizations are derived from observations with adults. Thus, the question arises as to whether, and in what ways, youths differ from adults in the expression of alcohol and other drug-related problems, and the implications that any such differences may have for the applicability of adult-based conceptualizations in preventing relapse among youth.

The treatment of adolescents as miniature adults has been viewed as not acceptable unless empirical validation reveals it justifiable to do so (for example, Deas, Riggs et al., 2000). However, despite comprising a significant proportion of those treated annually for SUDs in the United States (10–12%) youth have rarely been included in field trials investigating these disorders. In the DSM–III field trials, for example, there were no participants younger than age eighteen included, and only one in seven research sites involved in the DSM-IV field trials included any data pertaining to adolescents (Cottler, Schuckit, Helzer, Crowley, Woody, Nathan, et al., 1995).

Initial use and experimentation with substances most often begins during teenage years, with most adults with SUDs reporting onset of use beginning before age fifteen (Robins & Przybeck, 1985). For some, experimental substance use leads to rapid escalation resulting in recurrent psychological, physical, legal, academic, and interpersonal/familial consequences sufficient to require specific treatment. Moreover, substance misuse in youth tends to cluster with conduct disordered and delinquent behavior problems, and it is these individuals who consume much of the resources of the youth service system. A study by Aarons and colleagues (2001) examined the prevalence of SUDs among 12,662 adolescents who received treatment services in various public sectors in San Diego county, California. They found lifetime rates of 82.6% in alcohol and other drug services, 62.1% in juvenile justice, 40.8% in mental health, 23.6% in seriously emotionally disturbed, and 19.2% in child welfare with rates significantly higher among older youths and males. Thus, intervention efforts may be critical to improve concurrent functioning. In addition, early intervention may also prevent or significantly alter the trajectory of future problematic alcohol and other drug use and poor mental health outcomes shown to occur in adulthood (Bates & Labouvie, 1997; Brook, Brook, Zhang, Cohen, & Whiteman, 2002).

Adolescents in treatment for substance-related problems have been shown to differ from adults in several ways. Adolescence is a time of rapidly occurring biological, cognitive, and social change with large maturation differences observable across short age spans. This social-cognitive heterogeneity makes any broad conceptualization for approaching "youth treatment" difficult. The content and process of intervention may need to vary substantially within the same treatment program and be, ideally, tailored to the specific and variable needs of individual children. Adults, in contrast, although they also certainly vary in maturity levels, tend to be more disorder-homogeneous, making a uniform approach more feasible.

In terms of substance use topography, youth have been shown to differ along dimensions of frequency and severity of dependence, number of substances used,

TABLE 24.1.   TREATED ADOLESCENTS VERSUS TREATED ADULTS: LIFE-STAGE DIFFERENCES.

Comparison Dimension	Adolescents (More Heterogeneous)	Adults (More Homogeneous)
Substance use topography	Less frequent Concurrent use of multiple (3–4) substances Shorter history	More frequent Heavier use of primarily one or maybe two substances Longer history
Addiction severity	Less severe (less withdrawal/ secondary medical complications)	More severe (more withdrawal/secondary medical complications)
Nature of SUDs	Correlational or consequential nature of SUD (part of a "problem behavior syndrome")	Primary or causative
Motivation for change	Rarely enter treatment voluntarily (pre-contemplators) or recognize problem or extent of problem	More often enter treatment voluntarily (contemplators) and have greater recognition of substance-related problems
Autonomy	Dependent on parents/family Limited independent resources	Independent—free to make independent decisions More resources available
Psychiatric comorbidity	Externalizing disorders more common and clinically relevant	Internalizing disorders more common and clinically relevant
Twelve-step self-help groups	Few age-specific groups or participants	Adults comprise the mainstay of groups

types of substances used, and types of consequences encountered. The vast majority of adolescents tend to use multiple substances (Pollock & Martin, 1999; Brown, Vik, & Creamer, 1989) and have a significantly shorter duration of substance use than do adults (Brown, 1993). Brown and associates (1990) found that teens entering treatment had used alcohol regularly for only three years and harder drugs for only one to two years, on average. Compared to adults, youths have been found to use significantly less frequently and be less prone to alcoholic blackouts. However, they have been found to consume alcohol at the same intensity on average as some adult samples (Deas et al., 2000). Furthermore, although adolescent substance involvement has been associated with multiple psychological, social, and physical consequences, teens entering treatment generally have far fewer and less intense medical complications and dependence or withdrawal symptoms compared to adults (Brown et al., 1990; Pollock & Martin, 1999). Thus, the degree to which youths experience PAW symptoms would be less. Youths also seem not to suffer from the degree of psychological dependence observed among adults and may be less likely to experience symptoms related to cognitive preoccupation (such as obsessively ruminating about and planning substance use) or feel compelled to engage in prolonged substance use so as to suffer significant interference with daily activities (Deas et al., 2000).

One of the criticisms of adult-model approaches for use with adolescents is the singular emphasis on the primary causative role of the substance(s) of misuse in the clinical presentation, which may be more true of adults. This approach may ignore the markedly heterogeneous nature of adolescents with SUDs who present (or are presented) for treatment. As Jessor and Jessor (1977) and Newcomb and Bentler (1989) have posited, substance misuse in adolescence is correlated with, and constitutes only one part of a more intricate pattern of problem behavior which includes delinquency, precocious sexual behavior, deviant attitudes, and school dropout. Indeed, studies have revealed that adolescents in treatment for SUDs also meet criteria for other DSM-IV Axis I syndromes such as conduct disorder and attention-deficit/hyperactivity disorder (ADHD) (Bukstein, Glancy, & Kaminer, 1992; Crowley & Riggs, 1995), which are seldom observed among adults treated for SUDs.

Another critical consideration is related to the issue of legal status, independent resources, and decision making. Adolescents, unlike adults, are under the legal jurisdiction of parents until age eighteen, and depend on parents for resources fundamental to existence, including food, shelter, money and transportation. This developmental difference has a fundamental impact on the nature and temporal topography of both substance use and treatment.

A further difference between youths and adults treated for SUDs is related to addiction-focused self-help groups such as Alcoholics Anonymous (AA). Involvement in such groups appear beneficial for many adults (Project MATCH Research Group, 1997; 1998; Ouimette, Finney, & Moos, 1997; Miller, Ninonuevo et al., 1997; Morgenstern, Labouvie et al., 1997). However, even if adolescents are motivated to attend twelve-step groups, the predominantly adult composition of most groups may hinder identification and present a barrier to continued attendance and affiliation. Demographic data from AA's latest triennial survey (Alcoholics Anonymous Membership Survey, 1998), revealed the average age of membership to be forty-five years old, with only 2% under age twenty-one. Age similarity may be particularly important for youth due to the influence of variables tied to their developmental status (Deas et al., 2000). Youths who attend meetings may have lower perceived similarity to individual participants (Vik, Grizzle, & Brown, 1992) and difficulty identifying with issues central (such as severity of substance dependence) and peripheral (such as employment concerns or marital relations) to recovery. Consequently, sharing of specific experiences by older members may not be perceived by youth as helpful or relevant in dealing with their own life-stage recovery issues. Such differences may diminish therapeutic gains associated with youth twelve-step group attendance. (See Kelly et al., 2000; 2002.)

A further important developmental difference is the influence of the peer group during adolescence and the predominantly social precipitants of relapse for youth. Whereas negative affective states and interpersonal conflict may be the most often reported antecedents in adult relapse, the social environment is likely to be the principal determinant of relapse among youth and should be a critical component of any conceptualization of the youth relapse process. Consequently, adolescents may differ in the types of skills needed to avoid relapse.

Perhaps the most crucial difference between adolescents and adults in treatment for SUDs is that adolescents differ from adults in their motivation to cease alcohol or drug use because they rarely enter treatment due to an intrinsic desire to stop abusing substances. Instead, their motivation could be conceived as being more "extrinsic" in that they are usually coerced into treatment, to a lesser or greater degree, because of a variety of school, legal, or familial/interpersonal problems (Brown et al., 1989). One large-scale, randomized, controlled study with approximately 600 youths comparing a number of different outpatient intervention approaches (Dennis et al., 2000) found 80% of the adolescent sample did not perceive themselves as having an alcohol or other drug problem.

A critical assumption of both of the RP models explicated herein is the notion of an intrinsic desire to cease (or reduce) substance use. Consequently, RP approaches that focus on the "maintenance" stage of the recovery process may not be a good fit for adolescents, the majority of whom may not believe they have a problem in the first place (Dennis et al., 2000). It is more appropriate to view youth from a precontemplation or contemplation stage, rather than assuming that youth are ready and willing to change, but merely lack the skills.

Studies examining coping skills among youths stress the importance of avoiding high-risk social situations and using abstinent-specific social supports in terms of maintaining abstinence. However, it is important to realize that, although coping repertoires have been found to be predictive of substance use outcomes among youth, coping skills may be outweighed by motivational factors and commitment to change. These differences highlight the importance of interventions that are more explicitly and intently focused on both motivational and social components in attempting to prevent a return to substance use among youth. From a theoretical standpoint, it may be that self-regulation theory (the management of behavior based on the cognitive appraisal of anticipated, concurrent, or past events) (Kanfer & Gaelick, 1986) or its derivative, motivational enhancement theory (Miller & Rollnick, 1991) may be an important framework for explaining youth recovery/relapse, but this theory awaits more explicit testing.

Putative Targets of Treatment

Marlatt and Gordon

With regard to the Marlatt and Gordon RP paradigm, three broad areas of intervention arise. The first involves skills training in cognitive and behavioral strategies to deal with high-risk situations. The second involves cognitive reframing to help the individual understand the nature of the habit-change process (that is, to view it more as a learning process). In addition, coping imagery is used to deal with urges and warning signs and cognitively reframe reactions to lapses. Thus, former personally experienced or future anticipated high-risk situations are pictured while mentally rehearsing appropriate coping strategies to deal effectively with the threat of the situation. Furthermore, in a similar way, mental rehearsing is carried out in vitro and alternative more adaptive ways of viewing the event are rehearsed. The third target of intervention involves a broader focus on lifestyle intervention to increase individuals' general coping capacity and help reduce the frequency and intensity of urges or cravings.

In clinical practice, training in coping skills forms the mainstay of relapse prevention work. This includes identifying and coping with high-risk situations, coping with urges and cravings, implementing damage control procedures during a lapse, staying engaged in treatment even after relapses, and learning lifestyle balance (Parks & Marlatt, 1999).

Marlatt and Gordons' model was based on retrospective analysis of antecedent events. However, empirical evidence in adults has shown that certain elements of this model appear to be related to relapse when measured prospectively. A study conducted as part of the Relapse Replication and Extension Project (RREP) revealed that coping skills and belief in the disease model were the most robust predictors of relapse (Miller et al., 1996). However, this was based on the definition of a relapse as use after only a four-day period of abstinence. This is very different to the Gorski model described next, which describes a protracted dynamic trajectory characterized by various warning signs before a final return to substance use occurs.

Gorski and Miller

Gorski and Miller's clinical approach is to educate patients about the nature of PAW, help them to identify sources of stress, and develop skills in decision making and problem solving. In addition, proper diet, exercise, regular habits, relaxation training, and positive attitudes all play important parts in controlling PAW. This is similar to Marlatt and Gordon's model emphasizing lifestyle change and balance.

Gorski and Miller describe a specific nine-step approach to counteract the relapse process, referred to as "relapse prevention planning." The stages are: stabilization (acute withdrawal), self-assessment, relapse education, warning sign identification, warning sign management, inventory training, reviewing the recovery program, involving significant others, and follow-up/updating RP plan. These nine steps are designed to be implemented to ensure greater awareness and active management of relapse warning signs and PAW symptoms.

It may be that the two models apply to different aspects of the relapse process. The Marlatt and Gordon model appears to us to represent more of a short-term explication of the relapse process, whereas the Gorski and Miller model may be a better fit later in explaining relapse following longer periods of abstinence and prolonged period of adaptive behavior change.

The approaches of both Marlatt and Gordon and Gorski and Miller highlight the importance of a reconceptualization of the relapse process. First, relapse is a *process* and is more likely to occur early following the cessation of an intervention. Thus, (re)education is a critical component in clinical RP activity. Gorski and Miller emphasize targeting mistaken beliefs about the relapse process as an important component of their clinical approach. The Marlatt and Gordon RP approach would emphasize the difference between a lapse and relapse and use education and cognitive reframing to become aware of and understand the potential harm emanating from an individual's reaction to initial lapses. The Marlatt and Gordon approach attempts to increase the repertoire of coping skills and/or improve those coping skills already possessed.

Empirical Support and Applicability of Adult-Based RP Models with Youths

Given the observed developmental differences between youths and adults mentioned above, we now examine the applicability of these RP models for youth. First, we focus on the research specific to Marlatt and Gordon's RP model and related constructs, and then we briefly examine the appropriateness of Gorski and Miller's model for use with youth.

Marlatt and Gordon

Motivation

The most critical consideration in applying this RP model to youth is the discrepancy between youth and adults in their motivation or readiness to change their substance use behavior. Although in reference to adults, Marlatt and Gordon emphasize this critical construct: "An important constraint of the model is that it applies only to those cases in which the person has made a voluntary choice or decision to change; the implications of the theory for enforced or involuntary abstinence have yet to be determined" (Marlatt & Gordon, 1985, pg. 37). With as many as 80% of adolescents in treatment for a diagnosed SUD not perceiving themselves as having a problem with alcohol or drug use, it is difficult to imagine how such a paradigm might apply to youth. Thus, it would seem that an adult-derived assumption that youths are ready and willing to change but lack the skills to do so may lead to a premature focus on coping skills training, in the absence of any commitment or intrinsic desire to change. Related to this point, Marlatt and Gordon state:

> Those of us in the treatment field need to pay greater attention to the motivation and commitment stage of change in order to improve the "readiness" of clients to embark upon a specific program change. Unless the ground is firmly prepared and one's commitment to change is solid and based on sound decision making, premature commitment may lead to self-defeating experiences of failure and a reluctance to recommit oneself to the change process.

Although their emphasis is on adult relapse, the point may be *more* critical for youth and may be the prepotent target for RP among youth. One process-oriented study found that motivation, measured at three months post-treatment, was the most influential predictor of subsequent substance use in the following three months, outweighing level of coping skills (Kelly, Myers, & Brown, 2000). A study by Cady, Winters, Jordan, Solberg and Stichfield (1996) with 234 adolescents treated for SUDs in residential and outpatient settings found that high motivation for change predicted lower frequency of post-treatment drug use and more abstinence six months following treatment, although this study did not examine the relative contribution of motivation compared to other factors.

With increasing focus on motivation and motivational interviewing (Miller & Rollnick, 1991), motivational enhancement interventions have begun to be tested with youth. One randomized, controlled study of adolescents treated in an emergency room after an alcohol-related event found that, compared to standard care, a brief motivational interview (MI) was associated with greater reductions in alcohol-related consequences (Monti et al., 1999). A large-scale, randomized, controlled trial focusing on youth SUDs examined the efficacy of five different manualized interventions in a sample of 600 adolescents aged between twelve and eighteen (Dennis et al., 2000). One of the conditions consisted of two individual sessions of motivational enhancement therapy, followed by three group sessions of cognitive behavioral therapy (CBT). When compared to a community reinforcement (CR) and multidimensional family therapy intervention, outcomes were comparable to the CR and significantly better than the family intervention at three months.

Thus, the use of motivationally focused interventions appears promising in the treatment of youth SUDs. Motivational readiness should never be assumed, even when, and maybe especially when, youths are seen to easily "comply" with treatment recommendations. (See Florsheim et al., 2000.)

High-Risk Situations. Although relapse rates for both adults and teens following an index treatment episode look very similar (Hunt et al., 1971), there is evidence that developmentally specific social factors associated with adolescence are more influential precipitants of relapse.

Studies of adult relapse reveal a stronger association with negative affective states and interpersonal conflict (Marlatt & Gordon, 1985) while teen relapses are more often linked to direct or indirect social pressure in a peer context (Brown, Vik, & Creamer, 1989; Brown, Mott, & Myers, 1990). A study by Brown and colleagues (1989) specifically focusing on precipitants of adolescent relapse following an index inpatient treatment episode found social pressure to be the main precipitant accounting for 60% of youth relapses. In contrast, a study with adults found social pressure associated with only 20% of relapses (Cummings et al., 1980). Brown (1993) points out that by the time teens enter SUD treatment, their social resources are made up predominantly of substance abusing teens and, although the treated teens view these friends as helpful and supportive, the untreated teens are likely to be unsympathetic to any attempts to stop abusing psychoactive substances. Thus, while peer group influences are purported to affect clinical outcomes for adults and teens, they may be even more salient for youth treated for SUDs than adults.

Both Brown, and Marlatt and Gordon (1985) allude to the fact that these precipitants are not necessarily related to relapse in a *causal* way. Adults and youths with poorer prognoses may place themselves at high risk by self-selecting into these situations to begin with. In the Brown and associates (1989) study, the majority of youths were thinking about using alcohol or other drugs before entering a "relapse-inducing" situation. Thus, it is not clear whether youths relapse in response to overwhelming environmental demands, for which the available coping repertoire was insufficient, or whether there is intention and a desire to re-engage in substance use, obviating the need for deployment of alternative coping skills.

Coping Skills and Self-Efficacy. From a Marlatt and Gordon RP perspective, the greater the available coping repertoire, the greater the self-efficacy an individual will possess in meeting the demands of high-risk situations. As in many adult studies, coping and self-efficacy have been found to be significantly associated with

SUD treatment outcomes among youth (Myers, Brown, & Mott, 1993; Myers & Brown, 1996). In a study of fifty adolescents treated for SUDs, those with the poorest outcomes at a six-month follow-up reported use of significantly fewer coping strategies and lower self-efficacy (Myers & Brown, 1990). Also, a study by Kelly, Myers, and Brown (2000) found that greater coping and self-efficacy measured at treatment intake were significantly associated with abstinence and lower levels of substance use at three and six months following inpatient treatment.

Wills and Shiffman (1985) make a distinction between different types of coping strategies. They posit that coping strategies aimed at avoiding substance use (temptation coping) are distinct from strategies aimed at dealing with more general life events (coping with stress). Empirically, the specific type of coping skills has shown to be important. One prospective study found it was use of "wishful thinking" as a coping strategy that was associated with worse outcomes, while use of abstinent-specific social support as a coping mechanism was associated with longer period of initial abstinence (Myers, Brown, & Mott, 1993). A further study by Myers and Brown using the adolescent relapse coping questionnaire (Myers & Brown, 1996) found that, of the three subscales included in the measure (generic cognitive-behavioral coping, self-critical thinking, and abstinence-focused coping), it was abstinence-focused coping that was most strongly associated with alcohol and drug use both concurrently and in predicting substance use a year ahead.

Importantly, although coping repertoires have been found to be predictive of substance use outcomes among youth, they may be outweighed by motivational factors. A study by Kelly and colleagues (2000) on approximately 100 youths following inpatient treatment found that, whereas coping skills at three months post-treatment was predictive of substance use outcomes, they were no longer significant once motivation was considered. Thus, coping skills deficits, although important, may not be as important as helping youth to reach and maintain a commitment to change (such as to abstain). It may be that once such a commitment is reached, existing knowledge and skills about how to maintain behavior changes (such as abstinence) may be sufficient and successfully employed.

Gorski and Miller

The Gorski RP paradigm is less well known and consequently has been less extensively used and received little empirical attention compared to Marlatt and Gordon's RP conceptualization. However, preliminary investigations into the utility, reliability, and validity of the conceptualization have shown promise with adults. A large-scale multisite prospective study found that a measure of Gorski's relapse warning signs was predictive of future substance use (Miller, Westerberg,

Harris, & Tonigan, 1996). A further psychometric study of a measure of the thirty-seven warning signs found excellent internal consistency, test-retest reliability, and construct validity as it predicted both minor and major relapses prospectively at follow-up (Miller & Harris, 2000). To our knowledge, the paradigm has not been examined empirically among youth, although it is touted as generally applicable by the progenitors of the theory.

As mentioned previously, PAW primarily affects higher-level cognitive functioning (such as abstract thinking and memory), which may lead to faulty decision-making and maladaptive coping efforts, such as substance use. Given that this model was derived from observations made with chronic and severe alcohol-dependent adults, the purported CNS sequelae may not be as evident among youth. However, there is some preliminary evidence to suggest CNS differences may be present among youth with substantial substance use histories. One study found that protracted alcohol use was associated with poorer performance on verbal and nonverbal retention in the context of intact learning and recognition discriminability in alcohol-dependent adolescents when compared to non-dependent adolescents (Brown, Tapert, Granholm, & Delis, 2000). Although the quasi-experimental study design preludes a determination regarding direction of effect, alcohol use may affect neurocognitive functioning.

Regarding the prediction of relapse to substance use following treatment, Tapert and colleagues (1999) examined the relationship between coping skills and relapse and whether such a relationship may be moderated by level of neurocognitive functioning. An interaction was detected between coping and a measure of general intelligence. Adolescents with lower neurocognitive abilities used little or no alcohol or drugs if good coping skills were present. However, they did use more alcohol and drugs if their coping skills were poor. An association between coping skills and outcome did not exist for teens with better neurocognitive abilities. The authors suggest a possible treatment match where adolescents with poorer neurocognitive skills may benefit from coping skills training programs, whereas youth with higher neurocognitive abilities may benefit from a focus in other areas such as motivation.

Another investigation conducted by Knapp and colleagues (1991) suggests that mental functioning and neurological risk factors can predict relapse in adolescents with histories of alcohol and drug-related problems. This study found favorable outcomes were associated with higher verbal IQ, lower performance IQ, and fewer neurological risk factors (such as head injury, premature birth, or special education).

Current evidence suggests that neurocognitive functioning may play a role in adolescent relapse and that alcohol and other drug use may deleteriously influence such functioning. Deficits may be more evident among youth with longer and more severe substance use histories and, in such cases, Gorski and Miller's model may be a better fit. However, for youth on average, a clinical approach based on managing such symptoms may not be the most prudent use of resources. Conceptually, the use of a dynamic relapse progression paradigm could be useful for youth, but the applicability of the thirty-seven, adult-derived warning signs have not been systematically examined among youth. Given the prepotent influence of the social environment in youth relapse, the topography on the road to youth relapse (or recovery) could differ substantially.

In summary, specific empirical evidence for RP interventions with youths based on popular RP paradigms is lacking. In general, there is a dearth of good-quality research on the efficacy and effectiveness of youth SUD treatment and thus, optimal treatment strategies for youth are unknown. However, we believe an RP conceptual framework can be useful in approaching substance-related problems in youths, provided it takes into account developmental status. Next, we describe a specific case example, intended to illustrate how such an approach can be incorporated into youth treatment.

Personal Experiences and Cases

In this section, we provide a case example, which we believe highlights the issues most frequently encountered with youth SUDs and, within this broader context, describe how a developmentally sensitive RP approach might be applied to address some of these.

Background

Brandon, a white, male, seventeen-year-old, was referred to outpatient aftercare counseling by another therapist in a large outpatient clinic for help with problems specific to chronic heavy use of cannabis and alcohol. He also had a history of other sporadic drug use including inhalants, cocaine, methamphetamine, and LSD.

Brandon described a pattern of heavy alcohol use since his early teens with at least weekly heavy intoxication and related blackouts. He also described daily use of cannabis "four to five blunts" for the previous three years. He reported a long history of suicidal ideation, but with no tangible attempts. Brandon's mother reported that he was threatening to jump from a second floor window three weeks prior to treatment. Brandon reported a long history of conduct disordered and delinquent behaviors, including running away, destruction of property, lying, starting fights, and school truancy and related problems. He was currently on probation for breaking and entering, handling stolen goods, and possession of cannabis.

Brandon described a long history of mental health treatment since age nine for various behavioral and affective (depression) problems, but this was his first specifically focused on substance-related issues. Most recently, Brandon had been seeing a therapist for individual therapy on an outpatient basis and was followed for medication by a psychiatrist. He lived with his mother, who was emotionally and instrumentally supportive, and reported a good relationship with her. She rarely drank alcohol and denied use of other substances. Brandon's father had absconded at the time of his birth and he had only minimal contact with him since that time. Brandon's mother and the patient reported that Brandon's father was addicted to alcohol. Brandon had dropped out of school two years prior to treatment and was currently working to complete his GED. He had an active substance-using peer group, from which he was trying to extricate himself, and had few sober friends apart from a relatively new girlfriend who was a supportive, non-drinker/non-substance user and very supportive of his abstinence.

Brandon had no medical problems. He was prescribed Trazedone, Prozac, and Antabuse, but he was noncompliant and refused to take medication because of the side effects—he felt that they compromised his functioning, reporting that they made him tired and less alert.

Regarding his mental status, he was generally well dressed and groomed. His speech and thought processes and content were within normal limits and there was no reported history or observable evidence of psychosis. His attention, concentration, and memory were intact. His mood was initially depressed, but fluctuated throughout the course of treatment. He met criteria for cannabis dependence and alcohol abuse, major depressive disorder (MDD), and conduct disorder. Given his positive history of conduct disorder and the fact that he turned age eighteen during the course of treatment, there was a need to rule out antisocial personality disorder on Axis II. Brandon had obvious employment and academic problems and his global assessment of functioning was judged to approximately fifty at treatment entry.

Treatment Course

Brandon began outpatient therapy with a doctoral-level clinical psychologist specializing in the treatment of SUDs and dual diagnosis following discharge from an intensive evening program focusing on alcohol and other drug abuse or dependence. The treatment protocol included random urine toxicology screens as a therapeutic adjunct, to which the patient's mother, probation officer, and patient agreed. These were used consistently for the first six weeks of treatment followed by a more random protocol of approximately one every two weeks. Prior to entering outpatient treatment, Brandon had undergone a short inpatient detoxification stay of three days. He was required to attend some form of ongoing aftercare as part of his probation and a twelve-session aftercare treatment was recommended.

Therapeutic Alliance. Brandon initially appeared motivated for treatment and had positive outlook. The first author had met Brandon during his attendance at the evening program and, consequently, had some rapport established. One important aspect to building rapport with such youth is to not focus too prematurely on the issue at hand, especially when the patient may be sensitive to, or ambivalent about the substance use. Brandon was interested in computers, computer games, and music and enjoyed talking about them. Casual topics, such as these, were frequent areas of discussion in beginning each session and were returned to often. This was helpful to engage Brandon and build a therapeutic alliance.

Education About Addiction Relapse/Recovery. One critical aspect of both Marlatt's and Gorski's models of RP is to prepare individuals, realistically, for the road ahead, through education and dispelling myths. Thus, initially, some time was spent talking with Brandon about the nature of relapse and recovery and what to expect. Through a Socratic and interactive dialogue, Brandon was educated about the nature of addiction at a simplified behavioral, genetic, and neurophysiological level. Brandon was introduced to the "behavior chain" model of behavior (trigger–thoughts–feelings–actions–positive consequences–negative consequences) within the context of a behavioral functional analysis often used in cognitive behavioral interventions (McCrady, Dean, Dubreuil, & Swanson, 1985). Brandon was able to grasp these ideas well. He liked the behavior chain as a model of behavior and he made his own link and distinctions between triggers, and high-risk situations, and relapse warning signs. He was able to understand that relapse and recovery is a dynamic process.

Differential Diagnosis and Suicidality. There are many strategies for determining independence of syndromes, but this can still be a complex issue. For this patient, it was quite difficult to determine the extent to which the conduct behaviors and depressive symptoms were a result of alcohol and cannabis use or whether they occurred independently. The use of a timeline spanning the patient's life proved to be very helpful in this regard, with input from the patient and the patient's mother.

Of critical importance among youth with substance use problems is the issue of suicide. Suicide is the third leading cause of death among fifteen- to twenty-four-year-olds, and of the associated risk factors, SUDs have the strongest relationship (Fombone, 1998; Fowler, Rich, & Young, 1986). The frequency and intensity of suicidal ideation including any intent, plan, and means were monitored throughout treatment in collaboration with his mother and probation officer. He had reported some suicidal ideation during his residential detoxification stay. However, no suicidal ideation was reported during treatment.

Motivational Readiness. Given what has been discussed above with regard to motivational readiness among youth, the general therapeutic style used was motivational interviewing (Miller & Rollnick, 1991). The *motivational interviewing* approach is based on five general principles: expression of empathy, developing discrepancy between the patient's values or goals and current behaviors, avoiding argumentation, rolling with (instead of confronting and fighting) resistance, and supporting patients' self-efficacy. Given the weighty extrinsic reinforcement for this patient to comply with treatment (that is, on probation), the issue of motivation was explicitly, and frequently, raised. Ambivalence about being in treatment and the need to change substance use behavior was discussed openly, with use of reflective listening techniques outlined by Miller and Rollnick (1991). From a stages-of-change perspective, Brandon was probably in the contemplation stage—intrinsically ambivalent about change. Given his probationary status, the issue of "serving his time in treatment" was discussed, and reframed to be a time that Brandon could talk about issues relevant to him and his life values and goals. In this context, it was possible to "develop discrepancies" between his current behaviors and his stated objectives and goals. For example, Brandon valued his relationship with his new girlfriend very highly and also wanted to finish his GED and get a good job. More immediate was his goal to finish his probationary period successfully. Through empathic reflection, Brandon was often able to see that his (delinquent/ substance use) behavior was incompatible with these goals. This helped move him forward in the process of change toward adaptive action.

It is important to note that disseminating information about the negative effects of substance use without personalizing such effects is unlikely to yield any positive results (Farabee, Simpson, Dansereau, & Knight, 1995). Thus, Brandon was also asked to write out a list of the things he had lost or not gained as a direct or indirect result of his substance use. These were discussed during session. Having a written, patient-generated record for regular review was critical for maintaining motivation to change throughout treatment. This is similar to completing a written first step of the AA program, often required as a part of Minnesota model, twelve-step-based treatment.

Each session began with a check-in, including Brandon's evaluation of the last session and how helpful various aspects of it were. This was helpful in reducing resistance to treatment by giving Brandon a sense of inclusion and active participation in the treatment process.

The ability for self-reflection and self-determination will depend to a large degree on the maturity level of the youth. This patient was deemed to be quite mature, and able to consider and weigh the consequences of his actions in light of his goals and aspirations. With younger youth, or those less mature, a more directive or family systems approach may be optimal.

High-Risk Situations and Coping Skills. During the third session, the patient and therapist discussed "high risk" relapse situations. Subsequently, Brandon listed and ordered them from the most to the least risky. Rather than talk about relapse, as such, Brandon was asked about situations or emotional states encountered during the past year, which were very difficult for him to cope with in the absence of alcohol or other drugs. As has been found in study of relapse precipitants among youth (Brown et al., 1989), it was the social situations with his friends in the evening and on weekends that were the highest risk for this patient. In fact, there was seldom an instance when the patient would use alcohol, cannabis, or another drug when alone.

One important aspect of a motivational enhancement theory is to elicit solutions and alternative behaviors from the patient rather than have the therapist generate them. Brandon was able to identify two coping strategies to reduce the risk of relapse in these high-risk situations. First, if he decided to go to parties or social events at which alcohol or other drugs were likely to be present, he could bring a sober friend. (He had made such a friend during his time in the evening treatment program he had attended and who was currently attending Narcotics Anonymous [NA] meetings.) Second, he stated that he could avoid the event in favor of an alternative social event that would not put him under so much pressure, such as going on a date with his girlfriend, who was a non-substance user, and very supportive of his abstinence and recovery goals. Although asking the patient to generate feasible alternative behaviors may sometimes take more time (and adolescents may sometimes need suggestions), results are likely to be more effective and lasting than if these are generated or imposed by the therapist. Within this same context, drink and drug refusal skills were rehearsed and role-played during this and subsequent sessions to help increase skill level and self-efficacy in such situations. The patient and therapist played both the role of the "pusher" and the "resistor" so that the patient could generate his own coping strategies but also have other alternatives modeled by the therapist.

At the end of each of the twelve treatment sessions, Brandon was asked to describe his anticipated activities during the next week. During this time, potentially high-risk situations were identified by either Brandon or by the therapist and discussed. This helped facilitate recognition and anticipation of difficult situations. Appropriate relapse prevention/coping strategies were then formulated, discussed, cognitively rehearsed, or role-played. To gauge Brandon's level of self-efficacy in preparation of each anticipated event, Brandon was asked how confident (on a one to ten scale) he felt about coping effectively without using substances. This procedure is generally very useful to pinpoint particular subjectively challenging events, and became increasingly useful to Brandon during his treatment.

Abstinence Violation Effect. Abstinence as a SUD treatment outcome is related to better overall psychosocial adjustment and functioning at various follow-ups, for both youths and adults (Brown, D'Amico, McCarthy, & Tapert, 2001; Ouimette, Moos, & Finney, 1998). However, with a return to substance use more likely than not during early change attempts, the AVE was discussed implicitly with Brandon. First, Brandon was educated about the difference between a lapse and a relapse, as specified in Marlatt's RP theory. With the use of the behavior chain, two hypothetical individuals' cognitive interpretations of a substance use event were illustrated and shown to lead to two different trajectories emerging from the lapse: abstinence or continued use (relapse). Brandon was able to comprehend the importance of an individual's reaction to such an event well. In addition, during the first few sessions, Brandon was asked to imagine such a situation himself and how he would interpret it and react to it. These reactions were discussed in-session. Increasingly adaptive interpretations emerged as Brandon began to realize how harshly he judged himself and how such negativity could lead to greater use and "just giving up." Although a return to substance use was not reported, detected, or observed during Brandon's treatment, time spent in such "relapse intervention" may be helpful in minimizing the extent and severity of lapses for youths.

Substance Using Versus Abstinence-Oriented Peer Group. An important component of any treatment with substance-involved youth is the issue of the peer group. Brandon had a very good and subjectively valued support—his girlfriend. This relationship carried a great deal of weight in his mind. The patient also began attending self-help group meetings (NA) two to three times per week, with the friend he had met in treatment. NA is generally composed of a younger cohort than in AA. It is more focused on drugs other than alcohol (for which AA would be the fellowship of choice), but views alcohol as a drug from which one should abstain to minimize risks of relapse to other drugs and the development of a possible cross-addiction to alcohol. The patient also attended two regular meetings specifically for "young people," which are increasingly common in both NA and AA. The patient was actively directed to similar-age meetings, as this has been shown to be important in engaging youth in such groups (Kelly et al., 2002). Feedback about his self-help meeting experiences was elicited each week during check-in at the beginning of each session. This was done to address any barriers he may have experienced and to facilitate active involvement at meetings, which has been shown to be predictive of maintaining motivation for abstinence (Kelly et al., 2002). He reported that he liked attending the meetings and stated that some of the benefits of attending for him were that he felt that he was "not the only one with these problems," being "reminded of what it was like" and "the good things that can happen" if he maintained abstinence. One therapy session included both his girlfriend and his NA sober friend, in an attempt to enhance network support for abstinence.

From the outset, Brandon was strongly encouraged to replace his former, substance-using peer group with one more conducive to meeting his goals. This was not easy for Brandon, especially regarding one or two of his former friends, who he believed were "good friends" despite their alcohol and other drug use. Although Brandon was unable to completely sever ties to these individuals, he made progress during treatment in recognizing the high-risk nature of these interactions following three "near miss" experiences, where he felt he only narrowly escaped a relapse in a social context with them.

Social supports can be very helpful in RP efforts, although it is not explicitly emphasized in Marlatt's or Gorski's RP models. One important role supportive persons can play is to point out to the patient when they notice relapse warning signs emerging. This early warning system can be set up during treatment, when motivation for change is high. Brandon was able to list five behaviors or attitudes that, for him, would indicate a regression into old behavior patterns. He then asked his girlfriend, his mother, and his NA sponsor to point out to him when they observed any of these behaviors emerging. Such warnings can be very helpful in heading off potential substance use as, often, the insidious, gradual progressive nature of the relapse process is out of the patient's conscious awareness, but obvious to observers.

Probation Contact and Team Involvement. Contact with probation officer, psychiatrist, and mother was made on numerous occasions. We also had three entire team discussion meetings; twice by conference call and one at the hospital. These were critical to keeping all team members functioning as a more unified, and more effective, multisystemic support system as well as up to date with patient progress. So often in such cases, team efforts are difficult to coordinate because of geographical and scheduling barriers and, consequently, become fragmented and lose impact. Coordination efforts used in this case did involve some extra time commitment, but were therapeutic for both patient *and* treatment team members.

Discharge and Continuing Care. At time of discharge, Brandon had been seeing his psychiatrist for medication follow-up, and had agreed to begin taking Prozac to help with some residual depressed mood. He had acquired a job working at a local supermarket and was working toward completing his GED. He had also acquired an NA sponsor who was helping him get to other meetings including a meeting focused on completing work on the twelve steps. Brandon had been abstinent for more than three months, which was verified by parent corroboration and urine toxicology. He was referred back to his prior therapist for continued work on maintaining abstinence and for more in-depth examination surrounding issues about his relationship with his father.

Conclusion. Brandon made good progress during treatment. A developmentally sensitive RP framework was utilized as part of a multidimensional, multidisciplinary treatment package. Urine toxicology and probationary status, along with supportive attention from family, girlfriend, treatment team, and the self-help community served as important external reinforcers in treatment engagement, retention, and abstinence. He had attained an adequate understanding about the nature of addiction, relapse, and recovery. He was able to build motivation for abstinence and adaptive change through self-assessment of the deleterious impact alcohol and other drugs had on his life and how they prevented him from meeting his needs and achieving his goals. He was able to identify his own high-risk relapse situations and frequently generate his own adaptive coping strategies, which were deployed and practiced during treatment. Social supports were used to point out relapse warning signs to Brandon.

This case focused on an older adolescent. It was chosen because it contains the types of issues that are most likely to be present when dealing with these youth. Furthermore, because substance use and addiction severity increase with age, older youth tend to be more suited to these RP techniques. In fact, the notion of a "substance use disorder" among younger adolescents (ages twelve to fifteen) frequently requires a very different conceptualization and approach. These younger adolescents rarely use alcohol or other drugs intensively enough, or for a sufficient length of time, to possess the essential qualities of an actual "disorder" to which concepts such as "remission" and "relapse" can be meaningfully applied. Additionally, due to their social-cognitive level, and presence of psychiatric comorbidity (such as ADHD), such youth often lack the insight and decision-making ability that RP approaches require. Family-based secondary interventions and family therapy (Liddle, 2002) are often better suited to these cases because they can alter contingencies systemically without the need for individual insight and decisional processing.

Future Directions

During the past twenty years, several psychological and neurobiological RP models have been posited. The two most prominent, Marlatt and Gordon (1985) and Gorski and Miller (1986), have been discussed in this chapter. These RP paradigms have gained increasingly widespread acceptance and use in conceptualizations of treatment for SUDs. They have also been generalized for use with many other clinical and non-clinical problems. Given that these models were derived from adult observations, we considered their applicability for youth. A number of differences between youths and adults were highlighted and discussed, many of which may influence the fit of these models for adolescents. Available empirical evidence suggests some utility of these adult-derived models and constructs for use with youths. A case example was used to illustrate how one may adapt these adult paradigms to help effect salutary changes in youth.

◆ ◆ ◆

To our knowledge, there is no current, formal explication of a specific RP model for youth that attempts to take developmental differences into account. Low levels of substance-use problem-recognition and related readiness to change among youths affects fundamental assumptions and applicability of adult models. The issue of readiness and commitment to change is fundamental to any youth conceptualization. Although preliminary evidence suggests that substance-using adolescents may already be developing some of the neurophysiological changes formerly associated with more chronic use among adults (Tapert et al., 2001), which may compromise cognitive functioning, most youths do not have the kinds of damage or skills deficits associated with more intensive, chronic use. Thus, there may be less of a need to focus on managing post-acute withdrawal symptoms or increasing coping skills than to help youths reach an intrinsic commitment to change substance use that is reinforced by family and peers. Further study is needed to compare models to determine optimal conceptualizations for adolescent RP.

Some may argue that the very notion of "relapse" as a relevant construct for youth who misuse substances is questionable. This fairly weighty, medical model term implies the reoccurrence of a previously remitted SUD. However, as alluded to earlier, substance use may be only one piece of a general maladaptive behavior pattern that attracts acute interest from several concerned third parties (police and schools, for example) eventually forcing the adolescent into SUD treatment. Although use of any substances is worrisome for many parents, teachers, and clinicians, a narrow or exclusive focus on substance use as the primary cause of this general syndrome may be off target. Placing substance use in a broader behavioral and social context may require a conceptual shift, but bring greater rewards.

Future RP models and related clinical approaches designed for youth also would benefit from recognizing large within-group variability—that adolescents differ greatly from one another on multiple dimensions during this dynamic and multiphase stage of development. Future research should examine the implications of such heterogeneity for any broad youth conceptualization of RP, because the prodigious maturational range evident during adolescence may render the fit and application of a single paradigm or clinical approach questionable. Adult models might be more suited to more "adult-like" youth (older, more mature), whereas younger adolescents may need a completely different approach (such as family therapy). Patient-treatment matching is an area that has not been extensively pursued by adolescent researchers, but may prove valuable in discerning optimal treatment approaches.

References

Aarons, G. A., Brown, S. A., Stice, E., & Coe, M. T. (2002). Psychometric evaluation of the marijuana and stimulant effect expectancy questionnaires for adolescents. *Addictive Behaviors, 26*(2), 219–236.

Abrams, D. B., & Niaura, R. S. (1987). Social learning theory. In H. T. Blane & K. E. Leonard (Eds.), *Psychological theories of drinking and alcoholism* (pp. 131–178). New York: Guilford Press.

Alcoholics Anonymous. (1999). *1998 membership survey: A snapshot of A. A. membership.* New York: AA World Services.

Annis, H. M. (1990). Relapse to substance abuse: Empirical findings within a cognitive-social learning approach. *Journal of Psychoactive Drugs, 22*, 117–123.

Bandura, A. (1977a). *Social learning theory.* Englewood Cliffs, NJ: Prentice-Hall.

Bandura, A. (1977b). Self-efficacy: Toward a unifying theory of behavior change. *Psychological Review, 84*, 199–215.

Bates, M. E., & Labouvie, E. W. (1997). Adolescent risk factors and the prediction of persistent alcohol and drug use in to adulthood. *Alcoholism, Clinical and Experimental Research, 21*(5), 944–950.

Brook, D. W., Brook, J. S., Zhang, C., Cohen, P., & Whiteman, M. (2002). Drug use and the risk of major depressive disorder, alcohol dependence, and substance use disorders. *Archives of General Psychiatry, 59*, 1039–1044.

Brown, S. A. (1985). *Treating the alcoholic: A developmental model of recovery.* New York: John Wiley & Sons.

Brown, S. A. (1993). Recovery patterns in adolescent substance abuse. In J. S. Baer, G. A. Marlatt, & R. J. McMahon (Eds.), *Addictive behaviors across the lifespan: Prevention, treatment, and policy issues* (pp.161–183). Newbury Park, CA: Sage.

Brown, S. A., D'Amico, E. J., McCarthy, D. M., & Tapert, S. F. (2001). Four-year outcomes from adolescent alcohol and drug treatment. *Journal of Studies on Alcohol, 62*(3), 381–388.

Brown, S. A., Mott, M. A., & Myers, M. G. (1990). Adolescent alcohol and drug treatment outcome. In R. R. Watson (Ed.), *Drug and alcohol abuse prevention: Drug and alcohol abuse reviews* (pp. 373–403). Clifton, NJ: Humana.

Brown, S. A., Tapert, S. F., Granholm, E., & Delis, D. C. (2000). Neurocognitive functioning of adolescents: Effects of protracted alcohol use. *Alcoholism, Clinical and Experimental Research, 24*(2), 164–171.

Brown, S. A., Vik, P. W., & Creamer, V. A. (1989). Characteristics of relapse following adolescent substance abuse treatment. *Addictive Behaviors, 14,* 291–300.

Buckstein, O. G., Glancy, L. J., & Kaminer, Y. (1992). Patterns of affective comorbidity in a clinical population of dually diagnosed adolescent substance abusers. *Journal of the American Academy of Child and Adolescent Psychiatry, 31*(6), 1041–1045.

Cady, M. E., Winters, K. C., Jordan, D. A., Solberg, K. B., & Stinchfield, R. D. (1996). Motivation to change as a predictor of treatment outcome for adolescent substance abusers. *Journal of Child and Adolescent Substance Abuse, 5,* 73–91.

Connors, G. J., Maisto, S. A., & Donnovan, D. M. (1996). Conceptualizations of relapse: A summary of psychological and psychobiological models. *Addiction, 91,* S5–S13.

Cottler, L. B., Schuckit, M. A., Helzer, J. E., Crowley, T., Woody, G., Nathan, P., & Hughes, J. (1995). The DSM-IV field trial for substance use disorders: Major results. *Drug and Alcohol Dependence, 38*(1), 59–69.

Crowley, T., & Riggs, P. (1995). *Adolescent substance use disorder with conduct disorder and comorbid conditions.* Rockville, MD: National Institute of Drug Abuse.

Cummings, C., Gordon, J., & Marlatt, G. A. (1980). Relapse: Strategies of prevention and prediction. In W. R. Miller (Ed.), *The addictive behaviors: Treatment of alcoholism, drug abuse, smoking, and obesity* (pp. 291–321). New York: Pergamon.

Deas, D., Riggs, P., Langenbucher, J., Goldman, M., & Brown, S. (2000). Adolescents are not adults: Developmental considerations in alcohol users. *Alcoholism, Clinical and Experimental Research, 24*(2), 232–237.

Dennis, M. L., Diamond, G., Donaldson, J., Godley, S., Herrell, J., Kaminer, Y., et al. (2000). Cannabis youth treatment group. Washington, DC: Center for Substance Abuse Treatment.

Farabee, D., Simpson, D. D., Dansereau, D., & Knight, K. (1995). Cognitive inductions into treatment among drug users on probation. *Journal of Drug Issues, 24,* 669–682.

Florsheim, P., Shotorbani, S., Guest-Warnick, G., Barratt, T., & Hwang, W. C. (2000). Role of the working alliance in the treatment of delinquent boys in community-based programs. *Journal of Clinical Child Psychology, 29,* 94–107.

Fombonne, E. (1998). Suicidal behaviors in vulnerable adolescents: Time trends and their correlates. *British Journal of Psychiatry, 173,* 154–159.

Fowler, R.C., Rich, C. L., & Young, D. (1986). San Diego suicide study. II. Substance abuse in young cases. *Archives of General Psychiatry, 43*(10), 962–965.

Garber, J. (1984). Classification of childhood psychopathology: A developmental perspective. *Child Development, 55*(1), 30–48.

Gorski, T. (1979). *The neurologically-based alcoholism diagnostic system.* Hazel Crest, IL: Al-Press.

Gorski, T., & Miller, M. (1982). *Counseling for relapse prevention.* Independence, MO: Independence Press.

Gorski, T., & Miller, M. (1986). *Staying sober: A guide for relapse prevention.* Independence, MO: Independence Press.

Hser, Y. I., Grella, C. E., Hubbard, R. L., Hsieh, S. C., Fletcher, B. W., Brown, B. S., et al. (2001). An evaluation of drug treatments for adolescents in 4 US cities. *Archives of General Psychiatry, 58*(7), 689–695.

Hunt, W. A., Barnett, L. W., & Branch, L. G. (1971). Relapse rates in addiction programs. *Journal of Clinical Psychology, 27,* 455–456.

Jessor, R. (1982). Problem behavior and developmental transition in adolescence. *Journal of School Health, 52*(5), 295–300.

Jessor, R., & Jessor, S. L. (1977). *Problem behavior and psychosocial development: A longitudinal study of youth.* New York: Academic Press.

Kanfer, F. H., & Gaelick, L. (1986). Self-management methods. In F. H. Kanfer & A. P. Goldstein (Eds.), *Helping people change* (pp. 283–345). Elmsford, NY: Pergamon Press.

Kelly, J. F., Myers, M. G., & Brown, S. A. (2000). A multivariate process model of adolescent 12-step attendance and substance use outcome following inpatient treatment. *Psychology of Addictive Behaviors, 14,* 376–389.

Kelly, J. F., Myers, M. G., & Brown, S. A. (2002). Do adolescents affiliate with 12-step groups? A multivariate process model of effects. *Journal of Studies on Alcohol, 63*(3), 293–304.

Knapp, J. E., Templer, D. I., Cannon, W. G., & Dobson, S. (1991). Variables associated with success in an adolescent drug treatment program. *Adolescence, 26*(102), 306–317.

Liddle, H. A. (2002). Multidimensional Family therapy (MDFT) for adolescent cannabis users (Volume 5 for the Cannabis Youth Treatment manual series). Rockville, MD: CSAT/SAMHSA (http://www.samhsa.gov/csat/csat.htm.).

Marlatt, G. A., & Gordon, J. A. (Eds.). (1985). *Relapse prevention: Maintenance strategies in the treatment of addictive behaviors.* New York: Guilford Press.

McCrady, B. S., Dean, L., Dubreuil, E., & Swanson, S. (1985). The problem drinker's project: A programmatic application of social-learning based treatment. In G. A. Marlatt, & J. R. Gordon (Eds.), *Relapse Prevention.* New York: Guilford Press.

Miller, N. S., Ninonuevo, F. G., Klamen, D. L., & Hoffmann, N. G. (1997). Integration of treatment and posttreatment variables in predicting results of abstinence-based outpatient treatment after one year. *Journal of Psychoactive Drugs, 29,* 239–248.

Miller, W. R., & Harris, R. J. (2000). A simple scale of Gorski's warning signs for relapse. *Journal of Studies on Alcohol, 61,* 759–765.

Miller, W. R., & Rollnick, S. (1991). *Motivational interviewing: Preparing people to change addictive behavior.* New York: Guilford Press.

Miller, W. R., Westerberg, V. S., Harris, R. J., & Tonigan, J. S. (1996). What predicts relapse? Prospective testing of antecedent models. *Addiction, 91,* S155–S171.

Monti, P. M., Colby, S. M., Barnett, N. P., Spirito, A., Rohsenow, D. J., Myers, M., et al. (1999). Brief intervention for harm reduction with alcohol-positive older adolescents in a hospital emergency department. *Journal of Consulting and Clinical Psychology, 67,* 989–994.

Morgenstern, J., Labouvie, E., McCrady, B. S., & Kahler, C. W. (1997). Affiliation with Alcoholics Anonymous after treatment: A study of its therapeutic effects and mechanisms of action. *Journal of Consulting and Clinical Psychology, 65,* 768–777.

Myers, M. G., & Brown, S. A. (1990a). Coping responses and relapse among adolescent substance abusers. *Journal of Substance Abuse, 2,* 177–189.

Myers, M. G., & Brown, S. A. (1990b). Coping and appraisal in high risk for relapse situations among adolescent substance abusers following treatment. *Journal of Adolescent Chemical Dependency, 1,* 95–115.

Myers, M. G., & Brown, S. A. (1996). The Adolescent Relapse Coping Questionnaire: Psychometric validation. *Journal of Studies on Alcohol, 57,* 40–46.

Myers, M. G., Brown, S. A., & Mott, M. A. (1993). Coping as a predictor of adolescent substance abuse treatment outcome. *Journal of Substance Abuse, 5,* 15–29.

Newcomb, M. D., & Bentler, P. M. (1989). *Consequences of adolescent drug use.* Newbury Park, CA: Sage.

Ouimette, P. C., Finney, J. W., & Moos, R. H. (1997). Twelve-step and cognitive-behavioral treatment for substance abuse: A comparison of treatment effectiveness. *Journal of Consulting and Clinical Psychology, 65*(2), 230–240.

Ouimette, P. C., Moos, R. H., & Finney, J. W. (1998). Influence of outpatient treatment and 12-step group involvement on one-year substance abuse treatment outcomes. *Journal of Studies on Alcohol, 59*(9), 513–522.

Parks, G. A., & Marlatt, G. A. (1999). Relapse prevention therapy for substance-abusing offenders: A cognitive-behavioral approach. In L. E. Lanham (Ed.), *What works? Strategic solutions. The International Community Correction Association examines substance abuse,* OH: *American Correctional Association* (pp. 161–233).

Peters, R. H., & Schonfeld, V. (1993). Determinants of recent substance abuse among jail inmates referred to treatment. *Journal of Drug Issues, 23,* 101–117.

Pollock, N. K., & Martin, C. S. (1999). Diagnostic orphans: Adolescents with alcohol symptom who do not qualify for DSM-IV abuse or dependence diagnoses. *American Journal of Psychiatry, 156*(6), 897–901.

Prochaska, J. O., & DiClemente, C. C. (1982). Transtheoretical therapy: Toward a more integrative model of change. *The Journal of Psychotherapy Practice and Research, 19,* 276–288.

Project Match Research Group. (1997). Matching alcoholism treatments to client heterogeneity: Post-treatment drinking outcomes. *Journal of Studies on Alcohol, 58,* 7–29.

Project Match Research Group. (1998). Matching alcoholism treatments to client heterogeneity: Project Match three-tear drinking outcomes. *Alcoholism: Clinical and Experimental Research, 22,* 1300–1311.

Robins, L. N., & Przybeck, T. R. (1985). Age of onset of drug use as a factor in drug and other disorders. *NIDA Research Monograph, 56,* 178–192.

Substance Abuse and Mental Health Services Administration (SAMHSA). (2001). Center for Substance Abuse Treatment. Washington, DC: U.S. Department of Health and Human Services.

Substance Abuse and Mental Health Services Administration (SAMHSA). (2002). Center for Substance Abuse Treatment. Washington, DC: U.S. Department of Health and Human Services.

Tapert, S. F., Brown, G. G., Kindermann, S., Cheung, E. H., Frank, L. R., & Brown, S. A. (2001). FMRI measurement of brain dysfunction in alcohol-dependent young women. *Alcoholism: Clinical and Experimental Research, 25*(2), 236–245.

Tapert, S. F., Brown, S. A., Myers, M. G., & Granholm, E. (1999). Psychometric evaluation of the customer drinking and drug use record. *Journal of Studies On Alcohol, 60,* 500–508.

Vik, P. W., Grizzle, K. L., & Brown, S. A. (1992). Social resource characteristics and adolescent substance abuse relapse. *Journal of Adolescent Chemical Dependency, 2,* 59–74.

Wills, T. A., & Shiffman, S. (1985). Coping and substance use: A conceptual framework. In S. Shiffman & T. A. Wills (Eds.), *Coping and substance use* (pp. 3–24). Orlando, FL: Academic Press.

Wilson, P. H. (1992). *Principles and practice of relapse prevention.* New York: Guilford Press.

CHAPTER TWENTY-FIVE

MENTAL SKILLS TRAINING

Glenn S. Brassington, Ph.D.

Children are faced with challenges to perform in a variety of high-pressure situations, such as sports competitions, music recitals, and academic examinations. Critical to success in these endeavors is a child's ability to maintain focus and emotional control during performance situations. Although children spend countless hours preparing physically and intellectually to perform well in these domains, they spend relatively little time developing the ability to effectively regulate mental and physiological processes necessary for successful performance. As a result, many talented children experience decrements in their performance when they are in situations that they perceive as high-pressure. The frustration that children experience when they cannot effectively manage their thoughts, emotions, and behaviors during performance robs them of the success and enjoyment that they would otherwise experience as a result of long hours of commitment and practice. Hence, it is important for children to successfully develop the ability to manage mental and physiological processes in order to perform well during the pressure of performance. Further, mental skills training may reduce the likelihood that a child will employ pathological coping strategies (for example, substance use) in an attempt to manage performance situations.

Mental skills training consists of a series of interventions that teach performers how to create an optimal psychophysiological/mind-body state during practice and performance, which many performers call "The Zone." Mental Skills Training is derived from sports and performance psychology literature (Williams,

2001). Athletes have called upon mental health professionals and exercise scientists to help them deal more effectively with the pressure of athletic performance. Athletes are acutely aware that the mental state they are in during competition greatly affects the quality of their training and practice as well as how they perform during the pressure of competition. Over the past forty years, mental health practitioners, researchers, and sports scientists have developed strategies for teaching individuals involved in a variety of performance situations (sports, performing arts, pubic speaking, academics, business) three essential mental skills: (1) the ability to create the drive and motivation to develop the skills necessary to succeed (for example, to persist in practice, training, and learning), (2) the ability to create the optimal mental state for competition and performance, and (3) the ability to recover from errors and setbacks that are inevitably associated with striving for higher and higher levels of performance.

Mental skills training teaches performers how to focus their attention on the most relevant performance cues, modulate their emotional arousal, and create the optimal level of muscle tension before, during, and after performance situations. The training in focus, emotional control, and tension control results in the performer becoming the master rather than the servant of his/her mental state. Unfortunately, performers frequently spend countless hours learning and training to perfect their physical, intellectual, and creative skills only to find that they are in a less than optimal mental state during performances. However, this does not have to occur. Figure 25.1 illustrates the optimal performance state in which focus, energy, and relaxation converge.

Performers talk about this state (The Zone) in almost religious terms, with many feeling that being in The Zone, when it occurs, is bestowed on them by the gods. Conversely, those who teach mental skills training contend that

FIGURE 25.1. DIMENSION OF THE OPTIMAL PERFORMANCE STATE (THE ZONE).

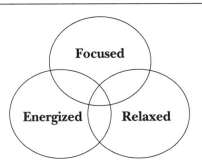

FIGURE 25.2. CENTRAL FACTORS INFLUENCED DURING MENTAL SKILLS TRAINING.

performers, through consistent practice, can learn to harness the power of their mind and consistently *create* the optimal mental state for performance.

What follows is a description of a mental skills training program typically employed by the author. Before the mental training program is implemented, the central goal for the training is explained to performers. Performers are told that they will learn techniques to help them use their thoughts, behaviors, and how they respond to the environment to perform at their best during practice and under pressure during performances. The ability to control and use one's thoughts, behaviors, and environment is the key to consistently achieving peak performances. Figure 25.2 illustrates the dynamic and reciprocally determined relationship among these three areas of focus for mental training.

Mental skills training interventions are usually conducted in four phases. First, mental attributes that have been show to be related to success are assessed. Second, performers are aided in increasing their awareness of factors that tend to facilitate and inhibit performance (such as thoughts, behaviors, environmental cues). Third, performers are taught a series of exercises designed to increase their awareness and ability to control cognitive and behavioral processes identified as being salient to performance. Fourth, the newly learned self-control abilities are transferred (that is, generalized) and tested in the performance setting. Interventions are refined based on in vivo effects, practice is reinforced and monitored, and post-intervention assessment is conducted. Each of these phases of a mental skills training program will be discussed in turn.

Phase 1. Several questionnaire measures are available for assessing mental attributes related to successful performance (Ostrow, 1996). Some of the measures were created to assess personality attributes in the non-athlete/performer population (such as the California Personality Inventory, 16PF) or psychopathology (MMPI, sentence completion). However, recently questionnaire measures have been developed to assess performance-specific mental attributes. For example, a questionnaire developed by the author of this chapter is the Mental Strengths Assessment (MSA) (Brassington, 2001). The MSA assesses thirty mental attributes and skills related to successful performance that are conceptually grouped into five categories: Drive, Attitude, Focus, Self-Regulation, and Mental Skills. (See Table 25.1 for a list of scales.)

For space considerations, each scale will not be described. Performers are encouraged to score within one-half standard deviation of the mean for an elite performers comparison group (n = 500) on each scale. However, the MSA provides performers with valuable information and insights about their mental strengths, and identifies areas in which mental training may have a positive effect on performance. Usually, troubled performers report using very few of the mental skills (such as goal setting or visualization) and report problems on several scales dealing with self-regulation, focus, attitude, and drive.

Phase 2. After assessing the attributes listed above, performers are asked to reflect on their profiles. Then performers identify factors associated with some of their best and worst practices and performances. Performers are asked to identify thoughts, behaviors, and the way they use the environment that are associated with an optimal mental state during performance and with less than optimal mental states. During this discovery process, performers discuss several memorable practice and performance situations in which they performed at their best and felt as if they were in an optimal mental state. Performers also examine times when they performed suboptimally. This process of exploration helps the clinician identify the client's mental strengths and weaknesses. Strategies that are often used in this phase include journal writing, discussions with coaches and teachers, and reviewing videotapes of significant performances. The level of awareness of cognitive and behavioral processes related to performance can vary greatly between one performer and another. Hence, it is not uncommon for one performer to gain valuable insights in as few as one session, while another performer takes weeks or even months to do so.

Phase 3. After the performer and clinician consensually validate the findings of the MSA, explore the performance issues, and gain significant insights about the performer's mental strengths and weakness, performers learn a series of exercises that teach them how to control their focus, control their emotional arousal, and effectively modulate their physical tension. The seven mental skills that performers learn are (1) goal setting, (2) relaxation response training, (3) emotional/arousal control, (4) focusing, (5) environmental management, (6) performance routines, and (7) cognitive restructuring.

To develop the *goal setting* skill, a performer learns how to set realistic but challenging goals for succeeding in upcoming performances (Locke, 1991; Locke & Latham, 1985; Locke, Shaw, Saari, & Latham, 1981; Weinberg, 1994). For goal setting to be effective, performers should be directed to set outcome goals

TABLE 25.1. MENTAL STRENGTHS ASSESSMENT SCALES.

Drive	Attitude	Focus	Self-Regulation	Mental Skills
Commitment	Optimism	Depth of focus	Optimal energy	Self-talk
Competitive orientation	Sport confidence	Duration of focus	Negative thinking*	Visualization
Intrinsic motivation	Mental confidence	Temporal focus	Pre-competition anxiety*	Goal setting
Extrinsic motivation	Sense of control	External distraction*	Emotional control	Social support
Will to win	Fear of failure*	Internal distraction*	Ability to relax	Relaxation/breathing
	Fear of success*		Ability to energize	Pre-event routines
			Ability to recover	Letting go
			Handling pressure	

*Lower scores are considered better on these scales.

(winning), process goals (focusing attention on important performance cues and strategies), and performance goals (personal best). Performers should also be counseled to set short- and long-term goals, breaking down long-term goals into achievable short-term goals. Other things that should be considered when setting goals include (1) setting specific measurable goals, (2) setting moderately difficult but realistic goals, (3) having a specific timeline for achieving each goal, (4) setting practice and competition goals, (5) recording goals, (6) writing an individual goal statement, (7) arranging for feedback about each goal, and (8) providing support and accountability for achieving each goal. In addition, performers are encouraged to keep their goals in view (such as on the refrigerator, on index cards, in the bedroom, or in the bathroom) and to read and visualize their goals throughout the day, before going to sleep, and upon awakening.

After developing and refining goals, performers learn how to voluntarily relax their muscles and reduce sympathetic nervous system activity. Clinicians have preferred methods for teaching clients how to create a relaxation response; however, the most commonly used methods are progressive muscle relaxation training, autogenic relaxation training, and diaphragmatic breathing. The technique that is most often used in the United State is progressive muscle relaxation training (Jacobson, 1974). In using this technique, the performer lies on the floor for approximately twenty minutes with her legs and arms uncrossed and systematically tenses (for five seconds) and relaxes (for fifteen seconds) each major muscle group in her body, beginning with the muscles of her feet and ending with the muscles of her face and head. With continued practice, the performer learns to create this deep state of relaxation in less and less time, gradually moving from a lying, to a sitting, to a standing position. Over the course of several months, the performer develops the ability to relax the major muscles of her body within minutes or seconds without using the tense-relax activity. Many performers report that the progressive muscle relaxation training was the first time that they had ever felt deeply relaxed and that this state of relaxation could be under their conscious control. This increased sense of control often translates into improved performance without the addition of the other mental training techniques. It should be noted that many performance enhancement consultants recommend that performers practice meditation techniques; however, it has not been established that these techniques help performers learn to relax. In some cases, meditation techniques may actually make the performer feel more anxious as they become even more aware of the lack of control they have over their thoughts during meditation.

After several weeks, performers are usually able to create a sufficiently relaxed state that they are ready to learn the second set of skills, Emotional/Arousal Control (Gould & Udry, 1994). In a deeply relaxed state, the performer is asked to imagine a past performance in which he was performing at his very best. He is asked to not only re-experience what he saw, but also what he felt, heard, touched, tasted, and smelled. He is asked to incorporate all of his senses as he re-experiences this peak performance. For example, a tennis player, while recalling himself serving exceptionally well during a match, re-experiences the feeling of the sun on his body, the taste of sweat in his mouth, the smell of the felt on the ball in his hand, the sound of his feet moving on the court, and so on. With continued practice, the performer is able to create the emotional arousal that he experienced during his peak performance while he is lying down, sitting in a chair, standing, or competing.

In addition to recalling past peak experiences, performers are asked to recall what they were thinking about and what they were saying to themselves (self-talk) during their peak performances. The addition of positive self-talk typically increased the positive emotional arousal that the performer experiences. This technique of re-experiencing one's best performance is not only used to teach the performer how to create an optimal level of emotion and arousal, but also to identify other aspects of the client's behaviors (such as what they were focused on in the environment, how they moved) that contribute to peak performance.

Although learning how to relax and create the optimal level of emotion and arousal is central to mental training, performers also need to learn how to consistently focus their attention on the most salient factors related to success in their particular performance activity (for example, the ball in tennis, the questions in an examination, and so on). The first step in helping the performer develop the appropriate focus (or what is often termed *concentration*) during practice and performance is to identify the most important elements of the activity on which the performer should focus (Boutcher & Crews, 1987; Ziegler, 1994). This is achieved by discussing where the performer's focus was during each moment of a peak performance. For example, a musician usually identifies three focal points when discussing her performance: the sheet music, the conductor, and the sound coming from the instrument they are playing. After identifying where the performer's attention is during peak performances, that performer is aided in identifying where her focus is when she is not in the optimal mental state during performance (such as when she is anxious, tense, or emotionally flat). It is common for a performer's focus to shift from the essential elements of the performance to her own thoughts during performances (internal distraction) or to non-performance relevant external factors (external distraction). Common internal distractions may be thoughts that the performer will make a mistake or fail, or disappoint a coach, teacher, or significant other. Common external distractions include sights and sounds such as those associated with the audience, other performers, or significant others.

After the performer gains some confidence manipulating his physical tension, emotions, arousal, and focus, and begins to see improvements in performance, he is taught how to manage his practice and performance environment. Because the environment in which a performer practices and performs has an impact on his performance, performers are taught how to create a performance-enhancing environment. Given that the performer cannot always control what might occur in his environment, he is also taught to prepare for and control his responses to uncontrollable environmental factors. For example, a student who is studying for an upcoming national examination may decide to go to a quiet part of the library where there are fewer distractions than at home. This strategy would likely lessen the external distractions that the student would encounter during his studying. Further, the student would identify what things he would put in his environment that would be conducive to studying. The student may determine that bringing a bag that contained only study materials (as opposed to a cell phone, electronic games, a magazine) and a laminated card containing the goals he has set for the upcoming examination would limit environmental distractions. The student identifies potential performance inhibiting environmental factors that are beyond his control such as friends coming to visit him in the library, getting hungry, being too cold, and so on. The student would develop a plan for how to use each of these environmental factors to help create the optimal focus, emotions, arousal, and physical relaxation during the study period.

In addition to identifying strategies that performers can use to manage their environment, they are encouraged to reinterpret environmental cues that typically inhibit their performance. For example, a performer may find herself getting overly anxious and worried when she has to perform before large audiences because she begins to think that, "All of the people expect me to be perfect. They're going to see that we're not really very good." To avoid this, performers can learn to interpret these situations in a much more calming, positive, and energizing way, such as, "Look at all of these people waiting to hear how well I play. I must be great to have so many interested people pulling for me." This latter interpretation would likely lead to a greater sense of confidence, positive arousal, and poise during performance.

The technique that integrates all of these mental skills is the use of performance routines. Performance routines consist of components of the techniques the performers had been practicing previously. Each routine should contain an explicit description of how the performer is going to use his thoughts, behaviors, and the environment to create the optimal focus, emotion/arousal, and physical tension prior to and during performances or following an error or setback. For example, a gymnast would develop and write down a script that describes what she is going to do the hour before her gymnastics performance. The script would include precisely what she will think about, say to herself, and imagine when she is getting changed and putting on her make up, warming up, waiting to perform, and moments before beginning her routine. The script would also include how she will behave (breathing and relaxation exercises), talk, move, and so on, as well as exactly what she will focus on (for example, the back of the beam prior to mounting as opposed to the coach or the crowd). Over time, performers refine their performance routines, integrating new insights and observations based on each successive performance.

The final technique that should be considered in a mental training program is cognitive restructuring. *Cognitive restructuring* consists of identifying core beliefs that performers have about themselves and the world that are inhibiting their ability to successfully implement the mental training program. Not every performer needs to work at the level of modifying core beliefs. Rather, it is the performer who is not able to effectively apply the mental skills discussed above who needs to examine core beliefs that may be inhibiting his mastery. Examples of common negative core beliefs include

I'm just not as talented as other people.
I'm a born choker.
There's something wrong with me that will not let me succeed.
I don't deserve to win.
Losing would be unbearable.
I must be perfect in every performance.
Losing or making an error is the worse thing that could ever happen to me.
I couldn't face my friends if I didn't do well.
I am unlucky.

External factors control my performance. As you can see, core beliefs that inhibit practice and performance tend to be associated with one's lack of confidence in oneself as a performer, the catastrophic consequences of failure or making mistakes, perfectionism, and having an external locus of control (believing that performance outcomes are determined by uncontrollable external factors rather than factors under one's control). Although these negative core beliefs can spur some performers to practice and perform with more intensity to avoid the agony of defeat, they generally lead other performers to become overly tense, anxious, inhibited, unfocused, and fatalistic, which leads to decrements in performance.

Phase 4. Critical to the success of mental skills training is the generalization of mental skills learned in the consultant's office or in the performer's training environment to the actual performance setting. This process requires a considerable amount of time and energy in order to be successful. As one can imagine, achieving a state of relaxation lying down in an office is likely to be much easier to do than under the pressure of an important performance. As mentioned above, the performance routines (pre-practice, preperformance, and post-error) provide a way to integrate the individual mental training techniques and become the focal point for transferring the skills learned in the "lab" to the performance setting.

It is important to emphasize to the performer that progress will be made over time, but not without setbacks. Performers who are looking for a quick fix with mental training will be disappointed; however, those performers who consistently practice the basic skills and integrate them into performance routines learn that they can create the optimal mental state for performance on demand. In order to encourage performers to continue to practice their skills and to effectively deal with relapse, it is suggested that traditional behavioral adherence strategies (such as assessment of progress, monitoring, reinforcement) be included in all mental training programs (O'Donohue & Krasner, 1997).

Putative Mechanisms of Efficacy

Mental skills training teaches children and adolescents to regulate their mental, emotional, and physiological responses to performance situations. Several mechanisms may account for improved performance following mental skills training. The mechanism that has received the most attention is self-efficacy (Bandura, 1986, 1997, 2001). Self-efficacy is one's confidence that one can carry out a chosen course of behavior. A considerable amount of research supports the notion that mental skills training increases self-efficacy and that increased self-efficacy is associated with improved performance (Garza & Feltz, 1998). Once performers have demonstrated to themselves that they can regulate their focus, emotional arousal, and muscle tension during mental training, they have an increased sense that they can better maintain poise during the pressure of performance. This increased sense of self-efficacy increases a performer's outcome expectations, desire to persist in practice, and desire to win in performances.

Other factors that may mediate the effect of mental skills training on performance have not received sufficient research attention for conclusions to be drawn. However, many of the factors assessed on the Mental Strengths Assessment (Brassington, 2001) are likely mediators. For example, improved focus would likely increase a performer's self-efficacy to perform his skills under increasing pressure, leading to improved performance. Correspondingly, performers learning how to better regulate themselves in the form of being able to relax, energize, and recover from errors would likely enhance their self-efficacy. Clearly, the effect of mental skills training is bi-directional in that the enhanced psychophysiological control causes an increase in his self-efficacy that in turn improves his performance. This enhanced performance reinforces the benefits of the mental skills training, causing the performer to anticipate greater control and performance success in the future. Figure 25.3 illustrates the proposed mediators of the effect of mental skills training on performance.

FIGURE 25.3. PROPOSED MEDIATORS OF THE EFFECT OF MENTAL SKILLS TRAINING ON PERFORMANCE.

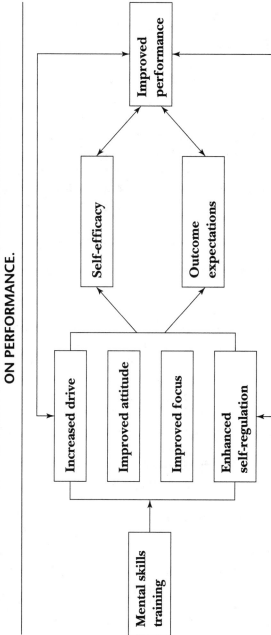

Future research should be conducted to determine the mediators that are most responsible for the performance gains that have been reported as a result of mental skills training. To do this, it would be necessary to assess the changes in the proposed mediators from baseline to the end of the mental skills training program, and then to correlate these changes with improvements in performance. To demonstrate true mediators, those performers who had positive changes in the mediators would have realized improvements in performance, while performers who did not have positive changes in the mediators would not realize performance gains. For example, self-efficacy would be considered a mediator of the effect of mental skills training on performance if children who increased their self-efficacy had improvements in performance, while children who did not increase their self-efficacy had not improved. This type of result would suggest that the mechanism through which mental skills training achieves its results is increasing self-efficacy.

Developmental Influences

Several important issues need to be addressed when implementing a mental training program with children, including (1) the cognitive development of the child, (2) the most appropriate role for parents in the training, (3) the influence of coaches, teachers, and peers, and (4) the importance of reinforcing adherence to the mental training techniques.

Cognitive development. A mental skills training program should focus on behavioral strategies for helping children younger than eleven years perform in performance situations and a combination of behavioral and cognitive strategies with older children. For example, an eight-year-old performer who frequently looks at her parents for approval during a gymnastics competition would likely benefit from controlling her attentions with visual cues as opposed to restructuring her thinking. Conversely, an older child may benefit from challenging his dysfunctional thinking about the consequences if his parents are disappointed with the performance as well as using behavioral techniques, such as preperformance routines.

Parent's involvement in training. Throughout mental skills training, it is critical that the parents be apprised of the training and included where appropriate. Several factors should be taken into consideration when deciding on how to involve the parent in mental skills training. First, the age and maturity of the child generally determines the appropriate involvement of the parents. Younger children can greatly benefit from the parents' involvement as they attempt to raise their awareness of the mental factors involved in their performance. Because younger children are generally involved in more concrete operations, they have difficulty generalizing what they have learned in mental training from one performance situation to another. Parents, if properly trained, can help the child apply what she has learned in one performance context to novel performance situations.

Parent involvement in mental skills training is not only beneficial to young children, but it can also provide older children and adolescents with valuable support and encouragement as they seek to integrate these new mental skills into their performances. Nevertheless, older children are often beginning to develop their autonomy, seeking to separate themselves from their parents. For this reason, it is important for the mental training professional to help parents find ways that foster their child's autonomy and self-efficacy, while reducing their child's feelings of being controlled or criticized. I often encourage parents to view themselves as supporters, whose job it is to focus on their child's mental and physical strengths and to leave corrections to the child's coaches, teachers, and mental training professionals. If parents try to take too active a role in getting their child to practice the mental training techniques or to be "mentally tough" during performances, the child may resent the parents and completely oppose mental training. Conversely, supportive parenting that encourages a child to practice the mental training techniques and reinforces gains that the child is making can greatly contribute to the success of the mental skills training program. (For more information about the role of the family in mental training, refer to the family systems model for addressing mental training issues in children and adolescents in Hellstedt, 1995.)

The influence of coaches, teachers, and peers. Like parents, coaches, teachers, and peers play a significant role in helping children prepare for and master the challenges of performing in school, sports, performing arts, and life. Although mental skills training does not specifically focus on working with the significant social relations in a performer's life, this does not mean that they cannot either act to facilitate or hinder the effects of a mental skills training program. If coaches, teachers, and peers value mental training, they will create space for the performer to practice the mental training exercises and encourage the development of mental skills. For example, behaviors such as listening with interest when a performer speaks about mental training or speaking confidently about the benefits of mental practice can positively affect a performer's confidence in mental training. This enhanced confidence can increase the performer's commitment to mental skills practice, thereby increasing the overall effectiveness of the mental skills training program.

Conversely, if a performer's coach, teacher, or peers believe that mental training is ineffective and a waste of time, it is likely that the performer will also doubt the effectiveness of the mental training. A chasm between the mind and the body still exists in this culture in that physical strength and techniques are seen as the royal road to success, while the mind is often viewed as an unpredictable, unruly beast that needs to be tamed through brute force and punishment. It is for this reason that it is not uncommon to hear coaches, teachers, and peers yelling epithets at performers such as, "You are mentally weak! Stop being a baby and stay in control!" These types of messages tend to only exacerbate the performers' problems by heightening their anxiety, lowering their self-confidence, and making them feel helpless and inadequate.

Reinforcing adherence to the mental training techniques. Like physical activity, mental skills need to be practiced consistently before a performer gains sufficient self-control and mastery to use the techniques in pressure situations. Hence, it is imperative that strategies be employed to encourage adherence and continued self-monitoring. Techniques that have been used in other types of behavioral therapy (Kazdin, 1994) and social cognitive theory (Bandura, 1997) can be applied to mental practice. The techniques that I have found most helpful include positive reinforcement by clinicians, parents, teachers, coaches, and performers; requiring performers to record their practice sessions; intermittent reminder calls and email messages; and the involvement of a performer's peers in mental practice (social support, norming).

Putative Targets of Treatment

Mental skills training focuses on teaching performers a series of self-regulation skills designed to help them create an optimal mental and emotional state during practice and performance. The target for the mental skills training interventions is the performers' mental strengths, their capacity to regulate their focus, control their arousal, and harness their drive to train intensely and perform with composure and confidence under pressure. The goal of this type of training is to build a reserve of mental energy and composure that can be accessed when needed under pressure. This approach to performance enhancement is consistent with the recent Positive Psychology movement (Seligman, 2002; Seligman & Csikszentmihalyi, 2000). As children age, they are faced with increasing pressure to perform well under pressure (exams, sports competitions, theatrical recitals, and so on). Mental skills training helps performers respond to performance situations in such a way as to minimize distress and promote healthy adaptation to performance pressure. It is believed that this healthy adaptation to pressure leads to personal growth and feelings of accomplishment and satisfaction. Hence, the goal of mental skills training is not to remove performers from stressful situations, but, rather, to help them express their talents and creative abilities in the "heat" of competition and performance. A story from the Zen tradition of Japan that has

been told in various forms by a number of authors illustrates the central aim of
mental skills training:

> A student came to a famous Zen sword master and requested that he teach him
> to be an expert swordsman. As is common in the Zen tradition, the student was
> instructed to do mundane chores around the master's house to show that he
> had sufficient discipline and commitment to deserve receiving the master's
> training. After several years of cooking and taking care of the master's house,
> the student asked the master when he was going to start his sword training. The
> master ignored the question, but that evening when the student was cooking
> dinner, the master came up behind him and hit the student on the head with a
> wooden stick and walked quietly away. The student jumped in surprise and
> didn't understand the master's action. During the days and weeks that followed,
> the master would sneak up behind the student and hit him with the stick when
> he was cooking, cleaning, and even sleeping. The student soon became so
> paranoid that he was going to be hit by the master that he could not keep his
> mind on his work for even a few minutes. He even had dreams of being
> attacked by the master. Nevertheless, the master continued to attack the student
> randomly throughout the day and night until one day when the master was
> striking the student from behind, the student moved gracefully to the side
> evading the staff and returning to his work undisturbed. Seeing this response,
> the master said, "Now it is time for you to learn to use the sword, because your
> mind will not be unsettled by your opponent or the unpredictability of the
> environment in which you find yourself."

This story illustrates the central target of mental skills training, which is to
teach performers how to maintain their poise and composure during the pressure
of competition and in the midst of an unpredictable and constantly changing
word. In many ways, mental skills training helps performers maintain their confidence and trust in their hard-earned skills and creativity regardless of what their
opponents and the world "throws" at them.

Empirical Support for Treatment Efficacy

A large number of studies have demonstrated the efficacy of mental skills training
on academic (Smith, 1989), athletic (Vealey, 1994), and musical performance among
children and adults. More than ten literature reviews have been conducted between
1966 and 1999 (Feltz & Landers, 1983; Gould & Udry, 1994; Greenspan & Feltz,
1989; Kirschenbaum, 1987; Martin, Moritz, & Hall, 1999; Murphy, 1994;

Petruzzello, Landers, & Salazar, 1991; Richardson, 1967a, 1967b; Vealey, 1994; Weinberg, 1994). Some of the reviews have examined the impact of individual mental-skill interventions, such as goal setting, imagery, and so on, while other studies have examined the impact of multi-skill interventions in which performers are taught several mental skills over the course of the study. Reviewers of these studies have generally suggested that multi-skill interventions are more effective than single-skill interventions. Also, the lengths of the mental skill training programs assessed in studies to date have varied from one hour to twelve months, with longer interventions yielding greater improvements in performance.

One of the limitations of research sited above is that fewer studies have been conducted with adolescents and children as compared to college students and adults (Bar-Eli, Dreshman, Blumenstein, & Weinstein, 2002; Bar-Eli, Tenenbaum, Pie, & Kudar, 1997; Barnett, 1977; Casby & Moran, 1998; Corbin, 1967; Crocker, Alderman, & Smith, 1988; Hollingsworth, 1975; Lanning & Hisanaga, 1983; Lee & Hewitt, 1987; Spink, 1988; Wanlin, Hrycaiko, Martin, & Mahon, 1997). Hence, based on the current scientific literature, it is unclear whether certain techniques are more appropriate for younger performers. It is the author's experience that behavioral techniques such as progressive muscle relaxation training, focusing drills, and preperformance routines are more effective than cognitive techniques such as goal setting, visualization, and cognitive restructuring for younger performers.

Personal Experience and Cases

Several case studies will be discussed to illustrate the application of mental skills training to children and adolescents. The first case involved a ten-year-old white, non-Hispanic, female gymnast whom I will call Ann. Ann was brought to me by her parents after she performed poorly in a national gymnastics competition. I met with Ann and her parents for an initial interview and had Ann complete the Mental Strengths Assessment (Brassington, 2001). The parents reported that Ann appeared to be getting progressively more nervous before competitions during the six months following her first national competition. Ann's parents described her as generally "relaxed and in good spirits" with the exception of the days leading up to competitions, during which Ann was nervous, irritable, and less cooperative at home and school. Ann's parents did not feel that this was currently a significant problem, but were concerned that Ann seemed to be having increasing difficulties handling competition at the national level. Their greatest concern was that the changes in Ann's attitudes and behavior, if not corrected, would continue to deteriorate along with her enjoyment and success in gymnastics. When asked how she was feeling about competing in a national competition, Ann stated that she enjoyed competing but wanted to perform better. She described feeling nervous before competition but did not like to think about it too much. She could not identify changes in her thinking or behavior since moving to a higher level of competition that might account for the recent decrements in her performance. She said that her parents were supportive of her during competitions as well as when she did not perform at her best.

This initial presentation by Ann and her parents is very typical and illustrates two significant points about assessing children who present for mental skills training. First, parents of younger children often become aware of changes in their child's attitude and behavior before their child is even aware. Typically, parents have been watching their child in performance situations for many years and are sensitive to subtle changes. Conversely, children have not, in general, reflected on cognitions or behaviors associated with competition—they performed on autopilot. Not until the pressure of performance has a negative effect does the child reflect on the mental dimensions of performance. Second, the majority of parents who bring their child for mental skills training consider their behavior toward their child to be supportive at best and benign at worst. However, it is not uncommon for this to be far from the truth. Hence, clinicians should be mindful that it may take some time to increase both the parents' and the child's awareness of how their attitudes and behavior are affecting the mental dimensions of the child's performance.

For nine sessions following the initial assessment, I met with Ann individually. During these sessions, I gave her age-appropriate feedback on the MSA. (See selected pre-scores in Figure 25.4.)

Of special note were her lower scores on optimism, mental confidence, and sense of control. They were significantly lower than the normative sample. Further, her scores on the scales reflecting focus, attitude, and self-regulation were well below the mean for the normative sample. Ann concurred with the results of the MSA. She said that she is feeling more and more afraid of losing. She said that she used to "just go out and compete," but then she began thinking about what mistakes to avoid (fear of failure). Ann described her mind as a "bunch of thoughts pinging around" in her brain distracting her during competitions. On several occasions during our assessment feedback session, she described feeling as though "it is more luck whether I feel mentally ready to perform at a competition." She denied having any real ability to regulate her muscle tension, emotions, or thoughts during competition. Ann stated that if she made a mistake in a competition she never recovers. During recent competitions she made errors early in the competitions leading to a steady decline in performance as the competition progressed.

FIGURE 25.4. MENTAL STRENGTH'S ASSESSMENT RESULTS (ANN).

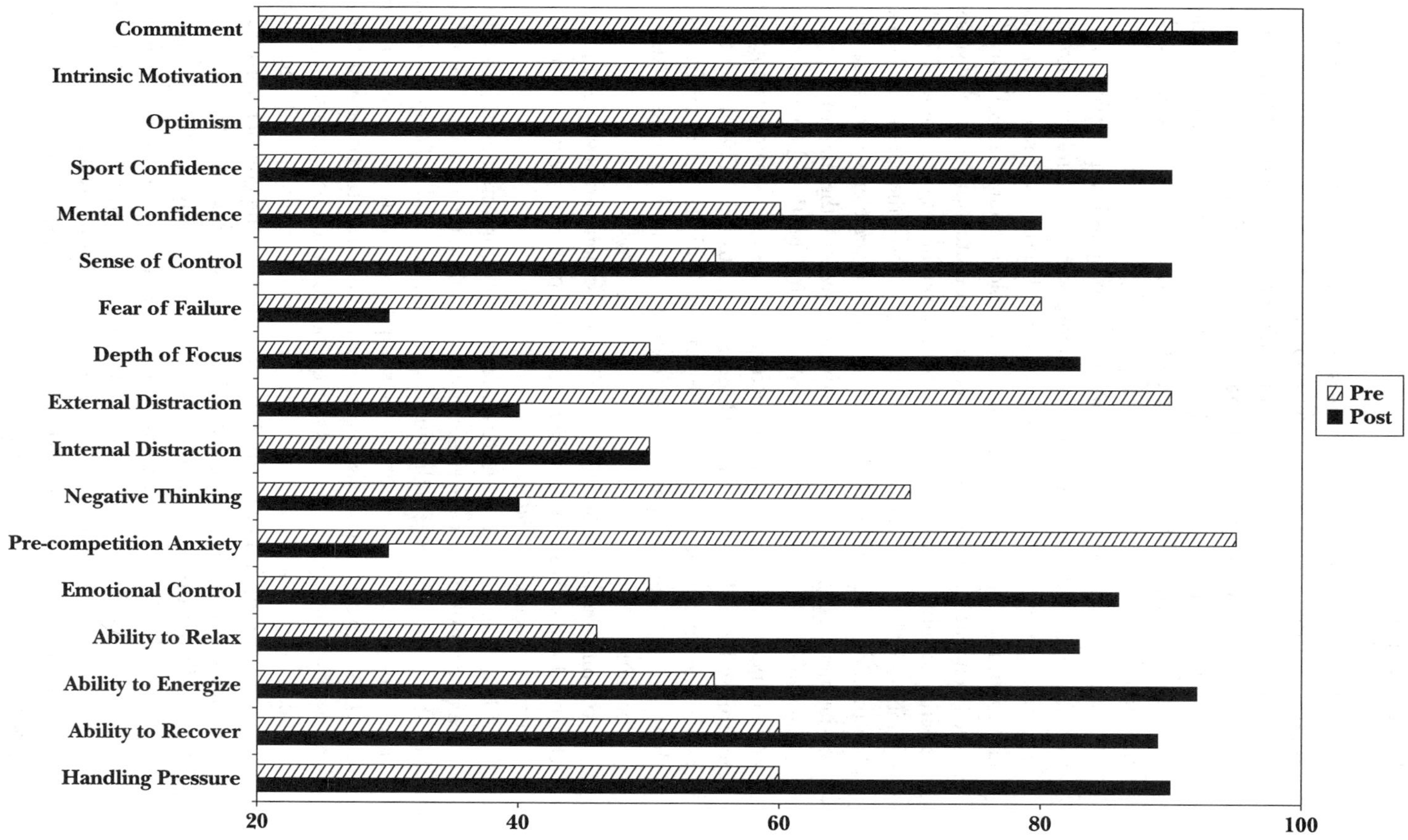

During the assessment feedback session, I took a great deal of time to normalize Ann's experience and to instill hope in her that she could learn to effectively manage the increased pressure associated with national competition. I explained that her experience was very common and that I had successfully worked with many young athletes who had experiences similar to hers. I told Ann that there are mental exercises that she can practice that would help her manage anxiety and worry before and during competitions. I emphasized that she would have to practice the mental exercises daily and with as much energy and commitment she practices her physical skills.

In the sessions that followed, Ann was taught progressive muscle relaxation training to increase her ability to reduce excess physical tension. She was asked to do two twenty-minute practice sessions each day. The records of her practice over the course of eight weeks indicated that she was able to create a deep state of relaxation in less and less time. Ann initially needed twenty minutes to achieve a deep state of relaxation; however, by the eighth week of practice, she was able to create this state in less than five minutes. Ann reported that this type of practice really gave her a sense that she could manage her "nervousness" before competitions. She said that the progressive muscle relaxation training not only helped her feel physically less tense, but it also helped quiet her mind.

After several weeks of practicing relaxation training, Ann was taught how to use visualization to create positive energy and emotions prior to practice and competitions. To do this, she was asked to recall several of her best performances. While recalling these performances, Ann was asked to involve all of her senses in the recollection. She was asked to pay special attention to what she was feelings, how she was using her body, and how she was responding to the environment. Ann recalled a balance beam performance several years earlier. She described her performance as effortless and flawless. Ann was able to recall staring at the center of the end of the balance beam before mounting the balance beam for her routine. She vividly recalled the smell of chalk and sweat in the gym, and the way she held her shoulders back and tensed the muscled of her eyes in a stare. It was interesting to watch Ann's reaction to practicing this recollection imagery exercise. I could clearly observe the look of joy on her face when she opened her eyes. She said that she would love to have the chance to compete "right now." I explained to her that with practice she would be able to create these feelings of excitement, confidence, and joy whenever she wished. She was instructed to add the imagery practice after she had finished her twice-daily relaxation training.

In the weeks that followed, Ann developed a pre-competition mental routine that she followed before each competition. Her pre-competition mental routine included the following elements and began approximately one hour before each competition. First, she would engage in ten minutes of progressive muscle relaxation lying down. Second, she would do five minutes of imagery in which she would see herself performing the upcoming gymnastics elements flawlessly. Third, she would warm up and stretch, using positive self-talk, positive images about the upcoming performance, and diaphragmatic breathing—focusing on her body (not external factors) throughout this period. Hence, the physical warm-up was also a mental warm-up and focusing activity. These strategies not only helped Ann increase positive emotions and expectations, they also reduced the likelihood that her thoughts would wander in a negative direction, leading to doubt and uncertainty about the upcoming performance. Fourth, Ann developed a series of external focal points that she would use to keep her focused on the present during the waiting period. She used breathing and self talk to modulate her emotions/energy while waiting. Finally, when it was her turn to demonstrate a skill, she would focus on a predetermined part of the apparatus, take a deep breath, and begin her performance.

Ann was able to produce an exceptional performance during a national competition after several weeks of mental training. Subsequently, she reported consistently strong performances, and, hence, we agreed to conclude training after eight weeks. Nevertheless, I counseled her to continue practicing the mental training skills if she wished to continue to reap the performance benefits she had seen. It is not uncommon for performers to diligently engage in Mental Skills Training and rigorous mental preparation for performances only to become complacent about mental practice when things begin to go well. It is important to continually emphasize the need to make mental practice as integral a part of one's training and performance regimen as is physical practice.

In order to identify and reinforce the most helpful parts of the mental skills training program for Ann, I asked her to reflect on what worked and what did not work for her. Ann attributed the gains in her performance to what she called the "getting quiet exercise," which referred to the progressive muscle relaxation training, the "getting psyched-up" imagery, and having a mental plan for competition day. Ann said that she found having something to do with her mind stopped her from worrying about what might go wrong or about what others might think about her performance. Ann's post-test scores on the MSA indicate that she experienced significant improvements in all of the MSA scales that she was low on before participating in the mental skills training program, with the exception of "internal distraction" that was at a relatively low level before the training. (See Figure 25.4.) She was more confident in her mental abilities. She reported increased emotional control, focus, and ability to self-regulate. Further, she reported a very large decrease in fear of failure and pre-competition anxiety.

   To illustrate the application of mental skills training in an academic setting, I will briefly describe a case of a sixteen-year-old whom I will call John. John came to me at the recommendation of his school counselor. John said he was having trouble getting himself motivated to study and had been getting progressively more anxious before examinations. John was in his junior year of a preparatory high school. He reported that since starting his junior year he had not been enjoying school as much as in past years. He stated that he was feeling a lot of pressure because the workload was increasing and the classes were becoming more difficult. He described high school as "a pressure cooker" and said that he was having trouble imagining how much pressure there must be in college. John was asked to take the Mental Strengths Assessment. As can be seen in Figure 25.5, John reported lower than desirable scores on several of the attitude, focus, and self-regulations scales.

   During the initial interview, it became clear to me and to John that before his junior year of high school, he was able to mange the demands of school and did not think much about whether he would do well in his classes; he just always did. At this point, he was starting to question his abilities, and this made him anxious about upcoming exams. He reported that he would avoid studying because he disliked how nervous he became when he sat down to do his homework. He also reported that his friends were constantly talking about college applications and the many requirements that the better schools had as part of their admissions policies. I worked with John for about five weeks. During our first session, we discussed his MSA profile and he felt that the profile he received was an accurate depiction of his approach to academic work. During the subsequent weeks, we discussed techniques that he could use to manage his anxiety and frame his academic work in a more positive and less frightening manner.

   John diligently practiced mental skills such as progressive muscle relaxation and visualization. He reported that these techniques immediately helped him feel more in control of his anxiety and that he was spending less time avoiding studying. He said that he did not realize how anxious he had become until he started to use the progressive muscles relaxation. During other sessions, John developed a mental script containing positive affirmations about his academic performance. These affirmations (cognitive restructuring) led John to feel more excited about his academic future. He described himself as having moved from fear about whether he could succeed in college to looking forward to the challenge of more rigorous academic standards. This new perspective led to John studying more, which in turn led to him doing better on several of his examinations.

   It is likely that John became involved in mental skills training at a very opportune time. He clearly had positive feelings about school until he found himself outside of his "comfort zone." However, with some training in how to take

FIGURE 25.5. MENTAL STRENGTH'S ASSESSMENT RESULTS (JOHN).

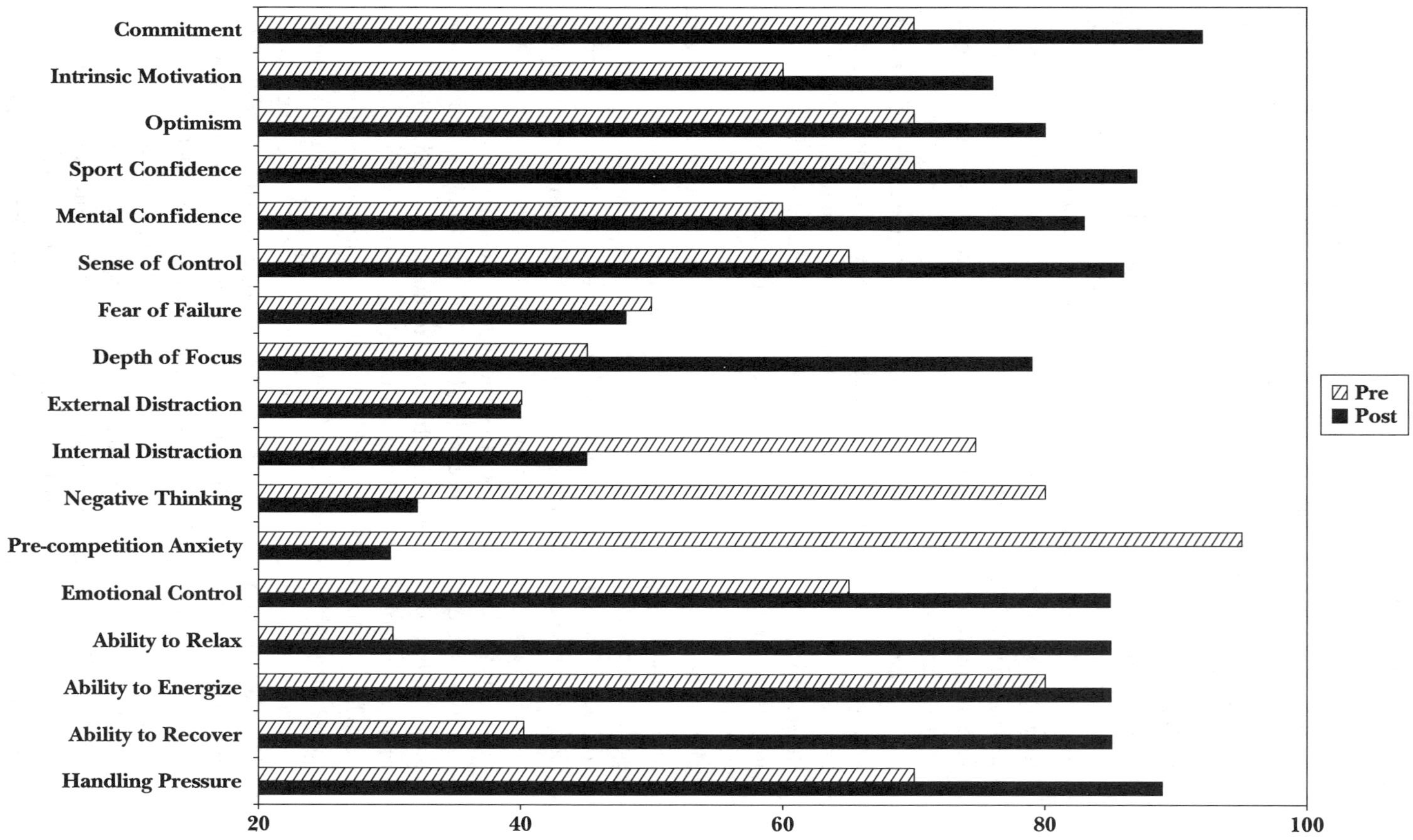

control of his focus, emotional arousal, and physical tension, he was able to alter his perspective and enhance his efficacy for managing the demands of his junior year of high school and the college application process. It is likely that a large number of children who find themselves at a crossroads in their development could be saved a lot of suffering and defeat if they could learn how to tap into their mental strengths as the performance demands increase thoughout the high school years and beyond.

Future Directions

Although current research supports the performance enhancing effects of mental skills training for children, the mediators (that is, the mechanisms by which this type of training achieves its results) still require significantly more research, and the moderators of treatment effects (such as sex, developmental stage, and ethnicity) remain unexplored. Hence, the future refinement of mental training techniques requires further investigation into exactly how these treatments work, for whom they work, and under what conditions they work most effectively.

◆ ◆ ◆

In conclusion, it is encouraging to observe the increasing interest and acceptance of mental skills training in Olympic, professional, college, and high school athletics because coaches and athletes are realizing the profound effects these techniques can have on performance. It is my hope that in the years to come, mental skills training will be embraced by everyone concerned with the success and healthy development of young performers, leading to a marked increase in the prevention of mental problems in children and the greater realization of each child's potential.

References

Bandura, A. (1986). *Social foundations of thought and action: A social cognitive theory.* Englewood Cliffs, NJ: Prentice-Hall.

Bandura, A. (1997). *Self-Efficacy: The exercise of control.* New York: W. H. Freeman & Company.

Bandura, A. (2001). Social cognitive theory: An agentic perspective. *Annual Review of Psychology, 52,* 1–26.

Bar-Eli, M., Dreshman, R., Blumenstein, B., & Weinstein, Y. (2002). The effect of mental training with biofeedback on the performance of young swimmers. *Applied Psychology: An International Review, 51*(4), 567–581.

Bar-Eli, M., Tenenbaum, G., Pie, J. S., & Kudar, K. (1997). Aerobic performance under different goal orientations and different goal conditions. *Journal of Sport Behavior, 20*(1), 3–15.

Barnett, M. L. (1977). Effects of two methods of goal setting on learning a gross motor task. *Research Quarterly, 48*(1), 19–23.

Boutcher, S. H., & Crews, D. J. (1987). The effect of a preshot attentional routine on a well-learned skill. *International Journal of Sport Psychology, 18*(1), 30–39.

Brassington, G. S. (2001). *Mental Strengths Assessment.* Retrieved from http://www.eliteperformers.com

Casby, A., & Moran, A. (1998). Exploring mental imagery in swimmers: A single-case study design. *Irish Journal of Psychology, 19*(4), 525–531.

Corbin, C. B. (1967). The effects of covert rehearsal on the development of a complex motor skill. *Journal of General Psychology, 76*(2), 143–150.

Crocker, P. R., Alderman, R. B., & Smith, M. R. (1988). Cognitive-affective stress management training with high performance youth volleyball players: Effects on affect, cognition, and performance. *Journal of Sport & Exercise Psychology, 10*(4), 448–460.

Feltz, D. L., & Landers, D. M. (1983). The effects of mental practice on motor skill learning and performance: A meta-analysis. *Journal of Sport Psychology, 5*(1), 25–57.

Garza, D. L., & Feltz, D. L. (1998). Effects of selected mental practice on performance, self-efficacy, and competition confidence of figure skaters. *Sport Psychologist, 12*(1), 1–15.

Gould, D., & Udry, E. (1994). Psychological skills for enhancing performance: Arousal regulation strategies. *Medicine & Science in Sports & Exercise, 26*(4), 478–485.

Greenspan, M. J., & Feltz, D. L. (1989). Psychological interventions with athletes in competitive situations: A review. *Sport Psychologist, 3*(3), 219–236.

Hellstedt, J. (1995). Invisible players: A family systems model. In S. M. Murphy (Ed.), *Sport Psychology Interventions.* Champaign, IL: Human Kinetics Press.

Hollingsworth, B. (1975). Effects of performance goals and anxiety on learning a gross motor task. *Research Quarterly, 46*(2), 162–168.

Jacobson, E. (1974). *Progressive relaxation: A physiological & clinical investigation of muscular states and their significance in psychology and medical practice.* University of Chicago Press.

Kazdin, A. E. (1994). *Behavior modification in applied settings* (5th ed.). Pacific Grove, CA: Brooks/Cole.

Kirschenbaum, D. S. (1987). Self-regulation of sport performance. *Medicine & Science in Sports & Exercise, 19*(5, Suppl), 106–113.

Lanning, W., & Hisanaga, B. (1983). A study of the relation between the reduction of competition anxiety and an increase in athletic performance. *International Journal of Sport Psychology, 14*(4), 219–227.

Lee, A. B., & Hewitt, J. (1987). Using visual imagery in a flotation tank to improve gymnastic performance and reduce physical symptoms. *International Journal of Sport Psychology, 18*(3), 223–230.

Locke, E. A. (1991). Problems with goal-setting research in sports—and their solution. *Journal of Sport & Exercise Psychology, 13*(3), 311–316.

Locke, E. A., & Latham, G. P. (1985). The application of goal setting to sports. *Journal of Sport Psychology, 7*(3), 205–222.

Locke, E. A., Shaw, K. N., Saari, L. M., & Latham, G. P. (1981). Goal setting and task performance: 1969–1980. *Psychological Bulletin, 90*(1), 125–152.

Martin, K. A., Moritz, S. E., & Hall, C. R. (1999). Imagery use in sport: A literature review and applied model. *Sport Psychologist, 13*, 245–268.

Murphy, S. M. (1994). Imagery interventions in sport. *Medicine & Science in Sports & Exercise,* *26*(4), 486–494.

O'Donohue, W., & Krasner, L. (Eds.). (1997). *Theories of behavior therapy: Exploring behavior change.* Washington DC: American Psychological Association.

Ostrow, A. C. (Ed.). (1996). *Directory of psychological tests in the sport and exercise sciences.* Morgantown: Fitness Information Technology, Inc.

Petruzzello, S. J., Landers, D. M., & Salazar, W. (1991). Biofeedback and sport/exercise performance: Applications and limitations. *Behavior Therapy, 22*(3), 379–392.

Richardson, A. (1967a). Mental practice: A review and discussion: I. *Research Quarterly, 38*(1), 95–107.

Richardson, A. (1967b). Mental practice: A review and discussion: II. *Research Quarterly, 38*(2), 263–273.

Seligman, M.E.P. (2002). Positive psychology, positive prevention, and positive therapy. In C. R. Snyder & S. J. Lopez (Eds.), *Handbook of positive psychology.* London: Oxford University Press.

Seligman, M.E.P., & Csikszentmihalyi, M. (2000). Positive psychology: An introduction. *American Psychologist, 55*(1), 5–14.

Smith, R. E. (1989). Effects of coping skills training on generalized self-efficacy and locus of control. *Journal of Personality & Social Psychology, 56,* 228–233.

Spink, K. S. (1988). Facilitating endurance performance: The effects of cognitive strategies and analgesic suggestions. *Sport Psychologist, 2*(2), 97–104.

Vealey, R. S. (1994). Current status and prominent issues in sport psychology interventions. *Medicine & Science in Sports & Exercise, 26*(4), 495–502.

Wanlin, C. M., Hrycaiko, D. W., Martin, G. L., & Mahon, M. (1997). The effects of a goal-setting package on the performance of speed skaters. *Journal of Applied Sport Psychology, 9*(2), 212–228.

Weinberg, R. S. (1994). Goal setting and performance in sport and exercise settings: A synthesis and critique. *Medicine & Science in Sports & Exercise, 26*(4), 469–477.

Williams, J. M. (2001). *Applied sport psychology: Personal growth to peak performance* (4 ed.). The McGraw-Hill Companies.

Ziegler, S. G. (1994). The effects of attentional shift training on the execution of soccer skills: A preliminary investigation. *Journal of Applied Behavior Analysis, 27*(3), 545–552.

CHAPTER TWENTY-SIX

EMPOWERING THE FAMILY AS A RESOURCE FOR RECOVERY: AN EXAMPLE OF FAMILY-BASED TREATMENT FOR ANOREXIA NERVOSA

James Lock, M.D, Ph.D.

Family therapy has evolved over the past quarter century to the extent that specialized training in "schools" of family therapy (for example, structural, Milan, Post-Milan, or Narrative) is now common for those who practice in this modality (Minuchin, Rosman, & Baker, 1978; Palazzoli, 1974). In addition, there are specialized credentials that attest to a skill base in family therapy, especially in Europe and the United Kingdom. In the United States, this trend is somewhat less pronounced. The focus of research and training in psychotherapy in the United States has been more individual approaches, notably cognitive behavioral therapy and interpersonal psychotherapy (Kazdin, 2000). In psychotherapy of children and adolescents, family therapy, in a generic sense, is commonly recommended and practiced. Like other psychotherapy modalities, family therapy is under-researched and evidence for its effectiveness is limited to case series, for the most part (Hoagwood, Burns, Kiser, Ringeisen, & Schoenwald, 2001).

Even those with limited exposure to family therapy recognize that anorexia nervosa (AN) is often the paradigmatic illness for family interventions. Structural family therapy used anorexia nervosa as an illness to explain problematic family processes, as well as an example of how these processes could be addressed in systematic family treatment (Minuchin et al., 1978). Strategic family therapy explored ways to produce change from within the family by using the families of adolescents with anorexia nervosa as examples (Haley, 1973; Palazzoli, 1974). Therefore, it is not surprising that one of the major sources of evidence for treatment efficacy of family therapy is in the context of AN.

Here we report on one of the few family therapy treatment approaches that has an evidence base. It is a family-based treatment of anorexia nervosa devised by family therapists at the Maudsley Hospital in London, which has been used in four randomized, controlled trials of psychotherapy to date (Dare, Eisler, Russell, Treasure, & Dodge, 2001; Eisler et al., 2000; Le Grange, Eisler, Dare, & Russell, 1992; Russell, Szmukler, Dare, & Eisler, 1987). The treatment combines elements of several of the main schools of family therapy—some might argue the best of each school. As a treatment, it is specific for anorexia nervosa, but the principles and main interventions are likely to be useful in other clinical situations and with other illnesses. By focusing in detail on this particular family therapy, we hope to highlight both the features of the treatment specific to anorexia nervosa, as well as identify those that may be applicable more generally. We hope this encourages systematic research in family therapy for other conditions, as such studies are needed to support the use of this form of intervention.

Family therapy was not the first type of treatment to be used with AN. Early treatment of AN was dominated by psychoanalysis and other psychodynamically oriented psychotherapies. Psychoanalytic theorists postulated that refusal to eat was a defense mechanism designed to avoid conscious understanding of sexual wishes such as oral impregnation fantasies (Waller, Kaufman, & Deutch, 1940a; 1940b). In this line, Thoma suggests that AN is symptomatic of regression to the oral stage and an abandonment of the genital stage during early adolescence (Thoma, 1967). Bruch (1973), employing a more developmental understanding of adolescents, suggested that the person with AN suffers from an inadequate sense of self that is the result of a parental failure to support independent thinking and behavior in early adolescence (Bruch, 1973). In a related formulation, Crisp contends that AN is a phobic avoidance of adolescence and that self-starvation and food and weight preoccupation are ways to cope with anxieties and fears associated with pubertal change and psychosocial immaturity (Crisp, 1980, 1997). Psychoanalytic and psychodynamic therapies emphasized the intra-personal problems of the adolescent and often disregard, exclude, or blame the family, particularly the parents, for their adolescent's predicament.

Family approaches to AN treatment have a long history of controversy, starting with the early pioneers in the field. For the English, Sir William Gull proposed that families were "the worst attendants" for their children with AN (Gull, 1874). In contrast, on the other side of the Channel, Charles Lasegue viewed families as necessary for recovery (Lasegue, 1883). The outcome of this early debate favored Gull's perspective and the intervening 100 years mostly aimed interventions at individual pathology. By the 1970s, AN became an interest by structural and strategic schools of family therapy (Liebman, Minuchin, & Baker, 1974; Minuchin et al., 1978; Palazzoli, 1974; Rosman, Minuchin, Baker, & Liebman, 1977; Selvini Palazzoli, 1974, 1988; Selvini Palazzoli & Viaro, 1988). These approaches view the family as a system whose processes affect usual adolescent development. It also emphasizes the family system as a potential solution for the dilemmas of AN in the adolescent patient, stressing family process, communication, and negotiation of adolescent developmental issues.

In contradistinction to psychodynamic individual therapies, family therapy for AN, as described by Salvador Minuchin and Mara Selvini Palazzoli, views the family as a system whose pathological processes are the target of therapeutic intervention. Although family systemic therapies have not been the subject of any randomized clinical trials, several non-controlled trials of family therapy suggest that the approach is helpful. For example, Minuchin and colleagues reported good outcomes in 86% of fifty-three adolescent patients he treated using structural family therapy (Liebman et al., 1974). In addition, Stierlin and Weber used strategic family therapy in forty-two patients with AN and found that approximately two-thirds had recovered weight and menstruation at follow-up (Stierlin & Weber, 1989).

Structural and strategic family therapy emphasize that changing how the family system generally operates is how therapy changes the behaviors of AN. The approach intervenes to address family process, communication, and the ways deficits in them interfere with adolescent development. Challenging coalitions that are problematic and supporting the appropriate roles of parents and children in the family hierarchy are classic ways family therapists orchestrate change. In the case of AN, the focus is on pathological processes within the family (such as enmeshment, overprotectiveness, and avoidance of conflict) that must be addressed in order for patients to recover from AN.

A more recent refinement of family therapy for AN is represented in the work of Dare and Eisler from the Maudsley Hospital in London (Dare & Eisler, 1997; Dare, Eisler, Russell, & Szmukler, 1990). We will refer to the Maudsley Approach as Family-Based Treatment (FBT). FBT amalgamates elements of both strategic and structural family therapy, but also incorporates more recent developments in family therapy, including both feminist and narrative perspectives. For example, FBT uses family meals, which were first recommended by Minuchin. However, unlike Minuchin and colleagues, Dare and Eisler do not view the target of their intervention as faulty family process; instead, they take an "agnostic" view as to the cause of AN. Such a non-pathologizing perspective is derivative of the family therapy formulations of Jay Haley (1973). In addition, families are seen as a resource to assist the adolescent with AN, rather than an impediment to recovery and development. This allows FBT to empower the family to find solutions to the problems that AN is causing. This stance is based in the non-authoritarian therapeutic position recommended by Milan systems therapy as well as feminist theory (Palazzoli, 1974; Mandanes, 1981). In order to help the family understand that they are dealing with an illness rather than a rebellious adolescent, the approach borrows a technique from narrative therapy designed to emphasize the difference between the adolescent and anorexia nervosa (White, 1987; White & Epston, 1990).

Putative Mechanisms of Efficacy

How might FBT for AN work? FBT contends that therapy works not by addressing family pathology, but instead by the following mechanisms:

1. increasing parental awareness and anxiety about the medical and psychological problems associated with anorexia nervosa
2. diminishing parental guilt to allow them to take action
3. increasing parental self-efficacy through focusing on their successes and abilities as opposed to liabilities
4. focusing on changing eating behavior and insisting on weight gain because perpetuation of these symptoms helps to maintain AN

The treatment's strong focus on weight gain and normalizing eating behaviors quickly and decisively undoubtedly is a key component of its success as well. Refeeding has long been accomplished on inpatient programs or residential programs without parental involvement with noteworthy decreases in preoccupations and behaviors of AN demonstrated in the short term. Moreover, weight gain and symptomatic control by parents at home are similar in function to the activities of nursing staff and counselors in inpatient and residential settings. Thus, if parents can act as effectively as nursing staff at home, progress is likely. Low weight and restrictive dieting are probably maintaining factors for the distorted thinking that accompanies anorexia nervosa, so early reversal of these is likely to lead to recovery more quickly and with more success—especially if this is accompanied by addressing the life-context (the family and school) in vivo. This "in vivo" process of weight restoration and normalization of eating processes can happen only at home and with the substantial and sustained efforts of parents to promote these changes.

Theoretically, FBT works, in large part, because parents are helped to become authoritative and able to manage a particular set of problems (dieting, caloric restriction, and related behaviors) while still being both warm and understanding, but firm in their attention to the problem and resolute in their determination to change the behaviors. This may relate to the FBT's ability to increase parental self-efficacy in the face of a problem that seemed initially to overwhelm, stymie, and defeat them (Bandura, 1977, 1997).

One of the main criticisms of FBT for anorexia nervosa is based on the fear that the adolescent is simply "made to eat" and "forced" to do what the parents demand. This is perceived as dismissing of the adolescent's need for autonomy and self-control. Such a formulation misses the crucial intervention the therapist makes throughout treatment that supports both parental and patient awareness that AN is an illness. Those who have AN might think alike and behave similarly. The individual adolescent's identity and ways of thinking and feeling have been reduced to the limited range allowed by the illness. In addition, the adolescent is respected in the process of treatment because she is not blamed for the illness—it is externalized. Further, the therapy ultimately aims to return control over eating and weight at the earliest opportunity to the patient. The insistence of this point throughout treatment diminishes guilt and responsibility on the part of both the parents—when they have to fight these distorted thoughts and behaviors—and the adolescent, who is helped to recognize that thoughts and desires she believes are her own actually are the result of an illness that has taken away her independence of thought and action.

Finally, FBT enables parents to use and develop their own skills in relation to their own capacities and family and social context. There is no formula that each family follows; instead, their creativity and use of their own perspectives and experiments are encouraged in order for them to find the way out of the dilemmas that anorexia nervosa poses for their family. The therapist is an expert consultant who does not overpower or direct these efforts, but provides continuous positive reinforcement, support, and critical review of these attempts. In these ways, FBT *empowers* family members. Through this empowerment, their sense of effectiveness generally increases, and this leads to the necessary persistence, imagination, and determination required to defeat the problems that AN is causing them. They are prepared to move forward as a united team to find strength rather than focus on past problems or failures. This practical and forward looking approach is similar to cognitive behavioral therapy in this way.

Developmental Influences

In examining the importance of developmental themes in family therapy for AN there are three questions we would like to answer:

1. Is anorexia nervosa a developmental illness?
2. Is family therapy appropriate for adolescents?
3. Is FBT appropriate for adolescents with AN?

These three questions are interrelated. If AN is a developmental illness, specifically of adolescent development, then this leads naturally to the next question of how it should be addressed (Steiner, Sanders, & Ryst, 1995). The third question is a refinement, albeit an important refinement, of the second question.

Is Anorexia Nervosa a Developmental Illness?

The answer to this question appears to be a resounding "yes" and "no" (Steiner & Lock, 1998). The main objection to seeing anorexia nervosa as a purely developmental illness is the growing body of evidence that suggests a substantial biological substrate for the disorder. There is a burgeoning interest in the neurobiology and genetic influence on the development of eating disorders. For example, studies (Kendler et al., 1995; Strober & Humphrey, 1987; Strober, Lambert, Morrell, & Burroughs, 1999) indicate that AN aggregates in the first-degree relatives of people with AN and bulimia nervosa (BN), and that greater than 50% of the risk for AN is attributable to additive genetic influences. In addition, there is new evidence that some symptoms such as binge eating, self-induced vomiting, dietary restraint, body dissatisfaction, and weight preoccupation are also moderately to highly heritable. Taken together, these findings suggest the existence of a broad eating disorder (ED) phenotype with possible shared genetic predisposition. In addition, more recent advances employing neuroimaging techniques suggest that bulimic patients and anorexic patients differ in serotonin activity; however, the significance of these findings remains unclear.

These studies suggest that there is a neurobiological substrate for AN, and this may account for why some adolescents are at greater risk than others for AN. This hypothesis goes against the view that individual intrapsychic deficits or family pathology causes the disorder. On the other hand, these studies suggest that personality and behavioral characteristics associated with AN, such as anxiety, perfectionism, being driven, and obsessionality, may be common in families. These patients may come by these traits genetically, but when applied to dieting (as opposed to other activities where they may indeed be helpful), they become an engine to support developing and maintaining the symptoms of AN.

On the "yes" side of this question is the extensive data base suggesting that pubertal onset, social factors, sexual abuse, and response to media are all risks for the development of AN that increase during adolescence. Our group has proposed a specific model along theses lines for this disorder (Steiner et al., 2003).

Many see AN as a paradigmatic illness of adolescence in line with Crisp's formulations suggesting that AN is a "phobic" avoidance of the challenges of adolescence itself, including separating from the family of origin, negotiating peer competition, and developing intimate and sexual relations. A number of studies suggest that adolescents with AN are more anxious about these issues than many others, and in this sense, appear to be more likely to turn to the behaviors and preoccupations of AN to skirt the developmental challenges of adolescence.

In addition to the overall developmental challenges of the adolescent period, it appears that puberty, and with it increased emphasis on body type and weight, especially as shaped by the increasing influence of media images, plays a role in increasing the appeal of dieting and thereby, the potential for AN. For example, pubertal onset and eating problems were examined by Attie and Brooks-Gunn (1989) prospectively by following 193 girls from seventh through tenth grade for two years (Attie & Brooks-Gunn, 1989). In their study, eating problems emerged in response to pubertal change, especially fat accumulation. However, in addition to the physical changes associated with puberty, the girls' attitudes were predictive. Those girls who felt most negatively about their bodies were at highest risk for the development of eating difficulties. The relationship of these attitudes about their bodies may sometimes be related to experiences of abuse. In a cross-sectional study of adolescents in a community high school, we found that boys with disordered eating had histories of increased sexual and physical abuse compared to their male peers, while girls with eating disorders were more likely to be more sexually active than their female peers (Lock, Reisel, & Steiner, 2001).

The emphasis on thinness begins early, though so do obesity and overweight problems, but become increasingly important during adolescence. Studies of the changes in body fat in female models (in the downward direction) appear to be correlated with increasing rates of AN in adolescent females (Lucas, Beard, & O'Fallon, 1991). Moreover, studies of the effect of media on adolescents in non-Western countries suggest that media may be a real risk factor. However, the media does not play a role simply in setting body types of the thin ideal. It also provides information on dieting, "healthy" eating, and exercise regimens, all aimed at influencing the behavior of young women in these regards. The role of the media as a trigger for the development of AN is probably even more significant for adolescents than for adults or younger children, as they turn to the media more consistently to inform them of socially accepted roles and behaviors.

Is Family Therapy Appropriate for Adolescents?

Strategic and structural family therapies supposedly work by addressing pathological processes in families that are interfering with adolescent development and supporting the continuation of symptoms of AN. According to some studies, families of patients with AN are more controlled and organized than average families. In contrast, families of bulimic patients often are more chaotic, conflicted, and critical than average families. These observations have been documented by observer-rated transactions (Humphrey, 1986, 1987). The etiology implicated in some family therapy approaches therefore remains unsettled. However, if one assumes for a moment that family processes are an appropriate target for intervention, certainly family therapy would be a logical way to proceed to address them.

However, more to the point is to challenge the idea that adolescent therapy should focus exclusively, or almost exclusively, on the adolescent as an individual. Although there is a popular idea that adolescence is a time of great upheaval and conflict, especially as conceived of by many psychoanalytic thinkers, these notions are generally rejected now based on empirical studies that suggest the majority of adolescents have good relationships with their parents (Blos, 1979; Erikson, 1950; Rutter, Graham, & Chadwick, 1976). The role of parents in a positive sense for adolescence has been somewhat neglected. The focus has been on the intrapsychic development of adolescents set in opposition to their parents rather than on the opportunity for parents to assist with the developmental challenges of the period. A number of reports suggest that parents can play a critical role in helping adolescents, especially those that use a particular style of parenting—authoritative parenting—is particularly advantageous in supporting adolescents (Steinberg, Lamborn, & Dornbusch, 1994). Such parenting is characterized as warm and involved, but also firm and consistent in establishing and enforcing guidelines, limits, and developmentally appropriate expectations. It also encourages and permits the adolescent to develop his own perspectives and opinions without unnecessary control or criticism. Thus, parental involvement in helping an adolescent with an eating disorder would seem appropriate to support. To think of it another way, if a child is deprived of parental support, he or she is deprived of a resource to support recovery that would normally be available to assist them in moving forward in adolescent development. Thus, it appears that family therapy is generally appropriate for adolescents.

Is Family Therapy of the Maudsley Type Developmentally Appropriate for Adolescents?

Based in part on the ideas that the adolescent with AN feels out of control as a result of excessive parental involvement and intrusiveness, parents being involved in treatment, especially in re-feeding itself, remains controversial. Interestingly, few treatments of children and adolescents currently take as strong a position of parental exclusion in treatment as do some advocates of individual treatment of adolescents with AN. For example, in treatments for anxiety, depression, and conduct disorder, family involvement is valued and contributes to a better outcome (Brent et al., 1997; March, 1995). FBT acknowledges that there are likely genetic and neurological processes that underlie the disorder and thus potentially frees families to address the problem without the guilt associated with being perceived as being "bad" parents. In addition, the fact that many of the medical problems associated with malnutrition that are secondary to anorexia nervosa are normalized by re-feeding and weight gain supports the emphasis that FBT places on correcting these deficiencies. In addition, FBT takes seriously the role of parents and family during adolescence and emphasizes the potential for positive support and influence, thereby encouraging authoritative parenting. Further, FBT does not ignore the individual adolescent's development, but focuses on it in the context of the family—where development would usually be taking place.

Although the emphasis on re-feeding early in treatment may seem out of sync with adolescent autonomy needs, therapists using FBT find that the thoughts and behaviors associated with AN so distort normal processes of adolescent development that initial treatment must confront this by paradoxically taking away adolescent autonomy in this single area in the service of weight restoration. This perspective is supported by the success of re-feeding inpatient programs and by the success of FBT in randomized controlled treatment trials (RCTs) (Russell et al., 1987).

Putative Targets of Treatment

Many authors have suggested that problems in familial relationships are associated with the development and maintenance of AN (Selvini Palazzoli, 1988; Stern, Dixon, & Jones, 1989; Stierlin & Weber, 1989; Strober & Humphrey, 1987; Yager, 1981). One of the main distinctions between FBT and that of the Philadelphia and Milan groups is that it begins with the view that the cause of AN is unknown. Further, this approach contends that families should specifically not be blamed for causing the illness, because guilty feelings in response to this blame are likely to impede their ability to help their affected child. In addition, FBT does not presume that these families are fundamentally flawed or pathological. By being held in a positive regard, these families are more easily empowered and motivated to take up the task of assisting their child.

FBT for adolescent AN proceeds through three phases. Initially, the therapist focuses on the dangers of severe malnutrition associated with AN and the need for parents to take action to reverse it. By focusing on these problems, the therapist increases parental anxiety to motivate them to take definitive action to re-feed their adolescent. To help parents accomplish this, the therapist illustrates how AN has altered their child's mood and behaviors. The therapist identifies and highlights the differences between their son or daughter with AN compared to how they were prior to its onset (White, 1987). When there are siblings, the therapist asks them to support their ill brother or sister by being kind supportive, less critical, and practically helpful with tasks unrelated to eating.

During the second session, the family brings a picnic to the office. This meal allows the therapist to observe how the family plans and orchestrates a meal together. During this session, the therapist asks the parent to try to encourage their adolescent with AN to eat more than he intended. The therapist actively coaches the parents to work together, set a plan, and be firm but caring in insisting that more is eaten. Success in this endeavor has more to do with parental empowerment than actual consumption of food. Still, if the parents do succeed, it is evidence that they can be effective. Subsequent treatment sessions in the first phase are focused on the patterns and problems associated with eating and weight gain. Although the specifics of how to re-feed are left up to the parents, the therapist reviews their attempts in detail in these subsequent sessions. Although dilemmas and frustrations are explored, the parents' efforts are consistently, positively reinforced as much as possible. Other problems in the family not related to re-feeding are deferred until later in treatment. The first phase of treatment usually lasts between two and four months.

When the patient is eating more normally and weight gain is steady, the second phase of treatment begins. Although disordered eating remains the focus of treatment, other issues related to re-feeding and weight can be brought forward as a subject in therapy insofar as these issues interfere with or support the parents in assuring continued progress. The ultimate goal of the second phase is to help parents to step back from being totally in charge of re-feeding and support the adolescent in taking this task on for herself. Parents experiment with handing back control of eating to the adolescent. A variety of strategies can be used to help to explore if and when the adolescent is ready to make more independent food choices, including allowing her to eat snacks or some meals alone, allowing her to serve herself, and so on. If parents are satisfied the adolescent can manage her meals and eating independently and the patient is at approximately 95% of ideal body weight (IBW), treatment enters the third phase. The Second phase usually lasts three to four months.

During the first two phases, FBT is focused on food and weight gain. During the third phase, treatment turns to a more general focus of adolescence. Therapy explores the ways that AN has affected adolescent development, comprising a discussion of the central issues of adolescence (for example, puberty, socialization, separation from parents, and sexuality). It also includes a focus on increased personal autonomy for the adolescent, if needed, as well as support for parents identifying how their own relationship changes as their children mature and are less dependent. The third phase usually lasts two to three months.

Empirical Support for Treatment Efficacy

Despite the seriousness of AN, only nine psychotherapy treatment trials have been published, with fewer than 500 total patients (Hall, 1987; Channon, 1989; Crisp, 1991; Le Grange et al., 1992; Treasure, 1995; Robin et al., 1999; Eisler et al., 2000; Russell, 1987). Only four RCTs have focused on adolescents with AN (Russell, 1987; Le Grange et al., 1992; Robin et al., 1999; Eisler et al., 2000).

Two of these RCTs compared forms of individual therapy to family therapy. In the 1987 seminal study by Russell and colleagues, a subgroup of twenty-one adolescent females with AN for less than one year were randomized to either family therapy or supportive individual therapy after being restored in-hospital to 90% of their IBW (Russell et al., 1987). Family therapy initially focused on the need for parental responsibility for managing food and weight progress of their child while deferring other adolescent developmental issues until later in treatment. Individual treatment was supportive in nature, conceived of as a non-specific treatment. At the end of one year of outpatient treatment, 90% (n = 9) of the adolescents in this subgroup who received family treatment had a good or intermediate outcome, and only 18% (n = 2) of patients assigned to individual therapy had good or intermediate outcome (Russell et al., 1987). At five years, these results were maintained, though there was evidence that the individual therapy cohort had also improved (Dare & Eisler, 1997). Ninety percent (n = 9) of early-onset patients receiving family therapy had good outcomes, while 55% (n = 6) had good or intermediate outcomes from the individual therapy cohort (Dare & Eisler, 1997).

In the most recent study, thirty-seven adolescent females were randomized to either behavioral family systems therapy (BFST) or psychodynamic individual therapy (ego-oriented individual therapy) (Robin et al., 1999). BFST is based in part on a family-systems model that incorporated parents being responsible for re-feeding their child. At the end of treatment, family therapy resulted in greater body mass index (BMI) changes and higher rates of return of menstruation. Both treatments demonstrated similar results in other measures (eating attitudes, body-shape concerns, and eating-related family conflicts). Each treatment type was associated with significant improvement in two-thirds of the patients. At the one-year follow-up, there were no significant differences between treatment groups on any measures (Robin et al., 1999).

A few studies have suggested baseline factors that may predict the outcome for AN, including degree of weight loss, duration of illness, age of onset, failure of previous treatment, gender, and comorbidity (Engel, Meyer, Henze, & Wittern, 1992; Field, Wolf, Herzog, Cheung, & Colditz, 1993). Degree of weight loss has been suggested to have an impact on outcome because of cognitive changes associated with severe malnutrition, evidence of behavioral success of restriction, and loss of hunger. In clinical trials, only Eisler and associates have explored this question. Their data, based on a study using the Maudsley approach, shows that adolescents who presented at lower weights responded less favorably to treatment (Eisler et al., 2000). Longer duration of illness also appears to predict poor outcome (Ratnasuriya, Eisler, & Szmukler, 1991; Steinhausen, Rauss-Mason, & Seidel, 1991, 1993). However, this has been explored in only two clinical trials. The 1987 study by Russell and colleagues compared the outcomes of patients with long versus short durations of illness in a study of the Maudsley FBT. They found that patients who had shorter durations of illness (less than three years) did better with FBT than those with longer durations of illness (greater than three years) (Russell et al., 1987). Eisler and associates found that patients with poorer outcomes were ill for significantly longer (15.8 months) than those who did well (5.7 months) (Eisler et al., 2000). The importance of age of onset of AN as a predictor of outcome is unclear. Age was specifically examined as a predictor in the study by Russell (1987) who found that for patients receiving FBT, younger patients (younger than age 18) fared better than older ones (Russell et al., 1987). Failure of previous treatment has also been suggested as leading to a poor outcome for psychotherapy treatment in general. As noted above, comorbid conditions are common with AN, especially anxiety and affective disorders. Current data suggest that comorbidity may complicate recovery, but has not been formally evaluated in any published trial for AN treatment (Herzog et al., 1996).

Familial Expressed Emotion (EE) (in particular, high levels of parental criticism toward their offspring) may moderate treatment outcome in adolescents treated with family therapy. Higher levels of parental criticism are associated with higher treatment dropout and a poorer response to treatment (Eisler et al., 2000; Le Grange, Eisler, Dare, & Hodes, 1992). In FBT, Eisler found that in families with higher levels of criticism, patients recovered better when the parents were seen separately from the adolescent (Eisler et al., 2000). The authors hypothesize that it may be important to treat families with high and low EE differently—that is, by treating the parents with high levels of EE separately from their children. Whether or not similar findings will occur in the treatment of patients who are treated with individual therapy is unknown. There are no published studies of mediators of treatment outcome in AN.

In summary, there are only four published RCTs of outpatient psychological treatments for adolescents with AN. These studies are small, with a total of 116 subjects with an average of fewer than fifteen subjects per cell (with a range of 9 to 20). Both family therapy and individual therapy appear to be helpful, though family therapy may produce its effects more quickly. Family criticism, clinical severity (degree of weight loss), and duration of illness may predict or moderate outcome, though there are no studies of moderators or mediators of treatment outcome for either family or individual therapy. Given the severity of the psychological and physical health problems associated with AN, there is a compelling need to address these deficiencies in our knowledge.

Personal Experience and Case Material

How does the FBT for anorexia nervosa unfold? We have manualized the overall approach, and in so doing, we have further defined the processes of therapy and provided illustrative case material. Here we describe an overall sense of how each of the phases of treatment unfolds and the kinds of "real life" questions that have arisen (Lock, 2001; Lock & Le Grange, 2001; Lock, Le Grange, Agras, & Dare, 2001). The overall context for these remarks is patient-involved in a large (86 adolescent patients) NIMH-funded RCT for adolescent AN treated with differing amounts of FBT.

The mean age of patients in the study is 15.1 years (range of 11.95 to 18.37). Ninety-one percent of patients are female. The mean duration of illness is 11.1 months (range of 2 to 48 months). The mean weight at presentation was 81% IBW or mean BMI of 17.5 (SD = 1.41). At baseline, 19% of patients exhibited binge eating or purging. The majority of patients were white (74%), but a substantial minority were from other racial or ethnic groups (9% Asian, 12% Hispanic, 1% American Indian, and 4% bi-racial). Seventy-five percent are nuclear families, while 14% are single-parent families, and 11% are reconstituted families. Outcomes of patients suggest that FBT is effective in reversing both the weight loss and psychological concerns about weight and shape associated with AN. At twelve-months, the mean BMI was 20.2 (SD = 1.38).

In my experience, the first phase is characterized by high anxiety, feelings of powerlessness, guilt, and anger in families, especially in parents. "I feel helpless" is a common quote at the beginning of treatment. "I don't know what to do" is another. To address these feelings, I must challenge the parents to take definitive action in the form of directly increasing their anxieties about the possibility of death and other morbidities (such as depression or osteoporosis) in the event that anorexic behaviors are not disrupted. However, common to most therapy, raising anxiety may increase motivation of treatment, but only if the patient also perceives that the therapist can assist them. Thus, I must also communicate warmth, understanding, and engender trust in ensuring that changes can be made.

In other words, while I aim to increase anxiety and instill the need for parental action, I also contain this anxiety to a certain extent so that it is not overwhelming and paralyzing. In the initial sessions, I am highly focused on each family member, but especially the parents, who are the initial agents for changing the behaviors of their child.

Early in treatment, there is a family meal, modeled after Minuchin's "lunches," but distinguished from them by a less critical, more inquiring attitude. I am often asked why we do this meal. Therapists often feel that the intervention is artificial and most are worried about what will happen. Indeed, I have seen a variety of things happen during family meals—everything from a five-course dinner with candles and tablecloths, to food being thrown at me across the room. I think that the meal offers an important opportunity for "joining" the family in their practical dilemma of re-feeding. Parents often think that the therapist "sees what it's really like" when they see the resistance at mealtime. In addition, it provides a concrete opportunity to actively coach the parents in vivo. I endeavor to learn the families' usual meal time processes (who cooks, who sets the table, when do they eat, and so on) and explore how the presence of AN has modified these usual practices. Usually, I learn that patients are cooking their own meals, eating alone, and avoiding the family at mealtime. I help the family to appreciate the difficulty these alterations pose for them in helping to make sure their child eats and ask them to consider how they might try to get things back to normal—or at least closer to normal. This often means that parents decide to monitor eating for a period, to set a predictable schedule of meals and snacks, to persist in the effort to encourage eating more. I sometimes say that AN is defeated one bite at a time and I mean this.

Related to this is one of the crucial interventions during the picnic—the therapist's request to the parents that they help their adolescent eat one more bite. When one reaches this point in the session, it is usually quite clear that the adolescent has eaten all that she has planned. Parents are usually like "deer in the headlights" when I ask them to help her eat more. I often gently suggest that they choose something they think will help their adolescent to gain weight. This can be anything from a grape (not as good a choice) to a bite of cheese (much better). Then parents usually ask (not a good way to proceed usually) their adolescent to do it. I encourage them to put it on the adolescent's plate. Next, I ask them to sit on either side and gently insist that she eat. Some parents are embarrassed by their seeming failure; others, use some slight (not sarcastic) humor, and others give up after only a few minutes. Throughout these efforts, I am focused more on getting the parents to work together and to see that talking and hoping are unlikely to lead to eating. Whether the adolescent eats or not is secondary, though this does happen most of the time.

Sessions during the initial phase are highly focused on eating and weight. I begin every session by showing how weight has changed on a graph. If weight has increased, we look for how that was accomplished. Usually, this means that parents have been successful in reinstating normal meal times and have increased overall consumption. When weight has decreased, we talk about what the challenges were during that week that might have led to this outcome. For example, meals were taken independently by the patient (particularly if they are in school without meal supervision), if they are over-exercising, and if the family varied its routine (went on a trip, or ate in restaurants more frequently). Any of these factors can derail weigh gain temporarily, and parents learn this and proceed to be increasingly methodical about their approach. At first, most parents find it helpful to just get their adolescent eating regularly, then eating more, and finally refining food choices to include those that include more protein and fat.

Common dilemmas I confront with families during this period include questions about nutrition, exercise, and school attendance. It has been a mainstay of treatment that nutritionists are involved in treating AN. This seems particularly relevant for adults with AN who need consultation about their choices (which are under their control) that are often distorted by anorexic concerns and that benefit from being challenged by an expert in nutrition. On the other hand, too much of a focus on calorie counting, weight gain, food amounts, and portions can lead inadvertently to increased preoccupation in these areas that is consistent with AN itself. I often advise parents who are anxious about their child's nutrition to consult a nutritionist themselves. What they should learn is that if they provide three well-balanced meals and two to three healthy snacks a day, they will be able to help their child gain weight. In the beginning, the amounts of food needed to gain weight will be larger than will be needed to maintain weight once it has returned to normal. More harmful, at least when using FBT, are individual meetings with a nutritionist and adolescent separate from the parents, where agreements are made that may limit and interfere with the parents' ability to carry out re-feeding according to their capacities and resources.

Similar dilemmas can arise with pediatricians who are anxious about exercise. Parents may well want to limit exercise in order to promote faster weight gain to minimize cardiac strain during acute weight restoration. Other parents may feel that small and focused exercise may help their child to be motivated to comply with eating. This is not an easy dilemma to resolve, but I recommend that parents attend carefully to the advice of their pediatricians, and to defer as much as possible to these recommendations, but I also emphasize that this is ultimately their decision. I have had parents who have not allowed any exercise until weight was fully restored because they felt that anything that delayed weight gain to normal levels was counterproductive. However, with some athletes with anorexia nervosa, parents have allowed exercise earlier and have remained successful in weight recovery.

Many adolescents with AN are exceptional students. I sometimes say that if they do not get straight A's, they probably do not have AN. This is true more than 90% of the time, not so much because these adolescents are smarter than others, but because they work very hard and are exceptionally invested in the evidence that an A gives them about their self-worth. Therefore, returning to school, or remaining in school is a priority for many of them. Parents, reasonably enough, see schoolwork as a good thing for the most part. Still, many of them correctly perceive that too much attention to schoolwork and anxiety about school performance can interfere with eating and weight gain. I ask families to consider a two- to four-week period of home schooling in the early part of treatment in order to reduce both the academic and social pressure of school, as well as to provide the parents with a twenty-four-hour-a-day opportunity to observe and support normal eating. This can be challenging for single parent families, and also for families in which both parents work, but options include grandparents, vacation time, or even a temporary leave of absence. Importantly, during this period, the adolescent is still encouraged to do some schoolwork, have friends visit (usually not a meal times), and to do things socially as much as possible. The transition back to school, when the parents are ready, often entails parents still coming to school for lunch and making sure after-school snacks are eaten for an additional four to six weeks after the adolescent has returned to school.

One other area I am often asked about is the role of siblings. They are definitely not supposed to help with the re-feeding process, but their presence in family sessions and at meal times involves them in helping with recovery. Siblings are important because they understand the family and its dilemmas and can be a source of support when affected adolescents are angry about being made to eat and gain weight. They also can help by providing distractions, by accompanying or being present at meals and after meals. Many times, simple gestures, like writing a card, asking the sibling to play a game, or taking a walk with the sibling can make things more tolerable. For siblings, the fact that they can be of help even in small ways makes them feel less worried about their brother or sister and can relieve their anxieties.

A final comment on the re-feeding phase has to do with how it differs for younger and older adolescents. In most respects, in my experience, what parents need to do does not vary and my approach to encouraging them does not either. Still, what I have learned is that parents are generally pretty smart and would not try the same things with older and younger adolescents. They respect the developmental capacities of their children, for the most part. Specifically, this means that parents of younger adolescents (ages twelve to fourteen or so) are more likely to employ much more directive efforts at re-feeding. Parents of older adolescents are more likely to need to influence behaviors through their relationship with their child, but also by providing more evidence to their adolescent that they understand the dilemma. In therapy with older adolescents, there is more talk about the thoughts and beliefs associated with AN and the adolescent herself tends to speak up more and be more articulate about the challenges they are experiencing. Although it might seem that the parents of older adolescents may have a tougher go, in fact, it is just different, in my opinion. The intellectual and verbal abilities of the older adolescents change the character of the therapy, but the tasks and responsibility remain the same.

Families move into the second phase when the adolescent has recovered most of the weight he has lost and is eating much more normally. This takes about two to four months in most cases. If I have not seen significant improvement by then, I worry that the family may not be able to use this approach; however, when I have persevered, some have recovered their weight, though much later. It is unclear to me at this time why some families seem to struggle. It does not appear to be anything as simple as the construct of the family, but may have more to do with the overall degree of other stresses that could distract the family from being able to focus on AN. For example, severe parental discord and imminent divorce, sexual or physical abuse, another child or family member with a severe medical or psychiatric problem, may decrease response to FBT. In addition, the adolescent may be more severely affected by anorexic thinking, have other psychiatric illnesses, or have been ill longer, any of which will likely make the work of parental re-feeding more challenging.

During the second phase, parents are asked to manage the anxiety of turning eating and weight control back to their adolescent. Some are relieved to do so because they feel confident that these issues are resolved enough that they are likely to succeed. Others, because they have struggled, or are uncertain, or remain highly anxious, are more cautious. I sometimes compare this to parents trying to decide when to allow their adolescent, who has had a major driving infraction, to start driving again. Often, in such a case, parents would suggest driving only when necessary (to school and back), then if that went well, to include all daytime and weekday driving. If that went well, back to full driving privileges. Returning eating control back to the adolescent is the goal of treatment, so parents are encouraged to find a way to do it without overstressing the adolescent or themselves. The usual pattern that parents adopt is to allow their child to eat snacks on their own first, then meals at school, and finally control over choices at meal time. Throughout this period, weights are monitored and parents, though less in charge, still keep an eye on things; again, much like the parent whose child has had a driving infraction will keep an eye on things even when they appear to be fine.

The third phase of treatment is a brief focus on adolescent development. I like to ask parents about their own adolescence. This provides an opportunity for the general themes of adolescent development to be highlighted cross-generationally. So, we discuss how each parent felt during puberty about how their bodies changed, what their hopes and fears were about this, and how they managed them. Next, we discuss how each parent developed a social identity and explored it with friends. Finally, we discuss how parents took risks during adolescence and what they learned. Naturally, parents are in charge of how much they divulge about any of these areas—no parent to date has been inappropriate in this regard.

This discussion of parental experiences with adolescence allows me to help the family and patient identify relevant issues for their adolescent with AN. These issues vary with the age of the adolescent. Younger adolescents are usually focused on early socialization and identity processes, whereas older adolescents are focused on leaving home, college, and dating. The point of this phase it to help the family see any dilemmas that AN may cause or have caused in terms of usual adolescent development. In the younger adolescents, there is often a need to encourage more socialization, and less focus on performance in school or sports to help balance their views with those of their peer group. With older adolescents, the focus is more on anxiety about leaving home in real terms—for college, usually. How ready is the family for this transition and how will they help make sure it is successful? An important part of the third phase is to look at the impact of AN on the parental dyad. I make one of the few directives during the treatment during this phase aimed at the parents. I tell them that they are to spend some specific time focused on one another. It is surprising how difficult this assignment turns out to be for many parents. I think this is the case, in part, because these are often parents who tend to defer their own interests in favor of their children, but also because they have been so focused on the problems that AN has caused them it is hard to turn away from them. On the other hand, when we have asked parents how they felt about treatment, one of the things they see as improved is the relationship between themselves. This is not surprising in some ways, because for the treatment to succeed, the parents must learn to work very closely together again and in so doing, they often spend more time together. In addition, when they succeed in the task they set, in this case helping their adolescent recover from AN, they feel closer together for this shared effort.

Termination of treatment in the FBT is surprisingly gentle, but moving. Usually, by this point, I see the family only once a month or so, so they are managing quite independently. There is, therefore, no steep cut off. Still, because I have been present for and assisted them with a severe and life-threatening problem, the connection is strong. I spend the last session going over the progress that has been

FIGURE 26.1. VENN DIAGRAMS BEFORE AND AT END
OF TREATMENT.

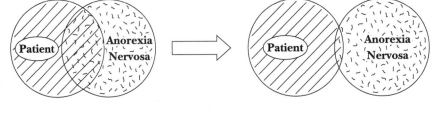

Before Treatment   **End of Treatment**

made, usually employing a changing Venn diagram to illustrate this process (see Figure 26.1). I try to normalize any remaining thought processes related to AN both in terms of usual adolescent dieting and body concerns (and adult concerns, for that matter), but also to allow for the idea that recovery does not necessary stop just because I am not there—something they have experienced all along if I have done my job right throughout the year or so that I have been treating them.

Future Directions

I suggested at the outset that FBT for AN is a paradigmatic illness for family therapy. I believe that this is true. That being the case, it seems that the future of the therapy could progress in several directions. The first direction would be its continued application and research exploration in the context of eating disorders.

Although the evidence for FBT for AN is the best we have to date, it must be emphasized that it is far from being confirmed as being the best approach to adolescent AN. It is important to better understand if FBT works, and if so and how for whom? Large RCTs that compare FBT to other treatments are needed. It seems unlikely that a "no treatment" or "placebo" treatment would be feasible giving the seriousness of the disorder. Once efficacy has been more established, it will be important to gain a better understanding about whether it is effective because parental behaviors are changed, as we have proposed here, or whether other factors lead to improvements. Further, it is clear that FBT does not work for everyone, and it would be good to know what it is about the differences in patients that would help us make the decision to use FBT or not.

FBT is generally conceived of as a "whole family" therapy. That is, the entire family is present for the sessions. However, in fact, two studies have examined the possible utility of employing the same type of therapy, but separating the parents from the affected child (Eisler et al., 2000; Le Grange, Eisler, Dare, & Russell, 1992). Based on these studies, it appears that familial EE (as expressed by high levels of parental criticism) may moderate the treatment's outcome in the family treatment approach to adolescent AN. Higher levels of parental criticism are associated with higher treatment dropout and a poorer response to treatment in that study. Eisler and associates (2000) found that in families with higher levels of criticism, patients recovered better when the parents were seen separately. The authors hypothesize that it may be important to treat highly critical families by using separated family treatment, and for those families that are less critical, in whole family treatment. Theoretically, in more critical families, it is more difficult to help parents succeed in re-feeding without creating additional tension and stress on the child. Thus, by seeing the parents separately, the therapist can provide the same interventions to assist them in their tasks, but without risking additional criticism of the child.

Yet another way of using the same principles in FBT, but in a different construct, is multi-family therapy. Multi-family therapy involves three- to four-day events in which three to five families meet together for the first several sessions, applied in all-day sessions. The early reports of this version of FBT suggest that it helps to motivate and provide additional support for families who are sharing common problems and dilemmas. It is too early to tell how effective the approach will be, however.

Another eating disorder that might respond to FBT is BN in adolescents. Some studies suggest that it does respond, and an RCT currently under way will likely give us data to better answer this question. Adolescents with BN often have similar struggles with food intake and meal regulation, and parental support for structuring meals and preventing binge eating and purging episodes might well be helpful. Data from the published trial on AN have included patients with binge/purge type AN and they appear to respond to these interventions as well as the purely restrictive type of AN. In addition, one small case series found that adolescents with BN improved using FBT. A trial is under way at the university of Chicago investigating this possibility and we must await its completion for a more definitive answer about FBT's usefulness in adolescent BN.

◆ ◆ ◆

Beyond eating disorders, the model of FBT has the potential for more general applicability to other disorders in adolescents. In particular, it bears some affinities with parent management training (PMT), which addresses a disorder on the entirely other spectrum—AN is an internalizing disorder, whereas, ODD and CD are externalizing disorders (see Chapter 27). What this suggests is that some of the basic principles of empowering parents, supporting the development of skills, while tracking and supporting adolescent developmental issues, may be useful for other disorders in which behaviors (either internalizing or externalizing) are problems (such as substance abuse, OCD, and phobias). One of the main advantages of FBT is that it likely reduces the need to employ more expensive inpatient and residential treatments. This is especially relevant for AN, a mental illness that has a high cost (Lock, in press). In two of the studies using FBT for AN, patients were never hospitalized and recovery was excellent in the overall cohort (Eisler et al., 2000; Le Grange, Eisler, Dare, & Russell, 1992). Besides cost, however, being able to assist an adolescent in the home and community is always a better alternative if the treatment is effective. Exploring these and other implications of the principles of FBT is an exciting area for further research and development in psychotherapy research involving the family.

References

Attie, I., & Brooks-Gunn, J. (1989). Development of eating problems in adolescent girls: A longitudinal study. *Developmental Psychology, 25,* 70–79.

Bandura, A. (1977). Self-efficacy: Toward a unifying theory of behavioral change. *Psychological Review, 84,* 191–215.

Bandura, A. (1997). *Self-efficacy: The exercise of control.* New York: Freeman.

Blos, P. (1979). *The adolescent passage.* Madison, CT: International Universities Press, Inc.

Brent, D., Holder, D., Kolko, D., Birmhaher, B., Baugher, M., Roth, C., et al. (1997). A clinical psychotherapy trial for adolescent depression comparing cognitive, family, and supportive therapy. *Archives of General Psychiatry, 54,* 877–885.

Bruch, H. (1973). *Eating disorders: Obesity, anorexia nervosa, and the person within.* New York: Basic Books.

Channon, S., De Silva, P., Helmsley, D., & Perkins, R. (1989). A controlled trial of cognitive-behavioral and behavioural treatment of anorexia nervosa. *Behavioural Research and Therapy, 27,* 529–535.

Crisp, A. H. (1980). *Anorexia nervosa: Let me be.* London: Academic Press.

Crisp, A. H. (1997). Anorexia nervosa as flight from growth: Assessment and treatment based on the model. In D. M. Garner & P. Garfinkel (Eds.), *Handbook of treatment for eating disorders* (pp. 248–277). New York: Guilford.

Crisp, A. H., Norton, K., Gowers, S., Halek, C., Bowyer, C., Veldhan, D., Levett, G., & Bhat, A. (1991). A controlled study of the effect of therapies aimed at adolescent and family psychopathology in anorexia nervosa. *British Journal of Psychiatry, 159,* 325–333.

Dare, C., & Eisler, I. (1997). Family therapy for anorexia nervosa. In D. M. Garner & P. Garfinkel (Eds.), *Handbook of treatment for eating disorders* (pp. 307–324). New York: Guilford Press.

Dare, C., Eisler, I., Russell, G., & Szmukler, G. I. (1990). Family therapy for anorexia nervosa: Implications from the results of a controlled trial of family and individual therapy. *Journal of Marital and Family Therapy, 16,* 39–57.

Dare, C., Eisler, I., Russell, G., Treasure, J. L., & Dodge, E. (2001). Psychological therapies for adults with anorexia nervosa: Randomized controlled trial of outpatient treatments. *British Journal of Psychiatry, 178,* 216–221.

Eisler, I., Dare, C., Hodes, M., Russell, G., Dodge, E., & Le Grange, D. (2000). Family therapy for adolescent anorexia nervosa: The results of a controlled comparison of two family interventions. *Journal of Child Psychology and Psychiatry, 41*(6), 727–736.

Engel, K., Meyer, A., Henze, M., & Wittern, M. (1992). Long-term outcome in anorexia nervosa inpatients. In W. Herzog & W. Vandereycken (Eds.), *The course of eating disorders* (pp. 167–181). Berlin: Springer-Verlag.

Erikson, E. (1950). Childhood and society. New York: W. W. Norton and Company.

Field, A., Wolf, A., Herzog, D. B., Cheung, L., & Colditz, G. (1993). The relationship of caloric intake to frequency of dieting among preadolescent and adolescent girls. *Journal of the American Academy of Child and Adolescent Psychiatry, 32,* 1246–1252.

Gull, W. (1874). Anorexia nervosa (apepsia hysterica, anorexia hysterica). *Transactions of the Clinical Society of London, 7,* 222–228.

Haley, J. (1973). *Uncommon therapy: The psychiatric techniques of Milton H. Erickson.* New York: Norton.

Hall, A., & Crisp, A. H. (1987). Brief psychotherapy in the treatment of anorexia nervosa: Outcome at one year. *British Journal of Psychiatry, 151,* 185–191.

Herzog, D. B., Field, A. E., Keller, M. B., West, J. C., Robbins, W. M., Staley, J., et al. (1996). Subtyping eating disorders: Is it justified? *Journal of the American Academy of Child and Adolescent Psychiatry, 35*(7), 928–936.

Hoagwood, K., Burns, B., Kiser, L., Ringeisen, H., & Schoenwald, S. (2001). Evidence-based practice in child and adolescent mental health services. *Psychiatric Services, 52,* 1179–1189.

Humphrey, L. (1986). Structural analysis of parent-child relationships in eating disorders. *Journal of Abnormal Psychology, 95,* 395–402.

Humphrey, L. (1987). Comparison of bulimic-anorexic and nondistressed families using structural analysis of behavior. *Journal of the American Academy of Child and Adolescent Psychiatry, 26,* 248–255.

Kazdin, A. (2000). Developing a research agenda for child and adolescent psychotherapy. *Archives of General Psychiatry, 57,* 829–835.

Kendler, K. S., Walters, E. E., Neale, M. C., Kessler, R. C., Heath, A. C., & Eaves, L. J. (1995). The structure of genetic and environmental risk factors for six major psychiatric disorders in women. *Archives of General Psychiatry, 52,* 374–383.

Lasegue, E. (1883). De l'anorexie hysterique. *Archives Generales De Medecine, 21,* 384–403.

Le Grange, D., Eisler, I., Dare, C., & Hodes, M. (1992). Family criticism and self-starvation: A study of expressed emotion. *Journal of Family Therapy, 14,* 177–192.

Le Grange, D., Eisler, I., Dare, C., & Russell, G. (1992). Evaluation of family treatments in adolescent anorexia nervosa: A pilot study. *International Journal of Eating Disorders, 12*(4), 347–357.

Liebman, R., Minuchin, S., & Baker, I. (1974). An integrated treatment program for anorexia nervosa. *American Journal of Psychiatry, 131,* 432–436.

Lock, J. (2001). What is the best way to treat adolescents with anorexia nervosa? *Eating Disorders, 9,* 299–302.

Lock, J. (in press). A health services perspective on anorexia nervosa. *Eating Disorders.*

Lock, J., & Le Grange, D. (2001). Can family-based treatment of anorexia nervosa be manualized? *Journal of Psychotherapy Practice and Research, 10,* 253–261.

Lock, J., Le Grange, D., Agras, W. S., & Dare, C. (2001). *Treatment manual for anorexia nervosa: A family-based approach.* New York: Guilford Publications.

Lock, J., Reisel, B., & Steiner, H. (2001). Associated health risks of adolescents with disordered eating: How different are they from their peers? Results from a high school survey. *Child Psychiatry and Human Development, 31,* 249–265.

Lucas, A. R., Beard, C. M., & O'Fallon, W. M. (1991). 50-year trends in the incidence of anorexia nervosa in Rochester, Minn: A population-based study. *American Journal of Psychiatry, 148,* 917–929.

Mandanes, C. (1981). *Strategic family therapy.* San Francisco: Jossey-Bass.

March, J. (1995). Cognitive-behavioral psychotherapy for adolescents with OCD: A review and recommendations for treatment. *Journal of the American Academy of Child and Adolescent Psychiatry, 34,* 7–18.

Minuchin, S., Rosman, B., & Baker, I. (1978). *Psychosomatic families: Anorexia nervosa in context.* Cambridge, MA: Harvard University Press.

Palazzoli, M. (1974). *Self-starvation: From the intrapsychic to the transpersonal approach to anorexia nervosa.* London: Chaucer Publishing.

Ratnasuriya, R., Eisler, I., & Szmukler, G. I. (1991). Anorexia nervosa: Outcome and prognostic factors after 20 years. *The British Journal of Psychiatry, 156,* 495–456.

Robin, A., Siegal, P., Moye, A., Gilroy, M., Dennis, A., & Sikand, A. (1999). A controlled comparison of family versus individual therapy for adolescents with anorexia nervosa. *Journal of the American Academy of Child and Adolescent Psychiatry, 38*(12), 1482–1489.

Rosman, B., Minuchin, S., Baker, L., & Liebman, R. (1977). A family approach to anorexia nervosa: Study, treatment and outcome. In R. A. Vigersky (Ed.), *Anorexia nervosa* (pp. 341–348). New York: Raven Press.

Russell, G. F., Szmukler, G. I., Dare, C., & Eisler, I. (1987). An evaluation of family therapy in anorexia nervosa and bulimia nervosa. *Archives of General Psychiatry, 44*(12), 1047–1056.

Rutter, M., Graham, P., & Chadwick, F. (1976). Adolescent turmoil: Fact or fiction? *Journal of Child Psychology and Psychiatry,* 35–56.

Selvini Palazzoli, M. (1974). *Self-starvation: From the intrapsychic to the transpersonal approach.* London: Chaucer.

Selvini Palazzoli, M. (1988). *The work of Mara Selvini Palazzoli.* New York: Jason Aronson.

Selvini Palazzoli, M., & Viaro, M. (1988). The anorectic process in the family: A six-stage model as a guide for individual therapy. *Family Process, 27,* 129–148.

Steinberg, L., Lamborn, S., & Dornbusch, S. (1994). Over-time changes in adjustment and competence among adolescents from authoritative, authoritarian, indulgent, and neglectful families. *Child Development,* 1266–1281.

Steiner, H., Kwan, W., Walker, S., Miller, S., Sagar, A., & Lock, J. (2003). Risk and protective factors for juvenile eating disorders. *European Child and Adolescent Psychiatry, 12,* Suppl 1, 38–46.

Steiner, H., & Lock, J. (1998). Anorexia nervosa and bulimia nervosa in children and adolescents: A review of the past 10 years. *Journal of the American Academy of Child and Adolescent Psychiatry, 37*(4), 352–359.

Steiner, H., Sanders, M., & Ryst, E. (1995). Precursers and risk factors for juvenile eating disorders. In H. Steinhausen (Ed.), *Eating disorders in children and adolescence: Anorexia and bulimia nervosa* (pp. 95–125). Berlin-New York: Walter de Gruyter.

Steinhausen, H., Rauss-Mason, C., & Seidel, R. (1991). Follow-up studies of anorexia nervosa: A review of four decades of outcome research. *Psychological Medicine, 21,* 447–454.

Steinhausen, H., Rauss-Mason, C., & Seidel, R. (1993). Short-term and intermediate term outcome in adolescent eating disorders. *Acta Psychiatrica Scandinavica, 88,* 169–173.

Stern, S., Dixon, K., & Jones, D. (1989). Family environment in anorexia nervosa and bulimia nervosa. *International Journal of Eating Disorders, 8,* 25–31.

Stierlin, H., & Weber, G. (1989). *Unlocking the family door: A systemic approach to the understanding and treatment of anorexia nervosa.* New York: Brunner/Mazel.

Strober, M., & Humphrey, L. (1987). Family contributions to the etiology and course of anorexia and bulimia. *Journal of Clinical Psychology, 55,* 654–659.

Strober, M., Lampert, C., Morrell, W., & Burroughs, J. (1990). A controlled family study of anorexia nervosa: Evidence of familial aggregation and of shared transmission of affective disorders. *International Journal of Eating Disorders, 9,* 239–253.

Thoma, H. (1967). *Anorexia nervosa.* New York: International Universities Press.

Treasure, J., Todd, G., Brolly, M., Tiller, J., Nehmed, A., & Denman, F. (1995). A pilot study of a randomized trial of cognitive analytical therapy versus educational behavioral therapy for adult anorexia nervosa. *Behavioral Research and Therapy, 33,* 363–367.

Waller, J., Kaufman, M., & Deutch, F. (1940a). Anorexia nervosa: A psychosomatic entity. *Psychosomatic Medicine, 2,* 3–16.

Waller, J., Kaufman, M., & Deutch, F. (1940b). *Evolution of psychosomatic concepts—anorexia nervosa: A paradigm.* New York: International Universities Press.

White, M. (1987). Anorexia nervosa: A cybernetic perspective. *Family Therapy Collections, 20,* 117–129.

White, M., & Epston, D. (1990). *Narrative means to therapeutic ends.* New York: W. W. Norton.

Yager, J. (1981). Anorexia nervosa in the family. In M. Lansky (Ed.), *Family therapy and major psychopathology* (pp. 249). New York: Grune and Stratton.

CHAPTER TWENTY-SEVEN

FROM THEORY TO PRACTICE: INCREASING EFFECTIVE PARENTING THROUGH ROLE-PLAY

The Oregon Model of Parent Management Training (PMTO)

Marion S. Forgatch, Bernadette Marie Bullock, Ph.D., and Gerald R. Patterson, Ph.D.

The Oregon Model of Parent Management Training (PMTO) is an intervention strategy that evolved over three decades of programmatic work integrating theory, research, and practical application. PMTO was developed primarily to benefit families with children and adolescents who exhibit antisocial, aggressive, and other externalizing behavior problems, including delinquency and substance abuse. In this chapter, we briefly describe the theoretical rational for PMTO, the effects of development on mechanisms related to the changing form and function of antisocial behavior, the PMTO intervention approach and related empirical findings, and the function of role-play as a tool to help parents apply the five core child-rearing strategies that serve as the foundation of PMTO.

Theoretical Foundation

The model underlying PMTO interventions is Social Interaction Learning (SIL), which represents the merging of two theoretical streams: social interaction and social learning. Both perspectives emphasize the influence of the social environment on an individual's overall adjustment. The social interactional dimension describes connections among family members at microsocial levels, primarily coercive parenting practices that promote youngsters' deviant behavior

FIGURE 27.1. SOCIAL INTERACTION LEARNING MODEL.

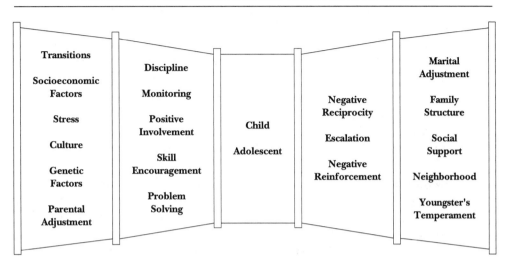

and interfere with their healthy development. The social learning dimension of the model addresses the question of how coercive behavioral patterns become established through reinforcing contingencies. A key assumption is that five core positive parenting practices control the reinforcing contingencies that occur in families. The SIL model incorporates contexts that influence parenting practices and thereby indirectly influence child outcomes. Background contexts are presumed to affect youngsters' adjustment through their impact on parenting practices. This ecological perspective is treated through mediational analyses.

Figure 27.1 illustrates the adjustment of youngsters as enveloped in two layers of context—one provided by parents and one by contextual factors. The inner layer consists of positive and coercive parenting practices, which are presumed to be proximal mechanisms of several domains of youngsters' adjustment. On the left-hand side are positive parenting practices (discipline, monitoring, positive involvement, skill encouragement, and problem solving). Each such parenting practice is presumed to make a unique contribution to adjustment, yet the five skills are presumed to operate in concert with one another. On the right-hand side are coercive parenting practices (negative reciprocity, escalation, and negative reinforcement) that erode healthy adjustment. The layer of parenting practices is surrounded by background contexts that can affect youngsters to the extent that they influence the quality of parenting. These background contexts are more distal to child and adolescent adjustment than are parenting practices.

Parents shape the social environment at home and influence the social settings their children will experience away from home. Parental management of social environments is composed of the set of positive practices that the interventions seek to strengthen. Cross-sectional and longitudinal analyses using multiple-method assessment and path modeling have shown that deficits in these parenting skills predict several adjustment difficulties for children and adolescents. These negative outcomes include antisocial behavior, substance abuse, academic failure, noncompliance, deviant peer association, delinquency, and depressed mood (Capaldi, 1992; Conger, Patterson, & Ge, 1995; DeGarmo, Forgatch, & Martinez, 1999; Dishion & Patterson, 1999; Patterson & Yoerger, 1993).

The positive parenting skills and their applications have been described in detail by various clinicians and researchers (Chamberlain, 1994; Dishion & Patterson, 1996; Forgatch & DeGarmo, 1999, 2002; Forgatch & Patterson, 1989; Patterson & Forgatch, 1987). Briefly, *skill encouragement* promotes prosocial development through teaching techniques (for example, breaking behavior into small steps, prompting appropriate behavior) and contingent positive reinforcement (Forgatch & DeGarmo, 1999). *Effective discipline* decreases deviant behavior through the appropriate and contingent use of mild sanctions (Patterson, 1986). *Monitoring* protects youngsters from involvement in risky and inappropriate activities and association with deviant peers. This skill requires keeping track of youngsters' activities, associates, and whereabouts and arranging for appropriate supervision (Patterson & Forgatch, 1987). *Problem-solving* skills help family members negotiate disagreements, establish rules, and specify consequences for following or violating rules (Forgatch & Patterson, 1989). *Positive involvement* reflects the many ways parents invest time and plan activities with their youngsters (Forgatch & DeGarmo, 1999).

Coercive parenting, shown on the right-hand side of the parenting practices layer in Figure 27.1, has a destructive effect on relationships in general, and child adjustment in particular. For this reason, the interventions attempt to provide alternative behaviors to decrease coercive family dynamics. Coercion is a complex process in which people are inadvertently shaped to become increasingly hostile. In distressed relationships, coercive processes become overlearned, automatic, and generally take place with little or no cognitive awareness (Patterson, 1982). Social interactional patterns are learned and practiced within families (such as between siblings, between parents, or between parent and child) (Bank, Patterson, & Reid, 1996). A balance favoring coercion can entrap family members in interactional styles that disrupt interpersonal relationships outside the family (with teachers, peers, coworkers). When parents tolerate and reinforce certain patterns of social interaction more than others, they provide the training grounds for habitual behavioral patterns. Coercive patterns then generalize from the settings in which they are learned to other social environments (from home to school) (DeBaryshe,

Patterson, & Capaldi, 1993; Patterson, 1982). Coercive parenting practices have been described in detail elsewhere (Forgatch & DeGarmo, 1999; Patterson, 1982; Snyder, Schrepferman, & St. Peter, 1997; Snyder, Edwards, McGraw, Kilgore, & Holton, 1994). More discussion of the development and function of coercive process follows later.

Putative Mechanisms of Efficacy

Theory promotes positive outcomes in interventions by indicating potent mechanisms of relevant outcomes. The SIL model specifies parenting practices as proximal mechanisms of child outcomes; thus SIL-based interventions focus on decreasing coercive parenting and increasing effective parenting practices.

Behavioral Research on the Etiology of Behavior Problems

The positive and coercive parenting practices that are the primary targets of PMTO interventions were identified through extensive research. Related investigations also identified contextual factors that made it difficult for parents to enact effective parenting strategies or change existing coercive patterns. For example, parental adjustment (antisocial behavior, substance abuse, depression) was associated with resistance to parent training procedures (Patterson & Chamberlain, 1988). Other aspects of the family social ecology such as divorce, social status, and neighborhood quality are also important in that they can enhance or detract from parenting quality. For example, if the family lives in a high-crime neighborhood, extraordinary levels of monitoring may be necessary to protect children from harm, deviant peer exposure, and delinquency (Wilson, 1980). Divorce is associated with increases in coercive discipline (Furstenberg & Seltzer, 1986; Hetherington, Cox, & Cox, 1985).

The culture or subculture in which families live can influence people's attitudes, beliefs, and parenting practices. A child's intra-individual qualities (genetic and temperamental) can challenge parenting skills that may have sufficed under ordinary circumstances (Lykken, 1993). Social advantage can benefit parenting quality through increased availability of resources (DeGarmo & Forgatch, 1999). The SIL model specifies that the effect of such contexts on a youngster's adjustment be mediated through parenting. Thus, each context can function as a direct risk to or enhancement for parenting practices and an indirect risk to or enhancement for child and adolescent adjustment.

Parenting strategies and family contexts have long been linked to child adjustment—particularly the prevalence of behavior problems. In turn, high rates of behavioral maladjustment, particularly at an early age, tend to be prognostic of persistent and chronic antisocial behavior and escalation to more serious problems such as delinquency and substance abuse (Fergusson, Horwood, & Lynskey, 1995; Nagin & Tremblay, 1999; Patterson, Shaw, Snyder, & Yoerger, 2003). Several studies have shown that given preschool identification as antisocial, the odds are about 50–60% of being so classified during adolescence (Kazdin, Mazurick, & Bass, 1993; Tremblay, Boulerice, Pihl, Vitaro, & Zoccolillo, 1996). During late childhood, very small numbers of new cases are added. It seems then that most chronic antisocial individuals begin this trajectory during preschool years (Fergusson et al., 1995; Nagin & Tremblay, 1999; Patterson et al., submitted).

While epidemiologists estimate that about 8% of boys and fewer than 3% of girls fit the definition of early emerging and persisting extreme antisocial behavior (Offord, Boyle, & Racine, 1991), early onset behavior problems often set the stage for a more virulent antisocial repertoire, substance use, academic problems, and difficulty with interpersonal relationships. Indeed, a multiple-method longitudinal study revealed that boys rated as being most disruptive in kindergarten and again seven years later exhibited the highest rates of substance abuse in early adolescence (Dobkin, Tremblay, & Sacchitelle, 1997). These findings and others suggest that antisocial behavior in young children is predictive of later substance problems and should be considered an important risk factor (Biglan, Mrazek, Carnine, & Flay, 2003; Dobkin et al., 1997; Duncan, Duncan, Biglan, & Ary, 1998; Mrazek & Haggerty, 1994; Patterson, 1993).

If left unchecked, the effects of early onset antisocial behavior can be pervasive and insidious. In addition to predicting escalations in behavior problems, childhood conduct problems are related to persistent, longitudinal deficits in academic achievement (Huesmann, Eron, & Yarmel, 1987; Olweus, 1983; Patterson, Reid, & Dishion, 1992). Antisocial behavior is also a major precursor for poor social relationships (Shortt, Capaldi, Dishion, Bank, & Owen, in press), poor health (Patterson & Yoerger, 1995), and an unsuccessful work history (Wiesner, Vondracek, Capaldi, & Porfeli, in press). The ensuing rejection and inability to function effectively in interpersonal and professional domains often results in the individual seeking out others who gravitate toward delinquency and substance abuse. Undeniably, deviant peer association during adolescence is one of the best predictors of escalations in antisocial behavior, including drug use (Dishion, 1990; Patterson, 1995).

Reinforcing Mechanisms for Antisocial Behavior

In the early 1960s, one-half to two-thirds of all referrals for child clinical services consisted of externalizing problems such as antisocial and hyperactive behavior. At that time, there were no interventions shown to be effective using well-designed (randomized trial, objective measures) studies. Consequently, the National Institutes of Health began funding research destined to fill the gaps through building effective models for both theory and intervention. In our work, we assumed that the extent to which a child employs aggressive responses reflects the extent to which these behaviors are reinforced. In poorly functioning families, the payoffs are higher for coercive than for prosocial responses. For well-functioning families, the payoffs are just the reverse, with prosocial behavior being more highly reinforced.

By the mid-1960s, the reinforcing mechanisms, who provided them, and what determined when or how they were bestowed remained elusive. To unravel this puzzle, observers at the Oregon Social Learning Center were trained to visit "natural" settings such as nursery schools, homes, and classrooms. A simple coding system was utilized that described each aggressive episode directed toward a nursery school child (Patterson, Littman, & Bricker, 1967). The child's reaction to the attack, together with the attacker's subsequent reaction, was also noted. These data revealed that roughly 80% of the 2,583 aggressive events were followed by such outcomes as "victim cries" or "victim gives up toy." From the attacker's view, these would seem to be positive reinforcers. Young children in a nursery school setting could find a rich supply of reinforcers for child aggression; the victim inadvertently supplied them. If victim acquiescence was reinforcing, it would be anticipated that the aggressor would be more likely to continue attacking the same victim or continue the same form of attack. Conversely, given a punishing consequence (victim hits back), the aggressor would be more likely to select a different victim or a different form of attack. Consistent with this prediction, the nine most aggressive boys provided evidence that consequences judged presumably to be positive or negative were reliable predictors of subsequent aggressive behavior.

Historically, developmental theorists assumed that the genesis for children's aggression was to be found in family process (Maccoby & Martin, 1983). A decade's effort to use self-report measures of parenting failed to establish a reliable connection between family interactions and child aversive behaviors (Maccoby & Martin, 1983; Schuck, 1974). We hypothesized that the inability to make this distinction was due, in part, to the lack of predictive validity of self-report measures in this context. Presumably, multi-method and multi-agent measures of parenting—particularly those based on direct observation—would provide more reliable and valid predictors for child outcomes.

It took three years to develop an observational code system that effectively described sequential family interactions among family members (Jones, Reid, & Patterson, 1975; Reid, 1978). Up to ten hours of baseline observations was collected in the homes of both clinical and non-clinical samples. The code was later updated to enable data collection in real time using a small handheld computer (Dishion, Gardner, Patterson, Reid, & Thibodeaux, 1983). The most current family observation system is the Family and Peer Process Code (FPPC) (Stubbs, Crosby, Forgatch, & Capaldi, 1998).

Home observation data provided a catalyst in our conceptualization of children's aggression (Patterson & Cobb, 1971, 1973). Hundreds of hours spent observing in the homes of successful and clinical families revealed that children from families referred for treatment of aggression learned to cope with very high rates of irritable interactions with other family members. Moreover, all family members, including the referred child, learned to employ aversive behaviors to terminate conflict bouts with other family members (Patterson, 1982). The data indicated that in clinically referred families, conflict bouts occurred about once every sixteen minutes, with 10–15% of all interactions tending to be aversive (Patterson et al., 1992). Whereas successful families engaged in conflict bouts at much lower rates, and these episodes were often terminated when the child displayed either prosocial (such as talking, negotiating, using humor) or coercive (such as yelling, arguing, hitting) reactions (Snyder & Patterson, 1995), this process was markedly different in referred families. Specifically, conflict bouts tended to terminate with coercive behaviors.

To further examine the phenomenon of coercive process, Snyder and Patterson (1995) collected observational data to assess the relative rate of negative reinforcement provided during conflict bouts for an at-risk sample of kindergarten boys interacting with their mothers. The relative rate of negative reinforcement for deviant child behavior correlated 0.83 with the coercive child behavior observed in the home a week later. In a different sample, the reinforcement variables were used to predict a composite (police arrest and out-of-home placement) clinical outcome two years later (Snyder et al., 1997). Boys who experienced higher relative rates of reinforcement for coercive behaviors when interacting with family members were at greater risk for police arrest and for out-of-home placement two years later. These findings are particularly compelling given the young age of the target boys.

Further refinement of this theoretical model developed with NIH support to develop effective multi-method, multi-agent measures to assess the five core parenting practices: monitoring, discipline, skill encouragement, problem solving, and positive involvement (Forgatch & DeGarmo, 1999, 2002; Patterson, 1982; Patterson et al., 1992). Using structural equation models from three different samples, Forgatch (1991) provided evidence that latent constructs for parenting practices accounted for 30–52% of the variance in latent constructs measuring child antisocial behavior. These findings suggest that intervention strategies must include provisions for altering parenting practices *as well as* the reinforcing contingencies supplied by family members. Additional models showed the impact on child outcomes of contextual variables such as neighborhood quality, social disadvantage, divorce, and parental depression to be mediated by its impact on parenting practices (Patterson et al., 1992). As such, parent effectiveness is central to child adjustment and provides the most proximal link to child outcomes.

In sum, coercive family processes in general and reinforcement contingencies in particular, are consistently linked with the etiology of child and adolescent behavior problems. If left unchecked, these insidious mechanisms can pave the way for antisocial behavior from early childhood into adulthood. The reinforcement of negative behaviors is, perhaps, one of the most formidable challenges to prevention and intervention scientists. More recent work suggests that the most effective way to measure family processes and outcomes is through multi-trait, multi-method assessment batteries. These approaches not only provide a greater breadth of information regarding the behavior in question, but also tend to be more sensitive to change (Bank, Dishion, Skinner, & Patterson, 1990).

Developmental Issues

We now turn to a review of the developmental sequelae of antisocial behavior and a discussion of the intra- and extra-familial concomitants of behavior problems. A number of investigations using the SIL theoretical framework indicate that expression of antisocial behavior evolves as a function of development, and that changes in the reinforcing contingencies within youngsters' social environment play a central role in the emergence of behavior problems (Patterson, 1992; Patterson & Yoerger, 1993; Reid, Patterson, & Snyder, 2002). From the ages of approximately eighteen months to preadolescence, reinforcement by family members is associated with overt forms of antisocial behavior. With school entrance, a gradual increase in covert forms often transpires (Patterson et al., submitted).

The mechanism for this growth is known to be positive reinforcement by siblings and deviant peers (Bank et al., 1996; Bullock & Dishion, 2002; Dishion et al., 1995; Patterson, 1984). Contact with deviant peers markedly accelerates this performance of covert forms (substance abuse, health-risking sexual behavior, delinquency) (Elliott, Huizinga, & Ageton, 1985). Observations of adolescent interactions show that those with a history of antisocial behavior exhibit interpersonal dynamics with their siblings and peers that are characterized by rich schedules of positive reinforcement for deviant talk and behavior (Bullock & Dishion, 2002; Dishion, Duncan, Eddy, Fagot, & Fetrow, 1994). Indeed, dynamics that support deviant talk are linked to concurrent antisocial behavior and substance use (Bullock & Dishion, 2002; Dishion et al., 1994) and predictive escalations in substance use and delinquency by middle adolescence, and involvement in serious offenses, high-risk sexual behavior, substance use, and aggression toward a partner during early adulthood (Capaldi, Dishion, Stoolmiller, & Yoerger,

2001; Dishion, Eddy, Haas, Li, & Spracklen, 1997; Snyder, West, Stockemer, Gibbons, & Almquist-Parks, 1996). The topography of antisocial behavior itself may start as noncompliance and temper tantrums in early childhood and transform during adolescence into more serious deviancy, such as delinquency and substance abuse (Patterson, 1982). In early and middle childhood, parents and siblings are the principal reinforcing agents; as youngsters mature, however, peer influences become increasingly salient (Bullock & Dishion, 2002; Dishion & Bullock, 2002; Elliott et al., 1985).

To explicate the role of development on trajectories of antisocial behavior, Patterson (1993) examined the changing form of deviancy over a four-year period (ages ten to fourteen) during the transition into adolescence. Problem behavior was represented by a latent construct composed of four indicators: antisocial behavior, academic failure, substance use, and police arrest. As the boys matured, the factor structure of deviancy shifted from delinquency and academic failure to increasingly serious problems (substance abuse, police arrests). In the next step, change in the predictors of deviancy was also examined. For childhood antisocial behavior and academic failure, disrupted parenting practices (monitoring, discipline) were the significant contributors to deviancy. As new forms of antisocial behavior evolved, however, friendships with deviant peers became the significant predictor.

More recent analyses revealed that antisocial behavioral repertoires tend to grow at the same rate in that the slopes are correlated (Patterson, Dishion, & Yoerger, 2000). For example, growth in deviancy was related to the amount of time spent with deviant peers and the relative amount of reinforcement provided by the peers for deviant behavior. Thus, peers became increasingly influential socializing agents during the transition to adolescence, especially if youngsters were poorly monitored or allowed to wander in the community without adult supervision (Dishion, Nelson, & Bullock, in press; Stoolmiller, 1994). These findings emphasize the importance of interventions that focus in part on parents' controlling access to deviant peer networks and teaching youngsters prosocial behaviors that facilitate entry into prosocial peer groups.

Putative Targets of Treatment

As mentioned previously, maturation from childhood to adolescence and early adulthood is directly related to important changes in forms of antisocial behavior. Recent developments in prevention science have made it possible to identify the causal mechanisms related to growth in problem behavior vis-à-vis experimental tests in which families randomly assigned to receive PMTO are compared to a no-treatment control group. In a series of such studies, changes in parenting were found to precede changes in child outcomes (Chamberlain & Reid, 1998; Dishion, Patterson, & Kavanagh, 1992; Forgatch & DeGarmo, 1999, 2002; Martinez & Forgatch, 2001). These findings also generalize to deviant peer involvement. In a prevention trial in which recently divorced single mothers were randomly assigned to either a PMTO or no-treatment control group, DeGarmo and Forgatch (2000) found a significant reduction in deviant peer association and delinquent behavior for the PMTO group versus no-treatment controls. Consistent with the SIL model, child delinquent behavior was mediated by improved parenting practices as well as reductions in involvement with deviant peers.

Having reviewed the theoretical foundation for PMTO, developmental considerations related to the constellation of antisocial behaviors, the proximal relationship of parenting effectiveness to child adjustment, and the empirical support for the efficacy of the intervention, we now turn to a more comprehensive discussion of the tenets of PMTO and the function of role-playing in the delivery of this intervention method.

Empirical Support for the Treatment

Oregon Social Learning Center (OSLC) interventions have been tailored for clinical problems related to externalizing behavior such as antisocial behavior, stealing, delinquency, child abuse, and substance abuse. In the last decade, the concepts have been tailored to fit prevention designs. The programs include manuals detailing the procedures: Chamberlain (1994) for treatment foster care; Dishion, Andrews, Kavanagh, and Soberman (1996) for youth at risk for substance abuse; Forgatch (1994) for single mothers and stepfamilies (Forgatch & Rains, 1997), and Reid's study for children at risk for antisocial behavior (Ramsey, Antoine, Kavanagh, & Reid, 1992a, 1992b; Ramsey, Lathrop, Tharp, & Reid, 1992a, 1992b). All the programs emphasize a common set of effective parenting practices (that is, discipline, encouragement, positive involvement, monitoring, and interpersonal problem solving). These parenting practices are the core components of the intervention.

In the 1970s, two small-scale randomized trial studies were successfully carried out and showed that parent training was more effective than a placebo condition (Walter & Gilmore, 1973) and more effective than a wait-list control condition (Wiltz & Patterson, 1974). The findings were replicated in larger-scale randomized trials by Patterson, Chamberlain, and Reid (1982) and by Bank and colleagues (1991). Several randomized PMTO studies provide direct support for the underlying theoretical model of PMTO because they find that the intervention produces significant benefits to the parenting practices for the experimental group compared to the control, and these changes are, in turn, mediators of change in externalizing and internalizing behavior, delinquency, and substance abuse (DeGarmo & Forgatch, 2000; DeGarmo, Patterson, & Forgatch, in press; Forgatch & DeGarmo, 1999; Knutson, DeGarmo, & Reid, in press; Martinez & Forgatch, 2001). In Montreal, a large-scale study replicated and extended the Oregon parent training model with randomized trials and long-term follow-up. The Montreal study demonstrated the generalizability of parent management training to a French-speaking culture (Tremblay et al., 1991).

What Is PMTO?

Perhaps one of the best ways to introduce PMTO is through the eyes of a parent who has benefited from the experience. We were fortunate to be given the audiotape of a radio interview with such a parent. As part of a nationwide PMTO implementation in Norway, this family received help for their kindergarten-aged child who was referred for externalizing behavior problems. The short interview has been translated. In it, you learn about the many dimensions of the parental experience, including the difficulty of living with an out-of-control child, perception of the treatment approach, and feelings about receiving tools needed to improve child behavior.

I = Interviewer
O = Ole (Father)
M = Marit (Mother)
TC = Their Child

I Parent Management Training came to Norway from the USA. Using role-plays, the parents are able to reach their children and to start communicating with them. Ole, his wife, and their son have become a happy family since they learned this method of communicating.

O It started early, way back when he wanted to hold his own baby bottle. And he also wanted to decide how the world should revolve—all around him! He was a restless child. He was relatively goal oriented. He was very active and had a tremendous imagination for finding things to do.

I How was life for you, the parents?

O Little by little—as TC learned to speak—he would try to push his friends, he would act big—all of this at an extremely high tempo. It was a very exhausting time—with friends and at home with the family.

I Was it possible to say no to this child?

O There was no such a thing as no in his vocabulary. He was a very determined child. With him, everything was dead ahead!

I How would you describe life for you—the parents?

O When our son started kindergarten, life became rather special. Every day when we picked him up, we were met at the door by, "This has been a terrible boy—no, I mean this has been a terrible day. Your boy has destroyed the atmosphere and the play for the other children." This, of course, transferred directly to our home, and it became rather difficult.

I How did this work out for you?

O It was terribly stressful. It wore mom and dad to exhaustion. It also wore out his sister who got her own dose from the circumstances, especially because she did not get her share of attention.

I Did you get any help to tackle this situation?

O Yes, at the kindergarten the PPT [school psychologist services] got involved. They gave very good guidance to the teachers in the kindergarten regarding how to deal with a restless child. They had the doctors test our son. The doctors found nothing physically wrong with him. Up to then, the teachers in the kindergarten suspected that TC was hard of hearing. That turned out not to be the case.

I Do you feel that you were ostracized by the teachers in the kindergarten and by other parents?

O It was taxing. It was especially hard on my wife, who took TC to kindergarten and picked him up every day. It became psychologically rather heavy for her.

I Then came the help in the form of Parent Management Training. Let us get back to what that really is. For now, I am wondering how you found out about this help.

O Again, it was the PPT who alerted us to the possibility for PMT. We got into the queue of getting a diagnosis—looking at ADHD. During that time, we were offered help by way of PMT, and we accepted.

I And now I want you to tell us what Parent Management Training is.

O PMT is a theory that is based on training the parents. It is organized into very specific details as to what we are to do in relation to our son in every situation. This is done by working on role-plays—where only the adults are present.

I What is the technique, and what do you learn?

O As an example, we learn how much praise we need to give him in relation to the corrections that we offer him. It teaches us when to act and react. We give him Time Out when he does not listen to us. Time Out is to give him a place to sit where there are no toys, whatsoever. He stays on a chair from five up to ten minutes. This gives him the chance to think through the situation. This is a rather effective tool. He gets time to reflect, he calms down, he becomes himself—again. From there we can get back to a dialogue instead of operating with anger and frustration—from his point of view—also from ours. Not like we practiced earlier.

I Since Ole and his wife learned the PMT strategies, the parents have been able to talk to their son in a more objective way. The son gets small rewards when he undresses all by himself and puts his clothes away neatly. When he does this, he gets a special trading card, which he collects and trades in for the real reward at the agreed-upon time. The parents have spent a great deal of time learning these strategies. This is no easy job.

O We go once a week to a one-hour training session. They use the teaspoon method on us. We get small doses each day that we practice there. Then we go home and put this to work during the week. We use a chart in order to track what went well and what did not.

I One typical family situation is a child who does not want to go to bed. Would you explain to me how this method would solve: "I do not want to go to bed."

O Earlier on this was a terrible problem. He did not want to go to bed; he did not want to sleep. He threatened with suicide and other deeds. After we started the reward charts, bedtime was no longer a hassle. He goes to bed all by himself. Even when he does not want to go to bed, we are able to talk about this rationally—the "carrot" is there in front of him and he knows it!

I Would you say that in this case it is you, the parents, that have been treated?

O Yes, directly. We got the treatment or instruction. We—as parents—were taught some very basic parenting skills that we have in us and find difficult to put into practice. We also learned to treat our son "in the same way." My wife and I had, up to then, used very different techniques. We are two separate people who have learned how to agree on cooperating in the raising of our son. In that respect one can say that we did the learning. But our son has also learned that we all get very good results from the consistency of cooperation and working together.

I You mentioned that you, the parents, agree. Is it a prerequisite that both of you are equally kind and equally strict?

O I believe that the cooperation is important during the training period. I think it is important for us that we treat him the same way. My wife and I have had a great deal of problems with that specific point, and we have learned to conquer it.

I As opposed to several other methods of treatments, the parents are viewed as the main resource in the Parent Management Program. Does this seems right, Ole?

O With the guiding that we have been through now, I feel confident that all situations can be straightened out, so I hope that a lot of parents get the chance to take part in this program.

I Are you and your wife your son's counselors now or are you his parents?

O Above all, we are his parents. We now have learned a number of techniques that have made it possible for us to have wonderful communications at home. This stability *(O uses the word ballast)* is a great addition and help to our whole family.

I I am wondering if you look to the future with confidence now—I am specifically thinking of your son entering the teenage years and what goes along with that.

O Yes, we can now reach our son. We can talk together with respect and understanding. In that manner I am easy about our future in that we can do a lot to prepare for his teenage years. He is a very active boy—he is continually planning things. I am convinced that he will have more than his share of challenges as a teenager, and that makes us feel even better about the advantages that we now have had.

Personal Experiences and Cases

In the 1960s and 1970s, we used behavioral language that was rather awkward. We had yet to learn the sophisticated teaching and process skills we needed to help parents change. One concept we have since added to our clinical tool box is to identify each family's storyline and gradually weave the threads of our PMTO story together with theirs, thus creating a new family fabric. This weaving process involves an integration of language, concepts, metaphors, and behavior. For example, notice that Ole talked about confirming and encouraging his child's behavior rather than using the behavioral phrase *contingent positive reinforcement.* It was our Norwegian colleagues who taught us to replace these words with confirmation, and we have since adopted this in our own work. In many ways, the difference in meaning is insignificant, yet perhaps that word *confirmation* contributed to Ole's formulation that PMTO helped him and his wife learn to use the basic parenting skills they already had within them.

In PMTO, we shape skills that empower parents to turn their children away from deviant paths toward more healthy trajectories. In many cases, families referred because of their children's externalizing behaviors have multiple problems; they are struggling with high levels of stress and low levels of resources. Telling parents what child-rearing strategies they *should* use does not effect change. We must help them learn the skills at a level of performance that becomes automatic. Because they had never learned effective parenting skills, or perhaps because they were overwhelmed by harsh environmental circumstances, these parents frequently engaged in dysfunctional behavior patterns. Our job is to facilitate the replacement of ineffective patterns with well-practiced effective strategies. To accomplish this, we systemati-cally engage the parents in the grueling process of reconstructing the social environment within the family. We are not talking about short-term therapy.

During the 1980s, we carried out studies of therapy process that revealed that therapist teaching, especially in concert with confrontation, increased client resistance tenfold (Patterson & Forgatch, 1985). Since then, we have spent years developing strategies that enable us to provide instruction unobtrusively and with-out confrontation. Role-play has become one of the most powerful strategies in our clinical toolbox. We use role-play to shape behavior change through behav-ior rehearsal. If you remember, Ole mentioned using role-play in the therapist's office to practice new techniques and then taking them home to use with their children.

Role-play in the hands of an expert PMTO therapist serves multiple func-tions. First, it enables family members to see that there *is* a pattern and that all participants in the interaction are contributors. Therapists use "wrong-way right-way" examples to demonstrate differences in sequences of behavior and the different outcomes these sequences produce. In follow-up debriefings, the thera-pist questions parents, helping them specify behaviors that promote or impede positive outcomes. In this sense, cognition is brought into play. Parents learn to verbalize behaviors and rules and rehearse putting ideas into practice until they know precisely what to do. Role-play can be used as a diagnostic tool to evaluate specific parental strengths and challenges, to determine what the parents have learned, and to identify targets for additional emphasis. A particularly important function of role-play is that it provides an opportunity to rehearse effective sequences with the guidance of a good coach.

Increasing Positives

In the next section, we present a transcript from a therapy session in which role-play was artfully applied by a gifted Norwegian psychologist who uses the PMTO model. During this session, the therapist was working on the topic of praise with special emphasis on helping the mother overcome her overlearned pattern of crit-icizing her children (a coercive pattern of behavior) with encouragement. The mother had grown up in an extremely abusive home and had experienced little, if any, praise, support, or encouragement as a child. Not only did this limit her ability to praise her own children, but also she had developed a pattern of coercive interactions with her children. Her unrealistic expectations for her children's performance, given their stage of development, further contributed to her problems praising them. Because the father was more comfortable with encouragement, the therapist used him as a resource. As you will see, however, he too had much to learn in the process. This family already had several PMTO sessions and they were well versed in the use of role-play. We enter the scene about halfway through the session. The mother had just completed a story regarding a recent visit with some friends. She was particularly impressed with the frequent praise her friend directed toward her children for their quiet play. The therapist seized this opportunity to practice praising.

T = Therapist
M = Mother
D = Dad

The children are Carl and Liv.

T And how do your children respond to praise?
M My children like praise, but I have to remind myself to do it. And I'm not always capable of doing that. *(Laughs, nervously)*
T Maybe we should practice this a little bit. *(Hands M some papers)* Okay, you are Carl now and you are drawing. And I am you. Pretend you are drawing a house.

T draws the mother into a role-play directly, without discussion, providing a prop (paper) and telling the mother what to do.

M Mom! See! I drew a house.
T *(Yawns—bored tone of voice)* Mm hmm. *(Looks away)*
M *(Wistfully)* You didn't like it?
T *(Out of role-play)* So that's one way I can respond to you. As Carl, how did that feel?
M Very rejecting. It's like, "Wait a while and maybe I'll look at it later."
T Right. That is a form of rejection. Okay, let's try once more. I will try to be a bit nicer.

T's "wrong way" role-play enabled the mother to experience the rejection from the child's perspective. Notice her punctuation of the mother's word, but also notice that T did not dwell on rejection; she simply agreed and moved on.

M See here, I have drawn something!
T *(Gets up, walks over to M, shows warm interest)* Oh, what have you drawn? A house?
M Mm hmm.
T Whose house is it?

M It is our house.

T I can see that. It looks a lot like our house. How nice! And we have the fireplace going!

M Mm hmm.

T You are really good at perspective in your drawings. *(pointing)* This looks like a real roof!

M It is! It is!

T That's great! Where have you learned that?

M I have learned it myself. From a book!

T That's great! Good job! I am excited to see what else you can draw.

(End of role-play)

T next engaged D by asking him, in his role as observer, to identify specific behaviors that differentiated the two role-plays. We will discuss the debriefing process later.

Next, M asked how to deal with the jealousy that emerges when M praises one child in front of the other.

M But another problem is that if you praise one child, the other one gets jealous.

T Yes.

M They should learn to compliment each other.

T Yes, that is right. They should also compliment each other.

Instead of talking about what to do, T sets up another role-play, in which T plays Mom, Mom plays daughter Liv, and Dad plays son Carl. T instructs the parents to criticize each other's artwork during the role-play and stands next to M.

T *(To M)* That's a nice drawing you created.

M Oh, yes!

D It's not that nice.

M Is too.

D Is not.

T *(Interrupting)* Very nice drawing Liv *(turns directly toward D)* and you Carl, you have also made a really nice drawing . . . *(stepping back to include both in vision)* You are both so talented! Look here at these two beautiful drawings. They are both very different, but they are both so nice!

D Maybe hers is okay.

M And I guess I like his, too.

T You are both so talented. And you did a great job of complimenting each other. It is nice to get complimented on your work, right? I'm proud of you both for playing so nicely together!

(End of role-play)

T demonstrated (1) that you can praise two children at once, (2) how to praise them both, (3) that you can refrain from joining in childish arguments, and (4) how to stay focused on the positive.

Next, T debriefs the role-play to help the parents verbalize the information in this experience. A primary goal is to punctuate specific behaviors that contribute to processes and outcomes of interpersonal exchanges, and thereby add to cognitive understanding. Pay particular attention to the manner in which T asks questions during the debriefing.

T Now think back on it . . . what did I do that made this a nice experience for you as my two lovely children?

M You complimented both of us and we learned to compliment each other.

T Yes.

D We complimented each other!

T Yes, that is right.

D *(D is looking down, thinking, placing his hand on his pretend drawing)* It worked well. It did!

T *(To M)* Yes, instead of scolding them for criticizing each other, you encouraged each of them, prompted them to compliment each other, and then you praised them for it.

Within this debrief, T used an extremely sophisticated empowering technique. She changed her use of pronouns from I to you, thus giving mom credit for the praising in the role play.

Next, notice how the debriefing provides an opportunity for discussion of principles.

M It just isn't natural for me.

T Yes . . . Right.

M But this change isn't natural, to just compliment people.

T Right, so when it isn't natural for you, try to practice so that it becomes more natural. When you learned to ride a bicycle for the first time, it wasn't natural, but you practiced and practiced until you could ride the bicycle and eventually, it felt natural.

M Yes.

T And it is like that with lots of things. It takes practice. And then we become better for the practice, too.

Further discussion could interfere with the level of revelation that has taken place here. By the way, one of the most common complaints from parents is that the new parenting techniques are not natural. Shouting, scolding, and criticizing, on the other hand, is natural. Not natural is no reason not to learn new skills.

In the next role-play, T draws D further into the action. And she provides M with the requested opportunity to practice using praise.

(Role-play begins—D is drawing and M is watching him)

M *(Sitting in her chair, with some, but not much, enthusiasm)* Will you show me your drawing?

T *(Coaching M)* Practice what we have just discussed. Remember to be enthusiastic, get out of your chair, be specific in praising what you see . . . just to get familiar with this, so you can do it more easily at home.

D Here Mommy. I have drawn a bird. Look!

M *(Gets up and looks at drawing)* Oh, that is great! Look at that nice beak! *(Laughing and covering mouth, embarrassed)*

T *(Encouraging)* Yes, good.

D Mommy, that is a crow.

M I see that. This is super! I like the colors that you have chosen.

D I got a book and looked at it.

M I see. Yes, that is super! We are going to hang this on the wall.

D Yes, near the bed!

(Role-play finished)

T Good, good! What kind of things made that so good? Let's write them down. *(T stands up, walks over to white board)* What was working well?

Although T had set up each person in the role-play with specific directions, M was timid. T simply coached her, reminding her of the specific behaviors to use and encouraging M in the process.

This next section is an excellent example of debriefing the role-play, asking the parents to specify behaviors that make children feel good about their efforts. The parents had some difficultly identifying behaviors. T gave them plenty of time, and when they clearly did not understand, she provided some ideas.

M I gave positive feedback.

D I was getting recognition for example.

T Mm hmmm.

D It could have been a bit more sincere, maybe.

T We can practice that, after we first talk about what was working well.

Couples commonly fall into the trap of identifying problems rather than specific positive behaviors. It is important not to follow the focus on problems when debriefing role-plays.

During debriefing, T elicits specific behaviors that the parents can use to encourage their children. All three of them, M, D, and T, are identifying behaviors. By writing the ideas on the board, the outcome reflects a group process. The words T writes on the board punctuate the concepts and strengthens them. This is a very empowering process for parents.

T Also M, when doing the role-play, you had a warm voice tone and a relaxed and easy expression on your face.

D You looked at the drawing and pointed out the things you liked.

T And then you made eye contact. When you had eye contact, you smiled. *(Writes warm voice, easy face, eye contact)*

M Yes.

T If you try one more time and build him up even more . . . You might feel embarrassed because this is new to you, but you can even go further with this. *(T walks back to chair)*

Repeated short role-plays are more effective than a marathon that covers all the information. Each role-play provides an opportunity for debriefing. This combines cognitive processing with behavioral rehearsal.

Engaging in a sequence of short role-plays enabled the therapist to prompt, coach, and shape appropriate behavior patterns in the minutia of praise. There was no need for a long and boring lecture. The parents had the opportunity to experience different perspectives, and they especially had a chance to rehearse and rehearse and rehearse uncomfortable new behavior patterns until they became less foreign. T used role-play to provide training while also being responsive to the parents' issues and questions.

Working Through Child Noncompliance

In the next section, role-play is used to teach the use of Time Out for noncompliance. Noncompliance is seen as a cornerstone in a sequence of behaviors that leads to increasingly serious externalizing problems (Patterson, 1982), and therefore we target it early on during PMTO intervention. The first step we take in reducing noncompliance is to teach parents to give their children clear, succinct, polite, specific, start-up directions. We use the neutral word direction rather than command (which is seen as being too authoritarian by many parents) or request (which suggests that the child has the option of refusing).

During one of the very first sessions in the intervention program, parents practice giving good directions and their home practice assignment is to keep track of their children's responses to their directions. Parents identify a set of child behaviors using the words they prefer (compliance/noncompliance, minding/not minding, cooperation/noncooperation, listening/not listening). Next, we teach parents to encourage cooperation by providing small tokens for doing as directed. Eventually, we teach parents to use Time Out for noncompliance.

In the next transcript, we enter Session 11 during the introduction of Time Out. Time Out is not the only negative sanction in the PMTO set of disciplinary actions, but it is usually the first one that we teach.

In prior sessions, these parents learned the foundation behaviors leading up to Time Out. They practiced giving good directions at home and used trading cards for cooperation. These trading cards can be easily produced in several formats that appeal to boys and girls. In this family, the children save them up until they have enough to exchange for a comic book. Rather than explaining the Time Out procedure to these parents, the therapist demonstrates it through role-play. And within minutes, he has the father rehearsing how to do it.

T = Therapist
M = Mom
D = Dad

T And now for the next step in this program. What we have talked about up to now is good and bad directions, encouragement and rewards, and now we talk about discipline or negative consequences. We have talked a little bit about this in the past. We use something called Time Out. So . . . I go to you and tell you *(gets up, walks over to D, uses assertive but friendly voice)* "D, go and hang your coat over there now please." *(Coaches D)* Refuse me.

D No, I am not going to do it.

T Go and hang up your coat now, or go to Time Out.

D No, I am not going to do it.

T That's 5 minutes in Time Out.

D No, I don't want to.

T 6 . . .

D I am not going to do it.

T 7 . .

D No.

T 8 . . . *(breaks out of role-play)* You will have explained all of this in advance. You know where to go and you know what Time Out means. You know all that in advance. We will practice how to explain Time Out to children a little later. So when I say to hang up your coat, you have the choice.

M To hang up the coat?

T Yes, or go to Time Out.

D Hmmm.

This quick demonstration is so much more concrete than telling the parents about the procedure. Stopping after this brief introduction invites the parents to ask questions.

Next, T adds a new piece of information, to label the behavior that earns Time Out, and then he demonstrates again.

T Actually, it is best to label the behavior that earns the Time Out. You say, "This is not minding. Go to Time Out." Let's do it one more time. *(Gets up and walks over to D, assertive but friendly voice)* D, hang up your swimming trunks now please.

D No.

T I call this not minding.

D I am not going to do it.

T Hang up your swimming trunks or go to Time Out.

D No!

T That's 5 minutes in Time Out.

D NO!

T 6 . . . *(breaks out of role)* What you already know is that when I count like that, I'm adding a minute. So you have the choice . . . Let's continue *(back in role-play)* . . 7. .

D NOOO!

T 8 . . .

D YOU CAN'T MAKE ME!

T 9 . .

D I HATE YOU!

T Go to Time Out now for 10 minutes or you won't be allowed to watch the Cartoon Network between 6 and 7 tonight.

D I don't care.

T Ok, no Cartoon Network between 6 and 7 tonight. *(out of role-play)* So that's how it goes. You, D, refuse to hang up your swim trunks, so I tell you to go to Time Out. You refuse Time Out and I count. And at this point, as the child you can decide what to do. You know what it means when I count. 6 . . . 7 . . . 8 . . . You can still save yourself by going to an 8 minute Time Out. 9 . . . 10. At that point, I tell you to you go to Time Out now for 10 minutes or there won't be any Cartoon Network.

M Explain that to me. He doesn't go to Time Out *and* now he loses Cartoon Network!

T What you are doing as parent is giving him a choice to take a short Time Out or to lose some privilege he takes for granted, like watching TV or riding his bike. Before we begin using Time Out, we will develop a list of privileges you may want to use to back up Time Out. In this example, I gave him the choice of going to Time Out for ten minutes or not watching the Cartoon Network. If he refuses Time Out, he'll lose that privilege.

M But when he refuses to go to Time Out and you remove a privilege such as TV time, is he still supposed to go to Time Out?

T No. You have confiscated the TV program. Privilege loss hurts a bit more than Time Out and it provides you with a back up to Time Out if he refuses to go. You must have control over any privilege you remove or it won't work. If you are not sure you can control the privilege, choose something else.

M & D *(Nodding)* Mm hmm.

The new piece of information here is that privilege removal backs up Time Out refusal. In our approach, we never have the parents make physical contact with the child, as this can lead to escalation that could become abusive. Children quickly learn that it is far easier to go to Time Out for five to ten minutes than it is to lose something they take for granted, such as watching cartoons.

Therapists spend at least a couple of sessions preparing parents to succeed at Time Out before they try out the procedure at home. Before they use Time Out, the parents will have practiced introducing it to their children, they will have lots of experience role-playing, and they will have a list of privileges they can use to back up Time Out refusal.

T Good. We can look closer at privileges to remove later. But when it comes to discipline, the point is to slow down negative behavior, and we use Time Out for that. The problem for us as parents is that we often threaten negative consequences, but we seldom follow through. And in part we don't follow through because we threaten consequences that are unrealistic: "If you don't hang up your coat now, you'll be grounded for four days!!" You might be able to go through with the grounding for a day or two, but you have, in effect, punished yourself with this consequence. And it turns out to be something you are incapable of following through with. We often do negative consequences with our children that are too unsystematic. The point is to be systematic. We let the children know in advance. And when I have introduced a consequence to you, I follow through with it. Why don't you, D, come over here and tell me to do something. I'll refuse. Then you tell me that this is not minding and tell me to go to Time Out.

This T is using outstanding pacing, providing small chunks of information one at a time. This makes it possible for the parents to absorb the information. A common error that many therapists make is to tell all in one long rap, thereby relieving them of the responsibility to cover the topic. The T feels effective, but the parents miss most of the points.

Now that the parents have observed T using Time Out, D takes a turn at playing parent.

D *(Gets up and walks over to T, in assertive but friendly voice)* Go and clear off the kitchen table now!

T No, why do I have to do this again? I do it all the time!!

D This is not cooperation.

T Not now! I want to finish reading this magazine!

D 5 . . .

T Tell me that I have to go to Time Out for five minutes.

Coaching parents in the midst of role-plays can be very smooth, and it enables the parents to be successful.

D Go to Time Out for five minutes.

T No, it isn't my turn to clean up!! *(Coaches D)* Start counting.

D 6 . . .

T NO!

D 7 . . .

T It isn't my turn to do it!! Tell my sister to do it!

D 8 . . .

T No, I don't want to do it!

D 9 . . .

T I'm not going.

D 10 . . .

T *(Out of role)* Great! Good job. You did it exactly by the book. You did not get into an argument with me. When I refused, you told me to go to Time Out for five minutes. You said, "This is not minding, go to Time Out for five minutes" When I protested, you just kept counting. And as child, I knew in advance what was happening. I could save myself by going to Time Out at 6 or 7.

Notice that T ended the role play before the more difficult procedure of backing up Time Out with privilege removal. In the debriefing, T punctuated the specific behaviors that D did correctly. It is not always necessary to draw the parents into the debriefing. It depends on your goal. In this case, the primary purpose was to introduce a new concept. In future sessions, both parents will have the opportunity to practice Time Out, and T will draw them both into the debriefing process, questioning them carefully on specific behaviors they experienced.

D Yes.

T But you just keep on counting, even though I might harass you. You maintain your calm and keep counting. Don't enter any discussion. It is so easy to do that. It is so easy to begin an argument, "Why are you doing this?" "It is too your turn" and so on. All you do is count and count.

M We shouldn't have to have a discussion with them, because they should know that when we give them a direction, they have to cooperate.

T The point is that you have a plan, a guideline to follow. You don't have the option of screaming out some sort of threat where we only follow up partly or not at all. Another thing is that the consequence will come right after the action.

M When I tell him that I am the one who makes the decisions, he jokes and says it is the king and I say no! *[Norway is a kingdom.]*
(Laughter)

T The reality is that we recognize some of the feelings around this. We are tired and stressed . . . whatever. But with this program, we're consistent. Another thing. When it comes to praise and negative consequences, there should much more praise than consequences . . .

The balance of five positives to one negative is a key principle in the training process. Families with externalizing children commonly provide attention for problem behavior and ignore prosocial behavior. Thus, we begin the therapy asking parents to identify their children's strengths, and ever after we help them notice these strengths and praise them.

Role-play is an integral part of our PMTO intervention because it is an effective tool for shaping family process. With role-play, therapists can help family members develop appropriate patterns of interaction to replace the old, overlearned, coercive patterns of behavior. People develop patterns of behavior that become automatic through repetition and reinforcement. Some situations are so well practiced that the patterns run off our tongues with no thought at all. One example is the common set of phrases we use to greet people: "Hi, how are you?" and "I'm fine, how about you?" In the midst of strong negative emotions, interactions have a tendency to become rigid. For example, when angered, people often use verbal and nonverbal signals that elicit predictable reactions, often with breathtaking speed. Unfortunately, the reactions are most likely to be coercive patterns of behavior, including negative reciprocity, escalation, and negative reinforcement (Patterson, 1982; Snyder, 2002). It is well known that frequent use of coercion within families leads to child deviancy. The use of role-play helps parents learn to replace coercive patterns with behavior patterns that promote positive outcomes.

Future Directions

The goal of the chapter was to present information regarding the foundation of PMTO, an intervention designed to treat and prevent externalizing behavior and concomitant problems in youngsters. We have discussed the developmental course of antisocial behavior, the theoretical model detailing mechanisms involved in the instantiation of child and adolescent behavior problems, and an intervention strategy designed to curtail coercive family interactions and replace them with effective parenting skills. The Oregon Model of Parent Management Training is an intervention with five core parenting practices specified as mechanisms of child outcomes. These putative mechanisms have been identified and evaluated over decades of theoretical model building and empirical research with passive and experimental longitudinal studies. The Social Interaction Learning model and the intervention programs based on it continue to be refined to accommodate variability in family circumstances and socio-cultural contexts. Competent adherence to PMTO principals has been shown to attenuate the progression of antisocial behavior in children and adolescents, especially when interventions are introduced before conduct problems become deeply entrenched in families. PMTO provides a positive, practical strategy to bolster parenting effectiveness and to stop the progression of coercive family processes and escalation of antisocial behavior in its tracks.

◆ ◆ ◆

In the past five or ten years, the OSLC group has focused increasingly on developing strategies to implement PMTO in community settings. With the move into the rough-and-tumble world of community intervention, we have begun to develop methods to study the relevant processes of training, adaptation, evaluating program fidelity, adoption, and other dimensions related to the dissemination of efficacious programs. When Chamberlain's multidimensional treatment foster care program (Chamberlain, 1994) was identified as a blue print program, she and her group had to develop training strategies for professionals all over the United States. More recently, Norway decided to implement PMTO nationwide, which has required the development of training strategies that could be carried out in another culture and language and from a distance of more than 6,000 miles. In the past year, NIMH has funded two Latina intervention scientists to implement PMTO with Latino populations. One tenet to which these PMTO extensions hold is the necessity of using direct observation to assess critical processes. We use observation methodology to examine family process through structured parent child interactions and intervention process through videotapes of therapy sessions. Testing the theory, methods, and PMTO intervention throughout the United States and internationally will provide an opportunity to study the extent to which the Social Interaction Learning model generalizes to differing cultures and subcultures.

References

Bank, L., Dishion, T., Skinner, M., & Patterson, G. R. (1990). Method variance in structural equation modeling: Living with "glop." In G. R. Patterson (Ed.), *Depression and aggression in family interaction* (pp. 247–279). Hillsdale, NJ: Erlbaum.

Bank, L., Marlowe, J. H., Reid, J. B., Patterson, G. R., & Weinrott, M. R. (1991). A comparative evaluation of parent-training interventions of families of chronic delinquents. *Journal of Abnormal Child Psychology, 19*(1), 15–33.

Bank, L., Patterson, G. R., & Reid, J. B. (1996). Negative sibling interaction patterns as predictors of later adjustment problems in adolescent and young adult males. In G. H. Brody (Ed.), *Sibling relationships: Their causes and consequences* (pp. 197–229). Norwood, NJ: Albex.

Biglan, A., Mrazek, P. J., Carnine, D., & Flay, B. R. (2003). The integration of research and practice in the prevention of youth problem behaviors. *American Psychologist, 58,* 433–440.

Bullock, B. M., & Dishion, T. D. (2002). Sibling collusion and problem behavior in early adolescence: Toward a process model for family mutuality. *Journal of Abnormal Child Psychology, 30*(2), 143–153.

Capaldi, D. M. (1992). Co-occurrence of conduct problems and depressive symptoms in early adolescent boys: A 2-year follow-up at grade 8. *Development and Psychopathology, 4,* 125–144.

Capaldi, D. M., Dishion, T. J., Stoolmiller, M., & Yoerger, K. (2001). Aggression toward female partners by at-risk young men: The contribution of male adolescent friendships. *Developmental Psychology, 37,* 61–73.

Chamberlain, P. (1994). *Family connections: A treatment foster care model for adolescents with delinquency* (Vol. 5). Eugene, OR: Castalia.

Chamberlain, P., & Reid, J. B. (1998). Comparison of two community alternatives to incarceration for chronic juvenile offenders. *Journal of Consulting and Clinical Psychology, 66*(4), 624–633.

Conger, R. D., Patterson, G. R., & Ge, X. (1995). It takes two to replicate: A mediational model for the impact of parents' stress on adolescent adjustment. *Developmental Psychology, 66,* 80–97.

DeBaryshe, B. D., Patterson, G. R., & Capaldi, D. M. (1993). A performance model for academic achievement in early adolescent boys. *Developmental Psychology, 29,* 795–804.

DeGarmo, D. S., & Forgatch, M. S. (1999). Contexts as predictors of changing parenting practices in diverse family structures: A social interactional perspective to risk and resilience. In E. M. Hetherington (Ed.), *Coping with divorce, single parenting and remarriage: A risk and resiliency perspective* (pp. 227–252). Mahwah, NJ: Erlbaum.

DeGarmo, D. S., & Forgatch, M. S. (2000). *Preventing the "early start" within transitional divorce families: An experimental test of precursors influencing antisocial behavior and delinquency.* Paper presented at the American Society of Criminology Annual Meeting: Crime and Criminology in the Year 2000, San Francisco.

DeGarmo, D. S., Forgatch, M. S., & Martinez, C. R., Jr. (1999). Parenting of divorced mothers as a link between social status and boys' academic outcomes: Unpacking the effects of SES. *Child Development, 70,* 1231–1245.

DeGarmo, D. S., Patterson, G. R., & Forgatch, M. S. (in press). How do outcomes in a specified parent training intervention maintain or wane over time? *Prevention Science.*

Dishion, T. J. (1990). The family ecology of boys' peer relations in middle childhood. *Child Development, 61,* 874–892.

Dishion, T. J., Andrews, D. W., & Crosby, L. (1995). Antisocial boys and their friends in early adolescence: Relationship characteristics, quality, and interactional processes. *Child Development, 66,* 139–151.

Dishion, T. J., Andrews, D. W., Kavanagh, K., & Soberman, L. H. (1996). Preventive interventions for high-risk youth: The Adolescent Transitions Program. In R. D. Peters & R. J. McMahon (Eds.), *Preventing childhood disorders, substance abuse, and delinquency* (pp. 184–214). Thousand Oaks, CA: Sage.

Dishion, T. J., & Bullock, B. M. (2002). Parenting and adolescent problem behavior: An ecological analysis of the nurturance hypothesis. In J. G. Borkowski, S. Ramey, & M. Bristol-Pwer (Eds.), *Parenting and the child's world: Influences on intellectual, academic, and social-emotional development* (pp. 231–249). Mahwah, NJ: Erlbaum.

Dishion, T. J., Duncan, T. E., Eddy, J. M., Fagot, B. I., & Fetrow, R. (1994). The world of parents and peers: Coercive exchanges and children's social adaptation. *Social Development, 3*(3), 255–268.

Dishion, T. J., Eddy, J. M., Haas, E., Li, F., & Spracklen, K. (1997). Friendships and violent behavior during adolescence. *Social Development, 6*(2), 207–223.

Dishion, T. J., Gardner, K., Patterson, G. R., Reid, J. B., & Thibodeaux, S. (1983). *Family process code: A multidimensional system for observing family interaction* (unpublished technical report). Eugene, OR: Oregon Social Learning Center.

Dishion, T. J., Nelson, S., & Bullock, B. M. (in press). Parenting disengagement in adolescence: Facilitating the trajectory to young adult problem behavior. *Journal of Research on Adolescence.*

Dishion, T. J., & Patterson, S. G. (1996). *Preventive parenting with love, encouragement, and limits: The preschool years.* Eugene, OR: Castalia.

Dishion, T. J., & Patterson, G. R. (1999). Model building in developmental psychopathology: A pragmatic approach to understanding and intervention. *Journal of Clinical Child Psychology, 28*(4), 502–512.

Dishion, T. J., Patterson, G. R., & Kavanagh, K. A. (1992). An experimental test of the coercion model: Linking measurement theory, and intervention. In J. McCord & R. Tremblay (Eds.), *The interaction of theory and practice: Experimental studies of intervention* (pp. 253–282). New York: Guildford Press.

Dobkin, P. L., Tremblay, R. E., & Sacchitelle, C. (1997). Predicting boys' early-onset substance abuse from father's alcoholism, son's disruptiveness, and mother's parenting behavior. *Journal of Consulting and Clinical Psychology, 65,* 86–92.

Duncan, S. C., Duncan, T. E., Biglan, A., & Ary, D. (1998). Contributions of the social context to the development of adolescent substance use: A multivariate latent growth modeling approach. *Drug and Alcohol Dependence, 50*(1), 57–71.

Elliott, D. S., Huizinga, D., & Ageton, S. S. (1985). *Explaining delinquency and drug use.* Beverly Hills, CA: Sage.

Fergusson, D., Horwood, L. J., & Lynskey, M. T. (1995). The stability of disruptive childhood behaviors. *Journal of Abnormal Child Psychology, 23*(3).

Forgatch, M. S. (1991). The clinical science vortex: A developing theory of antisocial behavior. In D. Pepler & K. H. Rubin (Eds.), *The development and treatment of childhood aggression* (pp. 291–315). Hillsdale, NJ: Erlbaum.

Forgatch, M. S. (1994). *Parenting through change: A programmed intervention curriculum for groups of single mothers.* Eugene, OR: Oregon Social Learning Center.

Forgatch, M. S., & DeGarmo, D. S. (1999). Parenting through change: An effective prevention program for single mothers. *Journal of Consulting and Clinical Psychology, 67,* 711–724.

Forgatch, M. S., & DeGarmo, D. S. (2002). Extending and testing the social interaction learning model with divorce samples. In J. B. Reid, G. R. Patterson, & J. Snyder (Eds.), *Antisocial behavior in children and adolescents: A developmental analysis and model for intervention* (pp. 235–256). Washington DC: American Psychological Association.

Forgatch, M. S., & Patterson, G. R. (1989). *Parents and adolescents living together: Vol. 2. Family problem solving.* Eugene, OR: Castalia.

Forgatch, M. S., & Rains, L. (1997). *MAPS: Marriage and Parenting in Stepfamilies* (parent training manual). Eugene, OR: Oregon Social Learning Center.

Furstenberg, F. F., Jr., & Seltzer, J. A. (1986). Divorce and child development. *Sociological Studies of Child Development, 1,* 137–160.

Hetherington, E. M., Cox, M., & Cox, R. (1985). Long-term effects of divorce and remarriage on the adjustment of children. *Journal of the American Academy of Child Psychiatry, 24*(5), 518–530.

Huesmann, L. R., Eron, L. D., & Yarmel, P. W. (1987). Intellectual functioning and aggression. *Journal of Personality and Social Psychology, 52*(1), 232–240.

Jones, R. R., Reid, J. B., & Patterson, G. R. (1975). Naturalistic observation in clinical assessment. In P. McReynolds (Ed.), *Advances in psychological assessment* (Vol. 3, pp. 42–95). San Francisco: Jossey-Bass.

Kazdin, A. E., Mazurick, J. L., & Bass, D. (1993). Risk for attrition in treatment of antisocial children and families. *Journal of Clinical Child Psychology, 22*(1), 2–16.

Knutson, J. F., DeGarmo, D. S., & Ried, J. B. (in press). Social disadvantage and neglectful parenting as precursors to the development of antisocial and aggressive child behavior: Testing a theoretical model. *Aggressive Behavior.*

Lykken, D. T. (1993). Predicting violence in the violent society. *Applied and Preventive Psychology, 2,* 13–20.

Maccoby, E. E., & Martin, J. A. (1983). *Handbook of child psychology* (Vol. IV). New York: Wiley.

Martinez, C. R., Jr., & Forgatch, M. S. (2001). Preventing problems with boys' noncompliance: Effects of a parent training intervention for divorcing mothers. *Journal of Consulting and Clinical Psychology, 69,* 416–428.

Mrazek, P. J., & Haggerty, R. J. (1994). Illustrative preventive intervention research programs. In P. J. Mrazek & R. J. Haggerty (Eds.), *Reducing risks for mental disorders: Frontiers for preventive intervention research* (pp. 215–313). Washington DC: National Academy Press.

Nagin, D., & Tremblay, R. E. (1999). Trajectories of boys' physical aggression, opposition, and hyperactivity on the path to physically violent and nonviolent juvenile delinquency. *Child Development, 70,* 1181–1196.

Offord, D. R., Boyle, M. C., & Racine, Y. (1991). The epidemiology of antisocial behavior in childhood and adolescence. In D. Pepler & K. H. Rubin (Eds.), *The development and treatment of childhood aggression* (pp. 31–54). Hillsdale, NJ: Erlbaum.

Olweus, D. (1983). Low school achievement and aggressive behavior in adolescent boys. In D. Magnusson & V. L. Allen (Eds.), *Human development: An interactional perspective* (pp. 353–365). New York: Academic Press.

Patterson, G. R. (1982). *Coercive family process.* Eugene, OR: Castalia.

Patterson, G. R. (1984). Siblings: Fellow travelers in a coercive system. In R. J. Blanchard & D. C. Blanchard (Eds.), *Advances in the study of aggression* (Vol. 1, pp. 173–215). New York: Academic Press.

Patterson, G. R. (1986). Performance models for antisocial boys. *American Psychologist, 41,* 432–444.

Patterson, G. R. (1992). Developmental changes in antisocial behavior. In R. D. Peters, R. J. McMahon, & V. L. Quinsey (Eds.), *Aggression and violence throughout the life span* (pp. 52–82). Newbury Park, CA: Sage.

Patterson, G. R. (1993). Orderly change in a stable world: The antisocial trait as a chimera. *Journal of Consulting and Clinical Psychology, 61*(6), 911–919.

Patterson, G. R. (1995). Orderly change in a stable world: The antisocial trait as a chimera. In J. Gottman & J. Sackett (Eds.), *The analysis of change* (pp. 84–100). Hillsdale, NJ: Erlbaum.

Patterson, G. R., & Chamberlain, P. (1988). Treatment process: A problem at three levels. In L. C. Wynne (Ed.), *The state of the art in family therapy research: Controversies and recommendations* (pp. 189–223). New York: Family Process Press.

Patterson, G. R., Chamberlain, P., & Reid, J. B. (1982). A comparative evaluation of a parent-training program. *Behavior Therapy, 13,* 638–650.

Patterson, G. R., & Cobb, J. A. (1971). A dyadic analysis of "aggressive" behaviors. In J. P. Hill (Ed.), *Minnesota Symposia on Child Psychology* (Vol. 5). Minneapolis, MN: University of Minnesota Press.

Patterson, G. R., & Cobb, J. A. (1973). Stimulus control for classes of noxious behaviors. In J. F. Knutson (Ed.), *The control of aggression: Implications from basic research.* Chicago: Aldine.

Patterson, G. R., Dishion, T. J., & Yoerger, K. (2000). Adolescent growth in new forms of problem behavior: Macro- and micro-peer dynamics. *Prevention Science, 1,* 3–13.

Patterson, G. R., & Forgatch, M. S. (1985). Therapist behavior as a determinant for client noncompliance: A paradox for the behavior modifier. *Journal of Consulting and Clinical Psychology, 53*(6), 846–851.

Patterson, G. R., & Forgatch, M. S. (1987). *Parents and adolescents living together: The basics* (Vol. I). Eugene, OR: Castalia.

Patterson, G. R., Littman, R. A., & Bricker, W. (1967). Assertive behavior in children: A step towards a theory of aggression. *Monographs of the Society of Research in Child Development, 32*(5), 1–43.

Patterson, G. R., Reid, J. B., & Dishion, T. J. (1992). *Antisocial boys* (Vol. 4). Eugene, OR: Castalia.

Patterson, G. R., Shaw, D. S., Snyder, J. J., & Yoerger, K. (2003). Maternal ratings of growth in children's overt and covert antisocial behavior. Manuscript submitted for publication.

Patterson, G. R., & Yoerger, K. (1993). Developmental models for delinquent behavior. In S. Hodgins (Ed.), *Crime and mental disorders* (pp. 140–172). Newbury Park, CA: Sage.

Patterson, G. R., & Yoerger, K. (1995). Two different models for adolescent physical trauma and for early arrest. *Criminal Behavior and Mental Health, 5,* 411–423.

Ramsey, E., Antoine, K., Kavanagh, K., & Reid, J. B. (1992a). LIFT Parent Education Component: Grade 1. OSLC Technical manual. (Available from Oregon Social Learning Center, 160 E. 4th Ave., Eugene, OR 97401).

Ramsey, E., Antoine, K., Kavanagh, K., & Reid, J. B. (1992b). LIFT Parent Education Component: Grade 5. OSLC Technical manual. (Available from Oregon Social Learning Center, 160 E. 4th Ave., Eugene, OR 97401).

Ramsey, E., Lathrop, M., Tharp, L., & Reid, J. B. (1992a). LIFT Classroom Social Skills Component: Grade 1. OSLC Technical manual. (Available from Oregon Social Learning Center, 160 E. 4th Ave., Eugene, OR 97401).

Ramsey, E., Lathrop, M., Tharp, L., & Reid, J. B. (1992b. LIFT Classroom Social Skills Component: Grade 5. OSLC Technical manual. (Available from Oregon Social Learning Center, 160 E. 4th Ave., Eugene, OR 97401).

Reid, J. B. (Ed.). (1978). *A social learning approach to family intervention: Observation in home settings.* Eugene, OR: Castalia.

Reid, J. B., Eddy, J. M., Fetrow, R. A., & Stoolmiller, M. (1999). Description and immediate impacts of a preventive intervention for conduct problems. *American Journal of Community Psychology, 27*(4), 483–517.

Reid, J. B., Patterson, G. R., & Snyder, J. (Eds.). (2002). *Antisocial behavior in children and adolescents: A developmental analysis and model for intervention.* Washington DC: American Psychological Association.

Schuck, J. R. (1974). The use of causal nonexperimental modes in aggression research. In J. DeWit & W. W. Hartup (Eds.), *Determinants and origins of aggressive behavior* (pp. 381–389). The Hague: Mouton.

Shortt, J. W., Capaldi, D. M., Dishion, T. J., Bank, L., & Owen, L. D. (in press). The role of adolescent peers, romantic partners, and siblings in the emergence of the adult antisocial lifestyle. *Journal of Family Psychology.*

Snyder, J. (2002). Reinforcement and coercion mechanisms in the development of antisocial behavior: Peer relationships. In J. B. Reid, J. Snyder, & G. R. Patterson (Eds.), *Antisocial behavior in children and adolescents: A developmental analysis and model for intervention* (pp. 101–122). Washington DC: American Psychological Association.

Snyder, J., Schrepferman, L., & St. Peter, C. (1997). Origins of antisocial behavior: Negative reinforcement and affect dysregulation of behavior as socialization mechanisms in family interaction. *Behavior Modification, 21*(2), 187–215.

Snyder, J., West, L., Stockemer, V., Gibbons, S., & Almquist-Parks, L. (1996). A social learning model of peer choice in the natural environment. *Journal of Applied Developmental Psychology, 17,* 215–237.

Snyder, J. J., Edwards, P., McGraw, K., Kilgore, K., & Holton, A. (1994). Escalation and reinforcement in mother-child conflict: Social processes associated with the development of physical aggression. *Development and Psychopathology, 6,* 305–321.

Snyder, J. J., & Patterson, G. R. (1995). Individual differences in social aggression: A reinforcement model of socialization in the natural environment. *Behavior Therapy, 26,* 371–391.

Stoolmiller, M. (1994). Antisocial behavior, delinquent peer association, and unsupervised wandering: Growth and change from childhood to early adolescence. *Multivariate Behavioral Research, 29*(3), 263–288.

Stubbs, J., Crosby, L., Forgatch, M. S., & Capaldi, D. M. (1998). Family and peer process code: A synthesis of three Oregon Social Learning Center behavior codes (Training manual, available from Oregon Social Learning Center; 160 East 4th Avenue, Eugene, OR 97401.)

Tremblay, R. E., Boulerice, B., Pihl, R. O., Vitaro, F., & Zoccolillo, M. (1996). *Male adolescent conduct disorder is predicted by kindergarten impulisivity, but there are moderating effects.* Paper presented at the Society of Research in Child and Adolescent Psychiatry, Santa Monica, CA.

Tremblay, R. E., Kurtz, L., Masse, L. C., Vitaro, F., & Pihl, R. O. (1995). A bimodal preventive intervention for disruptive kindergarten boys: Its impact through mid-adolescence. *Journal of Consulting and Clinical Psychology, 63*(4), 560–568.

Tremblay, R. E., McCord, J., Boileau, H., Charlebois, P., Gagnon, C., & LeBlanc, M. (1991). Can disruptive boys be helped to become competent? *Psychiatry, 54,* 148–161.

Vitaro, F., Brendgen, M., & Tremblay, R. E. (1999). Prevention of school dropout through the reduction of disruptive behaviors and school failure in elementary school. *Journal of School Psychology, 23*(1), 39–74.

Walter, G. J., & Gilmore, S. K. (1973). Placebo versus social learning effects in parent training procedures designed to alter the behaviors of aggressive boys. *Behavior Therapy, 4,* 361–377.

Wiesner, M., Vondracek, F. W., Capaldi, D. M., & Porfeli, E. (in press). Childhood and adolescent predictors of early adult career pathways. *Journal of Vocational Behavior.*

Wilson, H. (1980). Parental supervision: A neglected aspect of delinquency. *The British Journal of Criminology, 20,* 203–235.

Wiltz, N. A., Jr., & Patterson, G. R. (1974). An evaluation of parent training procedures designed to alter inappropriate aggressive behavior of boys. *Behavior Therapy, 5,* 215–221.

PART FOUR

SOCIOTHERAPY

CHAPTER TWENTY-EIGHT

SOCIOTHERAPIES FOR CHILDREN AND ADOLESCENTS: AN OVERVIEW

Jeffrey J. Wilson, M.D.

Sociotherapy, broadly defined, includes any type of treatment that has as its primary emphasis the socio-environmental and interpersonal factors in adjustment (Campbell, 1996). Sociotherapy is interwoven into most of what we do as child mental health professionals. With all of the remarkable advances in the neuropsychiatry of developmental disorders, and even among the most profoundly genetically based disorders, there is always, inevitably, the interface between genetics and environment through which we express ourselves pheno-typically. As such, sociotherapies occur "where the rubber meets the road," that is, at the intersection of individual biology, personal choice, and interpersonal action.

Within this "proximal zone of development" (Vygotsyky, 1978) we find our patients, and within this zone of development we intervene with our varied treatments and preventive efforts. At no point is an individual free of environmental influence, as all behaviors are embedded in their social context. In fact, many of the most common reasons for referral are interpersonal. The most common reason for referral is disruptive behavior, a disruption in an individual's interaction with the world around him or her. We have selected several "sociotherapies" that will be explored in detail in accord with the practical theme of this handbook. Although we will not cover all the possible forms of socio-therapy, we hope to lay out a practical guide to the practice of each of the specific areas covered.

Sociotherapies can include a wide variety of what we do in child/adolescent psychiatry, ranging from family therapy (described in the previous section on psychotherapy), to group therapy, to inpatient treatment, to consultation with various agencies (schools or courts) or fellow physicians, and preventive interventions. Inpatient psychotherapy, residential treatment, and the "therapeutic community" are among the most invasive and intense sociotherapies available. Yet all of these modalities emphasize aspects of intervention that are socially invasive in one way, shape, or form; they all emphasize varying degrees of social manipulation as a means of assessing and often changing individual behavior. These social manipulations can range from using the peer group guided by group therapists; to using consumer-driven peer support groups; to using intense, often locked, inpatient treatments; to using schools, pediatricians, or the legal system. We end the chapter by exploring methods of reducing high-risk sexual behaviors in a variety of social contexts, emphasizing the importance of integrating treatment and prevention for children in danger from high-risk sexual behavior as well as commonly comorbid psychiatric or substance-related problems.

Sarah Erickson and Laura Palmer introduce the concept of using the peer group as a mechanism of behavioral change in their chapter on group psychotherapy. The peer group deservedly receives a fair amount of attention in both risk and resiliency factors related to child and adolescent deviance. Drs. Erickson and Palmer explore several evidence-based indications for and approaches to group therapy with children and adolescents. The most effective group therapies are administered by trained therapists for specific indications, including: a variety of anxiety disorders, social skills deficits, parent-child relational problems, depression, self-injurious behavior, bereavement, anger management, and even severe pediatric illnesses.

Although group therapies are often administratively cost-effective, their effectiveness with some problems that youths commonly face remains to be established. Much of Erickson and Palmer's discussion of putative mechanisms of efficacy for group therapy is based on a scholarly review of the available literature, and much of this is based on adults. Particularly for adolescents with problem behaviors, it should be noted that the administration of group therapy itself can potentially be helpful as well as harmful, depending on the group and the positive and negative processes that arise during the treatment. This negative group process can be a major regulating factor in composing and monitoring groups for youths with disruptive or substance use disorders (Dishion, McCord, & Poulin, 1999). On the other hand, positive group processes, as those often fostered in well-managed therapeutic communities, can result in dramatic developments of self-restraint (DeLeon, 1999). Understanding the positive and negative processes that arise in peer groups, both in and out of treatment, are major social influences that have yet to be fully explored in developmental science. It is hoped that continued investigation of these social phenomena will complement and inform group psychotherapy such that these forces can be used in promoting healthier behaviors given group therapy's predominant social role in influencing vulnerable young people. Basic research into the mechanisms of effectiveness in adolescents, in particular the mediators and moderators of effectiveness, may pave the way in the future for maximizing the power of the peer group.

Colleen Loomis and Keith Humphreys expand on the potentially healing aspects of group process by examining processes of individual change within mutual help organizations, which function without the guidance of trained mental health professionals. They note that these organizations are more commonly used as a resource for distressed individuals and families than all mental health services combined. A plethora of such organizations is available for a broad variety of conditions ranging from alcoholism and drug addiction to groups that focus on helping parents of medically ill or disabled children. Loomis and Humphreys have focused on self-help groups that deal with child and adolescent psychiatric or social problems (such as divorce or sexuality). Loomis and Humphreys frame the utility of these groups to such children and their families from a developmental perspective, drawing heavily on the work of Vygotsky in this area. They argue that these groups go beyond the work of therapists, entering the zone of proximal development through associations with peers who are struggling with the same problems in a more relevant fashion than health care professionals.

Case examples are used to demonstrate how these groups can enhance life transitions, such as understanding a child's illness or an adolescent's sexual preference. The theory is compelling, but the evidence for these mechanisms of change is still early in development. Little research has focused on this area. While convincing effectiveness data are difficult to find, the popularity of these groups among families suffering from mental illness or other social stigmata is unquestionable. They go on to practically discuss the methods that some of the most popular of these groups use, and dispense information for providers and members to connect with groups such as the National Alliance for the Mentally Ill (NAMI). Nonetheless, much is yet to be learned about the practical interface between mental health workers and mutual help organizations, for both providers and participants. More research into the mechanisms by which these groups are effective can yield important information on how to tap into the valuable resource of mutual help.

Dan Becker and Mark DeAntonio then introduce one of the most intense interventions of psychiatry: inpatient treatment. The risks, benefits, and alternatives to inpatient treatment are discussed for a variety of psychiatric disorders. They describe the methods they use at their units in detail, including psychopharmacotherapy, group, individual, family, and milieu therapy. They briefly discuss the empirical basis for these treatments, considering both the potential stabilization of a patient's danger to self or others versus removing the child or adolescent from his or her environment. More research is needed regarding how to integrate these treatments into the community; that is, how to generalize benefits observed in intensive milieu therapies to less restricted outpatient settings.

Shashank Joshi describes one of the most important areas for children, families, and child/adolescent psychiatry: School. Our ability to observe how children interact is facilitated through our relationships with child study teams, teachers, and other educational personnel. This facilitates both diagnosis and treatment; some disorders, such as ADHD, should not even be diagnosed without input from school personnel. Yet, this is often difficult to obtain for mental health professionals unfamiliar with the structure and terminology of the educational world in which children, especially special education children, live. Dr. Joshi introduces the terms that mental health professionals need to understand, the roles of the various personnel, and the current basis for psychiatric interventions with students and school districts. He also outlines the model he and his colleagues have developed at Stanford. This should be of value to any mental health professional interested in facilitating effective feedback from schools, and helping students in one of their most important, and increasingly complex, areas of functioning.

Richard Shaw and Laura Palmer address the area of medical consultation, focusing on one of the most troubling aspects of pediatric, or for that matter, most types of care—adherence to treatment. In treating adherence itself as a remediable factor during treatment, they go beyond the unfortunate tendency of giving up on those that do not want to help themselves. Of course, in pediatrics the consent process is complicated by having a patient who is unable to consent for herself, and health care providers may recommend things that the family or the pediatric patient may disagree with. The most troubling aspect of their work is that although many of the treatments are toxic, they can save lives; hence, failing to understand the risk-benefit analysis can be life-threatening to the children involved. The extent of the problem is pandemic, with approximately 50% of families not adhering to their recommended treatments.

Shaw and Palmer go on to discuss several empirically validated factors that may contribute to non-adherence, including: developmental issues, treatment side effects, child maladaptation, parental maladaptation to the child's illness, peer group factors, parent-child conflict, and even adaptive non-adherence (for quality of life issues). Many of these issues are uniquely suited to intervention by a child/adolescent psychiatrist or psychologist, and a thorough assessment to rule out the presence of one or more of these factors can go a long way to improving adherence on a case by case basis. Moving beyond the general consultative role,

Shaw and Palmer have developed a manualized treatment that incorporates both educational and behavioral interventions; the target population includes patients, families, and even staff. Although this model is firmly grounded in developmental and behavioral theory, they go on to describe the developing nature of this field of research and the multiple obstacles investigators face in conducting this research. Currently, a careful assessment of the individual factors involved in a child's medical illness and the benefits derived from treatment must be considered, all in the developmental context of the child's ability to understand his illness, his family's ability to understand the same, and whether or not any treatable psychiatric or behavioral disorders exist. More research is needed to help to identify those youth at greatest risk of maladaptive non-adherence, and the benefits of earlier intervention. This might provide multiple benefits to the patients, because demonstration of reduced health care costs, reduced morbidity, and mortality would go a long way to arguing for the importance of integrated psychosocial treatment for severe pediatric illness.

Peter Ash takes on the relatively little researched, but legally well-defined, topic of legal consultations, building upon his extensive clinical experience in the area. Interactions with the legal system, from the point of view of a child or adolescent, can be frightening and can have extensive consequences in terms of the child's care. He begins the chapter by describing some of the key aspects of the difference between legal consultation and private practice. First and foremost, he emphasizes the need to focus on the forensic question, which defines the role of the consulting psychiatrist: to provide an opinion on the relative test. Dr. Ash goes on to recommend some specific questions that the consultant needs to clarify so that she can appropriately answer the question while respecting the rights of the minors and all parties involved. Specific recommendations are then given on approaching some common but different types of cases (divorce or custody cases, sexual abuse cases, and evaluations for waiver to adult court). The preparation of the report is then discussed in detail, because this writing process is different than preparing assessments for medical purposes. Finally, Dr. Ash walks the reader through the process of testifying in court or at a deposition. Although many child and adolescent psychiatrists may feel uncomfortable with such work, there remains a need for obtaining expert opinions in this area. Effective testimony in this setting can significantly improve a child's life.

Larry Brown and I wrote the final chapter in this section. In it, we emphasize the effectiveness of HIV-preventive interventions in a variety of community and clinical settings. We believe that prevention of high-risk behaviors, in general, among the children we see in practice is a key aspect of practice that may be overlooked. Because children, and adolescents in particular, commonly experiment with new, at times risky, behaviors that have not yet become routine or cemented as a part of their adaptation to their world, there is a unique opportunity for child and adolescent specialists to intervene with problem behaviors before they become disorders. We think it is important to assess the whole youth and her family, considering the wide variety of behaviors she may bring to treatment in an comprehensive fashion.

We have selected high-risk sexual behavior as our focus because we hope these strategies will convince the reader that effective preventions are available for a variety of risk behaviors, and demonstrate in a practical fashion some of the key aspects of prevention in working with adolescents. The main reasons we have selected high-risk sexual behavior as our representative preventive intervention are because of potential health consequences (e.g., HIV/AIDS), because it can be a normative part of development, and because sexual behavior is an interpersonal behavior that can be prevented with prolonged abstinence or adapted into safer sex behaviors with specific, empirically validated methods. A useful behavioral theory guides many of the most effective interventions, and is discussed in detail within this chapter. This theory considers developmental, psychiatric, and family influences in the development and maintenance of high-risk sexual behaviors. Some professionals and families shy away from the topic of sexuality with the obviously developing adolescent, yet we have found that when presented in the proper context, the information and the preventive strategies are helpful to adolescents.

◆ ◆ ◆

In summary, we hope to bring to the reader the existing evidence and clinical wisdom that exists in this sampling of sociotherapies. Almost no aspect of psychiatry is devoid of sociotherapy; even psychopharmacologists or neurologists must at some point discuss social behaviors to assess the patient or his response. Sociotherapies can be powerful interventions, and can be effective at a variety of levels. Working with developing adolescents, we have the unique opportunity to observe the interface between biology, psychology, and sociology. When we can find the place where the youth is developing, what Vygotsky (1978) referred to as the zone of proximal development, or what Bronfenbrenner and Ceci (1994) referred to as the social ecology of the individual, we can meet the youth where she *is*. We are also a part of the social context of the individual. To the extent we can connect with an adolescent, where they are, we can collaborate with them to assist them in finding themselves, an increasingly complicated developmental phase within our culture of mass media, information overload, and often unrealistic pressures from without as well as within.

References

Bronfenbrenner, U., & Ceci, S. J. (1994). Nature-nurture reconceptualized in developmental perspective: A bioecological model. *Psychological Review, 101*(4), 568–586.

Cambell, R. J. (1996). *Psychiatric Dictionary* (7th ed.). New York: Oxford University Press.

DeLeon, G. (1999). Therapeutic communities. In M. Galanter & H. D. Kleber (Eds.), *Textbook of substance abuse treatment* (pp. 447–462). Washington DC: American Psychiatric Press.

Dishion, T. J., McCord, J., & Poulin, F. (1999). When interventions harm: Peer groups and problem behavior. *American Psychologist 54*(9): 755–764.

Vygotsky, L. S. (1978). *Mind in society.* Cambridge, MA: Harvard University Press.

CHAPTER TWENTY-NINE

GROUP THERAPY AND INTERVENTIONS WITH CHILDREN AND ADOLESCENTS

Sarah J. Erickson, Ph.D., and Laura L. Palmer, M.Ed., Psy.D.

Group therapy is the most frequently employed therapy modality for children in inpatient and residential treatment (Sugar, 1993). Group therapy offers many advantages to mental health programs, perhaps most notably the economic advantage of having fewer therapists intervene with more patients. In addition, group therapy is often indicated for a variety of child and adolescent clinical problems, and may be the treatment of choice for some problems. Although there are many different types of group therapy used with children and adolescents, conducted in a variety of settings, most of these groups share some goals, procedures, and processes. Innovations in group therapy research and clinical experience have further delineated treatment-specific goals, the role of the leader, group membership, and relative emphasis on prevention, intervention, and psychological growth for a variety of problems.

In this chapter, we will review the basic rationale for group therapy, describe putative mechanisms of efficacy, review the empirical support for group therapy, describe developmental influences relevant to group treatment, outline putative targets of treatment, and then provide an illustration of group therapy for adolescents with cancer and their parents.

Basic Rationale for Group Therapy Treatment

Group therapy with children and adolescents offers several advantages beyond economical considerations. Because of the sociotherapeutic nature of the group, specific interventions can be implemented in groups that are difficult to implement in individual treatment. For both school-age children and adolescents, the group format can match their developmental needs and competencies. For example, group therapy mirrors the developmental task of finding, learning to integrate into, and maintaining a peer group. According to Schechtman's (2001) process research on group therapy with children, preadolescents seem to have a significant need for cathartic experiences and for sharing personal experiences and feelings. Self-disclosure in a group setting is one effective way to achieve such goals and may set the stage for a more direct generalization to extra-therapeutic peer group involvement. Group therapy may also be well-suited for adolescents, to the extent that their primary developmental challenges relate to identity formation and relationships and interactions with others: separation-individuation, independence/dependence, peer conflicts, and conformity/individuality.

Group therapy is unique because of a variety of processes inherent in this format, including: a recognition of the commonality of members' needs and conflicts, modeling of behaviors, assessment of social perceptions, normative peer support, interpersonal feedback, relationship development, reduced isolation, and enhanced self-esteem. These processes interact to provide clients with a new understanding of their problems and strengths, and how to make sense of them in relation to others. In addition, the supportive climate and special group activities characteristic of group therapy encourage children to share their distress and concerns with peers (Schechtman, 2001). These group therapy characteristics are conceptualized to be important mechanisms of change for children and adolescents. Because of their relatively greater dependency and lack of insight into interactional processes, groups with younger children often require more structure and leader facilitation compared with adolescent groups.

Group therapy with medically ill children is an excellent evidence-based example of the therapeutic benefits of the group modality (Stuber et al., 1995). For several reasons group therapy may be particularly beneficial to children who have shared concerns, for example, those with serious medical conditions. Children with medical conditions typically feel different and isolated from peers, as well as uncertain about how to cope with their condition. Group interventions for children and adolescents have been developed to increase knowledge of illness, to reduce their sense of isolation, to promote psychological adaptation, and to decrease physical symptoms and side effects (Erickson, Palmer, Achilles, Classen, & Spiegel, 2000; Palmer et al., 2000; Plante, Lobato, & Engel, 2001).

Although individual therapy continues to be the most common format for treatment in outpatient clinical settings, nearly half of all child and adolescent clinical treatment outcome studies have assessed the efficacy of treatments provided within a group context (Kazdin, Bass, Ayers, & Rodgers, 1990). The primary finding of these outcome studies is that, across diagnoses, individual and group therapy with children and adolescents yield positive outcome effects in the moderate to large range, which are comparable to the effects of therapy with adults (Kazdin, 2000; Kazdin et al., 1990; Weisz, Han, Granger, Weiss, & Morton, 1995).

Putative Mechanisms of Efficacy

Unfortunately, mediators and moderators of group therapy efficacy have not yet been empirically identified and evaluated. However, there are several ways in which group therapy with children and adolescents is hypothesized to benefit children. With well-trained group therapists, group members can learn more about their interpersonal style and ways to improve their interactions with others. Children can experiment with alternative behaviors in the group and receive feedback from one another about how they are experienced in the group. Because social competence is an important predictor of peer acceptance and long-term adjustment (Furman & Gavin, 1989), supporting its ongoing development is crucial.

Because theoretical models of group therapy with children and adolescents are in an early phase of development and evaluation, we utilize an integration of Yalom's (1985) adult group model and Brent and Kolko's (1998) child and adolescent individual model of therapeutic change. Within Yalom's (1985) existential framework, theoretically derived therapeutic factors have been identified that have not yet amassed empirical support with children. Yalom's therapeutic factors include: instillation of hope (members need to believe that their condition will improve), universality (members need to know that their situation and concerns are shared by others, thereby reducing isolation), imparting of information (leader and members impart new information and address misinformation or misperceptions), altruism (members experience satisfaction through assisting others); corrective recapitulation of the primary family group (members become aware of their family patterns and how patterns affect current functioning), development of social skills, imitative behavior (members learn from leader and other members), interpersonal learning (members develop positive relationships with one another); group cohesiveness (members experience a sense of belonging, thereby reducing isolation), catharsis (members express emotions without reprisal, producing self-acceptance and connectedness with others), and existential factors (members address existential concerns).

The therapy group may be conceptualized as a microcosm of the child's larger world, where the group process provides an illustration of the child's experience in the world. Conflicts and concerns within the group are believed to mirror those in the child's outside life. Members are exposed to discussions that foster new ways of dealing with situations and then are able to evaluate, within a supportive group context, the effectiveness of these techniques. When members have a common problem, sharing experiences and perceptions may lead to decreased feelings of isolation and feeling "different" than peers. This sense of belonging, or universalization, along with group cohesion, fosters members' willingness to express their emotions and explore emotionally laden issues. Group therapy experience may afford an opportunity for a child or adolescent to experience empathy, support, and understanding from peers, and develop warm, non-exploitive relationships with others. In addition, most older children and adolescents are able to other members' perspectives, an important step in developing one's empathic capacity. Group therapists may need to be more active in the beginning stages of a group in order to model supportive efforts, make connections between members' experience, support self-disclosure and emotional expression, and aid in perspective taking. For example, in group therapy with adolescents undergoing cancer treatment, a therapist may make connections between group members' experience by pointing out how one child's fear of going back to school after a long absence and physical changes (such as hair loss) is quite common, and likely similar to the fears of others in the group. The therapist may tie the child's current concern to another group member's previous concern about hair loss, appearance in general, feeling different, and fear of peer rejection.

In addition to these group therapy-specific mechanisms of change, mediators of individual therapy change may be salient for group members as well. Brent and Kolko (1998) enumerated a model of therapy change with children and adolescents wherein each potential mediator has garnered significant empirical support. Specifically, they identified the therapeutic relationship; the child's attitudes, thoughts, affect, and behavior; and the social context of development as potential mechanisms of change.

Among these potential mediators, the child's social context, most notably family variables including parenting style, parental psychopathology, and family adversity, has received the strongest empirical support regarding its significant contribution to child outcome. The school environment has also been shown to influence educational and behavioral outcomes. In brief, the efficacy of therapy with children and adolescents is often either enhanced or diminished depending on the larger social context: if parents, the school system, or the larger environment do not support therapeutic change in the child, then the group will necessarily have a limited impact. In fact, we recommend that group therapy with children be augmented with parent or family sessions in which parents are kept informed of the general issues addressed in the group and assisted in supporting the child's progress at home. Similarly, school teachers or counselors may be incorporated into therapy efforts in order to ensure continuity of expectations and consequences across settings. When parents or school personnel are included in therapeutic efforts, clear delineations regarding confidentiality must be addressed at the outset of therapy. We recommend informing all parties involved that specifics of child behavior or statements, unless representing a serious threat to the safety of the child or others, will not be shared, but general themes that are relevant to facilitating therapeutic change will be shared. In fact, we recommend meeting with parents approximately once per month to keep them apprised of their child's progress in general terms. Prior to the monthly parent meetings, we ask group members to help determine what sort of information would be important, permissible, and helpful to share. By involving the group members in this process, they collaborate with determining what and how information is shared with parents.

In addition, targeting child behavior change, including enhancing social competence and social-cognitive skills such as problem-solving, has received support from different lines of child therapy research. Group therapy is uniquely suited to act as a microcosm in which children can learn and experiment with alternative social behaviors in a safe, facilitated group environment. Finally, the literature suggests that age is an important moderator of treatment efficacy. For example, cognitive behavioral therapy is almost twice as effective with adolescents compared with younger children, and family management is more efficacious for younger children. The importance of other proposed mediators has only limited support in the child and adolescent therapy literature. However, the extant studies with children and adolescents, and the more extensive research with adults, suggest possible mediator roles in child therapy outcomes for

A. Therapist characteristics including empathy, enhancement of therapy involvement, good interpersonal skills, and provision of support and understanding
B. Affect regulation with a focus on anger management for disruptive disordered children
C. Peer relationships both within and outside of the group
D. Social-ecological factors such as exposure to violence, poverty, and criminality (See Brent & Kolko, 1998 for a review.)

Developmental Influences

The organizational perspective on development provides a theoretical framework for conceptualizing the hierarchical progression of qualitative reorganizations within and among biological, psychological, and social systems (Cicchetti, 1993). Conceptualizing developmental trends and reorganizations (that is, major developmental tasks; critical needs, issues, conflicts, and choices; domains of continuity and discontinuity; and the potential for developmental crises at each stage of development) is an essential component of group work with children. Attention to when during the developmental course and why a disorder occurred, how long a deviant trajectory has been in effect, and what precursors to the maladaptive functioning can be identified require a developmental framework to ensure developmentally timed and sensitive interventions (Toth & Cicchetti, 1999).

Because developmental competencies emerge and evolve over the course of development, no treatment is likely to be effective throughout childhood and adolescence. Appropriate intervention requires an understanding of children's developmental competencies. To the extent that pathological conditions may be associated with developmental delays or deviance, considering age alone is inadequate in determining a child's developmental competencies. Toth and Cicchetti (1999) identified causal reasoning, emotion understanding, self-understanding, and language ability as developmental domains that must be considered in designing interventions.

Causal reasoning abilities have direct implications for the child's ability to benefit from therapeutic processes. Because a child's ability to understand an event in relation to internal, non-observable sources rather than external situations increases with age, therapy with younger children needs to be concrete and not reliant on interpretations, metaphors, an understanding of internal issues, or an ability to make generalizations. In addition, past versus present orientation must be addressed. The ability to link past events with current behavior or affect emerges in middle childhood. Hence, early childhood interventions should focus on current correlates of behavior or affect. The conscious-unconscious dimension of interventions must also be considered. Prior to adolescence, children will typically have difficulty understanding explanations of unconscious behavior.

Children's understanding of emotion increases with age, with a shift from external to internal explanations. Considering developmental correlates of emotion understanding, such as the number of emotions that can be processed simultaneously and the ability to distinguish between emotions, must be taken into account when determining an intervention approach. For example, addressing conflicting feelings makes sense only if a child is aware of the feelings being simultaneously present and distinct.

According to Toth and Ciccetti (1999), changes in the content, organization, and structure of self-understanding unfold over development. Self-understanding evolves from a focus on external attributes to more psychological attributes. Children also become more accurate in their self-assessments over time, with an increasing ability to take into account others' evaluations. One implication is that, with increasing age, children become more sensitive to the evaluation of other group members. Over the course of childhood, with a significant peak in adolescence, children also become increasingly concerned with developing a coherent sense of self. They seek consistency among their beliefs, values, and behavior, and this can serve as a significant incentive for therapeutic change.

Finally, limitations in language skills must be considered in designing efficacious treatment strategies. Children's ability to encode (labeling affect) and decode (understanding verbal messages) is an important language ability that may either enhance or limit a child's ability to benefit from therapy. In addition, children's narrative or expressive abilities are relevant to group process and outcome. For example, children's ability to identify and express their feelings, often a goal of therapy, requires developmental competence in that arena. Cultural and gender considerations may also play a role in expressive abilities. For example, girls tend to feel more comfortable and have more experience with verbal expression of feelings compared with boys; and cultures in which verbal expression is not considered an important, or even positive, attribute, such as in Native American cultures, may produce members for whom increasing verbal expressiveness is not a culturally appropriate goal.

Erikson's (1963) psychosocial theory of human development is useful in conceptualizing the relevant psychosocial issues at various life stages, and their subsequent implications for group work. During the school age period (ages six to twelve years) children's principal task is to achieve a sense of industry and adequacy (Erikson, 1963). This is accomplished through achieving personally identified and meaningful goals. If this does not occur, a child is likely to feel inadequate and inferior. Some of the issues originating in this stage, with direct implications for group work, include members' negative self-concept, feelings of inadequacy and inferiority relating to personal abilities and social relationships, core value conflicts, fear of new challenges, and dependency and lack of initiative (Corey, 2000). With group support, an individual with these issues can make connections between current feelings and historical events, express previously disowned feelings, place historical events in perspective, and make choices about the future.

Group therapy is particularly suited to meet the developmental needs of adolescents, whose major psychological tasks are separation-individuation and identity formation. Conflicts and crises during this period include conflicts around independence/dependence, conformity/individuality, peer acceptance/rejection, and identity development. Affiliation to a peer group is a primary task of adolescence so that dependency can shift from parents to peers. In a group therapy setting, adolescents can experience this shift in dependency needs while they express their feelings and beliefs, modify their values, test limits, discover that they are not isolated in their conflicts, and practice social and communication skills. The therapy group provides a constructive transitional object to build ego development, question and modify values, learn social skills, and eventually achieve constructive independent functioning.

Putative Targets of Group Therapy

Targets of treatment vary depending on the purpose of the group and characteristics of its members. Group-specific targets of treatment include: developing an awareness of and sensitivity to the commonality of members' needs and conflicts, reduction of social skill deficits through group process, reduced isolation, interpersonal skill development, and enhanced self-esteem.

Because the vast majority of group therapies with children and adolescents employs a cognitive behavioral framework, targets of treatment typically include assisting group members in becoming aware of their thoughts, addressing cognitive distortions and deficiencies, learning how thoughts mutually interact with feelings and behaviors, developing problem-solving skills to cope with difficult situations, increasing engagement in behaviors that elicit positive reinforcement and avoid negative reinforcement from the environment, and learning to self-evaluate and self-reward. For a review of targets of cognitive behavioral therapy by childhood disorder, see Chapter 18.

Plante and colleagues (2001) reviewed group interventions for pediatric populations through a systematic literature review of 125 studies. Although the groups included in the review were pediatric populations, their findings may be generalized to other child and adolescent populations in relation to the relevant goals and targets of treatment. Group interventions were classified into one of five groups distinguished by their primary goals and treatment foci. Each type of group has different targets of treatment:

1. *Emotional support groups'* primary goal is to improve psychological adaptation by providing contact and discussion with others in similar situations. Emotional support groups explicitly and exclusively emphasize providing support, as opposed to providing information or modifying specific skills or symptoms.
2. *Psychoeducational groups'* primary goal is to enhance psychological adjustment by providing information about shared problems as well as discussion of social and psychological issues.
3. *Adaptation/skill development groups* are those with the dual goals of enhancing psychosocial adaptation and improving shared symptoms by enhancing specified skills. The skills targeted in these groups included family communication and functioning, social skills, problem-solving skills, symptom monitoring, and skills directly related to managing shared symptoms (for example, improving diet).

4. *Symptom reduction groups* are those in which the explicit and exclusive goal of treatment is to reduce or eliminate shared symptoms through behavior change. Psychological or social adaptation is neither a focus nor a goal of treatment.

5. *Summer camps* are residential or day programs designed for children with shared difficulties, such as chronic illness or disability, which include typical social-recreational activities. Unlike other forms of groups, camp programs may or may not include didactic activities or discussions focused explicitly on problem-related issues (Plante, Labato, & Engel, 2001).

Empirical Support for Group Therapies with Children and Adolescents

The empirical literature supports the efficacy of child and adolescent group therapy. In particular, cognitive-behavioral group therapy with a variety of anxiety disorders has amassed the strongest support. Controlled studies of cognitive-behavioral group therapy have shown significant improvement for a variety of anxiety disorders including: social phobia (Albano & Barlow, 1996; Barrett, 1998; Hayward et al., 2000; Silverman et al., 1999), overanxious disorder (Silverman et al., 1999), generalized anxiety disorder (Silverman et al., 1999), post-traumatic stress disorder (March, Amaya-Jackson, Murray, & Schulte, 1998), obsessive-compulsive disorder (Thienemann et al., 2001), and heterogeneous anxiety disorders (Flannery-Schroeder & Kendall, 2000; Lumpkin et al., 2002; Mendlowitz et al., 1999). Parent-child cognitive behavioral therapy has also been found to be helpful in decreasing symptoms in childhood anxiety disorders (Barrett, Dadds & Rapee, 1996; Mendlowitz et al., 1999; Toren et al., 2000). In addition to anxiety disorders, group CBT has also demonstrated efficacy with adolescents with depression (Lewinsohn, Clarke, Rohde, Hops & Seeley, 1996), in decreasing deliberate self-harm in adolescents (Wood et al., 2001), and in decreasing anxiety and depressive symptoms in children bereaved by the suicide of a relative (Pfeffer et al., 2002).

In addition to internalizing disorders, group therapy has been shown to be effective in improving social skills (Elliott & Gresham, 1993; Pfiffner & McBurnett, 1997; Varni, Katz, Colegrove & Dolgin, 1993; LaGreca & Satogrossi, 1980), in addressing specific problems in attention-deficit/hyperactivity disorder (Barkley, 1998; Hinshaw, 1996; Hinshaw, Klein, & Abicoff, 1998; Pelham & Hoza, 1996), and in treating aggressive children (Lochman, Whidby, & Fitzgerald, 2000). In addition, multifamily group therapy has demonstrated efficacy with children with diabetes (Satin, LaGreca, Zigo, & Skyler, 1989) and is commonly used with adolescent substance abusers (Polcin, 1992).

In some cases, however, therapists need to consider the potential harmful effects of group treatment. In particular, groups of young adolescents with disruptive behavior disorders or adolescents with substance-related disorders may inadvertently facilitate increased disruptive or drug-using behavior. Often called negative group processes, these include gaining peer acceptance and reinforcement for problem behavior, and fostering new deviant peer relationships (Dishion, McCord, & Poulin, 1999; Poulin, Dishion, & Burraston, 2001). For another ego-syntonic disorder, anorexia nervosa, the authors have observed negative group processes arise that may include competition for thinness and learning new methods of restrictive eating and compulsive exercising. Because of the severity of their symptoms and the subsequent attention required for symptom management (such as medication management), severely mentally ill populations such as psychotic or bipolar youth may not be able to benefit from group therapy. In addition, socially phobic youths may be unable to benefit from group therapy until their symptoms have stabilized and they can tolerate a group setting.

In addition to demonstrated overall efficacy with a variety of disorders and psychopathological conditions, meta-analyses of child and adolescent treatment outcome studies, both individual and group, have identified secondary findings. Specifically, results across individual and group outcome studies suggest: individual therapy typically shows greater effects than group therapy; behavioral therapies, including cognitive behavioral therapy, behavioral contracting, and behavioral rehearsal, demonstrate greater outcome effects than non-behavioral therapies such as insight-oriented therapy and client-centered therapy; targeted problems show greater improvement than overall adjustment; treatment effects appear to remain relatively stable from post-treatment to follow-up (approximately six months); treatment is equally effective for internalizing and externalizing problems; and outcome effects are related to the interaction of age and gender, with treatment effects particularly positive for adolescent girls (Kazdin, 2000; Weisz et al., 1995). Thus, similar to individual therapy, the positive benefits of group therapy can vary widely. Specific to the group modality, outcomes appear to depend in part on group membership, treatment orientation, and outcome measurement.

In order to demonstrate the broad range of empirically supported group therapies with children and adolescents, we have highlighted a selection of efficacious group therapies targeting diverse problem domains and child and adolescent populations.

Empirical Support for Group Cognitive Behavioral Therapy with Children and Adolescents with Anxiety Disorders

Group cognitive behavioral therapy (GCBT) for anxiety disordered youth has amassed more empirical support than group therapy for any other childhood disorder. In one study, Silverman and colleagues (1999) conducted a randomized, controlled trial of group CBT compared with a wait-list control group for children ages six to sixteen with a range of anxiety disorders. They employed an approach wherein control is gradually transferred from therapist to parent to child. Exposure is targeted as the primary change-producing mechanism, as exposure appears to be the most effective way of reducing anxious symptoms. They found that 61% of treatment completers no longer met diagnostic criteria at post-assessment, compared with 13% of those in the wait-list condition. Treatment gains were maintained at one-year follow-up. Lumpkin and colleagues (2002) reported similar results when they applied group CBT with a heterogeneous group of anxiety disordered children (ages six to sixteen). They found significant symptom abatement and remission rates post-treatment: 50% remission at immediate post-treatment, 83% remission at six months post-treatment, and 75% remission at twelve months post-treatment. Flannery-Schroeder and Kendall (2000) compared group and individual CBT, along with a wait-list control group, for eight- to fourteen-year-olds with a variety of anxiety disorders. At the end of treatment, 73% of children who completed individual CBT no longer met anxiety disorder criteria, 50% of children who completed group CBT no longer met criteria, and 8% of children in the wait-list group no longer met criteria. Although this study suggests that CBT is somewhat more effective in individual versus group format, a larger study with longer-term follow-up is necessary to determine long-term efficacy. Taken together, these findings support the application of group CBT for the range of anxiety disorders.

Two small randomized, controlled trials of group CBT versus a control condition for socially phobic adolescents found promising preliminary results (Albano & Barlow, 1995; Hayward et al., 2000). Primary goals were anxiety reduction and social functioning enhancement through identifying triggers to anxiety, recognizing anxious responses (cognitive, physiological, behavioral), employing appropriate anxiety management skills, and coping with normal levels of social anxiety. This preliminary work suggests that their small samples experienced significantly decreased anxiety symptoms.

The efficacy of group CBT for single episode trauma has preliminary support by the work of March and colleagues (1998). Fourteen children with post-traumatic stress disorder (PTSD) diagnoses from a variety of single exposure traumas, ranging in age from ten to fifteen years, were included in the eighteen-week, CBT-based group treatment. Results revealed PTSD diagnostic remission rates of 57% at immediate post-treatment and 86% at six months post-treatment. Symptoms of depression, anxiety, and anger also showed significant improvement.

In a group CBT trial for adolescents with obsessive-compulsive disorder (OCD), Thienemann and colleagues (2001) found that OCD symptoms improved both in statistical and clinical significance. Furthermore, adolescents consistently shared information and designed exposure interventions for themselves and others during sessions. Clinical improvement and patient satisfaction justify further investigation in a controlled study (Thienemann, Martin, Cregger, Thompson, & Dyer-Friedman, 2001).

Some recent studies incorporating parents in group therapy with their children have shown promising results. Mendlowitz and associates (1999) compared the efficacy of CBT in a parent-child group, children-only group, and parent-only group with children ages seven to twelve with a range of anxiety disorders. Children in all three treatment arms improved in self-reported anxiety and depression compared with wait-list controls. Preliminary evidence also suggests that children in groups with their parents reported more active coping than children in the other groups. Similarly, Toren and colleagues (2000) conducted a randomized, controlled trial of brief parent-child group CBT compared with a wait-list control group for preadolescents with anxiety disorders. Of the children in the treatment group, 70% no longer met diagnostic criteria immediately post-treatment, and 91% no longer met criteria at the three-year follow-up. These results suggest the importance of incorporating parents in group therapy with children.

Empirical Support for Group Cognitive Behavioral Therapy with Adolescents with Depression

Adolescents may more maximally utilize the group modality because of their increased capacity for abstraction and self-evaluation, as well as their search for identity. A protected social environment such as that supplied by group therapy also allows adolescents to consider the cognitive component of depression and how cognitions, behavior, and affect are interrelated. Cognitive-behavioral conceptualizations of depression were employed in two randomized controlled trials of the psychoeducational "Coping with Depression Course for Adolescents" (CWD–A) (Lewinsohn et al., 1996). The cognitive treatment component included assisting adolescents in recognizing and modifying their maladaptive thoughts and negative expectancies. Behavioral treatment focused on increasing pleasurable activities; learning communication, negotiation, and conflict-resolution skills; and developing social skills. Sixteen sessions were offered over eight weeks, with up to ten adolescents per group. Studies demonstrate that CWD–A was significantly more effective in reducing depressive symptoms than a wait-list control condition (with 33% and 52%, respectively, meeting depressive disorder diagnostic criteria). Treatment effects were maintained for two years. This study is particularly important in that adolescents with a depressive disorder diagnosis constituted the sample, thereby more closely mirroring clinical versus research cases. Treatment effects were broader than symptom reduction: coping, global adjustment, and symptoms were all affected positively.

Group Therapy for Repeated Deliberate Self-Harm in Adolescents

Wood and colleagues (2001) compared group treatment with routine care in adolescents who had deliberately harmed themselves on at least two occasions within a year. In this study, adolescents who had group treatment were less likely to repeat deliberate self-harm, when compared to adolescents who received routine care. Results also found that group members were less likely to use routine care, had better school attendance, and had a lower rate of behavioral disorder than adolescents given routine care alone. Group treatment shows promise as a treatment for adolescents who repeatedly harm themselves, but larger studies with appropriate controls are required to assess more accurately the efficacy of this intervention (Wood, Trainor, Rothwell, Moore, & Harrington, 2001).

Empirical Support for Bereavement Groups with Children

Bereavement groups for children who have lost a close family member have been found to be an effective means to help them cope with their trauma, and prevent subsequent pathology (Masterman & Reams, 1988; Aronson, 1994). A recent study found that group therapy was effective in decreasing anxiety and depressive symptoms among children bereaved by the suicide of a relative (Pfeffer et al., 2002).

Empirical Support for Social Skills Groups with Children

Children's social skills have been hypothesized to be important in eliciting and maintaining social support from peers and in enhancing social competence in general (Elliot & Gresham, 1993). The rationale for social support interventions is that children with positive peer relationships are more likely to experience benefits in such broad domains as school achievement, self-esteem, shyness, depressive symptoms, and long-term adjustment (Furman & Gavin, 1989). In contrast, children with peer relationship difficulties are at increased risk for long-term adjustment problems. Social skills training typically includes problem solving, behavioral rehearsal in the forms of modeling and role playing, feedback, broadening one's coping repetoire, and contingency management in the form of both internal and external reinforcement. Training situations are based on difficult situations encountered by the children and include behavioral rehearsal, corrective feedback, and reinforcement. Prosocial skills such as engaging in cooperative play, positive peer interactions, peer acceptance, and building friendships are particular targets of treatment (Elliot & Gresham, 1993).

Pfiffner and McBurnett (1997) developed a CBT social skills training program for boys and girls with ADHD. Goals included improving relationships with both peers and adults, and the targets of treatment included: remediating skills for knowledge deficits, remediating skills for performance deficits, fostering recognition of verbal and nonverbal social cues, teaching adaptive responding to new problem situations, and promoting generalization. The group includes a highly structured, high-intensity contingency management system. In the parent-mediated generalization treatment condition, parents meet in groups simultaneously with the child groups. Parents receive instruction that is similar to their children's instruction. Results suggest an incremental benefit of the additional parent intervention component in promoting generalization and maintaining the social skills gains of their children.

Beidel and colleagues (2000) developed a randomized, controlled trial of social effectiveness therapy for children (SET–C) for eight- to twelve-year-old children with social phobia. SET–C combines group social skills training, individual exposure, and homework assignments in twenty-four sessions over twelve weeks. Post-treatment remission rates were 67% of the treated children compared with 5% of control group children. Treatment gains were maintained for six months.

LaGreca and Santogrossi (1980) developed a behavioral group approach for social skills training with elementary school children in the third to fifth grades who showed difficulty relating to peers. Children participated in ninety-minute group sessions for four weeks. The following skill areas were selected for training based on the literature regarding correlates of peer acceptance in elementary school children: (1) smiling/laughing, (2) greeting others, (3) joining ongoing activities, (4) extending invitations, (5) conversational skills, (6) sharing and cooperation, (7) verbal complimenting, and (8) physical appearance/grooming (LaGreca & Mesibov, 1979). The treatment procedures included modeling, coaching, behavioral rehearsal with videotaped feedback, and homework assignments. Study results found that compared with control groups, children in the social skills training group demonstrated increased skills in role-playing, greater knowledge of how to interact with peers, and more initiation of peer interactions in school (LaGreca & Santogrossi, 1980).

Ecologically sensitive social skills training may prove efficacious with special populations as well. Varni and colleagues (1993) evaluated the efficacy of a CBT social skills intervention in a randomized, controlled trial with school-aged children with newly diagnosed cancer. The social skills and situations in the training represented situations identified as difficult for this population. Post-treatment assessment results suggest that this intervention benefited these children when they returned to school.

Empirical Support for Group Therapy with Children with Attention-Deficit/Hyperactivity Disorder

Hinshaw evaluated the efficacy of self-management group therapy with small groups of boys with ADHD (1996). The principal components included self-monitoring and self-evaluations skills, and anger management therapy. He found a reduction in negative and aggressive behaviors, promotion of prosocial behaviors, and improvement in social competence skills in general. However, Hinshaw (1996) notes that all current treatments for ADHD are insufficient to adequately address the constellation of problems associated with ADHD.

Pelham and Hoza (1996) developed and tested an intensive, multimodal eight-week summer treatment program for children and adolescents, ages five to fifteen, with ADHD. The intervention included: behavioral management, peer interventions, daily report cards, sports skills training, time out, classroom behavioral management, parent involvement, medication assessment, and long-term follow-up. Although uncontrolled, the study demonstrated short-term effectiveness in self, peer, academic, and home domains.

Empirical Support for Group CBT with Aggressive Children

Lochman and colleagues (2000) employed a group CBT model in a series of randomized, controlled trials to address the deficient and distorted social-cognitive processes in aggressive children. Fourth- and fifth-grade aggressive boys completed eighteen group sessions aimed at ameliorating the skill deficits documented in aggressive youth during conflictual situations that include affective arousal. Goals included enhancing awareness of anger arousal, self-reflection and self-control skills, social problem-solving skills, and behavioral strategies to address conflictual situations. This Anger Coping Program evidenced improvements in disruptive-aggressive off-task classroom behavior, aggression reduction, and improved self-esteem. Results regarding the maintenance of treatment gains over three years were mixed: self-esteem and problem-solving skills remained improved, with relatively lower substance use rates, but reductions in aggressive and off-task behavior were maintained only for boys who received booster treatment during the subsequent school year. Building on these findings, a multi-component Anger Coping Program was developed. Compared to control children, treated children demonstrated greater improvements in social competence, social information processing, and aggressive behavior, and their parents showed improved parenting practices and marital relationships (Lochman et al., 2000).

Empirical Support for Multi-Family Group Interventions

Multiple family group therapy combines the principles of family therapy and group therapy. This type of family group is common to several populations, including adolescent substance abusers and medically ill children. The basic theoretical assumption is that the individual (adolescent) lives in the system (family) and the system maintains the symptoms of the individual and the family. Satin and colleagues (1989) developed a multifamily group intervention for adolescents with diabetes. This intervention contains several components that are designed to increase family support and positive family interventions around diabetes management, and to improve metabolic status and overall psychological functioning. Facilitators focused on promoting independent problem-solving skills regarding managing diabetes. Family members were encouraged to discuss feelings and to communicate with each other in an assertive and positive manner. This study found that participants in the small multi-family groups, with and without the simulated experience component, exhibited improvements in metabolic functioning relative to controls at both the three- and six-month assessment periods. Adolescents in both intervention groups reported more positive perceptions of a "teenager with diabetes" at post-treatment than did the control group, but there were no significant changes post-intervention in either adolescents' or parents' perceptions of family functioning (Satin, LaGreca, Zigo, and Skyler, 1989; Thompson & Gustafson, 1999).

Empirical Support for Processes Underlying Child Group Therapy Efficacy

Although the effectiveness of group interventions with children has been well established, little is known about the processes that make child group therapy effective (Dagley et al., 1994; Hoag & Burlingame, 1997). Such research is essential for the development of a theory of group work with children. In a recent study of group interactions, Schechtman (2001) concluded that children primarily need support and encouragement in the group setting and may not have the ego strength to deal with criticism. They want to be listened to, requiring attention, encouragement, empowerment, and assistance with their emotional and practical difficulties. These results suggest that group leaders should discourage confrontation and encourage supportive feedback, a skill that most children do not naturally possess and in which they need to be trained. Letting children interact spontaneously is not inherently therapeutic and can be quite detrimental to the group process (Schechtman, 2001).

In a process research study focused on self-disclosure, Leichtentritt & Shechtman (1998) investigated children's verbal responses in three stages of group development (initial, working, and termination). The most frequent type of children's response (both for boys and girls) was self-disclosure, followed by feedback and questions. All other responses (such as encouragement, directives, and paraphrases) were rare. Interestingly, self-disclosure was relatively high from the initial stage of the group onward, mostly generated by structured therapeutic activities or games, and by questions. Findings suggest that preadolescent children have a high need for self-disclosure and little reservation about sharing private facts and experiences or expressing emotions. However, children need assistance in expressing themselves through structured questions, games, or activities. These results depart from adult group findings, for which structured activities or games are only rarely recommended. Meaningful self-disclosure is expected mostly in the working stage of adult groups, whereas in this study, children kept the level of self-disclosure high from the beginning stage onward. Thus, it is important to investigate group processes in children's groups, rather than draw conclusions from the experience and literature of adult groups (Shechtman, 2001). Many important therapy process issues, including therapeutic factors, the therapist's role, stages of group development, difficult situations, and cultural influences, are still awaiting investigation.

Group Therapy Illustration: Supportive Expressive Group Therapy with Adolescents with Cancer

Across all theoretical orientations, groups require meaningful goals. While specific goals are generally left for individual group members to identify, the parameters of group goals are often determined by common problems and issues. General goals shared by most groups include: increasing trust in oneself and others, fostering self-knowledge, increasing self-confidence and self-acceptance, expanding one's coping repertoire, increasing autonomy, making conscious one's choices and their consequences, improving social and communication skills, clarifying and expressing one's values, and taking initiative in one's life (Corey, 2000). Most theoretical perspectives exhort group members to formulate their individual goals in addition to any common overall group goals. This individual goal-setting is conceptualized as a process that requires ongoing re-evaluation and modification. Group leaders can assist members in identifying reasonable, clear, and specific goals and methods by which to attain their goals.

The role of the group leader is to facilitate interaction among group members by modeling behaviors conducive to interaction and cohesion, such as sensitive, active listening, initiating interactions, expressing interest and concern, asking questions to deepen discussion, and maintaining a nonjudgmental stance. A leader can foster independence by encouraging members to interact with each other directly and not simply through the group leader. Group leaders are also responsible for creating a safe climate in which members can reveal themselves, their concerns, and experiment with new behaviors or ways of being. As part of creating a safe environment, leaders must establish group rules, discuss issues of confidentiality, rights and responsibilities, and set limits in order to ensure the psychological safety of group members. A group leader assists members in changing their attitudes, beliefs, and feelings about themselves, others, and their world through techniques such as reflection of members' verbal and nonverbal communication, clarification of feelings and thoughts, role-playing, and offering interpretations.

With only a few exceptions, empirically supported group therapy with children and adolescents involves time-limited group therapy. Mooney and Schamess' (1991) review of time-limited group therapy with children found that short-term children's groups need to incorporate the following principles: rapid assessment, contracting, the therapist's willingness and ability to actively structure and focus the treatment process, and paying careful attention to the symbolic meaning inherent in pre-established time-limits (Lomonaco et al., 1994).

We employed these overarching principles regarding goals, group leader responsibilities, and time-limited therapy in our supportive-expressive group therapy for adolescents with cancer. Although supportive-expressive group therapy has not yet been empirically evaluated for use with adolescent patients with cancer, it is based on a broad set of principles related to aspects of these intervention approaches that have previously been used with adult women with cancer. It is guided by three theoretical principles: (1) social support, (2) coping responses, including developing a meaningful framework for making sense of the suffering experienced with illness, and (3) emotional expression and regulation. Supportive-expressive group therapy has been found to be effective in reducing pain (Spiegel & Bloom, 1983), alleviating distress (Spiegel, Morrow et al., 1996), and increasing survival (Spiegel et al., 1989) among breast cancer patients. This model was developed for primary and metastatic breast cancer patients (Classen et al., 1993) and has been adapted for use with adolescents with cancer and their parents (Erickson et al., 2000; Palmer et al., 2000).

The primary aims of supportive-expressive therapy include: encouraging social support among group members, encouraging members to take an active coping approach to solving problems, helping patients to derive greater life meaning from confronting their illness, helping patients to express painful emotions appropriately, and explicit training in self-hypnosis to develop skills in managing pain and other symptoms.

The targets of treatment include open expression of emotion, dealing with fears of pain and disability, exploring and sharing coping strategies, mobilization of social support, improving doctor-patient relationships, and training in self-hypnosis for anxiety and pain control. Each of these targets is described in our manual (Erickson et al., 2000), along with treatment strategies for working with this material. (See manual for examples of how each theme might present itself as a good therapeutic response and a poor response.) For example, in facilitating open expression of emotion, group members must explore disturbing fears and concerns. This exploration may frighten members if they believe that the feelings will overwhelm and engulf them. The therapist's role is to help patients modulate the extent to which they enter into their troubling experience. To some extent, this is done by helping them tolerate the strong emotion it elicits while stepping back in order to view it from a more objective vantage point. Similar to dealing with any extremely painful material, such as occurs in grieving someone's death, it can only be done in psychologically tolerable doses. There is a natural and adaptive tendency to allow oneself to experience only as much as can be tolerated. Thus, for normal individuals, both they and the facilitators can count on this built-in defense mechanism to protect the patients from being engulfed by terrifying thoughts and feelings. Patients will naturally pull back if it becomes too threatening. In addition to protecting the self, stepping back is also essential for viewing their experience more objectively and thereby developing a more adaptive perspective on this aspect of self.

The expression and exploration of all emotional states and thoughts gives members the sense that no thought or feeling is too frightening to face. It can also be validating to discover that negative feelings and disturbing thoughts are shared by others. Through open and honest sharing of feelings, concerns, thoughts, and ideas with others in a safe and supportive environment, patients come to recognize that they are not alone and, in fact, have a forum in which to express their full experience. Thoughts and emotions that are potentially overwhelming are detoxified as their experiences begin to feel more normalized. Participants are left with an enhanced sense of control and well-being, as well as expanded resources for mastery.

With regards to facilitating supportive interactions within the group, although it is important for the therapist to be supportive, it is even more important to facilitate members supporting each other. In this respect the therapist can take an active role in fully developing the healing potential within the group. For instance, if a member has revealed something painful, the therapist might ask the group what it was like to hear this. This kind of question frequently leads to supportive statements on the part of other members or, alternatively it can lead to others revealing similar pains. Both responses leave patients feeling supported because they are less alone with their pain.

The therapist facilitates working on a problem experientially and interactively. For example, if a child complains about difficulties at school since her diagnosis and treatments, and states repeatedly that absolutely no one could possibly understand her experience, the therapist could say, "It sounds like you feel extremely alone; I'm wondering if you feel that way here, too? What is the hardest part about what you're going through?" Or, "You must be feeling very alone, but I know some of you have experienced similar situations. How have others dealt with something like this?" Younger adolescents may need particular assistance with responding to others and may therefore benefit from active therapist facilitation. Experiencing the concern of others and learning through each other's experiences is an invaluable source of support.

Mutual support is derived from sharing meaningful personal experiences with others, as well as common concerns such as treatments, self-image, or doctor-patient relationships. It entails both receiving support and offering support to other group members. This fosters the development of rapport and mutual caring, which generally extends beyond the parameters of group meetings. The potential for receiving support outside the group increases as the members begin to share information, commonality of experiences, and help each other with both practical and emotional support.

All communication within a group affects other group members, whether or not the members acknowledge it. The therapist's task is to facilitate the expression of these effects and to encourage direct communication between members. The facilitation of interaction among group members is an ongoing and essential role that the therapist plays. Communication should proceed in all possible directions and not solely through the group leaders. The direct expression of members' thoughts and feelings to each other is critical for the establishment of trust and mutual support.

Therapists serve to guide the quality of discussion to be personal, specific, emotionally expressive, and relevant to others in the group. When necessary, the therapists suggest activities and topics for discussion as a means of ensuring that all important topics are covered. In our series of group therapy, group members were between eleven and nineteen years of age. Although this age span is quite large considering developmental differences within this age range, older adolescents helped younger ones express themselves and remarked repeatedly on the younger ones' bravery, and younger members looked up to the older members and appeared to appreciate the attention. Hence, we did not experience any difficulties related to this diverse age group. This modality may be slightly modified for use with other chronically ill pediatric populations. It could also be modified for use with traumatized populations. Applications with other populations has not yet been explored.

Future Directions

Additional research is needed to examine the relative utility of theoretically informed (such as cognitive restructuring, behavioral rehearsal) versus group-specific (such as group support, group cohesion) treatment components. In this way, an efficacious group treatment may be systematically deconstructed and varied in order to determine what components are necessary to achieve the most beneficial outcomes. Group process variables are infrequently addressed in childhood treatment outcome studies, and should be examined in terms of their independent effects. Treatment format (group versus individual treatment) could be a factor routinely investigated once a treatment has amassed considerable empirical support. In addition, mediators and moderators of treatment efficacy need to be identified so that we gain a better understanding of how and for whom group treatments effect change.

◆ ◆ ◆

The research in child development suggests that the role of effective parenting is critical in promoting children's cognitive and psychosocial development. Thompson and Gustafson (1999) espouse that parents play a critical role in supporting their children's active coping efforts to deal effectively with adaptive tasks and to maintain normative, age-appropriate interactions and functioning. Thus, similar to individual therapy, group therapy with children and adolescents may achieve additional benefit by incorporating a parent component. Another important area of future research, parent groups may allow parents to gain support from other parents with similar experience, normalize their feelings and experience, and expand their coping and parenting skills. A psycho-educational component might also assist parents in gaining a greater understanding of their child's problem and how they may best support their child, employ developmentally appropriate expectations, and create appropriate environmental contingencies.

Developmental, cultural, socioeconomic, and gender considerations are rarely addressed in the group therapy literature. Beyond sample descriptions, these variables present important information about what treatments work for whom and under what circumstances. Our experience suggests that some groups are more beneficial if they are homogeneous in membership (for example, traumatized children, medically ill children, or victims of prejudice or oppression), whereas other groups are more beneficial if they have heterogeneous membership (as with ADHD, CD/ODD). While further research is necessary to explore these hypotheses, if differential treatment gains were identified across such categories, this would aid clinicians in matching patients to the most effective treatments. In fact, these variables may help explain some equivocal findings and should be investigated in terms of their independent effects.

References

Albano, A. M., & Barlow, D. H. (1996). Breaking the vicious cycle: Cognitive behavioral group treatment for socially anxious youth. In E. D. Hibbs & P. Jensen (Eds.), *Psychosocial treatment research of child and adolescent disorders: Empirically based strategies for clinical practice* (pp. 109–135). Washington, DC: American Psychological Association.

Aronson, S. (1994). Group intervention with children of parents with AIDS. *Group, 18,* 133–140.

Barkley, R. A., (1998). *Attention deficit hyperactivity disorder: A handbook for diagnosis and treatment* (2nd ed.). New York: Guilford Press.

Barrett, P. M. (1998). Evaluation of cognitive-behavioral group treatments for childhood anxiety disorders. *Journal of Clinical Child Psychology, 27,* 459–468.

Barrett, P. M., Dadds, M. R., & Rapee, R. M. (1996). Family treatment for childhood anxiety: A controlled trial. *Journal of Consulting and Clinical Psychology, 64,* 333–342.

Beidel, D. C., Turner, S. M., & Morris, T. L. (2000). Behavioral treatment of childhood social phobia. *Journal of Consulting and Clinical Psychology, 68,* 1072–1080.

Brent, D. A., & Kolko, D. J. (1998). Therapy: Definitions, mechanisms of action, and relationship to etiological models. *Journal of Abnormal Child Psychology, 26*(1), 17–25.

Cicchetti, D. (1993). Developmental psychopathology: Reactions, reflections, projections. *Developmental Review, 13,* 471–502.

Classen, C., Diamond, S., Soleman, A., Fobair, P., Spira, J., & Spiegel, D. (1993). *Brief supportive-expressive group therapy for women with primary breast cancer: A treatment manual.* Stanford, CA: Stanford University School of Medicine.

Corey, G. (2000). *Theory and practice of group counseling (5th ed.).* Monterey, CA: Brooks/Cole Publishing.

Dagley, J. C., Gazda, G. M., Eppinger, S. J., & Stuwart, E. A. (1994). Group therapy research with children, preadolescents, and adolescents. In A. Fuhriman & G. M. Burlingame (Eds.), *Handbook of group therapy* (pp. 340–370). New York: Wiley.

Diagnostic and Statistical Manual (4th ed.). (1994). Washington, DC: American Psychiatric Association.

Dishion, T. J., McCord, J., & Poulin, F. (1999). When interventions harm: Peer groups and problem behavior. *American Psychologist, 54*(9), 755–764.

Elliott, G., & Gresham, J. (1993). Social skill interventions for children. *Behavioral Modification, 17,* 287–313.

Erickson, S. J., Palmer, L., Achilles, G. M., Classen, C., & Speigel, D. (2000). Brief supportive-expressive group therapy for adolescents with cancer and their families: A treatment manual. Unpublished manual.

Erikson, E. (1963). *Childhood and society* (2nd ed.). New York: Norton.

Flannery-Schroeder, E. C., & Kendall, P. C. (2000). Group and individual cognitive behavioral treatments for youth with anxiety disorders: A randomized controlled trial. *Cognitive Therapy and Research, 24,* 251–281.

Furman, W., & Gavin, L. (1989). Peers' influence on adjustment and development: A view from the intervention literature. In T. J. Berndt & G. W. Ladd (Eds.), *Peer relationships in child development*. New York: Wiley.

Hayward, C., Varady, A., Albano, A.M., Thienemann, M., Hernderson, L., & Schatzberg, A. F. (2000). Cognitive behavioral group therapy for social phobia in female adolescents: Results of a pilot study. *Journal of the American Academy of Child and Adolescent Psychiatry, 39*, 721–726.

Hinshaw, S. P. (1996). Enhancing social competence: Integrating self-management strategies with behavioral procedures for children with ADHD. In E. D. Hibbs & P. Jensen (Eds.), *Psychosocial treatment research of child and adolescent disorders: Empirically based strategies for clinical practice* (pp. 285–309). Washington, DC: American Psychological Association.

Hinshaw, S. P., Klein, R. G., & Abicoff, H. (1998). Childhood attention-deficit hyperactivity disorder: Nonpharmacologic and combination approaches. In P. E. Nathan & J. M. Gorman (Eds.), *A guide to treatments that work* (pp. 27–41). New York: Oxford University Press.

Hoag, M. J., & Burlingame, G. M. (1997). Evaluating the effectiveness of child and adolescent group treatment: A meta-analysis review. *Journal of Clinical Child Psychology, 26*, 234–246.

Kazdin, A. E. (2000). *Therapy for children and adolescents: Directions for research and practice*. New York: Oxford University Press.

Kazdin, A. E., Bass, D., Ayers, W. A., & Rodgers, A. (1990). Empirical and clinical focus of child and adolescent therapy research. *Journal of Consulting and Clinical Psychology, 58*, 729–740.

LaGreca, A. M., & Mesibov, G. B. (1979). Social skills intervention with learning disabled children: Selecting skills and implementing training. *Journal of Clinical Child Psychology, 8*, 234–241.

LaGreca, A. M., & Santogrossi, D. A. (1980). Social skills training with elementary school students: A behavioral group approach. *Journal of Consulting and Clinical Psychology, 48*, 220–227.

Leichtentritt, J., & Shechtman, Z. (1998). Therapist, trainees, and child verbal response modes in child group therapy. *Group Dynamics, 2*, 36–47.

Lewinsohn, P. M., Clarke, G. N., Rohde, P., Hops, H., & Seeley, J. R. (1996). A course in coping: A cognitive behavioral approach to the treatment of adolescent depression. In E. D. Hibbs & P. Jensen (Eds.), *Psychosocial treatment research of child and adolescent disorders: Empirically based strategies for clinical practice* (pp. 109–135). Washington, DC: American Psychological Association.

Lochman, J. E., Whidby, J. M., & Fitzgerald, D. P. (2000). Cognitive behavioral assessment and treatment with aggressive children. In P. C. Kendall (Ed.), *Child and adolescent therapy: Cognitive behavioral procedures* (2nd ed., pp. 31–87). New York: Guilford Press.

Lumpkin, P. W., Silverman, W. K., Weems, C. F., Markham, M. R., & Kurtines, W. M. (2002). Treating a heterogeneous set of anxiety disorders in youth with group cognitive behavioral therapy: A partially nonconcurrent multiple-baseline evaluation. *Behavior Therapy, 33*(1), 163–177.

March, J. S., Amaya-Jackson, L., Murray, M. C., & Schulte, A. (1998). Cognitive behavioral therapy for children and adolescents with post-traumatic stress disorder after a single incident stressor. *Journal of the American Academy of Child and Adolescent Psychiatry, 37*(5), 585–593.

Masterman, S., & Reams (1988). Support groups for bereaved preschool and school-age children. *American Journal of Orthopsychiatry, 58,* 562–570.

Mendlowitz, S. L., Manassis, K., Bradley, S., Scalpillato, D., Miezitis, S., & Shaw, B. F. (1999). Cognitive behavioral group treatments in childhood anxiety disorders: The role of parental involvement. *Journal of the American Academy of Child and Adolescent Psychiatry, 38,* 1223–1229.

Mooney, S., & Schamess, G. (1991). Focused time-limited, interactive group therapy with latency-age children: Theory and practice. *Journal of Child and Adolescent Group Therapy, 1,* 107–145.

Palmer, L., Erickson, S., Shaffer, T., Koopman, C., Amylon, M., & Steiner, H. (2000). Challenges and coping strategies identified in group therapy by adolescents with cancer and their parents. *International Journal of Rehabilitation and Health, 51*(1), 43–54.

Pelham, W. E., & Hoza, B. (1996). Intensive treatment: A summer treatment program for children with ADHD. In E. D. Hibbs & P. Jensen (Eds.), *Psychosocial treatment research of child and adolescent disorders: Empirically based strategies for clinical practice* (pp. 109–135). Washington, DC: American Psychological Association.

Pfeffer, C. R., Jiang, H., Kakuma, T., Hwang, J., & Metsch, M. (2002). Group intervention for children bereaved by the suicide of a relative. *Journal of the American Academy of Child and Adolescent Psychiatry, 41*(5), 505–513.

Pfiffner, L., & McBurnett, K. (1997). Social skills training with parent generalization: Treatment effects for children with attention deficit hyperactivity disorder. *Journal of Consulting and Clinical Psychology, 65,* 749–757.

Plante, W., Lobato, D., & Engel, R. (2001). Review of group interventions for pediatric chronic conditions. *Journal of Pediatric Psychology, 26,* 435–453.

Polcin, D. L. (1992). A comprehensive model for adolescent chemical dependency treatment. *Journal of Counseling and Development, 70*(3), 376–382.

Poulin, F., Dishion, T. J., & Burraston, B. (2001). Three year iatrogenic effects associated with aggregating high-risk adolescents in cognitive-behavioral preventative interventions. *Applied Developmental Science, 5*(4), 214–224.

Satin, W., LaGreca, A. M., Ziogo, M. A., & Skyler, J. S. (1989). Diabetes in adolescence: Effects of multifamily group intervention and parent simulation of diabetes. *Journal of Pediatric Psychology, 14,* 259–276.

Schechtman, Z. (2001). Process research in child group counseling/therapy. *The Group Circle, Feb March issue.*

Silverman, W. K., Kurtines, W. M., Ginsburg, G. S., Weems, D. F., Ravian, B., & Serafini, L. T. (1999). Treating anxiety disorders in children with group cognitive-behavioral therapy: A randomized controlled trial. *Journal of Consulting and Clinial Psychology, 67,* 995–1003.

Sourkes, B. (1995). *Armfuls of time.* Pittsburgh, PA: University of Pittsburgh Press.

Spiegel, D., & Bloom, J. R. (1983). Group therapy and hypnosis reduce metastatic breast carcinoma pain. *Psychosomatic Medicine, 45*(4), 333–339.

Spiegel, D., Bloom, J. R., Kraemer, H. C., & Gottheil, E. (1989). Effect of psychosocial treatment on survival of patients with metastatic breast cancer. *Lancet, 2,* 888–891.

Spiegel, D., Morrow, G., Classen, C., & Koopman, C. (1996). Effect of group therapy on women with primary breast cancer. *The Breast Journal, 2*(1), 104–116.

Stuber, M., Gonzales, S., Benjamin, H., & Golant, M. (1995). Fighting for recovery: Group intervention for adolescents with cancer and their parents. *Journal of Therapy Practice and Research, 4*(4), 286–296.

Sugar, M. (1993). Research in child and adolescent group therapy. *Journal of Child and Adolescent Group Therapy, 3,* 207–226.

Thienemann, M., Martin, J., Cregger, B., Thompson, H., & Dyer-Friedman, J. (2001). Manual-driven group cognitive behavioral therapy for adolescents with obsessive compulsive disorder: A pilot study. *Journal of the American Academy of Child and Adolescent Psychiatry, 40*(11),1254–1260.

Thompson, R. J., & Gustafson, K. E. (1999). *Adaptation to chronic childhood illness.* Washington, DC.: American Psychological Association.

Toren, P., Wolmer, L., Rosental, B., Eldar, S., Koren, S., Lask, M., Weizman, R., & Laor, N. (2000). Case series: Brief parent-child group therapy for childhood anxiety disorders using a manualized cognitive behavioral technique. *Journal of the American Academy of Child and Adolescent Psychiatry, 39,* 1309–1312.

Toth, S. L., & Cicchetti, D. (1999). Developmental approaches and child therapy. In S. W. Russ & T. H. Ollendick (Eds.), *Handbook of psychotherapies with children and adolescents.* New York: Kluwer.

Varni, J. W., Katz, E. R., Colegrove, R., Jr., & Dolgin, M. (1993). The impact of social skills training on the adjustment of children with newly diagnosed cancer. *Journal of Pediatric Psychology, 22,* 635–649.

Weisz, J. R., Han, S. S., Granger, D. A., Weiss, B., & Morton, T. (1995). Effects of therapy with children and adolescents revisited: A meta-analysis of treatment outcome studies. *Psychological Bulletin, 117,* 450–468.

Wood, A., Trainor, G., Rothwell, J., Moore, A., & Harringon, R. (2001). Randomized trial of group therapy for repeated deliberate self-harm in adolescents. *Journal of the American Academy of Child and Adolescent Psychiatry, 40*(11), 1246–1253.

Yalom, I. (1985). *The theory and practice of group therapy* (3rd ed.). New York: Basic Books.

CHAPTER THIRTY

MUTUAL HELP ORGANIZATIONS FOR DISTRESSED CHILDREN AND THEIR FAMILIES: A VYGOTSKIAN DEVELOPMENTAL PERSPECTIVE

Colleen Loomis, Ph.D., and Keith Humphreys, Ph.D.

"Every function in the child's cultural development appears twice: first on the social level and later, on the individual level; first between *people* (interpsychological), *and then* inside *the child* (intrapsychological)."

(VYGOTSKY, 1978, P. 57)

This volume attests to the broad range of professional interventions available for children, adolescents, and their parents. Yet the number of visits made by distressed families to all mental health professionals combined is far less than their attendance at peer-directed mutual help organizations such as National Alliance for the Mentally Ill (NAMI), Candlelighters, and Compassionate Friends (Kessler et al., 1997). Over seven million U.S. adults attend mutual help groups each year, but many professionals know little about the nature and impact of these organizations (Kessler, Mickelson, & Zhao, 1997). The purpose of this chapter is to provide an introduction to family mutual help organizations using Lev Vygotsky's

Support for preparation comes from the Department of Veterans Affairs Office of Academic Affairs and Health Services Research and Development Service and from The California Wellness Foundation. Please send all correspondence to Colleen Loomis at the Stanford University School of Medicine, VAPAHCS (MPD-152), 795 Willow Rd., Menlo Park, CA 94025; E-Mail: Colleen. Loomis@Stanford.edu developmental theory to illuminate their structure and mechanisms of action, and to highlight mutual help interventions through two case studies.

We begin by specifying our terminology and scope. By "mutual help organization" (or the synonymous term "self-help organization"), we refer to organizations that are entirely operated by peer members and thus are clearly distinguishable from family psychotherapy, and from professionally facilitated support groups and psycho-educational programs. Mutual help organizations are operated by individuals and families experiencing a shared challenge, and seek to provide support and information to others in the same situation, usually through self-help group meetings. Some organizations also engage in public education and advocacy (White & Madara, 2002).

We use the term mutual help *group* to refer to individual, supportive small group meetings (for example, "The NAMI group that meets every Wednesday at the community center"), and mutual help *organization* to refer to the larger network of activities and structures in which individual groups are embedded. Like members of these groups and organizations, sometimes we use the broader term *self-help* (without group or organization) to refer to general involvement in either structure.

Turning from mutual help terminology to topical areas of self-help groups and organizations, there are many. There is a group for almost any interest and the Internet accelerates the creation of new ones, allowing families in the same situation to easily find one another (Madara, 1997). Self-help for addiction disorders is the best known, and is addressed elsewhere (Humphreys, in press; Kelly, Myers, & Brown, 2000, 2002a). Another category of self-help organizations is medically focused groups, ones in which the child has a birth defect or disease that is causing long-term psychological strain for the child, siblings, and parents. A few example organizations include ABC (bladder exstrophy) and CLASS (liver disease/transplant). For more information about self-help organizations related to medical issues (such as premature birth) see *The Self-Help Group Sourcebook* (White & Madara, 2002); for a detailed case study of cancer and self-help, see the work of Chesler and Chesney (1995).

Here we focus on self-help organizations that address a psychiatric (for example, early-onset schizophrenia) or life transition (such as the death of a parent) crisis in a child or adolescent member of a family. Psychiatrically focused groups include those for psychotic-spectrum disorders and for attention-deficit/hyperactivity disorder (ADHD) in a child or adolescent. Stressful-event focused groups include those for coping with life transitions (such as divorce groups, Compassionate Friends groups for bereavement), stressful circumstances (such as Parents, Families, and Friends of Lesbians and Gays [PFLAG] groups for families in which a gay or lesbian adolescent has just "come out"), and catastrophic events (such as groups for children traumatized by war and natural disaster). The population we focus upon are those who probably benefit the most from such mutual help organizations: families that were not highly disordered prior to the onset of the psychiatric or life transition crisis.

Vygotsky's Conceptualization of Human Development

Vygotsky's conceptualization of human development informs our analysis of mutual help organizations as an intervention for children and adolescents. His integrated developmental approach for interventions is composed of multiple levels of analysis. This integration encompasses treatment at the individual level of analysis, the child. (See Sections I and II in this volume.) Other pieces of the developmental puzzle are the child's family (see Chapters 26 and 27 in this volume), as well as other institutions (such as self-help organizations or treatment settings and schools) and the broader society in which development occurs (Vygotsky, 1978). This conceptualization of *individual-in-context* is sometimes referred to as *social ecology* (Barker, 1968; Bronfenbrenner, 1977; Kelly, 1966).

Vygotsky's work on cognitive development as a social activity provides a theoretical framework for understanding self-help interventions. The developmental perspective of this chapter is threefold. First, illness, behavior problems, or stressful events in the life of child or adolescent typically pose long-term challenges to family functioning (Kurtz, 1994; Potasznik & Nelson, 1984). Second, self-help group interactions such as a member sharing a story and the group helping to reframe it—referred to as *cognitive antidotes* (Levine, Toro, & Perkins, 1993)—is linked to cognitive development. Third, we extend these applications of (seemingly) individual cognitive development to socially distributed cognition (Dillengourg & Self, 1992), in which cognition is a social process and achieved extra-individually.

Vygotsky's theory is particularly apposite here because it is based on his work with children who were largely excluded from society (children labeled as learning disabled). He worked to create services that would change the way researchers and educators understood childhood development and intervention. Some people consider Vygotsky the founding father of special education, although his version differs significantly from what exists in the United States today (Newman & Holzman, 1993). In the early 1900s, Lev Vygotsky stressed the importance of social context on children's development, particularly in the areas of language and communication. These ideas did not appeal to U.S. behavioral scientists until the 1970s or 1980s (Newman & Holzman, 1993). He envisioned special education as children working together to solve problems (that is, aiding each other's development). Because this approach is the philosophy of mutual help organizations, it seems particularly relevant to focus on mutual help as a social intervention.

A Vygotskian Perspective of Social Interventions' Mechanisms

For Vygotsky, the mechanisms of social interventions are participating in revolutionary activity, building a group, and establishing zones of proximal development (ZPD) (Newman & Holzman, 1993). Each is described below.

One of the clearest interpretations of Vygotsky's work, offered by Newman and Holzman (1993), presents Vygotsky's idea of revolutionary activity as a way of making meaning from an existing context or an activity that fills a practical and critical need missing in society. For Vygotsky, a revolutionary activity occurs in development when a response to a turn of events or change in circumstances results in new ideas, uses, or reorganization of existing resources. In other words, revolutionary activity is new activity in response to available resources in an environment.

A second mechanism that has cognitive benefits is the process of building a group (or activity setting). The formation of a group occurs through social interactions in which individuals are accountable to one another as well as responsible for their own behavior. In building a group, members create the meaning of their being together and establish a group identity. Within a particular group, activities belong to the group rather than to individuals. Thus, members work together developing practices that ensure the group's tasks are met. A primary goal in the development of an activity setting is to create an environment that fosters all members' development. Importantly, Vygotsky believed that cognitive benefits from group-building are achieved by peers or near-peers without outside help from a professionally skilled person. (For example, in classrooms students have to establish group procedures without help from a teacher.) This process of creating an activity setting, Vygotsky posited, generates cognitive development at two levels within an individual: what an individual accomplishes alone and what he accomplishes with group members.

Vygotsky (1978) believed that another mechanism of development is establishing a "zone of proximal development." He characterized the ZPD as a dynamic developmental region. The concept of ZPD is stated simply by Vygotsky:

"[The zone of proximal development is] the distance between the actual developmental level as determined by independent problem solving and the level of potential development as determined through problem solving under adult guidance or in collaboration with more capable peers." (Vygotsky, 1978, p. 86).

Vygotsky's Theory of Human Development and Mutual Help Organizations

Particularly in light of Vygotsky's theory of human development, encouraging the family to participate in a self-help group for treatment is a beneficial intervention for children and adolescents. As we know, children's functioning and environments are in constant interplay. Interventions such as self-help directed to the family environment thus invariably affect children's immediate social environment.

Mutual help provides a complementary intervention to psychotherapy and exists for families facing a variety of issues during various developmental stages of a child's life from birth (La Leche League, a group for mothers of newborns) through adolescence (Rainbow Room, a group for teens who are sexual minorities). Vygotsky conceptualized development as a life-long process. Thus, development may occur anywhere in the life span, and these mutual help interventions are relevant to children in need because their siblings, friends, family, and the broader society need to develop (change) along with them. Vygotsky understood well the role that social context plays in influencing developmental outcomes. Self-help groups are a social context and therefore are highly relevant to developmental interventions.

The nature of self-help is particularly well-suited to address these challenges because families will cope more poorly if they feel emotionally overwhelmed, are isolated, and lack information about the child's problem and available health care options. As mentioned above, self-help involvement can ameliorate all of these problems. For example, self-help groups' members provide emotional support to deal with crises and reduce social isolation. Moreover, some self-help organizations are also quite skilled at gathering medical information for members (e.g., what services are available, which providers are particularly expert in treating the condition of concern, what recent research has found, and so on).

Putative Targets of Change in Family Mutual Help Organizations

The targets of change vary in mutual help organizations depending on the problem addressed. However, four targets of change are prevalent across most family mutual help organizations: family and social networks, institutions, topical funds of knowledge, and societal stigma and discrimination.

The primary target of change is to enhance coping and reduce emotional overload for families. Crisis theory maintains that emotionally overwhelming events reduce the ability of otherwise mentally healthy people to cope with stressors (Caplan, 1964; Lindemann, 1944). This is certainly true of conditions like childhood cancer, birth defects, and family bereavement. Ineffective coping response, such as emotional withdrawal, aggressive outbursts, brooding, and increased consumption of alcohol exacerbate the original threat to family functioning. Mutual help groups teach and reinforce effective coping strategies (Humphreys, Finney, & Moos, 1994), and, provide an emotionally safe context for the catharsis of intense emotions such as grief and rage. These opportunities facilitate the resumption of healthy coping styles that were present prior to the current challenge.

Self-help groups also change members' social networks. Mutual help organizations, by definition, are social entities, and provide many opportunities for families to expand their social networks. This is particularly important for families who may have lost social ties as a result of their current challenge (for example, an adolescent comes out as gay in a conservative community). Self-help group members are often "swapped into" social networks to replace individuals who either contributed to the problem or were unsupportive (Humphreys & Noke, 1997).

Many groups go beyond targeting members and their social networks and work to change institutions such as the health care system. Engaging in the advocacy process and gaining information itself can be empowering and affect an individual's sense of community (Loomis & Dockett, under review). Many of the problems discussed in this chapter, for example, bring families into contact with the (managed) health care system, which requires them at times to fight for ethical treatment and high-quality care. Mutual help organizations typically support and encourage such efforts by families, and also engage in group-level advocacy where appropriate (for example, to pressure a hospital to improve care for pediatric cancer). (See Chesler & Chesney, 1995.)

Self-help initiatives also change the "funds of knowledge" (Moll & Greenberg, 1990) on topics. Families who experience a problem personally often become excellent students of the science and health resources relevant to it. Organizations are thus able to pool a large amount of information about their condition of interest (particularly for rare disorders) and may know far more about it than would any general practitioner. This information not only reduces anxiety, but also allows families to make better decisions about medical and psychiatric care options.

Finally, society in general, and the mental health professions in particular, have a long history of blaming families for misfortunes that befall children. One of the motivators for some early NAMI members, for example, was that psychoanalysts blamed mothers for childhood schizophrenia and autism. This stigma and consequent isolation increases the burden on families already experiencing significant challenges. By their very nature, mutual help organizations expose families to others in the same situation, which reduces shame and loneliness. Family members see that their problem is more prevalent than they realize, and, that it affects a wide range of families rather than being attributable to an idiosyncratic dysfunction particular to families like their own.

Vygotsky's conceptualization of activity, group building, and establishing a zone of proximal development as central to human development provides a theory for exploring the mechanisms of efficacy of mutual help groups and organizations. As mentioned above, we distinguish between mutual help organizations and mutual help groups. Because work accomplished at the organizational level grew from group level efforts, in the next section we focus mainly on self-help groups, or more generally, mutual help. Some recognized mechanisms of efficacy of mutual help are identification with others in a similar situation, de-stigmatization of the focal problem, achieving accomplishments, access to role models for learning effective coping strategies, and creation of resources.

Identification with others in a similar situation. A first step in identifying with other individuals is to "shop" for a self-help group or build one's own. (For more information on creating a new group, see White and Madara, 2002.) The voluntary nature of self-help groups implies individual volition in selecting or building a group (or in Vygotsky's terms, activity setting). Members choose to investigate a group, then choose whether to join a group. Within a group, members select with whom they socialize. In making each of these choices, the person is developing. Thus, the benefits derived from a self-help group intervention begin before a meeting is ever attended and likely extend well after attendance stops. In Vygotsky's model, the creation-of-an-activity setting is part of the learning process. The nature of self-help groups is self-directed as members come and go and meeting places change. No one particular person is in charge. Multiple people must be involved to sustain the group. Thus, the process of participating in a self-help group is a continuous production of an activity setting. Consequently, self-help groups for families, by their very nature, provide positive developmental consequences for the parents.

Another key aspect of the identification process is parents' experiential knowledge (Borkman, 1976; 1990). All self-help members are currently dealing (or previously have dealt) with the same issue and similar challenges that prospective parents face. Indeed, sharing a common problem defines membership status (Katz, 1970). This unifying experience, from a Vygotskian perspective, comes in part from members' activities of co-creating a group that engages in the revolutionary activity of making meaning out of their existing resources and circumstances. Members may be attracted to self-help in particular because the approach requires that they create meaning on their own with similar peers, rather than meaning being "handed down from on high" from a mental health provider or another expert person in an authoritarian position (for example, a church leader). Furthermore, a well-meaning, formally trained professional is more likely to be in a different ZPD from a parent in need than is another individual, increasing the likelihood of identification and subsequent related development.

De-stigmatization of the focal problem. The stigma that often faces children with psychiatric or stressful life events affects communication within and outside of families that subsequently affects children's cognitive and social development. During group meetings and other informal interactions with other self-help families, members confront their own previously held attitudes and beliefs and reframe them with new information and ideas. The degree of formality in this process varies.

Some groups de-stigmatize the focal issue through conversations and sharing information gathered. Other mutual help groups create and facilitate more formal education programs (such as with a curriculum or target audience) focused on decreasing stigma and increasing knowledge. In Vygotskian terms, engaging in the process of de-stigmatization at any level is participating in revolutionary activity—learning that leads to development. De-stigmatization is part of the mutual help process that fosters the development of children with special needs, as well as their families, peers, and other adults who interact with them.

Achieving accomplishments. Self-help parents support each other in various ways on many different tasks. Many of the tasks, such as gathering the most current information available on a topic, are beyond the developmental level of any one individual. Having tasks of this nature is an important aspect of Vygotsky's model of social learning. Specifically, he believed that in order to develop individually, group-tasks must be beyond all members' individual developmental level. The research of Moll and Greenberg (1990) is informative in this area. These researchers explored learning and development among Mexican households in Arizona, studying social relations among home, school, and community. They found that the households have "funds of knowledge." The synthesis of information among household members created the wealth in the fund, which was greater than any one individual's expertise or the sum of all household members' knowledge. This scenario is also true in the case of mutual help groups. No one person is an expert in therapeutic approaches or the illness or in life transitions confronting members.

Access to role models for learning effective coping strategies. Another important mechanism of self-help is learning effective coping strategies from role models who are highly accessible (Humphreys & Rappaport, 1994; Humphreys, in press). Vygotsky's ZPD concept generalizes well to a family's developmental trajectory when faced with a transitional event or illness. We can increase our understanding of how a family in transition copes by observing their ZPD, which is visible within a social context such as a self-help organization. Individual and collaborative accomplishments vary depending on a person's ZPD. Because self-help groups have several individuals at various stages of life-transition development, members have an opportunity to select one-on-one interactions and role models from more developmentally advanced peers within their ZPD. This access facilitates development to the next zone, where other self-help group members become more immediate peers. According to Vygotsky, we can only imitate behaviors that are within our zone. Vygotsky argued that individual assessment did not capture the full extent of a person's development, which appears only in relation to others. Therefore, we need to assess and understand how interventions in relation with others (such as within a self-help group) affect mental health outcomes.

Creation of resources. More generally, self-help groups are what Roger Barker referred to as an *undermanned setting* (literally, a setting with "not enough hands"). Undermanned settings provide members with opportunities for taking on valued roles within the group, which enhances their esteem and sense of control. In many ways, self-help organizations address how community resources (including attitudes and beliefs) affect the development of the socially marginalized. Vygotsky wrote: "It is necessary to formulate the categories and concepts that are specifically relevant—in other words, to create one's own Capital [capitalization in original text]" (Vygotsky, 1978, p. 8). Creating capital is important developmentally and particularly important within self-help because members' marginalization from the mainstream reduces resources available to them. The experiential basis of self-help (Borkman, 1976; 1990) is a necessary ingredient in creating capital, and this capital is consistent with Vygotsky's method for building a truly human science relevant to a specific phenomenon. Thus, not only do self-help members create capital for themselves, but (from a Vygotskian perspective) they also are revolutionary scientists challenging lay and professional knowledge, attitudes, and beliefs with their contemporary experiential knowledge.

Empirical Support for Treatment Efficacy

The slowly growing body of research on self-help began more than half a century ago, investigating a variety of foci and topical areas (Kurtz, 1994). Most of the studies focus on group effects on members and a few studies explore (internal) organizational effects (Maton, Leventhal, Madara, & Julien 1989; Wituk, Shepherd, Warren, & Meissen, 2002). Other examples of organizational studies of self-help research include studies of effects on social institutions (Humphreys & Moos, 1996; 2001) and the broader society (at the societal level of analysis) (Borkman, 1999). We are unaware of systematic research on the effects of self-help activism on non-members within the general public (Humphreys, 1997). Few studies have looked at the effects of self-help on individuals or family units not directly involved in self-help (although they are potentially affected by it) such as friendship networks (with the exception of Humphreys & Noke, 1997) and children and adolescents.

Much of the empirical evidence in self-help research has been conducted with addiction-related groups (Christo & Sutton, 1994; Emrick, Tonigan, Montgomery, & Little, 1993; Humphreys, in press; Humphreys & Moos, 2001). A second area includes in-depth studies of particular organizations. Research on the GROW organization for people with serious mental illness (Kennedy, 1990; Maton & Salem, 1995; Rappaport, 1993; Roberts et al., 1999), Alliance for the

Mentally Ill (Sommer, 1990; Sommer, Williams, & Williams, 1984), Recovery, Inc. (Wechsler, 1994), and Candlelighters cancer-focused mutual help groups (Chesler & Chesney, 1995) are examples of this kind of study. Of particular relevance to this chapter are studies of caregiver groups, especially care from an adult to a child (rather than adult to adult caregiving) (Toseland, Rossiter, & Labrecque, 1989).

Self-help participation enhances parent-child interactions and decreases parents' caregiving-related stress. In a case study of self-help group for families, adults reported that mutual help participation increased emotional expression, understanding, coping skills, and enhanced social environments (Kurtz, 1994). In a separate study of effects on children, a controlled clinical trial of parents of premature infants who remained in the hospital showed that parents involved in a self-help group visited more often and were more involved with their babies than parents who did not participate in a mutual help group. Furthermore, three months after discharge differences persisted in mothers' interactions with their infants during feedings, in favor of self-help group participation (Minde et al., 1980). In a different longitudinal study of support group effects, single young mothers who consistently participated in an online mutual support group had decreased levels of stress six months after initiating participation than before joining the group (Dunham et al., 1998). As a third example, in a study of NAMI researchers found that parents attending self-help group sessions experienced less caregiver-burden than similar parents who did not participate in a NAMI affiliate group (Cook, Heller, & Pickett-Schenk, 1999). Findings from these studies show that self-help involvement benefit a variety of parents and their children.

Research on family functioning is also relevant to our interests here as self-help groups for families intend to restore healthy family functioning, so we provide a few examples of this particular body of literature. Family functioning improves outcomes for children with medical needs or a disability. For example, family support is positively associated with treatment adherence among diabetic adolescents (LaGreca et al., 1995), and behavior problems with pediatric burn survivors (LeDoux, Meyer, Blakeney, & Herndon, 1998). One study of African American families found that well-adjusted families are correlated with higher levels of disability adjustment (Alston, McCowan, & Turner, 1994). The above mentioned studies mostly address a family's role in promoting or facilitating positive health outcomes. There are two additional ways that family functioning affects youth; it can be both a risk and a protective factor. In a sample of more than 1,500 adolescents, depression (past, current, and future) was associated with low family support (Lewinsohn et al., 1994). After controlling for depression, family support is inversely related to suicide attempts (Asarnow, 1992; Lewinsohn, Rohde, & Seeley, 1994). As findings from these studies suggest, lower functioning families add to child and adolescent risks. Thus, increasing family functioning can serve as a protective factor as well as promote healthy adjustment.

About self-help groups for distressed families, much remains to be learned. Limitations notwithstanding, findings from studies of effects on self-help group members, self-help effects on members' children, and research on family support combine to suggest that participation in mutual help makes a difference for the individual participant and positively influences child and adolescent developmental outcomes.

Case Examples

Self-help groups that benefit young people could be divided roughly into three types: (1) children or adolescents who have "X," (2) children whose parent has "X," and (3) parents or caregivers whose child has "X." There are few self-help groups specifically for children in the first category, perhaps because children face practical issues in starting their own groups (for example, they are too young to reserve public meeting places or have their own form of transportation). Adults of some self-help organizations have started youth groups such as Candlelighters and Rainbow Room. Candlelighters is for survivors of childhood cancer and Rainbow Room is for sixteen- to twenty-one-year-olds who identify as gay, lesbian, bisexual, or transgender. Because so few groups outside of the addiction area (Kelly 2002a; 2002b) exist for youth, and little is known about their effects, we do not directly address these types of self-help groups in this chapter. The second category, a child whose parent has X, primarily focuses on parents so we do not include these groups either. The focus of this chapter is on the third category, self-help organizations for families facing challenges related to a child's illness or stressful life event.

In self-help groups for families, caregivers provide developmentally appropriate information about the issues their children face, as well as receive emotional support and learn coping skills. In a self-help group parents can determine the developmental issues (such as increased risk-taking behavior in adolescents) and the symptoms of illness or coping tools. Parents also learn how to better communicate with their teenager about risk assessment and decision-making so young people dealing with a psychiatric or medical illness or a life transition can make some of these decisions like other non-affected teens. Within self-help groups, parents learn from each other the source of their overprotectedness and learn how to relax a little, allowing teens to feel some safe space for risk-taking that did not exist before, such as painting, creative writing, playing music, acting, or playing team sports. As mentioned above (in addition to families) peers, media, and the broader society influence the emotional and social development of children. For this reason, many self-help organizations go beyond parent-to-parent meetings (self-help groups) and create educational materials and practices that change society's perspective.

We present two case studies, one for each type of self-help organization. NAMI is used as an example of a psychiatrically focused groups, and PFLAG for families in which an adolescent has come out as gay, lesbian, or bi-sexual is used as an example of a life-transition focused group. The basic structure of each group is detailed and relevant research and case experience described.

Psychiatrically Focused Self-Help

For children and adolescents, being diagnosed with a mental illness such as OCD or ADHD affects emotional development beyond the effects of the illness. Not only is the development of youth with these psychiatric illnesses affected, but the development of their siblings, friends, and school peers is also affected. Therefore, in order to address the developmental issues for children and adolescents, mental health interventions must work together to form a holistic, complementary approach from an ecological framework that addresses an individual, the family, the schools, and the broader community and society. Several grassroots organizations complement clinicians' care by addressing the multidimensional context of children's lives (for example, the National Association for Retarded Citizens, formerly Association for the Help for Retarded Children). An organization that began as a grassroots movement in 1950s in the United States is the Association for Retarded Children (ARC). (For more information, visit their Web site at http://www.thearc.org/.) To illustrate the various kinds of interventions provided by these organizations, we present a brief case study of one of them, the NAMI, highlighting the following: history and mission, membership, self-help groups and other interventions (from the group or organizational level), and connections to professional services.

National Alliance for the Mentally Ill (NAMI). Millions of children and adolescents suffer from one or more kinds of serious mental illness, such as the most common psychiatric illnesses—obsessive-compulsive disorder (OCD) and ADHD. (For adults, NAMI also focuses on schizophrenia and bipolar disorder.) These disorders and other brain disorders (such as early onset depression and Tourette's syndrome) affect a youth's developmental outcomes, in school performance and socialization. Among adolescents, untreated severe mental illness increases the likelihood for health risk behaviors such as alcohol and drug abuse, early sexual activity, and school failure (American Psychological Association, 2002).

NAMI provides self-help groups for consumers, families, and friends having (or relating to someone with) known physical brain disorders, generally referred to as severe mental illnesses. The organization provides support, education, advocacy, and research functions, addressing mental illness across the life span from children to adults.

Overall, the mission of NAMI "is dedicated to the eradication of mental illnesses and to the improvement of the quality of life of all whose lives are affected by these diseases" (National Alliance for the Mentally Ill, 2003). A central tenet of the organization is that biological factors cause serious mental illnesses. Therefore, individuals and their families are not at fault for the illnesses and society has a moral obligation to care for its people in a way that includes and empowers affected families (Hatfield, 1991).

The organization was founded in 1979 and has affiliates in all fifty states (United States of America) and the territories of the District of Columbia, Puerto Rico, and American Samoa. NAMI is also in Canada. A few other countries—Australia, Japan, and the Ukraine—have started sister organizations with assistance from NAMI. NAMI in the United States has local, state, and national tiers, serving more than 220,000 members. Most members (referred to as *affiliate members*) are consumers (individuals with severe mental illness) or families and friends of consumers who join ($35 dues) through a local group and belong to NAMI at all three levels. NAMI also provides professional membership ($50 dues) for individuals who share NAMI's mission but who do not qualify as affiliate members (such as clinicians, researchers, and attorneys). This class of membership, *national associate member,* is attached only at NAMI's national level. Through the local, state, and national organizational levels, NAMI provides several forms of mental health interventions for children and adolescents, as well as their loved ones and treatment providers. (See also http://www.nami.org/youth/.) Following deinstitutionalization, the organization was instrumental in the social movement for improved quality of professional care, availability of services, and decreased stigmatization for individuals with mental illnesses (Hatfield, 1991).

In communities around the world, NAMI self-help group meetings are held for consumers and their families to share concerns, learn more about brain diseases, and receive emotional support and practical advice about health insurance, medical treatment, housing, employment, and community resources. For example, one focus is on respite care as a way to enrich family life. Self-help groups exist for various target groups: parents, young siblings age thirteen and under, teens (fourteen to nineteen) support group led by a child psychiatrist—the group meets at the same time their parents meet in a self-help (peer-led) group, and an entire family group.

As mentioned, to effectively treat children with severe mental illness, we need to address the multidimensional context of their lives (their parents, siblings, peers, schools, churches, and so on) as well as the children themselves. Part of NAMI's organizational level interventions include providing science-based information in books, pamphlets, and educational seminars as well as an outreach component to faith communities focusing on creating a place where people with mental illnesses can experience acceptance, love, and appreciation.

NAMI has two educational programs designed by families for families and two of these are focused on having a child with a mental illness: Hand-to-Hand and Visions for Tomorrow. Hand-to-Hand is an eight-week program with an overarching goal to empower parents. The curriculum provides information about their children's diagnosis and addresses families' emotional needs for healing, particularly from self-blaming for their child's illness and so forth. For more information, see www.namiohio.org or call Muriel Jeffries at NAMI Ohio (800-686-2646). The other program, Visions for Tomorrow, is similar in content to Hand-to-Hand and is taught by parents of children with brain disorders who have been trained to facilitate workshops. For more information, see the Web site www.texas.nami.org or contact Linda Zweifel by phone (800-633-3760) or e-mail (linda@texami.org).

Another important arena of self-help activities is the area of social stigma, which affects psychological and tangible resources. Reducing stigma and ignorance about severe mental illness helps eliminate discrimination and restrictions on access to essential treatments and life supports such as employment, housing, health insurance, and social contact. NAMI provides social support electronically through the "KnowHow" Listserv for consumers who are NAMI members and through face-to-face self-help group meetings.

NAMI also engages in advocacy. Legislation and policy affect the lives of individuals with mental illnesses, including children. The organization considers itself "The Nation's Voice on Mental Illness" and develops policy platforms. For example, the organization takes a position on the practice of custody relinquishment. Specifically, "NAMI declares that under no circumstances shall families be coerced or forced to relinquish custody of their dependent children with brain disorders in order to obtain care, treatment, and education" (www.nami.org/update/unitedchildren.html). Children who stay with their families fare better on developmental outcomes than their separated counterparts. Thus, NAMI's actions on this matter enhance developmental outcomes for youth with severe mental illnesses. NAMI's advocacy information is available to the public (including members, policy makers, media, and so on) at no cost through an electronic newsletter called NAMI E-News, to which more than 15,000 individuals subscribe (NAMI, 2003).

NAMI cooperates with professionals. NAMI self-help group members are a resource for referral to mental health professionals and treatment facilities that specialize in caring for children and adolescents. Another bridge is in the area of public education, research, and advocacy as well as critique. For example, NAMI's OCD pamphlet was reviewed by Judith Rapoport, M.D., chief, Child Psychiatry Branch, National Institute of Mental Health, and the brochure on early onset depression was reviewed by David G. Fassier, M.D., child and adolescent psychiatrist, Otter Creek Associates. In turn, NAMI provides expertise for professionals, such as when its report *Families on the Brink* (1999) identified critical weaknesses in the systems of mental health care for children and adolescents. Service providers were not able to recognize some of the systemic problems NAMI illuminated because providers are part of the system, focused on a small part that does not allow them to experience the system as a whole. If they do see the big picture it is usually be from the perspective of an administrator rather than from one using the system. For this reason, NAMI's report allowed professional treatment systems and settings to learn from an outside evaluation. The information gained from this evaluation shifts professional focus, addressing identified needs and resolving problems.

For more information or to join NAMI contact the organization on the toll-free HelpLine 1-800-950-NAMI (6264), the Web site at www.nami.org, by phone 703-524-7600, or through the mail at national headquarters in the U.S. at National Alliance for the Mentally Ill, Colonial Place Three, 2107 Wilson Blvd., Suite 300, Arlington, VA 22201.

Life Transition-Focused Self-Help

Many mutual help organizations address stressful life transitions. One life transition is the development of sexuality, which may be particularly stressful for adolescents exploring or identifying as gay, lesbian, or bisexual in a heterosexist-centric society (APA, 2002; D'Augelli, 1998). Such adolescents risk losing various forms of social support offered by family and friends, and, may be marginalized and victimized by their peers, communities, and society. Increased stressors (such as victimization and alienation) and decreased social resources (such as social isolation) are associated with decreased well-being and adjustment (Bontempo & D'Augelli, 2002; Hershberger & D'Augelli, 2000).

An immediate social context of adolescents is their family, and various mutual help organizations have been developed as a resource for families. Virtually all mutual help organizations for gay and lesbian people do not define same-sex attraction as a problem, but rather view it as a status which is distressing due to discrimination (Humphreys, in press, p. 18). The earliest of these mutual help organizations that is still in existence in the United States today is Dignity/USA, founded in 1969 as a support group for Catholic gay, lesbian, bisexual, or trans-gendered individuals and their families and friends (White & Madara, 2002). Similar groups established in the 1970s and 1980s include Family Pride Coalition, National Gay and Lesbian Task Force, and PFLAG. Among these organizations, the focus on support groups and advocacy varies, but most are involved in chang-ing societal views to some extent. One of the most highly visible organizations of this kind is PFLAG, which we present as a case study.

Parents, Families, and Friends of Lesbians and Gays (PFLAG). The roots of this mu-tual help organization began in 1972 when Jeanne Manford, the mother of gay son, watched with outrage as her gay son was attacked at a gay rights protest demonstration and police did not intervene. She marched with her son in the 1972 New York's Pride Day parade. Other gay and lesbian individuals seeing her alliance with her son asked Ms. Manford to talk with their parents. From this impetus more and more self-help groups focused on issues of sexual orientation developed. The following year the first family support group meeting was held. Over time similar groups developed throughout the United States and in 1981 a national organization was formed that supports, educates, and advocates for gay, lesbian, bisexual, and transgendered people and their families and friends. PFLAG headquarters now are located in Washington, D.C. (PFLAG, 2003).

These small group efforts have grown into a large organization (with more than 80,000 members) that provides support, education, and advocacy with a vision of promoting "respect, dignity and equality for all" (PFLGA, 2003); inter-national organizations also have developed. The mission statement of PFLAG follows:

> PFLAG promotes the health and well-being of gay, lesbian, bisexual and trans-gendered persons, their families and friends through: support, to cope with an adverse society; education, to enlighten an ill-informed public; and advocacy, to end discrimination and to secure equal civil rights. Parents, Families and Friends of Lesbians and Gays provides opportunity for dialogue about sexual orientation and gender identity, and acts to create a society that is healthy and respectful of human diversity.

As you can see from its roots and mission statement, PFLAG intends not only to meet individual and family needs, but also to reduce stigma and sexual prejudice.

Support groups address many challenging issues. For example, some individ-uals struggled with if and how to "come out" to their parents. Parents' responses vary. In a study of fourteen- to twenty-one-year-olds living at home, family members' response to disclosure of sexual orientation was sometimes verbal and physical abuse (D'Augelli, Hershberger, & Pilkington, 1998). A PFLAG member and mother confirms that many PFLAG members face this difficulty in determining whether disclosure would lead to increased family support or rejection (Henderson, 1998). This issue represents one example of support received in self-help group meetings.

The context of adolescents' lives includes pressure, support, and prejudice around sexual exploration (or not). For example, among adolescent boys, peer pressure to have sex with a girl is strong. In contrast, adolescents expressing same- or multiple-sex desires face sexual prejudice, stigma, and lack of peer support. A mutual help group can help youths and parents to identify sexual prejudice as well as provide coping skills to avoid responding to the prejudice.

PFLAG parent mutual help groups provide a setting for confronting members' own sexual prejudices and understanding their child's disclosure. In self-help group meetings, members explore various ways to integrate multiple dimensions of their parenting experience (religious traditions, ideas about grandchildren, and so on) in a way that promotes healthy development. With the support of PFLAG, parents learn how to foster youth identity development that has an extra task of integrating a sexual minority identity. In this growth process, many parents express a desire to continue protecting their child. Some parents worry about being unable to protect their child in a society that marginalizes and victimizes her because of sexual orientation; this latter awareness often leads parents to place an increased emphasis on education and activism as a way to benefit their children.

The educational component of PFLAG potentially affects the development of parents, families and friends, and school students. For example, the organization publishes many "support publications" such as *Our Daughters & Sons: Questions and Answers for Parents of Gay, Lesbian, Bisexual and Transgendered People* and *Faith in Our Families: Parents, Families & Friends Talk About Religion & Homosexuality* (PFLAG, 2003). In addition to published literature (available in English and Spanish), PFLAG develops educational programs designed to reduce stigmatization and victimization in schools (*From Our House to the School House: A Recipe for Safe School*). These educational efforts are important forms of support for families and create a less alienating, more inclusive and safe environment for adolescent development.

Another important form of support that PFLAG offers is advocacy for changes in policies and legislation to provide equal rights to all, including gay, lesbian, bisexual, and transgendered individuals. Press releases, newsletters, and policy statements are just a few of the ways that PFLAG supports its members in the public realm. Like other not-for-profit organizations, PFLAG does not endorse or oppose particular political parties or candidates. Primarily they focus on shaping the debates and encouraging civic participation to influence the outcome of legislation that ensures equal opportunities for all.

From the beginning, one purpose of PFLAG has been to raise awareness of and change sexual prejudice and discrimination through grassroots education and legislative lobbying efforts. In fact, many mutual help groups focus on participation if you find the support helpful. PFLAG, in contrast, insists that the organization needs you even if you do not need the organization or self-help meetings. (See Frequently Asked Questions on the Web site). This position on involvement is one example of how PFLAG is a mutual help organization involved in a social movement (for other aspects of social movements, see Broad, 2002).

Throughout the various aspects of the organization (support, education, and advocacy), PFLAG consistently sends the messages that "You're not alone" and "We understand." These sentiments and associated experiences are central to the mutual help phenomenon and Vygotsky's theory of human development in context with more capable peers. PFLAG fosters the development of adolescent members directly through affiliation with peers and the creation of resources (such as pamphlets for expanding an individual's thinking about "coming out" to family and friends) as well as indirectly through families, friends, school communities and society by working to de-stigmatize bisexual and gay and lesbian sexual orientation. Finally, PFLAG illustrates well the concept of members accomplishing much more together than could be accomplished on one's own.

Future Directions

The mutual help organizations presented in this chapter illustrate the importance of self-help interventions to address multiple dimensions of a child or adolescent's social world, including family, peers, and the broader societal context. Self-help group members often report psychological and social benefits from participation. Inherent characteristics of professional interventions, such as fee-for-service and a client's fixed role as a recipient of help, prohibit the activation of many healing properties available within social relations (for example, the dynamic roles as a recipient of help and helper). Like Vygotsky's learning goals, some mental health benefits are best achieved through group efforts rather than individual ones. Thus, future interventions with children and adolescents would benefit from addressing the social nature of their cognitive, emotional, and social development. This task may be accomplished by professionals suggesting to parents that they participate in a mutual help organization.

In our experience with members of self-help groups, we have learned that there are many paths in which self-help and professional treatment work together facilitating a person or family's return to well-being: independent uncombined, sequential (professional treatment then self-help, sequential) self-help then professional treatment, simultaneously both individual treatment and mutual help, and combined self-help group with a professionally led support group. The independent approach includes individuals who have experienced only one form or the other of intervention, but not both. In this case, professionals' clients are not self-help group members. In a sequential combination of interventions, some therapists refer their clients to self-help groups as a "maintenance" form for the post-professional intervention. Alternatively, some people who are initially uncomfortable with individual treatment come to value the benefits of individual treatment after hearing in a self-help meeting accounts of "what goes on in therapy." Still others when faced with a crisis simultaneously initiate mutual help and professional help. Finally, some self-help members find that they want to meet more frequently than the number of mutual help meetings available and use professionally led support groups as an alternative meeting format, so making these meetings accessible is important social intervention (Kurtz, 1994).

In addition to professionals understanding, accepting, and encouraging their clients' involvement in mutual help, future work also needs to address the dearth of research in this area. As we reviewed in this chapter, little systematic research exists on mutual help organizations for families, including their direct effects on parents as well as indirect effects on their children. We need more systematic research employing both quantitative and qualitative methods (Tebes & Kraemer, 1991) in order to examine the second- and third-degree effects of mutual help. Understanding both the social impact of these organizations as well as the mental health benefits members derive by engaging in these activities and making meaning in their lives will enhance our ability to foster child and adolescent development.

References

Alston, R. J., McCowan, C. J., & Turner, W. L. (1994). Family functioning as a correlate of disability adjustment for African Americans. *Rehabilitation Counseling Bulletin, 37*, 277–289.

Barker, R. G. (1968). *Ecological psychology.* Stanford, CA: Stanford University Press.

Bontempo, D. E., & D'Augelli, A. R. (2002). Effects of at-school victimization and sexual orientation on lesbian, gay, or bisexual youths' health risk behavior. *Journal of Adolescent Health, 30*, 364–374.

Borkman, T. J. (1976). Experiential knowledge: A new concept for the analysis of self-help groups. *Social Service Review, 50*, 445–456.

Borkman, T. J. (1990). Experimental, professional and lay frames of reference. In T. J. Powell (Ed.), *Working with self-help* (pp. 3–30). Silver Springs, MD: NASW Press.

Borkman, T. J. (1999). *Understanding self-help/mutual aid: Experiential learning in the commons.* New Brunswick, NJ: Rutgers University Press.

Borman, L. D. (1979). Characteristics of development and growth. In M. A. Lieberman & L. D. Borman (Eds.), *Self-help groups for coping with crisis* (pp. 13–42). San Francisco: Jossey-Bass.

Broad, K. L. (2002). Social movement selves. *Sociological perspectives, 45,* 317–336.

Brofenbrenner, U. (1977). Toward an experimental ecology of human development. *American psychologist, 32,* 513–531.

Caplan, G. (1964). *Principles of preventive psychiatry.* New York: Basic Books.

Chesler, M. A., & Chesney, B. K. (1995). Cancer and self-help: Bridging the troubled waters of childhood illness. Madison, WI: University of Wisconsin Press.

Christo, G., & S. Sutton (1994). Anxiety and self-esteem as a function of abstinence time among recovering addicts attending Narcotics Anonymous. *British Journal of Clinical Psychology, 33,* 198–200.

Cook, J. A., Heller, T., & Pickett-Schenk, S. A. (1999). The effect of support group participation on caregiver burden among parents of adult offspring with severe mental illness. *Family Relations, 48,* 405–410.

D'Augelli, A. R. (1998). Developmental implications of victimization of lesbian, gay, and bisexual youths. In G. M. Herek (Ed.), *Stigma and sexual orientation: Understanding prejudice against lesbians, gay men, and bisexuals* (pp. 187–210). Thousand Oaks, CA: Sage.

D'Augelli, A. R., Hershberger, S. L., & Pilkington, N. W. (1998). Lesbian, gay, and bisexual youth and their families: Disclosure of sexual orientation and its consequences. *American Journal of Orthopsychiatry, 68,* 361–371.

Developing adolescents: A reference for professionals. (2002). Washington, DC: American Psychological Association.

Dillengourg, P., & Self, J. A. (1992). A longitudinal approach to socially distributed cognition. *European Journal of Psychology of Education, 2,* 352–373.

Dunham, P. J., Hurshman, A., Litwin, E., Gusella, J., Ellsworth, C., & Dodd, P.W.D. (1998). Computer-mediated social support: Single young mothers as a model system. *American Journal of Community Psychology, 26,* 281–306.

Emrick, C. D., Tonigan, J. S., Montgomery, H., & Little, L. (1993). Alcoholics Anonymous: What is currently known? In B. S. McCrady & W. R. Miller (Eds.), *Research on Alcoholics Anonymous: Opportunities and alternatives* (pp. 41–75). Athens, GA: University of Georgia, Counseling & Testing Center.

Hatfield, A. B. (1991). The National Alliance for the Mentally Ill: A decade later. *Community Mental Health Journal, 27,* 95–103.

Henderson, M. G. (1998). Disclosure of sexual orientation: Comments from a parental perspective. *American Journal of Orthopsychiatry, 68,* 372–375.

Hershberger, S. L., & D'Augeli, A. R. (2000). Issues in counseling lesbian, gay, and bisexual adolescents. In R. M. Perez, K. A. DeBord, & K. J. Bieschke (Eds.), *Handbook of counseling and psychotherapy with lesbian, gay, and bisexual clients* (pp. 225–247). Washington, DC: American Psychological Association.

Humphreys, K. (1997). Self-help/mutual aid organizations: The view from Mars. *Substance Use & Misuse, 32,* 2105–2109.

Humphreys, K. (in press). *Circles of recovery: Self-help organizations for addictions.* Cambridge University Press.

Humphreys, K., Finney, J. W., & Moos, R. H. (1994). Applying stress and coping framework to research on mutual help organizations. *Journal of Community Psychology, 22,* 312–327.

Humphreys, K., & Moos, R. H. (1996). Reduced substance-abuse-related health care costs among voluntary participants in Alcoholics Anonymous. *Psychiatric Services, 47,* 709–713.

Humphreys, K., & Moos, R. H. (2001). Can encouraging substance abuse patients to participate in self-help groups reduce demand for health care? A quasi-experimental study. Alcoholism. *Clinical and Experimental Research, 25,* 711–716.

Humphreys, K., & Noke, J. M. (1997). The influence of post-treatment mutual help group participation on the friendship networks of substance abuse patients. *American Journal of Community Psychology, 25,* 1–16.

Humphreys, K., & Rappaport, J. (1994). Researching self-help/mutual aid groups and organizations: Many roads, one journey. *Applied and Preventive Psychology, 3,* 217–231.

Katz, A. H. (1970). Self-help orgnizations and volunteer participation in social welfare. *Social Work, 15,* 51–60.

Kelly, J. G. (1966). Ecological constraints on mental health services. *American Psychologist, 21,* 535–539.

Kelly, J. F., Myers, M. G., & Brown, S. A. (2000). A multivariate process model of adolescent 12-step attendance and substance use outcome following inpatient treatment. *Psychology of Addictive Behaviors, 14,* 376–389.

Kelly, J. F., Myers, M. G., & Brown, S. A. (2002a). Do adolescents affiliate with 12-step groups? A multivariate process model of effects. *Journal of Studies on Alcohol, 63,* 293–304.

Kelly, J. F., Myers, M. G., & Brown, S. A. (2002b). *The effects of age composition of 12-step groups on adolescent 12-step participation and substance use outcome.* Poster presented at the 25th Annual Research Society on Alcoholism Conference, San Francisco, California.

Kennedy, M. (1990). Psychiatric hospitalizations of GROWers. Paper presented at the Second Biennial Conference on Community Research and Action, East Lansing, MI.

Kessler, R. C., Frank, R. G., Edlund, M., Katz, S. J., Lin, E., & Leaf, P. (1997). Differences in the use of psychiatric outpatient services between the United States and Ontario. *New England Journal of Medicine, 326,* 551–557.

Kessler, R. C., Mickelson, K. D., & Zhao, S. (1997). Patterns and correlates of self-help group membership in the United States. *Social Policy, 27,* 27–46.

Kurtz, L. F. (1994). Self-help groups for families with mental illness or alcoholism. In T. J. Powell (Ed.), *Understanding the self-help organization: Frameworks and findings* (pp. 293–313). Thousand Oaks, CA: Sage.

Kyrouz, E. M., Humphreys, K., & Loomis, C. (2002). A review of research on the effectiveness of self-help mutual aid groups. In B. J. White & E. J. Madara (Eds.), *The self-help group sourcebook* (7th ed., pp. 71–86). Cedar Knolls, NJ: American Self-Help Group Clearinghouse.

LaGreca, A. M., Auslander, W. F., Greco, P., Spetter, D., Fisher, Jr. E. B., & Santiago, J. V. (1995). I get by with a little help from my family and friends: Adolescents' support for diabetes care. *Journal of Pediatric Psychology, 20,* 449–476.

LeDoux, J., Meyer, W. J., III, Blakeney, P. E., & Herndon, D. N. (1998). Relationship between parental emotional states, family environment and the behavioural adjustment of pediatric burn survivors. *Burns, 24,* 425–432.

Levine, M., Toro, P. A., & Perkins, D. V. (1993). Social and community interventions. *Annual Review of Psychology, 44,* 525–558.

Lewinsohn P. M., Roberts, R. E., Seeley, J. R., Rohde, P., Gotlib, I. H., & Hops, H. (1994). Adolescent psychopathology: II. Psychosocial risk factors for depression. *Journal of Abnormal Psychology, 103,* 302–315.

Lewinsohn, P. M., Rohde, P. l., & Seeley, J. R. (1994). Psychosocial risk factors for future adolescent suicide attempts. *Journal of Consulting & Clinical Psychology, 62,* 297–305.

Lindemann, E. (1944). Symptomatology and management of acute grief. *American Journal of Psychiatry, 101,* 141–148.

Loomis, C., & Dockett, K. H. (2003). Changes in sense of community: Empirical findings. Manuscript submitted for review.

Madara, E. (1997). The mutual aid self-help online revolution. *Social Policy, 27,* 20–26.

Marsh, D. T. (1998). Serious mental illness and the family: The practitioner's guide.

Marsh, D. T., & Dickens, R. M. (1998). *How to cope with mental illness in your family: A guide for siblings, offspring, and parents.* New York: Tarcher/Putnam.

Maton, K. I. (1988). Social support, organizational characteristics, psychological well-being, and group appraisal in three self-help group populations. *American Journal of Community Psychology, 16,* 53–77.

Maton, K. I. (1993). Moving beyond the individual level of analysis in mutual-help group research: An ecological paradigm.

Maton, K. I., Leventhal, G. S., Madara, E. J., & Julien, M. (1989). Factors affecting the birth and death of mutual-help groups: The role of national affiliation, professional involvement, and member focal problem. *American Journal of Community Psychology, 17,* 643–671.

Maton, K. I., & Salem, D. A. (1995). Organizational characteristics of empowering community settings: A multiple case study approach. *American Journal of Community Psychology, 23,* 631–656.

Minde, K., N. Shosenberg, N., Marton, P., Thompson, J., Ripley, J., & Burns S. (1980). Self-help groups in a premature nursery: A controlled evaluation. *Behavioral Pediatrics, 96*(5), 933–940.

Moll, L., & Greenberg, J. (1990). Creating zones of possibilities: Combining social contexts for instruction. In L. Moll (Ed.), *Vygotsky and education* (pp. 319–348). London: Cambridge University Press.

NAMI (2003). National Alliance for the Mentally Ill Web site. http://www.nami.org

Newman, F., & Holzman, L. (1993). *Lev Vygotsky: Revolutionary scientist.* London: Routledge.

PFLAG (2003). Parents, Families and Friends of Lesbians and Gays Web site. http://www.pflag.org

Potasznik, H., & Nelson, G. (1984). Stress and social support: The burden experienced by the family of a mentally ill person. *American Journal of Community Psychology, 12,* 589–607.

Rappaport, J. (1993). Narrative studies, personal stories, and identity transformation in the mutual help context. *Journal of Applied Behavioral Science, 29,* 239–256.

Rapping, E. (1997). There's self-help and then there's self-help: Women and the recovery movement. *Social Policy, 27,* 56–61.

Revenson, T., & Cassel, B. (1991). An exploration of leadership in a medical mutual help organization. *American Journal of Community Psychology, 19,* 683–698.

Riessman, F. (1965). The helper therapy principle. *Social Work, 10,* 26–32.

Riessman, F. (1990). Restructuring help: A human service paradigm for the 1990's. *American Journal of Community Psychology, 18,* 221–230.

Roberts, L. J., Salem, D., Rappaport, J., Toro, P. A., Luke, D. A., & Seidman, E. (1999). Giving and receiving help: Interpersonal transactions in mutual-help meetings and psychosocial adjustment of members. *American Journal of Community Psychology, 27,* 841–868.

Shepherd, M., Schoenberg, M., Slavich, S., Wituk, S., Warren, M., & Meissen, G. (1999). Continuum of professional involvement in self-help groups. *The Journal of Community Psychology, 27,* 39–53.

Sommer, R. (1990). Family advocacy and the mental health system: The recent rise of the alliance for the mentally ill. *Psychiatric Quarterly, 61,* 205–221.

Sommer, R., Williams, P., & Williams, W. A. (1984). Self-survey of family organizations. *Psychiatric Quarterly, 56,* 276–285.

Tebes, J. K., & Kraemer, D. T. (1991). Quantitative and qualitative knowing in mutual support research: Some lessons from the recent history of scientific psychology. *American Journal of Community Psychology, 19,* 739–756.

Toseland, R. W., Rossiter, C. M., & Labrecque, M. S. (1989). The effectiveness of two kinds of support groups for caregivers. *Social Service Review, September,* 415–432.

Vygotsky L. S. (1978). *Mind in society.* Cambridge, MA: Harvard University Press.

Watson, C. G., Hancock, M., Gearhart, L. P., Mendez, C. M., Malovrh, P., & Raden, M. (1997). A comparative outcome study of frequent, moderate, occasional, and non-attenders of Alcoholics Anonymous. *Journal of Clinical Psychology, 53,* 209–214.

Wechsler, H. (1994). The self-help organization in the mental health field: Recovery, Inc., a case study. In T. J. Powell (Ed.), *Understanding the self-help organization: Frameworks and findings* (pp. 187–212). Thousand Oaks, CA: Sage.

White, B. J., & Madara, E. J. (2002). *The self-help group sourcebook* (7th ed.). Cedar Knolls, NJ: American Self-Help Group Clearinghouse.

Wituk, S., Shepherd, M., Warren, M. L., & Meissen, G. J. (2002). Factors contributing to the survival of self-help groups. *American Journal of Community Psychology, 30,* 349–366.

Zimmerman, M. A., Reischl, T. M., Seidman, E., Rappaport, J., Toro, P. A., & Salem, D. A. (1991). Expansion strategies of a mutual help organization. *American Journal of Community Psychology, 19,* 251–278.

CHAPTER THIRTY-ONE

HOSPITAL TREATMENT OF ADOLESCENTS

Daniel F. Becker, M.D., and Mark DeAntonio, M.D.

T he treatment of adolescents in the most intensive, or acute, levels of care is diverse in its specific forms and theoretical approaches. This partly reflects the historical development of these modalities, and partly reflects economic necessity. Although, for a variety of reasons, clinicians hope to minimize the use of the most restrictive forms of treatment, such interventions are likely to be necessary in the cases of severest pathology, or when socioenvironmental supports are failing. In this chapter, we will review the inpatient treatment of adolescents, briefly considering partial hospitalization and residential treatment, for comparison. Although the hospital-level treatment of adolescents is likely never to be as common as it was a couple of decades ago, there is little doubt that it will continue to play a key role in the armamentarium of the adolescent psychiatrist.

Rationale for Treatment

The rationale for the inpatient treatment of adolescents has evolved considerably over the last three-quarters of a century. Historically, the psychiatric hospitalization of minors began in the United States during the 1920s. These early treatment facilities were primarily pediatric neurology units, serving a custodial function for post-encephalitic children. By mid-century, more sophisticated understandings of child psychopathology and psychotherapeutic intervention led to the increased involvement of child psychiatrists on inpatient psychiatric units. The mid-twentieth century also saw important developments in the orientation of residential programs for children and adolescents. Such programs—developing, over two centuries, from a tradition of orphanages, training schools, and detention centers—gradually shifted their focus to psychotherapeutic approaches (Jemerin & Philips, 1988). By the 1960s, inpatient psychiatric units and residential treatment centers provided similar treatment, except for the former's tendencies toward a shorter length of stay and toward more of a medical/nursing orientation. Also during the 1960s, a variety of legislative changes resulted in the origins of partial hospitalization for children and adolescents.

In the 1970s, societal trends favored reintegration of adolescents into families and communities, leading to a move away from residential treatment and toward inpatient treatment. This shift was also supported by burgeoning advances in child and adolescent psychopathology, and improved understandings of the biological underpinnings of psychiatric disorders (Jemerin & Philips, 1988). As a result, pharmacotherapy—and a medical approach—tended to be favored over the predominantly sociotherapeutic approaches used in residential settings. These changes led to a willingness of third-party payers to fund the hospital treatment of adolescents—and a dramatic rise in inpatient utilization during the 1970s and 1980s (Geraty, 1989; Strauss, Chassin, & Lock, 1995). The magnitude of the resulting costs led to a re-evaluation of adolescent hospitalization patterns by the end of the 1980s (Borchardt & Garfinkel, 1991). During the 1990s, well-established managed care techniques sought to reduce lengths of stay and to limit the clinical situations that would lead to inpatient care (Masters, 1997; Nurcombe, 1989).

Also beginning in the 1990s, and partly due to these managed care pressures, partial hospitalization was used much more frequently Although partial hospital programs had been in existence for two to three decades, they had largely been under-used until economic pressures lessened frequent or prolonged inpatient stays (Leibenluft & Leibenluft, 1988). These partial hospital programs were often seen as an alternative to inpatient hospitalization, or as a means of reducing inpatient lengths of stay by providing intensive outpatient treatment after the inpatient phase (Grizenko, 1997; Grizenko, Papineau, Sayegh, 1993; Hoge, Farrell, Munchel, & Strauss, 1988; Kiser, Culhane, & Hadley, 1995).

At present, the more intensive levels of care—such as inpatient treatment—are seen as components of a broader system of care. They are viewed less as definitive treatment interventions, than as interventions that serve specific, time-limited functions during the overall course of treatment. Specifically, hospitalization provides emergent management during times of psychiatric decompensation or environmental crisis. In the presence of significant danger to self or other, there is no other alternative for intensive evaluation and sufficient safety. Overall, the goal of such treatment is to move patients into the least restrictive settings that their symptoms will tolerate—thus affording them maximum integration into, and benefit from, their family environments, educational settings, and communities (Bickman, Foster, & Lambert, 1996; Foster, 1998; Leon, Uziel-Miller, Lyons, & Tracy, 1999; Masters, 1997; Nurcombe, 1989).

Mechanisms of Efficacy

The key component of the intensive treatment of adolescents—whether it is at the inpatient, residential, or partial hospital level—is containment, or additional external structure. Patients admitted to these care levels require added support—often due to the loss, through psychiatric decompensation, of internal, psychological structures—but also due to the deterioration of community and family structures. In this latter instance, the inpatient or residential setting can provide a short- or longer-term respite from stressful, or otherwise undesirable, environmental influences. In the novel environment—especially within the context of more protracted treatment programs, such as residential or partial hospital care—patients will have the opportunity to develop new relationships and new social competencies. These relatively non-specific milieu factors—the respite from environmental stressors and the opportunity to develop new competencies—underlie all hospital-level programs. In a related vein, the containment of the hospital or residential setting provides a much higher level of safety with respect to suicidality, aggression, and a wide variety of destructive behaviors. Also, the acute treatment setting allows for a more detailed evaluation than is typically possible in a less intensive setting. The data developed by the thorough multidisciplinary assessment can often lead to improved treatment specificity. Finally, the multi-modal approach of hospital-level programs allows for a broad series of therapeutic trials—pharmacologic and psychosocial—which can be conducted reasonably efficiently, given the opportunity for frequent observations of treatment efficacy by a wide range of clinical staff. Once the acute psychiatric symptomatology has abated—or when the environmental stressors that contributed to the crisis have been resolved—the results of these therapeutic trials can be utilized to develop an aftercare plan that may sustain the patient's clinical progress in a less intensive setting, and in a manner that provides for the individual's gradual reintegration into the family and community.

Developmental Considerations

Hospital-level treatment is relatively common in the adolescent age group, due to the relatively frequent onset of significant psychopathology during this developmental period, coupled with adolescents' lack of internal control structures and a frequent inability of parents or other guardians to exert effective external controls on their behalf (Pottick, Hansell, Gutterman, & White, 1995).

Although, historically, the hospital treatment of adolescents often occurred on units with patients of mixed ages—that is, along with either adults or younger children, program administrators in recent decades have tended to treat adolescents on specialized units designed for individuals of this developmental stage. In addition to the safety considerations, specialized adolescent units are likely to provide better treatment due to their ability to offer age-specific groups and therapeutic activities. Even so, it is often the case that patients at the younger end of the adolescent range will have treatment and developmental needs that diverge from those of their later-adolescent peers. When the developmental phases of the unit population are noticeably varied, clinical staff must take particular care to individualize patients' treatment plans. A negative group process can sometimes emerge when groups of delinquent or substance-abusing or even eating-disordered youth are sequestered without appropriate supervision. (See Erickson & Palmer, this volume.)

In general, adolescent units will need to provide more opportunity for physical activity than may be required on a similar unit for adults. Also, an active family treatment program is essential to the psychiatric care of this age group. Multi-family groups can be enormously valuable in helping family members cope with their child's illness. (See Chapters 29 and 30, in this book.) Because of the high level of experimentation with drugs and alcohol among adolescents, and the attendant risks associated with psychiatric comorbidity, most adolescent inpatient programs may benefit from a substance abuse education and treatment component (Tarter et al., 1999). We have found that this should be available to all patients and their families, not simply to those with identified comorbid substance-use disorders. This component is especially relevant to this age group, given adolescents' tendency to experiment with novel behaviors and their susceptibility to peer influences. Care should be used in applying the appropriate diagnostic criteria for substance-use disorders in this age group, because use does not equal abuse, and a "dependence" diagnosis can follow youths a long way, and even deter them from some placements (such as group homes, foster care). Conversely, given the high risk these youths face (Mattanah, Becker, Levy, Edell, & McGlashan, 1995), we would suggest that the absence of a substance use disorder in an adolescent at a given point in time does not render an individual immune from such difficulties in the future. Finally, nursing staff on an adolescent treatment unit must be particularly vigilant with respect to a variety of impulsive behaviors—ranging from self-mutilation to vandalism to sexual activity. For example, nursing rounds may be required more frequently than they may be on a similar adult unit—and "close observation" or "one-to-one" staffing may be used more often.

Overall Approach to Treatment: Targets and Empirical Support

As indicated, hospital-level treatment for adolescent patients aims at a range of developmental, symptomatic, behavioral, functional, and environmental factors. Priorities for intervention will vary from individual to individual, and will be determined through the evaluation process. In this section, we will outline the process of hospital-level treatment, indicating how potential targets of intervention are chosen, and indicating—wherever possible—the research literature that may support these specific treatment approaches.

Admission Criteria

Admission criteria to inpatient settings have become relatively well defined. Such definitions have come from third party payers (within the context of some of the managed care pressures mentioned above), from individual treatment facilities, and from various professional organizations—including the American Academy of Child and Adolescent Psychiatry (1987). In general, adolescent patients admitted to an inpatient unit must suffer from a psychiatric disorder as defined in the *Diagnostic and Statistical Manual* (DSM-IV) (American Psychiatric Association, 1994), and—as a result of this disorder—must be at imminent risk of harm to self or others, or must be gravely disabled (Dicker et al., 1997; Goldston et al., 1998; King, Hovey, Brand, & Ghaziuddin, 1997; Strauss et al., 1995). In addition, patients may be considered for inpatient admission if they are experiencing medical complications arising from a psychiatric disorder. The rationale for hospitalization should be explained to the adolescent, as well as to the parent or guardian. Although involuntary hospitalization is often necessary, every effort should be made to negotiate with the patient and family for a voluntary inpatient stay.

The admission criteria for partial hospital programs and residential treatment programs have not been so well defined. Again, most professionals would agree that a DSM-defined psychiatric disorder must be diagnosed, and that this disorder must be sufficiently severe to impair social or academic functioning. Patients are specifically admitted to residential settings because of the inadequacy of the home environment to maintain safety and to allow for reasonable treatment progress in an outpatient setting. Patients admitted to partial hospital programs, on the other hand, are often minimally able to be maintained in their home and community environments, but cannot do so safely or consistently without the added support and structure of the partial hospital. Although individual programs tend to have clear admission criteria, these vary from program to program based on the patient population served, the resources of the program, and the theoretical orientation of the program staff. As noted above, residential treatment facilities tend to be required when the adolescent's environment fails to contain him safely, and in a manner that allows for ongoing outpatient treatment. Partial hospital programs tend to be employed when an attempt is being made to avert an inpatient hospitalization—or, alternatively, as a means of facilitating transition from inpatient to outpatient care. Again, the underlying principle is that adolescents should be placed in the least restrictive environment that allows for their safety and for reasonable therapeutic progress (Bickman et al., 1996; Zimet, Farley, & Zimet, 1994).

Evaluation and Treatment Planning

All psychiatric patients will benefit from an assessment that is as thorough as possible. Due to the severity of their conditions, patients admitted to hospital-based levels of care require a comprehensive, multidisciplinary assessment, leading to a clear DSM diagnosis and a biopsychosocial formulation (Jemerin & Philips, 1988; Nurcombe, 1989)—and, finally, resulting in a detailed treatment plan, including a discharge plan.

For most adolescents admitted to a hospital facility, the non-psychiatric medical findings—including neurological and laboratory evaluations—do not contribute significantly to the diagnosis, formulation, or overall treatment plan (Ricciuti, Morton, Behar, & Delaney, 1987). Nonetheless, a significant minority of such patients do have neurological or other non-psychiatric medical findings that require attention (Woolston & Riddle, 1990). Urine toxicology screening may be helpful to the diagnostic process, but in and of itself does not diagnose substance use disorder given the high rates of use in this population. Moreover, the increasing frequency of pharmacologic intervention—along with the heightened complexity of medication combinations—necessitates some routine screening of hematological, hepatic, renal, thyroid, and perhaps cardiac functions, which will vary somewhat according to the particular medications prescribed. In addition, serum medication levels may be helpful, or necessary. It is important, in female patients, to determine pregnancy status before proceeding with pharmacotherapeutic intervention. Although a routine physical examination should be performed on all patients admitted to a hospital, discretion should be used in proceeding with pelvic or rectal examinations. In adolescents, such examinations should generally be performed only when specific complaints or behaviors necessitate them—or when sexual abuse is a concern. In the latter case, the examination should be done by a clinician specifically trained in sexual abuse examinations of adolescents. Other specific physical or laboratory examinations may be performed when they are necessitated by the medical history, the clinical presentation, or the proposed treatment plan.

Central to the psychiatric evaluation is the clinical interview. Most adolescent patients will be able to provide some account of the evolution of their symptoms and functional problems. As with any medical interview, the psychiatrist inquires about the frequency, intensity, duration, and circumstances of symptoms. Also, the clinician is interested in the ways in which symptoms may impair social and academic functioning. In addition to these functional deficits, it is equally important to gain an understanding of the patient's strengths and areas of positive adjustment. Also, support systems—as well as any environmental instability (Mundy, Robertson, Greenblatt, & Robertson, 1989)—should be noted. Finally, an account of the precipitating events, or recent stressors, is key (Kowitt et al., 1989). Using the direct interview of the patient, interview of the parents or caregivers, medical records, and consultation with outpatient clinicians and primary care providers, the psychiatrist forms an understanding of the course of the individual's development, and of the interplay between psychopathology and development throughout childhood and adolescence. Within the context of the clinical interview, the psychiatrist also performs a mental status examination, including formal testing of cognitive functions. Although standardized interviews and rating scales are indispensable to clinical research, they generally have limited usefulness in routine clinical evaluation. That being said, some scales can be quite helpful in establishing a pre-treatment baseline of symptom severity—or in tracking progress in response, for instance, to a psychopharmacologic agent. Psychological testing—both cognitive and projective—can also be useful in specific circumstances; however, such assessments are not generally necessary in the routine evaluation of inpatients.

All adolescent patients should have a family assessment—including an evaluation of family communication patterns, methods of conflict resolution, and ability to provide support to the identified patient. Educational assessment should be performed when academic functioning is impaired, or when psychiatric symptoms are manifested, especially in relation to the school setting (Woolston, 1989). In addition to the assessment of school functioning, a broader functional assessment is often helpful; as mentioned above, this evaluation should identify areas of strength as well as deficit.

One advantage of the hospital treatment setting is the richness of the multidisciplinary treatment team (American Psychiatric Association, 1994). In order to capitalize on this breadth of clinical knowledge and experience, it is best that the findings from the various discipline-specific assessments are shared in multidisciplinary treatment team meetings (Margo & Manring, 1989). The result of this process should be a clear DSM-based diagnosis, a developmentally focused biopsychosocial formulation (American Academy of Child and Adolescent Psychiatry, 1995; Harper, 1989), and a treatment plan leading to an aftercare plan.

The treatment plan should address the problems that led to the hospital admission as well as any additional problems that may have been noted during the course of the initial evaluation. These problems may be symptoms, behaviors, or environmental difficulties. The treatment plan may be expressed in terms of one or more specific treatment goals (Harper, 1989; Nurcombe, 1989). The patient and the family should be made aware of the treatment plan—and, optimally, they should participate actively in formulating the problem list and goals of treatment (Harper, 1989; Woolston, 1989). Just as the multidisciplinary treatment team must collaborate during the assessment phase, ongoing multidisciplinary teamwork is needed in constructing the treatment plan and goals.

The discharge plan is an important element of the overall treatment plan—not only to ensure an appropriately short length of stay, but primarily in order to ensure appropriate aftercare and continuity between acute care and outpatient or community functioning (Foster, 1998; King et al., 1997; Pfeiffer & Strzelecki, 1990). The discharge plan should be formulated in an approximate form at the time that the initial treatment plan is constructed, and should be complete, in every detail, a day or so prior to discharge. These details should include psychiatric follow-up, any adjunctive therapies (such as family therapy), living arrangements, school arrangements, transportation arrangements when necessary, and so forth. If the outpatient psychiatrist is different than the inpatient psychiatrist, direct verbal communication is the best way to ensure clinical continuity between levels of care.

Therapeutic Modalities

Any patient who requires hospital-level treatment is likely to have psychopathology severe enough, or complex enough, to warrant a multiplicity of treatment interventions. Given the powerful pharmacologic options currently available, all adolescents admitted to an acute level of care should be evaluated for pharmacotherapy. Recent decades have brought a revolution in child and adolescent psychopharmacotherapy. The hospital, residential, or partial hospital setting provides an excellent opportunity for patients' symptoms and behaviors to be observed by various staff members during a wide range of activities and interpersonal situations. Such intensive observation allows for a more refined diagnosis, as well as for careful monitoring of response to pharmacologic intervention. The rationale for pharmacotherapy should be explained to the adolescent as well as to parents or guardians, and—except in emergency situations—the psychiatrist should obtain assent from the adolescent, as well as consent from the responsible adult. For a variety of developmental reasons, adolescents are often especially hesitant to accept medication; therefore, considerable time must often be spent by medical and nursing staff to educate the patient and to support her in this form of treatment.

Individual psychotherapy is a key feature of most hospital treatment programs (Margo & Manring, 1989). Although the specific form of individual psychotherapy offered may be dictated by the theoretical orientation of the therapist, it is preferable for the therapeutic approach to be determined by the capacities and therapeutic needs of the patient. These capacities and needs may, of course, change over time. For example, patients who initially benefit most from a supportive or cognitive behavioral approach may later benefit most from insight-oriented or psychodynamic therapy.

Family therapy is an essential aspect of the treatment of the adolescent within an institutional setting. The therapeutic approach to the family will be determined by the family assessment, and by the capacities and needs of the family determined therein. In some instances, interventions aimed at dysfunctional family dynamics may lead to a significant improvement in the patient's living environment. At the very least, family members can be educated about the patient's illness, and can be recruited as supporters or facilitators of the overall treatment plan (Woolston, 1989).

Group psychotherapy is a particularly powerful tool in the treatment of adolescents. This therapeutic approach is helpful for addressing social and interpersonal issues in patients of all ages, but adolescent patients appear to be particularly helped by interactions with peers. Also, groups containing peers and therapy staff will often reflect the family dynamics of the individual patient participants. These issues can be discussed in group, and can also be carried back to family therapy for further work. Occupational therapy and recreational therapy groups are helpful in improving adaptive functioning. Also, it is easier for some patients to work on interpersonal and social issues within the context of a physical activity, as opposed to a verbal context.

Coordination with the educational system is another critical aspect of treating adolescents within a hospital setting (Woolston, 1989). In longer-stay inpatient settings and in residential centers, an educational program is often provided within the overall program. In short-stay hospital units, treatment staff may coordinate with teachers from the community-based school. Partial hospital programs may be designed to include a school program—or they may dovetail with separate school programming. Whichever approach is used, education is a fundamental developmental task for adolescents, and this aspect of the patient's life must be included within the overall treatment plan.

Finally, milieu therapy plays a central role in any hospital treatment program (Steiner, Haldipur, & Stack, 1982; Steiner, Marx, & Walton, 1991). Its theoretical approach may be psychodynamic, deriving from large-group analytic principles (Weiner & Lewis, 1984). Alternatively, it may be more behavioral—possibly incorporating aspects of a "token economy." Optimally, the sociotherapy staff will tailor their approach to the needs of the overall group of patients—and to the needs of the individual adolescents as well. Goals of milieu therapy are similar to those addressed in group therapy—including interpersonal and social problem-solving (Russakoff & Oldham, 1982).

Safety is a primary concern. In general, the safety of patients and staff can be ensured through interpersonal and behavioral techniques—and by addressing patients' developmental needs, deficient cognitive skills, and poor internalized controls (Kalogjera, Bedi, Watson, & Meyer, 1989; Rosen & Walsh, 1989; Vivona et al., 1995). On occasion, seclusion and/or physical restraint may also be necessary to prevent violent or self-destructive action (Antoinette, Iyengar, & Puig-Antich, 1990; Garrison et al., 1990; Millstein & Cotton, 1990). There is some evidence that the appropriate use of these interventions can reduce hospital lengths of stay, and that it can also improve the process of engaging patients in treatment (Troutman, Myers, Borchardt, Kowalski, & Bubrick, 1998). In considering the use of seclusion or restraints, it is important to be sure that other, less restrictive alternatives have already been attempted (Joshi, Capozzoli, & Coyle, 1988)—and, once seclusion or restraint has been initiated, it should be continued for as short a time as is necessary.

Discussion and Future Directions

The application of intensive treatments—including inpatient, residential, and partial hospital programs—for adolescents has evolved considerably over the past several decades. Although such interventions are generally used less now than previously, they are indispensable tools in the treatment of severely ill patients. While it is hoped that adolescent psychiatrists will continue to develop pharmacologic and psychosocial techniques that will reduce the need for hospital-level care, it is nonetheless likely that hospital treatment will always be a necessary part of the therapeutic repertory. Hospital-based treatments afford a unique opportunity to maintain patients' safety while performing a thorough evaluation, and while applying a series of therapeutic trials—pharmacologic, as well as psychosocial. Although alternative approaches—such as intensive outpatient management—do exist, patients with the severest pathology and the severest of environmental stressors will likely always require treatment within a contained setting. In the best of circumstances, this type of treatment resolves symptomatic crises and sets the course for a successful outpatient treatment plan.

While pharmacologic interventions can play an important role in acute care, psychological and sociotherapeutic interventions are equally important (Malone et al., 1997). For this reason, child and adolescent psychiatry training programs must continue to develop skills in psychosocial intervention that match the developing physician's abilities in the biological therapies. It is only through such a breadth of clinical skill that child and adolescent psychiatrists will be fully capable of functioning within, managing, and developing the hospital-based programs of tomorrow.

References

American Academy of Child and Adolescent Psychiatry. (1995). Practice parameters for the psychiatric assessment of children and adolescents. *Journal of the American Academy of Child and Adolescent Psychiatry, 34,* 1386–1402.

American Psychiatric Association. (1994). Guidelines for psychiatric practice in public sector psychiatric inpatient facilities. *American Journal of Psychiatry, 151,* 797–798.

Antoinette, T., Iyengar, S., & Puig-Antich, J. (1990). Is locked seclusion necessary for children under the age of 14? *American Journal of Psychiatry, 147,* 1283–1289.

Bickman, L., Foster, E. M., & Lambert, E. W. (1996). Who gets hospitalized in a continuum of care? *Journal of the American Academy of Child and Adolescent Psychiatry, 35,* 74–80.

Borchardt, C. M., & Garfinkel, B. D. (1991). Predictors of length of stay of psychiatric adolescent inpatients. *Journal of the American Academy of Child and Adolescent Psychiatry, 30,* 994–998.

Child and adolescent psychiatric illness: Guidelines for treatment resources, quality assurance, peer review and reimbursement. (1987). Washington, DC: American Academy of Child and Adolescent Psychiatry.

Diagnostic and statistical manual of mental disorders (4th ed.). (1994). Washington, DC: American Psychiatric Association.

Dicker, R., Morrissey, R. F., Abikoff, H., Alvir, J.M.J., Weissman, K., Grover, J., et al. (1997). Hospitalizing the suicidal adolescent: Decision-making criteria of psychiatric residents. *Journal of the American Academy of Child and Adolescent Psychiatry, 36,* 769–776.

Foster, E. M. (1998). Does the continuum of care improve the timing of follow-up services? *Journal of the American Academy of Child and Adolescent Psychiatry, 37,* 805–814.

Garrison, W. T., Ecker, B., Friedman, M., Davidoff, R., Haeberle, K., & Wagner, M. (1990). Aggression and counteraggression during child psychiatric hospitalization. *Journal of the American Academy of Child and Adolescent Psychiatry, 29,* 242–250.

Geraty, R. (1989). Administrative issues in inpatient child and adolescent psychiatry. *Journal of the American Academy of Child and Adolescent Psychiatry, 28,* 21–25.

Goldston, D. B., Daniel, S. S., Reboussin, B. A., Reboussin, D. M., Kelley, A. E., & Frazier, P. H. (1998). Psychiatric diagnoses of previous suicide attempters, first-time attempters, and repeat attempters on an adolescent inpatient psychiatry unit. *Journal of the American Academy of Child and Adolescent Psychiatry, 37,* 924–932.

Grizenko, N. (1997). Outcome of multimodal day treatment for children with severe behavior problems: A five-year follow-up. *Journal of the American Academy of Child and Adolescent Psychiatry, 36,* 989–997.

Grizenko, N., Papineau, D., & Sayegh, L. (1993). Effectiveness of a multimodal day treatment program for children with disruptive behavior problems. *Journal of the American Academy of Child and Adolescent Psychiatry, 32,* 127–134.

Harper, G. (1989). Focal inpatient treatment planning. *Journal of the American Academy of Child and Adolescent Psychiatry, 28,* 31–37.

Hoge, M. A., Farrell, S. P., Munchel, M. E., & Strauss, J. S. (1988). Therapeutic factors in partial hospitalization. *Psychiatry, 51,* 199–210.

Jemerin, J. M., & Philips, I. (1988). Changes in inpatient child psychiatry: Consequences and recommendations. *Journal of the American Academy of Child and Adolescent Psychiatry, 27,* 397–403.

Joshi, P. T., Capozzoli, J. A., & Coyle, J. T. (1988). Use of a quiet room on an inpatient unit. *Journal of the American Academy of Child and Adolescent Psychiatry, 27,* 642–644.

Kalogjera, I. J., Bedi, A., Watson, W. N., & Meyer, A. D. (1989). Impact of therapeutic management on use of seclusion and restraint with disruptive adolescent inpatients. *Hospital and Community Psychiatry, 40,* 280–285.

King, C. A., Hovey, J. D., Brand, E., & Ghaziuddin, N. (1997). Prediction of positive outcomes for adolescent psychiatric inpatients. *Journal of the American Academy of Child and Adolescent Psychiatry, 36,* 1434–1442.

Kiser, L. J., Culhane, D. P., & Hadley, T. R. (1995). The current practice of child and adolescent partial hospitalization: Results of a national survey. *Journal of the American Academy of Child and Adolescent Psychiatry, 34,* 1336–1342.

Kowitt, M. P., Sachs, J. S., Lowe, M. G., Schuller, R. B., Rubel, M., & Ellis, D. M. (1989). Predicting discharge and follow-up status of hospitalized adolescents. *Hospital and Community Psychiatry, 40,* 724–731.

Leibenluft, E., & Leibenluft, R. F. (1998). Reimbursement for partial hospitalization: A survey and policy implications. *American Journal of Psychiatry, 145,* 1514–1520.

Leon, S. C., Uziel-Miller, N. D., Lyons, J. S., & Tracy, P. (1999). Psychiatric hospital service utilization of children and adolescents in state custody. *Journal of the American Academy of Child and Adolescent Psychiatry, 38,* 305–310.

Malone, R. P., Luebbert, J. F., Delaney, M. A., Biesecker, K. A., Blaney, B. L., Rowan, A. B., et al. (1997). Nonpharmacological response in hospitalized children with conduct disorder. *Journal of the American Academy of Child and Adolescent Psychiatry, 36,* 242–247.

Margo, G. M., & Manring, J. M. (1989). The current literature on inpatient psychotherapy. *Hospital and Community Psychiatry, 40,* 909–915.

Masters, K. J. (1997). Using a coordinated treatment system to minimize child psychiatric hospitalization. *Journal of the American Academy of Child and Adolescent Psychiatry, 36,* 566–568.

Mattanah, J. J. F., Becker, D. F., Levy, K. N., Edell, W. S., & McGlashan, T. H. (1995). Diagnostic stability in adolescents followed up 2 years after hospitalization. *American Journal of Psychiatry, 152,* 889–894.

Millstein, K. H., & Cotton, N. S. (1990). Predictors of the use of seclusion on an inpatient child psychiatric unit. *Journal of the American Academy of Child and Adolescent Psychiatry, 29,* 256–264.

Mundy, P., Robertson, J., Greenblatt, M., & Robertson, M. (1989). Residential instability in adolescent inpatients. *Journal of the American Academy of Child and Adolescent Psychiatry, 28,* 176–181.

Nurcombe, B. (1989). Goal-directed treatment planning and the principles of brief hospitalization. *Journal of the American Academy of Child and Adolescent Psychiatry, 28,* 26–30.

Pfeiffer, S. I., & Strzelecki, S. C. (1990). Inpatient psychiatric treatment of children and adolescents: A review of outcome studies. *Journal of the American Academy of Child and Adolescent Psychiatry, 29,* 84–853.

Pottick, K., Hansell, S., Gutterman, E., & White, H. R. (1995). Factors associated with inpatient and outpatient treatment for children and adolescents with serious mental illness. *Journal of the American Academy of Child and Adolescent Psychiatry, 34,* 425–433.

Ricciuti, A., Morton, R., Behar, D., & Delaney, M. A. (1987). Medical findings in child psychiatric inpatients. *Journal of the American Academy of Child and Adolescent Psychiatry, 26,* 554–555.

Rosen, P. M., & Walsh, B. W. (1989). Patterns of contagion in self-mutilation epidemics. *American Journal of Psychiatry, 146,* 656–658.

Russakoff, L. M., & Oldham, J. M. (1982). The structure and technique of community meetings: The short-term unit. *Psychiatry, 45,* 38–44.

Steiner, H., Haldipur, C. V., & Stack, L. C. (1982). The acute admission ward as a therapeutic community. *American Journal of Psychiatry, 139,* 897–901.

Steiner, H., Marx, L., & Walton, C. (1991). The ward atmosphere of a child psychosomatic unit: A ten-year follow-up. *General Hospital Psychiatry, 13,* 246–252.

Strauss, G., Chassin, M., & Lock, J. (1995). Can experts agree when to hospitalize adolescents? *Journal of the American Academy of Child and Adolescent Psychiatry, 34,* 418–424.

Tarter, R., Vanyukov, M., Giancoila, P., Dawes, M., Blackson, T., Mezzich, A., et al. (1999). Etiology of early age onset substance use disorder: A maturational perspective. *Development and Psychopathology, 11,* 657–683.

Troutman, B., Myers, K., Borchardt, C., Kowalski, R., & Bubrick, J. (1998). When restraints are the least restrictive alternative for managing aggression. *Journal of the American Academy of Child and Adolescent Psychiatry, 37,* 554–558.

Vivona, J. M., Ecker, B., Halgin, R. P., Cates, D., Garrison, W. T., & Friedman, M. (1995). Self- and other-directed aggression in child and adolescent psychiatric inpatients. *Journal of the American Academy of Child and Adolescent Psychiatry, 34,* 434–444.

Weiner, J. A., & Lewis, L. (1984). Interpretive psychotherapy in the inpatient community meeting. *Psychiatry, 47,* 333–341.

Woolston, J. L. (1989). Transactional risk model for short and intermediate term psychiatric inpatient treatment of children. *Journal of the American Academy of Child and Adolescent Psychiatry, 28,* 38–41.

Woolston, J. L., & Riddle, M. A. (1990). The role of advanced technology in inpatient child psychiatry: Leading edge or useful aid? *Journal of the American Academy of Child and Adolescent Psychiatry, 29,* 905–908.

Zimet, S. G., Farley, G. K., & Zimet, G. D. (1994). Home behaviors of children in three treatment settings: An outpatient clinic, a day hospital, and an inpatient hospital. *Journal of the American Academy of Child and Adolescent Psychiatry, 33,* 56–59.

CHAPTER THIRTY-TWO

SCHOOL CONSULTATION AND INTERVENTION

Shashank V. Joshi, M.D.

Children and teens spend much of their lifetime in school settings, and schools are the major providers of mental health services for children (Hoagwood & Erwin, 1997), providing more than 75% of the care. (Bums et al., 1995; Costello et al., 1996). However, this seems to be more by default than by design, as the majority of school-based interventions have not been empirically tested (Hoagwood & Erwin, 1997). School-based mental health services are a logical choice to reach certain pediatric populations, especially socioeconomically disadvantaged children and teens, because these youngsters often have limited access to medical care. Furthermore, they may be at highest risk for certain disorders, and may need to be served via an alternative to the traditional clinic model.

History of School Consultation

Direct service and consultation models have been in existence for over 100 years. In 1898, the Chicago School Board initiated one of the first "school-labs" with its Saturday psycho-physical laboratories located in the District's central office.

Sincere thanks to Shalini Joshi, M.S., Lic. S.W., for her assistance in preparing and reviewing this manuscript.

Twenty such clinics were known to be running by 1914 (French, 1990). By 1930, the Pennsylvania Department of Education had developed a model for certifying school psychologists. Its primary purpose was to designate students who were candidates for special education. In general, psychological services at that time were focused on age-based cognitive assessments of the "abnormal" child (Fagan, 1992; Hoagwood & Erwin, 1997).

One of the first to outline a more consultation-oriented approach was Dr. Jules Coleman (1947). In his work on consulting to casework agencies (Coleman, 1947), he emphasized the importance of concentrating on the *why now* aspect of consultation. That is, rather than focusing on the student's problems as such, the consultant was to try and understand the reasons that a case worker would ask for consultation at a particular time. The task was to find out *how* one could be helpful, and *what feelings* need to be understood from the consultee (caseworker). Maddux expanded on this by concentrating on caseworkers' feelings of anxiety, anger, and hostility toward their supervisors, colleagues, and clients (Maddux, 1950). Gerald Caplan wrote extensively about the need to understand that consultee concerns stemmed from intrapsychic conflicts aroused by the problems that a particular client was asking about (Caplan, 1956, 1959, 1963). A consultant could best help the consultee by encouraging a focus on this self-understanding of their own issues, such that they could better help their clients. Irving Berlin expanded on this further, and recommended keeping in touch with consultees even after the initial consultation to emphasize a sense of continual support, validation, and interest on the part of the consultant (Berlin, 1956). Mattison (2000, 2001) has helped to reframe the Special Education setting as a sort of "Therapeutic Day School." His major recommendations will be outlined later in this chapter. Bostic and Rauch (1999) have outlined key aspects of getting started in school consultation psychiatry: gaining access to a school or district, building an alliance with both senior administration and teachers as well as more junior staff, protecting confidentiality, devising a framework to deal with consultee questions and concerns, and negotiating a payment structure. The psychiatrist's role is then to develop the three R's of school consultation: focus on *relationships* of the people allied around a particular pupil, foster the *recognition* of the dynamic forces (motivations and resistances) that may impede or advance a student's healthy progress in school or at home, and generate *responses* to problems (Bostic & Rauch, 1999).

This chapter will focus on some of the major models proposed by the above authors, and present specific case examples of how their specific principles may be applied. As this publication was going to press, the American Academy of Child and Adolescent Psychiatry was developing the *Practice Parameters for School Consultation,* scheduled for publication in early 2004, and readers are strongly encouraged to add this to the list of useful references at the end of this chapter.

Putative Mechanisms of Efficacy and Targets of Treatment

As others have noted, while some psychiatrists may think of themselves more as consultants than direct service providers, many blend their roles and function both as school psychiatrist, and as teacher or staff consultant (Bostic & Bagnell, 2004). The *school psychiatrist* or *school-based mental health practitioner* provides direct service to students (therapy and/or medication management) and to staff (direct treatment, support groups, professional development seminars). In this model, teachers and other staff focus more specifically on teaching, while leaving the mental health issues to the psychiatrist (Bostic & Bagnell, in press). However, as the psychiatrist usually has only a part-time school site presence (a few hours per week), he or she is often seen as having a "consultant role." The *school consultant* functions more as an advisor, nonjudgmental colleague, and professional with a sympathetic ear. Roles may include indirect services to pupils through direct contact (face-to-face, phone, or video) with teachers, school psychologists, guidance counselors, school aides, and more senior administrators (principals, directors of special education, or superintendents). Educational staff and school consultants report being most satisfied with their collaborative relationships when they view each other with mutual respect, and understand their respective roles and stressors well (Weist, Proescher, Prodente, Ambrose, & Waxman, 2001).

We will now outline some specific strategies that are used in working with schools. Six overall concepts are presented: Establishing a relationship with a school or district, identifying a framework for treatment and consultation, working specifically with students and educators in regular education settings (those with Section 504 plans), the approach to special education settings and personnel, suggested modifications and accommodations for youths with specific disorders, and a summary of our team's approach to consultation.

Establishing a Relationship with a School or District

One of the primary tasks for any consultant is to understand the needs of the consultee as well as possible. School personnel are often under great pressure to balance the tasks of teaching children how to think, how to socialize, how to learn appropriate academic, vocational, and life skills, and how to continuously meet expectations in the form of academic standards. Hence, it is important for the consultant to be familiar with general characteristics of a school: its population, priorities, strengths, and weaknesses. Months of relationship-building may need to occur before a school or district is ready to contract for services. General approaches include conducting needs assessments with teachers or school psychologists (where both quantitative and qualitative aspects are addressed). These may be done with teachers at the beginning of the school year, at the end of the year (with time during the summer to develop appropriate services, based on what the needs are), or more informally with senior administrators.

On the other hand, though many poorer school districts may desire consultant services, they may not be as able to pay as their better-funded counterparts in higher socioeconomic status (SES) districts. Ideas for funding such services are covered later in this chapter.

Setting a framework: The consultant needs to decide how she will approach cases. Consultee-centered approaches require a familiarity with the roles of various school personnel. Useful summaries have been delineated elsewhere. (See Bostic & Bagnell, in press.) We present an adapted version in Table 32.1.

TABLE 32.1. SCHOOL PERSONNEL.

Specific Personnel	Hours/day with Students	Number of Students	Years/Type of Training
Teachers*	6	20–35	Bachelor's degree, plus teacher certification Some have Master's degree
Special Education teachers*	6	Depends on number of classes in school and state-specific guidelines 6–28 pupils per teacher	Bachelor's degree, plus credentialing to provide instruction to those with special learning, emotional, or behavioral needs
School psychologists*	3–6	Usually 0.5–1 FTE psychologist for entire school (may be responsible for several hundred students at different schools within the same district) Poorer districts may have less than 0.25 FTE psychologist time for entire school	Master's degree, sometimes Doctoral degree
Guidance counselors*	6	Usually 1–2 counselors per grade Poorer districts may have only 0.25-1 FTE counselor for entire school	Master's degree
Classroom 1:1 aides	2–6	May be assigned to supervise 1–4 students in any particular school during a school day Often knows the pupil in question very well	May be in process of obtaining teacher credential High school degree or GED is sometimes a minimum requirement
*Resource specialists (Includes both staff and "RSP teachers" A.K.A. Special Education teachers)	2–6	Depends on number of classes in school 6–50 students per teacher These staff members may function as tutors, or may teach groups of students with similar learning difficulties in the special education setting	Bachelor's degree, plus credentialing to provide instruction to those with special learning, emotional, or behavioral needs May have earned Master's degree or certificate in Special Education

TABLE 32.1. (CONTINUED).

Specific Personnel	Hours/day with Students	Number of Students	Years/Type of Training
School adjustment specialists Social workers*	3–6	Depends on number of hours in school setting Often split time with other job setting Provide case management and/or psychosocial treatments to students and families	Master's degree, or special training
Psychology Social work MFT interns*	2–6	Usually 10–20 clients per school Provide individual and group therapy Often interested in learning empirically proven medication approaches and psychotherapies from psychiatric consultant	Bachelor's degree, in process of earning Master's degree
School nurses*	3–8	1 FTE RN or LVN per school, but could be 1 FTE for entire district Address acute health care needs of students, including administration of medications	Bachelor's degree Advanced Practice Nurse may have Master's degree (MSN) Includes Public Health Nurses, Nurse Practitioners (NP), Clinical Nurse Specialists (CNS)
Occupational therapists	3–6	0.25–1 FTE per district Often consults on contractual basis May run groups for teaching activities of daily living May design ergonomic modifications for schoolwork Work 1:1 to help students who have difficulty coping with sensory integration May design and run social skills groups and behavior modification plans, along with psychologist or intern	Advanced degree usually includes Master's degree
Speech therapists	36	0.25–1 FTE per school Help students with communication disorders and social skills problems	Master's degree

*denotes staff who often initiate consultation.

**All paraprofessionals hired after January 8, 2002 must have (1) completed two years of study at an institution of higher education, (2) obtained an associate's (or higher) degree, or (3) met a rigorous standard of quality and be able to demonstrate, through a formal state or local academic assessment, knowledge of and the ability to assist in instructing reading, writing, and mathematics (or, as appropriate, reading readiness, writing readiness, and mathematics readiness).

Vice Principals (one to two per middle or high school) are usually responsible for all aspects of disciplinary procedures and enforcement, and report to the Principal. The *Principal* is in charge of all services and personnel at each particular school site. The *Director of Special Education* of a district is in charge of all of the school psychologists and special education staff, and reports to the superintendent, as does the Principal. The *Superintendent,* in turn, is responsible for guiding all educational activities for a specific school district. He reports to an elected school board (public schools), or to an appointed school board (charter, private, or parochial schools) (Bostic & Bagnell, in press).

Recent authors (Bostic, 2004; Mattison, 1999) have promoted models that have been partly adapted for modern school contexts from Caplan's earlier work. Bostic's approach includes five components germane to each consultation:

Bostic's Five Components
1. Decide who the actual consultee is, and what the confidentiality parameters are.
2. Focus on the consultee question, and pay attention to what the needs and wishes of the consultee are.
3. How does this problem affect the system? (How does the system experience the problem?)
4. What are the legal and ethical factors to be considered?
5. What is the consultant's biopsychosocial understanding of the problem?

Further, this model promotes the building of alliances and sharing of information that can help school staff recognize, resolve, and in time (hopefully) prevent problems. The three goals of this model are

(1) Allying with the consultee through validation of her perceptions of the problem. Respect is created for all who are involved, and the anxiety around a particular case is pooled. The latter results in an *overall decrease in anxiety of the system,* as the more people who can share and understand the problem, the less anxious each member of the team will be.

(2) Clarification of consultee objectives.

(3) Mobilization of resources.

This third component involves much in the way of empowerment of school staff. For example, autonomy and self-esteem of the consultee can be enhanced by praise at efforts currently being made, and by trying to expand the consultee's skills as much as possible. Our team has found it helpful to additionally offer to get resources for the consultee which may not be available to those outside of a university system (for example, selected reference material from a campus library, or materials obtained online or from a conference that may be helpful in the classroom).

Staff can be further empowered when the consultant uses the consultee's own words to frame specific interventions. With this empowerment, teachers will feel that they are part of the solution and more invested in suggestions and interventions. Finally, we try to help consultees anticipate potential problems before they occur and to practice role-plays of sample interventions to decrease anxiety. All of these interventions serve to increase the options available in a consultee's "toolbox."

Developmental Influences on Consultation

The following section will review important developmental considerations in school consultation.

Preschool

For many parents, this period will be the first time they are entrusting the care of their most cherished possession to a group of total strangers. Young children may experience much uncertainty in the world outside of their homes and their parents' watchful eyes. Personality development is in its infancy, as are the skills required to master self-care and interactions within a group setting (Nelson, 2001). School psychiatry consultants must help the daycare or preschool staffs understand as much as possible about the developmental and emotional life of three- to five-year-olds, as well as in assisting the parents of these youngsters. Consultants can model interactions with parents of preschoolers, as well as provide brief seminars or workshops in temperament, attachment, separation-individuation, and impulse control, adapted for the education level of the audience. (Education levels of parents and staff may be quite different.) Staff development seminars on adult and parental development should also be considered (Nelson, 2001).

Elementary School

Clinicians will be most successful if they remain cognizant of the developmentally typical conflicts, anxieties, and behaviors of this age group (Shaw & Feldman, 1997). As with preschoolers, efforts must be made to educate staff regarding the importance of their roles as major adult figures in each child's life. During this school stage, the importance of attaining a sense of competence, effectiveness, and mastery in the Eriksonian sense ("industry versus inferiority") must be communicated to teachers and parents. If this stage develops successfully, so too will self-esteem. Parental relationships are especially crucial in this regard. Those who enjoy their child, are responsive to her needs, and are involved and interested in their child's achievements are most likely to promote and enhance healthy self-esteem development (Shaw & Feldman, 1997). Authoritative parenting (and teaching) styles, which feature frequent praise with warm and empathic (but consistent and firm) limit-setting, also foster self-worth and self-confidence. As these children grow into young adolescents, exciting cognitive, behavioral, and social-emotional changes take place. If major mood or behavior problems do occur, care must be taken to not attribute these simply to "raging hormones," as the majority of teens approach and enter puberty with relatively good functioning.

Middle School

Early (ages eleven to thirteen) and middle (fourteen to sixteen) adolescence are often identified as the periods of most intensive transition in cognitive, emotional, pubertal, and social domains. Although change, as a general theme, is the hallmark of the second decade of life, these six years in particular have generated a great deal of research interest within developmental psychology and psychopathology. (For an excellent discussion of the important themes of this age group for school consultants, see Feldman & Elliott, 1993 and Steiner & Feldman, 1996.) The young adolescent years are often filled with the greatest difficulty in adjustment for the *adults* involved in the early teen's life. Teachers and staff must resist becoming inadvertently "parentified." Developmental tasks for this age group include personality development, individuation from parents, and the establishment of peer groups and important relationships with members of the opposite sex (Conger, 1977).

High School

According to Kerr, within a high school setting the major goals of the consultant are to:

- Promote the students' well-being and safety in the context of their school setting and educational experience.
- Reduce problematic risk-taking behaviors so students can take full advantage of their school experiences (Kerr, 2001).

Further, she has described the essential features of the kind of caring high school community that can bring about the above results: The first component is developmental guidance, provided by all staff at the school. This is essentially how the school cares for all of its students, with the assistance of outside consultants. The second is how the school deals with those kids who might stumble along the way, or the "at-risk" population. The third component involves intervention. Examples include individual counseling and therapy, academic support for those in trouble, support groups, school mental health services, and staff support and professional development.

The final component involves crisis intervention for youths in acute need because of their own mental health issues, family problems, community events, threats of terrorism or other potential tragedy at the school. During these times, schools will likely seek help from the mental health community of psychiatrists, psychologists, family therapists, and social workers.

"Students receiving interventions are not merely at risk; they are in need . . ." (Kerr, 2001, p. 106)

Academic Modifications, Accommodations, and Service/Education Plans

When a child first presents with an academic or behavioral difficulty, the initial step is to gather the important school staff involved with the child and the parents, called a Student Support Team or Student Success Team (SST) meeting. It must be held within fifteen calendar days of the receipt of request by the school's SST site co-ordinator. It usually includes a teacher, counselor and/or psychologist, principal, parent, and outside professionals, such as a parent advocate or mental health consultant. If it is determined that the reason for difficulty is due to a *substantially limiting* mental or physical health disability, the student is eligible for services and/or special accommodations under Section 504 of the Rehabilitation Act of 1973. This federal statute stipulates that all schools that receive federal funding must provide an education to all children regardless of disability, in the *least restrictive setting.* A student with a disability is considered to be someone who has a physical or mental impairment that *substantially limits* one or more major life activities. The resultant intervention is an ISP, or Individualized Service Plan (A.K.A. 504 Plan), which specifies the types of accommodations that the school will provide. Because funding is not directly provided by the federal government, state and local districts vary widely on the degree to which they provide accommodations. Section 504 specifically excludes certain conditions from qualifying a student as disabled, including certain sexual disorders, gender identity disorders that do not result from a physical impairment, compulsive gambling, kleptomania, pyromania, and current psychoactive substance abuse disorders (Ravenswood City Unified School District Parent Handbook, 1996; Fullerton & Rollins, 1996). The Americans with Disabilities Act (ADA), 1990, applies the protections of Section 504 to public and private schools, but does not include parochial schools. If the ISP (504 plan) does not adequately address the student's educational needs, the next step is a referral to the local school district Committee on Special Education (CSE). Requests for an evaluation should be made in written form to the Director of the CSE for the specified district. Samples of letters can be found on the Parents Helping Parents Web site, www.php.com. The CSE has fifteen calendar days to respond in writing to the request, and to schedule an Individualized Education Plan (IEP) meeting. The parent must then sign an agreement to allow their child to be evaluated, and all assessments are to be completed within fifty calendar days of a signed assessment plan.

Bayer and Kaye (2002) have nicely summarized the major legal developments on special education that are relevant for school mental health practitioners. In the 1970s, several laws attempted to redress educational inequities for disabled children in the United States. Following the Rehabilitation Act of 1973, Congress passed the Education for All Handicapped Act, or PL 94-142, in 1975, which laid the groundwork for special education services. All persons aged six to twenty-one would be entitled to a *Free and Appropriate Education* (FAPE), regardless of handicapping condition. Furthermore, education must take place in the *Least Restrictive Environment,* whenever possible. This means that an otherwise qualified disabled student can be removed from the regular educational environment only if formalized classroom accommodations, supplementary aids, or other services fail to help educate the student satisfactorily (Fullerton & Rollins, 1996). A CSE is constituted in each school district to oversee an IEP for all students who qualify under this program because of a specific disability. (See Exhibit 32.1.) Later, the law was amended to apply to children as young as three (PL 99-457, 1986), and a Committee on Preschool Education would convene to develop an Individualized Family Service Plan (IFSP). Parents must participate with the components of the plan, must give informed consent, and have the right to due process whenever indicated. Re-evaluation of the IEP or IFSP must occur every year, and a full review (including retesting, if indicated) is required every three years ("triennial review"). In 1990, PL 94-142 was changed to emphasize the words "individual" over "education," and "disability" instead of "handicapped," and the IDEA ("Individuals with Disabilities Education Act"), PL 101-476, was born. Autism and traumatic brain injury were also added to the list of qualifying disabilities at that time, and ADHD and Tourette's disorder were added to the list in 1991. The latter two conditions may be classified under "Other Health Impaired," "Learning Disability," or "Emotional Disturbance," depending on the most debilitating symptoms. IDEA also required that IEP recommendations include "assistive technology" (alternative communication devices, occupational health assessments, and so on), "transition (to adulthood) services" (vocational training, rehabilitation, skills of daily living), and counseling where indicated. Finally, in 1997, IDEA was amended (PL 105-17, "IDEA 97") to include the following important additions: increased parent and student involvement in the IEP process, an emphasis on *inclusion* of special education students in the regular classroom setting, the need to plan for "transition services" beginning at age fourteen, focus on *positive behavioral strategies* in the classroom with a clear and consistent policy on discipline and consequences, and the option to wave retesting at the triennial review.

Note: An Individualized Program Plan (IPP) is similar to an IEP, applies to children and teens with developmental disabilities, and focuses on vocational and adaptive behavior strategies for those with cognitive limitations.

EXHIBIT 32.1. DETERMINING SPECIAL EDUCATION ELIGIBILITY.

(The categories listed below are general, and each state will have specific criteria to meet eligibility.)

1. DISABILITY CATEGORIES:

   Does the child have *one or more of the following types of disabilities* (documented by a psychiatric or medical evaluation/diagnosis, or educational/psychological testing)?

   ➢ Autism (AUT)
   ➢ Deafness (D)
   ➢ Deaf-Blindness (DB)
   ➢ Emotional Disturbance (ED)
   ➢ Hearing Impairment (HI)
   ➢ Mental Retardation (MR)
   ➢ Multiple Handicapped (MH)
   ➢ Other Health Impairment (OHI)
   ➢ Orthopedic Impairment (OI)
   ➢ Speech or Language Impaired (SLI)

      ○ Articulation Disorder
      ○ Fluency Disorder
      ○ Language Disorder
      ○ Voice Disorder

   ➢ Specific Learning Disability (SLD)
   ➢ Traumatic Brain Injury (TBI)
   ➢ Visual Impairment (VI)

   Note: Students with ADHD may receive IDEA services under SLD, OHI, or ED categories, depending on the clinical presentation and degree of impairment.

2. If one or more of the above disabilities is present, is the child *making effective progress in school?* If the student is being *re-evaluated* to determine if a disability is still affecting the child, would he/she continue to make progress in school without the currently provided special education services?

3. Is any lack of progress a *result of the child's disability?*

4. Does the child *require specially designed instruction in order to make effective progress in school* or does the child require related services in order to access the general curriculum?

Source: Adapted from Bostic and Bagnell, in press.

Mattison described the characteristics of 169 consultations performed during consultation to special education classrooms (Mattison, 2001). The vast majority of referred students were performing poorly academically. Questions from teachers included establishing a psychiatric diagnosis (56%); helping with classroom management strategies, especially for externalizing behaviors (51%); clarifying medication doses and need for medication (32%); recommending placement (31%); helping in understanding family issues (6%); and whether or not a child had a learning or language disorder (2%). Among diagnoses made, ADHD was the most common (79%), and 56% of the entire sample was classified as Learning Disabled. He recommends that the school consultant conceptualize the ED/SED (Emotionally Disturbed/Severe Emotional Disturbance) Classroom as a sort of "therapeutic day school," as these students tend to be the most psychiatrically ill among their peers in any community. Also, the graduation rate for SED students at about 40% provides further evidence for the need to have child psychiatrists in the milieu.

Tables 32.2 through 32.8 itemize some classroom-specific therapeutic techniques, based on recommendations from teachers and mental health experts.

Let us now turn to the work by various investigators that has shown empirical effectiveness. In a ten-year research review, Hoagwood and Erwin (1997) identified sixteen studies of school-based mental health services that met criteria for rigorously designed outcome studies (defined as use of random assignment to the intervention, inclusion of a control group, and use of standardized outcome measures). The three types of interventions that had the most empiric support were teacher consultation (TC), cognitive behavioral therapy (CBT), and social skills training. Positive outcomes were also associated with art therapy and relaxation training. TC intervention studies examined the effects of behavioral consultation on pre-referral (to special education placement) practices and reductions in problematic behaviors, and demonstrated positive results (Fuchs & Fuchs, 1989). Effective CBT approaches included those that focused on the prevention of affective disorders, the tertiary treatment of depression in the schools, and the prevention of drop-outs.

Clarke and associates (1995) examined 150 teens at risk for developing depressive disorders, who were randomly assigned to either a fifteen-session cognitive group prevention intervention or a control condition. Results strongly favored the prevention group, with affective disorder incidence rates of 14.5%, compared to 25.7% for the control group (Clarke et al., 1995).

Reynolds and Coats (1986) demonstrated statistically significant reductions in depressive symptoms on both self-report and clinical interviews during their intervention with thirty depressed high school teenagers. Random assignment was made to one of three interventions: CBT, relaxation training, or wait-list control.

TABLE 32.2. CLASS INTERVENTIONS FOR ATTENTION-DEFICIT/HYPERACTIVITY DISORDER (ADHD).

Elementary/Middle School

Inattention/Organizational difficulties
—Encourage firm policies such as, "Class participation is not optional."
—Be ready to closely monitor ADHD students for several months.
—Recommend a full line of organizational materials, and be prepared to teach students how to use them; encourage them to be creative with the art/design on its covers to make it uniquely "theirs."
—Systematically teach students to enter assignment information on calendars and memory joggers.
—Put list of materials needed for class on student's book.
—Have student keep separate set of classroom materials (such as pencil, paper, even texts whenever possible) in desk, with another set at home.
—Affix/Tape pen/pencil to desk.
—Place seat in location that limits distractions.
—Give signal for instructions (for example, "Sammy, when I squeeze your shoulder, you need to pay attention to the directions.").
—Have student repeat directions back to teacher.
—Provide check-in points during lesson (for example, every third problem).
—Use a timer to clarify time for task.
—Provide untimed tests or assignments.
—Provide information in small chunks.
—Pair preferred, easier tasks with more difficult ones.
—Provide visual cues to signal return to on-task behavior.
—Diminish external distractions. (Provide headphones, tennis balls on chair legs.)
—Provide temporary stopgap measures when necessary.
—Purchase a small supply of emergency materials.

   (". . . consider the purchase of extra pencils and a stack of notebook paper as an investment in stress management," Guyer, 2000, pg. 72)

—E-mail assignments to home.
—Consider home-school notebooks as a form of daily sign-offs/communication for parents and teachers.
—Encourage a class lesson that is not contingent on successful completion of last night's homework.
—Reward any efforts in positive direction, and provide continued encouragement and immediate feedback whenever possible.
   —Examples include public praise, such as, "I like the way Joey is sitting up and looking at the board."

Middle/High School

Inattention
—Place the student close to the teacher's desk.
—Present the material in several different media (chalkboard, overhead, pictures, video, small group discussions, and so on).
—Do not be critical of the student in front of his/her peers.
—Use a "buddy" system for peer-to-peer help, when appropriate.
—Give the student only one assignment at a time.

(Continued)

TABLE 32.2.   CLASS INTERVENTIONS FOR ATTENTION-DEFICIT/HYPERACTIVITY DISORDER (ADHD) (CONTINUED).

—Consider formal attention training, using cassette tapes with tones at regular intervals to remind the student to pay attention.
—Try shortening assignments, or giving extra time to complete assignments.
—Partial (predictable and time-dependent depreciable) credit should be given for late assignments.
—Build as much structure into the class as possible.
—Have one location for completed assignments to be placed, and established routines/schedules for the class day.
—Post expected assignments for the day/week in the same place.
—Allow student to audit class or attend previously before taking for credit.
—Call on student often.

Distractibility
—Suggest the use of earplugs if noises are distracting.
—Seat the student where it will be easy to get her back on task, and next to students who are relatively quiet.
—Give regular, positive feedback.
—Reward the student for attending. (Allow for tic-tac-toe, doodling, a quiet computer game.)
—Assign work that can be done independently.
—Encourage and provide opportunities for leadership when possible (handling out papers, going to main office for errands).
—Use nonverbal means to help the student focus.

Disorganization
—Encourage discussion of the lack of organization that you've observed.
—Get the student to admit that lack of organization is a problem.
—Send home a week's/month's worth of assignments at a time.
—A planner is key; encourage artwork/stickers/political statements to make the planner uniquely "theirs," and not merely a suggestion of adults.
—Partner with parents in helping the teen get organized at home as well.
   —Put a schedule on the disorganized student's door.
   —Select clothes for the next day before going to bed.
   —Put everything going to school at the front door before going to bed.
   —Be as specific as possible, and help to create the "action plan."
    (For example, "Clean out your desk" is less helpful than "Take out all the candy wrappers and crumpled papers from your desk.")
—Strategically plan study hall period to derive greatest benefit (such as at end of day, just after lunch, or first period).
—Schedule A.M. check-in and P.M. check-out to organize for school day and for homework.
—Allow extra time between classes for transition, or to organize backpack or locker.
—Increase frequency of feedback to both student and pupil in selected classes.
—Establish a regular parent conference frequency.
—Allow for parent input on selection of following year's teachers.
—Use praise as a reward as much as possible.

TABLE 32.2. (CONTINUED).

—Acknowledge your own disorganization (we all have some), and find ways for the teen to give you helpful hints.

Specific Test-Taking Modifications
—Allow for extra time.
—Arrange for short breaks during tests.
—Permit student to retake tests.
—Allow for alternate test room or day.
—Let student show competence through an alternate modality, such as an oral report or exam.
—Use short, frequent quizzes instead of long tests.
—Provide computer access during essay exams.
—Consider open book or take-home exams.
—Consider approved notes as prompts for recall during test.

Hyperactivity/Impulsivity (all ages)
—Devise behavioral contracts clarifying classroom expectations/alternatives.
—Arrange for/encourage exercise before class.
—Reinforce quiet behaviors with verbal praise.
—Provide a competing response for motoric activity (squeezeball, fabric to rub, finger exercises).
—Identify times and places student can move about within the class, and outside class (for example, take attendance sheets to office).
—Use movement as a reward.
  —If the student is quiet for a certain period of time, he will be rewarded by being able to use the computer, move around the room, or perform an errand that involves leaving the classroom.
—Provide cues to signal stop talking, and identify later opportunity to talk.
—Encourage cognitive behavior strategies, such as asking, "And what are you supposed to be doing right now?" to encourage self-monitoring.
—Clarify volume and activity level expectations before attempting games or less structured activities.
—Assign a specific place for student to stand, or a specific student to stand next to in line.
—Rotate active periods with inactive periods.
—Have student write down an answer before she raises her hand to answer aloud.
—Allow for non-disruptive calming techniques, such as listening to classical music with headphones on.
—Have student identify other students who are "ready."
—Establish waiting routine. (Count to five, then raise other hand.)
—For teens, consider allowing gum chewing in class. Guyer (2000) reports that when she allows it, the mouths moving with gum tend to talk less, and there is less body movement. Use guidelines about no popping, sticking under desk, and so on.
—Brainstorm, especially with teens, about innovative ways to quietly expend energy (repeated leg lifts, stretches in the back of the classroom).

Source: Adapted from Rief, 1993; Robin, 1998; Guyer, 2000; and Bostic and Bagnell, in press.

TABLE 32.3.   MOOD DISORDERS.

—Educate teachers and staff about mood disorders and CBT principles for addressing symptoms.
—Establish check-in plan to clarify mood status during school day.
—Connect academics and interests to increase motivation (such as reading an alternative novel, summarizing a current news event for the class).
—Base grade on work completed/attempted rather than expected, and allow for partial credit when work is turned in late.
—Break assignments into small, easily completed segments.
—Attempt opportunities for student to "fix mistakes" when work doesn't meet expectations.
—Start student's school day later or earlier consistent with student's circadian rhythm.
—Encourage snacks and exercise to minimize weight changes and improve energy.
—Provide a time and place beforehand to regroup if weepy, fatigued.
—Attend extracurricular clubs and activities to increase peer connections.
—Tape-record lectures.
—Identify activities student does more/less when mood is improving/worsening.
—Narrow choices to two when student becomes indecisive.
—Establish hierarchy of people to contact if student reports suicide ideation.
—Devise safety plan for crisis situations.
—Acknowledge student's feelings rather than dispute or argue feelings.
—Identify "evidence" surrounding negative perceptions of self or events.
—Reinforce efforts in the correct direction (such as "Wow, you did get half these problems done.").
—Focus on successive approximations toward goals (such as being able to stay in class twenty minutes today without crying).

Source: Adapted from Bostic and Bagnell, in press.

TABLE 32.4.   ANXIETY DISORDERS.

Devise protocol to diminish anxiety in classroom/school

—Educate teachers and staff about anxiety disorders and CBT principles for addressing symptoms, such as encouraging positive self-talk and problem solving.
—Provide steps student may take to relax (deep breathing, counting to ten, visualization).
—Provide alternative foci to distract from somatic symptoms (such as "mantras," calming activities).
—Identify safe place in school to de-escalate anxiety symptoms and guidelines for appropriate use.
—Model appropriate behavior in anxiety-provoking situation.
—If avoiding school, address cause and initiate immediate plan for return; may require gradual reintroduction.

Specific Phobias
—Identify desensitization approach agreeable to student.
—Identify alternatives to unnecessary exposure to phobic stimulus.

Social Phobia
—Identify staff person or peer to meet student on arrival.
—Modify stressful social situations (such as, eat lunch in small group, practice speaking one on one).

TABLE 32.4.   (CONTINUED).

—Encourage small group interaction, areas of competency.
—Avoid singling student out in classroom setting.

Separation Fears
—Identify staff person to meet student on arrival.
—Provide times for student to convey messages to family.
—Identify hierarchy of safe persons for student to access if parent unavailable.
—Have parent send notes to student to read as reward for staying in school.

Panic Attacks
—Identify relaxation ritual (breathing exercises, positive visualization).
—Establish parameters for meeting/measurements by school nurse.

Obsessive-Compulsive Symptoms
—Educate teachers and staff about DRO (Directed Reinforcement of Other
  Behaviors), and other CBT principles for OCD.
—Establish acceptable teacher comments to "unstick" student when obsessing.
—Personify obsessions and provide steps for student to resist uncomfortable
  thoughts.
—Allow student to dictate/tape record if cannot touch pencil or paper.
—Allow alternative activities if student cannot initiate particular task.
—Allow student to alter sequence of work (start on even-numbered problems,
  from end).
—Identify less school-intrusive compulsive behaviors (such as touching surface
  under desk to "short-circuit OCD").

Post-Traumatic Stress Disorder
—Avoid unnecessary exposures to evocative stimuli.
—Provide alternative schoolwork (such as a different story, film) to avoid eliciting
  past trauma.
—Identify cues (nonverbal, simple phrases) to signal student when shutting down.
—Follow general hints under Anxiety Disorders (above).

Source: Adapted from Bostic and Bagnell, 2004, and March and Mulle, 1999.

TABLE 32.5.   EATING DISORDERS.

—Help teachers and school staff be knowledgeable about the particular eating
  disorder, and encourage flexibility in both scheduling and types of food allowed
  in class/school.
—Identify student-acceptable comments that classroom personnel (teachers, aides,
  pupils) can employ during eating periods.
—Allow student to eat in more comfortable setting (for example, with a teacher or
  counselor, in a particular classroom away from peers if necessary, leaving campus
  to eat with a parent).
—Allow for eating or snacking while doing other activity (while reading,
  during P.E.).
—Allow student to go to bathroom before eating, and remain in classroom/activity
  for a specified time (for example sixty minutes) after eating.
—Identify alternative foods or snacks available for student if certain foods are
  unattractive.

Source: Adapted from Bostic and Bagnell, in press.

TABLE 32.6. CONDUCT DISORDER/OPPOSITIONAL DEFIANT DISORDER.

—Make each student feel welcome in the classroom.
—Start each lesson with enthusiasm.
—Take time to connect with each student.
—Take a disability perspective, and remember where these kids have trouble:
  —Processing information when frustrated.
  —Recognizing and communicating their frustrations appropriately.
  —Using effective problem solving and conflict negotiation skills.
—Focus on developing "thinking skills" for handling frustration more adaptively.
—Provide student opportunities to describe her perception of events (for example, write out incident).
—Avoid use of "standards" writing as punishment ("I must not curse at teachers" fifty times).
—Provide choices in completing tasks (such as, doing problems in different order).
—Identify alternative acceptable behavior.
—Be on the lookout for neutral or good behavior, and praise appropriately.
—Devise consistent cues or language (such as "reading time") to redirect student.
—Fix the problem rather than affix blame.
—Use incentives before punishments.
—Anticipate and *plan* for misbehavior.
—Reward appropriate behaviors at multiple intervals during the school day.
—Project alternatives and consequences with student.
—Effective praise is

Immediate, contingent on desired behavior, specific (describe behavior of student), and *credible* (personal, sincere, and focused on improvement).

"Praise will only be effective if the student believes that it is true." (Applebaum, 2001, p. 63)

—Identify good efforts even if ultimately behavior is unsuccessful.
—Remove the audience or the student if escalations emerge.
—Role-play alternative responses and plan for what to do "next time."
—Allow student to fix mistake (for example, following property destruction).
—Enlist friends and family to help student get to school.
—Identify where school may contact student if not in school.

Important *do nots*
—Return the anger.
—Avoid the student.
—Think the student is "spoiled."
—Walk on "eggshells."
—Be logical with an out-of-control student.
—Attempt to reason with an out-of-control student.
—Repeat your requests or commands more than once or twice.
—Use negatives when upset. ("How could you do something so stupid? How could you be so sneaky?")
—Be inconsistent.

"Grant freedom within limits. Stay in charge. You're the teacher." (Applebaum, 2001, p. 42)

Source: Adapted from Applebaum, 2001; Bostic and Bagnell, in press.

TABLE 32.7. PSYCHOTIC DISORDERS.

—Identify and avoid distressing stimuli.
—Allow alternative activities or content to avoid provoking delusions.
—Provide grounding activities (such as working with hands, non-emotional reading content).
—Devise steps to employ when delusional (for example, when paranoid, check in with teacher who provides safe/code words agreed to beforehand).
—Provide hierarchy of safe places to de-escalate if overstimulated.
—Identify safe subjects to discuss when delusional or hallucinating.
—Establish non-frightening protocol to respond to delusions or hallucinations. For example, (1) Change topic, (2) Change activity, (3) Change setting or room, (4) Involve additional, safe, familiar staff, (5) Access other stabilizing adult (counselor, parent), (6) PRN medication.

Source: Adapted from Bostic and Bagnell, in press.

TABLE 32.8. PERVASIVE DEVELOPMENTAL DISORDERS.

Communication
—Use one- or two-word command prompts (such as "laces" and then "shoes" instead of "Now tie your laces on top of the shoes.")
—Facilitate language use: model appropriate phrases with visual cues, match words to gestures.
—Structure situations to encourage language use.
—Provide pictures that allow communication for students to point to.
—Build social and emotional awareness: facilitate two-way communication by teaching awareness of others' thoughts or feelings, clarification of literal interpretations, and understanding of humor and jokes.

Social Interaction
—Identify situations in which the student can work with another student(s).
—Practice social acts in role-play with clearly outlined steps.
—Use a peer or adult to help student interact with others.
—Provide explicit teaching about how to start conversations, respond to other's comments, and end conversations.

Restrictive Routines/Interests
—Provide alternative tasks, particularly when sensory overloaded.
—Prioritize target behaviors (such as safety first).
—Identify more appropriate "one step up" routines (for example, pilot video game to replace violent combat video game).

Source: Adapted from Bostic and Bagnell, in press.

TABLE 32.9.   NONVERBAL AND SOCIAL COGNITION DISORDERS.

—Provide written material that is visually clear and simple.
—Allow more space and time for physical activities.
—Consider allowing the use of favorite restricted interest (Fantasy games, Pokemon cards, Anime, and the like) as incentives for adherence to a behavior plan.
—Recognize literal interpretations and explain multiple meanings of words/phrases.
—Point out generalizations that can be drawn from assignments.
—Verbally emphasize similarities, differences, and connections between past and current assignments.
—Provide a verbal map of the school the student can use to find rooms.
—Assist, simplify, or break down motor tasks such as using scissors.
—Rehearse transitions between classes.
—Specify daily routine, and use social stories when deviating.
—Allow the student to ask the two most important questions to begin work, and then check in after the student begins the assignment.
—Provide index cards to cover up written material unnecessary to immediate task.
—For those with very poor writing skills, focus on (and consider grading) readability rather than neatness.
—When necessary, limit handwriting and provide alternatives, such as computer typing and tape recording.
—Provide enlarged print tests, and extra space for handwritten answers.
—Provide directions in writing as well as verbally to connect modalities.
—Provide direct social skills instruction, and role-play appropriate social interactions.
—Provide direct instruction about what is communicated through facial expressions, intonation, gestures, and other mannerisms.

Source: Adapted from Bostic and Bagnell, in press.

Prominent symptom reductions were seen in both treatment groups, but not in the controls (Reynolds & Coates, 1986).

Rosal and colleagues (1993) examined thirty-six students in grades four through six with moderate to severe behavioral problems, and demonstrated significant functional improvement for those children who received either CBT or art therapy, compared to a group that received no therapy. Improved adaptive behaviors were demonstrated by use of the Connors Teacher Rating Scale, though none of the three groups showed any changes on measures of locus of control, pre- and post-intervention (Rosal, 1993).

Social skills training programs that have empiric support were those that focused on school adjustment and substance use problems. Bierman and colleagues (1987) were interested in developing a program to help socially rejected and negative boys become more socially and functionally adaptable. Boys in grades one through three who showed highly negative social behaviors were randomly assigned to one of four conditions: instructions and coaching in positive behaviors, prohibitions and response cost for negative behaviors, a combination of instructions and prohibitions, or no treatment. The interventions took place over ten sessions, which were thirty-minute, supervised, small group play sessions. Treatment effects were assessed using behavioral observations and teacher/peer ratings. The most robust effects were for boys receiving the combined program, who showed immediate post-treatment decreases in negative initiations, later decreases in negative peer responses, and stable positive peer interactions. This project showed both functional improvement and symptom reduction (Bierman, Miller, & Stabb, 1987).

Thorkildssen (1985) randomly assigned children in six elementary school special education settings to participate in an interactive videodisc social skills training program, or to continue in their resource room programs. Results showed significantly greater improvements for the experimental group on measures of peer acceptance.

Dupper and Krishef (1993) examined the effects of a social skills cognitive training program on locus of control for sixth and seventh graders with behavior problems. Significant differences were observed, favoring experimental over control groups on locus of control measures (functioning) and on teacher ratings of self-control (symptom reduction).

Henderson and colleagues (1992) examined locus-of-control orientation, self-concept, and appropriate coping skills development among sixty-five children from an inner-city school. The students were randomly assigned to a stress management group or control group, with the stress management group showing higher scores on measures of self-concept, and a more internal locus of control.

Lochman and colleagues (1993) examined the effect of social skills training program with aggressive, non-aggressive rejected, and rejected African-American children. Random assignment was used for selection to experimental or control group. Post-treatment and one-year follow-up studies showed the most improvements on non-impulsive problem solving for the aggressive and the rejected children, but not for the non-aggressive rejected group.

Most recent studies have looked at CBT interventions (with and without medication) specifically for anxiety and depression. Ginsburg and Drake (2002) evaluated the effectiveness of a manualized ten-session CBT group intervention for African-American teenagers. Twelve adolescents were randomly assigned to either CBT (n = 6) or a group attention-support control condition (n = 6). Post-treatment results showed that self- and clinician ratings of anxiety were significantly less in the CBT-treated group than in the control group. Teens in both groups reported lower rates of social anxiety at the end of the intervention (Ginsburg & Drake, 2002).

Bernstein and colleagues (2000) found that imipramine plus CBT was substantially more effective than placebo plus CBT for school refusal in an eight-week prospective randomized double-blind trial with sixty-three subjects participating (and forty-seven subjects completing). Subjects' mean age was 13.9 $+/-3.9$ years, and ethnic composition was 90% white, 8% African-American, and 2% Hispanic. Readers are encouraged to consult a recent comprehensive review of research on school refusal by King and Bernstein (2001), for further discussion of this topic.

For depressive disorders, work by Lewinson and associates (1990) and Gilham and associates (1995) have shown the effectiveness of CBT, and Freres and colleagues (2002) have demonstrated that a manualized CBT intervention can be useful for *prevention* of depressive symptoms in an at-risk population. The Penn Resiliency Project (PRP) utilizes a twelve-session twenty-four-hour manualized protocol, and it has recently added a parent component, the PRP for Parents Freres et al. (2002). The latter is a six-session, nine-hour manualized treatment in which parents are taught the core skills that their children are learning, but at an adult level. This manualized treatment is well-suited for school settings. Currently, a large scale NIMH-funded study is examining this treatment (parent plus child) versus the child-only version and a usual care control.

Mattison (2000) reviewed literature pertaining to four specific issues that consultants often get asked about: absenteeism, disciplinary referrals, retention, and dropping out. The summary of recommendations that consultants should consider is as follows:

Be attentive to excessive absences, frequent disciplinary referrals, signs that a retention recommendation is imminent, and focus on the underlying reasons.

Encourage early identification, specific diagnosis (preferred to the term "labeling"), and tailored treatment planning with sustained involvement of school staff.

Establish objective "at-risk" parameters and evaluate high risk students for which interventions are most appropriate for them.

Help the district choose an efficient screening instrument (or help them design one). It should include academic, behavioral, and family components. One suggestion by Mattison is the Critical Events Index and the Adaptive and Maladaptive Rating Scales of the Systematic Screening for Behavioral Disorders (Walker and Severson, 1992). A Child Behavior Checklist may be sufficient (Achenbach, 1991), as it also includes family and teacher components.

Help with implementation, ideally through the auspices of the SST or IEP.

Help the school staff intervene with the child, and be as specific as possible with what it can provide (versus simply referring to community resources).

"Ideally, a mental health team will emerge with whom the mental consultant can then collaborate." (Mattison, 2000, p. 412)

Recent work by Kataoka and colleagues (2003), Stein et al. (2002, 2003), and Jaycox (2003) have nicely demonstrated how CBT-oriented mental health programs may be developed specifically for certain populations (traumatized Latino immigrant children, for example), and then developed into a manual for broader use, also with empiric support (Jaycox, 2003; Kataoka et al., 2003; Stein, Jaycox et al., 2003; Stein, Kataoka et al., 2003; Stein et al., 2002).

Violent Students and Threat Assessments

Though the above scenarios represent the most frequent reasons for consultation, more and more, assistance is being sought from consultants regarding students' capacity to do harm to others. Rappaport (2000) presents a list of important considerations when making a threat assessment:

- Sharing responsibility is key. Psychiatrists acting alone deprive themselves and their consultee of crucial collaboration.
- Consultants must be aware of those adolescents who may be marginalized and have low frustration tolerance, yet not be the "Teenage Werewolf" (overtly externalizing, not subtle about their agitation). Though the marginalized may be more subtle in their presentation, they may still be capable of lethal violence.
- Help staff navigate the tasks of correctly estimating a student's harm potential, while being able to appropriately assess their own biases. One example is the troubled school athlete whose violence potential is overlooked, and about whom staff are overly optimistic due to their own investment in the student's potential school contributions. The opposite reaction can occur in response to overt verbal expressions of anger by a teen. Staff must be helped to differentiate normal frustration from potentially dangerous remarks. To not do so impairs useful student-staff relationship building.
- Students must be given an opportunity to give their perspective on events. Rappoport recommends an approach that overtly seeks a better understanding of the teen by the interviewer, in order to minimize perceptions of interrogation. Also, information to be shared with school personnel should be done with adolescent permission whenever possible.
- Key to the role of consultant is the aspect of providing an understanding, non-judgmental sanctuary for school staff. They should feel at ease enough to

be thoughtful and reflective, while the consultant supports their thinking and working through difficult situations (preferably aloud). As these situations are often very complex and the stakes high, clarity is critical. Rappoport concludes by referring the reader to James Garbarino's *Lost Boys* (1999), and by encouraging consultants to use their roles to advocate for systemic interventions that can make children and teens more resourceful. Some of these include the encouragement of parent education, of bully-proofing schools, and of making certain that structured extracurricular activities and mentoring exists (Rappaport, 2000).

"As collaborative consultants, we can assist in creating a safe learning space for students and staff, and share responsibility and contain affect so that educators can make good decisions." (Rappoport, 2000, p. 165)

Twemlow warns of a covert power dynamic (PD) that pervades all schools that experience violence (Twemlow, Fonagy, & Sacco, 2001). This PD is in reference to an overt or covert pattern in which an individual or group controls the thoughts or actions of others. The environment in school reveals this PD through high levels of disciplinary referrals and poor academic achievement. He advises that consultants ought to thoughtfully and carefully help school staff become aware of this PD in a way that does not demean or bully them. Examples include non-coercive discipline plans, creation of an awareness and zero-tolerance of the bully-victim-bystander cycle, using peer mentors and adult volunteers on school grounds for conflict resolution outside of the classroom, and utilizing physical education time to practice appropriate role-plays in conflict resolution. Goals of this sort of teaching include the softening of the power dynamic, while restoring a more peaceful and less humiliating climate to the school (Twemlow et al., 2001).

Diverse Roles for Consultants

Other authors have promoted the use of school consultants as direct implementers of psycho-education programs targeted toward prevention of violence, substance abuse, suicide, teen pregnancy, and sexually transmitted diseases (Walter, 2001), as consultants during crises (Arroyo, 2001), and as consultants to boarding schools (Gottlieb, 2001), as consultants to schools in rural communities (Adelsheim, Carrillo, & Coletta, 2001) and as consultants to facilities on remote islands (Campo, 2001). Others have examined consultation in large urban districts (Wang, 2001), to school administrators (Blader & Gallagher, 2001) and to schools of education (Berkovitz, 2001). These and other outstanding contributions to the school consultation literature appear together in a volume edited by Berkovitz (2001), and include a comprehensive review of current models of consultation and of successful school mental health centers (Rappaport, 2001).

The Stanford School Mental Health Team

Within the Stanford University School-based Mental Health Service, we have brought together the disciplines of child psychiatry, psychology, education, and pediatrics to try and best address the needs of several different school settings. As a consultation service, we are contracted with an organization that specializes in serving children and teens with developmental disabilities. We also serve as mental health consultants to an entire school district, with two high schools, three middle schools, and ten elementary schools. And through grant support, we work with a relatively poorer school district in targeting interventions that focus on youth development through life skills, group process, substance abuse education and violence prevention, and on prevention of "teacher dropout/burnout" through teacher and staff consultation. We shall describe our work with the school districts in more detail in the following sections.

Relationship Building

The initial part of our work in all districts begins with several months of relationship building. Through regular meetings with front line teachers and senior administrative officials, we first try to get a sense for what the strengths and limitations are of the school environment as a whole, and of the current mental health services specifically. In each of the communities that we serve, we believe that the school-based approach affords a unique opportunity to work with youths in the context and setting of their daily lives. Our team uses a culturally informed resiliency approach that focuses on the inherent strengths of consultee, student, and system. According to the resiliency model, schools can offer children experiences that enhance their self-esteem and competence, thereby reinforcing resilience (Brooks, 1991, 1992; Curwin, 1992; Rutter, 1985, 1987; Zunz, Turner, & Norman, 1993). Although the work of the School Mental Health Team is school-based, all of us work as clinicians in a university-based clinic as well, and many of us work with trainees (psychology interns, adult psychiatry residents, or child psychiatry fellows). We try to emphasize the importance of school in a child's life for and with our trainees by taking a thorough school history for clinic-based patients as well, and to assist parents, teachers, and staff to remember the resiliency and strengths of each child for whom consultation is being sought. Clearly, consultants are not sought out because things are going well, and this must be acknowledged from the start. However, a paradigm shift from looking at all referred behaviors as strictly maladaptive can be refreshing, and can also provide the team with new ways of looking at old problems. Examples include asking questions in ways to find out about strengths. When taking the school history from a referred client, for example, rather than asking, "How do you do in school?" we prefer to ask "What do you like in school?" or "What are you *good at* in school?" A response such as "recess" or "lunch" or "P.E." is answered back with, "Oh really? What is it about *fill in favorite non-academic period here* that makes it your favorite?" opens doors and builds a rapport in ways that parentified questions do not ("What kind of grades do you get?" "What's your teacher's name?"—both of which are important questions, but are not necessarily alliance-building).

Many of the schools we consult with have a large population of immigrant and refugee children. Guarnaccia and Lopez (1998) have highlighted some of the crucial issues regarding school services and the mental health needs of these youths and their families. Their recommendations are summarized as follows:

1. Pay special attention to the assessment of second language acquisition, not only for immigrant children, but also for children growing up in bicultural households.
2. Recommend culturally informed family interventions that will address the intergenerational tensions that often exist within immigrant families.
3. Promote teacher training to best understand and work with linguistically and culturally diverse children. Schools are uniquely poised to promote the value of cultural diversity and to counter prejudice against newly arrived students.
4. Help staff understand the special needs of immigrant parents in negotiating the complex systems of special education assessment.
5. Help staff to recognize the high levels of academic motivation among some immigrant parents as a valuable resource for their children and for the school.

Our Approach

We have found that a five-step process has worked well for us, and is similar to Mattison's seven-step model (Mattison, 1999). It works best with school districts that have the infrastructure to support a mental health team at the school.

1. A consultee initiates a question through the school psychologist, who then contacts the attending psychiatrist by e-mail. An intake packet is then sent to the parent's home, which contains information about our service, consent for evaluation and treatment, and several questionnaires and measures of child-hood functioning. These include a qualitative target symptom questionnaire for parents and children, Child Behavior Checklist (CBCL), Parent Stress Inventory (PSI), Columbia Scale of Functioning (CSF), and Family Assessment

Device (FAD). We believe the relationship starts with the packet—it must be easy to read, appropriate for the education of the parent (we modify the measures based on parent literacy level), and sent out in a timely fashion.

2. Next (after the packet has been filled out and returned, with a signed consent form to evaluate and treat), a call is placed to the parents and an e-mail message sent to the school psychologist and teacher to clarify the consultee questions in more detail. An initial school visit is scheduled. The goal is to meet with the teacher and other important staff in the classroom, and to observe the child in class (elementary school), or schedule an interview (middle or high school) with the student.

3. After this meeting, initial feedback is given to parents by phone, and to staff by e-mail, and a second child interview is scheduled, preferably within the next one to two weeks. Further history is obtained from the parent, and both teachers and parents are given (short) supplementary forms to fill out, which may be more specific for suspected conditions, such as a Connor's questionnaire for ADHD, Multidimensional Anxiety Scale for Children (MASC) for anxiety disorders, or a Children's Depression Inventory (CDI).

4. The second and third sessions are conducted with the youth, and impressions are shared with the consultee. Differential diagnoses are considered, and a formulation is constructed with the consultee based on the information known. At times, an evaluation known as a functional behavioral assessment (FBA) may be warranted. This can be an important tool in understanding the reasons for a particular problem behavior. FBAs are typically done by a clinician with specialized training in such assessments. For useful resources on this tool, see O'Neill, et al. (1997), and McComas, Hoch, and Mace (2000).

5. The data are presented orally to the parents, either in person (preferred), or over the phone. In our experience, the feedback often takes place in front of an IEP or SST team, as the initial consultation may be urgently requested in order to plan appropriately. In this case, it is especially crucial to give parents some clinical impressions prior to the meeting, in order to minimize surprises at the time of the actual meeting. Written summaries are provided if requested. Our recommendations always include timelines to closely follow up our treatment plan, especially when recommendations are made for community resources. Often, families prefer to have us become the providers of treatment, given that we have begun a relationship with them and their child/teen. Though medication management is what we are asked to do most frequently, we also provide individual treatment with various psychotherapies, employing manualized therapies such as those by Kendall, Jaycox, or Mufson whenever available (Jaycox, 2003; Kendall, 1992; Kendall, Choudhury, Hudson, & Webb, 2002; Mufson, Moreau, Weissman, & Klerman, 1993).

Funding Sources

Our team has a fee-for-service contract with the school district, and services are paid for through a combination of funding sources, one of which includes the federally funded "Safe and Drug-Free Schools Program." This program includes moneys given to schools and local providers to provide science-based prevention and early intervention programs to prevent violence and substance abuse in schools.

Adelsheim (2000) has proposed exploring the availability of other funds at respective local districts. These include the Federal "Medicaid in the Schools" program, which allows for schools to bill directly for services provided to special education students through their IEPs. City and County governments may have set money aside for "dropout prevention," and this money has been used to fund both consultative and direct services from child psychiatrists and other mental health professionals. Other sources of funding highlighted by Adelsheim include Title XI, a federal program that allows districts to use up to 5% of their federal education funds to coordinate services for schools. Some districts have combined these with county physical and mental health funds to create school-based health centers, which can also serve as training sites for adult psychiatry residents, child and adolescent psychiatry fellows, pre- and post-doctoral education and psychology students, and other mental health trainees.

Private foundations and federal grant agencies continue to be very interested in supporting innovative school intervention programs. Because the funding streams usually require outcome measurement, it encourages evidence-based practice while also promoting the development of new models. For a useful reference on granting agencies, see Stovell (1998).

Summary and Future Directions

Children and teens spend a good deal of their waking hours in school. Consultation about, and direct service to, students within the context and setting of their daily lives allows for greater staff and client empowerment, resiliency building, and both prevention and treatment of problematic behaviors and symptoms than similar services in an outside clinic. Many excellent models of school consultation and school-based health clinics exist, and recent papers have summarized these. We hope to continue to help train the next generation of psychiatric school consultants through involving mental health and education trainees from year one, and to promote continued research into the major issues of importance to school staff, students, and parents.

References

Achenbach, T. (1993). Child behavior checklist (CBCL). Burlington, VT: University Associates in Psychiatry.

Adelsheim, S. (2000). Financial issues in school mental health. *AACAP News* (May/June), 117, 120.

Adelsheim, S., Carrillo, K., & Coletta, E. (2001). Developing school mental health in a rural state: The New Mexico School Mental Health Initiative. *Child and Adolescent Psychiatric Clinics of North America: School Consultation/Intervention, 10*(1), 151–160.

Applebaum. (2001). *Working with angry and oppositional students.* Houston: Applebaum Training Institute.

Arroyo, W. (2001). *School crisis consultation. Child and Adolescent Psychiatric Clinics of North America: School Consultation/Intervention, 10*(1), 55–66.

Bayer, D. J., & Kaye, D. L. (2002). The school system. In D. L. Kaye, M. E. Montgomery, & S. W. Munson (Eds.), *Child and adolescent mental health* (pp. 95–114). Philadelphia: Lippincott, Williams and Wilkins.

Berkovitz, I. H. (Ed.). (2001). *Child and adolescent psychiatric clinics of North America: School consultation/intervention,* (Vol. 10, 1). Philadelphia: WB Saunders.

Berlin, I. N. (1956). Some learning experiences as psychiatric consultant in schools. *Mental Hygiene, 40,* 215–236.

Bierman, K. L., Miller, C. L., & Stabb, S. D. (1987). Improving the social behavior and peer acceptance of rejected boys: Effects of social skill training with instructions and prohibitions. *Journal of Consulting and Clinical Psychology, 55,* 194–200.

Blader, J. C., & Gallagher, R. (2001). Consultation to administrators. *Child and Adolescent Psychiatric Clinics of North America: School Consultation/Intervention, 10*(1), 185–198.

Bostic, J. Q., & Bagnell, A. (in press). School consultation. In B. J. Kaplan & V. A. Sadock (Eds.), *Comprehensive textbook of psychiatry, 8th ed.*

Bostic J. Q., & Rauch, P. K. (1999). The 3 R's of school consultation. *Journal of the American Academy of Child and Adolescent Psychiatry, 38*(3), 339–341.

Brooks, R. B. (1991). *The self-esteem teacher.* Cirlcle Pines, MN: American Guidance Service.

Brooks, R. B. (1992). Self-esteem during the school years: Its normal development and hazardous decline. *Pediatric Clinics of North America, 39,* 537–550.

Bums, B. J., Costello, E. J., Angold, A., Tweed, D., Stangl, D., Farmer, E.M.Z., et al. (1995). Children's mental health service use across service sectors. *Health Affairs, 14,* 147–159.

Campo, A. E. (2001). Psychiatric consultation to schools on remote islands. *Child and Adolescent Psychiatric Clinics of North America: School Consultation/Intervention, 10*(1), 161–168.

Caplan, G. (1956). Mental health consultation in the schools: Who can do it and why. *Community Mental Health Journal, 1,* 19–22.

Caplan, G. (1959). *Concepts of mental health and consultation.* Washington DC: U.S. Children's Bureau.

Caplan, G. (1963). Types of mental health consultation. *American Journal of Orthopsychiatry, 33,* 47–481.

Clarke, G. N., Hawkins, W., Murphy, M., Sheeber, L., Lewinsohn, P. M., & Seeley, J. R. (1995). Targeted prevention of unipolar depressive disorder in an at-risk sample of high school adolescents: A randomized trial of a group of cognitive intervention. *Journal of American Academy of Child and Adolescent Psychiatry, 34,* 312–321.

Coleman, J. R. (1947). Psychiatric consultation in casework agencies. *American Journal of Orthopsychiatry, 17,* 548–566.

Conger, J. J. (1977). *Adolescence and youth: Psychological development in a changing world.* New York: Harper.

Costello, E. J., Angold, A., Bums, B. J., Erkanli, A., Stangl, D., & Tweed, D. (1996). The Great Smokey Mountains study of youth: Goals, design, methods and the prevalence of DSM-III-R disorders. *Archives of General Psychiatry, 53,* 1129–1136.

Curwin, R. L. (1992). *Rediscovering hope: Our greatest teaching strategy.* Bloomington, IN: National Educational Service.

Dupper, D. R., & Krishef, C. H. (1993). School-based social-cognitive skills training for middle school students with school behavior problems. *Children and Youth Services Review, 15,* 131–142.

Fagan, T. K. (1992). Compulsory schooling, child study, clinical psychology, and special education: Origins of school psychology. Special Issue: The history of American psychology. *American Psychologist, 47,* 236–243.

Feldman, S. S., & Elliott, G. (1993). *At the threshold: The developing adolescent.* Cambridge, MA: Harvard University Press.

French, J. L. (1990). History of school psychology. In T. B. Gutkin & C. R. Reynolds (Eds.), *The handbook of school psychology* (2nd ed., pp. 3–20). New York: John Wiley.

Freres, D. R., Gillham, J. E., Hamilton, J. D., & Patton, K. (2002). *Preventing Depressive Symptoms in Early Adolescence: 2-Year Follow-Up of a Randomized Trial.* Paper presented at the 49th Annual Meeting of the American Academy of Child and Adolescent Psychiatry, San Francisco, CA.

Fuchs, D., & Fuchs, L. S. (1989). Exploring effective and efficient preferral interventions: A component analysis of behavioral consultation. *School Psychology Review, 18,* 260–279.

Fullerton, G., & Rollins, I. (1996). Palo Alto Unified School District Section 504 Policy and Procedure Manual. Palo Alto, CA.

Garbarino, J. (1999). *Lost boys: Why our sons turn violent and how we can save them.* New York: Free Press.

Gillham, J. E., Hamilton, J. D., Patton, K., & Freres, D. R. (2000). *Preventing depressive symptoms in early adolescence: A randomized trial.* Paper presented at the Annual Meeting of the American Academy of Child and Adolescent Psychiatry, New York, NY.

Ginsburg, G. S., & Drake, K. L. (2002). School-based treatment for anxious African-American adolescents: A controlled pilot study. *Journal of American Academy of Child and Adolescent Psychiatry, 41*(7), 768–775.

Gottlieb, R. M. (2001). Consultation and therapy in the boarding high school setting. *Child and Adolescent Psychiatric Clinics of North America: School Consultation/Intervention, 10*(1), 139–150.

Guarnaccia, P., & Lopez, S. (1998). The mental health and adjustment of immigrant and refugee children. *Child and Adolescent Psychiatric Clinics of North America: The Child Psychiatrist in the Community, 7*(3), 537–553.

Guyer, B. P. (2000). Reaching and teaching the adolescent with ADHD. In B. P. Guyer (Ed.), *ADHD: Achieving success in school and in life* (pp. 81–98). Boston: Allyn and Bacon.

Henderson, P. A., Kelbey, T. J., & Engebretson, K. M. (1992). Effects of stress-control program on children's locus of control, self-concept, and coping behavior. *School Counselor, 40,* 125–131.

Hoagwood, K., & Erwin, H. D. (1997). Effectiveness of school-based mental health services for children: A 10-year research review. *Journal of Child and Family Studies, 6*(4), 435–451.

Kendall, P. C. (1992). *Cognitive-behavioral therapy for impulsive children: Therapist manual* (2nd ed.). Ardmore, PA: Workbook Publishing.

Kendall, P. C., Choudhury, M., Hudson, J., & Webb, A. (2002). *The C.A.T. project workbook for the cognitive behavioral treatment of anxious adolescents.* Ardmore, PA: Workbook Publishing.

Kerr, M. M. (2001). High school consultation. *Child and Adolescent Psychiatric Clinics of North America: School Consultation/Intervention, 10*(1), 105–116.

King, N. J., & Bernstein, G. A. (2001). School refusal in children and adolescents: A review of the past 10 years. *Journal of American Academy of Child and Adolescent Psychiatry, 40*(2), 197–205.

Lewinsohn, P. M., Clarke, G. N., Hops, H., & Andrews, J. A. (1990). Cognitive-behavioral treatment for depressed adolescents. *Behavior Therapy, 21*(4), 385–401.

Lochman, J. E., Dunn, S. E., & Klimes-Dougan, B. (1993). An intervention and consultation model from a social cognitive perspective: A description of the Anger Coping Program. *School Psychology Review, 22,* 458–471.

Maddux, J. F. (1950). Psychiatric consultation in a public welfare agency. *American Journal of Orthopsychiatry, 20,* 754–764.

March, J., & Mulle, K. (1998). *OCD in children and adolescents: A cognitive-behavioral treatment manual.* New York: Guilford Press.

Mattison, R. E. (1999). School Consultation. In B. J. Kaplan & V. Sadock (Eds.), *Comprehensive Textbook of Psychiatry, 7th Ed.*

Mattison, R. E. (2000). School consultation: A review of research on issues unique to the school environment. *Journal of American Academy of Child and Adolescent Psychiatry, 39*(4), 402–413.

Mattison, R. E. (2001). Consultation interactions between special education teachers and child psychiatrists. *Child and Adolescent Psychiatric Clinics of North America: School Consultation/Intervention, 10*(1), 67–82.

McComas, J., Hoch, H., & Mace, F. C. (2000). Functional analysis. In E. Shapiro & T. Kratochwill (Eds.), *Conducting school-based assessments of child and adolescent behavior* (pp. 78–120). New York: Guilford Press.

Nelson, M. S. (2001). Mental Health Consultations in the Preschool Daycare Center. *Child and Adolescent Psychiatric Clinics of North America: School Consultation/Intervention, 10*(1), 45–54.

O'Neill, R., Horner, R., Albin, R., Sprague, J., Storey, R. & Newton, J. (1997). *Functional assessment and program development for problem behavior: A practical handbook.* Pacific Grove, CA: Brooks/Cole.

Rappaport, N. (2000). Missing the mark: School consultation-assessing students' potential for violence. *AACAP News, 31*(4), 164–165.

Rappaport, N. (2001). Emerging models. *Child and Adolescent Psychiatric Clinics of North America: School Consultation/Intervention, 10*(1), 13–24.

Ravenswood City School District. (1996). Parent guide to policies and procedures, Section 504 and IDEA; East Palo Alto, CA.

Reynolds, W. M., & Coates, K. I. (1986). A comparison of cognitive-behavioral therapy and relaxation training for the treatment of depression in adolescents. *Journal of Consulting and Clinical Psychology, 54,* 653–660.

Rief, S. F. (1993). *How to reach and teach ADD/ADHD children: Practical techniques, strategies, and interventions.* W. Nyack, NY: The Center for Applied Research in Education.

Robin, A. L. (1998). *ADHD in adolescents.* New York: Guilford Press.

Rosal, M. L. (1993). Comparative group art therapy research to evaluate changes in locus of control in behavior disordered children. *The Arts in Psychotherapy, 20,* 231–241.

Rutter, M. (1985). Resilience in the face of adversity. Protective factors and resistance to psychiatric disorder. *British Journal of Psychiatry, 147,* 598–611.

Rutter, M. (1987). Psychosocial resilience and protective mechanisms. *American Journal of Orthopsychiatry, 57,* 316–331.

Shaw, R. J., & Feldman, S. S. (1997). General principles and special problems. In H. Steiner & I. Yalom (Eds.), *Treating social-age children* (pp. 1–32). San Francisco: Jossey-Bass.

Steiner, J., & Feldman, S. S. (1996). General principles and special problems. In H. Steiner & I. Yalom (Eds.), *Treating Adolescents* (pp. 1–41). San Francisco: Jossey-Bass.

Stovell, K. (Ed.). (1998). Prevention programs for youth: *A guide to outcomes evaluation, best practices, and successful funding.* Providence, RI: Manisses Communications Group.

Thorkildssen, R. (1985). Using an interactive videodisc program to teach social skills to handicapped children. *American Annals of the Deaf, 130,* 383–385.

Twemlow, S. W., Fonagy, P., & Sacco, F. C. (2001). An innovative psychodynamically influenced approach to reduce school violence. *Journal of American Academy of Child and Adolescent Psychiatry, 40*(3), 377–379.

Walter, H. (2001). School-Based Prevention of Problem Behaviors. *Child and Adolescent Psychiatric Clinics of North America: School Consultation/Intervention, 10*(1), 117–128.

Wang, A.C.L. (2001). Opportunities within a large metropolitan school district. *Child and Adolescent Psychiatric Clinics of North America: School Consultation/Intervention, 10*(1), 179–184.

Weist, M. D., Proescher, E., Prodente, C., Ambrose, M. G., & Waxman, R. P. (2001). Mental health, health, and education staff working together in schools. *Child and Adolescent Psychiatric Clinics of North America: School Consultation/Intervention, 10*(1), 33–44.

Zunz, S. J., Turner, S., & Norman, E. (1993). Accentuating the positive: Stressing resiliency in school based substance abuse prevention programs. *Social Work in Education, 15,* 169–175.

Resources

http://www.schwablearning.org
A valuable online resource for families affected by learning disorders.

http://www.parentshelpingparents.com
User-friendly site for parents who want to know more about special education laws.

http://smph.psych.ucla.edu
Center for Mental Health in Schools is an outstanding online resource for school mental health specialists.

http://www.ericae.net/nav-lib.htm
Educational Resources Information Center Clearinghouse on Assessment and Evaluation (ERIC)—a useful source of information for all areas of educational, assessment, theory, and practice.

http://www.fape.org
Family and Advocates Partnership for Education (FAPE): Another useful resource for families and other advocates on the special education system.

CHAPTER THIRTY-THREE

CONSULTATION IN THE MEDICAL SETTING: A MODEL TO ENHANCE TREATMENT ADHERENCE

Richard J. Shaw, M.B., B.S., and Laura Palmer, M.Ed., Ph.D.

Although many important clinical problems are often identified in the course of pediatric psychiatric consultation, one critical and common concern for both medical and psychiatric providers is that of poor adherence to the medical treatment regimen. In this chapter, we will review some of the clinical and methodological issues related to treatment adherence, and then describe a conceptual model that can be used to enhance adherence in children with chronic illness. Our intent is to provide the reader with specific clinical tools to apply to the issue of adherence to medical treatment. For a more general review of the principles of pediatric psychiatric consultation, the reader is referred to Lewis (2002).

Basic Rationale for Treatment

Treatment compliance, also commonly referred to as *treatment adherence,* has been defined as the "extent to which a person's behavior . . . coincides with medical or health advice" (Haynes, 1979). Difficulties with treatment adherence, specifically the failure to follow through on prescribed medical treatments, is one of the most common reasons for psychiatric consultation in the medical setting. It is a particular issue for adolescents with chronic illnesses that require regular monitoring and dietary restrictions, such as diabetes mellitus. Another high-risk group includes organ transplant recipients who are required to take immunosuppressant medications that have undesirable cosmetic side effects (Shaw et al., in press). It is a problem that is likely to increase in importance as advances in medical technology often result in increasingly complicated treatment regimens that are more likely to engender treatment resistance (Rapoff, 1999). In addition, trends in health care have led to more of the burden of treatment being shifted to the family at the same time that access to mental health treatment, which is often needed for evaluation and treatment of non-adherence, has become more limited. As a result, hospital-based mental health providers face increasing pressure to intervene with patients whose non-adherence results in medical complications and morbidity.

Prevalence of Non-adherence

Rates of treatment adherence vary widely depending on the nature of the medical condition, the type of treatment prescribed, and the criteria used to define adherence (La Greca, 1990a). It is a common issue not only for more benign acute medical conditions, but also for patients for whom poor adherence to treatment may have life-threatening consequences. Studies of children with chronic physical illnesses, reviewed by Rapoff (1999), suggest rates of non-adherence that vary from 4–90%, although overall rates of non-adherence in this population are probably closer to 50% (Litt & Cuskey, 1980). Rates of adherence to more intrusive aspects of treatment, such as dietary restrictions in diabetes, or physical therapy in cystic fibrosis, may be even lower than for medication adherence. There is general consensus that the rate of non-adherence increases with the complexity of the treatment regimen and with side effects of treatment (Rapoff, 1999).

Consequences of Non-adherence

Non-adherence with medical treatment may result in adverse consequences that include medical, financial, and quality of life outcomes (Rapoff, 1999). Studies have shown a direct relationship between non-adherence and recurrent diabetic ketoacidosis in diabetic patients (Liss et al., 1998), as well as increased mortality rates in children with asthma (Sly, 1988). Ettenger and colleagues (1991) found that two-thirds of adolescent renal transplant recipients were non-adherent with their immunosuppressant medications, and of this group, 15% had graft rejection, while 26% had graft dysfunction. In adult patients, non-adherence has been cited as the third leading cause of graft loss after rejection and systemic infection (Didlake et al., 1988). In one study of pediatric heart transplant recipients, Cooper and associates (1984) reported that non-adherence accounted for up to 26% of deaths. This increased morbidity is often associated with higher health care costs, due to the need for hospital admissions or longer inpatient stays. Berg and colleagues (1993) have estimated that the financial cost of treatment non-adherence to the United States health care system may be as high as $100 billion per year. Children hospitalized for medical complications of non-adherence may also experience other negative consequences, including diminished quality of life due to missed school or social activities.

Correlates of Non-adherence

There has been fairly extensive research on the correlates of treatment adherence. (See Table 33.1.) For example, researchers have noted an association with age, complexity of the treatment regimen, and severity of medication side effects

TABLE 33.1. CORRELATES OF TREATMENT ADHERENCE.

Patient Factors
- Age
- Socioeconomic status
- Knowledge about illness
- Self-esteem
- Locus of control
- Behavioral and emotional problems
- Denial of illness

Family Factors
- Parental separation and divorce
- Family support and cohesion
- Family conflict
- Parental coping
- Parental psychopathology
- Parental monitoring of treatment

Disease Factors
- Nature of illness
- Duration of illness
- Course of illness
- Patient and parental perceptions of illness severity

Treatment Factors
- Complexity of treatment regimen
- Financial costs of treatment
- Side effects of treatment
- Perceptions of efficacy of treatment

Source: Adapted from Rapoff, 1999.

among others (Cole, 1994; Brownbridge & Fielding, 1994; La Greca & Schuman, 1995; Rapoff, 1999; Shemesh et al., 2000; Wolff et al., 1998). Results of these studies have been used both to identify subjects at particular risk, often based on their demographic characteristics, as well as to help develop treatment interventions (Rapoff, 1999).

Several studies have established a relationship between treatment adherence and the presence of individual psychopathology. For example, the presence of behavioral and emotional problems has been correlated with poor adherence in patients with both renal disease and diabetes (Brownbridge & Fielding, 1994; Kovacs et al., 1992). Patients who are less knowledgeable about their disease also tend in general to be less adherent with their treatment (La Greca et al., 1990). These studies suggest that adolescents are a high-risk group, particularly when there is comorbid psychiatric illness.

Many studies have shown that adaptation to chronic illness is closely related to different aspects of family functioning (Lorenz & Wysocki, 1991). For example, parental depression and anxiety have also been correlated with poor adherence in children and adolescents with renal disease and seizure disorders (Brownbridge & Fielding, 1994). Additional family variables include the presence or absence of family conflict, parental supervision and support, and communication style. These studies have led to different hypotheses about the relationship between treatment adherence and the family environment (Christiaanse et al., 1989; Friedman et al., 1986). More recently, treatment intervention studies have started to target some of these variables, such as parent adolescent conflict, in an effort to improve treatment adherence (Quittner et al., 2000; Wysocki et al., 1995).

Developmental Influences

Data from studies on treatment adherence suggest that specific developmental factors play an important role (Beck et al., 1980; La Greca, 1990b). For example, numerous studies have shown a close correlation between age and adherence. Difficulties in treatment adherence increase markedly during adolescence (Anderson, 1990; Dolgin et al., 1986; Johnson et al., 1986; Kovacs et al., 1992; La Greca et al., 1990; Quittner et al., 1996). These findings may be understood by considering the developmental issues in adolescence that may directly interfere with an adolescent's ability to adapt to the diagnosis of a chronic illness (Shaw, 2001). Three major developmental issues that may directly interfere with the adolescent's ability to adhere to their medical treatment are discussed next. (See Table 33.2.)

TABLE 33.2.   DEVELOPMENTAL AND PSYCHOPATHOLOGICAL ISSUES AFFECTING TREATMENT ADHERENCE.

Separation-Individuation Conflicts

Difficulties with Risk Assessment
- Cognitive maturity
- Adolescent omnipotence
- Cognitive limitations due to illness or treatment

Affiliation with the Peer Group

Adaptive Non-adherence

Psychiatric Comorbidity
- Depression
- Attention-deficit/hyperactivity disorder
- Post-traumatic stress disorder
- Personality pathology
- Parent-child conflict

Separation-Individuation

The developmental task of separation-individuation is one of the core issues for adolescents and one that often results in conflict within the parent-child relationship (Blos, 1967). Although there has been little empirical study of this issue in children with chronic illness, clinical observations suggest that adolescents may act out conflicts with their parents by either overt or covert refusal to adhere to medications or other prescribed treatments (Hamburg & Wortman, 1996; 1997; La Greca et al., 1990; La Greca & Schuman, 1995). Stein (1999) has also suggested that some adolescents may decide to limit or avoid treatment in an effort to reduce feelings of dependency on their parents.

Influence of Separation-Individuation Conflicts on Treatment Adherence

The diagnosis of a chronic medical illness may directly interfere with the adolescent's attempts to separate from his or her parents. The illness, for example, may result in significant physical limitations or require increased levels of parental involvement due to the demands of treatment. The result is often heightened conflict that may result in different patterns of behavior with respect to treatment adherence. It is not uncommon to see an overt struggle around the medical treatment, with blatant non-adherence. Lask (1994) has categorized this group of patients as "refusers." A second and more common pattern of behavior is that of adolescents who persistently maintain that they are fully adherent with their treatment, despite clear medical evidence to the contrary. Lask (1994) has categorized this group of patients as "deniers." A third dynamic is that of children who use the threat of refusing treatment as a way to manipulate their parents and situations to their own advantage. Nocon (1991) has described this behavior in children with asthma and described what he refers to as the "tyranny of the asthmatic child." In all of these cases, it is important to note that despite adolescent claims that they are able to take responsibility for their medical treatment, their behavior suggests, by contrast, that they require increased levels of parental supervision.

Influence of Illness on Caregivers

Parents often react to the diagnosis of a serious medical illness in their children in ways that may enhance the potential for conflict around adherence issues. Parents may experience feelings of "genetic guilt," particularly when their child's illness has a genetic component (Taylor & Eminson, 1994). In their efforts to compensate for these feelings, parents may fail to set limits on their child's behaviors and hence indirectly encourage acting out behaviors, including those of the failure to adhere to treatment. Another consequence is that of increased anxiety and hypervigilance in parents whose child has potentially life-threatening diseases such as asthma or leukemia. This may result in parents being reluctant to allow their child to participate in age-appropriate activities, for example, going away for camps or overnight trips due to the parents' concern about their safety. This phenomenon has been referred to as the Damocles syndrome (Koocher & O'Malley, 1981). This anxiety can foster a pattern of overprotectiveness that may further interfere with the adolescent's need for autonomy (Reynolds & Garralda, 1988). This dynamic may be particularly problematic in parents who develop symptoms of posttraumatic stress disorder (PTSD) related to their child's illness and treatment (Stuber et al., 1996). Wamboldt and associates (1995), for example, have shown a relationship between parental PTSD and poor treatment adherence in asthmatic children.

Difficulties with Risk Assessment

Several of the social-cognitive theories of treatment adherence describe the importance of risk assessment and its relationship with adherence. The ability of a patient to assess the risks of non-adherence clearly plays an important role. Adolescents generally have a limited capacity for risk assessment, and will engage in risk-taking behaviors in many areas of behavior, often with negative consequences. If the adolescent has a chronic illness that requires regular treatment, non-adherence becomes yet one other area in which to act out by missing medications. The adolescent feeling of omnipotence and the belief that they are in some way immune to the consequences of non-adherence may play a direct role in explaining their behavior. Both child and parent perceptions of the seriousness of their health condition as well as maternal perceptions of risks related to non-adherence have been shown to be related to treatment adherence (Riekert & Drotar, 2000). Other explanations given for the adolescent's difficulty in assessing risk include cognitive difficulties in assessing personal risk, lack of experience with the consequences of risk, ignorance, and denial (Brooks-Gunn, 1993).

Cognitive Maturity

Piaget's (1968) theory of cognitive development provides a model to understand some of the developmental issues that contribute to poor treatment adherence. The adolescent's level of cognitive development may have a strong influence on how they make decisions about their treatment (Campbell, 1975). Early adolescents are still likely to employ concrete operations in making these decisions, and even when formal reasoning has begun to develop, it may not be evident in decisions that involve emotionally charged material (Hamburg & Wortman, 1996; 1997). Younger adolescents in particular tend to have a narrow range of perceived solutions to difficulties related to their prescribed medical treatment. For example, they have a tendency to ignore long-term consequences, and rush to premature decisions when faced with the need to conform to family or peer pressures.

Adolescent Omnipotence

Invulnerability is a common belief of adolescents that may contribute to a sense that they are immune to the potential negative consequences of high-risk behavior (Elkind, 1967). This observation has led to speculation that poor adherence to medical treatment may be based, in part, on the adolescent belief that they can get away with not adhering to prescribed treatment (Harris & Linn, 1985). Elkind (1967) suggests that adolescents' belief that they are invulnerable is so strong that it "becomes a conviction that he will not die, that death will happen to others, but not to him," which in physical illness may translate into non-adherence. Theoretical support for this concept is also found in the work of Hauser (1991). Hauser defines a sequence of increasingly mature stages of functioning in several domains that include impulse control and cognitive style. According to this theory, ego development involves the greater ability to anticipate the consequences of behavior as well as the ability to take increased personal responsibility for one's actions. Hauser described six stages of ego development in which the overall progression is toward greater social conformity. During the impulsive stage, the early adolescent tends to be impulsive and present-focused with little ability to accept the need to conform to rules related to medical treatment. In addition, at this stage, adolescents are unable to consider the possibility of potentially negative future consequences of non-adherence, particularly in diseases from which there are no immediate or visible consequences of missing doses of medications (Litt & Cuskey, 1980). It is not until late adolescence, during Hauser's conscientious stage, that responsibility for treatment can be appropriately delegated to the adolescent, and even at this stage, some ongoing adult supervision is likely to be necessary.

Cognitive Limitations

The presence of cognitive limitations is another important factor that may interfere with the adolescent's ability to assess risk. These cognitive limitations may be related not only to the child's level of cognitive maturity, but also a consequence of both the disease and its treatment. Many of the chronic illnesses, for example, renal and liver failure, may directly affect cognitive and academic functioning. There may also be indirect effects as a result of the need to miss school days due to hospitalizations and medical appointments (Schweitzer & Hobbs, 1995). In addition, the medications used in the treatment of many chronic medical conditions, for example, anticonvulsant medications used in seizure disorders, or immunosuppressant used in organ transplant recipients, can impair cognitive functioning (DuPaul & Kyle, 1995). It is also important to assess parental knowledge and functioning, because it is usually the responsibility of parents and families to monitor treatment, especially in younger children. La Greca and colleagues (1990) emphasize the importance of this point in their finding that preadolescent but not adolescent treatment adherence is correlated with maternal knowledge in diabetic patients.

Affiliation with the Peer Group

Another adolescent issue that may interfere with treatment adherence is the developmental task of establishing social relationships with the peer group. The desire for acceptance and conformity with the peer group is often at odds with expectations for treatment adherence (Brooks-Gunn, 1993). One important issue is that of the stigma associated with chronic illness. The pressures for conformity may result in resistance to treatment recommendations, particularly those treatments that have cosmetic side effects (Dolgin et al., 1986; Friedman & Litt,

1987; Korsch, Fine, & Negrete, 1978). Examples include the antirejection medications used in organ transplant recipients that result in hair growth and corticosteroids used in the treatment of asthma and juvenile rheumatoid arthritis. Some individuals may avoid taking their medications in front of their peers, or stop taking them altogether in order to reduce the stigma of their illness (Conrad, 1985). Hauser's work, cited earlier, suggests that it is not until late adolescence that individuals develop the maturity to manage peer pressure and conform to needed medical treatments (Hamburg & Wortman, 1996; 1997).

Adaptive Non-adherence

Closely related to the issue of risk assessment is the individual's judgment of the benefits of following the prescribed treatment versus the perceived barriers and costs of treatment referred to in the literature as outcome expectancies (Riekert & Drotar, 2000). In their efforts to maintain a semblance of age-appropriate behavior and psychological functioning, adolescents may make "quality of life" decisions about how closely to follow treatment recommendations. This may translate into the periodic decision to take calculated risks about their treatment. Deaton (1995), in a study of asthmatic patients, has used the term "adaptive noncompliance" to describe this phenomenon. Similarly, Koocher and associates (1990), in their typology of non-adherence in patients with cystic fibrosis, use the term "educated non-adherence." Using the analogy of non-adherence as a risk-taking behavior, it may be helpful to differentiate adaptive non-adherence as a form of normal adolescent risk-taking behavior that promotes adolescent individuation and development (Shaw, 2001). By contrast, risk behaviors are those patterns of risk-taking that have predominantly negative consequences (Ponton, 1997).

Psychiatric Comorbidity

We have reviewed some of the common developmental issues that are related to treatment adherence in normal adolescents. However, a smaller subset of medically ill adolescents may engage in a spectrum of risk-taking behaviors, including non-adherence, which indicate the presence of comorbid psychopathology. A relationship between non-adherence and psychiatric comorbidity has been shown in several studies (Brownbridge & Fielding, 1994; Jacobson et al., 1987; Korsch et al., 1978; Kovacs et al., 1992). It is particularly important to identify these patients because they may require more intensive psychological interventions. In the following section, we will discuss some of the specific interactions between psychopathology and non-adherence.

Mood Disorders

Clinical observations suggest a strong relationship between the presence of a mood disorder and treatment adherence. Depressed patients may forget or ignore their medical treatment, or in severe cases, intentionally miss medications as an expression of their hopelessness or suicidality. Empirical support for these observations comes from studies of patients on renal dialysis showing an association between poor treatment adherence and depression (Brownbridge & Fielding, 1994) or suicidal behavior (Abram et al., 1971). Feelings of low self-esteem were also correlated with poor treatment adherence in renal transplant recipients (Korsch et al., 1978). As a result of terminal illness, patients may make deliberate decisions to refuse treatment, believing that the costs of treatment outweigh the potential benefits. This observation finds support in a study by Gudas and colleagues (1991) who found that greater pessimism was associated with non-adherence in patients with cystic fibrosis.

Attention-Deficit/Hyperactivity Disorder

Attention-deficit/hyperactivity disorder (ADHD) is one disorder that may place medically ill children at particular risk of non-adherence. It is an important group to consider given its relatively high prevalence of 3–5% in the general child population (American Psychiatric Association, 1987). Children with ADHD are particularly prone to forget their medications and require additional supervision. In addition, children with ADHD are more likely to have behavioral and emotional difficulties, including comorbid diagnoses of oppositional defiant disorder and conduct disorder that have also been associated with poor adherence (Shelton & Barkley, 1995). The associated hyperactivity can also create major obstacles to maintaining a safe environment for children who have a prescription of limited activity, for example, in patients with hemophilia or those recovering from trauma.

Posttraumatic Stress Disorder

There are a number of studies that have reported symptoms of post-traumatic stress disorder (PTSD) as a consequence of physical trauma and medical illness (Green et al., 1997). For example, studies have found significant rates of PTSD symptoms in both cancer survivors and their family members (Cella, Mahon, & Donovan, 1990; Stuber et al., 1996). Shemesh and colleagues (2000) found a direct relationship between symptoms of PTSD and non-adherence in pediatric liver transplant recipients, and suggested that the PTSD-avoidance symptom cluster may lead patients to avoid taking their medications so as not to remind themselves of their illness. There are also studies of diabetic patients suggesting that the aversive experience of hypoglycemia leads patients to deliberately run high glucose levels in order to avoid hypoglycemic episodes (Cox et al., 1987). Wamboldt and associates (1995) have suggested that parental histories of trauma and PTSD may also result in the greater likelihood of non-adherence in asthmatic patients.

Personality Pathology

Although the relationship between treatment adherence and personality pathology has been better examined in adult patients, many of the principles identified apply during adolescence. For example, patients with borderline personality traits have particular difficulties trusting their physicians and their pattern of impulsive and self-destructive behavior may directly affect their ability to cooperate with their medical treatment (Stoudemire & Thompson, 1993). Patients who engage in self-defeating patterns of behavior may also undermine and sabotage treatment interventions. These patients may have unconscious motivations to create despair in their doctors, or to provoke feelings of rejection and frustration (Elliot, 1987). Lipsitt (1970) has also suggested that this group of patients may unconsciously be requesting care rather than desiring cure for their illness.

Parent-Child Conflict

Aspects of family function play a crucial role in the adaptation of children and adolescents to chronic illness (Lorenz & Wysocki, 1991). For example, numerous studies have shown a direct relationship between family conflict and treatment adherence (Christiaanse et al., 1989; Friedman et al., 1986). Other family correlates of adherence include parental coping, family support, family cohesion, efficacy of family communication as well as parental supervision of the medical treatment (Beck et al., 1980; Bobrow, AvRuskin, & Siller, 1985; Hauser et al., 1990). Families with excessive levels of conflict are at particular risk since the support of the parents is critical to ensure adequate treatment adherence, particularly in younger adolescents.

Treatment Intervention

In spite of over three decades of research on the prevalence and correlates of non-adherence, there have been relatively few studies that attempt to validate interventions to improve treatment adherence (Rapoff, 1999). Drawing conclusions from these studies is also difficult since many of the interventions have several components to them and it is unclear which component is the one responsible for change. Sample sizes are often small, and may lack homogeneity, and many studies have been relatively short-term in nature with no good long-term follow-up data.

Advances regarding the efficacy of treatment interventions have been limited by several factors, one of which is the limited number of conceptual models used to explain non-adherence (Riekert & Drotar, 2000). Establishing conceptual models of treatment adherence is critical in the development of effective treatment interventions. Research on the correlates of non-adherence, described earlier, has been a useful first step and one that helps identify groups at particular risk, such as adolescents. It also helps suggest specific interventions, for example, treatment that is aimed at reducing family conflict, or improving family cohesion and communication. Conceptual models may also help identify factors that are likely to reduce the efficacy of treatment interventions, such as psychiatric comorbidity.

La Greca and Schuman (1995) and Rapoff (1999) have classified the treatment approaches used to address non-adherence in pediatric patients into several major categories. These include educational, organizational, behavioral, and psychotherapeutic interventions. (See Table 33.3.)

Educational interventions should be part of the routine care provided when patients are first diagnosed, or when the goal is a simple one such as helping

TABLE 33.3.   GENERAL APPROACHES TO THE MANAGEMENT OF TREATMENT ADHERENCE.

1. *Educational interventions*
   Education regarding illness and risks of non-adherence
   Education regarding appropriate levels of parental supervision

2. *Organizational interventions*
   Increased supervision by the medical team (more frequent medical visits or lab tests)
   The use of home-based visual cues or reminders (telephone calls, pagers, alarm clocks)

3. *Behavioral interventions*
   Reinforcement strategies using behavior modification principles
   Increased parental supervision and support
   Incentives for good treatment adherence

4. *Psychotherapy interventions*
   Treatment of comorbid psychiatric illness using individual or family therapy and psychiatric medications where indicated
   Family therapy to address specific issues, such as family conflicts

adolescents take on increased levels of responsibility. Used alone, however, these measures have very limited impact on improving adherence in children with chronic illness, particularly in higher-risk patients (La Greca & Skyler, 1991). Other helpful strategies rely on organizational changes, for example, simplifying the treatment regimen, and increasing the level of medical supervision (Eney & Goldstein, 1976; Rapoff et al., 1988). More data support the use of interventions that integrate behavioral approaches, for example, the use of incentives or other positive reinforcement strategies. These strategies are in general more effective than simple educational programs (Padgett et al., 1988). However, preliminary findings suggest that most success has been associated with programs that combine treatment strategies such as intensive education, parental involvement, self-monitoring, and reinforcement procedures. La Greca and Schuman (1995) also suggest the need to look at specific child and family characteristics that may influence the patient's ability to respond to interventions.

Rapoff (1999) has emphasized that one implication of this body of research is that the family needs to be the primary focus of interventions designed to improve adherence to therapeutic regimens in pediatric populations. Parents generally have the primary responsibility for ensuring good treatment adherence, especially in younger adolescents (La Greca et al., 1990). Interventions that aim to increase the level of parental involvement have been found to be successful in improving rates of adherence (Anderson et al., 1989; Satin et al., 1989). In addition, as reviewed earlier, there have been numerous studies showing a clear relationship between adherence and family functioning, which include conflict, communication style, and most importantly, parental support (Wysocki et al., 1995). More recent innovations include the use of peer-group interventions designed to enhance problem-solving techniques and social skills and the use of computer-based programs and video games in adolescents with diabetes (Brown et al., 1997; Horan et al., 1990; Kaplan et al., 1985).

Finally, an important focus for future research is the issue of psychiatric comorbidity, particularly how this may interact with interventions designed to enhance treatment adherence. These mediating variables may not only promote poor adherence, but also adversely affect efforts to improve adherence. Wysocki and colleagues (2000), for example, have conducted one of the first randomized controlled studies on non-adherence in adolescents with diabetes using an intervention based on the behavioral family systems therapy model of Robin and Foster (1989), in which the primary target for intervention was parent-adolescent conflict. Quittner and associates (2000) are currently testing a similar intervention for adolescents with cystic fibrosis in which the focus is on family-centered problem solving and education.

Enhanced Educational and Behavioral Intervention

We have recently developed a standardized treatment protocol to address the issue of non-adherence in children with chronic illness. (See Exhibit 33.1.) This is a nine-session program that consists of educational, behavioral, and family therapy components. Our treatment model is an integrated treatment model that incorporates a wide range of factors, but which is based predominantly on developmental principles (Hanson, 1992; Riekert & Drotar, 2000). Our treatment approach incorporates intensive education of the patient and family about both medical as well as the developmental issues that need to be considered in adolescent transplant recipients (Shaw, 2001). We also integrate behavior modification programs and regular family meetings as part of our treatment.

Education of the Medical Team

The first step in any hospital-based intervention program is to establish a working relationship and understanding with the primary medical team. It is important to educate the medical team about clinical populations at higher risk of non-adherence, such as adolescents, particularly those with comorbid psychiatric illness. Screening procedures and early referral for psychiatric assessment may help facilitate early identification of patients prior to the development of serious, potentially preventable medical complications. Simplification of the treatment regimen may be considered earlier for such high-risk patients. Education of the medical team regarding developmental or psychiatric issues that may contribute to non-adherence is important to help establish a cohesive approach to this issue. For example, it is important to come to a consensus on the age at which patients are expected to take responsibility for treatment because individual practitioners vary widely in terms of their own expectations. Although little is known about the optimal age at which adolescents should start to assume greater responsibility or how to intervene when there are the inevitable lapses in adherence, awareness of these issues is of great clinical value (Riekert & Drotar, 2000).

Education of the Family

Assessing the knowledge of the patient and family regarding the illness as well as its treatment are critical aspects of initiating any program to enhance adherence (La Greca et al., 1990). To facilitate this goal, the therapist observes the meeting between the medical team and the family in session one as the details of the illness and its treatment are explained. In addition to medical information, the family is given specific suggestions regarding the role of the parents in supervising and

EXHIBIT 33.1.   ENHANCED EDUCATIONAL AND BEHAVIORAL INTERVENTION (EEBI).

Session 1
Standard Medical Education.

The patient and his/her family and EEBI therapist meet with the medical team representative (physician, diabetic educator, transplant team coordinator) for standard medical education regarding the diagnosis and proposed treatment. Topics covered in this session include

- The nature of the illness including its course and prognosis.
- The proposed treatment interventions, including medications, surgery, dietary modifications, fluids, and exercise requirements.
- The likely complications and risks of non-adherence with treatment.
- The roles and responsibilities of parents and family members for providing supervision of the medical treatment.
- Explanation of role of EEBI therapist and review of the major components of EEBI, including schedule of appointments and behavior modification program.

Session 2
Assessment of the Family's Knowledge Base Regarding the Illness and Its Treatment.

The patient and family meet with the EEBI therapist to review the material from Session 1. All family members complete a short questionnaire to evaluate their understanding of the illness and its treatment, as well as the family's responsibility for providing supervision of the treatment.

- The EEBI therapist uses the results of the questionnaire to evaluate any major misconceptions on the part of the family and, if necessary, refers the family back to the medical team for further education.
- The EEBI therapist evaluates the patient's and family's emotional reaction to the diagnosis of the illness to assess their degree of acceptance as well as identify possible feelings of denial that may interfere with treatment.
- Patients or family members who manifest symptoms of comorbid psychiatric illness that seem serious or likely to persist (adjustment disorders, major depression) are referred for more comprehensive psychiatric evaluation and/or treatment.
- The EEBI therapist evaluates the self-efficacy beliefs of the patient and family to determine whether or not they believe that their behavior can influence the outcome of the illness.

Session 3
Family Education Regarding the Principles of Adolescent Development and Their Relationship with Treatment Adherence.

The patient and family meet with the EEBI therapist for a family educational session to review the common developmental issues of adolescence and how they may influence health care behavior with a particular emphasis on treatment adherence.

(Continued)

EXHIBIT 33.1.   ENHANCED EDUCATIONAL AND BEHAVIORAL INTERVENTION (EEBI) (CONTINUED).

Separation/Individuation
- Review of the adolescent's developmental need to separate and individuate from the parents.
- Discussion of the ways in which the diagnosis of a chronic physical illness interferes with the separation/individuation process (greater parental role in monitoring treatment, physical effects of illness, demands of treatment, effect on self-esteem, academic difficulties).
- Discussion of how parental anxiety about their child's health may result in restrictive or inflexible styles of parenting, which in turn exacerbates parent-child conflict.
- Explanation of how increased conflict with the parents may result in the adolescent acting out in the form of non-adherence.

Risk Assessment
- Review of the early adolescent tendency to use concrete operations in making decisions about treatment (narrow range of perceived solutions to problems, tendency to ignore long-term consequences; tendency to rush to premature decisions when faced with the need to conform to family or peer pressures).
- Review of the tendency of adolescents to believe that they are invulnerable to the potential negative consequences of high-risk behavior including non-adherence with their medical treatment.

Peer Pressure
- Discussion of the adolescent preoccupation with peer acceptance and how this is influenced by the diagnosis of a chronic illness (stigma about illness; heightened concern about body image during puberty; resistance to taking medications in front of peers; cosmetic side effects of medications; reluctance to miss school or social activities due to treatment).

Session 4
Introduction of the Behavioral Modification Program.

The EEBI therapist meets with the patient and family to discuss the principles of behavior modification and the use of a program to promote better treatment adherence. The following topics may be addressed:

- Why behavior modification is useful for adolescents to enhance adherence (principle of paying attention to positive and not just negative behavior; need for absolute consistency; discussion of parental concerns about using reinforcements for required behaviors).
- How to individualize the program to suit the needs of the family (choice of appropriate rewards; system to monitor adherence behavior; involvement of different family members; adaptation of program across multiple environments including home(s), overnights at friends' houses, and school).
- Discussion of how to implement the program over the following week. Ask patient to use the following techniques to assist with the integration of the behavioral modification plan into their daily routine: (1) self-monitoring—observation of what is happening during weeks when the patient has good adherence and

EXHIBIT 33.1. (CONTINUED).

what is happening when non-adherence occurs (such as family fighting, being overwhelmed by school work); (2) visual cues/reminders—encourage the adolescent to use visual cues to ensure the success of behavioral modification plan (such as cue sheets on bathroom mirror or the use of alarm or pager at medication times); and (3) encouragement of the parents to be consistent with their use of reinforcements.
- Discussion of potential barriers to implementing the behavior modification program.

Session 5
Review of the Behavior Modification Program.

The patient and family meet with the EEBI therapist to discuss the family's success in the use of the behavior modification program and the potential need to make changes to the program.

- Discussion of how well the program worked for the family (ability to monitor the adherence behavior, consistency of parents, effectiveness of incentives in motivating the patient).
- Further discussion on objective methods to assess treatment adherence rather than relying just on self-report (parent and teacher report, daily logs or medication diaries, use of signature sheet, laboratory tests, electronic monitoring of medication use).
- The EEBI therapist conducts a role-play in the session to illustrate how parents should respond to evidence of non-adherence with the behavior modification program (greater supervision, avoiding punitive "all-or-nothing" responses; how to give feedback on poor performance in a supportive manner).

Session 6
Individual Session with the Patient to Discuss Adolescent Developmental Issues.

The patient meets alone with the EEBI therapist to discuss common adolescent issues that may interfere with treatment adherence.

- Discussion of the major lifestyle adjustment resulting from the diagnosis of the illness (changes in physical appearance and its effect on body image and self-esteem; the need to modify exercise and eating patterns; changes in life expectancy or alterations in career goals). The EEBI therapist addresses each of these issues and assesses their emotional impact on the patient.
- Discussion of the impact of the illness on peer and sibling relationships (feelings of stigma and being different; changes in priorities as a result of illness; resentment of siblings due to special attention from parents due to illness; guilt about impact of illness on the family).
- Discussion of issues related to puberty and sexuality (changes in body appearance or growth due to illness and treatment; concerns that the opposite sex with not find the patient attractive).
- Assessment of other psychiatric issues including anxiety, depression, and substance abuse and their potential effects on treatment adherence.

(Continued)

EXHIBIT 33.1.   ENHANCED EDUCATIONAL AND BEHAVIORAL INTERVENTION (EEBI) (CONTINUED).

Session 7
Family Education Regarding School Reintegration.

The patient and family meet with the EEBI therapist to discuss common issues related to school reintegration.

- Discussion of how best to handle questions and curiosity about the patient's illness following the return to school (how much information to disclose and to whom; handling teasing and name-calling; how to handle absences and missed school work due to medical appointments and hospitalizations; dealing with overprotective parents).
- Discussion of how to handle academic concerns (scheduling a meeting with the school principal; establishing a plan to catch up on missed work; requesting an Individualized Education Program to ensure that necessary accommodations will be made by the school).

Session 8
Family Education Regarding How to Respond to Non-adherence with Treatment.

Because lapses in adherence are inevitable, the family meets with the EEBI therapist to discuss how to respond when these lapses occur.

- Discussion of when the parents should be concerned and intervene after having evidence of non-adherence (immediately versus after a pattern is established).
- Discussion of typical examples of effective and ineffective ways to deal with non-adherence. The EEBI therapist conducts a role-play for possible scenarios (patient forgets to take medications prior to going to a friend's house; patient starts to act out in a blatant and risky pattern of non-adherence).
- The EEBI therapist models how to question the patient about the treatment adherence in order to understand the behavior and respond in a supportive and non-punitive manner. Explanation that the reasons for non-adherence may be diverse (lapse in memory, denial of illness, desire not to miss an important social event, concern about reactions of peers, feelings of despair and hopelessness about illness).
- Discussion of how the family can problem-solve after the reason for the non-adherence is understood. Discussion of appropriate responses on the part of the parents with input from the adolescent (increased level of supervision, loss of privileges, change in the behavior modification program incentives).
- Ensure that non-adherence is not due to lack of understanding of the medical plan or miscommunication about instructions regarding the medications.

EXHIBIT 33.1.   (CONTINUED).

Session 9
Family Education on How to Negotiate Issues with the Medical Team.

Since treatment adherence may be affected by the nature of the doctor-patient relationship, the final session focuses on how to negotiate issues that come up with the medical team. The EEBI therapist meets separately with the medical team prior to this session to get an understanding of the team's perception of the patient and family.

- Review of any possible misconceptions that may have arisen due to miscommunication between family and the medical team, particularly those issues related to the treatment regimen.
- Discussion of how the patient and family can best communicate with the medical team when problems arise so as to be able to negotiate successful compromises (the treatment is too complicated or unrealistic; the patient does not feel supported or respected by the team; dissatisfaction with communication between the family and the team).

---

monitoring their child's treatment. The presence of the therapist at the first meeting not only provides a shared knowledge base between the family and the psychiatric consultant regarding the treatment, but also establishes the therapist as part of the medical team. In session two, the family members complete a questionnaire to assess their knowledge based on this first meeting. The results of the questionnaire establish to what degree the family is able to comprehend and retain important medical information at the beginning of their treatment. In session three, the therapist reviews the core principles of adolescent development and their relationship with adherence. This is an educational session that emphasizes the role of the family in supporting their child's treatment and in anticipating the difficulties that may interfere with adherence. Topics that are covered in this session include the need to anticipate periods at which children may be at greater risk for non-adherence as well as education about appropriate responses to episodes of non-adherence.

Behavioral Intervention

In session four, the family is introduced to the behavior modification program that will be used to reinforce treatment adherence. Because adolescents frequently receive attention only when they fail to take needed medications, the positive reinforcement of desired, rather than negative, behaviors is emphasized. A specific behavioral plan is tailored for each patient, choosing appropriate incentives and establishing an effective system to monitor and reward the patient's behavior. In session five, there is a review of the family's success in implementing the program and ways to overcome the barriers to its use.

Addressing Specific Developmental Issues

In session six, there is an individual meeting between the therapist and the patient to explore common adolescent developmental issues that may affect adherence and which were reviewed earlier. The impact of the adolescent's illness and treatment, including medication side effects, is discussed in this meeting. In session seven, the important topic of school reintegration is discussed with an emphasis on how to handle teasing and name calling, and how to handle academic issues related to missing school. In session eight, there is a problem-solving exercise on how patients and family members respond to inevitable episodes of non-adherence, with suggestions on how to continue to support the adolescent's need for autonomy while parents maintain their supervisory role over the treatment.

Treatment of Psychiatric Comorbidity

When psychiatric comorbidity is identified, it is important to institute prompt and appropriate treatment depending on the disorder in question. This may include medication treatment for depression, referral for substance abuse treatment, or family therapy for parent-child conflict. We have found that ongoing assessment and treatment of parental psychopathology is important at all stages of treatment. The presence of significant psychiatric illness may result in the family being unsuitable for our treatment intervention. However, when these important underlying comorbid disorders have been adequately treated, patients may become candidates for less intensive intervention programs that are targeted specifically at enhancing treatment adherence. The development of clinical pathways or treatment algorithms may be useful in determining what types of treatment are required for specific subgroups of patients. This approach is also likely to have important cost benefits if the screening of patients results in them being assigned to appropriate levels of intervention.

Future Directions

The study of treatment adherence is one that is still very much in its infancy. Research has been limited partly due to many logistic and methodological issues. These include, for example, difficulties establishing reliable and valid measures of adherence behavior, and problems with the recruitment of adequate sample sizes. In addition, as mentioned earlier, there is a lack of conceptual models to help guide intervention efforts, and only a few of the existing models have been subjected to rigorous scientific examination. One important focus of future research is that of the relationship between adherence itself and clinical outcome to establish whether or not improved adherence translates into better medical prognoses. This is an area that is likely to attract increasing scrutiny, particularly as the financial and health care costs of non-adherence become more apparent.

In terms of future directions, there is a strong need for large, well-designed, multi-site, placebo-controlled studies to examine both the factors that contribute to poor adherence as well as interventions to enhance adherence. These studies need to establish the types of intervention that are likely to be most effective in specific populations of medically ill children. Greater awareness of the factors that limit the efficacy of treatment interventions is needed so that patients in high-risk groups, for example, adolescents with severe psychiatric comorbidity, can be assigned to more appropriate levels of care. When appropriate treatment protocols have been tested in tertiary care settings, there is a need to develop treatment manuals that can be adapted and used by practitioners in other clinical settings. Finally, another critical area of research is the relationship between treatment adherence and quality of life outcome variables. The balance between the intensity of our medical treatments and quality of life is a factor that needs to be kept in mind in all decisions related to the care of children with medical illness.

In this chapter, we have described a treatment approach designed to help medically ill children who are referred for consultation due to problems with treatment adherence. The principles used in our intervention program are widely applicable to many areas of psychiatric consultation. These include education of the pediatric team to help with the identification and referral of high-risk patients in an effort to prevent medical and psychiatric illness. Second is the need to educate both patients and family members about how best to intervene to support children diagnosed with medical illness. Finally, there is the need to recognize the developmental issues unique to children and adolescence so as to tailor interventions and improve the likelihood of their success.

References

Abram, H. S., Gorden, L., Moore, M. E., & Westevelt, F. (1971). Suicidal behavior in chronic dialysis patients. *American Journal of Psychiatry, 127*, 9.

Anderson, B. J., Auslander, W. F., Jung, K. C., Miller, J. P., & Santiago, J. V. (1990). Assessing family sharing of diabetes responsibilities. *Journal of Pediatric Psychology, 15*, 477–492.

Anderson, B. J., Wolf, F. M., Burkhart, M. T., Cornell, R. G., & Bacon, G. E. (1989). Effects of peer-group intervention on metabolic control of adolescents with IDDM: Randomized outpatient study. *Diabetes Care, 3,* 179–183.

Beck, D. E., Fennell, R. S., Yost, R. L., Robinson, J. D., Geary, D., & Richards, G. A. (1980). Evaluation of an educational program on compliance with medication regimens in pediatric patients with renal transplants. *The Journal of Pediatrics, 96,* 1094–1097.

Berg, J. S., Dischler, J., Wagner, D. J., Raia, J., & Palmer-Shevlin, N. (1993). Medication compliance: A health care problem. *The Annals of Pharmacotherapy, 27(Suppl),* 2–21.

Blos, P. (1967). The second individuation process of adolescence. *Psychoanalytic Study of the Child, 22,* 162–186.

Bobrow, E. S., AvRuskin, T. W., & Siller, J. (1985). Mother-daughter interaction and adherence to diabetes mellitus. *Diabetes Care, 8,* 146–151.

Brooks-Gunn, J. (1993). *Why do adolescents have difficulties adhering to health regimes?* Hillsdale, NJ: Erlbaum.

Brown, S. J., Lieberman, D. A., Germeny, B. A., Fan, Y. C., Wilson, D. M., & Pasta, D. J. (1997). Educational video game for juvenile diabetes: Results of a controlled trial. *Medical Informatics, 22,* 77–89.

Brownbridge, G., & Fielding, D. M. (1994). Psychosocial adjustment and adherence to dialysis treatment regimens. *Pediatric Nephrology, 8,* 744–749.

Campbell, J. D. (1975). Illness is a point of view: The development of children's concepts of illness. *Child Development, 46,* 92–100.

Cella, D. F., Mahon, S. M., & Donovan, M. (1990). Cancer recurrence as a traumatic event. *Behavioral Medicine, 16,* 15–22.

Christiaanse, M. E., Lavigne, J. V., & Lerner, C. V. (1989). Psychosocial aspects of compliance in children and adolescents with asthma. *Journal of Developmental and Behavioral Pediatrics, 10,* 75–80.

Cole, B. R. (1994). Noncompliance to medical treatments. In A. H. Tejani (Ed.), *Pediatric Renal Transplantation* (pp. 397–408). New York: Wiley-Liss.

Conrad, P. C. (1985). The meanings of medication: Another look at compliance. *Social Science and Medicine, 20,* 29–37.

Cooper, D. K. C., Lanza, R. P., Barnard, C. N. (1984). Noncompliance in heart transplant recipients: The Cape Town Experience. *Heart Transplantation, 3,* 248–253.

Cox, D., Irvine, A., Gonder-Frederick, L., Nowacek, G., & Butterfield, J. (1987). Fear of hypoglycemia: Quantification, validation, and utilization. *Diabetes Care, 10,* 617–621.

Deaton, A. V. (1995). Adaptive noncompliance in pediatric asthma: The parent as expert. *Journal of Pediatric Psychology, 10,* 1–14.

Diagnostic and statistical manual of mental disorders (3rd ed.). (1987). Washington, DC: American Psychiatric Association.

Didlake, R. H., Dreyfus, K., Kerman, R. H., Van Buren, C. T., & Kahan, B. D. (1988). Patient noncompliance: A major cause of late graft failure in cyclosporine-treated renal transplants. *Transplantation Proceedings, 20,* 63–69.

Dolgin, M. J., Katz, E. R., Doctors, S. R., & Siegel, S. E. (1986). Caregivers' perceptions of medical compliance in adolescents with cancer. *Journal of Adolescent Health Care, 7,* 22–27.

DuPaul, G. J., & Kyle, K. E. (1995). *Pediatric pharmacology and psychopharmacology.* New York: Guilford Press.

Elkind, D. (1967). Egocentrism in adolescence. *Child Development, 38,* 1025–1034.

Elliot, R. L. (1987). The masochistic patient in consultation-liaison psychiatry. *General Hospital Psychiatry, 9,* 241–250.

Eney, R. D., & Goldstein, E. O. (1976). Compliance of chronic asthmatics with oral administration of theophylline as measure by serum and salivary levels. *Pediatrics, 57,* 513–517.

Ettenger, R. B., Rosenthal, J. T., Marik, J. L., Malekzadeh, M., Forsythe, S. B., Kamil, E. S., et al. (1991). Improved cadeveric renal transplant outcome in children. *Pediatric Nephrology, 5,* 137–142.

Friedman, I. M., & Litt, I. F. (1987). Adolescents' compliance with therapeutic regimens: Psychological and social aspects and intervention. *Journal of Adolescent Health Care, 8,* 52–65.

Friedman, I. M., Litt, I. F., King, D. R., Henson, R., Holtzman, D., Halverson, D., et al. (1986). Compliance with anticonvulsant therapy by epileptic youth. *Journal of Adolescent Health Care, 7,* 12–17.

Green, B. L., Epstein, S. A., Krupnick, J. L., & Rowland, J. H. (1997). *Trauma and medical illness: Assessing trauma-related disorders in the medical settings.* New York: Guilford.

Gudas, L. J., Koocher, G. P., & Wyplj, D. (1991). Perceptions of medical compliance in children and adolescents with cystic fibrosis. *Developmental and Behavioral Pediatrics, 12,* 236–247.

Hamburg, B. A., & Wortman, R. N. (Eds.). (1996/97). *Adolescent development and psychopathology* (Vol. 2, Chapter 4). Philadephia, New York: Lippincott-Raven Publishers.

Hanson, C. L. (1992). Developing systematic models of the adaptation of youths with diabetes. In A. M. La Greca, L. J. Siegel, J. L. Wallander, & C. E. Walker (Eds.), *Stress and coping in child health* (pp. 212–241). New York: Guilford Press.

Harris, R., & Linn, M. W. (1985). Health beliefs, compliance, and control of diabetes mellitus. *Southern Medical Journal, 78,* 162–166.

Hauser, S. T. (1991). *Adolescents and their families.* New York: Free Press.

Hauser, S. T., Jacobson, A. M., Lavori, P., Wolfsdorf, J. I., Herskowitz, R. D., Milley, J. E., et al. (1990). Adherence among children and adolescents with insulin-dependent diabetes mellitus over a four-year longitudinal follow-up: Immediate and long term linkages with the family milieu. *Journal of Pediatric Psychology, 15,* 527–542.

Haynes, R. B. (1979). *Introduction.* Baltimore: Johns Hopkins University Press.

Horan, P. P., Yarborough, M. C., Besigel, G., & Carlson, D. R. (1990). Computer-assisted self-control of diabetes by adolescents. *The Diabetes Educator, 16,* 205–216.

Jacobson, A. M., Hauser, S. T., Wolfsdorg, J. I., Houlihan, J., Milley, J. E., Herskowitz, R. D., et al. (1987). Psychologic predictors of compliance in children with recent onset diabetes mellitus. *Journal of Pediatrics, 110,* 805–811.

Johnson, S. B., Silverstein, J., Rosenbloom, A., Carter, R., & Cunningham, W. (1986). Assessing daily management of childhood diabetes. *Health Psychology, 5,* 545–564.

Kaplan, R. M., Chadwick, M. W., & Schimmel, L. E. (1985). Social learning intervention to promote metabolic control in type I diabetes mellitus: Pilot experimental results. *Diabetes Care, 8,* 152–155.

Koocher, G. P., McGrath, M. L., & Gudas, L. J. (1990). Typologies of nonadherence in cystic fibrosis. *Journal of Developmental & Behavioral Pediatrics, 11,* 353–358.

Koocher, G. E., & O'Malley, J. E. (1981). *The Damocles Syndrome.* New York: McGraw-Hill.

Korsch, B. M., Fine, R. N., & Negrete, V. F. (1978). Noncompliance in children with renal transplants. *Pediatrics, 61,* 872–876.

Kovacs, M., Goldston, D., Obrosky, D. S., & Iyengar, S. (1992). Prevalence and predictors of pervasive noncompliance with medical treatment among youths with insulin-dependent diabetes mellitus. *Journal of the American Academy of Child and Adolescent Psychiatry, 31,* 1112–1119.

La Greca, A. M. (1990a). Issue in adherence with pediatric regimens. *Journal of Pediatric Psychology, 15,* 423–436.

La Greca, A. M. (1990b). Social consequences of pediatric conditions: Fertile area for future investigation and intervention? *Journal of Pediatric Psychology, 15,* 423–436.

La Greca, A. M., Follansbee, D., & Skyler, J. S. (1990). Developmental and behavioral aspects of diabetes management in youngsters. *Child Health Care, 19,* 132–137.

La Greca, A. M., & Schuman, W. B. (1995). Adherence to prescribed medical regimes. In M. C. Roberts (Ed.), *Handbook of pediatric psychology* (2nd ed., pp. 55–83). New York: Guilford.

La Greca, A. M., & Skyler, J. S. (1991). *Psychological management of diabetes.* London: Chapman & Hall.

Lask, B. (1994). Non-adherence to treatment in cystic fibrosis. *Journal of the Royal Society of Medicine, 87,* S21, 25–27.

Lipsitt, D. R. (1970). Medical and psychological characteristics of "crocks." *Psychiatric Medicine, 1,* 15–25.

Liss, D. S., Waller, D. A., Kennard, B. D., McIntire, D., Capra, P., & Stephens, J. (1998). Psychiatric illness and family support in children and adolescents with diabetic ketoacidosis: A controlled study. *Journal of the American Academy of Child and Adolescent Psychiatry, 37,* 536–544.

Litt, I., & Cuskey, W. R. (1980). Compliance with medical regimens during adolescence. *Pediatric Clinics of North America, 27,* 1–15.

Lorenz, R. A., & Wysocki, T. (1991). The family and childhood diabetes. *Diabetes Spectrum, 4,* 261–292.

Nocon, A. (1991). Social and emotional impact of childhood asthma. *Archives of Disease in Childhood, 66,* 458–460.

Padgett, D., Mumford, E., Hynes, M., & Carter, R. (1988). Meta-analysis of the effects of educational and psychosocial interventions on management of diabetes mellitus. *Journal of Clinical Epidemiology, 41,* 1007–1030.

Piaget, J. (1968). *The growth of logical thinking.* New York: Basic Books.

Ponton, L. E. (1997). *The Romance of risk.* New York: Basic Books.

Quittner, A. L., Drotar, D., Ievers-Landis, C., Slocum, N., Seidner, D., & Jacobsen, J. (2000). Adherence to medical treatments in adolescents with cystic fibrosis: The development and evaluation of family-based interventions. In D. Drotar (Ed.), *Promoting adherence to medical treatment in childhood chronic illness: Concepts, methods, and interventions* (pp. 383–408). Mahwah, NJ: Erlbaum.

Quittner, A. L., Tolbert, V. E., Regoli, M. J., Orenstein, D., Hollingsworth, J. L., & Eigen, H. (1996). Development of the Role-play Inventory of Situations and Coping Strategies (RISCS) for parents of children with cystic fibrosis. *Journal of Pediatric Psychology, 21,* 209–235.

Rapoff, M. A. (1999). *Adherence to pediatric medical regimens.* New York: Kluwer Academic/Plenum Publishers.

Rapoff, M. A., Purviance, M. R., & Lindsley, C. B. (1988). Improving medication compliance for juvenile rheumatoid arthritis and its effect on clinical outcome: A single-subject analysis. *Arthritic Care Research, 1,* 12–16.

Reynolds, J. M., & Garralda, M. E. (1988). How parents and families cope with chronic renal failure. *Archives of Disease in Childhood, 63,* 821–826.

Riekert, K. A., & Drotar, D. (2000). Adherence to medical treatment in pediatric chronic illness: Critical issues and answered questions. In D. Drotar (Ed.), *Promoting adherence to medical treatment in chronic childhood illness: Concepts, methods and interventions* (pp. 1–32). Mahwah, NJ: Erlbaum.

Robin, A. L., & Foster, S. L. (1989). *Negotiating parent-adolescent conflict: A behavioral family systems approach.* New York: Guilford Press.

Satin, W., La Greca, A. M., Zigo, M. A., & Skyler, J. S. (1989). Diabetes in adolescence: Effects of multifamily group intervention and parent simulation of diabetes. *Journal of Pediatric Psychology, 14,* 259–276.

Schweitzer, J. B., & Hobbs, S. A. (1995). *Renal and liver disease: End-stage and transplantation issues.* New York: Guilford Press.

Shaw, R. J. (2001). Treatment adherence in adolescents: Development and psychopathology. *Clinical Child Psychology and Psychiatry, 6*(1), 137–150.

Shelton, T. L., & Barkley, R. A. (1995). *The assessment and treatment of attention-deficit/hyperactivity disorder in children.* New York: Guilford Press.

Shemesh, E., Lurie, S., Stuber, M. L., Emre, S., Patel, Y., Vohra, P., et al. (2000). A pilot study of post-traumatic stress and non adherence in pediatric liver transplant recipients. *Pediatrics,* 105, e129.

Sly, R. M. (1988). Mortality for asthma in children 1979–1984. *Annals of Allergy, 60,* 433–443.

Stein, M. T. (1999). An adolescent who abruptly stops his medication for attention deficit hyperactivity disorder. *Journal of Developmental & Behavioral Pediatrics, 20,* 106–110.

Stoudemire, A., & Thompson, T. L., II. (1993). Medication noncompliance: Systematic approaches to evaluation and intervention. *General Hospital Psychiatry, 5,* 233–239.

Stuber, M., Christakis, D., Houskamp, B., & Kazak, A. E. (1996). Post-traumatic symptoms in childhood leukemia survivors and their parents. *Psychosomatics, 37,* 254–261.

Taylor, D. C., & Eminson, D. M. (1994). *Psychological aspects of chronic physical sickness.* Oxford: Blackwell Science.

Wamboldt, M. Z., Weintraub, P., Krafchick, D., Berce, N., & Wamboldt, F. S. (1995). Links between past parental trauma and the medical and psychological outcome of asthmatic children: A theoretical model. *Family Systems Medicine, 13,* 129–149.

Wolff, G., Strecker, K., Vester, U., Latta, K., & Ehrich, J. H. H. (1998). Non-compliance following renal transplantation in children and adolescents. *Pediatric Nephrology, 12,* 703–708.

Wysocki, T., Harris, M. A., Greco, P., McDonell, K., Taylor, A. M., & White, N. H. (2000). Randomized, controlled trial of behavior therapy for families of adolescents with insulin-dependent diabetes mellitus. *Journal of Pediatric Psychology, 25*(1), 23–33.

Wysocki, T., White, N. H., Bubb, J., Harris, M. A., & Greco, P. (1995). *Family adaptation to diabetes: A model for intervention research.* New York: Guilford Press.

CHAPTER THIRTY-FOUR

LEGAL CONSULTATIONS

Peter Ash, M.D.

Forensic psychiatric consultations involve psychiatric questions that come before the courts. While many child and adolescent psychiatrists shy away from such work, often because of anxiety about providing in-court testimony, and particularly about being cross-examined by an attorney who is trying to find defects in the psychiatric expert's opinion, such work can be intellectually rewarding and be of enormous benefit to the children involved. In forensic work with adults, the psychiatric expert is usually retained by a party to the case (although some evaluations are court-ordered and the expert is an expert for the court). This typically places the expert on one side of an adversarial process. In the three most common forensic questions that child psychiatrists are called upon to answer, child custody questions in divorce, child placement issues in abuse or neglect cases, and disposition of delinquency cases in juvenile court, the child psychiatrist is more of an advocate for the well-being of the child. Such a role is somewhat above the fray, as the expert is not beholden to any of the parties in the case. This is a different role than is typical in adult forensic work, in which the expert typically provides an opinion to assist the court in reaching a just disposition, either with regard to how the evaluee should be handled in a criminal process (such as whether he should stand trial or be found not guilty by reason of insanity), or whether he should receive money in a civil case. In such cases, the well-being of the evaluee is not the prime consideration. The emphasis on what is good for the child gives child forensic work a more therapeutic thrust, similar in some ways to an expert's role in a civil commitment proceeding, and so much child forensic work is more congenial to those whose primary professional identification is as a therapist.

The Forensic Question

The aspect that most sharply distinguishes forensic consultation from diagnosis and treatment in most clinical contexts is that forensic evaluations are focused on the particular forensic question involved. Usually, there is a forensic test set out in legal language either by statute or in court precedents. These tests vary from state to state, and it is important for the consultant to be clear on the test used in his or her jurisdiction. Examples of commonly used forensic tests are listed in Table 34.1.

TABLE 34.1.   COMMONLY USED FORENSIC TESTS.

Issue	Typical Test
Custody in the context of divorce	Best interests of the child
Abuse or neglect proceedings	Varies according to the stage of the proceeding: Was the child abused or neglected? Are the parents fit to raise the child? Should protective services pursue reunification? Is termination of parental rights in the best interests of the child?
Delinquency: study and report	What mental health services will be useful?
Waiver to adult court	Risk of future dangerousness and amenability to rehabilitation
Competency to stand trial	Understand charges and nature of the proceedings and able to assist his or her attorney
Competency to waive a constitutional right (such as competency to confess, waive right to counsel, or plead guilty)	Is waiver knowing, intelligent, and voluntary?
Malpractice	Did the treating physician's care meet the standard of practice?
Personal injury	Nature of damages, their causes, and treatments to ameliorate them
Civil commitment	Dangerous to self or others or unable to care for self
Special education services	Is child "seriously emotionally disturbed"?
Consent to an abortion	Is girl a "mature minor"?

Source: Adapted from Ash, in press.

The consultant's role is to provide an opinion on the relevant test. Issues of diagnosis and treatment become relevant only to the extent that they help substantiate such a position.

Because the role of the evaluator is to provide an opinion to the person or agency requesting the consultation, the evaluator typically does not have a duty to treat the child or adolescent involved. In fact, when the evaluator does have a duty to treat the child because the child is the evaluator's patient, it is generally preferable to refer the forensic evaluation to another clinician.

Beginning the Case

Cases frequently begin with a telephone call from at attorney. As with any consultation, it is very important to be clear about the question to be answered and the role of the consultant. Because of the scrutiny forensic reports often undergo by attorneys and courts, it is especially important in forensic consultations that these issues be clear at the outset. The most common error of those inexperienced in forensic work is to become involved in a case without having clarified beginning issues, only to find, part way into the case, that the evaluator is trapped in a role that precludes an objective view of the situation. The two main issues that need to be clarified before accepting a case are

1. The forensic question to be answered
2. The role of the evaluator, including defining who the client is (the child, the court, a parent, and so on), payment issues (including who is responsible for payment), and to whom the report (if any) is to be sent.

The Forensic Question

In order to answer the forensic question, the consultation needs to be oriented so that it provides information relevant to the forensic test, and, as will be discussed further, the report should address the test in the specific legal language used in the jurisdiction. In the event the consultant is not sure of the forensic test to be utilized, he or she should clarify the question with the referring party (attorney, judge, client, and so on). In some instances, most commonly when the consultee is a party to the case, the consultee may not know the operative test, in which case the psychiatrist will need to determine it by other means. It is disheartening to spend a great deal of time and thought on a case only to have one's opinion set aside because the expert failed to address the relevant legal standard (for example, opining that removal from the home is in a child's best interests rather than addressing whether the parents are fit to raise the child).

Clarifying the Consultant's Role

For clinicians who do not have a great deal of forensic experience, consultations that go awry and result in considerable hair-pulling are frequently due to not getting the consultant's role clear in the beginning. In addition to understanding the forensic question, issues that need to be clarified before the case is begun include

1. Who is requesting the evaluation (a parent, an attorney, the school, or the court)?
2. Who is providing the requisite consent for the evaluation?
3. Who is to be interviewed?
4 To whom will the report be sent?
5. What are the arrangements for paying the fees?

These issues are frequently more complex in cases involving minors than in cases involving adults. First, minors have limited formal decision-making authority, and so, although the minor may be the subject of a case, others will often be speaking for the minor in court. Second, in custody cases, both divorce-related and in abuse or neglect proceedings, the child is typically not a formal party to the case at all. Some particulars of defining role will be discussed after the example cases.

Many experienced forensic evaluators obtain written fee contracts prior to beginning an evaluation, but some do not. Generally, unless the retaining agent is a corporate defendant or state agency, fees should be paid prior to conducting the work and in any event prior to completing the evaluation. It is quite tempting for a party who is disappointed in the evaluation not to pay, either to save money or to prevent the report from being sent. Wondering whether the retaining party will pay the fee can also be a subtle source of bias for the evaluator, which may be brought out on cross-examination. ("Now doctor, do you really think you'll be paid for your testimony today if it's not favorable to Mr. X?")

Forensic Evaluations on One's Own Patients

Not uncommonly, a child in treatment will become the subject of a legal proceeding. The attorney for either the child or a parent may wish to use the treating clinician as the expert on the grounds that the clinician knows the child best. For several reasons, it is almost always preferable to refer one's patient to another clinician for forensic evaluation. First, a forensic role usually is quite disruptive of the treatment. Once the child (or parent) knows that the therapist is a route to the judge, confidentiality goes out the window, and the parameters of the treatment change. Second, the clinician may not have a well-formed opinion on the particular forensic issue. For example, if the parents are divorcing and one parent wishes the clinician to give an opinion on post-divorce custody arrangements, the clinician may well not have assessed the parents' parenting capacity or compared their relationships with the child. To do so will generally require going beyond (and potentially threatening) the treatment relationship. This role conflict is known as the "double-agent problem" (that is, being the agent of the child, as therapist, and being an agent of the court or parent, as forensic evaluator). Finally, treating doctors are frequently seen by courts as advocating for their patients, and in some cases such advocacy will be seen as bias. An attorney for a parent may nevertheless subpoena the treating psychiatrist out of a sense of efficiency. Such actions can sometimes be discouraged. For example, in a child custody case in which a parent's attorney threatens to subpoena the treating psychiatrist, the therapist may point out that such an action is likely to disrupt the child's treatment, and this may be evidence that the parent is not acting in the best interest of the child.

Conducting the Evaluation

Different types of evaluations require different approaches. Several examples of common child forensic psychiatric evaluations will be discussed to illustrate some of the general principles involved. If a clinician is inexperienced in forensic evaluations, he should seriously consider obtaining consultation or supervision from a more experienced evaluator for at least his first several cases. It is not uncommon that inexperienced evaluators find themselves in unforeseen dilemmas that might otherwise have been avoided.

Child Custody in Divorce

Custody evaluations in the context of divorce (either pre-divorce or post-judgment) are among the most taxing, both in time and in emotion, evaluations in forensic psychiatry. A number of professional organizations have published practice parameters for conducting them (American Academy of Child and Adolescent Psychiatry, 1997; American Psychological Association Committee on Professional Practice and Standards, 1994). Unlike many adult forensic evaluations, which involve assessing one person, child custody evaluations typically involve assessing the child (or children) in the family, each parent, possibly new spouses who will be part of the proposed custodial environment, *and* the relationships between all these people. Most experts agree that it is best, although not always possible, to structure the evaluation so that the evaluator is not beholden to one side, but free to advocate for the child's best interests. In order to have access to all relevant information, it is best if the evaluator is able to interview children and all adults involved in the case. This is most easily accomplished by having the evaluation be court-ordered rather than conducted at the request of just one party. Many experienced evaluators accept cases only on court order. If a parent or attorney for a parent requests an evaluation, they recommend obtaining such an order to ensure that both sides will participate. (There is a further benefit to conducting evaluations on court order: the evaluator then typically has the immunity of the court, and is therefore immune to a malpractice suit brought by a disgruntled parent, although he is not immune to grievances of professional organizations or state boards of medicine.)

While there are different perspectives on how to conduct such evaluations, the author recommends accepting cases only under the following ground rules:

1. Evaluations are accepted only on court order.
2. Both parents, all children, and new spouses agree to participate.
3. There is no confidentiality within the confines of the evaluation—the evaluator is free to discuss with any person involved or put in the report any material he or she believes is relevant and received from whatever source.
4. The report will go to the attorneys for both parties and to the court. (One side will not be able to bury an unfavorable report.)
5. The evaluator will be an advocate for the best interests of the child(ren).

It is beyond the scope of this chapter to discuss all the possible parameters in conducting such an evaluation. Clinicians who are interested should obtain supervision or consultation with an experienced evaluator until they have some experience. The following is the basic structure for a pre-divorce custody evaluation. The sessions indicated are typically double sessions:

1. The evaluation does not begin until a copy of the court order is received. It is unwise to assume that a parent's or attorney's characterization of the existence or contents of the order is accurate.
2. A letter is sent to each parent covering the ground rules of the evaluation, and includes a questionnaire about some basic demographic information, the nature of the issue, and a symptom checklist for each parent to fill out about each child.
3. The initial interview session is conducted with both parents. Doing this interview jointly makes clear to each parent that the evaluator is not on one

parent's side, and allows for cross-checking of basic background information. A central goal of the session is to obtain an understanding of why the
parents are unable to work out a custody/access arrangement by themselves
or with the help of a mediator. In about one-seventh of cases, this author is
able to help parents settle their dispute in this first session, the main difficulty
having been that no one previously ever tried (Ash & Guyer, 1986). The second goal is to focus on the best interests of the children, and ascertain what
each parent thinks is in the child's best interest. Many custody cases arise when
parents focus on what the parent is entitled to (and what the spouse should be
deprived of). There are many aspects of this adversarial system that encourage and reinforce such feelings of entitlement. Parents who can be helped to
refocus on the child's best interest (rather than feeling they are giving in to a
hated spouse) often reach agreement.

The interviewer begins with a review of the ground rules of the evaluation, and solicits any questions the parents may have. The interview should remain child-focused: extended criticisms of the other parent, or a detailed
history of the deterioration of the relationship, should be actively curtailed.
The evaluator is trying to get the general lay of the land: the details of why
the spouses are furious with each other are counterproductive in a joint interview. The idea is to learn what facts the parents can agree on and the areas
in which the disputes remain. Releases are obtained for school records, speaking to the child's therapist, and other records, as appropriate.

4. Individual assessment of each parent. This allows the evaluator to understand
each parent's perspective and concerns, evaluate their thinking, and obtain
information along the two major axes that need to be assessed: the parenting
capacity of each parent, and the nature of the child's attachment to each parent.
Psychological testing of each parent (such as the Minnesota Multiphasic
Personality Inventory [MMPI-2]) is used routinely by many evaluators. There is
a tendency for parents to "fake good" in such testing, but lack of such testing
is frequently used to attack the "completeness" of the evaluation in court. Regarding mental health treatment of a parent, the author generally asks for a release to speak with outpatient therapists, but does not solicit written records of
outpatient treatment. The reason for this is to attempt to retain some confidentiality in their individual treatment. Any record the evaluator sees is discoverable
(can be reviewed by a party to the case) and can be entered as evidence. What
the evaluator typically wants to learn from the therapist is what problems the
evaluator might have overlooked; the evaluator should *not* rely on conclusions of
others (How does he know they're valid?), but use the information gained to more
efficiently make his own inquiries of the parent. In the event a parent has been
hospitalized, reading the discharge summary is generally useful.

(As an aside, therapists in private practice who are contacted by one parent to provide treatment of a child during a contentious separation or divorce should be aware of the potential limitations of their point of view. Parents who refuse a therapist the consent to even contact the other parent may be driven by a variety of factors that are not always in the best interest of the child. Similarly, reports for schools are discoverable by either parent and may become part of a child's record, so potentially biased sources of information and their attendant limitations should be carefully documented. In short, in any case, it is important to be aware of who has custody, and whether this is full, joint or partial, especially when treatment decisions are being made.)

5. Direct observation and assessment of the parent-child relationship and individual assessment of the child. In a typical case involving two elementary school-aged children, the author would typically structure a two-hour appointment as follows:

   • One parent and both children are shown into a room with some toys and drawing material and told, "I would like you to act as you might at home if you were waiting to go out together and had some extra time. I realize this is a strange place, and you're being observed, but try to act natural."

     [If a one-way vision mirror is being used] "I'll be watching on the other side of the mirror."

     [If the evaluator remains in the room] "Just pretend I'm a fly on the wall."

     The evaluator then watches for about twenty minutes. If the interaction becomes repetitive or not useful (for example, the group starts playing a game and has no conversation other than the mechanics of the game), the evaluator can intervene after a few minutes and give the group a task, such as to make up a story.

   • The evaluator returns to the room and begins with, "I realize this was an unusual situation. How typical do you think it was of what actually goes on at home?" (Surprisingly, most families say the interaction was typical or better than usual. The author recalls one interview in which the mother, step-father, and step-siblings immediately started berating one of the children, and continued non-stop until the author could not stand it any longer. When asked how typical this interaction was, everyone in the family, including the scapegoated child, agreed this was the best they had gotten along in the previous three months!) Family discussion of the interaction leads into a twenty- to thirty-minute discussion of how the children and parent relate, and should cover the good times and the difficult times ("How does discipline work in your family?"), as well as provide more direct observation of interaction. The evaluator should attempt to have everyone join in the discussion, not just listen to the parent give his or her view.

- The parent is sent out of the room, and the children are seen together for a period (say ten minutes) and then individually for at least twenty-five minutes each. The previously observed interactions make a useful springboard for discussion of how members of the family relate to each other.

The above sequence is repeated on a different day with the other parent.

6. In post-divorce cases, the proposed living groups (new spouses, step-siblings) are included for a portion of the time.
7. The evaluator takes stock of what is known. If she feels confident of her recommendation, she proceeds to write a draft of the report. (Reports are discussed more fully below.) If more information is needed, additional sessions are set up or information is obtained. Depending on the particulars of the case, this may include additional interviews with family members, interviews with collateral subjects (such as grandparents, teachers), or obtaining documents. Generally speaking, the evaluator should resist the temptation to play detective. Relatively few cases turn on ascertaining the truth of allegations about disputed events that the children did not witness. There is little reason to think that a mental health expert brings much expertise to the detective process. Parties to an evaluation are not under oath (evaluators new to forensic evaluations are often surprised by how frequently people lie), and recommendations will be more compelling if based on evidence the evaluator gathered directly through observations and assessment.

   The judgment of what to recommend to the court is complex. The evaluator should generally give fairly specific recommendations as to who should decide what (sole or joint decision-making on issues such as education, religion, and medical care) and how much the child should be with each parent (physical custody, visitation, or access issues). Whether the legal label of sole custody or joint legal custody is applied is generally less critical. In some cases, recommendations regarding future methods of dispute resolution are appropriate. (For example, the parents should identify a mediator to whom they will go in the event of disagreements, appointment of a special master, or recommendations for treatment.) The limited research regarding the outcomes of child custody decisions is unfortunately not of sufficient power to determine most decisions in individual cases. There is some research evidence that imposing joint custody on unwilling and acrimonious parents is likely to be problematic, and that better mental health of the custodial parent is associated with better outcomes for children following an acrimonious divorce (Johnston, 1994). However, recommendations remain a clinical judgment, based on applying theories to the particulars of the case. The most difficult cases include those in which the child is more attached to the less capable parent and those in which both parents appear quite good but a difficult choice must be made. (For example, parents of a two-year-old are in the military; one is to be transferred to Japan and the other to Germany.)

8. After a draft of the report is prepared, the evaluator should meet with each parent separately to discuss the findings. The interview with the disappointed parent is not one evaluators look forward to, but is very important for a number of reasons. First, it is humane, having subjected two parents to a very difficult evaluation that carries enormous implications for them, to allow some feedback on one's findings. Second, the evaluator should encourage the parent to express negative and disappointed feelings, in part to decrease their being acted out negatively toward the child or through the legal system. Third, the evaluator can give his impression of the case thus far: in some instances, the parent will give further information or correct a misunderstanding of the evaluator. Finally, the parent's reaction may provide further data substantiating the evaluator's recommendation. In cases involving adolescents, the evaluator should consider conducting a separate feedback session with the adolescent. (In one evaluation, the adolescent refused to provide any information to the author, a decision which was respected. The author conducted the first feedback session with the adolescent, and laid out a summary of his findings and recommendations. "Wrong!" announced the adolescent, who went on to provide data that led to changing the recommendations.)

9. The evaluator completes the report and sends it to the court and the parents' attorneys.

Evaluations in Sexual Abuse Cases

Sexual abuse allegations are among the most heated and contentious evaluations in forensic psychiatry. When a clinician has a reasonable suspicion that a child has been abused or neglected, in all states he has a legal duty to make a report to the state's child protective service agency. The child projective service agency is charged with investigating the case. A full investigation involves ascertaining whether or not the child was abused, and if so, what harm the child suffered, the parents' current parenting capacity, and the prognosis (Barnum, 1997). A child psychiatrist will most often attempt to ascertain whether or not abuse took place when a case is referred to him for a second opinion, or when he is treating a patient and the question of whether or not abuse occurred is clinically relevant. Sexual abuse issues occur so frequently in a treatment practice that it behooves all clinicians to be aware of the general principles of a sexual abuse evaluation. The stakes are high. Abuse cases frequently involve removal of children from their homes and criminal prosecution of perpetrators, and a good deal of litigation has dealt with the adequacy and correctness of sexual abuse evaluations (Ceci, 1995).

The evaluator's primary concern in interviewing should be to obtain relevant data without contaminating the memories of the child involved. This is particularly important when a preschool child is involved, because the younger the child, the more susceptible she is to suggestion (Ceci & Huffman, 1997). Interviews in an evaluation for sexual abuse take place over a number of sessions, and include evaluations of the child and collateral sources.

Evaluations of Adults

It is important to interview both of the child's parents, any other adult to whom an allegation was communicated by the child, and the alleged perpetrator. It is especially important to understand how the allegation first arose from the person who first heard the child's allegation, in as much detail as possible. What was the context? How did the subject come up? What did the adult (most often a parent) say? The less evidence of suggestion in the initial report, the more credible the allegation. A mother who reports that her three-year-old son came home from nursery school very upset and volunteered, "A big boy on the playground made me kiss his wee-wee," generates a much higher index of suspicion than a mother who reports that her three-year-old son was fondled while on visitation with her ex-husband, and who reports, when asked why she thinks this, that when her son returns from a visit, she always asks if his father touched his wee-wee and this time, he giggled and said, "When I was in the bath."

The psychiatrist should also attempt to obtain a comprehensive picture of the parents' and family's functioning. Interviews with the adults should include obtaining a developmental history of the child, the child's general functioning, and the child's current symptoms. Sexual abuse may cause a wide variety of symptoms. There is no "sexually abused child syndrome," a constellation of symptoms from which abuse can be deduced.

Although it is useful to have background information before the child is seen, there is also fairly clear evidence that knowledge of the particulars of the allegation can bias interviewers toward confirming what is suspected (Ceci & Huffman, 1997).

Interview of the Child

The interview of a preschool child who may have been sexually abused is a delicate balancing act. On the one hand, repetitive, suggestive, or leading questioning run a high risk both of obtaining inaccurate information, and since such questioning changes memory, of contaminating future investigations as well (Ceci & Bruck, 1995). On the other hand, young children may not provide spontaneous accounts of what happened, and require some structured questioning. Videotaping of the child interviews should be done to preserve the record of what took place. A number of protocols have been proposed, but there is no settled consensus about the one correct way to proceed. A number of authors describe beginning in an unstructured manner, and then progressing toward more structured questioning (American Academy of Child & Adolescent Psychiatry, 1997; Quinn, 2002; Yuille, Hunter, Joffe, & Zaparniuk, 1993). One approach to structuring the interview is as follows:

1. An unstructured portion of the interview in which the clinician develops rapport with the child and assesses the child's developmental level. Assessment of whether the child knows the difference between the truth and a lie, and telling the child the interview will focus on what really happened and "not pretend."
2. Introduce issue of sexual information and action.
   - Does the child know why she is being seen? Has anything happened to make the child uncomfortable?
   - Assessment of child's level of sexual knowledge, including the child's words for sex organs. This may be done with the assistance of drawings or anatomically correct dolls. (See cautions, below.)
3. If the child brings up an incident of abuse, encourage the child to provide more details in a non-leading manner: "Do you remember anything else about what happened?" It is important that such questions not be repeated over and over, thus communicating to the child that a "No" is the wrong answer.
4. Follow-up questions to delineate details of the event. It is crucial that the interviewer remain unbiased, and that both potentially confirming and disconfirming details be obtained. For example, if a three-year-old says that her father touched her "hiney" in the bath, the interviewer needs to attempt to determine whether this occurred as part of normal bathing of a small child or for the parent's sexual gratification.
5. Questions aimed at assessing the child's susceptibility to suggestion. These may include asking misleading questions about irrelevant events: "You came here by taxi today, didn't you?"

The use of aids to interviewing children, such as anatomically correct dolls or figure drawing with genitalia, is controversial. Some argue that they may help young children talk or show what happened (Everson & Boat, 1994), but there is also evidence that the use of dolls is suggestive and increases the risk of a false positive allegation (Bruck, Ceci, & Francoeur, 2000).

Assessing the data in a sexual abuse case can be extremely difficult. While many cases present data with which most clinicians would agree, when the data are not clear-cut, experts looking at the same data may well reach different conclusions as to whether abuse took place. In one of the few studies of expert decision-making in these cases (Horner, Guyer, & Kalter, 1993), forty-eight experts reviewed the same clinical data and videotaped interviews. Not only did the experts reach very different conclusions as to whether abuse took place, their confidence in their opinions varied from very low to almost certain.

Evaluations for Waiver to Adult Court

When a minor is arrested on a criminal charge, he typically comes under the jurisdiction of the juvenile court. In some instances involving serious charges, especially murder, the minor may be waived to adult court. State law governs the type of waiver that will apply to an individual case. Waiver statutes typically take the form of "Youth over the age of X, who are charged with one of the following offenses . . . , may [or shall] be waived to adult court if . . ." Psychiatrists are most often involved in conducting an evaluation for a judicial waiver. The U.S. Supreme Court has held that a judge cannot waive a youth without a hearing (Kent v United States, 1966). Other types of waiver either automatically place youth facing serious charges in adult court (mandatory or legislative waiver), or allow the prosecutor to decide to move the case to adult court (direct file or prosecutorial waiver).

Juvenile judges commonly make use of mental health evaluations to assist them in making a determination at a waiver hearing. Judges have considerable discretion in what factors they consider and how they weigh each factor. These proceedings are governed by state law, but the statutory criteria for waiver to federal court (18 USCS §5032) are typical and include the age and social background of the juvenile, the nature of the alleged offense, the extent and nature of the juvenile's prior delinquency record, the juvenile's present intellectual development and psychological maturity, the nature of past treatment efforts and the juvenile's response to such efforts, and the availability of programs designed to treat the juvenile's behavioral problems. From the perspective of the evaluating psychiatrist, the two most relevant dimensions are the risk of future dangerousness and amenability of rehabilitation.

As is the case in psychiatry generally, the prediction of dangerousness, which in these cases is essentially a prediction of recidivism, turns on the assessment of risk factors. Grisso (1998) recommends that the evaluator not provide the court with an opinion as to whether the defendant youth will or will not be violent, but rather provide the court with a risk estimate, an analysis of how the risk factors of this particular youth compare to those of some relevant population, such as youths who come before the court. Although a full discussion of the evaluation of risk assessment in delinquents is beyond the scope of this chapter (see Loeber & Farrington, 1998; Satcher, 2001; Steiner & Dunne, 1997), several points that distinguish evaluations of juveniles from other risk assessments (such as for hospitalization or civil commitment) will be made. Although past behavior is the best predictor of future behavior, in the context of a delinquency proceeding, obtaining an accurate past history may be difficult. It is important to be clear about whether or not what the youth tells the evaluator can be used to prosecute the youth, either for current or past offenses. Even if the material may not be formally admissible in court, the defense attorney may advise his client not to talk about illegal acts out of a concern that such information may lead the prosecutor to other evidence, or prejudice the judge against his client. Second, the developmental course of delinquent behavior needs to be considered. Youths arrested for a serious violent offense have typically committed numerous previous offenses (Elliott, 1994); however, the persistence of violent behavior into adulthood is fairly low (less than 20%) with those who were violent prior to adolescence at considerably greater risk than those who first became violent in adolescence (Loeber & Farrington, 2000; U.S. Department of Health and Human Services, 2001). Personality factors (sociopathic/predatory versus affective/reactive aggression) or substance abuse (its presence, absence, or remission) are relevant to estimating rates of recidivism (Steiner, Cauffman, & Duxbury, 1999; Wilson, Rojas, Haapanen, Duxbury, & Steiner, 2001). Finally, the psychiatrist should keep in mind that risk assessments developed in the context of evaluating a mentally ill person for danger to others, with their emphasis on homicidal or suicidal ideation and the existence of a plan, are of very limited use in predicting predatory violence.

Assessing amenability to rehabilitation requires an assessment of the youth's psychosocial treatment needs and in many jurisdictions, an assessment of available resources to treat the identified problems. The assessment of treatment needs includes a good diagnostic assessment, generally with a particular focus on antisocial traits, substance abuse, and conduct disorder (Steiner & Dunne, 1997). Social factors, especially the defendant's peer group, need to be assessed. The connection between the crime and identified problems should be made explicit. For example, the relevance of depression in a youth with no prior criminal record who attempted a murder-suicide at school is much greater than depression which occurred secondary to arrest and detention. Finally, making a judgment about the availability of interventions requires knowledge of the juvenile justice system's resources.

Other Forensic Evaluations

Many different sorts of cases involving children and adolescents can come before a court. Many of these evaluations are discussed in forensic textbooks (Melton, Petrila, Poythress, & Slobogin, 1997; Nurcombe & Partlett, 1994; Rosner, 2003; Schetky & Benedek, 2002). For example, if a youth is waived to adult court, the full panoply of adult criminal process comes into play, including issues of competency to stand trial and insanity or other diminished capacity defenses. These evaluations call for clear understanding of the forensic tests and issues involved (Grisso & Schwartz, 2000). Insanity defenses are rare in waived youths because the incidence of psychosis is considerably lower in adolescents than in adults and because serious mental illness is a compelling reason not to waive a youth to adult jurisdiction.

If a youth remains under juvenile court jurisdiction and emotional disturbance is thought to play a role in the youth's behavior, the juvenile court judge will often order a mental health evaluation. This is often referred to as a *study and report,* and is intended to assist in formulating a disposition. A study and report is a general psychological evaluation that often includes psychological testing and concludes with recommendations for mental health interventions.

Child psychiatrists may also be asked to participate in a wide range of civil cases, including child psychiatry malpractice (Ash, 2002), special education (Dalton, 2002), and psychiatric trauma related to accidents (Lubit, Hartwell, van Gorp, & Eth, 2002).

Reports

Because the audience and purpose of a forensic report is different from a psychiatric treatment record, information and opinions need to be presented in a different manner.

1. Focus on the forensic question. In the introduction, the evaluator should indicate what the forensic question is (in legal language). Rather than having a "history of present illness," the report should outline the history of the problem.
2. The ground rules of the evaluation should be made explicit. This includes who referred the case, to whom the report is going, and what consent, notification, or assent was obtained for the evaluation.
3. The basis of the opinion should be laid out. This begins with a list of the sources of information (interviews, including dates and duration, documents, records and videotapes reviewed, and so on). The general rule in organizing the report is to keep the data and opinion sections separate: the data section should not contain opinions, and the opinion section should not contain any new data. It is not necessary to put in all data obtained during the evaluation; rather, the report should focus on the data relevant to the forensic opinion. Psychiatric evaluations can be wide-ranging, and frequently a great deal of highly personal information is obtained. Remember that in many instances, the report becomes a public court record. Therefore, the inclusion of potentially embarrassing or

highly personal information not necessary for formulating the opinion is generally inappropriate.

4. The conclusion should address the specific prongs of the legal test. For example, if evaluating competency to stand trial, the conclusion of the report should explicitly address the defendant's knowledge of the charges *and* discuss his ability to assist his attorney (plus whatever other components the particular jurisdiction requires). The reasoning from the data to the opinion should be made explicit.
5. Remember that the primary audience for the report is the judge and attorneys involved in the case. The report should be written in language aimed at the intelligent layperson. Professional jargon should be avoided, and when used, should be defined. The class of medications listed should be identified (for example, "Risperdal, an antipsychotic medication, . . ."). Remember, too, that you may have to defend the report under cross-examination. You should make sure the facts are correct and the report is written grammatically. Many a cross-examination proceeds by rubbing the expert's nose in incorrect dates and sloppily worded facts, leaving the impression that the expert is so thoughtless and careless that his opinion—which may not even be challenged—may safely be ignored by the jury. Any bias in the report will seriously weaken the persuasiveness of the expert's opinion. It is important, therefore, to explicitly address that data that provide support for a contrary opinion. Few cases are black and white, and making explicit a careful weighing of the evidence goes a long way toward demonstrating impartial expertise. Finally, a well-reasoned report becomes a large bargaining chip in pre-trial settlement negotiations. The vast majority of cases do not go to trial. Trials occur when there is sufficient uncertainty about the outcome. (If everyone agrees on how the judge or jury will rule, why go through the time and expense of trial?) A persuasive report, particularly if issued by a court-appointed expert, markedly reduces uncertainty about the outcome.

Testimony

If the expert was court-appointed (for example, in a custody case), one or both of the attorneys may wish to discuss the expert's findings. Generally, it is appropriate for a court-appointed expert to do so. For an expert retained by one party to the case, discussion with the other party's attorney is not appropriate. In civil cases, a non-retaining attorney generally has the right to request a discovery deposition to find out more about the expert's opinion (and to assess what sort of witness the expert is likely to be). The underlying concept is that in a civil trial, there should not be too many surprises at trial. In most jurisdictions, criminal cases do not allow for discovery depositions.

Depositions

Depositions are scheduled at the expert's convenience, and may take place at his office, at an attorney's office, or at another location of the expert's choosing. The expert should bring several copies of his current curriculum vitae and all notes and records pertaining to the case.

Before a discovery deposition, the expert should meet with the retaining attorney to discuss what is likely to come up at the deposition. The expert should discuss with the retaining attorney whether that conversation is itself discoverable (that is, whether the expert needs to answer questions of the form: "What did you and the retaining attorney discuss?"). In a discovery deposition, the retaining attorney typically asks very few questions, so the deposition takes on the character of a cross-examination without a preceding direct examination. The general rule is to limit one's answers to the questions posed, and not offer information that is not explicitly asked about. If the answer is "No," just say, "No." Do not explain why "No" is the answer. Inexperienced experts too often attempt to persuade the questioning attorney of the correctness of their opinion, or feel that if they do not address every nuance, they will be falling into some clever cross-examiner's trap. Such behavior more often gives away more than it gains.

The expert should try to remain calm and collected, and consider each question carefully before answering. This also gives the retaining attorney a chance to object. Even if an objection is raised, the expert must ordinarily answer the question unless directed not to answer by the retaining attorney, under the theory that the judge could rule later on the objection if the deposing attorney attempts to have the answer entered as evidence.

Avoid becoming defensive ("What? You've only done *two* custody evaluations in your entire career?" . . . "Yes." . . . "And yet you expect us to give any weight *at all* to your opinion?" . . . "My expectation of your opinion about my opinion is not a medical question, and I don't have a professional opinion about it.") Don't get caught up in the attorney's pace. Rapid-fire questions do not require rapid-fire answers. Only a transcript of a discovery deposition is prepared, so pauses and tone of voice are not recorded. The recommended readings include references that more fully address expert testimony (e.g., Gutheil & Simon, 2002).

Occasionally, an attorney will use the absence of a judge to ask questions the expert thinks are overly personal. The general test is whether the question is relevant to the issue at hand. Questions that go to bias or competence are relevant. For example, questions about fees in this case need to be answered; questions about total income generally do not. Board status, license restrictions, loss of privileges, and so on, are considered relevant. The answers to other questions ("Have you ever been sued? Arrested?") are already in the public domain. More problematic are issues such as whether the expert, as a child, was sexually abused. This might be relevant in a sexual abuse case, but would not be relevant in a delinquency case. If the expert anticipates such problems or feels especially vulnerable in a particular area, this should be discussed with the retaining attorney in advance of the deposition.

In a discovery deposition in which the expert is court-appointed, the approach is less adversarial. Often both attorneys will ask questions, and the expert tries to communicate his findings, explain any unclarities in his report, and lay out his qualifications.

A second type of deposition is called a deposition *de bene esse*. This is a deposition that occurs in lieu of the expert's appearance at trial, which generally occurs if, for some reason, the expert will be unavailable for a live appearance. Such depositions are generally videotaped, and are then shown to the judge or jury at trial. The expert treats such a deposition as trial testimony.

Trial Testimony

Although a "Perry Mason" cross-examination in which the witness is ultimately reduced to confessing perjury is what most people fear when they imagine trial testimony, the direct testimony is usually considerably more difficult. On direct examination, the expert lays out his case before the judge or jury. If the direct testimony is not clear and coherent, the cross-examination need do nothing. It is crucial, therefore, that the expert meet with the attorney who will be conducting the direct examination and discuss how the relevant material will be presented. It is, unfortunately, all too common that attorneys skip this meeting, for example, say, they'll go over it with the expert for a few minutes in the hall before trial, and the resulting direct examination suffers drastically. Many attorneys do not understand mental health concepts very well, and discussion with the attorney is the only way to rectify this situation. An expert report that is thought through well can often serve as a template for the direct examination. I generally ask attorneys what the style of the direct examination will be: do they want to ask questions that call for short answers to lead me through testimony in small steps, or will they ask relatively open-ended questions that allow me to structure the material and emphasize what I think is important. ("What did Mr. Jones tell you about his work history?" versus "What information about Mr. Jones' background did you find important in reaching an opinion?")

It is important to remember that a trial is a very human process. If the jury gains an impression of an expert as accomplished, thoughtful, impartial, and caring, they will use her testimony very differently than if they see her as biased and money-grubbing. The expert should dress conservatively. Most experienced experts recommend a calm and composed approach, although the personality of the expert has a great deal to do with witness style, and some experts have been quite successful using more emotional and confrontational styles. Audiovisual materials such as portions of videotapes, blow-ups of pages from the medical chart, and posters with a time line listing the chronology of key events are often helpful in bringing the material alive to a jury.

The expert should be well-prepared and familiar with his opinions and with the data that support them. It is not, however, necessary to memorize every detail. The witness may bring written materials with him to the witness stand (most commonly his report, notes, curriculum vitae, records he may want to cite—the full file has usually been admitted into evidence and does not need to be lugged up—and a copy of the *DSM*), and the expert will be allowed to "refresh his recollection" from these documents. The cross-examining attorney has the right to inspect any document the witness brings to the stand.

After the direct examination is completed, the opposing attorney has the opportunity to cross-examine. A well-prepared expert with a coherent opinion should have little to fear on cross-examination, although this is the portion of the trial that is generally most anxiety-laden for inexperienced experts. It is important to try to remain calm and consider each question carefully. For inexperienced experts, one of the more common problems is becoming overly adversarial, and refusing to grant any ambiguity in the issues. The answer to questions that begin, "Doctor, isn't it possible that . . . " is almost always affirmative, with perhaps a thrown-in qualifier, such as, "Possible, but very unlikely." Being overly defensive or long-winded in responding to such questions tends to make the expert look biased, and once the judge or jury thinks the witness is biased, they find it easy to discount the entire opinion. It is better to adopt a stance that recognizes that this is a complex issue with at least some evidence on both sides, but an impartial consideration of the evidence leads to the expert's conclusion being by far the most likely. A natural reaction to being questioned is to look at the attorney asking the questions, but it is the jury, or if no jury, the judge, who is the trier of fact and will take the opinion into account. It is generally useful to make eye contact with the trier of fact for much of the time when responding.

If the expert has been appointed by the court, and in some cases even when retained by one party, the judge may also have some questions. This is especially common in cases in which the child is not formally a party to the case, but has important interests at stake, such as in cases involving divorce and abuse or neglect.

◆ ◆ ◆

The legal system has great need of child psychiatric expertise. Although many psychiatrists feel that the legal arena is fraught with anxiety, a clinician with a well-considered, carefully reasoned opinion, has little to fear from hostile cross-examination. Court decisions often have an enormous impact on a child's life: they may decide with whom the child will live, whether he will be able to see one of his parents, or whether he will spend years in an adult prison rather than much more limited time in juvenile detention. The forensic consultant can take great satisfaction in helping courts make such decisions correctly.

References

American Academy of Child and Adolescent Psychiatry (Bernet W. principal author). (1997). Practice parameters for the forensic evaluation of children and adolescents who may have been physically or sexually abused. AACAP Official Action. American Academy of Child and Adolescent Psychiatry. *Journal of the American Academy of Child and Adolescent Psychiatry, 36,* 423–442.

American Academy of Child and Adolescent Psychiatry (Herman S. P. principal author). (1997). Practice parameters for child custody evaluation. *Journal of the American Academy of Child and Adolescent Psychiatry, 36,* 57S–68S.

American Psychological Association Committee on Professional Practice and Standards (COPPS). (1994). Guidelines for child custody evaluations in divorce proceedings. *American Psychologist, 49,* 677–680.

Ash, P. (in press). Children and adolescents. In R. I. Simon & L. H. Gold (Eds.), *Forensic Psychiatry for the Clinician: Guidelines for assessment, APPI.*

Ash, P. (2002). Malpractice in child and adolescent psychiatry. *Child and Adolescent Psychiatric Clinics of North America, 11,* 869–886.

Ash, P., & Guyer, M. (1986). The functions of psychiatric evaluations in contested child custody and visitation cases. *Journal of the American Academy of Child Psychiatry, 25,* 554–561.

Barnum, R. (1997). A suggested framework for forensic consultation in cases of child abuse and neglect. *Journal of the American Academy of Psychiatry and the Law, 25,* 581–593.

Bruck, M., Ceci, S. J., & Francoeur, E. (2000). Children's use of anatomically detailed dolls to report genital touching in a medical examination: Developmental and gender comparisons. *Journal of Experimental Psychology: Applied, 6,* 74–83.

Ceci, S. J., & Bruck, M. (1995). *Jeopardy in the courtroom: A scientific analysis of children's testimony.* Washington DC: American Psychological Association.

Ceci, S. J., & Huffman, M. L. (1997). How suggestible are preschool children? Cognitive and social factors. *Journal of the American Academy of Child and Adolescent Psychiatry, 36,* 948–958.

Dalton, M. A. (2002). Education rights and the special needs child. *Child and Adolescent Psychiatric Clinics of North America, 11,* 859–868.

Elliott, D. S. (1994). Serious violent offenders: Onset, developmental course, and termination—The American Society of Criminology 1993 Presidential Address. *Criminology, 32,* 1–21.

Everson, M. D., & Boat, B. W. (1994). Putting the anatomical doll controversy in perspective: An examination of the major uses and criticisms of the dolls in child sexual abuse evaluations. *Child Abuse and Neglect, 18,* 113–129.

Grisso, T. (1998). *Forensic evaluation of juveniles.* Sarasota, FL: Professional Resource Press.

Grisso, T., & Schwartz, R. G. (Eds.). (2000). *Youth on trial: A developmental perspective on juvenile justice.* University of Chicago Press.

Gutheil, T. G., & Simon, R. I. (2002). *Mastering forensic psychiatric practice: Advanced strategies for expert witness:* Washington, DC: American Psychiatric Association.

Horner, T. M., Guyer, M. J., & Kalter, N. M. (1993). Clinical expertise and the assessment of child sexual abuse. *Journal of the American Academy of Child and Adolescent Psychiatry, 32,* 925–931.

Johnston, J. R. (1994). High-conflict divorce. *Future of Children, 4,* 165–182.

Kent v United States (1966). 383 U.S. 541.

Loeber, R., & Farrington, D. P. (Eds.). (1998). *Serious and violent juvenile offenders: Risk factors and successful interventions.* Thousand Oaks, CA: Sage.

Loeber, R., & Farrington, D. P. (2000). Young children who commit crime: Epidemiology, developmental origins, risk factors, early interventions, and policy implications. *Development and Psychopathology, 12,* 737–762.

Lubit, R., Hartwell, N., van Gorp, W. G., & Eth, S. (2002). Forensic evaluation of trauma syndromes in children. *Child and Adolescent Psychiatric Clinics of North America, 11,* 823–858.

Melton, G. B., Petrila, J., Poythress, N. G., & Slobogin, C. (1997). *Psychological evaluations for the courts: A handbook for mental health professionals and lawyers* (2nd ed.). New York: Guilford Press.

Nurcombe, B., & Partlett, D. F. (1994). *Child mental health and the law.* New York: Macmillan.

Quinn, K. M. (2002). Interviewing children for suspected sexual abuse. In D. H. Schetky & E. P. Benedek (Eds.), *Principles and practice of child and adolescent forensic psychiatry* (pp. 149–159). Washington, DC: American Psychiatric Association.

Rosner, R. (Ed.). (2003). *Principles and practice of forensic psychiatry* (2nd ed.). London: Hodder Arnold.

Schetky, D. H., & Benedek, E. P. (Eds.). (2002). *Principles and practice of child and adolescent forensic psychiatry.* Washington, DC: American Psychiatric Association.

Steiner, H., Cauffman, E., & Duxbury, E. (1999). Personality traits in juvenile delinquents: Relation to criminal behavior and recidivism. *Journal of the American Academy of Child and Adolescent Psychiatry, 38,* 256–262.

Steiner, H., & Dunne, J. E. (1997). Summary of the practice parameters for the assessment and treatment of children and adolescents with conduct disorder. *Journal of the American Academy of Child and Adolescent Psychiatry, 36,* 1482–1485.

U.S. Dept. Health and Human Services. (2001). *Youth violence: A report of the surgeon general.* Rockville, MD: U.S. Dept. Health and Human Services, Centers for Disease Control and Prevention, National Center for Injury Prevention and Control; Substance Abuse and Mental Health Services Administration, Center for Mental Health Services; and National Institutes of Health, National Institute of Mental Health.

Wilson, J. J., Rojas, N., Haapanen, R., Duxbury, E., & Steiner, H. (2001). Substance abuse and criminal recidivism: A prospective study of adolescents. *Child Psychiatry and Human Development, 31,* 297–312.

Yuille, J. C., Hunter, R., Joffe, R., & Zaparniuk, J. (1993). Interviewing children in sexual abuse cases. In G. S. Goodman & B. L. Bottoms (Eds.), *Child victims, child witnesses: Understanding and improving testimony* (pp. 95–115). New York: Guilford Press.

CHAPTER THIRTY-FIVE

PREVENTING HIGH-RISK SEXUAL BEHAVIORS AMONG CHILDREN AND ADOLESCENTS

Jeffrey J. Wilson, M.D., and Larry K. Brown, M.D.

Prevention is a cardinal hope of child and adolescent treatment. Adolescents commonly experiment with a variety of risky behaviors, perhaps the most socially complex of these involving their budding sexuality (King 2002; Yates 2002). The developmental phase of adolescence is pivotal in determining future health habits. Hence, those of us privileged to work with adolescents have a unique window in which to influence healthy behaviors in *status nascendi*. While many adolescents experiment with risky behaviors, these most commonly do not become part of their permanent character structure (except perhaps for the most deviant adolescent). Intervening before these patterns are incorporated into their permanent character holds the most promise in reducing the risk of life-course persistent deviant behavior (Vermeiren 2003). The following chapter demonstrates effective preventive interventions to reduce high-risk sexual behavior. The authors have selected the issue of high-risk sexual behaviors among children and adolescents because of the significant developmental risks associated with HIV and related sexually transmitted diseases. Moreover, we feel that the practical prevention of high-risk sexual behavior for the child mental health provider or educator involves representatively complex social interactions between normal

This research is supported by NIH grant DA14572 (JJW) and a grant from the Carmel Hill Foundation (JJW).

adolescent development, public health, and (at times) psychopathology. We hope that clinicians may find these useful to other areas of preventive intervention, and that this chapter will offer generalizable insights into how prevention can be used effectively in a variety of adolescent risk behaviors. For a more general review of preventive methods in child and adolescent psychiatry, please refer to Offord and Bennet, 2003.

Basic Rationale and Theory for Prevention of High Risk Sexual Behavior

Abstinence versus "Safer" Sex Initiatives

Some people may argue that any sexual behavior is a high-risk for an adolescent. We believe this is an important consideration, but one that is best answered by an individual family and their adolescent. One area of concern since the development of the HIV/AIDS epidemic is how to provide adolescents with what many consider vital information about protecting themselves without implicitly or explicitly encouraging sexual behaviors. These discussions prove rather intense between Parent Teacher Associations (PTAs) and school boards across the country, with discussions ranging from the extent of sexual education to whether abstinence or harm-reduction is more appropriate. This chapter will review our clinical and empirical experiences with trying to stem the tide of the HIV epidemic, considering particularly some of the most well-designed studies of the subject. It is our intent to help child health care professionals guide patients and their parents through this morally and emotionally charged issue with the latest and most relevant scientific research.

Some groups have questioned whether so-called "safe sex" initiatives would increase adolescent proclivity toward high-risk sexual behaviors. They argue that providing alternatives would implicitly give permission to adolescents to engage in high-risk sexual behavior. There is no empirical support for this view. Two independent controlled studies with safer-sex alternatives have demonstrated that adolescent groups that offer skills-based safer sex alternatives increase abstinence, not sexual behavior or high risk sexual behavior. This is true when safer-sex interventions are compared to either abstinence interventions (Jemmott & Jemmott, 2000), or straightforward psycho-education (St. Lawrence et al., 1995, 2002).

Significance of Preventing HIV/AIDS during Adolescence

Worldwide, forty-two million people are currently living with HIV/AIDS, and in 2002 alone 3.1 million people died from AIDS. The World Health Organization estimates that sixty-five million more people will die worldwide from HIV/AIDS before 2025; young people will account for many of these deaths (UNAIDS/World Health Organization, 2002). The incidence of this disease has been declining in many populations, but not among adolescents: the incidence of this devastating illness increased just over a third (35%) in young people during the last decade. Most individuals acquire HIV and AIDS because of high-risk behaviors that begin during adolescence (e.g., Kalichman, 1998; Rotheram-Borus, 2000). HIV and the development of AIDS remains an important, preventable, cause of death in adolescents (CDC, 1999). At least half of the new seroconversions to HIV+ status occurs in young people under the age of twenty-five. Of note, relatively few young people with HIV know when they are affected (that is, HIV seropositive), making it much more likely that they will contribute to the spread of this epidemic. For example, in one study of young people at urban dance clubs, 77% of those who were seropositive, between the ages of fifteen and twenty-nine, were not aware that they were infected with HIV (AIDS World Conference 2002, Barcelona).

High-Risk Sexual Behavior

High-risk sexual behavior among adolescents has a number of other valid public health concerns associated with it besides the devastating epidemic of HIV/AIDS. Pregnancy at an early age can significantly impede development for both the teenage parent and the child (Woodward & Fergusson, 1999). Teenage mothers and fathers are at risk, although by far the developmental impact tends to be levied on mothers (Fagot et al., 1998). Age at onset of sexual behavior is in itself a major risk factor for later high-risk sexual behaviors associated with HIV/AIDS (Capaldi et al., 2002). Perhaps even more commonly, sexual behavior without serious adverse sequelae can also have significant interpersonal consequences. The consequences of sexual relationships going wrong in some fashion are also not uncommon reasons for referral to mental health professionals, for both boys and girls.

Developmental Issues

While life-prolonging treatments have been developed, a cure for HIV/AIDS has remained beyond the reach of modern medicine. In the absence of life-saving treatments or an effective vaccine, prevention remains the only public health intervention to prevent the spread of AIDS. Paradoxically, these very treatments may contribute to the not uncommonly encountered myth among adolescents, especially those at the highest risk: that HIV/AIDS is curable. Some developmentally appropriate factors that make HIV prevention among adolescents more challenging than with adults include: the adolescent search for identity and intimacy, developing "formal" or abstract reasoning abilities, experimentation with drugs and alcohol, other risk-taking and sexual exploration. Moreover, an exaggerated sense of invulnerability may result from high levels of sensation-seeking and developmentally exaggerated egocentrism (Greene et al., 2000). All of these factors are described in further detail, with examples and references for further reading, in Table 35.1.

In a naturalistic study, Capaldi and colleagues (2002) reported heterosexual risk behaviors in adolescents and young adult men over a ten-year period. Both distal and proximal risk factors contributed to the contraction of sexually transmitted diseases during adolescence, most particularly early onset sexual behavior and substance use. While both antisocial behaviors and specific drug use behaviors increase the risk of sexual risk behaviors, substance use appeared to be a stronger predictor of sexual risk behaviors. This could be explained by both direct and indirect mechanisms associated with substance use. An example of a direct mechanism is disinhibition via direct psychopharmacological action (substance use); indirect mechanisms include social cue effects, greater exposure to deviant peers, or a general problem behavior syndrome such as conduct disorder (indirect).

High-Risk Groups

When psychiatric or social problems are added to normative developmental issues, the incidence of high-risk sexual behavior increases greatly. Several groups of adolescents are at particular risk for high-risk sexual behavior. These groups include adolescents with severe mental illness (Smith, 2001), adolescents with substance use disorders (Malow et al., 2001), runaway or homeless adolescents (Rotheram-Borus et al., 2000) sexually abused (Brown et al., 2000), delinquent adolescents, and adolescents with conduct disorders or other disorders of impulse control (Devieux et al., 2002, Steiner & Wilson, 1999). These adolescents are commonly referred to some sort of mental health or substance abuse treatment for a variety of behavior problems. Hence, child mental health or substance abuse professionals are potential resources for the developing young man or woman to turn to—an adult other than a parent with whom an adolescent can explore these complex developmental issues.

High-Risk Sexual Behavior as a Preventive Target

Potential targets of HIV prevention are summarized in Table 35.2 and described in the text following. Even in community samples, alcohol problems are a significant predictor of unprotected sexual behavior (NIMH Multisite HIV Prevention Trial Group, 2002). Young people under the age of twenty-five years had the highest rates of relapse to high-risk sexual behaviors and were less than half as

TABLE 35.1. DEVELOPMENTAL CONSIDERATIONS IN PREVENTING HIV AMONG ADOLESCENTS.

Developmental Domain	Relevant Stage or Task	Examples	References for Further Reading
Biological development	Puberty impulse control	Sexual development can sometimes outpace social development. Girls with early-onset sexual behavior are at particularly high risk.	Woodward & Fergusson (1999) Yates (2002)
Cognitive development	Concrete versus formal operations	Difficulty understanding abstractions, such as a. Having medicines that help but do not cure AIDS. b. Having HIV but being healthy.	Piaget (1969) King (2002)
Personality development	Identity versus role diffusion	Early in adolescent development, adolescents strive to find an identity in a culture where they are barraged with what's "cool" and what's not. One's sexual identity is a major component of this struggle.	Erikson (1968)
	Self-restraint versus impulsivity	Low restraint and conduct problems place adolescents at particularly high risk for sexually risky behavior.	Steiner & Wilson (1999)
	Invulnerability versus power-lessness	The sense of invulnerability that adolescents experience can interfere with their ability to make "good" or "safer" sexual decisions.	Greene et al. (2000)
	Intimacy versus isolation	It seems that the desire for intimacy and the fear of isolation haunt adolescents at earlier and earlier ages in our high-paced culture.	Erikson (1968)

(Continued)

TABLE 35.1. DEVELOPMENTAL CONSIDERATIONS IN PREVENTING HIV AMONG ADOLESCENTS (CONTINUED).

Developmental Domain	Relevant Stage or Task	Examples	References for Further Reading
Social development	Autonomy versus dependence	The developmental task of achieving an autonomous identity is perhaps the central feature of adolescence.	Erikson (1968) King (2002)
	Parent/guardian relations	Breaking away from parental control is a normal part of development; yet parents are still necessary to help adolescents navigate this complicated phase of development. Parents may react to this in a variety of ways that are conducive or maladaptive.	Dishion et al. (1995)
	Authority relations: teachers, therapists, counselors	This strife for autonomy also plays out in classrooms. When forced into a therapist's office, these issues require careful navigation such that autonomy can be encouraged but relationships maintained.	Patterson (1982)
	Peer relations	Often eclipse parental influences during adolescence.	La Greca et al. (2001)
	Group process	The microcosm of an adolescent group brings out many of these issues, and can be an excellent way of helping adolescents define themselves independently within a peer context.	Group issues in treating adolescents are explored further in Chapter 29.

TABLE 35.2.   CLINICAL TARGETS FOR PREVENTION OF HIGH-RISK SEXUAL BEHAVIOR.

Community Samples	High-Risk Samples
Delay age at onset of sexual behavior	Substance abuse treatment
Peer group affiliations	Psychiatric treatment (especially impulse
Enhance parental monitoring	control disorders, such as conduct
and parent-child communication	disorder, ADHD)
Reduce substance use	Psychosocial interventions (homelessness,
Education about HIV, STDs, and	availability of services)
"safer" sex	Multimodal treatment of comorbid
Specific safer-sex skills training	problems

likely as older participants to demonstrate protected or improved patterns of sexual behavior. The direct effects of the most commonly abused substance of abuse during adolescence, alcohol, include disinhibition, impulsivity, and poor judgment, all of which may lead to poor sexual decisions such as reduced condom use or sex with multiple partners (Tapert et al., 2001).

The most compelling indirect mechanism that may explain this association is the "problem behavior syndrome"—that the most common problem behaviors are commonly found together (Jessor, 1998). These behaviors may be explained by fundamental developmental deficits in self-regulation, which may explain a variety of conduct problems, including substance use, sexual behavior, physical and verbal aggression, and so on (Tarter, 1999). In fact, adolescents who exhibit early onset of substance use, as well as adolescents who exhibit early onset of sexual behaviors, tend to have a poorer prognosis in a variety of domains, including a higher degree of exposure to unsafe sexual practices (Capaldi et al., 2002). As substance use proceeds to disorder, which is more common among adolescents with this constellation of behavior problems, developmental deficits in self-regulation may further unravel, leading to severe developmental dysfunction and failure to complete developmentally appropriate tasks of adolescence (Clark, 1998, 1999; Reebeye, 1995; Steiner & Wilson, 1999). However, it is increasingly clear that treatment of one aspect of this developmental dysfunction, adolescent substance abuse, for example, ASA, does not necessarily improve other aspects, condom use, such as (Flisher et al., 2001). An integrated, multifaceted approach appears necessary to reduce high-risk sexual behavior in high-risk groups (CDC, 1999).

Of particular relevance to child and adolescent mental health professionals is that adolescents with severe mental illness are also at serious risk for early onset of sexual behavior and high-risk sexual behavior. (See Brown et al., 1987; Smith, 2001 for a recent comprehensive review.) An adolescent whose psychopathology interferes with self-restraint, or exacerbates developmentally normative risk-taking, may have a limited ability to engage in HIV-preventive behaviors. Indirect effects may also be responsible for this association. For example, adolescents experiencing severe mental illness more commonly have serious family problems (including abuse or neglect), maladaptive peer networks, and more delinquent behavior. In fact, studies of HIV+ adolescents demonstrate that the majority of these individuals report sexual or physical abuse, and many have been in foster care or in the criminal justice system. Several studies reviewed by Smith (2001) demonstrated the association between HIV risk and severe mental illness among adolescents. While the etiology of this association is unclear, variables that may explain this association include early onset of sexual behavior, higher numbers of sexual partners, and less condom use than their peers without severe mental illness.

Putative Mechanisms of Efficacy

One of the most useful theoretical models of high-risk sexual behavior is the Information-Motivation-Behavior (IMB) model (Fisher & Fisher, 1992, 2000). This is a commonly used model with demonstrated efficacy and effectiveness in a variety of populations. According to this model, information directly relevant to HIV transmission and prevention is a prerequisite of preventive behavior. This information should be culturally relevant, developmentally appropriate, and readily applicable to the target population, in their particular social setting. Motivation to engage in HIV-preventive behavior is a second prerequisite for change in sexual risk behavior. Motivation can be considered from both personal and social perspectives. Personal motivation involves favorable attitudes toward performance of HIV-preventive acts (such as abstinence, attitudes toward sexual alternatives to intercourse, attitudes toward condom use, and so on). Social motivation involves the support that an adolescent perceives for performing these acts (for example, peer norms or attitudes of partners). Finally, HIV-preventive behavior depends heavily on an adolescent's ability or specific skills to perform specific HIV-preventive acts. These skills include both objective skills (such as effective condom use) as well as a sense of self-efficacy in carrying these out. Skills-based HIV preventive interventions are the most effective, and involve a variety of role-playing exercises geared toward assessing risky situations, negotiating risky sexual situations, and the demonstration of specific skills such as condom use skills (CDC, 2000; also see Effective HIV-Preventive Interventions, following).

Addressing the contextual factors in an adolescent's environment that may maintain high-risk sexual behavior are also key elements of any effective HIV prevention. For example, in high-risk samples, failure to address substance use may preclude HIV-preventive behaviors due to the direct consequences of drug or alcohol use (NIDA, 2002). Addressing family factors that may inadvertently or actively maintain high-risk sexual behaviors is also highly relevant to effecting changes in problem behaviors, including high-risk sexual behavior. Effective parental monitoring is clearly negatively correlated with a variety of adolescent problem behaviors, including high-risk sexual behavior (Li et al., 2000). Addressing issues related to past sexual abuse may be particularly important. A recent study found that among adolescents with psychiatric disorders (already at high risk for HIV) those with histories of sexual abuse were three times more likely than their peers to use condoms inconsistently (Brown et al., 2000). Similarly, sex trade workers, homeless adolescents, or sexually or physically abused adolescents commonly require comprehensive interventions that may address multiple risk factors in their environment or in their adjustment to their environment for HIV-preventive behaviors to be developed. Finally, it is clear from several studies of adolescents that the more culturally appropriate and population-specific an intervention is, the more effective it is found to be in controlled studies (Johnson et al., 2003; Ramirez et al., 2000; Mullen et al., 2002).

A model, based on information from Capaldi and colleagues (2002) and our literature search of high-risk adolescents is presented in Figure 35.1. Distal risk and resiliency factors are found more to the left, while proximal risk and resiliency

FIGURE 35.1. A DEVELOPMENTAL MODEL OF HIGH-RISK SEXUAL BEHAVIOR.

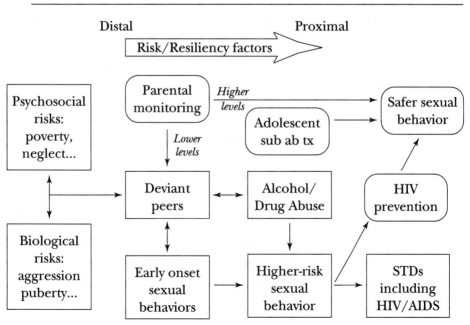

factors are found more to the right. Risk factors are denoted by squares, while protective and potentially protective factors are denoted by squares with slightly rounded edges. The latter indicate developmental pathways away from risk—potential targets for preventive interventions. In reviewing this model, it should become clear that assessment, prevention, or treatment of high-risk sexual behavior involves evaluation of multiple factors that may maintain or otherwise contribute to high-risk sexual behavior in adolescents.

Effective HIV Preventive Interventions

Despite the existence of scientifically proven, evidence-based treatments, many states rely on information-only approaches to HIV prevention. While many governing bodies are to be applauded for including mandated HIV/AIDS education for these high-risk groups, such as adolescents and adults abusing drugs or alcohol, the precise interventions administered by programs vary widely within and between those states requiring a minimum of HIV education in clinical treatment programs. It should be noted that even *manualized* psycho-education is of little value in reducing actual risk behavior in the majority of controlled studies (CDC, 2000; NIDA, 2002). On a clinical note, we think that it is clear from the literature that simply educating (or lecturing at) adolescents about the dangers of HIV/AIDS is not sufficient in reducing high-risk sexual behaviors, especially among many of our high-risk adolescents.

On the other hand, dozens of effective preventive interventions for HIV/AIDS have been published over the past decade, in terms of both adolescents and adults. Shoveller and Pietersma (2002) proposed criteria by which they evaluated their recent meta-analysis of HIV-preventive interventions for adolescents. These criteria are scientifically valid and represent the developing body of research on HIV-prevention in adolescents. We recommend that these criteria be applied to the science upon which any preventive intervention is based, when a program is considering to use such an intervention.

1. HIV/AIDS is the *primary focus* of intervention, and not part of or included as a package including general health, mental health, or substance abuse treatment.
2. Quantitative *study design* with attention and activity control. Some studies of HIV prevention in the past have had questionable external validity because of design issues, including: small sample size, lack of appropriate control group, and so on (Jemmott & Jemmott, 2000).
3. Must include sufficient numbers of *adolescents*. Studies of adult sexual behavior are not necessarily generalizable to adolescents for a variety of reasons,

particularly developmental issues (see Table 35.1) and issues related to duration and frequency of sexual behaviors.

4. Outcome measures focus on *behavioral change;* not solely on information and attitudes. That is, studies assessed sexual behavior (frequency of clearly defined sexual acts over time) and risk-reduction behavior change (frequency of unprotected vaginal or anal intercourse over time).

The Centers for Disease Control and Prevention (CDC) composed a compendium of effective HIV preventions (CDC, 2000), and other federal agencies have distilled principles of effective HIV prevention from the most effective, evidence-based interventions (NIDA, 2000). Table 35.3 provides examples of these evidence-based interventions. All of these studies pass the scientific criteria of that of Shoveller and Pietersma (2002). All of these interventions share many components in common, which will be described below, but the interested reader is referred to either of the above publications or Web sites (see References at the end of this chapter) for more information. It should be noted that as a general rule, the more high-risk the population, the more intensive the HIV/AIDS-preventive intervention will need to be.

According to the Center for Disease Control (2000), for HIV preventions to be effective, they must

- Be accessible to the target population
- Be culturally competent for the target population
- Include clearly defined target groups
- Focus on specific behavioral skills
- Achieve lasting behavioral change
- Be offered as part of a continuum of care

Accessible to Target Population

There are multiple levels of accessibility. First, the intervention must be affordable and reachable. Reaching those at the highest risk for HIV infection may be the greatest challenge, yet a number of programs have used homeless shelters and case work to enhance accessibility and retention (for example, Rotheram-Borus et al. [1997] "Street Smart"). The interventions should also be offered in such a way that the participants are able to access the intervention in a non-threatening way. For example, the authors recommend that these interventions are best offered in small groups to enhance processes whereby individuals can explore their own values and experiences. In such small groups, adolescents have the rare opportunity to role-play difficult-to-manage sexual situations with the guidance of a trained

TABLE 35.3. EXAMPLES OF EFFECTIVE HIV-PREVENTION INTERVENTIONS FOR ADOLESCENTS.

Intervention	Population	Behavioral Findings	Investigators
Community Interventions			
Be Proud! Be Responsible! 8 × 1-hour sessions incorporating knowledge, skills development (delaying onset of intercourse, condom use), and empowerment.	Adolescents recruited from low-income area middle schools	Compared to an abstinence-only intervention, adolescent in the intervention group had increased condom use and increased abstinence.	Jemmott and Jemmott (2000)
Focus on Kids 8 sessions at local recreation centers and one at a campsite. In addition to HIV information, multiple delivery formats were used, including videos, games, role-playing, acting, storytelling.	Adolescents recruited from community recreation centers	Sexually active adolescent in the intervention reported greater condom use than in the control (attention control with HIV information, discussion and condom access) condition.	Stanton et al. (1996)
High-Risk Groups			
Street Smart 10 group sessions over 3 weeks emphasizing 1. HIV knowledge 2. Social skills 3. Resource access 4. Personalized beliefs, attitudes and norms.	Homeless adolescent Included incentive: $1 for carrying condoms and arriving to program on time	Adolescents who participated in the intervention reduced both the frequency of unprotected sex acts and their substance use more than adolescents in comparison shelters.	Rotheram-Borus et al. (1997)
IMB Model for Adolescent in Substance Abuse Treatment 12 weekly group sessions empha-sizing 1. HIV education 2. Motivation 3. Specific "safer sex" skills.	Adolescent substance abusers completing treatment	I + B and I + B + M groups (as opposed to I only) reduced unprotected sex acts, increased behavioral skill performance, and even increased abstinence.	St. Lawrence et al. (2002)

Note: More information on effective HIV interventions and other studies can be found on the CDC Web site (CDC, 1999). The studies above were selected primarily because they had attention controls or dealt with extremely high risk adolescents (as in Street Smart). Additional examples of HIV-preventive interventions in inpatient hospitals are found in Smith (2001).

facilitator. Such groups are also more conducive for group members to discuss socially complex or controversial material such as sexual diversity. Gender-specific groups or groups for traumatized adolescent may also be helpful in making groups more accessible. Groups of adolescent with high degrees of attrition, such as those with substance use disorders, may be better engaged with fewer sessions of longer duration (two four-hour sessions versus eight one-hour sessions).

Culturally Competent for Target Population

We have also found in trying to design effectiveness trials for HIV prevention interventions, that a "bottom-up" (versus a "top-down") approach is nearly always more effective. Understanding the community and the counselors in which the program will be based is a necessary component of implementing any intervention. Including the population (both adolescents and their families) during the design of the intervention is invaluable to the process of designing or adapting an intervention for use in ethnically diverse populations. (See Malow et al., 2000 for further reading.)

Include Clearly Defined Target Groups

What is "effective" may vary widely across populations of adolescents. For examples, homeless adolescents may require a range of services that would be of little utility to a group of private high school students. Substance abusing adolescents require concomitant substance abuse treatment as well as groups that focus on the relationship between drug use and risky sexual behavior. Since risk factors are likely to differ between these groups, identifying risky situations and behaviors can vary between groups (Capaldi et al., 2002).

Focus on Specific Behavioral Skills

These guidelines universally subscribe that skills-based interventions are necessary components of effective HIV-preventive efforts for adolescents, especially those high-risk adolescents most mental health professionals are likely to come into contact with. Effective skills-based interventions often include enhancing a adolescent's sense of self-efficacy in sexual situations. (Examples range from promoting abstinence to safer sexual, non-penetrative alternatives, to effective condom use.) Studies that emphasize a cognitive-behavioral, skills-based curriculum related to safer sex consistently have the highest degree of effectiveness in reducing unsafe sex episodes, and can also increase abstinence (Jemmott & Jemmott, 2000; St. Lawrence et al., 1995, 2002).

Achieve Lasting Behavioral Change

One of the greatest indicators of effectiveness is maintaining change over time. If change is effected only during, or shortly after, the intervention, it may be hard for programs to justify the expense of HIV prevention. However, this may be one of the most difficult outcome measures among the highest-risk groups, who tend to be highly mobile and highly non-adherent to recommendations for follow-up. Whenever possible, outcomes should be followed as long as possible, preferably to a year, but at least six-months among difficult-to-follow populations. Comprehensive follow-up information can be used to assess whether or not "booster" sessions are needed.

Are Offered as a Part of a Continuum of Care

If substance abuse drives high-risk sexual behavior, any intervention that fails to address the substance abuse component is likely doomed. Similarly, if homelessness and poverty drives prostitution, any intervention that fails to address homelessness in a concrete fashion is similarly doomed. Far from being unreachable, both of these populations of at-risk adolescents have been reached through comprehensive HIV-preventive interventions offered as an overall continuum of care. (See St. Lawrence et al., 2002; Rotheram-Borus et al., 1997, respectively.) Identifying key risk factors such as mental illness or substance abuse or homelessness are vital aspects to effective HIV prevention.

As a cautionary note, the peer group can be a powerful intervention for high-risk sexual behavior. However, negative group processes can emerge during peer treatment. Until we identify those factors that are most helpful and most harmful, group interventions need to be carefully monitored to reduce the negative group processes that can emerge (Dolcini & Adler, 1994). Grouping high-risk adolescents together for prevention, good intentions notwithstanding, is not without risk, and can at times be harmful (Dishion et al., 1999). Hence, many of the most effective prevention groups are small, highly structured skills-based programs, often with two co-leaders to facilitate positive change. In one study of the IMB model among inner city adolescents that compared classroom-based versus peer-based interventions, peer-based interventions fared poorly at the one-year follow-up, even when coupled with the classroom-based intervention (Fisher et al., 2002). Only the classroom-based intervention group (without peer-based intervention) maintained positive HIV-preventive behavioral change at the one-year follow-up period. This study suggests that there may be time by intervention effects for peer-based interventions, which can be negative, and which must be carefully monitored so as to *do no harm*. More research is clearly needed to understand how their effects deteriorate over time.

Recommendations for Office-Based Practice

The Relevance of Prevention in Adolescent Psychiatry

It is imperative that clinicians unite in stopping HIV infection and AIDS. This is particularly so among those of us who commonly see adolescents at the highest risk—adolescent with substance use disorders, disruptive behavior disorders, severe mental illness or histories of sexual abuse. The overlap between psychiatric factors and sexual behavior can be demonstrated by considering a clinical example of a sexually abused adolescent. Sexuality may be complicated by a history of sexual abuse, which leads to feelings of powerlessness and, sometimes, repetitive counter-phobic risk behavior. The current context of sexuality may thus include perceived lack of power in sexual relationships, partner coercion, and intimate partner violence. Therapy is the ideal setting to address these influential factors (Brown et al., 1997). Because of the stigma surrounding sex and HIV/AIDS in our culture, many clinicians find discussion of these issues uncomfortable and defer these issues to "other clinicians," who may or may not be involved in the adolescent's care related to sexual issues. Several strategies exist for incorporating discussion of these issues in both medical and psychiatric settings. For example, Schreibman and Friedland (2003) recommend supportive and nonpunitive counseling in a comfortable setting; interactive counseling and motivational interviewing; repeated sessions and incorporation at every clinical encounter; promotion and distribution of condoms; use of HIV infection-prevention posters, fact sheets, and brochures; partner counseling and notification; and referral services for substance abuse treatment and psychiatric treatment.

Assessing HIV Risk Behavior

There are various standardized paper-and-pencil questionnaires, computerized questionnaires, and standardized psychiatric interviews that can be used to assess HIV risk behavior. For some adolescents, these paper-and-pencil or computerized measures can be easier to complete and at times have greater external validity. A summary of many of these measures can be found at http://chipts.ucla.edu/assessment/topic.html. One measure we have found to be particularly useful, which follows the IMB model, is the Teen Health Survey (Dolcini & Adler, 1994). We have found that measures should be carefully selected with the target population in mind. For example, if one commonly works with adolescents who have substance abuse problems, which are a major risk factor for high-risk behavior, the relationship between these behaviors is important. One measure that assesses the relationship between high-risk sexual behavior and substance use, using the time line follow back (TLFB) method of Sobel and Sobel (1990), has been developed by Carey and colleagues (2001). This method can be of particular value when trying to develop connections between socially unacceptable behaviors such as high-risk sexual behavior and substance abuse and related sequelae.

However, as the therapeutic relationship develops with time between an adolescent and a therapist, the ability of an adolescent to discuss initially difficult material can improve drastically. A major advantage to therapeutic understanding of high-risk sexual behavior is the ability to explore the context and personal meanings of these behaviors, considering the conflicts over sexuality, autonomy, and individuality that often attend these. One of the major obstacles that is relatively unique to child and adolescent psychiatry is that it is uncommon for the adolescents to enter treatment of their own accord. A complex set of issues surrounds the confidentiality of adolescent treatment. We have found in individual adolescent treatment that these issues are best approached in an individualized, psychologically tolerable, but consistent matter. As trust develops, some adolescents are able to fully explore these issues, when relevant. Over time, it is a good clinical rule of thumb to ask about the full range of these high-risk behaviors. Similar to substance abuse treatment, adolescents can be quite concrete in their answers. That is to say, if you do not ask questions about specific sexual behaviors, they are unlikely to be answered.

Countertransference and Confidentiality

It is worth considering how our presentation (as child health care professionals) may make it more or less difficult for some adolescents to talk about these sexual issues. In supervising residents and psychology interns, it is often important to emphasize the importance of discussing these issues. Younger health care professionals often can find it difficult to discuss these issues with adolescents closer to their age, yet this very obstacle can often make the discussion of these issues all the more valuable to the adolescent, bridging the distance between generations. Older HCPLs may feel paternalistic or maternalistic, and adolescents may find it difficult to discuss high-risk sexual behaviors with a father- or mother-figure. Whatever our age, we find that confidentiality is a major factor in how well we can explore these issues with kids. The authors find that an open approach to confidentiality, with carefully delineated boundaries for the adolescent and the parent(s), often helps adolescents to discuss these issues more openly.

DiClemente and Prochaska's (1998) "transtheoretical model of change" is a useful clinical model with which to approach the development of change in high-risk sexual behavior, just as it is in substance abuse treatment. In their model, patients progress through a series of stages: precontemplation, contemplation, preparation, action, and maintenance. Most adolescents, often presented by their parents for any of a variety of conduct problems, are in the precontemplative "I don't know why I'm here" phase. Brown and Lourie (2001) have developed a model that applies to motivational interviewing to adolescents with high-risk sexual behaviors. Using a non-confrontational and engaging approach, adolescents are encouraged to explore their own values and how they relate to their behaviors, with the initial goal being increasing the perceived susceptibility of adolescents to the dangers of high-risk sexual behaviors. By reflecting the dissonance between an adolescent's ideals and his/her behaviors, a foundation for change, or contemplation of change is set. A variety of techniques described in detail by Brown and Lourie can be used to effect change (2001), including: asking open-ended questions, using affirming language, reframing the issues, and encouraging the development of a "menu of strategies" or a "cluster of options" rather than a coercive solution enforced by the therapist and the adolescent's family.

Future Directions

The main concern is bringing "effective" interventions from research centers to communities, and testing their "real-world" effectiveness in a variety of populations. To the extent these interventions are made more available, HIV/STD prevention can improve the health of youth. In order to maximize generalizability and effectiveness of HIV prevention programs, Rotheram-Borus and Daihua (2003) recently suggested that marketing strategies could be utilized to maximize intervention in the "next generation" of effectiveness research. This article offers practical, business-world solutions to addressing the implementation of effectiveness trials in a variety of settings. Although comprehensive discussion of this article is beyond the scope of this chapter, the authors' highly recommend this article to the interested reader. As a summary, we offer Jensen's thoughtful commentary on this article. He outlines three areas of obstacles to effectiveness trials: (1) child and family factors, (2) provider factors, and (3) systemic and societal factors (Jensen, 2003). We suggest that in administering an effective ("bottom-up") intervention, or in designing your own, that you follow a strategy that incorporates community involvement from the beginning, including particularly potential participants and community treatment providers, as well as investigators familiar with your field and effectiveness research. Incorporating a comprehensive team of experienced investigators, community treatment providers and community members from the beginning can go a long way to overcoming these obstacles.

◆ ◆ ◆

On a broader level, we hope that the future directions of HIV prevention move beyond individual-level interventions. That is to say, to move toward a more effective use of the peer group in preventive intervention, and on a broader policy level, increase the awareness of the existence of these effective HIV-prevention strategies on a community level. Even though most HIV-prevention strategies for adolescents focus on the individual level, clinical emphasis on interventions at multiple levels (individual, family, community) may be more effective, particularly for high-risk groups (DiClemente & Wingood, 2000). As preventive technology is developing rapidly in the field of individual HIV prevention, we hope that this can be applied on a broader social axis that includes family and community interventions as part of a comprehensive policy to reduce HIV transmission among adolescents. In the long run, as prevention science develops, it is our hope that preventive strategies for a variety of adolescent risk behaviors can be slowly moved from appendices or afterthoughts to the forefront of textbooks and handbooks such as these.

References

Brown, L., Danovsky, M., & Lourie, K. (1997). Adolescents with psychiatric disorders and their risk for HIV. *Journal of the American Academy of Child and Adolescent Psychiatry, 36,* 1005–1009.

Brown, L. K., & Lourie, K. J. (2001). Motivational interviewing and the prevention of HIV among adolescents. In P. M. Monti, S. M. Colby, & T. A. O'Leary (Eds.), *Adolescents, alcohol, and substance abuse.* New York: Guilford Press.

Brown, L., Lourie, K., Zlotnick, C., & Cohn, J. (2000). Impact of sexual abuse on the HIV-risk-related behavior of adolescents in intensive psychiatric treatment. *American Journal of Psychiatry, 157,* 1413–1415.

Brown, L. K., Kessel, S. M., Lourie, K. J., Ford, H. H., & Lipsitt, L. P. (1999). Influence of sexual abuse on HIV-related attitudes and behaviors in adolescent psychiatric inpatients. *Journal of the American Academy of Child and Adolescent Psychiatry, 36,* 316–322.

Capaldi, D. M., Stoolmiller, M., Clark, S., & Owen, L. D. (2002). Heterosexual risk behaviors in at-risk young men from early adolescence to young adulthood: Prevalence, prediction and association with STD contraction. *Developmental Psychology, 38*(3), 394–406.

Carey, M. P., Carey, K. B., Maisto, S. A., Gordon, C. M., & Weinhardt, L. S. (2001). Assessing sexual risk behavior with the Timeline Followback (TLFB) approach: Continued development and psychometric evaluation with psychiatric outpatients. *International Journal of STD & AIDS, 12,* 365–375.

Centers for Disease Control and Prevention. AIDS cases in 13–19 year olds reported in 1996 and 1996 population estimates by race and ethnicity. United States, available at http://www.cdc.gov/nchstp/HIV-AIDS/stats.

Center for Disease Control (2000). Compendium of HIV Prevention Interventions with Evidence of Effectiveness, National Center for HIV/AIDS Prevention–Intervention Research and support, Atlanta, GA. Also available @http://www.cdc.gov

Devieux, J., Malow, R., Stein, J. A., Jennings, T. E., Lucenko, B. A., Averhart, C., & Kalichman, S. (2002). Impulsivity and HIV risk among adjudicated alcohol- and other drug-abusing adolescents. *AIDS Education and Prevention, 14,* 24–35.

DiClemente, R. J., & Prochaska, J. O. (1998). Toward a comprehensive, transtheoretical model of change. In W. R. Miller & N. Heather, *Treating addictive behaviors (2nd ed.).* New York: Plenum Press.

DiClemente, R. J., & Wingwood, G. M. (2000). Expanding the scope of HIV prevention for adolescents: Beyond individual-level interventions. *Journal of Adolescent Health, 26,* 377–378.

Dishion, T. J., French, D. C., & Patterson, G. R. (1995). The development and ecology of antisocial behavior. In D. Cicchetti, & D. J. Cohen (Eds.), *Developmental psychopathology (Vol. 2,* pp. 421–471). New York: Wiley and Sons.

Dishion, T. J., McCord, J., Poulin, F. (1999). When interventions harm: Peer groups and problem behavior. *American Psychologist, 54*(9), 755–764.

Erikson, E. H. (1968). *Identity: Adolescent in crisis.* New York: WW Norton and Co., Inc.

Fagot, B. I., Pears, K. C., Capaldi, D. M., Crosby, L., & Leve, C. S. (1998). Becoming an adolescent father: Precursors and parenting. *Developmental Psychopathology, 34*(6), 1209–1219.

Fisher, J. D., & Fisher, W. A. (2000). Theoretical approaches to individual-level change in HIV-risk behavior. In J. Peterson & R. J. DiClemente (Eds.), *HIV Prevention Handbook.* New York: Kluwer Academic/Plenum Press.

Fisher, J. D., Fisher, W. A., Bryan, A. D., & Misovich, S. J. (2002). Information-motivation-behavioral skills model-based HIV risk behavior change intervention for inner-city high school adolescent. *Health Psychology, 21*(2), 177–186.

Greene, K., Krcmar, M., Walters, L. H., Rubin, D. L., Hale, J., & Hale, L. (2000). Targeting adolescent risk-taking behaviors: The contributions of egocentrism and sensation-seeking. *Journal of Adolescence, 23,* 439–461.

Jensen, P. S. (2003). Commentary: The next generation is long overdue. *Journal of the American Academy of Child and Adolescent Psychiatry, 42*(5), 527–530.

Jessor, R. (1998). *New Perspectives on adolescent risk behavior.* New York: Cambridge University Press.

Johnson, B. T., Carey, M. P., Marsh, K. L., Levin, K. D., & Scott-Sheldon, L.A.J. (2003). Interventions to reduce sexual risk for HIV in adolescents, 1985–2000. *Archives of Pediatrics and Adolescent Medicine, 157*(4), 381–388.

Kalichman, S., Stein, J. A., Malow, R., Averhart, C., Devieux, J., Jennings, T., et al. (2002). Predicting protected sexual behaviour using the Information-Motivation-Behaviour skills model among adolescent substance abusers in court-ordered treatment. *Health & Medicine, 7*(3), 327–338.

Karon, J., Rosenburg, P., McQuillan, G., Khare, M., Gwinn, M., & Peterson, L. (1996). Prevalence of HIV infection in the United States 1984–1992. *Journal of the American Medical Association, 276,* 126–131.

King, R. A. (2002). Adolescence. In M. Lewis (Ed.), *Child & Adolescent psychiatry* (pp. 332–342). Philadelphia: Lippincott Williams & Wilkins.

La Greca, A. M., Prinstein, M. J., & Fetter, M. (2001). Adolescent peer crowd affiliation: Linkages with health-risk behaviors and close friendships. *Journal of Pediatric Psychology, 26,* 145–159.

Li, X., Stanton, B., & Fiegelman, S. (2000). Impact of perceived parental monitoring on adolescent risk behavior over 4 years. *Journal of Adolescent Health, 27,* 49–56.

Lyon, M., Richmand, D., & D'Angelo, L. (1995). Is sexual abuse in childhood or adolescence a predisposing factor for HIV infection during adolescence. *Pediatrics AIDS HIV Infection, 6,* 271–275.

Malow, R. M., Devieux, J. G., Jennings, T., Lucenko, B., & Kalichman, S. C. (2001). Substance-abusing adolescents at varying levels of HIV risk: Psychosocial characteristics, drug use, and sexual behavior. *Journal of Substance Abuse, 13*(1–2), 103–117.

Malow, R. M., Rosenberg, R., & Devieux, J. (2000). Translating primary HIV prevention intervention in diverse groups: The AIDS Prevention Center (APC) in Miami. *Psychology and AIDS Exchange, 28,* 1–8.

NIMH Multisite HIV Prevention Trial Group (2002). Predictors of sexual behavior patterns over one year among persons at high risk for HIV. *Archives of Sexual Behavior, 31*(2), 165–176.

Offord, D. R., & Bennett, K. J. (2003). Prevention. In M. Rutter & E. Taylor (Eds.), *Child & adolescent psychiatry (4th ed.).* Malden, MA: Blackwell Science.

Patterson, G. (1982). *Coercive family process.* Eugene, OR: Castalia.

Piaget, J. (1969). *The psychology of the child.* New York: Basic Books.

Ramirez, J. I., Gossett, D. R., Ginsburg, K. R., Taylor, S. L., & Slap, G. P. (2000). Preventing HIV transmission: The perspective of inner-city Puerto Rican adolescents. *Journal of Adolescent Health, 26,* 258–267.

Riggs, P., & Whitmore, E. (1999). Substance use disorders and disruptive behavior disorders. In R. Henderen (Ed.), *Disruptive behavior disorders in children and adolescents* (pp. 133–173). Washington DC: American Psychiatric Press.

Rotheram-Borus, M. J., & Naihua, D. (2003). Next generation of preventive interventions. *Journal of the American Academy of Child and Adolescent Psychiatry, 42*(5), 518–526.

Rotheram-Borus, M. J., O'Keefe, Z., Kracker, R., & Foo, H. H. (2000). Prevention of HIV among adolescents. *Prevention Science, 1,* 48–59.

Schreibman, T., & Friedland, G. (2003). Human immunodeficiency virus prevention: Strategies for clinicians. *Clinical Infectious Diseases, 36,* 1171–1176.

Shoveller, J. A., & Pietersma. (2002). Preventing HIV/AIDS risk behavior among adolescent. *AIDS and Behavior, 6*(2), 123–129.

Smith, M. D. (2001). HIV risk in adolescents with severe mental illness: A literature review. *Journal of Adolescent Health, 29,* 320–329.

Sobell, L., Kwan, E., & Sobell, M. (1995). Reliability of a drug history questionnaire (DHQ). *Addictive Behavior, 20,* 233–241.

Society for Adolescent Medicine. (2000). Expanding the scope of HIV prevention for adolescents: Beyond individual level interventions. *Journal of Adolescent Health, 26,* 377–378.

Steiner, H., & Wilson, J. J. (1999). Conduct disorder. In R. Hendren (Ed.), *Disruptive behavior disorders in children and adolescents* (pp. 47–98). Washington DC: American Psychiatric Press.

Tapert, S. F., Aarons, G. A., Sedlar, G. R., & Brown, S. A. (2001). Adolescent substance use and risk-taking behavior. *Journal of Adolescent Health, 28,* 181–189.

UNAIDS and World Health Organization (2002). AIDS Epidemic Update.

Vermeiren, R. (2003). Psychopathology and delinquency in adolescents: A descriptive and developmental perspective. *Clinical Psychology Review, 23*(2), 277–318.

Woodard, L. J., & Fergusson, D. M. (1999). Early conduct problems and later risk of teenage pregnancy in girls. *Development and Psychopathology, 11,* 127–141.

Yates, A. (2002). Childhood sexuality. In M. Lewis (Ed.), *Child & adolescent psychiatry* (pp. 274–286). Philadelphia: Lippincott Williams & Wilkins.

CHAPTER THIRTY-SIX

INTEGRATING TREATMENT: THE DEVELOPMENTAL PERSPECTIVE

Dr. med. univ. Hans Steiner, Leena A. Khanzode, M.D., Michelle King, B.A., and Don Mordecai, M.D.

In this final chapter, we will take on the challenging task of helping the practitioner decide when and how to use which of the many interventions we have presented. The data base supporting our treatments is steadily increasing and we are now to a point where we can expand our questions to include those that ask not only how our treatments work (Hager, 2002), but also precisely in what combination.

Most of our knowledge regarding the efficacy of interventions comes from controlled clinical trials featuring head to head comparisons of single interventions against placebo or inactive treatment. However, in clinical practice, it is quite apparent that our young patients commonly require several interventions at the same time in order to be restored to a healthier developmental trajectory. How do we decide what packages to use and when to apply them? Using the scientific data base and the expert consensus of practice guidelines, we will try to answer this question.

The first step will be to define integrated treatment and its components. At the present time, several labels are used in psychiatry to denote the fact that combinations of treatments are used for maximum effectiveness. In order to stimulate discussion and research, and unify practices, we will introduce definitions of single and combined treatments to keep the nomenclature clear and consistent.

Second, we will review the empirical literature backing up the practice of combined treatment. Our empirical data base is limited, but growing, and there are many relevant studies in adults and youths. Additionally, where gold standard studies are not available, we can base some of our recommendations on existing practice parameters from national expert consensus.

Third, we wish *to* provide the reader with a method to organize interventions for children and adolescents based on developmental principles. Combining the accumulated wisdom from practice guidelines and data, we suggest using, as much as practicable an algorithm-driven, evidence-based approach. We will describe a method of formulating a case that has been discussed in great detail elsewhere (Steiner & Hayward, 2004). We have applied this method in several case series (Smith et al., 1993; Steiner, 2003), which confirms its clinical value by means of prospective follow-up for over thirteen years.

Finally, we will use some cases to illustrate the principles we have introduced. The cases permit the construction of some reasonable algorithms for interventions in youths, which ultimately will have to be tested in rigorous designs.

Defining Integrated Treatment and Its Components

Integrated treatment refers to the use of comprehensive mental health interventions, which target putative, causal, precipitating, and perpetuating processes in the pathogenesis of mental disorders. Integrated treatment is assembled in rational packages that account for the developmental needs and potentials of the patient. The package is tailored to the patient according to the formulation of the particular case (Connor & Fisher, 1997; Greenspan & Greenspan, 2003; Steiner & Hayward, 2004), which takes into account symptoms, syndromal status, a person's more permanent traits and characteristics, strengths and weaknesses, and developmental progress. Causal processes to be targeted for treatment can be described on three familiar levels—social, psychological, or biological—for most forms of psychopathology. (See section "Preparing for Integrated Treatment" in this chapter.) Treatments and their putative processes of efficacy can also be described on these same three levels of abstraction, and they have been presented this way in this handbook.

Interventions can be simultaneously or sequentially applied, depending on the problem and patient characteristics. First and foremost, integrated treatment refers to a type of practice in which the clinician is committed to non-reductionist thinking, applying efficacious and effective interventions from a wide array of possible treatments based on a rational theory, and, ideally, tested in rigorous trials according to evidence-based medical standards. There is no a priori assumption that one of these forms of intervention is superior to or subsumes the others. We do not subscribe to therapeutic reductionism. We propose therapeutic emergentism, which can be paraphrased, following the words of Rose (1998), as trying to find "the appropriate level of organization of matter at which to seek causally effective determinants of the behavior of individuals" and methods to influence these determinants therapeutically. We believe the ultimate utility of any or all of these interventions will become evident with controlled clinical trials in head-to-head comparisons. Until such comparisons become available, it is advisable to keep any efficacious intervention in our armamentarium.

Monomodal therapy refers to treatment with one agent, be that an antidepressant, cognitive behavior therapy (CBT), or group therapy. Usually, but not always, monotherapy targets specific deficiencies and symptoms and is probably applicable in fairly uncomplicated and less severe cases with minimal or moderate developmental delay in adaptive functioning.

Multimodal therapy refers to the simultaneous application of several treatments. There are two important subcategories: combination treatment and augmentation, which are differently defined.

Combination therapy refers to a treatment regimen in which two or more therapeutic agents with either the same or different processes of efficacy are used. More often than not, the two agents will be a combination of top-down and bottom-up efficacious intervention (such as a combination of psychotherapy and pharmacotherapy; see below in section, "Personal Experiences"), as the literature suggests that such a combination is more efficacious than either treatment alone (see below in section, "Review of Empirical Evidence for Integrated or Combined Treatment"). All treatments are delivered at optimal dosing. They are assumed to be synergistic. More often than not, we are probably employing combinations of treatment if we wish to target multiple or complex problems, face problems of greater severity and/or wish to accelerate the effects of treatment to provide more immediate relief. Usually, but not always, we may encounter high acuity, and/or multiple diagnoses—true comorbidity and/or severe developmental delay in the patient.

Finally, we wish to reserve the term *augmentation treatment* for those instances in which low or even suboptimal doses of two therapeutic agents with similar processes of efficacy (two medications, two psychotherapies) are employed to improve treatment efficacy while avoiding problematic side effects. The two agents "augment"—i.e., help each other achieve a desired effect. Figure 36.1 summarizes these definitions in graphic form.

Types of treatment can be defined by the major processes of efficacy they bring to the intervention, as they are outlined in the three major subsections of this handbook. To briefly recapitulate, we have the following at our disposal, each with its own set of advantages and disadvantages:

Sociotherapy (such as hospitalization, residential treatment)–the processes of efficacy include environmental manipulation, which targets cultures, groups,

FIGURE 36.1. INTEGRATED TREATMENT: SUBTYPES.

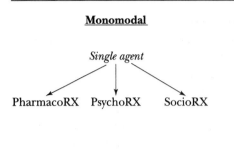

Monomodal	**Multimodal**
Single agent	*Multiple agent*

PharmacoRX   PsychoRX   SocioRX

Combinaiton:
Different or same
process of efficacy
(POE)
Optimal doses
Synergistic
Interactive?

Augmentation:
Same POE
Suboptimal doses
Boosting effects
Avoid side effects
Synergistic
Interactive

interpersonal processes. Interventions in this class are among the most immediately potent in psychiatry, but have the drawback that they are usually vulnerable to rapid decay of effects once they are stopped. They have mostly a palliative and therapeutic profile.

Psychotherapy–the processes of efficacy here include therapeutic discourse and behavioral intervention, which work through communication and target mental states (motives, beliefs, attitudes, conflicts, and cognitions) and behaviors (visible and objectively observable action patterns, habits and skills). These techniques generally work slowly, are of intermediate potency, but seem to have the greatest potential for long-term impact. Psychotherapies are palliative, therapeutic, and in some cases (as in exposure techniques in simple phobias) curative.

Pharmacotherapy–the use of medications altering central nervous system functioning. Medication achieves its processes of efficacy through altering neuronal functioning. Its potency profile is mixed, but most of our compounds work relatively quickly (days to weeks), though not as quickly as sociotherapeutic (i.e., hospitalization, residential treatment) interventions. Many of these agents have only therapeutic and palliative efficacy, although there is a promise that we might have curative agents soon in the form of neuroprotection.

Within the category of combined treatment, we have several possible combinations of interventions:

1. Sociotherapy/psychotherapy/pharmacotherapy. An example would be the residential treatment of highly comorbid conduct disorder.
2. Pharmacotherapy/psychotherapy. An example would be the outpatient treatment of relatively severe obsessive-compulsive disorder.

3. Sociotherapy/psychotherapy. This treatment early in patient treatment of anorexia nervosa, during which psychopharmacological agents are usually not helpful.

4. Sociotherapy/pharmacotherapy. This treatment is used for acute psychosis in an inpatient setting.

Top-Down Interventions

Top-down interventions would be treatments that use in their process of efficacy alterations in high-level emergent structures of the brain-mind system—working with the whole person to affect change and influence lower level systemic components: self-observation, emotion expression and management, correction of cognitive distortions in attitudes and belief and expectations, exploration of internal conflict and identity issues, and examination of interpersonal relationships and cultures and subcultures. They would be expected to penetrate downward in the mind-brain system, changing behaviors, skills, systems of self-regulation and habits, or perhaps even lower level features of the brain-mind system, such as hormonal and neuronal functioning (Kandel, 1998; Gabbard & Kay, 2001; Searle, 2002).

Bottom-Up Interventions

Bottom-up interventions would be treatments that use in their process-of-efficacy alterations in lower level structures of the mind-brain system, such as neurons and other anatomical brain structures, hormones, neurotransmitters, and receptors and their genetic regulation and expression. Currently, most bottom-up efficacious agents are psychopharmacological in nature. Processes of action would be receptor blockade and enhancements, the facilitation of new synaptic potentiation and formations, even the influence of sub-cellular components, such as factors, which control gene expression. Bottom-up interventions would also aim at upward penetration toward more complex states of mental functioning.

At the present time, we have no systematic data on how deeply downward or upward treatments penetrate through the cascade that constitutes the brain-mind system. A cautious, conservative, but reasonable, assumption now is that the level of penetration is moderate. For instance, being motivated to seek pleasurable experiences and enlarge one's interpersonal circle in some cases of depression might be not sufficient to normalize sleep and appetite; conversely, having an efficacious agent on board that corrects basic mood state, sleep, appetite, and circadian rhythms might not be sufficient to equip a patient with new and more effective strategies for making friends if they did not exist prior to the onset of depression. However, patients relieved of their vegetative symptoms might look at the world in a fundamentally different way, thus making them amenable to learning and applying new social skills. In such a case, the combination of both therapies might be the most reasonable choice.

Review of the Empirical Evidence for Integrated or Combined Treatment

A review of the existing data will show that we have much work ahead of us. Many of the existing studies combine late adolescent and adult findings—probably not helpful given the importance to integrated treatment of considering the different developmental phases in which the patients find themselves. A few studies with pure pediatric samples exist; most are relatively short term, assessment instruments and other methods vary widely, and there are multiple methodological problems. Most studies use a limited number of interventions, and in principle, most are designed as competitive comparisons rather than examinations of efficacy on the basis of pretreatment moderators of outcomes. Table 36.1 summarizes the findings in randomized controlled studies. Table 36.2 summarizes the findings from open studies without randomization.

In the studies on bulimia nervosa in the eighteen to forty age group by Mitchell and colleagues (1990), who compared a combination of imipramine and CBT with placebo; Agras, Rossiter, and Arnow (1992), who compared desipramine–CBT combination with placebo; Walsh and associates (1997), who compared a combination of CBT and psychodynamically oriented, supportive therapy with or without active pharmacotherapy using desipramine or, if it was ineffective or intolerable, fluoxetine, and Goldbloom, Olmsted, and Davis (1997), who compared fluoxetine, CBT, and a combination of the two; all found that combined treatment with medication and psychotherapy was superior to placebo, medication alone, or psychotherapy alone on specific parameters such as binge eating, vomiting episodes, depression, and anxiety symptoms. In 2000, Pamela, James, and Traci assessed the long-term impact of short-term treatment with an imipramine–CBT combination and placebo in bulimic patients studied by Mitchell and colleagues (1990), and found that women who received combined treatment showed improved social adjustment at long-term follow-up compared with women randomized to the placebo condition.

There have been a few randomized clinical trials in ADHD, as cited in Table 36.1. Klein and Abikoff (1997) studied eighty-nine children ages six to twelve years who were randomly assigned to three groups: behavior therapy alone, methylphenidate alone, and a combination of behavior therapy and methylphenidate for eight weeks. Children on combined treatments were switched

TABLE 36.1. DOUBLE-BLIND PLACEBO-CONTROLLED RANDOMIZED CLINICAL TRIALS OF COMBINED TREATMENT IN CHILDREN AND ADOLESCENTS/YOUNG ADULTS WITH PSYCHIATRIC DIAGNOSES SINCE 1990.

Study	N	Age	DX	Agents	Duration	Measures	Outcomes
Mitchell et al., 1990	254	18–40	Bulimia nervosa	Imipramine Intensive group therapy	12 weeks	EDI, HDRS, HARS	Imipramine + group therapy > placebo + group therapy in depression and anxiety symptoms
Agras et al., 1992	71	Mean age 18–65	Bulimia nervosa	Desipramine CBT and combined	32 weeks	BDI, EDI, EAT	Desipramine for 24 weeks + CBT > Desipramine alone for 16 weeks
Walsh et al., 1997	120	18–45	Bulimia nervosa	Desipramine for first 8 weeks and fluoxetine later + CBT	16 weeks	Eating attitudes test, the Beck Depression Inventory, SCL-90	Drug + CBT > placebo + CBT in binge eating and depression
Goldbloom et al., 1997	76	18–45	Bulimia nervosa	Fluoxetine, CBT, and combined	16 weeks	EDI, HRSD, BDIRSE	Fluoxetine + CBT > CBT alone on specific parameters like binge eating and vomiting episodes
Pamela et al., 2000	101	18–40	Bulimia nervosa	Long-term follow-up of patients treated with Imipramine + Intensive behavior therapy	10 years	HDRS, EDI, EDQ	Imipramine + behavior therapy > placebo + Behavior therapy in long-term outcome of improved social adjustment
Klein et al., 1997	89	6–12	ADHD	Methlyphenidate + behavior therapy	8 weeks	Ratings from parents, teacher, and clinician	Methylphenidate + behavior therapy > placebo + BT
The MTA GROUP, 1999	579	7–9.9	ADHD	4 groups—Medication, psychosocial treatment, combined treatment, and community treatment	14 months	Parent, teacher, and child ratings	Combined treatment > intensive behavior treatment and/or community treatment in several domains of expanded functioning and combined treatment = behavioral treatment > community treatment in the core symptoms of ADHD

(Continued)

TABLE 36.1. DOUBLE-BLIND PLACEBO-CONTROLLED RANDOMIZED CLINICAL TRIALS OF COMBINED TREATMENT IN CHILDREN AND ADOLESCENTS/YOUNG ADULTS WITH PSYCHIATRIC DIAGNOSES SINCE 1990 (CONTINUED).

Study	N	Age	DX	Agents	Duration	Measures	Outcomes
Bernstein et al., 2000	63	13–16	School refusal with comorbid anxiety and depression	Imipramine + CBT	8 weeks	ARC-R, CDRS-R, RCMAS, BDI	Imipramine + CBT > placebo + CBT
Pelham et al., 2000 (MTA group)-STP	117	7–9	ADHD	Medication + behavioral treatment or behavioral treatment		Parents and teachers ratings	Medication + behavioral treatment > only behavioral treatment
MTA Group, 2002	579	7–9.9	ADHD with comorbidity	Behavior therapy, medication and combined treatment	14 months	Parents and clinician ratings	Combined treatment > medication or behavior therapy alone, mainly for ADHD/CD-ODD/Anx
Neziroglu et al., 2000	10	10–17	OCD	Fluvoxamine alone or with behavior therapy	10 weeks	CY-BOCS	Fluvoxamine + behavior therapy > Fluvoxamine alone in reducing OCD symptoms
Pine et al., 2001	128	6–17	Social phobia, separation anxiety disorder, Generalized anxiety disorder	Supportive and psycho-educational therapy (3 weeks) followed by fluvoxamine (8 weeks)	8 weeks	PARS, CGI-I	Psychotherapy + fluvoxamine > psychotherapy + placebo

to placebo, double-blind, after the period of active treatment. The results of this study showed that both methylphenidate and combination treatments were significantly superior to behavior therapy alone, and in a few instances, such as normalization of behavior, combination was superior to methylphenidate.

An important recent multicenter study was done by the MTA group in 1999, in which 579 children with ADHD Combined type, ages 7 to 9.9 years, were randomly assigned to four treatment groups: fourteen months of medication management, intensive behavioral treatment, the previous two combined, or standard community care (medication management provided by community physicians). Outcomes were assessed in multiple domains. For most ADHD symptoms, children in the combined treatment and medication management groups showed significantly greater improvement than those given behavioral treatment or community care. Combined and medication management treatments did not differ significantly in direct comparisons of efficacy on core symptoms of ADHD, but in several domains of expanded functioning such as oppositional or aggressive symptoms, internalizing symptoms, teacher-related social skills, parent-child relations, and reading achievement, combined treatment was superior to intensive medication management.

As part of the behavioral intervention segment in the MTA study, another small study called the intensive Summer Treatment Programme (STP), was carried out. This study examined the differences between fifty-seven children in the combined treatment group, who were medicated and sixty children in the behavioral treatment group, who were unmedicated. Results showed that combined group children were significantly better than behavioral treatment group on five measures: rule following, good sportsmanship, peer negative nominations, and STP teacher post-treatment ratings of inattention and over activity.

Another randomized clinical trial by the same MTA group tested children with ADHD alone and with comorbid anxiety (ADHD/Anx), conduct or oppositional defiant disorder (ADHD/CD-ODD), and both anxiety and behavior disorders (ADHD/Anx/CD-ODD) with three different modalities of treatment: behavior therapy, medication management, and both combined. They found that in children with ADHD/Anx/CD-ODD, combined intervention offered substantial advantages over the other treatments alone.

Bernstein, Borchardt, and Perwein (2000) studied sixty-three adolescents (ages 13.9 to 17 years) that had a diagnosis of school refusal with comorbid anxiety and depression and compared them on a combination of imipramine and CBT with a combination of placebo and CBT for eight weeks using outcome measures such as weekly school attendance rates and anxiety and depression rating scales. This study concluded that imipramine plus CBT is significantly more efficacious than placebo plus CBT in improving school attendance and decreasing symptoms of anxiety and depression.

Neziroglu, Yaryura, and Jose (2000) studied ten patients (ages ten to seventeen) with obsessive-compulsive disorder who had not previously responded to behavior therapy. Subjects were randomly assigned to two groups: fluvoxamine alone or fluvoxamine with behavior therapy. All received fluvoxamine for ten weeks; five of them continued the medication for one year, and the remaining five engaged in behavior therapy for twenty sessions along with fluvoxamine and subsequently continued the medication for one. They were then rated on Children's Yale-Brown Obsessive Compulsive Scale (CY-BOCS), Clinical Global Impression—Improvement (CGI–I), and Clinical Global Impression—Severity (CGI–S) scales. Those who received the combination of fluvoxamine and exposure with response prevention showed the most improvement on the CY-BOCS, a finding that was also noted on two-year follow-up.

Another recent randomized controlled trial conducted by Pine and Walkup (2001) potentially supports the conclusion that combined treatment is more effective than single treatment in another diagnostic subgroup. He studied 128 children (ages six to seventeen years) who met the criteria for social phobia, separation anxiety disorder, or generalized anxiety disorder, and who had received other diverse psychological treatment for three weeks without improvement. These children were randomly assigned to receive fluvoxamine or placebo for eight weeks and were evaluated by using different measures, including the Pediatric Anxiety Rating Scale (PARS) and CGI–I. Results showed that the mean decrease in symptoms of anxiety in fluvoxamine group was 9.7 points compared with 3.1 points in the placebo group, a significant discrepancy.

In sum, these ten controlled clinical trials of combination treatment tested about 1,608 subjects in various designs. This number is inflated by the fact that a great portion of the eating disorder samples contained adults and smaller unknown numbers of late adolescents. The real number of subjects in these studies is probably closer to a range of 700 to 900, children/adolescents from six to nineteen years of age. Diagnoses are diverse and include externalizing and internalizing disorders such as eating disorders, anxiety and mood disorders, school refusal, disruptive behavior disorders, and ADHD. The therapeutic agents tested are also diverse, but not comprehensive: tricyclic antidepressants (TCAs), selective-serotonin reuptake inhibitors (SSRIs), and stimulants as the psychopharmacological agents (no mood stabilizers or anti-psychotics); and group therapy. It is not always clear from the study descriptions which sociotherapeutic agents were applied, and how controlled this component of the treatment was. Thus, it is probably that day treatments, after-school programs, coordination with school settings, or even inpatient interventions were applied in these studies, and most likely contributed to outcomes, but they are not accounted for, a regrettable omission that characterizes almost all clinical trials in child and adolescent psychiatry at the present time.

CBT, behavior therapy, and psychodynamic therapy are the psychotherapeutic modalities tested. The range of lengths of these trials is wide, from eight weeks to fourteen months. Separate outcomes are usually assessed at exit from protocol, but some studies provide long-term outcomes over several years. Generally, the studies report the greater efficacy of combined treatments, especially in internalizing disorders. In externalizing disorders, these effects seem to become evident only if one examines functioning beyond core symptom domains or if one includes comorbid internalizing disorders.

Open-label studies can be useful to determine the effectiveness and adverse effects of various treatments prior to the testing of these treatments in more costly and complicated controlled clinical trials. There are five such studies of multimodal treatment in children and adolescents, described in Table 36.2.

Dawson studied sixteen inpatients (ages six to fourteen) that received combined medical and psychological treatment for encopresis between 1984 and 1986, and he found significant reduction in the frequency of encopretic episodes at the one-year follow-up. Steiner, Mazer, and Litt (1990) assessed forty-one adolescents with mixed eating disorders who were treated in a standardized integrated program (Steiner, Marx, & Walton, 1991) an average of 32.4 months after discharge. Seventy percent improved considerably, 24% were still symptomatic and 5% remained in

TABLE 36.2.   OPEN LABEL CLINICAL TRIALS OF COMBINED TREATMENT IN CHILDREN AND ADOLESCENTS WITH PSYCHIATRIC DIAGNOSES SINCE 1990.

Study	N	Age	Diagnosis	Agents	Duration	Measures	Outcome
Dawson et al., 1990	16	6–14	Encopresis (inpatient)	Combined medical and psychological treatment	2 years		Decrease in the frequency of encopretic episodes
March et al., 1994	15	7–18	OCD	SSRI + CBT	22 weeks	YBOCS, CGI–I	Significant reduction in OCD symptoms, and no relapse on 18 month follow-up
Chavira et al., 2002	12	8–17	Social anxiety disorder	Citalopram + counseling sessions	12 weeks	CGI, SASC-R, SPAI-C, CDI, SSQ-P	Significant reduction in social anxiety, depression with improvement in social skills

poor condition. In a longer follow-up study of another cohort, Smith and colleagues (1993) studied twenty-three adolescent patients who were treated six years prior by the same carefully coordinated intervention package of sociotherapy (Steiner, Marx, & Walton, 1991), individual and family psychotherapy, and pharmacotherapy after weight rehabilitation. Although outcomes after six years were less impressive than after two and a half years, they still were better compared to the outcomes in a strongly behaviorally based program (Halmi, 1995)—43% still had eating disorders, versus 73% in the behavioral program. March, Mulle, and Herbel (1994), in his open trial of CBT concluded that adding CBT to SSRI treatment in cases of partial response is effective in reducing OCD symptoms. Chavira and Stein (2002) studied generalized anxiety disorder in twelve children and adolescents (eight to seventeen years) with twelve weeks of citalopram and eight brief counseling sessions, which included psycho-education about social anxiety, skills coaching, and behavioral exercises. He found significant reduction in social anxiety and depressive symptoms as well as improvement in parent's perception of social skills. In sum, these open trials treated about 116 patients between the ages of seven and eighteen who were diagnosed with anorexia nervosa and bulimia, OCD, encopresis, or social anxiety; the agents tested were inpatient treatment, SSRIs, CBT, and individual and family therapy and counseling. Treatments lasted between twelve weeks and two years. Positive effects were described for all combined interventions up to six years later.

These data are interesting and suggestive, encouraging us to expand our efforts to document efficacy and effectiveness. In comparison to adult data on multimodal treatment, the child literature is of comparable quality. We are not too far off the mark. In the adult literature, there are about forty studies of multimodal treatment (Gabbard, Markowitz, & Clemens, 2000; Sammons & Schmidt, 2001) with similar limitations as the data on young patients. Overall, they show similar results in favor of combination interventions. Interestingly, in at least two diagnoses (schizophrenia and substance abuse) multimodal treatment is the standard of care, as stated in the practice parameters for these conditions.

This leads us to a discussion of another source of data on how to make decisions regarding mono- versus multimodal treatment in children and adolescents: practice parameters are available for a whole range of internalizing and externalizing disorders. (See www.aacap.org for detailed information.) The most recent ones (Steiner & AACAP 1997; Steiner, Remsing, & AACAP 2004) clearly emphasize the need for integrated treatment in a variety of externalizing and internalizing (AACAP, 1998; AACAP, 2001) disorders. While such practice parameters cannot replace clinical trials, they do represent a nationwide clinical consensus, which can be valuable. In general, almost all practice parameters in children and adolescents support careful consideration of integrated treatment, although the exact admixtures of the integrated treatment package usually vary from disorder to disorder. In the next section, we will propose rational ways of approaching the issue of how to assemble an appropriate treatment package for a patient.

Preparing for Integrated Treatment

This portion of the chapter will provide a pragmatic, hands-on way of mapping treatments onto existing problems. Ideally, we diagnose a patient and treat with the one treatment, which has been shown to be curative, correcting the pathogenetic process. At our current stage of knowledge in psychiatry, we are far removed from this scenario. Our diagnoses are not confined: they are comorbid. We know relatively little about the pathogenetic process, which brings about a variety of diagnoses. Our treatments are not specific, but work for a wide range of conditions—they are relatively nonspecific to the nomenclature in our possession. Many of our treatments are of unknown efficacy and effectiveness.

In such a limited state of knowledge, we can be pragmatic, using several principles that are informed by the following: (1) Occam's razor—parsimony, (2) *primum nil nocere*, and (3) use of a developmental orientation: expect complexity, examine continuity, prepare for context, and look for data supporting your approach.

Establish a Principal Descriptive Diagnosis If Possible

The current gold standard is our phenomenological Diagnostic and Statistical Manual (DSM) or International Classification Diagnosis (ICD) system, which provides algorithms for appropriate diagnosis based on a clustering of symptoms. The value of establishing a principal diagnosis becomes increasingly evident as our treatments become more specific and refined, and target particular problems. The CBT used to treat PTSD and phobias and depression, for instance, is based on similar principles; however, the content of the treatment varies according to diagnosis. Social-skills building for socially phobic children and oppositional defiant children also demands different content and focus (Steiner & Remsing, in press).

In the case of emergency child psychiatric care, we have some evidence that the establishment of a diagnosis adds beneficial information incrementally to broad symptomatic assessment, such as danger to others and self (Gutterman, 1998; Bickman, 1996; Petti, 1998).

One of the problems with the DSM system is that in children it routinely leads to multiple diagnoses, known as comorbidity (Steiner, Carrion, Plattner, & Koopman, 2003). The DSM system allows comorbidity, as patients fulfill criteria. Quite often, in the case of children and adolescents, and probably also with adults, this practice leads to bizarre situations in which a child has six or more diagnoses, which sometimes are treated with six to ten different psychopharmacological agents without any psychotherapeutic or sociotherapeutic interventions provided. In reality, when we speak to expert clinicians, they usually select a principal diagnosis on the basis of severity and focus of concern, even if they practice according to the DSM criteria. This is much preferable to us and fits better with a rational approach to treatment. In the absence of comparative data, we are not able to firmly recommend one approach over the other (Rutter, Taylor, & Hersov, 1994). From a pragmatic point of view, we recommend to err on the side of simplicity and caution.

The DSM system only weakly embraces the approach of establishing a principal diagnosis: there is a provision to select a diagnosis on the basis of the reason for the current visit and the major concern. This method for establishing a principal diagnosis is much too vulnerable to many factors unrelated to the disorder, especially in children and adolescents (who usually are not there for any reason at all, especially if externalizing disorders are involved). We prefer the ICD's approach (Croudace, et al., 2003), which in its clinical version specifies that the clinician is to select a principal diagnosis based on the mapping of symptom patterns onto disease criteria. While this is certainly not an easy task and sometimes will not be possible, we should at least attempt to do it, in the interest of developing rational treatment.

Assess Developmental Status

Because the developmental approach to psychopathology is not narrowly symptom focused, we also assess the phase of development of the patient, along with mastery of normative tasks. We check for delays in the important domains of functioning—social, cognitive, and academic, basic biological functioning and self-care (sleeping, eating, physical activity), and play. We attempt to ascertain if this patient reached the completion of a skill or task in the past and, under the impact of the current disorder lost that capacity, as in regression. Another possibility to consider is whether this patient never mastered this skill at all, as in fixation. A more complex situation arises when the patient skipped ahead to another phase of development, but never firmly established a base in the previous phase (the definition of pseudomaturity and precocious progression). Assessing these phase-specific achievements is a hallmark of the developmental approach. Usually, complex tasks and skills are involved (such as forming and maintaining age-appropriate relationships or being motivated to do school work) that require sophisticated clinical assessment. There are many scales and instruments available for cognitive development, but social-emotional tasks are highly complex and many times can be captured only clinically.

At the same time, such developmental information can be crucial to treatment. Take, for instance, a child whose principal disorder is anorexia nervosa but who has entered puberty, has experimented sexually, and subsequently becomes phobic of dating. Such a patient requires very different interventions from a patient with anorexia who never has experienced any sexual contact at all and is too shy and inhibited to spend time with peers. Separation from the family of origin is a primary concern (Steiner & Hayward, 2004). In the latter case, family therapy will address these issues effectively. In the former case, a psychoeducational intervention about dating and sexual practices, and perhaps an adolescent medicine consultation is indicated, preparing the child for the physical realities of adolescence and the management of sexual practices.

Expand the Data to Include All Domains of Functioning, Assessing Assets and Strengths

Practitioners of the developmental approach are keenly aware that there is considerable "within diagnostic category" heterogeneity in a whole range of domains of functioning, which all may have therapeutic and prognostic implications (Steiner & Hayward, 2004; Smith et al., 1993; Steiner, Cauffman, & Duxbury, 1999).

This expanded assessment is not yet another symptom tally, but obtains information that may help tailor interventions to personal habitual modes of functioning (potential moderators of treatment), and examines an array of strengths that can be used to promote recovery of a normal developmental trajectory.

The literature has found such protective factors in the individual, the family, and the community of the child. These factors interact dynamically with the patient to create a resilience profile that can be used to overcome risk, adversity and even syndromal illness (Smith et al., 1993; Leckman, 2002). For a detailed account of these variables, see Rutter, 1989. We examine basic health and biological functioning, interpersonal functioning, academic and vocational functioning, and recreational patterns (Steiner & Hayward, in press).

Describe the Pathway by Which This Patient Arrived at the Current State

The clinician needs to plot risk and protective factors from all relevant domains, interpunctuating them with a record of life events that affect the patient along the way. (See Figure 36.2.) It is quite likely that obtaining all this information will take some time.

But the clinician needs to be prepared to track all these facts, as they may add important new information to the next step and the formulation of the case, and will likely inform treatment options.

FIGURE 36.2. THE DEVELOPMENTAL TIMELINE.

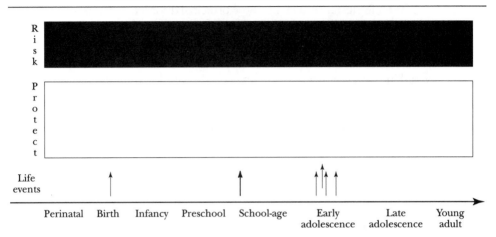

Such a description builds on a family and maturational history, but does not stop there. As the phases of development and the functioning are described, we take into account life events, which had an impact on the patient and the family, be they normative or non-normative. We assess the family's understanding of these events, their "story" of what happened. We note the social, psychological, and biological forces, which interact to produce the outcome we are assessing. The particular pathway by which our patients end up in their current predicament is especially valuable in those diagnoses, which represent final common pathways, because appropriate treatments may vary. At our current level of knowledge of pathogenesis, this would be a majority of diagnoses applicable to children and adolescents. Figure 36.3 shows the major pathways in the case of conduct disorder. Other similar complex paths have been proposed by Loeber (2000) and Burke (2002) for ODD, CD, and depression.

Because the DSM and ICD types are not exclusive, that they are highly "comorbid," it is extremely unlikely that we will find single specific treatments for them. Perhaps in the future, we will have a better understanding of diagnostic types, allowing us to treat with a higher degree of specificity. On the other hand, it is quite possible that descriptive diagnoses will always remain a fuzzy type that delineates major domains of disturbance, requiring us to still look for the many pathways to disorder (Rutter & Sroufe, 1984). In our description of the pathways, we must aim to describe causal processes, broadly and comprehensively defined. This description prepares us for the formulation. (See Figure 36.4)

FIGURE 36.3. FINAL COMMON PATHWAYS: ASSESSING CAUSAL PROCESSES OVER PHENOMENOLOGY.

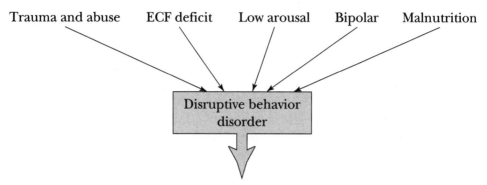

Trauma and abuse   ECF deficit   Low arousal   Bipolar   Malnutrition

Disruptive behavior disorder

Looks the same, but treatment needs to be different

FIGURE 36.4. SETTING UP INTEGRATED TREATMENT: THE FORMULATION.

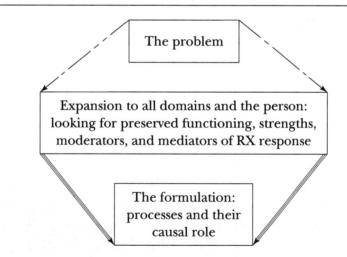

The problem

Expansion to all domains and the person: looking for preserved functioning, strengths, moderators, and mediators of RX response

The formulation: processes and their causal role

Formulate the Case

Take into account the most relevant social, psychological, and biological levels of description of the problem and causal forces that bring about symptoms and developmental delays. (See also the section on personal experiences for sample formulations of cases, and Steiner & Hayward, 2004, for extensive discussion.)

Treatment from a developmental point of view targets causal processes—not descriptive clusters of symptoms. Descriptive symptom clusters are an initial step in looking for causal processes. Descriptions from all levels of abstraction may be relevant. Through our formulation—the summary of the causal descriptors and processes involved in a particular case, we prepare ourselves for the next step—the mapping of specific interventions onto causal processes. The formulation then details a plan for specific interventions aimed at specific causal processes. The formulation should consider whether or not one will encounter synergism, independent efficacy, antagonism, or augmentation in the combination of treatments prescribed. The formulation should end with an estimate of how much progress will be achieved, and a set time interval for the evaluation of progress.

By formulating the case, the clinician commits to a selection of variables, which she thinks are the most important causal determinants in the pathogenesis of a case. She proposes an explanatory developmental trajectory with a specific set of causal descriptors. A formulation should be looked upon as a working hypothesis, a work in progress. It is highly likely that the array of causal forces, and therefore our treatment of the case, will change as we (1) get to know the patient better in the course of treatment and acquire more facts, and (2) begin to see how treatments are effective or not, and how much change they bring about. The developmental clinician is open to new additions or subtractions of highly relevant data, which usually cannot be obtained in a brief initial interview.

A formulation is to the patient as a scientific hypothesis is to the empirical study. Clinicians need to construct a plausible explanatory scenario for a case. One is then in a much better position to know when treatment is effective or not, similar to the scientist whose results are more meaningful when driven by a theory and a hypothesis. In science, exploratory studies are sometimes necessary to pave the way for more informed ones. Cases without formulation have a similar position in clinical practice. But they should be the exception and not the norm. The current comorbidity model does not encourage such hypothesis-driven thinking, as it "treats" all conditions diagnosed. As there is no commitment to a particular scenario, and as one applies multimodal pharmacological treatment, it is very difficult to know when one is wrong and when right, when treatment is effective and when not.

Being able to prescribe the most appropriately matched intervention presupposes a familiarity on the part of the practitioner with what causal descriptors are relevant in a particular case, additional familiarity with specific intervention techniques, and realistic appraisal of what he can and cannot achieve.

But precisely how do we map treatments onto the causal processes? In the absence of definitive data on the comparative efficacy of all treatments available to us in psychiatry, we need alternatives to decide on the treatment of a particular case from a rational point of view. Two important concepts that will facilitate treatment selection are top-down and bottom-up treatments, and mediators and moderators of treatment.

Top-Down and Bottom-Up Treatments

At the beginning of this chapter, we defined bottom-up and top-down efficacious treatments. One helpful way to approach a particular case is to match method of intervention and putative process of efficacy with level of abstraction of the causal determinant or descriptor. For example, we know that in the case of conduct problems, working on a patient's peer associations and environment (Snyder & Stoolmiller, 2002; Reid et al., 2003; Forgatch & Patterson, 1989), moral development (Arbuthnot, 1992), enhancing gabaergic neurotransmission (Steiner et al., 2003a) and blocking dopaminergic receptors with atypical antipsychotics (Findling et al., 2000) all have therapeutic efficacy. These interventions range from sociotherapy to psychotherapy to pharmacotherapy. Relevant causal processes encompass societal forces all the way down to neurotransmission and neuronal functioning. In any given case, we most likely would find different admixtures of these causal processes at work, producing problems and disorder. Depending on our assessment of the relative potency of these causal processes, we would then match intervention to the causal forces we believe to be most influential in a particular case.

Thus, if there are pronounced problems with adequate parenting, we would focus on parent effectiveness training. If this is a case of a maladaptively aggressive child who shows evidence of chronic traumatization and reactive and affectively charged aggressive patterns, we probably would use medications enhancing gabaergic neuronal functioning or decreasing dopaminergic reactivity. A child who repeatedly gets into problems with maladaptive aggression predominantly under the influence of antisocial peer associations would best be exposed to a prosocial peer group, which addresses moral development (Arbuthnot, 1992). From a developmental perspective, it would be problematic to think that giving medications or group therapy or psychotherapy would always be the best intervention. This stance would amount to therapeutic reductionism.

In Chapter 1, we introduced the idea that in psychopathology we are routinely dealing with a mixture of very complex states relevant to the description and causation of psychopathology. This brief statement now needs to be elaborated to provide more extensive justification for our advocating a comprehensive stance in the treatment of mental health problems in children and adolescents. This special state of affairs is due to the special status of the brain as an organ, which produces mental states, which have special ontological status. Mental states are emergent features of brain functioning, which ontologically cannot be reduced to neuronal functioning (Searle, 1990). Mental states are core to the descriptions of many psychopathological syndromes (for example, reliving flashbacks in PTSD, anhedonia in depression, body image distortions in eating disorders, and disregarding societal rules in conduct disorder). They have "causal" force in the sense that they are legitimate, empirically tested descriptors of processes and states implicated in the causation of certain disorders. Sometimes mental states possess a feature of *Intentionality* (Searle, 1983)—they are about something in this person's life, have meaning and significance—sometimes they do not. To distinguish when one is the case and not the other is one of the core tasks in the assessment of mental disorders. Any a priori assumption that mental states are always about something (as was the case in psychoanalysis in the 1950s) or that they are not (as is the case today in the descriptive diagnostic system) is untenable in the long run.

Adding to our difficulties is the fact that some of these states are accessible only to the individual who has them; they are "subjective." This, of course, does not preclude us from studying them scientifically, although to do so will be more complicated (Searle, 1995). But what it does mean is that in order to access them we will need methods that skillfully use the patient's ability to convey them to us. We propose that as long as these mental states are shown to be relevant in the causation of disorders, we will need methods of intervention that manipulate them, such as the different forms of psychotherapy that examine mental content, and sociotherapies that seek to influence mental states (attitudes and beliefs) via interpersonal relationships and the creation of certain cultures.

The "reliving of traumatic events" criterion for PTSD is a good example to elaborate. The symptom clearly possesses Intentionality—it clearly is about a highly significant event in the person's life. It is this "Intentionality" that in fact defines it. For an external observer, it is impossible to completely define whether this patient has this symptom or not. We cannot unfold a screen and ask him to play the "reliving" for us like a movie. We have to ask him whether he in fact is going through this experience and ask him to describe it. We might some day be able to plot brain activation patterns in some form of functional imaging as they relive the event, but this still would not constitute the actual reliving—it is a subjective and irreducible state that is biologically based on the activity of the brain, but ontologically irreducible to those brain states (Searle, 1995). This symptom also gives us the opportunity for a special kind of intervention. To ask the patient to relate to us what has happened (in some exposure or flooding paradigm) is again a powerfully top-down efficacious intervention (we use the patient's narration and remembrance, two complex mental states) that has been shown to produce good to excellent outcomes in PTSD (Pitman et al., 1996).

We can provide another top-down treatment, which works through group cohesion: we can put a patient suffering from post-combat PTSD into a group of war veterans who will share their experiences, help the patient understand his symptoms better, provide a culture of normalization of the experience, help him purge the traumatic aspects, and so on. Finally, we can work in a bottom-up paradigm and mute the physiological arousal that accompanies the terrifying remembrances, thus perhaps preventing them from becoming overwhelming and debilitating and perhaps prevent them from even recurring (Post et al., 1998).

To make matters even more complicated, we encounter yet another additional complexity—the fact that some of the mental states presuppose the presence of a shared socially constructed reality between individuals (Searle, 2002). Examples would be the violation of social rules of conviviality as is the case in disruptive behavior disorders, or the dissatisfaction with one's body as compared to cultural ideals, as found in eating disorders. In order for someone to exhibit maladaptive aggression, which violates rules, we have to have a shared culture that imposes such rules (Searle, 2002); and in order for someone to feel deficient in appearance we have to know that there are such things as commonly agreed upon ideals for appearance. Both these symptoms are what Searle has referred to as "observer dependent"—they exist only if humans who construct social norms and ideals exist. These symptoms relate to a shared social background without which the symptoms would not exist. Without the social context we would not be able to explain the symptoms and we would not be able to intervene. By contrast, the social context of a particular patient with cancer of the liver is almost completely irrelevant in symptom description, diagnosis of disorder, and intervention.

Subjective symptoms and symptoms that require a socially constructed reality would be emergent features of the brain. They would be top-down causal descriptors. A priori, we would expect that in all likelihood they would require a top-down efficacious treatment. We would not presume a priori, that giving such a patient anti-anxiety agents would automatically translate into a correction of their body image. Such an assumption would constitute a therapeutic reductionism, paralleling reductionism in the explanation of behavioral phenomena, of which we have good reasons to be suspicious (Rose, 2002).

On the other hand, as we assess psychopathology, we also must consider factors that would be readily assessed by objective measures, such as brain scans and EEG, and which exist independent of any shared social assumptions. We would group these factors into bottom-up causal descriptors. These would be factors that are observer-independent properties of the brain organ itself—faulty synaptic transmission, defective wiring of brain lobes, damage to existing wiring patterns, and pathological formation of altered pathways. These are objectively observable entities that do not rely on the patient telling us anything at all, but which can be detected by us in a more or less accurate fashion. These causal processes also could be targeted with increasing precision and efficacy by means of medications and novel treatments such as electric stimulation of neuronal circuits and other currently unimaginable interventions. Bottom-up treatments, such as medications, are quite successful in controlling lower level causal descriptors such as sleep and mood in depression. But it is also well accepted that successful medication treatment for depression can alter behavior permanently after correcting the mood state without any appeal to the patient's conscious efforts at change.

Pragmatically speaking, these causal descriptors should lead to interventions that match the level of abstraction of the descriptor. For instance, if we have a disorder that has been ascribed to the immersion of women in the unrealistic ideals of beauty of Westernized culture, we cannot dismiss this causal descriptor in our treatment planning. We will need to address it by correcting our patients' misperceptions of their appearance, by group therapy focusing on women's issues, and psycho-education or cognitive behavioral techniques.

Figure 36.5 gives us the full array of interventions relevant to today's mental health practice, grouped along the top-down, bottom-up continuum. The relevant causal descriptors for each intervention described in this volume is presented in each chapter under the rubric of "rationale and putative mechanisms of efficacy." These levels map onto Figure 1.1 (Chapter 1), giving a list of abstractions relevant to psychopathology. The arrows indicate putative levels of penetration of the two major treatment pathways.

Ultimately, from an pragmatic—empirical point of view, the main criterion for deciding which level is relevant in a particular case is evidence that this level of causal description has received support in the literature, and that treatments conceptualized along the lines suggested by the causal descriptor have been shown to be efficacious.

Another important consideration in treatment selection is how deeply treatments penetrate this continuum, an issue that we know little about. Ideally, we would find treatments with deep penetration, in order to be parsimonious. But, as we have seen in the respective chapters on treatment, most interventions produce comparable response rates in clinical trials, as far as core symptoms of psychopathology are concerned.

The age of a child most likely will also aid in selecting treatments along the top-down to bottom-up continuum in a particular case. The younger the patient, the more dependent on her social context she is and the less complex and differentiated her mental states we will encounter. This would suggest that the younger the patient, the more likely it is that we will be more effective using sociotherapeutic approaches, such as dyadic treatment in the case of infants and toddlers,

FIGURE 36.5. LEVELS OF INTERVENTIONS IN DEVELOPMENTAL TREATMENT.

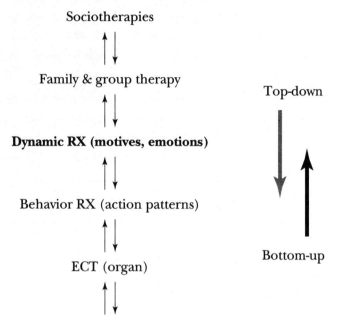

and family therapy for school-age children. Almost all patients in this age range should receive some family therapy, at least for helping alliance building and psycho-educational purposes. It would be the rare late adolescent whose family was not seen in at least periodic supportive sessions. With decreasing age, dependence on the family increases and can help and hinder profoundly with our treatment packages. Psychotherapies using self-observation and reflection would not be efficacious in very young patients. Medications also should be effective in these youngest age groups, as they are relatively independent from intra-individual psychological variables at a younger age, which can interfere with compliance with medication regimens (that is, motivation and ability of others to control the child—for example, parental supervision for compliance).

Another reasonable assumption as we decide on treatment strategies would be that perhaps a preponderance of complex mental states in any given diagnoses would be an indication that top-down efficacious treatments are indicated. A good example would be a clustering of problems with identity (such as in certain forms of dissociation). By contrast, a clustering of basic biological disturbances (appetite, sleep, mood) would be an indication for bottom-up efficacious interventions. From the adult literature we know that pharmacotherapy appears to provide rapid, reliable relief from acute distress, and psychotherapy appears to provide broad and enduring change (Sammons & Schmidt, 2001), especially as far as interpersonal relationships are concerned. Similar patterns might hold for children and adolescents. Acute psychiatric problems presenting a danger to the patient or others will usually be handled first by sociotherapeutic interventions (isolation, restraints hospitalization, placement) before consideration of psychopharmacological interventions (TRAAY, 2002; Steiner, Saxena, & Chang, 2003a).

An additional consideration is important: specific treatments rarely operate in an interpersonal vacuum. Non-specific factors apply to treatment efficacy across the board. Building and maintaining a good therapeutic alliance with patient and family is essential in all cases. We would advocate a minimum of five sessions to achieve such a working alliance, with routine assessment that such an alliance has been achieved. Standardized instruments are available to assess Helping Alliance (Luborsky et al., 1996). We recommend that periodic checks of the formation and maintenance of the alliance be performed, especially in cases in which psychopharmacology or behavior therapy is used as a monomodal therapy. As we discuss in great detail in Chapter 15, there is no such thing as a psychologically inert intervention. But while all other interventions have an inbuilt automatic check for helping alliance, these techniques do not. Problems with treatments do not always reside in the treatment technique itself, but often in the context in which it is delivered.

Having matched intervention to targets, we suggest that, if possible, monomodal therapy is applied and optimized until we either see progress, or lack thereof, or side effects. The exact dosing of each intervention is highly intervention-dependent, and we refer the reader to the various chapters in this handbook. We propose that as we approach treatment, we select the most cost-effective, empirically proven intervention first for monomodal therapy if at all possible. If there are two interventions that are equally effective, but operate on quite different levels of causal description, we select the one that matches most closely the patient moderator characteristics that predict better outcomes with one or the other. (See the discussion following on moderators and their influence on the treatment process.)

Adding Treatments Together

How do we decide to go from monotherapy to multimodal treatment and then how do we decide on combinations or augmentation strategies? Clearly, some of these decisions will depend on diagnosis and treatment modality, but in general, we propose the following. These recommendations are based on the assumption that we wish to rapidly restore health and developmental progress.

If there is no efficacy in the maximum amount of time allotted for a particular treatment to work, we suggest to switch to another monotherapy trial with an agent of a different mechanism of action. If side effects interfere (problems with sleep or appetite on an SSRI, or lack of compliance with a complex CBT regimen), we propose to augment the treatment by lowering the dose, reducing the amount of medicine taken, stretching out the CBT sessions, and interspersing either family sessions or individual sessions where the origin of the non-compliance can be explored.

If the response is still suboptimal, we then are ready to consider combination treatments. Here, the first step should be the combination of psychotherapy with pharmacotherapy, as most of the literature in adults, children, and adolescents suggests these combinations to be the most beneficial, but age of the patient and exact targets are major considerations. In our experience, and this seems to be reflected in the adult and child literature on combinations of interventions, a top-down and bottom-up strategy is usually superior than simple add-ons of the same interventions. To diversify the treatment program is an important consideration in treating children and adolescents, and treatment should be done in such a manner that it preserves their everyday world as much as possible. But, as mentioned before, acuteness and safety considerations would tip the balance to massive environmental manipulations, such as hospitalization and other higher levels of care, such as day treatment, residential care, and partial programs.

Alternatives for Matching Patients to Modes of Interventions: Moderators and Mediators of Treatment

The second set of concepts relevant as we are preparing to intervene would be the influence of moderator and mediator variables on treatment outcomes (Kraemer et al., 2002). Knowing about these variables might enable us to more rationally match patients to interventions, especially at those times when data about differential efficacy are not available or not clear. We have just begun to define relevant variables and there are only a few controlled studies assessing the impact of these in children and adolescents (Saxena et al., 2003).

Moderators "identify on whom and under what circumstances treatments have different effects" (Kraemer et al., 2002). Moderators can be thought of as characteristics that the patient brings to treatment, which can potentially affect the outcome of treatment. These would include fairly straightforward factors such as age, sex, and socioeconomic status as well as educational level.

Moderators also include more complicated and interesting factors such as adaptive style and modes of self-regulation, two concepts that operate at the heart of many psychotherapeutic interventions. We have previously described a simplified model of a personality typology by Weinberger and Schwartz (1990), which seems to capture important relevant aspects of emotion regulation in adults, adolescents, and children. The typology is built on the five factor trait model of McCrae and Costa and examines patients' self-report of what emotions they habitually feel (distress) and how they control impulses and emotions (restraint), two large super-ordinate variables that capture the essence of four of the five variables representing personality, as distilled by McCrae and Costa (1987).

General emotional affective tone and patterns of restraint are important to consider as we plan treatment. Interventions that have as their aim such diverse targets as expression of emotion, disciplined exercising of complex tasks, practicing new skills in the real world with real peers or parents, or examination of developmental progress in certain adaptive phases would call for very different skill sets to be successful. As clinicians, we would like to know in advance how easy or difficult it will be for a patient to explore and express their emotional life, and refrain from impulsive action when stressed.

In Weinberger's modified typology (Erickson & Steiner, 2003) we have the patients describe patterns of habitual emotional activation (distress) and patterns of inhibition (restraint) through a series of eighty-four questions. The two dimensions are then used to create a four-quadrant typology. (See Figure 36.6; Erickson & Steiner, 2003; Steiner, Cauffman, & Duxbury, 1999 for discussion.)

FIGURE 36.6. ADAPTIVE STYLE BY DISTRESS AND RESTRAINT: AGES 31–60.

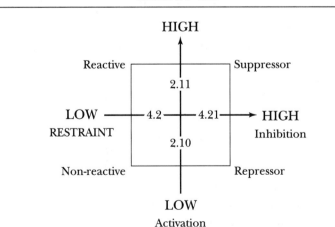

The axes of distress (vertical) and restraint (horizontal) are plotted by intersecting them at the age-appropriate means (2.4/2.41 for distress; 4.2/4.21 for restraint). This creates four types, labeled reactive, suppressive, non-reactive, and repressive. These types have been shown to manage emotions very differently under duress (a paradigm for mental disorder and for treatment). The two types high in distress (reactive and suppressive) habitually express much emotionality, negative, and positive. Between themselves, they differ in the degree to which they simultaneously inhibit themselves (restrain themselves): reactives usually do not, tending to be impulsive. Suppressives are cognizant of their emotions, but restrain and manage them carefully, showing much higher capacity for self-restraint, even when stressed. They are quite capable of expressing a wide and diverse range of emotions appropriately and in measured doses.

Both these types in our clinical experience tend to use treatment modalities well where explicit and detailed examination of emotions is called for. Reactives may need extra structure in their treatment to protect themselves from their tendency to be impulsive under stress (perhaps some sociotherapeutic interventions or behavioral skill building along with the expressive psychotherapy). Suppressives generally are not in need of such structured approaches. But the uniting characteristic between them is their capacity for emotional expression and examination.

In the lower stratum, we encounter two types who habitually de-emphasize the emotional aspect of experience: non-reactives and repressives. As in the upper stratum, these two types again differ between themselves in the capacity to self-restrain: non-reactives are more impulsive, possibly requiring structure as we begin treatment, while repressives are quite capable of self-control and restraint, sometimes to a fault. Both of these types tend to prefer interventions in which examination of emotions is not immediately required, like for instance, psychopharmacology. Both of them are in fact also more prone to drug abuse and dependence (Steiner et al., 2003; Wilson et al., 2001). With the non-reactive type, motivation can be a problem in treatment, and often sociotherapeutic and structured interventions precede the use of others. The repressive type does poorly in psychotherapies, which emphasize emotional expression, as they do not seem to have easy access to them, especially if they are negative emotions (Weinberger & Schwartz, 1990). The repressive's habitual ignoring of negative affect makes describing such emotions in any detail very difficult. In fact, repressors often insist that they are quite content and happy, despite all evidence to the contrary, and despite an accumulation of stressful events, which would constitute a significant allostatic load (McEwen and Wingfield, 2003) that would call for re-examination of life trajectories and decisions regarding alternative pathways. Supportive interventions are helpful to pair with medications. If expressive treatment techniques are needed (as would be for instance in the case of acute PTSD), clinicians should be aware that treatment should proceed in small steps, accompanied by psychoeducation along the way. A model that provides reasonable therapeutic access to these patients is a stress diathesis model, which emphasizes accumulated allostatic load, education regarding the signal function of negative emotions and their usefulness in navigating stressful life circumstances. These types are almost equally common in samples of non-clinical subjects (Erickson & Steiner, 2003). In juveniles, there tends to be a skew to the left, in older populations a skew to the right. Women are somewhat over-represented in the upper stratum, men in the lower one.

The description of these types suggests that certain treatment combinations would produce better outcomes according to type, regardless of syndromal disorder, if treatments have been shown to possess equal efficacy. The act of matching the type of intervention (top-down versus bottom-up efficacious) should optimize the chances that patients will use treatments offered because the treatment matches their habitual style of self-regulation. Thus, in two cases of depression, bottom-up treatments (medication) should better match those patients not particularly good at examining and expressing emotions, while top-down interventions would probably be most useful in those who fear that medication would "alter their personality" and prefer to be in more explicit control of psychological processes.

Preliminary empirical data suggest that these assumptions are valid. We have found that exposure to standardized treatments results in differential outcomes in cohorts of youths (Steiner, Cauffman, & Duxbury, 1999; Smith et al., 1993). We are currently testing these assumptions in fully randomized controlled clinical trials. In the meantime, this set of moderators provides a reasonable way to decide on necessary treatment combinations. Reactives should benefit from interventions that provide structure and emotional expressivity, such as combinations of bottom-up and top-down procedures. The latter would focus on emotion expression, the former on impulse containment. Non-reactives would most likely benefit from structure and bottom-up procedures, which do not require much expressivity, such as psychopharmacological approaches. On the right hand of the typology, patients would not require structure, but instead would be better fitted to techniques that decrease inhibition and restraint. Explorative approaches, which examine hidden motives, assumptions, conflicts, and goals, would be more suitable. These patients present with high degrees of inner structure and would benefit from greater expressivity and spontaneity. The two types would differ among themselves in terms of how natural it would seem to them to express emotion. The highly restrained repressor would probably be more accessible to a cognitively based approach to an examination of their problems, while the suppressor, once convinced that it is safe to express emotions, would be more available to expressive techniques.

Mediators are defined as "identifying why and how treatments have effects." These are characteristics of the treatment itself that affect treatment outcomes. They describe specific processes that alter the causal processes, which generate psychopathology. Some examples would be: receptor density in response to drug administration, brain level of serotonin after application of SSRIs, compliance with treatment as a function of helping alliance, the shift in negative attribution bias under the impact of CBT, the application of emotional control in stressful situations as a function of successful Dialectical Behavior Therapy (DBT). Our chapters have presented a whole range of mediators of treatment. Still, in our clinical trials, we have only a few examples (Kraemer et al., 2002) in which these have been measured and linked to application of technique and changes in outcome (Forgatch & Patterson, 1989). Is very likely that individuals with particular disorders such as depression will have special response rates to interventions depending on these variables. We currently know very little regarding the predictors of outcomes of interventions in children and adolescents. We anticipate that the literature in the next five to ten years will address these deficiencies. Still, it is useful to track what we know in this regard, as the developmental model of psychopathology weighs in heavily on the side of causal and curative processes, and because a continued refinement of our case formulations will depend entirely on us acquiring more and more accurate information of moderators and mediators of treatment. Ultimately, such knowledge will allow us to map with treatments of greater precision onto pathogenic process and thus lead to improved outcomes.

Personal Experiences

To illustrate our personal experience with this method of practice, we will describe three cases: (1) an inborn "bottom-up" disorder complicated by environmental factors (bipolar), (2) a difficult, but normal range, temperament complicated by the environment (oppositional defiant disorder), and (3) normal at birth, confronted by a persistently toxic environment (chronic abuse).

A case of a recently referred fifteen-year-old teenage girl will elucidate. She arrived for the evaluation of lack of progress and Figure 36.7 shows her DSM diagnostic profile given by the practitioner: diagnoses of anorexia, bulimia, obsessive-compulsive disorder (OCD), oppositional defiant disorder (ODD), ADHD, kleptomania, panic disorder, and bipolar NOS. Her treatment was as follows: paroxetine, sertraline, risperidone, methylphenidate, trazodone, divalproex sodium, and lithium. All of these were given at small doses, targeting the syndromes listed. She saw a "counselor" at school every other month. Parents and she saw the prescribing psychiatrist once a month, where the girl spent twenty

FIGURE 36.7. PSYCHOPATHOLOGY: THE DSM COMORBIDITY VIEW.

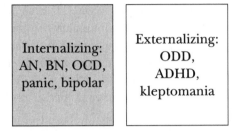

Internalizing: AN, BN, OCD, panic, bipolar

Externalizing: ODD, ADHD, kleptomania

to thirty minutes talking about the medications, and the parents subsequently talked about her eating problems. She saw a nutritionist every week for her diet plan and weight. On this regimen, she had lost another ten pounds in three months, bringing her close to hospitalization. The parents and the practitioner wondered why.

The problem became somewhat clearer when we simply ordered the various syndromes in time of appearance, and rather than have them do so in a vacuum, we examined and plotted the social context in which these symptoms appeared. This generated a clinical formulation that provided a more reasonable working model for the problems found in this patient. Figure 36.8 summarizes this time line. The girl's problems started with a somewhat moody, difficult temperament.

FIGURE 36.8. COMPLEX PSYCHOPATHOLOGY: THE DEVELOPMENTAL VIEW.

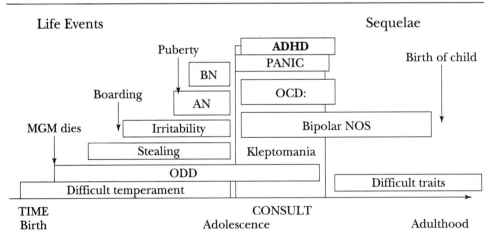

Following a beloved grandmother's death she became stubbornly oppositional, and as nobody wondered about her grieving for her grandmother, she began to steal items, including money from her parents. The temporal ordering and juxtaposition of symptom onset to life events provided more diverse and useful intervention strategies to succeed in this case. This patient's symptoms possessed a relationship to events in her life that implied an Intentionality (Searle, 1985) on her part that needed to be addressed in communications about her sentiments regarding the grandmother's death, her sorrow, the feeling of emptiness and depletion felt in her absence, and so on through a series of top-down interventions, rather than the simplistic and ineffective piling on of psychopharmacological agents.

As there was now much tension in the home and nobody still thought of her being aggrieved, more conflict ensued, she became irritable and persisted in her stealing, to the point where the family decided to place her in a boarding school. This increased the already considerable emotional distance to her mother, and as she approached pubertal development, which, in her case was rapid and premature and pronounced, she was completely unprepared for its consequences—the unwarranted advances and mockery of her boy classmates. She began severe dietary restriction, which resulted in rapid weight loss, but also brought on breakthrough binge and purge episodes, which went undetected for some time. Pressure increased for her to normalize her weight, and she became increasingly panicky around her meal times, especially when she thought she would not be able to throw up after a meal. She obsessed with counting calories in order not to gain too much weight. While under the threat to be hospitalized because of her weight, she became more irritable, her mood fluctuated, and her attention in class suffered.

In our clinic we saw the mood problem as the predominant problem, worsened by the loss of the grandmother. Our general approach was that none of her problems occurred in an interpersonal or experiential vacuum, that delineating the pathway to her current complex situation required asking her and her parents about events that happened along the way, their understanding of it and a thoughtful mapping of emerging symptom patterns on this pathway. Because of the history of affective disorder and alcoholism in the family of both parents, we felt justified in calling her problem Bipolar NOS. We saw oppositionality, stealing, and eating problems as attempts to help herself regulate her affective state, although none of them were successful and led to a secondary layer of problems with panic, obsessions, and attention as she tried to deal with the consequences of her unsuccessful attempts at handling her dysphoric state and disposition. She was treated with weight rehabilitation, binge prevention CBT, an SSRI and a mood stabilizer. After she reached stabilization, she finished school at home and came more or less regularly for individual exploratory psychotherapy sessions in which we carefully dissected the exact pathway that got her into her predicament, and where we shaped her understanding of how it led to such a confusing intermediate outcome. Parents were not much involved or interested in treatment, but managed also not to interfere with treatment and supported it financially. Ten years after her treatment she is the mostly happy, still irritable married mother of a three-year-old. She is off all medications, but periodically inquires about returning to the mood stabilizer.

The problems in treating this case were mostly driven by our current DSM comorbidity model. The high comorbidity rate in this and other patients has lead to some highly unusual and irrational practices, whereby patients who suffer from five disorders will appear on five different medications, which supposedly target specific disorders. Of the referrals we receive in our tertiary care setting, 80% fit this profile. Such practice is generally not in keeping with the ideal of medicine, in which diagnostic certainty or simplicity is a treasured goal. By contrast, in our own clinics at Stanford, a tertiary care center, we find very different practice profiles. Most of our referrals come after having failed community treatment or looking for second opinions. In a highly specialized second opinion professor's clinic, just looking at the use of psychiatric medication, 80% of patients are on monomodal therapy, employing one agent; 25% on combinations of medications; 5% on augmentation treatment; all in one integrated treatment. In a general intake clinic at Stanford, 40% receive psychopharmacological monotherapy; 50% on combination treatment; 10% augmentation therapy. This is a pronounced contrast.

We suggest that if a patient fulfills diagnostic criteria for more than one disorder, that we use *developmental ordering* as an aid in deciding how and with what to treat this patient. Embedding the appearance of symptoms and syndromes in a certain context and examining the causal forces active at the times of symptom emergence may help us select a principal diagnosis, which directs our treatment. We are essentially recreating the developmental trajectory for this particular person coming to understand as clinicians, and helping the patient to understand how they have left a healthy developmental path and how to find their way back.

A single causal process can produce different descriptive diagnoses at different points of time in development (see Figure 36.2), a classical case of *non-isomorphic presentation* of a disorder, such as we think will explain many cases of juvenile bipolar disorder (Chang, Steiner, & Ketter, 2002) (see Figure 36.9). Recent studies suggest that bipolar offspring present with high levels of comorbidity yielding different presentations in different phases of development. Attention and hyperactivity problems tend to appear first in children who are described as temperamentally difficult from birth (Chang et al., 2000). These problems usually are

FIGURE 36.9. PSYCHOPATHOLOGY AS NON-ISOMORPHIC SERIES OF DISTURBANCES.

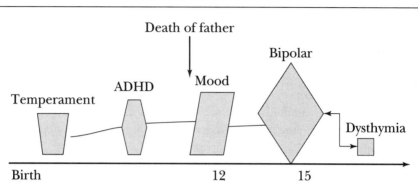

followed by problems with aggression and disruptive behavior, followed by mood and anxiety problems. These mood problems, mostly depression, usually begin after a serious loss or disappointment, as has been noted by Kraepelin (Chang et al., 2000).

In the current DSM model, we would target all these comorbidities as separate illnesses, leading to a whole host of psychopharmacological interventions. In the principal disorder model, developmentally ordered, we will conceptualize these various disorders as manifestations of what presumably is juvenile presyndromal bipolar disorder (caused by unstable mood regulation that is triggered and precipitated by developmental transitions and adverse stressful life events), regardless of whether current problems are oppositionality or depression. Evidently, treatment of bipolar offspring with mood stabilizers usually controls presenting symptoms the patients presents with (Chang et al., 2003), although not always completely. In many cases we need to add other therapies to appropriately treat all problems. CBT has recently been shown to increase compliance in adult bipolars (Lam et al., 2003; Miklowitz et al., 2000). Add-on treatment with an atypical antipsychotic seems to be helpful in times of high allostatic load in the life of a patient (Saxena et al., 2003), as are techniques diffusing family conflict and improving communication, structure, and predictability, as well as (Chang et al., 2001) improving personal stress management skill. At times, antidepressants (used judiciously) may be necessary to normalize a depressive phase, and stimulants can be added (with care) on to provide symptomatic relief from troubles with attention.

The main point is that the mainstay of intervention is mood stabilization, since this is the most likely underlying pathological process that drives the morbidity and comorbity, symptoms that arise de novo are approached from the vantage point of the principal diagnosis. We will, for instance assume that the patient's oppositionality will improve with the successful treatment of his mood, and we would not start a complicated parent effectiveness training program as would be helpful if we thought that ODD was truly a separate condition, and as parent training is one of the main successful interventions for this problem (Steiner, Remsing, & AACAP, 2004). As much as possible we will apply monotherapy—mood stabilization, but also tailor other interventions to what is known about the treatment of bipolar disorder, simplifying our interventions as much as possible and optimizing the treatment. Only if treatment is not successful do we shift gears and examine the possibility that there are two truly independent processes and disorders that need attention and intervention.

Another example in which the developmental, principal-diagnosis approach would be helpful is a case in which the causal process that brings about the patient's diagnosis is also unrelenting, but rather than just simply leading to an accumulation of disorders in a variety of domains, there is a transformation of the presenting disorders as a function of increasing psychosocial stressors. An example would be the progression from acute stress disorder to post-traumatic stress disorder to dissociative disorder to multiple personality disorder and substance use dependence in the case of severe, unrelenting untreated abuse in the family (see Figure 36.10). Figure 36.3 shows us such a clinical scenario in the case of disorders following abuse—a case in which the causal process (abuse) resides in the environment of the patient (Steiner et al., 2003b; Plattner et al., 2003).

The unrelenting nature of the abuse gradually transforms the psychopathology into more and more severe variants, which indicate increasing fragmentation

FIGURE 36.10. PRINCIPAL DIAGNOSIS FROM A DEVELOPMENTAL PERSPECTIVE: SEQUENTIALLY DEVELOPING TRANSFORMED MORBIDITY.

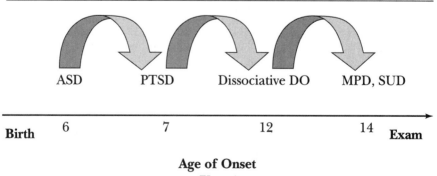

of complex levels of functioning, such as personality integration. In such a case, we probably would have to work rapidly to gain control of the situation, to avoid self-harm and non-compliance. We would start from the most fragmented state, target the last appearing psychopathology first, multiple personality disorder, in order to stabilize the patient and make her accessible to treatment. Interventions initially would be psychotherapeutic, with potential add-on atypical agents to control fragmentation of functioning under stress. Once a helping alliance is established, we would be in a better position to eliminate drug use, which in all likelihood is a form of self-medication. As the patient retains longer and longer periods of intactness, we can begin to prepare for more complex interventions that require some compliance and will to cooperate, such as the use of mood stabilizers for the treatment of chronic PTSD, SSRIs for irritability and dysthymia, and abuse survivor support group abuse issues.

Finally, we present a relatively uncomplicated case of true comorbidity (Figure 36.3) where the situation led to sequential irrational polypharmacy, which was eventually eliminated by establishing a principal diagnosis, optimizing existing treatment, and adding a sociotherapeutic intervention. Figure 36.11 summarizes this case.

This is a case of an eight-year-old boy who was diagnosed with ADHD and subsequently successfully treated with Ritalin monotherapy. One year after his diagnosis, he did well in terms of attention and school work, but became increasingly aggressive at home and at school to the point where he was on the

FIGURE 36.11. PRINCIPAL DIAGNOSIS FROM A DEVELOPMENTAL PERSPECTIVE: A CASE OF TRUE COMORBIDITY.

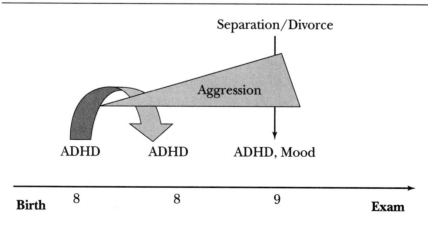

verge of being expelled. He was switched, in rapid order to racemic mixtures of stimulants, long-acting stimulants and Wellbutrin, each employed less than two weeks, but at adequate doses. He did not respond in terms of his aggression, threatened siblings with weapons in the home and finally was expelled. Home schooling made him worse. At this point, risperidone was added, which provided some relief from aggression. He returned to school, but the medication was discontinued after three months because he was doing well. He almost immediately started having problems with aggression, especially at school with his male teacher. At that point he was switched to divalproex sodium, which was ineffective and he again was expelled from school. This is the time of consultation. Examination revealed that the parents had been having serious marital problems in the previous year. This had never been examined at the brief "med checks" the boy was receiving from his pediatrician. We reinstated methylphenidate at his old effective dose, risperidone at night for treatment of acute aggression to enable him to return to school immediately and added family therapy sessions to explain the marital problems and the pending divorce to the boy. His mood worsened and there was some discussion of perhaps adding an SSRI; however, the parents were reluctant to add another medication. After six weeks, his mood improved, aggression subsided. We discontinued risperidone slowly, checking continued aggression control at school. As the parents decided to divorce and as the visitation schemes were clarified, the boy's mood improved to the point at which no further consideration was given to adding an antidepressant. On the one-year follow up, the child was at school doing well academically and socially. He visits parents on alternate days and his relationship with his siblings is age appropriate.

This case illustrates a patient's fairly uncomplicated clinical trajectory, which was inadequately treated by serial prescriptions of multiple agents, some of them effective, some not, because a major life event complication was not elucidated and dealt with by the most appropriate intervention, family therapy. The child clearly suffered from ADHD, which actually responded well to methylphenidate. The increasing aggression was not due to the ADHD worsening or not responding, thus the multiple switching between stimulant agents was ineffective and should have called for a broadening of the scope of inquiry. It seems that the worsening of aggression was the early manifestation of his mood problem in reaction to marital discord, a combination that is common in young patients. As soon as it was addressed properly, the mood and the aggression problem subsided, having been controlled immediately by risperidone, which allowed for the boy's rapid return to school before school avoidance could set in. This child suffered from the principal diagnosis of ADHD, which later was complicated by the comorbid mood problem, which encompassed the child's difficulty with aggression.

Open Questions and the Future

We have reached the end of a long, but exciting journey. Many questions were raised, many answered, and many remain. Is integrated treatment really better? We have reason to believe so (Steiner et al., 2003). But which forms, which combinations? For which diagnoses and diagnostic clusters? Which treatments are synergistic, which antagonistic? How do they really work in children and adolescents? Are they better or worse in the short or long run? Should we prepare single clinician experts to provide integrated treatment or train carefully composed mental health teams? How will these multimodal treatments fare in naturalistic settings? Are they cost effective?

Most of these questions we cannot answer now. But in line with our concept of the scientist/practitioner team moving the field along in a perennial dialectical process, this book should better prepare us to hold up our end of the bargain. In determining "how" these treatments work, we will also be helping to bridge the gap between brain and mind.

◆ ◆ ◆

Finally, speaking entirely pragmatically, we also must be prepared for the possibility that we never will bridge the gap at all, that brain and mind will forever remain distinct concepts, as some pessimists seem to think, because of limits intrinsic to human knowledge (McGinn, 1999). We do not share this pessimism. But should this indeed be the case, we then perhaps can rest easy in the knowledge that we never have stopped providing help and care in an efficient, humane manner to those who needed it, while at the same time doing no harm.

References

Agras, W. S., Rossiter, E. M., & Arnow, B. (1992). Pharmacologic and cognitive—behavioral treatment for bulimia nervosa: A controlled comparison. *American Journal of Psychiatry, 149*(1), 82–87.

American Academy of Child and Adolescent Psychiatry. (1997a). Practice parameters for the assessment and treatment of children, adolescents, and adults with attention-deficit/hyperactivity disorder. *Journal of the American Academy of Child and Adolescent Psychiatry, 36*(Suppl. 10).

American Academy of Child and Adolescent Psychiatry. (1997b). Practice parameters for the assessment and treatment of children and adolescents with anxiety disorders. *Journal of the American Academy of Child and Adolescent Psychiatry, 36*(Suppl. 10).

American Academy of Child and Adolescent Psychiatry. (1997c). Practice parameters for the assessment and treatment of children and adolescents with substance use disorders. *Journal of the American Academy of Child and Adolescent Psychiatry, 36*(Suppl. 10).

American Academy of Child and Adolescent Psychiatry. (1998a). Practice parameters for the assessment and treatment of children and adolescents with obsessive-compulsive disorder. *Journal of the American Academy of Child and Adolescent Psychiatry, 37*(Suppl. 10).

American Academy of Child and Adolescent Psychiatry. (1998b). Practice parameters for the assessment and treatment of children and adolescents with post-traumatic stress disorder. *Journal of the American Academy of Child and Adolescent Psychiatry, 37*(Suppl. 10).

American Academy of Child and Adolescent Psychiatry. (2001). Practice parameter for the prevention and management of aggressive behavior in child and adolescent psychiatric institutions with special reference to seclusion and restraint. *Journal of the American Academy of Child and Adolescent Psychiatry.*

American Academy of Child and Adolescent Psychiatry. (2001). Practice parameters for the assessment and treatment of children and adolescents with schizophrenia. *Journal of the American Academy of Child and Adolescent Psychiatry.*

Arbuthnot, J. (1992). Sociomoral reasoning in behavior-disordered adolescents: Cognitive and behavioral change. In J. McCord & R. E. Tremblay (Eds.), *Preventing antisocial behavior: Interventions from birth through adolescence* (pp. 283–310). New York: Guilford.

Barlow, D. H., Shear, M. K., & Woods, S. W. (2000). Cognitive-behavioral therapy, imipramine, or their combination for panic disorder: A randomized controlled trial. *Journal of American Medical Association, 283*(19), 2529–2536.

Barondes, S. H. (1999). An agenda for psychiatric genetics. *Archives of General Psychiatry, 56,* 549–552.

Bernstein, G. A., Borchardt, C. M., & Perwein, A. R. (2000). Imipramine plus cognitive–behavioral therapy in treatment of school refusal. *American Academy of Children and Adolescent Psychiatry, 39*(3), 276–283.

Bickman, L. (1996). A continuum of care: More is not always better. *American Psychologist, 51*(7), 689–701.

Boyce, W. T., Frank, E., Jensen, P., Kessler, R. C., Nelson, C. A., & Steinberg, L. (in press). *Social context in developmental psychopathology: Recommendations for future research from the MacArthur Network on Psychopathology and Development. Development and Psychopathology.*

Broadwell, R. D. (1995). Neuroscience, memory, and language. In *Decade of the Brain,* Vol. 1. Washington DC: Library of Congress.

Chang, K., Blasey, C., Ketter, T., & Steiner, H. (2001). Family environment of children and adolescents with bipolar parents. *Journal of Affective Disorders, 3,* 73–78.

Chang, K., Steiner, H., & Ketter, T. (2000). Psychiatric phenomenology of child and adolescent bipolar offspring. *Journal of the American Academy of Child and Adolescent Psychiatry, 39*(4), 453–460.

Chang, K., Steiner, H., & Ketter, T. (2003). Studies of offsprings of parents with bipolar disorder. *American Journal of Medical Genetics, 123c*(1), 26–35.

Chavira, D. A., & Stein, M. B. (2002). Combined psychoeducation and treatment with selective serotonin reuptake inhibitors for youth with generalized social anxiety disorder. *Journal of Child and Adolescent Psychopharmacology, 12*(1), 47–54.

Connor, D. F., & Fisher, S. G. (1997). An interactional model of child and adolescent mental health clinical case formulation. *Clinical Child Psychology and Psychiatry, 2*(3), 353–368.

Croudace, T., Evans, J., Harrison, G., Sharp, D., Wilkinson, E., McCann, G., et al. (2003). Impact of the ICD-10 Primary Health Care (PHC) diagnostic and management guidelines for mental disorders on detection and outcome in primary care: Cluster randomized controlled trial, *British Journal of Psychiatry, 182*(1), 20–30.

Dawson, P. M., Griffith, K., & Boeke, K. M. (1990). Combined medical and psychological treatment of hospitalized children with encopresis. *Child Psychiatry and Human Development, 20*(3), 181–190.

Erickson, S., & Steiner, H. (2003). Predicting adolescent's global functioning from personality typologies. *Child Psychiatry and Human Development, 33*(4), 63–80.

Findling, R. L., McNamara, N. K., Branicky, L. A., Schluchter, M. D., Lemon, E., & Blumer, J. L. (2000). A double-blind pilot study of risperidone in the treatment of conduct disorder. *Journal of the American Academy of Child and Adolescent Psychiatry, 39*(4), 509–516.

Forgatch, M. S., & Patterson, G. R. (1989). *Parents and adolescents living together Part 2: Family problem solving.* Eugene, OR: Castalia.

Gabbard, G. O. (1992). Psychodynamic psychiatry in the "Decade of the Brain." *American Journal of Psychiatry, 149,* 991–998.

Gabbard, G. O., & Kay, J. (2001). The fate of integrated treatment: Whatever happened to the biopsychosocial psychiatrist? *American Journal of Psychiatry, 158*(12), 1956–1963.

Gabbard, G. O., Markowitz, J. C., & Clemens, N. A. (2000). Cost-effectiveness of psychiatrists. *American Journal of Psychiatry, 157*(2), 306.

Goldbloom, D. S., Olmsted, M., & Davis, R. (1997). A randomized controlled trial of fluoxetine and cognitive behavioral therapy for bulimia nervosa: Short-term outcome. *Behavioral Research and Therapy, 35*(9), 803–811.

Greenspan, S. I., & Greenspan, N. T. (2003). *The clinical interview of the child.* (3rd ed.). Washington, DC: American Psychiatric Publishing, Inc.

Group for the Advancement of Psychiatry Committee on the Family. (1989). The challenge of relational diagnoses: Applying the biopsychosocial model in DSM-IV. *American Journal of Psychiatry, 146,* 1492–1494.

Gutterman, E. M. (1998). Is diagnosis relevant in the hospitalization of potentially dangerous children and adolescents? *Journal of the American Academy of Child and Adolescent Psychiatry, 37*(10), 1030–1037.

Hager, M. (Ed.). (2002). *Modern psychiatry: Challenges in educating health professionals to meet new needs.* New York: Josiah Macy, Jr. Foundation.

Halmi, K. A. (1995). Eating disorders. In Gabbard, G., (Ed.), *Treatments of psychiatric disorders* (2nd ed., Vols. 1 & 2, pp. 2081–2239), Washington, DC: American Psychiatric Association.

James, E. M., Richard, L. P., Elke, D. E. (1990). A comparison study of antidepressants and structured intensive group psychotherapy in the treatment of bulimia nervosa. *Archives of General Psychiatry, 47,* 149–157.

Jensen, P. S., & Hoagwood, K. (1997). The book of names: DSM-IV in context. *Development and Psychopathology, 9,* 231–249.

Jensen, P. S., & Members of MTA Cooperative Group. (2002). ADHD comorbidity findings from the MTA study: New diagnostic subtypes and their optimal treatments. In J. E. Helzer (Ed.). *Defining psychopathology in the 21st century: DSM-V and beyond* (pp. 169–192). Washington, DC: American Psychiatric Association.

Jones, D., & Elcock, J. (2001). *History and theories of psychology: A critical perspective.* New York: Oxford University Press.

Kandel, E. (1998). A new intellectual framework for psychiatry. *American Journal of Psychiatry, 155,* 457–469.

Klein, R. G., & Abikoff, H. (1997). Behavior therapy and methyl phenidate in treatment of children with ADHD. *Journal of Attention Disorders, 2*(2), 89–114.

Kraemer, H., Kazdin, A., Offord, D., Kessler, R., Jensen, P., & Kupfer, D. (1997). Coming to terms with the terms of risk. *Archives of General Psychiatry, 54,* 337–343.

Kraemer, H., Stice, E., Kazdin, A., Offord, D., & Kupfer, D. (2001). How do risk factors work together? Mediators, moderators, and independent, overlapping, and proxy risk factors. *American Journal of Psychiatry, 158,* 848–856.

Kraemer, H., Wilson, G., Fairburn, C., & Agras, W. (2002). Mediators and moderators of treatment effects in randomized clinical trials. *Archives of General Psychiatry, 59*(10), 877–883.

Lam, D. H., Edward, R., Hayward, P., Bright, J., Wright, K., Kerr, N., et al. (2003). A randomized controlled study of cognitive therapy for relapse prevention for bipolar affective disorder. *Archives of General Psychiatry, 60,* 145–152.

Leckman, J. F. (2002). Tourette's syndrome, *The Lancet,* 360 (Issue 9345), 1577.

Ledoux, J. (2002). *Synaptic self: How our brains become who we are.* New York: The Penguin Group.

Li, X., Ketter, T. A., & Frye, M. A. (2002). Synaptic, intracellular, and neuroprotective mechanisms of anticonvulsants: Are they relevant for the treatment and the course of bipolar disorders? *Journal of Affective Disorders, 69*(1–3), 1–14.

Loeber, R., Burke, J., Jeffrey, D., & Laney, B. (2002). What are adolescent antecedents to antisocial personality disorder? *Criminal Behavior and Mental Health, 12*(1), 24–36.

Loeber, R., & Famington, D. P. (2000). Young children who commit crime: Epidemiology, developmental origins, risk factors, early interventions, and policy implications. *Development and Psychopathology, 12*(4), 737–762.

Luborsky, L., Barber, J., Siqueland, L., Johnson, S., Najavitis, L., Franck, A., et al. (1996). The revised helping alliance questionnaire (Haq II). *Journal of Psychotherapy Practice Res., 5,* 260–271.

McCrae, R. R., & Costa, P. T., Jr. (1987). Validation of the five-factor model of personality across instruments and observers. *Journal of Personality and Social Psychology, 52,* 81–90.

Magnusson, D. (1999). Individual developmental: Toward a developmental science. *Proceedings of the American Philosophical Society, 143*(1), 86–96.

Manji, H. K., Moore, G. J., & Chen, G. (2000). Clinical and preclinical evidence for the neurotrophic effects of mood stabilizers: Implications for the pathophysiology and treatment of manic-depressive illness. *Biological Psychiatry, 48*(8), 740–754.

March, J., Mulle, K., & Herbel, B. (1994). Behavioral psychotherapy for children and adolescents with obsessive-compulsive disorder: An open trial of a new protocol-driven treatment package. *Journal of the American Academy of Child and Adolescent Psychiatry, 33*(3), 333–341.

May, R. (1998). Levels of organization in ecological systems. In Novartis Foundation Symposium 213, *The limits of reductionism in biology.* (pp. 193–202). Chichester: John Wiley & Sons.

McEwen, B. S., & Wingfield, J. C. (2003). The concept of allostasis in biology and biomedicine. *Hormones and Behavior, 43*(1), 2–15.

McGinn, C. (1999). *The character of mind: An introduction to the philosophy of mind.* (2nd ed.). New York: Oxford University Press.

Miklowitz, D. J., Simoneau, T. L., George, E. L., Richards, J. A., Kalbag, A., Ericsson, N. S., et al. (2000). *Biological Psychiatry, 48,* 582–592.

Mitchell, J., Pyle, R., Eokert, E., Hatsukani, D., Domeay, C., & Zimmerman, R. (1990). A comparison study of antidepressants and structured intensive group psychotherapy in the treatment of bulemia nervosa. *Archives of General Psychiatry, 47,* 149–157.

MTA Cooperative Group. (1999). A 14-month randomised clinical trial of treatment strategies for attention-deficit/hyperactivity disorder. *Archives of General Psychiatry, 56*(12), 1073–1086.

Neziroglu, F., Yaryura, T., & Jose, A. (2000). The effect of fluvoxamine and behavior therapy on children and adolescents with obsessive-compulsive disorder. *Journal of Child and Adolescent Psychopharmacology, 10*(4), 295–306.

Noam, G. G. (in press). Clinical-developmental psychology: Towards developmentally differentiated interventions. In I. Sigel, & K. A. Renninger (Eds.), *Handbook of child psychology: Vol. 4, Child psychology in practice.* Cambridge, Mass, Harvard University Press.

Pamela, K. K., James, E. M., & Traci, L. D. (2000). Long-term impact of treatment in women diagnosed with bulimia nervosa. *International Journal of Eating Disorder, 31,* 151–158.

Pelham, W. E., Gnagy, E. M., & Greiner, A. R. (2000). Behavioral versus behavioral and pharmacological treatment in ADHD children attending a summer treatment program. *Journal of Abnormal Child Psychology, 28*(6), 507–525.

Petti, Theodore A. (1998). Discussion: Diagnosis is relevant to psychiatric hospitalization. *Journal of the American Academy of Child and Adolescent Psychiatry, 37*(10), 1038–1040.

Pine, D. S., & Walkup, J. T. (2001). Fluvoxamine for the treatment of anxiety disorders in children and adolescents. *New England Journal of Medicine, 344*(17), 1279–1285.

Pitman, R. K., Orr, S. P., Altman, B., & Longpre, R. R. (1996). Emotional processing during eye movement desensitization and reprocessing therapy of Vietnam veterans with chronic post-traumatic stress disorder. *Comprehensive Psychiatry, 37*(6), 419–429.

Plattner, B., Silverman, M., Redlich, A., Carrion, V., Feucht, B., Friedrich, M., et al. (in print). Pathways to dissociation: Intrafamilial versus extrafamilial trauma in juvenile delinquents. *Journal of Nervous and Mental Diseases.*

Post, R. M. (1992). Transduction of psychosocial stress into the neurobiology of recurrent affective disorder. *American Journal of Psychiatry, 149,* 999–1010.

Post, R. M., Weiss, S. R., Li, H., Smith, M. A., Zhang, L. X., Xing, G., Osuch, E. A., & McCann, U. D. (1998). Neural plasticity and emotional memory. *Developmental Psychopathology, 10*(4), 829–855.

Putnam, H. (1967). The nature of mental states. In W. H. Captian and D. D. Merrill (Eds.). *Art, Mind and Religion.* University of Pittsburgh Press.

Reid, J. B., Patterson, G. R., & Snyder, J. (2003). Antisocial behavior in children and adolescents: A developmental analysis and model for intervention. *American Journal of Psychiatry, 160*(4), 805.

Reiss, D., Plomin, R., & Hetherington, M. (1991). Genetics and psychiatry: An unheralded window on the environment. *American Journal of Psychiatry, 148,* 283–291.

Rose, S. (1998). What is wrong with reductionist explanations behaviour? In: Novartis Foundation Symposium, 213. The limits of reductionism in biology, Chichester, Wiley, pp. 176–192.

Rose, G. J., Fortune, E. S. (2002). Roles for short-term synaptic plasticity in behavior. *Journal of Physiology of Paris, 96*(5–6), 539–545.

Rosenthal, D. (Ed.). (1991). *The Nature of Mind.* New York: Oxford University Press.

Rutter, M. (Ed.). (1995). *Psychosocial disturbances in young people: Challenges for prevention.* New York: Cambridge University Press.

Rutter, M. (1989). Pathways from childhood to adult life. *Journal of Child Psychology and Psychiatry, 30*(1), 23–51.

Rutter, M., & Sroufe, L. (1984). The domain of developmental psychopathology. *Child Development, 55*(1), 17–29.

Rutter, M., Taylor, E., & Hersov, L. (1994). *Child and adolescent psychiatry.* New York: Oxford University Press.

Sameroff, A. J. (1995). General systems theories and developmental psychopathology. In D. Cicchetti & D. Cohen (Eds.), *Manual of Developmental Psychopathology,* (Vol. 1, pp. 659–695). New York: Wiley.

Sammons, M. T., & Schmidt, N. (Eds.). (2001). *Combined treatments for mental disorders.* Washington, DC: American Psychological Association.

Saxena, K., Chang, K., Steiner, H. (2003). Psychopharmacologic strategies for the treatment of aggression in juveniles. *CNS Spectrums, 8*(4), 298–308.

Searle, J. (1983). *Intentionality: An Essay in the Philosophy of Mind.* New York: Cambridge University Press.

Searle, J. (1995). *The construction of social reality.* New York: The Free Press.

Searle, J. (1995). *The rediscovery of the mind.* London: The MIT Press.

Searle, J. (1997). *The mystery of consciousness.* New York Review.

Searle, J. (2002). *Consciousness and language.* New York: Cambridge University Press.

Smith, C., Feldman, S., & Steiner, H. (1993). Psychological characteristics and DSM-III-R diagnoses at 6 year follow-up of adolescent anorexia nervosa. *Journal of the American Academy of Child and Adolescent Psychiatry, 32*(6), 1237–1245.

Snyder, J., & Stoolmiller, M. (2002). Reinforcement and coercion mechanisms in the development of antisocial behavior: Peer relationships. In J. B. Reid, G. R. Patterson, & J. Snyder (Eds.), *Antisocial behavior in children and adolescents: A developmental analysis and model for intervention* (pp. 45–64). Washington, DC: American Psychological Association.

Solnit, A. J., Neubauer, P., Abrams, S., & Dowling, S. (Eds.). (1996). *The psychoanalytic study of the child.* Vol. 51. New Haven, CT: Yale University Press.

Sroufe, L. A. (1990). Considering normal and abnormal together: The essence of developmental psychopathology. *Development and Psychopathology, 2,* 335–347.

Sroufe, L. A. (1997). Psychopathology as an outcome of development. *Development and Psychopathology, 9,* 251–268.

Sroufe, L. A., & Rutter, M. (1984). The domain of developmental psychopathology. *Child Development, 55,* 17–29.

Steiner, H. (Ed.). (1996). *Treating adolescents.* San Francisco: Jossey-Bass.

Steiner, H. (Ed.). (1997a). *Treating Preschool Children.* San Francisco: Jossey-Bass.

Steiner, H. (Ed.). (1997b). *Treating school-age children.* San Francisco: Jossey-Bass.

Steiner, H., & AACAP Workgroup on Quality Issues. (Principal Author: Steiner, H.). (1997). Practice parameters for the assessment and treatment of children and adolescents with conduct disorder. *Journal of the American Academy of Child and Adolescent Psychiatry, 36*(10).

Steiner, H. (Chair, Symposium). (2003). Integrated treatment: Psychotherapy and psychopharmacology. *Annual meeting of the American Psychiatric Association.* San Francisco, CA.

Steiner, H., Carrion, V., Plattner, B., & Koopman, C. (2003b). Dissociative symptoms in post-traumatic stress disorder: Diagnosis and treatment. In N. Laor (Ed.), *Child and Adolescent Psychiatric Clinics of North America, 12,* 231–249.

Steiner, H., Cauffman, E., & Duxbury, E. (1999). Personality traits in juvenile delinquents: Relation to criminal behavior and recidivism. *Journal of the American Academy of Child and Adolescent Psychiatry, 38*(3), 256–262.

Steiner, H., & Hayward C. (2004). *Change, complexity, continuity and context: Developmental approaches to diagnosis and treatment.* New York: Guilford.

Steiner, H., Marx, L., Walton, C. (1991). The ward atmosphere of a child psychosomatic unit: A ten-year follow-up. *General Hospital Psychiatry, 13,* 246–252.

Steiner, H., Mazer, C., & Litt, I. F. (1990). Compliance and outcome in anorexia nervosa. *Western Journal of Medicine, 153,* 133–139.

Steiner, H., & Remsing, L., and AACAP. (2004). Practice parameters for the assessment and treatment of children and adolescents with oppositional defiant disorder. *Journal of the American Academy of Child and Adolescent Psychiatry.*

Steiner, H., Saxena, K., & Chang, K. (2003a). Psychopharmacological strategies for the treatment of aggression in youth. *CNS Spectrums, 8*(4), 298–308.

Tharinger, D. (2000). The complexity of development and change: The need for the integration of theory and research findings in psychological practice with children. *Society for the Study of School Psychology,* 383–388.

Walkup, J. T., Labellarte, M. J., & Riddle, M. A. (2001). Fluvoxamine for the treatment of anxiety disorders in children and adolescents. *The New England Journal of Medicine, 344*(17), 1279–1285.

Walsh, T., Wilson, T., Loeb, K., Derlin, M., Pike, K., Roose, et al. (1997). Medication and psychotherapy in the treatment of bulimia nervosa. *American Journal of Psychiatry, 154*(4), 523–531.

Weinberger, D. A. (1997). Distress and self-restraint as measures of adjustment across the life span: Confirmatory factor analyses in clinical and nonclinical samples. *Journal of Psychological Assessment, 9*(2), 132–135.

Weinberger, D. A., & Schwartz, G. E. (1990). Distress and restraint as superordinate dimensions of self-reported adjustment: A typological perspective. *Journal of Personality, 58*(2), 382–417.

Wilson, J., Rojas, N., Haapanen, R., & Steiner, H. (2001). Substance abuse and criminal recidivism: A prospective study of adolescents. *Child Psychiatry and Human Development, 31*(4), 297–312.

Winston, A. (2003). Integrated Psychotherapy. *Psychiatric Services, 54,* 152–154.

ABOUT THE EDITOR

Dr. med. univ. *Hans Steiner* is Professor of Psychiatry and Behavioral Sciences at the Stanford University School of Medicine, where he has taught at the graduate and undergraduate level since 1978. In the Division of Child Psychiatry and Child Development, he is currently the Director of Education. He has authored over 300 published articles, abstracts, and book chapters. He is the editor of three volumes on Treating Preschool Children, School-Age Children, and Adolescents, respectively, published by Jossey-Bass. He is one of three editors of the *Lehrbuch der Kinder und Jugendlichenpsychiatrie,* published by Hogrefe, Gottingen, Germany. He serves on the editorial boards of over forty scientific journals and publishing houses, and is very active in public service, sitting on advisory boards of several organizations and national task forces dealing with issues concerning troubled youth. He has lectured widely in the United States, Europe, and Australia and regularly provides keynote addresses at national and international professional meetings on topics of his core research interests. He is particularly interested in increasing diversity among mental health clinicians and researchers.

He is a Distinguished Fellow of the American Psychiatric Association (APA), a Fellow of the American Academy of Child and Adolescent Psychiatry (AACAP) and the Academy of Psychosomatic Medicine (APM). He is an invited member of the Group for the Advancement of Psychiatry (GAP). In 2002, he was named Pfizer Visiting Professor to the Department of Psychiatry at Brown University and Visiting Scholar to Loyola University's Department of Pediatrics by the

American Psychosomatic Society. In 2003, he was named visiting professor to Howard University and provided the keynote address at the Annual National Capitol Lectures Series on Mental Health; was visiting professor at the Free University at Amsterdam, Holland; and was closing plenary speaker at the Joint Scientific Congress of the German, Austrian, and Swiss Societies for Child and Adolescent Psychiatry in Vienna, Austria.

As a clinician, he provides frequent second opinions and expert forensic testimony. He was cited in 2003 in *America's Top Psychiatrists* by the Consumer's Research Council of America; in 2002 in *Kingston's National Registry of Who is Who*, 2002 edition, Lifetime Member, #128962; from 2001 to present in Castle & Conolly *America's Top Doctors;* since 2001 in *Who is Who*, #14879; since 1996 in *Best Doctors Inc.;* in 1995 in *International Who is Who in Medicine;* and in 1994 in Good Housekeeping, one of 327 best mental health experts.

He has won numerous national awards for his research, teaching, and mentorship of young physicians and mental health researchers. In 1996, he received the Goldberger Award of the American Medical Association for his work in eating disorders. In 1990, 1992, 1993, 1995, 1996, 1998, and 1999 he was the recipient of the Outstanding Mentor Award of the American Academy of Child and Adolescent Psychiatry. In 1993, he won the Dlin/Fisher Award of the Academy of Psychosomatic Medicine for achievements in clinical research.

Dr. Steiner was born in Vienna, Austria, and received his M.D. (Doctor medicinae universalis—Dr. med. univ.) from the University of Vienna, Austria, in 1972. He completed his residency in adult psychiatry at SUNY Upstate Medical Center, and his child and adolescent psychiatry residency at the University of Michigan in Ann Arbor.

Dr. Steiner is considered an expert in three areas: (1) Aggression and its relationship to psychopathology. He is regarded as a national and international expert on the overlap between psychopathology, aggression, and antisocial behavior. He has extensive experience in consulting to juvenile justice. A related interest is his research and consultancy in the mental health dimensions of sports and elite athletes. (2) Psychopathologies associated with trauma and victimization. Abuse and child victimization are important precursors of disorders related to aggression. (3) Pediatric and psychiatric comorbidity (that is, the overlap between pediatric and psychiatric diseases). He has conducted extensive research in juvenile eating disorders, somatoform disorders, the psychiatric sequelae of pediatric disease and intensive treatment systems for pediatric psychiatric comorbidity.

Dr. Steiner's research is based on developmental approaches to psychopathology that emphasize the conjoint study of normative and non-normative phenomena, and the complex interaction of biological, psychological, and social variables in the etiology, pathogenesis, diagnosis, and treatment of mental disorders.

ABOUT THE SECTION EDITORS

Kiki D. Chang, M.D., is Assistant Professor of Psychiatry and Behavioral Sciences at the Stanford University School of Medicine, Division of Child and Adolescent Psychiatry. He is Director of the Pediatric Bipolar Disorders Clinic, where he specializes in pediatric psychopharmacology and treatment of depression and bipolar disorder in children and adolescents. Dr. Chang is the recipient of the Eli Lilly Pilot Research Award from the American Academy of Child and Adolescent Psychiatry, the Klingenstein Third Generation Foundation Fellowship in Child and Adolescent Depression, and the American Psychiatric Association/ AstraZeneca Young Minds in Psychiatry Award. He has been the recipient of two National Alliance for Research on Schizophrenia and Depression (NARSAD) Young Investigator Awards and has received a five-year Career Development Award from the National Institutes of Health.

As Director of the Pediatric Bipolar Disorders Program, Dr. Chang conducts research into various facets of bipolar disorder. He is currently conducting phenomenologic, biologic, pharmacologic, and genetic studies of bipolar disorder in adults and children. These studies include brain imaging (MRI, MRS, fMRI) and medication trials. He is particularly interested in detecting prodromal bipolar disorder in children who might then be treated to prevent the development of full bipolar disorder. To do this, he has been studying children of parents with bipolar disorder who are at high risk for developing the disorder themselves.

Dr. Chang is the author of numerous papers and book chapters regarding bipolar disorder and has presented widely at national and international scientific conferences and meetings.

James Lock, M.D., Ph.D. is Associate Professor of Child Psychiatry and Pediatrics in the Department of Psychiatry and Behavioral Sciences at Stanford University School of Medicine, where he has taught since 1993. In the Division of Child Psychiatry and Child Development, he is currently Director of the Eating Disorders Program, which consists of both inpatient and outpatient treatment facilities. His major research and clinical interests are in psychotherapy research, especially in children and adolescents, and specifically for those with eating disorders. In addition, he is interested in the psychosexual development of children and adolescents and related risks for psychopathology.

Dr. Lock has published over 100 articles, abstracts, and book chapters. He is the author, along with Drs. Le Grange, Agras, and Dare, of the only evidenced-based treatment manual for anorexia nervosa, *Treatment Manual for Anorexia Nervosa: A Family-Based Approach.* He serves on the editorial panel of many scientific journals, especially focused on psychotherapy and eating disorders related to child and adolescent mental health. He has lectured widely in the United States, Europe, and Australia.

Dr. Lock is the recipient of a National Institute of Mental Health (NIMH) Career Development Award focused on enhancing psychosocial treatments of eating disorders in children and adolescents.

Jeffrey J. Wilson, M.D., is Assistant Professor of Clinical Psychiatry at the College of Physicians and Surgeons at Columbia University. Dr. Wilson is Board Certified in Adult and Child and Adolescent Psychiatry, and he has also completed a National Institute of Drug Abuse-sponsored clinical research fellowship in Addiction Psychiatry. Dr. Wilson has received several awards for teaching, clinical research, and administration. Dr. Wilson's main research interest is related to the developmental psychopathology of addictive vulnerability. This research interest began while Chief Resident in Child/Adolescent Psychiatry at Stanford University, under the mentorship of Dr. Steiner. He is currently researching parent-child interactions between opiate dependent parents and their children, and is working toward the development of interventions to prevent the development of substance use disorders among these high-risk children. Dr. Wilson is also an Associate Research Scientist with the Clinical Trials Network of the National Institute on Drug Abuse. He is currently working on community-based effectiveness trials for smoking cessation and HIV prevention among adults and adolescents in substance abuse treatment. A Patient-Oriented Career Development Award from the National

Institute on Drug Abuse coupled with a Ruane Scholar's Award, funds Dr. Wilson's research activities.

Dr. Wilson has published numerous peer-reviewed publications and book chapters in areas related to delinquency, adolescent substance abuse treatment, language disorders, ADHD, and children of addicted parents. He has also presented findings from his research at national meetings of the American Academy of Child and Adolescent Psychiatry, the American Academy of Addiction Psychiatry, the American Society of Addiction Medicine, the College of Problems on Drug Dependence, and the American Psychiatric Association.

ABOUT THE CONTRIBUTORS

Georgianna Achilles, Ph.D.
Post-doctoral Research Fellow, Institute for the Study of Exceptional Children and Youth, Department of Special Education, University of Maryland

Peter Ash, M.D.
Associate Professor and Director, Psychiatry and Law Services, Department of Psychiatry and Behavioral Sciences, Emory University School of Medicine, Atlanta

Daniel F. Becker, M.D.
Associate Clinical Professor of Psychiatry at the University of California, San Francisco, and Medical Director of Behavioral Health Services, Mills-Peninsula Medical Center, Burlingame, California

Christine Blasey, Ph.D.
Division of Child and Adolescent Psychiatry, Stanford University

Glenn S. Brassington, Ph.D.
Assistant Professor of Psychology, Sonoma State University Adjunct Clinical Instructor, Department of Psychiatry and Behavioral Sciences, Stanford University

Larry K. Brown, M.D.
Clinical Instructor, Brown University

Bernadette Marie Bullock, Ph.D.
Research Associate, Oregon Social Learning Center

Kiki D. Chang, M.D.
Assistant Professor of Psychiatry and Behavioral Sciences, Division of Child
and Adolescent Psychiatry, Stanford University

Mark DeAntonio, M.D.
Associate Clinical Professor of Psychiatry at the University of California,
Los Angeles, and Director of the Adolescent Inpatient Service, UCLA
Neuropsychiatric Hospital, Los Angeles

Sandra DeJong, M.D.
McLean Hospital, Pediatric Psychotic Disorders Program, Department of
Child Psychiatry, Department of Psychiatry, Harvard Medical School, Boston

Graham J. Emslie, M.D.
Professor, Director, Bob Smith, M.D. Center for Pediatric Psychiatry Research,
Department of Psychiatry, University of Texas Southern Medical Center at
Dallas, and Children's Medical Center of Dallas

Sarah J. Erickson, Ph.D.
Assistant Professor, Psychology Department, The University of New Mexico

Brandi C. Fink
The University of New Mexico

John H. Flavell, Ph.D.
Professor Emeritus, Department of Psychology, Stanford University

Peter Fonagy, Ph.D., F.B.A.
Freud Memorial Professor of Psychoanalysis, University College, London,
Director, Child Family Center, Menninger Clinic, Kansas Director of Research,
Anna Freud Centre, London

Marion S. Forgatch, Ph.D.
Senior Scientist, Oregon Social Learning Center

Jean A. Frazier, M.D.
Director, Pediatric Psychotic Disorders Research Program, McLean Hospital and Harvard Medical School

Anthony J. Giuliano, Ph.D.
Department of Psychiatry, Harvard Medical School

Joachim Hallmayer, M.D.
Associate Professor (Research), Division of Child and Adolescent Psychiatry, Stanford University

Judith H. Hume, M.S.
Department of Psychiatry, University of Texas, Southwestern Medical Center at Dallas, and Children's Medical Center of Dallas

Keith Humphreys, Ph.D.
Veterans Affairs and Stanford University Medical Centers

Shashank V. Joshi, M.D.
Director, School-based Mental Health Services, Division of Child and Adolescent Psychiatry, Stanford University

Niranjan S. Karnik, M.D., Ph.D.
Resident in Psychiatry, Stanford Hospital and Clinics, Palo Alto, California

John F. Kelly, Ph.D.
Research Scientist, VA Palo Alto Health Care System, and Consulting Assistant Professor of Psychiatry and Behavioral Sciences, Stanford University

Leena A. Khanzode, M.D.
Stanford University School of Medicine

Michelle King, B.A.
Stanford University School of Medicine

E. Chandini Kumar, B.A.
Department of Psychiatry, University of Texas, Southwestern Medical Center at Dallas, and Children's Medical Center of Dallas

James Lock, M.D., Ph.D.
Associate Professor of Psychiatry and Behavioral Sciences, Division of Child
and Adolescent Psychiatry, Stanford University

Coleen Loomis, Ph.D.
Veterans Affairs and Stanford University Medical Centers

Linda Lotspeich, M.D.
Assistant Professor of Psychiatry and Behavioral Sciences, Division of Child
and Adolescent Psychiatry, Stanford University

Michael J. Loughran, Ph.D.
Associate Clinical Professor of Psychiatry, Stanford University, Advanced
Candidate, San Francisco Psychoanalytic Institute

David M. Lyons, Ph.D.
Associate Professor (Research) of Psychiatry and Behavioral Sciences,
Stanford University

Don Mordeci, M.D.
Stanford University School of Medicine

Alec L. Miller, Psy.D.
Associate Professor of Psychiatry and Behavioral Sciences, Chief, Child and
Adolescent Psychology, Albert Einstein College of Medicine, Montefiore
Medical Center

Laura Mufson, Ph.D.
Director, Department of Clinical Psychology, New York State Psychiatric
Institute, Associate Professor of Clinical Psychology in Psychiatry, Columbia
University College of Physicians and Surgeons

Laura L. Palmer, M.Ed., Ph.D.
Stanford University School of Medicine

Gerald R. Patterson, Ph.D.
Senior Scientist, Founding Director, Oregon Social Learning Center

Andrew M. Portteus, M.D., M.P.H.
Department of Psychiatry, University of Texas Southwestern Medical Center at Dallas, and Children's Medical Center of Dallas

Robert M. Post, M.D.
Chief, Biological Psychiatry Branch, National Institute of Mental Health, National Institutes of Health, DHHS

Susan L. W. Post, L.C.S.W.
Private Practice

Luis Puelles, M.D., Ph.D.
Department of Morphological Sciences, School of Medicine, University of Murcia, Spain

Jill H. Rathus, Ph.D.
Associate Professor of Psychology, Clinical Psychology Program, Long Island University

Ethan Remmel, Ph.D.
Assistant Professor, Western Washington University

John L. R. Rubenstein, M.D., Ph.D.
Professor and Nina Ireland Endowed Chair in Child Psychiatry, Nina Ireland Laboratory of Developmental Neurobiology, Department of Psychiatry, University of California at San Francisco

Kirti Saxena, M.D.
APA Research Fellow, Division of Child and Adolescent Psychiatry, Stanford University

Richard J. Shaw, M.B., B.S.
Assistant Professor of Psychiatry and Pediatrics, Stanford University

Diana I. Simeonova-Lennon, Dipl.-Psych.
Division of Child and Adolescent Psychiatry, Stanford University

Dr. med. univ. Hans Steiner
Professor of Psychiatry and Behavioral Sciences, Division of Child Psychiatry, Stanford University

Margo Thienemann, M.D.
Assistant Professor of Psychiatry and Behavioral Sciences, Stanford University

Stephen W. Tracy, M.A.
Center for Healthcare Evaluation, Veterans Affairs, Palo Alto Healthcare System

Elizabeth E. Wagner, Ph.D.
Assistant Professor of Psychiatry and Behavioral Sciences, Assistant Director, Adolescent Depression and Suicide Program, Montefiore Medical Center

Jeffrey J. Wilson, M.D.
Assistant Professor of Clinical Psychiatry at the College of Physicians and Surgeons at Columbia University

Jami F. Young, Ph.D. (Finkelson)
Post-doctoral Fellow, Department of Child Psychiatry, Columbia University

Marina Zelenko, M.D.
Voluntary Clinical Instructor, Department of Psychiatry, Stanford University, Current position and primary affiliation: Kaiser Santa Clara Child and Adolescent Services, Child Psychiatrist

NAME INDEX

SUBJECT INDEX